AF700892

ADMINISTRATIVE LAW

A Casebook

EDITORIAL ADVISORS

Rachel E. Barkow
Vice Dean and Charles Seligson Professor of Law
Segal Family Professor of Regulatory Law and Policy
Faculty Director, Center on the Administration of Criminal Law
New York University School of Law

Erwin Chemerinsky
Dean and Jesse H. Choper Distinguished Professor of Law
University of California, Berkeley School of Law

Richard A. Epstein
Laurence A. Tisch Professor of Law
New York University School of Law
Peter and Kirsten Bedford Senior Fellow
The Hoover Institution
Senior Lecturer in Law
The University of Chicago

Ronald J. Gilson
Charles J. Meyers Professor of Law and Business
Stanford University
Marc and Eva Stern Professor of Law and Business
Columbia Law School

James E. Krier
Earl Warren DeLano Professor of Law Emeritus
The University of Michigan Law School

Tracey L. Meares
Walton Hale Hamilton Professor of Law
Director, The Justice Collaboratory
Yale Law School

Richard K. Neumann, Jr.
Alexander Bickel Professor of Law
Maurice A. Deane School of Law at Hofstra University

Robert H. Sitkoff
Austin Wakeman Scott Professor of Law
John L. Gray Professor of Law
Harvard Law School

David Alan Sklansky
Stanley Morrison Professor of Law
Faculty Co-Director, Stanford Criminal Justice Center
Stanford Law School

ASPEN CASEBOOK SERIES

ADMINISTRATIVE LAW

A Casebook

TENTH EDITION

Bernard Schwartz

Late Chapman Distinguished Professor of Law
University of Tulsa College of Law

Roberto L. Corrada

Mulligan Burleson Chair in Modern Learning and Professor of Law
University of Denver Sturm College of Law

J. Robert Brown, Jr.

Professor of Law
University of Denver Sturm College of Law

Jessica L. West

Assistant Dean of Academic Success Programs
University of Washington School of Law

ASPEN PUBLISHING

Copyright © 2022 Aspen Publishing. All Rights Reserved.

No part of this publication may be reproduced or transmitted in any form or by any means, electronic or mechanical, including photocopy, recording, or utilized by any information storage or retrieval system, without written permission from the publisher. For information about permissions or to request permissions online, visit us at www.AspenPublishing.com.

To contact Customer Service, e-mail customer.service@aspenpublishing.com, call 1-800-950-5259, or mail correspondence to:

Aspen Publishing
Attn: Order Department
PO Box 990
Frederick, MD 21705

Printed in the United States of America.

1 2 3 4 5 6 7 8 9 0

ISBN 978-1-5438-4615-7

Library of Congress Cataloging-in-Publication Data

Names: Schwartz, Bernard, 1923-1997 author. | Corrada, Roberto L., 1960- author. | Brown, J. Robert, Jr., 1957- author. | West, Jessica L., author.
Title: Administrative law : a casebook / Bernard Schwartz, Late Chapman Distinguished Professor of Law University of Tulsa College of Law ; Roberto L. Corrada, Mulligan Burleson Chair in Modern Learning and Professor of Law, University of Denver Sturm College of Law; J. Robert Brown, Jr., Professor of Law, University of Denver Strum College of Law; Jessica L. West, Assistant Dean of Academic Success Programs, University of Washington School of Law.
Description: Tenth edition. | Frederick, MD : Aspen Publishing, 2022. | Series: Aspen casebook series | Includes bibliographical references and index. | Summary: "A casebook for law students of Administrative Law"—Provided by publisher.
Identifiers: LCCN 2021051599 | ISBN 9781543846157 (hardcover) | ISBN 9781543846164 (ebook)
Subjects: LCSH: Administrative law--United States. | Casebooks (Law) lcgft
Classification: LCC KF5402 .S343 2022 | DDC 342.73/06—dc23/eng/20211109
LC record available at https://lccn.loc.gov/2021051599

About Aspen Publishing

Aspen Publishing is a leading provider of educational content and digital learning solutions to law schools in the U.S. and around the world. Aspen provides best-in-class solutions for legal education through authoritative textbooks, written by renowned authors, and breakthrough products such as Connected eBooks, Connected Quizzing, and PracticePerfect.

The Aspen Casebook Series (famously known among law faculty and students as the "red and black" casebooks) encompasses hundreds of highly regarded textbooks in more than eighty disciplines, from large enrollment courses, such as Torts and Contracts to emerging electives such as Sustainability and the Law of Policing. Study aids such as the *Examples & Explanations* and *Glannon Guide* series, both highly popular collections, help law students master complex subject matter.

Major products, programs, and initiatives include:

- **Connected eBooks** are enhanced digital textbooks and study aids that come with a suite of online content and learning tools designed to maximize student success. Designed in collaboration with hundreds of faculty and students, the Connected eBook is a significant leap forward in the legal education learning tools available to students.
- **Connected Quizzing** is an easy-to-use formative assessment tool that tests law students' understanding and provides timely feedback to improve learning outcomes. Delivered through CasebookConnect.com, the learning platform already used by students to access their Aspen casebooks, Connected Quizzing is simple to implement and integrates seamlessly with law school course curricula.
- **PracticePerfect** is a visually engaging, interactive study aid to explain commonly encountered legal doctrines through easy-to-understand animated videos, illustrative examples, and numerous practice questions. Developed by a team of experts, PracticePerfect is the ideal study companion for today's law students.
- The **Aspen Learning Library** enables law schools to provide their students with access to the most popular study aids on the market across all of their courses. Available through an annual subscription, the online library consists of study aids in e-book, audio, and video formats with full text search, note-taking, and highlighting capabilities.
- Aspen's **Digital Bookshelf** is an institutional-level online education bookshelf, consolidating everything students and professors need to ensure success. This program ensures that every student has access to affordable course materials from day one.
- **Leading Edge** is a community centered on thinking differently about legal education and putting those thoughts into actionable strategies. At the core of the program is the Leading Edge Conference, an annual gathering of legal education thought leaders looking to pool ideas and identify promising directions of exploration.

This book is dedicated
by Bernard Schwartz to Brian, who persuaded him to undertake this casebook;
by Roberto Corrada to Cándido and Vilma, his parents;
by J. Robert Brown, Jr., to Allison Herren Lee, his inspiration for all things in life;
and by Jessica West to all the lawyers (and aspiring lawyers) who fight for greater justice.

SUMMARY OF CONTENTS

PREFACE TO THE 10TH EDITION

Administrative law continues to be one of the most dynamic, interesting, and impactful areas of the law. Since the last edition, the U.S. Supreme Court has been quite active re-envisioning the relationship between administrative agencies and the judicial branch. As a consequence, this edition has substantially updated materials relating to separation of powers (Chapter 1), nondelegation (Chapter 2), and judicial review (Chapter 7). We have also tightened up and shortened some of the material regarding evidentiary hearings (Chapter 6). Regrettably, this edition is produced without the labor of Jay Brown, who, in 2017, was appointed a Commissioner of the Public Company Accounting Oversight Board (PCAOB). We expect to tap into Jay's deepened expertise in administrative law for the next edition when he returns to the fold of academia.

We continue to be guided by Bernard Schwartz's thinking on administrative law, as evidenced by his text and his many articles on the subject. As mentioned in a prior preface, Bernard Schwartz was dedicated to the advancement of administrative law. This casebook contains bits and pieces of his work in virtually every facet of administrative law, demonstrating his enormous commitment and contribution to the development of the area. While it may not have started as such, his casebook eventually came to be a showcase for his thinking on administrative law. We have endeavored to preserve the casebook as a legacy and testament to the force of his ideas on this subject. The following tributes to Bernard Schwartz attest to his extraordinary life in the law: Symposium, *The Life and Legacy of Bernard Schwartz*, 34 Tulsa L.J. 651-711 (1999); *In Memoriam: Bernard Schwartz*, 33 Tulsa L.J. 1041-1096 (1998); *Bernard Schwartz*, 73 N.Y.U. L. Rev. 701 (1998).

We are, of course, indebted to a number of people for their advice and assistance in producing this casebook. At Aspen Publishing, thanks to Anton Yakovlev for his oversight of this project. At the University of Denver Sturm College of Law, Roberto thanks Trevor Klein for his substantial and invaluable contributions with respect to the chapters on separation of powers and judicial review. He also thanks Kit Longnecker for her edits and research assistance with respect to chapters on nondelegation and rulemaking. Jessica owes thanks to her family for putting up with her while she worked on the update without student support as well as Roberto, who pulled the laboring oar on the 10th Edition.

Roberto L. Corrada
Jessica L. West

January 2022

ADMINISTRATIVE LAW

A CASEBOOK

CHAPTER 1

Administrative Agencies and Administrative Law

A WHAT IS ADMINISTRATIVE LAW?

GILMORE v. LUJAN

947 F.2d 1409 (9th Cir. 1991)

THOMAS G. NELSON, Circuit Judge. Appellant Reed Gilmore appeals a rejection of his oil and gas lease offer by the Bureau of Land Management ("BLM"). BLM refused the offer because it did not contain a personal handwritten signature and the Interior Board of Land Appeals ("IBLA") upheld that rejection. . . . This district court summarily affirmed the IBLA's decision. We affirm.

FACTUAL AND PROCEDURAL BACKGROUND

This appeal arises out of a failure of our postal system. Reed Gilmore filed an oil and gas application for Parcel NV-148 in the June 1987 simultaneous filing of the BLM. His application was selected in the computerized random drawing. BLM sent its decision, dated August 26, which stated in part:

> Enclosed is the original and two copies of Form No. 3100-11, "Offer to Lease and Lease for Oil and Gas" for your execution. The applicant (or the applicant's attorney-in-fact, as provided by 43 CFR [§]3112.6-1(a) and (b) [(1986)]) must manually sign and date each copy on the reverse side of the form.
>
> All copies of the lease form must be properly executed and filed in this office within thirty (30) days from your receipt of this decision, which constitutes a compliance period. Failure to do so will result in the rejection of your offer without further notice.

The decision was sent certified mail, with a return receipt requested, from the Reno, Nevada office of the BLM. Gilmore received the decision on August 29, 1987; therefore, to comply with the deadline, he was to file the completed forms no later than Sept. 28, 1987.

Gilmore signed the copies of the lease form and sent them by certified mail from his office in Kimball, Nebraska, with a return receipt requested, to the Reno office on September 21. Gilmore states that his secretary, Debra Bohac, noticed on the morning of the deadline, Monday, Sept. 28, that they had not yet received the return receipt card from the envelope containing the signed forms. Bohac called the Reno office to inquire whether the forms had been received. She spoke with Joan Woodin, Supervisory Land Law Examiner for the Nevada State Office. While the text of the entire conversation is disputed, Woodin did inform Bohac that the forms had not yet arrived.

Bohac states that she then investigated whether Gilmore could travel to Reno that day. She allegedly found no commercial airline that could transport Gilmore to Reno by the close of the BLM's business day. Bohac called Woodin again. Her call was returned on Woodin's behalf by Bernita Dawson, a Land Law Examiner in the Reno office. Both parties to this second call agree that Bohac informed Dawson that Gilmore's office would arrange for a telecopied (i.e., "faxed") lease form to be delivered to the Reno BLM office that day, September 28. Bohac also states, "I asked Ms. Dawson if they (BLM) would consider the telecopied signed lease form for acceptance as the signed lease offer and she told me they would." However, Dawson claimed that she told Bohac that telecopying "would not do any good because it would merely be a copy and not the original and two copies as required by our Aug. 26, 1987 decision."

Gilmore sent a telecopy to Robert McCarthy, a Reno attorney, who delivered it to the BLM at 11:15 A.M., September 28. The mailed original and copies of the signed lease form were received by the Reno office the next day, September 29. On that day, BLM informed Gilmore that his offer was rejected.

Gilmore appealed the decision, and on Jan. 26, 1989, the IBLA affirmed the BLM's rejection on the grounds that the telecopied lease offer did not bear a personal, handwritten signature as required by 43 CFR §3122.6-1(a) and §3102.4 (1986). Reed Gilmore (On Reconsideration), 107 IBLA 37 (1989). The IBLA concluded that Gilmore's "failure to submit the signed lease offer and stipulations within 30 days was a violation of a substantive rule that justified per se rejection of the offer." *Id.* at 45. The IBLA also concluded that it did not need to decide the facts of the disputed phone conversations on two grounds: (1) "[p]arties dealing with the Government are chargeable with knowledge of duly promulgated regulations" and therefore Gilmore "knew that the law required his lease offer to be returned to BLM within 30 days and could not have justifiably relied on any possible misstatement by Woodin"; and (2) assuming that Dawson promised to consider the telecopied form, "the only commitment made by BLM was to consider whether the telecopied lease offer constituted a proper lease offer," which BLM did before rejecting it. *Id.* at 45-46.

Gilmore sought judicial review and the United States District Court for the District of Nevada summarily affirmed the decision on Sept. 14, 1989. Gilmore filed a timely appeal to this court. . . .

DISCUSSION

For what would seem a minor detail to the uninitiated, there is an abundance of administrative decisions involving the requirement of a holographic signature on lease applications. Of particular significance to this case is *W. H. Gilmore*, 41 IBLA 25 (1979) (no apparent relation to appellant here) published prior to the regulations in effect in this case. *W. H. Gilmore*, who was the second priority applicant, protested the award of the lease to the first applicant who had used a rubber-stamped signature in his filing. The Board refused Gilmore's petition because the only pertinent regulation in effect at that time, 43 CFR §3102.6-1 (1979) coupled with a prior Board decision, clearly allowed rubber-stamped signatures. . . .

As the result of *W. H. Gilmore*, the BLM promptly amended the regulations. In June 1980, the BLM added 43 CFR §3102.4 which read in part, "[a]ll applications [and] the original offers . . . shall be holographically signed in ink by the potential lessee. . . . Machine or rubber stamped signatures shall not be used."

The BLM regulation . . . gave fair notice to all applications that failure to comply should result in denial of their application. Such is the case here. The telefaxed application submitted by the appellant was not holographic, and it was created by a machine — both violations of the plain language of the regulation. It was within the discretion of the Secretary not to depart from the regulation in this case.

While in this instance, denial produces a harsh result, a telefaxed signature is a machine-produced signature. It is the exact situation the amended regulations sought to address. . . .

The decision we reach here is compelled by the narrow scope of the court's review of agency decisions. Obviously the equities favor Gilmore, as he is guilty of no omission but use of the United States mails. Eight days for delivery of mail from Nebraska to Nevada far exceeds the time it should take. Indeed, the Pony Express could have covered the distance with time to spare.

Justice Holmes observed that citizens dealing with their government must turn square corners. *Rock Island, AK, and Louisiana Railway Co. v. United States*, 254 U.S. 141, 143 (1920). Gilmore turned all but the last millimeter, but that millimeter, whose traverse is jealously guarded by the BLM, was his undoing. Relief to Gilmore in this narrow case would expose BLM to no fraud or risk of fraud, as his bona fides are beyond question. If Gilmore and those other few luckless applicants whose documents are stored rather than delivered by the Postal Service are to get any relief, it must come at the hands of the BLM. As shown by this case, those hands are more iron than velvet. We can only suggest to BLM that the body politic would not be put at risk by the granting of relief in these narrow and rare situations.

Affirmed.

NOTES

1. What is the purpose of administrative law? Is it to prevent decisions like that in Gilmore v. Lujan? Or, if it cannot do that, is its function to provide a legal remedy to people like Gilmore?

2. What do you make of the need to turn "square corners" when dealing with the government? The approach suggests a rigid application of the bureaucratic process. Should this always be the case? For example, should judges take into account the "manifest injustice" of the result? See Thomas Jefferson University v. Shalala, 512 U.S. 504, 529 (1994) (Thomas, J., dissenting, joined by Stevens, O'Connor, and Ginsburg, JJ.) ("Although '[m]en must turn square corners when they deal with the Government,' Rock Island, A. & L.R. Co. v. United States, 254 U.S. 141, 143 (1920) (Holmes, J.), the manifest injustice of the Court's result should be apparent."). Given these tensions between the approaches, what should be the general rule in the context of administrative action, "square corners" or "manifest injustice"?

3. Should the need for "square corners" also apply to the government? See Heckler v. Community Health Services of Crawford Cty., Inc., 467 U.S. 51, 61, n.13 (1984) ("It is no less good morals and good law that the Government should turn square corners in dealing with the people than that the people should turn square corners in dealing with their government."). What exactly would this mean in practice? Can, for example, the government be required to make payments in violation of congressional appropriations where it failed to turn "square corners"?

Kenneth F. Warren

ADMINISTRATIVE LAW IN THE POLITICAL SYSTEM*

16-17 (5th ed. 2011)

Broadly speaking, administrative law deals with (1) the ways in which power is transferred from legislative bodies to administrative agencies, (2) how administrative agencies use power, and (3) how the actions taken by administrative agencies are reviewed by the courts. More specifically, administrative law is concerned with the legal developments which have so dramatically increased the power and scope of the administrative branch. The law-making (technically, quasi-legislative or rule-making) and judicial (technically, quasi-judicial or order-making) powers, which have been delegated to administrators by the legislative branch at both the national and state levels, have created an extremely powerful administrative branch, thus changing the meaning we have traditionally attributed to the separation of powers doctrine.

---

* Reprinted by permission. Copyright © 2011 Westview Press, a member of the Perseus Books Group.

NOTES

1. The primary purpose of administrative law is to keep administrative powers within their legal bounds and to protect individuals against abuse of those powers. As such it may be defined as the branch of the law that controls the administrative operations of government. It sets forth the powers that may be exercised by administrative agencies, lays down the principles governing the exercise of those powers, and provides legal remedies to those aggrieved by administrative action. This definition divides administrative law into three parts:

(1) the powers vested in administrative agencies;
(2) the requirements imposed by law upon the exercise of those powers; and
(3) remedies against unlawful administrative action.

2. A major part of the administrative law course is devoted to administrative procedure. This is a natural reflection of growing concern with the procedural aspects of administrative action. This concern is a recent development. At the turn of the last century, administrative law was divided into the subjects of powers and remedies. Administrative law was thought of as "that part of the public law which fixes the organization and determines the competence of the administrative authorities, and indicates to the individual remedies for the violation of his rights." 1 Goodnow, Comparative Administrative Law 8-9 (1893). Delegation of authority and judicial review alone were stressed. More recently there has come the realization that of equal, if not greater, importance is the exercise of administrative power. With this realization has come the emphasis on procedural safeguards to ensure the proper exercise of administrative authority — an emphasis that found legislative articulation in the Federal Administrative Procedure Act (APA) of 1946, a law laying down the basic procedures that must be followed by federal agencies. (5 U.S.C. §§551-559, 701-706, 1305, 3105, 3344, 5362, 7521.) The APA is now the foundation of federal administrative law. Pertinent portions of it are contained throughout this book. For the student of administrative law, understanding the APA provisions is as important as understanding the Uniform Commercial Code provisions for students of commercial law.

3. Administrative procedure legislation has also been enacted in the states. The state laws have, in the main, been based on the Model State Administrative Procedure Act (Model Act) approved by the American Bar Association and the National Conference of Commissioners on Uniform State Laws in 1946. A Revised Model State Act was approved in 1961, and a newer Model Act in 1981. Though acceptance of the Model Act was slow at first (with only five states adopting it by 1959), the Act now serves as the basis of administrative procedure legislation in twenty-seven states and the District of Columbia. In addition, eleven states, including the District of Columbia, have enacted APAs based upon the 1981 revision and twenty others have also enacted administrative procedure legislation.

B ADMINISTRATIVE AGENCIES

Federal Administrative Procedure Act

5 U.S.C. §551 (1946)

§ 551. Definitions

For the purpose of this subchapter—

(1) "Agency" means each authority of the Government of the United States, whether or not it is within or subject to review by another agency, but does not include—

(A) the Congress;

(B) the courts of the United States;

(C) the governments of the territories or possessions of the United States;

(D) the government of the District of Columbia.

NOTES

1. Virtually every administrative law case arises out of a controversy between a private party and an administrative agency. What is an administrative agency under the APA definition? Is the APA definition too inclusive for purposes of administrative law? Consider that the legislative history of the APA indicates that Congress "wanted to avoid a formalistic definition of 'agency' that might exclude any authority within the executive branch that should appropriately be subject to" its requirements. Armstrong v. Bush, 924 F.2d 282, 289 (D.C. Cir. 1991).

2. Are all federal governmental acts subjected to APA requirements, except those included within the four specific exceptions contained in §551(1)?

3. What about action of the President? Is the President an agency within the meaning of the APA? See Franklin v. Massachusetts, 505 U.S. 788 (1992) (holding that the President is not an agency under the APA); Meyer v. Bush, 981 F.2d 1288, 1297 (D.C. Cir. 1993) (holding that a presidential task force was not an agency because it lacked substantial independent authority).

The definition of an agency matters for purposes of the application of the Administrative Procedure Act. Is there also a constitutional dimension to the definition?

DEPARTMENT OF TRANSPORTATION v. ASSOCIATION OF AMERICAN RAILROADS

575 U.S. 43 (2015)

Justice Kennedy delivered the opinion of the Court.

In 1970, Congress created the National Railroad Passenger Corporation, most often known as Amtrak. Later, Congress granted Amtrak and the Federal

Railroad Administration (FRA) joint authority to issue "metrics and standards" that address the performance and scheduling of passenger railroad services. Alleging that the metrics and standards have substantial and adverse effects upon its members' freight services, respondent — the Association of American Railroads — filed this suit to challenge their validity. The defendants below, petitioners here, are the Department of Transportation, the FRA, and two individuals sued in their official capacity.

Respondent alleges the metrics and standards must be invalidated on the ground that Amtrak is a private entity and it was therefore unconstitutional for Congress to allow and direct it to exercise joint authority in their issuance. . . .

. . .

I

A

Amtrak is a corporation established and authorized by a detailed federal statute enacted by Congress for no less a purpose than to preserve passenger services and routes on our Nation's railroads. . . . Congress recognized that Amtrak, of necessity, must rely for most of its operations on track systems owned by the freight railroads. So, as a condition of relief from their common-carrier duties, Congress required freight railroads to allow Amtrak to use their tracks and facilities at rates agreed to by the parties — or in the event of disagreement to be set by the Interstate Commerce Commission (ICC). See 45 U.S.C. §§561, 562 (1970 ed.). The Surface Transportation Board (STB) now occupies the dispute-resolution role originally assigned to the ICC. See 49 U.S.C. §24308(a) (2012 ed.). Since 1973, Amtrak has received a statutory preference over freight transportation in using rail lines, junctions, and crossings. See §24308(c).

The metrics and standards at issue here are the result of a further and more recent enactment. Concerned by poor service, unreliability, and delays resulting from freight traffic congestion, Congress passed the Passenger Rail Investment and Improvement Act (PRIIA) in 2008. See 122 Stat. 4907. Section 207(a) of the PRIIA provides for the creation of the metrics and standards:

> "Within 180 days after the date of enactment of this Act, the Federal Railroad Administration and Amtrak shall jointly, in consultation with the Surface Transportation Board, rail carriers over whose rail lines Amtrak trains operate, States, Amtrak employees, nonprofit employee organizations representing Amtrak employees, and groups representing Amtrak passengers, as appropriate, develop new or improve existing metrics and minimum standards for measuring the performance and service quality of intercity passenger train operations, including cost recovery, on-time performance and minutes of delay, ridership, on-board services, stations, facilities, equipment, and other services." Id., at 4916.

Section 207(d) of the PRIIA further provides:

> "If the development of the metrics and standards is not completed within the 180-day period required by subsection (a), any party involved in the development of those standards may petition the Surface Transportation Board to appoint an arbitrator to assist the parties in resolving their disputes through binding arbitration." Id., at 4917.

The PRIIA specifies that the metrics and standards created under §207(a) are to be used for a variety of purposes. Section 207(b) requires the FRA to "publish a quarterly report on the performance and service quality of intercity passenger train operations" addressing the specific elements to be measured by the metrics and standards. Id., at 4916-4917. Section 207(c) provides that, "[t]o the extent practicable, Amtrak and its host rail carriers shall incorporate the metrics and standards developed under subsection (a) into their access and service agreements." Id., at 4917. And §222(a) obliges Amtrak, within one year after the metrics and standards are established, to "develop and implement a plan to improve on-board service pursuant to the metrics and standards for such service developed under [§207(a)]." Id., at 4932.

Under §213(a) of the PRIIA, the metrics and standards also may play a role in prompting investigations by the STB and in subsequent enforcement actions. For instance, "[i]f the on-time performance of any intercity passenger train averages less than 80 percent for any 2 consecutive calendar quarters," the STB may initiate an investigation "to determine whether and to what extent delays . . . are due to causes that could reasonably be addressed . . . by Amtrak or other intercity passenger rail operators." Id., at 4925-4926. While conducting an investigation under §213(a), the STB "has authority to review the accuracy of the train performance data and the extent to which scheduling and congestion contribute to delays" and shall "obtain information from all parties involved and identify reasonable measures and make recommendations to improve the service, quality, and on-time performance of the train." Id., at 4926. Following an investigation, the STB may award damages if it "determines that delays or failures to achieve minimum standards . . . are attributable to a rail carrier's failure to provide preference to Amtrak over freight transportation." Ibid. The STB is further empowered to "order the host rail carrier to remit" damages "to Amtrak or to an entity for which Amtrak operates intercity passenger rail service." Ibid.

B

In March 2009, Amtrak and the FRA published a notice in the Federal Register inviting comments on a draft version of the metrics and standards. App. 75-76. The final version of the metrics and standards was issued jointly by Amtrak and the FRA in May 2010. Id., at 129-144. The metrics and standards address, among other matters, Amtrak's financial performance, its scores on consumer satisfaction surveys, and the percentage of passenger-trips to and from underserved communities.

Of most importance for this case, the metrics and standards also address Amtrak's on-time performance and train delays caused by host railroads. The standards associated with the on-time performance metrics require on-time performance by Amtrak trains at least 80% to 95% of the time for each route, depending on the route and year. Id., at 133-135. With respect to "host-responsible delays" — that is to say, delays attributed to the railroads along which Amtrak trains travel — the metrics and standards provide that "[d]elays must not be more than 900 minutes per 10,000 Train-Miles." Id., at 138. Amtrak conductors determine responsibility for particular delays. Ibid., n.23.

. . .

II

In holding that Congress may not delegate to Amtrak the joint authority to issue the metrics and standards — authority it described as "regulatory power," ibid. — the Court of Appeals concluded Amtrak is a private entity for purposes of determining its status when considering the constitutionality of its actions in the instant dispute. That court's analysis treated as controlling Congress' statutory command that Amtrak "'is not a department, agency, or instrumentality of the United States Government.'" Id., at 675 (quoting 49 U.S.C. §24301(a)(3)). The Court of Appeals also relied on Congress' pronouncement that Amtrak "'shall be operated and managed as a for-profit corporation.'" 721 F.3d, at 675 (quoting §24301(a)(2)); see also id., at 677 ("Though the federal government's involvement in Amtrak is considerable, Congress has both designated it a private corporation and instructed that it be managed so as to maximize profit. In deciding Amtrak's status for purposes of congressional delegations, these declarations are dispositive"). Proceeding from this premise, the Court of Appeals concluded it was impermissible for Congress to "delegate regulatory authority to a private entity." Id., at 670; see also ibid. (holding Carter v. Carter Coal Co., 298 U.S. 238, 56 S. Ct. 855, 80 L. Ed. 1160 (1936), prohibits any such delegation of authority).

That premise, however, was erroneous. Congressional pronouncements, though instructive as to matters within Congress' authority to address, see, e.g., United States ex rel. Totten v. Bombardier Corp., 380 F.3d 488, 491-492 (C.A.D.C. 2004) (Roberts, J.), are not dispositive of Amtrak's status as a governmental entity for purposes of separation of powers analysis under the Constitution. And an independent inquiry into Amtrak's status under the Constitution reveals the Court of Appeals' premise was flawed.

It is appropriate to begin the analysis with Amtrak's ownership and corporate structure. The Secretary of Transportation holds all of Amtrak's preferred stock and most of its common stock. Amtrak's Board of Directors is composed of nine members, one of whom is the Secretary of Transportation. Seven other Board members are appointed by the President and confirmed by the Senate. 49 U.S.C. §24302(a)(1). These eight Board members, in turn, select Amtrak's president. §24302(a)(1)(B); §24303(a). Amtrak's Board members are subject to salary limits set by Congress, §24303(b); and the Executive Branch has concluded that all appointed Board members are removable by the President without cause, see 27 Op. Atty. Gen. 163 (2003).

Under further statutory provisions, Amtrak's Board members must possess certain qualifications. Congress has directed that the President make appointments based on an individual's prior experience in the transportation industry, §24302(a)(1)(C), and has provided that not more than five of the seven appointed Board members be from the same political party, §24302(a)(3). In selecting

Amtrak's Board members, moreover, the President must consult with leaders of both parties in both Houses of Congress in order to "provide adequate and balanced representation of the major geographic regions of the United States served by Amtrak." §24302(a)(2).

In addition to controlling Amtrak's stock and Board of Directors the political branches exercise substantial, statutorily mandated supervision over Amtrak's priorities and operations. Amtrak must submit numerous annual reports to Congress and the President, detailing such information as route-specific ridership and on-time performance. §24315. The Freedom of Information Act applies to Amtrak in any year in which it receives a federal subsidy, 5 U.S.C. §552, which thus far has been every year of its existence. Pursuant to its status under the Inspector General Act of 1978 as a "'designated Federal entity,'" 5 U.S.C. App. §8G(a)(2), p. 521, Amtrak must maintain an inspector general, much like governmental agencies such as the Federal Communications Commission and the Securities and Exchange Commission. Furthermore, Congress conducts frequent oversight hearings into Amtrak's budget, routes, and prices. . . .

It is significant that, rather than advancing its own private economic interests, Amtrak is required to pursue numerous, additional goals defined by statute. To take a few examples: Amtrak must "provide efficient and effective intercity passenger rail mobility," 49 U.S.C. §24101(b); "minimize Government subsidies," §24101(d); provide reduced fares to the disabled and elderly, §24307(a); and ensure mobility in times of national disaster, §24101(c)(9).

In addition to directing Amtrak to serve these broad public objectives, Congress has mandated certain aspects of Amtrak's day-to-day operations. Amtrak must maintain a route between Louisiana and Florida. §24101(c)(6). When making improvements to the Northeast corridor, Amtrak must apply seven considerations in a specified order of priority. §24902(b). And when Amtrak purchases materials worth more than $1 million, these materials must be mined or produced in the United States, or manufactured substantially from components that are mined, produced, or manufactured in the United States, unless the Secretary of Transportation grants an exemption. §24305(f).

Finally, Amtrak is also dependent on federal financial support. In its first 43 years of operation, Amtrak has received more than $41 billion in federal subsidies. In recent years these subsidies have exceeded $1 billion annually. See Brief for Petitioners 5, and n.2, 46.

Given the combination of these unique features and its significant ties to the Government, Amtrak is not an autonomous private enterprise. Among other important considerations, its priorities, operations, and decisions are extensively supervised and substantially funded by the political branches. A majority of its Board is appointed by the President and confirmed by the Senate and is understood by the Executive to be removable by the President at will. Amtrak was created by the Government, is controlled by the Government, and operates for the Government's benefit. Thus, in its joint issuance of the metrics and standards with the FRA, Amtrak acted as a governmental entity for purposes of the Constitution's separation of powers provisions. And that exercise of governmental power must be consistent with the design and requirements of the Constitution, including those provisions relating to the separation of powers.

Respondent urges that Amtrak cannot be deemed a governmental entity in this respect. Like the Court of Appeals, it relies principally on the statutory directives that Amtrak "shall be operated and managed as a for profit corporation" and "is not a department, agency, or instrumentality of the United States Government." §§24301(a)(2)-(3). In light of that statutory language, respondent asserts, Amtrak cannot exercise the joint authority entrusted to it and the FRA by §207(a).

[Ed. Note: The Court describes another case, Lebron v. Nat'l Railroad Passenger Corp., 513 U.S. 374 (1995), in which it held that Amtrak was a governmental entity for the purpose of determining the First Amendment rights of citizens affected by Amtrak's actions. On this basis, the Court reasons that the federal government's control and supervision over Amtrak prevails over Congress' description of Amtrak's status.]

. . . Treating Amtrak as governmental for these purposes, moreover, is not an unbridled grant of authority to an unaccountable actor. The political branches created Amtrak, control its Board, define its mission, specify many of its day-to-day operations, have imposed substantial transparency and accountability mechanisms, and, for all practical purposes, set and supervise its annual budget. Accordingly, the Court holds that Amtrak is a governmental entity, not a private one, for purposes of determining the constitutional issues presented in this case.

. . .

It is so ordered.

NOTES

1. Amtrak is not unique. Congress has created other entities that have regulatory responsibilities yet are excluded from the definition of "agency" of the U.S. government. See 15 U.S.C. §7211(b) ("The [Public Company Accounting Oversight] Board shall not be an agency or establishment of the United States Government, and, except as otherwise provided in this Act, shall be subject to, and have all the powers conferred upon a nonprofit corporation by, the District of Columbia Nonprofit Corporation Act."). The PCAOB has significant regulatory responsibility, as will be discussed later in this chapter. What is the reason for the creation of these types of entities? Why doesn't Congress simply create a new government agency? Justice Alito in his concurring opinion seemed concerned with stealth regulation by Congress and concomitant concerns over accountability. See 575 U.S. at 57 ("One way the Government can regulate without accountability is by passing off a Government operation as an independent private concern.").

2. The Court did not, for constitutional purposes, give definitive weight to the decision by Congress that Amtrak was not a department, agency, or instrumentality of the U.S. government. What factors seemed to matter most to the

Court? See, e.g., United States v. Ackerman, 831 F.3d 1292, 1297-1298 (10th Cir. 2016) (holding that an organization was a federal entity given, *inter alia*, the origin of its funding and mandates in statute, statutory control over its day-to-day operations, and the significant presence of government officials on its board); Jefferson Cmty. Health Care Ctrs., Inc. v. Jefferson Par. Gov't, No. 16-12910, 2016 U.S. Dist. LEXIS 98117, at *46-47 (E.D. La. July 26, 2016) (holding that plaintiff was unlikely to prevail on its argument for treatment as a federal entity despite its reliance on federal funds and being subject to substantial federal oversight), rev'd in part on other grounds, 849 F.3d 615 (5th Cir. 2017).

3. What are the consequences of this decision? What requirements apply and what requirements do not apply to Amtrak? For a more detailed discussion of the implications of this decision, see note 5, infra at 120-121.

4. The finding that Amtrak was "a federal actor or instrumentality" and not a private entity left unanswered a raft of additional issues. On remand, for example, the Court noted that the designation of the president of Amtrak by the board of directors had been challenged under the Appointments Clause, a provision that we will address later in this chapter. To the extent the president is an officer, but not an inferior officer, appointment rests with the President and requires advice and consent of the Senate. Moreover, even assuming the president is an inferior officer, appointment by the board is possible only if the board is considered the "Head of a Department." A separate issue exists as to whether Amtrak constitutes a "Department" of the government for constitutional purposes.

5. With respect to Amtrak, what do you make of the "for profit" status of the entity? Does this raise any concerns with respect to Amtrak's regulatory responsibilities? Other "for profit" entities with regulatory responsibilities exist in our system of government. Stock exchanges are an example. They have the ability to adopt rules and regulations and to discipline companies that violate their listing standards. The NYSE converted to a for-profit company in 2005. How might this case apply to that entity?

C TYPES OF AGENCIES

Administrative agencies have been a part of the U.S. system of government since the very beginning. The consistency of their presence, however, masks a significant evolution in their duties and responsibilities. Congress often adopts legislation that amounts to a template and assigns to the agencies the authority to develop the specific requirements. Moreover, in an era when issues addressed by the government have become increasingly complex, the responsibilities of the administrative agencies have grown significantly.

Despite their longstanding nature, administrative agencies continue to raise unique constitutional questions. As will be developed in this chapter, there is a category of administrative agency that has been deliberately designed to be more "independent" of the President. The constitutional basis for these "independent" agencies has shifted over time and is not entirely resolved. Similarly, efforts to create new types of "independent" agencies have not been met with judicial approval, as the *PCAOB* case excerpted later in this chapter shows.

NOTES

1. Administrative agencies are as old as American government itself. The very first session of the first Congress enacted three statutes conferring important administrative powers. Two of them were antecedents of statutes now administered by the Bureau of Customs in the Treasury Department, and the third initiated the program of benefits now operated by the Veterans Administration. The latter statute provided for pensions to be paid to disabled veterans "under such regulations as the President of the United States may direct" — the first express delegation of rulemaking powers by Congress. Under the other two laws, port collectors were vested with adjudicatory authority, including licensing powers, and the power to decide the amount of duties payable.

2. The delegations made by the first Congress were repeated by later legislatures. The Interstate Commerce Commission (ICC) was created in 1887 — the date usually considered the beginning of our administrative law. Well before the ICC, the courts recognized the existence of agencies vested with legislative and judicial-type powers. In 1813, the Supreme Court dealt with the question of whether legislative authority could be transferred by Congress and, twelve years later, Chief Justice Marshall acknowledged that Congress could delegate rulemaking power. Before the ICC was given comparable authority, the federal courts upheld the establishment of agencies with the legislative power to fix rates. Other pre-ICC cases recognized the administrative exercise of "quasi-judicial functions." Even the form of independent commission was not original in the ICC. The first federal independent commission was created in 1822, and similar commissions existed in the states before the ICC was established.

3. The establishment of the ICC was, nevertheless, a quantum step forward in the development of American administrative law. With the ICC, the modern instrument of administrative regulation was first created. To enable the new commission to perform its specialized tasks, it was vested with broad powers of rulemaking and adjudication, as well as the more traditional types of executive power. Extensive authority that was later conferred made the ICC a virtual combined executive, Congress, and Supreme Court over the railroad industry. The ICC has been the archetype of the modern administrative agency. It has served as the model for a host of federal and state agencies, patterned in their essentials on the first federal regulatory commission. In countless instances, specialization to deal with particularized problems of administration has been provided in the same way it was in 1887. The result has been a proliferation of federal and state agencies endowed with the power to determine, by rule or by decision, private rights and obligations.

Kenneth F. Warren

ADMINISTRATIVE LAW IN THE POLITICAL SYSTEM

*40-41 (5th ed. 2011)**

According to James Q. Wilson, . . . there were four periods in our history when the political climate favored the rapid growth of regulatory agencies. . . . He asserted that each wave

> was characterized by progressive or liberal Presidents in office (Cleveland, T. R. Roosevelt, Wilson, F. D. Roosevelt, Johnson); one was a period of national crisis (the 1930s); three were periods when the President enjoyed extraordinary majorities of his own party in both houses of Congress (1914-1916, 1932-1940, and 1964-1968); and only the first preceded the emergence of the national mass media of communication. These facts are important because of the special difficulty of passing any genuinely regulatory legislation. . . . Without specific political circumstances — a crisis, a scandal, extraordinary majorities, an especially vigorous President, the support of the media — the normal barriers to legislative innovation . . . may prove insuperable.

These periods are sketched in Table [1.1]. I have added to Table [1.1] a fifth stage, the "deregulation stage," which took place mostly during the Reagan and George H. W. Bush years, reflecting the sentiment that bureaucracy is "too fat and even illegitimate."

TABLE [1.1]**

JAMES Q. WILSON'S FOUR PERIODS OF BUREAUCRATIC GROWTH

Period	Focus	Key Acts Passed
1887-90	Control monopolies and rates	Interstate Commerce Act Sherman Act
1906-15	Regulate product quality	Pure Food and Drug Act Meat Inspection Act Federal Trade Commission Act Clayton Act
1930-40	Extend regulation to cover various socioeconomic areas, especially new technologies	Food, Drug, and Cosmetic Act Public Utility Holding Company Act National Labor Relations Act Securities and Exchange Act Natural Gas Act

---

* Reprinted by permission. Copyright © 2011 Westview Press, a member of the Perseus Books Group.

** This table is based on Wilson, The Rise of the Bureaucratic State, The Public Interest 41 (1975), reprinted in F. Rourke, Bureaucratic Power in National Policy Making 125-148 (4th ed. 1986), but table categories and descriptions were created and supplemented by K. F. Warren.

Period	Focus	Key Acts Passed
1960-79	Expand regulation to make America a cleaner, healthier safer, and fairer place to live and work	Economic Opportunity Act Civil Rights Acts of 1960, 1964, and 1968 National Environmental Policy Act Clean Air Act Occupational Safety and Health Act
1978-93	Deregulation movement as a reaction to bureaucratic overexpansion	Paperwork Reduction Act Air Deregulation Act Radio and TV deregulation Banking deregulation
1993-present	Deregulation, reregulation, or more regulation	Communication Decency Act of 1996 Telecommunications Act of 1996 USA Patriot Act of 2001

REGULATORY PROGRAM OF THE UNITED STATES GOVERNMENT

xiv, xviii, Apr. 1, 1985 through Mar. 31, 1986

Federal regulations serve a variety of functions, and generalizations concerning them can be so abstract that their implications may be difficult to discern. Nonetheless, by sorting regulatory programs according to the functions they serve, similar programs at different agencies can be analyzed and compared and general principles can be established.

One of the most important regulatory functions is the protection of public health and safety and the environment. The Environmental Protection Agency and the Occupational Safety and Health Administration of the Department of Labor regulate to these ends. The Food and Drug Administration of the Department of Health and Human Services and various elements of the Departments of Agriculture and Transportation also issue regulations to protect public health and safety and the environment. The intended benefits of these programs include improved health and longevity and a cleaner environment. The costs often take the form of higher costs to producers and higher prices to consumers for goods and services of all types. Virtually every production activity is affected in some way by Federal health, safety, and environmental regulations.

A second function of regulation is the direct control of commerce and trade, i.e., traditional "economic" regulation. This involves regulating entry, prices, production, or other aspects of business and industry — not for safety reasons, but for economic reasons. For the most part, the United States relies on free enterprise and competition in the marketplace to determine prices and production levels, although we use some generic (not industry-specific) regulation to encourage competition. Antitrust regulation is a good example; patent and trademark regulation is another. Generally, economic regulation of specific industries is justified, however, only where unregulated competition is not appropriate. For example, the local "public utility" industries — electricity, gas, and telephone service — are natural monopolies, and they have traditionally been regulated as such by the states. Other industries, especially in interstate transportation and communications, have long been regulated at the Federal level — usually by independent regulatory commissions. . . .

Economic regulation of industry is the oldest form of Federal regulatory activity, having originated with the establishment of the Interstate Commerce Commission (ICC) in 1887. A rationale for establishing the ICC was that the existence of a natural monopoly (the railroads) warranted government intervention, a rationale which — where it applies — still finds general acceptance today. Actions to deregulate transportation over the past decade have come about not because the natural monopoly rationale has been rejected, but because it came to be recognized that economic regulation was being applied to transportation modes that never were natural monopolies, such as airlines, trucks, and intercity buses, or that had since been subjected to effective competition from other modes, as railroads have been for much of their traffic. The most recent steps in this development were the passage of the Motor Carrier Act of 1980, the Staggers Rail Act of 1980, the Administration's bill to deregulate intercity buses in 1982, and the closing of the Civil Aeronautics Board on January 1, 1985.

For a detailed analysis of the paradigmatic shift toward deregulation and its causes, see Joseph D. Kearney & Thomas W. Merrill, The Great Transformation of Regulated Industries Law, 98 Colum. L. Rev. 1323 (1998).

NOTES

1. To the administrative lawyer, there are two principal kinds of governmental organ.

- **a.** Present-day administrative agencies are vested with authority to prescribe generally what shall or shall not be done in a given situation (just as legislatures do); to determine whether the law has been violated in particular cases and to proceed against the violators (just as prosecutors and courts do); to admit people to privileges not otherwise open to members of the public (as the Crown once could do); and even to impose fines and render what amount to money judgments. Agencies vested with these powers are usually called "regulatory agencies" because their activities impinge on private rights and regulate the manner in which those rights may be exercised. To administrative lawyers, this is the best-known type of agency; its prototype was the Interstate Commerce Commission, the first of an entirely new family of governmental bodies.

b. There is another group of agencies vested with the authority to dispense benefits for promoting social and economic welfare, such as pensions, disability and welfare grants, and government insurance. They exist at both the state and federal levels. The federal system of social welfare includes programs of old age, survivors, disability insurance, Medicare and Medicaid, aid to families with dependent children, supplementary security income, veterans' pensions and other benefits, and workers' compensation. The federal agencies that administer these programs are the Department of Health and Human Services, the Veterans Administration, and the Department of Labor.

2. Administrative lawyers have concentrated primarily on the regulatory agency — for the natural reason that it serves to restrict private rights. It is in this area, accordingly, that the law is more fully developed. An imposing edifice of formal administrative procedure has been constructed, patterned on the adversary procedure of the courtroom. When people speak of the judicialization of the administrative process, it is essentially the regulatory process to which they are referring.

3. Recent decades have, however, seen a substantial shift in the center of gravity toward the nonregulatory area. The welfare state has converted an ever-growing portion of the community into government clients. The Affordable Care Act represents perhaps the most recent example. Pub. L. No. 111-148, Mar. 23, 2010. Quantitatively, the work of the Department of Health and Human Services typically dwarfs that of a regulatory agency like the Federal Trade Commission.

4. Nonetheless, this should not understate the role of the traditional regulatory agencies. In the aftermath of the financial crisis of 2008, Congress adopted the Dodd-Frank Wall Street Reform and Consumer Protection Act, a law that consisted of 848 pages of statutory text. Pub. L. No. 111-203, 124 Stat. 1376 (July 21, 2010). By July 2013, this legislative total had been dwarfed by the actions of the relevant regulatory agencies such as the Securities and Exchange Commission, the Federal Reserve, and the Commodities Futures Trading Commission. Agencies had produced 13,789 pages of regulation (more than 15 million words). Moreover, this represented only 39 percent of the "required" rulemaking contained in the Act. See Davis Polk & Wardwell LLP, Dodd-Frank Progress Report, July 15, 2013.

D AGENCIES AND ACCOUNTABILITY

The growth of the bureaucracy, particularly since the Great Depression, has been nothing short of explosive. Moreover, Congress has delegated to the agencies broad regulatory authority, with few areas of social and economic policy exempt from some level of agency oversight. The role played by agencies raises serious issues of accountability. Who ensures that the unelected bureaucracy engages in a proper exercise of authority?

1. Agency Accountability and Congress

IMMIGRATION AND NATURALIZATION SERVICE v. CHADHA

462 U.S. 919 (1983)

CHIEF JUSTICE BURGER delivered the opinion of the Court.

I

Chadha is an East Indian who was born in Kenya and holds a British passport. He was lawfully admitted to the United States in 1966 on a nonimmigrant student visa. His visa expired on June 30, 1972. On October 11, 1973, the District Director of the Immigration and Naturalization Service ordered Chadha to show cause why he should not be deported for having "remained in the United States for a longer time than permitted." App. 6. Pursuant to §242(b) of the Immigration and Nationality Act (Act), 8 U.S.C. §1252(b), a deportation hearing was held before an Immigration Judge on January 11, 1974. Chadha conceded that he was deportable for overstaying his visa and the hearing was adjourned to enable him to file an application for suspension of deportation under §244(a)(1) of the Act, 8 U.S.C. §1254(a)(1). . . .

The June 25, 1974, order of the Immigration Judge suspending Chadha's deportation remained outstanding as a valid order for a year and a half. For reasons not disclosed by the record, Congress did not exercise the veto authority reserved to it under §244(c)(2) until the first session of the 94th Congress. This was the final session in which Congress, pursuant to §244(c)(2), could act to veto the Attorney General's determination that Chadha should not be deported. The session ended on December 19, 1975. 121 Cong. Rec. 42014, 42277 (1975). Absent congressional action, Chadha's deportation proceedings would have been canceled after this date and his status adjusted to that of a permanent resident alien. . . .

On December 12, 1975, Representative Eilberg, Chairman of the Judiciary Subcommittee on Immigration, Citizenship, and International Law, introduced a resolution opposing "the granting of permanent residence in the United States to [six] aliens," including Chadha. H. Res. 926, 94th Cong., 1st Sess.; 121 Cong Rec. 40247 (1975). . . .

The resolution was passed without debate or recorded vote. Since the House action was pursuant to §244(c)(2), the resolution was not treated as an Art. I legislative act; it was not submitted to the Senate or presented to the President for his action....

...

III

A

We turn now to the question whether action of one House of Congress under §244(c)(2) violates strictures of the Constitution....

Explicit and unambiguous provisions of the Constitution prescribe and define the respective functions of the Congress and of the Executive in the legislative process. Since the precise terms of those familiar provisions are critical to the resolution of these cases, we set them out verbatim. Article I provides:

> "All legislative Powers herein granted shall be vested in a Congress of the United States, which shall consist of a Senate *and* House of Representatives." Art. I, §1. (Emphasis added.)
>
> "Every Bill which shall have passed the House of Representatives *and* the Senate, *shall*, before it becomes a law, be presented to the President of the United States ...." Art. I, §7, cl. 2. (Emphasis added.)
>
> "*Every* Order, Resolution, or Vote to which the Concurrence of the Senate and House of Representatives may be necessary (except on a question of Adjournment) *shall be* presented to the President of the United States; and before the Same shall take Effect, *shall be* approved by him, or being disapproved by him, *shall be* repassed by two thirds of the Senate and House of Representatives, according to the Rules and Limitations prescribed in the Case of a Bill." Art. I, §7, cl. 3. (Emphasis added.)

These provisions of Art. I are integral parts of the constitutional design for the separation of powers....

B. The Presentment Clauses

The records of the Constitutional Convention reveal that the requirement that all legislation be presented to the President before becoming law was uniformly accepted by the Framers. Presentment to the President and the Presidential veto were considered so imperative that the draftsmen took special pains to assure that these requirements could not be circumvented. During the final debate on Art. I, §7, cl. 2, James Madison expressed concern that it might easily be evaded by the simple expedient of calling a proposed law a "resolution" or "vote" rather than a "bill." 2 Farrand 301-302. As a consequence, Art. I, §7, cl. 3, *supra*, at 945-946, was added. 2 Farrand 304-305.

The decision to provide the President with a limited and qualified power to nullify proposed legislation by veto was based on the profound conviction of the Framers that the powers conferred on Congress were the powers to be most carefully circumscribed. It is beyond doubt that lawmaking was a power to be shared by both Houses and the President. . . .

The President's role in the lawmaking process also reflects the Framers' careful efforts to check whatever propensity a particular Congress might have to enact oppressive, improvident, or ill-considered measures. . . .

C. Bicameralism

The bicameral requirement of Art. I, §§1, 7, was of scarcely less concern to the Framers than was the Presidential veto and indeed the two concepts are interdependent. By providing that no law could take effect without the concurrence of the prescribed majority of the Members of both Houses, the Framers reemphasized their belief, already remarked upon in connection with the Presentment Clauses, that legislation should not be enacted unless it has been carefully and fully considered by the Nation's elected officials. . . .

However familiar, it is useful to recall that apart from their fear that special interests could be favored at the expense of public needs, the Framers were also concerned, although not of one mind, over the apprehensions of the smaller states. Those states feared a commonality of interest among the larger states would work to their disadvantage; representatives of the larger states, on the other hand, were skeptical of a legislature that could pass laws favoring a minority of the people. See 1 Farrand 176-177, 484-491. It need hardly be repeated here that the Great Compromise, under which one House was viewed as representing the people and the other the states, allayed the fears of both the large and small states.

We see therefore that the Framers were acutely conscious that the bicameral requirement and the Presentment Clauses would serve essential constitutional functions. The President's participation in the legislative process was to protect the Executive Branch from Congress and to protect the whole people from improvident laws. The division of the Congress into two distinctive bodies assures that the legislative power would be exercised only after opportunity for full study and debate in separate settings. The President's unilateral veto power, in turn, was limited by the power of two-thirds of both Houses of Congress to overrule a veto thereby precluding final arbitrary action of one person. See *id.*, at 99-104. It emerges clearly that the prescription for legislative action in Art. I, §§1, 7, represents the Framers' decision that the legislative power of the Federal Government be exercised in accord with a single, finely wrought and exhaustively considered, procedure.

IV

The Constitution sought to divide the delegated powers of the new Federal Government into three defined categories, Legislative, Executive, and Judicial, to assure, as nearly as possible, that each branch of government would confine itself to its assigned responsibility. The hydraulic pressure inherent within each of the separate Branches to exceed the outer limits of its power, even to accomplish desirable objectives, must be resisted.

Although not "hermetically" sealed from one another, *Buckley v. Valeo*, 424 U.S., at 121, the powers delegated to the three Branches are functionally identifiable. When any Branch acts, it is presumptively exercising the power the Constitution has delegated to it. When the Executive acts, he presumptively acts in an executive or administrative capacity as defined in Art. II. And when, as here, one House of Congress purports to act, it is presumptively acting within its assigned sphere.

Beginning with this presumption, we must nevertheless establish that the challenged action under §244(c)(2) is of the kind to which the procedural requirements of Art. I, §7, apply. Not every action taken by either House is subject to the bicameralism and presentment requirements of Art. I. See *infra*, at 955, and nn. 20, 21. Whether actions taken by either House are, in law and fact, an exercise of legislative power depends not on their form but upon "whether they contain matter which is properly to be regarded as legislative in its character and effect." S. Rep. No. 1335, 54th Cong., 2d Sess., 8 (1897).

Examination of the action taken here by one House pursuant to §244(c)(2) reveals that it was essentially legislative in purpose and effect. In purporting to exercise power defined in Art. I, §8, cl. 4, to "establish an uniform Rule of Naturalization," the House took action that had the purpose and effect of altering the legal rights, duties, and relations of persons, including the Attorney General, Executive Branch officials and Chadha, all outside the Legislative Branch. Section 244(c)(2) purports to authorize one House of Congress to require the Attorney General to deport an individual alien whose deportation otherwise would be canceled under §244. The one-House veto operated in these cases to overrule the Attorney General and mandate Chadha's deportation; absent the House action, Chadha would remain in the United States. Congress has *acted* and its action has altered Chadha's status.

The legislative character of the one-House veto in these cases is confirmed by the character of the congressional action it supplants. Neither the House of Representatives nor the Senate contends that, absent the veto provision in §244(c)(2), either of them, or both of them acting together, could effectively require the Attorney General to deport an alien once the Attorney General, in the exercise of legislatively delegated authority, had determined the alien should remain in the United States. Without the challenged provision in §244(c)(2), this could have been achieved, if at all, only by legislation requiring deportation. Similarly, a veto by one House of Congress under §244(c)(2) cannot be justified as an attempt at amending the standards set out in §244(a)(1), or as a repeal of §244 as applied to Chadha. Amendment and repeal of statutes, no less than enactment, must conform with Art. I.

The nature of the decision implemented by the one-House veto in these cases further manifests its legislative character. After long experience with the clumsy, time-consuming private bill procedure, Congress made a deliberate choice to delegate to the Executive Branch, and specifically to the Attorney General, the authority to allow deportable aliens to remain in this country in certain specified circumstances. It is not disputed that this choice to delegate authority is precisely the kind of decision that can be implemented only in accordance with the procedures set out in Art. I. Disagreement with the Attorney General's decision on Chadha's deportation — that is, Congress' decision to deport Chadha — no less than Congress' original choice to delegate to the Attorney General the authority to make that decision, involves determinations of policy that Congress can implement in only one way: bicameral passage followed by presentment to the President. Congress must abide by its delegation of authority until that delegation is legislatively altered or revoked.

Finally, we see that when the Framers intended to authorize either House of Congress to act alone and outside of its prescribed bicameral legislative role, they narrowly and precisely defined the procedure for such action. There are four provisions in the Constitution, explicit and unambiguous, by which one House may act alone with the unreviewable force of law, not subject to the President's veto:

- **(a)** The House of Representatives alone was given the power to initiate impeachments. Art. I, §2, cl. 5;
- **(b)** The Senate alone was given the power to conduct trials following impeachment on charges initiated by the House and to convict following trial. Art. I, §3, cl. 6;
- **(c)** The Senate alone was given final unreviewable power to approve or to disapprove Presidential appointments. Art. II, §2, cl. 2;
- **(d)** The Senate alone was given unreviewable power to ratify treaties negotiated by the President. Art. II, §2, cl. 2.

Clearly, when the Draftsmen sought to confer special powers on one House, independent of the other House, or of the President, they did so in explicit, unambiguous terms. These carefully defined exceptions from presentment and bicameralism underscore the difference between the legislative functions of Congress and other unilateral but important and binding one-House acts provided for in the Constitution. These exceptions are narrow, explicit, and separately justified; none of them authorize the action challenged here. On the contrary, they provide further support for the conclusion that congressional authority is not to be implied and for the conclusion that the veto provided for in §244(c)(2) is not authorized by the constitutional design of the powers of the Legislative Branch.

Since it is clear that the action by the House under §244(c)(2) was not within any of the express constitutional exceptions authorizing one House to act alone, and equally clear that it was an exercise of legislative power, that action was subject to the standards prescribed in Art. I. The bicameral requirement, the Presentment Clauses, the President's veto, and Congress' power to override a veto were intended to erect enduring checks on each Branch and to protect the people from the improvident exercise of power by mandating certain prescribed steps. To preserve those checks, and maintain the separation of powers, the carefully defined limits on the power of each Branch must not be eroded. To accomplish what has been attempted by one House of Congress in this case requires action in conformity with the express procedures of the Constitution's prescription for legislative action: passage by a majority of both Houses and presentment to the President.

The veto authorized by §244(c)(2) doubtless has been in many respects a convenient shortcut; the "sharing" with the Executive by Congress of its authority over aliens in this manner is, on its face, an appealing compromise. In purely practical terms, it is obviously easier for action to be taken by one House without submission to the President; but it is crystal clear from the records of the Convention, contemporaneous writings and debates, that the Framers ranked other values higher than efficiency. The records of the Convention and debates in the States preceding ratification underscore the common desire to define and limit the exercise of the newly created federal powers affecting the states and the people. There is unmistakable expression of a determination that legislation by the national Congress be a step-by-step, deliberate and deliberative process.

The choices we discern as having been made in the Constitutional Convention impose burdens on governmental processes that often seem clumsy, inefficient, even unworkable, but those hard choices were consciously made by men who had lived under a form of government that permitted arbitrary governmental acts to go unchecked. There is no support in the Constitution or decisions of this Court for the proposition that the cumbersomeness and delays often encountered in complying with explicit constitutional standards may be avoided, either by the Congress or by the President. With all the obvious flaws of delay, untidiness, and potential for abuse, we have not yet found a better way to preserve freedom than by making the exercise of power subject to the carefully crafted restraints spelled out in the Constitution.

V

We hold that the congressional veto provision in §244(c)(2) is severable from the Act and that it is unconstitutional. Accordingly, the judgment of the Court of Appeals is

Affirmed.

JUSTICE WHITE, dissenting.

Today the Court not only invalidates §244(c)(2) of the Immigration and Nationality Act, but also sounds the death knell for nearly 200 other statutory provisions in which Congress has reserved a "legislative veto." For this reason, the Court's decision is of surpassing importance....

The prominence of the legislative veto mechanism in our contemporary political system and its importance to Congress can hardly be overstated. It has become a central means by which Congress secures the accountability of executive and independent agencies. Without the legislative veto, Congress is faced with a Hobson's choice: either to refrain from delegating the necessary authority, leaving itself with a hopeless task of writing laws with the requisite specificity to cover endless special circumstances across the entire policy landscape, or in the alternative, to abdicate its law-making function to the Executive Branch and independent agencies. To choose the former leaves major national problems unresolved; to opt for the latter risks unaccountable policymaking by those not elected to fill that role. Accordingly, over the past five decades, the legislative veto has been placed in nearly 200 statutes. The device is known in every field of governmental concern: reorganization, budgets, foreign affairs, war powers, and regulation of trade, safety, energy, the environment, and the economy.

NOTES

1. The majority opinion makes the outcome seem almost obvious; yet, as Justice White notes in his dissent, there were over 200 statutes that included some type of congressional veto provision, whether unicameral or bicameral. Was Congress flouting the Constitution, or is there a serious argument that these veto provisions are in fact constitutional?

2. What is the consequence of this case with respect to agency accountability? What residual role does Congress have in the oversight process? Does it ensure agency accountability?

3. Congress could have avoided the issue in *Chadha* by not delegating the authority to suspend deportations to the Attorney General in the first place. Is that a practical way of solving the problem of agency accountability? How might this case affect the amount of authority Congress is willing to delegate to agencies?

4. Note the wide sweep of the *Chadha* opinion. Under it, is any room now left for use of the legislative veto technique?

5. The White dissent asserts that the Court's decision that all "lawmaking" must be shared by Congress and the President "ignores that legislative authority is routinely delegated to the executive branch, to the independent regulatory agencies." If congressional action under the legislative veto technique is "lawmaking" that must be shared by Congress and the President, why is the same not true of the agency action that the technique attempts to control? See, e.g., United States v. Seluk, 691 F. Supp. 525, 533 (D. Mass. 1988) (explaining that "[t]o read *Chadha* in this way . . . would be to disregard the Court's explicit recognition of Congress' authority to delegate portions of its power").

6. Despite *Chadha*, within three years of the decision Congress had passed bills containing 102 legislative veto provisions. Berns, Locke and the Legislative Principle, The Public Interest 147 (Summer 1990). Compare Executive Office Appropriations Act, 103 Stat. 790 (1991) (no funds from the appropriation "shall be used to implement, administer or enforce any regulation which has been disapproved pursuant to a [congressional] resolution"). See also Louis Fisher, The Legislative Veto: Invalidated, It Survives, 56 L. & Contemp. Probs. 273 (1993) (describing various "informal and nonstatutory" ways the legislature has used to circumvent *Chadha*'s holding.

7. What about the situation in the states? At the time *Chadha* was decided, at least twenty-eight states had adopted some form of legislative review of administrative rulemaking. In New Jersey, the legislature adopted a legislative veto in 1981, overriding the governor's veto. See General Assembly v. Byrne, 90 N.J. 376, 378-379, 448 A.2d 438 (1982) (striking down authority as a violation of separation of powers). In response to the ruling in *Byrne*, the state constitution was amended to provide:

> The Legislature may review any rule or regulation to determine if the rule or regulation is consistent with the intent of the Legislature as expressed in the language of the statute which the rule or regulation is intended to implement. Upon a finding that an existing or proposed rule or regulation is not consistent with legislative intent, the Legislature shall transmit this finding in the form of a concurrent resolution to the Governor and the head of the Executive Branch agency which promulgated, or plans to promulgate, the rule or regulation. The agency shall have 30 days to amend or withdraw the existing or proposed rule or regulation. If the agency does not amend or withdraw the existing or proposed rule or regulation, the Legislature may invalidate that rule or regulation, in whole or in part, or may prohibit that proposed rule or regulation, in whole or in part, from taking effect by a vote of a majority of the authorized membership of each House in favor of a concurrent resolution providing for invalidation or prohibition, as the case may be, of the rule or regulation.

N.J.S.A. Const. Art. 5, §4. What do you make of this provision? Will it significantly increase the role of the legislature in ensuring agency accountability? Consider the fact that the final amendment confers much narrower review powers than the New Jersey legislature had originally envisioned. See Commc'n Workers of America, AFL-CIO v. N.J. Civ. Serv. Comm'n, 191 A.3d 643, 660-61 (N.J. 2018). See also Jonathan L. Marshfield, Popular Regulation? State Constitutional Amendment and the Administrative State, 8 Belmont L. Rev. 342 (2021).

How does *Chadha* affect these state uses of the legislative veto?

2. Congressional Review Act

In the aftermath of the Supreme Court's decision in *Chadha*, Congress sought to retain an active role in the review of agency regulations. In doing so, however, it had to stay within the confines of the Supreme Court's analysis. The result was the Congressional Review Act, codified at 5 U.S.C. §801 et seq.

UNITED STATES v. NASIR

2013 U.S. Dist. LEXIS 138622 (E.D. Ky. Sept. 25, 2013)

JOSEPH M. HOOD, SENIOR DISTRICT JUDGE. This matter is before the Court on the Motion to Dismiss Indictment. . . .

Defendants argue that they cannot be held criminally liable for distribution of the synthetic cannabinoids JWH-122 and AM 2201, as analogues of the substance JWH-018 because JWH-018 was not properly scheduled as a controlled substance by the Drug Enforcement Administration (DEA). Specifically, Defendants concede that the DEA followed the proper procedures under 21 U.S.C. §811(h) for the emergency scheduling of JWH-018, but argue that the DEA's failure to comply with the Congressional Review Act (CRA) during that process meant that the rule scheduling JWH-018 did not go into effect. The Court agrees with the government that the DEA complied with the CRA when JWH-018 was scheduled. Accordingly, for the reasons fully described herein, Defendants' motion will be denied.

I. BACKGROUND

A. The Congressional Review Act

The Small Business Regulatory Enforcement Fairness Act of 1996, 5 U.S.C. §§801-808, more commonly known as the Congressional Review Act (CRA), "requires congressional review of agency regulations by directing agencies to submit the rule before it takes effect to the Comptroller General and each house of Congress." *Liesegang v. Sec'y of Veterans Affairs*, 312 F.3d 1368, 1373 (Fed. Cir. 2002). Regulations that qualify as a "major rule" are subject to additional conditions but for non-major rules, such as the one at issue, notice is all that is required.

B. The Controlled Substances Act

The Controlled Substances Act (CSA) classifies into five "schedules" those drugs and other substances that have a "potential for abuse." 21 U.S.C. §812(b)(1)-(5). Drugs in Schedule I are subject to the strictest controls, and violations involving Schedule I substances are subject to the most severe penalties because they are believed to present the most serious threat to public safety. *Touby v. United States*, 500 U.S. 160, 162, 111 S. Ct. 1752, 114 L. Ed. 2d 219 (1991). Schedule I drugs (1) have "a high potential for abuse," (2) do not have a "currently accepted medical use in treatment in the United States," and (3) lack "accepted safety for use . . . under medical supervision." 21 U.S.C. §812(b)(1).

The DEA may control a drug by adding it to one of the schedules, transferring it between schedules, or removing a drug from the schedules altogether. 21 U.S.C. §§802(5), 811(a). Typically, the DEA controls a substance with a potential for abuse by making "the findings prescribed by [21 U.S.C. §812(b)] for the schedule in which [the] drug is to be placed[.]" 21 U.S.C. §811(a)(1). Prior to initiating rulemaking, the DEA must gather "the necessary data" and request a scientific and medical evaluation and recommendation as to whether the drug should be controlled from the Secretary of the U.S. Department of Health and Human Services. 21 U.S.C. §811(b). The Secretary's recommendations are binding on the DEA with respect to scientific and medical matters. *Id.* Additionally, the DEA must also consider the eight factors listed in §811(c), and comply with the notice and hearing provisions of the Administrative Procedure Act (APA).

The Dangerous Drug Diversion Control Act of 1984, Pub. L. 98-73, 98 Stat. 1837, amended the CSA to add the temporary scheduling provision found at 21 U.S.C. §811(h) in order to make the process more responsive to the emerging "designer" drug market by providing a temporary scheduling provision, see *Touby*, 500 U.S. at 163.

To temporarily schedule a drug on an emergency basis pursuant to §811(h), the DEA must find that it is necessary to temporarily schedule a substance in schedule I "to avoid an imminent hazard to the public safety." 21 U.S.C. §811(h)(1). Instead of the eight factors required for permanent scheduling under the standard §811(c) rulemaking procedures, §811(h)(3) only requires the DEA to consider three factors before reaching an "imminent hazard" determination, specifically: (1) the drug's "history and current pattern of abuse"; (2) "[t]he scope, duration, and significance of abuse"; and (3) "[w]hat, if any, risk there is to the public health." In addition, the DEA considers "actual abuse, diversion from legitimate channels, and clandestine importation, manufacture, or distribution." *Id.* §811(c)(4), (5), (6); *id.* §811(h)(3). "Rather than comply with the APA notice-and-hearing provisions, the Attorney General need provide only a 30-day notice of the proposed scheduling in the Federal Register." *Touby*, 500 U.S. at 163. The DEA scheduled JWH-018 under this emergency scheduling authority. *See* Notice of Intent to Temporarily Schedule, 75 Fed. Reg. 71635, [DE 235-1 (DEA Letter to HHS); DE 235-2 (HHS Letter responding to DEA)].

On March 1, 2011, the DEA published a Final Order temporarily placing five synthetic cannabinoids in Schedule I on an emergency basis for a period of one year. *See* Final Order, 76 Fed. Reg. 11075 (Mar. 1, 2011); 21 U.S.C. §811(h). In connection with this Order, the DEA invoked an exception to the procedural requirements of the Congressional Review Act (CRA) in order to avoid any delay. *See* 5 U.S.C. §808(2).

On February 29, 2012, DEA published an order extending the temporary scheduling of JWH-018 to August 29, 2012, or until the final rulemaking proceedings were complete, whichever came first. *See* Final Rule, 77 Fed. Reg. 12201 (Feb. 29, 2012). On July 9, 2012, President Barack Obama signed the Synthetic Drug Abuse Prevention Act of 2012, Pub. L. No. 112-144, into law. The Act bans several specific synthetic cannabinoids (including JWH-018) and an entire class of "cannabimimetic agents" as Schedule I substances, thereby obviating the need for the DEA to publish a Final Rule.

The indictment in this matter covers activity involving JWH-018 analogues during the time span of fall, 2011 to October, 2012, in other words, during the time period that JWH-018 was included on Schedule I through the temporary scheduling authority described above.

II. ANALYSIS

The issue, Defendants argue, is whether "the DEA's failure to notify Congress and the Comptroller General before issuing the March 1, 2011 order adding JWH-018 to Schedule I pursuant to 21 U.S.C. §811(h) precludes prosecution of this defendant with regard to the alleged conspiracy to distribute JWH-122 and AM 2201, as analogues of JWH-018." [DE 219 at # 775.] To be clear, the defendants do not challenge the DEA's compliance with the temporary scheduling process set forth in 21 U.S.C. §811(h), only the DEA's compliance with the notifications required by the CRA.

The government contends, first, that the DEA did notify Congress and the Comptroller General prior to issuing the March 1, 2011 order as required by the CRA, under 5 U.S.C. §801(a)(1)(A); second, that the DEA properly invoked the "good cause" exemption to compliance with the CRA under 5 U.S.C. §808(2); and, finally, that the CRA, specifically, 5 U.S.C. §805, bars judicial review of an agency's compliance with the CRA. This Court agrees that the DEA clearly provided notice to Congress and the Comptroller General as required under the CRA, thus, this Court need not reach the government's remaining arguments.

A. Compliance with CRA

Pursuant to 5 U.S.C. §801(a)(1)(A), prior to taking effect, the federal agency promulgating the rule shall provide to each House of Congress and to the Comptroller General a report with: (1) a copy of the rule; (2) a concise general statement relating to the rule, including whether it is a major rule; and (3) the proposed effective date of the rule. 5 U.S.C. §801(a)(1)(A). The CRA makes distinction based on whether a rule is a "major" rule, as defined in 5 U.S.C. §804(2), or a "non-major" rule. Major rules are subjected to additional procedures and a delay in the effective date of the rule, as proscribed in the CRA. The DEA designated the rule at issue as a "non-major" rule. In the case of a "non-major" rule, as here, the rule "shall take effect as otherwise provided by law after submission to Congress." 5 U.S.C. §801(4).

On or about November 24, 2010, the DEA published its Notice of Intent, dated November 15, 2010, to place JWH-018 on Schedule I under the temporary scheduling provisions. The Notice of Intent included a statement regarding the CRA in which the DEA noted that this was not a major rule. Subsequently, the DEA published a correction on or about January 13, 2011 in which it clarified that the certification regarding the CRA was prematurely included in the Notice of Intent and struck that paragraph from the Notice of Intent. 76 Fed. Reg. 2287.

The DEA provided its Final Order, dated February 18, 2011, scheduling JWH-018 as a Schedule I drug for publication in the March 1, 2011, Federal Register. With respect to the CRA, the DEA stated that it was invoking the exception to the CRA under 5 U.S.C. §808(2) because it was making a good faith finding that "notice and public procedure [on the final rule] are impracticable, unnecessary, or contrary to the public interest." Notwithstanding the DEA's reliance on §808(2), and despite the Defendants' assertions, the DEA still went forward with the requirements of 5 U.S.C. §801(a)(1)(A). A copy of the rule, a concise statement and the proposed effective date, as required under the CRA, were provided to the President of the Senate on February 28, 2011 [DE 235-3]. The same information under the CRA was provided to the Speaker of the House of Representatives on February 28, 2011. [DE 235-4]; 157 CONG. REC. H2212 (Mar. 31, 2011). The U.S.

Government Accountability Office ("GAO") also received a copy on February 28, 2011. [DE 235-5]; also available at www.gao.gov/fedrules/165353.

As explained by defendants, "the DEA merely has to go through the perfunctory steps of presentation to Congress and the Comptroller General to place a substance on the list of controlled substances" [DE 219-1 at 9], and that is precisely what the DEA did in this instance.

This Court's research revealed that this challenge to the DEA's procedure for temporarily scheduling JWH-018 has only been made in one prior case, *United States v. Reece*, No. 6:12-cr-146 (W.D. La. 2012). The *Reece* Court determined that it was not necessary for the DEA to comply with the CRA, 5 U.S.C. §801; rather, the DEA's compliance with 21 U.S.C. §811(h) was sufficient. *United States v. Reece*, No. 6:12-cr-146, 2013 WL 3327913 *8-9 (W.D. La. July 1, 2013). The conclusion in *Reece* may be correct, however, this Court chooses to decide the issue on the most narrow ground possible. Since this Court finds that the DEA complied with the CRA, 5 U.S.C. §801, there is no need to determine whether the DEA was required to comply with the CRA or not.

. . .

C. Judicial Review of Compliance with CRA

It is beyond cavil that the DEA's temporary scheduling of JWH-018 under the CSA, pursuant to the procedure in 21 U.S.C. §811, is subject to judicial review. *Touby*, 500 U.S. at 168. However, in its Reply, the government argues that "[n]o determination, finding, action or omission under [the CRA] shall be subject to judicial review." 5 U.S.C. §805. The government does not argue, as Johnston suggests, that the scheduling of JWH-018 is not subject to review. Instead, this Court understands the United States' position to be that this Court may review the scheduling of JWH-018 by the DEA pursuant to §811 but the collateral aspect of the DEA's compliance, or lack thereof, with the CRA, i.e. the statute providing for notification to and any necessary action by Congress in reviewing the DEA's rulemaking, is not subject to judicial review under the plain language of §805.

Despite the plain language of the statute, at least two courts have concluded that judicial review is permitted to determine whether a rule has gone into effect. *Reece*, 2013 WL 3327913 at *8-9 (finding judicial review of temporary scheduling of JWH-018 proper, without significant discussion of 5 U.S.C. §805); *United States v. Southern Ind. Gas and Elec. Co.*, No. IP99-1962-C-M/S, 2002 WL 31427523 (S.D. Ind. October 24, 2002). In *Southern Indiana*, the Court found that the statute was ambiguous because it was susceptible to two meanings: (1) that "Congress did not intend for courts to have any judicial review of an agency's compliance with the CRA"; or (2) that Congress only intended to foreclose review of its own determinations, findings, actions or omissions made under the CRA after a rule is submitted. *Southern Ind.*, 2002 WL 31427523 at *5. In finding that §805 should be read in keeping with the second interpretation, the *Southern Indiana* court noted that the sponsors of the CRA had stated "the major rule determinations made by the Administrator of the Office of Information and Regulatory Affairs of the Office of Management and Budget are not subject to judicial review. Nor may a court review whether Congress complied with the congressional review procedures in this chapter" but had not indicated a similar prohibition for judicial review of agency compliance with the CRA. *Id.* (quoting 142 Cong. Rec. S3686 (daily ed. Apr. 18, 1996)) (joint statement of Senate sponsors).

Nonetheless, the majority of courts considering this issue have noted, at least in passing, that the CRA precludes any judicial review. *See Montanans for Multiple Use v. Barbouletos*, 568 F.3d 225, 229 (D.C. Cir. 2009) (noting that §805 denies courts the power to void rule on the basis of agency noncompliance with the CRA); *Via Christi Reg. Med. Ctr., Inc. v. Leavitt*, 509 F.3d 1259, 1271 n. 11 (10th Cir. 2007) (same); *United States v. Ameren Missouri*, No. 4:11-cv-77-RWS, 2012 WL 2821928, *3-4 (E.D. Mo. July 12, 2012) (noting that the court lacked jurisdiction to review CRA challenge); *Forsyth Memorial Hosp. Inc. v. Sebelius*, 667 F. Supp. 2d 143, 150 (D.D.C. 2009); *United States v. Amer. Elec. Power Serv. Corp.*, 218 F. Supp. 2d 931, 949 (S.D. Ohio 2002) (same).

This Court need not weigh in on this debate in this instance, however, because it is clear from the face of the documents presented and the arguments before it that the DEA complied with the provisions of the CRA. Thus, this Court need look no further — there is no determination, finding, action or omission for this Court to review. *See* 5 U.S.C. §805.

NOTES

1. The concept of congressional review was included in the Contract for America, an agenda developed by Republicans that contributed to the party's retaking control of the House of Representatives in 1994. They were a direct response to the ruling in *Chadha* and an attempt by Congress to reassert itself in the oversight of federal agencies.

2. As the case notes, it matters whether the rule at issue is a "major" rule. In the case of a major rule, the provision cannot become effective for at least sixty days. During that time period, Congress can act to repeal the rule. To facilitate rapid action, §802 limits the amount of debate that can occur in the Senate over any resolution designed to overturn an agency rule (although there are no parallel provisions with respect to debate in the House of Representatives).

3. What do you make of the discussion of judicial review? The CRA provides in a relatively unequivocal fashion that "[n]o determination, finding, action, or omission under this chapter shall be subject to judicial review." 5 U.S.C. §805. Yet the court suggests that some form of review may be preserved. See Kan. Natural Res. Coalition v. United States Dep't of Interior, 971 F.2d 1222 (10th Cir. 2020) (DOI rule not submitted to Congress could nonetheless be subject to judicial review by "the plain language of the CRA." Kansas Natural Resources Coalition February 2021 cert. petition asks "whether agency violations of the CRA's rule-submission requirements are subject to judicial review); Tugaw Ranches, L.L.C. v. United States Dep't of Interior, 362 F. Supp. 3d 879, 889 (D. Idaho 2019) ("blanket prohibition on all judicial review of *any* actions taken by anyone under the CRA . . . does not make sense, defeats the general purpose of the act, is contradicted by the legislative history, and ultimately leaves third parties without any remedy at law against violations of the act itself."). Assuming some form of review is preserved, when should courts examine compliance under the CRA? Could, for example, the categorization of a rule as not "major" be challenged? What implication would this have for administrative lawyers? See also Michael Cole, Interpreting the Congressional Review Act: Why the Courts Should Assert Judicial Review, Narrowly Construe "Substantially the Same," and Decline to Defer to Agencies Under Chevron, 70 Admin L. Rev. 53 (2018).

4. How effective do you think these provisions have been? At one time, the provision was generally viewed as ineffective. According to one study by the Congressional Research Quarterly, only forty-seven joint resolutions of disapproval were introduced between April 1996 and April 2008, with only one passing. During the same period, 47,540 rules, including 731 major rules, became effective. See Morton Rosenberg, Congressional Review of Agency Rulemaking: An Update and Assessment of the Congressional Review Act After a Decade, CRS Report for Congress, Order Code RL30116, May 8, 2008, at 6. That changed, however, in 2017. Congress in the first half of the year overturned fourteen agency rules. See Daniel Lyons, The Administrative Law of Deregulation: The Long Road for the Trump Administration to Undo Obama-Era Regulation, 61 Bos. B.J. 18 (2017). See also Paul Larkin, The Trump Administration and the Congressional Review Act, 16 Geo. J.L. & Pub. Pol'y 505, 506-508, 512 (2018) (praising early use of the CRA by the Trump administration to reform the administrative state and urging the CRA's continued use to pursue this goal).

5. Congress employed the CRA more frequently in 2017 as a response, in part, to the issuance of numerous "midnight regulations" or "midnight rules" by administrative agencies near the end of the Obama administration. Paul J. Larkin, Jr., Reawakening the Congressional Review Act, 41 Har. J.L. & Pub. Pol'y 187, 190-191 (2018). "Midnight regulations" are new rules issued at the end of an outgoing administration that will be followed by a new administration belonging to a different political party, such as during the "lame duck" period following a presidential election. Id. at 190 n. 6. Many criticize midnight rules on a wide variety of grounds, arguing, *inter alia*, that they represent the outgoing administration's attempt to extend its agenda beyond its term, that they reduce the administration's accountability for the impacts of the new rules, and that they contravene basic democratic principles when enacted after a presidential election. Jack M. Beerman, Midnight Rules: A Reform Agenda, 2 Mich. J. Env't & Admin. L. 285, 313 (2013). Others defend midnight rules, asserting that outgoing administrations can legitimately issue new rules until their terms end and that increased rulemaking at the end of an administration merely reflects that administration's rush to accomplish its agenda. Id. at 314.

6. As Brito and de Rugy describe, the Bush administration attempted to avoid the midnight regulation phenomenon. Jerry Brito & Veronique de Rugy, Midnight Regulations and Regulatory Review, 61 Admin. L. Rev. 163 (2009). The chief of staff, Joshua Bolten, sent a memorandum to agencies telling them that new regulations needed to be proposed by June 1 and adopted by November 1, with exceptions allowed only for extraordinary circumstances. The result? Agencies largely ignored the edict. The number of significant regulations issued by agencies in the last few months of President Bush's term differed little from the number issued for the prior administration. Why do you think this was the case? Strategically, if you were in charge of an agency, how might you avoid the impact of the CRA? How realistic are these strategies?

7. Given the use of the CRA in 2017, would it surprise you to know that legislation was introduced the same year to repeal the CRA? See S. 1140, 115th Cong., 1st Sess. (2017) ("Sunset the CRA and Restore American Protections Act of 2017" or the "SCRAP Act"). At the same time, would it also surprise you that legislation was proposed that would expand the sixty-day period to six months? H.R. 21, 115th Cong. (2017). Should Congress adopt either of these approaches? What would be the consequence of repeal of the CRA?

The effort to undo regulations when an administration changes is not limited to the federal government. Governors at the state level may want to undo efforts initiated by their predecessor. In the absence of a statutory framework like the CRA, the legal authority to do so may be less clear, depending upon the circumstances.

NEW ENERGY ECONOMY INC. v. MARTINEZ

247 P.3d 286 (N.M. 2011)

CHAVEZ, J. Does the State Records Administrator have a clear, indisputable, and mandatory duty to publish regulations filed with the State Records Center and Archives (Records Center) by the Environmental Improvement Board (EIB) and the Water Quality Control Commission (WQCC), despite a request by the Acting Secretary of the New Mexico Environment Department to delay publication for ninety days? We answer this question in the affirmative for four reasons. First, the powers and duties of the EIB, the WQCC, and the Records Center do not fall under either the Governor's or the Secretary's authority. Second, Executive Order 2011-001, relied upon by the acting secretary in his request to the records Center, did not apply to the subject regulations because the Executive Order applies only to regulations under the Governor's authority. Third, rules promulgated by the State Records Administrator mandate that regulations filed with the Records Center must be published within a specified time frame after being properly submitted by the issuing authority. Fourth, the Records Center erred in not publishing the regulations that the issuing authorities, the EIB, and the WQCC submitted for publication. Accordingly, we issued a writ of mandamus ordering the State Records Administrator to publish the regulations.

BACKGROUND

On December 6, 2010, after a two-year rule-making process, the EIB adopted a regulation pursuant to the Environmental Improvement Act, NMSA 1978,

§§74-1-1 to -15 (1971) (as amended through 2009), and the Air Quality Control Act, NMSA 1978, §§74-2-1 to -17 (1967) (as amended through 2009), to be codified as Regulation 20.2.100 NMAC. On December 13, 2010, EIB Chair Gay Dillingham transmitted Regulation 20.2.100 to the Records Center for filing and publication pursuant to Section 14-4-3 of the State Rules Act, NMSA 1978, §§14-4-1 to -11 (1967) (as amended through 1995). The regulation was filed with the Records Center at 10:40 A.M. on December 27, 2010. The Records Center scheduled the regulation for publication in the January 14, 2011 edition of the New Mexico Register.

On December 15, 2010, following a year-long rule-making process, the WQCC, pursuant to its authority under the Water Quality Act, NMSA 1978, §§74-6-1 to -17 (1967) (as amended through 2009), adopted a new set of regulations for discharges from dairy facilities, to be codified as Regulation 20.6.6 NMAC. On December 21, 2010, WQCC Chair Sarah Cottrell transmitted the regulations for filing to the Records Center; and the Records Center accepted the regulations for filing on December 23, 2010 at 10:07 a.m. These regulations were also scheduled to be published in the January 14, 2011 edition of the New Mexico Register.

On January 1, 2011, newly elected Governor Susana Martinez issued Executive Order 2011-001, which formed a small business-friendly task force and suspended all proposed and pending rules and regulations under the Governor's authority for a ninety-day review period. On January 4, 2011, John Martinez, the director of the Administrative Law Division (ALD) of the Records Center, sent an e-mail to the Governor's general counsel, Jessica Hernandez, drawing her attention to a number of rules and regulations that were filed and scheduled for publication in the January 14, 2011 edition of the New Mexico Register. Mr. Martinez stated:

> I have read Executive Order 2011-001 which establishes a 90-day freeze on rulemaking. I am writing you because there are 34 rules that were filed during the last administration but will not be published in the New Mexico Register until January 14, 2011. We plan on publishing these rules unless we receive written notification from the issuing authorities in the respective agencies that these rule filings should be pulled back. The major issue for the ALD is that today is the rule filing deadline meaning that we will have to know by the end of today if any of these rule filings will not be published. Beginning tomorrow, the text will be type set and cannot be changed after that point.
>
> I have attached a report of the 34 rule filings that are slated to be published on January 14, 2011. Please note that the State Records Center and Archives (noted in the report as the Commission of Public Records) is an independent agency not under the authority of the Governor.

Ms. Hernandez responded by telling Mr. Martinez that the regulations should not be published because the Governor's executive order applied to the regulations. She also asked him to identify the "point people" for the issuing agencies. Mr. Martinez replied to Ms. Hernandez that the Records Center would "need written notification from the respective *Issuing Agencies* stating the desire to cancel the rule filing[s] that occurred last month" and attached a list of the issuing authorities. (Emphasis added.) The issuing authority for the EIB was identified as Gay Dillingham, Chair of the EIB. The issuing authority for the WQCC was identified as Sarah Cottrell, Chair of the WQCC.

During the afternoon of January 4, 2011, Ms. Hernandez sent a high priority e-mail to the contact persons for various administrative agencies and departments requesting that they send written notification to Mr. Martinez to suspend publication of the regulations listed. Soon afterward, Acting Cabinet Secretary of the New Mexico Environment Department Raj Solomon e-mailed Mr. Martinez, requesting suspension of the publication of the two environmental regulations at issue in this case. Soon after that Respondent F. David Martin was nominated to be the Department Secretary and is awaiting confirmation.

After learning that publication of the regulations was suspended, Petitioners, as proponents of the adoption of Regulations 20.6.6 and 20.2.100, each filed a petition for writ of mandamus under Rule 12-504 NMRA against Governor Martinez, the Secretary of the New Mexico Environment Department (Secretary), and the State Records Administrator. Petitioners sought an order compelling the State Records Administrator to reinstate the filing of Regulations 20.6.6 and 20.2.100 and to then publish them. Petitioners also sought an order compelling the Governor and the Secretary to rescind their cancellation of the filings and to refrain from interfering with the lawful process by which final administrative regulations are filed with and published by the Records Center. In their respective petitions, Petitioners alleged that Governor Martinez and Secretary-designate Martin exceeded the limits of their constitutional authority in violation of the separation of powers doctrine and that the State Records Administrator had a non-discretionary ministerial duty to publish the regulations.

EIB POWERS AND DUTIES THAT ARE INDEPENDENT OF THE GOVERNOR

The Legislature created the Department of Environment in the executive branch under Section 9-7A-4 of the Department of Environment Act. NMSA 1978, §§9-7A-1 to -15 (1991) (as amended through 2005). The administrative head of the Department is the Secretary, who is responsible to the Governor for the Department's operation. Sections 9-7A-5 to -6. By contrast, under Section 74-1-4 of the Environmental Improvement Act, the Legislature created the EIB. Each of the seven members of the EIB is appointed by the Governor with the Senate's advice and consent. *Id.* However, under Section 9-7A-12 of the statutes that empowered it to promulgate regulations, the EIB's powers, duties, and responsibilities are explicitly exempt from the authority of the Secretary.

The EIB is required to promulgate all regulations applying to persons and entities outside the Environment Department, Section 74-1-5, and in specified areas of the law, Section 74-1-8. Specifically as it relates to this matter, the EIB has the responsibility to "adopt, promulgate, publish, amend and repeal regulations consistent with the Air Quality Control Act." Section 74-2-5(B)(1). The process for the EIB's rule-making authority under the Air Quality Control Act is outlined in Section 74-2-6. Subsection A permits any person to recommend or propose regulations to the EIB. *Id.* Under Subsection F, regulations adopted by the EIB shall become effective thirty days after their filing under the State Rules Act. *Id.* Any appeal of the regulations must be made to the New Mexico Court of Appeals within thirty days of the date of the EIB's filing of the regulation with the Records Center. Section 74-2-9(A)-(B); §14-4-5.

WQCC POWERS AND DUTIES THAT ARE INDEPENDENT OF THE GOVERNOR

The WQCC was created under Section 74-6-3 of the Water Quality Act. Only four of its fourteen members are appointed by the Governor. *Id.* Like the EIB, under the statutes that empowered it to promulgate regulations, the WQCC's powers, duties, and responsibilities are explicitly exempt from the authority of the Secretary. Section 9-7A-13. The WQCC is responsible for, among other things, adopting, promulgating, and publishing regulations to prevent or abate water pollution, Section 74-6-4(E); and it is specifically mandated to adopt regulations for the dairy industry, Section 74-6-4(K). The process for the WQCC's rulemaking authority is outlined in Section 74-6-6. Under Subsection B, "[a]ny person may petition in writing to have the commission adopt, amend or repeal a regulation or water quality standard." *Id.* Under Subsection E, any regulation, standard, or amendment adopted by the WQCC becomes effective thirty days after its filing under the State Rules Act. *Id.* Any appeal of the regulations must be made to the New Mexico Court of Appeals within thirty days of the date of the regulation's filing by the WQCC with the Records Center. Section 74-6-7(A); §14-4-5.

RECORDS CENTER POWERS AND DUTIES THAT ARE INDEPENDENT OF THE GOVERNOR

The State Rules Act requires any agency that promulgates a regulation to submit the regulation to the Records Center. Section 14-4-2(A) defines "agency" as including boards and commissions. Section 14-4-2(C) defines "rule" as including "any rule, regulation, order, standard, statement of policy, including amendments thereto or repeals thereof issued or promulgated by any agency and purporting to affect one or more agencies besides the agency issuing such rule or to affect persons not members or employees of such issuing agency." The Records Center was created under the Public Records Act, NMSA 1978, Sections 14-3-1 to -25 (1959) (as amended through 2005), and is under the supervision and control of the State Records Administrator, who in turn is employed by and serves at the pleasure of the State Commission of Public Records. Section 14-3-4; §14-3-8. Once the Records Center receives a regulation, it must (1) note on the filed document the date and hour of filing, (2) maintain the original copy as a permanent record, (3) publish the regulation in a timely manner in the New Mexico Register, and (4) compile the regulation into the New Mexico Administrative Code (NMAC). Section 14-4-3. The New Mexico Register must be published at least twice a month. Section 14-4-7.1(A). The State Records Administrator is required by law to adopt and promulgate rules necessary for the implementation and administration of the publication of rules in the New Mexico Register and which set forth the procedures for compiling the rules in the NMAC. Section 14-4-7.1(E).

Chapter 24 of Title 1 sets forth the procedures for compiling rules in the NMAC and Title 1, Chapter 24, Part 15 sets forth the rules pertaining to the New Mexico Register. The objective of the New Mexico Register is to inform the public regarding rule-making activity within the executive branch. 1.24.15.6 NMAC. The objective of the NMAC is to establish standards for uniform rule filings to ensure that rules are readily identifiable and available for public inspection. 1.24.10.6 NMAC.

The following administrative rules inform our decision. First, "[t]he records center shall not accept a rule filing signed by other than the issuing authority, or a formally appointed designee." 1.24.10.10(C) NMAC. Second,

> [n]o rule shall be valid and enforceable until it is filed with the records center and published in the New Mexico register as provided by the State Rules Act. If properly submitted and not published as a result of error, the rule shall be deemed to have been published three weeks after filing with the records center.

1.24.10.16(E) NMAC. Third, "[t]he records center shall refuse to file written material if it is not a rule as defined in 1.24.1.7 NMAC or if the materials submitted for rule filing do not conform to the style and format requirements detailed in 1.24.10 NMAC." 1.24.10.17(A) NMAC. Fourth, "[m]aterial that is filed after the cut-off date for publication shall be published in the next issue, and, if necessary, the effective date shall be modified." 1.24.15.11(D)(2) NMAC. The Records Center publishes a submittal deadlines and publication dates schedule on its website at http://www.nmcpr.state.nm.us/nmregister/. In this case, the EIB Chair was the issuing authority for regulations adopted by the EIB. Mr. Martinez, on behalf of the Records Center, specifically identified the EIB Chair as the issuing authority. Respondents do not contend that the Secretary was formally designated as the issuing authority for regulations adopted by the EIB. The Secretary is not the issuing authority since the law clearly provides that the EIB's powers, duties, and responsibilities under Section 74-2-5 and other statutes are explicitly exempt from the Secretary's authority. Section 9-7A-12. Therefore, the Records Center should have declined to recognize the Acting Secretary's request to suspend publication of Regulation 20.2.100.

With respect to publication in the New Mexico Register, it is uncontradicted that the Records Center accepted Regulation 20.2.100 for filing on December 27, 2010. Section 14-4-3 requires the Records Center to publish a regulation in a timely manner. Without more, the requirement to publish in a timely manner would not be the type of clear and indisputable duty that would warrant issuance of a writ of mandamus. However, Regulation 1.24.15.11(D)(2) NMAC, adopted to specifically address publication in the New Mexico Register, states that "[m]aterial that is filed after the cut-off date for publication shall be published in the next issue. . . ." Under the 2010 submittal and publication schedule published by the Records Center, regulations submitted to the Records Center between December 16, 2010 and January 4, 2011 were to be published in the January 14, 2011 edition of the New Mexico Register. Because Regulation 20.2.100 was submitted after December 16, 2010 and before January 4, 2011, the Records Center was required to publish it in the January 14, 2011 edition of the New Mexico Register. The Records Center did not have discretion to delay publication. We note that there is no provision in the NMAC that specifically permits an agency to withdraw publication of a regulation that had been accepted for filing by the Records Center. Although Regulation 1.24.10.17 of the Administrative Code specifically addresses when a regulation is to be rejected for filing and publication, Respondents do not contend that this provision applies in this case. We do not need to answer whether an issuing authority may withdraw its request to publish a filed regulation because in this case the issuing authority did not make such a request and the Records Center did not have discretion to delay publication.

The same analysis applies with respect to Regulation 20.6.6 filed with the Records Center by the WQCC on December 23, 2010. The WQCC Chair was the issuing authority for regulations adopted by the WQCC and was identified as such by Mr. Martinez of the Records Center. Respondents do not contend that the Secretary was formally designated as the issuing authority for regulations adopted by the WQCC. The Secretary is not the issuing authority because the law clearly provides that the powers, duties, and responsibilities of the WQCC under Section 74-6-4 and other statutes are explicitly exempt from the Secretary's authority. Section 9-7A-13. Therefore, the Records Center should have declined to recognize the Acting Secretary's request to suspend publication of Regulation 20.6.6. Because Regulation 20.6.6 was submitted after December 16, 2010 but before January 4, 2011, the Records Center was required to publish the regulation in the January 14, 2011 edition of the New Mexico Register. It was error for the Records Center not to publish these regulations in the New Mexico Register on January 14, 2011.

CONCLUSION

The State Records Administrator breached a clear, indisputable, and non-discretionary duty to publish regulations accepted for filing with the Records Center. Therefore, a writ of mandamus ordering the Records Center to publish Regulations 20.6.6 and 20.2.100 forthwith has been issued. To the extent the attorney for Governor Martinez, acting as her agent, and Acting Secretary Solomon ordered the Records Center not to publish these regulations, they were without constitutional or statutory authority to do so. On its face, Executive Order 2011-001 only applies to rules and regulations under the Governor's authority; therefore, a writ of mandamus compelling the Governor to refrain from further interference with the proper and lawful filing and publication of regulations under the State Rules Act is denied. Finally, a writ against Secretary-designate Martin is also not warranted since Secretary-designate Martin did not issue the order to temporarily suspend publication of the regulations.

NOTES

1. The case foremost illustrates that the issue of Midnight Regulations is not an entirely federal phenomenon.

2. The case involved rules submitted by two different state agencies. Does the structure of the two agencies (specifically the governor's authority to appoint board members) make any difference in the ultimate outcome of this matter?

3. Is this the right outcome? Should a new executive coming into office have the right to suspend "Midnight Rules" and establish his or her own priorities? Would a state statute duplicating the CRA adequately address these issues?

3. Agency Accountability and the Courts

Courts generally have a right to review agency actions. To the extent that agencies violate statutory or constitutional requirements, courts can overturn actions or enjoin agency behavior. What, however, if the agencies simply ignore, or "nonacquiesce," to the court's decision?

JOHNSON v. UNITED STATES RAILROAD RETIREMENT BOARD

969 F.2d 1082 (D.C. Cir. 1992)

MIKVA, Chief Judge:

In a bold challenge to judicial authority, the United States Railroad Retirement Board argues that it is free, when it chooses, to ignore the decisions of United States courts of appeals. Since 1981, the Board has cut off benefits for the spouses and widows of railroad workers after their dependent children turn sixteen, even though the Railroad Retirement Act of 1974 says that they are entitled to benefits until the children turn eighteen. In 1985, the Court of Appeals for the Eighth Circuit rejected the Board's position that an amendment to the Social Security Act required the change. The Board, however, refused to apply the *Costello* decision, even within the Eighth Circuit, and continued to deny benefits at the administrative level. In March 1991, the Court of Appeals for the Eleventh Circuit rejected the Board's position for the same reasons as the Eighth Circuit. The Board still refuses to acquiesce. Since individual challenges have been ineffective, Nancy Johnson, whose spousal benefits were denied, tried to bring a class action in district court challenging the Board's interpretation of the Railroad Act and its policy of intracircuit nonacquiescence.

Because we think that Mrs. Johnson has not been denied "meaningful" access to judicial review, we uphold the district court's conclusion that the Railroad Act vests exclusive jurisdiction in the courts of appeals. But we join the Eighth and Eleventh Circuits and reject the Board's interpretation of the Railroad Act for the third time. We also think that the Board's unapologetic policy of nonacquiescence is inconsistent with the Board's own jurisdictional arguments and troubling on statutory and constitutional grounds. If the Board continues to deny benefits after our decision today, we expect that the policy itself can be directly challenged in an appropriate action before this court.

I. BACKGROUND

Nancy Johnson is the wife of Edward Johnson, a former railroad employee. As the mother and stepmother of his five children, the Board found her eligible for a spousal annuity effective September 10, 1976. In late 1986, the Board notified her that the Tier I component of her annuity would be cut off on April 1, 1987, when her youngest child turned sixteen. (The Railroad Act divides the benefit into two tiers, with separate eligibility criteria.) On reconsideration, Mrs. Johnson's claim was denied, and her monthly payment was reduced from $391.11 to $84.11. She filed an administrative appeal, and was told that the issue presented "was solely a matter of law," and did not require a hearing. The first appeals referee denied Mrs. Johnson's claim, and came to the remarkable conclusion that the *Costello* case requires her benefits to be terminated, even though the case explicitly requires the opposite result. A second appeals referee reopened the decision and again rejected her argument, noting that "*Costello* was not a class action case and the Board did not pursue it further." Mrs. Johnson appealed again, and on May 16, 1989, a three-member panel of the Board issued its final decision, affirming the decision of the second appeals referee in a one-sentence order. The third panel member dissented vigorously, calling the Board's policy of nonacquiescence "grossly unjust" and urging payment of Tier I benefits to all widows and spouses with children between sixteen and eighteen.

Having exhausted her administrative remedies, Mrs. Johnson filed a class action in district court, suing individually and on behalf of similarly situated beneficiaries under the Act. She claimed that the Board's denial of full benefits to those in her circumstances violated the Act and the Fifth Amendment's Due Process clause. She also claimed that the Board's policy of intracircuit nonacquiescence violated the statutory and constitutional rights of her class....

II. ANALYSIS

A. District Court Jurisdiction

[W]e reject Mrs. Johnson's jurisdictional claim. Mrs. Johnson does not suggest that defendants whose benefits have been cut off could not be joined in a single proceeding before the court of appeals, as in *Linquist*, 813 F.2d at 888. She does not suggest that the administrative record in her case is inadequate, as in *McNary*; nor does she suggest that claimants in her position have no access to judicial review because they fear a heavy penalty like deportation, or because the government refuses to deport them, as in *Ayuda*, 948 F.2d at 751.

Mrs. Johnson does argue forcefully that the Board's policy of nonacquiescence forecloses meaningful judicial review. The Board refuses to petition for

Supreme Court review of adverse circuit court rulings in individual appeals, and at the same time, it continues to apply the rejected interpretation not only in other circuits, but to other individuals' claims in the same circuit. The practical effect of this policy, Mrs. Johnson says, is to insure that few claimants will actually obtain the relief to which federal courts say they are entitled by law. We agree that the Board's policy raises grave constitutional and statutory questions, and we will address them below. But we are not persuaded that the policy is "tantamount to a complete denial of judicial review" for most claimants, as in *McNary*; especially because if the nonacquiescence policy is unlawful, we think it can be directly challenged before our court. Because we can provide meaningful review to spouses and widows who have the patience and means to seek it, we affirm the district court's conclusion that it lacked jurisdiction over the class action, and we turn to the merits of Mrs. Johnson's claim.

B. Mrs. Johnson's Entitlement

Two circuit courts have reviewed the "tortuous" history of the relationship between the Railroad Act and the Social Security Act, and rejected the Board's interpretation. *See Costello v. United States R.R. Retirement Bd.*, 780 F.2d 1352 (8th Cir. 1985); *Johnson v. United States R.R. Retirement Bd.*, 925 F.2d 1374 (11th Cir. 1991). We join the Eighth and Eleventh Circuits and reject the Board's position once more.

The Railroad Act says clearly that a qualified spouse "shall . . . be entitled to a spouse's annuity . . . in the amount provided under 231c of this title" if, "in the case of a wife, [she] has in her care . . . a child who meets the qualifications prescribed in (iii) of section (d)(1). . . ." 45 U.S.C. §231(a)(c) (1988). Section (d)(1)(iii) defines "child" as one who is under 18 years of age. Section 231c(a), in turn, defines the amount of the entitlement:

> (1) The annuity of a spouse . . . shall be in an amount equal to the amount . . . of the wife's insurance benefit . . . to which such spouse *would have been entitled* under the Social Security Act . . . if such individual's service as an employee after December 31, 1936, had been included in the term "employment" as defined in the [Social Security] Act.

5 U.S.C. §231c(a) (1988) (emphasis added).

There was no conflict between the Railroad and Social Security Acts before 1981, since the eligibility requirements in both were the same. In 1981, however, as part of the Omnibus Budget Reconciliation Act, Congress cut Social Security Benefits by lowering the age of termination for children's benefits under the Social Security Act from 18 to 16. Pub. L. No. 97-35, §2205, 95 Stat. 357 (amending 42 U.S.C. §402(s)(1)). It did not amend the parallel provision in the Railroad Act. The question, therefore, is whether Congress intended spousal annuitants under the Railroad Act, like the Social Security Act, to lose their benefits once their children turn sixteen.

The Board's initial response to the question was remarkably wooden. In 1981, it issued a legal opinion insisting that "the eligibility provisions of the Railroad Retirement Act were not affected by" the Omnibus Budget Act and that spouses and widows remain "entitled to a benefit as long as they have a minor child of the employee under age 18 in their care and custody." Legal Opinion L-81-193. The Opinion interpreted the amended Social Security Act, however, to reduce the Tier I *amount* due to widows and spouses with children between sixteen and eighteen to "zero." Those whose Tier II benefits were calculated as 30% of Tier I would receive "zero" Tier II benefits as well. *Id.*

In *Costello*, the Eighth Circuit held that the Board's interpretation lacked a reasonable basis in law because it forces annuitants to meet the eligibility requirements of *both* statutes, even though the Railway Act refers to the Social Security Act only for the purpose of determining the *amount* an eligible Social Security annuitant *would have received*. . . .

In response to the *Costello* decision, the Board issued a new policy in 1986, which Mrs. Johnson now challenges. The Board continues to maintain that widows and spouses are entitled to "zero" Tier I benefits after their children turn sixteen, even though *Costello* requires the opposite. But in an abrupt change, it has agreed to pay Tier II benefits to all widows until their children turn eighteen, even those whose Tier II benefits are required to be calculated as 30% of Tier I. Legal Opinion L-86-112.

[Ed. Note: At this point, the court addresses the Board's assertion that it is entitled to deference because it is interpreting its own governing statute, the Railroad Act. The court concludes that the Board is in fact interpreting the relationship between the Railroad Act and the Social Security Act, an area that is "outside of its expertise." Therefore, the Board was not entitled to deference by the court.]

C. Nonacquiescence

"We have been grossly unjust," the dissenting Board member wrote, in refusing to follow the *Costello* case, even within the Eighth Circuit. "Moreover," he added, "the Court may severely criticize us for our handling of these cases." He was correct.

In response to the *Costello* case, the Board refused to pay Tier I benefits even within the Eighth Circuit, unless claimants complete the administrative process, which includes an initial decision, reconsideration, a hearing before a referee, and a final decision by the three-member Board itself. 20 C.F.R. §259. At oral argument before this court, furthermore, the Board repeated its extraordinary position that an agency is not bound to respect the pronouncements of a U.S. Court of Appeals, even within its own circuit. Mrs. Johnson challenged the constitutionality of the nonacquiescence policy in her complaint, and asked for, among other things, mandamus relief. We think such a dramatic step would be premature, since the Board has not announced definitively that it will refuse to acquiesce in our decision today; and in the interest of judicial restraint, we will give the Board a chance to reconsider its position in light of our opinion. To inform the Board's response, however, we think it useful to suggest why the Board's policy is inconsistent with the Board's jurisdictional arguments and troubling on statutory and constitutional grounds.

First, the Board's entire jurisdictional argument is based on the claim that Congress put great stock on the efficiency and expertise of appellate review. But the same legislative history the Board quotes to suggest that Congress intended to preclude district court jurisdiction also suggests that Congress expected the Board to respect circuit court decisions rather than to defy them. The Board put particular emphasis on the testimony of Mr. Schoene, the labor representative, who showed a special concern for avoiding the "further expense" of additional appeals that would be forced on a claimant if she lost in the district court. *House Hearings* at 1083-93 (1946). Yet the Board itself has put claimants to further expense and meaningless appeals by forcing them to exhaust their administrative remedies before they can receive benefits. Mr. Schoene also noted that "more careful consideration will be given to the entire case . . . in the circuit court of appeals," *id.*; and the Board took great pains to argue that Congress intended appellate judges to apply their expertise to legal challenges to the Board's policies. Now, however, the Board refuses to respect the "expert" judgments of appellate courts.

The Board's refusal to acquiesce, in short, undermines all of the advantages of appellate review that the Board insists Congress intended to recognize. To the degree that the Board's policy clashes with the intent of the framers of the Railroad Act, it cannot be sustained. More generally, defenders of nonacquiescence rely heavily on the premise that the "current administrative landscape" suggests an "implicit authorization of nonacquiescence," Estreicher & Revesz, *Nonacquiescence by Federal Administrative Agencies*, 98 Yale L.J. 679, 729 (1989). Evidence that Congress intended the opposite in this case leaves the argument without a foundation.

The Board's position also ignores basic rules of legal precedent, which are governed not by an inherent judicial hierarchy, but by the mechanisms of review provided by Congress. State courts, for example, are bound to follow Supreme Court precedent because if they do not, they can be reversed. Federal courts of appeals, by contrast, do not review state decisions, so their decisions are not generally considered binding precedent in state courts. In the current tax court, similarly, identical cases on the merits may receive different dispositions, because they are appealable to different federal circuits. Amar, *A Neo-Federalist View of Article III: Separating the Two Tiers of Federal Jurisdiction*, 65 B.U. L. Rev. 205, 258-59 n.170 (1985). The Board's refusal to acquiesce even in cases it knows will be appealed to the Eighth Circuit defies Congress's plan in making decisions under the Railroad Act reviewable by the courts of appeals in which the injury arose.

On the broadest level, the Board's position raises serious statutory and constitutional questions. Intracircuit nonacquiescence has been condemned by almost every circuit court of appeals that has confronted it. . . .

Several courts have questioned the constitutionality of intracircuit nonacquiescence with broad references to *Cooper v. Aaron*, 358 U.S. 1, 3 L. Ed. 2d 5, 78 S. Ct. 1401 (1958), and *Marbury v. Madison*, 5 U.S. 137, 177, 2 L. Ed. 60 (1803). . . . But it is not necessary to accept the *Cooper* analogy to criticize the Board's policy in this case. In *Cooper*, the Supreme Court said that its interpretations of the Constitution are binding on state officials, even on those who were not parties to the case or bound by a court order. *Marbury*, according to the *Cooper* Court, "declared the basic principle that the federal judiciary is supreme in the exposition of the law of the Constitution"; therefore, the Court concluded, judicial interpretations of the Constitution are the "supreme law of the land," and state officials are bound by oath to follow them. 358 U.S. at 18. Circuit courts, for their part, have compared the nonacquiescence of federal agencies to the defiance of Governor Faubus at Little Rock, noting that "what the [*Cooper*] Court said with regard to the Constitution applies with full force with regard to federal statutory law." *Lopez*, 725 F.2d at 1497 n.5.

Defenders of nonacquiescence argue that the *Cooper* analogy is inexact. Although *Cooper* speaks not of the Supreme Court but of "*the federal judiciary* [as] supreme in the exposition of the law of the Constitution," 348 U.S. at 18 (emphasis added), the decision seems to assume that "the law forming the basis for the obligation to acquiesce is no longer in flux." Estreicher & Revesz, 98 Yale L.J. at 725. Supreme Court decisions, the argument goes, should be followed in the interests of national uniformity; but until the Supreme Court has spoken, agencies have argued that their responsibility to formulate "uniform and orderly national policy in adjudications" allows them to refuse to acquiescence in the conflicting views of U.S. Courts of Appeals....

But even if we assume, for the sake of argument, that an interest in national uniformity might justify nonacquiescence in *some* cases, the sincerity of the Railroad Board's interest in uniformity is open to question. When an agency honestly believes a circuit court has misinterpreted the law, there are two places it can go to correct the error: Congress or the Supreme Court. The Railroad Retirement Board has done neither. It has not asked Congress to clarify its intentions, even after two circuits said it had misunderstood Congress's intentions. More remarkably, it has failed to petition the Supreme Court for certiorari, even in the decisions it claims to believe were wrongly decided. The Board appears, as a result, to be less interested in national uniformity than in denying benefits one way or another.

The Board, in the end, can hardly defend its policy of selective nonacquiescence by invoking national uniformity. The policy has precisely the opposite effect, since it results in very different treatment for those who seek and who do not seek judicial review....

Conceding the lack of vertical uniformity — similar treatment of all claimants in the same circuit — defenders of nonacquiesence have tried to point to the benefits of what they call horizontal uniformity — similar treatment of all national claimants in initial agency proceedings. At the same time, they acknowledge that horizontal uniformity is not an end in itself, but a means to other values, such as fairness. *See, e.g.*, Estreicher & Revesz, 98 Yale L.J. at 748. It is a peculiar view of fairness, however, that treats all claimants equally poorly by depriving them of benefits they will eventually receive if they have the fortitude to run an administrative gauntlet. This looks uncomfortably like the frivolous and obstructionistic litigation that the Supreme Court has severely criticized in the context of habeas corpus....

Because of the venue provisions of the Railroad Act, furthermore, *any* claimant who is denied Tier I benefits in the future can eventually receive benefits by seeking review in our circuit. *See* 45 U.S.C. §355(f) (1988). It is hard to see the fairness of a policy that guarantees benefits to those who cannot. Under these circumstances, the interests of both fairness and national uniformity suggest that the Board should consider reinstating Tier I benefits in all jurisdictions.

Ordinarily, of course, the arguments against *inter*circuit nonacquiescence (which occurs when an agency refuses to apply the decision of one circuit to claims that will be reviewed by another circuit) are much less compelling than the arguments against *intra*circuit nonacquiescence. Although the decision of one circuit deserves respect, we have recognized that "it need not be taken by the Board as the law of the land." ... When the Board's position is rejected in one circuit, after all, it should have a reasonable opportunity to persuade other circuits to reach a contrary conclusion. And there is an additional value to letting important legal issues "percolate" throughout the judicial system, so the Supreme Court can have the benefit of different circuit court opinions on the same subject.... But now that three circuits have rejected the Board's position, and not one has accepted it, further resistance would show contempt for the rule of law. After ten years of percolation, it is time for the Board to smell the coffee.

In light of our decision today, we hope that the Board will choose to abandon its policy of intracircuit nonacquiescence, as the Social Security Administration did after being severely criticized by the Courts and by Congress. *See, e.g.*, H.R. Conf. Rep. No. 1039, 98th Cong., 2d Sess. 38 (1984), *reprinted in* 1984 U.S.C.C.A.N. 3080, 3095. But if the Board persists, we expect that the policy of nonacquiescence itself could be considered a "final decision of the Board" under 45 U.S.C. §355(f) that could be challenged by a spouse or widow in an appropriate action before this court....

III. CONCLUSION

We affirm the district court's dismissal of the complaint for lack of jurisdiction. We reverse the Board's order and remand with directions to award Mrs. Johnson a Tier I spouse's annuity for the period which began with the termination of her annuity and which ended when her youngest child turned eighteen.

It is so ordered.

BUCKLEY, Circuit Judge, concurring in part and dissenting in part:

III. NONACQUIESCENCE

... Nor should we suggest a rigid rule of "three strikes and out," as the majority does in the case of intercircuit nonacquiescence. It is easy enough to say that when an agency is reversed on an important issue, its proper course is to appeal to Congress or the Supreme Court. Catching Congress's ear, however, is more easily said than done; and given the huge volume of petitions for certiorari that flood the Supreme Court, it is often necessary to establish a split among the circuits before the Court will examine an issue. If an agency is confident enough of its own position, I would be reluctant to establish an arbitrary limit on the intercircuit waters it would be allowed to test.

NOTES

1. Does this case involve intra- or inter-circuit nonacquiescence? What difference, if any, would it make to the analysis? According to one commentator, "Practically no one objects to the first category of nonacquiescence the intercircuit variety." Ross E. Davies, Remedial Nonacquiescence, 89 Iowa L. Rev. 65 (2003). Do you agree with this view? Is it consistent with Judge Mikva's analysis in *Johnson*?

2. What are the disadvantages of nonacquiescence? What are the benefits? Is it clear that the disadvantages of nonacquiescence outweigh the benefits?

3. Judge Mikva seems highly critical of the nonacquiescence process. Do you agree with the views expressed? Some view agency nonacquiescence as part of an interactive relationship between agencies and courts. See Todd S. Aagaard, Factual Premises of Statutory Interpretation in Agency Review Cases, 77 Geo. Wash. L. Rev. 366, 406 (2009) ("When a court sets aside an agency decision and remands, the agency has the opportunity to reconsider its decision in light of the court's ruling. Even when a court upholds an agency decision, the agency considers the court's decision as precedent that may be relevant to other agency actions. In considering this precedent, the agency is not merely a passive recipient of judicial dictates. The agency must decide, for example, whether to follow the court's precedent.") (footnotes omitted).

4. What limits, if any, are there on an agency's decision to not acquiesce? Should any such limits differ for intracircuit and intercircuit nonacquiescence? One answer can be found in Samuel Estreicher & Richard L. Revesz, Nonacquiescence by Federal Administrative Agencies, 98 Yale L.J. 679, 735 (1989), an article cited several times in the *Johnson* case:

> We conclude that intracircuit nonacquiescence can be justified only as an interim measure that allows the agency to maintain a uniform administration of its governing statute following an adverse decision by a court of appeals while the agency reasonably seeks in the courts a national validation of its position. For the other two categories, we do not believe that limitations would advance the proper functioning of the administrative lawmaking system.

5. To the extent that a circuit rules against an agency, how can an agency use nonacquiescence to induce the circuit court to change its ruling? Can it simply obtain a contrary view from the next panel of judges in the same circuit who considers the issue? One of the potential benefits of intracircuit nonacquiescence is that it encourages "intercircuit dialogue" if an agency convinces a circuit court to change its position based on the reasoning of another circuit. See Brian Gumz, Administrative Nonacquiescence and the EPA, 10 Geo. Wash. J. Energy and Env't L. 1, 5 (2019). However, "[a]s some commentators have suggested, circuit reconsideration of past precedent is so rare that only marginal intercircuit dialogue is produced by intracircuit nonacquiescence." Id.

6. The practical difficulties in this area can be seen from a series of cases in the Fourth Circuit. Plaintiffs sued the Social Security Administration (SSA) because of its failure to consider certain types of evidence. The trial court found that SSA had not acquiesced to controlling precedent in the Fourth Circuit and enjoined the Agency's position. The Fourth Circuit agreed that SSA had refused to acquiesce to controlling precedent, but overturned the injunction and invited the Agency to reconsider its position. See Hyatt v. Heckler, 757 F.2d 1455, 1460 (4th Cir. 1985) (denying injunctive relief as judicial overreach while rejecting the SSA's policy of nonacquiescence), vacated and remanded, 476 U.S. 1167 (1986); Hyatt v. Heckler, 807 F.2d 376, 380-381, (4th Cir. 1986) (on remand, rejecting reconsideration of denial of injunction as beyond the scope of remand, but holding that SSA's nonacquiescence constituted exceptional circumstances entitling claimants to reconsideration of their claims despite procedural errors). SSA, however, continued its refusal to acquiesce. The Fourth Circuit issued yet another decision in the case, upholding the lower court's order requiring SSA to distribute Fourth Circuit law "to all administrative law judges and all others within this circuit who look to the Secretary for authority or advice" on such matters. See Hyatt v. Sullivan, 899 F.2d 329, 336 (4th Cir. 1990). Ultimately, SSA did acquiesce and, as part of a settlement entered in 1994, agreed to reevaluate disability claims denied under the improper standard. See Hunter v. Sullivan, 993 F.2d 31, 34-35 (4th Cir. 1992) (concluding that the SSA denied a disability claim through application of the proper standard). Even then, however, the litigation did not come to an end. Battles over fees lasted into the new millennium. See Hyatt v. Barnhart, 315 F.3d 239, 248, 250-251 (4th Cir. 2002) (affirming district court's decision to award claimants attorneys' fees because SSA's position was not substantially justified, but capping the award at the statutory maximum).

7. The court in this case was hesitant to issue a nationwide injunction against the agency. That hesitancy may be a thing of the past. See Hawaii v. Trump, 859 F.3d 741, 788 (9th Cir. 2017) (finding that lower court "did not abuse its discretion in entering a nationwide preliminary injunction" against executive order "temporarily suspending for 90 days entry of nationals from six majority-Muslim countries, suspending for 120 days the United States Refugee Admissions Program (USRAP), and decreasing refugee admissions for 2017 fiscal year by more than half"), vacated and remanded with instructions to dismiss as moot, 138 S. Ct. 377 (2017); see also Texas v. United States, 809 F.3d 134 (5th Cir. 2015) (upholding nationwide injunction by district court against implementation of Deferred Action for Parents of Americans and Lawful Permanent Residents), as revised (Nov. 25, 2015), aff'd by an equally divided Court, 136 S. Ct. 2271 (2016). However, in a recent concurring opinion, Justice Gorsuch, joined by Justice Thomas, expressed strong opinions against the increasing use of nationwide injunctions:

> Universal injunctions have little basis in traditional equitable practice. Their use has proliferated only in very recent years. And they hardly seem an innovation we should rush to embrace. By their nature, universal injunctions tend to force judges into making rushed, high-stakes, low-information decisions. . . . The rise of nationwide injunctions may just be a sign of our impatient times. But good judicial decisions are usually tempered by older virtues.

Dep't of Homeland Sec. v. New York, 140 S. Ct. 599, 600 (2020) (Gorsuch, J., concurring) (citations omitted). Others have described further negative effects of nationwide injunctions, including how to handle conflicting decisions among circuits on the same substantive case and a "balance of power between the executive and legislative branches and the judicial branch that is . . . more than slightly off kilter." *Ramos v. Wolf*, 975 F.3d 872, 903 (9th Cir. 2020) (Nelson, J., concurring). To the extent that courts are more willing to issue nationwide injunctions against actions of agencies, what impact might that have? Do you see this as a positive development, or do you share the negative views of Justice Gorsuch and Judge Nelson?

4. Agency Accountability and the President

The administrative bodies addressed in this casebook are primarily located in the executive branch and subject to the oversight of the President. The size of the federal government and the myriad of tasks performed by the assorted agencies and departments (some of which overlap) make oversight logistically difficult. The oversight process involves two separate and sometimes conflicting goals. On the one hand, the President has the goal of efficiency. This may entail the elimination of redundant offices or unnecessary regulations. The President also typically wants to control the policies emanating from these agencies.

In the executive branch, the Office of Management and Budget (OMB) acts as a centralized review office. Executive branch agencies (but not independent agencies) are subject to review of their budgets by OMB. Similarly, the Office of Information and Regulatory Affairs (OIRA), an office within OMB, reviews significant rulemaking proposals submitted by executive branch agencies (but again, not independent agencies). Therefore, ORIA is at the center of the regulatory review process. See Identifying and Reducing Regulatory Burdens, Executive Order 13610, May 10, 2012 (requiring agencies to conduct "retrospective analyses of existing rules" and to "report on the status of their retrospective review efforts to OIRA").

NOTES

1. Even with information about the actions of the various agencies, control over policy by the President has not always been straightforward. The authority of the President to command agencies to act is unclear. See Robert V. Percival,

Who's in Charge? Does the President Have Directive Authority over Agency Regulatory Decisions?, 79 Fordham L. Rev. 2487, 2538 (2011) ("Although it is unlikely that the debate over whether the President has the legal authority to dictate the substance of regulatory decisions entrusted by statute to agency heads ever will be definitively resolved, the view most widely accepted by scholars is that the President does not."). Of course, the President can dismiss heads of agencies and departments that act in a manner inconsistent with his or her policies. Does this represent an adequate form of control over agency policies? See also David Driesen, The Unitary Executive Theory in Comparative Context, 72 Hastings L.J. 1, 41, 49 (2020) (comparing American practices under the unitary executive theory to the evolution of similar practices in Hungary, Turkey, and Poland, asserting that "the unitary executive provides a pathway to autocracy," and arguing that the Supreme Court's decision in Seila Law LLC v. Consumer Fin. Prot. Bureau, 140 S. Ct. 2183 (2020) embraces the unitary executive theory and, as a result, erodes Congress's ability to consider the potential for authoritarianism to which Driesen's foreign examples suggest this theory can lead.); Kathryn E. Kovacs, The Supersecretary in Chief, 94 S. Cal. L. Rev. Postscript 61 (2020) (To correct the "impermissibl[e] shift[] [in] the balance of powers toward the President" embodied in the unitary executive theory, Kovacs recommends applying APA requirements to the President when they are "exercising another officer's statutory authority" (i.e., when they act as Supersecretary in Chief), criticizing the Supreme Court's contrary decision in Franklin v. Massachusetts); Cary Coglianese, The Emptiness of Decisional Limits: Reconceiving Presidential Control of the Administrative State, 69 Admin. L. Rev. 43, 80 (2017) (arguing for a bright-line rule by which administrative actions would take legal effect only after the administrator of the agency has "sign[ed] off" on the action, thus limiting presidential power by forcing the president to convince an official with signing authority to take action that comports with the president's own views.)

2. Eloise Pasachoff argues that "OMB's budget and management authority provides the opportunity for significant control over agency policymaking." Eloise Pasachoff, The President's Budget as a Source of Agency Policy Control, 125 Yale L.J. 2182, 2207 (2019). According to Pasachoff, OMB "affects how agencies prioritize, justify, and make decisions about the policies under their purview" through its role in budget preparation and execution. Id. Do you agree that centralized review of the budget could be an effective method of controlling agency policies? How might this process provide such control?

3. What other roles might OMB play in the coordination of, and control over, agencies in the executive branch? In 2017, President Trump ordered OMB to propose a plan for the reorganization of the executive branch that would include "as appropriate, recommendations to eliminate unnecessary agencies, components of agencies, and agency programs, and to merge functions." Presidential Executive Order on a Comprehensive Plan for Reorganizing the Executive Branch, 2017 WL 955932, Mar. 13, 2017. In 2018, OMB issued a "reform plan" that included thirty-two dramatic cross-agency reorganization proposals, such as merging the departments of education and labor, moving the policymaking functions of the Office of Personnel Management to the Executive Office of the President, and restructuring the U.S. Postal Service. Congressional Research Service, The Trump Administration's Reform Plan and Reorganization Recommendations 1-2 (2018). Implementing these proposals would have required changes to statutes and budgetary changes, many of which would have also required congressional approval. Id. at 2-3.

4. What about control over the number of regulations? See Presidential Executive Order on Reducing Regulation and Controlling Regulatory Costs, 2017 WL 394070, Jan. 30, 2017 (in order to manage "costs associated with the governmental imposition of private expenditures" order requiring that "for every one new regulation issued, at least two prior regulations be identified for elimination"). How might this approach be effective? How might the approach be ineffective? Does your answer change knowing that the goal was to control the costs of regulation? See id. ("any new incremental costs associated with new regulations shall, to the extent permitted by law, be offset by the elimination of existing costs associated with at least two prior regulations"). Should regulations be examined entirely based upon cost? What about the benefits resulting from the efforts? For a detailed discussion of the appropriate role of cost-benefit analysis in regulatory decision making, see Paul R. Noe and John D. Graham, The Ascendancy of the Cost-Benefit State?, 5 ALR Accord 85 (2020) ("Reasonable minds can agree that the goal of regulation is to enhance, not undermine, societal well-being. [Benefit-cost analysis], despite its limitations, is the best decision-making [sic] tool to ensure that regulations are evidence-based and actually do enhance societal well-being.").

5. We will revisit the Office of Information and Regulatory Affairs later in this casebook. Suffice it to say that OIRA reviews agency regulations and is sometimes called the most powerful office no one has ever heard of. OIRA has the ability to affect the regulatory process. Pasachoff, The President's Budget, *supra*, at 2182, 2201-2202 ("OIRA's review can result in a regulation being significantly delayed, never being published at all, or being published in a dramatically different form."). How might OIRA affect regulatory policy? See Kathryn A. Watts, Controlling Presidential Control, 114 Mich. L. Rev. 683, 699-700 (2016) (discussing use of delay by OIRA during Obama administration as a "means of aggressively controlling the regulatory state" and noting that average review time at OIRA in the first half of 2013 increased to 140 days, "nearly three times the average for the period from 1994 through 2011").

The President may or may not have the authority to order agencies to act in a certain manner or adopt particular policies. To the extent that he or she is lacking the authority, the President nonetheless has the authority to remove heads of agencies and departments at will. Persons can be appointed who are more likely to reflect the policy choices of the President. As a result, heads of agencies know that if they do not conform to the President's agenda, they are susceptible to removal at will. At the same time, the public knows that the President has some ability to control administrative agencies, creating a degree of political accountability. Agency policies can therefore be attributed, to some extent, to the President, and he or she may suffer or benefit from them at the ballot box.

Reducing the authority of the President therefore necessarily means reducing the authority to hire (appoint) and fire (remove) those running departments and agencies. The power of appointment is set out in Article II, Section 2, Paragraph 2 of the U.S. Constitution. The Court's imposition of restrictions on the right of the President to remove officials (beyond impeachment, of course) is not explicitly found in the language of the Constitution.

a. Appointment

LUCIA v. SECURITIES AND EXCHANGE COMMISSION

___ U.S. ___, 138 S.Ct. 2044 (June 21, 2018)

JUSTICE KAGAN delivered the opinion of the Court:

The Appointments Clause of the Constitution lays out the permissible methods of appointing "Officers of the United States," a class of government officials distinct from mere employees. Art. II, §2, cl. 2. This case requires us to decide whether administrative law judges (ALJs) of the Securities and Exchange Commission (SEC or Commission) qualify as such "Officers." In keeping with *Freytag* v. *Commissioner*, 501 U.S. 868, 111 S. Ct. 2631, 115 L. Ed. 2d 764 (1991), we hold that they do.

I.

The SEC has statutory authority to enforce the nation's securities laws. One way it can do so is by instituting an administrative proceeding against an alleged wrongdoer. By law, the Commission may itself preside over such a proceeding. But the Commission also may, and typically does, delegate that task to an ALJ. The SEC currently has five ALJs. Other staff members, rather than the Commission proper, selected them all. . . .

This case began when the SEC instituted an administrative proceeding against petitioner Raymond Lucia and his investment company. Lucia marketed a retirement savings strategy called "Buckets of Money." In the SEC's view, Lucia used misleading slideshow presentations to deceive prospective clients. The SEC charged Lucia under the Investment Advisers Act, and assigned ALJ Cameron Elliot to adjudicate the case. After nine days of testimony and argument, Judge Elliot issued an initial decision concluding that Lucia had violated the Act and imposing sanctions, including civil penalties of $300,000 and a lifetime bar from the investment industry. . . .

On appeal to the SEC, Lucia argued that the administrative proceeding was invalid because Judge Elliot had not been constitutionally appointed. According to Lucia, the Commission's ALJs are "Officers of the United States" and thus subject to the Appointments Clause. Under that Clause, Lucia noted, only the President, "Courts of Law," or "Heads of Departments" can appoint "Officers." See Art. II, §2, cl. 2. And none of those actors had made Judge Elliot an ALJ. To be sure, the Commission itself counts as a "Head[ ] of Department[ ]." But the Commission had left the task of appointing ALJs, including Judge Elliot, to SEC staff members. As a result, Lucia contended, Judge Elliot lacked constitutional authority to do his job.

The Commission rejected Lucia's argument. It held that the SEC's ALJs are not "Officers of the United States." Instead, they are "mere employees" — officials with lesser responsibilities who fall outside the Appointments Clause's ambit. The Commission reasoned that its ALJs do not "exercise significant authority independent of [its own] supervision." Because that is so (said the SEC), they need no special, high-level appointment.

Lucia's claim fared no better in the Court of Appeals for the D.C. Circuit. That decision [agreeing with the Commission and denying Lucia's claim] conflicted with one from the Court of Appeals for the Tenth Circuit. See *Bandimere v. SEC*, 844 F. 3d 1168, 1179 (2016).

Lucia asked us to resolve the split by deciding whether the Commission's ALJs are "Officers of the United States within the meaning of the Appointments Clause." Up to that point, the Federal Government (as represented by the Department of Justice) had defended the Commission's position that SEC ALJs are employees, not officers. But in responding to Lucia's petition, the Government switched sides. So when we granted the petition, we also appointed an *amicus curiae* to defend the judgment below. We now reverse.

II.

The sole question here is whether the Commission's ALJs are "Officers of the United States" or simply employees of the Federal Government. The Appointments Clause prescribes the exclusive means of appointing "Officers." Only the President, a court of law, or a head of department can do so. See Art. II, §2, cl. 2. And as all parties agree, none of those actors appointed Judge Elliot before he heard Lucia's case; instead, SEC staff members gave him an ALJ slot. So if the Commission's ALJs are constitutional officers, Lucia raises a valid Appointments Clause claim. The only way to defeat his position is to show that those ALJs are not officers at all, but instead non-officer employees — part of the broad swath of "lesser functionaries" in the Government's workforce. *Buckley v. Valeo*, 424 U.S. 1, 126, n. 162 (1976) (*per curiam*). For if that is true, the Appointments Clause cares not a whit about who named them. See *United States v. Germaine*, 99 U.S. 508, 510 (1879).

Two decisions set out this Court's basic framework for distinguishing between officers and employees. *Germaine* held that "civil surgeons" (doctors hired to perform various physical exams) were mere employees because their duties were "occasional or temporary" rather than "continuing and permanent."

Id., at 511-512. Stressing "ideas of tenure [and] duration," the Court there made clear that an individual must occupy a "continuing" position established by law to qualify as an officer. *Id.*, at 511. *Buckley* then set out another requirement, central to this case. It determined that members of a federal commission were officers only after finding that they "exercis[ed] significant authority pursuant to the laws of the United States." 424 U.S., at 126. The inquiry thus focused on the extent of power an individual wields in carrying out his assigned functions.

Both the *amicus* and the Government urge us to elaborate on *Buckley*'s "significant authority" test, but another of our precedents makes that project unnecessary. The standard is no doubt framed in general terms, tempting advocates to add whatever glosses best suit their arguments. . . . And maybe one day we will see a need to refine or enhance the test *Buckley* set out so concisely. But that day is not this one, because in *Freytag v. Commissioner*, 501 U.S. 868 (1991), we applied the unadorned "significant authority" test to adjudicative officials who are near-carbon copies of the Commission's ALJs. As we now explain, our analysis there (sans any more detailed legal criteria) necessarily decides this case.

The officials at issue in *Freytag* were the "special trial judges" (STJs) of the United States Tax Court. The authority of those judges depended on the significance of the tax dispute before them. In "comparatively narrow and minor matters," they could both hear and definitively resolve a case for the Tax Court. *Id.*, at 873. In more major matters, they could preside over the hearing, but could not issue the final decision; instead, they were to "prepare proposed findings and an opinion" for a regular Tax Court judge to consider. The proceeding challenged in *Freytag* was a major one, involving $1.5 billion in alleged tax deficiencies. See *id.*, at 871, n. 1. After conducting a 14-week trial, the STJ drafted a proposed decision in favor of the Government. A regular judge then adopted the STJ's work as the opinion of the Tax Court. See *id.*, at 872. The losing parties argued on appeal that the STJ was not constitutionally appointed.

This Court held that the Tax Court's STJs are officers, not mere employees. Citing *Germaine*, the Court first found that STJs hold a continuing office established by law. See 501 U.S. at 881. They serve on an ongoing, rather than a "temporary [or] episodic[,] basis"; and their "duties, salary, and means of appointment" are all specified in the Tax Code. The Court then considered, as *Buckley* demands, the "significance" of the "authority" STJs wield. 501 U.S. at 881. In addressing that issue, the Government had argued that STJs are employees, rather than officers, in all cases (like the one at issue) in which they could not "enter a final decision." But the Court thought the Government's focus on finality "ignore[d] the significance of the duties and discretion that [STJs] possess." Describing the responsibilities involved in presiding over adversarial hearings, the Court said: STJs "take testimony, conduct trials, rule on the admissibility of evidence, and have the power to enforce compliance with discovery orders." *Id.*, at 881-82. And the Court observed that "[i]n the course of carrying out these important functions, the [STJs] exercise significant discretion." *Id.*, at 882. That fact meant they were officers, even when their decisions were not final.

Freytag says everything necessary to decide this case. To begin, the Commission's ALJs, like the Tax Court's STJs, hold a continuing office established by law. Indeed, everyone here — Lucia, the Government, and the *amicus* — agrees on that point. Far from serving temporarily or episodically, SEC ALJs "receive[] a career appointment." And that appointment is to a position created by statute, down to its "duties, salary, and means of appointment." *Freytag*, 501 U.S., at 881.

Still more, the Commission's ALJs exercise the same "significant discretion" when carrying out the same "important functions" as STJs do. *Freytag*, 501 U.S. at 882. Both sets of officials have all the authority needed to ensure fair and orderly adversarial hearings — indeed, nearly all the tools of federal trial judges. See *Butz*, 438 U.S. at 513. Consider in order the four specific (if overlapping) powers *Freytag* mentioned. First, the Commission's ALJs (like the Tax Court's STJs) "take testimony." More precisely, they "[r]eceiv[e] evidence" and "[e]xamine witnesses" at hearings, and may also take pre-hearing depositions. Second, the ALJs (like STJs) "conduct trials." As detailed earlier, they administer oaths, rule on motions, and generally "regulat[e] the course of" a hearing, as well as the conduct of parties and counsel. Third, the ALJs (like STJs) "rule on the admissibility of evidence." They thus critically shape the administrative record (as they also do when issuing document subpoenas). And fourth, the ALJs (like STJs) "have the power to enforce compliance with discovery orders." In particular, they may punish all "[c]ontemptuous conduct," including violations of those orders, by means as severe as excluding the offender from the hearing. So point for point — straight from *Freytag*'s list — the Commission's ALJs have equivalent duties and powers as STJs in conducting adversarial inquiries.

And at the close of those proceedings, ALJs issue decisions much like that in *Freytag* — except with potentially more independent effect. As the *Freytag* Court recounted, STJs "prepare proposed findings and an opinion" adjudicating charges and assessing tax liabilities. Similarly, the Commission's ALJs issue decisions containing factual findings, legal conclusions, and appropriate remedies. And what happens next reveals that the ALJ can play the more autonomous role. In a major case like *Freytag*, a regular Tax Court judge must always review an STJ's opinion. And that opinion counts for nothing unless the regular judge adopts it as his own. By contrast, the SEC can decide against reviewing an ALJ decision at all. And when the SEC declines review (and issues an order saying so), the ALJ's decision itself "becomes final" and is "deemed the action of the Commission." That last-word capacity makes this an *a fortiori* case: If the Tax Court's STJs are officers, as *Freytag* held, then the Commission's ALJs must be too.

The *amicus* offers up two distinctions to support the opposite conclusion. His main argument relates to "the power to enforce compliance with discovery orders" — the fourth of *Freytag*'s listed functions. The Tax Court's STJs, he states, had that power "because they had authority to punish contempt" (including discovery violations) through fines or imprisonment. By contrast, he observes, the Commission's ALJs have less capacious power to sanction misconduct. The *amicus*'s secondary distinction involves how the Tax Court and Commission, respectively, review the factfinding of STJs and ALJs. The Tax Court's rules state that an STJ's findings of fact "shall be presumed" correct. Tax Court Rule 183(d). In comparison, the *amicus* notes, the SEC's regulations include no such deferential standard.

But those distinctions make no difference for officer status. To start with the *amicus*'s primary point, *Freytag* referenced only the general "power to enforce compliance with discovery orders," not any particular method of doing so. True enough, the power to toss malefactors in jail is an especially muscular means of enforcement — the nuclear option of compliance tools. But just as armies can often enforce their will through conventional weapons, so too can administrative judges. As noted earlier, the Commission's ALJs can respond to discovery violations and other contemptuous conduct by excluding the wrongdoer (whether party or lawyer) from the proceedings — a powerful disincentive to resist a court order. Similarly, if the offender is an attorney, the ALJ can "[s]ummarily suspend" him from representing his client — not something the typical lawyer wants to invite. And finally, a judge who will, in the end, issue an opinion complete with factual findings, legal conclusions, and sanctions has substantial informal power to ensure the parties stay in line. Contrary to the *amicus*'s view, all that is enough to satisfy *Freytag*'s fourth item (even supposing, which we do not decide, that each of those items is necessary for someone conducting adversarial hearings to count as an officer).

The only issue left is remedial. This Court has held that the "appropriate" remedy for an adjudication tainted with an appointments violation is a new "hearing before a properly appointed" official. *Id.*, at 183, 188. And we add today one thing more. That official cannot be Judge Elliot, even if he has by now received (or receives sometime in the future) a constitutional appointment. Judge Elliot has already both heard Lucia's case and issued an initial decision on the merits. He cannot be expected to consider the matter as though he had not adjudicated it before. To cure the constitutional error, another ALJ (or the Commission itself) must hold the new hearing to which Lucia is entitled.

We accordingly reverse the judgment of the Court of Appeals and remand the case for further proceedings consistent with this opinion.

JUSTICE BREYER, with whom JUSTICE GINSBURG and JUSTICE SOTOMAYOR join as to Part III, concurring in the judgment in part and dissenting in part:

I agree with the Court that the Securities and Exchange Commission did not properly appoint the Administrative Law Judge who presided over petitioner Lucia's hearing. But I disagree with the majority in respect to two matters. First, I would rest our conclusion upon statutory, not constitutional, grounds. I believe it important to do so because I cannot answer the constitutional question that the majority answers without knowing the answer to a different, embedded constitutional question, which the Solicitor General urged us to answer in this case: the constitutionality of the statutory "for cause" removal protections that Congress provided for administrative law judges. Cf. *Free Enterprise Fund v. Public Company Accounting Oversight Bd.*, 561 U.S. 477 (2010). Second, I disagree with the Court in respect to the proper remedy.

I

The relevant statute here is the Administrative Procedure Act. That Act governs the appointment of administrative law judges. It provides (as it has, in substance, since its enactment in 1946) that "[e]ach agency shall appoint as many administrative law judges as are necessary for" hearings governed by the Administrative Procedure Act. 5 U.S.C. §3105; see also Administrative Procedure Act, §11, 60 Stat. 244 (original version, which refers to "examiners" as administrative law judges were then called). In the case of the Securities and Exchange Commission, the relevant "agency" is the Commission itself. But the Commission did not appoint the Administrative Law Judge who presided over Lucia's hearing. Rather, the Commission's staff appointed that Administrative Law Judge, without the approval of the Commissioners themselves.

I do not believe that the Administrative Procedure Act permits the Commission to delegate its power to appoint its administrative law judges to its staff. We have held that, for purposes of the Constitution's Appointments Clause, the Commission itself is a "'Hea[d]'" of a "'Departmen[t].'" *Free Enterprise Fund, supra,* at 512-513. Thus, reading the statute as referring to the Commission itself, and not to its staff, avoids a difficult constitutional question, namely, the very question that the Court answers today: whether the Commission's administrative law judges are constitutional "inferior Officers" whose appointment Congress may vest only in the President, the "Courts of Law," or the "Heads of Departments." Art. II, §2, cl. 2; see *United States v. Jin Fuey Moy,* 241 U.S. 394, 401 (1916) ("A statute must be construed, if fairly possible, so as to avoid not only the conclusion that it is unconstitutional but also grave doubts upon that score").

I have found no other statutory provision that would permit the Commission to delegate the power to appoint its administrative law judges to its staff. The statute establishing and governing the Commission does allow the Commission to "delegate, by published order or rule, any of its functions to a division of the Commission, an individual Commissioner, an administrative law judge, or an employee or employee board." 15 U.S.C. §78d-1(a). But this provision requires a "published order or rule," and the Commission here published no relevant delegating order or rule. Rather, Lucia discovered the Commission's appointment system for administrative law judges only when the Commission's enforcement division staff filed an affidavit in this case describing that staff-based system. Regardless, the same constitutional-avoidance reasons that should inform our construction of the Administrative Procedure Act should also lead us to interpret the Commission's general delegation authority as excluding the power to delegate to staff the authority to appoint its administrative law judges, so as to avoid the constitutional question the Court reaches in this case.

The analysis may differ for other agencies that employ administrative law judges. Each agency's governing statute is different, and some, unlike the Commission's, may allow the delegation of duties without a published order or rule. See, e.g., 42 U.S.C. §902(a)(7) (applicable to the Social Security Administration). Similarly, other agencies' administrative law judges perform distinct functions, and their means of appointment may therefore not raise the constitutional questions that inform my reading of the relevant statutes here.

The upshot, in my view, is that for statutory, not constitutional, reasons, the Commission did not lawfully appoint the Administrative Law Judge here at issue. And this Court should decide no more than that.

II

A

The reason why it is important to go no further arises from the holding in a case this Court decided eight years ago, Free Enterprise Fund v. Public Corporation Accounting Oversight Board, 561 U.S. 477 (2010). [see infra pp. 92-104] Because, in the Court's view, the relevant statutes (1) granted the Securities and Exchange Commissioners protection from removal without cause, (2) gave the Commissioners sole authority to remove Board members, and (3) protected Board members from removal without cause, the statutes provided Board members with two levels of protection from removal and consequently violated the Constitution. Id., at 495-498. . . .

[T]he implications of *Free Enterprise Fund*'s technical-sounding holding about "multilevel protection from removal" remain potentially dramatic. 561 U.S., at 484, 130 S. Ct. 3138, 177 L. Ed. 2d 706. The same statute, the *Administrative Procedure Act*, that provides that the "agency" will appoint its administrative law judges also protects the administrative law judges from removal without cause. . . . And the President may, in turn, remove members of the Merit Systems Protection Board [which can find good gause to remove ALJs] only for "inefficiency, neglect of duty, or malfeasance in office." §1202(d). Thus, Congress seems to have provided administrative law judges with two levels of protection from removal without cause — just what *Free Enterprise Fund* interpreted the Constitution to forbid in the case of the Board members. . . .

[I]t should be clear why the application of *Free Enterprise Fund* to administrative law judges is important. If that decision does not limit or forbid Congress' statutory "for cause" protections, then a holding that the administrative law judges are "inferior Officers" does not conflict with Congress' intent as revealed in the statute. But, if the holding is to the contrary, and more particularly if a holding that administrative law judges are "inferior Officers" brings with it application of *Free Enterprise Fund*'s limitation on "for cause" protections from removal, then a determination that administrative law judges are, constitutionally speaking, "inferior Officers" would directly conflict with Congress' intent, as revealed in the statute. In that case, it would be clear to me that Congress did not intend that consequence, and that it therefore did not intend to make administrative law judges "inferior Officers" at all.

III

Separately, I also disagree with the majority's conclusion that the proper remedy in this case requires a hearing before a *different* administrative law judge. *Ante*, at 12-13. The Securities and Exchange Commission has now itself appointed the Administrative Law Judge in question, and I see no reason why he could not rehear the case. After all, when a judge is reversed on appeal and a new trial ordered, typically the judge who rehears the case is the same judge who heard it the first time. The reversal here is based on a technical constitutional question, and the reversal implies no criticism at all of the original judge or his ability to conduct the new proceedings. For him to preside once again would not violate the structural purposes that we have said the Appointments Clause serves, see *Freytag*, 501 U.S., at 878, nor would it, in any obvious way, violate the Due Process Clause.

Regardless, this matter was not addressed below and has not been fully argued here. I would, at a minimum, ask the Court of Appeals to examine it on remand rather than decide it here now. That is especially so because the majority seems to state a general rule that a different "Officer" must *always* preside after an Appointments Clause violation. In a case like this one, that is a relatively minor imposition, because the Commission has other administrative law judges. But in other cases — say, a case adjudicated by an improperly appointed (but since reappointed) Commission itself — the "Officer" in question may be the *only* such "Officer," so that no substitute will be available. The majority suggests that in such cases, the "rule of necessity" may excuse compliance with its newfound different-"Officer" requirement. But that still does not explain why the Constitution would require a hearing before a different "Officer" at all. . . .

The Court's decision to address the Appointments Clause question separately from the constitutional removal question is problematic. By considering each question in isolation, the Court risks (should the Court later extend *Free Enterprise Fund*) unraveling, step-by-step, the foundations of the Federal Government's administrative adjudication system as it has existed for decades, and perhaps of the merit-based civil-service system in general. And the Court risks doing so without considering that potential consequence. For these reasons, I concur in the judgment in part and, with respect, I dissent in part.

[A concurrence by Justices Thomas and Gorsuch has been omitted.]

[A dissent by Justices Sotomayor and Ginsburg has been omitted.]

NOTES

1. As the *Lucia* Court explains, *Freytag* mandates the ultimate result in the case. Nonetheless, all of the prior lower court cases in this area purported to rely on *Freytag* yet came to opposite conclusions. There is little question that the Court in *Freytag* placed significant reliance on the absence of final decision-making authority by the special trial judges at issue in that case. See 501 U.S. 868, 874-875 ("Petitioners appear not to appreciate the distinction between the special trial judges' authority to hear cases and prepare proposed findings and opinions under subsection (b)(4) and their lack of authority actually to decide those cases, which is reserved exclusively for judges of the Tax Court. Because they do not distinguish between hearing a case and deciding it, petitioners advance two arguments that, it seems to us, miss the mark."). What is still unclear after *Lucia* is whether final decision-making authority is merely one factor or a necessary factor in determining inferior officer status. The *Lucia* opinion strongly suggests it is one factor. The fact that SEC ALJs in *Lucia* have "last word capacity," though, seems to have made the case much easier for the majority. Indeed, the dissent would have held that "the ability to make final, binding decisions on behalf of the Government" *is* required to conclude that a person or multimember body wields the "significant authority" necessary to operate as an officer. *Lucia*, 138 S. Ct. at 2065 (Sotomayor, J., dissenting). See also Samuel A. Schwartz, Lucia v. SEC: The Ambiguity of the Appointments Clause Continues, Sending Tremors Coursing Throughout the Administrative State, 14 J. Bus. & Tech L. Proxy 1 (2019).

2. The Supreme Court received two petitions for certiorari raising the Appointment Clause issue. In addition to *Lucia*, the 10th Circuit, in Bandimere v. Securities and Exchange Commission, 844 F.3d 1168 (10th Cir. 2016), had found the SEC ALJ appointment process unconstitutional. Had the Supreme Court used *Bandimere* as the vehicle for resolving the constitutional question, the composition of the participating Justices would have likely changed. Justice Gorsuch was on the 10th Circuit at the time the government petitioned for rehearing en banc, a petition ultimately denied. He therefore may have been ineligible to participate in the Supreme Court's consideration of *Bandimere*, a limitation that did not apply to *Lucia*. Indeed, the Supreme Court eventually denied certiorari in *Bandimere* without the participation of Justice Gorsuch. See No. 17-475 (June 28, 2018) ("The petition for a writ of certiorari is denied. Justice Gorsuch took no part in the consideration or decision of this petition.").

3. *Lucia* will increase the focus on the definition of "Head of Department." The Justices were split on a related issue in *Freytag*; while the majority strongly implied that only "Cabinet-level entities" constituted "departments," 501 U.S. 868 at 887, three others joined Justice Scalia's concurrence, in which he defined "department" to mean "all independent executive establishments." Id. at 919 (Scalia, J., concurring in part and dissenting in part). The Court later adopted this view, writing that a department is a "freestanding component of the Executive Branch not subordinate to or contained within any other such component." Free Enteprise Fund v. Public Corporation Accounting Oversight Board, 561 U.S. 477, 511 (2010). Under this understanding of "department," the administrator of the EPA would likely be considered a "Head of Department" empowered to appoint inferior officers under the Appointments Clause. William Funk, Is the Environmental Appeals Board Unconstitutional or Unlawful?, 49 Env't L. 737, 740-741 (2019). The Commissioner of the Internal Revenue Service, however, might not be. David Hahn, Late for an Appointment: Balancing Impartiality and Accountability in the IRS Office of Appeals, 103 Minn. L. Rev. 385, 402 (2018). Shortly after *Lucia*, the Solicitor General released a guidance memo to agency general counsels identifying a Department Head as one who has "authority derived from statute (or from a valid regulation promulgated through statutory authority)" to make an appointment. U.S. Dep't of Justice, Guidance on Administrative Law Judges after *Lucia* (2018) at 3-4. Regardless, ambiguities remain.

4. How will the SEC and other agencies have to change the appointment process for ALJs? While *Lucia* was pending before the U.S. Supreme Court, the SEC issued an order ratifying the appointment of ALJs that had been undertaken by staff. See In re Pending Administrative Orders, Exchange Act Release No. 82178 (Nov. 30, 2017) (issuing an order ratifying the appointment of ALJs at the agency in order "[t]o put to rest any claim that administrative proceedings pending before, or presided over by, Commission administrative law judges violate the Appointments Clause."). Whether this approach was sufficient, however, was not made clear by the Court. The opinion contained one obscure reference to the possibility of agency cure; in establishing a remedy of rehearing, the Court said, "[The] official [who rehears the case] cannot be Judge Elliot, even if he has by now received (or receives sometime in the future) a constitutional appointment." Notably, Justice Breyer in dissent does suggest that the SEC has already cured the violation. Do you think ratification by the SEC of the appointment actions of its staff is enough to meet the requirements of the Appointments Clause? The Solicitor General's guidance memo suggests it is; it advises agencies "to arrange prompty for the appropriate Department Head to ratify and approve the appointment of existing ALJs and similarly situated adjudicatory officers," having concluded that "the final appointment [of ALJs] must be made *or approved* by the Department head personally." U.S. Dep't of Justice, Guidance on Administrative Law Judges after *Lucia* (2018) at 1, 4 (emphasis added). The memo even recommends specific ratification language. Id. at 5. In addition, the memo identifies "the multi-member body itself, acting by majority vote," as the Head of Department for the SEC and similar agencies for purposes of the Appointments Clause. Id. at 4. See also Paul Verkuil, Presidential Administration, the Appointment of ALJs, and the Future of For Cause Protection, 72 Admin. L. Rev. 461 (2020); Roberta S. Karmel, Little Power Struggles Everywhere: Attacks on the Administrative State at the Securities and Exchange Commission, 72 Admin. L. Rev. 207 (2020).

5. The decision also raises questions about requirements imposed on departments with respect to the appointment process. Until the decision in *Lucia*, ALJs were selected through a "merit-selection" process run by the Office of Personnel Management. See *Bandimere*, at 1176. Agencies selected ALJs from the "top three candidates" submitted by OPM. Id. at 1177. Shortly after the *Lucia* decision, the President issued an executive order altering the appointment process to reduce the role of OPM and increase the discretion by the agencies actually appointing the ALJs at least in part because of perceived concern over the constitutionality of the OPM process.*See* Executive Order Excepting Administrative Law Judges from the Competitive Service, July 10, 2018 ("As evident from recent litigation, *Lucia* may also raise questions about the method of appointing ALJs, including whether competitive examination and competitive service selection procedures are compatible with the discretion an agency head must possess under the Appointments Clause in selecting ALJs."). The order sought to permit appointment "without proceeding through complicated and elaborate examination processes or rating procedures that do not necessarily reflect the agency's particular needs. . . ." What might be some consequences of the altered appointment process?

6. The status of ALJs as inferior officers raises other constitutional questions. ALJs typically cannot be removed except "for cause." To the extent the Head of the Department also cannot be removed except for cause (as is the case with commissioners of the SEC), the double layer of removal restrictions raises the question addressed in Free Enterprise Fund v. PCAOB, 561 U.S. 477 (2010) (see infra). As Justice Breyer noted in *Lucia,* one possible interpretation is that ALJs, as inferior officers, will "lose their 'for cause' removal protections. . . ." What would be the consequence of such a determination? See Michael A. Sabino, "Liberty Requires Accountability": The Appointments Clause, Lucia v. SEC, and the Next Constitutional Controversy, 11 Wm. & Mary Bus. L. Rev. 173 (2019).

7. Since the decision in *Lucia,* the Court has begun to define some of its limits. For example, in Fin. Oversight & Mgmt. Bd. For P.R. v. Aurelius Inv., L.L.C., 140 S. Ct. 1649 (2020), the Supreme Court declined to apply *Lucia* to members of the board that Congress created to "represent[] Puerto Rico in bankruptcy decisions and supervis[e] aspects of Puerto Rico's fiscal and budgetary policies." Id. at 1655. While the Court recognized that the Appointments Clause applies to "Officers of the United States," even in Puerto Rico and similar areas (such as the District of Columbia), it concluded that members of the board at-issue have "primarily local duties such that their selection [was] not subject to the constraints of the Appointments Clause." Id. at 1661-1663. In this way, the Court established a new test for the applicability of the Appointments Clause: whether the officials in question exercise power in primarily local or primarily federal matters. Without this test, the majority concluded, it would be "significantly more difficult for local residents . . . to share responsibility for the implementation of (statutorily created) primarily local duties," thereby undermining democratic accountability. Id. at 1663.

UNITED STATES v. ARTHREX, INC.

___ U.S. ___, 141 S. Ct. 1970 (June, 2021)

CHIEF JUSTICE ROBERTS delivered the opinion of the Court with respect to Parts I and II.

The validity of a patent previously issued by the Patent and Trademark Office can be challenged before the Patent Trial and Appeal Board, an executive tribunal within the PTO. The Board, composed largely of Administrative Patent Judges appointed by the Secretary of Commerce, has the final word within the Executive Branch on the validity of a challenged patent. Billions of dollars can turn on a Board decision.

Under the Constitution, "[t]he executive Power" is vested in the President, who has the responsibility to "take Care that the Laws be faithfully executed." Art. II, §1, cl. 1; §3. The Appointments Clause provides that he may be assisted in carrying out that responsibility by officers nominated by him and confirmed by the Senate, as well as by other officers not appointed in that manner but whose work, we have held, must be directed and supervised by an officer who has been. §2, cl. 2. The question presented is whether the authority of the Board to issue decisions on behalf of the Executive Branch is consistent with these constitutional provisions.

I

A

. . .

The present [patent registration] system is administered by the Patent and Trademark Office (PTO), an executive agency within the Department of Commerce "responsible for the granting and issuing of patents" in the name of the United States. 35 U. S. C. §§1(a), 2(a)(1). Congress has vested the "powers and duties" of the PTO in a sole Director appointed by the President with the advice and consent of the Senate. §3(a)(1). As agency head, the Director "provid[es] policy direction and management supervision" for PTO officers and employees. §3(a)(2)(A).

This suit centers on the Patent Trial and Appeal Board (PTAB), an executive adjudicatory body within the PTO established by the Leahy-Smith America Invents Act of 2011. 125 Stat. 313. The PTAB sits in panels of at least three members drawn from the Director, the Deputy Director, the Commissioner for Patents, the Commissioner for Trademarks, and more than 200 Administrative Patent Judges (APJs). 35 U. S. C. §§6(a), (c). The Secretary of Commerce appoints the members of the PTAB (except for the Director), including the APJs at issue in this dispute. §§3(b)(1), (b)(2)(A), 6(a). The Board decides whether an invention satisfies the standards for patentability on review of decisions by primary examiners. §§6(b)(1), 134(a).

Through a variety of procedures, the PTAB can also take a second look at patents previously issued by the PTO. §§6(b)(2)–(4). One such procedure is inter partes review. Established in 2011, inter partes review is an adversarial process by which members of the PTAB reconsider whether existing patents satisfy the novelty and nonobviousness requirements for inventions. See §6(a) of the America Invents Act, 125 Stat. 299. Any person — other than the patent owner himself — can file a petition to institute inter partes review of a patent. 35 U. S. C. §311(a). The Director can institute review only if, among other requirements, he determines that the petitioner is reasonably likely to prevail on at least one challenged patent claim. §314(a). Congress has committed the decision to institute inter partes review to the Director's unreviewable discretion. . . . By regulation, the Director has delegated this authority to the PTAB itself. . . .

The Director designates at least three members of the PTAB (typically three APJs) to conduct an inter partes proceeding. 35 U. S. C. §6(c). The PTAB then assumes control of the process, which resembles civil litigation in many respects.

§316(c). The PTAB must issue a final written decision on all of the challenged patent claims within 12 to 18 months of institution. §316(a)(11).... A party who disagrees with a decision may request rehearing by the PTAB. 35 U. S. C. §6(c); 37 CFR §42.71(d).

The PTAB is the last stop for review within the Executive Branch. A party dissatisfied with the final decision may seek judicial review in the Court of Appeals for the Federal Circuit. 35 U. S. C. §319. At this stage, the Director can intervene before the court to defend or disavow the Board's decision. §143. The Federal Circuit reviews the PTAB's application of patentability standards *de novo* and its underlying factual determinations for substantial evidence.... Upon expiration of the time to appeal or termination of any appeal, "the Director shall issue and publish a certificate canceling any claim of the patent finally determined to be unpatentable, confirming any claim of the patent determined to be patentable, and incorporating in the patent by operation of the certificate any new or amended claim determined to be patentable." §318(b).

B

Arthrex, Inc. develops medical devices and procedures for orthopedic surgery. In 2015, it secured a patent on a surgical device for reattaching soft tissue to bone without tying a knot, U. S. Patent No. 9,179,907 ('907 patent). Arthrex soon claimed that Smith & Nephew, Inc. and ArthroCare Corp. (collectively, Smith & Nephew) had infringed the '907 patent, and the dispute eventually made its way to inter partes review in the PTO. Three APJs formed the PTAB panel that conducted the proceeding and ultimately concluded that a prior patent application "anticipated" the invention claimed by the '907 patent, so that Arthrex's patent was invalid....

On appeal to the Federal Circuit, Arthrex raised for the first time an argument premised on the Appointments Clause of the Constitution. That Clause specifies how the President may appoint officers who assist him in carrying out his responsibilities. *Principal* officers must be appointed by the President with the advice and consent of the Senate, while *inferior* officers may be appointed by the President alone, the head of an executive department, or a court. Art. II, §2, cl. 2. Arthrex argued that the APJs were principal officers and therefore that their appointment by the Secretary of Commerce was unconstitutional. The Government intervened to defend the appointment procedure.

The Federal Circuit agreed with Arthrex that APJs were principal officers. 941 F. 3d 1320, 1335 (2019). Neither the Secretary nor Director had the authority to review their decisions or to remove them at will. The Federal Circuit held that these restrictions meant that APJs were themselves principal officers, not inferior officers under the direction of the Secretary or Director.

To fix this constitutional violation, the Federal Circuit invalidated the tenure protections for APJs. Making APJs removable at will by the Secretary, the panel held, prospectively "renders them inferior rather than principal officers." The Federal Circuit vacated the PTAB's decision and remanded for a fresh hearing before a new panel of APJs, who would no longer enjoy protection against removal.

This satisfied no one. The Government, Smith & Nephew, and Arthrex each requested rehearing en banc, which the Court of Appeals denied. 953 F. 3d 760, 761 (2020) (*per curiam*). The parties then requested review of different aspects of the panel's decision in three petitions for certiorari.

We granted those petitions to consider whether the PTAB's structure is consistent with the Appointments Clause, and the appropriate remedy if it is not.

II

A

The President is "'responsible for the actions of the Executive Branch'" and "'cannot delegate [that] ultimate responsibility or the active obligation to supervise that goes with it.'" *Free Enterprise Fund v. Public Company Accounting Oversight Bd.*, 561 U.S. 477, 496-497 (2010) (quoting *Clinton v. Jones*, 520 U.S. 681, 712-713 (1997) (BREYER, J., concurring in judgment)). The Framers recognized, of course, that "no single person could fulfill that responsibility alone, [and] expected that the President would rely on subordinate officers for assistance." *Seila Law LLC v. Consumer Financial Protection Bureau*, 591 U.S. ___, ___ (2020) (plurality opinion) (slip op., at 2).

Today, thousands of officers wield executive power on behalf of the President in the name of the United States. That power acquires its legitimacy and accountability to the public through "a clear and effective chain of command" down from the President, on whom all the people vote. *Free Enterprise Fund*, 561 U.S., at 498. James Madison extolled this "great principle of unity and responsibility in the Executive department," which ensures that "the chain of dependence [will] be preserved; the lowest officers, the middle grade, and the highest, will depend, as they ought, on the President, and the President on the community." 1 Annals of Cong. 499 (1789).

The Appointments Clause provides:

> "[The President] shall nominate, and by and with the Advice and Consent of the Senate, shall appoint Ambassadors, other public Ministers and Consuls, Judges of the supreme Court, and all other Officers of the United States, whose Appointments are not herein otherwise provided for, and which shall be established by Law: but Congress may by Law vest the Appointment of such inferior Officers, as they think proper, in the President alone, in the Courts of Law, or in the Heads of Departments." Art. II, §2, cl. 2.

Assigning the nomination power to the President guarantees accountability for the appointees' actions because the "blame of a bad nomination would fall upon the president singly and absolutely." The Federalist No. 77, p. 517 (J. Cooke ed. 1961) (A. Hamilton). As Hamilton wrote, the "sole and undivided responsibility of one man will naturally beget a livelier sense of duty and a more exact regard to reputation." *Id.*, No. 76, at 510–511. The Appointments Clause adds a degree of accountability in the Senate, which shares in the public blame "for both the making of a bad appointment and the rejection of a good one." *Edmond* v. *United States*, 520 U.S. 651, 660 (1997).

Only the President, with the advice and consent of the Senate, can appoint noninferior officers, called "principal" officers as shorthand in our cases. See *id.*, at 659. The "default manner of appointment" for inferior officers is also nomination by the President and confirmation by the Senate. *Id.*, at 660. But the Framers foresaw that "when offices became numerous, and sudden removals necessary, this mode might be inconvenient." *United States* v. *Germaine*, 99 U.S. 508, 510 (1879). Reflecting this concern for "administrative convenience," the Appointments Clause permits Congress to dispense with joint appointment, but only for inferior officers. *Edmond*, 520 U.S., at 660. Congress may vest the appointment of such officers "in the President alone, in the Courts of Law, or in the Heads of Departments."

B

Congress provided that APJs would be appointed as inferior officers, by the Secretary of Commerce as head of a department. The question presented is whether the nature of their responsibilities is consistent with their method of appointment. As an initial matter, no party disputes that APJs are officers — not "lesser functionaries" such as employees or contractors — because they "exercis[e] significant authority pursuant to the laws of the United States." *Buckley v. Valeo*, 424 U.S. 1, 126, and n. 162 (1976) (*per curiam*); see *Lucia v. SEC*, 585 U.S. ___, ___-___ (2018) (slip op., at 8-9). APJs do so when reconsidering an issued patent, a power that (the Court has held) involves the adjudication of public rights that Congress may appropriately assign to executive officers rather than to the Judiciary. . . .

The starting point for each party's analysis is our opinion in *Edmond*. There we explained that "[w]hether one is an 'inferior' officer depends on whether he has a superior" other than the President. 520 U.S., at 662. An inferior officer must be "directed and supervised at some level by others who were appointed by Presidential nomination with the advice and consent of the Senate." *Id.*, at 663.

In *Edmond*, we applied this test to adjudicative officials within the Executive Branch — specifically, Coast Guard Court of Criminal Appeals judges appointed by the Secretary of Transportation. See *id.*, at 658. We held that the judges were inferior officers because they were effectively supervised by a combination of Presidentially nominated and Senate confirmed officers in the Executive Branch: first, the Judge Advocate General, who "exercise[d] administrative oversight over the Court of Criminal Appeals" by prescribing rules of procedure and formulating policies for court-martial cases, and could also "remove a Court of Criminal Appeals judge from his judicial assignment without cause"; and second, the Court of Appeals for the Armed Forces, an executive tribunal that could review the judges' decisions under a *de novo* standard for legal issues and a deferential standard for factual issues. *Id.*, at 664–665. "What is significant," we concluded, "is that the judges of the Court of Criminal Appeals have no power to render a final decision on behalf of the United States unless permitted to do so by other Executive officers." *Id.*, at 665.

Congress structured the PTAB differently, providing only half of the "divided" supervision to which judges of the Court of Criminal Appeals were subject. *Id.*, at 664. Like the Judge Advocate General, the PTO Director possesses powers of "administrative oversight." *Ibid.* The Director fixes the rate of pay for APJs, controls the decision whether to institute inter partes review, and selects the APJs to reconsider the validity of the patent. 35 U.S.C. §§3(b)(6), 6(c), 314(a). The Director also promulgates regulations governing inter partes review, issues prospective guidance on patentability issues, and designates past PTAB decisions as "precedential" for future panels. §§3(a)(2)(A), 316(a)(4).... He is the boss, except when it comes to the one thing that makes the APJs officers exercising "significant authority" in the first place — their power to issue decisions on patentability. *Buckley*, 424 U.S., at 126. In contrast to the scheme approved by *Edmond*, no principal officer at any level within the Executive Branch "direct[s] and supervise[s]" the work of APJs in that regard. 520 U. S., at 663.

Edmond goes a long way toward resolving this dispute. What was "significant" to the outcome there — review by a superior executive officer — is absent here: APJs have the "power to render a final decision on behalf of the United States" without any such review by their nominal superior or any other principal officer in the Executive Branch. *Id.*, at 665. The only possibility of review is a petition for rehearing, but Congress unambiguously specified that "[o]nly the Patent and Trial Appeal Board may grant rehearings." §6(c). Such review simply repeats the arrangement challenged as unconstitutional in this suit.

This "diffusion of power carries with it a diffusion of accountability." *Free Enterprise Fund*, 561 U. S., at 497. The restrictions on review relieve the Director of responsibility for the final decisions rendered by APJs purportedly under his charge. The principal dissent's observation that "the Director alone has the power to take final action to cancel a patent claim or confirm it," (opinion of THOMAS, J.), simply ignores the undisputed fact that the Director's "power" in that regard is limited to carrying out the ministerial duty that he "shall issue and publish a certificate" canceling or confirming patent claims he had previously allowed, as dictated by the APJs' final decision. §318(b); see §§131, 153. The chain of command runs not from the Director to his subordinates, but from the APJs to the Director.

The Government and Smith & Nephew assemble a catalog of steps the Director might take to affect the decisionmaking process of the PTAB, despite his lack of any statutory authority to review its decisions.... The Government reminds us that it is the Director who decides whether to initiate inter partes review. §314(a). The Director can also designate the APJs who will decide a particular case and can pick ones predisposed to his views. §6(c). And the Director, the Government asserts, can even vacate his institution decision if he catches wind of an unfavorable ruling on the way. The "proceeding will have no legal consequences" so long as the Director jumps in before the Board issues its final decision....

If all else fails, the Government says, the Director can intervene in the rehearing process to reverse Board decisions. The Government acknowledges that only the PTAB can grant rehearing under §6(c). But the Director, according to the Government, could manipulate the composition of the PTAB panel that acts on the rehearing petition. For one thing, he could "stack" the original panel to rehear the case with additional APJs assumed to be more amenable to his preferences. See *Oil States*, 584 U.S., at ___ (GORSUCH, J., dissenting) (slip op., at 3). For another, he could assemble an entirely new panel consisting of himself and two other officers appointed by the Secretary — in practice, the Commissioner for Patents and the APJ presently designated as Chief Judge — to decide whether to overturn a decision and reach a different outcome binding on future panels. The Government insists that the Director, by handpicking (and, if necessary, repicking) Board members, can indirectly influence the course of inter partes review.

That is not the solution. It is the problem. The Government proposes (and the dissents embrace) a roadmap for the Director to evade a statutory prohibition on review without having him take responsibility for the ultimate decision. (BREYER, J., concurring in judgment in part and dissenting in part); (opinion of THOMAS, J.). Even if the Director succeeds in procuring his preferred outcome, such machinations blur the lines of accountability demanded by the Appointments Clause. The parties are left with neither an impartial decision by a panel of experts nor a transparent decision for which a politically accountable officer must take responsibility. And the public can only wonder "on whom the blame or the punishment of a pernicious measure, or series of pernicious measures ought really to fall." The Federalist No. 70, at 476 (A. Hamilton).

The Government contends that the Director may respond after the fact by removing an APJ "from his judicial assignment without cause" and refusing to designate that APJ on *future* PTAB panels. *Edmond*, 520 U.S., at 664. Even assuming that is true, reassigning an APJ to a different task going forward gives the Director no means of countermanding the final decision already on the books. Nor are APJs "meaningfully controlled" by the threat of removal from federal service entirely, *Seila Law*, 591 U.S., at ___ (slip op., at 23), because the Secretary can fire them after a decision only "for such cause as will promote the efficiency of the service," 5 U.S.C. §7513(a). In all the ways that matter to the parties who appear before the PTAB, the buck stops with the APJs, not with the Secretary or Director.

Review outside Article II — here, an appeal to the Federal Circuit — cannot provide the necessary supervision. While the duties of APJs "partake of a Judiciary quality as well as Executive," APJs are still exercising executive power and must remain "dependent upon the President." 1 Annals of Cong., at 611-612 (J. Madison); see *Oil States*, 584 U.S., at ___ (slip op., at 8). The activities of executive officers may "take 'legislative' and 'judicial' forms, but they are exercises of — indeed, under our constitutional structure they *must be* exercises of — the 'executive Power,'" for which the President is ultimately responsible. *Arlington v. FCC*, 569 U.S. 290, 305, n. 4 (2013) (quoting Art. II, §1, cl. 1).

Given the insulation of PTAB decisions from any executive review, the President can neither oversee the PTAB himself nor "attribute the Board's failings to those whom he *can* oversee." *Free Enterprise Fund*, 561 U.S., at 496. APJs accordingly exercise power that conflicts with the design of the Appointments Clause "to preserve political accountability." *Edmond*, 520 U.S., at 663.

The principal dissent dutifully undertakes to apply the governing test from *Edmond*, see (opinion of THOMAS, J.), but its heart is plainly not in it. For example, the dissent rejects any distinction between "inferior-officer power" and "principal-officer power," but *Edmond* calls for exactly that: an appraisal of how much power an officer exercises free from control by a superior. The dissent pigeonholes this consideration as the sole province of the Vesting Clause, but *Edmond* recognized the Appointments Clause as a "significant structural safeguard[ ]" that "preserve[s] political accountability" through direction and supervision of subordinates — in other words, through a chain of command. 520 U.S., at 659, 663. The dissent would have the Court focus on the location of an officer in the agency "organizational chart," but as we explained in *Edmond*, "[i]t is not enough that other officers may be identified who formally maintain a higher rank, or possess responsibilities of a greater magnitude," 520 U.S., at 662-663. The dissent stresses that "at least two levels of authority" separate the President from PTAB decisions, but the unchecked exercise of executive power by an officer buried many layers beneath the President poses more, not less, of a constitutional problem. Conspicuously absent from the dissent is any concern for the President's ability to "discharge his own constitutional duty of seeing that the laws be faithfully executed." *Myers v. United States*, 272 U.S. 52, 135 (1926).

The other dissent charges that the Court's opinion has "no foundation" in past decisions (opinion of BREYER, J.). Of course, we have a different view on the proper application of *Edmond* in this dispute. As for other past decisions, it is the dissent that expressly grounds its analysis in dissenting opinions from *Free Enterprise Fund* and *Seila Law*, while frankly acknowledging that the *Court's* opinions in those cases support the principles that guide us here. *Post*, at 5–7.

C

History reinforces the conclusion that the unreviewable executive power exercised by APJs is incompatible with their status as inferior officers. Since the founding, principal officers have directed the decisions of inferior officers on matters of law as well as policy. Hamilton articulated the principle of constitutional accountability underlying such supervision in a 1792 Treasury circular. Writing as Secretary of the Treasury to the customs officials under his charge, he warned that any deviations from his instructions "would be subversive of uniformity in the execution of the laws." 3 Works of Alexander Hamilton 557 (J. Hamilton ed. 1850). "The power to superintend," he explained, "must imply a right to judge and direct," thereby ensuring that "the responsibility for a wrong construction rests with the head of the department, when it proceeds from him." *Id.*, at 559. . . .

Congress has carried the model of principal officer review into the modern administrative state. As the Government forthrightly acknowledged at oral argument, it "certainly is the norm" for principal officers to have the capacity to review decisions made by inferior adjudicative officers. Tr. of Oral Arg. 23. The Administrative Procedure Act, from its inception, authorized agency heads to review such decisions. 5 U.S.C. §557(b). And "higher-level agency reconsideration" by the agency head is the standard way to maintain political accountability and effective oversight for adjudication that takes place outside the confines of §557(b). Walker & Wasserman, The New World of Agency Adjudication, 107 Cal. L. Rev. 141, 157 (2019). To take one example recently discussed by this Court in *Free Enterprise Fund*, the Public Company Accounting Oversight Board can issue sanctions in disciplinary proceedings, but such sanctions are reviewable by its superior, the Securities and Exchange Commission. 15 U.S.C. §§7215(c)(4), 7217(c).

. . .

When it comes to the patent system in particular, adjudication has followed the traditional rule that a principal officer, if not the President himself, makes the final decision on how to exercise executive power. . . . The history of the Board of Appeals . . . has little to say about the present provision expressly ordering the Director to undo his prior patentability determination when a PTAB panel of unaccountable APJs later disagrees with it. See 35 U.S.C. §318(b).

We hold that the unreviewable authority wielded by APJs during inter partes review is incompatible with their appointment by the Secretary to an inferior office. The principal dissent repeatedly charges that we never say whether APJs are principal officers who were not appointed in the manner required by the Appointments Clause, or instead inferior officers exceeding the permissible scope of their duties under that Clause. (opinion of THOMAS, J.). But both formulations describe the same constitutional violation: Only an officer properly appointed to a principal office may issue a final decision binding the Executive Branch in the proceeding before us.

In reaching this conclusion, we do not attempt to "set forth an exclusive criterion for distinguishing between principal and inferior officers for Appointments Clause purposes." *Edmond*, 520 U.S., at 661. Many decisions by inferior officers do not bind the Executive Branch to exercise executive power in a particular manner, and we do not address supervision outside the context of adjudication. Cf. (opinion of THOMAS, J.). Here, however, Congress has assigned APJs "significant authority" in adjudicating the public rights of private parties, while also insulating their decisions from review and their offices from removal. *Buckley*, 424 U.S., at 126.

III

We turn now to the appropriate way to resolve this dispute given this violation of the Appointments Clause. In general, "when confronting a constitutional flaw in a statute, we try to limit the solution to the problem" by disregarding the "problematic portions while leaving the remainder intact." *Ayotte v. Planned*

Parenthood of Northern New Eng., 546 U.S. 320, 328-329 (2006). This approach derives from the Judiciary's "negative power to disregard an unconstitutional enactment" in resolving a legal dispute. *Massachusetts v. Mellon*, 262 U.S. 447, 488 (1923). In a case that presents a conflict between the Constitution and a statute, we give "full effect" to the Constitution and to whatever portions of the statute are "not repugnant" to the Constitution, effectively severing the unconstitutional portion of the statute. *Bank of Hamilton v. Lessee of Dudley*, 2 Pet. 492, 526 (1829) (Marshall, C. J.). This principle explains our "normal rule that partial, rather than facial, invalidation is the required course." *Brockett v. Spokane Arcades, Inc.*, 472 U.S. 491, 504 (1985).

Arthrex asks us to hold the entire regime of inter partes review unconstitutional. In its view, any more tailored declaration of unconstitutionality would necessitate a policy decision best left to Congress in the first instance. Because the good cannot be separated from the bad, Arthrex continues, the appropriate remedy is to order outright dismissal of the proceeding below. The partial dissent, similarly forswearing the need to do anything beyond "identifying the constitutional violation," would grant full relief to Arthrex. (GORSUCH, J., concurring in part and dissenting in part).

In our view, however, the structure of the PTO and the governing constitutional principles chart a clear course: Decisions by APJs must be subject to review by the Director. Congress vested the Director with the "powers and duties" of the PTO, 35 U.S.C. §3(a)(1), tasked him with supervising APJs, §3(a)(2)(A), and placed the PTAB "in" the PTO, §6(a). A single officer has superintended the activities of the PTO since the Commissioner of Patents assumed the role of "chief officer" of the Patent Office in 1836. §1, 5 Stat. 117-118. The Commissioner long oversaw examiners-in-chief, see 12 Stat. 246-247, just as the Director today has the responsibility to oversee APJs. While shielding the ultimate decisions of the 200-plus APJs from review, Congress also provided the Director means of control over the institution and conduct of inter partes review. 35 U.S.C. §§314(a), 316(a). In every respect save the insulation of their decisions from review within the Executive Branch, APJs appear to be inferior officers — an understanding consistent with their appointment in a manner permissible for inferior but not principal officers.

The America Invents Act insulates APJs from supervision through two mechanisms. The statute provides that "each . . . inter partes review shall be heard by at least 3 members of the [PTAB]" and that "only the [PTAB] may grant rehearings." §6(c). The upshot is that the Director cannot rehear and reverse a final decision issued by APJs. If the Director were to have the "authority to take control" of a PTAB proceeding, APJs would properly function as inferior officers. *Go-Bart Importing Co. v. United States*, 282 U.S. 344, 354 (1931).

We conclude that a tailored approach is the appropriate one: Section 6(c) cannot constitutionally be enforced to the extent that its requirements prevent the Director from reviewing final decisions rendered by APJs. Because Congress has vested the Director with the "power and duties" of the PTO, §3(a)(1), the Director has the authority to provide for a means of reviewing PTAB decisions.

See also §§3(a)(2)(A), 316(a)(4). The Director accordingly may review final PTAB decisions and, upon review, may issue decisions himself on behalf of the Board. Section 6(c) otherwise remains operative as to the other members of the PTAB.

This does not result in an incomplete or unworkable statutory scheme. Cf. *United States v. Treasury Employees*, 513 U.S. 454, 479 (1995). To the contrary, review by the Director would follow the almost-universal model of adjudication in the Executive Branch, and aligns the PTAB with the *other* adjudicative body in the PTO, the Trademark Trial and Appeal Board, see §228 of the Trademark Modernization Act of 2020, 134 Stat. 2209.

The Government defends the different approach adopted by the Federal Circuit. The Court of Appeals held unenforceable APJs' protection against removal except "for such cause as will promote the efficiency of the service," 5 U.S.C. §7513(a), which applies through 35 U.S.C. §3(c). See 941 F. 3d, at 1337, 1340. If the for-cause provision were unenforceable, the Secretary could remove APJs at will. See *Ex parte Hennen*, 13 Pet. 230, 259-260 (1839). The Government contends that APJs would then be inferior officers under *Free Enterprise Fund*. But regardless whether the Government is correct that at-will removal by the Secretary would cure the constitutional problem, review by the Director better reflects the structure of supervision within the PTO and the nature of APJs' duties, for the reasons we have explained.

In sum, we hold that 35 U.S.C. §6(c) is unenforceable as applied to the Director insofar as it prevents the Director from reviewing the decisions of the PTAB on his own. The Director may engage in such review and reach his own decision. When reviewing such a decision by the Director, a court must decide the case "conformably to the constitution, disregarding the law" placing restrictions on his review authority in violation of Article II. *Marbury v. Madison*, 1 Cranch 137, 178 (1803). We add that this suit concerns only the Director's ability to supervise APJs in adjudicating petitions for inter partes review. We do not address the Director's supervision over other types of adjudications conducted by the PTAB, such as the examination process for which the Director has claimed unilateral authority to issue a patent.

We also conclude that the appropriate remedy is a remand to the Acting Director for him to decide whether to rehear the petition filed by Smith & Nephew. Although the APJs' appointment by the Secretary allowed them to lawfully adjudicate the petition in the first instance, see *Freytag*, 501 U.S., at 881-882, they lacked the power under the Constitution to finally resolve the matter within the Executive Branch. Under these circumstances, a limited remand to the Director provides an adequate opportunity for review by a principal officer. Because the source of the constitutional violation is the restraint on the review authority of the Director, rather than the appointment of APJs by the Secretary, Arthrex is not entitled to a hearing before a new panel of APJs. Cf. *Lucia*, 585 U.S., at ___-___ (slip op., at 12–13).

. . .

Today, we reaffirm and apply the rule from *Edmond* that the exercise of executive power by inferior officers must at some level be subject to the direction and supervision of an officer nominated by the President and confirmed by the Senate. The Constitution therefore forbids the enforcement of statutory restrictions on the Director that insulate the decisions of APJs from his direction and supervision. To be clear, the Director need not review every decision of the PTAB. What matters is that the Director have the discretion to review decisions rendered by APJs. In this way, the President remains responsible for the exercise of executive power — and through him, the exercise of executive power remains accountable to the people.

The judgment of the United States Court of Appeals for the Federal Circuit is vacated, and the cases are remanded for further proceedings consistent with this opinion.

It is so ordered.

[A dissent by JUSTICE GORSUCH maintaining that he would opt to set aside the decision involving Arthrex rather than severing §6(c) from the rest of the statute, is omitted.]

JUSTICE THOMAS, with whom JUSTICE BREYER, JUSTICE SOTOMAYOR, and JUSTICE KAGAN join as to Parts I and II, dissenting.

For the very first time, this Court holds that Congress violated the Constitution by vesting the appointment of a federal officer in the head of a department. Just who are these "principal" officers that Congress unsuccessfully sought to smuggle into the Executive Branch without Senate confirmation? About 250 administrative patent judges who sit at the bottom of an organizational chart, nestled under at least two levels of authority. Neither our precedent nor the original understanding of the Appointments Clause requires Senate confirmation of officers inferior to not one, but *two* officers below the President.

I

On appeal, Arthrex argued that the Federal Circuit must vacate the Board's decision. According to Arthrex, administrative patent judges are constitutionally defective because they are principal officers who were neither appointed by the President nor confirmed by the Senate. The Federal Circuit agreed in part. The court held that administrative patent judges *are* principal officers. 941 F. 3d 1320, 1335 (2019). But the court professed to transform these principal officers into inferior ones by withdrawing statutory removal restrictions. *Id.*, at 1338.

The Court now partially agrees with the Federal Circuit. Although it cannot quite bring itself to say so expressly, it too appears to hold that administrative patent judges are principal officers under the current statutory scheme. But it concludes that the better way to judicially convert these principal officers to inferior ones is to allow the Director to review Board decisions unilaterally. *Ante*, at 21 (plurality opinion); *ante*, at 7 (BREYER, J., concurring in part and dissenting in part).

That both the Federal Circuit and this Court would take so much care to ensure that administrative patent judges, appointed as inferior officers, would remain inferior officers at the end of the day suggests that perhaps they were inferior officers to begin with. Instead of rewriting the Director's statutory powers, I would simply leave intact the patent scheme Congress has created.

II

The Constitution creates a default process to appoint all officers: The President "by and with the Advice and Consent of the Senate, shall appoint Ambassadors, other public Ministers and Consuls, Judges of the supreme Court, and all other Officers of the United States." Art. II, §2. But Congress has discretion to change the default process for "inferior" officers: "Congress may by Law vest the Appointment of such inferior Officers, as they think proper, in the President alone, in the Courts of Law, or in the Heads of Departments."

A

The Court has been careful not to create a rigid test to divide principal officers — those who must be Senate confirmed — from inferior ones. See, *e.g., Edmond v. United States*, 520 U.S. 651, 661 (1997) (the Court has "not set forth an exclusive criterion"); *Morrison v. Olson*, 487 U.S. 654, 671 (1988) ("We need not attempt here to decide exactly where the line falls between the two types of officers"). Instead, the Court's opinions have traditionally used a case-by-case analysis. And those analyses invariably result in this Court deferring to Congress' choice of which constitutional appointment process works best. No party (nor the majority) has identified any instance in which this Court has found unconstitutional an appointment that aligns with one of the two processes outlined in the Constitution.

Our most exhaustive treatment of the inferior-officer question is found in *Edmond*. There, we evaluated the status of civilian judges on the Coast Guard Court of Criminal Appeals who were appointed by the Secretary of Transportation. As in all previous decisions, the Court in *Edmond* held that the Secretary's appointment of the judges complied with the Appointments Clause.

Recognizing that no "definitive test" existed for distinguishing between inferior and principal officers, the Court set out two general guidelines. 520 U.S., at 661-662. First, there is a formal, definitional requirement. The officer must be lower in rank to "a superior." *Id.*, at 662. But according to the Court in *Edmond*, formal inferiority is "not enough." So the Court imposed a functional requirement: The inferior officer's work must be "directed and supervised at some level by others who were appointed by Presidential nomination with advice and consent of the Senate." *Id.*, at 663. Because neither side asks us to overrule our precedent, I would apply this two-part guide.

There can be no dispute that administrative patent judges are, in fact, inferior: They are lower in rank to at least two different officers. As part of the Board, they serve in the Patent and Trademark Office, run by a Director "responsible for providing policy direction and management supervision for the Office and for the issuance of patents and the registration of trademarks." 35 U.S.C. §3(a)(2)(A). That Office, in turn, is "[w]ithin the Department of Commerce" and "subject to the policy direction of the Secretary of Commerce." §1(a). The Secretary, in consultation with the Director, appoints administrative patent judges. §6(a).

As a comparison to the facts in *Edmond* illustrates, the Director and Secretary are also functionally superior because they supervise and direct the work administrative patent judges perform. In *Edmond*, the Court focused on the supervision exercised by two different entities: the Judge Advocate General and the Court of Appeals for the Armed Forces (CAAF). The Judge Advocate General exercised general administrative oversight over the court on which the military judges sat. *Edmond*, 520 U.S., at 664. He possessed the power to prescribe uniform rules of procedure for the court and to formulate policies and procedure with respect to the review of court-martial cases in general. And he could remove a Court of Criminal Appeals judge from his judicial assignment without cause, a "powerful tool for control."

The Court noted, however, that "[t]he Judge Advocate General's control over Court of Criminal Appeals judges is . . . not complete." This was so for two reasons. He could "not attempt to influence (by threat of removal or otherwise) the outcome of individual proceedings." And, he had "no power to reverse decisions of the court." But this lack of complete control did not render the military judges principal officers. That is because one of the two missing powers resided, to a limited degree, in a different entity: the CAAF. CAAF could not "reevaluate the facts" where "there [was] some competent evidence in the record to establish each element of the offense beyond a reasonable doubt." *Id.*, at 665. Still, it was "significant . . . that the judges of the Court of Criminal Appeals ha[d] no power to render a final decision on behalf of the United States unless permitted to do so by other Executive officers." Having recounted the various means of supervision, the Court held that the military judges were inferior officers. Consistent with the Constitution, Congress had the power to vest the judges' appointments in the Secretary of Transportation. *Id.*, at 665-666.

The Director here possesses even greater functional power over the Board than that possessed by the Judge Advocate General. Like the Judge Advocate General, the Director exercises administrative oversight over the Board. Because the Board is within the Patent and Trademark Office, all of its powers and duties are ultimately held by the Director. 35 U.S.C. §3(a)(1). He "direct[s]" and "supervis[es]" the Office and "the issuance of patents." §3(a)(2)(A). He may even "fix the rate of basic pay for the administrative patent judges." §3(b)(6). And ultimately, after the Board has reached a decision in a specific case, the Director alone has the power to take final action to cancel a patent claim or confirm it. §318(b).

Also like the Judge Advocate General in *Edmond*, the Director prescribes uniform procedural rules and formulates policies and procedures for Board proceedings. Among other things, he has issued detailed regulations that govern "Trial Practice and Procedure" before the Board. 37 CFR pt. 42 (2020) (prescribing regulations governing, *inter alia*, discovery, oral argument, termination of trial, notice, privilege, filing fees, etc.); see also 35 U.S.C. §§2(b)(2), 316(a)(4), 326(a)(4). He has designed a process to designate and de-designate Board decisions as precedential. Patent Trial and Appeal Board, Standard Operating

Procedure 2 (Revision 10), pp. 1–2 (Sept. 20, 2018) (SOP2). He may issue binding policy directives that govern the Board. §3(a)(2)(A). And he may release "instructions that include exemplary applications of patent laws to fact patterns, which the Board can refer to when presented with factually similar cases." 941 F. 3d, at 1331. His oversight is not just administrative; it is substantive as well. §3(a)(2)(A).

The Director has yet another "powerful tool for control." *Edmond*, 520 U.S., at 664. He may designate which of the 250-plus administrative patent judges hear certain cases and may remove administrative patent judges from their specific assignments without cause. See §6(c). So, if any administrative patent judges depart from the Director's direction, he has ample power to rein them in to avoid erroneous decisions. And, if an administrative patent judge consistently fails to follow instructions, the Secretary has the authority to fire him. 5 U.S.C. §7513(a); 35 U.S.C. §3(c); *Cobert* v. *Miller*, 800 F. 3d 1340, 1351 (CA Fed. 2015) (interpreting §7513(a) to allow removal for "'[f]ailure to fol- low instructions or abide by requirements [that] affec[t] the agency's ability to carry out its mission'").

To be sure, the Director's power over administrative patent judges is not complete. He cannot singlehandedly reverse decisions. Still, he has two powerful checks on Board decisions not found in *Edmond.*

Unlike the Judge Advocate General and CAAF in *Edmond*, the Director *may* influence individual proceedings.

The Director decides in the first instance whether to institute, refuse to institute, or de-institute particular reviews, a decision that is "final and nonappealable." 35 U.S.C. §314(d); see also §314(a). If the Director institutes review, he then may select which administrative patent judges will hear the challenge. §6(c). Alternatively, he can avoid assigning *any* administrative patent judge to a specific dispute and instead designate himself, his Deputy Director, and the Commissioner of Patents. In addition, the Director decides which of the thousands of decisions issued each year bind other panels as precedent. No statute bars the Director from taking an active role to ensure the Board's decisions conform to his policy direction.

But, that is not all. If the administrative patent judges "(somehow) reach a result he does not like, the Director can add more members to the panel — including himself — and order the case reheard." *Oil States Energy Services, LLC v. Greene's Energy Group, LLC*, 584 U.S. ___, ___ (2018) (GORSUCH, J., dissenting). There is a formalized process for this type of review. The Director may unilaterally convene a special panel — the Precedential Opinion Panel — to review a decision in a case and determine whether to order rehearing *sua sponte.* (Any party to a proceeding or any Board member can also recommend rehearing by the Precedential Opinion Panel.) The default members of the panel are the Director, the Commissioner for Patents, and the Chief Administrative Patent Judge. *Id.*, at 4. So even if *all* administrative patent judges decide to defy the Director's authority and go their respective ways, the Director and the Commissioner for Patents can still put a stop to it. And, if the Commissioner for Patents is running amuck, the Director may expand the size of the panel or may replace the Commissioner with someone else, including his Deputy Director. Further, this panel is not limited to reviewing whether there is "competent evidence" as the CAAF was. It can correct anything that may "have been misapprehended or overlooked" in the previous opinion. 37 CFR §41.79(b)(1). This broad oversight ensures that administrative patent judges "have no power to render a final decision on behalf of the United States unless permitted to do so by other Executive officers." *Edmond*, 520 U.S., at 665.

B

The Court today appears largely to agree with all of this. "In every respect" save one, the plurality says, "[administrative patent judges] appear to be inferior officers." But instead of finding it persuasive that administrative patent judges seem to be inferior officers — "an understanding consistent with their appointment" — the majority suggests most of *Edmond* is superfluous: All that matters is whether the Director has the statutory authority to individually reverse Board decisions. . . .

C

[T]he majority's new Appointments Clause doctrine, though, has nothing to do with the validity of an officer's appointment. Instead, it polices the dispersion of executive power among officers. Echoing our doctrine that Congress may not mix duties and powers from different branches into one actor, the Court finds that the constitutional problem here is that Congress has given a specific power — the authority to finally adjudicate inter partes review disputes — to one type of executive officer that the Constitution gives to another. [S]ee also, *e.g., Stern v. Marshall*, 564 U.S. 462, 503 (2011) (assignment of Article III power to Bankruptcy Judge); *Bowsher v. Synar*, 478 U.S. 714, 728-735 (1986) (assignment of executive power to a legislative officer). That analysis is doubly flawed.

For one thing, our separation-of-powers analysis does not fit. The Constitution recognizes executive, legislative, and judicial power, and it vests those powers in specific branches. Nowhere does the Constitution acknowledge any such thing as "inferior-officer power" or "principal-officer power." And it certainly does not distinguish between these sorts of powers in the Appointments Clause.

More broadly, interpreting the Appointments Clause to bar any nonprincipal officer from taking "final" action poses serious line-drawing problems. The majority assures that not every decision by an inferior officer must be reviewable by a superior officer. But this sparks more questions than it answers. Can a line prosecutor offer a plea deal without sign off from a principal officer? If faced with a life-threatening scenario, can an FBI agent use deadly force to subdue a suspect? Or if an inferior officer temporarily fills a vacant office tasked with making final decisions, do those decisions violate the Appointments Clause? And are courts around the country supposed to sort through lists of each officer's (or employee's) duties, categorize each one as principal or inferior, and then excise any that look problematic?

Beyond those questions, the majority's nebulous approach also leaves open the question of how much "principal-officer power" someone must wield before he becomes a principal officer. What happens if an officer typically engages in normal inferior-officer work but also has several principal-officer duties? Is he a hybrid officer, properly appointed for four days a week and improperly appointed for the fifth? And whatever test the Court ultimately comes up with to sort through these difficult questions, are we sure it is encapsulated in the two words "inferior officer"?

III

In the end, the Court's remedy underscores that it is ambivalent about the idea of administrative patent judges *actually* being principal officers. Instead of holding as much explicitly, the Court rewrites the statutory text to ensure that the Director can directly review Board decisions. Specifically, the Court declares unenforceable the statutory provision that "prevents the Director from reviewing the decisions of the [Board] on his own." And as a remedy, the Court "remand[s] to the Acting Director for him to decide whether to rehear the petition." In that way, the Court makes extra clear what should already be obvious: Administrative patent judges are inferior officers.

But neither reading of the majority's opinion — (1) that administrative patent judges are principal officers that the Court has converted to inferior officers, or (2) that administrative patent judges are inferior officers whose decisions must constitutionally be reversible by the Director alone — supports its proposed remedy.

Take the principal officer view. If the Court truly believed administrative patent judges are principal officers, then the Court would need to vacate the Board's decision. As this Court has twice explained, "the 'appropriate' remedy for an adjudication tainted with an appointments violation is a new 'hearing before a properly appointed' official." *Lucia*, 585 U.S., at ___ (slip op., at 12) (quoting *Ryder v. United States*, 515 U.S. 177, 183, 188 (1995)). If administrative patent judges are (or were) constitutionally deficient principal officers, then surely Arthrex is entitled to a new hearing before officers untainted by an appointments violation. But, the Court does not vacate the Board's decision. In fact, it expressly disavows the existence of an appointments violation.

JUSTICE BREYER, with whom JUSTICE SOTOMAYOR and JUSTICE KAGAN join, concurring in the judgment in part and dissenting in part.

I

I agree with JUSTICE THOMAS' discussion on the merits and I join Parts I and II of his dissent. Two related considerations also persuade me that his conclusion is correct.

First, in my view, the Court should interpret the Appointments Clause as granting Congress a degree of leeway to establish and empower federal offices.

Neither that Clause nor anything else in the Constitution describes the degree of control that a superior officer must exercise over the decisions of an inferior officer. To the contrary, the Constitution says only that "Congress may by Law vest the Appointment of such inferior Officers, as they think proper, . . . in the Heads of Departments." Art. II, §2, cl. 2. The words "by Law . . . as they think proper" strongly suggest that Congress has considerable freedom to determine the nature of an inferior officer's job, and that courts ought to respect that judgment. See *Lucia v. SEC*, 585 U.S. ___, (2018) (BREYER, J., concurring in judgment in part and dissenting in part). In a word, the Constitution grants to Congress the "authority to create both categories of offices — those the President must fill with the Senate's concurrence and 'inferior' ones. . . . That constitutional assignment to Congress counsels judicial deference." *In re Sealed Case*, 838 F. 2d 476, 532 (CADC) (R. Ginsburg, J., dissenting), rev'd *sub nom. Morrison v. Olson*, 487 U.S. 654 (1988). Article I's grant to Congress of broad authority to enact laws of different kinds concerning different subjects — and to implement those laws in ways that Congress determines are "necessary and proper" — suggests the same. Art. I, §8, cl. 18.

Even a small degree of "judicial deference" should prove sufficient to validate the statutes here. For one, the provisions at issue fall well within Article I's grant to Congress of the patent power. Nothing in them represents an effort by the "Legislative Branch [to] aggrandize itself at the expense of the other two branches." *Buckley v. Valeo*, 424 U.S. 1, 129 (1976) (*per curiam*). There is accordingly no general separation-of-powers defect that has arisen in other cases. See, *e.g., Metropolitan Washington Airports Authority v. Citizens for Abatement of Aircraft Noise, Inc.*, 501 U.S. 252, 277 (1991). . . .

Even were I to assume, with the majority, that the Director must have power to "control" the APJs, the statutes grant the Director considerable control. As the Court recognizes, the Director "fixes" their "rate[s] of pay," decides "whether to institute inter partes review," "selects the APJ's" who will preside at each particular proceeding, "promulgates regulations governing inter partes review," "issues prospective guidance on patentability issues," and "designates past PTAB decisions as 'precedential' for future panels." All told, the Director maintains control of decisions insofar as they determine policy. The Director cannot rehear and decide an individual case on his own; but Congress had good reason for seeking independent Board determinations in those cases — cases that will apply, not create, Director-controlled policy.

Finally, Congress' judgment is unusually clear in this suit, as there is strong evidence that Congress designed the current structure specifically to address constitutional concerns. See *In re DBC*, 545 F. 3d 1373, 1377-1380 (CA Fed. 2008) (explaining amendment to address defects in prior appointment process).

Second, I believe the Court, when deciding cases such as these, should conduct a functional examination of the offices and duties in question rather than a formalist, judicial-rules-based approach. In advocating for a "functional approach," I mean an approach that would take account of, and place weight on, why Congress enacted a particular statutory limitation. It would also consider the practical consequences that are likely to follow from Congress' chosen scheme....

In this suit, a functional approach, which considers purposes and consequences, undermines the Court's result. Most agencies (and courts for that matter) have the power to reconsider an earlier decision, changing the initial result if appropriate. Congress believed that the PTO should have that same power and accordingly created procedures for reconsidering issued patents. Congress also believed it important to strengthen the reconsideration power with procedural safeguards that would often help those whom the PTO's initial decision had favored, such as the requirement that review be available only when there is a "reasonable likelihood" that the patent will be invalid. 35 U.S.C....

More broadly, I see the Court's decision as one part of a larger shift in our separation-of-powers jurisprudence. The Court applied a similarly formal approach in *Free Enterprise Fund v. Public Company Accounting Oversight Bd.*, 561 U.S. 477 (2010), where it considered the constitutional status of the members of an accounting board appointed by the Securities and Exchange Commission. It held that Congress could not limit the SEC's power to remove those members without cause. The Court also applied a formalist approach in *Seila Law LLC v. Consumer Financial Protection Bureau*, 591 U.S. ___ (2020), where it held that Congress could not protect from removal without cause the (single) head of the Consumer Financial Protection Bureau....

I continue to believe that a more functional approach to constitutional interpretation in this area is superior. As for this particular suit, the consequences of the majority's rule are clear. The nature of the PTAB calls for technically correct adjudicatory decisions. And, as in *Wiener*, that fact calls for greater, not less, independence from those potentially influenced by political factors. The Court's decision prevents Congress from establishing a patent scheme consistent with that idea.

But there are further reasons for a functional approach that extend beyond the bounds of patent adjudication. First, the Executive Branch has many different constituent bodies, many different bureaus, many different agencies, many different tasks, many different kinds of employees. Administration comes in many different shapes and sizes. Appreciating this variety is especially important in the context of administrative adjudication, which typically demands decisionmaking (at least where policy made by others is simply applied) that is free of political influence. Are the President and Congress, through judicial insistence upon certain mechanisms for removal or review, to be denied the ability to create independent adjudicators?

Second, the Constitution is not a detailed tax code, and for good reason. The Nation's desires and needs change, sometimes over long periods of time. In the 19th century the Judiciary may not have foreseen the changes that produced the New Deal, along with its accompanying changes in the nature of the tasks that Government was expected to perform. We may not now easily foresee just what kinds of tasks present or future technological changes will call for. The Founders wrote a Constitution that they believed was flexible enough to respond to new needs as those needs developed and changed over the course of decades or centuries. At the same time, they designed a Constitution that would protect certain basic principles. A principle that prevents Congress from affording inferior level adjudicators some decisionmaking independence was not among them.

Finally, the Executive Branch and Congress are more likely than are judges to understand how to implement the tasks that Congress has written into legislation. That understanding encompasses the nature of different mechanisms of bureaucratic control that may apply to the many thousands of administrators who will carry out those tasks. And it includes an awareness of the reasonable limits that can be placed on supervisors to ensure that those working under them enjoy a degree of freedom sufficient to carry out their responsibilities. Considered as a group, unelected judges have little, if any, experience related to this kind of a problem.

This is not to say that the Constitution grants Congress free rein. But in this area of the law a functional approach, when compared with the highly detailed judicial-rules-based approach reflected in the Court's decision, is more likely to prevent inappropriate judicial interference. It embodies, at least to a degree, the philosopher's advice: "Whereof one cannot speak, thereof one must be silent."

NOTES

1. In Morrison v. Olson, 487 U.S. 654 (1988), the Court addressed both appointment and removal challenges to the constitutionality of the independent counsel provisions of the Ethics in Government Act of 1978. The majority found that independent counsel appointed under the Ethics Act were clearly inferior officers. The majority based its determination on a thorough analysis of the duties and powers of the independent counsel vis-à-vis his appointment by the Attorney General. The Court found first that the independent counsel is subject to removal by a higher Executive Branch official, the Attorney General, even though it could not be said that independent counsel was a subordinate to the Attorney General given the degree of independent discretion left to the independent counsel under the Act. The Court then found that the independent counsel could perform only certain limited duties and also that the scope of its office was limited. Scholars have deemed this to be a "functional" approach to the question of whether someone is a principal or inferior officer. Dissenting in *Morrison*, Justice Scalia argued that the independent counsel was not inferior because the independent counsel did not answer to any superior, not even the President. Scalia maintained that it is not clear that the factors analyzed by the majority are determinative of the question of inferior officer status. In what has been deemed a "formalist" approach, Scalia argued that the only relevant question based on the Constitution is whether the independent counsel is inferior, which Scalia concluded he is, simply because he "is not subordinate to another officer." Later in Edmond v. United States, 520 U.S. 651 (1997), Justice Scalia wrote the majority opinion in which he emphasized in his analysis whether judges of the Coast Guard Court of Military Appeals were subordinate to anyone but the President. Justice Scalia, writing for the Court in *Edmond*, concluded that the judges were inferior officers "by reason of the supervision over their work exercised by the General Counsel of the Department of Transportation in his capacity as Judge Advocate General and the Court of Appeals for the Armed Forces." Id. at 666. Take another look at the *Arthrex* case. Does the Court rely on *Morrison* or *Edmond* to reach a decision? What might this mean for the continued validity of the other approach?

2. Justice Breyer dissenting in *Arthrex* argues for a more functional approach in questions relating to the Appointments Clause. One of the reasons, he argues, is that the Constitution,

> is not a detailed tax code, and for good reason. The Nation's desires and needs change, sometimes over long periods of time. In the 19th century the Judiciary may not have foreseen the changes that produced the New Deal, along with its accompanying changes in the nature of the tasks that Government was expected to perform. We may not now easily foresee just what kinds of tasks present or future technological changes will call for. The Founders wrote a Constitution that they believed was flexible enough to respond to new needs as those needs developed and changed over the course of decades or centuries. At the same time, they designed a Constitution that would protect certain basic principles. A principle that prevents Congress from affording inferior level adjudicators some decisionmaking independence was not among them.

Arthrex, ___U.S. ___, 141 S. Ct. at 1988. But is there really a formalist/functional split in *Arthrex*? The Court seems to focus more on whether the APJs involved exercise "unreviewable executive power" rather than whether they answer to a superior officer below the President. In *Arthrex* it certainly seems to be more of a mixed bag, perhaps explaining the coalition of votes in the dissent and concurrence spanning the conservatice Justice Thomas to the more progressive Justice Breyer.

b. Removal

HUMPHREY'S EXECUTOR v. UNITED STATES

295 U.S. 602 (1935)

[The Federal Trade Commission is a five-person body that oversees the Federal Trade Agency. The Federal Trade Commission Act provides that commissioners shall be appointed for a term of five years. No commissioner may be removed by the President during his or her term except for "inefficiency, neglect of duty, or malfeasance in office."]

William E. Humphrey, the decedent, on December 10, 1931, was nominated by President Hoover to succeed himself as a member of the Federal Trade

Commission, and was confirmed by the United States Senate. He was duly commissioned for a term of seven years expiring September 25, 1938; and, after taking the required oath of office, entered upon his duties. On July 25, 1933, President Roosevelt addressed a letter to the commissioner asking for his resignation, on the ground "that the aims and purposes of the Administration with respect to the work of the Commission can be carried out most effectively with personnel of my own selection," but disclaiming any reflection upon the commissioner personally or upon his services....

Humphrey never acquiesced in this action, but continued thereafter to insist that he was still a member of the commission, entitled to perform its duties and receive the compensation provided by law at the rate of $10,000 per annum. Upon these and other facts set forth in the certificate, which we deem it unnecessary to recite, the following questions are certified:

1. Do the provisions of section 1 of the Federal Trade Commission Act, stating that "any commissioner may be removed by the President for inefficiency, neglect of duty, or malfeasance in office," restrict or limit the power of the President to remove a commissioner except upon one or more of the causes named?

...

To support its contention that the removal provision of §1 as we have just construed it, is an unconstitutional interference with the executive power of the President, the government's chief reliance is *Myers v. United States*, 272 U.S. 52 [holding that an 1876 law requiring Senate approval before the President can appoint or remove a postmaster was unconstitutional, and that the President has unilateral authority to remove such officers]....

The office of a postmaster is so essentially unlike the office now involved that the decision in the *Myers* case cannot be accepted as controlling our decision here. A postmaster is an executive officer restricted to the performance of executive functions. He is charged with no duty at all related to either the legislative or judicial power. The actual decision in the *Myers* case finds support in the theory that such an officer is merely one of the units in the executive department and, hence, inherently subject to the exclusive and illimitable power of removal by the Chief Executive, whose subordinate and aid he is. Putting aside dicta, which may be followed if sufficiently persuasive but which are not controlling, the necessary reach of the decision goes far enough to include all purely executive officers. It goes no farther; much less does it include an officer who occupies no place in the executive department and who exercises no part of the executive power vested by the Constitution in the President.

The Federal Trade Commission is an administrative body created by Congress to carry into effect legislative policies embodied in the statute in accordance with the legislative standard therein prescribed, and to perform other specified duties as a legislative or as a judicial aid. Such a body cannot in any proper sense be characterized as an arm or an eye of the executive. Its duties are performed without executive leave and, in the contemplation of the statute, must be free from executive control. In administering the provisions of the statute in respect of "unfair methods of competition" — that is to say in filling in and administering the details embodied by that general standard — the commission acts in part quasi-legislatively and in part quasi-judicially. In making investigations and reports thereon for the information of Congress under §6, in aid of the legislative power, it acts as a legislative agency. Under §7, which authorizes the commission to act as a master in chancery under rules prescribed by the court, it acts as an agency of the judiciary. To the extent that it exercises any executive function — as distinguished from executive power in the constitutional sense — it does so in the discharge and effectuation of its quasi-legislative or quasi-judicial powers, or as an agency of the legislative or judicial departments of the government.

If Congress is without authority to prescribe causes for removal of members of the trade commission and limit executive power of removal accordingly, that power at once becomes practically all-inclusive in respect of civil officers with the exception of the judiciary provided for by the Constitution. The Solicitor General, at the bar, apparently recognizing this to be true, with commendable candor, agreed that his view in respect of the removability of members of the Federal Trade Commission necessitated a like view in respect of the Interstate Commerce Commission and the Court of Claims. We are thus confronted with the serious question whether not only the members of these quasi-legislative and quasi-judicial bodies, but the judges of the legislative Court of Claims, exercising judicial power . . . continue in office only at the pleasure of the President.

We think it plain under the Constitution that illimitable power of removal is not possessed by the President in respect of officers of the character of those just named. The authority of Congress, in creating quasi-legislative or quasi-judicial agencies, to require them to act in discharge of their duties independently of executive control cannot well be doubted; and that authority includes, as an appropriate incident, power to fix the period during which they shall continue in office, and to forbid their removal except for cause in the meantime. For it is quite evident that one who holds his office only during the pleasure of another, cannot be depended upon to maintain an attitude of independence against the latter's will . . .

The power of removal here claimed for the President falls within this principle, since its coercive influence threatens the independence of a commission, which is not only wholly disconnected from the executive department, but which, as already fully appears, was created by Congress as a means of carrying into operation legislative and judicial powers, and as an agency of the legislative and judicial departments. . . .

To the extent that, between the decision in the *Myers* case, which sustains the unrestrictable power of the President to remove purely executive officers, and our present decision that such power does not extend to an office such as that here involved, there shall remain a field of doubt, we leave such cases as may fall within it for future consideration and determination as they may arise.

The significance of the distinction is this: While Congress has power to create an executive political office, control of that office should be in the hands of the President in order not to circumscribe the power of the President to control his agents. But in the case of an office such as the Federal Trade Commission, the nature of which is not political, the function of which is quasi-judicial and quasi-legislative, in order to safeguard its independence of political domination it is necessary and proper to enact legislative standards which the President must follow.

NOTES

1. Administrative agencies typically have both legislative and judicial powers concentrated in them. They have authority to issue rules and regulations that have the force of law (power that is legislative in nature) and authority to decide cases (power that is judicial in nature). It is through its exercise of rulemaking and adjudicatory authority that an administrative agency is able to determine private rights and obligations. To the private individual and the bar that advises her, rulemaking and adjudication are the substantive weapons in the administrative armory.

2. What do you make of the authority of administrative agencies and the reduced level of accountability to the President? According to one judge, they represent a "headless fourth branch of the U.S. Government." See PHH Corp. v. Consumer Financial Protection Bureau, 889 F.3d 75, 165 (D.C. Cir. 2018) (en banc) (Kavanaugh, J., dissenting) ("The independent agencies collectively constitute, in effect, a headless fourth branch of the U.S. Government. They exercise enormous power over the economic and social life of the United States. Because of their massive power and the absence of Presidential supervision and direction, independent agencies pose a significant threat to individual liberty and to the constitutional system of separation of powers and checks and balances."). Do you agree with this characterization?

3. "Independence" is often used in more than one way. It can describe stand-alone agencies. Thus, the Environmental Protection Agency, a free-standing agency, is sometimes called independent. In a constitutional sense, however, independent agencies are those toward which the President's right of removal is restricted. Independence, therefore, means independent of the President.

4. Are these limitations on the President's right to remove the only way to create an agency that is independent of the President? According to one Justice on the Supreme Court, "[a]gency independence is a function of several different factors, of which 'for cause' protection is only one. Those factors include, *inter alia*, an agency's separate (rather than presidentially dependent) budgeting authority, its separate litigating authority, its composition as a multimember bipartisan board, the use of the word 'independent' in its authorizing statute, and, above all, a political environment, reflecting tradition and function, that would impose a heavy political cost upon any President who tried to remove a commissioner of the agency without cause." Free Enterprise Fund v. PCAOB, 561 U.S. 477 (2010) (Breyer, J., dissenting, joined by Stevens, Ginsburg, and Sotomayor, JJ.). In the same opinion, Justice Breyer identified practical limitations that are likely to limit presidential control over agencies, regardless of the scope of the President's removal powers. Id. at 524 ("[A] legislative decision to place ultimate administrative authority in, say, the Secretary of Agriculture rather than the President, the way in which the statute defines the scope of the power the relevant administrator can exercise, the decision as to who controls the agency's budget requests and funding, the relationships between one agency or department and another, as well as more purely political factors (including Congress' ability to assert influence) are more likely [than for-cause removal] to affect the President's power to get something done.") Do you agree with this assessment? For example, assuming that there were no limits on the President's ability to remove the head of the agency, would the presence of separate budget authority provide true independence from the influence of the President?

5. Why were "independent" agencies created? Can their purpose be explained entirely by a need for technical, depoliticized management? See Elena Kagan, Presidential Administration, 114 Harv. L. Rev. 2245, 2270 (2000) ("The courts . . . have promoted vigorously the control of administrative policy by bureaucratic experts . . . by requiring that agency action bear the indicia of essentially apolitical, 'expert' process and judgment . . . [Judicial] requirements both express a vision of an expert-driven, technocratic administration and attempt to force that vision on the agencies."). Has independence served this purpose? As Justice Scalia observed: "The independent agencies are sheltered not from politics but from the President, and it has often been observed that their freedom from presidential oversight (and protection) has simply been replaced by increased subservience to congressional direction." FCC v. Fox TV Stations, Inc., 556 U.S. 502, 523 (2009). Indeed, Justice Scalia underscores the reach of congressional control by suggesting that Congress' "clear . . . wishes for stricter enforcement" would be "an adequate explanation" for an independent agency's decision to make a substantive change to its policies without additional rationale. Id. at 524. Do you agree with Justice Scalia's view?

6. The existence of overlapping regulatory authority among independent and executive branch agencies can generate anomalous results. In the case In re Aiken County, 645 F.3d 428 (D.C. Cir. 2011), Judge Kavanaugh wrote a concurring opinion pointing out some of the implications of *Humphrey's Executor*. The case involved a challenge to the decision of the Department of Energy (DOE) to abandon development of the Yucca Mountain nuclear waste repository. Although the President had made the decision, the "final word" on the matter was not held by DOE, but by the Nuclear Regulatory Commission (NRC), an "independent" agency. See id. at 439 ("The Secretary of Energy is removable by the President at will, meaning the Department of Energy is an executive agency that the President has authority to direct and supervise. By statute, the Commissioners of the Nuclear Regulatory Commission are removable by the President only for cause, not at will, meaning that the Commission is an independent agency that operates free of presidential direction and supervision."). To the extent, therefore, that the NRC rejected "the President's policy decision and legal interpretation — by rejecting the pending application by the Department of Energy (the President's subordinate) to withdraw the licensing application for Yucca Mountain — then the President may be forced to continue with the Yucca Mountain project simply because the Nuclear Regulatory Commission has told him so." Id. at 443. The conflict was hypothetical. At the time of the case, the NRC had not ruled in a manner inconsistent with DOE. Moreover, the conflict arose out of the decision by Congress to give two agencies overlapping responsibility. Is the "fix" for this "conflict," therefore, something that requires reconsideration of *Humphrey's Executor* or a change in Congress' approach to delegating responsibilities such that such conflicts are avoided? *See* Seila Law LLC v. CFPB, reproduced below.

7. Independent agencies may nonetheless be subject to considerable influence by the President. For example, most agencies, including the independent ones, cannot litigate directly in the U.S. Supreme Court. Instead, they must rely on the Solicitor General's Office in the Department of Justice within the executive branch. See Neal Devins, Unitariness and Independence: Solicitor General Control over Independent Agency Litigation, 82 Cal. L. Rev. 255 (1994). This allows the executive branch to maintain control over litigation positions taken in the Supreme Court. It also, however, allows the branch to override and take views contrary to the positions of the independent agencies.

8. Independent agencies are for the most part run by commissions. In 2010, Congress created the Consumer Financial Protection Bureau (CFPB) headed by a single director with a five-year term. See 12 U.S.C. §5491. The President appoints the director with the advice and consent of the Senate. Removal, however, can only be for "inefficiency, neglect of duty, or malfeasance in office." Does the replacement of a commission with a single director matter? The Supreme Court concluded that the structure was unconstitutional. See Seila Law LLC v. Consumer Financial Protection Bureau, 140 S. Ct. 2183, 2197 (2020). The Court first recognized that *Humphrey's Executor* alone could not resolve the constitutionality of CFPB's structure because, unlike CFPB, the official in *Humphrey's Executor* was one member of a multimember body that did not wield "executive power." Id. at 2200. Instead, the question before the Court was "whether to extend those precedents to . . . an independent agency led by a single Director and vested with significant executive power." Id. at 2201. The Court answered in the negative. Id. It concluded that CFPB's structure was unconstitutional for three main reasons: (1) the single Director structure is a historical anomaly in light of the fact that only four other agencies have a similar structure, and all four examples can be dismissed because of historical context, controversy around their structure, and/or relative lack of authority; (2) it contravenes the "carefully calibrated system" of separation of powers by "vesting significant governmental power in the hands of a single individual accountable to no one"; and (3) other features, such as a five-year term and an independent funding stream, "foreclose[] certain indirect methods of Presidential control." Id. at 2201-2204. What do you make of this analysis? In his concurring opinion, Justice Clarence Thomas suggested that the Court should have gone a step further, writing in favor of completely overruling *Humphrey's Executor*. Id. at 2218-2219 (Thomas, J., concurring in part and dissenting in part) ("*Humphrey's Executor* . . . sidesteps the President's removal power[] and encourages the exercise of executive power by unaccountable officers. . . . Continued reliance on *Humphrey's Executor* to justify the existence of independent agencies creates a serious, ongoing threat to our Government's design.") Do you agree with Justice Thomas?

9. Many scholars have criticized the Supreme Court's decision in *Seila Law.* For example, Howard Schweber wrote that the majority opinion fails to recognize the importance of checks and balances relative to separation of powers, ignores the fact that the existing system of independent agencies was crafted through compromise among government and private stakeholders to ensure consistency with the Constitution, and relies on an outdated understanding of presidential accountability. *See* Howard Schweber, The Roberts Court's Theory of Agency Accountability: A Step in the Wrong Direction, 8 Belmont L. Rev. 460, 489 (2021). Others have written that the decision is particularly notable for its embrace of the unitary executive theory, suggesting that it could have broad political consequences for management strategies in government and the actual and perceived influence of independent agencies. See generally Ganesh Sitaraman, The Political Economy of the Removal Power, 134 Harv. L. Rev. 352 (2020); Richard Murphy, The DIY Unitary Executive, 63 Ariz. L. Rev. 439 (2021). What are the likely consequences of the Court's decisions in *Seila Law*? Could it significantly increase presidential power? Richard Murphy suggests that any increase in presidential power flowing from decisions subsequent to *Seila Law* could be partially controlled by requiring that the President follow statutory procedural requirements whenever she acts as an agency head. Murphy, 63 Ariz. L. Rev. at 488. Does this seem like a reasonable approach? For a detailed discussion and analysis of *Seila Law* and the removal power in general, see Ilan Wurman, The Removal Power: A Critical Guide, 2019-2020 Cato Sup. Ct. Rev. 157 (2020).

10. The Supreme Court, applying its decision in *Seila Law*, found yet another "for cause" removal provision unconstitutional in Collins v. Yellen, 141 S. Ct. 1761 (2021). There, the court found that the head of the Federal Housing Finance Agency [FHFA] (an agency created in 2008 by the Housing and Economic Recovery Act of 2008), a single Director who could only be removed "for cause," was unconstitutionally protected by "for cause" removal because the FHFA is undistinguishable from the CFPB, the subject of its decision in *Seila Law*, notwithstanding the scope and breadth of the FHFA's authority nor its being labeled in legislation an "independent agency." The fact that the agency had a single director made *Seila Law* "all but dispositive" as a precedent. Importantly, it is evident that *Seila Law* and *Collins* only apply to removal provisions of agencies headed by a single director. The underlying reason is simply that under constitutional notions of separation of powers, the President, directly accountable to the people, should be unfettered in their ability to control subordinates.

MORRISON v. OLSON

487 U.S. 654 (1988)

CHIEF JUSTICE REHNQUIST delivered the opinion of the Court.

[The case involved the constitutionality of a statute that permitted the appointment by a "special court" of an independent counsel to investigate "high ranking government officials." The statute provided that independent counsel could be removed only for "good cause, physical disability, mental incapacity, or any other condition that substantially impairs the performance of such independent counsel's duties," by the Attorney General.]

Two terms ago we had occasion to consider whether it was consistent with the separation of powers for Congress to pass a statute that authorized a government official who is removable only by Congress to participate in what we found to be "executive powers." Bowsher v. Synar, 478 U.S. 714, 730 (1986). We held in *Bowsher* that "Congress cannot reserve for itself the power of removal of an officer charged with the execution of the laws except by impeachment." Id. at 726. A primary antecedent for this ruling was our 1925 decision in Myers v. United States, 272 U.S. 52 (1926). *Myers* had considered the propriety of a federal statute by which certain postmasters of the United States could be removed by the President only "by and with the advice and consent of the Senate." There too, Congress' attempt to involve itself in the removal of an executive official was found to be sufficient grounds to render the statute invalid. As we observed in *Bowsher*, the essence of the decision in *Myers* was the judgment that the Constitution prevents Congress from "draw[ing] to itself . . . the power to remove or the right to participate in the exercise of that power. To do this would be to go beyond the words and implications of the [Appointments Clause] and to infringe the constitutional principle of the separation of governmental powers." *Myers, supra*, at 161.

Unlike both *Bowsher* and *Myers*, this case does not involve an attempt by Congress itself to gain a role in the removal of executive officials other than its established powers of impeachment and conviction. The Act instead puts the removal power squarely in the hands of the Executive Branch; an independent counsel may be removed from office, "only by the personal action of the Attorney General, and only for good cause." §596(a)(3). In our view, the removal provisions of the Act make only this case more analogous to Humphrey's Executor v. United States, 295 U.S. 602 (1935), and Wiener v. United States, 357 U.S. 349 (1958), than to *Myers* or *Bowsher.*

In *Humphrey's Executor*, the issue was whether a statute restricting the President's power to remove the commissioners of the Federal Trade Commission only for "inefficiency, neglect of duty, or malfeasance in office" was consistent with the Constitution. 295 U.S. at 619. We stated that whether Congress can "condition the [President's power of removal] by fixing a definite term and precluding a removal except for cause, will depend upon the character of the office." Id. at 631. Contrary to the implication of some dicta in *Myers*, the President's power to remove government officials simply was not "all-inclusive in respect of civil officers with the exception of the judiciary provided for by the Constitution." 295 U.S. at 629. At least in regard to "quasi-legislative" and "quasi-judicial" agencies such as the FTC, "[t]he authority of Congress, in creating [such] agencies, to require them to act in discharge of their duties independently of executive control . . . includes, as an appropriate incident, power to fix the period during which they shall continue in office, and to forbid their removal except for cause in the meantime." Ibid. In *Humphrey's Executor*, we found it "plain" that the Constitution did not give the President "illimitable power of removal" over the officers of independent agencies. Ibid. Were the President to have the power to remove FTC commissioners at will, the "coercive influence" of removal power would "threate[n] the independence of [the] commission." Id. at 630.

Similarly, in *Wiener* we considered whether the President had unfettered discretion to remove a member of the War Claims Commission, which had been established by Congress in the War Claims Act of 1948, 62 Stat. 1240. The Commission's function was to receive and adjudicate certain claims for compensation from those who had suffered personal injury or property damage at the hands of the enemy during World War II. Commissioners were appointed by the President, with the advice and consent of the Senate, but the statute made no provision for the removal of officers, perhaps because the Commission itself was to have limited existence. As in *Humphrey's Executor*, however, the Commissioners were entrusted by Congress with adjudicatory powers that were to be exercised free from executive control. In this context, "Congress did not wish to have hang over the Commission the Damocles' sword of removal by the President for no reason other than that he preferred to have on that Commission men of his own choosing." 357 U.S. at 356. Accordingly, we rejected the President's attempt to remove a Commissioner "merely because he wanted his own appointees on [the] Commission," stating that "no such power is given to the President directly by the Constitution, and none is impliedly conferred upon him by statute." Ibid.

Appellees contend that *Humphrey's Executor* and *Wiener* are distinguishable from this case because they did not involve officials who performed a "core executive function." They argue that our decision in *Humphrey's Executor* rests on a distinction between "purely executive" officials and officials who exercise "quasi-legislative" and "quasi-judicial" powers. In their view, when a "purely executive" official is involved, the governing precedent is *Myers*, not *Humphrey's Executor.* See *Humphrey's Executor*, 295 U.S. at 628. And, under *Myers*, the President must have absolute discretion to discharge "purely" executive officials at will. See *Myers*, 272 U.S. at 132-134.

We undoubtedly did rely on the terms "quasi-legislative" and "quasi-judicial" to distinguish the officials involved in *Humphrey's Executor* and *Wiener* from these in *Myers*, but our present considered view is that the determination of whether the Constitution allows Congress to impose a "good cause"-type restriction on the President's power to remove an official cannot be made to turn on whether or not that official is classified as "purely executive." The analysis contained in our removal cases is designed not to define rigid categories of those officials who may or may not be removed at will by the President, but to ensure that Congress does not interfere with the President's exercise of the "executive power" and his constitutionally appointed duty to "take care that the laws be faithfully executed" under Article II. *Myers* was undoubtedly correct in its holding, and in its broader suggestion that there are some "purely executive" officials who must be removable by the President at will if he is to be able to accomplish his constitutional role.... At the end of the spectrum from *Myers*, the characterization of the agencies in *Humphrey's Executor* and *Wiener* as "quasi-legislative" and "quasi-judicial" in large part reflected our judgment that it was not essential to the President's proper execution of his Article II powers that these agencies be headed up by individuals who were removable at will. We do not mean to suggest that an analysis of the functions served by the officials at issue is irrelevant. But the real question is whether the removal restrictions are of such a nature that they impede the President's ability to perform his constitutional duty, and the functions of the officials in question must be analyzed in that light.

Considering for the moment the "good cause" removal provision in isolation from the other parts of the Act at issue in this case, we cannot say that the imposition of a "good cause" standard for removal by itself unduly trammels on executive authority. There is no real dispute that the functions performed by the independent counsel are "executive" in the sense that they are law enforcement functions that typically have been undertaken by officials within the Executive Branch. As we noted above, however, the independent counsel is an inferior officer under the Appointments Clause, with limited jurisdiction and tenure and lacking policymaking or significant administrative authority.[1] Although the counsel exercises no small amount of discretion and judgment in deciding how to carry out her duties under the Act, we simply do not see how the President's need to control the exercise of that discretion is so central to the function of the Executive Branch as to require as a matter of constitutional law that the counsel be terminable at will by the President.

Nor do we think that the "good cause" removal provision at issue here impermissibly burdens the President's power to control or supervise the independent counsel, as an executive official, in the execution of her duties under the Act. This is not a case in which the power to remove an executive official has been completely stripped from the President, thus providing no means for the President to ensure the "faithful execution" of the laws. Rather, because the independent counsel may be terminated for "good cause," the Executive, through the Attorney General, retains ample authority to assure that the counsel is competently performing her statutory responsibilities in a manner that comports with the provisions of the Act. Although we need not decide in this case exactly what is encompassed within the term "good cause" under that Act, the legislative history of the removal provision also makes clear that the Attorney General may remove an independent counsel for "misconduct." . . . Here, as with the provision of the Act conferring the appointment authority of the independent counsel on the special report, the congressional determination to limit the removal power of the Attorney General was essential, in the view of Congress, to establish the necessary independence of the office. We do not think that this limitation as

1. [Ed. Note: Article II, Section 2 of the Constitution gives the president the power to appoint (with Senate approval) certain principal officers, but reserves for Congress the power to determine who can appoint "inferior" officers. In this case, the Court first addressed whether the officer in question is "inferior" to evaluate the constitutionality of the appointment component of the statute. The Court concluded that the officer was inferior because she was "subject to removal by a higher Executive Branch official," had only "certain, limited duties," and held an office that was "limited in jurisdiction." *Morrison*, 487 U.S. at 670-672.]

it presently stands sufficiently deprives the President of control over the independent counsel to interfere impermissibly with his constitutional obligation to ensure the faithful execution of the laws.

NOTES

1. Chief Justice Rehnquist specifically disavowed the language in *Humphrey's Executor* that relied on the quasi status of the FTC. What difference does this make? See Morrison v. Olson, 487 U.S. 654, 725, 108 S. Ct. 2597, 2637 (1988) (Scalia, J., dissenting) ("It has often been observed, correctly in my view, that the line between 'purely executive' functions and 'quasi-legislative' or 'quasi-judicial' functions is not a clear one or even a rational one."). What does that tell us about the position of the FTC in our system of government?

2. How does this case change the analysis set out in *Humphrey's Executor*? Why didn't the Court simply overrule *Humphrey's Executor*? As we learned in *Seila Law*, some on the Court today would like to see *Humphrey's Executor* overruled. See supra note 8, p. 85. Indeed, those who are critical of the decision in *Seila Law* question the extent to which *Humphrey's* can still exert influence. *See* Richard Murphy, *The DIY Unitary Executive*, 63 Ariz. L. Rev. 439, 466 (2021) ("By expressly refusing to overrule its (new) versions of *Humphrey's Executor* and *Morrison*, the *Seila* Court nominally left space to continue to uphold the constitutionality of the traditionally recognized independent agencies. . . . Nonetheless, *Seila* contains language and themes that store up trouble for the future of these agencies even if the Court continues to leave *Humphrey's Executor* and *Morrison* damaged but in place."). Others have leveraged the *Seila* Court's reluctance to overrule *Humphrey's* to argue that agencies retain, and should protect, a measure of independence given its importance to agency functions. *See* Joshua D. Wright & Alexander Krzepicki, *What Is an Independent Agency to Do? The Trump Administration's Executive Order on Preventing Online Censorship and the Federal Trade Commission*, 6 ALR Accord 29, 45 (2020) ("In our view, the FTC must also protect whatever *Seila Law* leaves of its independence. Not just for the sake of independence itself, but because its independence is a critical asset that helps the under resourced agency achieve its core objectives in protecting consumers and competition across the modern economy.").

3. The opinion in *Morrison* asserts that the case does not turn on "the functions served by the officials at issue" but instead on the limits imposed on the President's ability to perform his or her constitutional duties. But doesn't the performance of constitutional duties in part depend upon the functions of the official at issue? How much does the function actually matter? The *PCAOB* case will shed some light on that subject.

4. It is clear that the Supreme Court would not permit restrictions that made it impossible to remove an executive branch employee. The standard in the statute allows for removal "for good cause, physical disability, mental incapacity, or any other condition that substantially impairs the performance of such independent counsel's duties." The phrase "good cause" was undefined. The Court noted, however, that the legislative history clarified that good cause allowed removal for "misconduct." Under this standard, according to the Chief Justice, the President "retains ample authority to assure that the counsel is competently performing his or her statutory responsibilities in a manner that comports with the provisions of the Act." Is this tantamount to a constitutionally acceptable definition of good cause? Do you agree with this? Can the President perform his or her constitutional functions if allowed to remove only under this standard?

5. According to the Chairman of the Administrative Conference (an agency set up by Congress to study and make recommendations on federal agencies), *Bowsher* illustrates the "formalist" approach to separation of powers. *Morrison* represents a "functionalist" approach. As the article described:

> Under the formalist view, each branch of our government has been assigned different powers, and it violates the constitutional road map if one branch undertakes tasks assigned to any other. Thus, under this model, separation of powers means that the executive branch is exclusively responsible for executive activity, the legislative power is limited to those powers specifically enumerated in the Constitution, and the judiciary retains the judicial power. . . .
>
> [On the other hand, opponents] of "formalism" advocate an alternative model which allows for permeability between the branches. This "functionalist" approach argues that Congress may, by statute, adjust or alter the tripartite division of federal power so long as it does not undermine a core function or responsibility of one of the branches.
>
> [Morrison v. Olson was said to follow such an approach.] In *Morrison*, the Court ruled that the congressional restrictions on the executive power were not "of such a nature that they impede[d] the President's ability to perform his constitutional duty." Placing itself firmly in a "functionalist" posture, the Court held that the "analysis contained in our removal cases is designed not to define rigid categories . . . but to ensure that Congress does not interfere with the President's exercise of the 'executive power' and his constitutionally appointed duty to 'take care that the laws be faithfully executed' under Article II."

Breger, Comments on Bernard Schwartz's Essay, 5 Admin. L.J. 347, 350 (1991).* Discuss the merits of these two approaches.

6. What was the effect of the "functionalist" *Morrison* approach on the President's position as Chief Executive? Did the Court in fact reach a conclusion about the Ethics in Government Act that interfered with the President's exercise of the "executive power"? Consider the views of Robert W. Gordon, Imprudence

* Reprinted with permission of the Administrative Law Journal. Chairman Breger's article was a comment on Schwartz, Recent Administrative Law Issues and Trends, 3 Admin. L.J. 543 (1990).

and Partisanship: Starr's OIC and the Clinton-Lewinsky Affair, 68 Fordham L. Rev. 639, 639 (1999):

> The Independent Counsel Act expired on June 30, 1999, largely unmourned. The performance of independent counsels, it was widely said, had shown the prescience of Justice Scalia's dissent in Morrison v. Olson. The statute gave the counsel's office no other job than to investigate and prosecute a designated target. The counsel was unconstrained by budget, other tasks compelling a sense of priorities or proportion, competing political concerns, or any time-table to complete his work. He had access to the full terrifying machinery of the criminal process: to subpoena individuals to testify before grand juries; to threaten indictments or grant or withhold immunity; to prosecute witnesses for perjury or false statements if not told what he wanted to hear; and to call upon FBI agents and private investigators without limit and turn them into great armored tanks to run the state's investigative authority through the lives of targets, witnesses and their families and friends, shattering their privacy and their reputations and bankrupting them with lawyers' fees. The appointing judges of the Special Division might select as counsel a political enemy of the Administration he was supposed to investigate. If he ran amok the Attorney General would risk a "firestorm" of public criticism if she tried to remove him for cause. Yet so concerned was the statute to make him independent that he could operate without any real supervision or check on his abuse of office.

7. In *Seila Law*, the Supreme Court held that both *Morrison* and *Humphrey's Executor* are merely exceptions to the President's general removal power. See 140 S. Ct. 2183, 2198 (2020). The Court explicitly narrowed the holdings of these cases, describing *Humphrey's Executor* as permitting for-cause removal protections only for "multimember expert agencies that do not wield substantial executive power," and *Morrison* as allowing the same for "inferior officers with limited duties and no policymaking or administrative authority." *Id.* at 2199-2200. What are the potential implications of narrowing these holdings? *See supra* note 2, p. 90.

Morrison changed the analysis; the location of "independent" agencies no longer matters. Instead, the central issue is the degree to which the restrictions interfere with the President's ability to perform his or her constitutional responsibilities. The difference in approach can be seen in the next case.

FREE ENTERPRISE FUND v. PCAOB

561 U.S. 477 (2010)

CHIEF JUSTICE ROBERTS wrote the opinion for the Court.

Our Constitution divided the "powers of the new Federal Government into three defined categories, Legislative, Executive, and Judicial." *INS v. Chadha*, 462 U.S. 919, 951 (1983). Article II vests "[t]he executive Power . . . in a President of the United States of America," who must "take Care that the Laws be faithfully executed." Art. II, §1, cl. 1; §3. In light of "[t]he impossibility that one man should be able to perform all the great business of the State," the Constitution provides for executive officers to "assist the supreme Magistrate in discharging the duties of his trust." 30 Writings of George Washington 334 (J. Fitzpatrick ed. 1939).

Since 1789, the Constitution has been understood to empower the President to keep these officers accountable — by removing them from office, if necessary. See generally *Myers v. United States*, 272 U.S. 52 (1926). This Court has determined, however, that this authority is not without limit. In *Humphrey's Executor v. United States*, 295 U.S. 602 (1935), we held that Congress can, under certain circumstances, create independent agencies run by principal officers appointed by the President, whom the President may not remove at will but only for good cause. Likewise, in *United States v. Perkins*, 116 U.S. 483 (1886), and *Morrison v. Olson*, 487 U.S. 654 (1988), the Court sustained similar restrictions on the power of principal executive officers — themselves responsible to the President — to remove their own inferiors. The parties do not ask us to reexamine any of these precedents, and we do not do so.

We are asked, however, to consider a new situation not yet encountered by the Court. The question is whether these separate layers of protection may be combined. May the President be restricted in his ability to remove a principal officer, who is in turn restricted in his ability to remove an inferior officer, even though that inferior officer determines the policy and enforces the laws of the United States?

We hold that such multilevel protection from removal is contrary to Article II's vesting of the executive power in the President. The President cannot "take Care that the Laws be faithfully executed" if he cannot oversee the faithfulness of the officers who execute them. Here the President cannot remove an officer who enjoys more than one level of good-cause protection, even if the President determines that the officer is neglecting his duties or discharging them improperly. That judgment is instead committed to another officer, who may or may not agree with the President's determination, and whom the President cannot remove simply because that officer disagrees with him. This contravenes the President's "constitutional obligation to ensure the faithful execution of the laws." *Id.*, at 693.

A

After a series of celebrated accounting debacles, Congress enacted the Sarbanes-Oxley Act of 2002 (or Act), 116 Stat. 745. Among other measures, the Act introduced tighter regulation of the accounting industry under a new Public Company Accounting Oversight Board. The Board is composed of five members, appointed to staggered 5-year terms by the Securities and Exchange Commission. It was modeled on private self-regulatory organizations in the securities industry — such as the New York Stock Exchange — that investigate and discipline their own members subject to Commission oversight. Congress created the Board as a private "nonprofit corporation," and Board members and employees are not considered Government "officer[s] or employee[s]" for statutory purposes. 15 U.S.C. §§7211(a), (b). The Board can thus recruit its members and employees from the private sector by paying salaries far above the standard Government pay scale. See §§7211(f)(4), 7219.

Unlike the self-regulatory organizations, however, the Board is a Government-created, Government-appointed entity, with expansive powers to govern an entire industry. Every accounting firm — both foreign and domestic — that participates in auditing public companies under the securities laws must register with the Board, pay it an annual fee, and comply with its rules and oversight. §§7211(a), 7212(a), (f), 7213, 7216(a)(1). The Board is charged with enforcing the Sarbanes-Oxley Act, the securities laws, the Commission's rules, its own rules, and professional accounting standards. §§7215(b)(1), (c)(4). To this end, the Board may regulate every detail of an accounting firm's practice, including hiring and professional development, promotion, supervision of audit work, the acceptance of new business and the continuation of old, internal inspection procedures, professional ethics rules, and "such other requirements as the Board may prescribe." §7213(a)(2)(B).

The Board promulgates auditing and ethics standards, performs routine inspections of all accounting firms, demands documents and testimony, and initiates formal investigations and disciplinary proceedings. §§7213-7215 (2006 ed. and Supp. II). The willful violation of any Board rule is treated as a willful violation of the Securities Exchange Act of 1934, 48 Stat. 881, 15 U.S.C. §78a *et seq.* — a federal crime punishable by up to 20 years' imprisonment or $25 million in fines ($5 million for a natural person). §§78ff(a), 7202(b)(1) (2006 ed.). And the Board itself can issue severe sanctions in its disciplinary proceedings, up to and including the permanent revocation of a firm's registration, a permanent ban on a person's associating with any registered firm, and money penalties of $15 million ($750,000 for a natural person). §7215(c)(4). Despite the provisions specifying that Board members are not Government officials for statutory purposes, the parties agree that the Board is "part of the Government" for constitutional purposes, *Lebron v. National Railroad Passenger Corporation*, 513 U.S. 374, 397 (1995), and that its members are "'Officers of the United States'" who "exercis[e] significant authority pursuant to the laws of the United States," *Buckley v. Valeo*, 424 U.S. 1, 125-126 (1976) (*per curiam*) (quoting Art. II, §2, cl. 2); cf. Brief for Petitioners 9, n. 1; Brief for United States 29, n. 8.

The Act places the Board under the SEC's oversight, particularly with respect to the issuance of rules or the imposition of sanctions (both of which are subject to Commission approval and alteration). §§7217(b)-(c). But the individual members of the Board — like the officers and directors of the self-regulatory organizations — are substantially insulated from the Commission's control. The Commission cannot remove Board members at will, but only "for good cause shown," "in accordance with" certain procedures. §7211(e)(6).

Those procedures require a Commission finding, "on the record" and "after notice and opportunity for a hearing," that the Board member

> (A) has willfully violated any provision of th[e] Act, the rules of the Board, or the securities laws;

(B) has willfully abused the authority of that member; or

(C) without reasonable justification or excuse, has failed to enforce compliance with any such provision or rule, or any professional standard by any registered public accounting firm or any associated person thereof. §7217(d)(3).

Removal of a Board member requires a formal Commission order and is subject to judicial review. See 5 U.S.C. §§554(a), 556(a), 557(a), (c)(B); 15 U.S.C. §78y(a)(1). Similar procedures govern the Commission's removal of officers and directors of the private self-regulatory organizations. See §78s(h)(4). The parties agree that the Commissioners cannot themselves be removed by the President except under the *Humphrey's Executor* standard of "inefficiency, neglect of duty, or malfeasance in office," 295 U.S., at 620, 55 S.Ct. 869 (internal quotation marks omitted); see Brief for Petitioners 31; Brief for United States 43; Brief for Respondent Public Company Accounting Oversight Board 31 (hereinafter PCAOB Brief); Tr. of Oral Arg. 47, and we decide the case with that understanding.

B

Beckstead and Watts, LLP, is a Nevada accounting firm registered with the Board. The Board inspected the firm, released a report critical of its auditing procedures, and began a formal investigation. Beckstead and Watts and the Free Enterprise Fund, a nonprofit organization of which the firm is a member, then sued the Board and its members, seeking (among other things) a declaratory judgment that the Board is unconstitutional and an injunction preventing the Board from exercising its powers. App. 71.

III

We hold that the dual for-cause limitations on the removal of Board members contravene the Constitution's separation of powers.

B

As explained, we have previously upheld limited restrictions on the President's removal power. In those cases, however, only one level of protected tenure separated the President from an officer exercising executive power. It was the President — or a subordinate he could remove at will — who decided whether the officer's conduct merited removal under the good-cause standard.

The Act before us does something quite different. It not only protects Board members from removal except for good cause, but withdraws from the President any decision on whether that good cause exists. That decision is vested instead in other tenured officers — the Commissioners — none of whom is subject to the President's direct control. The result is a Board that is not accountable to the President, and a President who is not responsible for the Board.

The added layer of tenure protection makes a difference. Without a layer of insulation between the Commission and the Board, the Commission could remove a Board member at any time, and therefore would be fully responsible for what the Board does. The President could then hold the Commission to account for its supervision of the Board, to the same extent that he may hold the Commission to account for everything else it does.

A second level of tenure protection changes the nature of the President's review. Now the Commission cannot remove a Board member at will. The President therefore cannot hold the Commission fully accountable for the Board's conduct, to the same extent that he may hold the Commission accountable for everything else that it does. The Commissioners are not responsible for the Board's actions. They are only responsible for their own determination of whether the Act's rigorous good-cause standard is met. And even if the President disagrees with their determination, he is powerless to intervene — unless that determination is so unreasonable as to constitute "inefficiency, neglect of duty, or malfeasance in office." *Humphrey's Executor*, 295 U.S., at 620, 55 S. Ct. 869 (internal quotation marks omitted).

This novel structure does not merely add to the Board's independence, but transforms it. Neither the President, nor anyone directly responsible to him, nor even an officer whose conduct he may review only for good cause, has full control over the Board. The President is stripped of the power our precedents have preserved, and his ability to execute the laws — by holding his subordinates accountable for their conduct — is impaired.

That arrangement is contrary to Article II's vesting of the executive power in the President. Without the ability to oversee the Board, or to attribute the Board's failings to those whom he *can* oversee, the President is no longer the judge of the Board's conduct. He is not the one who decides whether Board members are abusing their offices or neglecting their duties. He can neither ensure that the laws are faithfully executed, nor be held responsible for a Board member's breach of faith. This violates the basic principle that the President "cannot delegate ultimate responsibility or the active obligation to supervise that goes with it," because Article II "makes a single President responsible for the actions of the Executive Branch." *Clinton v. Jones*, 520 U.S. 681, 712-713 (1997) (Breyer, J., concurring in judgment).

Indeed, if allowed to stand, this dispersion of responsibility could be multiplied. If Congress can shelter the bureaucracy behind two layers of good-cause tenure, why not a third? At oral argument, the Government was unwilling to concede that even *five* layers between the President and the Board would be too many. Tr. of Oral Arg. 47-48. The officers of such an agency — safely encased within a Matryoshka doll of tenure protections — would be immune from Presidential oversight, even as they exercised power in the people's name.

Perhaps an individual President might find advantages in tying his own hands. But the separation of powers does not depend on the views of individual Presidents, see *Freytag v. Commissioner*, 501 U.S. 868, 879-880 (1991), nor on whether "the encroached-upon branch approves the encroachment," *New York v. United States*, 505 U.S. 144, 182 (1992). The President can always choose to restrain himself in his dealings with subordinates. He cannot, however, choose to bind his successors by diminishing their powers, nor can he escape responsibility for his choices by pretending that they are not his own.

The diffusion of power carries with it a diffusion of accountability. The people do not vote for the "Officers of the United States." Art. II, §2, cl. 2. They instead look to the President to guide the "assistants or deputies . . . subject to his superintendence." The Federalist No. 72, p. 487 (J. Cooke ed.1961) (A. Hamilton). Without a clear and effective chain of command, the public cannot "determine on whom the blame or the punishment of a pernicious measure, or series of pernicious measures ought really to fall." *Id.*, No. 70, at 476 (same). That is why the Framers sought to ensure that "those who are employed in the execution of the law will be in their proper situation, and the chain of dependence be preserved; the lowest officers, the middle grade, and the highest, will depend, as they ought, on the President, and the President on the community." 1 Annals of Cong., at 499 (J. Madison).

By granting the Board executive power without the Executive's oversight, this Act subverts the President's ability to ensure that the laws are faithfully executed — as well as the public's ability to pass judgment on his efforts. The Act's restrictions are incompatible with the Constitution's separation of powers.

C

Respondents and the dissent resist this conclusion, portraying the Board as "the kind of practical accommodation between the Legislature and the Executive that should be permitted in a 'workable government.'" *Metropolitan Washington Airports Authority v. Citizens for Abatement of Aircraft Noise, Inc.*, 501 U.S. 252, 276 (1991) (*MWAA*) (quoting *Youngstown Sheet & Tube Co. v. Sawyer*, 343 U.S. 579, 635 (1952) (Jackson, J., concurring)); see, *e.g.*, *post*, at 6 (opinion of Breyer, J.). According to the dissent, Congress may impose multiple levels of for-cause tenure between the President and his subordinates when it "rests agency independence upon the need for technical expertise." *Post*, at 18. The Board's mission is said to demand both "technical competence" and "apolitical expertise," and its powers may only be exercised by "technical professional experts." *Post*, at 18 (internal quotation marks omitted). In this respect the statute creating the Board is, we are told, simply one example of the "vast numbers of statutes governing vast numbers of subjects, concerned with vast numbers of different problems, [that] provide for, or foresee, their execution or administration through the work of administrators organized within many different kinds of administrative structures, exercising different kinds of administrative authority, to achieve their legislatively mandated objectives." *Post*, at 8.

No one doubts Congress's power to create a vast and varied federal bureaucracy. But where, in all this, is the role for oversight by an elected President? The Constitution requires that a President chosen by the entire Nation oversee the execution of the laws. And the "'fact that a given law or procedure is efficient, convenient, and useful in facilitating functions of government, standing alone, will not save it if it is contrary to the Constitution,'" for "'[c]onvenience and efficiency are not the primary objectives — or the hallmarks — of democratic government.'" *Bowsher*, 478 U.S., at 736 (quoting *Chadha*, 462 U.S., at 944).

One can have a government that functions without being ruled by functionaries, and a government that benefits from expertise without being ruled by experts. Our Constitution was adopted to enable the people to govern themselves, through their elected leaders. The growth of the Executive Branch, which now wields vast power and touches almost every aspect of daily life, heightens the concern that it may slip from the Executive's control, and thus from that of the people. This concern is largely absent from the dissent's paean to the administrative state.

For example, the dissent dismisses the importance of removal as a tool of supervision, concluding that the President's "power to get something done" more often depends on "who controls the agency's budget requests and funding, the relationships between one agency or department and another, . . . purely political factors (including Congress' ability to assert influence)," and indeed whether particular *unelected* officials support or "resist" the President's policies. *Post*, at 11, 13 (emphasis deleted). The Framers did not rest our liberties on such bureaucratic minutiae. As we said in *Bowsher, supra*, at 730, "[t]he separated powers of our Government cannot be permitted to turn on judicial assessment of whether an officer exercising executive power is on good terms with Congress."

In fact, the multilevel protection that the dissent endorses "provides a blueprint for extensive expansion of the legislative power." *MWAA, supra*, at 277. In a system of checks and balances, "[p]ower abhors a vacuum," and one branch's handicap is another's strength. 537 F.3d, at 695, n. 4 (Kavanaugh, J., dissenting) (internal quotation marks omitted). "Even when a branch does not arrogate power to itself," therefore, it must not "impair another in the performance of its constitutional duties." *Loving v. United States*, 517 U.S. 748, 757 (1996). Congress has plenary control over the salary, duties, and even existence of executive offices. Only Presidential oversight can counter its influence. That is why the Constitution vests certain powers in the President that "the Legislature has no right to diminish or modify." 1 Annals of Cong., at 463 (J. Madison). The Framers created a structure in which "[a] dependence on the people" would be the "primary control on the government." The Federalist No. 51, at 349 (J. Madison). That dependence is maintained, not just by "parchment barriers," *id.*, No. 48, at 333 (same), but by letting "[a]mbition . . . counteract ambition," giving each branch "the necessary constitutional means, and personal motives, to resist encroachments of the others," *id.*, No. 51, at 349. A key "constitutional means" vested in the President — perhaps *the* key means — was "the power of appointing, overseeing, and controlling those who execute the laws." 1 Annals of Cong., at 463. And while a government of "opposite and rival interests" may sometimes inhibit the smooth functioning of administration, The Federalist No. 51, at 349, "[t]he Framers recognized that, in the long term, structural protections against abuse of power were critical to preserving liberty." *Bowsher, supra*, at 730.

Calls to abandon those protections in light of "the era's perceived necessity," *New York*, 505 U.S., at 187, are not unusual. Nor is the argument from bureaucratic expertise limited only to the field of accounting. The failures of accounting regulation may be a "pressing national problem," but "a judiciary that licensed extraconstitutional government with each issue of comparable gravity would, in the long run, be far worse." *Id.*, at 187-188. Neither respondents nor the dissent explains why the Board's task, unlike so many others, requires *more* than one layer of insulation from the President — or, for that matter, why only two. The point is not to take issue with for-cause limitations in general; we do not do that. The question here is far more modest. We deal with the unusual situation, never before addressed by the Court, of two layers of for-cause tenure. And though it may be criticized as "elementary arithmetical logic," *post*, at 23, two layers are not the same as one.

The President has been given the power to oversee executive officers; he is not limited, as in Harry Truman's lament, to "persuad[ing]" his unelected subordinates "to do what they ought to do without persuasion." *Post*, at 11 (internal quotation marks omitted). In its pursuit of a "workable government," Congress cannot reduce the Chief Magistrate to a cajoler-in-chief.

D

The United States concedes that some constraints on the removal of inferior executive officers might violate the Constitution. It contends, however, that the removal restrictions at issue here do not.

To begin with, the Government argues that the Commission's removal power over the Board is "broad," and could be construed as broader still, if necessary to avoid invalidation. See, *e.g.*, *id.*, at 51, and n. 19; cf. PCAOB Brief 22-23. But the Government does not contend that simple disagreement with the Board's policies or priorities could constitute "good cause" for its removal. See Tr. of Oral Arg. 41-43, 45-46. Nor do our precedents suggest as much. *Humphrey's Executor*, for example, rejected a removal premised on a lack of agreement "'on either the policies or the administering of the Federal Trade Commission,'" because the FTC was designed to be "'independent in character,'" "free from 'political domination or control,'" and not "'subject to anybody in the government'" or "'to the orders of the President.'" 295 U.S., at 619, 625. Accord, *Morrison*, 487 U.S., at 693 (noting that "the congressional determination to limit the removal power of the Attorney General was essential . . . to establish the necessary independence of the office"); *Wiener v. United States*, 357 U.S. 349 (1958) (describing for-cause removal as "involving the rectitude" of an officer). And here there is judicial review of any effort to remove Board members, see 15 U.S.C. §78y(a)(1), so the Commission will not have the final word on the propriety of its own removal orders. The removal restrictions set forth in the statute mean what they say.

Indeed, this case presents an even more serious threat to executive control than an "ordinary" dual for-cause standard. Congress enacted an unusually high standard that must be met before Board members may be removed. A Board member cannot be removed except for willful violations of the Act, Board rules, or the securities laws; willful abuse of authority; or unreasonable failure to enforce compliance — as determined in a formal Commission order, rendered on the record and after notice and an opportunity for a hearing. §7217(d)(3); see §78y(a). The Act does not even give the Commission power to fire Board members for violations of *other* laws that do not relate to the Act, the securities laws, or the Board's authority. The President might have less than full confidence in, say, a Board member who cheats on his taxes; but that discovery is not listed among the grounds for removal under §7217(d)(3).

The rigorous standard that must be met before a Board member may be removed was drawn from statutes concerning private organizations like the New York Stock Exchange. Cf. §§78s(h)(4), 7217(d)(3). While we need not decide the question here, a removal standard appropriate for limiting Government control over private bodies may be inappropriate for officers wielding the executive power of the United States.

Alternatively, respondents portray the Act's limitations on removal as irrelevant, because — as the Court of Appeals held — the Commission wields "at-will removal power over Board *functions* if not Board members." 537 F.3d, at 683 (emphasis added); accord, Brief for United States 27-28; PCAOB Brief 48. The Commission's general "oversight and enforcement authority over the Board," §7217(a), is said to "blun[t] the constitutional impact of for-cause removal," 537 F.3d, at 683, and to leave the President no worse off than "if Congress had lodged the Board's functions in the SEC's own staff," PCAOB Brief 15.

Broad power over Board functions is not equivalent to the power to remove Board members. The Commission may, for example, approve the Board's budget, §7219(b), issue binding regulations, §§7202(a), 7217(b)(5), relieve the Board of authority, §7217(d)(1), amend Board sanctions, §7217(c), or enforce Board rules on its own, §§7202(b)(1), (c). But altering the budget or powers of an agency as a whole is a problematic way to control an inferior officer. The Commission cannot wield a free hand to supervise individual members if it must destroy the Board in order to fix it.

Even if Commission power over Board activities could substitute for authority over its members, we would still reject respondents' premise that the Commission's power in this regard is plenary. As described above, the Board is empowered to take significant enforcement actions, and does so largely independently of the Commission. See *supra*, at 3-4. Its powers are, of course, subject to some latent Commission control. See *supra*, at 4-5. But the Act nowhere gives the Commission effective power to start, stop, or alter individual Board investigations, executive activities typically carried out by officials within the Executive Branch.

The Government and the dissent suggest that the Commission could govern and direct the Board's daily exercise of prosecutorial discretion by promulgating new SEC rules, or by amending those of the Board. Brief for United States 27; *post*, at 15. Enacting general rules through the required notice and comment procedures is obviously a poor means of micromanaging the Board's affairs. See §§78s(c), 7215(b)(1), 7217(b)(5); cf. 5 U.S.C. §553, 15 U.S.C. §7202(a), PCAOB Brief 24, n. 6. So the Government offers another proposal, that the Commission require the Board by rule to "secure SEC approval for any actions that it now may take itself." Brief for United States 27. That would surely constitute one of the "limitations upon the activities, functions, and operations of the Board" that the Act forbids, at least without Commission findings equivalent to those required to fire the Board instead. §7217(d)(2). The Board thus has significant independence in determining its priorities and intervening in the affairs of regulated firms (and the lives of their associated persons) without Commission preapproval or direction.

Finally, respondents suggest that our conclusion is contradicted by the past practice of Congress. But the Sarbanes-Oxley Act is highly unusual in committing substantial executive authority to officers protected by two layers of for-cause removal — including at one level a sharply circumscribed definition of what constitutes "good cause," and rigorous procedures that must be followed prior to removal. . . .

The Constitution that makes the President accountable to the people for executing the laws also gives him the power to do so. That power includes, as a general matter, the authority to remove those who assist him in carrying out his duties. Without such power, the President could not be held fully accountable for discharging his own responsibilities; the buck would stop somewhere else. Such diffusion of authority "would greatly diminish the intended and necessary responsibility of the chief magistrate himself." The Federalist No. 70, at 478.

While we have sustained in certain cases limits on the President's removal power, the Act before us imposes a new type of restriction — two levels of protection from removal for those who nonetheless exercise significant executive power. Congress cannot limit the President's authority in this way.

The judgment of the United States Court of Appeals for the District of Columbia Circuit is affirmed in part and reversed in part, and the case is remanded for further proceedings consistent with this opinion.

It is so ordered.

NOTES

1. In creating the PCAOB, Congress sought to achieve a delicate balance. On the one hand, Congress wanted the PCAOB to be independent of the bureaucracy. As a result, the PCAOB was set up as a nonprofit organization that was funded by industry rather than tax revenue. On the other hand, Congress did not want the PCAOB to become dominated by the very industry it was designed to regulate. As a result, Congress gave the SEC some oversight authority, including the right to remove directors in the event that the PCAOB failed to enforce its own rules. The legislative history of the Sarbanes-Oxley Act, which created the PCAOB, sheds light on Congress's reasoning:

> Congress's intention to insulate the PCAOB from political influence and partisan forces would be thwarted if the PCAOB could, in the words of the D.C. Circuit, be

> "micromanag[ed]" by the SEC. Recognizing that the past is prologue, Congress feared that its own members and the President might be tempted to persuade the SEC to adopt positions favored by their powerful constituents and contributors. Congress also may have surmised that the SEC, headed by a Chairman who serves at the pleasure of the President, and composed (at the time) of a majority of members from the President's political party, would be more inclined to favor the President's policy preferences. Accordingly, fueled with bipartisan spirit in the wake of the collapses of Enron and WorldCom, Congress designed the PCAOB to be doubly insulated from political and partisan pressure.

Donna M. Nagy, Is the PCAOB a "Heavily Controlled Component" of the SEC?: An Essential Question in the Constitutional Controversy, 71 U. Pitt. L. Rev. 361, 384 (2010). By striking down the restrictions imposed on the SEC's ability to remove members of the PCAOB, the Supreme Court disrupted the balance by effectively giving the SEC plenary control over the Board. What impact, if any, is the decision likely to have on the decisions of the PCAOB? Does this decision suggest an end to the experiment of assigning regulatory responsibility to a nongovernment entity?

2. Compare the PCAOB to the New York Stock Exchange. The NYSE is a for-profit company that also has regulatory responsibility. The SEC has the authority to review the rules and decisions of the NYSE but has no authority to replace the entity's management. Stock exchanges have often been criticized for failing to enforce their own rules with sufficient vigor. What do you make of this model of regulation? What problems or concerns might it raise? The stock exchanges were given regulatory authority in the 1930s. Would Congress be likely to duplicate this model today?

3. The majority treats the SEC as an independent agency. To the extent that independence arises from restrictions on the president's ability to remove the heads of an agency (in this case the five commissioners), can you make an argument that, in fact, the SEC is not independent? The statute creating the agency gives each commissioner a five-year term but includes no explicit restriction on the President's right of removal. Take a look at the language in the Securities Exchange Act of 1934 that created the Commission. 15 U.S.C.S. §78d. Was the omission deliberate? Some on the Supreme Court think so, given that the statute was passed before the Court's decision in *Humphrey's Executor* that for-cause removal protections for the heads of independent agencies were constitutional. See Free Enterprise Fund v. PCAOB, 561 U.S. 477, 546-547 (2010) (Breyer, J., dissenting, joined by Stevens, Ginsburg, and Sotomayor, JJ.) (explaining the historical context in which the statute was passed and noting that "the absence of a 'for cause' provision in the statute that created the Commission [was not] likely to have been inadvertent"). Nevertheless, the dissenting justices in *Free Enterprise* state that the absence of statutory for-cause removal protections "does not mean [that Congress] intended to create a dependent, rather than an independent agency." Id. at 547. What other factors should a court consider in determining the independent status of an agency? See *supra* note 4, p. 50; see also Wiener v. United States, 357 U.S. 349, 353 (1958) (describing "the nature of the function that Congress" vests in an agency as "the most reliable factor for drawing an inference regarding the President's power of removal in our case"); *See also* Daniel Richardson, Congressional Control of Agency Expertise, 105 Va. L. Rev. 173, 223 (2019) ("Congress has not adopted an all-or-nothing approach to agency independence.").

4. One consequence of the use of a nonprofit company rather than a government agency is that the PCAOB is not subject to the traditional pay scale for government employees. See Free Enterprise Fund v. PCAOB, 561 U.S. 477 n. 1 (2010) ("The current salary for the Chairman is $673,000. Other Board members receive $547,000."). This is substantially more than the Chair of the SEC (base salary of $165,300 in 2013) and even the President of the United States ($400,000). What difference might this make in the operation of the PCAOB?

5. In the case of the independent counsel in *Morrison*, the President had no direct removal authority. As a practical matter, however, a President wanting counsel removed could simply dismiss an unwilling Attorney General. In fact, this occurred in connection with the so-called Saturday Night Massacre when President Nixon dismissed two Attorney Generals (Elliot Richardson and William Ruckelshaus) before the third one (Robert Bork) would carry out his instructions to fire Archibald Cox, the Watergate special prosecutor. See Senator Carl Levin (with assistance from Elise J. Bean), A Symposium on Special Prosecutions and the Role of the Independent Counsel: The Independent Counsel Statute: A Matter of Public Confidence and Constitutional Balance, 16 Hofstra L. Rev. 11, 12 (1987). Is there an argument to be made that the President could do the same thing with respect to the SEC? If the President wanted members of the PCAOB removed, could he or she remove unwilling commissioners of the SEC, contending that their refusal constituted good cause?

6. One of the judges on the panel that decided the PCAOB case at the D.C. Circuit viewed the Supreme Court's decision as "in tension" with *Humphrey's Executor*. See In re Aiken County, 645 F.3d 428, 446 (D.C. Cir. 2011) (Kavanaugh, J., concurring) ("But there can be little doubt that the *Free Enterprise* Court's wording and reasoning are in tension with *Humphrey's Executor* and are more in line with Chief Justice Taft's majority opinion in *Myers*."). Do you agree with this? Does this suggest the possibility that the reasoning in *Free Enterprise* may eventually be extended to all independent agencies? One article, published before a final decision in PCAOB, suggested as much. See Donna M. Nagy, Is the PCAOB a "Heavily Controlled Component" of the SEC?: An Essential Question in the Constitutional Controversy, 71 U. Pitt. L. Rev. 361, 363-364 (2010) ("A broad holding by the Court [in PCAOB] could raise questions about the level of independence asserted by even long-standing federal agencies such as the Federal Reserve, an entity often described as the most independent of all federal agencies and the least subject to congressional oversight." (internal quotation marks omitted)).

7. *Free Enterprise* permitted a challenge by a private party to the constitutionality of the PCAOB directly and not as part of a challenge to a final order by the PCAOB. Subsequent lower court decisions, however, have been less willing to permit these types of challenges, at least against the Securities and Exchange

Commission. See Tilton v. SEC, 824 F.3d 276 (2d Cir. 2016) ("By enacting the SEC's comprehensive scheme of administrative and judicial review, Congress implicitly precluded federal district court jurisdiction over the appellants' constitutional challenge" to the appointment process for administrative law judges). Other circuits have agreed with the approach in *Tilton*. See Bennett v. SEC, 844 F.3d 174 (11th Cir. 2016) (following the reasoning of the "Second, Seventh, Eleventh, and D.C. Circuits that have addressed the issue"). Instead, the challenges must first be adjudicated by the Commission, and only then can the courts review the issue. What is the consequence of this approach? Given that these cases involve challenges to the appointment process of administrative law judges, is it reasonable to ask ALJs in the first instance to resolve the issue? *Free Enterprise, Humphrey's Executor*, and *Morrison* all address restrictions on the removal of executive branch employees. What about the appointment process? At least here there is a specific provision addressing appointments, yet the provision sometimes fits uncomfortably within the administrative state.

CHAPTER 2

Delegation of Powers

One of the first books on American administrative law was Ernst Freund's Administrative Powers over Persons and Property (1928). Inquiry into the powers possessed by agencies is the natural starting point in the study of administrative law.

The basic principle governing administrative power is that of limiting agencies to the authority delegated by statute. In the words of one court, an administrative "agency is but a creature of statute. Any and all authority pursuant to which an agency may act ultimately must be grounded in an express grant from Congress." Killip v. Office of Personnel Management, 991 F.2d 1564, 1569 (Fed. Cir. 1993). The relationship of any agency to its governing statute is comparable to that of a corporation to its charter; as the corporation is to its charter, the agency is to its enabling legislation.

This means that the basic doctrine of administrative law, as of corporation law, is the doctrine of *ultra vires*. The jurisdictional principle is the root principle of administrative power. The statute is the source of agency authority as well as of its limits. If an agency act is within the statutory limits (or *vires*) its action is valid; if it is outside them (*ultra vires*), it is invalid. No statute is needed to establish this; it is inherent in the constitutional positions of agencies and courts.

If an agency possesses substantive powers, it does so because of a statutory delegation from the legislature. It is from this point of view that there is a legal basis for the common assertion on Capitol Hill that administrative agencies are "arms of Congress."

What powers may be delegated by the legislature to agencies? What, if any, limits are there on delegations?

Administrative agencies might be distinguished by their possession of the power to determine, either by rule or by decision, private rights and obligations. In effect this defines agencies by their possession of legislative and/or judicial authority — the legislative power to promulgate rules and regulations having the force of law and/or the judicial power to decide individual cases. How can these powers be conferred on nonlegislative and nonjudicial organs? Doesn't Doesn't the separation of powers mean that only the legislature may exercise legislative powers and only the courts may exercise judicial powers?

These are the questions to which this chapter will be devoted.

A LEGISLATIVE POWER

According to the famous Steel Seizure case, the Constitution is inconsistent with the notion of executive lawmaking authority: "In the framework of our Constitution, the President's power to see that the laws are faithfully executed refutes the idea that he is to be a lawmaker. . . . The founders of this Nation entrusted the law making power to the Congress alone in both good and bad times." Youngstown Sheet and Tube Co. v. Sawyer, 343 U.S. 579, 587-589 (1952).

Despite this categorical judicial assertion, it can hardly be denied that the administrative agency today is a lawmaking agency. More and more, the legislature has delegated significant powers of lawmaking to agencies. Indeed, as Justice Scalia has explained, "Broad delegation . . . is the hallmark of the modern administrative state[.]" Scalia, Judicial Deference to Administrative Interpretations of Law, 1989 Duke L.J. 511, 516. The administrative agency is characterized by its possession of authority to make rules and regulations having the force of law. "[A]gency rulemaking powers are the rule rather than, as they once were, the exception[.]" Id. Nor should it be thought that the lawmaking powers vested in agencies are powers of slight import. On the contrary, administrative lawmaking powers have become fully comparable (both quantitatively and qualitatively) to those exercised directly by the legislature.

From a quantitative point of view, the administrative exercise of rulemaking power dwarfs the direct exercise of legislative authority by the elected representatives of the people. "For some time, the sheer amount of law — the substantive rules that regulate private conduct and direct the operation of government — made by the agencies has far outnumbered the lawmaking engaged in by Congress through the traditional process." INS v. Chadha, 462 U.S. 919, 985-986 (1983) (White, J., dissenting). The Federal Register (in which federal regulations are published) since its beginning in 1935 has vastly exceeded in size the Statutes at Large (in which laws enacted by Congress are published).

Also, what is often not realized is that, qualitatively speaking, administrative lawmaking powers are comparable to the powers exercised by the legislative branch. As a retired federal judge tells us, "Agencies . . . are legislating, in any conventional sense of the term, when they engage in rulemaking. . . . It is over a century too late to suggest that legislating is done only by Congress." Gibbons, The Court's Role in Interbranch Disputes over Oversight of Agency Rulemaking, 14 Cardozo L. Rev. 957, 985 (1993).

The authority of agencies to make rules and regulations is thus a power of enormous consequence. Rules and regulations, no less than statutes, lay down patterns of conduct to which those affected must conform. As Chief Justice Stone once pointed out,

> [u]nlike an administrative order or a court judgment adjudicating the rights of individuals, which is binding only on the parties to the particular proceeding, a valid exercise of the rule-making power is addressed to and sets a standard of conduct for all to whom its terms apply. It operates as such in advance of the imposition of

> sanctions upon any particular individual. It is common experience that men conform their conduct to regulations by governmental authority so as to avoid the unpleasant legal consequences which failure to conform entails.

Columbia Broadcasting System v. United States, 316 U.S. 407, 418 (1942).

Inevitably, the rise and growth of rulemaking power have played a predominant part in the great shift in the center of gravity of lawmaking that has occurred in modern times. Originally, the shift was entirely one from the courts to the legislative process. Case law had, prior to the nineteenth century, been the matrix of the common law. When Jeremy Bentham thundered his philippics against judge-made law, he urged that it was the elected representatives of the people who rightfully had the primary responsibility for the making of law. After Bentham, the growing point of law shifted from Her Majesty's Judges to the Lords and Commons, in Parliament assembled. And the same development occurred on the western side of the Atlantic.

But Bentham and his disciples greatly oversimplified the process of legislative lawmaking in a complicated industrial society. Quite correctly, they grasped the occasion to use the legislature to sweep aside the archaisms that had become encrusted in the common law. Yet negative reform of this type has by itself not proved adequate. Modern public opinion has more and more required the state to assume a positive duty to eliminate the excesses and injustices that are the inevitable concomitants of a wholly unrestrained industrial economy. Such a positive role could hardly be assumed by mere prohibitions enacted by legislative fiat. On the contrary, the state has been required not only to prohibit by legislative decree but also to assume a continuing duty to regulate those subject to its authority. In addition, the state has had to bring ever-increasing parts of the population directly under its fostering guardianship. The representative legislative assembly is peculiarly inappropriate itself to perform these continuous tasks of regulation and guardianship. It has had to delegate their performance to the administrative process. Indeed, the need for an effective instrument through which these tasks could be performed has been perhaps the primary reason for the growth of that process.

1. Separation and Delegation

The Supreme Court has referred to the doctrine of separation of powers as one that is "at the heart of our Constitution[.]" Buckley v. Valeo, 424 U.S. 1, 119 (1976). If the doctrine were (in Cardozo's phrase) a doctrinaire concept to be made use of with pedantic rigor, the rise of the modern agency would have been an impossibility, for the outstanding characteristic of such agency is the possession by it of powers that are both legislative and judicial in nature. The powers so vested in these agencies are comparable to those traditionally exercised by the legislature and the courts. They have, however, been vested in organs outside the legislative and judicial branches because without such powers, those organs could not effectively perform the manifold tasks entrusted to them by the legislature.

Even at this late date, there may be those who deny that, in a system dominated by the separation of powers, any governmental organ outside the legislature or the courts can exercise legislative or judicial authority. Such constitutional purism is wholly out of line with the facts of contemporary governmental life.

To be sure, if we think of the separation of powers as carrying out the distinction between legislation and administration with mathematical precision and as dividing the branches of government into watertight compartments, we would probably have to conclude that any exercise of lawmaking authority by an agency is automatically invalid. Such a rigorous application of the constitutional doctrine is neither desirable nor feasible; the only absolute separation that has ever been possible was that in the theoretical writings of a Montesquieu, who looked across at foggy England from his sunny Gascon vineyards and completely misconstrued what he saw.

In classic constitutional theory, the separation-of-powers notion requires the exclusive character of the powers conferred on the three branches of government. "It may be stated then, as a general rule inherent in the American constitutional system, that, . . . the Legislature cannot exercise either executive or judicial power; the executive cannot exercise either legislative or judicial power; the judiciary cannot exercise either executive or legislative power." Springer v. Government of the Philippine Islands, 277 U.S. 189, 201-202 (1928). Under this approach, only the legislature itself can exercise lawmaking authority; organs outside the legislative branch cannot be vested with legislative power.

This result is reinforced by the maxim against the delegation of power (delegata potestas non potest delegari). As explained by Justice Story, "It is a general rule of law that a delegated authority cannot be delegated." Shankland v. Washington, 30 U.S. (5 Pet.) 390, 391 (U.S. 1831). This rule, originally a principle of the private law of agency, has played an important part in public law theory.

The basis of governmental authority is delegation from some ultimate source of power. "We the people of the United States," declares the Preamble to the Federal Constitution, "do ordain and establish this Constitution. . . ." U.S. Const. pmbl. The legislative, executive, and judicial branches possess power only because it has been delegated to them by the people. But, if this is true, since the three branches are the recipients of *the* legislative, executive, and judicial power delegated by the people, it follows, from the maxim against delegation, that they must be the *sole* repositories of such power.

If we apply this theory more specifically to legislative power, we see that, under it, Congress itself is only a delegatee; its possession of legislative power stems from the delegation to it of that power in the Constitution. As a delegatee, Congress cannot redelegate any of its legislative authority to anyone else. In its essentials, this approach is derived from John Locke, who, more than any other political philosopher, influenced the framers of the Constitution. Said Locke, in a passage often cited by American jurists: "The legislative cannot transfer the power of making laws to any other hands: for it being but a delegated power from the people, they who have it cannot pass it over to others." John Locke, Second

Treatise of Civil Government §141 (1690). Or, as it was put in a leading case that relies expressly on this passage:

> That a power conferred upon an agent because of his fitness and the confidence reposed in him cannot be delegated by him to another, is a general and admitted rule. Legislatures stand in this relation to the people whom they represent. Hence it is a cardinal principle of representative government, that the legislature cannot delegate the power to make laws to any other body or authority.

Locke's Appeal, 72 Pa. 491, 494 (1873).

Under such an approach, delegated legislation, in the sense of the exercise by a subordinate authority, such as an administrative agency, of the legislative power delegated by the legislature, becomes impossible. How then has our law been able to accommodate the practical necessity for delegated legislation with the constitutional doctrine against the delegation of legislative power?

To understand the cases on delegation of legislative power, one must first realize the impossibility of a rigid, inflexible employment of the maxim against delegation. Noting that there are powers of a doubtful classification (powers that analytically or historically or from both standpoints might be assigned to either of two departments), Chief Justice Marshall, very early on, saw that a literal application of the maxim was undesirable, and held that it was within the legislative competence to assign exercise of these powers to the executive branch: "The line has not been exactly drawn which separates those important subjects, which must be entirely regulated by the legislature itself, from those of less interest, in which a general provision may be made, and power given to those who are to act under such general provisions to fill up the details." Wayman v. Southard, 23 U.S. (10 Wheat.) 1, 43 (U.S. 1825). See also generally Mortenson & Bagley, Delegation at the Founding, 121 Colum. L. Rev. 277 (2021) (refuting claims that the Constitution was originally understood to contain a nondelegation principle).

But there were few who, like the great Chief Justice, could so early openly admit that the constitutional maxim was not inflexible. The resulting judicial dilemma, when the courts were confronted with delegation cases, was resolved by the judicious choice of words to describe the delegated power. The authority transferred was, in Justice Holmes's felicitous phrase, "softened by a quasi," and the courts were thus able to admit the fact of delegated legislation and still to deny the name.

This result is well put in Professor R. E. Cushman's syllogism. *Major premise:* Legislative power cannot be constitutionally delegated by Congress. *Minor premise:* It is essential that certain powers be delegated to administrative officers and regulatory commissions. *Conclusion:* Therefore the powers thus delegated are not legislative powers. R. E. Cushman, The Independent Regulatory Commissions 429 (1941). They are instead "administrative" or "quasi-legislative" powers. This approach was affirmed by the Supreme Court in the *Whitman* case, *infra* p. 106, but note the concurrence by Justices Stevens and Souter arguing that the power delegated is actual legislative power, *infra* p. 109 (Stevens, J., concurring).

During this century, however, the Supreme Court has followed a more realistic approach. The law has shifted from an unworkable rule prohibiting *any* delegation of *legislative* power to one prohibiting *excessive* delegation — one that does not contain any defined standard, or what the Court calls an "intelligible principle" in Mistretta v. United States, 488 U.S. 361, 372 (1989) (citing J.W. Hampton, Jr. & Co. v. U.S., 276 U.S. 394, 409 (1928)).

2. The *Panama Refining* and *Schechter Poultry* Cases

In only two cases has the Supreme Court struck down delegations, and both were decided in 1935. The first was Panama Refining Co. v. Ryan, 293 U.S. 388 (1935). Section 9(c) of the National Industrial Recovery Act empowered the President to prohibit the transportation in interstate commerce of so-called hot oil (oil produced or withdrawn from storage in excess of the amount permitted by state law). The Court held the delegation invalid because the statute contained only the bare delegation: Congress had not stated whether or in what circumstances or under what conditions the President was to exercise the prohibitory authority. Though the authority delegated was clearly defined, Congress had not set up a standard for the President's action. Instead, it gave the President an unlimited authority to lay down the prohibition or not, as he might see fit.

Justice Cardozo dissented. He found the required standard in §1 of the statute, which declared the policy of Congress that the Act was intended to promote: to remove obstructions to commerce, promote industry organization, eliminate unfair competition, avoid restriction of production, increase consumption, reduce unemployment, rehabilitate industry, and conserve natural resources. According to Cardozo, the President was intended to exercise the prohibitory authority whenever satisfied that doing so would effectuate the policy declared in §1. This, the dissent urged, was a sufficient definition of a standard to make the statute valid.

The majority held that §1 was too broad to constitute an adequate standard. The goals stated were too general to furnish any real guide on whether and under what conditions the delegated authority should be exercised. The broad outline of §1 was simply an introduction of the statute, leaving the legislative policy as to particular subjects to be declared by subsequent sections — which §9(c) failed to do.

The division in *Panama Refining* turns on the adequacy of the standard in a statute delegating legislative power. Both the majority and the dissent agreed that the statute must contain a standard. They differed on how detailed the standard must be. The majority refused to accept a standard so broad that it did not limit or guide the delegate in any meaningful way. Cardozo maintained that, properly construed, the statute contained a sufficient standard. Congress could not circumscribe more closely a power granted to deal with pressing economic problems.

As we shall see, the federal cases since *Panama Refining* have moved in the direction of the Cardozo dissent. They continue to assert the need for standards, but uphold, as adequate, standards at least as broad as those in §1 of the National Industrial Recovery Act. This tends to reduce the standards requirement itself to an empty form and raises the question whether the law still imposes meaningful restrictions upon congressional delegations.

Four months after its *Panama Refining* decision, the Supreme Court again struck down a congressional delegation in A.L.A. Schechter Poultry Corp. v. United States, 295 U.S. 495 (1935). At issue was §3 of the National Industrial Recovery Act, which authorized the President to approve "codes of fair competition" for the governance of trades and industries. When a code was approved, its provisions were to be the "standards of fair competition" for the trade or industry concerned, and any violation was punishable penally.

The Court, composed of the same Justices who had decided *Panama Refining*, ruled unanimously that the delegation was invalid. For the majority voiding the far narrower *Panama Refining* delegation, such a result was easy. Even Justice Cardozo found the delegation too broad. Cardozo's concurrence is explained by the extent of power delegated. Though the statutory phrase "codes of fair competition" was similar to that in the Federal Trade Commission Act, the codes promulgated had not been limited by any such concept. If the Act was given the same construction as had been given to it by its administrators, the terms "codes of fair competition" became a euphemism; the statutory term *fair competition* was not a limiting standard. The President's power was not restricted to proscription of "unfair" methods of competition alone. Instead, it included whatever ordinances were deemed desirable in the trade or industry affected. The code at issue, for example, regulated virtually every aspect of the poultry business, including hours, number of employees, labor relations, working conditions, and trade practices. The President's power was as wide as the field of industrial regulation and permitted the imposition of any regulatory requirement on the business concerned.

Schechter Poultry stands apart in any discussion of delegation. It involved the broadest delegation Congress has ever made, for it involved nothing less than abdication of the commerce power. Under the statute, anything that Congress might do under its commerce power for the betterment of business might be done by the President. The President was thus given virtually unlimited legislative authority over the economic system. This was delegation running riot. The breadth of delegation rendered irrelevant the "standards" that Cardozo, in his *Panama Refining* opinion, had found in §1 of the act. No standard could save a delegation virtually as sweeping as the Commerce Clause itself.

3. Post-1935 Federal Cases

The *Panama Refining* and *Schechter Poultry* cases are the only cases in which delegations have been invalidated by the Supreme Court. Since these two cases, however, the Supreme Court has upheld, "without deviation, Congress' ability to delegate power under broad standards." Mistretta v. United States, 488 U.S. 361, 373 (1989). And, it remains true today, more than twenty years after the Court's decision in *Mistretta.* This has been true despite the fact that the past half-century has seen increasingly broad delegations of legislative power — those during the later New Deal, World War II, the cold war period, the Korean and Vietnam wars, environmental concerns, the economic downturn, the energy crisis, and the post-9/11 war on terror. If crisis has become endemic in our day, delegation has been the normal legislative response.

What is the present status of the delegation doctrine? Are the *Panama Refining* and *Schechter Poultry* decisions still good law?

The *Schechter Poultry* delegation still stands apart as the widest delegation in American history. Even during war emergencies, Congress has never conferred so broad a power as that in the National Industrial Recovery Act, giving the President legislative power over the economic system virtually coextensive with that delegated to Congress itself by the Commerce Clause. Whatever else may be the current status of the delegation doctrine, *Schechter Poultry* remains as a warning that there is still a line beyond which Congress may not go in delegating power. The Supreme Court itself has implied that "the requirement of *Schechter Poultry*" was still a hurdle for statutes to overcome. National Cable Television Ass'n, Inc. v. United States, 415 U.S. 336, 342 (1974).

The *Panama Refining* decision is a different matter. The dividing line between the *Panama Refining* majority and the Cardozo dissent, as already noted, was over the adequacy of the standards contained in the delegating statute. The post-1935 federal cases move from the majority *Panama Refining* view to that expressed in Cardozo's dissent: "the Court has upheld statutes containing only vague standards and statements of policy and delegating very broad discretion." National Farmers' Org., Inc. v. Block, 561 F. Supp. 1201, 1205 (E.D. Wis. 1983). While the Supreme Court has continued to assert the need for standards, it has upheld standards at least as broad as those involved in *Panama* and, in at least one case, upheld a delegation without any standard.

Among the cases usually cited to illustrate the post-1935 Supreme Court approach to delegation are the following:

(a) Yakus v. United States, 321 U.S. 414 (1944). This case dealt with the validity of the Emergency Price Control Act of 1942. Under that statute, the Price Administrator was given the authority, when, in his judgment, commodity prices rose or threatened to rise "to an extent or in a manner inconsistent with the purposes" of the act, to establish such maximum price or prices as "in his judgment will be generally fair and equitable and will effectuate the purposes" of the act. Id. at 420. The purposes of the Act referred to were contained in §1:

> to stabilize prices and to prevent speculative, unwarranted, and abnormal increases in prices and rents; to eliminate and prevent profiteering, hoarding, manipulation, speculation, and other disruptive practices resulting from

> abnormal market conditions or scarcities caused by or contributing to the national emergency; to assure that defense appropriations are not dissipated by excessive prices; to protect persons with relatively fixed and limited incomes, consumers, wage earners, investors, and persons dependent on life insurance, annuities, and pensions, from undue impairment of their standard of living; to prevent hardships to persons engaged in business . . . and to the Federal, State, and local governments, which would result from abnormal increases in prices; to assist in securing adequate production of commodities and facilities; to prevent a post emergency collapse of values[.]

Id. at 420.

In addition, the administrator was told that in establishing any price he should, "[s]o far as practicable," give due consideration to prices prevailing between October 1 and October 15, 1941. Id. at 421. If he fixed other prices, he had to make a "statement of the considerations" that led him to choose them instead of the base period prices. Id. at 422.

The Court sustained the statute on the ground that sufficiently precise standards were prescribed to confine the administrator's regulations and orders within fixed limits. According to Chief Justice Stone,

> The standards prescribed by the present Act, with the aid of the "statement of the considerations" required to be made by the Administrator, are sufficiently definite and precise to enable Congress, the courts and the public to ascertain whether the Administrator, in fixing the designated prices, has conformed to those standards. . . . Hence we are unable to find in them an unauthorized delegation of legislative power.

Id. at 426.

The Court's decision called forth a vigorous dissent by Justice Roberts, who asserted that the standards laid down in the Price Control Act were no more definite than those prescribed in the National Industrial Recovery Act:

> Reflection will demonstrate that in fact the Act sets no limits upon the discretion or judgment of the Administrator. His commission is to take any action with respect to prices which he believes will preserve what he deems a sound economy during the emergency and prevent what he considers to be a disruption of such a sound economy in the post war period. His judgment, founded as it may be, on his studies and investigations, as well as other economic data, even though contrary to the great weight of current opinion or authority, is the final touchstone of the validity of his action.

Id. at 451-452.

The discretion vested in the Price Administrator was, in Justice Roberts' view, no more canalized within banks that kept it from overflowing than was that delegated in the *Schechter* case. Hence, he concluded, the *Yakus* case "leaves no doubt that the [*Schechter*] decision is now overruled." Id. at 452.

Did §1 of the Price Control Act really do more to guide the administrator than section 1 of the National Industrial Recovery Act in the *Panama Refining* case? Does that, however, necessarily mean that the Roberts dissent was correct in its conclusion that *Yakus* overruled *Schechter*?

(b) Lichter v. United States, 334 U.S. 742 (1948). This case arose out of a claim that the Renegotiation Act of 1942 unlawfully attempted to delegate legislative power. That law provided for the renegotiation of war contracts and authorized administrative officers to recover profits they determined to be "excessive." But the Act did not define the term "excessive profits" other than to state that it "means any amount of a contract or subcontract price which is found as a result of renegotiation to represent excessive profits" — which does not really say more than that excessive means excessive. Id. at 777.

Despite this lack of specificity, the Court upheld the Act:

> The statutory term "excessive profits," in its context, was a sufficient expression of legislative policy and standards to render it constitutional. . . . It is not necessary that Congress supply administrative officials with a specific formula for their guidance in a field where flexibility and the adaptation of the congressional policy to infinitely variable conditions constitute the essence of the program. . . .

Id. at 783-785.

Though the 1942 Renegotiation Act did not contain more than the solipsistic guide to the meaning of "excessive profits" referred to, the agencies administering the statute developed a list of the factors they would take into account in determining whether profits had been excessive. Congress amended the statute in 1944 expressly to include these agency-developed standards. The amendment provided that "[i]n determining excessive profits there shall be taken into consideration the following factors:

> (i) efficiency of contractor . . . ;
> (ii) reasonableness of costs and profits, with particular regard to volume of production, normal pre-war earnings, and comparison of war and peacetime products;
> (iii) amount and source of public and private capital employed and net worth;
> (iv) extent of risk assumed, including the risk incident to reasonable pricing policies;
> (v) nature and extent of contribution to the war effort, including inventive and developmental contribution and cooperation with the Government and other contractors in supplying technical assistance;
> (vi) character of business, including complexity of manufacturing technique, character and extent of subcontracting, and rate of turn-over;
> (vii) such other factors the consideration of which the public interest and fair and equitable dealing may require. . . ."

58 Stat. 78, 79 (1944). (Note that this amendment did not affect the *Lichter* decision, since it turned only on the validity of the original 1942 delegation.)

Does the 1944 amendment rebut the argument in the *Lichter* opinion that Congress did all it could, since it was not practical for it to "supply administrative officials with a specific formula for their guidance in a field where flexibility and the adaptation of the congressional policy to infinitely variable conditions constitute the essence of the program"? 334 U.S. at 785.

Can both *Yakus* and *Lichter* be distinguished on the ground that they involved wartime delegations? The Supreme Court has held that whatever restrictions there are on delegation do not apply to delegations that relate solely to foreign affairs. United States v. Curtiss-Wright Export Corp., 299 U.S. 304 (1936). Should the same be true of delegations under the war power?

(c) Fahey v. Mallonee, 332 U.S. 245 (1947). Under the Home Owners' Loan Act of 1933, the Federal Home Loan Bank Board was empowered to issue regulations prescribing the terms and conditions on which a conservator might be appointed to take over a mismanaged federal savings and loan association. The district court had held that this constituted an invalid delegation, since no criterion was established to guide the exercise of the authority conferred. The Supreme Court candidly conceded that there was no express legislative standard, but that did not lead it to declare the law at issue invalid:

> It may be that explicit standards in the Home Owners' Loan Act would have been a desirable assurance of responsible administration. But the provisions of the statute under attack are not penal provisions. . . . The provisions are regulatory. . . . A discretion to make regulations to guide supervisory action in such matters may be constitutionally permissible while it might not be allowable to authorize creation of new crimes in unchartered fields.

Id. at 250.

Couldn't the Court's reasoning be applied to most regulatory delegations, at least those where regulatory power is not backed by penal sanctions for violations?

The *Fahey* opinion also stressed that the delegation dealt

> with a single type of enterprise and with the problems of insecurity and mismanagement which are as old as banking enterprise. . . . It is one in which accumulated experience . . . has established well-defined practices for the appointment of conservators, receivers and liquidators. Corporate management is a field, too, in which courts have experience and many precedents have crystallized into well-known and generally acceptable standards.

Id.

Is this a valid basis on which delegation without express statutory standards may be upheld?

The cases that follow demonstrate the point that delegation of legislative power continues to be an issue that can surface in any case involving a comprehensive federal regulatory scheme, and is even more likely to surface in states as a challenge to state legislation. In 1980, for example, despite a sense that legislative delegation issues involving post-1935 legislative regulatory schemes had been resolved by the Supreme Court, Justice Rehnquist's concurrence in the *Benzene* case, in which he maintained that the legislative delegation to the Secretary of Labor in the Occupational Safety and Health Act of 1970 (OSHA) was constitutionally infirm, once again brought the issue of delegation to the forefront of administrative law. Industrial Union Dep't v. American Petroleum Inst., 448 U.S. 607, 671 (1980) (Rehnquist, J., concurring).

The *Benzene* case involved a challenge to the Secretary of Labor's promulgated safety standard limiting benzene exposure under OSHA. The OSHA statute provided that in setting standards "dealing with toxic materials or harmful physical agents," like benzene, the Secretary of Labor "shall set the standard which most adequately assures, *to the extent feasible*, on the basis of the best available evidence, that no employee will suffer material impairment of health. . . ." Id. at 612 (emphasis added). The Secretary of Labor had aggressively interpreted the statutory language to mean that the safety standard should be the lowest level that can be attained at bearable cost with available technology. Id. at 613. The Court invalidated the benzene standard. Id. at 653. The plurality opinion (Justices Stevens, Burger, and Stewart) found the standard was not supported by appropriate findings. Id. at 653-662. Justice Powell concurred, concluding however that the statute required a cost-benefit analysis. Id. at 664-671.

Justice Rehnquist also concurred but found the legislature's OSHA delegation to the Secretary of Labor invalid. Id. at 671. According to Justice Rehnquist,

> [r]ead literally, the relevant portion of §6(b)(5) is completely precatory, admonishing the Secretary to adopt the most protective standard if he can, but excusing him from that duty if he cannot. In the case of a hazardous substance for which a "'safe'" level is either unknown or impractical, the language of §6(b)(5) gives the Secretary absolutely no indication where on the continuum of relative safety he should draw his line. Especially in light of the importance of the interests at stake, I have no doubt that the provision at issue, standing alone, would violate the doctrine against uncanalized delegations of legislative power.

Id. at 675.

Rehnquist then proceeded to distinguish the *Benzene* case from other post-1935 cases like *Lichter* and *Curtiss-Wright*, both discussed *supra*, before adding the following important policy insight about the foundations of the nondelegation doctrine:

> As formulated and enforced by this Court, the nondelegation doctrine serves three important functions. First, and most abstractly, it ensures to the extent consistent with orderly governmental administration that important choices of social policy are made by Congress, the branch of our Government most responsive to the popular will. . . . Second, the doctrine guarantees that, to the extent Congress finds it necessary to delegate authority, it provides the recipient of that authority with an "intelligible principle" to guide the exercise of the delegated discretion. . . . Third, and derivative of the second, the doctrine ensures that courts charged with reviewing the exercise of delegated legislative discretion will be able to test that exercise against ascertainable standards. . . .
>
> I believe the legislation at issue here fails on all three counts. The decision whether the law of diminishing returns should have any place in the regulation of toxic substances is quintessentially one of legislative policy. For Congress to pass that decision on to the Secretary in the manner it did violates, in my mind, John Locke's caveat . . . that legislatures are to make laws, not legislators. Nor, as I think the prior discussion amply demonstrates, do the provisions at issue

> or their legislative history provide the Secretary with any guidance that might lead him to his somewhat tentative conclusion that he must eliminate exposure to benzene as far as technologically and economically possible. Finally, I would suggest that the standard of "feasibility" renders meaningful judicial review impossible.
>
> We ought not to shy away from our judicial duty to invalidate unconstitutional delegations of legislative authority solely out of concern that we should thereby reinvigorate discredited constitutional doctrines of the pre-New Deal era. If the nondelegation doctrine has fallen into the same desuetude as have substantive due process and restrictive interpretations of the Commerce Clause, it is, as one writer has phrased it, "a case of death by association." . . . Indeed, a number of observers have suggested that this Court should once more take up its burden of ensuring that Congress does not unnecessarily delegate important choices of social policy to politically unresponsive administrators. Other observers, as might be imagined, have disagreed. . . .

Id. at 685-687.

In Mistretta v. United States, 488 U.S. 361 (1989), the U.S. Supreme Court upheld against a nondelegation challenge sentencing guidelines promulgated by the United States Sentencing Commission, an agency of the judicial branch of the United States. Only Justice Scalia had an issue with Congress delegating rulemaking authority to a branch other than the executive branch. According to Scalia, rulemaking delegation to the executive branch is more or less tolerated because certain ability to make rules is critical for the executive branch to carry out its enforcement function. However, in the case of a pure rulemaking delegation to the judicial branch, Congress is doing nothing more than creating a junior varsity Congress to make laws. Id. at 416-421. The majority restated the law of nondelegation to reflect the state of the doctrine in more modern times. In the following excerpt from *Mistretta*, notice especially in footnote 1 the characterization by the Court of the earlier *Panama Refining* and *Schechter Poultry* precedents.

> So long as Congress "shall lay down by legislative act an intelligible principle to which the person or body authorized to [exercise the delegated authority] is directed to conform, such legislative action is not a forbidden delegation of legislative power."
>
> Applying this "intelligible principle" test to congressional delegations, our jurisprudence has been driven by a practical understanding that in our increasingly complex society, replete with ever changing and more technical problems, Congress simply cannot do its job absent an ability to delegate power under broad general directives. . . . Accordingly, this Court has deemed it "constitutionally sufficient if Congress clearly delineates the general policy, the public agency which is to apply it, and the boundaries of this delegated authority." American Power & Light Co. v. SEC, 329 U.S. 90, 105 (1946).
>
> Until 1935, this Court never struck down a challenged statute on delegation grounds. After invalidating in 1935 two statutes as excessive delegations, see A.L.A. Schechter Poultry Corp. v. United States, 295 U.S. 495 (1935), and Panama Refining Co. v. Ryan, supra, we have upheld, again without deviation, Congress' ability to

> delegate power under broad standards.[1] See, e.g., Lichter v. United States, 334 U.S. 742, 785-786 (1948) (upholding delegation of authority to determine excessive profits); American Power & Light Co. v. SEC, 329 U.S. at 105 (upholding delegation of authority to Securities and Exchange Commission to prevent unfair or inequitable distribution of voting power among security holders); Yakus v. United States, 321 U.S. 414, 426 (1944) (upholding delegation to Price Administrator to fix commodity prices that would be fair and equitable, and would effectuate the purposes of Emergency Price Control Act of 1942); FPC v. Hope Natural Gas Co., 320 U.S. 591, 600 (1944) (upholding delegation to Federal Power Commission to determine just and reasonable rates); National Broadcasting Co. v. United States, 319 U.S. 190, 225-226 (1943) (upholding delegation to Federal Communications Commission to regulate broadcast licensing "as public interest, convenience, or necessity" require).

Id. at 372-373.

In his dissent in *Mistretta,* Justice Scalia wrote openly about the breadth of some legislative delegations since *Panama Refining* and *Schechter Poultry*, and the Court's unwillingness to strike them down.

> But while the doctrine of unconstitutional delegation is unquestionably a fundamental element of our constitutional system, it is not an element readily enforceable by the courts. Once it is conceded, as it must be, that no statute can be entirely precise, and that some judgments, even some judgments involving policy considerations, must be left to the officers executing the law and to the judges applying it, the debate over unconstitutional delegation becomes a debate not over a point of principle but over a question of degree. As Chief Justice Taft expressed the point . . . , the limits of delegation "must be fixed according to common sense and the inherent necessities of the governmental co-ordination." Since Congress is no less endowed with common sense than we are, and better equipped to inform itself of the "necessities" of government; and since the factors bearing upon those necessities are both multifarious and (in the nonpartisan sense) highly political . . . it is small wonder that we have almost never felt qualified to second-guess Congress regarding the permissible degree of policy judgment that can be left to those executing or applying the law. As the Court points out, we have invoked the doctrine of unconstitutional delegation to invalidate a law only twice in our history, over half a century ago. . . . What legislated standard, one must wonder, can possibly be too vague to survive judicial scrutiny, when we have repeatedly upheld, in various contexts, a "public interest" standard? . . .

Id. at 415-416 (Scalia, J., dissenting).

---

1. In *Schechter Poultry* and *Panama Refining* the Court concluded that Congress had failed to articulate any policy or standard that would serve to confine the discretion of the authorities to whom Congress had delegated power. No delegation of the kind at issue in those cases is present here. The Act does not make crimes of acts never before criminalized, see Fahey v. Mallonee, 332 U.S. 245, 249 (1947) (analyzing *Panama Refining*), or delegate regulatory power to private individuals, see Yakus v. United States, 321 U.S. 414, 424 (1944) (analyzing *Schechter*). In recent years, our application of the nondelegation doctrine principally has been limited to the interpretation of statutory texts, and, more particularly, to giving narrow constructions to statutory delegations that might otherwise be thought to be unconstitutional. See, e.g., Industrial Union Dept. v. American Petroleum Institute, 448 U.S. 607, 646 (1980); National Cable Television Assn. v. United States, 415 U.S. 336, 342 (1974).

Commentators have concluded that the post-1935 federal cases, culminating in Mistretta v. United States, "rang a virtual death knell for the nondelegation doctrine." Eskridge & Ferejohn, Making the Deal Stick: Enforcing the Original Constitutional Structure of Lawmaking in the Modern Regulatory State, 8 J.L. Econ. & Org. 165, 172 (1992). Even today, however, it may be erroneous to assume that the old law on delegation is, in Justice Scalia's phrase, "dead, or at least 'moribund,'" Synar v. United States, 626 F. Supp. 1374, 1384 (D.D.C. 1986), and to assert that there are no longer any constitutional restrictions on delegation. The post-1935 federal cases discussed may go far to support such an assertion. But the federal law is not the only law on delegation. State judges may still follow a stricter approach to delegation than their federal confreres.

Even so far as federal administrative law is concerned, it may not be accurate to contend that there are no longer any limitations on delegation and that consequently all congressional delegations, no matter how extreme, would now be valid. Despite the post-1935 decisions discussed, federal judges continue to use the traditional language, as the following newer cases show; they continue to assert the need for standards in statutes delegating legislative power.

WHITMAN v. AMERICAN TRUCKING ASS'NS

531 U.S. 457 (2001)

JUSTICE SCALIA delivered the opinion of the Court.

These cases present the following questions: (1) Whether §109(b)(1) of the Clean Air Act (CAA) delegates legislative power to the Administrator of the Environmental Protection Agency (EPA). . . .

I.

Section 109(a) of the CAA, as added, 84 Stat. 1679, and amended, 42 U.S.C. §7409(a), requires the Administrator of the EPA to promulgate NAAQS for each air pollutant for which "air quality criteria" have been issued under §108, 42 U.S.C. §7408. Once a NAAQS has been promulgated, the Administrator must review the standard (and the criteria on which it is based) "at five-year intervals" and make "such revisions . . . as may be appropriate." CAA §109(d)(1), 42 U.S.C. §7409(d)(1). These cases arose when, on July 18, 1997, the Administrator revised the NAAQS for particulate matter and ozone. See NAAQS for Particulate Matter, 62 Fed. Reg. 38652 (codified in 40 CFR §50.7 (1999)); NAAQS for Ozone, id., at 38856 (codified in 40 CFR §§50.9, 50.10 (1999)). American Trucking Associations, Inc., and its co-respondents in No. 99-1257 — which include, in addition to other private companies, the States of Michigan, Ohio, and West Virginia — challenged the new standards in the Court of Appeals for the District of Columbia Circuit, pursuant to 42 U.S.C. §7607(b)(1). . . .

III.

Section 109(b)(1) of the CAA instructs the EPA to set "ambient air quality standards the attainment and maintenance of which in the judgment of the Administrator, based on [the] criteria [documents of §108] and allowing an adequate margin of safety, are requisite to protect the public health." 42 U.S.C. §7409(b)(1). The Court of Appeals held that this section as interpreted by the Administrator did not provide an "intelligible principle" to guide the EPA's exercise of authority in setting NAAQS. "[The] EPA," it said, "lack[ed] any determinate criteria for drawing lines. It has failed to state intelligibly how much is too much." 175 F.3d, at 1034. The court hence found that the EPA's interpretation (but not the statute itself) violated the nondelegation doctrine. Id., at 1038. We disagree.

In a delegation challenge, the constitutional question is whether the statute has delegated legislative power to the agency. Article I, §1, of the Constitution vests "[a]ll legislative Powers herein granted . . . in a Congress of the United States." This text permits no delegation of those powers, Loving v. United States, 517 U.S. 748, 771 (1996); see id., at 776-777 (Scalia, J., concurring in part and concurring in judgment), and so we repeatedly have said that when Congress confers decision-making authority upon agencies Congress must "lay down by legislative act an intelligible principle to which the person or body authorized to [act] is directed to conform." J.W. Hampton, Jr., & Co. v. United States, 276 U.S. 394, 409 (1928). We have never suggested that an agency can cure an unlawful delegation of legislative power by adopting in its discretion a limiting construction of the statute. Both Fahey v. Mallonee, 332 U.S. 245, 252-253, 67 S. Ct. 1552 (1947), and Lichter v. United States, 334 U.S. 742, 783, 68 S. Ct. 1294 (1948), mention agency regulations in the course of their nondelegation discussions, but *Lichter* did so because a subsequent Congress had incorporated the regulations into a revised version of the statute, *ibid.*, and *Fahey* because the customary practices in the area, implicitly incorporated into the statute, were reflected in the regulations. 332 U.S. at 250. The idea that an agency can cure an unconstitutionally standardless delegation of power by declining to exercise some of that power seems to us internally contradictory. The very choice of which portion of the power to exercise — that is to say, the prescription of the standard that Congress had omitted — would *itself* be an exercise of the forbidden legislative authority. Whether the statute delegates legislative power is a question for the courts, and an agency's voluntary self-denial has no bearing upon the answer.

We agree with the Solicitor General that the text of §109(b)(1) of the CAA at a minimum requires that "[f]or a discrete set of pollutants and based on published air quality criteria that reflect the latest scientific knowledge, [the] EPA must establish uniform national standards at a level that is requisite to protect public health from the adverse effects of the pollutant in the ambient air." . . . Requisite, in turn, "mean[s] sufficient, but not more than necessary." . . . These limits on the EPA's discretion are strikingly similar to the ones we approved in Touby v. United States, 500 U.S. 160 (1991), which permitted the Attorney General to designate a drug as a controlled substance for purposes of criminal drug enforcement if doing so was "'necessary to avoid an imminent hazard to the public safety.'" Id., at 163, 111 S. Ct. 1752. They also resemble the Occupational Safety and Health Act of 1970 provision requiring the agency to "'set the standard which most adequately assures, to the extent feasible, on the basis of the best available evidence, that no employee will suffer any impairment of health'" — which the Court upheld in Industrial Union Dept., AFL-CIO v. American Petroleum Institute, 448 U.S. 607, 646 (1980). . . .

The scope of discretion §109(b)(1) allows is in fact well within the outer limits of our nondelegation precedents. In the history of the Court we have found the requisite "intelligible principle" lacking in only two statutes, one of which provided literally no guidance for the exercise of discretion, and the other of which conferred authority to regulate the entire economy on the basis of no more precise a standard than stimulating the economy by assuring "fair competition." See Panama Refining Co. v. Ryan, 293 U.S. 388 (1935); A.L.A. Schechter Poultry Corp. v. United States, 295 U.S. 495 (1935). We have, on the other hand, upheld the validity of §11(b)(2) of the Public Utility Holding Company Act of 1935, 49 Stat. 821, which gave the Securities and Exchange Commission authority to modify the structure of holding company systems so as to ensure that they are not "unduly or unnecessarily complicate[d]" and do not "unfairly or inequitably distribute voting power among security holders." American Power & Light Co. v. SEC, 329 U.S. 90, 104 (1946). We have approved the wartime conferral of agency power to fix the prices of commodities at a level that "'will be generally fair and equitable and will effectuate the [in some respects conflicting] purposes of th[e] Act.'" Yakus v. United States, 321 U.S. 414, 420 (1944). And we have found an "intelligible principle" in various statutes authorizing regulation in the "public interest." See, e.g., National Broadcasting Co. v. United States, 319 U.S. 190, 225-226 (1943) (Federal Communications Commission's power to regulate airwaves); New York Central Securities Corp. v. United States, 287 U.S. 12, 24-25 (Interstate Commerce Commission's power to approve railroad consolidations). In short, we have "almost never felt qualified to second-guess Congress regarding the permissible degree of policy judgment that can be left to those executing or applying the law." Mistretta v. United States, 109 S. Ct. 647 (1989) (Scalia, J., dissenting); see id., at 373, 109 S. Ct. 647 (majority opinion).

It is true enough that the degree of agency discretion that is acceptable varies according to the scope of the power congressionally conferred. See Loving v. United States, 517 U.S., at 772-773; United States v. Mazurie, 419 U.S. 544, 556-557 (1975). While Congress need not provide any direction to the EPA regarding the manner in which it is to define "country elevators," which are to be exempt from new-stationary-source regulations governing grain elevators, see 42 U.S.C. §741 1(i), it must provide substantial guidance on setting air standards that affect the entire national economy. But even in sweeping regulatory schemes we have never demanded, as the Court of Appeals did here, that statutes provide a "determinate criterion" for saying "how much [of the regulated harm] is too much." 175 F.3d, at 1034. In *Touby*, for example, we did not require the statute to decree how "imminent" was too imminent, or how "necessary" was necessary enough, or even — most relevant here — how "hazardous" was too hazardous. 500 U.S., at 165-167. Similarly, the statute at issue in *Lichter* authorized agencies to recoup "excess profits" paid under wartime Government contracts, yet we did not insist that Congress specify how much profit was too much. 334 U.S., at 783-786. It is therefore not conclusive for delegation purposes that, as respondents argue, ozone and particulate matter are "nonthreshold" pollutants that inflict a continuum of adverse health effects at any airborne concentration greater than zero, and hence require the EPA to make judgments of degree. "[A] certain degree of discretion, and thus of lawmaking, inheres in most executive or judicial action." Mistretta v. United States, supra, at 417 (Scalia, J., dissenting) (emphasis deleted); see 488 U.S., at 378-379 (majority opinion). Section 109(b)(1) of the CAA, which to repeat we interpret as requiring the EPA to set air quality standards at the level that is "requisite" that is, not lower or higher than is necessary — to protect the public health with an adequate margin of safety, fits comfortably within the scope of discretion permitted by our precedent.

We therefore reverse the judgment of the Court of Appeals remanding for reinterpretation that would avoid a supposed delegation of legislative power. . . .

JUSTICE STEVENS, with whom JUSTICE SOUTER joins, concurring in part and concurring the judgment.

Section 109(b)(1) delegates to the Administrator of the Environmental Protection Agency (EPA) the authority to promulgate national ambient air quality standards (NAAQS). In Part III of its opinion, ante, at 911-914, the Court explains why the Court of Appeals erred when it concluded that §109 effected "an unconstitutional delegation of legislative power." American Trucking Ass'ns, Inc. v. EPA, 175 F.3d 1027, 1033 (C.A.D.C. 1999) (per curiam). I wholeheartedly endorse the Court's result and endorse its explanation of its reasons, albeit with the following caveat.

The Court has two choices. We could choose to articulate our ultimate disposition of this issue by frankly acknowledging that the power delegated to the EPA is "legislative" but nevertheless conclude that the delegation is constitutional because adequately limited by the terms of the authorizing statute. Alternatively, we could pretend, as the Court does, that the authority delegated to the EPA is somehow not "legislative power." Despite the fact that there is language in our opinions that supports the Court's articulation of our holding . . . , I am persuaded that it would be both wiser and more faithful to what we have actually done in delegation cases to admit that agency rulemaking authority is "legislative power . . . " (footnotes omitted).

The proper characterization of governmental power should generally depend on the nature of the power, not on the identity of the person exercising it. See Black's Law Dictionary 899 (6th ed. 1990) (defining "legislation" as, inter alia, "[f]ormulation of rule[s] for the future"); 1 K. Davis & R. Pierce, Administrative Law Treatise §2.3, p. 37 (3d ed. 1994) ("If legislative power means the power to make rules of conduct that bind everyone based on resolution of major policy issues, scores of agencies exercise legislative power routinely by promulgating what are candidly called 'legislative rules.'"). If the NAAQS that the EPA promulgated had been prescribed by Congress, everyone would agree that those rules would be the product of an exercise of "legislative power." The same characterization is appropriate when an agency exercises rulemaking authority pursuant to a permissible delegation from Congress.

My view is not only more faithful to normal English usage, but is also fully consistent with the text of the Constitution. In Article I, the Framers vested "All legislative Powers" in the Congress, Art. I, §1, just as in Article II they vested the "executive Power" in the President, Art. II, §1. Those provisions do not purport to limit the authority of either recipient of power to delegate authority to others. See Bowsher v. Synar, 478 U.S. 714, 752 (1986) (Stevens, J., concurring in judgment) ("Despite the statement in Article I of the Constitution that 'All legislative powers herein granted shall be vested in a Congress of the United States,' it is far from novel to acknowledge that independent agencies do indeed exercise legislative powers"); INS v. Chadha, 462 U.S. 919, 985-986 (1983) (White, J., dissenting) ("[L]egislative power can be exercised by independent agencies and Executive departments . . . "); 1 Davis & Pierce, Administrative Law Treatise §2.6, p. 66 ("The Court was probably mistaken from the outset in interpreting Article I's grant of power to Congress as an implicit limit on Congress' authority to delegate legislative power."). Surely the authority granted to members of the Cabinet and federal law enforcement agents is properly characterized as "Executive" even though not exercised by the President. Cf. Morrison v. Olson, 487 U.S. 654, 705-706 (1988) (Scalia, J., dissenting) (arguing that the independent counsel exercised "executive power" unconstrained by the President).

It seems clear that an executive agency's exercise of rulemaking authority pursuant to a valid delegation from Congress is "legislative." As long as the delegation provides a sufficiently intelligible principle, there is nothing inherently unconstitutional about it. Accordingly, while I join Parts I, II, and IV of the Court's opinion, and agree with almost everything said in Part III, I would hold that when Congress enacted §109, it effected a constitutional delegation of legislative power to the EPA.

NOTES

1. On remand, the United States Court of Appeals for the D.C. Circuit upheld the EPA's 0.08 standard as not arbitrary or capricious, stating that "[a]lthough we think Petitioners' individual criticisms have some force, we are satisfied that in selecting a level of 0.08 rather than 0.07 (or, for that matter, 0.09), EPA 'engaged in reasoned decision-making.'" See ATA v. EPA, 283 F.3d 355, 379 (D.C. Cir. 2002).

2. For an involved discussion of *American Trucking* and its various effects, see Lisa Schultz Bressman, Disciplining Delegation After *Whitman v. American Trucking Ass'ns*, 87 Cornell L. Rev. 452 (2002).

3. In 2015, the United States Supreme Court faced and dodged another substantial delegation challenge. In Dep't of Transportation v. Ass'n of American Railroads, 575 U.S. 43 (2015), the Court reviewed an appeal from a D.C. Circuit opinion holding that Congress's grant of regulatory authority to allow Amtrak jointly with the Surface Transportation Board to determine standards for Amtrak's own performance was unconstitutional as a delegation of legislative authority to a private entity. According to the D.C. Circuit, Congress's "statutory command that Amtrak 'is not a department, agency, or instrumentality of the United States Government'" was controlling in determining Amtrak's status. Id. at 50. The U.S. Supreme Court reversed the D.C. Circuit, finding that Amtrak was not a private entity, but a governmental one. According to the Court, congressional pronouncements about Amtrak's status are not controlling for purposes of separation of powers analysis under the Constitution.

GUNDY v. UNITED STATES

588 U.S. ___, 139 S. Ct. 2116 (2019)

JUSTICE KAGAN delivered the opinion of the Court.

The nondelegation doctrine bars Congress from transferring its legislative power to another branch of Government. This case requires us to decide whether . . . the Sex Offender Registration and Notification Act (SORNA), violates that doctrine. We hold it does not. Under §20913(d), the Attorney General must apply SORNA's registration requirements as soon as feasible to offenders convicted before the statute's enactment. That delegation easily passes constitutional muster.

I

Congress has sought, for the past quarter century, to combat sex crimes and crimes against children through sex-offender registration schemes. In 1994, Congress first conditioned certain federal funds on States' adoption of registration laws meeting prescribed minimum standards. Two years later, Congress strengthened those standards, most notably by insisting that States inform local communities of registrants' addresses. By that time, every State and the District of Columbia had enacted a sex-offender registration law. But the state statutes varied along many dimensions, and Congress came to realize that their "loopholes and deficiencies" had allowed over 100,000 sex offenders (about 20% of the total) to escape registration.

SORNA makes "more uniform and effective" the prior "patchwork" of sex-offender registration systems. The Act's express "purpose" is "to protect the public from sex offenders and offenders against children" by "establish[ing] a comprehensive national system for [their] registration." §20901. To that end, SORNA covers more sex offenders, and imposes more onerous registration requirements, than most States had before. The Act also backs up those requirements with new criminal penalties. Any person required to register under SORNA who knowingly fails to do so (and who travels in interstate commerce) may be imprisoned for up to ten years.

The basic registration scheme works as follows. A "sex offender" is defined as "an individual who was convicted of" specified criminal offenses: all offenses "involving a sexual act or sexual contact" and additional offenses "against a minor." 34 U.S.C. §§20911(1), (5)(A), (7). Such an individual must register — provide his name, address, and certain other information — in every State where he resides, works, or studies. See §§20913(a), 20914. And he must keep the registration current, and periodically report in person to a law enforcement office, for a period of between fifteen years and life (depending on the severity of his crime and his history of recidivism). See §§20915, 20918.

Section 20913 — the disputed provision here — elaborates the "[i]nitial registration" requirements for sex offenders. §§20913(b), (d). Subsection (b) sets out the general rule: An offender must register "before completing a sentence of imprisonment with respect to the offense giving rise to the registration requirement" (or, if the offender is not sentenced to prison, "not later than [three] business days after being sentenced"). Two provisions down, subsection (d) addresses (in its title's words) the "[i]nitial registration of sex offenders unable to comply with subsection (b)." The provision states:

> "The Attorney General shall have the authority to specify the applicability of the requirements of this subchapter to sex offenders convicted before the enactment of this chapter . . . and to prescribe rules for the registration of any such sex offenders and for other categories of sex offenders who are unable to comply with subsection (b)."

Subsection (d), in other words, focuses on individuals convicted of a sex offense before SORNA's enactment — a group we will call pre-Act offenders. Many of these individuals were unregistered at the time of SORNA's enactment, either because pre-existing law did not cover them or because they had successfully evaded that law (so were "lost" to the system). And of those potential new registrants, many or most could not comply with subsection (b)'s registration rule because they had already completed their prison sentences. For the entire group of pre-Act offenders, once again, the Attorney General "shall have the authority" to "specify the applicability" of SORNA's registration requirements and "to prescribe rules for [their] registration."

Under that delegated authority, the Attorney General issued an interim rule in February 2007, specifying that SORNA's registration requirements apply in full to "sex offenders convicted of the offense for which registration is required prior to the enactment of that Act." 72 Fed. Reg. 8897. The final rule, issued in December 2010, reiterated that SORNA applies to all pre-Act offenders. 75 Fed. Reg. 81850. That rule has remained the same to this day.

Petitioner Herman Gundy is a pre-Act offender. The year before SORNA's enactment, he pleaded guilty under Maryland law for sexually assaulting a minor. After his release from prison in 2012, Gundy came to live in New York. But he never registered there as a sex offender. A few years later, he was convicted for failing to register. He argued below (among other things) that Congress unconstitutionally delegated legislative power when it authorized the Attorney General to "specify the applicability" of SORNA's registration requirements to pre-Act offenders. §20913(d). The District Court and Court of Appeals for the Second Circuit rejected that claim, as had every other court (including eleven Courts of Appeals) to consider the issue. We nonetheless granted certiorari. Today, we join the consensus and affirm.

II.

Article I of the Constitution provides that "[a]ll legislative Powers herein granted shall be vested in a Congress of the United States." §1. Accompanying that assignment of power to Congress is a bar on its further delegation. Congress, this Court explained early on, may not transfer to another branch "powers which are strictly and exclusively legislative." *Wayman v. Southard*, 23 U.S. (10 Wheat.) 1, 42-43. But the Constitution does not "deny[ ] to the Congress the necessary resources of flexibility and practicality [that enable it] to perform its function[s]." *Yakus v. United States*, 321 U.S. 414, 425 (1944). Congress may "obtain[ ] the assistance of its coordinate Branches" — and in particular, may confer substantial discretion on executive agencies to implement and enforce the laws. *Mistretta v. United States*, 488 U.S. 361, 372 (1989). "[I]n our increasingly complex society, replete with ever changing and more technical problems," this Court has understood that "Congress simply cannot do its job absent an ability to delegate power under broad general directives." *Ibid.* So we have held, time and again, that a statutory delegation is constitutional as long as Congress "lay[s] down by legislative act an intelligible principle to which the person or body authorized to [exercise the delegated authority] is directed to conform." *Ibid.*

Given that standard, a nondelegation inquiry always begins (and often almost ends) with statutory interpretation. The constitutional question is whether Congress has supplied an intelligible principle to guide the delegee's use of discretion. So the answer requires construing the challenged statute to figure out what task it delegates and what instructions it provides. See, *e.g.*, *Whitman v. American Trucking Assns.*, Inc., 531 U.S. 457, 473 (2001) (construing the text of a delegation to place constitutionally adequate "limits on the EPA's discretion.") Only after a court has determined a challenged statute's meaning can it decide whether the law sufficiently guides executive discretion to accord with Article I. And indeed, once a court interprets the statute, it may find that the constitutional question all but answers itself.

That is the case here, because §20913(d) does not give the Attorney General anything like the "unguided" and "unchecked" authority that Gundy says. The provision, in Gundy's view, "grants the Attorney General plenary power to determine SORNA's applicability to pre-Act offenders — to require them to register, or not, as she sees fit, and to change her policy for any reason and at any time." *Id.*, at 42. If that were so, we would face a nondelegation question. But it is not. This Court has already interpreted §20913(d) to say something different — to require the Attorney General to apply SORNA to all pre-Act offenders as soon as feasible. See *Reynolds*, 565 U.S. at 442-443. And revisiting that issue yet more fully today, we reach the same conclusion. The text, considered alongside its context, purpose, and history, makes clear that the Attorney General's discretion extends only to considering and addressing feasibility issues. Given that statutory meaning, Gundy's constitutional claim must fail. Section 20913(d)'s delegation falls well within permissible bounds.

A

This is not the first time this Court has had to interpret §20913(d). In *Reynolds*, the Court considered whether SORNA's registration requirements applied of their own force to pre-Act offenders or instead applied only once the Attorney General said they did. We read the statute as adopting the latter approach. But even as we did so, we made clear how far SORNA limited the Attorney General's authority. And in that way, we effectively resolved the case now before us.

B

Recall again the delegation provision at issue. Congress gave the Attorney General authority to "specify the applicability" of SORNA's requirements to pre-Act offenders. §20913(d). And in the second half of the same sentence, Congress gave him authority to "prescribe rules for the registration of any such sex offenders . . . who are unable to comply with" subsection (b)'s initial registration requirement. *Ibid.* What does the delegation in §20913(d) allow the Attorney General to do?

The different answers on offer here reflect competing views of statutory interpretation. As noted above, Gundy urges us to read §20913(d) to empower the Attorney General to do whatever he wants as to pre-Act offenders: He may make them all register immediately or he may exempt them from registration forever (or he may do anything in between). Gundy bases that argument on the first half of §20913(d), isolated from everything else — from the second half of the same section, from surrounding provisions in SORNA, and from any conception of the statute's history and purpose. *Reynolds* took a different approach (as does the Government here), understanding statutory interpretation as a "holistic endeavor" which determines meaning by looking not to isolated words, but to text in context, along with purpose and history.

This Court has long refused to construe words "in a vacuum," as Gundy attempts. *Davis v. Michigan Dept. of Treasury*, 489 U.S. 803, 809 (1989). "It is a fundamental canon of statutory construction that the words of a statute must be read in their context and with a view to their place in the overall statutory scheme." *National Assn. of Home Builders v. Defenders of Wildlife*, 551 U.S. 644, 666 (2007) (internal quotation marks omitted); see *Utility Air Regulatory Group v. EPA*, 573 U.S. 302, 321, 134 S.Ct. 2427, 189 L.Ed.2d 372 (2014) ("[R]easonable statutory interpretation must account for both the specific context in which . . . language is used and the broader context of the statute as a whole."). And beyond context and structure, the Court often looks to "history [and] purpose" to divine the meaning of language.

So begin at the beginning, with the "[d]eclaration of purpose" that is SORNA's first sentence. §20901. There, Congress announced that "to protect the public," it was "establish[ing] a comprehensive national system for the registration" of "sex offenders and offenders against children." §20901. The term "comprehensive" has a clear meaning — something that is all-encompassing or sweeping. See, *e.g.*, Webster's Third New International Dictionary 467 (2002) ("covering a matter under consideration completely or nearly completely"); New Oxford American Dictionary 350 (2d ed. 2005) ("complete; including all or nearly all elements or aspects of something"). That description could not fit the system SORNA created if the Attorney General could decline, for any reason or no reason at all, to apply SORNA to all pre-Act offenders. After all, for many years after SORNA's enactment, the great majority of sex offenders in the country would be pre-Act offenders. If Gundy were right, all of those offenders could be exempt from SORNA's registration requirements. So the mismatch between SORNA's statement of purpose and Gundy's view of §20913(d) is as stark as stark comes. Responding to that patent disparity, Gundy urges us to ignore SORNA's statement of purpose because it is "located in the Act's preface" rather than "tied" specifically to §20913(d). But the placement of such a statement within a statute makes no difference. See A. Scalia & B. Garner, Reading Law: The Interpretation of Legal Texts 220 (2012). Wherever it resides, it is "an appropriate guide" to the "meaning of the [statute's] operative provisions." *Id.*, at 218. And here it makes clear that SORNA was supposed to apply to all pre-Act offenders — which precludes Gundy's construction of §20913(d).

The Act's definition of "sex offender" makes the same point. Under that definition, a "sex offender" is "an individual who was convicted of a sex offense." §20911(1). Note the tense: "was," not "is." This Court has often "looked to Congress' choice of verb tense to ascertain a statute's temporal reach," including when interpreting other SORNA provisions. *Carr v. United States*, 560 U.S. 438, 447–448 (2010) (holding that because SORNA "sets forth [its] travel requirement in the present tense," the statute's criminal penalties do not apply to a person whose interstate travel predated enactment). . . . Here, Congress's use of the past tense to define the term "sex offender" shows that SORNA was not merely forward-looking. The word "is" would have taken care of all future offenders. The word "was" served to bring in the hundreds of thousands of persons previously found guilty of a sex offense, and thought to pose a current threat to the public. The tense of the "sex offender" definition thus confirms that the delegation allows only temporary exclusions, as necessary to address feasibility issues. Contra Gundy, it does not sweep so wide as to make a laughingstock of the statute's core definition.

The Act's legislative history backs up everything said above by showing that the need to register pre-Act offenders was front and center in Congress's thinking. Recall that Congress designed SORNA to address "loopholes and deficiencies" in existing registration laws. And no problem attracted greater attention than the large number of sex offenders who had slipped the system. According to the House Report, "[t]he most significant enforcement issue in the sex offender program is that over 100,000 sex offenders" are " 'missing,' meaning that they have not complied with" then-current requirements. H. R. Rep. No. 109-218, at 26. There is a "strong public interest," the Report continued, in "having [those offenders] register with current information to mitigate the risks of additional crimes against children." *Id.*, at 24. Senators struck a similar chord in the debates preceding SORNA's passage, repeatedly stressing that the new provisions would capture the missing offenders. See, *e.g.*, 152 Cong. Rec. 15338 (2006) (statement of Sen. Kyl) ("The penalties in this bill should be adequate to ensure that [the 100,000 missing offenders] register"); *id.*, at 13050 (statement of Sen. Frist) ("Every day that we don't have this national sex offender registry, these missing sex predators are out there somewhere"). Imagine how surprising those Members would have found Gundy's view that they had authorized the Attorney General to exempt the missing "predators" from registering at all.

With that context and background established, we may return to §20913(d). As we have noted, Gundy makes his stand there (and there only), insisting that the lonesome phrase "specify the applicability" ends this case. But in so doing, Gundy ignores even the rest of the section that phrase is in. Both the title and the remaining text of that section pinpoint one of the "practical problems" discussed above: At the moment of SORNA's enactment, many pre-Act offenders were "unable to comply" with the Act's initial registration requirements. §20913(d). That was because, once again, the requirements assumed that offenders would be in prison, whereas many pre-Act offenders were on the streets. In identifying that issue, §20913(d) itself reveals the nature of the delegation to the Attorney General. It was to give him the time needed (if any) to address the various implementation issues involved in getting pre-Act offenders into the registration system. "Specify the applicability" thus does not mean "specify *whether* to apply SORNA" to pre-Act offenders at all, even though everything else in the Act commands their coverage. The phrase instead means "specify *how* to apply SORNA" to pre-Act offenders if transitional difficulties require some delay. In that way, the whole of §20913(d) joins the rest of SORNA in giving the Attorney General only time-limited latitude to excuse pre-Act offenders from the statute's requirements. Under the law, he had to order their registration as soon as feasible.

And no Attorney General has used (or, apparently, thought to use) §20913(d) in any more expansive way. To the contrary. Within a year of SORNA's enactment (217 days, to be precise), the Attorney General determined that SORNA would apply immediately to pre-Act offenders. See Interim Rule, 72 Fed. Reg. 8897. That rule has remained in force ever since (save for a technical change to one of the rule's illustrative examples). See Final Rule, 75 Fed. Reg. 81850. And at oral argument here, the Solicitor General's office — rarely in a hurry to agree to limits on the Government's authority — acknowledged that §20913(d) does not allow the Attorney General to excuse a pre-Act offender from registering, except for reasons of "feasibility." We thus end up, on close inspection of the statutory scheme, exactly where *Reynolds* left us. The Attorney General's authority goes to transition-period implementation issues, and no further.

C

Now that we have determined what §20913(d) means, we can consider whether it violates the Constitution. The question becomes: Did Congress make an impermissible delegation when it instructed the Attorney General to apply SORNA's registration requirements to pre-Act offenders as soon as feasible? Under this Court's long-established law, that question is easy. Its answer is no.

As noted earlier, this Court has held that a delegation is constitutional so long as Congress has set out an "intelligible principle" to guide the delegee's exercise of authority. *J. W. Hampton, Jr., & Co.*, 276 U.S. at 409. Or in a related formulation, the Court has stated that a delegation is permissible if Congress has made clear to the delegee "the general policy" he must pursue and the "boundaries of [his] authority." *American Power & Light*, 329 U.S. at 105. Those standards, the Court has made clear, are not demanding. "[W]e have 'almost never felt qualified to second-guess Congress regarding the permissible degree of policy judgment that can be left to those executing or applying the law.'" *Whitman*, 531 U.S. at 474-475, 121 S.Ct. 903 (quoting *Mistretta*, 488 U.S. at 416, 109 S.Ct. 647 (Scalia, J., dissenting)). Only twice in this country's history (and that in a single year) have we found a delegation excessive — in each case because "Congress had failed to articulate *any* policy or standard" to confine discretion. *Mistretta*, 488 U.S. at 373, n. 7 (emphasis added); see *A. L. A. Schechter Poultry Corp. v. United States*, 295 U.S. 495 (1935); *Panama Refining Co. v. Ryan*, 293 U.S. 388 (1935). By contrast, we have over and over upheld even very broad delegations. Here is a sample: We have approved delegations to various agencies to regulate in the "public interest." See, *e.g.*, *National Broadcasting Co.*, 319 U.S. at 216; *New York Central Securities Corp. v. United States*, 287 U.S. 12, 24 (1932). We have sustained authorizations for agencies to set "fair and equitable" prices and "just and reasonable" rates. *Yakus*, 321 U.S. at 422, 427; *FPC v. Hope Natural Gas Co.*, 320 U.S. 591 (1944). We more recently affirmed a delegation to an agency to issue whatever air quality standards are "requisite to protect the public health." *Whitman*, 531 U.S. at 472, 121 S.Ct. 903 (quoting 42 U.S.C. §7409(b)(1)). And so forth.

In that context, the delegation in SORNA easily passes muster (as all eleven circuit courts to have considered the question found). The statute conveyed Congress's policy that the Attorney General require pre-Act offenders to register as soon as feasible. Under the law, the feasibility issues he could address were administrative — and, more specifically, transitional — in nature. Those issues arose from the need to "newly register[ ] or reregister[ ] 'a large number' of pre-Act offenders" not then in the system. And they arose, more technically, from the gap between an initial registration requirement hinged on imprisonment and a set of pre-Act offenders long since released. See 565 U.S. at 441. Even for those limited matters, the Act informed the Attorney General that he did not have forever to work things out. By stating its demand for a "comprehensive" registration system and by defining the "sex offenders" required to register to include pre-Act offenders, Congress conveyed that the Attorney General had only temporary authority. Or again that he could prevent "*instantaneous* registration" and impose some "implementation delay." That statutory authority, as compared to the delegations we have upheld in the past, is distinctly small-bore. It falls well within constitutional bounds.

Indeed, if SORNA's delegation is unconstitutional, then most of Government is unconstitutional — dependent as Congress is on the need to give discretion to executive officials to implement its programs. Consider again this Court's longtime recognition: "Congress simply cannot do its job absent an ability to delegate power under broad general directives." *Mistretta*, 488 U.S. at 372. Or as the dissent in that case agreed: "[S]ome judgments . . . must be left to the officers executing the law." 488 U.S. at 415 (opinion of Scalia, J.); see *Whitman*, 531 U.S. at 475, 121 S.Ct. 903 ("[A] certain degree of discretion[ ] inheres in most executive" action). Among the judgments often left to executive officials are ones involving feasibility. In fact, standards of that kind are ubiquitous in the U.S. Code. See, *e.g.*, 12 U.S.C. §1701z-2(a) (providing that the Secretary of Housing and Urban Development "shall require, to the greatest extent feasible, the employment of new and improved technologies, methods, and materials in housing construction[ ] under [HUD] programs"); 47 U.S.C. §903(d)(1) (providing that "the Secretary of Commerce shall promote efficient and cost-effective use of the spectrum to the maximum extent feasible" in "assigning frequencies for mobile radio services"). In those delegations, Congress gives its delegee the flexibility to deal with real-world constraints in carrying out his charge. So too in SORNA.

It is wisdom and humility alike that this Court has always upheld such "necessities of government." *Mistretta*, 488 U.S. at 416, 109 S.Ct. 647 (Scalia, J., dissenting); see *ibid.* ("Since Congress is no less endowed with common sense than we are, and better equipped to inform itself of the 'necessities' of government; and since the factors bearing upon those necessities are both multifarious and (in the nonpartisan sense) highly political . . . it is small wonder that we have almost never felt qualified to second-guess Congress regarding the permissible degree of policy judgment that can be left to those executing or applying the law"). We therefore affirm the judgment of the Court of Appeals.

It is so ordered.

JUSTICE ALITO, concurring in the judgment.

The Constitution confers on Congress certain "legislative [p]owers," Art. I, §1, and does not permit Congress to delegate them to another branch of the Government. See *Whitman v. American Trucking Assns., Inc.*, 531 U.S. 457, 472 (2001). Nevertheless, since 1935, the Court has uniformly rejected nondelegation arguments and has upheld provisions that authorized agencies to adopt important rules pursuant to extraordinarily capacious standards. See *ibid.*

If a majority of this Court were willing to reconsider the approach we have taken for the past 84 years, I would support that effort. But because a majority is not willing to do that, it would be freakish to single out the provision at issue here for special treatment.

Because I cannot say that the statute lacks a discernable standard that is adequate under the approach this Court has taken for many years, I vote to affirm.

JUSTICE GORSUCH, with whom THE CHIEF JUSTICE and JUSTICE THOMAS join, dissenting.

The Constitution promises that only the people's elected representatives may adopt new federal laws restricting liberty. Yet the statute before us scrambles that design. It purports to endow the nation's chief prosecutor with the power to write his own criminal code governing the lives of a half-million citizens. Yes, those affected are some of the least popular among us. But if a single executive branch official can write laws restricting the liberty of this group of persons, what does that mean for the next?

Today, a plurality of an eight-member Court endorses this extraconstitutional arrangement but resolves nothing. Working from an understanding of the Constitution at war with its text and history, the plurality reimagines the terms of the statute before us and insists there is nothing wrong with Congress handing off so much power to the Attorney General. But Justice Alito supplies the fifth vote for today's judgment and he does not join either the plurality's constitutional or statutory analysis, indicating instead that he remains willing, in a future case with a full Court, to revisit these matters. Respectfully, I would not wait.

I

For individuals convicted of sex offenses *after* Congress adopted the Sex Offender Registration and Notification Act (SORNA) in 2006, the statute offers detailed instructions. It requires them "to provide state governments with (and to update) information, such as names and current addresses, for inclusion on state and federal sex offender registries." The law divides offenders into three tiers based on the seriousness of their crimes: Some must register for 15 years, others for 25 years, and still others for life. The statute proceeds to set registration deadlines: Offenders sentenced to prison must register before they're released, while others must register within three business days after sentencing. The statute explains when and how offenders must update their registrations. And the statute specifies particular penalties for failing to comply with its commands. On and on the statute goes for more than 20 pages of the U. S. Code.

But what about those convicted of sex offenses *before* the Act's adoption? At the time of SORNA's enactment, the nation's population of sex offenders exceeded 500,000, and Congress concluded that something had to be done about these "pre-Act" offenders too. But it seems Congress couldn't agree what that should be. The treatment of pre-Act offenders proved a "controversial issue with major policy significance and practical ramifications for states." Among other things, applying SORNA immediately to this group threatened to impose unpopular and costly burdens on States and localities by forcing them to adopt or overhaul their own sex offender registration schemes. So Congress simply passed the problem to the Attorney General. For all half-million pre-Act offenders, the law says only this, in 34 U. S. C. §20913(d):

> "The Attorney General shall have the authority to specify the applicability of the requirements of this subchapter to sex offenders convicted before the enactment of this chapter . . . and to prescribe rules for the registration of any such sex offender."

Yes, that's it. The breadth of the authority Congress granted to the Attorney General in these few words can only be described as vast. As the Department of Justice itself has acknowledged, SORNA "does not require the Attorney General" to impose registration requirements on pre-Act offenders "within a certain time frame or by a date certain; it does not require him to act at all." If the Attorney General does choose to act, he can require all pre-Act offenders to register, or he can "require some but not all to register." For those he requires to register, the Attorney General may impose "some but not all of [SORNA's] registration requirements," as he pleases. And he is free to change his mind on any of these matters "at any given time or over the course of different [political] administrations." Congress thus gave the Attorney General free rein to write the rules for virtually the entire existing sex offender population in this country — a situation that promised to persist for years or decades until pre-Act offenders passed away or fulfilled the terms of their registration obligations and post-Act offenders came to predominate.

Unsurprisingly, different Attorneys General have exercised their discretion in different ways. For six months after SORNA's enactment, Attorney General Gonzales left past offenders alone. Then the pendulum swung the other direction when the Department of Justice issued an interim rule requiring pre-Act offenders to follow all the same rules as post-Act offenders. A year later, Attorney General Mukasey issued more new guidelines, this time directing the States to register some but not all past offenders. Three years after that, Attorney General Holder required the States to register only those pre-Act offenders convicted of a new felony after SORNA's enactment. Various Attorneys General have also taken different positions on whether pre-Act offenders might be entitled to credit for time spent in the community before SORNA was enacted.

These unbounded policy choices have profound consequences for the people they affect. Take our case. Before SORNA's enactment, Herman Gundy pleaded guilty in 2005 to a sexual offense. After his release from prison five years later, he was arrested again, this time for failing to register as a sex offender according to the rules the Attorney General had then prescribed for pre-Act offenders. As a result, Mr. Gundy faced an additional 10-year prison term — 10 years more than if the Attorney General had, in his discretion, chosen to write the rules differently.

II

A

Our founding document begins by declaring that "We the People . . . ordain and establish this Constitution." At the time, that was a radical claim, an assertion that sovereignty belongs not to a person or institution or class but to the whole of the people. From that premise, the Constitution proceeded to vest the authority to exercise different aspects of the people's sovereign power in distinct entities. In Article I, the Constitution entrusted all of the federal government's legislative power to Congress. In Article II, it assigned the executive power to the President. And in Article III, it gave independent judges the task of applying the laws to cases and controversies.

To the framers, each of these vested powers had a distinct content. When it came to the legislative power, the framers understood it to mean the power to adopt generally applicable rules of conduct governing future actions by private persons — the power to "prescrib[e] the rules by which the duties and rights of every citizen are to be regulated," or the power to "prescribe general rules for the government of society." The framers understood, too, that it would frustrate "the system of government ordained by the Constitution" if Congress could merely announce vague aspirations and then assign others the responsibility of adopting legislation to realize its goals. Through the Constitution, after all, the people had vested the power to prescribe rules limiting their liberties in Congress alone. No one, not even Congress, had the right to alter that arrangement. As Chief Justice Marshall explained, Congress may not "delegate . . . powers which are strictly and exclusively legislative." Or as John Locke, one of the thinkers who most influenced the framers' understanding of the separation of powers, described it:

> "The legislative cannot transfer the power of making laws to any other hands; for it being but a delegated power from the people, they who have it cannot pass it over to others. The people alone can appoint the form of the commonwealth, which is by constituting the legislative, and appointing in whose hands that shall be. And when the people have said we will submit to rules, and be governed by laws made by such men, and in such forms, nobody else can say other men shall make laws for them; nor can the people be bound by any laws but such as are enacted by those whom they have chosen and authorised to make laws for them."

Why did the framers insist on this particular arrangement? They believed the new federal government's most dangerous power was the power to enact laws restricting the people's liberty. An "excess of law-making" was, in their words, one of "the diseases to which our governments are most liable." To address that tendency, the framers went to great lengths to make lawmaking difficult. In Article I, by far the longest part of the Constitution, the framers insisted that any proposed law must win the approval of two Houses of Congress — elected at different times, by different constituencies, and for different terms in office — and either secure the President's approval or obtain enough support to override his veto. Some occasionally complain about Article I's detailed and arduous processes for new legislation, but to the framers these were bulwarks of liberty.

Nor was the point only to limit the government's capacity to restrict the people's freedoms. Article I's detailed processes for new laws were also designed to promote deliberation. "The oftener the measure is brought under examination," Hamilton explained, "the greater the diversity in the situations of those who are to examine it," and "the less must be the danger of those errors which flow from want of due deliberation, or of those missteps which proceed from the contagion of some common passion or interest."

. . .

If Congress could pass off its legislative power to the executive branch, the "[v]esting [c]lauses, and indeed the entire structure of the Constitution," would "make no sense." Without the involvement of representatives from across the country or the demands of bicameralism and presentment, legislation would risk becoming nothing more than the will of the current President. And if laws could be simply declared by a single person, they would not be few in number, the product of widespread social consensus, likely to protect minority interests, or apt to provide stability and fair notice. Accountability would suffer too. Legislators might seek to take credit for addressing a pressing social problem by sending it to the executive for resolution, while at the same time blaming the executive for the problems that attend whatever measures he chooses to pursue. In turn, the executive might point to Congress as the source of the problem. These opportunities for finger-pointing might prove temptingly advantageous for the politicians involved, but they would also threaten to "'disguise . . . responsibility for . . . the decisions.'"

. . .

B

Accepting, then, that we have an obligation to decide whether Congress has unconstitutionally divested itself of its legislative responsibilities, the question follows: What's the test? Madison acknowledged that "no skill in the science of government has yet been able to discriminate and define, with sufficient certainty, its three great provinces — the legislative, executive, and judiciary." Chief Justice Marshall agreed that policing the separation of powers "is a subject of delicate and difficult inquiry." Still, the framers took this responsibility seriously and offered us important guiding principles. First, we know that as long as Congress makes the policy decisions when regulating private conduct, it may authorize another branch to "fill up the details." In *Wayman v. Southard*, this Court upheld a statute that instructed the federal courts to borrow state-court procedural rules but allowed them to make certain "alterations and additions." Writing for the Court, Chief Justice Marshall distinguished between those "important subjects, which must be entirely regulated by the legislature itself," and "those of less interest, in which a general provision may be made, and power given to those who are to act . . . to fill up the details." The Court upheld the statute before it because Congress had announced the controlling general policy when it ordered federal courts to follow state procedures, and the residual authority to make "alterations and additions" did no more than permit courts to fill up the details. Second, once Congress prescribes the rule governing private conduct, it may make the application of that rule depend on executive fact-finding. Here, too, the power extended to the executive may prove highly consequential.

During the Napoleonic Wars, for example, Britain and France each tried to block the United States from trading with the other. Congress responded with a statute instructing that, if the President found that either Great Britain or France stopped interfering with American trade, a trade embargo would be imposed against the other country. Half a century later, Congress likewise made the construction of the Brooklyn Bridge depend on a finding by the Secretary of War that the bridge wouldn't interfere with navigation of the East River. The Court held that Congress "did not abdicate any of its authority" but "simply declared that, upon a certain fact being established, the bridge should be deemed a lawful structure, and employed the secretary of war as an agent to ascertain that fact." Third, Congress may assign the executive and judicial branches certain non-legislative responsibilities. While the Constitution vests all federal legislative power in Congress alone, Congress's legislative authority sometimes overlaps with authority the Constitution separately vests in another branch. So, for example, when a congressional statute confers wide discretion to the executive, no separation-of-powers problem may arise if "the discretion is to be exercised over matters already within the scope of executive power."

C

Before the 1930s, federal statutes granting authority to the executive were comparatively modest and usually easily upheld. But then the federal government began to grow explosively. And with the proliferation of new executive programs came new questions about the scope of congressional delegations. Twice the Court responded by striking down statutes for violating the separation of powers. [Since *Schecter Poultry* and *Panama Refining*, the Court has not struck down any law for unconstitutional delegation of legislative power. Why?]

[M]aybe the most likely explanation . . . lies in the story of the evolving "intelligible principle" doctrine. This Court first used that phrase in 1928 in *J. W. Hampton, Jr., & Co. v. United States*, where it remarked that a statute "lay[ing] down by legislative act an intelligible principle to which the [executive official] is directed to conform" satisfies the separation of powers. No one at the time thought the phrase meant to effect some revolution in this Court's understanding of the Constitution. While the exact line between policy and details, lawmaking and fact-finding, and legislative and non-legislative functions had sometimes invited reasonable debate, everyone agreed these were the relevant inquiries. And when Chief Justice Taft wrote of an "intelligible principle," it seems plain enough that he sought only to explain the operation of these traditional tests; he gave no hint of a wish to overrule or revise them. Tellingly, too, he wrote the phrase seven years before *Schechter Poultry* and *Panama Refining*, and it did nothing to alter the analysis in those cases, let alone prevent those challenges from succeeding by lopsided votes.

[I]t's undeniable that the "intelligible principle" remark eventually began to take on a life of its own. We sometimes chide people for treating judicial opinions as if they were statutes, divorcing a passing comment from its context, ignoring all that came before and after, and treating an isolated phrase as if it were controlling. But that seems to be exactly what happened here. For two decades, no one thought to invoke the "intelligible principle" comment as a basis to uphold a statute that would have failed more traditional separation-of-powers tests. In fact, the phrase sat more or less silently entombed until the late 1940s. Only then did lawyers begin digging it up in earnes t and arguing to this Court that it had somehow displaced (*sub silentio* of course) all prior teachings in this area.

This mutated version of the "intelligible principle" remark has no basis in the original meaning of the Constitution, in history, or even in the decision from which it was plucked. Judges and scholars representing a wide and diverse range of views have condemned it as resting on "misunderst[ood] historical foundations." They have explained, too, that it has been abused to permit delegations of legislative power that on any other conceivable account should be held unconstitutional.

. . .

To determine whether a statute provides an intelligible principle, we must ask: Does the statute assign to the executive only the responsibility to make factual findings? Does it set forth the facts that the executive must consider and the criteria against which to measure them? And most importantly, did Congress, and not the Executive Branch, make the policy judgments? Only then can we fairly say that a statute contains the kind of intelligible principle the Constitution demands.

III

A

. . .

[SORNA] sounds all the alarms the founders left for us. Because Congress could not achieve the consensus necessary to resolve the hard problems associated with SORNA's application to pre-Act offenders, it passed the potato to the Attorney General. And freed from the need to assemble a broad supermajority for his views, the Attorney General did not hesitate to apply the statute retroactively to a politically unpopular minority. Nor could the Attorney General afford the issue the kind of deliberative care the framers designed a representative legislature to ensure. Perhaps that's part of the reason why the executive branch found itself rapidly adopting different positions across different administrations. And because SORNA vested lawmaking power in one person rather than many, it should be no surprise that, rather than few and stable, the edicts have proved frequent and shifting, with fair notice sacrificed in the process. Then, too, there is the question of accountability. In passing this statute, Congress was able to claim credit for "comprehensively" addressing the problem of the entire existing population of sex offenders (who can object to that?), while in fact leaving the Attorney General to sort it out.

It would be easy enough to let this case go. After all, sex offenders are one of the most disfavored groups in our society. But the rule that prevents Congress from giving the executive *carte blanche* to write laws for sex offenders is the same rule that protects everyone else. Nor is it hard to imagine how the power at issue in this case — the power of a prosecutor to require a group to register with the government on pain of weighty criminal penalties — could be abused in other settings. To allow the nation's chief law enforcement officer to write the criminal laws he is charged with enforcing — to "'unit[e]'" the "'legislative and executive powers . . . in the same person'" — would be to mark the end of any meaningful enforcement of our separation of powers and invite the tyranny of the majority that follows when lawmaking and law enforcement responsibilities are united in the same hands.

Nor would enforcing the Constitution's demands spell doom for what some call the "administrative state." The separation of powers does not prohibit any particular policy outcome, let alone dictate any conclusion about the proper size and scope of government. Instead, it is a procedural guarantee that requires Congress to assemble a social consensus before choosing our nation's course on policy questions like those implicated by SORNA. What is more, Congress is hardly bereft of options to accomplish all it might wish to achieve. It may always authorize executive branch officials to fill in even a large number of details, to find facts that trigger the generally applicable rule of conduct specified in a statute, or to exercise non-legislative powers. Congress can also commission agencies or other experts to study and recommend legislative language. Respecting the separation of powers forecloses no substantive outcomes. It only requires us to respect along the way one of the most vital of the procedural protections of individual liberty found in our Constitution.

. . .

B

. . .

In a future case with a full panel, I remain hopeful that the Court may yet recognize that, while Congress can enlist considerable assistance from the executive branch in filling up details and finding facts, it may never hand off to the nation's chief prosecutor the power to write his own criminal code. That "is delegation running riot."

NOTES

1. Many scholars think that, based on Justice Gorsuch's dissent and Justice Alito's concurrence in *Gundy*, the traditional "intelligible principle" nondelegation test will be challenged and changed in the near future. See e.g., Bamzai, Delegation and Interpretive Discretion: *Gundy*, *Kisor*, and the Formation and Future of Administrative Law, 133 Harv. L. Rev. 164 (2019) ("It is hard not to view *Gundy* . . . as [a proxy] for larger battles about the nature of stare decisis and the place of the administrative state in American society. Hard, yes, but not impossible. For at their core, *Gundy* [is] ultimately [a] case[] about the proper rules for interpreting the Constitution and statutes. . . ."); Phillips, Slaying "Leviathan" (or Not): The Practical Impact (or Lack Thereof) of a Return to a "Traditional" Nondelegation Doctrine, 107 Va. L. Rev. 919 (2021); Klein, Nondelegating Death, 81 Ohio St. L.J. 923 (2020); Postell, The Nondelegation Doctrine After *Gundy*, 13 NYU J.L. & Liberty 280 (2020); Lawson, "I'm Leavin' It (All) Up to You": *Gundy* and the (Sort-of) Resurrection of the Subdelegation Doctrine, 2019 Cato Sup. Ct. Rev. 31 (2019).

2. Justices Kavanaugh and Barrett were not involved in the *Gundy* case. What about them? Do you think that they would be willing to change the traditional nondelegation test? It may depend on how strong their feelings are about *stare decisis* principles. *See* Wharton, *Gundy v. United States*: Breathing New (and Unexpected) Life Into the Nondelegation Doctrine, 79 Md. L. Rev. 1086 (2020) (arguing *Gundy* was correctly decided based on statutory and constitutional *stare decisis*). There has been some speculation about Justice Kavanaugh's position. See generally Lawson, *Subdelegation Doctrine*, at 63. In 2019, Justice Kavanaugh commented on *Gundy* in a statement accompanying denial of certiorari in Paul v. United States, 140 S. Ct. 342 (2019), suggesting that he might be open to a changed test, at least with respect to legislation related to major national policy decisions. Justice Kavanaugh wrote:

> I agree with the denial of certiorari because this case [Paul v. U.S.] ultimately raises the same statutory interpretation issue that the Court resolved last Term in Gundy v. United States, 588 U.S. ___, 139 S. Ct. 211 (2019). I write separately because Justice Gorsuch's scholarly analysis of the Constitution's nondelegation doctrine in his *Gundy* dissent may warrant further consideration in future cases. Justice Gorsuch's opinion built on views expressed by then-Justice Rehnquist some 40 years ago in Industrial Union Dept., AFL-CIO v. American Petroleum Institute, 448 U.S. 607, 685-686 (1980) (Rehnquist, J., concurring in judgment). In that case, Justice Rehnquist opined that major national policy decisions must be made by Congress and the President in the legislative process, not delegated by Congress to the Executive Branch.
>
> In the wake of Justice Rehnquist's opinion, the Court has not adopted a nondelegation principle for major questions. But the Court has applied a closely related statutory interpretation doctrine: In order for an executive or independent agency to exercise regulatory authority over a major policy question of great economic and political importance, Congress must either: (i) expressly and specifically decide the major policy question itself and delegate to the agency the authority to regulate and enforce; or (ii) expressly and specifically delegate to the agency the authority both to decide the major policy question and to regulate and enforce. See, e.g., Utility Air Regulatory Group v. EPA, 573 U.S. 302, 134 S. Ct. 2427, 189 L. Ed. 2d 372 (2014); FDA v. Brown & Williamson Tobacco Corp., 529 U.S. 120, 120 S. Ct. 1291, 146 L. Ed. 2d 121 (2000); MCI Telecommunications Corp. v. American Telephone & Telegraph Co., 512 U.S. 218, 114 S. Ct. 2223, 129 L. Ed. 2d 182 (1994); Breyer, Judicial Review of Questions of Law and Policy, 38 Admin. L. Rev. 363, 370 (1986).
>
> The opinions of Justice Rehnquist and Justice Gorsuch would not allow that second category — congressional delegations to agencies of authority to decide

> major policy questions — even if Congress expressly and specifically delegates that authority. Under their approach, Congress could delegate to agencies the authority to decide less-major or fill-up-the-details decisions.
>
> Like Justice Rehnquist's opinion 40 years ago, Justice Gorsuch's thoughtful *Gundy* opinion raised important points that may warrant further consideration in future cases."

Id. at 342. Justice Kavanaugh's statement opens the possibility that the nondelegation doctrine may be split in the future. There might be a separate more rigid test for major national policy decisions, like the Clean Air Act, but the "intelligible principle" test for more minor legislative efforts. See Summers, Nondelegation of Major Questions, 74 Ark. L. Rev. 83 (2021). Might there even be more than two nondelegation standards? See Milner, Into the Multiverse: Replacing the Intelligible Principle Standard With a Modern Multi-Theory of Nondelegation, 28 Geo. Mason L. Rev. 395, 398 (2020) ("[W]hy should American jurisprudence restrain itself to a single nondelegation standard to test the varied types of delegation? Since Congress delegates authority along a wide spectrum of issues, why should the Court not consider creating multiple, different nondelegation standards that correspond to the scope of authority delegated? This Comment considers these questions and proposes a new method of nondelegation inquiry: the Multi-Theory."); Hessick & Hessick, Nondelegation and Criminal Law, 107 Va. L. Rev. 281 (2021).

3. If the test for nondelegation does indeed change, is Gorsuch's alternative formulation a good one? Think of its application in the *Mistretta* or in the *Whitman* case. Does it work well in those contexts? Do you reach a different result in each case? See Coglianese, Dimensions of Delegation, 167 U. Pa. L. Rev. 1849, 1882 (2019) (while the dissent "correctly recognize[s] the inability of the intelligible principle test to provide a coherent standard," the dissent does not propose a more manageable standard); Logan, *Gundy v. United States*: Gunning for the Administrative State, 17 Ohio St. J. Crim. L. 185 (2019).

4. In oral argument in *Gundy*, Justice Breyer raised the question regarding whether a new nondelegation standard would require reviewing the constitutionality of hundreds of thousands of administrative rules. Certainly the constitutionality of a rule can be raised in defense when the rule is applied. Wouldn't there exist the potential for substantial amounts of litigation over these questions? See Hall, The Gorsuch Test: *Gundy v. United States*, Limiting the Administrative State, and the Future of Nondelegation, 70 Duke L.J. 175 (2020) (new test could bring into question many statutes); but see Phillips, Slaying "Leviathan" (or Not): The Practical Impact (or Lack Thereof) of a Return to a "Traditional" Nondelegation Doctrine, 107 Va. L. Rev. 919, 957-958 (2021) ("To be sure, the tests [put forth by Justice Gorsuch] are at least moderately more restrictive than the toothless "intelligible principle" test, and statutes that have been upheld under that standard may face increased scrutiny under a reinvigorated approach. Nonetheless, the alarmist concerns articulated in the wake of the decision largely are without merit — applying the traditional tests does not unwind "most of Government" as we know it. The traditional approach to which Justice Gorsuch advocates returning is not some hyperrestrictive, formalist approach that prohibits Congress from delegating authority in any and all circumstances. Rather, it is a recognition that the principle of separation of powers places meaningful boundaries on the respective branches of government.").

5. *Individual rights and liberties.* Should administrative agencies be allowed broad leeway, even within the context of fairly restrictive "intelligible principles," to legislate in the arena of individual rights and liberties? Should these agencies, for example, be able to set up regimes of criminal punishment? Should they be able to restrict the ability of citizens to march in a parade or to travel abroad? Compare Marshall, J., concurring, in National Cable Television Ass'n v. United States, 415 U.S. 336, 352-353 (1974):

> The notion that the Constitution narrowly confines the power of Congress to delegate authority to administrative agencies, which was briefly in vogue in the 1930s, has been virtually abandoned by the Court for all practical purposes, at least in the absence of a delegation creating "the danger of overbroad, unauthorized, and arbitrary application of criminal sanctions in an area of [constitutionally] protected freedoms."

See Kent v. Dulles, 357 U.S. 116 (1958). The Passport Act of 1926 authorized the Secretary of State to "grant and issue passports . . . under such rules as the President shall designate and prescribe." Id. at 123. The secretary issued a regulation that provided that no passport should be issued to members of the Communist Party or persons who engaged in activities supporting the Communist movement or were going abroad to advance the Communist movement. Kent was refused a passport on the ground that he was a Communist and had had "a consistent and prolonged adherence to the Communist Party line." Id. at 118. His petition for declaratory relief was denied by the lower courts. The Supreme Court reversed. It interpreted the statute narrowly, as not giving the secretary the discretion to deny a passport for any reason he might choose but instead as limiting him to the grounds for refusal that had governed administrative practice prior to the 1926 statute: (1) lack of citizenship and (2) illegal conduct by the applicant. Congress had intended to incorporate these two grounds as the basis for passport denials, rather than to give the secretary unbridled discretion.

The Court was led to its restrictive interpretation by the constitutional implications inherent in a broader delegation. The opinion noted that freedom to travel was an important aspect of liberty:

> The right to travel is a part of the "liberty" of which the citizen cannot be deprived without due process of law under the Fifth Amendment. . . . If that "liberty" is to be regulated, it must be pursuant to the law-making functions of the Congress. And if that power is delegated, the standards must be adequate to pass scrutiny by the accepted tests. See Panama Refining Co. v. Ryan, 294 U.S. 388, 420-430. Where activities or enjoyment, natural and often necessary to the well-being of an American citizen, such as travel, are involved, we will construe narrowly all delegated powers that curtail or dilute them. We hesitate to find in this broad generalized power an authority to trench so heavily on the rights of the citizen.

Id. at 125, 129.

Although the implications of the original *Kent* case have been diminished somewhat, especially with respect to those that may have been gleaned from the Court's broad statements about the right to travel, see, e.g., Regan v. Wald, 468 U.S. 222 (1984); Hutchins v. District of Columbia, 188 F.3d 531 (D.C. Cir. 1999), it remains clear that agencies acting in the arena of an individual citizen's constitutional freedoms should continue to face tougher scrutiny by federal courts. This may be especially true for those agencies acting in the criminal law arena or with respect to rules with criminal implications. See, e.g., Hessick & Hessick, Nondelegation and Criminal Law, 107 Va. L. Rev. 281 (2021); Klein, Nondelegating Death, 81 Ohio St. L.J. 923 (2020).

4. State Delegation of Legislative Power

KRIELOW v. LA. DEP'T OF AGRIC. & FORESTRY

125 So. 3d 384 (La. 2013)

JOHNSON, C.J. This case is before us on direct appeal from a judgment of the district court declaring La. R.S. 3:3534(G)(2), (3) and La. R.S. 3:3544(E)(2), (3) unconstitutional. For the following reasons, we amend and affirm the ruling of the district court.

FACTS AND PROCEDURAL HISTORY

Plaintiffs are producers of rice in Louisiana. In 1972, the Louisiana Legislature enacted La. R.S. 3:3531, et seq. and La. R.S. 3:3541, et seq. This statutory scheme established the Louisiana Rice Promotion Board and the Louisiana Rice Research Board ("the Rice Boards"), with the stated purpose to promote the growth and development of the rice industry in Louisiana by promotion of rice and expanded research of rice, thereby promoting the general welfare of the people of Louisiana. The Rice Statutes obligate rice producers to pay an assessment on rice produced in Louisiana "not to exceed three cents per hundredweight."[4] However, the assessment is not imposed unless the rice producers approve it by majority referendum vote. The question of whether to impose the assessment and the amount of the assessment, subject to the "maxima" provided in the statutes, must be submitted to and approved by a majority of the rice producers who vote in the referenda. To be eligible to vote, a producer must have produced a rice crop in the year immediately preceding each referendum. If approved, the assessment is effective for five years, but may be extended indefinitely in increments of five years, by ratification and approval by a majority vote of all the rice producers who voted in the referenda. After collection, the Commissioner of Agriculture is required to pay over the funds to the Rice Boards as instructed

4. La. R.S. 3:3534(A)(1), 3544(A)(1).

in the Rice Statutes. The Rice Statutes originally provided any rice producer with the opportunity to request and receive a refund of the amount paid for the assessment. However, the statutes were amended in 1992 to provide that the refund is not available if the voting majority of rice producers vote to abolish the refund provisions.

Since the Rice Statutes went into effect, rice producers voting in the periodic referendums have approved the levy of an assessment. The refund provisions were abolished in the 1992 referendum. Plaintiffs, approximately forty rice producers, filed suit against the Louisiana Department of Agriculture and Forestry ("LDAF") and the Rice Boards, challenging the constitutionality of the Rice Statutes ... on their face....

Thereafter, plaintiffs filed a motion for summary judgment seeking to declare La. R.S. 3:3534 and La. R.S. 3:3544 facially unconstitutional on the ground those statutes permit an improper delegation of legislative authority, in violation of La. Const. art. III, §1. Plaintiffs argued the Rice Statutes permit a small group of private citizens to determine by majority vote whether the LDAF shall enforce and collect statutory assessments on rice, and whether the refund provisions will be abolished.

The district court granted plaintiffs' motion for summary judgment in part, declaring those sections of the Rice Statutes relative to abolishment of the refunds ... unconstitutional. The LDAF, State of Louisiana and the Rice Boards directly appealed to this court. The Plaintiffs answered the appeal, asserting [the Rice Statutes] are facially unconstitutional in their entirety.

DISCUSSION

... The Louisiana Constitution divides the powers of government into three separate branches: legislative, executive and judicial. Our constitution further provides that no branch may exercise power belonging to another. The legislative power of the State rests exclusively in the Legislature. Thus, it is axiomatic that the legislature is vested with the sole law-making power of the State.

Because of the constitutional separation of powers, delegation of legislative power is generally prohibited. We have recognized "that legislative power, conferred under constitutional provisions, cannot be delegated by the Legislature either to the people or to any other body of authority." However, as an exception to this rule, this court has recognized that the legislative branch has the authority to delegate to administrative boards and agencies of the State the power to ascertain and determine the facts upon which the laws are to be applied and enforced. We have noted that "delegation of certain administrative functions is necessary because of the vast amount of governmental functions that are vested in the legislative branch, which cannot possibly enact and re-enact detailed laws to cover every situation during rapidly changing times." ...

... The LDAF ... argues the Legislature may delegate to state boards, such as the Rice Boards, the power to ascertain and determine the facts upon which the laws are to be applied and enforced. In directing by statute how the Rice Boards must be composed, the Legislature ensured that the board members would have the specialized expertise necessary to carry out the vital public interests of rice research and rice promotion. The LDAF argues the Rice Statutes do not allow anyone to "make law." The vote of the rice producers only implements the law as the Legislature has dictated it. The LDAF asserts the Rice Statutes are complete in the expression of legislative will and the statutory scheme enacted to carry it out....

By contrast, the plaintiffs argue that on facial examination, the Rice Statutes clearly violate the Louisiana Constitution. The assessments established by the Rice Statutes are only imposed, extended, or refundable based on an election of private citizens, certain rice producers. Those private elections determine the very existence of the assessment, as well as its duration and character. The Legislature cannot delegate to private citizens the power to create or repeal laws....

Further, Plaintiffs argue the Legislature cannot create regulations or delegate actions that require officials or administrative bodies to exercise primary and independent discretion. The Rice Statutes go far beyond a delegation of ministerial authority because they expressly empower private citizens to decide whether to impose or nullify the assessments. Here, neither the Legislature nor the Rice Boards retained any discretion to approve, disapprove or modify the assessment decisions reached by the selected rice producers....

... First, we find the Legislature does not have the authority to delegate the question of imposition of the assessment to the rice producers. La. R.S. 3:3534(B)(1) and La. R.S. 3:3544(A)(3) allow private citizens the right to determine whether the Legislature's assessment provision will take effect. The vote is not subject to review by the Legislature or by any administrative agency, such as the Rice Boards. The sole decision on whether the assessments will be imposed is made by private persons, the rice producers....

... The Rice Statutes also violate the non-delegation doctrine by giving a private group the power to decide whether the law governing the refunds will change. La. R.S. 3:3534(G)(2) and La. R.S. 3:3544(E)(2) grant to a majority of the rice producers the power to repeal the Legislature's grant of a refund. In particular, the use of the term "abolish," indicates the power to actually repeal legislation. Further, this power is expansive in that it allows the rice producers to permanently repeal this legislation by voiding the Legislature's refund provisions such that they "thereafter have no effect."

Finally, the Rice Statutes unconstitutionally delegate legislative power to the rice producers to set the rate of the assessment. La. R.S. 3:3534(B)(1) and La. R.S. 3:3544(A)(3) provide that the assessment shall not be imposed until the "question of its imposition" and "the amount thereof" has been submitted to and voted on by a majority of the rice producers who vote at the referendum. As with the imposition of the assessment itself, the amount of the assessment is voted on by the rice producers. Because the legislature did not set the amount of the assessment in the statute, it has delegated to the rice producers the power to determine what the law will be. Presumably the Rice Boards have the power to choose the amount of the assessment placed on the ballot, subject to the three-cent maxima. Such a delegation of power to the Rice Boards does not satisfy constitutional requirements.

To determine whether a particular delegation of legislative authority is unconstitutional, we rely on the rule established by this Court in *Schwegmann Brothers Giant Super Markets v. McCrory, Commissioner of Agriculture*:

> So long as the regulation or action of the official or board authorized by statute does not in effect determine what the law shall be, or involve the exercise of primary and independent discretion, but only determines within prescribed limits some fact upon which the law by its own terms operates, such regulation is administrative and not legislative in its nature.

This rule requires courts to distinguish between "delegations of purely *legislative* authority, which necessarily violate the separation of powers, and delegations of *ministerial or administrative authority*, which do not." Guided by these principles, this Court has developed a three-part test to ascertain whether a statute unconstitutionally delegates legislative authority. A delegation of authority to an administrative agency is constitutionally valid if the statute: 1) contains a clear expression of legislative policy; 2) prescribes sufficient standards to guide the agency in the execution of that policy; and 3) is accompanied by adequate procedural safeguards to protect against abuse of discretion by the agency. This test serves two functions vital to preserving the separation of powers required by the Constitution:

> First, it insures that the fundamental policy decisions in our society will be made not by an appointed official but by the body immediately responsible to the people. Second, it prevents judicial review from becoming merely an exercise at large by providing the courts with some measure against which to judge the official action that has been challenged.

Moreover, we have explained the importance and necessity of each part of the test:

> Application of the *Schwegmann* three-prong test ensures the elected members of the Louisiana Legislature retain all legislative power by insisting that they, not their delegates in the executive branch, make the difficult policy choices for which they are accountable to the public through the democratic process. Furthermore, by insisting that the enabling statute prescribe not only the legislative policy to be enforced by the agency but also sufficient standards to guide or "canalize" the agency's execution of the legislative will, the test ensures the statute delegates only administrative or ministerial authority and guards against delegations of unbridled legislative discretion and the danger of "delegation running riot." Additionally, because even delegations of administrative or ministerial authority require agencies to exercise some discretion in executing the legislative will, the requirement of adequate procedural safeguards ensures the agency exercises that discretion in accordance with the policy and standards prescribed in the enabling statute and consistent with democratic values served by public participation and judicial review.

Application of the three-prong test set forth in *Schwegmann* and *All Pro Paint* compels us to conclude that the Rice Statutes fail to establish a constitutionally valid delegation of power to the Rice Boards to set the amount of the assessments. Examining the first prong of the test, we do find the Rice Statutes contain a sufficient expression of legislative policy. La. R.S. 3:3532 provides: "The purpose of this Chapter is to promote the growth and development of the rice industry in Louisiana by expanded research of rice, thereby promoting the general welfare of the people of this state." Similarly, La. R.S. 3:3542 provides: "The purpose of this Chapter is to promote the growth and development of the rice industry in Louisiana by promotion of rice, thereby promoting the general welfare of the people of this state." There is no question that the Legislature clearly expressed the policy behind the Rice Statutes. Thus, we find the Act sets forth a defined statement of legislative policy sufficient to satisfy the first prong of the test.

However, the Rice Statutes do not meet prongs two and three of the test. Other than setting a maximum assessment of three cents per hundredweight, the Rice Statutes contain no standards and provide no guidelines for the Rice Boards to consider in setting the amount of the assessment. Moreover, the Legislature did not retain any discretion to review, approve, disapprove or modify the assessment decision reached by the Board. This is not a case where the Legislature has merely delegated ministerial authority to the Rice Boards to determine the amount of the assessment by providing a blueprint for action or supplying factors or formulas. Thus, the Rice Statutes fail to provide sufficient safeguards or standards by which the amount of the assessment can be measured.

We have recognized that to successfully challenge a legislative act as unconstitutional on its face, the challenger must establish that no set of circumstances exists under which the Act would be valid. Here, because we find the text and structure of the Rice Statutes themselves impermissibly delegate legislative authority to private persons and to the Rice Boards, there are necessarily no circumstances under which application of the Rice Statutes can operate constitutionally.

CONCLUSION

In sum, we hold La. R.S. 3:3534 and La. R.S. 3:3544 are facially unconstitutional. The Rice Statutes delegate the power to impose the assessment, determine the amount of the assessment, and repeal the refund provisions, entirely to the rice producers. And, to the extent the power to set the amount of the assessment is delegated to the Rice Boards, the Rice Statutes do not contain sufficient standards and safeguards to satisfy the test set forth in *Schwegmann* and *All Pro Paint.* The Legislature improperly transferred its assessment power to a particular group of private voters who can impose, maintain or revoke the assessment and right to refunds through private elections. . . . Thus, we affirm and amend the district court's judgment to declare La. R.S. 3:3534 and La. R.S. 3:3544 unconstitutional in their entirety.

DECREE

AFFIRMED AS AMENDED.

NOTES

1. It's hard to know the exact reasons for opposition to the Louisiana Rice Boards and Rice Statutes based solely on a reading of the facts in the opinion itself. The following press release about the case from the U.S. Rice Producers Association may help to provide needed context:

> Supreme Court of Louisiana Finds State Rice Statutes Unconstitutional, Reports USRPA
>
> BATON ROUGE, La., Oct. 17, 2013/PRNewswire-USNewswire/ — In an astounding reaffirmation of individual producer rights, the Supreme Court of Louisiana declared unconstitutional the "Rice Statutes" authorizing the research and promotion of Louisiana rice. For many years there has been widespread rice producer dissatisfaction with the manner in which the rice research and promotion statutes have been implemented and their inability to seek a refund of the mandatory assessments levied solely on producers. After many attempts to negotiate compromise, frustrated rice producers initiated the suit which resulted in the statute being declared unconstitutional.
>
> One of the producers involved in the suit, Carl Krielow, stated, "The rice farmers that brought this constitutional challenge are certainly pleased that the Supreme Court has agreed with our position. It has always been our position that the Rice Promotion and Research Boards deserve the support of the rice industry in Louisiana. Our complaint has simply been that the process and procedures being followed by the Boards have not been transparent, fair, or consistent. We will support new legislation that will correct these problems pointed out in the litigation. Hopefully, we can resolve our differences with the two Boards."
>
> Many of the producers involved in the suit are members of the Louisiana Independent Rice Producers Association (LIRPA) and have long objected to the Louisiana Rice Promotion Board (the board that controls the use of rice producer funds for promotion) sending producer funds to the USA Rice Federation based in Arlington, VA. Many of the producers involved in the suit would prefer to see their dollars support a producer only organization such as the US Rice Producers Association (USRPA), an affiliate of LIRPA which does not include mills or processors.
>
> Dwight Roberts, President and CEO of USRPA said this case is definitely not a repudiation of rice promotion and research. Farmers clearly understand and support the use of their funding for those purposes. The funding provided to the LSU AgCenter Rice Research Station in Crowley, Louisiana, is vital to the operation of the facility and its research, especially during these times of reduced state funding. The AgCenter has developed new rice varieties that have dramatically increased the rice yield per acre. The outcome of this suit should be interpreted as repudiation by rice farmers to the manner in which the "Rice Statutes" were implemented. Now is the time for all Louisiana rice producers to work together to reinstate the rice research and promotion statutes in a constitutional manner. Certainly, USRPA will work with all parties to achieve this outcome.

2. *Adequate standards?* In *Krielow*, the court states a third prong of a test analyzing legislative delegation. That prong requires that there be adequate standards to check the agency's use of the power. However, the court does not provide much by way of analysis in the *Krielow* decision. The court does, however, cite its earlier decision in State v. All Pro Paint & Body Shop, 639 So. 2d 707 (La. 1994). There, the court said the following about the "adequate standards" prong of the test:

> In our third and final inquiry under the *Schwegmann* three-prong test, we find the [Louisiana Hazardous Waste and Control Law (HWCL)] is accompanied by adequate procedural safeguards to protect against abuse of discretion by [the Department of Environmental Quality] DEQ. First, the HWCL requires DEQ to promulgate regulations "after public hearing thereon in accordance with the Administrative Procedure Act" (APA).... The APA prescribes detailed procedures which administrative agencies must follow in adopting, amending, or repealing any regulation, including provisions for public notice and comment, ... and publication and distribution.
>
> Perhaps more importantly for purposes of ensuring the agency exercises its discretion in accordance with the policy and standards embodied in the enabling statute, the APA provides for judicial review of the validity or applicability of rules "in an action for declaratory judgment in the district court of the parish in which the agency is located." ... "The court shall declare the rule invalid or inapplicable if it finds that it violates constitutional provisions or exceeds the statutory authority of the agency or was adopted without substantial compliance with required rulemaking procedures." ... Judicial review thus provides a remedy where a regulation fails to implement faithfully the legislative will.

Id. at 720.

This probably means, does it not, that the delegation in *Krielow* did not satisfy the third prong of the test because there was no way judicially to review or challenge the determinations of the Rice Board with respect to votes on assessments or refunds. For a more recent application of the *Schwegmann* test, see Mid-City Auto, LLC v. State, 267 So. 3d 165, 178 (La. Ct. App. 2018) (Office of State Police Schedule of Fines unconstitutional under *Schwegmann* second prong because the legislative delegation places "no limits on the amount of administrative fines that may be assessed.").

3. How exactly does the nondelegation doctrine in the states differ from the federal version? Is the "adequate safeguards" requirement found in Louisiana law qualitatively different from inquiries at the federal level? The court in *Krielow* takes great pains to mention the strictures of the Louisiana Constitution, but does it really differ all that much from the U.S. Constitution, at least with respect to separation of powers? If you don't think so, would the binding arbitration process approved in the *Union Carbide* case, *infra* at p. 154, under federal constitutional law survive a constitutional challenge under Louisiana law if it had been enacted by the Louisiana legislature?

4. *Delegation of the ability to set criminal fines and penalties.* The typical statute contains a catch-all sanction provision, under which

> any violation of this Act shall be punished as a [misdemeanor], by imprisonment for not more than [ninety days] or a fine of not more than [$500].

When the statute delegates legislative power, the sanction provision may read:

> any violation of this Act *or of a rule or regulation promulgated thereunder* shall be punished as a [misdemeanor], by imprisonment for not more than [ninety days] or a fine of not more than [$500].

Such a provision was upheld in the leading case of United States v. Grimaud, 220 U.S. 506 (1911). Acting under a statute authorizing him to make rules regulating use of the federal forests, the Secretary of Agriculture issued regulations prohibiting grazing without a permit. Defendants were indicted for grazing sheep without a permit under the statutory provision that any violation of the statute, or of the rules and regulations promulgated thereunder, should be punishable as an offense. They claimed that Congress could not thus give an administrative officer the power to define crimes. According to the Court, however, a violation of the regulations "is made a crime, not by the Secretary, but by Congress. The statute, not the Secretary, fixes the penalty." Id. at 522. So long as the legislature sets the penalty, concerns about defining violations seem to ease if not vanish.

5. The *Krielow* case involved legislative delegation to a private industry group to allow it to raise funds using assessments to advance the industry's interests. Although the delegation involved a much smaller group than those empowered by the legislature through the executive in *Schechter Poultry*, the legislative impetus to empower a private industry or use private entities to help do the work of government may be something to be wary of. In Dep't of Transportation v. Ass'n of Am. R.R. 575 U.S. 43 (2015), the U.S. Supreme Court reversed a D.C. Circuit opinion finding the delegation of regulatory authority to Amtrak unconstitutional because Amtrak was a private entity. Although the Supreme Court disagreed and found that Amtrak was a governmental entity and therefore that the delegation was not unconstitutional, Justice Alito in concurrence raised other constitutional concerns about the statute's use of binding arbitration through an ostensibly private arbitrator to handle disputes concerning metrics and standards required by the law. According to Justice Alito:

> I entirely agree with the Court that Amtrak is "a federal actor or instrumentality," as far as the Constitution is concerned. "Amtrak was created by the Government, is controlled by the Government, and operates for the Government's benefit." The Government even "specif[ies] many of its day-to-day operations" and "for all practical purposes, set[s] and supervise[s] its annual budget." The District of Columbia Circuit understandably heeded 49 U.S.C. §24301(a)(3), which proclaims that Amtrak "is *not* a department, agency, or instrumentality of the United States Government," but this statutory label cannot control for constitutional purposes. (Emphasis added). I therefore join the Court's opinion in full. I write separately to discuss what follows from our judgment. . . .
>
> The principle that Congress cannot delegate away its vested powers exists to protect liberty. Our Constitution, by careful design, prescribes a process for making law, and within that process there are many accountability checkpoints. See *INS v. Chadha*, 462 U.S. 919, 959, 103 S. Ct. 2764, 77 L. Ed. 2d 317 (1983). It would dash the whole scheme if Congress could give its power away to an entity that is

> not constrained by those checkpoints. The Constitution's deliberative process was viewed by the Framers as a valuable feature, see, *e.g.*, Manning, Lawmaking Made Easy, 10 Green Bag 2d 202 (2007) ("[B]icameralism and presentment make lawmaking difficult *by design*" (citing, *inter alia*, The Federalist No. 62, p. 378 (J. Madison), and No. 63, at 443-444 (A. Hamilton))), not something to be lamented and evaded.
>
> Of course, this Court has "'almost never felt qualified to second-guess Congress regarding the permissible degree of policy judgment that can be left to those executing or applying the law.'" *Whitman v. American Trucking Assns., Inc.*, 531 U.S. 457, 474-475, 121 S. Ct. 903, 149 L. Ed. 2d 1 (2001) (quoting *Mistretta, supra*, at 416, 109 S. Ct. 647, 102 L. Ed. 2d 714 (Scalia, J., dissenting)). . . .
>
> When it comes to private entities, however, there is not even a fig leaf of constitutional justification. Private entities are not vested with "legislative Powers." Art. I, §1. . . . By any measure, handing off regulatory power to a private entity is "legislative delegation in its most obnoxious form." *Carter v. Carter Coal Co.*, 298 U.S. 238, 311, 56 S. Ct. 855, 80 L. Ed. 1160 (1936).
>
> For these reasons, it is hard to imagine how delegating "binding" tie-breaking authority to a private arbitrator to resolve a dispute between Amtrak and the [Federal Railroad Administration] could be constitutional. No private arbitrator can promulgate binding metrics and standards for the railroad industry. Thus, if the term "arbitrator" refers to a private arbitrator, or even the *possibility* of a private arbitrator, the Constitution is violated. See 721 F.3d, at 674 ("[T]hat the recipients of illicitly delegated authority opted not to make use of it is no antidote. It is *Congress's* decision to delegate that is unconstitutional" (citing *Whitman, supra*, at 473, 121 S. Ct. 903, 149 L. Ed. 2d 1)).

Id. at 56-62.

5. Delegation and Standards: Coda

If virtually all delegations of legislative power are upheld by the judiciary, why should so much time be devoted to the study of delegation? The answer is that the law on delegation has a vital relationship to the proper diffusion of power in a democratic system. The foundation of representative government is the position of the legislature as *the* lawmaking organ of the polity. Laws are made by the elected representatives of the people, who are subject to direct control through the electoral process. There is no comparable control when law is made by agencies. Perhaps the famous 1937 characterization of federal agencies by the President's Committee on Administrative Management as "a headless 'fourth branch' of the Government, a haphazard deposit of irresponsible agencies and uncoordinated powers," is exaggerated. Yet all too many agencies are not responsible for the details of their operations to either of the political departments, and certainly not to the control of the ballot box.

Delegation of lawmaking power is, of course, a categorical imperative in modern government. But it is essential that the people's representatives retain the primary legislative function, even while delegating secondary power to legislate to agencies. In a representative system, it is the job of the people's representatives to make the hard choices that are necessary to set meaningful policies. When Congress delegates wholesale powers, confined only by a vague "public interest" standard, it abdicates its job of making the difficult policy decisions. If the policy choices are thereby removed from the political process, they are also removed from popular control. To let the people's representatives pass the buck on policy choices to the administrative experts is to let them cast their vote for paternalism and against democracy.

See Minnesota Commission on Reform and Efficiency (CORE), Reforming Minnesota's Administrative Rulemaking System, Summary Report 19, 23 (1993):

> The biggest problem associated with rulemaking is the scope of authority for policymaking that the legislature grants to agencies. [CORE found that the legislature has often delegated its policymaking responsibilities to agencies to be carried out through rulemaking. Consequently, agencies may spend many months or years in rulemaking trying to resolve issues that should have been settled by elected officials. CORE recommends, therefore, that the legislature limit its delegations of rulemaking powers.] . . .
>
> Transferring policymaking to an agency shifts policy choices to an organization designed to administer the law, not make it. Political discussions are moved out of the legislature and into the rulemaking process.
>
> The lack of firm direction from the legislature or governor often results in agency rules that are prescriptive and based on inputs, rather than expected outcomes. A familiar analogy is that rules tend to include in excruciating detail how a plane should be built but not necessarily that it must also fly. . . .
>
> RECOMMENDATIONS
>
> 1. The legislature should limit and focus future delegations of rulemaking powers. . . .

Compare the following comment:

> The decline of Congress, whatever the causes, has produced a quiet crisis in constitutional law. The Constitution clearly presupposes that Congress is the most important policymaking institution. The reality is that Congress has become subordinate to the Executive and for many purposes even to the courts. The result is a growing gap between the law on the books and the law in action. Nowhere do we see this gap more clearly than with respect to the allocation of legislative power. The official line, as we have seen, is that Congress has a monopoly on the legislative power. The reality, as we have also seen, is that the Court has stood aside while Congress has delegated legislative power at will.
>
> Gaps between law on the books and law in action are not uncommon. Why should we be concerned about this one? One reason is that it exacerbates cynicism about government. Congress is declared to be the exclusive organ of legislation. But courts, perceiving the impracticality of this proposition, refuse to enforce it. Since the courts will not enforce it, legislators will not abide by it either, since they feel the demands of practicality even more insistently than the courts. The net result is that our system of government is seen as resting on a kind of massive constitutional violation. Agencies are depicted as exercising unconstitutional powers. Courts are regarded as lacking the courage to enforce the Constitution. Legislators are condemned for shirking the duty they were elected to perform.

> A second reason to be concerned about such a gap is that it is dangerous. Gaps between law on the books and law in action can give rise to sudden avulsions in legal understanding, as the tension between official doctrine and everyday practice becomes too great to tolerate any longer. At some point, official doctrine is apt to be wrenched aside and replaced with some new conception more consonant with institutional reality. Such avulsions are dangerous, especially when we are talking about basic constitutional architecture.

Merrill, Rethinking Article 1, Section 1: From Nondelegation to Exclusive Delegation, 104 Colum. L. Rev. 2097, 2162 (2004).

B JUDICIAL POWER

1. The United States Constitution and Judicial Power

DEBATE ON FEDERAL TRADE COMMISSION ACT*

U.S. Senate, July 1914

Mr. Sutherland: . . . Section 5 provides "That unfair competition in commerce is hereby declared unlawful." I have not any doubt that "unfair competition" is a term well known to the law. It occurs where one person attempts to impose upon the public his goods or his business as the goods or business of another.

I think that all the cases of unfair competition the courts have dealt with fall within that definition, the attempt of a person to impose on the public his goods or his business as the goods or the business of another. For example, we have a mineral water which is called "White Rock," and it is a well-known brand. Somebody undertakes to sell another mineral water, giving it a name resembling White Rock and pretending that it is White Rock. That is unfair competition. The violation of a trade-mark is a form of unfair competition.

Mr. Weeks: Let me ask the Senator from Utah, whose opinion is worth very much more than mine on any such question, if in his judgment there is not now sufficient law to protect a trader in such matters?

Mr. Sutherland: Oh, undoubtedly. I say "undoubtedly." I mean that that is my opinion. The point I was going to make about that is this: If "unfair competition" as used in this proposed law is to be construed as I have stated it, it is a matter within the jurisdiction of the courts; it presents purely a judicial question. In other words, if we were to write into this law "that unfair

---

* Reprinted from 3 Schwartz, The Economic Regulation of Business and Industry: A Legislative History of U.S. Regulatory Agencies 1776-1778 (1973).

competition in commerce is hereby declared unlawful" and provided that a violation of the provision should be punishable by fine and imprisonment, there could be no doubt that the court would lay hold of that question, and whenever a violation of that provision of the statutes occurred a proceeding would be brought in the court. That, it seems to me, demonstrates that it presents a judicial question.

If section 5 means that and nothing more, then it seems to me there is a clear attempt to vest in this legislative commission judicial power — power that we can not exercise ourselves, and that a legislative body can not devolve upon a committee of itself or a commission created by it. We can only devolve upon any such commission the power which we ourselves have, and that is the legislative power.

Mr. Weeks: Then I assume the Senator from Utah thinks this law which we are proposing to put on the statute books is unconstitutional?

Mr. Sutherland: I think it is utterly void, Mr. President, in that view. . . .

Mr. Lewis: . . . Do I understand correctly the Senator from Utah to assert as a legal proposition that it is not in the power of this body to vest judicial power in an administrative body?

Mr. Sutherland: I say so most emphatically, Mr. President. . . . [I]f we have the right to confer a power upon an administrative body we have the right to make the power effectual, but my contention is that we have no right to confer this power at all upon the administrative body; that it is a judicial power and belongs to the courts; that Congress itself can not exercise it. Suppose, for example, that Congress instead of undertaking to devolve this power upon an administrative body were itself to make an investigation of some particular case where it is claimed that unfair competition existed and Congress was to come to the conclusion that there existed unfair competition, does the Senator from Illinois think that Congress could issue an injunction against the continuance of that practice?

Mr. Lewis: No.

Mr. Sutherland: If Congress could not issue it, it would be because it would not be a legislative power; it would be because it was a judicial power; and if Congress could not itself issue the injunction in that case by what rule of law, by what provision of the Constitution, can it devolve that same power upon a legislative commission? . . .

NOTES

1. Despite Senator Sutherland's constitutional strictures, the Federal Trade Commission Act of 1914 was enacted. The FTC set up under it is vested with authority to hear and decide cases in which businessmen are charged with "methods of unfair competition." How does the power of the FTC to decide these cases differ from the power of the federal district courts to try cases under the antitrust laws?

2. Twenty years later, having become a member of the Supreme Court, Justice Sutherland wrote the opinion in Humphrey's Executor v. United States, 295 U.S. 602 (1935), the leading case upholding the independent status of the FTC. The Sutherland opinion expressed no doubt at all about the commission's constitutional position, though it expressly recognized that it "was created by Congress as a means of carrying into operation legislative and judicial powers. . . ." Id. at 630.

Why was *Justice* Sutherland's view on the delegation of judicial power to the FTC so different from that of *Senator* Sutherland?

THOMAS v. UNION CARBIDE AGRICULTURAL PRODUCTS CO.

473 U.S. 568 (1985)

JUSTICE O'CONNOR delivered the opinion of the Court.

This case requires the Court to revisit the data-consideration provision of the Federal Insecticide, Fungicide, and Rodenticide Act (FIFRA). [The statute provides for binding arbitration on compensation to be paid for EPA use of data submitted for pesticide registration.] . . .

Appellees are 13 large firms engaged in the development and marketing of chemicals used to manufacture pesticides. Each has in the past submitted data to EPA in support of registrations of various pesticides. [They] were engaged in litigation in the Southern District of New York challenging the constitutionality under Article I and the Fifth Amendment of the provisions authorizing data-sharing and disclosure of data to the public. In response to this Court's decision in Northern Pipeline Construction Co. v. Marathon Pipe Line Co., 458 U.S. 50 (1982), appellees amended their complaint to allege that the statutory mechanism of binding arbitration for determining the amount of compensation due them violates Article III of the Constitution. Article III, §1, provides that "[t]he judicial Power of the United States, shall be vested" in courts whose judges enjoy tenure "during good Behaviour" and compensation that "shall not be diminished during their Continuance in Office." Appellees allege Congress in FIFRA transgressed this limitation by allocating to arbitrators the functions of judicial officers and severely limiting review by an Article III court. . . .

An absolute construction of Article III is not possible in this area of "frequently arcane distinctions and confusing precedents." . . . "[N]either this Court nor Congress has read the Constitution as requiring every federal question arising under the federal law . . . to be tried in an Art. III court before a judge enjoying life tenure and protection against salary reduction." . . . Instead, the Court has long recognized that Congress is not barred from acting pursuant to its powers under Article I to vest decisionmaking authority in tribunals that lack the attributes of Article III courts. . . . Many matters that involve the application of legal standards to facts and affect private interests are routinely decided by agency action with limited or no review by Article III courts. . . .

. . . [A]ppellees contend that FIFRA confers a "private right" to compensation, requiring either Article III adjudication or review by an Article III court sufficient to retain "the essential attributes of the judicial power." . . . This "private right" argument rests on the distinction between public and private rights drawn by the plurality in *Northern Pipeline.* The *Northern Pipeline* plurality construed the Court's prior opinions to permit only three clearly defined exceptions to the rule of Article III adjudication: military tribunals, territorial courts, and decisions involving "public" as opposed to "private" rights. Drawing upon language in Crowell v. Benson [285 U.S. 22 (1932)], the plurality defined "public rights" as "matters arising between the Government and persons subject to its authority in connection with the performance of the constitutional functions of the executive or legislative departments." *Northern Pipeline Co., infra,* at 110. It identified "private rights" as "'the liability of one individual to another under the law as defined.'" Id., at 69-70, quoting Crowell v. Benson, [*supra*] at 51.

This theory that the public rights/private rights dichotomy of *Crowell* . . . provides a bright line test for determining the requirements of Article III did not command a majority of the Court in *Northern Pipeline.* Insofar as appellees interpret that case and *Crowell* as establishing that the right to an Article III forum is absolute unless the federal government is a party of record, we cannot agree. . . . Nor did a majority of the Court endorse the implication of the private right/public right dichotomy that Article III has no force simply because a dispute is between the Government and an individual. . . .

Chief Justice Hughes, writing for the Court in *Crowell,* expressly rejected a formalistic or abstract Article III inquiry, stating:

> In deciding whether the Congress, in enacting the statute under review, has exceeded the limits of its authority to prescribe procedure . . . , *regard must be had, as in other cases where constitutional limits are invoked, not to mere matters of form but to the substance of what is required.* 285 U.S., at 53 (emphasis added).

Crowell held that Congress could replace a seaman's traditional negligence action in admiralty with a statutory scheme of strict liability. In response to practical concerns, Congress rejected adjudication in Article III courts and instead proposed that claims for compensation would be determined in an administrative proceeding by a deputy commissioner appointed by the United States Employees' Compensation Commission. . . . Although such findings clearly concern obligations among private parties, this fact did not make the scheme invalid under Article III. Instead, after finding that the administrative proceedings satisfied due process, id., at 45-48, *Crowell* concluded that the judicial review afforded by the statute, including review of matters of law, "provides for the appropriate exercise of the judicial function in this class of cases." Id., at 54.

The enduring lesson of *Crowell* is that practical attention to substance rather than doctrinaire reliance on formal categories should inform application of Article III. . . . The extent of judicial review afforded by the legislation reviewed in *Crowell* does not constitute a minimal requirement of Article III without regard to the origin of the right at issue or the concerns guiding the selection by Congress of a particular method for resolving disputes. In assessing the degree of judicial involvement required by Article III in this case, we note that the statute considered in *Crowell* is different from FIFRA in significant respects. Most importantly, the statute in *Crowell* displaced a traditional cause of action and affected a pre-existing relationship based on a common-law contract for hire. Thus it clearly fell within the range of matters reserved to Article III courts under the holding of *Northern Pipeline.* See 458 U.S., at 70-71, and n.25 (plurality opinion) (noting that matters subject to a "suit at common law or in equity or admiralty" are at "protected core" of Article III judicial powers); id., at 90 (opinion concurring in judgment) (noting that state law contract actions are "the stuff of the traditional actions at common law tried by the courts at Westminster in 1789").

If the identity of the parties alone determined the requirements of Article III, under appellees' theory the constitutionality of many quasi-adjudicative activities carried on by administrative agencies involving claims between individuals would be thrown into doubt. . . .

The Court has treated as a matter of "public right" an essentially adversary proceeding to invoke tariff protections against a competitor, as well as an administrative proceeding to determine the rights of landlords and tenants. . . . These proceedings surely determine liabilities of individuals. Such schemes would be beyond the power of Congress under appellees' interpretation of *Crowell.* In essence, the public rights doctrine reflects simply a pragmatic understanding that when Congress selects a quasi-judicial method of resolving matters that "could be conclusively determined by the Executive and Legislative Branches," the danger of encroaching on the judicial powers is reduced. . . .

Our holding is limited to the proposition that Congress, acting for a valid legislative purpose pursuant to its constitutional powers under Article I, may create a seemingly "private" right that is so closely integrated into a public regulatory scheme as to be a matter appropriate for agency resolution with limited involvement by the Article III judiciary. To hold otherwise would be to erect a rigid and formalistic restraint on the ability of Congress to adopt innovative measures such as negotiation and arbitration with respect to rights created by a regulatory scheme. For the reasons stated in our opinion, we hold that arbitration of the limited right created by FIFRA §3(c)(1)(D)(ii) does not contravene Article III. The judgment of the District Court is reversed and the case is remanded for further proceedings consistent with this opinion. So ordered.

NOTES

1. At issue in Northern Pipeline Construction Co. v. Marathon Pipe Line Co., 458 U.S. 50 (1982) — the case discussed by Justice O'Connor — was whether the statute establishing bankruptcy courts staffed by judges not protected by Article

III safeguards (particularly those governing tenure and salaries) was consistent with Article III. The argument in favor of the statute had relied on the cases upholding the constitutionality of administrative agencies created to adjudicate cases.

The plurality opinion of Justice Brennan conceded that Congress had the power to create agencies to adjudicate cases involving "public rights," i.e., cases arising between the government and others. The opinion distinguished those cases from cases concerning the liability of one individual to another and involving only "private rights." According to Justice Brennan, "Our precedents clearly establish that *only* controversies in the former category may be removed from Art. III courts and delegated to . . . administrative agencies for their determination." Id. at 70. Note how Justice O'Connor repudiates the *Northern Pipeline* notion that "the identity of the parties . . . determined the requirements of Article III." 473 U.S. 568 at 587.

The Brennan opinion relied on the public rights/private rights distinction as the criterion on which delegations of adjudicatory authority might rest. But that distinction was rendered obsolete years ago by the establishment of workers' compensation agencies, for, as recognized in Crowell v. Benson, 285 U.S. 22, 51 (1932), the employee compensation case "is one of private right, that is, of the liability of one individual to another under the law as defined." The point under discussion is more than a matter of mere semantics. If agencies may be given only the power to adjudicate matters of public right, the implication is that the whole host of agencies vested with adjudicatory authority over cases arising between private parties, starting with workers' compensation, is somehow constitutionally suspect.

2. But compare State v. Mechem, 316 P.2d 1069, 1070-1071 (N.M. 1957) (citations omitted), where the constitutionality of the New Mexico Workmen's Compensation Act was at issue:

> The attack on the Act is multiple but the main question is whether it confers an unlawful delegation of judicial power on the commission. We think it does. . . .
>
> . . . This is not to say that the legislature, in the exercise of its police powers, may not confer "quasi-judicial" power on administrative boards for the protection of the rights and interest of the public in general whose orders are not to be overruled if supported by substantial evidence. For instance, boards regulating common carriers, transportation, telephone rates, Barber Boards, Medical Boards, Boards of Registration, Tax Boards, Division of Liquor Control, etc. . . . But nowhere does this power extend to a determination of rights and liabilities between individuals. . . .
>
> We think the function to be performed by the commission is clearly a judicial one. The commission is called upon to decide questions of fact between private litigants and is empowered to render decisions that have the force and effect of judgments. Being of the opinion that the commission is clothed with judicial power, the next question to be answered is, is this expressly permitted by our constitution? A reexamination of Article 6, Section 1, supplies an instant answer. The framers of the New Mexico Constitution in this section limited the creation of courts to those

named therein, and "such courts inferior to the district courts as may be established by law from time to time in any county or municipality of the state, including juvenile courts." Here the legislature has attempted to create an executive agency, clothe it with judicial power, on a parity with district courts, and invest it with state-wide jurisdiction. This cannot be done.

Is the New Mexico court correct in the assumption that there are cases so inherently judicial that they must be decided by courts alone? Is the line drawn between cases of public right and those of private right valid? If not, what other valid line can be drawn? Consider the reasoning in the New Mexico Supreme Court's later decision to overturn its precedent in *Mechem*:

> Additionally, we would take exception to the characterization in *Mechem*'s majority opinion of the commission for hearing workmen's compensation claims as a "clearly . . . judicial" rather than a "quasi-judicial" body. . . . The distinction attempted simply does not withstand examination of the two definitions. In the context of voluminous New Mexico case law, a workmen's compensation commission is no more "purely judicial" — as opposed to "quasi-judicial" — than is New Mexico's Public Service Commission, Environmental Improvement Board, Employment Security Department, Human Rights Commission, Alcoholic Beverage Control Commission, or many other administrative agencies. All of them operate unhindered under the same constitutional provision which the *Mechem* court found so constraining when applied to a worker's compensation board.
>
> Secondly, the effort to classify "judicial" and "quasi-judicial" activities in *Mechem* by looking to the public or private rights sought to be adjudicated ignored the longstanding and oft-repeated recognition in New Mexico case law of the public's stake in the worker's remedies: Public policy demands minimum financial security for the injured worker and his family. . . . Workmen's compensation benefits were enacted to prevent the workman from becoming dependent upon the public welfare. . . . Within the policy considerations of the Workmen's Compensation Act, the interests of the claimant and the public are paramount. . . . The underlying purpose of the Workmen's Compensation Act is to protect the workman from becoming a public charge upon the welfare rolls. . . . The consuming public, in the final analysis, bears the expense of workmen's compensation, as a charge included in the sale price of the service or commodity offered by the industry. . . . Moreover, as the *Mechem* dissent observed again and again, administrative boards and agencies have been upheld as properly created by state and federal legislative bodies for nearly a hundred years. Justice Sadler felt the *Mechem* decision to be fifty years behind the times when it was decided, and an "anachronism" when written thirty years ago. It has not gained more favor nor become more palatable, legally or logically, in the intervening years. . . .

Wylie v. Mowrer, 726 P.2d 1381, 1382-1383 (N.M. 1986).

3. *Judicial relief — the civil monetary penalty.* "Virtually every major administrative regulatory program authorized today contains some type of civil monetary penalty sanction." Project, The Decriminalization of Administrative Law Penalties, 45 Admin. L. Rev. 367, 387 (1993). The cases increasingly permit delegations to agencies of power to impose money penalties in individual cases.

The Supreme Court accepted the constitutionality of such grants of authority as early as Oceanic Steam Navigation Co. v. Stranahan, 214 U.S. 320 (1909). Since then, numerous federal statutes have empowered agencies to impose money penalties. This has been particularly true of federal statutes in the fields of environmental protection and industrial safety. For a long list of federal statutes delegating penalty power, see Atlas Roofing Co. v. Occupational Safety & Health Review Comm'n, 518 F.2d 990 (5th Cir. 1975), aff'd, 430 U.S. 442 (1977).

See Palmer, Administrative Hearings for the General Practitioner, 73 A.B.A. J. 86, 88 (1987):

> During 1977 . . . federal agencies collected more than $52 million in some 360,000 cases. By 1979, [the Administrative Conference] reported that the "civil money penalty has become one of the most widely used techniques in the enforcement programs of federal administrative agencies." 1 C.F.R. 305.79-3 (1984).
>
> The maximum authorized civil penalty, typically $500 per violation under older statutes, is now $10,000 under most recent ones. Some recently enacted statutes set maximums as high as $100,000.

Compare the delegation to the Interstate Commerce Commission under 49 U.S.C. §§13(1), 16(1) (1940):

> Any person, firm, corporation, company, or association, or any mercantile, agricultural, or manufacturing society or other organization, or any body politic or municipal organization, or any common carrier complaining of anything done or omitted to be done by any common carrier subject to the provisions of this chapter in contravention of the provisions thereof, may apply to said commission by petition, which shall briefly state the facts; whereupon a statement of the complaint thus made shall be forwarded by the commission to such common carrier, who shall be called upon to satisfy the complaint, or to answer the same in writing, within a reasonable time, to be specified by the commission. If such common carrier within the time specified shall make reparation for the injury alleged to have been done, the common carrier shall be relieved of liability to the complainant only for the particular violation of law thus complained of. If such carrier or carriers shall not satisfy the complaint within the time specified, or there shall appear to be any reasonable ground for investigating said complaint, it shall be the duty of the commission to investigate the matters complained of in such manner and by such means as it shall deem proper.
>
> If, after hearing on a complaint made as provided in section 13 of this chapter, the commission shall determine that any party complainant is entitled to an award of damages under the provisions of this chapter for a violation thereof, the commission shall make an order directing the carrier to pay to the complainant the sum to which he is entitled on or before a day named.

The Supreme Court has affirmed that such a "reparations scheme itself is of unquestioned constitutional validity." CFTC v. Schor, 478 U.S. 833, 856 (1986).

May agencies be given power to enforce their money awards by administrative execution? If not, how can agency money awards be enforced? See, e.g., 49 U.S.C. §16(2) (1940):

> If a carrier does not comply with an order for the payment of money within the time limit in such order, the complainant, or any person for whose benefit such order was made, may file in the district court of the United States for the district in which he resides or in which is located the principal operating office of the carrier, or through which the road of the carrier runs, or in any State court of general jurisdiction having jurisdiction of the parties, a complaint setting forth briefly the causes for which he claims damages, and the order of the commission in the premises. Such suit in the district court of the United States shall proceed in all respects like other civil suits for damages, except that on the trial of such suit the findings and order of the commission shall be prima facie evidence of the facts therein stated, and except that the plaintiff shall not be liable for costs in the district court nor for costs at any subsequent stage of the proceedings unless they accrue upon his appeal.

Can agencies go too far even though within proper statutory money penalty constraints? Consider United States v. Bajakajian, 524 U.S. 321 (1998), where a traveler was detained by the U.S. Customs Service for boarding a flight carrying some $357,000 in undeclared cash. It is a violation not to declare cash in excess of $10,000. The traveler pleaded guilty to the offense, but the Customs Service declared the entire amount forfeited because it was an instrumentality of a crime. The Supreme Court held that such a forfeiture violated the Excessive Fines Clause of the U.S. Constitution's Eighth Amendment because such forfeitures are fines if they constitute a punishment for an offense, and they are excessive if they are grossly disproportionate to the nature of the offense.

For penalty power to exist in an agency, there must, of course, be an express legislative delegation. Athlone Industries v. CPSC, 707 F.2d 1485 (D.C. Cir. 1983).

4. See Green v. United States Coast Guard, 642 F. Supp. 638, 644 (N.D. Ill. 1986), a case involving a money penalty imposed by an agency where it was claimed that

> this proceeding should have been conducted in a District Court, and he should have been afforded the protections of a criminal trial. The court rejects both of these arguments as meritless. First, Congress delegated the initial determination of civil penalties to the Coast Guard. It would be contrary to its expressed legislative intent to bypass the agency and allow adjudication in the District Courts in the first instance.... Second, these proceedings bear no resemblance to a criminal trial. For this reason, constitutional rights of a criminal defendant are inapplicable to these agency hearings.

Although agency civil money penalties are commonplace, agencies and criminal sanctions are anathema to one another. The Supreme Court, in Hudson v. United States, 522 U.S. 93, 103 (1997), held that criminal prosecution of persons earlier found in violation of banking laws by an administrative agency that fined and debarred them did not violate the Constitution's Double Jeopardy Clause. According to the Court:

> While the provision authorizing debarment contains no language explicitly denominating the sanction as civil, we think it significant that the authority to issue

> debarment orders is conferred upon the "appropriate Federal banking agencies." That such authority was conferred upon administrative agencies is prima facie evidence that Congress intended to provide for a civil sanction.

(Citations omitted.)

5. *Judicial injunctive power/administrative "cease and desist" authority.* In addition to their power to award damages, courts have the power to issue injunctions. Injunctive authority is, indeed, the hallmark of the Anglo-American judiciary; it is the most far-reaching power possessed by any civil courts. May an agency be given power to issue "injunctions"? May it be given authority to issue orders less powerful than injunctions yet still directing that specified acts be stopped or carried out?

See Federal Trade Commission Act, 15 U.S.C. §45(b):

> Whenever the Commission shall have reason to believe that any such person, partnership, or corporation has been or is using any unfair method of competition or unfair or deceptive act or practice in or affecting commerce, and if it shall appear to the Commission that a proceeding by it in respect thereof would be to the interest of the public, it shall issue and serve upon such person, partnership, or corporation a complaint stating its charges in that respect and containing a notice of a hearing upon a day and at a place therein fixed at least thirty days after the service of said complaint. The person, partnership, or corporation so complained of shall have the right to appear at the place and time so fixed and show cause why an order should not be entered by the Commission requiring such person, partnership, or corporation to cease and desist from the violation of the law so charged in said complaint.

Similar power to issue cease and desist orders has been delegated to most regulatory agencies. The cease and desist order is the administrative equivalent of the prohibitory or negative injunction.

6. *Contempt authority.* Without agency contempt power, how can cease and desist orders and other injunctive orders be enforced? The first and still the traditional enforcement method was that provided in the Federal Trade Commission Act of 1914, 38 Stat. 717, 720:

> If such person, partnership, or corporation fails or neglects to obey such order of the commission while the same is in effect, the commission may apply to the circuit court of appeals of the United States, within any circuit where the method of competition in question was used or where such person, partnership, or corporation resides or carries on business, for the enforcement of its order. . . .

Violation of the court order directing enforcement is punishable as a contempt, not of the commission, but of the court. Could Congress go further and provide a criminal penalty for violation of an FTC order?

7. *Immigration authority and judicial power.* The widest agency powers over the person are delegated in connection with the administration of immigration laws. Such powers are vested in the Immigration and Naturalization Service of the Department of Justice (now Immigration and Customs Enforcement (ICE), part of the Border and Transportation Security directorate within the Department of Homeland Security). The substantive powers conferred on ICE include the authority to determine whether particular undocumented persons should be excluded or deported from the United States. Few powers over the person in our legal system may be more drastic in their impact than that exercised in individual exclusion and deportation cases. Particularly in the latter, the consequences may be even more severe than the decisions in criminal cases; deportation may, in Justice Brandeis' famous phrase, "result . . . in loss of both property and life; or of all that makes life worth living." Ng Fung Ho v. White, 259 U.S. 276, 284 (1922).

ICE possesses power not only to make decisions that drastically affect the persons of those subject to its jurisdiction but also has the power directly to execute its own decisions. An exclusion decision is executed by a physical bar to entry by the relevant immigration officials. After a deportation order is issued, the undocumented person is given an opportunity to leave the country voluntarily. If he refuses to do so, ICE has the authority to execute the order by physically ejecting the person, i.e., by placing him on a plane or ship to the country to which he is deported. Is the immigration exception to the rule that the interposition of a court is required before an agency order has coercive consequences justified?

Congress may provide that specified classes of undocumented persons (e.g., those who have entered the country unlawfully) shall be deported and may delegate the determination of individual deportation cases to an agency. May Congress go further and enact a statute that provides the following?

> Any person whom ICE determines to have entered the United States unlawfully may be ordered by the said Service to be imprisoned at hard labor for a period not exceeding one year, and thereafter deported from the United States.

As stated in Wong Wing v. United States, 163 U.S. 228, 237 (1896), such a statute would be invalid. According to the Court, Congress may provide for deportation of persons by administrative decision and even may declare the act of such person in remaining unlawfully within the United States an offense, punishable by fine or imprisonment after a criminal trial and conviction. But it may not provide for imposition of imprisonment as a penalty by an agency: "[W]hen Congress sees fit to further promote such a policy by subjecting the persons of such aliens to infamous punishment at hard labor . . . we think such legislation, to be valid, must provide for a judicial trial to establish the guilt of the accused." For a statute to punish unlawful residence by deprivation of liberty "would be to pass out of the sphere of constitutional legislation, unless provision were made that the fact of guilt should first be established by a judicial trial." In the course of its *Wong Wing* opinion, the Court declared:

> We think it clear that detention, or temporary confinement, as part of the means necessary to give effect to the provisions for the exclusion or expulsion of aliens would be valid. Proceedings to exclude or expel would be vain if those accused

> could not be held in custody pending the inquiry into their true character and while arrangements were being made for their deportation.

Id. at 235.

Even if temporary detention authority is necessary, does that justify its delegation to administrative officials?

STERN v. MARSHALL

564 U.S. 462 (2011)

CHIEF JUSTICE ROBERTS delivered the opinion of the Court.

This "suit has, in course of time, become so complicated, that . . . no two . . . lawyers can talk about it for five minutes, without coming to a total disagreement as to all the premises. Innumerable children have been born into the cause: innumerable young people have married into it"; and, sadly, the original parties "have died out of it." A "long procession of [judges] has come in and gone out" during that time, and still the suit "drags its weary length before the Court." Those words were not written about this case, see C. Dickens, Bleak House, in 1 Works of Charles Dickens 4-5 (1891), but they could have been. This is the second time we have had occasion to weigh in on this long-running dispute between Vickie Lynn Marshall and E. Pierce Marshall over the fortune of J. Howard Marshall II, a man believed to have been one of the richest people in Texas. The Marshalls' litigation has worked its way through state and federal courts in Louisiana, Texas, and California, and two of those courts — a Texas state probate court and the Bankruptcy Court for the Central District of California — have reached contrary decisions on its merits. The Court of Appeals below held that the Texas state decision controlled, after concluding that the Bankruptcy Court lacked the authority to enter final judgment on a counterclaim that Vickie brought against Pierce in her bankruptcy proceeding. To determine whether the Court of Appeals was correct in that regard, we must resolve two issues: (1) whether the Bankruptcy Court had the statutory authority under 28 U.S.C. §157(b) to issue a final judgment on Vickie's counterclaim; and (2) if so, whether conferring that authority on the Bankruptcy Court is constitutional.

Although the history of this litigation is complicated, its resolution ultimately turns on very basic principles. Article III, §1, of the Constitution commands that "[t]he judicial Power of the United States, shall be vested in one supreme Court, and in such inferior Courts as the Congress may from time to time ordain and establish." That Article further provides that the judges of those courts shall hold their offices during good behavior, without diminution of salary. Those requirements of Article III were not honored here. The Bankruptcy Court in this case exercised the judicial power of the United States by entering final judgment on a common law tort claim, even though the judges of such courts enjoy neither tenure during good behavior nor salary protection. We conclude that, although the Bankruptcy Court had the statutory authority to enter judgment on Vickie's counterclaim, it lacked the constitutional authority to do so.

I.

... Of current relevance are two claims Vickie filed in an attempt to secure half of J. Howard's fortune. Known to the public as Anna Nicole Smith, Vickie was J. Howard's third wife and married him about a year before his death. Although J. Howard bestowed on Vickie many monetary and other gifts during their courtship and marriage, he did not include her in his will. Before J. Howard passed away, Vickie filed suit in Texas state probate court, asserting that Pierce — J. Howard's younger son — fraudulently induced J. Howard to sign a living trust that did not include her, even though J. Howard meant to give her half his property. Pierce denied any fraudulent activity and defended the validity of J. Howard's trust and, eventually, his will.

After J. Howard's death, Vickie filed a petition for bankruptcy in the Central District of California. Pierce filed a complaint in that bankruptcy proceeding, contending that Vickie had defamed him by inducing her lawyers to tell members of the press that he had engaged in fraud to gain control of his father's assets. The complaint sought a declaration that Pierce's defamation claim was not dischargeable in the bankruptcy proceedings. Pierce subsequently filed a proof of claim for the defamation action, meaning that he sought to recover damages for it from Vickie's bankruptcy estate. Vickie responded to Pierce's initial complaint by asserting truth as a defense to the alleged defamation and by filing a counterclaim for tortious interference with the gift she expected from J. Howard. As she had in state court, Vickie alleged that Pierce had wrongfully prevented J. Howard from taking the legal steps necessary to provide her with half his property.

On November 5, 1999, the Bankruptcy Court issued an order granting Vickie summary judgment on Pierce's claim for defamation. On September 27, 2000, after a bench trial, the Bankruptcy Court issued a judgment on Vickie's counterclaim in her favor. The court later awarded Vickie over $400 million in compensatory damages and $25 million in punitive damages....

III

Although we conclude that §157(b)(2)(C) permits the Bankruptcy Court to enter final judgment on Vickie's counterclaim, Article III of the Constitution does not.

A

Article III, §1, of the Constitution mandates that "[t]he judicial Power of the United States, shall be vested in one supreme Court, and in such inferior Courts as the Congress may from time to time ordain and establish." The same section provides that the judges of those constitutional courts "shall hold their Offices during good Behaviour" and "receive for their Services[ ] a Compensation[ ] [that] shall not be diminished" during their tenure.

As its text and our precedent confirm, Article III is "an inseparable element of the constitutional system of checks and balances" that "both defines the power and protects the independence of the Judicial Branch." *Northern Pipeline*, 458 U.S. at 58 (plurality opinion). Under "the basic concept of separation of powers . . . that flow[s] from the scheme of a tripartite government" adopted in the Constitution, "the 'judicial Power of the United States' . . . can no more be shared" with another branch than "the Chief Executive, for example, can share with the Judiciary the veto power, or the Congress share with the Judiciary the power to override a Presidential veto." United States v. Nixon, 418 U.S. 683 (1974).

In establishing the system of divided power in the Constitution, the Framers considered it essential that "the judiciary remain[ ] truly distinct from both the legislature and the executive." The Federalist No. 78, p. 466 (C. Rossiter ed. 1961) (A. Hamilton). As Hamilton put it, quoting Montesquieu, "'there is no liberty if the power of judging be not separated from the legislative and executive powers.'" We have recognized that the three branches are not hermetically sealed from one another . . . , but it remains true that Article III imposes some basic limitations that the other branches may not transgress. Those limitations serve two related purposes. "Separation-of-powers principles are intended, in part, to protect each branch of government from incursion by the others. Yet the dynamic between and among the branches is not the only object of the Constitution's concern. The structural principles secured by the separation of powers protect the individual as well." Bond v. United States, 564 U.S. [211] (2011).

Article III protects liberty not only through its role in implementing the separation of powers, but also by specifying the defining characteristics of Article III judges. The colonists had been subjected to judicial abuses at the hand of the Crown, and the Framers knew the main reasons why: because the King of Great Britain "made Judges dependent on his Will alone, for the tenure of their offices, and the amount and payment of their salaries." The Declaration of Independence P11. The Framers undertook in Article III to protect citizens subject to the judicial power of the new Federal Government from a repeat of those abuses. By appointing judges to serve without term limits, and restricting the ability of the other branches to remove judges or diminish their salaries, the Framers sought to ensure that each judicial decision would be rendered, not with an eye toward currying favor with Congress or the Executive, but rather with the "[c]lear heads . . . and honest hearts" deemed "essential to good judges." 1 Works of James Wilson 363 (J. Andrews ed. 1896).

Article III could neither serve its purpose in the system of checks and balances nor preserve the integrity of judicial decisionmaking if the other branches of the Federal Government could confer the Government's "judicial Power" on entities outside Article III. That is why we have long recognized that, in general, Congress may not "withdraw from judicial cognizance any matter which, from its nature, is the subject of a suit at the common law, or in equity, or admiralty." Murray's Lessee v. Hoboken Land & Improvement Co., 59 U.S. 272 (1856). . . .

B

This is not the first time we have faced an Article III challenge to a bankruptcy court's resolution of a debtor's suit. In *Northern Pipeline*, we considered whether bankruptcy judges serving under the Bankruptcy Act of 1978 — appointed by the President and confirmed by the Senate, but lacking the tenure and salary guarantees of Article III — could "constitutionally be vested with jurisdiction to decide [a] state-law contract claim" against an entity that was not otherwise part of the bankruptcy proceedings. The Court concluded that assignment of such state law claims for resolution by those judges "violates Art. III of the Constitution." . . .

The plurality in *Northern Pipeline* recognized that there was a category of cases involving "public rights" that Congress could constitutionally assign to "legislative" courts for resolution. That opinion concluded that this "public rights" exception extended "only to matters arising between" individuals and the Government "in connection with the performance of the constitutional functions of the executive or legislative departments . . . that historically could have been determined exclusively by those" branches. . . . A full majority of the Court, while not agreeing on the scope of the exception, concluded that the doctrine did not encompass adjudication of the state law claim at issue in that case. . . .

After our decision in *Northern Pipeline*, Congress revised the statutes governing bankruptcy jurisdiction and bankruptcy judges. In the 1984 Act, Congress provided that the judges of the new bankruptcy courts would be appointed by the courts of appeals for the circuits in which their districts are located. 28 U.S.C. §152(a). And . . . Congress permitted the newly constituted bankruptcy courts to enter final judgments only in "core" proceedings.

With respect to such "core" matters, however, the bankruptcy courts under the 1984 Act exercise the same powers they wielded under the Bankruptcy Act of 1978 (1978 Act), 92 Stat. 2549. . . .

C

Vickie and the dissent argue that the Bankruptcy Court's entry of final judgment on her state common law counterclaim was constitutional, despite the similarities between the bankruptcy courts under the 1978 Act and those exercising core jurisdiction under the 1984 Act. We disagree. It is clear that the Bankruptcy Court in this case exercised the "judicial Power of the United States" in purporting to resolve and enter final judgment on a state common law claim, just as the court did in *Northern Pipeline*. No "public right" exception excuses the failure to comply with Article III in doing so, any more than in *Northern Pipeline*. . . . Here Vickie's claim is a state law action independent of the federal bankruptcy law and not necessarily resolvable by a ruling on the creditor's proof of claim in bankruptcy. *Northern Pipeline* . . . rejected the application of the "public rights" exception in such cases. . . .

1

Vickie's counterclaim cannot be deemed a matter of "public right" that can be decided outside the Judicial Branch. As explained above, in *Northern Pipeline* we rejected the argument that the public rights doctrine permitted a bankruptcy court to adjudicate a state law suit brought by a debtor against a company that had not filed a claim against the estate. . . . Although our discussion of the public rights exception since that time has not been entirely consistent, and the exception has been the subject of some debate, this case does not fall within any of the various formulations of the concept that appear in this Court's opinions.

We first recognized the category of public rights in *Murray's Lessee.* That case involved the Treasury Department's sale of property belonging to a customs collector who had failed to transfer payments to the Federal Government that he had collected on its behalf. The plaintiff, who claimed title to the same land through a different transfer, objected that the Treasury Department's calculation of the deficiency and sale of the property was void, because it was a judicial act that could not be assigned to the Executive under Article III.

"To avoid misconstruction upon so grave a subject," the Court laid out the principles guiding its analysis. . . . It confirmed that Congress cannot "withdraw from judicial cognizance any matter which, from its nature, is the subject of a suit at the common law, or in equity, or admiralty." The Court also recognized that "[a]t the same time there are matters, involving public rights, which may be presented in such form that the judicial power is capable of acting on them, and which are susceptible of judicial determination, but which congress may or may not bring within the cognizance of the courts of the United States, as it may deem proper."

As an example of such matters, the Court referred to "[e]quitable claims to land by the inhabitants of ceded territories" and cited cases in which land issues were conclusively resolved by Executive Branch officials. In those cases "it depends upon the will of congress whether a remedy in the courts shall be allowed at all," so Congress could limit the extent to which a judicial forum was available. *Murray's Lessee,* 59 U.S. 272, 284. The challenge in *Murray's Lessee* to the Treasury Department's sale of the collector's land likewise fell within the "public rights" category of cases, because it could only be brought if the Federal Government chose to allow it by waiving sovereign immunity. The point of *Murray's Lessee* was simply that Congress may set the terms of adjudicating a suit when the suit could not otherwise proceed at all.

Subsequent decisions from this Court contrasted cases within the reach of the public rights exception — those arising "between the Government and persons subject to its authority in connection with the performance of the constitutional functions of the executive or legislative departments" — and those that were instead matters "of private right, that is, of the liability of one individual to another under the law as defined." Crowell v. Benson, 285 U.S. 22, 50-51 (1932) (other citations omitted).

Shortly after *Northern Pipeline*, the Court rejected the limitation of the public rights exception to actions involving the Government as a party. The Court has continued, however, to limit the exception to cases in which the claim at issue derives from a federal regulatory scheme, or in which resolution of the claim by an expert Government agency is deemed essential to a limited regulatory objective within the agency's authority. In other words, it is still the case that what makes a right "public" rather than private is that the right is integrally related to particular Federal Government action....

Our decision in *Thomas v. Union Carbide Agricultural Products Co.*, for example, involved a data-sharing arrangement between companies under a federal statute providing that disputes about compensation between the companies would be decided by binding arbitration. This Court held that the scheme did not violate Article III, explaining that "[a]ny right to compensation ... results from [the statute] and does not depend on or replace a right to such compensation under state law."

... Vickie's counterclaim ... does not fall within any of the varied formulations of the public rights exception in this Court's cases. It is not a matter that can be pursued only by grace of the other branches, as in *Murray's Lessee*, or one that "historically could have been determined exclusively by" those branches, *Northern Pipeline*. The claim is instead one under state common law between two private parties. It does not "depend[ ] on the will of congress,"; Congress has nothing to do with it.

In addition, Vickie's claimed right to relief does not flow from a federal statutory scheme, as in *Thomas*.... It is not "completely dependent upon" adjudication of a claim created by federal law.... [P]ierce did not truly consent to resolution of Vickie's claim in the bankruptcy court proceedings. He had nowhere else to go if he wished to recover from Vickie's estate....

Furthermore, the asserted authority to decide Vickie's claim is not limited to a "particularized area of the law," as in *Crowell*, *Thomas*, and *Schor*. We deal here not with an agency but with a court, with substantive jurisdiction reaching any area of the *corpus juris*. This is not a situation in which Congress devised an "expert and inexpensive method for dealing with a class of questions of fact which are particularly suited to examination and determination by an administrative agency specially assigned to that task." The "experts" in the federal system at resolving common law counterclaims such as Vickie's are the Article III courts, and it is with those courts that her claim must stay....

We recognize that there may be instances in which the distinction between public and private rights — at least as framed by some of our recent cases — fails to provide concrete guidance as to whether, for example, a particular agency can adjudicate legal issues under a substantive regulatory scheme. Given the extent to which this case is so markedly distinct from the agency cases discussing the public rights exception in the context of such a regime, however, we do not in this opinion express any view on how the doctrine might apply in that different context.

What is plain here is that this case involves the most prototypical exercise of judicial power: the entry of a final, binding judgment *by a court* with broad substantive jurisdiction, on a common law cause of action, when the action neither derives from nor depends upon any agency regulatory regime. If such an exercise of judicial power may nonetheless be taken from the Article III Judiciary simply by deeming it part of some amorphous "public right," then Article III would be transformed from the guardian of individual liberty and separation of powers we have long recognized into mere wishful thinking....

D

... We do not think the removal of counterclaims such as Vickie's from core bankruptcy jurisdiction meaningfully changes the division of labor in the current statute; we agree with the United States that the question presented here is a "narrow" one.

If our decision today does not change all that much, then why the fuss? Is there really a threat to the separation of powers where Congress has conferred the judicial power outside Article III only over certain counterclaims in bankruptcy? The short but emphatic answer is yes. A statute may no more lawfully chip away at the authority of the Judicial Branch than it may eliminate it entirely. "Slight encroachments create new boundaries from which legions of power can seek new territory to capture." Although "[i]t may be that it is the obnoxious thing in its mildest and least repulsive form," we cannot overlook the intrusion: "illegitimate and unconstitutional practices get their first footing in that way, namely, by silent approaches and slight deviations from legal modes of procedure." We cannot compromise the integrity of the system of separated powers and the role of the Judiciary in that system, even with respect to challenges that may seem innocuous at first blush.

Article III of the Constitution provides that the judicial power of the United States may be vested only in courts whose judges enjoy the protections set forth in that Article. We conclude today that Congress, in one isolated respect, exceeded that limitation in the Bankruptcy Act of 1984. The Bankruptcy Court below lacked the constitutional authority to enter a final judgment on a state law counterclaim that is not resolved in the process of ruling on a creditor's proof of claim. Accordingly, the judgment of the Court of Appeals is affirmed.

It is so ordered.

Justice Scalia, concurring.

I agree with the Court's interpretation of our Article III precedents, and I accordingly join its opinion. I adhere to my view, however, that — our contrary precedents notwithstanding — "a matter of public rights ... must at a minimum arise between the government and others[.]" ...

[L]eaving aside certain adjudications by federal administrative agencies, which are governed (for better or worse) by our landmark decision in *Crowell*, ... in my view an Article III judge is required in *all* federal adjudications, unless there is a firmly established historical practice to the contrary. For that reason — and not because of some intuitive balancing of benefits and harms — I agree that Article III judges are not required in the context of territorial courts, courts-martial, or true "public rights" cases. See *Northern Pipeline.* Perhaps historical practice permits non-Article III judges to process claims against the bankruptcy estate, see, *e.g.*, Plank, Why Bankruptcy Judges Need Not and Should Not Be Article III Judges, 72 Am. Bankr. L. J. 567, 607-609 (1998); the subject has not been briefed, and so I state no position on the matter. But Vickie points to no historical practice that authorizes a non-Article III judge to adjudicate a counterclaim of the sort at issue here.

JUSTICE BREYER, with whom JUSTICE GINSBURG, JUSTICE SOTOMAYOR, and JUSTICE KAGAN, join, dissenting.

Pierce Marshall filed a claim in Federal Bankruptcy Court against the estate of Vickie Marshall. His claim asserted that Vickie Marshall had, through her lawyers, accused him of trying to prevent her from obtaining money that his father had wanted her to have; that her accusations violated state defamation law; and that she consequently owed Pierce Marshall damages. Vickie Marshall filed a compulsory counterclaim in which she asserted that Pierce Marshall had unlawfully interfered with her husband's efforts to grant her an *inter vivos* gift and that he consequently owed her damages.

The Bankruptcy Court adjudicated the claim and the counterclaim. In doing so, the court followed statutory procedures applicable to "core" bankruptcy proceedings. And ultimately the Bankruptcy Court entered judgment in favor of Vickie Marshall. The question before us is whether the Bankruptcy Court possessed jurisdiction to adjudicate Vickie Marshall's counterclaim. I agree with the Court that the bankruptcy statute authorizes a bankruptcy court to adjudicate the counterclaim. But I do not agree with the majority about the statute's constitutionality. I believe the statute is consistent with the Constitution's delegation of the "judicial Power of the United States" to the Judicial Branch of Government. Consequently, it is constitutional.

I

My disagreement with the majority's conclusion stems in part from my disagreement about the way in which it interprets, or at least emphasizes, certain precedents. In my view, the majority overstates the current relevance of statements this Court made in an 1856 case, *Murray's Lessee*, and it overstates the importance of an analysis that did not command a Court majority in *Northern Pipeline*, and that was subsequently disavowed. At the same time, I fear the Court understates the importance of a watershed opinion widely thought to demonstrate the constitutional basis for the current authority of administrative agencies to adjudicate private disputes, namely, *Crowell v. Benson*.... And it fails to follow the analysis that this Court more recently has held applicable to the evaluation of claims of a kind before us here, namely, claims that a congressional delegation of adjudicatory authority violates separation-of-powers principles derived from Article III. *See Thomas v. Union Carbide; CFTC v. Schor*....

D

Rather than leaning so heavily on the approach taken by the plurality in *Northern Pipeline*, I would look to this Court's more recent Article III cases *Thomas* and *Schor* — cases that commanded a clear majority. In both cases the Court took a more pragmatic approach to the constitutional question. It sought to determine whether, in the particular instance, the challenged delegation of adjudicatory authority posed a genuine and serious threat that one branch of Government sought to aggrandize its own constitutionally delegated authority by encroaching upon a field of authority that the Constitution assigns exclusively to another branch.

1

In *Thomas*, the Court focused directly upon the nature of the Article III problem, illustrating how the Court should determine whether a delegation of adjudicatory authority to a non-Article III judge violates the Constitution. The statute in question required pesticide manufacturers to submit to binding arbitration claims for compensation owed for the use by one manufacturer of the data of another to support its federal pesticide registration. After describing *Northern Pipeline*'s holding . . . , the Court stated that "*practical attention to substance* rather than doctrinaire reliance on formal categories should inform application of Article III." It indicated that Article III's requirements could not be "determined" by "the identity of the parties alone," or by the "private rights"/"public rights" distinction. . . . And it upheld the arbitration provision of the statute.

The Court pointed out that the right in question was created by a federal statute, it "represent[s] a pragmatic solution to the difficult problem of spreading [certain] costs," and the statute "does not preclude review of the arbitration proceeding by an Article III court." . . .

NOTES

1. Does the Court take a "formalist" or "functionalist" approach to judicial power in the *Stern* case? Do you agree with the majority's characterization that the case will not have much of an effect, or are you persuaded by the dissent that the decision will impact judicial efficiency?

2. What about the bottom line here? Does Congress effectively diminish the judicial power by giving it to Article I bankruptcy judges? Why doesn't Congress get the same deference in the creation of a bankruptcy system as it does in creating independent regulatory agencies?

3. Is the "public rights" doctrine clearer to you now after *Stern*? It seems that Congress is allowed to create causes of action within the context of agency creation and public rights, but must steer clear of creating inferior courts to deal with common law actions. Is that a correct statement of the law after *Stern*? In

Stern, the parties voluntarily submitted claims to the bankruptcy court. The dissent felt that voluntary submission to jurisdiction was significant in deciding the constitutional question. Is it, or should it be? Compare the following case involving the right to a jury trial.

GRANFINANCIERA S.A. v. NORDBERG

492 U.S. 33 (1989)

JUSTICE BRENNAN delivered the opinion of the Court.

The question presented is whether a person who has not submitted a claim against a bankruptcy estate has a right to a jury trial when sued by the trustee in bankruptcy to recover an allegedly fraudulent monetary transfer. We hold that the Seventh Amendment entitles such a person to a trial by jury, notwithstanding Congress' designation of fraudulent conveyance actions as "core proceedings" in 28 U.S.C. §157(b)(2)(H) (1982 ed., Supp. IV).

I.

The Chase & Sanborn Corporation filed a petition for reorganization under Chapter 11 in 1983. A Plan of Reorganization approved by the United States Bankruptcy Court for the Southern District of Florida vested in respondent Nordberg, the trustee in bankruptcy, causes of action for fraudulent conveyances. In 1985, respondent filed suit against petitioners Granfinanciera, S.A. and Medex, Ltda. in the United States District Court for the Southern District of Florida. The complaint alleged that petitioners had received $1.7 million from Chase & Sanborn's corporate predecessor within one year of the date its bankruptcy petition was filed, without receiving consideration or reasonably equivalent value in return. Respondent sought to avoid what it alleged were constructively and actually fraudulent transfers and to recover damages, costs, expenses, and interest under 11 U.S.C. §§548(a)(1) and (a)(2), 550(a)(1) (1982 ed. and Supp. V).

The District Court referred the proceedings to the Bankruptcy Court. Over five months later, and shortly before the Colombian Government nationalized Granfinanciera, respondent served a summons on petitioners in Bogota, Colombia. In their answer to the complaint following Granfinanciera's nationalization, both petitioners requested a "trial by jury on all issues so triable." The Bankruptcy Judge denied petitioners' request for a jury trial, deeming a suit to recover a fraudulent transfer "a core action that originally, under the English common law, as I understand it, was a non-jury issue." Following a bench trial, the court dismissed with prejudice respondent's actual fraud claim but entered judgment for respondent on the constructive fraud claim in the amount of $1,500,000 against Granfinanciera and $180,000 against Medex. The District Court affirmed, without discussing petitioners' claim that they were entitled to a jury trial.

The Court of Appeals for the Eleventh Circuit also affirmed. 835 F.2d 1341 (1988). The court found that petitioners lacked a . . . right to a jury trial. . . .

We granted certiorari to decide whether petitioners were entitled to a jury trial, . . . and now reverse. . . .

III.

Petitioners rest their claim to a jury trial on the Seventh Amendment alone. The Seventh Amendment provides: "In Suits at common law, where the value in controversy shall exceed twenty dollars, the right of trial by jury shall be preserved. . . ." We have consistently interpreted the phrase "Suits at common law" to refer to "suits in which *legal* rights were to be ascertained and determined, in contradistinction to those where equitable rights alone were recognized, and equitable remedies were administered." . . .

The form of our analysis is familiar. "First, we compare the statutory action to 18th-century actions brought in the courts of England prior to the merger of the courts of law and equity. Second, we examine the remedy sought and determine whether it is legal or equitable in nature." . . . If, on balance, these two factors indicate that a party is entitled to a jury trial under the Seventh Amendment, we must decide whether Congress may assign and has assigned resolution of the relevant claim to a non-Article III adjudicative body that does not use a jury as fact-finder. . . .

B

The nature of the relief respondent seeks strongly supports [a] finding that the right he invokes should be denominated legal rather than equitable. . . .

. . . Respondent's fraudulent conveyance action plainly seeks relief traditionally provided by law courts or on the law side of courts having both legal and equitable dockets. Unless Congress may and has permissibly withdrawn jurisdiction over that action by courts of law and assigned it exclusively to non-Article III tribunals sitting without juries, the Seventh Amendment guarantees petitioners a jury trial upon request.

IV.

. . . The sole issue before us is whether the Seventh Amendment confers on petitioners a right to a jury trial in the face of Congress' decision to allow a non-Article III tribunal to adjudicate the claims against them.

A

In [Atlas Roofing Co. v. OSHRC, 430 U.S. 442 (1977)], we noted that "when Congress creates new statutory 'public rights,' it may assign their adjudication to an administrative agency with which a jury trial would be incompatible, without violating the Seventh Amendment's injunction that jury trial is to be 'preserved' in 'suits at common law.'" 430 U.S., at 455 (footnote omitted). We emphasized, however, that Congress' power to block application of the Seventh Amendment to a cause of action has limits. Congress may only deny trials by jury in actions at law, we said, in cases where "public rights" are litigated: "Our prior cases support administrative factfinding in only those situations involving 'public rights,' *e.g.*, where the Government is involved in its sovereign capacity under an otherwise valid statute creating enforceable public rights. Wholly private tort, contract, and property cases, as well as a vast range of other cases, are not at all implicated." Id., at 458.

We adhere to that general teaching. As we said in *Atlas Roofing:* "'On the common law side of the federal courts, the aid of juries is not only deemed appropriate but is required by the Constitution itself.'" Id., at 450, n.7, quoting Crowell v. Benson, 285 U.S. 22, 51 (1932). Congress may devise novel causes of action involving public rights free from the strictures of the Seventh Amendment if it assigns their adjudication to tribunals without statutory authority to employ juries as factfinders. But it lacks the power to strip parties contesting matters of private right of their constitutional right to a trial by jury. As we recognized in *Atlas Roofing*, to hold otherwise would be to permit Congress to eviscerate the Seventh Amendment's guarantee by assigning to administrative agencies or courts of equity all causes of action not grounded in state law, whether they originate in a newly fashioned regulatory scheme or possess a long line of common-law forebears. 430 U.S., at 457-458. The Constitution nowhere grants Congress such puissant authority. "[L]egal claims are not magically converted into equitable issues by their presentation to a court of equity," . . . nor can Congress conjure away the Seventh Amendment by mandating that traditional legal claims be brought there or taken to an administrative tribunal.

In certain situations, of course, Congress may fashion causes of action that are closely *analogous* to common-law claims and place them beyond the ambit of the Seventh Amendment by assigning their resolution to a forum in which jury trials are unavailable. See e.g., *Atlas Roofing*, 430 U.S., at 450-461 (workplace safety regulations); Block v. Hirsh, 256 U.S. 135, 158, (1921) (temporary emergency regulation of rental real estate). See also . . . Murray's Lessee v. Hoboken Land and Improvement Co., 18 How. 272, 284 (1856) (Congress "may or may not bring within the cognizance of the courts of the United States, as it may deem proper," matters involving public rights). Congress' power to do so is limited, however, just as its power to place adjudicative authority in non-Article III tribunals is circumscribed. . . . Unless a legal cause of action involves "public rights," Congress may not deprive parties litigating over that such a right of the Seventh Amendment's guarantee to a jury trial.

In *Atlas Roofing, supra*, [430 U.S.,] at 458, we noted that Congress may effectively supplant a common-law cause of action carrying with it a right to a jury trial with a statutory cause of action shorn of a jury trial right if that statutory cause of action inheres in or lies against the Federal Government in its sovereign capacity. Our case law makes plain, however, that the class of "public rights" whose adjudication Congress may assign to administrative agencies or courts of equity sitting without juries is more expansive than *Atlas Roofing*'s discussion suggests. Indeed, our decisions point to the conclusion that, if a statutory cause of action is legal in nature, the question whether the Seventh Amendment permits Congress to assign its adjudication to a tribunal that does not employ juries as factfinders requires the same answer as the question whether Article III allows Congress to assign adjudication of that cause of action to a non-Article III tribunal. For if a statutory cause of action, such as respondent's right to recover a fraudulent conveyance under 11 U.S.C. §548(a)(2), is not a "public right" for Article III purposes, then Congress may not assign its adjudication to a specialized non-Article III court lacking "the essential attributes of the judicial power." . . . And if the action must be tried under the auspices of an Article III court, then the Seventh Amendment affords the party a right to a jury trial whenever the cause of action is legal in nature. Conversely, if Congress may assign the adjudication of a statutory cause of action to a non-Article III tribunal, then the Seventh Amendment poses no independent bar to the adjudication of that action by a nonjury factfinder. . . . In addition to our Seventh Amendment precedents, we therefore rely as well on our decisions exploring the restrictions Article III places on Congress' choice of adjudicative bodies to resolve disputes over statutory rights to determine whether petitioners are entitled to a jury trial.

In our most recent discussion of the "public rights" doctrine as it bears on Congress' power to commit adjudication of a statutory cause of action to a non-Article III tribunal, we rejected the view that "a matter of public rights must at a minimum arise 'between the government and others.'" . . . We held, instead, that the Federal Government need not be a party for a case to revolve around "public rights." . . . The crucial question, in cases not involving the Federal Government, is whether "Congress, acting for a valid legislative purpose pursuant to its constitutional powers under Article I, [has] create[d] a seemingly 'private' right that is so closely integrated into a public regulatory scheme as to be a matter appropriate for agency resolution with limited involvement by the Article III judiciary." . . . If a statutory right is not closely intertwined with a federal regulatory program Congress has power to enact, and if that right neither belongs to nor exists against the Federal Government, then it must be adjudicated by an Article III court.[1] If the right is legal in nature, then it carries with it the Seventh Amendment's guarantee of a jury trial.

---

1. In *Atlas Roofing*, 430 U.S., at 442, 450, n.7, we stated that "[i]n cases which do involve only 'private rights,' this Court has accepted factfinding by an administrative agency, without intervention by a jury, only as an adjunct to an Art. III court, analogizing the agency to a jury or a special master and permitting it in admiralty cases to perform the function of the special master." That statement, however, must be read in context. First, we referred explicitly only to Congress' power, where disputes concern private rights, to provide administrative factfinding instead of jury trials in *admiralty* cases. Civil causes of action in admiralty, however, are not suits at common law for Seventh Amendment purposes, and thus no constitutional right to a jury trial attaches. . . . Second, our statement should not be taken to mean that Congress may assign at least the initial factfinding in all cases involving controversies entirely between private parties to administrative agencies or other tribunals not involving juries, so long as they are established as adjuncts to Article III courts. If that were so, Congress could render the Seventh Amendment a nullity. Rather, that statement, citing Crowell v. Benson, 285 U.S., at 51-65, means only that in *some* cases involving "private rights" as *that term was defined in* Crowell

B

Although the issue admits of some debate, a bankruptcy trustee's right to recover a fraudulent conveyance under 11 U.S.C. §548(a)(2) seems to us more accurately characterized as a private rather than a public right as we have used those terms in our Article III decisions. [Therefore,] we hold . . . that . . . the Seventh Amendment entitles petitioners to the jury trial they requested. Accordingly, the judgment of the Court of Appeals is reversed, and the case is remanded for further proceedings consistent with this opinion.

It is so ordered.

JUSTICE SCALIA, concurring in part and concurring in the judgment.

I join all but Part IV of the Court's opinion. I make that exception because I do not agree with the premise of its discussion: that "the Federal Government need not be a party for a case to revolve around 'public rights.'" . . . In my view a matter of "public rights," whose adjudication Congress may assign to tribunals lacking the essential characteristics of Article III courts, "must at a minimum arise 'between the government and others.'" . . .

NOTES

1. Does administrative exercise of adjudicatory authority violate the constitutional right to trial by jury in civil cases? For a recent negative answer, see Sasser v. EPA, 990 F.2d 127 (4th Cir. 1993) (EPA proceeding assessing penalties for reimpounding wetlands without a permit did not violate Seventh Amendment right to jury trial).

2. How does the Supreme Court answer the above question? Does its answer constitute a revival of the public rights/private rights distinction as the criterion for determining whether adjudicatory power may be exercised by a non-Article III tribunal such as an administrative agency? How should *Granfinanciera* be read after *Stern*? Does the Court seem only to have issues with bankruptcy judges, given that bankruptcy proceedings are more like traditional judicial proceedings? Does that mean that exercise of judicial power within a regulatory agency may be more constitutionally permissible than previously thought?

---

and used in Atlas Roofing — namely, as encompassing all disputes to which the Federal Government is not a party in its sovereign capacity — may Congress dispense with juries as factfinders through its choice of adjudicative forum. Those cases in which Congress may decline to provide jury trials are ones involving statutory rights that are integral parts of a public regulatory scheme and whose adjudication Congress has assigned to an administrative agency or specialized court of equity. Whatever terminological distinctions *Atlas Roofing* may have suggested, we now refer to those rights as "public" rather than "private."

2. State Constitutions and Judicial Power

MCHUGH v. SANTA MONICA RENT CONTROL BOARD

777 P.2d 91 (Cal. 1989)

LUCAS, Chief Justice.

In this appeal we consider whether a provision of the Santa Monica Rent Control Charter Amendment (art. XVIII, Santa Monica City Charter, hereafter Charter Amendment) which provides for administrative adjudication of excess rent claims . . . is unconstitutional because it permits the Santa Monica Rent Control Board (Board) to exercise judicial powers in violation of article VI, section 1 of the California Constitution.

We will conclude that administrative adjudication of excess rent claims under the Charter Amendment does not, in and of itself, violate the judicial powers clause. . . .

I. FACTS

. . .

Two tenants, Smith and Plevka, filed an administrative complaint under the Charter Amendment, asserting plaintiff McHugh had charged them excess rent. After a hearing officer made initial determinations and orders, all parties appealed to the Board. The Board held the tenants had been overcharged, and awarded restitution of excess rent. . . .

Plaintiff filed a petition for a writ of mandate (Code Civ. Proc., §1094.5) pursuant to section 1808. . . . Plaintiff's petition sought to compel the Board to set aside its decision on the ground that administrative adjudication of "excess rents" . . . violates, inter alia, the judicial powers clause of the California Constitution. (Art. VI. §1.) Plaintiff also sought to enjoin the Board from acting on any complaints for excess rent. . . .

After a hearing, the trial court granted plaintiff's and interveners' motions for summary judgment and entered judgment granting the petition for writ of mandate. It issued a peremptory writ ordering the Board to vacate the Plevka and Smith decisions, and declared former section 1809, subdivision (b), of the Charter Amendment "invalid because it requires the . . . Board to exercise judicial powers which fall within the ambit of Article VI, Section 1, of the California Constitution." . . . The Board appealed.

II. ANALYSIS

A. Background

Article VI, section 1 of the California Constitution provides: "The judicial power of this State is vested in the Supreme Court, courts of appeal, superior courts, municipal courts, and justice courts. . . ."

We have often noted that agencies not vested by the Constitution with judicial powers may not exercise such powers. "[A]rticle VI disposes of *all* judicial power not expressly disposed of elsewhere in the Constitution. . . . [Although] the Legislature retains the authority to grant a multitude of powers to local bodies pursuant to article XI, powers of a *judicial* nature are no longer at its disposal." . . . In this case we must determine whether the challenged Charter Amendment provision unconstitutionally authorizes the Board to exercise "judicial powers" within the meaning of article VI, section 1. . . .

C. Constitutional Propriety of the Powers at Issue in This Case

. . .

1. The Power to Make "Restitutive" Money Awards

. . . [P]rior California cases provide no direct guidance on the propriety of administrative restitutive money awards. Cases dealing with administrative licensing agencies, however, suggest that such agencies may properly order reparations as a probationary condition of a licensee, and hence these cases shed some light on the issue posed here. Moreover, the decisions of our sister states provide helpful guidance. The out-of-state decisions unanimously hold that an administrative agency may — consistently with the "judicial powers" doctrine — make restitutive money awards provided (i) doing so is reasonably necessary to effectuate the administrative agency's primary, legitimate regulatory purposes, and (ii) the "essential" judicial power remains ultimately in the courts, through review of agency determinations. We will conclude that these limitations on agency adjudication provide a reasoned and workable test by which to measure challenges under our Constitution's judicial powers clause, and will adopt that test as our own. . . .

b. Sister-State Cases

Our constitutional provision confining "judicial powers" to the courts (Cal. Const., art. VI, §1) has counterparts in most other state constitutions, as well as the federal Constitution. . . . Modern courts, however, have not rigidly construed these provisions. Instead, a more tolerant approach to the delegation of judicial powers has emerged out of a perceived necessity to accommodate administrative adjudication of certain disputes and thereby to cope with increasing demands on our traditional judicial system. . . .

At least nine states, all of which have constitutional provisions substantially identical to California Constitution, article VI, section 1, have considered the propriety of administrative adjudication of restitutive and compensatory "damages." The decisions unanimously hold such remedial power as is involved here does not constitute an impermissible exercise of judicial power . . . . We explain below the guiding principles we glean from these decisions.

c. Guiding Principles: Substantive and Procedural Limitations on the Remedial Power of Administrative Agencies

We conclude . . . that the veritable tidal wave of decisions against plaintiff's view cannot be ignored, and that our sister states' decisions on this issue suggest a workable solution to the constitutional problem posed here.

The better analyzed and more thoughtful decisions, as we read them, set out the following guidelines: An administrative agency may constitutionally hold hearings, determine facts, apply the law to those facts, and order relief—including certain types of monetary relief—so long as (i) such activities are authorized by statute or legislation and are *reasonably necessary* to effectuate the administrative agency's *primary, legitimate regulatory purposes*, and (ii) the "*essential*" *judicial power* (i.e., the power to make enforceable, binding judgments) *remains ultimately in the courts, through review of agency determinations* . . . .

(i) Substantive Limitations on the Remedial Power of Administrative Agencies The view of the judicial powers doctrine embraced by our sister states has the advantage of avoiding meaningless, wooden distinctions (used in a number of older cases) between "quasi-judicial" and "judicial" powers, and at the same time remaining true to the fundamental teaching of the various constitutional judicial powers clauses. The decisions forthrightly recognize that administrative agencies do indeed exercise "judicial-like" powers, and accept the need for broad administrative powers in our increasingly complex government. At the same time, the view espoused by our sister states includes a crucial and workable limiting principle: The agency may exercise *only those powers that are reasonably necessary to effectuate the agency's primary, legitimate regulatory purposes.* Thus, contrary to plaintiff's suggestions, we perceive no danger that the view of judicial power embraced by our sister states will lead to a proliferation of agencies created to adjudicate specialized private disputes, thereby undermining the traditional role of the courts. Plaintiff's fears have not materialized in other states, and many of the decisions expressly caution against any such intrusion.

Practical considerations also militate against a less accommodating view of the judicial powers doctrine. If nonconstitutional administrative agencies were barred from adjudicating all money claims between private individuals who are subject to administrative regulation, such agencies would be precluded from exercising powers routinely employed, and not previously challenged. For example, the authority of the FEHC to award backpay might thereby be called in doubt and the authority of licensing agencies to adjudicate and conditionally order restitution might also be questioned.

(ii) Procedural Limitations on the Remedial Powers of Administrative Agencies In addition to placing reasoned and workable substantive limitations on the remedial powers of administrative agencies, the view of the judicial powers doctrine embraced by our sister states also reserves to the courts the "true" judicial power. Consistently with our prior cases dealing with administrative revocation of professional licenses, the decisions uphold an agency's authority to exercise a challenged remedial power only if the administrative scheme also respects the "principle of check" by providing for judicial review of administrative determinations. It remains, of course, to resolve in different categories of cases, the procedures for and scope of judicial review necessary to fulfill the goal of reserving to the courts this essential attribute of judicial power.

(iii) Conclusion As observed above, there is no modern decision of this state addressing the precise administrative remedial power challenged here. . . . We believe our sister states' approach (i.e., embracing substantive as well as procedural limitations on administrative power) reflects a practical and reasoned understanding of the judicial powers doctrine. With the following considerations and concerns in mind, we, like our sister states, conclude that administrative adjudication and awarding of restitution does not offend our Constitution's judicial powers clause when these substantive and procedural limitations are respected.

We too will carefully apply the "reasonable necessity/legitimate regulatory purpose" requirements in order to guard against unjustified delegation of authority to decide disputes that otherwise belong in the courts. Specifically, we will inquire whether the challenged remedial power is authorized by legislation, and reasonably necessary to accomplish the administrative agency's regulatory purposes. Furthermore, we will closely scrutinize the agency's asserted regulatory purposes in order to ascertain whether the challenged remedial power is merely incidental to a proper, primary regulatory purpose, or whether it is in reality an attempt to transfer determination of traditional common law claims from the courts to a specialized agency whose primary purpose is the processing of such claims. Thus, for example, we would not approve the Board's adjudication of a landlord's common law counterclaims (extraneous to the Board's regulatory functions) against a tenant. Such adjudication would (i) not reasonably effectuate the Board's regulatory purposes — ensuring enforcement of rent levels — and (ii) it would shift the Board's primary purpose from one of ensuring the enforcement of rent levels, to adjudicating a broad range of landlord-tenant disputes traditionally resolved in the courts. Finally, we will continue to apply the "principle of check" in order to reserve to the courts the "true" judicial power.

d. Application of the Limiting Principles to the Facts of this Case

(i) The "Reasonable Necessity/Legitimate Regulatory Purpose" Requirement As noted above, the Board held hearings, heard testimony, and determined that plaintiff charged excess rents of $1,068 to tenant Plevka, and $600.50 to tenant Smith. We conclude that such actions, although judicial in nature, are both authorized by the Charter Amendment and reasonably necessary to accomplish the administrative agency's primary, legitimate regulatory purposes, i.e., setting and regulating maximum rents in the local housing market. The Board's legitimate regulatory authority, and hence its incidental remedial authority, is circumscribed. It may not, and does not, hear and adjudicate all manner of disputes between landlords and tenants. Its authority is derived from the local police powers . . . and extends only so far as necessary to set and regulate rents.

Incidental to that legitimate primary purpose — and "in order to produce an efficient and effective administrative enforcement of the public interest" . . . , the Board may review the rents actually charged, and order necessary adjustments to assure compliance with its price control regulations.

The trial court erred therefore in concluding that the Board exercised judicial powers in violation of the Constitution by adjudicating (subject to judicial review) tenants' claims for excess rents, and ordering restitution of the excess amounts. . . .

3. Right to a Jury Trial

Plaintiff interveners assert that administrative adjudication of monetary relief claims violates the state constitutional right to jury trial (Cal. Const., art. I, §16). They reason that such relief is available only in a court action at which, under the common law, a party has a right to a jury trial. Because we uphold the Board's authority to adjudicate "restitutive" excess rent claims, we also address plaintiff interveners' jury trial contention.

Our Constitution states: "Trial by jury is an inviolate right and shall be secured to all. . . ." We have long observed, "It is the right to trial by jury as it existed at common law which is preserved [by article I, section 16]." . . . We have not, however, previously considered the application of this provision to administrative adjudication.

A number of our sister states have addressed state constitutional jury trial challenges to similar administrative schemes. These decisions, which involve money awards by "antidiscrimination" commissions . . . and by a "landlord-tenant" board . . . unanimously hold that no jury trial right exists as to adjudication of a matter otherwise properly within the regulatory power of an administrative agency.

Our sister courts have emphasized aspects of the federal courts' "public rights" concept as well as other concerns, such as the existence of the action at common law, and the nexus between the challenged power and the agency's regulatory purpose. Read together with their discussions of the judicial powers issue, we adduce from these decisions the following proposition: Once a court has determined that exercise of a challenged administrative power meets the "substantive limitations" requirement imposed by the state constitution's judicial powers doctrine — i.e., the challenged activities are authorized by statute or legislation, and are reasonably necessary to, and primarily directed at, effectuating the administrative agency's primary, legitimate regulatory purposes — then the state constitution's jury trial provision does not operate to preclude administrative adjudication. . . .

We agree with the approach of our sister states. Having previously determined that the Board's adjudication of excess rents meets the substantive-limitations requirement imposed by our judicial powers clause . . . we further conclude that such adjudication is not precluded by article I, section 16. . . .

Plaintiff interveners suggest there is or should be a state constitutional right to jury trial if . . . (ii) the rights involved are "private" rather than "public," and (iii) the "private" right is grounded in the common law. Their argument fails . . . because, according to the very cases on which plaintiff interveners rely, the interests at issue here would be deemed "public" rights properly adjudicable by an administrative agency without a jury.

The "public" versus "private" rights distinction is drawn not from California jurisprudence, but from the federal cases addressing similar issues under, inter alia, the Seventh Amendment of the federal Constitution. That provision states: "In suits at common law, where the value in controversy shall exceed twenty dollars, the right of jury trial shall be preserved. . . ."

Under federal law, the right to jury trial does not attach to the administrative adjudication of "public rights." . . . Behind the "public rights" doctrine lies the idea that when a legislative body acts by statute to promote the general welfare, it is not precluded from establishing administrative enforcement of its statutory scheme — even if some incidental "private" interests (e.g., a money judgment made payable by one private party to another) are thereby affected. Contrary to plaintiff interveners' position, it is quite clear that the rent control matters involved here fall within the traditional scope of the federal "public rights" doctrine. . . .

Considering the [Supreme Court's] statements in [different cases] — it seems clear that the high court would view the matters at issue in this case (a claim of excess rent and adjudication thereof under the ordinance) as involving "public rights," and hence properly resolved by an administrative agency without a jury. . . .

In summary, we conclude that when, as here, a rent control board's adjudication of excess rent meets the substantive-limitations requirement imposed by our judicial powers clause, the Constitution's jury trial provision does not operate to preclude administrative adjudication. We do not adopt plaintiff interveners' suggested test incorporating the high court's "public rights" doctrine. We observe, however, that even under that approach, plaintiff was not entitled to a jury trial under article I, section 16 of the California Constitution.

III. DISPOSITION

For the reasons discussed above, we conclude former section 1809 is not constitutionally infirm. . . .

The judgment is reversed with directions to recall and/or set aside the peremptory writ of mandate issued by the court on November 15, 1983, . . . to deny the petition for writ of mandate in all other respects, and to deny the motions of plaintiff and interveners for summary judgment.

NOTES

1. Does *McHugh* involve "public rights" or only private rights between the landlord and the tenant? Note the California court's rejection of the "suggested test incorporating the high court's 'public rights' doctrine." Which test is better to handle disputes about judicial delegation and jury trial rights — federal or state? Why?

2. *Judicial remedial and penalty power.* The basic remedy in the law courts is the judgment for money damages. May the power to award damages be delegated to an agency? If the answer is yes, what types of damages?

In an early case, State v. Public Service Comm'n, 259 S.W. 445, 447 (Mo. 1924), the court answered no. The statute authorized the state agency to award reparations to a shipper injured by a railroad's exaction of excessive rates. Acting under the statute the agency had ordered defendant railroads to pay a shipper "the sum of $201.52, as damages by reason of the charging and collecting of the unlawful rate." The court held the delegation invalid:

> To determine whether one person is entitled to recover money from another by way of damages cannot be anything but a judicial question, and as such must be determined by the courts. The Public Service Commission is not, and under our Constitution cannot be a court. . . . If the Legislature under-took to empower the Public Service Commission to hear and determine a lawsuit, its act would be void. Such is a judicial function, and must be assigned to the judiciary under our state government. . . . The claim involved in this case is a pure claim for damages. It had no place before the Public Service Commission.

The trend since the 1960s, however, has been to uphold delegation to agencies of power to award damages. A leading case is Jackson v. Concord Co., 253 A.2d 793, 800 (N.J. 1969), where the court in sustaining the authority of a civil rights agency to order reimbursement for out-of-pocket loss suffered in a housing discrimination case, stated: "[A]t this advanced date in the development of administrative law, we see no constitutional objection to legislative authorization to an administrative agency to award, as incidental relief in connection with a subject delegable to it, money damages, ultimate judicial review thereof being available."

3. Although the *McHugh* court upheld agency power to award restitutive damages consistent with the statutory delegation in question, the court did not reach the question of agency ability to award compensatory or punitive damages. In 1991, however, the California Supreme Court struck down as unconstitutional a state agency award of damages for emotional distress and punitive damages. The court stated that "[t]he award of unlimited general compensatory damages is neither necessary [to the housing act's] purpose[, a streamlined and efficient procedure to make a victim of housing discrimination whole,] nor merely incidental thereto; its effect, rather, is to shift the remedial focus . . . to compensating the injured party . . . for the intangible and nonquantifiable injury to his or her psyche suffered as a result of the respondent's unlawful acts, in the manner of a traditional private tort action in a court of law." Walnut Creek Manor v. Fair Employment and Housing Commission, 814 P.2d 704, 715 (Cal. 1991).

In 2002, the California Supreme Court distinguished *Walnut Creek Manor* in upholding an award of emotional distress damages by the state agency. The California court was persuaded that 1992-1993 amendments in the state's fair housing law making state remedies "substantially equivalent" to federal remedies and providing a judicial option to potential claimants allowing them to choose a judicial rather than an administrative route eliminated separation of powers concerns. In so holding, the court stated, "we find persuasive the high court's decision in *CFTC* [*v. Schor*], which predates both *Walnut Creek Manor* and *McHugh*. Using *CFTC*'s rationale, the Commission and its amici curiae maintain that with the available alternative of a civil action and the requirement that all parties must consent to the Commission's jurisdiction, 'separation of powers concerns are diminished.'" Konig v. Fair Employment and Housing Commission, 50 P.3d 718, 751-752 (Cal. 2002). Do you agree that merely providing a court option is sufficient to eliminate concerns about the executive and/or legislative branches encroaching upon judicial power?

Courts not only possess power to award damages, but their money judgments may be enforced by execution. See, e.g., N.Y. Civil Practice Law §5230(b):

> At any time before a judgment is satisfied or vacated, an execution may be issued from the [court], in the county in which the judgment was first docketed, . . . to the sheriffs of one or more counties of the state, directing each of them to satisfy the judgment out of the real and personal property of the judgment debtor . . . and the debts due to him or her.

Another possible method of enforcing agency orders to pay money is illustrated by N.Y. Laws 1975, ch. 329(4)(2):

> The environmental control board shall have power to enforce its final decisions and orders imposing civil penalties, not to exceed ten thousand dollars for each respondent, for violations of laws, rules and regulations enforced by it pursuant to subdivision three of this section as if they were money judgments, without court proceedings, in the manner described herein. After four months from the issuance of such a final decision and order by the board, a copy of such decision and order shall be filed in the office of the clerk of any county within the city. In the event that the decision and order was issued as a result of the respondent being in default, a notice of default shall be mailed to such respondent at least seven days before such filing, and a copy of such notice and a receipt of mailing there for shall be filed with the copy of such decision and order. Upon such filing, such county clerk shall enter and docket such decision and order, in the same manner and with the same effect as a money judgment. Upon such entry and docketing, such decision and order may be enforced as provided in article fifty-two of the civil practice law and rules.

4. *Judicial injunctive relief.* Consider the following:

> Court injunctions are, of course, enforced by the contempt power. Since the [federal] *Brimson* case a century ago, it has been assumed that contempt power is limited to courts and may not be conferred upon administrative agencies. According to the Court in *Brimson*, a body such as the ICC, "could not, under our system of government, and consistently with due process of law, be invested with" contempt power. This was also the view taken by a Louisiana court, which held that "the powers of adjudicating and punishing for contempt are essentially judicial in nature. . . . An administrative agency does not have power to impose punishment for contempt, unless constitutional provisions expressly give the agency that power."

> The established *Brimson* rule notwithstanding, two state cases during the decade [late 1980s to 1990s] uphold agency exercises of contempt power. In the first case, a California statute empowered the Workers' Compensation Appeals Board or any member to "issue . . . all necessary process in proceedings for contempt, in like manner and to the same extent as courts of record." [Morton v. Workers' Compensation Appeals Bd., 238 Cal. Rptr. 651, 653 (Cal. Ct. App. 1987).] The delegation was ruled valid. The second case goes even further. . . . The Rhode Island court ruled that a workers' compensation commissioner possessed criminal contempt power even without any statutory delegation: "We believe that the power to hold persons in criminal contempt is also inherent in performing the duties of the workers' compensation trial commissioner." [Kennedy v. Kenney Mfg. Co., 519 A.2d 585, 586 (R.I. 1987).] This holding was supported by no reasoning or authority; neither *Brimson* nor any other case was cited. Instead, by its *laconic ipse dixit*, the Rhode Island court rejected one of the fundamental limitations on administrative power that has heretofore prevailed in our system.
>
> The conclusion of the California and Rhode Island courts that agencies may be vested with contempt power is contrary to our basic public law conceptions. The contempt power itself is so drastic that legal systems outside the common-law world have refused to confer anything like it even on courts. To vest it in administrative officials utterly ignores the separation of powers by allowing agencies to exercise a power that is so inherently judicial.

Bernard Schwartz, A Decade of Administrative Law: 1987-1996, 32 Tulsa L.J. 493, 512-513 (1997). Do you agree with Schwartz that contempt power should be circumscribed and limited as applied to administrative agencies? Consider the following case.

PEOPLE v. DAVIS

912 N.E.2d 1004 (N.Y. 2009)

CIPARICK, J.

In this appeal arising out of defendant's conviction for failure to comply with a posted sign indicating a New York City park's closing time, we conclude that Criminal Procedure Law §350.20, which permits class B misdemeanors to be tried and determined by judicial hearing officers (JHOs) "upon agreement of the parties," is constitutional and that the parties' agreement to engage in JHO adjudication here — as evidenced by a signed consent form and defense counsel's participation in the JHO proceeding — was valid. . . .

I.

An information charged defendant with violating New York City Parks and Recreation Department Rules (56 RCNY) §1-03(c)(2), which prohibits persons from being in city parks after their posted closing times. Although the Rule contains qualifying language stating that a person may disregard a park sign "upon order by a Police Officer or designated Department employee," the information — which was prepared by a police officer — did not state whether that portion of the Rule applied to defendant. Rather, it indicated that the officer had observed defendant in Brooklyn's Betsy Head Park at 2:06 A.M., on December 15, 2005, despite the fact that a park sign stated a closing time of 9 P.M. Violation of Rule 1-03(c)(2) is punishable as a class B misdemeanor the maximum penalty for which is 90 days' imprisonment and a $1,000 fine.

On February 16, 2006, defendant — represented by counsel — was arraigned and pleaded not guilty. The court informed defendant that he would need to return for trial and that he would receive certain "paper work." Contained in defendant's Criminal Court file is a form entitled "CONSENT TO ADJUDICATION BEFORE A JUDICIAL HEARING OFFICER (JHO)." Although the form explains that defendant's case was being referred to a JHO for "trial and/or final disposition and sentence," it explicitly stated that defendant had "the right to adjudicate this case before a Criminal Court judge." Further, the form listed the scope of the JHO's authority. . . .

> "The Judicial Hearing Officer who adjudicates this case will:
> a) determine all questions of law; and
> b) act as the exclusive trier of all issues of fact; and
> c) render a verdict; and
> d) impose a sentence if required."

Accordingly, the form indicated that the JHO presiding over defendant's class B misdemeanor trial "shall have the same powers as a Criminal Court judge and any action taken by the Judicial Hearing Officer shall be deemed the action of the Criminal Court." The form also stated that defendant would have the right to seek an appeal from the JHO's decision in his case in the same manner as he would had it been tried by a Criminal Court judge. Finally, immediately above its signature line, the form clarified that "[b]y signing this form[,] you hereby consent to having your case adjudicated before a Judicial Hearing Officer."

Defendant apparently signed the JHO consent form. With the assistance of counsel, he proceeded to trial before a JHO and was convicted of violating the relevant Parks Department rule based on the testimony of the observing officer. During trial, defendant did not attempt to prove that he had been granted permission by a police officer or Parks Department employee to remain in Betsy Head Park past its posted closing time. On April 17, 2006, he was sentenced to a $75 fine or ten days in jail. Approximately nine months later, he was resentenced to time served.

The Appellate Term affirmed. . . . A Judge of this Court granted defendant leave to appeal and we now affirm.

II.

. . . The goal of this legislation was to utilize the services of highly-qualified retired judges, or JHOs, to alleviate the backlog and delay that had begun to "seriously cripple[ ]" our State's court system and had "undermine[d] public confidence in the fairness of justice in our state" (*see* Report of the Committee to Utilize the Services of Retired Judges, Bill Jacket, L. 1983, ch. 840, at 60 [hereinafter Retired Judges Report]). One of the ways in which the Legislature sought to alleviate these problems was by granting judges the discretionary authority to assign class B and unclassified misdemeanors to JHOs for adjudication "upon agreement of the parties[.]" In such capacity, JHOs would act as a court. Thus, with consent of the litigants, JHOs would be empowered to "(a) determine all questions of law; (b) act as the exclusive trier of all issues of fact; and (c) render a verdict." Consensual JHO adjudication was intended to contribute to the goal of reducing pernicious calendar congestion, thereby fostering the more efficient administration of criminal justice. The question we must now decide is whether . . . pursuit of this worthy goal comports with the State and Federal Constitutions. For the reasons set forth below, we hold that it does.

III.

Defendant mounts two facial attacks against the constitutionality of CPL 350.20. He contends that it violates New York Constitution Article VI, §15(a), which provides for the establishment of the New York City Criminal Court and sets certain qualifications for that court's judges. Defendant also argues that he has both a federal and state due process right to adjudicate his class B misdemeanor case before a Criminal Court judge and that CPL 350.20 improperly abridges that right. . . .

Defendant's Article VI, §15(a) argument is premised almost entirely on our decision in *Scalza*. In that case, we dealt with CPL 255.20(4), which permits a court to refer any pretrial motion in a criminal case to a JHO for the preparation of a report setting forth the JHO's proposed findings of fact and conclusions of law. . . .

At its outset, *Scalza* held that because the trial court retained the ultimate authority to determine a suppression motion after referral to a JHO "no unauthorized or unconstitutional diversion of the trial court's exclusive jurisdiction and responsibility to decide is threatened[.]" Thus, the *Scalza* Court was not confronted, as we are here, with a situation in which the Legislature acted expressly to permit JHOs to exercise jurisdiction concurrent with that of a Criminal Court judge in cases where the litigants expressly agree to JHO adjudication of a class B misdemeanor.

As noted earlier, a key piece of section 350.20's legislative history is the Retired Judges Report. In that report, the Committee, under the direction of then-Chief Judge Lawrence Cooke, recognized that "the hearing of more minor matters in their entirety by retired judges would free lower-court judges to try more significant matters." It thus recommended that JHOs "be authorized to hear and determine, with the consent of the parties, minor criminal matters not requiring a jury." When JHOs were utilized in "this restrictive fashion," the Committee did "not foresee any constitutional problems."

. . .

It is clear that "[l]egislation which affects the jurisdiction" of a trial court is "not necessarily void." Indeed, in *Matter of Dolce v. Nassau County Traffic & Parking Violations Agency* (7 N.Y.3d 492, 859 N.E.2d 469, 825 N.Y.S.2d 663 [2006]), we held that the Legislature had authority to confer jurisdiction over certain traffic and parking prosecutions to an administrative arm of the Nassau County District Court staffed by JHOs. Such jurisdiction was proper even though JHO adjudication was permitted "without consent of the parties[.]" Thus, here, where consent is a prerequisite to JHO adjudication, we have little difficulty concluding that nothing in Article VI, §15(a) prohibited the Legislature from enacting CPL 350.20.

[The court's discussion of federal and state due process claims and other criminal defenses has been omitted.] . . .

It is important to emphasize that the nature of this case requires us to leave certain questions for another day. Among the issues not now before us is whether the Legislature could empower a non-judge, without a defendant's consent, to adjudicate even a petty criminal case in which — as in this one — imprisonment is a possible outcome (*cf. Matter of Rosenthal v. Hartnett*, 36 N.Y.2d 269, 271, 326 N.E.2d 811, 367 N.Y.S.2d 247 [1975] [approving administrative adjudication of traffic infractions "where such determination may result in the imposition of a fine but not imprisonment"]). Nor do we decide whether trials of felony or class A misdemeanors may be assigned to a non-judge even though a defendant has consented to such adjudication and waived the right to a jury trial. Although we hold that C.P.L. 350.20 is constitutionally valid, our holding is necessarily limited by the particular statutory and factual context that we consider here. There are unquestionably constitutional limits on the extent to which the Legislature can assign the task of adjudicating criminal cases to individuals who are not judges or justices. We have never decided, and do not now decide, exactly what those limits are; we only hold that they have not been exceeded here . . .

. . . Accordingly, the order of the Appellate Term should be affirmed.

NOTES

1. In the 1970s, the problem of traffic offenses congesting state criminal courts led to decriminalization of traffic violations in various states, and in New York City traffic violations were actually delegated to an administrative agency. See State v. Webb, 335 So. 2d 826, 827-828 (Fla. 1976); Force, Administrative Adjudications of Traffic Violations Confronts the Doctrine of Separation of Powers, 49 Tul. L. Rev. 84 (1974). A constitutional challenge to the New York delegation was resolved in favor of the action. See Rosenthal v. Hartnett, 326 N.E.2d 811 (N.Y. 1975). See also Carrow & Reese, State Problems of Mass Administrative Justice: The Administrative Adjudication of Traffic Violations — A Case Study, 28 Admin. L. Rev. 223 (1976). This early move to decriminalize and then remove a class of violations to an administrative agency caused some to worry about whether it signaled a trend that might not be deterred by the constitutional reasoning employed in *Rosenthal.* See Force, Administrative Adjudications, *supra,* at 131: "If administrative agencies can be given authority to adjudicate traffic violations, why can they not be given the power to adjudicate murder cases?" Does the court's reasoning in People v. Davis, above, prevent the delegation of a class of misdemeanors to an agency? What if the agency was run by the court system? What would prevent a legislature from creating such an agency based on the reasoning in *Davis*? Is the *Davis* case an example of *Rosenthal's* chickens coming home to roost? Is it inevitable that administrative agencies will be created to handle claims that are congesting criminal courts?

2. The *Davis* court states toward the end of its opinion:

> Among the issues not now before us is whether the Legislature could empower a non-judge, without a defendant's consent, to adjudicate even a petty criminal case in which — as in this one — imprisonment is a possible outcome. . . . Nor do we decide whether trials of felony or class A misdemeanors may be assigned to a non-judge even though a defendant has consented to such adjudication and waived the right to a jury trial.

912 N.E.2d at 1052 (citation omitted). Based on the *Davis* court's reasoning, how might those questions be answered? Is it enough that there is a problem with court congestion? Must there be an explicit directive in the Constitution preventing such delegation? What is the relationship of agency jurisdiction over criminal cases and the Bill of Rights and comparable state guaranties? Could agency jurisdiction be provided for in all criminal cases where a jury trial right does not apply? Could an agency ever imprison an individual even when the length of imprisonment has been determined in advance by the Legislature?

CHAPTER 2 PROBLEM

Assume that Congress three years ago created the Genetic Regulatory Administration (GRA) to address the growth of genetic engineering firms experimenting with "recombinant DNA." Section I ("Purpose") of the Genetic Regulatory Administration Act (GRAA) states the following:

> Genetic engineering is an important development at the very cusp of scientific advances. More than two decades ago scientists discovered a method for transplanting deoxyribonucleic acid (DNA), the principal substance of genes. Although exchanges and mutations of DNA occur in nature, genetic engineering provides the ability to control these fundamental processes of life and evolution. DNA segments can be recovered and cloned from one organism and inserted into another. The result is known as "recombinant DNA."
>
> Broad claims are made about both the potential benefits and the potential hazards of genetically engineered organisms. Use of recombinant DNA may lead to welcome advances in such areas as food production and disease control. At the same time, however, the environmental consequences of dispersion of genetically engineered organisms are far from clear. The potential environmental risks associated with the deliberate release of genetically engineered organisms or the translocation

> of any new organism into an ecosystem are best described as "low probability, high consequence risk." That is, while there is only a small possibility that damage could occur, the damage that could occur is great. Therefore, it is hereby declared to be the policy of the United States to ensure that organisms with recombinant DNA are released into the environment or any ecosystem only after careful review by the Genetic Regulatory Administration.

In addition to the preceding statement of purpose, Section III(B) ("Procedure") of the GRAA states:

> [A]ll aggrieved persons injured by recombinant DNA release must file a charge with the GRA. The GRA has full authority to adjudicate any charges by a full and complete hearing on the record. Appeals of GRA decisions shall be to the Secretary of the GRA and then to the U.S. Court of Appeals for the Federal Circuit.

Assume that last year, the GRA issued a series of regulations, through proper means under the Act, relating to the production, labeling, and care of Genetically Modified Organisms (GMOs) used in food. The GRA requires broadly that any issues involving injury of any kind related to GMOs must first be presented to the GRA in the form of an administrative complaint. Injury was defined by the GRA to include any kind of claim of fraud in labeling and negligence in production methods, including uncontrolled dispersal of GMO-treated plants or seeds.

Early this year, Tele-Tex Corporation began using GMOs in its various multistate operations involved in food processing. Tele-Tex's subsidiary, TT Foods, is involved in every facet of food production, from seed harvesting and seed production to the actual manufacturing of food products. TT Foods produces a line of foods called "100% Natural." This line had always in fact been composed of natural food products, but this year some products, including its vegetable oils, were made with GMO plants whose genes had been altered by laboratory scientists to exhibit traits that the seeds did not produce naturally. TT Foods began early this year to ask its farmers to plant GMO seeds but did not instruct these farmers how to grow the GMO crops in a way that would prevent spread of GMO seeds to neighboring farms that plant natural, non-GMO seeds for their crops. Both of these actions by TT Foods arguably violate GRA rules related to GMO labeling and use. Evaluate the legality of the GRA. If consumers and farmers wanted to sue Tele-Tex and TT Foods in court for violating GRA rules, how would you advise them?

CHAPTER 3

Investigations and Privacy

Most agencies are assigned the role of enforcing the statutory scheme they administer. As part of the process of enforcement, agencies require information, and they can obtain that information in a number of ways, including requiring that records be kept, conducting inspections and searches, and compelling the production of testimony or documents. Generally, agencies obtain information by pursuing two broad avenues: the agency can obtain voluntary disclosure of information, or it can seek to compel disclosure.

With respect to voluntary disclosure, an agency is free to request, and parties will often provide, information on a voluntary basis. To the extent agencies are seeking uncontroversial, empirical, or benign data, the benefits of cooperation will almost undoubtedly outweigh the consequences of disclosure. Where, however, agencies are seeking information that has the potential to result in an enforcement action, the decision to voluntarily cooperate is more complicated. Some agencies, such as the Securities and Exchange Commission, provide incentives to voluntary disclosure by taking cooperation into account when deciding whether to bring an action or in determining the appropriate sanctions.

With respect to compulsory disclosure, agencies have a number of tools to force compliance, though they face some constraints as well. When an agency seeks to conduct a search, the agency is bound by constitutional constraints, including the Fourth Amendment warrant requirement. As students of criminal procedure learn, however, the warrant requirement is perhaps most notable for its exceptions, and one of those exceptions is particularly important in searches by agencies. Courts have recognized that industries that are pervasively regulated — such as banks, liquor stores, pharmacies, gun stores, brokers, and investment advisers — have a lower expectation of privacy, and that agencies, therefore, often can conduct inspections without the need for a warrant. In addition to conducting searches or inspections, an agency can compel testimony from individuals as well as the production of documents. Although agencies are often permitted discretion to determine the level of formality they apply to investigations, compelled disclosures are generally mandated through the issuance of subpoenas.

Once an agency acquires information, whether voluntarily disclosed or not, privacy issues can arise. An agency may be compelled to disclose the acquired information under the Federal Freedom of Information Act (FOIA) or state counterparts. The FOIA contains discrete exemptions from disclosure, but they may not apply to the acquired information. In addition, use of any FOIA exemptions is discretionary. The agency may waive an exemption if it sees fit, whether the party from whom the information was obtained agrees or not.

Privacy and information collection by agencies can have a constitutional dimension. While agencies are allowed to collect information including data that raises privacy concerns, the Supreme Court has imposed at least modest limits, among them that collection must be reasonable and must be accompanied by "substantial protections against disclosure to the public." Privacy Act, 5 U.S.C.A. §552a. This chapter deals with the powers that enable agencies to secure needed information. It should be noted at the outset, however, that agency power to acquire information is both a necessity and a power that may be exercised oppressively. As the Supreme Court has put it: "Officious examination can be expensive, so much so that it eats up men's substance. It can be time consuming, clogging the processes of business. It can become persecution when carried beyond reason." Oklahoma Press Publishing Co. v. Walling, 327 U.S. 186 (1946). To be exercised properly, administrative investigatory power should be used, not as an end, but only as a means by which an agency can secure the information needed to enable it to make rational use of its substantive powers. When investigatory power becomes a method of harassment through officious intermeddling or even as a coercive device with substantive impact, it has been perverted from its proper purpose. This chapter will explore the limits on an agency's authority to use these tools to compel information.

A INVESTIGATIONS AND INSPECTIONS

Most agencies have broad authority to conduct investigations to determine whether violations of the statutory framework have occurred. Before conducting its investigation, however, an agency need not have particularized knowledge or belief that a violation has occurred. Indeed, an agency may launch an investigation "merely on suspicion that the law is being violated, or even just because it wants assurance that it is not." United States v. Morton Salt Co., 338 U.S. 632, 642-643 (1950).

Once an investigation begins, courts have construed an agency's investigatory authority broadly. In Dow Chem. Co. v. United States, 476 U.S. 227 (1985), a case better known for the Fourth Amendment challenge to aerial photographs taken by the EPA, defendants also challenged the agency's statutory authority to engage in the action. The Court made short shrift of the argument:

> Congress has vested in EPA certain investigatory and enforcement authority, without spelling out precisely how this authority was to be exercised in all the myriad circumstances that might arise in monitoring matters relating to clean air and water standards. When Congress invests an agency with enforcement and investigatory authority, it is not necessary to identify explicitly each and every technique

> that may be used in the course of executing the statutory mission. Aerial observation authority, for example, is not usually expressly extended to police for traffic control, but it could hardly be thought necessary for a legislative body to tell police that aerial observation could be employed for traffic control of a metropolitan area, or to expressly authorize police to send messages to ground highway patrols that a particular over-the-road truck was traveling in excess of 55 miles per hour. Common sense and ordinary human experience teach that traffic violators are apprehended by observation.

Id. at 233.

When an agency investigation is contemplated or underway, stringent limitations may require the safeguarding of material and prohihit the destruction of documents. The Sarbanes-Oxley Act, adopted in the wake of the Enron and Worldcom scandals, substantially changed the consequences of document destruction that occurs in the wake of an investigation. Known as the anti-shredding provision, §802 of Sarbanes-Oxley amended the law to broaden the circumstances when document destruction can be criminally prosecuted. See 18 U.S.C. §1519. The provision criminalizes the knowing destruction (or alteration) of "tangible objects" used to record or preserve information, "with the intent" to impede an investigation. See Yates v. U.S., 574 U.S. 528 (2015) (holding that the disposal of undersized fish did not involve a tangible object). The provision does not require that an agency investigation actually be underway; it is enough that the destruction occur in contemplation of an investigation.

1. Voluntary Disclosure

In obtaining information during an investigation, an agency may simply request and receive the necessary documents and testimony without resort to a compulsory process. Voluntary disclosure is quite common as a regulated party has a number of incentives to cooperate with an agency, especially one with which it has an ongoing regulatory relationship. The agency, too, may have incentives for seeking voluntary disclosure as it may lack the statutory authority (i.e., the Postal Rate Commission cannot issue subpoenas), time, or motivation to compel disclosure.

More commonly, though, even if the agency has the authority to compel information disclosure, it may choose the simpler and less formal method of requesting the information voluntarily. If an agency wants to take a look at a particular transaction or situation to determine whether anything improper occurred, a request for certain documents or for testimony may result in quick resolution of the matter. In addition, voluntary disclosure avoids a sometimes time-consuming internal process that must be undertaken before the staff of an agency can use compulsory methods of compelling information. See 17 C.F.R. §202.5 (2004) (requiring approval of a formal order of investigation by the Securities and Exchange Commission before staff can issue subpoenas).

Voluntary disclosure also occurs where the agency requests information it could otherwise not compel. An important issue in the area of voluntary disclosure concerns the impact on the attorney-client and work product privileges. Ordinarily, materials subject to these privileges can be withheld from disclosure to an agency, but sometimes companies give them to the agency voluntarily. As the case below indicates, the risk of these voluntary disclosures may be their dissemination not just within the agency, but also beyond the agency to which they were originally provided.

IN RE PACIFIC PICTURES CORP.

679 F.3d 1121 (9th Cir. 2012)

O'SCANNLAIN, Circuit Judge:

We must decide whether a party waives attorney-client privilege forever by voluntarily disclosing privileged documents to the federal government.

I

In the 1930s, writer Jerome Siegel and illustrator Joe Shuster joined forces to create the character that would eventually become Superman. They ceded their intellectual property rights to D.C. Comics when they joined the company as independent contractors in 1937. Since the Man of Steel made his first appearance in 1938, he has been fighting for "truth, justice, and the American way." Shuster, Siegel, their heirs ("Heirs"), and D.C. Comics have been fighting for the rights to his royalties for almost as long.

Marc Toberoff, a Hollywood producer and a licensed attorney, stepped into the fray around the turn of the millennium. As one of his many businesses, Toberoff pairs intellectual property rights with talent and markets these packages to movie studios. Having set his sights on Superman, Toberoff approached the Heirs with an offer to manage preexisting litigation over the rights Siegel and Shuster had ceded to D.C. Comics. He also claimed that he would arrange for a new Superman film to be produced. To pursue these goals, Toberoff created a joint venture between the Heirs and an entity he owned. Toberoff served as both a business advisor and an attorney for that venture. The ethical and professional concerns raised by Toberoff's actions will likely occur to many readers, but they are not before this court.

While the preexisting litigation was pending, Toberoff hired a new lawyer to work for one of his companies. This attorney remained in Toberoff's employ for only about three months before allegedly absconding with copies of several documents from the Siegel and Shuster files. Unsuccessful in his alleged attempt to use the documents to solicit business from the Heirs, this attorney sent the documents to executives at D.C. Comics. While he did not include his name with the package, he did append a cover letter, written in the form of a timeline, outlining in detail Toberoff's alleged master plan to capture Superman for himself.

This happened no later than June 2006, and the parties have been battling over what should be done with these documents ever since. Rather than exploiting the documents, D.C. Comics entrusted them to an outside attorney and sought to obtain them through ordinary discovery in the two ongoing lawsuits over Superman. Considering every communication he had with the Heirs to be privileged — regardless of whether the communication was in his capacity as a business advisor or an attorney — Toberoff resisted all such efforts. Ultimately, in April 2007, a magistrate judge ordered certain documents, including the attorney's cover letter, turned over to D.C. Comics. A few months later, Toberoff at long last reported the incident to the authorities (specifically the Federal Bureau of Investigation). In December 2008, Toberoff finally produced at least some of the documents.

In 2010, D.C. Comics filed this lawsuit against Toberoff, the Heirs, and three entities in which Toberoff owned a controlling interest (collectively, the "Petitioners"), claiming that Toberoff interfered with its contractual relationships with the Heirs. The attorney's cover letter formed the basis of the lawsuit and was incorporated into the complaint. Toberoff has continued to resist the use of any of the documents taken from his offices, including those already disclosed to D.C. Comics and especially the cover letter.

About a month after the suit was filed, Toberoff asked the Office of the United States Attorney for the Central District of California to investigate the theft. In response to a request from Toberoff, the U.S. Attorney's Office issued a grand jury subpoena for the documents as well as a letter stating that if Toberoff voluntarily complied with the subpoena the Government would "not provide the . . . documents . . . to non-governmental third parties except as may be required by law or court order." The letter also confirmed that disclosure would indicate that "Toberoff has obtained all relevant permissions and consents needed (if any) to provide the . . . documents . . . to the government." Armed with this letter, Toberoff readily complied with the subpoena, making no attempt to redact anything from the documents.

D.C. Comics immediately requested all documents disclosed to the U.S. Attorney, claiming that the disclosure of these unredacted copies waived any remaining privilege. Examining the weight of authority from other circuits, the magistrate judge agreed that a party may not selectively waive attorney-client privilege. . . .

III

Under certain circumstances, the attorney-client privilege will protect communications between clients and their attorneys from compelled disclosure in a court of law. See Upjohn Co. v. United States, 449 U.S. 383, 389 (1981). Though this in some way impedes the truth-finding process, we have long recognized that "the advocate and counselor [needs] to know all that relates to the client's reasons for seeking representation" if he is to provide effective legal advice. Trammel v. United States, 445 U.S. 40, 51(1980); *see also* 8 John Henry Wigmore,

Evidence §2290 (John T. McNaughton, ed. 1961). As such, we recognize the privilege in order to "encourage full and frank communication between attorneys and their clients and thereby promote broader public interests in the observance of law and administration of justice. *Upjohn Co.*, 449 U.S. at 389.

Nonetheless, because, like any other testimonial privilege, this rule "contravene[s] the fundamental principle that the public has a right to every man's evidence," *Trammel*, 445 U.S. at 50 (internal alterations and quotation marks omitted), we construe it narrowly to serve its purposes, see, e.g., United States v. Martin, 278 F.3d 988, 999 (9th Cir. 2002). In particular, we recognize several ways by which parties may waive the privilege. See, e.g., Hernandez v. Tanninen, 604 F.3d 1095, 1100 (9th Cir. 2010). Most pertinent here is that voluntarily disclosing privileged documents to third parties will generally destroy the privilege. *Id.* The reason behind this rule is that, "'[i]f clients themselves divulge such information to third parties, chances are that they would also have divulged it to their attorneys, even without the protection of the privilege.'" Comment, *Stuffing the Rabbit Back into the Hat: Limited Waiver of the Attorney—Client Privilege in an Administrative Agency Investigation*, 130 U. Pa. L. Rev. 1198, 1207 (1982). Under such circumstances, there simply is no justification to shut off judicial inquiry into these communications.

Petitioners concede that this is the general rule, but they assert a number of reasons why it should not apply to them.

A

Petitioners' primary contention is that because Toberoff disclosed these documents to the government, as opposed to a civil litigant, his actions did not waive the privilege as to the world at large. That is, they urge that we adopt the theory of "selective waiver" initially accepted by the Eight Circuit, Diversified Indus., Inc. v. Meredith, 572 F.2d 596 (8th Cir. 1978) (en banc), but rejected by every other circuit to consider the issue since, see In re Qwest Communications, 450 F.3d 1179 (10th Cir. 2006); Burden-Meeks v. Welch, 319 F.3d 897, 899 (7th Cir. 2003); In re Columbia/HCA Healthcare Corp. Billing Practices Litig., 293 F.3d 289, 295 (6th Cir. 2002) [hereinafter "In re Columbia"]; United States v. Mass. Inst. of Tech., 129 F.3d 681, 686 (1st Cir. 1997); Genentech, Inc. v. United States Int'l Trade Comm'n, 122 F.3d 1409, 1416-18 (Fed. Cir. 1997); In re Steinhardt Partners, L.P., 9 F.3d 230, 236 (2d Cir. 1993); Westinghouse Elec. Corp. v. Republic of Philippines, 951 F.2d 1414, 1425 (3d Cir. 1991); In re Martin Marietta Corp., 856 F.2d 619, 623-24 (4th Cir. 1988); Permian Corp. v. United States, 665 F.2d 1214, 1221 (D.C. Cir. 1981).

As the magistrate judge noted, we have twice deferred judgment on whether we will accept a theory of selective waiver. United States v. Bergonzi, 403 F.3d 1048, 1050 (9th Cir. 2005) (per curiam); Bittaker v. Woodford, 331 F.3d 715, 720 n. 5 (9th Cir. 2003) (en banc). But we share the concerns expressed by many of our sister circuits about the cursory analysis behind the *Diversified* rule. The Eighth Circuit—the first court of appeals to consider the issue—adopted what has become a highly controversial rule only because it concluded that "[t]o hold otherwise may have the effect of thwarting the developing procedure of corporations to employ independent outside counsel to investigate and advise them in order to protect stockholders." *Diversified*, 572 F.2d at 611. This apprehension has proven unjustified. Officers of public corporations, it seems, do not require a rule of selective waiver to employ outside consultants or voluntarily to cooperate with the government. See, e.g., *Westinghouse Elec. Corp.*, 951 F.2d at 1426.

More importantly, such reasoning does little, if anything, to serve the public good underpinning the attorney-client privilege. That is, "selective waiver does not serve the purpose of encouraging full disclosure to one's attorney in order to obtain informed legal assistance; it merely encourages voluntary disclosure to government agencies, thereby extending the privilege beyond its intended purpose." Id. at 1425.

It may well be that encouraging cooperation with the government is an alternative route to the ultimate goal of promoting adherence to the law. *In re Columbia*, 293 F.3d at 311 (Boggs, J., dissenting). And there are those who assert that "an exception to the third-party waiver rule need [not] be moored to the justifications of the attorney-client privilege." Id. at 308 (emphasis omitted). We disagree. If we were to unmoor a privilege from its underlying justification, we would at least be failing to construe the privilege narrowly. Cf. Univ. of Pa. v. EEOC, 493 U.S. 182, 189 (1990) (citing *Trammel*, 445 U.S. at 50; United States v. Bryan, 339 U.S. 323, 331 (1950). And more likely, we would be creating an entirely new privilege. *In re Qwest Commc'ns Int'l*, 450 F.3d 1179; *Westinghouse*, 951 F.2d at 1425.

It is not beyond our power to create such a privilege. *Univ. of Pa.*, 493 U.S. at 189 (noting that Fed. R. Evid. 501 provides certain flexibility to adopt privilege rules on a case-by-case basis). But as doing so requires balancing competing societal interests in access to evidence and in promoting certain types of communication, the Supreme Court has warned us not to "exercise this authority expansively." Id.; see also United States v. Nixon, 418 U.S. 683, 710, 94 S. Ct. 3090, 41 L. Ed. 2d 1039 (1974). Put simply, "[t]he balancing of conflicting interests of this type is particularly a legislative function." *Univ. of Pa.*, 493 U.S. at 189, 110 S. Ct. 577.

Since *Diversified*, there have been multiple legislative attempts to adopt a theory of selective waiver. Most have failed. Report of the Advisory Committee on Evidence Rules, May 15, 2007, at 4, *available at* http://www.uscourts.gov/uscourts/RulesAndPolicies/rules/Reports/2007-05-Committee_Report-Evidence.pdf (reporting the selective waiver provision separately from the general proposed rule); *SEC Statement in Support of Proposed Section 24(d) of the Securities Exchange Act of 1934*, 16 Sec. Reg. & L. Rep. 461 (Mar. 2, 1984). *But see* H.R. Rep. No. 870, 96th Cong., 1st Sess. (1980), 1980 U.S.C.C.A.N. 2716, codified at 15 U.S.C. §1312. Given that Congress has declined broadly to adopt a new privilege to protect disclosures of attorney-client privileged materials to the government, we will not do so here. *Univ. of Pa.*, 493 U.S. at 189, 110 S. Ct. 577 (requiring federal courts to be particularly cautious when legislators have "considered the relevant competing concerns but [have] not provided the privilege").

B

Petitioners next assert that even if we reject selective waiver as a general matter, we should enforce a purported confidentiality agreement based upon the letter from the U.S. Attorney's Office. Though no circuit has officially adopted such a rule, at least two have "left the door open to selective waiver" where there is a confidentiality agreement.*In re Columbia*, 293 F.3d at 301 (discussing *Steinhardt* and Dellwood Farms, Inc. v. Cargill, 128 F.3d 1122 (7th Cir. 1997)); see also *In re QwestCommc'ns Int'l*, 450 F.3d at 1192-94 (describing such a rule as a "leap" but declining to reject it completely).

Assuming that this letter constitutes a confidentiality agreement, Petitioners have provided no convincing reason that post hoc contracts regarding how information may be revealed encourage frank conversation at the time of the advice. Indeed, as the Sixth Circuit has noted, while this approach "certainly protects the expectations of the parties to the confidentiality agreement, it does little to serve the 'public ends' of adequate legal representation that the attorney-client privilege is designed to protect." *In re Columbia*, 293 F.3d at 303. Instead, recognizing the validity of such a contract "merely [adds] another brush on an attorney's palette [to be] utilized and manipulated to gain tactical or strategic advantage." *Steinhardt*, 9 F.3d at 235; *cf. Permian Corp.*, 665 F.2d at 1221. And it would undermine the public good of promoting an efficient judicial system by fostering uncertainty and encouraging litigation. *Upjohn*, 449 U.S. at 393 (noting that an "uncertain privilege . . . is little better than no privilege at all").

The only justification behind enforcing such agreements would be to encourage cooperation with the government. But Congress has declined to adopt even this limited form of selective waiver. *See Statement of Congressional Intent Regarding Rule 502 of the Federal Rules of Evidence*, 154 Cong. Rec. H. 7817 (2008), *reprinted in* Fed. R. Evid. 502 addendum to comm. n subdivision (d) (noting that Rule 502 "does not provide a basis for a court to enable parties to agree to a selective waiver of the privilege, such as to a federal agency conducting an investigation"). As such, we reject such a theory here.

. . .

IV

Because Petitioners have not established error, we need not discuss the other *Bauman* factors. The petition for mandamus is DENIED.

NOTES

1. Why would anyone voluntarily disclose information to a government agency that results in a waiver of the attorney-client and work product privilege? For at least a partial answer, see Report of Investigation Pursuant to Section 21(a) of the Securities Exchange Act of 1934 and Commission Statement on the Relationship of Cooperation to Agency Enforcement Decisions, Exchange Act Release No. 44969 (Oct. 23, 2001) (noting that company would not be charged in part because of cooperation with staff of SEC; cooperation included its willingness not to "invoke the attorney-client privilege, work product protection or other privileges or protections with respect to any facts uncovered in the investigation").

2. How will this decision and others like it impact agency investigations? Why was this particular type of information so important to the private parties involved?

3. The underlying issue here of whether a "selective waiver" is cognizable percolated in the courts for a few years but has mostly resolved consistent with the reasoning of *Pacific Pictures*. Stepping back from the court's holding, though, what are the arguments in favor of continuing to recognize a privilege with regard to material disclosed to an agency? What would be the benefits of such a privilege? Is the existence of the privilege an appropriate topic for the courts or is there another option for determination of the issue? For example, if the courts or Congress were to allow disclosure without waiving the privilege, who would benefit the most from that approach, the government or the company under investigation? At a minimum, it would make it harder for companies to resist "voluntary" disclosure of privileged information to the government.

4. Interaction with an agency on a voluntary basis does not change the rules with respect to the obligation of truthfulness. False statements made to an agency may be criminally prosecuted, even if given voluntarily and not under oath. See 18 U.S.C. §1001. Martha Stewart was convicted under this provision for giving false statements to SEC officials. See United States v. Stewart, 323 F. Supp. 2d 606 (S.D.N.Y. 2004). Similarly, materials voluntarily disclosed to an agency may be obtained by third parties (even competitors) under the FOIA, although trade secrets or confidential commercial information may be protected.

2. Compulsory Disclosure

An agency can seek the compulsory disclosure of information either in addition to or in lieu of pursuing voluntary disclosure of information. The particular methods available to an agency are limited to those statutorily granted to the agency. Nothing in the APA provides the substantive authority to compel disclosure. Methods of compelling disclosure most commonly include on-site visits, searches, inspections, and examinations; and the compelling of testimony or documents, usually pursuant to a subpoena. Of course, in addition to statutory and procedural constraints, agencies, as government actors, are also subject to constitutional limitations.

a. Administrative Searches and Their Scope

Agencies can conduct searches, including inspections, examinations, and other on-site visits from agency personnel. The nature and breadth of the inspection depends upon the authority granted to the agency by statute. In some cases, the inspection is limited to a review of required books, records, and other documents. See §17(b), 15 U.S.C. §78q(b) (authorizing Securities and Exchange Commission to examine required records for broker-dealers and other entities that operate in the securities markets). In other cases, the scope is substantially broader. See 42 U.S.C. §263a(g) (noting that for inspection of certain laboratories, "Secretary shall have access to all facilities, equipment, materials, records, and information that the Secretary determines have a bearing on whether the laboratory is being operated in accordance with this section").

Generally, agencies need not provide advance notice of an inspection, although they sometimes do so as a courtesy. Advance notice can facilitate the agency's task by allowing the company to have the relevant material ready for inspection. On the other hand, of course, advance notice poses the risk of thwarting the agency's ability to expose violations.

Of course, government agencies conducting searches or inspections are not exempt from the Constitution's warrant requirement. U.S. Const. amend. IV. See Michigan v. Clifford, 464 U.S. 287, 291 (1984) ("administrative searches generally require warrants"). However, the standards may be different from those required of local police investigating crimes. Reasoning that the purposes underlying administrative searches are distinct from those motivating criminal searches, courts only require that such searches meet the Fourth Amendment's "reasonableness" requirement. In the context of administrative searches, reasonableness will likely require a lower quantum of probable cause to justify an administrative warrant for the search.

The next case, *Camara*, settled the question of whether administrative searches required warrants and articulated the foundational standards for agency searches.

CAMARA v. MUNICIPAL COURT OF THE CITY AND COUNTY OF SAN FRANCISCO

387 U.S. 523 (1967)

Justice White delivered the opinion of the Court. [A San Francisco housing inspector was conducting a routine health and safety inspection to locate possible housing code violations when he developed a suspicion that Roland Camara was using his space impermissibly. The inspector asked Camara for permission to inspect the premises but Camara refused to allow the warrantless inspection. The inspector left but returned two additional times without a warrant; Camara denied entry each time. The housing department filed a complaint against Camara for refusing to permit a lawful inspection and Camara was arrested. Camara claimed that, in the absence of a warrant, the inspection was not lawful as it would have violated his rights under the Fourth and Fourteenth Amendments.] . . .

II

The Fourth Amendment provides that "no Warrants shall issue, but upon probable cause." Borrowing from more typical Fourth Amendment cases, appellant argues not only that code enforcement inspection programs must be circumscribed by a warrant procedure, but also that warrants should issue only when the inspector possesses probable cause to believe that a particular dwelling contains violations of the minimum standards prescribed by the code being enforced. We disagree.

In cases in which the Fourth Amendment requires that a warrant to search be obtained, "probable cause" is the standard by which a particular decision to search is tested against the constitutional mandate of reasonableness. To apply this standard, it is obviously necessary first to focus upon the governmental interest which allegedly justifies official intrusion upon the constitutionally protected interests of the private citizen. . . .

Unlike the search pursuant to a criminal investigation, the inspection programs at issue here are aimed at securing city-wide compliance with minimum physical standards for private property. The primary governmental interest at stake is to prevent even the unintentional development of conditions which are hazardous to public health and safety. Because fires and epidemics may ravage large urban areas, because unsightly conditions adversely affect the economic values of neighboring structures, numerous courts have upheld the police power of municipalities to impose and enforce such minimum standards even upon existing structures. In determining whether a particular inspection is reasonable — and thus in determining whether there is probable cause to issue a warrant for that inspection — the need for the inspection must be weighed in terms of these reasonable goals of code enforcement.

There is unanimous agreement among those most familiar with this field that the only effective way to seek universal compliance with the minimum standards required by municipal codes is through routine periodic inspections of all structures. It is here that the probable cause debate is focused, for the agency's decision to conduct an area inspection is unavoidably based on its appraisal of conditions in the area as a whole, not on its knowledge of conditions in each particular building. Appellee contends that, if the probable cause standard urged by appellant is adopted, the area inspection will be eliminated as a means of seeking compliance with code standards and the reasonable goals of code enforcement will be dealt a crushing blow.

. . . The second argument is in effect an assertion that the area inspection is an unreasonable search. Unfortunately, there can be no ready test for determining reasonableness other than by balancing the need to search against the invasion which the search entails. But we think that a number of persuasive factors combine to support the reasonableness of area code-enforcement inspections. First, such programs have a long history of judicial and public acceptance. See Frank v. Maryland, 359 U.S., at 367-371. Second, the public interest demands that all dangerous conditions be prevented or abated, yet it is doubtful that any other canvassing technique would achieve acceptable results. Many such conditions — faulty wiring is an obvious example — are not observable from outside the building and indeed may not be apparent to the inexpert occupant himself. Finally, because the inspections are neither personal in nature nor aimed at the discovery of evidence of crime, they involve a relatively limited invasion of the urban citizen's privacy. . . .

Having concluded that the area inspection is a "reasonable" search of private property within the meaning of the Fourth Amendment, it is obvious that "probable cause" to issue a warrant to inspect must exist if reasonable legislative or administrative standards for conducting an area inspection are satisfied with respect to a particular dwelling. Such standards, which will vary with the municipal program being enforced, may be based upon the passage of time, the nature of the building (*e.g.*, a multi-family apartment house), or the condition of the entire area, but they will not necessarily depend upon specific knowledge of the condition of the particular dwelling. . . .

NOTES

1. *Camara* sets the standard for obtaining an administrative search warrant. The standard does not require evidence of a specific violation but authorizes an "area inspection" designed to protect public health and safety. Does that mean that there are no standards that must be met to obtain an administrative warrant?

2. In Marshall v. Barlow's Inc., 436 U.S. 307 (1978), the Supreme Court explained the standard for an administrative warrant:

> For purposes of an administrative search such as this, probable cause justifying the issuance of a warrant may be based not only on specific evidence of an existing violation but also on a showing that "reasonable legislative or administrative standards for conducting an . . . inspection are satisfied with respect to a particular [establishment]." Camara v. Municipal Court, 387 U.S., at 538. A warrant showing that a specific business has been chosen for an OSHA search on the basis of a general administrative plan for the enforcement of the Act derived from neutral sources such as, for example, dispersion of employees in various types of industries across a given area, and the desired frequency of searches in any of the lesser divisions of the area, would protect an employer's Fourth Amendment rights.

Id. at 320-321. What does this standard mean? What does an agency need to show to constitutionally conduct an inspection or search?

3. In the criminal context, probable cause generally requires evidence of individualized wrongdoing. How is this different than in the administrative context? Why are the two standards different? Could an administrative search warrant ever be used solely to acquire evidence of criminal violations? Why not? For a case where an administrative warrant was suppressed as pretextual, see United States v. Johnson, 994 F.2d 740 (10th Cir. 1993). However, as New York v. Burger, *infra*, 482 U.S. 691, 712 (1987), shows, these cases can be exceedingly difficult to prove. In *Burger*, though, the police, rather than agency personnel, conducted the inspection, the Court upheld the constitutionality of the search.

4. From a practical perspective, what is the benefit of obtaining an administrative warrant? What protection does it provide to the recipient?

5. What do you make of the Court's conclusion that these types of inspections "involve a relatively limited invasion" of privacy? Assuming a warrant has been properly issued (or an exception to the warrant requirement exists, something we will explore in *Burger, infra*), are there any limits on the scope of the search?

6. Applying a standard as if in an administrative context, in 2009, the Supreme Court addressed the reasonableness of a warrantless search in a case in which school officials subjected a 13-year-old student to a search of her bra and underpants based on suspicion that the girl had brought to school prohibited prescription and over-the-counter medication. In Safford Unified School District #1 v. Redding, 557 U.S. 364 (2009), the Court articulated that a determination of the reasonableness of a search requires a balancing between the danger and the intrusion. "Th[e] suspicion [present in the case] was enough to justify a search of [the student's] backpack and outer clothing" but did not justify the intrusive search of the girl's undergarments. The Court held that the scope of a search will be permissible only when it is "not excessively intrusive in light of the age and sex of the student and the nature of the infraction."

> We do mean, though, to make it clear that . . . to limit a school search to reasonable scope requires the support of reasonable suspicion of danger or of resort to underwear for hiding evidence of wrongdoing before a search can reasonably make the quantum leap from outer clothes and backpacks to exposure of intimate parts. The meaning of such a search, and the degradation its subject may reasonably feel, place a search that intrusive in a category of its own demanding its own specific suspicions.

If you were counsel to a public school district and you received a call from the principal of a high school asking whether he or she could search a student's apparel for drugs, what advice would you give? How would you distinguish the *Safford* case? Whatever your advice, could you be certain that it would cause the search to remain within constitutional boundaries? If not, what would be the potential consequences to the district based upon this case?

The next case, *Platteville*, addresses the potential that an agency might use its investigative authority as a pretext to conduct a wider search.

PLATTEVILLE AREA APARTMENT ASS'N v. CITY OF PLATTEVILLE

179 F.3d 574 (7th Cir. 1999)

POSNER, Chief Judge.

Owners and tenants of rental housing in the City of Platteville, Wisconsin, brought this suit in federal district court to enjoin, primarily as a violation of the Fourth Amendment, the enforcement of a city ordinance that authorizes periodic searches of rental housing to determine compliance with the city's housing code. The district court gave the plaintiffs some of the relief they sought but not all, and both sides have appealed. The principal issue concerns the propriety of searching for violations not only of the health and safety provisions of the code, but also of the limits that the code places on multiple occupancy of a single dwelling unit.

Platteville is a college town that several years ago became concerned about the deterioration of its rental housing stock. The deterioration was believed to be caused by landlords' neglect of health and safety regulations. Their neglect was thought in turn due to the ineffectiveness of the procedure for enforcing the regulations. It required a complaint, and tenants rarely complained, either because they feared retaliation by their landlord or because they were unaware of the code violations that existed (no doubt they were usually unaware of the code's contents). To deal with the problem, the City in 1997 promulgated two ordinances that amended chapter 23 of the housing code. Ordinance 97-2 adopted with modifications a standard housing maintenance code, the Building Officials & Code Administrators International, Inc.'s (BOCA's) 1996 National Property Maintenance Code; this became section 23.16(b) of chapter 23. The second ordinance, 97-3, created a procedure for the periodic inspection and licensure of rental property. It added to chapter 23 section 23.13(b), which forbids landlords to rent out residential property that does not comply with the minimum standards established by the BOCA code to which we just referred "and any other standards adopted by the City of Platteville, as provided in [section] 23.16."

Chapter 22 of the housing code, which was not amended, contains a provision limiting the number of unrelated persons who may live in a single-family dwelling to four. Although this provision is not referred to in either section 23.13 or section 23.16, the sections directly affected by the two 1997 ordinances, a "Commentary" that was promulgated with the amended section 23.13 contains a list of "Duties of the Tenant" which quotes the multiple occupancy provision of chapter 22. The bulk of the commentary consists of requirements concerning smoke detectors, ventilation, electrical fixtures, plumbing, carpeting, and other fixtures and furnishings, and is interpretation or extension of the BOCA code. The section on "Duties of the Tenant" is unrelated to anything else in the commentary.

The amended chapter 23 divides rental property into three classes. . . . Class A properties are those found to be fully compliant with the housing code. Licenses permitting the rental of units in such properties are issued for three years. Class B properties are those with only minor infractions of the ordinance's minimum standards, and such properties are licensed for one year. Class C properties are in serious violation of the standards, and they may not be licensed for rental purposes at all.

To determine classification, the City's building inspector inspects each rental property in Platteville. If a landlord or tenant refuses to permit the inspection, the building inspector can apply to a Wisconsin court for a "special inspection warrant" for real property. . . . The application for the warrant, and the warrant itself, declare the search to be for the purpose of determining compliance with sections 23.13(b) and 23.16 of the housing code. But the inspector's practice in executing such warrants is to search for violations of the multiple occupancy provision as well, and this may involve his looking in closets or bureau drawers for evidence that more than four unrelated persons are living in the apartment. (The City's concern with multiple occupancy arises from suspicion that landlords have been packing more than four college students into an apartment.) Before this suit was brought, the building inspector dealt with landlords who refused to permit inspection simply by placarding the building with notices that it was unfit to be inhabited, but he has now abandoned this practice (which the plaintiffs had also challenged) in favor of utilizing the warrant procedure.

The plaintiffs argued in the district court unavailingly that searches by the building inspector violate the Fourth Amendment because they are not supported by probable cause to believe that the specific landlords whose premises are being searched are violating any municipal or other law. As an original matter, one might think that a landlord's refusal to permit an inspection that would not, after all, invade *his* privacy, but merely that of his tenants, would be pretty good evidence that he had something to hide — namely violations of the housing code — and so would supply the probable cause that the plaintiffs are demanding. (It is the refusal that triggers the application for a search warrant.) But that argument, though it finds some support in the case law, see references in 2 Wayne R. LaFave, *Search and Seizure: A Treatise on the Fourth Amendment* sec. 3.6(f), pp. 330-31 (3d ed. 1996), is not pressed here. Anyway, the warrants issued to determine compliance with Platteville's housing code contain no finding of probable cause to believe that a violation is occurring, and sometimes it was the tenants rather than the landlord who had refused entry to the inspector and thus precipitated the obtaining of a warrant.

The City seeks to justify the warrants by reference to the Supreme Court's decision in Camara v. Municipal Court, 387 U.S. 523 . . . (1967) . . . , which allowed the issuance of warrants unsupported by probable cause when necessary to enforce a local housing code. It is difficult to enforce such a code without occasional inspections; the tenants cannot be counted upon to report violations, because they may be getting a rental discount to overlook the violations, or, as we noted earlier, may be afraid of retaliation by the landlord or unaware of what conditions violate the code. And it is impossible to rely on a system of inspections to enforce the code without making them compulsory, since violators will refuse to consent to being inspected. In these circumstances the Fourth Amendment's requirement that all search warrants be supported by "probable cause" can be satisfied by demonstrating the reasonableness of the regulatory package that includes compulsory inspections, . . . and the reasonableness of Platteville's scheme, including such features as the exclusion of owner-occupied housing, is not questioned. The inspections are authorized only at yearly intervals in the case of Class B properties, and only triennially in the case of Class A properties.

So what is the fuss about here?

. . . The hostility to general warrants that underlies the Fourth Amendment's requirement of particularity was expressly related to a concern with privacy in

Horton v. California, *supra*, 496 U.S. at 141, and it is a solid ground for requiring that administrative search warrants describe the scope of the search with particularity.

Even if there were no constitutional requirement of particular description . . . a valid warrant would have to specify the object of the search, and that specification would operate to particularize the scope of the search. For the object determines the reasonable scope of the search, and all searches, to pass muster under the Fourth Amendment, must be reasonable. If you are looking for an adult elephant, searching for it in a chest of drawers is not reasonable. The principle that this example illustrates is that a search for a given body of evidence or contraband implies a limitation of the parts of the premises that may be searched. . . .

All that the warrants at issue in the present case specify with regard to the object or scope of the search is that the building inspector is to search for violations of sections 23.13(b) and 23.16 of the housing code. The multiple occupancy limitation is in a different chapter of the housing code altogether and so is not encompassed by the reference to sections 23.13(b) and 23.16. Nevertheless, were someone appealing to us from his conviction for violation of the multiple occupancy provision and seeking to suppress evidence of that violation obtained in the course of executing one of these warrants, the appeal would probably fail. For if while looking for violations of sections 23.13(b) and 23.16, as the warrant had properly authorized him to do, the inspector happened to see signs that there were more than four unrelated persons in a single-family apartment, the evidence of what he had seen would be admissible under the plain view doctrine, applied to administrative warrants in Michigan v. Clifford, *supra*, 464 U.S. at 294 (plurality opinion). But if the signs were not in plain view—if the inspector found them by opening drawers and closets even though such intrusions were not authorized by the warrant because evidence of violations of sections 23.13(b) and 23.16 would not be found in such places (one doesn't put a smoke detector in a bureau drawer)—then the plain view doctrine would be inapplicable and the evidence would have to be suppressed.

The plaintiffs claim that none of the building inspector's discoveries of violations of the limitations on multiple occupancy would be sheltered by the plain view doctrine, because his intent is to search for multiple occupancy violations. But his intent is irrelevant; the *Horton* decision forbids inquiry into the subjective intentions of the searcher.

So there would be nothing to argue over if the building inspector could always discover the telltale signs of multiple occupancy without looking into places where no evidence of a violation of section 23.13(b) or section 23.16 could be found. But apparently he cannot, for the City wants to preserve his right to rummage in closets and bureau drawers. To that end it argues that sections 23.13(b) and 23.16 incorporate chapter 22 by reference, and therefore a warrant's reference to those sections authorizes the more intrusive search. The incorporation by reference is oblique, to say the least.

. . . Granted that section 23.13 comes with a commentary that does refer to that chapter, the commentary is long and detailed and its legal significance obscure, as we have seen. Nor is it obvious that anyone requesting authorization to search for violations of chapter 22 must be intending to rummage through drawers and closets. It would be an extreme fiction to assume that the judges who issue these warrants know that this is what they are authorizing.

So the district judge was right to hold that the warrants for inspections by Platteville's building inspector do not authorize the intrusive searches conducted pursuant to them.

. . . Inspections for compliance with the standards referred to in the commentary, including the limitation on multiple occupancy, are therefore authorized by local law. But the *warrant* must authorize such inspections specifically. Thus, if the building inspector wants to search for violations of the multiple occupancy limitation, he should say in his application for a search warrant that he wants to search the specified rental property not only for evidence of violations of sections 23.13(b) and 23.16 but also "for evidence, including evidence contained in closets, cabinets, trunks, bureau drawers, and other closed or contained spaces, that more than four unrelated persons are living in a single-family dwelling unit, in violation of chapter 22 of the Platteville housing code," or words to that effect.

This is not to say that such a warrant should be granted, or even that it could be granted without infringing the Fourth Amendment. When the Supreme Court authorized administrative searches of residential housing, it didn't grant state and local governments carte blanche. The requirement of reasonableness that the Fourth Amendment imposes on all searches, whether or not pursuant to warrant, entails the striking of a balance between the benefits of an administrative search in implementing valid governmental programs and its costs to the property and privacy interests of the persons whose homes (whether owned or rented . . .) are searched. . . . Counting articles of underwear to determine how many people are living in an apartment may intrude on privacy further than the public interest in limiting apartment crowding justifies. But that is a separate issue from the question of the particularity of a warrant's description, and an issue insufficiently argued to require our reaching it. For, so far as the impact of the inspection program on privacy is concerned, the plaintiffs have been content to make a broadside attack upon the entire program and it is apparent from the case law that such an attack cannot succeed. An inspection that did not involve rummaging through closets and bureau drawers would clearly be a reasonable method of enforcing the housing code. Another issue that is not before us is whether consent to the inspection without a warrant should be thought to encompass an inspection of drawers and closets.

NOTES

1. One issue raised by *Platteville* is the possibility of agencies conducting something akin to a pretextual search. City officials here obtained warrants to conduct safety inspections but in reality wanted to assess whether there were violations of the occupancy limits. How does the court address this issue? Could, for example, the police use a traffic violation as a means of stopping a car suspected of involvement in drug activity? The U.S. Supreme Court addressed pretextual stops in Whren v. United States, 517 U.S. 806 (1996), holding unanimously that the personal subjective motives of an officer are not a factor in a Fourth Amendment analysis. The case is widely criticized for providing legal cover for police discrimination and a number of states have held that their state constitutions do not permit police to rely on pretext in the same manner that the federal constitution apparently allows.

2. Once an agency properly obtains a warrant and gains access to the premises, what are the limits on the area that can be searched? The area searched has to be reasonably related to the scope of the warrant. In this case, city officials wanted to use the warrant for a health and safety inspection to search "closets or bureau drawers." What is Judge Posner's view of this? What if the incriminating evidence had not been in a drawer but instead in "plain view?"

3. Judge Posner notes that an objection by a landlord to a warrantless search provides "pretty good evidence that he has something to hide" and, therefore, arguably provides the necessary evidence of wrongdoing necessary to obtain a warrant. What do you think of this reasoning? What are the practical implications of making such assumptions?

4. Had the City obtained a warrant to search for violations of the occupancy limits, would officials have been allowed to search closets and drawers? Unlike the health and safety inspections, evidence of violations could reasonably be expected to be found in a chest of drawers. Judge Posner, however, suggests that there may be other limits that restrict searches of these areas. Does the balancing test set out in *Safford* (note 6 *supra* on p. 203) help in analyzing reasonableness?

5. Does an agency have to get a warrant to search space otherwise open to the public? The issue was discussed at length in Dow Chemical Co. v. United States, 476 U.S. 227 (1986). Petitioner denied an EPA request for an on-site inspection of its chemical plant. The EPA did not seek a search warrant, but instead employed an aerial photographer to take photographs of the facility from various altitudes, all of which were within lawful navigable airspace. The Court held that the aerial photography of the plant complex without a warrant was not a search prohibited by the Fourth Amendment. The open areas of an industrial plant complex are not analogous to the "curtilage" of a dwelling, where the occupants have a legitimate expectation of privacy that society is prepared to accept. For purposes of aerial surveillance, the open areas of an industrial complex are more comparable to an "open field" in which an individual may not legitimately demand privacy. See also Air Pollution Variance Bd. v. Western Alfalfa Corp., 416 U.S. 861 (1974). Would the decision have been any different had the EPA used a thermal imaging device to assess the heat radiating from the inside of the plant? See Kyllo v. United States, 533 U.S. 27, 40 (2001) (noting that "Where, as here, the Government uses a device that is not in general public use, to explore details of the home that would previously have been unknowable without physical intrusion, the surveillance is a 'search' and is presumptively unreasonable without a warrant"). The same decision characterized the search in *Dow Chemical* as one involving "'visual observation' that is not a 'search' at all." Do you agree with this distinction? Nonetheless, the practical reality is that agency inspections often do not require a warrant. Why might that be the case?

b. Warrantless Searches and Inspections

Generally, the Fourth Amendment requires that government searches be authorized by a warrant. Given the large number of exceptions, however, the "warrant requirement" can be said to be recognized more in the breach than in the observance. The next two cases, *Burger* and *Patel*, set out the requirements and scope of a warrant exception particularly applicable to agencies.

NEW YORK v. BURGER

482 U.S. 691 (1987)

JUSTICE BLACKMUN delivered the opinion of the Court: This case presents the question whether the warrantless search of an automobile junkyard, conducted pursuant to a statute authorizing such a search, falls within the exception to the warrant requirement for administrative inspections of pervasively regulated industries. The case also presents the question whether an otherwise proper administrative inspection is unconstitutional because the ultimate purpose of the regulatory statute pursuant to which the search is done — the deterrence of criminal behavior — is the same as that of penal laws, with the result that the inspection may disclose violations not only of the regulatory statute but also of the penal statutes.

I

Respondent Joseph Burger is the owner of a junkyard in Brooklyn, N.Y. His business consists, in part, of the dismantling of automobiles and the selling of their parts. His junkyard is an open lot with no buildings. A high metal fence surrounds it, wherein are located, among other things, vehicles and parts of vehicles. At approximately noon on November 17, 1982, officer Joseph Vega and four other plainclothes officers, all members of the Auto Crimes Division of the New York City Police Department, entered respondent's junkyard to conduct an inspection pursuant to N.Y. Veh. & Traf. Law §415-a5 (McKinney 1986). On any given day, the Division conducts from 5 to 10 inspections of vehicle dismantlers, automobile junkyards, and related businesses.

Upon entering the junkyard, the officers asked to see Burger's license and his "police book" — the record of the automobiles and vehicle parts in his possession. Burger replied that he had neither a license nor a police book. The officers then announced their intention to conduct a §415-a5 inspection. Burger did not object. In accordance with their practice, the officers copied down the Vehicle

Identification Numbers (VINs) of several vehicles and parts of vehicles that were in the junkyard. After checking these numbers against a police computer, the officers determined that respondent was in possession of stolen vehicles and parts. Accordingly, Burger was arrested and charged with five counts of possession of stolen property and one count of unregistered operation as a vehicle dismantler, in violation of §415-a1.

In the Kings County Supreme Court, Burger moved to suppress the evidence obtained as a result of the inspection, primarily on the ground that §415-a5 was unconstitutional. After a hearing, the court denied the motion. . . .

The New York Court of Appeals, however, reversed. 67 N.Y.2d 338, 493 N.E.2d 926 (1986). In its view, §415-a5 violated the Fourth Amendment's prohibition of unreasonable searches and seizures. . . .

II

A

The Court long has recognized that the Fourth Amendment's prohibition on unreasonable searches and seizures is applicable to commercial premises, as well as to private homes. See v. City of Seattle, 387 U.S. 541, 543, 546 (1967). An owner or operator of a business thus has an expectation of privacy in commercial property, which society is prepared to consider to be reasonable, see Katz v. United States, 389 U.S. 347, 361 (1967) (Harlan, J., concurring). This expectation exists not only with respect to traditional police searches conducted for the gathering of criminal evidence but also with respect to administrative inspections designed to enforce regulatory statutes. See Marshall v. Barlow's, Inc., 436 U.S. 307, 312-313 (1978). An expectation of privacy in commercial premises, however, is different from, and indeed less than, a similar expectation in an individual's home. See Donovan v. Dewey, 452 U.S. 594, 598-599 (1981). This expectation is particularly attenuated in commercial property employed in "closely regulated" industries. The Court observed in Marshall v. Barlow's, Inc.: "Certain industries have such a history of government oversight that no reasonable expectation of privacy, see Katz v. United States, 389 U.S. 347, 351-352 (1967), could exist for a proprietor over the stock of such an enterprise." 436 U.S. at 313.

The Court first examined the "unique" problem of inspections of "closely regulated" businesses in two enterprises that had "a long tradition of close government supervision." In Colonnade Corp. v. United States, 397 U.S. 72 (1970), it considered a warrantless search of a catering business pursuant to several federal revenue statutes authorizing the inspection of the premises of liquor dealers. Although the Court disapproved the search because the statute provided that a sanction be imposed when entry was refused, and because it did not authorize entry without a warrant as an alternative in this situation, it recognized that "the liquor industry [was] long subject to close supervision and inspection." Id. at 77. We returned to this issue in United States v. Biswell, 406 U.S. 311 (1972), which involved a warrantless inspection of the premises of a pawnshop operator, who was federally licensed to sell sporting weapons pursuant to the Gun Control Act of 1968, 18 U.S.C. §921 et seq. While noting that "federal regulation of the interstate traffic in firearms is not as deeply rooted in history as is governmental control of the liquor industry," 406 U.S. at 315, we nonetheless concluded that the warrantless inspections authorized by the Gun Control Act would "pose only limited threats to the dealer's justifiable expectations of privacy." Id. at 316. We observed: "When a dealer chooses to engage in this pervasively regulated business and to accept a federal license, he does so with the knowledge that his business records, firearms, and ammunition will be subject to effective inspection." The "Colonnade-Biswell" doctrine, stating the reduced expectation of privacy by an owner of commercial premises in a "closely regulated" industry, has received renewed emphasis in more recent decisions. In Marshall v. Barlow's, Inc., we noted its continued vitality but declined to find that warrantless inspections, made pursuant to the Occupational Safety and Health Act of 1970, 84 Stat. 1598, 29 U.S.C. §657(a), of all businesses engaged in interstate commerce fell within the narrow focus of this doctrine. 436 U.S. at 313-314. However, we found warrantless inspections made pursuant to the Federal Mine Safety and Health Act of 1977, 91 Stat. 1290, 30 U.S.C. §801 et seq., proper because they were of a "closely regulated" industry. Donovan v. Dewey, *supra.* Indeed, in Donovan v. Dewey, we declined to limit our consideration to the length of time during which the business in question — stone quarries — had been subject to federal regulation. 452 U.S. at 605-606. We pointed out that the doctrine is essentially defined by "the pervasiveness and regularity of the federal regulation" and the effect of such regulation upon an owner's expectation of privacy. See id. at 600, 606. We observed, however, that "the duration of a particular regulatory scheme" would remain an "important factor" in deciding whether a warrantless inspection pursuant to the scheme is permissible. Id. at 606.

B

Because the owner or operator of commercial premises in a "closely regulated" industry has a reduced expectation of privacy, the warrant and probable-cause requirements, which fulfill the traditional Fourth Amendment standard of reasonableness for a government search . . . have lessened application in this context. Rather, we conclude that, as in other situations of "special need," . . . where the privacy interests of the owner are weakened and the government interests in regulating particular businesses are concomitantly heightened, a warrantless inspection of commercial premises may well be reasonable within the meaning of the Fourth Amendment. This warrantless inspection, however, even in the context of a pervasively regulated business, will be deemed to be reasonable only so long as three criteria are met. First, there must be a "substantial" government interest that informs the regulatory scheme pursuant to which the inspection is made. See Donovan v. Dewey, 452 U.S. at 602 ("substantial federal interest in improving the health and safety conditions in the Nation's underground and surface mines"); United States v. Biswell, 406 U.S. at 315 (regulation of firearms is "of central importance to federal efforts to prevent violent crime and to assist the States in regulating the firearms traffic within their borders"); Colonnade Corp. v. United States, 397 U.S. at 75 (federal interest "in protecting the revenue against various types of fraud").

Second, the warrantless inspections must be "necessary to further [the] regulatory scheme." Donovan v. Dewey, 452 U.S. at 600. For example, in *Dewey* we recognized that forcing mine inspectors to obtain a warrant before every inspection might alert mine owners or operators to the impending inspection, thereby frustrating the purposes of the Mine Safety and Health Act—to detect and thus to deter safety and health violations. Id. at 603.

Finally, "the statute's inspection program, in terms of the certainty and regularity of its application, [must] provid[e] a constitutionally adequate substitute for a warrant." In other words, the regulatory statute must perform the two basic functions of a warrant: it must advise the owner of the commercial premises that the search is being made pursuant to the law and has a properly defined scope, and it must limit the discretion of the inspecting officers. See Marshall v. Barlow's, Inc., 436 U.S. at 323; see also id. at 332 (Stevens, J., dissenting). To perform this first function, the statute must be "sufficiently comprehensive and defined that the owner of commercial property cannot help but be aware that his property will be subject to periodic inspections undertaken for specific purposes." Donovan v. Dewey, 452 U.S. at 600. In addition, in defining how a statute limits the discretion of the inspectors, we have observed that it must be "carefully limited in time, place, and scope." United States v. Biswell, 406 U.S. at 315.

III

A

Searches made pursuant to §415-a5, in our view, clearly fall within this established exception to the warrant requirement for administrative inspections in "closely regulated" businesses. First, the nature of the regulatory statute reveals that the operation of a junkyard, part of which is devoted to vehicle dismantling, is a "closely regulated" business in the State of New York. The provisions regulating the activity of vehicle dismantling are extensive. An operator cannot engage in this industry without first obtaining a license, which means that he must meet the registration requirements and must pay a fee. Under §415-a5(a), the operator must maintain a police book recording the acquisition and disposition of motor vehicles and vehicle parts, and make such records and inventory available for inspection by the police or any agent of the Department of Motor Vehicles. The operator also must display his registration number prominently at his place of business, on business documentation, and on vehicles and parts that pass through his business. §415-a5(b). Moreover, the person engaged in this activity is subject to criminal penalties, as well as to loss of license or civil fines, for failure to comply with these provisions. See §§415-a1, 5, and 6. That other States besides New York have imposed similarly extensive regulations on automobile junkyards further supports the "closely regulated" status of this industry....

Accordingly, in light of the regulatory framework governing his business and the history of regulation of related industries, an operator of a junkyard engaging in vehicle dismantling has a reduced expectation of privacy in this "closely regulated" business.

B

The New York regulatory scheme satisfies the three criteria necessary to make reasonable warrantless inspections pursuant to §415-a5. First, the State has a substantial interest in regulating the vehicle-dismantling and automobile-junkyard industry because motor vehicle theft has increased in the State and because the problem of theft is associated with this industry. In this day, automobile theft has become a significant social problem, placing enormous economic and personal burdens upon the citizens of different states. . . . Because contemporary automobiles are made from standardized parts, the nationwide extent of vehicle theft and concern about it are understandable.

Second, regulation of the vehicle-dismantling industry reasonably serves the State's substantial interest in eradicating automobile theft. It is well established that the theft problem can be addressed effectively by controlling the receiver of, or market in, stolen property. . . . Thus, the State rationally may believe that it will reduce car theft by regulations that prevent automobile junkyards from becoming markets for stolen vehicles and that help trace the origin and destination of vehicle parts.

Moreover, the warrantless administrative inspections pursuant to §415-a5 "are necessary to further [the] regulatory scheme." Donovan v. Dewey, 452 U.S. at 600. In this respect, we see no difference between these inspections and those approved by the Court in United States v. Biswell and Donovan v. Dewey. We explained in *Biswell*:

> If inspection is to be effective and serve as a credible deterrent, unannounced, even frequent, inspections are essential. In this context, the prerequisite of a warrant could easily frustrate inspection; and if the necessary flexibility as to time, scope, and frequency is to be preserved, the protections afforded by a warrant would be negligible. 406 U.S. at 316.

See also Donovan v. Dewey, 452 U.S. at 603. Similarly, in the present case, a warrant requirement would interfere with the statute's purpose of deterring automobile theft accomplished by identifying vehicles and parts as stolen and shutting down the market in such items. Because stolen cars and parts often pass quickly through an automobile junkyard, "frequent" and "unannounced" inspections are necessary in order to detect them. In sum, surprise is crucial if the regulatory scheme aimed at remedying this major social problem is to function at all.

Third, §415-a5 provides a "constitutionally adequate substitute for a warrant." Donovan v. Dewey, 452 U.S. at 603. The statute informs the operator of a vehicle dismantling business that inspections will be made on a regular basis. Id. at 605. Thus, the vehicle dismantler knows that the inspections to which he is subject do not constitute discretionary acts by a government official but are conducted pursuant to statute. See Marshall v. Barlow's, Inc., 436 U.S. at 332 (dissenting opinion). Section 415-a5 also sets forth the scope of the inspection and, accordingly, places the operator on notice as to how to comply with the statute. In addition, it notifies the operator as to who is authorized to conduct an inspection.

Finally, the "time, place, and scope" of the inspection is limited, United States v. Biswell, 406 U.S. at 315, to place appropriate restraints upon the discretion of the inspecting officers. See Donovan v. Dewey, 452 U.S. at 605. The officers are allowed to conduct an inspection only "during [the] regular and usual business hours." §415-a5. The inspections can be made only of vehicle-dismantling and related industries. And the permissible scope of these searches is narrowly defined: the inspectors may examine the records, as well as "any vehicles or parts of vehicles which are subject to the record keeping requirements of this section and which are on the premises."

IV

A search conducted pursuant to §415-a5, therefore, clearly falls within the well-established exception to the warrant requirement for administrative inspections of "closely regulated" businesses. . . .

Nor do we think that this administrative scheme is unconstitutional simply because, in the course of enforcing it, an inspecting officer may discover evidence of crimes, besides violations of the scheme itself. In *United States v. Biswell*, the pawnshop operator was charged not only with a violation of the recordkeeping provision, pursuant to which the inspection was made, but also with other violations detected during the inspection, see 406 U.S. at 313, n.2, and convicted of a failure to pay an occupational tax for dealing in specific firearms, id. at 312-313. The discovery of evidence of crimes in the course of an otherwise proper administrative inspection does not render that search illegal or the administrative scheme suspect. . . .

Finally, we fail to see any constitutional significance in the fact that police officers, rather than "administrative" agents, are permitted to conduct the §415-a5 inspection. The significance respondent alleges lies in the role of police officers as enforcers of the penal laws and in the officers' power to arrest for offenses other than violations of the administrative scheme. It is, however, important to note that state police officers, like those in New York, have numerous duties in addition to those associated with traditional police work. . . . As a practical matter, many States do not have the resources to assign the enforcement of a particular administrative scheme to a specialized agency. So long as a regulatory scheme is properly administrative, it is not rendered illegal by the fact that the inspecting officer has the power to arrest individuals for violations other than those created by the scheme itself. In sum, we decline to impose upon the States the burden of requiring the enforcement of their regulatory statutes to be carried out by specialized agents.

V

Accordingly, the judgment of the New York Court of Appeals is reversed, and the case is remanded to that court for further proceedings not inconsistent with this opinion.

It is so ordered.

[JUSTICES BRENNAN, MARSHALL, and O'CONNOR dissented.]

NOTES

1. On remand, in People v. Scott, 593 N.E.2d 1328 (N.Y. 1992), the New York Court of Appeals found that the junkyard search in question violated the provisions against unreasonable search and seizure under article 1, §12 of the New York State Constitution. Despite the U.S. Supreme Court's finding of constitutionality under the U.S. Constitution's Fourth Amendment in *Burger*, the New York court explained that administrative searches undertaken solely to help police uncover evidence of a crime cannot pass constitutional muster under the New York Constitution. Moreover, the New York court found that the administrative search exception to a warrant would have constitutional difficulty also because junkyards are not subject to the kind of pervasive governmental supervision that the exception truly requires.

2. The Court in *Burger* noted that "closely regulated industries" had a reduced expectation of privacy. Earlier decisions had recognized this in the context of industries that had a "long tradition of close government supervision" such as liquor (*Colonnade*), and guns (*Biswell*). How are these industries different from the industry subject to regulation in *Burger*? What does the analysis in *Burger* suggest about the types of industries that can be subjected to warrantless searches?

3. Pervasively regulated industries often are required to submit to periodic inspections by regulators without the protections of a warrant. One example is found in the Sarbanes-Oxley Act, which created the Public Company Accounting Oversight Board (PCAOB) and gave it the authority to adopt a "continuing program" of inspecting public accounting firms in order to "assess the degree of compliance" with applicable laws. The statute does limit inspections to audits conducted by the firm and the accounting firm's quality control system.

CITY OF LOS ANGELES v. PATEL

576 U.S. 409 (2015)

JUSTICE SOTOMAYOR delivered the opinion of the Court. Respondents brought a Fourth Amendment challenge to a provision of the Los Angeles Municipal Code that compels "[e]very operator of a hotel to keep a record" containing specified information concerning guests and to make this record "available to any officer of the Los Angeles Police Department for inspection" on demand. . . . The questions presented are whether facial challenges to statutes can be brought under the Fourth Amendment and, if so, whether this provision of the Los Angeles Municipal Code is facially invalid. We hold facial challenges can be brought under the Fourth Amendment. We further hold that the provision of the Los Angeles Municipal Code that requires hotel operators to make their registries available to the police on demand is facially unconstitutional because it penalizes them for declining to turn over their records without affording them any opportunity for precompliance review.

I

A

Los Angeles Municipal Code (LAMC) §41.49 requires hotel operators to record information about their guests, including: the guest's name and address; the number of people in each guest's party; the make, model, and license plate number of any guest's vehicle parked on hotel property; the guest's date and time of arrival and scheduled departure date; the room number assigned to the guest; the rate charged and amount collected for the room; and the method of payment. §41.49(2). Guests without reservations, those who pay for their rooms with cash, and any guests who rent a room for less than 12 hours must present photographic identification at the time of check-in, and hotel operators are required to record the number and expiration date of that document. §41.49(4). For those guests who check in using an electronic kiosk, the hotel's records must also contain the guest's credit card information. §41.49(2)(b). This information can be maintained in either electronic or paper form, but it must be "kept on the hotel premises in the guest reception or guest check-in area or in an office adjacent" thereto for a period of 90 days. §41.49(3)(a).

Section 41.49(3)(a) — the only provision at issue here — states, in pertinent part, that hotel guest records "shall be made available to any officer of the Los Angeles Police Department for inspection," provided that "[w]henever possible, the inspection shall be conducted at a time and in a manner that minimizes any interference with the operation of the business." A hotel operator's failure to make his or her guest records available for police inspection is a misdemeanor punishable by up to six months in jail and a $1,000 fine. §11.00(m) (general provision applicable to entire LAMC).

B

In 2003, respondents, a group of motel operators along with a lodging association, sued the city of Los Angeles (City or petitioner) in three consolidated cases challenging the constitutionality of §41.49(3)(a). They sought declaratory and injunctive relief. The parties "agree[d] that the sole issue in the . . . action [would be] a facial constitutional challenge" to §41.49(3)(a) under the Fourth Amendment. App. 195. They further stipulated that respondents have been subjected to mandatory record inspections under the ordinance without consent or a warrant. Id., at 194-195.

Following a bench trial, the District Court entered judgment in favor of the City, holding that respondents' facial challenge failed because they lacked a reasonable expectation of privacy in the records subject to inspection. A divided panel of the Ninth Circuit affirmed on the same grounds. 686 F.3d 1085 (2012). On rehearing en banc, however, the Court of Appeals reversed. 738 F.3d 1058, 1065 (2013).

The en banc court first determined that a police officer's nonconsensual inspection of hotel records under §41.49 is a Fourth Amendment "search" because "[t]he business records covered by §41.49 are the hotel's private property" and the hotel therefore "has the right to exclude others from prying into the[ir] contents." Id., at 1061. Next, the court assessed "whether the searches authorized by §41.49 are reasonable." Id., at 1063. Relying on Donovan v. Lone Steer, Inc., 464 U.S. 408, 104 S. Ct. 769, 78 L. Ed. 2d 567 (1984), and See v. Seattle, 387 U.S. 541, 87 S. Ct. 1741, 18 L. Ed. 2d 930 (1967), the court held that §41.49 is facially unconstitutional "as it authorizes inspections" of hotel records "without affording an opportunity to 'obtain judicial review of the reasonableness of the demand prior to suffering penalties for refusing to comply.'" 738 F.3d, at 1065 (quoting *See*, 387 U.S., at 545, 87 S. Ct. 1737).

Two dissenting opinions were filed. The first dissent argued that facial relief should rarely be available for Fourth Amendment challenges, and was inappropriate here because the ordinance would be constitutional in those circumstances where police officers demand access to hotel records with a warrant in hand or exigent circumstances justify the search. 738 F.3d, at 1065-1070 (opinion of Tallman, J.). The second dissent conceded that inspections under §41.49 constitute Fourth Amendment searches, but faulted the majority for assessing the reasonableness of these searches without accounting for the weakness of the hotel operators' privacy interest in the content of their guest registries. Id., at 1070-1074 (opinion of Clifton, J.).

We granted certiorari, and now affirm.

. . .

Rather than arguing that §41.49(3)(a) is constitutional under the general administrative search doctrine, the City and Justice Scalia contend that hotels are "closely regulated," and that the ordinance is facially valid under the more relaxed standard that applies to searches of this category of businesses. . . . They are wrong on both counts.

Over the past 45 years, the Court has identified only four industries that "have such a history of government oversight that no reasonable expectation of privacy . . . could exist for a proprietor over the stock of such an enterprise," *Barlow's, Inc.*, 436 U.S., at 313, 98 S. Ct. 1816. Simply listing these industries refutes petitioner's argument that hotels should be counted among them. Unlike liquor sales, Colonnade Catering Corp. v. United States, 397 U.S. 72, 90 S. Ct. 774, 25 L. Ed. 2d 60 (1970), firearms dealing, United States v. Biswell, 406 U.S. 311, 311-312, 92 S. Ct. 1593, 32 L. Ed. 2d 87 (1972), mining, Donovan v. Dewey, 452 U.S. 594, 101

S. Ct. 2534, 69 L. Ed. 2d 262 (1981), or running an automobile junkyard, New York v. Burger, 482 U.S. 691, 107 S. Ct. 2636, 96 L. Ed. 2d 601 (1987), nothing inherent in the operation of hotels poses a clear and significant risk to the public welfare. See, e.g., id., at 709, 107 S. Ct. 2636 ("Automobile junkyards and vehicle dismantlers provide the major market for stolen vehicles and vehicle parts"); *Dewey*, 452 U.S., at 602, 101 S. Ct. 2534 (describing the mining industry as "among the most hazardous in the country").

Moreover, "[t]he clear import of our cases is that the closely regulated industry . . . is the exception." *Barlow's, Inc.*, 436 U.S., at 313. To classify hotels as pervasively regulated would permit what has always been a narrow exception to swallow the rule. The City wisely refrains from arguing that §41.49 itself renders hotels closely regulated. Nor do any of the other regulations on which petitioner and Justice Scalia rely — regulations requiring hotels to, inter alia, maintain a license, collect taxes, conspicuously post their rates, and meet certain sanitary standards — establish a comprehensive scheme of regulation that distinguishes hotels from numerous other businesses. See Brief for Petitioner 33-34 (citing regulations); post, at 2460 (same). All businesses in Los Angeles need a license to operate. LAMC §§21.03(a), 21.09(a). While some regulations apply to a smaller set of businesses, see e.g. Cal. Code Regs., tit. 25, §40 (2015) (requiring linens to be changed between rental guests), online at http://www.oal.ca.gov/ccr.htm, these can hardly be said to have created a "'comprehensive'" scheme that puts hotel owners on notice that their "'property will be subject to periodic inspections undertaken for specific purposes,'" *Burger*, 482 U.S., n. 16. Instead, they are more akin to the widely applicable minimum wage and maximum hour rules that the Court rejected as a basis for deeming "the entirety of American interstate commerce" to be closely regulated in *Barlow's, Inc.*, 436 U.S., at 314. If such general regulations were sufficient to invoke the closely regulated industry exception, it would be hard to imagine a type of business that would not qualify.

Petitioner attempts to recast this hodgepodge of regulations as a comprehensive scheme by referring to a "centuries-old tradition" of warrantless searches of hotels. . . . History is relevant when determining whether an industry is closely regulated. See, e.g., *Burger*, 482 U.S., at 707, 107 S. Ct. 2636. The historical record here, however, is not as clear as petitioner suggests. The City and Justice Scalia principally point to evidence that hotels were treated as public accommodations. . . . For instance, the Commonwealth of Massachusetts required innkeepers to "'furnish[ ] . . . suitable provisions and lodging, for the refreshment and entertainment of strangers and travellers, pasturing and stable room, hay and provender . . . for their horses and cattle.'" . . . But laws obligating inns to provide suitable lodging to all paying guests are not the same as laws subjecting inns to warrantless searches. Petitioner also asserts that "[f]or a long time, [hotel] owners left their registers open to widespread inspection." Setting aside that modern hotel registries contain sensitive information, such as driver's licenses and credit card numbers for which there is no historic analog, the fact that some hotels chose to make registries accessible to the public has little bearing on whether government authorities could have viewed these documents on demand without a hotel's consent.

Even if we were to find that hotels are pervasively regulated, §41.49 would need to satisfy three additional criteria to be reasonable under the Fourth Amendment: (1) "[T]here must be a 'substantial' government interest that informs the regulatory scheme pursuant to which the inspection is made"; (2) "the warrantless inspections must be 'necessary' to further [the] regulatory scheme"; and (3) "the statute's inspection program, in terms of the certainty and regularity of its application, [must] provid[e] a constitutionally adequate substitute for a warrant." *Burger*, 482 U.S., at 702-703. We assume petitioner's interest in ensuring that hotels maintain accurate and complete registries might fulfill the first of these requirements, but conclude that §41.49 fails the second and third prongs of this test.

The City claims that affording hotel operators any opportunity for precompliance review would fatally undermine the scheme's efficacy by giving operators a chance to falsify their records. The Court has previously rejected this exact argument, which could be made regarding any recordkeeping requirement. See *Barlow's, Inc.*, 436 U.S., at 320 ("[It is not] apparent why the advantages of surprise would be lost if, after being refused entry, procedures were available for the [Labor] Secretary to seek an ex parte warrant to reappear at the premises without further notice to the establishment being inspected"); cf. *Lone Steer*, 464 U.S., at 411, 415, 104 S. Ct. 769 (affirming use of administrative subpoena which provided an opportunity for precompliance review as a means for obtaining "payroll and sales records"). We see no reason to accept it here.

As explained above, nothing in our decision today precludes an officer from conducting a surprise inspection by obtaining an ex parte warrant or, where an officer reasonably suspects the registry would be altered, from guarding the registry pending a hearing on a motion to quash. Justice Scalia's claim that these procedures will prove unworkable given the large number of hotels in Los Angeles is a red herring. While there are approximately 2,000 hotels in Los Angeles, there is no basis to believe that resort to such measures will be needed to conduct spot checks in the vast majority of them.

Section 41.49 is also constitutionally deficient under the "certainty and regularity" prong of the closely regulated industries test because it fails sufficiently to constrain police officers' discretion as to which hotels to search and under what circumstances. While the Court has upheld inspection schemes of closely regulated industries that called for searches at least four times a year, *Dewey*, 452 U.S., at 604 or on a "regular basis," *Burger*, 482 U.S., at 711, §41.49 imposes no comparable standard.

...

For the foregoing reasons, we agree with the Ninth Circuit that §41.49(3)(a) is facially invalid insofar as it fails to provide any opportunity for precompliance review before a hotel must give its guest registry to the police for inspection. Accordingly, the judgment of the Ninth Circuit is affirmed.

It is so ordered.

SCALIA, J., ROBERTS, C.J., and THOMAS, J., dissenting.

The city of Los Angeles, like many jurisdictions across the country, has a law that requires motels, hotels, and other places of overnight accommodation (hereinafter motels) to keep a register containing specified information about their guests. Los Angeles Municipal Code (LAMC) §41.49(2) (2015). The purpose of this recordkeeping requirement is to deter criminal conduct, on the theory that criminals will be unwilling to carry on illicit activities in motel rooms if they must provide identifying information at check-in. Because this deterrent effect will only be accomplished if motels actually do require guests to provide the required information, the ordinance also authorizes police to conduct random spot checks of motels' guest registers to ensure that they are properly maintained. §41.49(3). The ordinance limits these spot checks to the four corners of the register, and does not authorize police to enter any nonpublic area of the motel. To the extent possible, police must conduct these spot checks at times that will minimize any disruption to a motel's business.

The parties do not dispute the governmental interests at stake. Motels not only provide housing to vulnerable transient populations, they are also a particularly attractive site for criminal activity ranging from drug dealing and prostitution to human trafficking. Offering privacy and anonymity on the cheap, they have been employed as prisons for migrants smuggled across the border and held for ransom, and rendezvous sites where child sex workers meet their clients on threat of violence from their procurers.

Nevertheless, the Court today concludes that Los Angeles's ordinance is "unreasonable" inasmuch as it permits police to flip through a guest register to ensure it is being filled out without first providing an opportunity for the motel operator to seek judicial review. Because I believe that such a limited inspection of a guest register is eminently reasonable under the circumstances presented, I dissent.

NOTES

1. Can *Patel* be reconciled with *Burger*? For example, the Court lists four industries that have been found to be "closely regulated." Three of them (liquor, firearms, and mining) are clear enough, but what about the fourth one? While hotels may not resemble the first three, is it really the case that they bear no similarities to the junkyards found to be closely regulated in *Burger*?

2. In characterizing the industries subject to the exception, the majority noted that there was "nothing inherent in the operation of hotels" that posed "a clear and significant risk to the public welfare." How might this analysis apply, for example, to a warrantless search of a taxidermy shop? See United Taxidermists Ass'n v. Illinois Dep't of Natural Resources, 436 Fed. Appx. 692 (7th Cir. Aug. 25, 2011) (plaintiff conceded that *Burger* "controlled the case").

3. Even assuming an industry is closely regulated, the warrantless search must still be "necessary." The majority reject the argument that the right is necessary because otherwise a hotel could refuse to voluntarily turn over records pursuant to a surprise inspection and, while law enforcement officials obtained a warrant, could "falsify their records." In *Burger*, the Court indicated that the delay in obtaining a warrant was harmful "[b]ecause stolen cars and parts often pass quickly through an automobile junkyard." Can these cases be reconciled? If not, how would you explain the Court action to not extend the *Burger* holding to hotels?

c. *Subpoenas*

The main compulsory device used by agencies to acquire information during investigations is the subpoena. Without authority to issue subpoenas, agency investigatory power is essentially a power to obtain information only with consent. The subpoena is an official order directing an individual to give information, either in the form of testimony or documents. The subpoena ad testificandum is the ordinary subpoena that orders a witness to appear and give testimony; the "subpoena duces tecum is an order to produce documents or to show cause why they need not be produced." Nixon v. Sirica, 487 F.2d 700 (D.C. Cir. 1973). A statutory delegation is necessary for agencies to possess subpoena power. Such statutory delegations are widespread; virtually all agencies of consequence are given subpoena power by the legislature. This is particularly true of regulatory agencies, which are vested with subpoena power as a necessary adjunct of effective regulation.

Statutes delegating subpoena power to agencies are of two kinds. The most common is the delegation in the enabling legislation setting up a particular agency. See, e.g., 15 U.S.C. §49 (derived from Federal Trade Commission Act, 1914, §9): "[T]he Commission shall have power to require by subpoena the attendance and testimony of witnesses and the production of all such documentary evidence relating to any matter under investigation."

The other type of delegating statute is a general grant to agencies in the jurisdiction. See, e.g., N.Y. Civil Practice Law §2302(a): "Subpoenas may be issued without a court order by . . . any member of a board, commission authorized by law to hear, try or determine a matter or to do any other act, in an official capacity, in relation to which proof may be taken or the attendance of a person as a witness may be required."

Subdelegation. Statutes delegating subpoena power to agencies normally confer the authority to issue subpoenas on the heads of the agencies concerned, e.g., one of the commissioners in the Federal Trade Commission (15 U.S.C. §49) or the Administrator of the Wage and Hour Division under the Fair Labor Standards Act (29 U.S.C. §209). Sometimes the statutes expressly permit the heads to delegate their subpoena power to subordinates.

Right to subpoenas. Does a party in an administrative proceeding have a right to demand the issuance of subpoenas? The question does not arise so far as the agency itself as a party is concerned. The agency staff responsible for a case normally has available to it as many subpoenas as it deems necessary; the common practice is for agency attorneys to have access to an ample supply of subpoenas signed in blank by the appropriate official. Without a right to the subpoenas he needs, the private party in the agency proceeding may be at a serious disadvantage.

Should the agency subpoena be treated like a court subpoena, with issuance at the request of a party as a matter of right? See Federal Rules of Civil Procedure 45(a) (clerks of district courts have mandatory duty to issue subpoenas "signed and sealed but otherwise in blank" to a party on request).

Compare Del Vecchio v. White Plains Unit, 408 N.Y.S.2d 802 (2d Dep't 1978) (under New York law, attorney has right to issue subpoena in administrative, as well as judicial, proceeding).

The Federal APA provides:

> Agency subpoenas authorized by law shall be issued to a party on request and, when required by rules of procedure, on a statement or showing of general relevance and reasonable scope of the evidence sought.
> 5 U.S.C. §555(d).

In what ways does this provision permit agencies to limit private parties' right to subpoenas? What is the practical effect of the limitation? In considering whether private parties should have the same unrestricted right to agency subpoenas as they have to court subpoenas, note that federal agency subpoenas, unlike federal court subpoenas, are usually valid throughout the country, contributing to the potential possibility for abuse. See National Labor Relations Act, as amended in 1947, 29 U.S.C. §161(1):

> The Board, or any member thereof, shall upon application of any party to such proceedings, forthwith issue to such party subpoenas requiring the attendance and testimony of witnesses or the production of any evidence in such proceeding or investigation requested in such application.

This provision imposes a mandatory duty to issue subpoenas requested by parties in NLRB proceedings. Lewis v. NLRB, 357 U.S. 10 (1958). The Board is given the power, on petition of the person subpoenaed, to revoke the subpoena "if in its opinion the evidence whose production is required does not relate to any matter under investigation, or any matter in question in such proceedings." See NLRB v. Consolidated Vacuum Co., 395 F.2d 416 (2d Cir. 1968). Compare N.Y. Civil Practice Law §2302(a) ("Subpoenas may be issued without a court order by . . . an attorney of record for a party to an administrative proceeding.").

Unlike warrants, subpoenas may be challenged in a judicial proceeding prior to enforcement. The actions are initiated by a refusal of the subpoenaed party to comply. The agency typically files an action seeking enforcement. See 15 U.S.C. §78h(c) (authorizing the SEC to bring subpoena enforcement actions). In general, it is the objecting party who has the burden of showing a basis for quashing the warrant, although this is not always the case. See EEOC v. Dillon Cos., 310 F.3d 1271, 1274 (10th Cir. 2002) (noting that statutory scheme places burden of establishing relevancy on EEOC).

Can a party receiving the subpoena ever initiate a legal challenge? What if the statute provides that the failure to comply can result in the imposition of penalties by the agency?

FTC v. AMERICAN TOBACCO CO.

264 U.S. 298 (1924)

[The FTC petitioned the district court to require the defendant company to produce "all letters and telegrams received by the Company from, or sent by it to all of its jobber customers, between January 1, 1921 to December 31, 1921, inclusive." The commission claimed the documents were needed in connection with an investigation of the tobacco industry called for by a Senate resolution. The district court denied the petition.]

MR. JUSTICE HOLMES delivered the opinion of the Court.

The mere facts of carrying on a commerce not confined within State lines and of being organized as a corporation do not make men's affairs public, as those of a railroad company now may be. . . . Anyone who respects the spirit as well as the letter of the Fourth Amendment would be loath to believe that Congress intended to authorize one of its subordinate agencies to sweep all our traditions into the fire (Interstate Commerce Commission v. Brimson, 154 U.S. 447, 479) and to direct fishing expeditions into private papers on the possibility that they may disclose evidence of crime. We do not discuss the question whether it could do so if it tried, as nothing short of the most explicit language would induce us to attribute to Congress that intent. The interruption of business, the possible revelation of trade secrets, and the expense that compliance with the Commission's wholesale demand would cause are the least considerations. It is contrary to the first principles of justice to allow a search through all the respondents' records, relevant or irrelevant, in the hope that something will turn up. . . .

The right of access given by the statute is to documentary evidence — not to all documents, but to such documents as are evidence. The analogies of the law do not allow the party wanting evidence to call for all documents in order to see if they do not contain it. Some ground must be shown for supposing that the documents called for do contain it. Formerly in equity the ground must be found in admissions in the answer. . . . We assume that the rule to be applied here is more liberal but still a ground must be laid and the ground and the demand must be reasonable. . . . A general subpoena in the form of these petitions would be bad. Some evidence of the materiality of the papers demanded must be produced. . . .

We have considered this case on the general claim of authority put forward by the Commission. The argument for the Government attaches some force to the investigations and proceedings upon which the Commission had entered. The investigations and complaints seem to have been only on hearsay or suspicion — but even if they were induced by substantial evidence under oath the rudimentary principles of justice that we have laid down would apply. We cannot attribute to Congress an intent to defy the Fourth Amendment or even to come so near to doing so as to raise a serious question of constitutional law.

Judgments affirmed.

NOTES

1. Compare the following from the opinion in a later case involving FTC investigatory authority, United States v. Morton Salt Co., 338 U.S. 632, 642 (1950):

> The respondents argue that since the Commission made no charge of violation either of the decree or the statute, it is engaged in a mere "fishing expedition" to see if it can turn up evidence of guilt. We will assume for the argument that this is so. Courts have often disapproved the employment of the judicial process in such an enterprise. Federal judicial power itself extends only to adjudication of cases and controversies and it is natural that its investigative powers should be jealously confined to these ends. The judicial subpoena power not only is subject to specific constitutional limitations, which also apply to administrative orders, such as those against self-incrimination, unreasonable search and seizure, and due process of law, but also is subject to those limitations inherent in the body that issues them because of the provisions of the Judiciary Article of the Constitution.
>
> We must not disguise the fact that sometimes, especially early in the history of the federal administrative tribunal, the courts were persuaded to engraft judicial limitations upon the administrative process. The courts could not go fishing, and so it followed neither could anyone else. Administrative investigations fell before the colorful and nostalgic slogan "no fishing expeditions."

2. Is the *American Tobacco* decision based on an accurate analogy? Compare the following from the Supreme Court's more recent statement on the matter, in the previously cited *Morton Salt* case:

> The only power that is involved here is the power to get information from those who best can give it and who are most interested in not doing so. Because judicial power is reluctant if not unable to summon evidence until it is shown to be relevant to issues in litigation, it does not follow that an administrative agency charged with seeing that the laws are enforced may not have and exercise powers of original inquiry. It has a power of inquisition, if one chooses to call it that, which is not derived from the judicial function. It is more analogous to the Grand Jury, which does not depend on a case or controversy for power to get evidence but can investigate merely on suspicion that the law is being violated, or even just because it wants

> assurance that it is not. When investigative and accusatory duties are delegated by statute to an administrative body, it, too, may take steps to inform itself as to whether there is probable violation of the law.

338 U.S. at 643.

3. "At the investigatory stage, the Commission does not seek information necessary to prove specific charges; it merely has a suspicion that the law is being violated and wants to determine whether a complaint should be filed." FTC v. Invention Submission Corp., 965 F.2d 1086 (D.C. Cir. 1992).

4. For state cases approving what would once have been condemned as impermissible "fishing expeditions," see Atchison, T. & S.F. Ry. v. Lopez, 531 P.2d 455 (Kan. 1975); Myers v. Holshouser, 214 S.E.2d 630 (N.C. Ct. App. 1975), cert. denied, 216 S.E.2d 907 (N.C. 1975). For a more recent federal case rejecting a claim that a subpoena was unenforceable because the agency was on a fishing expedition, see SEC v. Blackfoot Bituminous, Inc., 622 F.2d 512 (10th Cir. 1980). To the extent agencies are to be denied the authority to engage in "fishing expeditions," the most appropriate method is to impose limits on subpoena authority in the enabling statute. See Bowsher v. Merck & Co., 460 U.S. 824, 838 n.12 (1983).

5. The leading Supreme Court case on the scope of agency subpoenas is Civil Aeronautics Bd. v. Hermann, 353 U.S. 322 (1957). The board there sought enforcement of subpoenas duces tecum served on a small nonscheduled airline and its officers and principal employees. The subpoenas called for production of virtually all the books and records of the airline during a period of thirty-eight months. The district court decreed enforcement, but the court of appeals reversed, limiting enforcement to those documents relevant and material to the proceeding before the board and holding that the district court must determine materiality and relevancy of the documents sought as a judicial question. The Supreme Court, per curiam, reinstated the district court's enforcement order. The *Hermann* decision upholds an agency subpoena that calls for production of all the books and records of the airline during a period of over three years. The production called for might not have imposed an undue burden on a giant company, which had many sets of records. But, at a time before the Xerox copier, the CAB requirement could have utterly disrupted the operation of a small airline, which might have only one copy of some of its most important records, especially those needed to operate the business. Under cases like *Hermann,* the unduly broad scope of an administrative subpoena may no longer be set up as a defense in the enforcement proceeding. "Broadness alone is not sufficient justification to refuse enforcement of a subpoena." FTC v. Texaco, 555 F.2d 862 (D.C. Cir.), cert. denied, 431 U.S. 974 (1977).

6. Could an administrative agency go so far as to require that records not only be produced but that records also be created in response to an agency subpoena? See EEOC v. Citicorp Diners Club, 985 F.2d 1036 (10th Cir. 1993). The EEOC issued a subpoena requiring the employer, Citicorp, to search its personnel files, interview employees, and provide written summaries of the findings. In response to Citicorp's claim that the information did not exist and would take hundreds of hours to compile, the court stated that the EEOC's subpoena power is not limited to the production of documents already in existence and that the EEOC may compel an employer to compile information within its control in order to respond to a subpoena. But see, E.E.O.C. v. Royal Caribbean Cruises, Ltd., 771 F.3d 757, 763 (11th Cir. 2014) (rejecting the EEOC subpoena as unreasonable and oppressive).

7. What defenses are still available in subpoena enforcement proceedings? According to Burlington Northern v. Office of Inspector General, 983 F.2d 631, 638 (5th Cir. 1993), "As a general rule, courts will enforce an administrative subpoena if: (1) the subpoena is within the statutory authority of the agency; (2) the information sought is reasonably relevant to the inquiry; and (3) the demand is not unreasonably broad or burdensome. . . . Courts will not enforce an administrative subpoena [only] if the above requirements are not met or if the subpoena was issued for an improper purpose, such as harassment." In addition, certain categories of information may not be subject to disclosure. Privileged information, whether attorney-client or work product, generally need not be produced. See Upjohn Co. v. United States, 449 U.S. 383 (1981). Some, but not all courts, have imposed a higher standard for subpoenas seeking information that implicates personal privacy. See McVane v. FDIC (In re McVane), 44 F.3d 1127, 1138 (2d Cir. 1995) ("Accordingly, we conclude that administrative subpoenas issued pursuant to an agency investigation into corporate wrongdoing, which seek personal records of persons who are not themselves targets of the investigation and whose connection to the investigation consists only of their family ties to corporate participants, must face more exacting scrutiny than similar subpoenas seeking records solely from corporate participants."). Not all courts, however, agree. See Doe v. United States (In re Admin. Subpoena), 253 F.3d 256 (6th Cir. 2001) (notwithstanding heightened privacy interests, court applied standard of reasonable relevance).

8. What about subpoenas to third parties to obtain records about those under investigation? Subpoenas might be issued to a bank for financial records or to a credit card company for expense records. There is no constitutional right to notice. See SEC v. Jerry T. O'Brien, Inc., 467 U.S. 735, 742-743 (1984). Instead, any requirement of notice would emanate from statutory requirements. Thus, the Right to Financial Privacy Act requires notice to customers of administrative subpoenas issued to banks, see 12 U.S.C. §3405, although there are numerous exceptions to the provision. See 12 U.S.C. §3413; see also 15 U.S.C. §78u(h)(2) (exceptions applicable to the SEC).

TEXAS LAWYERS INSURANCE EXCHANGE v. RESOLUTION TRUST CORP.

822 F. Supp. 380 (W.D. Tex. 1993)

NOWLIN, District Judge.

Before the Court is the above numbered and styled cause of action. Also before the Court is the Defendant Resolution Trust Corporation's Motion to Dismiss, filed July 9, 1992.

The U.S. Magistrate Judge was requested to make a Report and Recommendation in this matter pursuant to 28 U.S.C. §636(b) and Rule 1(d) of Appendix C of the Local Rules of the United States District Court for the Western District of Texas, as amended, effective July 1, 1990.

The Magistrate Judge filed his Report and Recommendation on March 31, 1993. The plaintiff Texas Lawyers Insurance Exchange filed its objections thereto and its motion to stay this action on April 15, 1993.

The Court has undertaken a de novo review of the entire file in this cause. The Court is of the opinion and finds that the Report and Recommendation filed by the Magistrate Judge in this cause is correct and should in all things be approved and adopted by the Court. . . .

This Court does hold that the Plaintiff, and all other similarly situated individuals and entities, shall not be subject to any sanctions, criminal penalties, or fines, until such a party fails to comply with a court order from a judicial enforcement proceeding that has been instituted by the Resolution Trust Corporation. . . .

REPORT AND RECOMMENDATION OF THE UNITED STATES MAGISTRATE JUDGE

CAPELLE, U.S. Magistrate Judge. The Magistrate Court submits this Report and Recommendation to the District Court pursuant to 28 U.S.C. §636(b) and Rule 1(d) of Appendix C of the Local Court Rules of the United States District Court for the Western District of Texas, Local Rules for the Assignment of Duties to United States Magistrates, as amended, effective July 1, 1990.

Before the Court is the Complaint filed on June 19, 1992 by Texas Lawyer's Insurance Exchange ("TLIE") to Quash, or in the Alternative, Modify Administrative Subpoena issued to it by the Resolution Trust Corporation ("RTC"). The RTC has filed a Motion to Dismiss Pursuant to Federal Rule of Civil Procedure 12(b)(1) and a Brief in support thereof on July 9, 1992. . . .

I. TLIE'S COMPLAINT

TLIE is a legal malpractice insurance company which has issued policies of legal malpractice insurance to the law firm of Eikenburg & Stiles. TLIE asserts that it has twelve (12) claims files in connection with this law firm and that it maintains a total of twenty-seven (27) files which relate to the firm. TLIE asserts that the files contain privileged communications from the insured and their counsel, as well as TLIE's own attorney-client communications, attorney work product, and consultant expert reports. TLIE states that Eikenburg & Stiles is currently a defendant in a lawsuit filed by the RTC in Civil Action No. H-92-1364, styled RTC v. Eikenburg & Stiles, et al., pending in the United States District Court, Southern District, Houston Division, and that a number of TLIE's files relate directly to this pending lawsuit. The plaintiff states that on or about June 7, 1992, the RTC telecopied the subpoena duces tecum at issue to TLIE's custodian of records, requesting the production of nine categories of documents by June 19, 1992.

TLIE sued to quash or modify this administrative subpoena duces tecum issued by the RTC to it under 12 U.S.C. §§1818(n) and 1821(d)(2)(I).... The RTC asserts that the subpoena issued is not self-executing, i.e., the RTC can only enforce compliance with the subpoena by filing an appropriate motion with a federal district court and with an opportunity to respond provided to TLIE. Therefore, the RTC asserts that this Court does not have jurisdiction to entertain this pre-enforcement challenge to the administrative subpoena.

TLIE [argues] that this Court does have jurisdiction to consider this motion to quash or modify the subpoena. TLIE asserts that §1818(n) grants the RTC the extraordinary power to fine or imprison those who do not produce subpoenaed documents. It alleges that the penalties and fines are self-executing because the statute does not require the RTC to first initiate a court action to compel compliance with the subpoena. TLIE asserts that this exposure to criminal penalties vests the district court with jurisdiction....

TLIE argues that "[f]ederal courts have long held that exposure to criminal penalties based upon the mere refusal to comply with a regulatory scheme vests the district court with jurisdiction to enjoin enforcement of the regulations." For this position, TLIE cites Ex Parte Young, 209 U.S. 123 (1908), in which a party's only avenue to contest state railroad rates was to refuse to comply with the rates, but this refusal subjected the party to fines and imprisonment regardless of the willfulness of the refusal to comply. In *Young*, the Supreme Court held that the federal district court had jurisdiction to enjoin enforcement of the rates. TLIE cites another case, Oklahoma Operating Co. v. Love, 252 U.S. 331 (1920), for a similar proposition. In that case, the laundry rate fixed by the Oklahoma Corporation Commission could be tested only by contempt with a daily penalty for each day of noncompliance. The Supreme Court held that the federal district court had jurisdiction to enjoin enforcement of the rate statute.

TLIE additionally argues that the main case supporting the RTC's position, Reisman v. Caplin, 375 U.S. 440 (1964), is distinct from the situation here in that the taxpayer with the subpoena in *Reisman* was not immediately subject to criminal penalties. Thus, the Supreme Court's ruling that the taxpayers' suit for declaratory and injunctive relief should be dismissed because they had an adequate remedy at law, i.e., they could raise their argument in any proceeding brought by the IRS to enforce the subpoena, is not applicable here. Instead, TLIE argues, §1818(n) gives the RTC power to enforce criminal penalties without need to first pursue a judicial action to enforce compliance; thus, TLIE's immediate subjugation to prosecution provides this court with jurisdiction to entertain this motion.

However, this argument propounded by TLIE has been considered and found unpersuasive by other courts. The *Reisman* court did consider the taxpayer's argument that he could be prosecuted under a section of the Internal Revenue Code for failing to produce the required documentation and thus be subject to a fine and/or imprisonment, as supported by the holdings of *Young* and *Oklahoma Operating Company*. Id., 375 U.S. at 446. However, the Court, in denying the declaratory and injunctive relief requested by the accounting firm from which the IRS subpoenaed financial records of certain taxpayers, concentrated on the ability of the taxpayer to challenge the subpoena before being subject to penalty. Id. In both *Young* and *Oklahoma Operating Company*, the Court decided that jurisdiction was present because the risk of penalty for refusing to comply with the subpoena was "so severe that the statutory procedure amounts to a denial of judicial review." Id. However, in a situation such as the subject "tax enforcement proceeding, the hearing officer has no power of enforcement or right to levy any sanctions." Id. Further, even if the taxpayer fails to produce the required documentation, the sanctions section would not be applicable "where the witness appears and interposes good faith challenges to the summons." Id., 375 U.S. at 447.

The Fifth Circuit Court of Appeals has not yet been presented with a situation similar to the one at hand involving §1818(n). However, in cases involving other types of administrative subpoenas, the Court has ruled that pre-enforcement challenges to such subpoenas must be dismissed for lack of subject matter jurisdiction. See Atlantic Richfield Co. v. FTC, 546 F.2d 646 (5th Cir. 1977) (declaratory and injunctive relief denied against enforcement of subpoena because, like the IRS subpoena in *Reisman*, FTC subpoenas are not self-executing and may only be enforced by a district court); United States v. Ramirez, 905 F.2d 97 (5th Cir. 1990) (following *Reisman*, the appellate court reversed the district court because it had no jurisdiction to entertain a motion to quash an administrative subpoena issued by the Immigration and Naturalization Service).

Thus, the question here is whether 12 U.S.C. §1818(n) requires the RTC to seek judicial enforcement of the subpoena issued thereunder before TLIE can be subject to sanctions for failure to comply or whether TLIE is immediately subject to sanctions without need for an independent court action. In pertinent part, §1818(n) provides

> Any such agency or any party to proceedings under this section may apply to the United States District Court for the District of Columbia, or the United States district court for the judicial district . . . in which such proceeding is being conducted, or where the witness resides or carries on business, for enforcement of any subpoena or subpoena duces tecum issued pursuant to this subsection, and such courts shall have jurisdiction and power to order and require compliance therewith.

12 U.S.C. §1818(n) (1989).

A court in the Fifth Circuit has construed a subpoena issued under §1818(n) to not be "self-executing and can only be enforced by an order of a district court." Ramirez v. Resolution Trust Corp., 798 F. Supp. 415, 416 (S.D. Tex. 1992). This court was faced with a situation nearly identical to this one presented. The RTC issued an administrative subpoena in order to facilitate an investigation of a failed savings institution, and the recipient filed a complaint to prevent enforcement thereof. The RTC then filed a motion to dismiss under Rule 12(b)(1) alleging the court's lack of subject matter jurisdiction to entertain a pre-enforcement judicial review of an administrative subpoena. The *Ramirez* court, citing the Fifth Circuit, stated: "Where an agency must resort to judicial enforcement of its subpoenas, courts generally dismiss anticipatory actions filed by parties challenging such subpoenas as not being ripe for review because of the availability of an adequate remedy at law if, and when, the agency files an enforcement action."...

In *Ramirez,* the court considered the plaintiff's argument that 1818(n) subjected him to immediate sanctions. Id. at 416-17. The court found that "noncompliance is not subject to prosecution when the summons is attacked in good faith." Id.... The plaintiff was afforded but failed to act on several opportunities to protect himself during the pre-enforcement stage: the subpoena itself allowed him to withhold any document considered privileged or protected from discovery, and he did not attempt to negotiate with the RTC for modification of the subpoena's scope before filing his complaint. Id., 798 F. Supp. at 417. Finding unpersuasive the plaintiff's sanctions argument, the court determined it had no jurisdiction to hear the pre-enforcement challenge. Id. at 417.

In addition to *Ramirez,* other courts reviewing §1818(n) have determined that subpoenas issued thereunder are not self-executing but require the agency to seek enforcement in federal court. See *Dobbs,* 931 F.2d at 957 ("In the context of an administrative subpoena, the administrative agency must request a district court to enforce its subpoenas."); Chandler v. RTC, Civ. No. J91-0691(W)(C), (S.D. Miss., Jackson Division, Dec. 16, 1991) (attached as Exhibit 1 to RTC's Brief) (court lacks subject matter jurisdiction over plaintiff's motion to quash because RTC's subpoena was not self-executing and can only be enforced by a federal district court)....

Here, the RTC issued its administrative subpoena pursuant to §1818(n) and §1821(d)(2)(I). Following Ramirez v. RTC, this Court concludes that the subpoena at issue is not self-executing and the RTC must resort to district court action to compel enforcement thereof. If such an action is initiated, if ever, TLIE will then be afforded an opportunity to respond and assert its reasons for noncompliance. If a district court then determines that TLIE has interposed a good faith challenge to the subpoena and follows *Reisman* and *Ramirez,* TLIE should not be subject to prosecution.

In light of the foregoing, the Magistrate Court RECOMMENDS that the District court GRANT the Defendant RTC's Motion to Dismiss the Case under Fed. R. Civ. P. 12(b)(1) filed on July 9, 1992 (#3) and DISMISS TLIE's complaint against the RTC for lack of subject matter jurisdiction....

NOTES

1. Subpoenas often end with a warning, such as "FAIL NOT AT YOUR PERIL." What is the peril run by a person who fails to obey an agency subpoena? Compare N.Y. Civil Practice Law §2308(a):

> Failure to comply with a subpoena issued by a judge, clerk or officer of the court shall be punishable as a contempt of court.

2. May agencies be vested with contempt power, so that they can punish directly disobedience of their subpoenas? Compare the following statements:

> Congress has never attempted, however, to confer upon an administrative agency itself the power to compel obedience to such a subpoena. . . . That Congress should so consistently have withheld powers of testimonial compulsion from administrative agencies discloses a policy that speaks with impressive significance.

Frankfurter, J., dissenting in Penfield Co. v. SEC, 330 U.S. 585, 603-604 (1947).

> *Brimson* is the basis of the well-established principle that agencies do not have power to enforce their own subpoenas. . . . [But] *Brimson* was decided in 1894, long before the advent of the "modern administrative state."

Atlantic Richfield Co. v. Department of Energy, 769 F.2d 771, 793 (D.C. Cir. 1984).

> Congress might well consider whether the long record of frustration and less restrictive modern notions of the separation of powers might not make it wise to empower at least some administrative agencies to enforce subpoenas without having to resort to the courts in every case.

Friendly, J., in Federal Maritime Comm'n v. New York Terminal Conference, 373 F.2d 424, 426 n.2 (2d Cir. 1967).

3. May the legislature make failure to obey an agency subpoena a criminal offense, punishable by fine or imprisonment? Of course, the individual who refuses to obey a court order enforcing an agency subponea may still be punished for contempt.

4. Congress has the ability to grant administrative agencies exceedingly broad subpoena authority. Section 215 of the Patriot Act, 50 U.S.C. §1861, allows the FBI to seek an order requiring production of "tangible things" to obtain "foreign intelligence information not concerning a United States person or to protect against international terrorism or clandestine intelligence activities. . . ." The order must be approved by a judge sitting on the Foreign Intelligence Surveillance Court, a court appointed by the Chief Justice that, for the most part, operates in secrecy. See 50 U.S.C. §1803(a). According to published reports, the NSA obtained an order from the FISA court that allowed it to collect telephone numbers, call times, and call durations (but apparently not the contents of the conversations) on all U.S. telephone calls.

5. The federal Administrative Procedure Act (APA) provision on subpoena enforcement reads as follows:

> On contest, the court shall sustain the subpoena or similar process or demand to the extent that it is found to be in accordance with law.
>
> Section 6(c), 5 U.S.C. §555(d).

Is the APA subpoena provision different from the law discussed in the prior pages? See Tobin v. Banks & Rumbaugh, 201 F.2d 223, 226 (5th Cir. 1953), cert. denied, 345 U.S. 942 (1953):

> Appellee urges that the phrase "in accordance with law" connotes that the court has jurisdiction, in an action to enforce the requirements of a subpoena to determine whether the person and the subject matter to which the subpoena is directed are within the jurisdiction of the agency, and in so doing, may adjudicate the issue of coverage. . . . There is nothing in the Administrative Procedure Act which suggests that the duty and burden of determining the question of coverage in the first instance was intended to be shifted from the administrative agency to the courts. To give effect to appellee's contention would, in most instances, sterilize the investigative powers of the Administrator and force him to trial without the benefit of the very evidence which the subpoena is designed to secure. Refusal of the courts to refrain from adjudicating the issue of coverage in the enforcement proceeding would result in a maelstrom of confusion, for by their refusal to permit investigation, employers would be enabled to secure a premature judgment on that issue and the very evil which Congress sought to overcome would prevail over the guardian appointed to correct it.

d. The Role of the Fifth Amendment

As the following case illustrates, The Fifth Amendment protection against compelled self-incrimination can also play a role in agency attempts to obtain information.

SHAPIRO v. UNITED STATES

335 U.S. 1 (1948)

MR. CHIEF JUSTICE VINSON delivered the opinion of the Court.

The petitioner, a wholesaler of fruit and produce, on September 29, 1944, was served with a subpoena *duces tecum* and *ad testificandum*, issued by the Price Administrator under authority of the Emergency Price Control Act. The subpoena directed petitioner to appear before designated enforcement attorneys of the Office of Price Administration and to produce "all duplicate sales invoices, sales books, ledgers, inventory records, contracts and records relating to the sale of all commodities from September 1, 1944 to September 28, 1944." In compliance with the subpoena, petitioner appeared and, after being sworn, was requested to turn over the subpoenaed records. Petitioner's counsel inquired whether petitioner was being granted immunity "as to any and all matters for information obtained as a result of the investigation and examination of these records." The presiding official stated that the "witness is entitled to whatever immunity which flows as a matter of law from the production of these books and records which are required to be kept pursuant to MPRs 271 and 426." Petitioner thereupon produced the records, but claimed constitutional privilege. . . .

It may be assumed at the outset that there are limits which the Government cannot constitutionally exceed in requiring the keeping of records which may be inspected by an administrative agency and may be used in prosecuting statutory violations committed by the record-keeper himself. But no serious misgiving that those bounds have been overstepped would appear to be evoked when there is a sufficient relation between the activity sought to be regulated and the public concern so that the Government can constitutionally regulate or forbid the basic activity concerned, and can constitutionally require the keeping of particular records, subject to inspection by the Administrator. It is not questioned here that Congress has constitutional authority to prescribe commodity prices as a war emergency measure, and that the licensing and record-keeping requirements of the Price Control Act represent a legitimate exercise of that power. Accordingly, the principle enunciated in the *Wilson* case, and reaffirmed as recently as the *Davis* case, is clearly applicable here: namely, that the privilege which exists as to private papers cannot be maintained in relation to "records required by law to be kept in order that there may be suitable information of transactions which are the appropriate subjects of governmental regulation and the enforcement of restrictions validly established."

Even the dissenting Justices in the *Davis* case conceded that there is an important difference in the constitutional protection afforded their possessors between papers exclusively private and documents having public aspects, a difference whose essence is that the latter papers, "once they have been legally obtained, are available as evidence." In the case at bar, it cannot be doubted that the sales record which petitioner was required to keep as a licensee under the Price Control Act has "public aspects." Nor can there be any doubt that when it was obtained by the Administrator through the use of a subpoena, as authorized specifically by §202 (b) of the statute, it was "legally obtained" and hence "available as evidence." The record involved in the case at bar was a sales record required to be maintained under an appropriate regulation, its relevance to the lawful purpose of the Administrator is unquestioned, and the transaction which it recorded was one in which the petitioner could lawfully engage solely by virtue of the license granted to him under the statute.

In the view that we have taken of the case, we find it unnecessary to consider the additional contention by the Government that, in any event, no immunity attaches to the production of the books by the petitioner because the connection between the books and the evidence produced at the trial was too tenuous to justify the claim.

For the foregoing reasons, the judgment of the Circuit Court of Appeals is *Affirmed.*

MR. JUSTICE FRANKFURTER, dissenting.

The Court this day decides that when Congress prescribes for a limited Governmental purpose, enforceable by appropriate sanctions, the form in which some records are to be kept, not by corporations but by private individuals, in what in everyday language is a private and not a Governmental business, Congress thereby takes such records out of the protection of the Constitution against self-incrimination and search and seizure. . . .

Instead of respecting "serious doubts of constitutionality" by giving what is at the least an allowable construction to the Price Control Act which legitimately avoids these doubts, the Court goes out of its way to make a far-reaching pronouncement on a provision of the Bill of Rights. In an almost cursory fashion, the Court needlessly decides that all records which Congress may require individuals to keep in the conduct of their affairs, because they fall within some regulatory power of Government, become "public records" and thereby, *ipso facto*, fall outside the protection of the Fifth Amendment that no person "shall be compelled in any criminal case to be a witness against himself." . . .

In conferring powers of investigation upon the Administrator, Congress designed to secure the promptest disclosure of the books and records of the millions of private enterprises subjected to the regulations of the Office of Price Administration. . . .

Subsections (a), (b), (c) and (e) impose these four requirements: persons engaged in the vast range of business subject to the Act may be required to (1) make and keep records, (2) make reports and (3) permit the inspection and copying of records and other documents; such persons as well as others may be required to (4) "appear and testify or to appear and produce documents, or both, at any designated place." An unconstrained reading of subsection (g) insured prompt compliance with all these requirements by removing any excuse based on the privilege against self-crimination.

Here the Administrator required the petitioner to "keep and make available for examination by the Office of Price Administration . . . records of the same kind as he has customarily kept. . . ." The Government contends that because the records of petitioner's own business, those that he "customarily kept," were required to be so kept by the Administrator, he was compelled to disclose their contents even though they may have incriminated him, and that he was afforded no immunity under subsection (g) because he was not disclosing what were really his records. . . .

If records merely because required to be kept by law *ipso facto* become public records, we are indeed living in glass houses. Virtually every major public law enactment — to say nothing of State and local legislation — has record-keeping provisions. In addition to record-keeping requirements, is the network of provisions for filing reports. Exhaustive efforts would be needed to track down all the statutory authority, let alone the administrative regulations, for record-keeping and reporting requirements. Unquestionably they are enormous in volume. The Congress began its history with such legislation. Chapter I of the Laws of the First Session of the First Congress — "An Act to regulate the Time and Manner of administering certain Oaths" — contained a provision requiring the maintenance of records by persons administering oaths to State officials. 1 Stat. 23, 24. . . . Every Congress since 1789 has added record-keeping and reporting requirements. Indeed, it was the plethora of such provisions that led President Roosevelt to establish the Central Statistical Board in 1933 and induced the enactment, in 1942, of the Federal Reports Act, 56 Stat. 1078. . . .

I do not intend by the above exposition to cast any doubt upon the constitutionality of the record-keeping or reporting provisions of the Emergency Price Control Act or, in general, upon the vast number of similar statutory requirements. Such provisions serve important and often indispensable purposes. But today's decision can hardly fail to hamper those who make and those who execute the laws in securing the information and data necessary for the most effective and intelligent conduct of Government.

The underlying assumption of the Court's opinion is that all records which Congress in the exercise of its constitutional powers may require individuals to keep in the conduct of their affairs, because those affairs also have aspects of public interest, become "public" records in the sense that they fall outside the constitutional protection of the Fifth Amendment. The validity of such a doctrine lies in the scope of its implications. The claim touches records that may be required to be kept by federal regulatory laws, revenue measures, labor and census legislation in the conduct of business which the understanding and feeling of our people still treat as private enterprise, even though its relations to the public may call for governmental regulation, including the duty to keep designated records.

If the records in controversy here are in fact *public*, in the sense of publicly owned, or governmental, records, their non-privileged status follows.... No one has a private right to keep for his own use the contents of such records. But the notion that whenever Congress requires an individual to keep in a particular form his own books dealing with his own affairs his records cease to be his when he is accused of crime, is indeed startling.

A public record is a public record. If the documents in controversy are "public records" and as such non-privileged in a prosecution under the Price Control Act, why are they not similarly public and non-privileged in any sort of legal action? There is nothing in either the Act or the Court's construction of it to qualify their "public" nature....

Moreover, the Government should be able to enter a man's home to examine or seize such public records, with or without a search warrant, at any time. If an individual should keep such records in his home, as millions do, instead of in his place of business, why is not his home for some purposes and in the same technical sense, a "public" library?... This is not "a parade of horribles." If a man's records are "public" so as to deprive him of his privilege against self-crimination, their publicness inheres in them for many other situations.

Violators should be detected, tried, convicted, and punished — but not at the cost of needlessly bringing into question constitutional rights and privileges. While law enforcement officers may find their duties more arduous and crime detection more difficult as society becomes more complicated, the constitutional safeguards of the individual were not designed for short-cuts in the administration of criminal justice.

And so I conclude that the Court has misconstrued the Fifth Amendment by narrowing the range and scope of the protection it was intended to afford. The privilege against self-incrimination is, after all, "as broad as the mischief against which it seeks to guard." If Congress by the easy device of requiring a man to keep the private papers that he has customarily kept can render such papers "public" and non-privileged, there is little left to either the right of privacy or the constitutional privilege. . . .

NOTES

1. Mandatory recordkeeping requirements are a pervasive element of the regulatory system, even more so now than at the time of the *Shapiro* opinion.

2. Justice Frankfurter wrote a vigorous dissent. As he noted, "If records merely because required to be kept by law *ipso facto* become public records, we are indeed living in glass houses." Do you agree with Justice Frankfurter about the possible implications of the majority decision, or do you think his objections and concerns are overblown?

3. *Shapiro* set out a standard for what has become known as the "required records" exception to the Fifth Amendment. Critics of the exception, including Justice Frankfurter in his dissent in *Shapiro*, note that the impact of allowing a statute or regulation requiring the maintainance of records to defeat the privilege, essentially allows a federal agency to override the Constitution's protection against compelled self-incrimination simply by prescribing recordkeeping requirements.

The next case addresses a related issue regarding the Fifth Amendment.

UNITED STATES v. HUBBELL

530 U.S. 27 (2000)

JUSTICE STEVENS delivered the opinion of the Court.

The two questions presented concern the scope of a witness' protection against compelled self-incrimination: (1) whether the Fifth Amendment privilege protects a witness from being compelled to disclose the existence of incriminating documents that the Government is unable to describe with reasonable particularity; and (2) if the witness produces such documents pursuant to a grant of immunity, whether 18 U.S.C. §6002 prevents the Government from using them to prepare criminal charges against him.

This proceeding arises out of the second prosecution of respondent, Webster Hubbell, commenced by the Independent Counsel appointed in August 1994 to investigate possible violations of federal law relating to the Whitewater Development Corporation. The first prosecution was terminated pursuant to a plea bargain. In December 1994, respondent pleaded guilty to charges of mail fraud and tax evasion arising out of his billing practices as a member of an Arkansas law firm from 1989 to 1992, and was sentenced to 21 months in prison. In the plea agreement, respondent promised to provide the Independent Counsel with "full, complete, accurate, and truthful information" about matters relating to the Whitewater investigation.

The second prosecution resulted from the Independent Counsel's attempt to determine whether respondent had violated that promise. In October 1996, while respondent was incarcerated, the Independent Counsel served him with a subpoena *duces tecum* calling for the production of 11 categories of documents before a grand jury sitting in Little Rock, Arkansas. See Appendix, *infra*. On November 19, he appeared before the grand jury and invoked his Fifth Amendment privilege against self-incrimination. In response to questioning by the prosecutor, respondent initially refused "to state whether there are documents within my possession, custody, or control responsive to the Subpoena." Thereafter, the prosecutor produced an order, which had previously been obtained from the District Court pursuant to 18 U.S.C. §6003(a), directing him to respond to the subpoena and granting him immunity "to the extent allowed by law." Respondent then produced 13,120 pages of documents and records and responded to a series of questions that established that those were all of the documents in his custody or control that were responsive to the commands in the subpoena, with the exception of a few documents he claimed were shielded by the attorney-client and attorney work-product privileges.

The contents of the documents produced by respondent provided the Independent Counsel with the information that led to this second prosecution....

II

It is useful to preface our analysis of the constitutional issue with a restatement of certain propositions that are not in dispute. The term "privilege against self-incrimination" is not an entirely accurate description of a person's constitutional protection against being "compelled in any criminal case to be a witness against himself."

The word "witness" in the constitutional text limits the relevant category of compelled incriminating communications to those that are "testimonial" in character. As Justice Holmes observed, there is a significant difference between the use of compulsion to extort communications from a defendant and compelling a person to engage in conduct that may be incriminating. Thus, even though the act may provide incriminating evidence, a criminal suspect may be compelled to put on a shirt, to provide a blood sample or handwriting exemplar, or to make a recording of his voice. The act of exhibiting such physical characteristics is not the same as a sworn communication by a witness that relates either express or implied assertions of fact or belief.... Similarly, the fact that incriminating evidence may be the byproduct of obedience to a regulatory requirement, such as filing an income tax return, maintaining required records, or reporting an accident, does not clothe such required conduct with the testimonial privilege.

More relevant to this case is the settled proposition that a person may be required to produce specific documents even though they contain incriminating assertions of fact or belief because the creation of those documents was not "compelled" within the meaning of the privilege. Our decision in *Fisher v. United*

States, 425 U.S. 391 (1976), dealt with summonses issued by the Internal Revenue Service (IRS) seeking working papers used in the preparation of tax returns. Because the papers had been voluntarily prepared prior to the issuance of the summonses, they could not be "said to contain compelled testimonial evidence, either of the taxpayers or of anyone else." Accordingly, the taxpayer could not "avoid compliance with the subpoena merely by asserting that the item of evidence which he is required to produce contains incriminating writing, whether his own or that of someone else." 425 U.S. at 409-410; see also *United States v. Doe*, 465 U.S. 605 (1984). It is clear, therefore, that respondent Hubbell could not avoid compliance with the subpoena served on him merely because the demanded documents contained incriminating evidence, whether written by others or voluntarily prepared by himself.

On the other hand, we have also made it clear that the act of producing documents in response to a subpoena may have a compelled testimonial aspect. We have held that "the act of production" itself may implicitly communicate "statements of fact." By "producing documents in compliance with a subpoena, the witness would admit that the papers existed, were in his possession or control, and were authentic." Moreover, as was true in this case, when the custodian of documents responds to a subpoena, he may be compelled to take the witness stand and answer questions designed to determine whether he has produced everything demanded by the subpoena. The answers to those questions, as well as the act of production itself, may certainly communicate information about the existence, custody, and authenticity of the documents. Whether the constitutional privilege protects the answers to such questions, or protects the act of production itself, is a question that is distinct from the question whether the unprotected contents of the documents themselves are incriminating.

Finally, the phrase "in any criminal case" in the text of the Fifth Amendment might have been read to limit its coverage to compelled testimony that is used against the defendant in the trial itself. It has, however, long been settled that its protection encompasses compelled statements that lead to the discovery of incriminating evidence even though the statements themselves are not incriminating and are not introduced into evidence. Thus, a half-century ago we held that a trial judge had erroneously rejected a defendant's claim of privilege on the ground that his answer to the pending question would not itself constitute evidence of the charged offense....

Compelled testimony that communicates information that may "lead to incriminating evidence" is privileged even if the information itself is not inculpatory. *Doe v. United States*, 487 U.S. 201, 208, n.6 (1988). It is the Fifth Amendment's protection against the prosecutor's use of incriminating information derived directly or indirectly from the compelled testimony of the respondent that is of primary relevance in this case.

III

... The "compelled testimony" that is relevant in this case is not to be found in the contents of the documents produced in response to the subpoena. It is, rather, the testimony inherent in the act of producing those documents. The disagreement between the parties focuses entirely on the significance of that testimonial aspect.

IV

The Government correctly emphasizes that the testimonial aspect of a response to a subpoena *duces tecum* does nothing more than establish the existence, authenticity, and custody of items that are produced. We assume that the Government is also entirely correct in its submission that it would not have to advert to respondent's act of production in order to prove the existence, authenticity, or custody of any documents that it might offer in evidence at a criminal trial; indeed, the Government disclaims any need to introduce any of the documents produced by respondent into evidence in order to prove the charges against him. It follows, according to the Government, that it has no intention of making improper "use" of respondent's compelled testimony.

The question, however, is not whether the response to the subpoena may be introduced into evidence at his criminal trial. That would surely be a prohibited "use" of the immunized act of production. See *In re Sealed Case*, 791 F.2d 179, 182 (CADC 1986) (Scalia, J.). But the fact that the Government intends no such use of the act of production leaves open the separate question whether it has already made "derivative use" of the testimonial aspect of that act in obtaining the indictment against respondent and in preparing its case for trial. It clearly has.

It is apparent from the text of the subpoena itself that the prosecutor needed respondent's assistance both to identify potential sources of information and to produce those sources. See Appendix, *infra*. Given the breadth of the description of the 11 categories of documents called for by the subpoena, the collection and production of the materials demanded was tantamount to answering a series of interrogatories asking a witness to disclose the existence and location of particular documents fitting certain broad descriptions. The assembly of literally hundreds of pages of material in response to a request for "any and all documents reflecting, referring, or relating to any direct or indirect sources of money or other things of value received by or provided to" an individual or members of his family during a 3-year period is the functional equivalent of the preparation of an answer to either a detailed written interrogatory or a series of oral questions at a discovery deposition. Entirely apart from the contents of the 13,120 pages of materials that respondent produced in this case, it is undeniable that providing a catalog of existing documents fitting within any of the 11 broadly worded subpoena categories could provide a prosecutor with a "lead to incriminating evidence," or "a link in the chain of evidence needed to prosecute."

Indeed, the record makes it clear that that is what happened in this case. The documents were produced before a grand jury sitting in the Eastern District of Arkansas in aid of the Independent Counsel's attempt to determine whether respondent had violated a commitment in his first plea agreement. The use of those sources of information eventually led to the return of an indictment by a grand jury sitting in the District of Columbia for offenses that apparently are unrelated to that plea agreement. What the District Court characterized as a "fishing expedition" did produce a fish, but not the one that the Independent Counsel expected to hook. It is abundantly clear that the testimonial aspect of respondent's act of producing subpoenaed documents was the first step in a chain of evidence that led to this prosecution. The documents did not magically appear in the prosecutor's office like "manna from heaven." They arrived there only after respondent asserted his constitutional privilege, received a grant of immunity, and — under the compulsion of the District Court's order — took the mental and physical steps necessary to provide the prosecutor with an accurate inventory of the many sources of potentially incriminating evidence sought by the subpoena. It was only through respondent's truthful reply to the subpoena that the Government received the incriminating documents of which it made "substantial use . . . in the investigation that led to the indictment." Brief for United States 3.

For these reasons, we cannot accept the Government's submission that respondent's immunity did not preclude its derivative use of the produced documents because its "possession of the documents [was] the fruit *only* of a simple physical act — the act of producing the documents." *Id.* at 29. It was unquestionably necessary for respondent to make extensive use of "the contents of his own mind" in identifying the hundreds of documents responsive to the requests in the subpoena. . . . The assembly of those documents was like telling an inquisitor the combination to a wall safe, not like being forced to surrender the key to a strongbox. 487 U.S. at 210, n.9. The Government's anemic view of respondent's act of production as a mere physical act that is principally non-testimonial in character and can be entirely divorced from its "implicit" testimonial aspect so as to constitute a "legitimate, wholly independent source" (as required by *Kastigar*) for the documents produced simply fails to account for these realities.

In sum, we have no doubt that the constitutional privilege against self-incrimination protects the target of a grand jury investigation from being compelled to answer questions designed to elicit information about the existence of sources of potentially incriminating evidence. That constitutional privilege has the same application to the testimonial aspect of a response to a subpoena seeking discovery of those sources. Before the District Court, the Government arguably conceded that respondent's act of production in this case had a testimonial aspect that entitled him to respond to the subpoena by asserting his privilege against self-incrimination. See 167 F.3d at 580 (noting District Court's finding that "Hubbell's compelled act of production required him to make communications as to the existence, possession, and authenticity of the subpoenaed documents"). . . .

Given our conclusion that respondent's act of production had a testimonial aspect, at least with respect to the existence and location of the documents sought by the Government's subpoena, respondent could not be compelled to produce those documents without first receiving a grant of immunity under

§6003. As we construed §6002 in *Kastigar*, such immunity is co-extensive with the constitutional privilege. *Kastigar* requires that respondent's motion to dismiss the indictment on immunity grounds be granted unless the Government proves that the evidence it used in obtaining the indictment and proposed to use at trial was derived from legitimate sources "wholly independent" of the testimonial aspect of respondent's immunized conduct in assembling and producing the documents described in the subpoena. The Government, however, does not claim that it could make such a showing. Rather, it contends that its prosecution of respondent must be considered proper unless someone — presumably respondent — shows that "there is some substantial relation between the compelled testimonial communications implicit in the act of production (as opposed to the act of production standing alone) and some aspect of the information used in the investigation or the evidence presented at trial." Brief for United States 9. We could not accept this submission without repudiating the basis for our conclusion in *Kastigar* that the statutory guarantee of use and derivative-use immunity is as broad as the constitutional privilege itself. This we are not prepared to do.

Accordingly, the indictment against respondent must be dismissed. The judgment of the Court of Appeals is affirmed.

It is so ordered.

NOTES

1. The *Fisher* case cited in *Hubbell* involved papers prepared by accountants in connection with the defendants' tax returns and given to the defendants' lawyers. The IRS knew the whereabouts of the documents and obtained testimony about the nature of the documents from the accountants. In declining to extend Fifth Amendment protection to the production of the documents, the Court had this to say:

> It is doubtful that implicitly admitting the existence and possession of the papers rises to the level of testimony within the protection of the Fifth Amendment. The papers belong to the accountant, were prepared by him, and are the kind usually prepared by an accountant working on the tax returns of his client. Surely the Government is in no way relying on the "truthtelling" of the taxpayer to prove the existence of or his access to the documents. . . . The existence and location of the papers are a foregone conclusion and the taxpayer adds little or nothing to the sum total of the Government's information by conceding that he in fact has the papers.

While the government in *Hubbell* had less knowledge about what he possessed, couldn't the government assume that certain business records were in his possession? The government, for example, sought a variety of specific documents such as tax returns, bank records, and employment contracts.

2. What kind of evidence would the government need to produce to avoid the Fifth Amendment problem raised by this case?

3. One of the sources cited by the majority in *Hubbell* was an article written by a Deputy Assistant Attorney General by the name of Samuel Alito. See 530

U.S. 27, 42, n.23. As the article notes, "When a witness turns over documents in response to a subpoena, he tacitly says two things of potential significance. First he says: 'I have these documents.' Second, he says: 'These seem to be the documents you want.' Because a witness producing documents makes these testimonial communications, there is logic in the theory that they should be protected by the Fifth Amendment privilege." Do you think now-Justice Alito would agree with the outcome of this case?

4. Justice Scalia, in a concurring opinion joined by Justice Thomas, had this to say about the Court's reasoning:

> I join the opinion of the Court because it properly applies this doctrine, but I write separately to note that this doctrine may be inconsistent with the original meaning of the Fifth Amendment's Self-Incrimination Clause. A substantial body of evidence suggests that the Fifth Amendment privilege protects against the compelled production not just of incriminating testimony, but of any incriminating evidence.

What is he suggesting in this concurring opinion? If his opinion were the law, how would it change the approach under the Fifth Amendment with respect to the act-of-production doctrine?

B PRIVACY AND ACCESS TO INFORMATION

Government agencies often possess large amounts of information about individuals and businesses. Questions as to what information held by agencies is open to public disclosure pits concerns about governmental openness against concerns about privacy. In some instances, disclosure could cause harm, for example to business interests, or invade personal privacy. Agencies feel this tension acutely as they may be under obligation to disclose information and yet limited in the permissible disclosures. At least three broad areas of law govern agency disclosures: the Freedom of Information Act (FOIA), 5 U.S.C. §552; the Privacy Act of 1974, 5 U.S.C. §552a; and the U.S. Constitution. The FOIA is a mechanism for compelling agencies to release information. The FOIA, however, contains exemptions from the requirement of mandatory disclosure, including, for example, one for personal privacy, another for trade secrets and another for confidential information. The Privacy Act contains restrictions on an agency's ability to disclose information. The Privacy Act also allows individuals to access agency records and ensure their accuracy. Finally, the U.S. Constitution to some degree protects informational privacy. The law around these constitutional proscriptions is not, however, well developed.

1. The Freedom of Information Act

Congress adopted the first iteration of the Freedom of Information Act (FOIA) in 1967, although it was amended significantly in the 1970s during the Watergate era.

> In enacting the FOIA . . . Congress sought "to open agency action to the light of public scrutiny." . . . Congress did so by requiring agencies to adhere to "a general philosophy of full agency disclosure." Congress believed that this philosophy, put into practice, would help "ensure an informed citizenry, vital to the functioning of a democratic society."

United States Department of Justice v. Tax Analysts, 492 U.S. 136, 142 (1989).

The Act requires federal agencies to disclose records upon request. The right to make such requests is "available to *any person*," not merely to *a party* in an agency proceeding. For the first time the individual was given a legally enforceable right of access to government files and documents that was not limited to those needed for litigation in an actual case. In this respect FOIA has made for a profound alteration in the position of the citizen vis-à-vis government. No longer is the individual seeking information from an agency in the position of a mere suppliant.

FOIA gives a person whose request for identifiable records is refused by an agency a right of action in a federal district court. The court is given jurisdiction to enjoin the agency from withholding records and to order production of agency records improperly withheld from complainant.

Although containing a presumption of disclosure, the FOIA contains a diverse number of exemptions from this requirement. They include matters classified as secret and involving national defense/foreign policy, certain internal agency matters, and documents compiled in connection with an investigation. In addition, several exemptions seek to protect privacy rights. Specifically, Exemption 4 allows an agency to withhold documents that contain trade secrets and confidential commercial or financial information. Exemption 2 applies to agency personnel policies, and Exemption 6 to personnel and medical and similar files, the disclosure of which would constitute a clearly unwarranted invasion of privacy. And, Exemption 7(C) protects documents compiled for law enforcement purposes that could reasonably be expected to constitute an unwarranted invasion of privacy.

How well do these exemptions work at balancing privacy and confidentiality with the benefits of an open government?

NATIONAL ARCHIVES AND RECORDS ADMINISTRATION v. FAVISH

541 U.S. 157 (2004)

JUSTICE KENNEDY delivered the opinion of the Court.

This case requires us to interpret the Freedom of Information Act (FOIA), 5 U.S.C. §552. FOIA does not apply if the requested data fall within one or more exemptions. Exemption 7(C) excuses from disclosure "records or information compiled for law enforcement purposes" if their production "could reasonably be expected to constitute an unwarranted invasion of personal privacy." §552(b)(7)(C)....

I

Vincent Foster, Jr., deputy counsel to President Clinton, was found dead in Fort Marcy Park, located just outside Washington, D.C. The United States Park Police conducted the initial investigation and took color photographs of the death scene, including 10 pictures of Foster's body. The investigation concluded that Foster committed suicide by shooting himself with a revolver. Subsequent investigations by the Federal Bureau of Investigation, committees of the Senate and the House of Representatives, and independent counsels Robert Fiske and Kenneth Starr reached the same conclusion. Despite the unanimous finding of these five investigations, a citizen interested in the matter, Allan Favish, remained skeptical. Favish is now a respondent in this proceeding. In an earlier proceeding, Favish was the associate counsel for Accuracy in Media (AIM), which applied under FOIA for Foster's death-scene photographs....

II

It is common ground among the parties that the death-scene photographs in OIC's possession are "records or information compiled for law enforcement purposes" as that phrase is used in Exemption 7(C).... This leads to the question whether disclosure of the four photographs "could reasonably be expected to constitute an unwarranted invasion of personal privacy."

Favish contends the family has no personal privacy interest covered by Exemption 7(C). His argument rests on the proposition that the information is only about the decedent, not his family. FOIA's right to personal privacy, in his view, means only "the right to control information about oneself." ... He quotes from our decision in *Reporters Committee*, where, in holding that a person has a privacy interest sufficient to prevent disclosure of his own rap sheet, we said "the common law and the literal understandings of privacy encompass the individual's control of information concerning his or her person." 489 U.S. 749, at 763, 103 L. Ed. 2d 774, 109 S. Ct. 1468. This means, Favish says, that the individual who is the subject of the information is the only one with a privacy interest.

We disagree. The right to personal privacy is not confined, as Favish argues, to the "right to control information about oneself." ... Favish misreads the quoted sentence in *Reporters Committee* and adopts too narrow an interpretation of the case's holding. To say that the concept of personal privacy must "encompass" the individual's control of information about himself does not mean it cannot encompass other personal privacy interests as well. *Reporters Committee* had no occasion to consider whether individuals whose personal data are not contained in the requested materials also have a recognized privacy interest under Exemption 7(C).

Reporters Committee explained, however, that the concept of personal privacy under Exemption 7(C) is not some limited or "cramped notion" of that idea. 489 U.S., at 763. . . . Records or information are not to be released under the Act if disclosure "could reasonably be expected to constitute an unwarranted invasion of personal privacy. 5 U.S.C. §552(b)(7). This provision is in marked contrast to the language in Exemption 6, pertaining to "personnel and medical files," where withholding is required only if disclosure "would constitute a clearly unwarranted invasion of personal privacy." §552(b)(6). The adverb "clearly," found in Exemption 6, is not used in Exemption 7(C). In addition, "whereas Exemption 6 refers to disclosures that 'would constitute' an invasion of privacy, Exemption 7(C) encompasses any disclosure that 'could reasonably be expected to constitute'such an invasion."*Reporters Committee*, 489 U.S. 749, at 756. Exemption 7(C)'s comparative breadth is no mere accident in drafting. We know Congress gave special consideration to the language in Exemption 7(C) because it was the result of specific amendments to an existing statute. See id., 489 U.S. 749, at 756, n. 9, *777*, n. 22.

Law enforcement documents obtained by Government investigators often control information about persons interviewed as witnesses or initial suspects but whose link to the official inquiry may be the result of mere happenstance. There is special reason, therefore, to give protection to this intimate personal data, to which the public does not have a general right of access in the ordinary course. Id., 489 U.S. 749, at 773. In this class of cases where the subject of the documents "is a private citizen," "the privacy interest . . . is at its apex." Id., 489 U.S. 749, at 780. . . .

As we shall explain below, we think it proper to conclude from Congress' use of the term "personal privacy" that it intended to permit family members to assert their own privacy rights against public intrusions long deemed impermissible under the common law and in our cultural traditions. This does not mean that the family is in the same position as the individual who is the subject of the disclosure. We have little difficulty, however, in finding in our case law and traditions the right of family members to direct and control disposition of the body of the deceased and to limit attempts to exploit pictures of the deceased family member's remains for public purposes.

Burial rites or their counterparts have been respected in almost all civilizations from time immemorial. See generally 26 Encyclopedia Britannica 851 (15th ed. 1985) (noting that "[t]he ritual burial of the dead" has been practiced "from the very dawn of human culture and . . . in most parts of the world"); 5 Encyclopedia of Religion 450 (1987) ("[F]uneral rites . . . are the conscious cultural forms of one of our most ancient, universal, and unconscious impulses"). They are a sign of the respect a society shows for the deceased and for the surviving family members. The power of Sophocles' story in Antigone maintains its hold to this day because of the universal acceptance of the heroine's right to insist on respect for the body of her brother. See Antigone of Sophocles, 8 Harvard Classics: Nine Greek Dramas 255 (C. Eliot ed. 1909). The outrage at seeing the bodies of American soldiers mutilated and dragged through the streets is but a modern instance of the same understanding of the interests decent people have for those whom they have lost. Family members have a personal stake in honoring and mourning their dead and objecting to unwarranted public exploitation that, by intruding upon their own grief, tends to degrade the rites and respect they seek to accord to the deceased person who was once their own.

In addition this well-established cultural tradition acknowledging a family's control over the body and death images of the deceased has long been recognized at common law. Indeed, this right to privacy has much deeper roots in the common law than the rap sheets held to be protected from disclosure in *Reporters Committee*. . . .

We can assume Congress legislated against this background of law, scholarship, and history when it enacted FOIA and when it amended Exemption 7(C) to extend its terms. Those enactments were also against the background of the Attorney General's consistent interpretation of the exemption to protect "members of the family of the person to whom the information pertains," U.S. Dept. of Justice, Attorney General's Memorandum on the Public Information Section of the Administrative Procedure Act 36 (June 1967), and to require consideration of the privacy of "relatives or descendants" and the "possible adverse effects [from disclosure] upon [the individual] or his family," U.S. Dept. of Justice Memorandum on the 1974 Amendments to the Freedom of Information Act 9-10 (Feb. 1975), reprinted in House Committee on Government Operations and Senate Committee on the Judiciary, Freedom of Information Act and Amendments of 1974 (Pub. L. 93-502), Source Book, App. 5, pp. 519-520, 94th Cong., 1st Sess. (Joint Comm. Print. 1975).

We have observed that the statutory privacy right protected by Exemption 7(C) goes beyond the common law and the Constitution. See *Reporters Committee*, 489 U.S. 749, at 762, n. 13, 103 L. Ed. 2d 774, 109 S. Ct. 1468 (contrasting the scope of the privacy protection under FOIA with the analogous protection under the common law and the Constitution); see also Marzen v. Department of Health and Human Servs., 825 F.2d 1148, 1152 (CA7 1987) ("[T]he privacy interest protected under FOIA extends beyond the common law"). It would be anomalous to hold in the instant case that the statute provides even less protection than does the common law.

The statutory scheme must be understood, moreover, in light of the consequences that would follow were we to adopt Favish's position. As a general rule, withholding information under FOIA cannot be predicated on the identity of the requester. See *Reporters Committee, supra*, 489 U.S. 749, at 771. We are advised by the Government that child molesters, rapists, murderers, and other violent criminals often make FOIA requests for autopsies, photographs, and records of their deceased victims. Our holding ensures that the privacy interests of surviving family members would allow the Government to deny these gruesome requests in appropriate cases. We find it inconceivable that Congress could have intended a definition of "personal privacy" so narrow that it would allow convicted felons to obtain these materials without limitations at the expense of surviving family members' personal privacy.

For these reasons, in agreement with the Courts of Appeals for both the District of Columbia and the Ninth Circuit, see Accuracy in Media v. National Park Serv., 338 U.S. App. D.C. 330, 194 F.3d 120 (CADC 1999); 217 F.3d 1168 (CA9 2000), we hold that FOIA recognizes surviving family members' right to personal privacy with respect to their close relative's death-scene images....

III

Our ruling that the personal privacy protected by Exemption 7(C) extends to family members who object to the disclosure of graphic details surrounding their relative's death does not end the case. Although this privacy interest is within the terms of the exemption, the statute directs nondisclosure only where the information "could reasonably be expected to constitute an unwarranted invasion" of the family's personal privacy. The term "unwarranted" requires us to balance the family's privacy interest against the public interest in disclosure. See *Reporters Committee*, 489 U.S. 749, at 762.

FOIA is often explained as a means for citizens to know "what the Government is up to." Id., 489 U.S. 749, at 773. This phrase should not be dismissed as a convenient formalism. It defines a structural necessity in a real democracy. The statement confirms that, as a general rule, when documents are within FOIA's disclosure provisions, citizens should not be required to explain why they seek the information. A person requesting the information needs no preconceived idea of the uses the data might serve. The information belongs to citizens to do with as they choose. Furthermore, as we have noted, the disclosure does not depend on the identity of the requester. As a general rule, if the information is subject to disclosure, it belongs to all.

When disclosure touches upon certain areas defined in the exemptions, however, the statute recognizes limitations that compete with the general interest in disclosure, and that, in appropriate cases, can overcome it. In the case of Exemption 7(C), the statute requires us to protect, in the proper degree, the personal privacy of citizens against the uncontrolled release of information compiled through the power of the state. The statutory direction that the information not be released if the invasion of personal privacy could reasonably be expected to be unwarranted requires the courts to balance the competing interests in privacy and disclosure. To effect this balance and to give practical meaning to the exemption, the usual rule that the citizen need not offer a reason for requesting the information must be inapplicable.

Where the privacy concerns addressed by Exemption 7(C) are present, the exemption requires the person requesting the information to establish a sufficient reason for the disclosure. First, the citizen must show that the public interest sought to be advanced is a significant one, an interest more specific than having the information for its own sake. Second, the citizen must show the information is likely to advance that interest. Otherwise, the invasion of privacy is unwarranted.

We do not in this single decision attempt to define the reasons that will suffice, or the necessary nexus between the requested information and the asserted public interest that would be advanced by disclosure. On the other hand, there must be some stability with respect to both the specific category of personal privacy interests protected by the statute and the specific category of public interests that could outweigh the privacy claim. Otherwise, courts will be left to balance in an ad hoc manner with little or no real guidance. Id., 489 U.S. 749, at 776. In the case of photographic images and other data pertaining to an individual who died under mysterious circumstances, the justification most likely to satisfy Exemption 7(C)'s public interest requirement is that the information is necessary to show the investigative agency or other responsible officials acted negligently or otherwise improperly in the performance of their duties. . . .

We hold that, where there is a privacy interest protected by Exemption 7(C) and the public interest being asserted is to show that responsible officials acted negligently or otherwise improperly in the performance of their duties, the requester must establish more than a bare suspicion in order to obtain disclosure. Rather, the requester must produce evidence that would warrant a belief by a reasonable person that the alleged Government impropriety might have occurred. . . . Given FOIA's pro-disclosure purpose, however, the less stringent standard we adopt today is more faithful to the statutory scheme. Only when the FOIA requester has produced evidence sufficient to satisfy this standard will there exist a counterweight on the FOIA scale for the court to balance against the cognizable privacy interests in the requested records. Allegations of government misconduct are "'easy to allege and hard to disprove,'" Crawford-El v. Britton, 523 U.S. 574, 585 (1998), so courts must insist on a meaningful evidentiary showing. It would be quite extraordinary to say we must ignore the fact that five different inquiries into the Foster matter reached the same conclusion. As we have noted, the balancing exercise in some other case might require us to make a somewhat more precise determination regarding the significance of the public interest and the historical importance of the events in question. We might need to consider the nexus required between the requested documents and the purported public interest served by disclosure. We need not do so here, however. Favish has not produced any evidence that would warrant a belief by a reasonable person that the alleged Government impropriety might have occurred to put the balance into play. . . .

NOTES

1. As already noted, FOIA reverses the normal presumption of validity for agency action by placing the burden on the agency in an FOIA action to sustain its action in withholding information. When complainant alleges that the agency refused his request for identifiable records, he has made out a case under FOIA. The burden now shifts to the agency to justify its refusal. How is this agency burden met?

The governing principle in this respect was stated by one federal court:

> The purpose of the Act, seen in the statutory language and the legislative history, was to reverse the self-protective attitude of the agencies under which they had found that the public interest required, for example, that the names of unsuccessful contract bidders be kept from the public. The Act made disclosure the general rule and permitted only information specifically exempted to be withheld; it required the agency to carry the burden of sustaining its decision to withhold information in a de novo equity proceeding in a district court. Disclosure is thus the guiding star for this court in construing the Act.

Consumers Union v. Veterans Admin., 301 F. Supp. 796 (S.D.N.Y. 1969), app. dismissed, 436 F.2d 1363 (2d Cir. 1971).

2. The agency can normally meet its FOIA burden only by showing that the records involved come within one of the nine exemptions listed in FOIA, which are expressly excluded from the disclosure requirement. One such exception is the "deliberative process" privilege, which allows the government to withhold documents that are generated as part of an agency's process of formulating a new policy. In her first Supreme Court opinion, Justice Amy Coney Barrett, writing for a 7-2 majority in 2021, addressed the question of whether FOIA's deliberative process privilege exempts from disclosure documents created during a statutorily required interagency consultation between the U.S. Fish and Wildlife Service, the National Marine Fisheries Service, and the Environmental Protection Agency. United States Fish & Wildlife Serv. v. Sierra Club, Inc., 141 S. Ct. 777 (2021). The Court protected from disclosure under FOIA documents created during interagency consultation that are "predecisional" and "deliberative." Further, the Court held that agency inactions remain predecisional and protected from disclosure if they "die on the vine," and are not adopted.

3. The power given the court by the 1974 amendments to examine records in camera to determine whether they may be withheld also extends to the other eight FOIA exemptions. With regard to them, however, the court must still take the exemptions as written. The matter to be determined in an FOIA action is whether the records at issue come within any of the eight exemptions.

4. For example, Milner v. Department of the Navy, 562 U.S. 562 (2011), addressed FOIA Exemption 2, which protects from disclosure material that is "related solely to the internal personnel rules and practices of an agency." The federal government had urged the Court to allow federal agencies to withhold not only records relating to employee relations and human resources but also those records whose disclosure could risk circumvention of the law. In an opinion joined by eight Justices, the Court criticized the lower court's expansive reading of what the Court considered plain unambiguous language as well as its practice of construing FOIA exemptions narrowly. In dissent, Justice Breyer noted that the more expansive definition had been relied upon by courts and agencies for thirty years. Although it rejected the application of Exemption 2 to protect the documents in this case, the Court noted that the government had "other tools at hand to shield national security information and other sensitive materials," including Exemption 1, which prevents access to classified documents, and Exemption 7, which protects information "compiled for law enforcement purposes" whose release "could reasonably be expected to endanger the life or physical safety of any individual."

5. It is the agency that decides whether to invoke an exemption. Yet in the case of personal privacy or the disclosure of trade secrets, the harm of disclosure falls on the person or entity who provided the agency with the records. Is there any way persons other than the agency can prevent disclosure under the FOIA? For example, what if an agency has a policy of always disclosing information requested under the FOIA, irrespective of the impact on privacy or the harm to the business? The short answer under the FOIA is no. In Chrysler v. Brown, 441 U.S. 281 (1979), the Supreme Court dealt with an effort by a government contractor to enjoin release under the FOIA of detailed employment data it had submitted to the Department of Labor. Known as a "reverse FOIA" suit since the purpose was to prevent rather than require disclosure, the Supreme Court rejected the cause of action. The Court held that the FOIA is exclusively a disclosure statute and affords no private right of action to enjoin agency disclosure. The FOIA protects the interests in confidentiality and privacy only to the extent that this interest is endorsed by the agency collecting the information. FOIA *ex proporio vigore* does not forbid agencies to disclose any information to the public. Does that mean companies or individuals must sit idly by while agencies disclose confidential or private information? No. They can allege that disclosure violates other statutes. In *Chrysler*, the disclosure may have violated the Trade Secrets Act. In addition, companies or individuals can argue that the agency decision to disclose was arbitrary and capricious. See McDonnell Douglas Corp. v. U.S. Dep't of the Air Force, 375 F.3d 1182 (D.C. Cir. 2004).

6. Do corporations have any "personal privacy" rights under the FOIA? AT&T argued that documents could be withheld under Exemption 7(C) because disclosure would result in an "unwarranted invasion" of its personal privacy. 5 U.S.C. §552(b)(7)(C). The Supreme Court, however, disagreed. See SEC v. AT&T, 562 U.S. 397 (2011) (finding that phrase "personal privacy" contained in Exemption 7(C) did not apply to corporations).

7. The Electronic FOIA (EFOIA) amendments adopted in 1996 were designed to clarify the application of FOIA to electronic records and to require agencies to set up electronic reading rooms where disclosed documents can be posted and available to the public. The FBI routinely adds additional material to its reading room, some involving very well known individuals. See http://vault.fbi.gov/recently-added

8. Perhaps most interesting, the 2007 amendments evince an attempt to provide greater oversight and centralization of the FOIA process. The amendments required each agency to establish a Chief FOIA Officer (of assistant director rank or its equivalent) to oversee the FOIA process within the agency, and FOIA Public Liaisons, who field complaints from requesters and participate "in reducing delays, increasing transparency and understanding of the status of requests, and assisting in the resolution of disputes." Finally, the amendments created the Office of Government Information Services within the National Archives and assigned it the task of verifying compliance by agencies with FOIA and offering "mediation services" to help resolve disputes between requestors and agencies.

AMERICAN IMMIGRATION LAWYERS ASS'N v. EXECUTIVE OFFICE FOR IMMIGRATION REVIEW

830 F.3d 667 (D.C. Cir. 2016)

Judge SRINIVASAN, Circuit Court Judge:

Immigration judges are employees of the Department of Justice. The American Immigration Lawyers Association submitted a request to the Department under the Freedom of Information Act (FOIA) seeking disclosure of records related to complaints about the conduct of immigration judges. In response to the request, the government disclosed thousands of pages of records. The government, however, redacted information in those records that it believes is either statutorily exempt from disclosure or non-responsive to the request. The district court upheld both categories of redactions. We disagree as to each.

First, the government invoked one of FOIA's statutory exemptions in redacting the immigration judges' names from all of the disclosed records. The government reasoned that, as a blanket matter, the privacy interest of immigration judges in avoiding disclosure of their names necessarily outweighs the public's interest in learning any of the judges' names. We conclude that the government's across-the-board approach cannot be sustained in light of the variety of privacy and public interests that may be at stake in connection with the disclosure of an immigration judge's name. We therefore remand for a more individualized inquiry into the propriety of redacting judges' names. . . .

I.

A.

Immigration judges are career civil-service employees in the Department of Justice's Executive Office of Immigration Review (EOIR). They preside over "deportation, exclusion, removal, recission, and bond" proceedings for noncitizens charged with violating the immigration laws. . . .

. . .

B.

The Freedom of Information Act generally requires government agencies to make information available to the public, subject to nine enumerated exemptions. For certain types of government records, the FOIA imposes an affirmative obligation — regardless of any request — to publish the information. Other records must be disclosed to the public upon request unless they fall within one of the statutory exemptions.

In November 2012, the American Immigration Lawyers Association (AILA) submitted a FOIA request to the Department of Justice seeking information about complaints filed against immigration judges. AILA took that action in light of ongoing concerns about immigration judges' conduct and questions about the transparency and efficacy of the complaint process. AILA's request sought the following information:

(1) All complaints filed against immigration judges;
(2) All records that reflect the resolution of complaints filed against immigration judges, including the type of informal action taken, if any, or formal discipline imposed, if any;
(3) All records that reflect the reasons for resolving complaints against immigration judges and/or findings relied on to resolve complaints against immigration judges, including any reports or memoranda from the Department of Justice Office of Professional Responsibility (OPR) or Office of the Inspector General (OIG);
(4) All records incorporated by reference in documents that reflect the resolution of complaints filed against immigration judges; and
(5) An index of the records described in paragraphs (2), (3), and (4) to the extent that those records constitute final opinions, including concurring and dissenti[n]g opinions, as well as orders, made in the adjudication of cases . . .

In June 2013, after more than six months had gone by without a response, AILA filed this lawsuit in the district court. Shortly thereafter, EOIR began a series of rolling disclosures, providing to AILA many responsive records including complaint files and other documents. By April 2014, EOIR had disclosed some 16,000 pages of documents encompassing 767 complaint files (including both substantiated and unsubstantiated complaints). The complaint files contained information about the date, nature, and resolution of each complaint, copies of relevant documents (e.g., the immigration judge's written decisions and hearing transcripts), emails, and documentation of the disposition and any other action taken in response to the complaint.

EOIR redacted from those records information it deemed exempt from disclosure under FOIA Exemptions 5 and 6. Exemption 5 covers information that would be privileged from disclosure in litigation, and the redactions under that exemption are not at issue here. Exemption 6 covers "personnel and medical files and similar files the disclosure of which would constitute a clearly unwarranted invasion of personal privacy." Invoking that exemption, EOIR redacted immigration judges' names and other identifying information from the disclosed complaint files. EOIR also, however, identified each immigration judge by a unique three-digit code in order to permit AILA to connect complaints to a particular judge and to identify patterns or track the progress of discipline.

. . .

In the district court, AILA challenged both EOIR's redaction under Exemption 6 and its redaction of non-responsive information in responsive records. In addition, AILA argued that FOIA's affirmative-disclosure obligation required publication of OCIJ's complaint resolution decisions. The district court rejected each of AILA's arguments and ultimately granted summary judgment to the government. AILA now appeals.

II.

AILA challenges the district court's decisions concerning: (a) the validity of the categorical redaction of immigration judges' names pursuant to Exemption 6. . . . We disagree with the district court's resolution [. . .] and remand for further proceedings. . . .

A.

We first consider EOIR's blanket redaction of immigration judges' names under FOIA's Exemption 6. The Supreme Court has explained that FOIA's exemptions are "explicitly made exclusive and must be narrowly construed." The agency bears the burden to establish the applicability of a claimed exemption to any records or portions of records it seeks to withhold.

Our review calls for us to "ascertain whether the agency has sustained its burden of demonstrating that the documents requested are . . . exempt from disclosure." . . .

FOIA's Exemption 6 enables the government to withhold "personnel and medical files and similar files the disclosure of which would constitute a clearly unwarranted invasion of personal privacy." We generally follow a two-step process when considering withholdings or redactions under Exemption 6. First, we "determine whether the [records] are personnel, medical, or 'similar' files covered by Exemption 6." There is no dispute that the records sought by AILA meet that criterion. Second, if, as here, the records are covered by the exemption, we "determine whether their disclosure 'would constitute a clearly unwarranted invasion of personal privacy.'" The dispute in this case concerns that second step.

In assessing whether the disclosure of the information at issue — immigration judges' names and identifying information — would rise to the level of a "clearly unwarranted invasion of personal privacy," we "'balance the public interest in disclosure against the interest Congress intended [Exemption 6] to protect.'" Here, we follow another two-step process. The first step, which, again, no one disputes is satisfied here, requires determining that "disclosure would compromise a substantial, as opposed to a *de minimis*, privacy interest."

"[T]he only relevant 'public interest in disclosure' to be weighed in this balance is the extent to which disclosure would serve the 'core purpose of the FOIA,' which is 'contributing significantly to public understanding of the operations or activities of the government.'" In other words, disclosure of government records under FOIA is meant to help the public stay informed about "what their government is up to."

AILA argues that ongoing concerns about the complaint process and disciplinary action (or lack thereof) imposed on immigration judges are relevant to understanding what the agency "is up to." We agree with AILA as a general matter, and have recognized similar public interests in our prior cases. We also note that EOIR has disclosed a substantial amount of information concerning the complaint system and the substance of actual complaints, and has made efforts to ensure that its disclosures are accessible and useful (including establishing a system to identify judges by anonymous three-digit codes, thereby enabling AILA — and the public — to track repeat offenders even without knowing the names of individual judges).

The relevant question, then, is not whether disclosing immigration judges' names would serve the public interest in disclosure in the abstract. Instead, the question is whether, given the information already disclosed by EOIR, the "incremental value" served by disclosing an immigration judge's name outweighs that person's privacy interest. Even given that more targeted inquiry, we conclude that EOIR's across-the-board redaction of all judges' names from all responsive documents was inadequately justified.

In an affidavit . . . EOIR outlined the rationale for its Exemption 6 redactions in categorical terms. It explained its view that all immigration judges have a privacy interest in withholding their names, and that their privacy interest, as a blanket matter, necessarily outweighs any public interest in learning any judge's name. . . . None of EOIR's materials addresses the privacy interests of individual immigration judges, or any potential public interest in learning individual immigration judges' names in particular circumstances. . . .

Exemption 6, we have explained, "does not categorically exempt individuals' identities . . . because the 'privacy interest at stake may vary depending on the context in which it is asserted.'" To be sure, in certain situations we have allowed an agency to justify withholding or redacting records "category-of-document by category-of-document" rather than "document-by-document." But we have permitted such an approach only if the documents within each category are sufficiently similar — and the categories are sufficiently well-defined and distinct — "to allow a court to determine whether the specific claimed exemptions are properly applied."

In other words, "the range of circumstances included in [a] category [must] 'characteristically support[ ] an inference' that the statutory requirements for exemption are satisfied." The question, then, is whether there has been a sufficient showing that the balancing analysis under Exemption 6 would yield a uniform answer across the entire proffered category, regardless of any variation among the individual records or persons falling within it. We cannot say that is true here.

The records at issue encompass all complaints OCIJ received during the relevant time period: whether substantiated or unsubstantiated, whether related to serious issues or comparatively trivial ones, and whether about immigration judges' conduct on the bench or their conduct outside the workplace. Moreover, the privacy interests at stake encompass those of each immigration judge subjected to any of the wide variety of types of complaints: whether a sitting immigration judge or someone no longer on the bench, whether a judge who has faced only one complaint or a judge who has repeatedly been the target of complaints, and whether the judge has been subjected to some type of discipline or has avoided disciplinary action (and the reasons why). Given the variety in types of complaints and circumstances of individual immigration judges, not every judge has the same privacy interests at stake and not every complaint would equally enlighten the public about "what their government is up to."

The interests on both sides of the Exemption 6 balancing test might vary in substantial measure with respect to different immigration judges (and perhaps different complaints). A retired immigration judge — who, after all, is a private citizen — presumably would have a greater privacy interest in avoiding disclosure of her name than would an immigration judge who sits on the bench today. Similarly, the public interest likely would be more pronounced in the case of a sitting immigration judge, who continues to make decisions as an employee of the Department of Justice, than in the case of a former judge. Additionally, disclosing the name of an immigration judge subject to numerous and/or serious substantiated complaints might shed considerable light on matters of public interest, whereas disclosing the name of an immigration judge subject to a single, unsubstantiated complaint might not. For instance, in the case of a sitting judge with a substantial number of serious and substantiated complaints, knowledge of her identity would enable the public to examine her official actions (including decisions), both past and future, and to assess any possible implications of those complaints for the conduct of her official responsibilities. By enabling the public to make such connections, knowing the identity of that judge could shed considerably more light on "what the[ ] government is up to," than simply knowing about the existence of some anonymous judge with a certain number of complaints against her.

"If it [were] always true that the damage to a[n] [immigration judge's] privacy interest from a [complaint file]'s production outweigh[ed] the FOIA-based public value of such disclosure, then it [would be] perfectly appropriate to conclude as a categorical matter that" disclosing immigration judges' names would constitute a clearly unwarranted invasion of personal privacy. But here, variations in the privacy and public interests at stake leave us unable to find, at least as a blanket matter, that the Exemption 6 balance tips in favor of withholding immigration judges' names in all circumstances. That is not to say, necessarily, that EOIR could not ultimately support redacting identifying information in all cases if its justifications for doing so were framed in a more targeted manner. That question is not before us, however. Because EOIR here sought to justify its withholding of immigration judges' names in purely categorical, across-the-board terms, it has not carried its burden to justify the Exemption 6 redactions.

On remand, if EOIR continues to claim that Exemption 6 warrants withholding the names of all immigration judges, it should make a more particularized showing for defined subgroups of judges or for individual judges. The district court would then "engage in ad hoc balancing of the competing interests at stake" for each subgroup of immigration judges or for each judge. The court, upon conducting the Exemption 6 balancing, might determine that the balance tips towards withholding in some, many, or all instances. And of course, if EOIR allocates immigration judges into subgroups and the grouping methodology is inadequate, the court may require EOIR to further separate the judges or make individual showings for each judge. At this stage, it suffices for us to conclude that "a categorical rule is inappropriate." . . .

NOTES

1. What were the AILA lawyers looking for? In your opinion, was this a valid use of the FOIA? Might there be circumstances in which the request for details about agency processes or actions would be inappropriate?

2. The court in *AILA* was critical of the "categorical approach" employed by the agency in redacting the material sought. What is the problem with allowing an agency to take a categorical approach to the FOIA request, and what interest is served in requiring the agency to take an individualized approach to the redactions? Aside from ease, why might the agency have preferred the categorical approach?

3. Most states have some version of the FOIA (usually labeled an "open records act"). For the most part, state open record acts (ORAs) track the FOIA in that they typically provide for a presumption of disclosure but also contain a number of exemptions. Often, language of the state ORA will track language of the FOIA and, where the state language tracks the federal, it is not unusual for state courts to rely on federal cases in interpreting their ORAs.

2. The Privacy Act

Agencies collect and maintain records, often on individuals. Those records may sometimes be inaccurate. Moreover, to the extent disclosed, the information may result in a violation of an individual's privacy or otherwise cause harm. Congress grappled with these issues by adopting the Privacy Act in 1974, another Watergate-era piece of legislation. The Act imposes limitations on the public disclosure of information by agencies. Unless subject to an exemption, information can only be disclosed after notifying the affected individual and obtaining written consent. In addition, the Act gives individuals the right to access records and have any inaccuracies corrected.

The Privacy Act contains numerous limitations and restrictions. For one thing, it only applies to materials maintained as part of a "system of records." The Act also contains a dozen exceptions from the prohibition on disclosure. Most significantly, however, while the Act contains a private right of action for violations, see 5 U.S.C. §552a(g)(4), the Supreme Court has severely limited the ability to show and obtain damages. In Doe v. Chao, 540 U.S. 614 (2004), the Court held that plaintiffs had to establish at least some "actual damages" in order to recover the minimum award of $1,000 guaranteed in the statute. In FAA v. Cooper, 132 S. Ct. 1441, 1453 (2012), the Court held that actual damages required a showing of pecuniary or economic hardship and did not, therefore, permit recovery for emotional distress.

NOTES

1. The Privacy Act is designed to prevent inappropriate disclosure. The Act allows "individuals on whom information is being compiled and retrieved the opportunity to review the information and request that the agency correct any inaccuracies." Henke v. United States Dep't of Commerce, 317 U.S. App. D.C. 405, 83 F.3d 1453, 1456-1457 (D.C. Cir. 1996).

2. Some view the Privacy Act as ineffective. They point to the limitation of the Act to information contained in a system of records. The phrase is defined as "a group of any records under the control of any agency from which information is retrieved by the name of the individual or by some identifying number, symbol, or other identifying particular assigned to the individual." 5 U.S.C. §552a(a)(5). Thus, not all records in the possession of the agency are subject to the prohibition on disclosure contained in the Act. See Bechhoefer v. United States DOJ, 312 F.3d 563, 566 (2d Cir. 2002) (disclosure of letter written by plaintiff to DEA did not violate Privacy Act because letter did not become part of agency's record-keeping system; letter had been kept in desk drawer by DEA agent).

3. In addition, the Privacy Act contains a number of exceptions. The broadest may be the "routine use" exception. See Fattahi v. BATF, 328 F.3d 176, 178 (4th Cir. 2003). See also Bechhoefer v. United States DOJ, 312 F.3d 563, 566 (2d Cir. 2002) ("It follows that the prescriptions of the Act do not come into play whenever a document falls into the possession of an employee of a covered agency. It is only when the document becomes incorporated into a record-keeping system under the agency's control that the Act's prescriptions apply.").

4. What about a record received by one agency from a system maintained by another agency? See Orekoya v. Mooney, 330 F.3d 1, 13-14 (1st Cir. 2003) ("The language does not support the view that an agency may immunize itself from liability by obtaining information from a different agency's system of records and then saying its further unauthorized disclosure is protected because its own system of records was not the original source. Such a reading would create a tremendous loophole in privacy protection, one surely not intended by Congress.").

3. Privacy and the U.S. Constitution

Privacy rights to personal information also emanate from the U.S. Constitution, although, after more than thirty years, the extent of the rights remains uncertain.

WHALEN v. ROE

429 U.S. 589 (1977)

JUSTICE STEVENS delivered the opinion of the Court. . . .

II

Appellees contend that the statute invades a constitutionally protected "zone of privacy." The cases sometimes characterized as protecting "privacy" have in fact involved at least two different kinds of interests. One is the individual interest in avoiding disclosure of personal matters,[1] and another is the interest in independence in making certain kinds of important decisions.[2] Appellees argue that both of these interests are impaired by this statute. The mere existence in readily available form of the information about patients' use of Schedule II drugs creates a genuine concern that the information will become publicly known and that it will adversely affect their reputations. This concern makes some patients reluctant to use, and some doctors reluctant to prescribe, such drugs even when their use is medically indicated. It follows, they argue, that the making of decisions about matters vital to the care of their health is inevitably affected by the statute. Thus, the statute threatens to impair both their interest in the nondisclosure of private information and also their interest in making important decisions independently.

We are persuaded, however, that the New York program does not, on its face, pose a sufficiently grievous threat to either interest to establish a constitutional violation. . . .

Unquestionably, some individuals' concern for their own privacy may lead them to avoid or to postpone needed medical attention. Nevertheless, disclosures of private medical information to doctors, to hospital personnel, to insurance companies, and to public health agencies are often an essential part of modern medical practice even when the disclosure may reflect unfavorably on the character of the patient. Requiring such disclosures to representatives of the State having responsibility for the health of the community, does not automatically amount to an impermissible invasion of privacy. . . .

JUSTICE STEWART, concurring.

In Katz v. United States, 389 U.S. 347, the Court made clear that although the Constitution affords protection against certain kinds of government intrusions

---

1. In his dissent in Olmstead v. United States, 277 U.S. 438, 478, Mr. Justice Brandeis characterized "the right to be let alone" as "the right most valued by civilized men"; in Griswold v. Connecticut, 381 U.S. 479, 483, the Court said: "[T]he First Amendment has a penumbra where privacy is protected from governmental intrusion." See also Stanley v. Georgia, 394 U.S. 557; California Bankers Assn. v. Shultz, 416 U.S. 21, 79 (Douglas, J., dissenting); id., at 78 (Powell, J., concurring).

2. Roe v. Wade, *supra*; Doe v. Bolton, 410 U.S. 179; Loving v. Virginia, 388 U.S. 1; Griswold v. Connecticut, *supra*; Pierce v. Society of Sisters, 268 U.S. 510; Meyer v. Nebraska, 262 U.S. 390; Allgeyer v. Louisiana, 165 U.S. 578. In Paul v. Davis, 424 U.S. 693, 713, the Court characterized these decisions as dealing with "matters relating to marriage, procreation, contraception, family relationships, and child rearing and education. In these areas, it has been held that there are limitations on the States' power to substantively regulate conduct."

into personal and private matters, there is no "general constitutional 'right to privacy.' . . . [T]he protection of a person's general right to privacy — his right to be let alone by other people — is, like the protection of his property and of his very life, left largely to the law of the individual States." Id., at 350-351 (footnote omitted).

Justice Brennan's concurring opinion states that "[b]road dissemination by state officials of [the information collected by New York State] . . . would clearly implicate constitutionally protected privacy rights. . . ." *Ante*, at 606. The only possible support in his opinion for this statement is its earlier reference to two footnotes in the Court's opinion, ibid., citing *ante*, at 598-600, and nn. 24-25 (majority opinion). The footnotes, however, cite to only two Court opinions, and those two cases do not support the proposition advanced by . . . Justice Brennan.

The first case referred to, Griswold v. Connecticut, 381 U.S. 479, held that a State cannot constitutionally prohibit a married couple from using contraceptives in the privacy of their home.

The other case referred to, Stanley v. Georgia, 394 U.S. 557, held that an individual cannot constitutionally be prosecuted for possession of obscene materials in his home. Although Stanley makes some reference to privacy rights, id., at 564, the holding there was simply that the First Amendment — as made applicable to the States by the Fourteenth — protects a person's right to read what he chooses in circumstances where that choice poses no threat to the sensibilities or welfare of others, id., at 565-568.

Upon the understanding that nothing the Court says today is contrary to the above views, I join its opinion and judgment.

NASA v. NELSON

562 U.S. 134 (2011)

JUSTICE ALITO delivered the opinion of the Court. In two cases decided more than 30 years ago, this Court referred broadly to a constitutional privacy "interest in avoiding disclosure of personal matters." Whalen v. Roe, 429 U.S. 589, 599-600 (1977); Nixon v. Administrator of General Services, 433 U.S. 425, 457(1977). Respondents in this case, federal contract employees at a Government laboratory, claim that two parts of a standard employment background investigation violate their rights under *Whalen* and *Nixon*. Respondents challenge a section of a form questionnaire that asks employees about treatment or counseling for recent illegal-drug use. . . .

I

A

The National Aeronautics and Space Administration (NASA) is an independent federal agency charged with planning and conducting the Government's "space activities." 51 U.S.C. §20112(a)(1). NASA's workforce numbers in the tens of thousands of employees. While many of these workers are federal civil servants, a substantial majority are employed directly by Government contractors. Contract employees play an important role in NASA's mission, and their duties are functionally equivalent to those performed by civil servants. . . . The Department of Commerce implemented this directive by mandating that contract employees with long-term access to federal facilities complete a standard background check, typically the National Agency Check with Inquiries (NACI). . . .

B

The NACI process has long been the standard background investigation for prospective civil servants. The process begins when the applicant or employee fills out a form questionnaire. Employees who work in "non-sensitive" positions (as all respondents here do) complete Standard Form 85 (SF-85).

Most of the questions on SF-85 seek basic biographical information: name, address, prior residences, education, employment history, and personal and professional references. The form also asks about citizenship, selective-service registration, and military service. The last question asks whether the employee has "used, possessed, supplied, or manufactured illegal drugs" in the last year. *Id.*, at 94. If the answer is yes, the employee must provide details, including information about "any treatment or counseling received." *Ibid.* A "truthful response," the form notes, cannot be used as evidence against the employee in a criminal proceeding. *Ibid.* The employee must certify that all responses on the form are true and must sign a release authorizing the Government to obtain personal information from schools, employers, and others during its investigation.

Once a completed SF-85 is on file, the "agency check" and "inquiries" begin. The Government runs the information provided by the employee through FBI and other federal-agency databases. It also sends out form questionnaires to the former employers, schools, landlords, and references listed on SF-85. . . .

All responses to SF-85 are . . . subject to the protections of the Privacy Act. The Act authorizes the Government to keep records pertaining to an individual only when they are "relevant and necessary" to an end "required to be accomplished" by law. 5 U.S.C. §552a(e)(1). Individuals are permitted to access their records and request amendments to them. §§552a(d)(1), (2). Subject to certain exceptions, the Government may not disclose records pertaining to an individual without that individual's written consent. §552a(b).

C

About two months before the October 2007 deadline for completing the NACI, respondents brought this suit, claiming, as relevant here, that the background-check process violates a constitutional right to informational privacy. . . .

As noted, respondents contend that portions of SF-85 . . . violate their "right to informational privacy." Brief for Respondents 15. This Court considered a similar claim in *Whalen*, 429 U.S. 589, which concerned New York's practice of collecting "the names and addresses of all persons" prescribed dangerous drugs with both "legitimate and illegitimate uses." *Id.*, at 591, 97 S. Ct. 869. In discussing that claim, the Court said that "[t]he cases sometimes characterized as protecting 'privacy'" actually involved "at least two different kinds of interests": one, an "interest in avoiding disclosure of personal matters"; the other, an interest in "making certain kinds of important decisions" free from government interference. The patients who brought suit in *Whalen* argued that New York's statute "threaten[ed] to impair" both their "nondisclosure" interests and their interests in making healthcare decisions independently. The Court, however, upheld the statute as a "reasonable exercise of New York's broad police powers."

. . .

III

As was our approach in *Whalen*, we will assume for present purposes that the Government's challenged inquiries implicate a privacy interest of constitutional significance. 429 U.S., at 599, 605. We hold, however, that, whatever the scope of this interest, it does not prevent the Government from asking reasonable questions of the sort included on SF-85 . . . in an employment background investigation that is subject to the Privacy Act's safeguards against public disclosure.

. . .

A

1

As an initial matter, judicial review of the Government's challenged inquiries must take into account the context in which they arise. When the Government asks respondents and their references to fill out SF-85 . . . it does not exercise its sovereign power "to regulate or license." Rather, the Government conducts the challenged background checks in its capacity "as proprietor" and manager of its "internal operation." Time and again our cases have recognized that the Government has a much freer hand in dealing "with citizen employees than it does when it brings its sovereign power to bear on citizens at large." This distinction is grounded on the "common-sense realization" that if every "employment decision became a constitutional matter," the Government could not function.

An assessment of the constitutionality of the challenged portions of SF-85 . . . must account for this distinction. The questions challenged by respondents are part of a standard employment background check of the sort used by millions of private employers. The Government itself has been conducting employment investigations since the earliest days of the Republic. . . . And the particular investigations challenged in this case arose from a decision to extend that requirement to federal contract employees requiring long-term access to federal facilities.

Respondents argue that, because they are contract employees and not civil servants, the Government's broad authority in managing its affairs should apply with diminished force. But the Government's interest as "proprietor" in managing its operations, *Cafeteria & Restaurant Workers*, does not turn on such formalities. See *Board of Comm'rs, Wabaunsee Cty. v. Umbehr*, 518 U.S. 668, 678, 679 (1996) (formal distinctions such as whether a "service provider" has a "contract of employment or a contract for services" with the government is a "very poor proxy" for constitutional interests at stake). The fact that respondents' direct employment relationship is with Cal Tech — which operates JPL under a Government contract — says very little about the interests at stake in this case. The record shows that, as a "practical matter," there are no "[r]elevant distinctions" between the duties performed by NASA's civil-service workforce and its contractor workforce. App. 221. The two classes of employees perform "functionally equivalent duties," and the extent of employees' "access to NASA . . . facilities" turns not on formal status but on the nature of "the jobs they perform." *Ibid.* . . .

2

With these interests in view, we conclude that the challenged portions of . . . SF-85 . . . consist of reasonable, employment-related inquiries that further the Government's interests in managing its internal operations. See *Engquist*, 553 U.S., at 598-599; *Whalen*, 429 U.S., at 597-598. As to SF-85, the only part of the form challenged here is its request for information about "any treatment or counseling received" for illegal-drug use within the previous year. The "treatment or counseling" question, however, must be considered in context. It is a follow-up to SF-85's inquiry into whether the employee has "used, possessed, supplied, or manufactured illegal drugs" during the past year. The Government has good reason to ask employees about their recent illegal-drug use. Like any employer, the Government is entitled to have its projects staffed by reliable, law-abiding persons who will "'efficiently and effectively'" discharge their duties. Questions about illegal-drug use are a useful way of figuring out which persons have these characteristics.

In context, the follow-up question on "treatment or counseling" for recent illegal-drug use is also a reasonable, employment-related inquiry. The Government, recognizing that illegal-drug use is both a criminal and a medical issue, seeks to separate out those illegal-drug users who are taking steps to address and overcome their problems. The Government thus uses responses to the "treatment or counseling" question as a mitigating factor in determining whether to grant contract employees long-term access to federal facilities.

This is a reasonable, and indeed a humane, approach, and respondents do not dispute the legitimacy of the Government's decision to use drug treatment as a mitigating factor in its contractor credentialing decisions. Respondents' argument is that, if drug treatment is only used to mitigate, then the Government should change the mandatory phrasing of SF-85 — "Include [in your answer] any treatment or counseling received" — so as to make a response optional. As it stands, the mandatory "treatment or counseling" question is unconstitutional, in respondents' view, because it is "more intrusive than necessary to satisfy the government's objective."

We reject the argument that the Government, when it requests job-related personal information in an employment background check, has a constitutional burden to demonstrate that its questions are "necessary" or the least restrictive means of furthering its interests. So exacting a standard runs directly contrary to *Whalen*. The patients in *Whalen*, much like respondents here, argued that New York's statute was unconstitutional because the State could not "demonstrate the necessity" of its program. The Court quickly rejected that argument, concluding that New York's collection of patients' prescription information could "not be held unconstitutional simply because" a court viewed it as "unnecessary, in whole or in part."

That analysis applies with even greater force where the Government acts, not as a regulator, but as the manager of its internal affairs. SF-85's "treatment or counseling" question reasonably seeks to identify a subset of acknowledged drug users who are attempting to overcome their problems. The Government's considered position is that phrasing the question in more permissive terms would result in a lower response rate, and the question's effectiveness in identifying illegal-drug users who are suitable for employment would be "materially reduced." That is a reasonable position, falling within the "'wide latitude'" granted the Government in its dealings with employees.....

B

1

Not only [is] SF-85 . . . reasonable in light of the Government interests at stake, they are also subject to substantial protections against disclosure to the public. Both *Whalen* and *Nixon* recognized that government "accumulation" of "personal information" for "public purposes" may pose a threat to privacy. But both decisions also stated that a "statutory or regulatory duty to avoid unwarranted disclosures" generally allays these privacy concerns. . . .

Respondents in this case, like the patients in *Whalen*, and former President Nixon, attack only the Government's *collection* of information on SF-85. . . . And here, no less than in *Whalen*, and *Nixon*, the information collected is shielded by statute from "unwarranted disclosur[e]." The Privacy Act, which covers all information collected during the background-check process, allows the Government to maintain records "about an individual" only to the extent the records are "relevant and necessary to accomplish" a purpose authorized by law. 5 U.S.C. §552a(e)(1). The Act requires written consent before the Government may disclose records pertaining to any individual. §552a(b). And the Act imposes criminal liability for willful violations of its nondisclosure obligations. §552a(i)(1). These requirements, as we have noted, give "forceful recognition" to a Government employee's interest in maintaining the "confidentiality of sensitive information . . . in his personnel files." *Detroit Edison Co. v. NLRB*, 440 U.S. 301 (1979). Like the protections against disclosure in *Whalen* and *Nixon*, they "evidence a proper concern" for individual privacy.

2

Notwithstanding these safeguards, respondents argue that statutory exceptions to the Privacy Act's disclosure bar, see §§552a(b)(1)-(12), leave its protections too porous to supply a meaningful check against "unwarranted disclosures." Respondents point in particular to what they describe as a "broad" exception for "routine use[s]," defined as uses that are "compatible with the purpose for which the record was collected." §§552a(b)(3), (a)(7).

Respondents' reliance on these exceptions rests on an incorrect reading of both our precedents and the terms of the Privacy Act. As to our cases, the Court in *Whalen* and *Nixon* referred approvingly to statutory or regulatory protections against "*unwarranted* disclosures" and "*undue* dissemination" of personal information collected by the Government. Neither case suggested that an ironclad disclosure bar is needed to satisfy privacy interests that may be "root[ed] in the Constitution." . . . Thus, the mere fact that the Privacy Act's nondisclosure requirement is subject to exceptions does not show that the statute provides insufficient protection against public disclosure. . . .

Citing past violations of the Privacy Act, respondents note that it is possible that their personal information could be disclosed as a result of a similar breach. But data breaches are a possibility any time the Government stores information. As the Court recognized in *Whalen*, the mere possibility that security measures will fail provides no "proper ground" for a broad-based attack on government information-collection practices. Respondents also cite a portion of SF-85 that warns of possible disclosure "[t]o the news media or the general public." By its terms, this exception allows public disclosure only where release is "in the public interest" and would not result in "an unwarranted invasion of personal privacy." Respondents have not cited any example of such a disclosure, nor have they identified any plausible scenario in which their information might be unduly disclosed under this exception.

In light of the protection provided by the Privacy Act's nondisclosure requirement, and because the challenged portions of the forms consist of reasonable inquiries in an employment background check, we conclude that the Government's inquiries do not violate a constitutional right to informational privacy.

. . .

For these reasons, the judgment of the Court of Appeals is reversed, and the case is remanded for further proceedings consistent with this opinion.

It is so ordered.

JUSTICE KAGAN took no part in the consideration or decision of this case.

JUSTICE SCALIA, with whom JUSTICE THOMAS joins, concurring in the judgment.

I agree with the Court, of course, that background checks of employees of government contractors do not offend the Constitution. But rather than reach this conclusion on the basis of the never-explained assumption that the Constitution requires courts to "balance" the Government's interests in data collection against its contractor employees' interest in privacy, I reach it on simpler grounds. Like many other desirable things not included in the Constitution, "informational privacy" seems like a good idea — wherefore the People have enacted laws at the federal level and in the states restricting the government's collection and use of information. But it is up to the People to enact those laws, to shape them, and, when they think it appropriate, to repeal them. A federal constitutional right to "informational privacy" does not exist.

NOTES

1. Most cases testing the constitutional boundaries of information privacy involve allegations of improper disclosure by government officials. This case, however, challenged the collection of data. What is the Court's view on this type of challenge? At least on the federal level, what limits, if any, exist on the ability of the government to collect personal information?

2. Initially, some courts of appeals were resistant to the establishment of a constitutional right to informational privacy. See J.P. v. DeSanti, 653 F.2d 1080, 1089 (6th Cir. 1981) ("Absent a clear indication from the Supreme Court we will not construe isolated statements in Whalen and Nixon more broadly than their context allows to recognize a general constitutional right to have disclosure of private information measured against the need for disclosure."). Gradually, however, courts addressing the issue have acknowledged the right. Even the Sixth Circuit seems to have reversed course. See Kallstrom v. City of Columbus, 136 F.3d 1055, 1062 (6th Cir. 1998) (undercover police officers had privacy interest in the personal information contained in their personnel records). Lower courts in general have not favored this constitutional protection and have sought to construe the right narrowly. See, e.g., Wade v. Goodwin, 843 F.2d 1150, 1153 (8th Cir. 1988) (right applied only to "most intimate aspects of human affairs"). Even where the courts find a violation of the constitutional right to privacy, they often dismiss on the grounds that the state actor was covered by qualified immunity. While some on the Supreme Court likewise question the right to informational privacy, only two Justices (Scalia and Alito) were willing to take that position in NASA v. Nelson.

3. What are some other kinds of information that if disclosed might violate a constitutional right to informational privacy? What about Social Security numbers? Compare Ferm v. United States Trustee (In re Crawford), 194 F.3d 954, 958 (9th Cir. 1999) ("the indiscriminate public disclosure of SSNs, especially when accompanied by names and addresses, may implicate the constitutional right to informational privacy") and Beacon Journal Publishing Co. v. Akron, 640 N.E.2d 164, 166 (Ohio 1994) ("the disclosure of the SSNs would violate the federal constitutional right to privacy") with Dodge v. Trustees of the National Gallery of Art, 326 F. Supp. 2d 1 (D.D.C. 2004) ("A privacy interest in the protection of one's Social Security number does not rise to the level of a fundamental right protected under the Fifth Amendment's substantive due process clause."). Which view is correct?

4. What about sexual orientation? See Sterling v. Borough of Minersville, 232 F.3d 190 (3d Cir. 2000) (police officer threatened to disclose to minor's grandmother about his homosexuality; minor committed suicide; "We can, therefore, readily conclude that [the minor's] sexual orientation was an intimate aspect of his personality entitled to privacy protection under Whalen"). Pregnancy? See Gruenke v. Seip, 225 F.3d 290 (3d Cir. 2000) (complaint alleged that high school swim team coach compelled team member to take pregnancy test then failed "to take appropriate steps to keep the information confidential").

5. What about disclosure of an ongoing investigation by a government agency that is otherwise confidential of a candidate for office? The answer, according to Judge Posner, is no. See Wolfe v. Schaeffer, 619 F.3d 782, 786 (7th Cir. 2010) ("The fact that a candidate for public office is under investigation for legal and ethical violations is likewise a matter of substantial public interest.").

6. Another provision designed to encourage greater transparency in the government is the Sunshine Act. See 90 Stat. 1241 (1976), 5 U.S.C. §552b. The provision requires most agency meetings to be open to the public. The provision in principle seems beneficial. Nonetheless, its application in practice may be otherwise. Because the definition of "meeting" includes any deliberation attended by "at least the number of individual agency members required to take action on behalf of the agency," a "meeting" can occur where, for example, a majority of the commissioners at the SEC discuss matters over lunch. As a result, the Act potentially impedes internal discussion and compromise.

7. The big exception to the open meeting requirement is the executive session. All the sunshine laws have provisions allowing executive sessions. Others authorize executive sessions where other listed subjects are discussed; typical subjects in these laws are labor negotiations; pardon and parole; national security; and acquisition, use, and disposition of real property. See Fla. Stat. §286.011(8) (board/commission may meet in private to discuss pending litigation). Note the executive session exceptions in the federal statute. How do they compare with those in the FOIA? Are they so broad as to defeat the law's purpose?

C GOVERNMENT IN SUNSHINE

Government in Sunshine Act

90 Stat. 1241 (1976), 5 U.S.C. §552b

Sec. 3. (a) Title 5, United States Code, is amended by adding after section 552a the following new section:

§552B Open meetings

(a) For purposes of this section—

(1) the term "agency" means any agency, as defined in section 552(e) of this title, headed by a collegial body composed of two or more individual members, a majority of whom are appointed to such position by the President with the advice and consent of the Senate, and any subdivision thereof authorized to act on behalf of the agency;

(2) the term "meeting" means the deliberations of at least the number of individual agency members required to take action on behalf of the agency where such deliberations determine or result in the joint conduct or disposition of official agency business, but does not include deliberations required or permitted by subsection (d) or (e); and

(3) the term "member" means an individual who belongs to a collegial body heading an agency.

(b) Members shall not jointly conduct or dispose of agency business other than in accordance with this section. Except as provided in subsection (c), every portion of every meeting of an agency shall be open to public observation.

(c) Except in a case where the agency finds that the public interest requires otherwise, the second sentence of subsection (b) shall not apply to any portion of an agency meeting, and the requirements of subsections (d) and (e) shall not apply to any information pertaining to such meeting otherwise required by this section to be disclosed to the public, where the agency properly determines that such portion or portions of its meeting or the disclosure of such information is likely to—

(1) disclose matters that are (A) specifically authorized under criteria established by an Executive order to be kept secret in the interests of national defense or foreign policy and (B) in fact properly classified pursuant to such Executive order;

(2) relate solely to the internal personnel rules and practices of an agency;

(3) disclose matters specifically exempted from disclosure by statute (other than section 552 of this title), provided that such statute (A) requires that the matters be withheld from the public in such a manner as to leave no discretion on the issue, or (B) establishes particular criteria for withholding or refers to particular types of matters to be withheld;

(4) disclose trade secrets and commercial or financial information obtained from a person and privileged or confidential;

(5) involve accusing any person of a crime, or formally censuring any person;

(6) disclose information of a personal nature where disclosure would constitute a clearly unwarranted invasion of personal privacy;

(7) disclose investigatory records compiled for law enforcement purposes, or information which if written would be contained in such records, but only to the extent that the production of such records or information would

(A) interfere with enforcement proceedings,

(B) deprive a person of a right to a fair trial or an impartial adjudication,

(C) constitute an unwarranted invasion of personal privacy,

(D) disclose the identity of a confidential source and, in the case of a record compiled by a criminal law enforcement authority in the course of a criminal investigation, or by an agency conducting a lawful national security intelligence investigation, confidential information furnished only by the confidential source,

(E) disclose investigative techniques and procedures, or

(F) endanger the life or physical safety of law enforcement personnel;

(8) disclose information contained in or related to examination, operating, or condition reports prepared by, on behalf of, or for the useof an agency responsible for the regulation or supervision of financial institutions;

(9) disclose information the premature disclosure of which would—

(A) in the case of an agency which regulates currencies, securities, commodities, or financial institutions, be likely to

(i) lead to significant financial speculation in currencies, securities, or commodities, or

(ii) significantly endanger the stability of any financial institution; or

(B) in the case of any agency, be likely to significantly frustrate implementation of a proposed agency action, except that subparagraph (B) shall not apply in any instance where the agency has already disclosed to the public the content or nature of its proposed action, or where the agency is required by law to make such disclosure on its own initiative prior to taking final agency action on such proposal; or

(10) specifically concern the agency's issuance of a subpena, or the agency's participation in a civil action or proceeding, an action in a foreign court or international tribunal, or an arbitration, or the initiation, conduct, or disposition by the agency of a particular case of formal agency adjudication pursuant to the procedures in section 554 of this title or otherwise involving a determination on the record after opportunity for a hearing.

(d) (1) Action under subsection (c) shall be taken only when a majority of the entire membership of the agency (as defined in subsection (a)(1)) votes to take such action. A separate vote of the agency members

> shall be taken with respect to each agency meeting a portion or portions of which are proposed to be closed to the public pursuant to subsection (c), or with respect to any information which is proposed to be withheld under subsection (c). A single vote may be taken with respect to a series of meetings, a portion or portions of which are proposed to be closed to the public, or with respect to any information concerning such series of meetings, so long as each meeting in such series involves the same particular matters and is scheduled to be held no more than thirty days after the initial meeting in such series. The vote of each agency member participating in such vote shall be recorded and no proxies shall be allowed. . . .

NOTES

1. "Open government" has become an increasingly popular battle cry. In response, two types of laws have been enacted. The first is the Freedom of Information Act (which has its counterpart in many states), which provides for public access to government records. The second is the open meeting law (popularly called "sunshine" law), of which the 1976 federal statute is the outstanding example. According to Goldman, The Sunshine Laws Do Not Uniformly Let Sunshine In, N.Y. Times, April 10, 1977, section 4, p. 7, "With passage in New York last summer, all 50 states have some form of sunshine law on the books."

2. The open meeting statutes in the different states range from the relatively simple requirement that all meetings of governmental bodies shall be open to the public, to complex laws that contain numerous definitions and express exclusions.

3. Note the scope of the "meeting" definition in the federal statute. Does it include informal as well as formal gatherings? Can agencies defeat the law's intent by dealing with, though not formally "disposing" of, business at informal sessions? (The California statute was expressly amended in 1961 to include informal meetings, Cal. Gov't Code §54953; Sacramento Newspaper Guild v. Board of Supervisors, 430 P.2d 43 (Cal. 1968).)

4. The big exception to the open meeting requirement is the executive session. All the sunshine laws have provisions allowing executive sessions. Others authorize executive sessions where other listed subjects are discussed; typical subjects in these laws are labor negotiations, pardon and parole, national security, and acquisition, use, and disposition of real property. See Fla. Stat. §286.011(8) (board/commission may meet in private to discuss pending litigation). Note the executive session exceptions in the federal statute. How do they compare with those in the FOIA? Are they so broad as to defeat the law's purpose?

5. Many of the sunshine laws also contain an exception for meetings connected with the judicial process, such as grand jury meetings. What about meetings of agencies exercising adjudicatory functions? Should the meetings of such agencies, particularly those deciding cases, be open to the public?

6. Compare Canney v. Board of Public Instruction, 278 So. 2d 260 (Fla. 1973) (Florida open meetings law applicable to county school board's "quasi-judicial" student suspension decision; strong dissent urged that open adjudicatory decision making was analogous to public jury deliberations).

See Board of Health v. State Journal-Gazette Co., 619 N.E.2d 273 (Ind. 1993) (open meetings law applicable only to meetings of agency heads, not meetings of agency employees).

CHAPTER 3 PROBLEM

You are outside counsel to Tele-Tex Corporation. About a year ago, the general counsel at Tele-Tex asked you to conduct an internal investigation to determine whether employees in the international division of Tele-Tex were adequately complying with environmental statutes and regulations. After an extensive investigation, you wrote a report that concluded that, over an eight-month period last year, the company was significantly in violation of the Clean Water Act as well as a number of other environmental regulations. Your report has been classified by the company as privileged. The Environmental Protection Agency (EPA) has notified Tele-Tex that it intends to conduct an inspection to examine books, records, and other materials necessary to determine whether the Company is in compliance with environmental regulations. The inspection is apparently part of a routine program of reviewing large companies for environmental compliance. The EPA has indicated that it would like to conduct the inspection tomorrow.

The general counsel has asked your opinion as to whether last year's violation should be voluntarily reported to the EPA. Even if Tele-Tex chooses to report the violations, the general counsel has asked your advice on whether to voluntarily turn over your report and whether, if given to the EPA, it could be obtained by private litigants or persons using the Freedom of Information Act. To buy some additional time, the general counsel would like to postpone tomorrow's inspection and wants to know if there is any legal basis for refusing to allow EPA officials to enter the Tele-Tex premises. Finally, the report contains highly personal information about some personnel at Tele-Tex (allegations of drug use on the part of some maintenance workers as well as sexual relationships between employees that may have contributed to the company's failure to discover the problem sooner). The general counsel is worried about the possibility that the report, if given to the EPA, will be leaked to the press. The general counsel has asked whether, in the event of a leak, there would be any recourse against the government. Prepare to respond to the general counsel on each of these issues.

Rules and Rulemaking

A TERMINOLOGY AND RULEMAKING

Bernard Schwartz

ADMINISTRATIVE TERMINOLOGY AND THE ADMINISTRATIVE PROCEDURE ACT*

48 Mich. L. Rev. 57-70 (1949)

The confusion of terminology in our administrative law is a natural result of the manner in which that branch of law has developed. "The use of terms in administrative law exemplifies its most characteristic element — that it did not spring from a single source but has its roots in many places." The administrative process has not evolved according to a fixed plan. . . . With the haphazard habit characteristic of our political life, individual administrative agencies have been created as and when the need for them arose, without any logical system. The form of agency chosen, the kinds of power delegated to it, and the safeguards imposed for the protection of private parties, appear often to have been dictated by opportunist considerations peculiar to the occasion. "As a natural consequence the choice of terminology has also been accidental"; and the terms employed have been neither consistent nor scientific. . . .

The most significant attempt to define basic administrative law terms is that made by the Federal Administrative Procedure Act of 1946. Section 2 of that act [now 5 U.S.C. §551] prescribes the meaning of the following key terms for the purposes of the act: Agency; Person and party; Rule and rule making; Order and adjudication; License and licensing; Sanction and relief; Agency proceeding and action.

The definitions in section 2 are fundamental to the operation of the Administrative Procedure Act. The act is carefully drawn so as to subject to its requirements only those cases specified by the relevant section. In determining the effect of any portion of the act upon specific administrative action, one must refer back to the definitions in section 2 to determine the scope of any of the

* Reprinted with permission of the Michigan Law Review Association © 1949.

terms defined in that section as they are used in any subsequent portion of the act. The operation of the Administrative Procedure Act thus depends upon the definitions in section 2. . . .

RULE AND RULE MAKING

The Administrative Procedure Act is based upon a fundamental dichotomy between rule making and adjudication. . . .

The definitions of "rule" and "order" in sections 2(c) and 2(d) of the Administrative Procedure Act [now 5 U.S.C. §551(4), (6); for the text of these definitions, see Appendix *infra*] are thus of cardinal significance, for they determine whether, in any given case, the agency concerned must conform to the formal adjudicatory procedures prescribed in sections 5, 7, and 8 of the act or whether it need only comply with the antecedent publicity requirements of section 4. In this respect, the definition of "rule" in section 2(c) is the more important, since, as we shall see, the definition of "order" in section 2(d) is a residuary one — "other than rule making but including licensing" — and thus turns upon the meaning of "rule."

Prior to the Administrative Procedure Act, the distinction between the legislative or rule making functions of administrative agencies and their judicial or adjudicative functions was one which had caused a great deal of difficulty. The distinction here was not merely a semantic one, for, even before the Administrative Procedure Act, the courts had imposed much less onerous procedural requirements in cases which concerned the exercise of functions which were legislative in nature.

Probably the most famous pre-Administrative Procedure Act attempt to explain the difference between legislative and judicial functions is that made by Justice Holmes in Prentis v. Atlantic Coast Line. [211 U.S. 210 (1908).] "A judicial inquiry," said he, "investigates, declares, and enforces liabilities as they stand on present or past facts and under laws supposed already to exist. That is its purpose and end. Legislation on the other hand looks to the future and changes existing conditions by making a new rule to be applied thereafter to all or some part of those subject to its power." The key factor in Justice Holmes' analysis is the element of time: A rule prescribes *future* patterns of conduct; a decision determines liabilities upon the basis of *present* or *past* facts. . . .

[T]he approach . . . will enable one to distinguish between rule making and adjudication in the great majority of cases. There are, however, certain situations which cause difficulty. Thus, under Justice Holmes' test, an administrative determination which is future in effect is a rule. This would lead to the conclusion that licensing or the issuance of injunctive orders, such as a cease and desist order of the National Labor Relations Board, are instances of rule making, which would be undesirable from the point of view of the procedural requirements which should be necessary in such cases. On the other hand, if the test of applicability be adopted, a function such as rate making would be classified as judicial, although most of the authority on the point indicates that it is legislative in character.

Section 2(c) of the Administrative Procedure Act seems to follow Justice Holmes in its definition of "rule." Under it, the key factor in determining the nature of any agency determination is that of "future effect." Aside from the element of time, a good part of the definition might be applicable as well to administrative adjudications. Thus, a judicial decision is normally of particular applicability and implements or interprets law. The difficulty noted above, under the time test, with regard to licensing and injunctive orders is, as we shall see, avoided by the express inclusion of them in section 2(d) of the act.

It should be emphasized that under the definition in section 2(c), rules are not limited to statements of *general* applicability. They also include statements of *particular* applicability — rules which apply only to specific individuals or situations. This is the portion of the definition of "rule" which, at first glance, causes the greatest difficulty, for particular applicability is usually thought to be the most characteristic feature of an adjudicatory decision. The original draft of the bill which became the Administrative Procedure Act limited rules to "statements of general applicability." "The change of the language to embrace specifically rules of 'particular' as well as 'general' applicability is necessary in order to avoid controversy and assure coverage of rule making addressed to named persons."

It has been suggested that this change in wording "may have the effect of very greatly increasing the scope of what is included as rule making, and, since the definition of adjudication is residual, of correspondingly drastically narrowing the scope of adjudication." The difficulty here is, however, largely avoided by the express limitation of section 2(c) to statements of "future effect." There can thus be no confusion with regard to the great majority of administrative adjudications, for, though particular in applicability, they do not meet the requirement of "future effect." The difficulty that arises with regard to certain types of adjudications which are future in effect is minimized by the express inclusion of injunctive and declaratory orders and licensing in the definition of "order and adjudication" in section 2(d).

Difficulties can, it is true, still arise with regard to certain types of administrative action. For example, any award requiring the payment of money is technically of future effect and hence a "rule." But a literal interpretation here is obviously undesirable. Indeed, as Professor Davis points out, the possible confusion inherent in section 2(c) can be avoided by assuming that, apart from the express examples given in that section, the term "rule" is intended by the Administrative Procedure Act to have its traditional meaning. "The words 'or particular' were not intended to change into rule making what has heretofore been regarded as adjudication; those words mean no more than what is otherwise rule making does not become adjudication merely because it applies only to particular parties or to a particular situation."

ORDER AND ADJUDICATION

The definition of "adjudication" in section 2(d) of the Administrative Procedure Act is primarily a residuary one. "Order" (which is the end result of an "adjudication") means the final agency disposition "in any matter other than rule making but including licensing." The scope of the term "adjudication" in section 2(d) of the act is thus dependent upon the content of the term "rule" as defined in section 2(c). The logical approach in any particular case would be to determine first whether the function concerned comes within the definition of "rule making" in section 2(c). If it does not, then it must come within section 2(d), for adjudication under the Administrative Procedure Act is determined by what is not rule making. As we have already discussed in some detail the scope of the definition in section 2(c) of the act, it will not be necessary to devote much space to section 2(d) at this time.

A word should, however, be said of the express inclusions in that section. Thus, it is expressly stated that an agency disposition comes within the definition of "order" whether it is "affirmative or negative . . . in form." The language here seems to be intended as a legislative restatement of the repudiation of the so-called "negative order" doctrine by Rochester Telephone Corp. v. United States [307 U.S. 125 (1939).] Under the Administrative Procedure Act, as under that decision, it is the effect rather than the form of administrative action that is determinative. If a matter before an agency is finally disposed of, and a rule making proceeding is not involved, the disposition is an "adjudication," even though it is negative in form. "Any distinction, as such, between 'negative' and 'affirmative' orders . . . serves no useful purpose, and insofar as earlier decisions have been controlled by this distinction, they can no longer be guiding."

The other express inclusions in section 2(d) take care of cases which might otherwise come within the definition of "rule" in section 2(c). Thus, as we have seen, agency action that is injunctive in form, for example, a cease and desist order of the Federal Trade Commission, might otherwise be considered a rule, a result that would manifestly be undesirable from the point of view of procedural requirements. The express addition of the term "injunctive" to section 2(d) was "prompted by the fact that some people interpret 'future effect' as used in defining rule making, to include injunctive action, whereas the latter is traditionally and clearly adjudication. It is made even more necessary that this matter be clarified because of the amendment of section 2(c) to embrace clearly particularized rule making. . . ." Like considerations apply to the express inclusion in section 2(d) of "declaratory orders," such as are authorized by section 5(d) of the Administrative Procedure Act, and "licensing." As we shall see, the question whether licensing is a legislative or an adjudicative function is one which has caused great difficulty.

The provisions of sections 2(c) and 2(d) of the Administrative Procedure Act represent an attempt to resolve one of the most troublesome problems of administrative terminology — whether a particular administrative function is legislative or judicial in nature. One may disagree with particular aspects of the act's definitions in this respect, but one must admit that they do result in consistency of nomenclature, if only for the purposes of the act itself. The effect of the Administrative Procedure Act in this respect is, of course, limited. Though the act employs the basic rule-order distinction, federal agencies continue to use the terminology to which they are accustomed, with confusing results such as have already been adverted to. "Thus, although the Act provides that wages and rate making determinations are 'rules,' the Wage and Hour Division and the Interstate Commerce Commission have designated them and continue to designate them as 'orders.' The Treasury Department uses the term 'decision' to describe amendments to its regulations."

Kenneth F. Warren

ADMINISTRATIVE LAW IN THE POLITICAL SYSTEM*

137 (6th ed. 2020)

There have been frustrating definitional and usage problems with rules and rulemaking. Scholars and courts have often used the terminology of rules and rulemaking differently, especially confusing the distinction between rulemaking and ordermaking (adjudication). Despite the need to make a sharper distinction between the meanings and applications of rules and orders, public agencies, courts, and legislators continue to employ the terminology inconsistently, confusing administrative law students and even themselves. For instance, the Treasury Department has a tradition of referring to rules as decisions, which it publishes as "Treasury Decisions," while regulatory commissions such as the FTC and FCC like to shape public policy through "orders," which they apply as general rules or regulations. Confusion over the status of rules and orders motivated Bernard Schwartz to write: "Today the administrative law student too often feels like Alice after going through her looking glass; [yearning] for that *other* room where chairs are actually chairs and tables, tables — and rules and regulations are rules and regulations and orders, orders."

For more in-depth discussion of the issues with the definition of "rule" and "rulemaking" in the APA, see Croston, It Means What It Says: Deciphering and Respecting the APA's Definition of "Rule", 53 Washburn L.J. 27 (2013) (looking at legislative history and past interpretations of "rule" in the APA); Levin, The Case for (Finally) Fixing the APA's Definition of "Rule", 56 Admin. L. Rev. 1007 (2004) (arguing that the APA's definition of "rule" does not comport with our everyday understanding of the term; suggests removal of "or particular" and "and future effect" from the definition).

* Reprinted with permission of Routledge (Taylor & Francis Group) © 2020.

MORALES v. CALIFORNIA DEP'T OF CORRECTIONS AND REHABILITATION

85 Cal. Rptr. 3d 724 (Cal. App. 2008)

SIMONS, Acting P.J.

The treatment and management of condemned inmates from the time an execution date is set through completion of the execution is subject to a protocol issued on May 15, 2007, by the California Department of Corrections and Rehabilitation (CDCR) and CDCR Secretary James E. Tilton (Tilton) (collectively appellants). The protocol, Operational Procedure No. 0-770, is formally titled "STATE OF CALIFORNIA SAN QUENTIN OPERATIONAL PROCEDURE NUMBER 0-770: EXECUTION BY LETHAL INJECTION" (hereafter OP 770). Two condemned inmates, respondents Michael Morales and Mitchell Sims, challenged the validity of OP 770, arguing it had been adopted without compliance with the requirements of the [California] Administrative Procedure Act (APA) (Gov. Code, §11340 et seq.). The trial court agreed, granted respondents' summary judgment motion and enjoined appellants from carrying out the lethal injection of any condemned inmates under OP 770 unless and until that protocol is promulgated in compliance with the APA.

Appellants raise . . . challenges to the trial court's ruling. They argue OP 770 is not subject to the APA because it is not a rule of "general application." . . .

BACKGROUND

San Quentin State Prison (San Quentin) is the only prison authorized to execute California inmates. (§3603.) Pursuant to section 3604, unless a condemned inmate affirmatively elects to be executed by lethal gas, executions are performed by lethal injection. OP 770 was adopted by the CDCR to implement section 3604. The protocol states the following purposes and objectives:

> "**A.** The purpose of this procedure is to establish appropriate guidelines for the execution of condemned inmates in compliance with the laws of the State of California and the United States.
>
> "**B.** The objectives of this procedure are:
>
> 1. To establish the care, treatment and management of condemned inmates from the time an execution date is set through the completion of the execution.
>
> "2. To establish criteria for the selection, training, and oversight of the Lethal Injection Team.
>
> "3. To delineate specific duties and responsibilities of personnel in preparation for and completion of the execution by lethal injection of condemned inmates.
>
> "4. To ensure direct supervision and managerial oversight of the Lethal Injection Process."

OP 770 states the procedure is subject to the approval of the San Quentin Warden (Warden) and the CDCR Secretary. It provides, "The Warden is responsible for the recruitment, selection, retention, and training of all staff involved in the Lethal Injection process" and "for managerial oversight and overall implementation of this procedure."

OP 770 provides that, upon receipt of the execution order, the Warden and certain other designated officials interview the condemned inmate and serve the warrant of execution. The inmate is informed of "the choices of execution method," and is instructed to indicate his choice within 10 days on a prescribed form. Further, he is informed that "if no choice is made, lethal injection will be the method of execution."

As to the recruitment, screening and selection of lethal injection team members, OP 770 provides in part:

> "a. With the assistance of the Director, Division of Adult Institutions (DAI), the Warden will coordinate the recruitment and selection of Lethal Injection Team Members. The Lethal Injection Team will consist of a minimum of 20 members. The total number of Lethal Injection Team Members will be determined by the Warden.
>
> "b. In the event the Warden is unable to field a sufficient number of qualified Lethal Injection Team Members, the Warden will contact the Director, DAI, to coordinate the identification of additional potential candidates for team membership. Prospective team members will be selected from departmental locations as determined appropriate by the Director, DAI.
>
> "c. The hiring authorities from designated locations will select prospective team members from personnel assigned to their respective areas of responsibility consistent with selection criteria [enumerated in OP 770]. The hiring authorities will forward the names and classifications of prospective team members to the Director, DAI."

OP 770 provides that the DAI Director will ensure that a sufficient number of lethal injection team members will be maintained.

As to news media witnesses at executions, OP 770 provides, "When an execution is scheduled, the CDCR, Assistant Secretary, Office of Public and Employee Communications, will notify the media and establish a 10-day filing period in which media may request to witness the execution." It further provides, "The Assistant Secretary, Office of Public and Employee Communications, and the San Quentin Public Information Officer will consult with the Warden to select the members of the news media to witness an execution." OP 770 also provides: "The San Quentin Public Information Officer and Assistant Secretary, Office of Public and Employee Communications will be responsible for all CDCR press releases prior to, during and after an execution and for the developing of all information releases."

As to the chronology of events prior to an execution, OP 770 provides that approximately 30 days prior to an execution, the CDCR Secretary will notify the Governor's legal affairs secretary in writing of all referrals made to the Marin County District Attorney's office for sanity review requests under section 3701. Approximately 10 days before an execution, the Warden will compile and send a final seven-day report regarding any changes to the inmate's mental condition to the DAI Director, whose office will forward it to the Governor's legal affairs secretary.

OP 770 is available for review by condemned inmates at San Quentin and by the general public....

DISCUSSION

Appellants contend the trial court erred in its rulings on the dueling summary judgment motions. "The rules of review are well established. If no triable issue as to any material fact exists, the [moving party] is entitled to a judgment as a matter of law. In ruling on the motion, the court must view the evidence in the light most favorable to the opposing party. We review the record and the determination of the trial court de novo."

I. The APA

Section 5058, subdivision (a) requires the CDCR Secretary to promulgate rules and regulations for the administration of prisons pursuant to the APA, unless enumerated exceptions apply. The APA was enacted to establish basic minimum procedural requirements for the adoption, amendment, or repeal of administrative regulations promulgated by administrative agencies. (Gov. Code, §11346; *Grier v. Kizer* (1990) 219 Cal. App. 3d 422, 431 [268 Cal. Rptr. 244], disapproved on other grounds in *Tidewater Marine Western, Inc. v. Bradshaw* (1996) 14 Cal. 4th 557, 577 [59 Cal. Rptr. 2d 186, 927 P.2d 296] (*Tidewater*).) A major purpose of the APA is to provide a procedure for persons or entities affected by a regulation to be heard on the merits in its creation, and to have notice of the law's requirements so they can conform their conduct accordingly. (*Tidewater*, at pp. 568-569.) Because of this, any doubt as to the applicability of the APA's requirements should be resolved in favor of the APA. (*United Systems of Arkansas, Inc. v. Stamison* (1998) 63 Cal. App. 4th 1001, 1010 [74 Cal. Rptr. 2d 407]; *Grier*, at p. 438.)

"If a rule constitutes a 'regulation' within the meaning of the APA (other than an 'emergency regulation,' which may not remain in effect more than 120 days) it may not be adopted, amended, or repealed except in conformity with 'basic minimum procedural requirements'" (Gov. Code, §11346, subd. (a)) that are exacting....

The APA defines "'[r]egulation'" as "every rule, regulation, order, or standard of general application or the amendment, supplement, or revision of any rule, regulation, order, or standard adopted by any state agency to implement, interpret, or make specific the law enforced or administered by it, or to govern its procedure." (Gov. Code, §11342.600.) "'A regulation subject to the APA ... has two principal identifying characteristics. [Citation.] First, the agency must intend its rule to apply generally, rather than in a specific case. The rule need not, however, apply universally; a rule applies generally so long as it declares how a certain class of cases will be decided. [Citation.] Second, the rule must "implement, interpret, or make specific the law enforced or administered by [the agency], or . . . govern [the agency's] procedure." [Citation.]'" (*Morning Star, supra*, 38 Cal. 4th at pp. 333-334, quoting *Tidewater, supra*, 14 Cal. 4th at p. 571.) Appellants do not dispute that OP 770 implements the statutory directive in section 3604, thus satisfying *Tidewater*'s second identifying characteristic of a "regulation."

II. OP 770 Is a Rule of General Application

. . . Appellants assert that because OP 770 applies only to certain condemned inmates housed at San Quentin and execution team members who are trained at San Quentin and perform their duties there, OP 770 does not affect a broad range of prisoners. . . .

The *Garcia* case [on which appellants rely] . . . directly addresses whether a prison regulation of more limited scope . . . is governed by the APA. If we agreed with *Garcia*'s analysis of this issue, appellant would prevail; but we do not.

In *Garcia*, an inmate (Garcia) incarcerated at a California medical facility sought habeas corpus relief after his request for permission to correspond with an inmate at another prison, Richard J. Donovan Correctional Facility (Donovan prison), was denied by that prison, in reliance upon its correspondence policy. That policy limited correspondence between Donovan prison inmates and inmates housed at other institutions. (*Garcia, supra*, 67 Cal. App. 4th at p. 843.) Garcia challenged the Donovan prison policy on the ground it was a regulation of general application not promulgated pursuant to the APA. (*Garcia*, at pp. 843, 845.) The prison authorities made two separate arguments as to why the APA did not apply: First, they argued the Donovan prison policy was not one of "general application," and second, even if it were, the policy was exempt from compliance with the APA under section 5058(c)(1) because it applied to only one prison facility. In its analysis of "general application," the *Garcia* court noted that the APA does not define this term, but suggested, in dicta, that in the prison context a rule is of general application where it significantly affected a "broad range of prisoners." (*Garcia*, at pp. 844-845.) *Garcia* then concluded a correspondence policy that applied to a single prison did not have this effect and, so, was not a rule of general application. (*Id.* at p. 845.)

The flaw in *Garcia*'s reasoning results from conflating the APA's definition of a subject regulation (one of general application) and the Penal Code's subsequent creation of an exception to the APA for regulations affecting only one prison. If, categorically, a regulation applicable to a single prison lacked general applicability, there would have been no need for the Legislature to enact the single prison exception contained in section 5058(c)(1). That said, the result in *Garcia* seems correct. The Donovan prison regulation appears to apply to a broad range of prisoners, *all* those at Donovan prison, but was exempt from the APA because it *only* applied to inmates at that facility.

Thus, the prison case principally relied upon by appellants fail[s] to assist us in refining the ambit of the term "general application" as utilized in the APA. In reviewing cases decided in other states on the applicability of their administrative procedures acts to a lethal injection protocol similar to OP 770, we find one case apt. In *Evans v. State* (2006) 396 Md. 256 [914 A.2d 25], a state prison inmate sentenced to death sought an injunction against application of the Maryland Department of Correction's protocols governing the use of lethal injection because they were not enacted in accordance with the procedures mandated by the Maryland Administrative Procedure Act (MAPA). (*Evans*, 914 A.2d at pp. 33-34.) At issue in *Evans*, as here, was whether the protocols were subject to the MAPA. (*Evans*, at pp. 78-79.) Title 10, subtitle 1 of the State of Maryland Government Article section 10-101(g)(1), "defines a regulation as including, in pertinent part, a statement that has general application." (*Evans*, at p. 78.) *Evans* rejected the argument that the protocols were not regulations because they did not have a general application. "The State's argument to the contrary notwithstanding, there can be no legitimate doubt that the portion of the [protocols] that govern the method of and procedure for administering the lethal injection have general application. . . . They have general application . . . because they comprehensively govern the manner in which every death sentence is implemented." (*Ibid.*)

We agree with *Evans*. The record reflects that as of September 11, 2006, there were 644 condemned inmates in California; no evidence was submitted to the trial court as to the precise number of inmates who have had an execution date scheduled. But those numbers are not determinative. All condemned inmates who have received an execution date are covered by OP 770 until a method of execution is selected. Unless the inmate affirmatively selects the use of lethal gas, all death sentences will be by lethal injection and will be carried out consistently with the remainder of the challenged protocol. Thus, the protocol "'declares how a certain class'" of inmates, those whose execution dates have been set, will be treated. (*Morning Star, supra*, 38 Cal. 4th at pp. 333-334, quoting *Tidewater, supra*, 14 Cal. 4th at p. 571.) Therefore, the protocol is subject to the APA, even if it does not apply to all inmates, or even to all inmates sentenced to death. . . .

III. Conclusion

The procedural requirements designated by the APA for administrative regulations are applicable to OP 770. Appellants' failure to comply with them invalidates the challenged protocol.

NOTES

1. "Determining whether an agency's statement is what the APA calls a 'rule' can be a difficult exercise." Lincoln v. Vigil, 508 U.S. 182, 196-197 (1993). The *Morales* case discusses the scope of "general" application. How many must be affected by a rule in order to say that it has general applicability?

Compare the method of another noted lexicographer: "'When *I* use a word,' Humpty Dumpty said, in rather a scornful tone, 'it means just what I choose it to mean — neither more nor less.'" L. Carroll, Through the Looking Glass, ch. 6. Compare the statement in the following case: "The title placed upon an administrative pronouncement does not determine whether or not the agency is engaging in rule making." State Board of Equalization v. Sierra Pacific Power Co., 634 P.2d 461, 464 (Nev. 1981). Or, as the Supreme Court has put it, the cases have "rejected the notion that the nature of the agency's proceedings might depend on their form[.]" New Orleans Public Service v. Council of New Orleans, 491 U.S. 350, 371 (1989). If terminology does not control, what *is* the difference between "rules" and other agency acts?

2. With respect to the *Morales* case, following state court proceedings regarding the revised protocol's legality under California's Administrative Procedures Act, a new lethal injection protocol became effective August 29, 2010. See Cal. Code Regs. tit. 15, §3349, et seq. On September 20, 2010, the California Court of Appeal, First District, held that the new procedure was presumptively valid, and authorized the resumption of executions. See Cal. Dep't of Corr. and Rehab. v. Superior Court, 2010 Cal. App. Unpub. LEXIS 7417, 2010 WL 3621873 at *4-5 (Sept. 20, 2010). However, another California court subsequently invalidated that protocol for its substantial failure to meet the substantive requirements of the APA. See Sims v. Cal. Dep't. of Corr. and Rehab., 157 Cal. Rptr. 3d 409 (Cal. App. 2013). In the end, it appears that a provision of the California Penal Code, enacted by voter resolution (Prop 66) in 2016, provides an exemption from the California APA for "standards, procedures, or regulations" governing administration of the death penalty. Briggs v. Brown, 400 P.3d 29, 221 Cal. Rptr. 3d 465 (Cal. 2017).

B DISTINGUISHING RULES AND ORDERS

PARALYZED VETERANS OF AMERICA v. SECRETARY OF VETERANS AFFAIRS

308 F.3d 1262 (Fed. Cir. 2002)

FRIEDMAN, Senior Circuit Judge.

A veterans' organization filed in this court a petition to review an opinion of the General Counsel of the Department of Veterans Affairs (["VA" or] "Department"). The opinion was rendered to, and in response to a request by, the Chairman of the Department's Board of Veterans' Appeals ("Board") for legal advice on issues involved in a pending case before the Board. . . .

I

The Chairman of the Board made a written request, in the form of a memorandum, to the Department's General Counsel. The Chairman described the facts in "this case," which involved a claim to compensation under 38 U.S.C. §1151. The claim was that the Department's failure to diagnose a veteran's cardiac illness in examining him at an outpatient clinic resulted in the veteran's subsequent death of a heart attack. The Chairman requested the General Counsel's "opinion" on two questions: (1) "does 38 U.S.C. §1151 . . . contemplate compensation for the absence or failure (by omission) of VA to diagnose or treat an underlying disease or injury, or does [it] only contemplate compensation for medical treatment or submission to an examination which involves acts of commission by VA?"; (2) if the former standard applies, "what are the essential elements of such a claim which must be established in order for a claimant to prevail?"

The Chairman acted pursuant to a Department regulation that authorized specified officials to request formal legal advice from the General Counsel, including the interpretation of statutes or regulations. 38 C.F.R. §14.502 (2001). A statute provides that "the Board shall be bound in its decisions by the regulations of the Department, instructions of the Secretary, and the precedent opinions of the chief legal officer of the Department," 38 U.S.C. §7104(c) (2000), and the Department treats such opinions as precedential and requires that its officials and employees follow them. 38 C.F.R. §14.507 (2001).

Almost two years later, the General Counsel responded in an 11-page single-spaced memorandum to the Chairman, which, after the extensive legal analysis, answered the two questions the Chairman had posed. The Paralyzed Veterans of America then filed in this court a petition to review "the validity of" the General Counsel's opinion. It described that opinion "as a final rule." . . .

II

Under 38 U.S.C. §502, "[an] action of the Secretary to which section 552(a)(1) refer[s] is subject to judicial review. . . . Those two references to title 5 are to provisions of [the Administrative Procedure] Act. The first reference — Section 552(a) — requires agencies to make public specified information, including publication in the Federal Register, of "substantive rules of general applicability adopted as authorized by law, and statements of general policy or interpretations of general applicability formulated and adopted by the agency." 5 U.S.C. §552(a)(1)(D) (2000). Section 553 specifies the procedures to be followed in "rule making." *Id.* §553 (2000).

As this court explained in LeFevre v. Secretary, Department of Veterans Affairs, 66 F.3d 1191, 1196 (Fed. Cir. 1995):

> Section 551(4) . . . defines a rule as the "whole or a part of an agency statement of general or particular applicability and future effect designed to implement, interpret, or prescribe law or policy or describing the organization, procedure, or practice requirements of an agency."
>
> As our predecessor court explained: "rule making is legislative in nature, is primarily concerned with policy considerations for the future rather than the evaluation of past conduct, and looks not to the evidentiary facts but to policy-making conclusions to be drawn from the facts." [Citation omitted.]

Thus, for the General Counsel's opinion to be directly reviewable by this court, it must constitute a "rule" within section 552(a)(1)(D).

Although the definition of "rule" is broad, the opinion of the Department's General Counsel does not come within its coverage. That opinion, rather, is a part of the Department's administrative quasi-judicial procedure for adjudicating veterans' claims.

The General Counsel rendered his opinion in response to a written request from the Chairman of the Board of Veterans' Appeals. The Chairman requested the opinion to aid him in deciding the case before the Board, and the opinion, which was addressed to him, would be used for that purpose. The rendering of the opinion was an integral part of the Board's adjudicatory process. The opinion itself had no immediate or direct impact upon any veteran. Whatever impact it had resulted from the Board's application of it in the particular case. The fact that the General Counsel's opinion is a precedent that binds the Department's officials and employees does not change its inherent nature or make it a rule.

The appropriate procedure for challenging the opinion's statutory interpretation would be for the veteran to await the decision of the Board in his case and, if that decision were adverse, to challenge it before the Court of Appeals for Veterans Claims ("Veterans Court") and then, if the veteran lost there, to seek further review in this court. . . .

Since Veterans Court review of the decision of the Board, with possible further review by this court, would permit full judicial consideration of the conclusions of the General Counsel's opinion, it is unlikely that Congress intended to permit direct review in this court of the General Counsel's opinion rendered for the Board.

Apparently the Department itself does not view the General Counsel's formal opinions as rules. As noted previously, the Administrative Procedure Act requires "agencies," which include departments . . . to "separately state and currently publish in the Federal Register . . . substantive rules of general applicability. . . ." The Department, however, did not publish the 11-page General Counsel's opinion in the Federal Register.

Instead, it published there a 58-line, single column summary of that opinion, together with summaries of 14 other opinions of the General Counsel and an announcement that a particular prior opinion of that official was being withdrawn. It stated that it "is publishing a summary of legal interpretations issued by the Department's Office of General Counsel involving veterans' benefits under laws administered by VA . . . to provide the public, and, in particular, veterans' benefit claimants and their representatives, with notice of VA's interpretations regarding the legal matters at issue." In contrast, apparently the Department customarily publishes in the Federal Register the full text of its rules and regulations. Indeed, five days after publishing the summaries the Department published the full text of an "Interim Final Rule" governing certain grants to states. . . .

The General Counsel's opinion in this case is different from the document that we held in *LeFevre* to be a rule and therefore directly reviewable. That case involved a determination by the Secretary that, pursuant to the Agent Orange Act of 1991 . . . certain diseases but not others were entitled to a presumption of causation by exposure to herbicides in Vietnam. The Secretary's determination followed and reflected a lengthy study of the problem and recommendations by the National Academy of Science, and a review of the Academy's report by an expert task force the Secretary had appointed. "The Secretary adopted the task force's recommendations, and published a detailed explanation of his decision in the Federal Register." *LeFevre*, 66 F.3d at 1196 (citation omitted). We held:

> The determination was a rule because it was a "statement of general . . . applicability and future effect designed to implement . . . or prescribe . . . law or policy. . . ." It prescribed the basis on which the Department would adjudicate every claim seeking disability or survivor benefits for specified diseases allegedly caused by exposure to herbicides in Vietnam. It reflects the result of a process that was "legislative in nature, [was] primarily concerned with policy considerations for the future . . . , and looked to policy-making conclusions to be drawn from the facts." Congress delegated to the Secretary the authority to determine whether or not to create a presumption of service connection between certain diseases and military service in Vietnam, and that determination would control the decisions in all subsequent cases involving the issue. *Id.* at 1196-97.

The differences between the two cases are significant, and call for a different result here. There the Secretary made his determination pursuant to and in implementation of, a statutory directive. Here the General Counsel's opinion was rendered in response to a request from a Department official in connection with the Board of Veterans' Appeal's consideration of an appeal by a particular veteran. There the process through which the Secretary made his determination was "legislative in nature . . . primarily concerned with policy considerations for the future." Here the General Counsel appears to have engaged in no more than the usual process of statutory interpretation. There the determination was made by the Secretary himself and the full and lengthy text of it was published in the Federal Register. Here the action was taken not by the Secretary but by an official of the Department, and only a relatively brief summary of the opinion was published in the Federal Register. There the Secretary's determination took the form of a general and detailed explanation of his decision. Here the General Counsel's opinion was rendered as a memorandum to the Chairman of the Board of Veterans' Appeals that responded to the Chairman's request for an opinion.

In sum, unlike the Secretary's determination in *LeFevre*, the General Counsel's opinion in this case was not a "rule" because it was not "a 'statement of general . . . applicability and future effect designed to implement . . . or prescribe . . . law or policy.'" It was only an integral part of the Department's adjudicatory proceedings. Indeed, were we to review directly the General Counsel's opinion in this case, which was rendered to aid the chairman in adjudicating an appeal to the Board by a particular veteran, we might be issuing an advisory opinion — which we may not do.

DISMISSED

CORDERO v. CORBISIERO

599 N.E.2d 670 (N.Y. 1992)

MEMORANDUM

The judgment of the Appellate Division, 170 A.D.2d 216, 565 N.Y.S.2d 109, should be modified, without costs, by annulling so much of respondent's determination as directed that the penalty be served during Saratoga racing days, and the matter should be remitted to respondent [State Racing and Wagering] Board for further proceedings in accordance with this memorandum.

As framed by the parties, the controlling question in this case is whether respondent's so-called "Saratoga policy" — which requires that, following an administrative appeal, a suspension imposed for an infraction committed at the Saratoga racetrack be served at the Saratoga meet the following year — has the attributes of a "rule" as that term is defined by State Administrative Procedure Act §102(2)(a)(i). The parties agree that, if it has such attributes, the Saratoga policy could not be applied in this case because it was not formally promulgated by the respondent pursuant to the rulemaking procedures set forth in State Administrative Procedure Act §202. Significantly, no argument has been made that the procedural requirements of State Administrative Procedure Act §202 are inapplicable to a policy, like this one, which was formulated by the Board in its adjudicatory capacity (cf., National Labor Relations Bd. v. Bell, Aerospace Co., 416 U.S. 267; Securities Commn. v. Chenery Corp., 332 U.S. 194, 202).

The Saratoga policy, according to the Board's brief on appeal, applies "to every jockey . . . who elect[s] to race at Saratoga, commit[s] an infraction there, and unsuccessfully appeal[s] to the Board." Such a policy seems clearly to fit the definition of what constitutes a rule, i.e., a fixed, general principle applied without regard to the facts and circumstances of the individual case. The Board argues, nonetheless, that the Saratoga policy does not fit the definition of a rule because it only affects the implementation of a penalty, not the jockey's conduct.

We reject this argument. The Saratoga policy does not relate to the penalty as such; it does not purport to control the Board's discretion as to what the suspension should be for a particular infraction. Rather, according to the Board's own description of the policy in this case, it establishes a mandatory procedure that pertains only to *when* and *where* a Saratoga suspension must be served in the event of an appeal. . . .

We conclude, therefore, that the Saratoga policy fits State Administration Procedure Act §102(2)(a)(i)'s definition of a rule — an agency's stated policy of general applicability which prescribes a procedure or practice requirement of the agency. . . .

NOTES

1. In determining whether a position taken by the agency constitutes a rule, does it matter who within the agency articulated the position? Amoco Prod. Co.

v. Watson, 410 F.3d 722, 732 (D.C. Cir. 2005) (agency personnel issued a letter; in finding the letter was not a legislative rule, court noted that the letter "is not an agency statement with future effect because nothing under [Department of the Interior] DOI regulations vests the Letter's author . . . with the authority to announce rules binding on DOI").

2. Under the Federal APA, a "rule" is the end result of an exercise of a legislative or rulemaking function, "and an order" that of a judicial or adjudicatory function. Why is the difference between rules and orders important? What difference does it make if, in the given case, an agency is exercising legislative, rather than judicial functions — or vice versa? Justice Scalia has acknowledged that, as pointed out in the Schwartz article, *supra* p. 271, "the most significant portions of the APA are based" upon the rulemaking-adjudication dichotomy. Bowen v. Georgetown University Hospital, 488 U.S. 204 (1988) (*infra* p. 297). This means that different procedural requirements under the APA govern, depending on whether the agency is engaged in rulemaking or adjudication in the given case. In this respect, the APA follows the traditional administrative law approach, grounded on the distinction between legislative and judicial functions. Later in this chapter, we shall note that the procedure prescribed for rulemaking is normally informal in character. As will be seen in the next two chapters, the requirements prescribed for adjudications, on the other hand, are more formal in nature, modeled in essentials on the procedure of the judicial process. This is what makes the characterization of an administrative act as rulemaking (legislative) instead of as adjudication (judicial) — or vice versa — of great importance.

3. A federal court has confirmed that there is no "'bright line' between adjudication and rule-making." Bell Telephone Co. v. FCC, 503 F.2d 1250, 1268 (3d Cir. 1974). As indicated in the Schwartz article, *supra*, the most noted attempt to explain the difference between legislative and judicial functions was made by Justice Holmes in Prentis v. Atlantic Coast Line Co., 211 U.S. 210 (1911). As pointed out there, the key factor according to Holmes is time: a rule prescribes *future* patterns of conduct; a decision determines liabilities upon the basis of *present* or *past* facts. For a more recent statement, see Scalia, J., concurring in *Bowen*, *supra* note 2: "Adjudication deals with what the law was; rulemaking deals with what the law will be." Compare the statement of Chief Justice Burger, while a circuit judge, in his dissent in American Airlines, Inc. v. CAB, 359 F.2d 624, 636 (D.C. Cir.), cert. denied, 385 U.S. 843 (1966): "Rulemaking is normally directed toward the formulation of requirements having a general application to all members of a broadly identifiable class." This is the approach followed in the *Morales* case, above. Note from the Schwartz article how the APA definition of rule adopts both the *Holmes* time test and the *Burger* applicability test.

4. Compare the APA definition of "order" (the final disposition in an agency adjudication). Note that it is a residual definition: if the given agency act is not a "rule," it must be an order. Under the APA, "adjudication" is determined by what is *not* rulemaking.

Note that this residual approach does not apply to the types of orders specifically mentioned in the APA definition: negative, injunctive, and declaratory orders, as well as orders in licensing cases. They are expressly included in the "order" definition, since otherwise (with the exception of so-called negative orders, see *supra* p. 274), they might fall within the definition of "rules." Note also that the APA terminology is binding only for purposes of the APA. Agencies may continue to use the terminology to which they are accustomed, as in the examples at the beginning of the Schwartz article.

C SUBSTANTIVE/LEGISLATIVE RULES: THE FORCE AND EFFECT OF LAW

1. Defining Legislative Rules

Robert A. Anthony

INTERPRETIVE RULES, POLICY STATEMENTS, GUIDANCES, MANUALS, AND THE LIKE — SHOULD FEDERAL AGENCIES USE THEM TO BIND THE PUBLIC?*

41 Duke L.J. 1321-1323 (1992)

[L]EGISLATIVE AND NONLEGISLATIVE RULES

Rules are broadly classified as "legislative" and "nonlegislative. . . ."[37] The United States Court of Appeals for the District of Columbia Circuit has stated: "The distinction between legislative rules and interpretative rules or policy statements [i.e., the main categories of nonlegislative rules] has been described at various

---

* Reprinted with permission of Duke Law Journal © 1992.

37. The courts, unfortunately, sometimes confusingly use the term "substantive rule" to mean "legislative rule." Compare United Technologies Corp. v. EPA, 821 F.2d 714, 719 (D.C. Cir. 1987) ("distinguish[] interpretive from legislative rules") and American Hosp. Ass'n v. Bowen, 834 F.2d 1037, 1045 (D.C. Cir. 1987) ("whether a given agency action is interpretive or legislative") with id. at 1045 ("the spectrum between a clearly interpretive rule and a clearly substantive one is a hazy continuum") and Cabais v. Egger, 690 F.2d 234, 237 (D.C. Cir. 1980) ("distinguishing between substantive and interpretative rules"); see also Batterton v. Marshall, 648 F.2d 694, 701 (D.C. Cir. 1980) (equating "'legislative' or 'substantive' rules"); Chrysler Corp. v. Brown, 441 U.S. 281, 302-303 (1979). Reasons for the preferred usage, observed in this Article, were well expressed in Metropolitan School Dist. of Wayne Township v. Davila, 969 F.2d 485, 488 (7th Cir. 1992): "We find the use of the term 'substantive' in this context misleading; an interpretation which explains the meaning of the statute can be just as 'substantive' as a legislative rule. We prefer the interpretive/legislative terminology because it avoids any potential confusion." As used in this Article, the term "substantive rule" contrasts with "procedural rule," and has a meaning parallel to the concept of "substantive law" — that is, a rule that creates or affects private rights, duties or obligations. See Black's Law Dictionary 1429 (6th ed. 1990). This is correct usage under the APA. See 5 U.S.C. §553(d) (1988). The term "substantive rule," therefore, embraces legislative rules, interpretive rules, and policy statements other than those concerned with procedure, practice, or agency organization. See id. §§553(b)(A), 553(d); see also Joseph v. United States Civil Serv. Comm'n, 554 F.2d 1140, 1153 n.24 (D.C. Cir. 1977) ("Interpretative rules may be substantive in the sense of addressing a substantive rather than a procedural issue of law. . . ."). This Article also follows the widespread modern usage of substituting the word "interpretive" for the statutory term "interpretative." See 5 U.S.C. §553(b)(A), (d)(2). For brevity, the term "policy statements" is used in place of the statute's "general statements of policy." Id.

times as 'tenuous,' 'fuzzy,' 'blurred,' and, perhaps most picturesquely, 'enshrouded in considerable smog.' As Professor Davis puts it, 'the problem is baffling.'"

With respect, the distinction is very clear. Legislative rules can readily be differentiated from those that are nonlegislative. The fundamental idea is that a "legislative rule is the product of an exercise of delegated legislative power to make law through rules." More particularly, a rule qualifies as legislative if all of the following requirements are met (1) The agency must possess delegated statutory authority to act with respect to the subject matter of the rule. (2) Promulgation of the rule must be an intentional exercise of that delegated authority. (3) The agency must also possess delegated statutory authority to make rules with the force of law. (4) Promulgation of the rule must be an intentional exercise of the authority to make rules with the force of law. (5) Promulgation of the rule must be an effective exercise of that authority. (6) The promulgation must observe procedures mandated by the agency's organic statute and by the APA. Particularly, unless it falls within an exemption in the organic legislation or in the APA, the rule must be developed through public notice-and-comment procedures and be published in the Federal Register. . . . [T]he most important of the requirements is the sixth. An agency's issuance is a valid legislative rule if and only if it meets all six of these requirements. All substantive rules that do not fit this template are nonlegislative. They are either interpretive rules (if they interpret specific statutory or regulatory language) or policy statements (if they do not). . . .

2. The Authority to Promulgate Legislative Rules

IN RE PERMANENT SURFACE MINING REGULATION LITIGATION

653 F.2d 514 (D.C. Cir. 1981)

MIKVA, J. This case presents a narrow question concerning the relative authority of the Secretary of the Interior . . . in the administration of the Surface Mining Control and Reclamation Act of 1977 (Surface Mining Act, or Act), 30 U.S.C. §§1201-1328 (Supp. I 1977). The United States District Court for the District of Columbia held that the Act gives the Secretary rulemaking power to prescribe minimum information requirements for permit applications submitted to the state regulatory agencies. We conclude that the Act does give the Secretary this authority, and accordingly affirm the judgment of the district court.

I. THE ISSUE PRESENTED

The Surface Mining Act embodies Congress' recognition that

> the expansion of coal mining to meet the Nation's energy needs makes even more urgent the establishment of appropriate standards to minimize damage to the

> environment and to productivity of the soil and to protect the health and safety of the public.

Act §101(d). After an initial period of direct regulation by the Secretary, the Act contemplates a continuing partnership between the states and the federal government, with the Secretary providing oversight, advice, and back-up authority, and the states bearing the major responsibility for implementation of the Act. The crucial step in accomplishing this transition is a state's submission of its proposed regulatory program to the Secretary for his approval. The Secretary may only approve the state program if he finds it capable of carrying out the exacting provisions of the Act, and consistent with his own regulations. Act §503(a). . . .

The Secretary's regulations for the permanent regulatory program, issued in March 1979, include rules concerning the content of acceptable state program submissions. See 44 Fed. Reg. 14,902, 15,312 (1979) (codified at 30 C.F.R. pts. 700-890 (1979)). These regulations specify minimum information that a state must require in a permit application, information which extends beyond the explicit information requirements detailed in the Act itself. See 30 C.F.R. pts. 778-784 (1979).

Various interested persons filed actions in the United States District Court for the District of Columbia, challenging the permanent regulations. Appellant attacked the Secretary's information requirements in sweeping terms, denying that the Secretary possessed any power to promulgate regulations on that subject. . . .

Our inquiry is narrow. We are called upon to determine only whether the Secretary has rulemaking authority to require that permit applicants submit *any* items of information beyond those enumerated in the Act. . . .

III. THE SOURCE OF THE SECRETARY'S RULEMAKING POWER

The Secretary identifies two grants of rulemaking power in the Act as the source of his authority to promulgate regulations expanding the list of information required to be submitted in permit applications. The first of these provisions is a general rulemaking grant typical of statutes that, like the Act, delegate extensive responsibilities to administrative agencies. It provides that the Secretary shall

> publish and promulgate such rules and regulations as may be necessary to carry out the purposes and provisions of this Act,

Act §201(c)(2). The second source is a more specific rulemaking grant, tied to the provisions of title V of the Act, in which the permit provisions are found. It requires the Secretary to

> *promulgate and publish in the Federal Register regulations* covering a permanent regulatory procedure for surface coal mining and reclamation operations performance standards based on and conforming to provisions of title V and *establishing procedures and requirements for preparation, submission, and approval of State programs* and development, and implementation of Federal programs under the title.

Act §501(b) (emphasis added).

A. The Secretary's Interpretation

The Secretary has cited sections 201(c) and 501(b) of the Act as authority for his rulemaking, and has viewed them as empowering him to expand the permit information requirements beyond those specified in the Act. As Congress recognized, "[t]he informational and environmental requirements of this [act] are its most vital provisions." S. Rep. No. 128, 95th Cong., 1st Sess. 53 (1977). The importance of an adequate data base to state decisionmaking, federal supervision, and citizen oversight makes the state program's information-gathering provisions crucial to the success of the Act. The Secretary has concluded that the explicit information provisions included in the Act should be supplemented to guarantee its effective implementation. As the interpretation favored by the agency responsible for administering the Act, this conclusion is entitled to some deference. See Miller v. Youakim, 440 U.S. 125, 145 n.25 (1979). Absent a contrary indication in the statute, we should accept the Secretary's judgment....

B. Interpretation of the Rulemaking Provisions

Appellant argues that the sections of the Act on which the Secretary relies for his rulemaking powers confer no substantive authority at all, and must instead be interpreted as routine housekeeping and procedural provisions. We disagree.

Section 201(c)(2) of the Act empowers the Secretary to

> publish and promulgate such rules and regulations as may be necessary to carry out the purposes and provisions of this Act.

Appellant urges that the Secretary's interpretation of section 201(c)(2) would give him unlimited power to enact rules, destroying the intended structure of the Act by drowning the states in a sea of irrelevant and time-consuming regulations. But as this court observed of the Clean Air Act's similar rulemaking grant, "[s]uch a provision does not provide the Administrator with carte blanche authority to promulgate any rules, on any matter relating to the ... Act, in any manner that the Administrator wishes." Citizens to Save Spencer County v. E.P.A., 600 F.2d 844, 873 (D.C. Cir., 1979). The Secretary's regulations must not be arbitrary, capricious, or inconsistent with the Act, and section 526(a)(1) of the Act provides for review of the individual regulations on that basis in the district court. Appellant is participating in that process in the district court, and nothing we decide today forecloses appellant's challenges to individual regulations.

Appellant's other argument against the Secretary's interpretation of section 201(c)(2) is a quantitative one. Because the Act contains, in addition to section 201(c)2, twenty-one *specific* grants of rulemaking power, appellant maintains, either those specific grants or section 201(c)(2)'s general grant must be redundant — and the 21:1 ratio in favor of the specific grants demonstrates that it is the interpretation of section 201(c)(2) that is erroneous. Rather than conferring general rulemaking power, in appellant's view, that section merely empowers the Secretary to engage in "routine housekeeping," such as setting up rules for distribution of government funds, and allocating authority among his employees. Appellant urges as a proposition of administrative law that the existence of specific grants must eviscerate a general grant of rulemaking power. That proposition cannot be squared with recent Supreme Court decisions relying on general rulemaking grants to uphold rulemaking authority despite the presence of specific grants in the statutes scrutinized....

In National Petroleum Refiners Assn. v. F.T.C., 482 F.2d 672 (D.C. Cir. 1973), cert. denied, 415 U.S. 951 (1974), this court upheld the power of the FTC to issue substantive rules governing its adjudications.... [T]he court recognized an "obvious judicial willingness to permit substantive rulemaking to undercut the primacy of adjudication in the development of agency policy." 482 F.2d at 679. The court praised the agency's use of rulemaking as a method for announcing new norms of conduct:

> [T]here is little question that the availability of substantive rule-making gives any agency a valuable resource-saving flexibility in carrying out its task of regulating parties subject to its statutory mandate. More than merely expediting the agency's job, use of substantive rule-making is increasingly felt to yield significant benefits to those the agency regulates. Increasingly, courts are recognizing that use of rule-making to make innovations in agency policy may actually be fairer to regulated parties than total reliance on case-by-case adjudication.

Id. at 681. This approbation may also be seen in a large body of cases that have rejected claims that a given agency may operate only on a case-by-case basis, and have likewise rejected crabbed interpretations of those agencies' rulemaking powers....

The rationale of *National Petroleum* and kindred cases lends additional strength to our conclusion that... section 201(c)(2)... of the Surface Mining Act authorize[s] the Secretary to issue rules governing approval of state programs. Appellant's arguments in favor of a trivializing construction of these provisions are wholly without merit....

IV. CONCLUSION

The Surface Mining Control and Reclamation Act of 1977 enacts a national plan to alleviate the harmful effects of surface mining. Because of past failures on the state level, the Act provides for national standards relating to environmental performance, and federal oversight of the state programs applying those standards to local geographic conditions. Before the Secretary may approve a state program, he must conclude that the program is sufficient to carry out the purposes of the Act. We hold that the Act does grant the Secretary rulemaking power enabling him to specify by regulation criteria necessary for his approval of a proposed state program.

We hold that the Act's explicit listings of information required of permit applicants are not exhaustive, and do not preclude the Secretary from requiring the states to secure additional information needed to ensure compliance with the Act. This question concerning the existence of the Secretary's authority is the only question decided and appellant is free to continue to contest the specific regulations in the district court. The judgment of the district court is affirmed.

NOTES

1. Rulemaking power is, of course, an essential feature of the modern administrative agency. "[A]gency rulemaking powers are the rule rather than, as they once were, the exception[.]" Scalia, Judicial Deference to Administrative Interpretations of Law, 1989 Duke L.J. 511, 516.

2. Note Judge Mikva's emphasis on the advantages of substantive/legislative rulemaking as compared with total reliance on case-by-case adjudication. The agency will be able to proceed more expeditiously, give greater certainty, and deploy its internal resources more efficiently with a mixed system of rulemaking and adjudication than with adjudication alone. To deny it rulemaking power would render the agency only partly effective.

3. Does substantive/legislative rulemaking power exist in the absence of a statutory delegation to the agency? See Respect, Inc. v. Committee on Status of Women, 815 F. Supp. 1112, 1123 (N.D. Ill. 1993): "It remains a fundamental principle of administrative law that agencies may not self-levitate their power to promulgate regulations — they must rather find any such power in a source conferred by Congress." But what about where the agency has the authority to adopt rules "in the public interest"? See 15 U.S.C. §78n(a). Is that tantamount to unlimited discretion? What about the absence of "explicit" rulemaking authority in a particular area? The Supreme Court has apparently recognized that agencies, "even without express authority to fill a specific statutory gap," may have an "implicit congressional delegation" of authority. United States v. Mead Corp., 533 U.S. 218, 237 (2001). How much does the language of the statute really limit what agencies can do?

4. Rulemaking power is, of course, a necessary characteristic of the administrative agency. The promulgation of regulations has been a normal feature of American government from the beginning. Like other aspects of governmental power it has tended to grow by leaps and bounds during the present century. "For some time, the sheer amount of law — the substantive rules that regulate private conduct . . . — made by the agencies has far outnumbered the lawmaking engaged in by Congress through the traditional process." INS v. Chadha, 462 U.S. 919, 985-986 (1983).

The situation in this respect was described some years ago by Chief Justice Vanderbilt:

> The volume of our administrative regulations is even more appalling. To check all of the federal administrative regulations one must search the 41 volumes of the Code of Federal Regulations of 1949 containing 22,055 pages and its annual pocket parts, as well as the current Federal Register, which in 1954 alone contained 9,910 pages. These figures for federal administrative regulations, moreover, are exclusive

> of specific legislation, such as is common in rate making and in banking matters, and of administrative interpretations of particular cases, none of which appear in the Federal Register and which are often very extensive.

A. T. Vanderbilt, The Challenge of Law Reform 138 (1955). Thirty-seven years later the situation had become much worse. The Federal Register for 1992 contained 62,920 pages. The Code of Federal Regulations (C.F.R.) (a codification of federal regulations currently in effect) in 1993 had grown to 198 volumes, containing well over 100,000 pages. Some years ago it was estimated C.F.R. contained over 50 million words — over 70 times as many as in the Bible and 60 times as many as in the complete works of Shakespeare.

3. The Force and Effect of Legislative Rules

REUTERS LTD. v. FCC

781 F.2d 946 (D.C. Cir. 1986)

STARR, Circuit Judge. A precept which lies at the foundation of the modern administrative state is that agencies must abide by their rules and regulations. We have frequently been called upon to apply that venerable principal of law and common sense, and the appeal before us today fits squarely into that long line of cases. We hold that the Federal Communications Commission ["FCC" or "Commission"] improperly breached this fundamental precept of administrative law in what turns out to have been a misguided effort to achieve a fair resolution of a dispute between two competing license applicants.

The warring contestants are Reuters Limited, who appeals from the FCC's adverse action, and Associated Information Services Corporation, the successful intervenor. The regulatory prize in question consists of thirteen microwave radio station licenses which had officially been granted to Reuters but which, in the face of Associated's strenuous protests, were rescinded by the Commission.

The background of the dispute can be briefly stated. Following a lengthy period when its earlier applications lay dormant at the Commission, Reuters filed new applications, pursuant to the Commission's order, for microwave radio licenses for a single channel in each of thirteen cities across the Nation. The applications were duly accepted for filing and listed on a Public Notice dated August 12, 1983. In the following month, on September 23, 1983, the Commission's Private Radio Bureau approved all thirteen applications.

On that same day, as coincidence would have it, Associated submitted thirty-nine applications for each of the available channels in the same thirteen cities for which Reuters had applied the preceding month. Associated's applications, as it turned out, were misfiled, having been submitted to the Commission's offices in Washington, D.C., whereas applicable FCC rules required that such applications be filed eighty miles to the north at the FCC's offices in Gettysburg, Pennsylvania.

Thus it was that Associated's competing applications were not effectively filed until five days later—on September 28, 1983—when its thirty-nine applications found their way to Gettysburg. As *a result, at the time of the grant to Reuters, no competing applications had been effectively filed.* In due course, on October 12, 1983, the FCC mailed Reuters the thirteen licenses which bore the following words: "Effective Date—September 23, 1983."

With its competitor thus in possession of the thirteen licenses, Associated vehemently protested the grant. Associated contended that the Commission acted improperly in granting the licenses prior to the expiration of sixty days following the date on which new applications were accepted. In Associated's view, the Commission had represented quite clearly in a rulemaking proceeding that a full sixty-day period for filing applications would be allowed. Associated had specifically relied, it maintained, upon the Commission's statements to that effect in timing its thirty-nine applications. As Associated therefore saw it, the Private Radio Bureau had jumped the gun in issuing Reuters the thirteen licenses before the requisite sixty days had expired.

In stark contrast to this view, Reuters maintained that the Commission's rules governing microwave radio licenses expressly permitted licenses to be awarded after the expiration of *thirty days* following an application. At the time the Private Radio Bureau acted on Reuters' application, two critical factors were present: *first*, more than thirty days had expired from the initial date for accepting applications, as provided by the Commission's rules; and *second*, no competing applications were on file as of the date of the grant. In Reuters' view, therefore, Associated's complaints were belied by the Commission's express rules which spoke with crystalline clarity to the question at hand.

With the issue thus joined, the Private Radio Bureau resolved the dispute in favor of Associated. Rejecting outright Associated's broad contention that the Commission's rules and pronouncements did not admit of a license grant prior to expiration of the sixty-day period, the Bureau nonetheless concluded that Associated's applications were, in fact, mutually exclusive to those of Reuters inasmuch as the former's applications were on file in Gettysburg prior to the time the licenses were actually issued by and mailed from the Commission. While thus rejecting the thrust of Associated's arguments, the Bureau set aside Reuters' thirteen licenses and designated Associated's applications as mutually exclusive.

Reuters appealed to the full Commission. Invoking the FCC's rules with respect to the effective dates of licenses, Reuters maintained that the Private Radio Bureau had expressly designated an effective date for the licenses of September 23, 1983, not the date of mailing. As it had before the Bureau, Reuters won the specific legal battles but lost the war. Specifically, the FCC agreed that the Bureau could lawfully issue a license any time after thirty days following the Commission's announced date on which applications would be received. So too, the Commission rejected Associated's argument that the FCC's more recent pronouncements in its rulemaking proceeding had altered the longstanding rules governing the timing of license grants. Reuters likewise won the point that the effective date of its licenses was September 23, 1983, as opposed to a date tied to the later mailing of the licenses by the FCC, and that Associated's applications were not effectively filed until they reached Gettysburg, five days after the effective date of Reuters' licenses.

But Reuters' arguments, tied in lawyerly fashion to the Commission's pertinent rules, in the end fell short. The Commission concluded that considerations of fairness required evisceration of the Reuters license grants and that Associated be permitted to stand alongside Reuters as a full competitor for these licenses.

Both to understand the Commission's rationale and to set the stage for our resolution of this appeal, we pause to enter the somewhat labyrinthine paths of the Commission's rules and pronouncements which guided these two contenders along rather different roads in the application process. It will be recalled that Reuters' applications lay dormant at the Commission for some considerable period prior to the events which generated the case at hand. The reason for this period of Commission inaction, it would appear, was regulatory uncertainty over the uses to which microwave radio stations could properly be put. As we understand it, the Commission had for some time harbored rather restrictive views about such usages, but this regulatory narrowness was under assault from various quarters, including those anxious to employ such stations in the purveying of video entertainment programming, as opposed to the traditional use of these frequencies for point-to-point internal communications relating to the licensee's business. FCC Brief at 4. While the Commission was wrestling internally with these broad questions, Reuters' applications, filed initially in the early weeks of 1980, languished.

At length, the Commission came to rest in the rulemaking proceeding, identified as Docket No. 19671. The Commission's Memorandum Opinion and Order in that docket FCC No. 83-245, 48 Fed. Reg. 32,578 (July 18, 1983), opened up these particular channels for *point-to-multi-point* systems, subject to a two-year period when only applicants seeking to provide data and other information-type services would be licensed in this particular part of the spectrum (2.5 GHz band). To carry out this new approach, the Commission returned all pending applications (including Reuters') and established a new filing period — to begin August 1, 1983 — for applicants seeking to employ these channels for data or information distribution services.

In language which was destined to sow seeds of confusion, the rulemaking Memorandum Opinion and Order stated that the Commission would "strictly apply the cut-off procedures detailed in §1.227(b)(4) of the Commission's Rules." 48 Fed. Reg. 32,578, 32,584 (July 18, 1983). This provision . . . listed alternative dates for Commission action. In explaining its invocation of this provision, the Commission stated: "This means that there will be a new 60-day filing period opened up for competing applications for each of the three 2.5 GHz channels in each locale, commencing with the first such application which we accept for filing in each area." Id. The Memorandum Opinion and Order did not refer to the portion of its rules, Section 1.962(f), governing applications for point-to-point microwave service (as opposed to point-to-multipoint service as involved here). And thus it came to be that Reuters invoked the latter procedure, which permits the Private Radio Bureau to award a license after a thirty-day period following issuance of public notice of the acceptance of an application for filing, whereas Associated relied upon the sixty-day period specified in the rulemaking opinion and order and in the then-applicable version of Section 1.227(b)(4).

Faced with these divergent approaches, the Commission concluded that considerations of fairness warranted rescission of Reuters' licenses. While the award to Reuters was entirely in keeping with applicable rules, the Commission determined that its own pronouncements had been misleading and could have led unsuspecting applicants to the erroneous view that no licenses would be granted prior to expiration of the sixty-day period. Consistent with this conclusion, the Commission on this appeal continues to admit to unfortunate draftsmanship in its rulemaking opinion:

> The Commission recognized . . . that, notwithstanding its subjective intent not to guarantee to every applicant a full sixty-day filing period . . . a contrary intent was inadvertently conveyed to potential applicants. The processing procedures that were intended to govern applicants in the 2.5 GHz band were ambiguous and, as a result, parties reasonably could have construed Section 1.227(b)(4) of the Commission's rules to allow a sixty-day filing period for mutually exclusive applications in the 2.5 GHz band.

We are constrained to disagree with the Commission's understandable effort to achieve a just resolution of this unfortunate turn of events. The reason for our disagreement is simple but emphatic: the Commission properly granted licenses to Reuters pursuant to the express provisions of its rules. What is more, neither the Private Radio Bureau nor the Commission itself embraced the proposition that the Memorandum Opinion and Order was intended to alter the FCC's long-standing rules governing applications. . . .

As we stated at the outset, it is elementary that an agency must adhere to its own rules and regulations. Ad hoc departures from those rules, even to achieve laudable aims, cannot be sanctioned . . . for therein lie the seeds of destruction of the orderliness and predictability which are the hallmarks of lawful administrative action. Simply stated, rules are rules, and fidelity to the rules which have been properly promulgated, consistent with applicable statutory requirements, is required of those to whom Congress has entrusted the regulatory missions of modern life.

Associated's invocation of well-settled principles of judicial deference to agency interpretations . . . is therefore quite beside the point. What is before us is not an agency interpretation of its own rules which Reuters is inviting us to override. Quite to the contrary. *The agency has authoritatively interpreted its rules in a manner which favors entirely Reuters' position.* What Associated would thus have us do, on analysis, is to permit the agency to deviate from its rules in order to achieve what it deems to be justice in the individual case. The agency has, in effect, said that its rules permitted the license awards granted to Reuters, but that the circumstances at hand warrant the Commission's walking away from the metes and bounds which otherwise contain it. This we cannot sanction. . . .

We are therefore obligated to reject the various arguments proffered to buttress the Commission's action in this case. Under these circumstances, we hold that the Commission erred in rescinding Reuters' licenses and that the Commission is therefore bound by its previous, lawful grant. In sum, Reuters is entitled to its previously issued thirteen licenses.

Judgment accordingly.

NOTES

1. The basic principle reaffirmed by the *Reuters* case is "the black-letter principle that properly enacted regulations have the force of law," Flores v. Bowen, 790 F.2d 740, 742 (9th Cir. 1986), which means that a rule or regulation has the same force and effect as a statute. "It has been established in a variety of contexts that properly promulgated . . . agency regulations have the 'force and effect of law.'" Chrysler Corp. v. Brown, 441 U.S. 281, 295 (1979).

2. What does the rule that an agency regulation has the legal effect of a statute mean in practice? Simply that "an agency issuing a legislative rule is itself bound by the rule until that rule is amended or revoked." National Family Planning v. Sullivan, 979 F.2d 227, 234 (D.C. Cir. 1992).

3. How does an agency go about changing a rule it doesn't like? For example, can an agency announce in an adjudicatory proceeding that it no longer intends to follow one of its rules? That issue arose in Tunik v. MSPB, 407 F.3d 1326 (Fed. Cir. 2005). There, the court held that a legislative rule could only be repealed through notice and comment, not through an adjudicatory proceeding.

4. What if there is reason to question the rule's validity? Can an agency unilaterally disregard a rule that is inconsistent with the relevant statute?

BOWEN v. GEORGETOWN UNIVERSITY HOSPITAL

488 U.S. 204 (1988)

JUSTICE KENNEDY delivered the opinion of the Court.

Under the Medicare program, health care providers are reimbursed by the Government for expenses incurred in providing medical services to Medicare beneficiaries. . . . Congress has authorized the Secretary of Health and Human Services to promulgate regulations setting limits on the levels of Medicare costs that will be reimbursed. The question presented here is whether the Secretary may exercise this rulemaking authority to promulgate cost limits that are retroactive.

I

The Secretary's authority to adopt cost-limit rules is established by §223(b) of the Social Security Amendments of 1972, 86 Stat. 1393, amending 42 U.S.C. §1395x(v)(1)(A). This authority was first implemented in 1974 by promulgation of a cost-limit schedule for hospital services; new cost-limit schedules were issued on an annual basis thereafter.

On June 30, 1981, the Secretary issued a cost-limit schedule that included technical changes in the methods for calculating cost limits. One of these changes affected the method for calculating the "wage index," a factor used to reflect the salary levels for hospital employees in different parts of the country. Under the prior rule, the wage index for a given geographic area was calculated by using the average salary levels for all hospitals in the area; the 1981 rule provided that wages paid by Federal Government hospitals would be excluded from that computation. 46 Fed. Reg. 33637, 33638-33639 (1981).

Various hospitals in the District of Columbia brought suit in United States District Court seeking to have the 1981 schedule invalidated. On April 29, 1983, the District Court struck down the 1981 wage-index rule, concluding that the Secretary had violated the Administrative Procedure Act (APA), 5 U.S.C. §551 et seq., by failing to provide notice and an opportunity for public comment before issuing the rule. See District of Columbia Hospital Assn. v. Heckler, No. 82-2520, App. to Pet. for Cert. 49a (hereinafter DCHA). The court did not enjoin enforcement of the rule, however, finding it lacked jurisdiction to do so because the hospitals had not yet exhausted their administrative reimbursement remedies. The court's order stated:

> If the Secretary wishes to put in place a valid prospective wage index, she should begin proper notice and comment proceedings; any wage index currently in place that has been promulgated without notice and comment is invalid as was the 1981 schedule.

DCHA, App. to Pet. for Cert. 64a.

The secretary did not pursue an appeal. Instead, after recognizing the invalidity of the rule, the Secretary settled the hospitals' cost reimbursement reports by applying the pre-1981 wage-index method.

In February 1984, the Secretary published a notice seeking public comment on a proposal to reissue the 1981 wage-index rule, retroactive to July 1, 1981, 49 Fed. Reg. 6175 (1984). Because Congress had subsequently amended the Medicare Act to require significantly different cost reimbursement procedures, the readoption of the modified wage-index method was to apply exclusively to a 15-month period commencing July 1, 1981. After considering the comments received, the Secretary reissued the 1981 schedule in final form on November 26, 1984, and proceeded to re-coup sums previously paid as a result of the District Court's ruling in DCHA. 49 Fed. Reg. 46495 (1984). In effect, the Secretary had promulgated a rule retroactively, and the net result was as if the original rule had never been set aside.

Respondents, a group of seven hospitals who had benefited from the invalidation of the 1981 schedule, were required to return over $2 million in reimbursement payments. After exhausting administrative remedies, they sought judicial review under the applicable provisions of the APA, claiming that the retroactive schedule was invalid under both the APA and the Medicare Act.

The United States District Court for the District of Columbia . . . held that retroactive application was not justified under the circumstances of the case.

The Secretary appealed to the United States Court of Appeals for the District of Columbia Circuit, which affirmed. 261 U.S. App. D.C. 262, 821 F.2d 750 (1987). The court based its holding on the alternative grounds that the APA, as a general matter, forbids retroactive rulemaking and the Medicare Act, by specific terms, bars retroactive cost-limit rules. We granted certiorari, . . . and now we affirm.

II

It is axiomatic that an administrative agency's power to promulgate legislative regulations is limited to the authority delegated by Congress. In determining the validity of the Secretary's retroactive cost-limit rule, the threshold question is whether the Medicare Act authorizes retroactive rulemaking.

Retroactivity is not favored in the law. Thus, congressional enactments and administrative rules will not be construed to have retroactive effect unless their language requires this result. . . . By the same principle, a statutory grant of legislative rulemaking authority will not, as a general matter, be understood to encompass the power to promulgate retroactive rules unless that power is conveyed by Congress in express terms. . . . Even where some substantial justification for retroactive rulemaking is presented, courts should be reluctant to find such authority absent an express statutory grant.

The Secretary contends that the Medicare Act provides the necessary authority to promulgate retroactive cost-limit rules in the unusual circumstances of this case. He rests on alternative grounds: first, the specific grant of authority to promulgate regulations to "provide for the making of suitable retroactive corrective adjustments," 42 U.S.C. §1395x(v)(1)(A)(ii); and second, the general grant of authority to promulgate cost-limit rules, §§1395x(v)(1)(A), 1395hh, 1395ii. We consider these alternatives in turn.

A

The authority to promulgate cost reimbursement regulations is set forth in §1395x(v)(1)(A). That subparagraph also provides that:

> Such regulations shall . . . (ii) provide for the making of suitable retroactive corrective adjustments where, for a provider of services for any fiscal period, the aggregate reimbursement produced by the methods of determining costs proves to be either inadequate or excessive.

Id.

This provision on its face permits some form of retroactive action. We cannot accept the Secretary's argument, however, that it provides authority for the retroactive promulgation of cost-limit rules. To the contrary, we agree with the Court of Appeals that clause (ii) directs the Secretary to establish a procedure for making case-by-case adjustments to reimbursement payments where the regulations prescribing computation methods do not reach the correct result in individual cases. The structure and language of the statute require the conclusion that the retroactivity provision applies only to case-by-case adjudication, not to rulemaking....

These are the only regulations that expressly contemplate the making of retroactive corrective adjustments. The 1984 reissuance of the 1981 wage-index rule did not purport to be such a provision; indeed, it is only in the context of this litigation that the Secretary has expressed any intent to characterize the rule as a retroactive corrective adjustment under clause (ii).

Despite the novelty of this interpretation, the Secretary contends that it is entitled to deference [citing] Chevron U.S.A. Inc. v. Natural Resources Defense Council, Inc., 467 U.S. 837, 842-844 (1984) [*infra* p. 730, and other cases]. We have never applied the principle of those cases to agency litigating positions that are wholly unsupported by regulations, rulings, or administrative practice. To the contrary, we have declined to give deference to any agency counsel's interpretation of a statute where the agency itself has articulated no position on the question, on the ground that "Congress has delegated to the administrative official and not to appellate counsel the responsibility for elaborating and enforcing statutory commands." ... Even if we were to sanction departure from this principle in some cases, we would not do so here. Far from being a reasoned and consistent view of the scope of clause (ii), the Secretary's current interpretation of clause (ii) is contrary to the narrow view of that provision advocated in past cases, where the Secretary has argued that clause (ii) "merely contemplates a year-end balancing of the monthly installments received by a provider with the aggregate due it for the year." ... Deference to what appears to be nothing more than an agency's convenient litigating position would be entirely inappropriate. Accordingly, the retroactive rule cannot be upheld as an exercise of the Secretary's authority to make retroactive corrective adjustments.

B

The statutory provisions establishing the Secretary's general rulemaking power contain no express authorization of retroactive rulemaking. Any light that might be shed on this matter by suggestions of legislative intent also indicates that no such authority was contemplated. In the first place, where Congress intended to grant the Secretary the authority to act retroactively, it made that intent explicit. As discussed above, §1395x(v)(1)(A)(ii) directs the Secretary to establish procedures for making retroactive corrective adjustments; in view of this indication that Congress considered the need for retroactive agency action, the absence of any express authorization for retroactive cost-limit rules weighs heavily against the Secretary's position....

The Secretary nonetheless suggests that, whatever the limits on his power to promulgate retroactive regulations in the normal course of events, judicial invalidation of a prospective rule is a unique occurrence that creates a heightened need, and thus a justification, for retroactive curative rulemaking. The Secretary warns that congressional intent and important administrative goals may be frustrated unless an invalidated rule can be cured of its defect and made applicable to past time periods. The argument is further advanced that the countervailing reliance interests are less compelling than in the usual case of retroactive rulemaking, because the original, invalidated rule provided at least some notice to the individuals and entities subject to its provisions.

Whatever weight the Secretary's contentions might have in other contexts, they need not be addressed here. The case before us is resolved by the particular statutory scheme in question. Our interpretation of the Medicare Act compels the conclusion that the Secretary has no authority to promulgate retroactive cost-limit rules.

The 1984 reinstatement of the 1981 cost-limit rule is invalid. The judgment of the Court of Appeals is affirmed.

JUSTICE SCALIA, concurring.

. . . I agree with the District of Columbia Circuit that the APA independently confirms the judgment we have reached.

The first part of the APA's definition of "rule" states that a rule

> "means the whole or a part of an agency statement of general or particular applicability *and future effect* designed to implement, interpret, or prescribe law or policy or describing the organization, procedure, or practice requirements of an agency. . . ."

5 U.S.C. §551(4) (emphasis added). The only plausible reading of the italicized phrase is that rules have legal consequences only for the future. It could not possibly mean that merely *some* of their legal consequences must be for the future, though they may also have legal consequences for the past, since that description would not enable rules to be distinguished from "orders," see 5 U.S.C. §551(6), and would thus destroy the entire dichotomy upon which the most significant portions of the APA are based. (Adjudication — the process for formulating orders, see §551(7) — has future as well as past legal consequences, since the principles announced in an adjudication cannot be departed from in future adjudications without reason. . . .)

Nor could "future effect" in this definition mean merely "*taking effect* in the future," that is, having a future effective date even though, once effective, altering the law applied in the past. That reading, urged by the [Government], produces a definition of "rule" that is meaningless, since obviously *all* agency statements have "future effect" in the sense that they do not take effect until after they are made. . . . Thus this reading, like the other one, causes §551(4) to fail in its central objective, which is to distinguish rules from orders. All orders have "future effect" in the sense that they are not effective until promulgated.

In short, there is really no alternative except the obvious meaning, that a rule is a statement that has legal consequences only for the future. If the first part of the definition left any doubt of this, however, it is surely eliminated by the second part. . . . After the portion set forth above, the definition continues that a rule "includes the approval or prescription *for the future* of rates, wages, corporate or financial structures or reorganizations thereof, prices, facilities, appliances, services or allowances therefor or of valuations, costs, or accounting, or practices bearing on any of the foregoing." 5 U.S.C. §551(4). It seems to me clear that the phrase "for the future"—which even more obviously refers to future operation rather than a future effective date—is not meant to add a requirement to those contained in the earlier part of the definition, but rather to repeat, in a more particularized context, the prior requirement "of future effect." And even if one thought otherwise it would not matter for purposes of the present case, since the HHS "cost-limit" rules governing reimbursement are a "prescription" of "practices bearing on" "allowances" for "services." . . .

This case cannot be disposed of, as the [Government] suggests, by simply noting that retroactive rulemaking is similar to retroactive legislation, and that the latter has long been upheld against constitutional attack where reasonable. . . . The issue here is not constitutionality, but rather whether there is any good reason to doubt that the APA means what it says. For purposes of resolving that question, it does not at all follow that, since Congress itself possesses the power retroactively to change its laws, it must have meant agencies to possess the power retroactively to change their regulations. Retroactive legislation has always been looked upon with disfavor . . . and even its constitutionality has been conditioned upon a rationality requirement beyond that applied to other legislation. . . . It is entirely unsurprising, therefore, that even though Congress wields such a power itself, it has been unwilling to confer it upon the agencies. Given the traditional attitude towards retroactive legislation, the regime established by the APA is an entirely reasonable one: Where quasi-legislative action is required, an agency cannot act with retroactive effect without some special congressional authorization. That is what the APA says, and there is no reason to think Congress did not mean it. . . .

NOTES

1. According to General Motors Corp. v. NHTSA, 898 F.2d 165 (D.C. Cir. 1990), *Bowen* sends a clear signal that, absent congressional authorization for retroactive rulemaking, it is invalid. Similarly, an agency determination that it has the statutory authority to adopt retroactive rules is entitled to no deference on review. See Combs v. Commissioner, 400 F.3d 353, 357 (6th Cir. 2005).

2. *Bowen*'s harsh holding regarding retroactive application of rules has been applied somewhat uncomfortably by courts confronting the issue. The U.S. Supreme Court itself, in a somewhat unclear decision, seems to depart from *Bowen* in Smiley v. Citibank, 517 U.S. 735 (1996). In *Smiley*, the Court upheld the Comptroller of the Currency's substantive rule under the National Bank Act that late payment fees charged by credit card companies constitute "interest" for the Act's purposes. Ordinarily, the Court's deferral to the agency's determination would be appropriate, but the rule was promulgated long after the dispute between the parties in the *Smiley* case. The Court could only defer to the agency's determination if it gave the rule retroactive effect, which it did. However, the Court applied the rule retroactively without a finding of clear congressional intent to allow retroactive application, seemingly in contradiction of *Bowen*'s clear mandate. In Catholic Social Services v. Shalala, 12 F.3d 1123 (D.C. Cir. 1994), the D.C. Circuit minimized the overall impact of *Bowen* by finding that a rule with both retroactive and prospective features should be severed and invalidated only with respect to retroactive application. For an analysis regarding when a rule has primary versus secondary retroactive effects, see Recent Case: Administrative Law — Retroactive Rules — Arkema v. EPA, 124 Harv. L. Rev. 1805 (2011) (critiquing D.C. Circuit decision in *Arkema* for failing to distinguish between primary (new sanctions on past conduct) and secondary (upsetting expectations) retroactivity in striking down EPA rule).

3. After *Bowen*, can an agency apply rules retroactively when Congress has stated a specific deadline for promulgation of rules that the agency has missed? In Nat'l Petrochemical & Refiners Ass'n v. EPA, 630 F.3d 145 (D.C. Cir. 2010), the D.C. Circuit said yes because Congress had authorized new rules to begin on a particular date and the regulated had statutory notice. See also Chris Schmitter, Going Back in Time: The Search for Retroactive Rulemaking Power in Statutory Deadlines, 97 Minn. L. Rev. 1114 (2013).

4. Retroactive application of legislation is also disfavored. In Landgraf v. USI Film Products, 511 U.S. 244 (1994), and in Rivers v. Roadway Express, Inc., 511 U.S. 298 (1994), the Court refused to apply legislation retroactively when it held that two provisions of the Civil Rights Act of 1991 do not apply retroactively. The Court found that there was a strong presumption against retroactive applicability that could only be overcome by "clear evidence" of congressional intention to have the legislation apply retroactively.

D NONLEGISLATIVE RULES

1. Defining Nonlegislative Rules

Robert A. Anthony

INTERPRETIVE RULES, POLICY STATEMENTS, GUIDANCES, MANUALS, AND THE LIKE — SHOULD FEDERAL AGENCIES USE THEM TO BIND THE PUBLIC?*

41 Duke L.J. 1324-1326 (1992)

[I]NTERPRETIVE RULES AND POLICY STATEMENTS

... Because they are both nonlegislative, interpretive rules and policy statements are often usefully discussed together.... The critical difference is that the courts do not treat interpretations as making new law, on the theory that they merely

* Reprinted with permission of Duke Law Journal © 1992.

restate or explain the preexisting legislative acts and intentions of Congress. By contrast policy statements, although within the agency's authority, do not rest upon existing positive legislation that has tangible meaning. Neither Congress nor the agency, acting legislatively, has already made the law that the policy statements express. Thus these documents are looked upon as creating new policy, albeit not legally binding policy as the documents were not promulgated legislatively.

An interpretive rule is an agency statement that was not issued legislatively and that interprets language of a statute (or of an existing legislative rule) that has some tangible meaning.

A policy statement is an agency statement of substantive law or policy, of general or particular applicability and future effect, that was not issued legislatively and is not an interpretive rule.

If the document goes beyond a fair interpretation of existing legislation, it is not an interpretive rule. Because it was not promulgated legislatively, it cannot be a legislative rule; it therefore is a policy statement. This is not merely the logical classification, but the proper one, as the agency is making policy in an area not specifically governed by the existing law.

All substantive nonlegislative issuances that are not interpretive rules are policy statements — whether they are captioned or issued as policy statements or manuals or guidances or memoranda or circulars or press releases or even as interpretations.

The cases are replete with statements to the effect that policy statements are "designed to inform rather than to control." But many policy statements — and manuals, guidances memoranda and the like that fall within the category of policy statements — manifestly are "designed to control. . . ." I have said that a substantive nonlegislative rule must be either an interpretive rule or a policy statement. Rather surprisingly, this perhaps self-evident proposition has eluded most courts and commentators, at least in the terminology they have chosen.

COMMENT: PROCEDURAL RULES

What exactly is a procedural rule? Does it include anything that involves "procedure"? In Tunik v. MSPB, 407 F.3d 1326 (Fed. Cir. 2005), the Merit Systems Protection Board took the position that a rule allowing an administrative law judge to file a complaint for constructive discharge was procedural and could therefore be repealed without notice and comment. In disagreeing, the D.C. Circuit reasoned that procedural requirements could sometimes affect individual rights and have the force of law. The court had little trouble concluding that this was the case with a rule that provided a right to bring an action for constructive discharge.

A key test for deciding whether a rule is procedural versus legislative/substantive is whether the rule was intended to confer significant procedural rights on parties or instead was intended merely to create an orderly method of doing business. For this distinction, agency intent is key. See Colorado Environmental Coalition v. Wenker, 353 F.3d 1221 (10th Cir. 2004) (rule requiring letter of reference to accompany nomination to advisory committee merely a procedural rule); American Farm Lines v. Black Ball Freight Service, 397 U.S. 532, 539 (1970) ("[I]t is always within the discretion of a court or an administrative agency to relax or modify its procedural rules adopted for the orderly transaction of business before it when in a given case the ends of justice require it. The action of either in such a case is not reviewable except upon a showing of substantial prejudice to the complaining party." (citing NLRB v. Monsanto Chemical Co., 205 F.2d 763, 764 (1953)).

Consider the following statement about procedural rules:

> Importantly, the D.C. Circuit has . . . warned that the procedural-rule exception "should not be deemed to include any action which goes beyond formality" because procedural rules are intended simply to "deal[] with the method of operation utilized by the [agency] in the dispatch of its business." It is instructive to consider a few examples of agency rules that the D.C. Circuit has found to be procedural in nature. For example, the circuit has concluded that rules that create or modify deadlines for regulated entities to notify the agency of their choice to exercise certain substantive rights are procedural rules. Similarly, regulations regarding how the agency is going to receive petitions from regulated entities, or the internal steps that the agency will take to screen such applications, have been considered procedural. The circuit has also concluded that regulations that govern an agency's internal procedures with respect to its processing of incomplete or objected-to petitions filed by regulated entities satisfy the procedural-rule exception. And, lastly, procedural rules include agency regulations organizing the agency's internal procedures to meet its own legal duties. Thus, it is fair to say that D.C. Circuit's precedents, as well as its more general pronouncements regarding the scope and meaning of the procedural-rule exception, suggest that procedural rules primarily concern the agency's internal operations, even if such rules also occasionally create expectations for regulated entities with respect to the timeframe, means, and methods by which those entities assert their substantive rights vis-à-vis the agency. *Moreover, where . . . a plaintiff challenges a rule provision that is plainly not directed to internal agency processes, the APA seemingly requires the agency to demonstrate that its rulemaking action nevertheless relates to "agency organization, procedure, or practice" to such a degree that it cannot be fairly characterized as having a substantive impact on the parties.*

AFL-CIO v. NLRB, 466 F. Supp. 3d 68, 92-95 (D.D.C. 2020) (citations omitted) (emphasis added).

WARSHAUER v. SOLIS

577 F.3d 1330 (11th Cir. 2009)

WILSON, Circuit Judge:

This appeal requires us to engage in an interpretation of the Labor-Management Reporting and Disclosure Act of 1959 ("LMRDA" or "Act"), and examine the Secretary of the United States Department of Labor's ("Secretary") authority under it. The case concerns certain website advisories the Secretary issued regarding reporting obligations under the Act, and the extent to which a designated legal counsel ("DLC") must file annual reports of payments the DLC makes over a designated dollar amount to a union or union officer or employee. A DLC is an attorney recommended by a labor union to its members for representation in personal injury lawsuits, who usually does not play a role in labor relations and is not in an actual or potential bargaining relationship with the labor organization. Our consideration of the plain language of the LMRDA leads us to conclude that the Secretary's interpretation is not arbitrary and capricious, such that the appellant, Michael Warshauer, a DLC, is required to file the annual reports. We also find that the Secretary was not required to engage in notice and comment rulemaking when she issued the website advisories.

I. BACKGROUND

A. Relevant LMRDA Provisions

Finding that "there ha[d] been a number of instances of breach of trust, corruption, disregard of the rights of individual employees, and other failures to observe high standards of responsibility and ethical conduct," in 1959 Congress enacted the LMRDA to protect the rights of employees and the public. 29 U.S.C. §401(b). An important component of this protection were reporting requirements which would shed light on certain financial transactions. The instant case concerns one of these reporting requirements: §203 of the LMRDA. Section 203(a)(1) of the LMRDA requires the filing of a financial report from "[e]very employer who in a fiscal year made — (1) any payment or loan, direct or indirect of money or other thing of value (including reimbursed expenses), or any promise or agreement therefor, to any labor organization or officer. . . ." 29 U.S.C. §433(a)(1).

Section 203(a)(1)'s reporting requirement applies only to "employers." The LMRDA defines an "employer" as: [A]ny employer or any group or association of employers engaged in an industry affecting commerce (1) which is, with respect to employees engaged in an industry affecting commerce, an employer within the meaning of any law of the United States relating to the employment of any employees. . . . 29 U.S.C. §402(e).

To implement the LMRDA, Congress authorized the Secretary "to issue, amend, and rescind rules and regulations prescribing the form and publication of reports required to be filed under this [subchapter] and such other reasonable rules and regulations . . . as [the Secretary] may find necessary to prevent the circumvention or evasion of such reporting requirements." 29 U.S.C. §438.

B. Relevant Department of Labor Regulations

In 1963, the Department of Labor promulgated regulations to implement the employer reporting requirements of the LMRDA, specifying that "every employer required to file an annual report by section 203(a) of the Act and §405.2 shall file such report on the United States Department of Labor Form LM-10 . . . in the detail required by the instructions accompanying such form and constituting a part thereof." 29 C.F.R. §405.3. The Instructions require employers to report only "certain transactions":

> Only those employers as defined in the [LMRDA] who have been involved in certain financial transactions or arrangements with labor organizations, union officials, employees, or labor relations consultants, or who have made expenditures for certain objects relating to employees' or unions' activities.

The Instructions also exempt from reporting "sporadic or occasional gifts, gratuities, or favors of insubstantial value, given under circumstances and terms unrelated to the recipient's status in a labor organization; e.g., traditional Christmas gifts."

The LMRDA Interpretive Manual ("Manual") was also published in 1963, giving guidance on implementing the statute and regulations. Like the Instructions, the Manual explained that certain payments need not be reported. It used a discretionary "subjective standard" to determine what payments qualified as of "insubstantial value," requiring that "each case . . . be considered on its own facts." The Secretary's decision not to enforce the reporting requirements for payments of "insubstantial value" is known as the *de minimis* exemption.

Warshauer introduced testimony of former Department of Labor officials, suggesting that historically the Secretary interpreted the LM-10 reporting requirement to apply only to employers who engaged in persuader activities. Moreover, it is clear that historically, "insubstantial value" was determined on a case-by-case basis, rather than a fixed dollar amount. The issues in this case arose when the Secretary allegedly departed from these historical practices by publishing advisories on her website regarding the application of §203(a)(1) to DLCs and the *de minimis* exemption.

C. Website Advisories

In 2005, the Secretary issued website advisories pertaining to Form LM-10 filers. A list of rules, called "Frequently Asked Questions," or "FAQs," detailed the reports to be filed, records to be kept, and calculations to be made annually by employers. In November 2005, the Secretary posted an FAQ, which specifically identified DLCs as falling within the definition of "employer" under the LMRDA, essentially directing DLCs to file the LM-10. Another FAQ stated that the *de minimis* rule for exempting transactions of "insubstantial value" from reporting would depend on a fixed dollar amount. In March 2006, the website announced that the fixed amount was $ 250 — "gifts and gratuities with an aggregate value of $250 or less provided by an employer will be considered insubstantial for the purposes of LM-10 reporting."

The Secretary published these website advisories without giving notice to the public or offering an opportunity for public comment.

D. Application to Warshauer

Michael Warshauer, an attorney who practices in Atlanta, Georgia, specializes in actions under the Federal Employers Liability Act ("FELA"). A rail labor union, the United Transportation Union ("UTU"), appointed him as a DLC. As a DLC, the UTU recommends Warshauer to its members for representation in workers' compensation cases, personal injury cases, and other matters. Warshauer offers this legal counsel to UTU members at a reduced fee of 25% of the recovery. Warshauer engages in normal business entertaining of potential UTU clients. In October 2002, the Department of Labor sent Warshauer a letter informing him that "payments made or promised to the UTU, . . . either directly or indirectly, by each DLC that is an 'employer' within the meaning of section 3(e) of the LMRDA, must be disclosed on Employer Report, Form LM-10, in accordance with the statute and with Department of Labor Interpretive Regulations. . . ." However, Warshauer did not file the Form LM-10, based on his belief that he does not qualify as an "employer" under §203(a)(1) of the LMRDA. . . .

III. DISCUSSION

Warshauer argues that . . . (3) the application of the Form LM-10 reporting requirement to DLCs and the setting of a $250 threshold for the *de minimis* exemption require notice and comment rulemaking. . . .

B. Notice and Comment Rulemaking

Warshauer claims that the advisories applying the Form LM-10 reporting requirements to DLCs and setting a numeric threshold for the *de minimis* exemption require notice and comment rulemaking. The Secretary argues that the advisories do not require notice and comment because they are interpretive rules.

Congress directed the Secretary to follow the APA, 5 U.S.C. §553, when issuing or amending rules and regulations pursuant to the LMRDA. 29 U.S.C. §526. The APA requires all federal agencies to publish proposed rules in the Federal Register in order to provide the public with notice and an opportunity to comment. However, notice and comment rulemaking is not required when an agency issues an "interpretive rule." Courts generally refer to two categories of rules — interpretive rules and legislative rules. A legislative rule creates new law, rights, or duties. An interpretive rule, on the other hand, "typically reflects an agency's construction of a statute that has been entrusted to the agency to administer" and does not "*modif[y]* or *add[]* to a legal norm based on the agency's *own authority*." *Syncor Int'l Corp. v. Shalala*, 127 F.3d 90, 94-95, 326 U.S. App. D.C. 422 (D.C. Cir. 1997) (emphasis in original). "[T]he distinction between an interpretative rule and a substantive rule . . . likely turns on how tightly the agency's interpretation is drawn linguistically from the actual language of the statute." *Id.* at 94 (internal quotation marks and citations omitted).

The DC Circuit has set out general principles to be used in determining whether a rule is interpretive. *See General Motors Corp. v. Ruckleshaus*, 742 F.2d 1561, 1565, 239 U.S. App. D.C. 408 (D.C. Cir. 1984) (en banc). First, although not dispositive, the agency's characterization of the rule is relevant to the determination. *Id.* Second, "[a]n interpretative rule simply states what the administrative agency thinks the statute means, and only 'reminds affected parties of existing duties.' On the other hand, if by its action the agency intends to create new law, rights or duties, the rule is properly considered to be a legislative rule." *Id.* (quoting *Citizens to Save Spencer County v. EPA*, 600 F.2d 844, 876 n.153, 195 U.S. App. D.C. 30 (D.C. Cir. 1979)). The Seventh Circuit has pointed out that "legislative rules have effects *completely independent* of the statute." *Metro. Sch. Dist. of Wayne Twp. v. Davila*, 969 F.2d 485, 490 (7th Cir. 1992) (emphasis in original) (internal quotation marks and citations omitted).

1. Applying the Form LM-10 Reporting Requirements to DLCs

Warshauer argues that the Secretary's advisory applying the Form LM-10 reporting requirement to DLCs requires notice and comment rulemaking because it is a new rule that changes the substantive state of the existing law. The Secretary argues that notice and comment is not required because the advisory is an interpretive rule that merely states what the Department of Labor thinks §203(a)(1) means.

The rule applying the Form LM-10 reporting requirements to DLCs is an interpretive rule. First, it is relevant that the Secretary characterizes the rule as interpreting §203(a)(1). Second, the Secretary's interpretation is drawn directly from the plain language of the statute.... Third, the rule "only reminded affected parties of existing duties" required by the plain language of the statute. It did not create any new law, right, duty, or have any effect independent of the statute. Thus, the rule "is a prototypical example of an interpretive rule issued by an agency to advise the public of the agency's construction of the statutes and rules which it administers." *Shalala v. Guernsey Mem'l Hosp.*, 514 U.S. 87, 99, 115 S. Ct. 1232, 131 L. Ed. 2d 106 (1995) (quoting *Chrysler Corp. v. Brown*, 441 U.S. 281, 302 n.31, 99 S. Ct. 1705, 60 L. Ed. 2d 208 (1979)) (internal quotation marks omitted). *See also Caraballo v. Reich*, 11 F.3d 186, 195, 304 U.S. App. D.C. 142 (D.C. Cir. 1993) ("A statement seeking to interpret a statutory or regulatory term is . . . the quintessential example of an interpretive rule."). The Secretary was authorized not to create a duty for DLCs but to *explain* the duty created by §203(a)(1).

. . .

2. The De Minimis Exemption and Annual Threshold for Reporting

Warshauer argues that the Secretary's advisory addressing the *de minimis* exemption and setting a $250 threshold for reporting requires notice and comment rulemaking because it imposes new reporting duties and is inconsistent with the Department of Labor's prior applications of the *de minimis* exemption.

The Secretary argues that the advisory does not require notice and comment because it is an interpretive rule.

In 1963 the Department published the Instructions to the Form LM-10. The Instructions exempt "sporadic or occasional gifts, gratuities, or favors of insubstantial value" from §203(a)(1) reporting obligations. The Department did not fix dollar amounts to define "insubstantial value," instead choosing to follow a subjective approach to the exemption. In 2005, the Secretary changed this subjective approach to an objective standard — $250 for everyone.

The Secretary's rule is interpretive. The advisory informs the public about the agency's current view of "insubstantial value" in its application of the *de minimis* exemption; in other words, it merely clarifies how the Secretary intends to enforce the long-standing exemption to the reporting requirement. It does not create any new law, right, or duty, but rather provides guidance as to how the Secretary will exercise her enforcement discretion.

That the rule contains a numeric value does not prevent it from being an interpretive rule. While a rule that turns on a number is likely legislative because it is an arbitrary choice among possible methods of implementing a statute, not every rule with a numeric component is legislative. *Hoctor*, 82 F.3d at 171 ("We are not saying that an interpretive rule can never have a numerical component," as "the use of a number as a rule of thumb to guide the application of a general norm will often be legitimately interpretive."). Here, the Secretary interpreted the phrase "insubstantial value" as $250 or less. Her decision not to enforce the statute against those who make only such trivial payments is within her discretionary power.

Warshauer is incorrect in claiming that the advisory imposed new reporting duties. On the contrary, such duties derive from the statute itself; the advisory simply provides additional guidance. That the Secretary has informed the public of her judgment does not render the rule legislative.

Furthermore, contrary to Warshauer's assertions, the Secretary's change in position on what constitutes "insubstantial value" does not trigger notice and comment procedures. "[S]o long as a new guidance document can reasonably be interpreted as consistent with prior documents, it does not significantly revise a previous authoritative interpretation." *MetWest*, 560 F.3d at 510 (internal quotations omitted). Although the Secretary has set and altered the numerical value of the *de minimis* threshold, the Secretary's advisories may be reasonably interpreted as consistent. There has been no significant departure from or revision of the policy of exempting gifts of "insubstantial value."

Accordingly, since the Secretary's advisory setting a $250 threshold is an interpretive rule, the district court did not err in holding that the Secretary was not required to engage in notice and comment rulemaking.

NOTES

1. To what extent is an agency bound by its interpretive regulations? An answer to this query must start by recognizing that, unlike substantive/legislative regulations, interpretive regulations do not automatically have the force of law. United States v. Evans, 712 F. Supp. 1435 (D. Mont. 1989). They represent only the agency's view of what the law means, Seldovia Native Ass'n v. Lujan, 904 F.2d 1335 (9th Cir. 1990), and do not, of themselves, affect anyone's legal rights and obligations; in legal theory, the statutes, not the interpretive regulations, remain the criterion of what the law authorizes and compels or what it forbids. Despite this, the Secretary's changed position in *Warshauer*, above, resulted in a new category of people, DLCs, having to file an LM-10. If the change does not result in new binding law, why is Warshauer suing? Does the fact that the guidance is merely interpretive mean that Warshauer can fail to file an LM-10 with impunity?

Compare the following statement by Chief Justice Burger, while a circuit judge, about an interpretive rule:

> Whatever practical or psychological effect this rule may have on the conduct of petitioners — and we do not doubt that it may have some pragmatic consequences — its legal effect is essentially that of an opinion of the legal staff.

American President Lines v. Federal Maritime Comm'n, 316 F.2d 419, 422 (D.C. Cir. 1963). Does this mean that an interpretive rule should be flouted only at one's peril? Are additional steps necessary to give an interpretive rule the force of law? If so, what would they be?

2. As suggested, an interpretive regulation may be more than a mere piece of paper without any consequences. In practice, interpretive rules tend to acquire all but substantive weight because of the deference paid to them by the courts. The judicial attitude is shown by the following quote from a leading case, Skidmore v. Swift & Co., 323 U.S. 134, 140 (1944):

> The fact that the Administrator's policies and standards are not reached by trial in adversary form does not mean that they are not entitled to respect. This Court has long given considerable and in some cases decisive weight to Treasury Decisions and to interpretive regulations of the Treasury and of other bodies that were not of adversary origin.
>
> We consider that the rulings, interpretations and opinions of the Administrator under this Act, while not controlling upon the courts by reason of their authority, do constitute a body of experience and informed judgment to which courts and litigants may properly resort for guidance.

ELECTRONIC PRIVACY INFO. CTR. v. UNITED STATES DEP'T OF HOMELAND SECURITY

653 F.3d 1 (D.C. Cir. 2011)

GINSBURG, Circuit Judge. The Electronic Privacy Information Center (EPIC) and two individuals petition for review of a decision by the Transportation Security Administration to screen airline passengers by using advanced imaging technology [AIT] instead of magnetometers. They argue this use of AIT violates various federal statutes and the Fourth Amendment to the Constitution of the United

States and, in any event, should have been the subject of notice-and-comment rulemaking before being adopted. Although we are not persuaded by any of the statutory or constitutional arguments against the rule, we agree the TSA has not justified its failure to issue notice and solicit comments. We therefore grant the petition in part.

I. BACKGROUND

By statute, anyone seeking to board a commercial airline flight must be screened by the TSA in order to ensure he is not "carrying unlawfully a dangerous weapon, explosive, or other destructive substance." 49 U.S.C. §§44901(a), 44902(a)(1). The Congress generally has left it to the agency to prescribe the details of the screening process, which the TSA has documented in a set of Standard Operating Procedures not available to the public. In addition to the SOPs, the agency has promulgated a blanket regulation barring any person from entering the so-called "sterile area" of an airport, the area on the departure side of the security apparatus, "without complying with the systems, measures, or procedures being applied to control access to, or presence or movement in, such area[]." 49 C.F.R. §1540.105(a)(2). The Congress did, however, in 2004, direct the TSA to "give a high priority to developing, testing, improving, and deploying" at airport screening checkpoints a new technology "that detects nonmetallic, chemical, biological, and radiological weapons, and explosives, in all forms." Intelligence Reform and Terrorism Prevention Act of 2004, Pub. L. No. 108-458, §4013(a), 118 Stat. 3719 (codified at 49 U.S.C. §44925(a)).

The TSA responded to this directive by contracting with private vendors to develop AIT for use at airports. The agency has procured two different types of AIT scanner, one that uses millimeter wave technology, which relies upon radio frequency energy, and another that uses backscatter technology, which employs low-intensity X-ray beams. Each technology is designed to produce a crude image of an unclothed person, who must stand in the scanner for several seconds while it generates the image. That image enables the operator of the machine to detect a nonmetallic object, such as a liquid or powder — which a magnetometer cannot detect — without touching the passengers coming through the checkpoint.

The TSA began to deploy AIT scanners in 2007 in order to provide additional or "secondary" screening of selected passengers who had already passed through a magnetometer. In 2009 the TSA initiated a field test in which it used AIT as a means of primary screening at a limited number of airports. Based upon the apparent success of the test, the TSA decided early in 2010 to use the scanners everywhere for primary screening. By the end of that year the TSA was operating 486 scanners at 78 airports; it plans to add 500 more scanners before the end of this year.

No passenger is ever required to submit to an AIT scan. Signs at the security checkpoint notify passengers they may opt instead for a patdown, which the TSA claims is the only effective alternative method of screening passengers. A passenger who does not want to pass through an AIT scanner may ask that the patdown be performed by an officer of the same sex and in private. Many passengers nonetheless remain unaware of this right, and some who have exercised the right have complained that the resulting patdown was unnecessarily aggressive.

The TSA has also taken steps to mitigate the effect a scan using AIT might have upon passenger privacy: Each image produced by a scanner passes through a filter to obscure facial features and is viewable on a computer screen only by an officer sitting in a remote and secure room. As soon as the passenger has been cleared, moreover, the image is deleted; the officer cannot retain the image on his computer, nor is he permitted to bring a cell phone or camera into the secure room. In addition to these measures to protect privacy, the agency has commissioned two studies of the safety of the scanners that use backscatter technology, each of which has found the scanners emit levels of radiation well within acceptable limits. Millimeter wave scanners are also tested to ensure they meet accepted standards for safety.

The petitioners, for their part, have long been unsatisfied with the TSA's efforts to protect passengers' privacy and health from the risks associated with AIT. In May 2009 more than 30 organizations, including the petitioner EPIC, sent a letter to the Secretary of Homeland Security, in which they objected to the use of AIT as a primary means of screening passengers. They asked that the TSA cease using AIT in that capacity pending "a 90-day formal public rulemaking process." The TSA responded with a letter addressing the organizations' substantive concerns but ignoring their request for rulemaking.

Nearly a year later, in April 2010, the EPIC and a slightly different group of organizations sent the Secretary and her Chief Privacy Officer a second letter, denominated a "petition for the issuance, amendment, or repeal of a rule" pursuant to 5 U.S.C. §553(e). They argued the use of AIT for primary screening violates the Privacy Act; a provision of the Homeland Security Act requiring the Chief Privacy Officer upon the issuance of a new rule to prepare a privacy impact assessment; the Religious Freedom Restoration Act (RFRA); and the Fourth Amendment. In May the TSA again responded by letter, clarifying some factual matters, responding to the legal challenges, and taking the position it is not required to initiate a rulemaking each time it changes screening procedures. In July, the EPIC, joined by two members of its advisory board who travel frequently and have been subjected to AIT screening by the TSA, petitioned this court for review.

II. ANALYSIS

■ ■ ■

A. Notice and Comment

In their opening brief, the petitioners argue the TSA "refus[ed] to process" and "effectively ignored" their 2010 letter, which was "explicitly marked as a 'petition'" for rulemaking under §553. The TSA responds that the petitioners did not petition "for the issuance, amendment, or repeal of a rule," as authorized by §553(e), because "the relief actually sought [was] . . . the immediate suspension of the AIT program." A construction of §553(e) that excludes any petition with a goal beyond mere process is dubious at best, and the agency offers no authority for it. The petitioners were clearly seeking "amendment[] or repeal of a rule"; that their aim was expressed in terms of the substance of the rule surely does not work against them. Indeed, we would be surprised to find many petitions for rulemaking that do not identify the substantive outcome the petitioner wants the agency to reach.

Anticipating this conclusion, the TSA next argues it responded appropriately to the petition by denying it. We will set aside an agency's decision to deny a petition for rulemaking only if it is "arbitrary, capricious, an abuse of discretion, or otherwise not in accordance with law." 5 U.S.C. §706(2)(A). Moreover, "an agency's refusal to institute rulemaking proceedings is at the high end of the range of levels of deference we give to agency action under our arbitrary and capricious review." Defenders of Wildlife v. Gutierrez, 532 F.3d 913, 919, 382 U.S. App. D.C. 312 (D.C. Cir. 2008) (internal quotation marks omitted). Here, however, the TSA denied the petition on the ground it "is not required to initiate APA rulemaking procedures each time the agency develops and implements improved passenger screening procedures." Because this position rests upon an interpretation of the Administrative Procedure Act, the crux of our review turns upon our analysis of that statute. See Am. Horse Prot. Ass'n, Inc. v. Lyng, 812 F.2d 1, 5, 258 U.S. App. D.C. 397 (D.C. Cir. 1987) (court may overturn decision to deny petition for rulemaking if based upon "plain errors of law" (internal quotation marks omitted)).

We turn, then, to §§553(b) and (c) of the APA, which generally require an agency to publish notice of a proposed rule in the Federal Register and to solicit and consider public comments upon its proposal. See U.S. Telecom Ass'n v. FCC, 400 F.3d 29, 34, 365 U.S. App. D.C. 149 (D.C. Cir. 2005) ("This court and many commentators have generally referred to the category of rules to which the notice-and-comment requirements do apply as 'legislative rules'"). As the TSA points out, however, the statute does provide certain exceptions to this standard procedure; in particular, as set forth in §553(b)(3)(A), the notice and comment requirements do not apply "to interpretative rules, general statements of policy, or rules of agency organization, procedure, or practice." The TSA argues its decision to use AIT for primary screening comes within all three listed categories and therefore is not a "legislative rule" subject to notice and comment.

1. Procedural Rule

We consider first the TSA's argument it has announced a rule of "agency organization, procedure, or practice," which our cases refer to as a "procedural rule." In general, a procedural rule "does not itself 'alter the rights or interests of parties, although it may alter the manner in which the parties present themselves or their viewpoints to the agency.'" Chamber of Commerce of U.S. v. DOL, 174 F.3d 206, 211, 335 U.S. App. D.C. 370 (D.C. Cir. 1999). As we have noted before, however, a rule with a "substantial impact" upon the persons subject to it is not necessarily a [legislative/]substantive rule under §553(b)(3)(A). See Pub. Citizen v. Dep't of State, 276 F.3d 634, 640-41, 349 U.S. App. D.C. 291 (2002). Further, the distinction between substantive and procedural rules is "one of degree" depending upon "whether the substantive effect is sufficiently grave so that notice and comment are needed to safeguard the policies underlying the APA." Lamoille Valley R.R. Co. v. ICC, 711 F.2d 295, 328, 229 U.S. App. D.C. 17 (D.C. Cir. 1983). In order to further these policies, the exception for procedural rules "must be narrowly construed." United States v. Picciotto, 875 F.2d 345, 347, 277 U.S. App. D.C. 312 (D.C. Cir. 1989).

Of course, stated at a high enough level of generality, the new policy imposes no new substantive obligations upon airline passengers: The requirement that a passenger pass through a security checkpoint is hardly novel, the prohibition against boarding a plane with a weapon or an explosive device even less so. But this overly abstract account of the change in procedure at the checkpoint elides the privacy interests at the heart of the petitioners' concern with AIT. Despite the precautions taken by the TSA, it is clear that by producing an image of the unclothed passenger, an AIT scanner intrudes upon his or her personal privacy in a way a magnetometer does not. Therefore, regardless whether this is a "new substantive burden," see Aulenback, 103 F.3d at 169, the change substantively affects the public to a degree sufficient to implicate the policy interests animating notice-and-comment rulemaking. Cf. Pickus v. Bd. of Parole, 507 F.2d 1107, 1113-14, 165 U.S. App. D.C. 284 (D.C. Cir. 1974) (rules governing parole hearings not procedural because they went "beyond formality and substantially affect[ed]" prisoners' liberty). Indeed, few if any regulatory procedures impose directly and significantly upon so many members of the public. Not surprisingly, therefore, much public concern and media coverage have been focused upon issues of privacy, safety, and efficacy, each of which no doubt would have been the subject of many comments had the TSA seen fit to solicit comments upon a proposal to use AIT for primary screening. To confirm these issues were relevant to the TSA's deliberations about AIT, we need look no further than its assurances to that effect in its response to the petitioners' 2010 letter: "AIT screening has proven effective in addressing ever-changing security threats, and numerous independent studies have addressed health concerns. TSA has carefully considered the important . . . privacy issues." For these reasons, the TSA's use of AIT for primary screening has the hallmark of a substantive rule and, therefore, unless the rule comes within some other exception, it should have been the subject of notice and comment.

2. Interpretive Rule

The TSA next tries to justify having proceeded without notice and comment on the ground that it announced only an "interpretative" rule advising the public of its current understanding of the statutory charge to develop and deploy new technologies for the detection of terrorist weapons. For their part, the petitioners argue the rule is legislative rather than interpretive because it "effectively amends a prior legislative rule," Am. Mining Congress v. Mine Safety & Health Admin., 995 F.2d 1106, 1112, 302 U.S. App. D.C. 38 (D.C. Cir. 1993), to wit, the secondary use of AIT only to back-up primary screening performed with magnetometers. See also Sprint Corp. v. FCC, 315 F.3d 369, 374, 354 U.S. App. D.C. 288 (D.C. Cir. 2003) ("an amendment to a legislative rule must itself be legislative" (internal quotation marks omitted)).

The practical question inherent in the distinction between legislative and interpretive regulations is whether the new rule effects "a substantive regulatory change" to the statutory or regulatory regime. U.S. Telecom Ass'n, 400 F.3d at 34-40 (FCC effected substantive change when it required wireline telephone carriers to permit customers to transfer their telephone numbers to wireless carriers). For the reasons discussed in Part II.A.1, we conclude the TSA's policy substantially changes the experience of airline passengers and is therefore not merely "interpretative" either of the statute directing the TSA to detect weapons likely to be used by terrorists or of the general regulation requiring that passengers comply with all TSA screening procedures. . . . Concedely, there is some merit in the TSA's argument it has done no more than resolve an ambiguity inherent in its statutory and regulatory authority, but the purpose of the APA would be disserved if an agency with a broad statutory command (here, to detect weapons) could avoid notice-and-comment rulemaking simply by promulgating a comparably broad regulation (here, requiring passengers to clear a checkpoint) and then invoking its power to interpret that statute and regulation in binding the public to a strict and specific set of obligations.

3. General Statement of Policy

Finally, the TSA argues notice and comment is not required because, rather than promulgating a legislative rule, the agency, in announcing it will use AIT for primary screening, made a "general statement[] of policy." The question raised by the policy exception "is whether a statement is . . . of present binding effect"; if it is, then the APA calls for notice and comment. McLouth Steel Prods. Corp. v. Thomas, 838 F.2d 1317, 1320, 267 U.S. App. D.C. 367 (D.C. Cir. 1988). Our cases "make clear that an agency pronouncement will be considered binding as a practical matter if it either appears on its face to be binding, or is applied by the agency in a way that indicates it is binding." Gen. Elec. Co. v. EPA, 290 F.3d 377, 383, 351 U.S. App. D.C. 291 (D.C. Cir. 2002) (internal citation omitted); see also *Chamber of Commerce*, 174 F.3d at 212-13. It is enough for the agency's statement to "purport to bind" those subject to it, that is, to be cast in "mandatory language" so "the affected private parties are reasonably led to believe that failure to conform will bring adverse consequences." *Gen. Elec.*, 290 F.3d at 383-84 (internal quotation marks omitted).

The TSA seems to think it significant that there are no AIT scanners at some airports and the agency retains the discretion to stop using the scanners where they are in place. More clearly significant is that a passenger is bound to comply with whatever screening procedure the TSA is using on the date he is to fly at the airport from which his flight departs. 49 C.F.R. §1540.105(a)(2). To be sure, he can opt for a patdown but, as the TSA conceded at oral argument, the agency has not argued that option makes its screening procedures nonbinding and we therefore do not consider the possibility. We are left, then, with the argument that a passenger is not bound to comply with the set of choices presented by the TSA when he arrives at the security checkpoint, which is absurd.

In sum, the TSA has advanced no justification for having failed to conduct a notice-and-comment rulemaking. We therefore remand this matter to the agency for further proceedings. Because vacating the present rule would severely disrupt an essential security operation, however, and the rule is, as we explain below, otherwise lawful, we shall not vacate the rule, but we do nonetheless expect the agency to act promptly on remand to cure the defect in its promulgation. See Allied-Signal, Inc. v. Nuclear Regulatory Comm'n, 988 F.2d 146, 150-51, 300 U.S. App. D.C. 198 (D.C. Cir. 1993).

The agency asks us to "make clear that on remand, TSA is free to invoke the APA's 'good cause' exception" to notice-and-comment rulemaking, 5 U.S.C. §553(b)(B) (exception "when the agency for good cause finds . . . that notice and public procedure thereon are impracticable, unnecessary, or contrary to the public interest"). We have no occasion to express a view upon this possibility other than to note we do not reach it. . . .

III. CONCLUSION

To sum up, first, we grant the petition for review insofar as it claims the TSA has not justified its failure to initiate notice-and-comment rulemaking before announcing it would use AIT scanners for primary screening. None of the exceptions urged by the TSA justifies its failure to give notice of and receive comment upon such a rule, which is legislative and not merely interpretive, procedural, or a general statement of policy. . . . Finally, due to the obvious need for the TSA to continue its airport security operations without interruption, we remand the rule to the TSA but do not vacate it, and instruct the agency promptly to proceed in a manner consistent with this opinion.

So ordered.

NOTES

1. Compare *Warshauer* and *EPIC*. What exactly is the difference in the two cases that leads one court to find an interpretive rule and the other to find a legislative one?

2. The *EPIC* court cites United States v. Telecom for the proposition that a legislative rule is one that imposes a "substantive regulatory change." But, what exactly does that mean? Almost any change can be viewed as "substantive." The better distinction would seem to be whether the agency intends the rule to "bind" regulated parties, no? See, e.g., GE v. EPA, *infra*, p. 319. Or, to create new legal rights, duties, or obligations? See, e.g., *Warshauer, supra*, p. 305. Some judges and scholars believe that the *EPIC* case may suggest whether a rule is substantive/legislative can also depend on the rule's *impact* on the public. See National Security Counselors v. CIA, 931 F. Supp. 2d 77, 111, 112 ("*EPIC* stands for the proposition that, even where a rule does not change the behavior expected of people, [a rule] may still be subject to notice and comment if it intrudes upon other, important or fundamental rights or interests held by affected parties."); Renan, The Fourth Amendment as Administrative Governance, 68 Stan. L. Rev. 1039, 1099-1100 (2016) ("The [*EPIC*] court concluded that the new TSA search policy "affects the public to a degree sufficient to implicate the policy interests animating notice-and-comment rulemaking." The rule at issue bound the agency and the public, and it "substantially changed the experience of airline passengers.").

2. Is It Binding? Distinguishing Between Legislative and Nonlegislative Rules

Robert A. Anthony

INTERPRETIVE RULES, POLICY STATEMENTS, GUIDANCES, MANUALS, AND THE LIKE — SHOULD FEDERAL AGENCIES USE THEM TO BIND THE PUBLIC?*

41 Duke L.J. 1327 (1992)

Although [agency] documents [may be] plainly nonlegislative (because they were not promulgated by notice-and-comment procedures), courts nevertheless in many cases have regularly asked whether such documents "are" legislative rules rather than interpretive rules or policy statements. This method of framing the issue begs the real question and seems to me to have bred unending confusion. For precision's sake, we must insist that these documents cannot "be" legislative rules, as they were not issued legislatively. What the courts in these cases plainly were looking for was whether the agency was trying to issue a rule that was legislative in nature. Did the agency, for example, attempt to "implement a general statutory mandate" or "intend [] to create new law, rights or duties" or "impose an obligation . . . not found in the statute itself" or "attempt[] . . . to supplement the Act, not simply to construe it" or "conclusively determine [] the . . . trigger [for] the . . . program allocations"? In short, did the agency's nonlegislative action bind or attempt to bind the affected public?

Thus, the proper question in these cases is not whether the policy document is a legislative rule. Rather, the proper question is whether the nonlegislative

* Reprinted with permission of Duke Law Journal © 1992.

document should have been issued as a legislative rule in the circumstances. The key to that question is, I believe, quite clear, based on analysis of the APA and of the many decided cases: Did the agency intend the document to bind? Has the agency given it binding effect? If the answer to either of these questions is "yes," the document should have been issued as a legislative rule.

A good example of what the excerpt above means is demonstrated in GE v. EPA, 290 F.3d 377 (D.C. Cir. 2002). There, the D.C. Circuit applied this thinking in determining whether an EPA "guidance document" was legislative or nonlegislative (i.e., a policy statement or an interpretation). The GE case involved the Toxic Substances Control Act (TSCA), which prohibits the use, manufacture, or distribution of polychlorinated biphenyls (PCBs) subject to several exceptions. The EPA promulgated a Guidance Document (Document) setting forth two methods to calculate the cancer risk under the exceptions. GE challenged the Document's promulgation. GE believed the Document was a legislative rule and therefore that the promulgation process was improper. Specifically, GE noted that the EPA did not publish a notice of proposed rulemaking, allow interested parties an opportunity to comment, or hold an informal hearing.

The court determined that the distinction between a legislative rule and a nonlegislative rule, in this case a policy statement, is whether the action has the force of law (i.e., is binding). The court stated that an agency action may be binding if it appears on its face to be binding. The court further stated that if an agency action expresses a change in law or policy that is intended to be binding on the agency and other parties, the agency may not rely on the policy statement exemption and must comply with the Administrative Procedure Act's rulemaking procedures. Although the Document allowed entities to seek an exception under the TSCA, entities were required to use one of the two permissible calculation methods. Thus, the court concluded that the Document was a binding agency action. Furthermore, the court determined that because the Document contained fixed rates of impermissible PCB levels, the Document purported to bind entities to the Document's guidelines. The court concluded that because the Document binds entities in addition to the EPA, the Document appears to have the force of law. The court also concluded that this appearance rendered the Document a legislative rule. The court vacated the guidelines within the Document because the EPA did not comply with the APA's requirements for legislative rules. See also Center for Auto Safety v. NHTSA, 452 F.3d 798 (D.C. Cir. 2006) (policy guidelines held to be nonbinding policy statement where formal legal consequences not intended and promulgated by an official lacking rulemaking authority); Consolidated Edison v. FERC, 315 F.3d 316 (D.C. Cir. 2003) (as contrasted with a legislative rule, an agency may refuse to follow an applicable policy statement so long as the agency offers a reasonable explanation for so doing); Interstate Natural Gas Ass'n v. FERC, 285 F.3d 18 (D.C. Cir. 2002) (the consequences of an agency choosing to characterize a rule as a policy statement is to forfeit the automatically binding nature of the promulgation).

The position of the D.C. Circuit was explained further in Securities Industry & Financial Markets Ass'n v. United States CFTC, 67 F. Supp. 3d 373 (D.D.C. 2014):

> Indeed, because each agency action is unique, determining whether a given agency action is a legislative rule, interpretive rule, or policy statement "is an extraordinarily case-specific endeavor." *Am. Hosp. Ass'n v. Bowen*, 834 F.2d 1037, 1045, 266 U.S. App. D.C. 190 (D.C. Cir. 1987).
>
> Courts, however, are not without some guidance. In distinguishing between legislative rules and general statements of policy, the D.C. Circuit has long been guided by two important factors: "the actual legal effect (or lack thereof) of the agency action in question on regulated entities," and the "agency's characterization" of the agency action. . . . The first "'focuses on the effects of the agency action,' asking whether the agency has '(1) impose[d] any rights and obligations, or (2) genuinely [left) the agency and its decisionmakers free to exercise discretion.'" . . . The second looks to the agency's expressed intentions: "'(1) the [a]gency's own characterization of the action; (2) whether the action was published in the Federal Register or the Code of Federal Regulations; and (3) whether the action has binding effects on private parties or on the agency.'" . . . Both factors ultimately cut to whether "the agency action binds private parties or the agency itself with the 'force of law.'" . . . Thus, "an agency pronouncement will be considered binding as a practical matter" — and thus a legislative rule — "If it either appears on its face to be binding . . . or is applied by the agency in a way that indicates it is binding."

Id. at 415-16 (citations omitted).

COMMENTS

1. Whether a rule is legislative or nonlegislative matters. Legislative rules are subject to the requirement of notice and comment under the APA, nonlegislative rules are not. In addition, the process used to articulate an agency position may matter in determining the amount of deference given to it by a court. See United States v. Mead Corp., 533 U.S. 218, 236 n.17 (2001) (noting that policy statements may not be entitled to judicial deference).

2. The application of law in this area is confused and confusing. Judge Patricia Wald of the U.S. Court of Appeals for the D.C. Circuit has written:

> Determining whether a given agency action is interpretive or legislative is an extraordinarily case-specific endeavor. As in the area of federal preemption jurisprudence, analogizing to prior cases is often of limited utility in light of the exceptional degree to which decisions in this doctrinal area turn on their precise facts.

American Hosp. Ass'n v. Bowen, 834 F.2d 1037, 1045 (D.C. Cir. 1987).

One helpful opinion, now followed in a number of different federal circuit courts, is the U.S. Court of Appeals for the D.C. Circuit decision in American Mining Congress v. MSHA, 995 F.2d 1106 (D.C. Cir. 1993). There, the court went back to first principles in defining substantive (referred to now in this casebook as "legislative") and interpretive rules as well as statements of policy:

The distinction between those agency pronouncements subject to APA notice-and-comment requirements and those that are exempt has been aptly described as "enshrouded in considerable smog," General Motors Corporation v. Ruckelshaus, 742 F.2d 1561, 1565 (D.C. Cir. 1984) (en banc); see also American Hospital Association v. Bowen, 834 F.2d 1037, 1046 (D.C. Cir. 1987) (calling the line between interpretive and legislative rules "fuzzy"); Community Nutrition Institute v. Young, 818 F.2d 943, 946 (D.C. Cir. 1987) (quoting authorities describing the present distinction between legislative rules and policy statements as "tenuous," "blurred" and "baffling").

Given the confusion, it makes some sense to go back to the origins of the distinction in the legislative history of the Administrative Procedure Act. Here the key document is the *Attorney General's Manual on the Administrative Procedure Act* (1947), which offers "the following working definitions":

> *Substantive[/Legislative] rules* — rules, other than organizational or procedural under section 3(a)(1) and (2), issued by an agency pursuant to statutory authority and which implement the statute, as, for example, the proxy rules issued by the Securities and Exchange Commission pursuant to section 14 of the Securities Exchange Act of 1934. . . . Such rules have the force and effect of law.
>
> *Interpretative rules* — rules or statements issued by an agency to advise the public of the agency's construction of the statutes and rules which it administers. . . .
>
> *General statements of policy* — statements issued by an agency to advise the public prospectively of the manner in which the agency proposes to exercise a discretionary power.

Id. at 30 n.3. See also Michael Asimow, *Public Participation in the Adoption of Interpretive Rules and Policy Statements*, 75 Mich. L. Rev. 520, 542 & n.95 (1977) (reading legislative history of Administrative Procedure Act as "suggesting an intent to adopt the legal effect test" as marking the line between substantive [legislative] and interpretive rules). 995 F.2d at 1108-1109. The *American Mining Congress* decision then set out a concise rule (no pun intended here) for distinguishing between legislative and interpretive rules:

> Accordingly, insofar as our cases can be reconciled at all, we think it almost exclusively on the basis of whether the purported interpretive rule has "legal effect," which in turn is best ascertained by asking (1) whether in the absence of the rule there would not be an adequate legislative basis for enforcement action or other agency action to confer benefits or ensure the performance of duties, (2) whether the agency has published the rule in the Code of Federal Regulations, (3) whether the agency has explicitly invoked its general legislative authority, or (4) whether the rule effectively amends a prior legislative rule. If the answer to any of these questions is affirmative, we have a legislative, not an interpretive rule.

995 F.2d at 1112. See also Securities Industry & Financial Markets Ass'n v. United States CFTC, 67 F. Supp. 3d 373, 416 (D.D.C. 2014) ("In distinguishing between legislative and interpretive rules, "[t]he practical question inherent in the distinction . . . is whether the new rule effects 'a substantive regulatory change' to the statutory or regulatory regime." . . . "On the margins, the distinction between legislative and interpretive rules "likely turns on how tightly the agency's interpretation is drawn linguistically from the actual language of the statute or rule.").

3. Why is an agency bound by its procedural rules, even though the procedure provided is more generous than the Constitution or a statute requires? See, e.g., United States *ex rel.* Accardi v. Shaughnessy, 347 U.S. 260 (1954). Consider the following two statements by Felix Frankfurter:

(a) As counsel for petitioners in Colyer v. Skeffington, 265 F. 17, 48 (D. Mass. 1920), rev'd, 277 F. 129 (1st Cir. 1922):

> Now, if there is one thing that is established in the law of administration, I take it that it is that a rule cannot be repealed specifically to affect a case under consideration by the administrative authorities; that is, if there is an existing rule which protects certain rights, it violates every sense of decency, which is the very heart of due process, to repeal that protection, just for the purpose of accomplishing the ends of the case which comes before the administrative authority.

(b) Concurring, in Vitarelli v. Seaton, 359 U.S. 535, 546-547 (1959):

> An executive agency must be rigorously held to the standards by which it professes its action to be judged. . . . Accordingly, if dismissal from employment is based on a defined procedure, even though generous beyond the requirements that bind such agency, that procedure must be scrupulously observed. . . . This judicially evolved rule of administrative law is now firmly established and, if I may add, rightly so. He that takes the procedural sword shall perish with that sword.

Compare the cases applying Vitarelli v. Seaton to agency procedures not embodied in formal rules. See, e.g., Garner v. FCC, 530 F.2d 1086 (D.C. Cir. 1976) (procedure established by agency's "usual practice"); United States v. Heffner, 420 F.2d 809 (4th Cir. 1969) (procedure announced in "News Release").

4. What about agency statements of policy? Can they ever be found to bind agencies? See Stinson v. United States, 508 U.S. 36 (1993) (policy statements issued by agencies serve to bind courts if they interpret substantive rules and are not inconsistent with the rules themselves, the statute, or the Constitution). Federal courts have generally resisted *Stinson* by finding, consistent with the Court's decision, that policy statements at issue do not interpret substantive rules and thus are only persuasive in effect. See, e.g., United States v. Hill, 48 F.3d 228 (7th Cir. 1995). In Professionals and Patients for Customized Care v. Shalala, 56 F.3d 592 (5th Cir. 1995), the Fifth Circuit found that a "Compliance Guide" issued by the FDA was only a policy statement and not a rule. The Guide set out nine factors the agency would consider in deciding whether a drug manufacturer was engaged in illegal and unlicensed manufacture of drugs. The plaintiffs urged that the Guide was a defective substantive rule because it had been promulgated without public notice and comment. The court's holding that the guide was a policy statement rather than a rule was premised both on the agency's characterization of the Guide and, perhaps more importantly, on the agency's retention of discretion regarding whether to apply the Guide or not in a particular circumstance. According to the court, a policy statement is not a rule if the agency retains discretion regarding its applicability.

5. The D.C. Circuit shifted its approach to policy statements in 2000, deciding to accord less deference to agencies' characterizations of their own rules and place more of an emphasis on whether the "*practical effect*" of the rule is to bind. See Appalachian Power v. EPA, 208 F.3d 1015 (D.C. Cir. 2000). Is this the same test applied by the court in the *EPIC* case, as discussed above? For criticism of the practical effect test, see Sunstein, "Practically Binding": General Policy Statements and Notice and Comment Rulemaking, 68 Admin. L. Rev. 491 (2016); Funk, When Is a "Rule" a Regulation? Marking a Clear Line Between Nonlegislative Rules and Legislative Rules, 54 Admin. L. Rev. 659 (2002).

E COST-BENEFIT ANALYSIS

Executive Order 13563 — Improving Regulation and Regulatory Review

76 Fed. Reg. 3821 (Jan. 21, 2011)

By the authority vested in me as President by the Constitution and the laws of the United States of America, and in order to improve regulation and regulatory review, it is hereby ordered as follows:

Section 1. General Principles of Regulation

(a) Our regulatory system must protect public health, welfare, safety, and our environment while promoting economic growth, innovation, competitiveness, and job creation. It must be based on the best available science. It must allow for public participation and an open exchange of ideas. It must promote predictability and reduce uncertainty. It must identify and use the best, most innovative, and least burdensome tools for achieving regulatory ends. It must take into account benefits and costs, both quantitative and qualitative. It must ensure that regulations are accessible, consistent, written in plain language, and easy to understand. It must measure, and seek to improve, the actual results of regulatory requirements.

(b) This order is supplemental to and reaffirms the principles, structures, and definitions governing contemporary regulatory review that were established in Executive Order 12866 of September 30, 1993. As stated in that Executive Order and to the extent permitted by law, each agency must, among other things: (1) propose or adopt a regulation only upon a reasoned determination that its benefits justify its costs (recognizing that some benefits and costs are difficult to quantify); (2) tailor its regulations to impose the least burden on society, consistent with obtaining regulatory objectives, taking into account, among other things, and to the extent practicable, the costs of cumulative regulations; (3) select, in choosing among alternative regulatory approaches, those approaches that maximize net benefits (including potential economic, environmental, public health and safety, and other advantages; distributive impacts; and equity); (4) to the extent feasible, specify performance objectives, rather than specifying the behavior or manner of compliance that regulated entities must adopt; and (5) identify and assess available alternatives to direct regulation, including providing economic incentives to encourage the desired behavior, such as user fees or marketable permits, or providing information upon which choices can be made by the public.

(c) In applying these principles, each agency is directed to use the best available techniques to quantify anticipated present and future benefits and costs as accurately as possible. Where appropriate and permitted by law, each agency may consider (and discuss qualitatively) values that are difficult or impossible to quantify, including equity, human dignity, fairness, and distributive impacts.

Sec. 2. Public Participation

(a) Regulations shall be adopted through a process that involves public participation. To that end, regulations shall be based, to the extent feasible and consistent with law, on the open exchange of information and perspectives among State, local, and tribal officials, experts in relevant disciplines, affected stakeholders in the private sector, and the public as a whole.

(b) To promote that open exchange, each agency, consistent with Executive Order 12866 and other applicable legal requirements, shall endeavor to provide the public with an opportunity to participate in the regulatory process. To the extent feasible and permitted by law, each agency shall afford the public a meaningful opportunity to comment through the Internet on any proposed regulation, with a comment period that should generally be at least 60 days. To the extent feasible and permitted by law, each agency shall also provide, for both proposed and final rules, timely online access to the rulemaking docket on regulations.gov, including relevant scientific and technical findings, in an open format that can be easily searched and downloaded. For proposed rules, such access shall include, to the extent feasible and permitted by law, an opportunity for public comment on all pertinent parts of the rulemaking docket, including relevant scientific and technical findings.

(c) Before issuing a notice of proposed rulemaking, each agency, where feasible and appropriate, shall seek the views of those who are likely to be affected, including those who are likely to benefit from and those who are potentially subject to such rulemaking.

Sec. 3. Integration and Innovation

Some sectors and industries face a significant number of regulatory requirements, some of which may be redundant, inconsistent, or overlapping. Greater coordination across agencies could reduce these requirements, thus reducing costs and simplifying and harmonizing rules. In developing regulatory actions and identifying appropriate approaches, each agency shall attempt to promote such coordination, simplification, and harmonization. Each agency shall also seek to identify, as appropriate, means to achieve regulatory goals that are designed to promote innovation.

Sec. 4. Flexible Approaches

Where relevant, feasible, and consistent with regulatory objectives, and to the extent permitted by law, each agency shall identify and consider regulatory approaches that reduce burdens and maintain flexibility and freedom of choice for the public. These approaches include warnings, appropriate default rules, and disclosure requirements as well as provision of information to the public in a form that is clear and intelligible.

Sec. 5. Science

Consistent with the President's Memorandum for the Heads of Executive Departments and Agencies, "Scientific Integrity" (March 9, 2009), and its implementing guidance, each agency shall ensure the objectivity of any scientific and technological information and processes used to support the agency's regulatory actions.

Sec. 6. Retrospective Analyses of Existing Rules

(a) To facilitate the periodic review of existing significant regulations, agencies shall consider how best to promote retrospective analysis of rules that may be outmoded, ineffective, insufficient, or excessively burdensome, and to modify, streamline, expand, or repeal them in accordance with what has been learned. Such retrospective analyses, including supporting data, should be released online whenever possible.

(b) Within 120 days of the date of this order, each agency shall develop and submit to the Office of Information and Regulatory Affairs a preliminary plan, consistent with law and its resources and regulatory priorities, under which the agency will periodically review its existing significant regulations to determine whether any such regulations should be modified, streamlined, expanded, or repealed so as to make the agency's regulatory program more effective or less burdensome in achieving the regulatory objectives.

Sec. 7. General Provisions

(a) For purposes of this order, "agency" shall have the meaning set forth in section 3(b) of Executive Order 12866.

(b) Nothing in this order shall be construed to impair or otherwise affect:

(i) authority granted by law to a department or agency, or the head thereof; or

(ii) functions of the Director of the Office of Management and Budget relating to budgetary, administrative, or legislative proposals.

(c) This order shall be implemented consistent with applicable law and subject to the availability of appropriations.

(d) This order is not intended to, and does not, create any right or benefit, substantive or procedural, enforceable at law or in equity by any party against the United States, its departments, agencies, or entities, its officers, employees, or agents, or any other person.

BARACK OBAMA
THE WHITE HOUSE,
January 18, 2011.

NOTES

1. President Reagan issued the first executive order that imposed a mandatory cost-benefit analysis on executive branch agencies. See Executive Order 12291, 46 Fed. Reg. 13193 (Feb. 17, 1981). President Reagan set the precedent that all subsequent presidents followed, including the decision to exclude the independent agencies and the disclaimer of any private right of action. However, Executive Order 13579, following this one by six months, extended Executive Order 13563 to independent regulatory agencies. See Executive Order 13579, 76 Fed. Reg. 41587 (July 11, 2011).

2. The order issued by President Obama referenced not only the requirement of a cost-benefit analysis but also the need to adopt a regulatory framework that "impose[d] the least burden on society" and took into consideration "alternatives to direct regulation." Since more than just a cost-benefit analysis is required, the executive order suggests that sometimes regulatory solutions are not warranted or preferred. What do you make of this language?

3. What are some of the inherent problems associated with cost-benefit analysis? Ought the analysis employed by agencies be subject to review?

For a time, cost-benefit analysis was largely an exercise imposed on agencies but was subject to little oversight in the courts. For one thing, the executive order specifically disclaimed any private right to seek judicial review of the analysis. For another, the order did not initially apply to independent agencies. In some cases, however, the cost-benefit requirement emanates not from an executive order but from a statute. This is true, for example, with respect to the Securities and Exchange Commission. The SEC must assess the impact of new rules on efficiency, competition, and capital formation. Parties have used the language to bring challenges, alleging that the failure to adequately perform the cost-benefit analysis rendered the rule arbitrary and capricious.

4. An executive order issued during the early days of the Trump administration suggested a different approach to cost-benefit analysis, one that focused not on individual rules or regulations but on those issued in the aggregate by the agency. See Reducing Regulation and Controlling Regulatory Costs, Executive Order 13771, Jan. 30, 2017 ("For fiscal year 2017 . . . the heads of all agencies are directed that the total incremental cost of all new regulations, including repealed regulations, to be finalized this year shall be no greater than zero, unless otherwise required by law or consistent with advice provided in writing by the Director of the Office of Management and Budget (Director)."). What do you make of this approach? How might this affect an agency's approach to regulation? Perhaps not surprisingly, this was one of the very first Executive Orders revoked by newly elected President Joe Biden on his first day in office. See Executive Order 13992, 86 Fed. Reg. 7049 (Jan. 20, 2021).

BUSINESS ROUNDTABLE v. SEC

647 F.3d 1144 (D.C. Cir. 2011)

GINSBURG, Circuit Judge: The Business Roundtable and the Chamber of Commerce of the United States, each of which has corporate members that issue publicly traded securities, petition for review of Exchange Act Rule 14a-11. The rule requires public companies to provide shareholders with information about, and their ability to vote for, shareholder-nominated candidates for the board of directors. The petitioners argue the Securities and Exchange Commission promulgated the rule in violation of the Administrative Procedure Act, 5 U.S.C. §551 et seq., because, among other reasons, the Commission failed adequately to consider the rule's effect upon efficiency, competition, and capital formation, as required by Section 3(f) of the Exchange Act and Section 2(c) of the Investment Company Act of 1940, codified at 15 U.S.C. §§78c(f) and 80a-2(c), respectively. For these reasons and more, we grant the petition for review and vacate the rule.

I. BACKGROUND

The proxy process is the principal means by which shareholders of a publicly traded corporation elect the company's board of directors. Typically, incumbent directors nominate a candidate for each vacancy prior to the election, which is held at the company's annual meeting. Before the meeting the company puts information about each nominee in the set of "proxy materials" — usually comprising a proxy voting card and a proxy statement — it distributes to all shareholders. The proxy statement concerns voting procedures and background information about the board's nominee(s); the proxy card enables shareholders to vote for or against the nominee(s) without attending the meeting. A shareholder who wishes to nominate a different candidate may separately file his own proxy statement and solicit votes from shareholders, thereby initiating a "proxy contest."

Rule 14a-11 provides shareholders an alternative path for nominating and electing directors. Concerned the current process impedes the expression of shareholders' right under state corporation laws to nominate and elect directors, the Commission proposed the rule, *see* Facilitating Shareholder Director Nominations, 74 Fed. Reg. 29,024, 29,025-26 (2009) (hereinafter Proposing Release), and adopted it with the goal of ensuring "the proxy process functions, as nearly as possible, as a replacement for an actual in-person meeting of shareholders," 75 Fed. Reg. 56,668, 56,670 (2010) (hereinafter Adopting Release). After responding to public comments, the Commission amended the proposed rule and, by a vote of three to two, adopted Rule 14a-11. *Id.* at 56,677. The rule requires a company subject to the Exchange Act proxy rules, including an investment company (such as a mutual fund) registered under the Investment Company Act of 1940 (ICA), to include in its proxy materials "the name of a person or persons nominated by a [qualifying] shareholder or group of shareholders for election to the board of directors." *Id.* at 56,682-83, 56,782/3.

To use Rule 14a-11, a shareholder or group of shareholders must have continuously held "at least 3% of the voting power of the company's securities entitled to be voted" for at least three years prior to the date the nominating shareholder or group submits notice of its intent to use the rule, and must continue to own those securities through the date of the annual meeting. *Id.* at 56,674-75. The nominating shareholder or group must submit the notice, which may include a statement of up to 500 words in support of each of its nominees, to the Commission and to the company. *Id.* at 56,675-76. A company that receives notice from an eligible shareholder or group must include the proffered information about the shareholder(s) and his nominee(s) in its proxy statement and include the nominee(s) on the proxy voting card. *Id.* at 56,676/1.

The Commission did place certain limitations upon the application of Rule 14a-11. The rule does not apply if applicable state law or a company's governing documents "prohibit shareholders from nominating a candidate for election as a director." *Id.* at 56,674/3. Nor may a shareholder use Rule 14a-11 if he is holding the company's securities with the intent of effecting a change of control of the company. *Id.* at 56,675/1. The company is not required to include in its proxy materials more than one shareholder nominee or the number of nominees, if more than one, equal to 25 percent of the number of directors on the board. *Id.* at 56,675/2.

The Commission concluded that Rule 14a-11 could create "potential benefits of improved board and company performance and shareholder value" sufficient to "justify [its] potential costs." *Id.* at 56,761/1. The agency rejected proposals to let each company's board or a majority of its shareholders decide whether to incorporate Rule 14a-11 in its bylaws, saying that "exclusive reliance on private ordering under State law would not be as effective and efficient" in facilitating shareholders' right to nominate and elect directors. *Id.* at 56,759-60. The Commission also rejected the suggestion it exclude investment companies from Rule 14a-11. *Id.* at 56,684/1. The two Commissioners voting against the rule faulted the Commission on both theoretical and empirical grounds. See Commissioner Troy A. Paredes, Statement at Open Meeting to Adopt the Final Rule Regarding "Proxy Access" (Aug. 25, 2010), *available at* http://www.sec.gov/news/speech/2010/spch082510tap.htm; Commissioner Kathleen L. Casey, Statement at Open Meeting to Adopt Amendments Regarding "Proxy Access" (Aug. 25, 2010), *available at* http://www.sec.gov/news/speech/2010/spch082510klc.htm (faulting Commission for failing to act "on the basis of empirical data and sound analysis").

The petitioners sought review in this court in September 2010. The Commission then stayed the final rule, which was to have been effective on November 15, pending the outcome of this case.

II. ANALYSIS

Under the APA, we will set aside agency action that is "arbitrary, capricious, an abuse of discretion, or otherwise not in accordance with law." 5 U.S.C. §706(2)(A). We must assure ourselves the agency has "examine[d] the relevant data and articulate[d] a satisfactory explanation for its action including a rational connection between the facts found and the choices made." *Motor Vehicle Mfrs. Ass'n of U.S., Inc. v. State Farm Mut. Auto. Ins. Co.*, 463 U.S. 29, 43, 103 S. Ct. 2856, 77 L. Ed. 2d 443 (1983) (internal quotation marks omitted). The Commission also has a "statutory obligation to determine as best it can the economic implications of the rule." *Chamber of Commerce v. SEC*, 412 F.3d 133, 143 (D.C. Cir. 2005).

Indeed, the Commission has a unique obligation to consider the effect of a new rule upon "efficiency, competition, and capital formation," 15 U.S.C. §§78c(f), 78w(a)(2), 80a-2(c), and its failure to "apprise itself—and hence the public and the Congress—of the economic consequences of a proposed regulation" makes promulgation of the rule arbitrary and capricious and not in accordance with law. *Chamber of Commerce*, 412 F.3d at 144; *Pub. Citizen v. Fed. Motor Carrier Safety Admin.*, 374 F.3d 1209, 1216 (D.C. Cir. 2004) (rule was arbitrary and capricious because agency failed to consider a factor required by statute).

The petitioners argue the Commission acted arbitrarily and capriciously here because it neglected its statutory responsibility to determine the likely economic consequences of Rule 14a-11 and to connect those consequences to efficiency, competition, and capital formation. They also maintain the Commission's decision to apply Rule 14a-11 to investment companies is arbitrary and capricious.

We agree with the petitioners and hold the Commission acted arbitrarily and capriciously for having failed once again—as it did most recently in *American Equity Investment Life Insurance Company v. SEC*, 613 F.3d 166, 167-68 (D.C. Cir. 2010), and before that in *Chamber of Commerce*, 412 F.3d at 136—adequately to assess the economic effects of a new rule. Here the Commission inconsistently and opportunistically framed the costs and benefits of the rule; failed adequately to quantify the certain costs or to explain why those costs could not be quantified; neglected to support its predictive judgments; contradicted itself; and failed to respond to substantial problems raised by commenters. For these and other reasons, its decision to apply the rule to investment companies was also arbitrary. Because we conclude the Commission failed to justify Rule 14a-11, we need not address the petitioners' additional argument the Commission arbitrarily rejected proposed alternatives that would have allowed shareholders of each company to decide for that company whether to adopt a mechanism for shareholders' nominees to get access to proxy materials.

A. Consideration of Economic Consequences

In the Adopting Release, the Commission predicted Rule 14a-11 would lead to "[d]irect cost savings" for shareholders in part due to "reduced printing and postage costs" and reduced expenditures for advertising compared to those of a "traditional" proxy contest. 75 Fed. Reg. at 56,756/2. The Commission also identified some intangible, or at least less readily quantifiable, benefits, principally that the rule "will mitigate collective action and free-rider concerns," which can discourage a shareholder from exercising his right to nominate a director in a traditional proxy contest, *id.*, and "has the potential of creating the benefit of improved board performance and enhanced shareholder value," *id.* at 56,761/1. The Commission anticipated the rule would also impose costs upon companies and shareholders related to "the preparation of required disclosure, printing and mailing . . . , and [to] additional solicitations," *id.* at 56,768/3, and could have "adverse effects on company and board performance," *id.* at 56,764/3, for example, by distracting management, *id.* at 56,765/1. The Commission nonetheless concluded the rule would promote the "efficiency of the economy on the whole," and the benefits of the rule would "justify the costs" of the rule. *Id.* at 56,771/3.

The petitioners contend the Commission neglected both to quantify the costs companies would incur opposing shareholder nominees and to substantiate the rule's predicted benefits. They also argue the Commission failed to consider the consequences of union and state pension funds using the rule and failed properly to evaluate the frequency with which shareholders would initiate election contests.

1. Consideration of Costs and Benefits

In the Adopting Release, the Commission recognized "company boards may be motivated by the issues at stake to expend significant resources to challenge shareholder director nominees." 75 Fed. Reg. at 56,770/2. Nonetheless, the Commission believed a company's solicitation and campaign costs "may be limited by two factors": first, "to the extent that the directors' fiduciary duties prevent them from using corporate funds to resist shareholder director nominations for no good-faith corporate purpose," they may decide "simply [to] include the shareholder director nominees . . . in the company's proxy materials"; and second, the "requisite ownership threshold and holding period" would "limit the number of shareholder director nominations that a board may receive, consider, and possibly contest." *Id.* at 56,770/2-3.

The petitioners object that the Commission failed to appreciate the intensity with which issuers would oppose nominees and arbitrarily dismissed the probability that directors would conclude their fiduciary duties required them to support their own nominees. The petitioners also argue it was arbitrary for the Commission not to estimate the costs of solicitation and campaigning that companies would incur to oppose candidates nominated by shareholders, which costs commenters expected to be quite large. The Chamber of Commerce submitted a comment predicting boards would incur substantial expenditures opposing shareholder nominees through "significant media and public relations efforts, advertising . . . , mass mailings, and other communication efforts, as well as the hiring of outside advisors and the expenditure of significant time and effort by the company's employees." *Id.* at 56,770/1. It pointed out that in recent proxy contests at larger companies costs "ranged from $14 million to $4 million" and at smaller companies "from $3 million to $800,000." *Id.* In its brief the Commission maintains it did consider the commenters' estimates of the costs, but reasonably explained why those costs "may prove less than these estimates."

We agree with the petitioners that the Commission's prediction directors might choose not to oppose shareholder nominees had no basis beyond mere speculation. Although it is possible that a board, consistent with its fiduciary duties, might forgo expending resources to oppose a shareholder nominee — for example, if it believes the cost of opposition would exceed the cost to the company of the board's preferred candidate losing the election, discounted by the probability of that happening — the Commission has presented no evidence that such forbearance is ever seen in practice. To the contrary, the American Bar Association Committee on Federal Regulation of Securities commented:

> If the [shareholder] nominee is determined [by the board] not to be as appropriate a candidate as those to be nominated by the board's independent nominating committee . . . , then the board will be compelled by its fiduciary duty to make an appropriate effort to oppose the nominee, as boards now do in traditional proxy contests.

Letter from Jeffrey W. Rubin, Chair, Comm. on Fed. Regulation of Secs., Am. Bar Ass'n, to SEC 35 (August 31, 2009), *available at* http://www.sec.gov/comments/s7-10-09/s71009-456.pdf.

The Commission's second point, that the required minimum amount and duration of share ownership will limit the number of directors nominated under the new rule, is a reason to expect election contests to be infrequent; it says nothing about the amount a company will spend on solicitation and campaign costs when there is a contested election. Although the Commission acknowledged that companies may expend resources to oppose shareholder nominees, *see* 75 Fed. Reg. at 56,770/2, it did nothing to estimate and quantify the costs it expected companies to incur; nor did it claim estimating those costs was not possible, for empirical evidence about expenditures in traditional proxy contests was readily available. Because the agency failed to "make tough choices about which of the competing estimates is most plausible, [or] to hazard a guess as to which is correct," *Pub. Citizen*, 374 F.3d at 1221, we believe it neglected its statutory obligation to assess the economic consequences of its rule, *see Chamber of Commerce*, 412 F.3d at 143.

The petitioners also maintain, and we agree, the Commission relied upon insufficient empirical data when it concluded that Rule 14a-11 will improve board performance and increase shareholder value by facilitating the election of dissident shareholder nominees. *See* 75 Fed. Reg. at 56,761-62. The Commission acknowledged the numerous studies submitted by commenters that reached the opposite result. *Id.* at 56,762/2 & n. 924. One commenter, for example, submitted an empirical study showing that "when dissident directors win board seats, those firms underperform peers by 19 to 40% over the two years following the proxy contest." Elaine Buckberg, NERA Econ. Consulting, & Jonathan Macey, Yale Law School, Report on Effects of Proposed SEC Rule 14a-11 on Efficiency, Competitiveness and Capital Formation 9 (2009), *available at* www.nera.com/upload/Buckberg_Macey_Report_FINAL.pdf. The Commission completely discounted those studies "because of questions raised by subsequent studies, limitations acknowledged by the studies' authors, or [its] own concerns about the studies' methodology or scope." 75 Fed. Reg. at 56,762-63 & n. 926-28.

The Commission instead relied exclusively and heavily upon two relatively unpersuasive studies, one concerning the effect of "hybrid boards" (which include some dissident directors) and the other concerning the effect of proxy contests in general, upon shareholder value. *Id.* at 56,762 & n. 921 (citing Chris Cernich et al., IRRC Inst. for Corporate Responsibility, Effectiveness of Hybrid Boards (May 2009), *available at* www.irrcinstitute.org/pdf/IRRC_05_09_EffectiveHybridBoards.pdf, and J. Harold Mulherin & Annette B. Poulsen, *Proxy Contests & Corporate Change: Implications for Shareholder Wealth*, 47 J. Fin. Econ. 279 (1998)). Indeed, the Commission "recognize[d] the limitations of the Cernich (2009) study," and noted "its long-term findings on shareholder value creation are difficult to interpret." *Id.* at 56,760/3 n. 911. In view of the admittedly (and at best) "mixed" empirical evidence, *id.* at 56,761/1, we think the Commission has not sufficiently supported its conclusion that increasing the potential for election of directors nominated by shareholders will result in improved board and company performance and shareholder value, *id.* at 56,761/1; *see id.* at 56,761/3.

Moreover, as petitioners point out, the Commission discounted the costs of Rule 14a-11 — but not the benefits — as a mere artifact of the state law right of shareholders to elect directors. For example, with reference to the potential costs of Rule 14a-11, such as management distraction and reduction in the time a board spends "on strategic and long-term thinking," the Commission thought it "important to note that these costs are associated with the traditional State law right to nominate and elect directors, and are not costs incurred for including shareholder nominees for director in the company's proxy materials." *Id.* at 56,765/1-2. As we have said before, this type of reasoning, which fails to view a cost at the margin, is illogical and, in an economic analysis, unacceptable. *See Chamber of Commerce*, 412 F.3d at 143 (rejecting Commission's argument that rule would not create "costs associated with the hiring of staff because boards typically have this authority under state law," and assuming that "whether a board is authorized by law to hire additional staff in no way bears upon" the question whether the rule would "in fact cause the fund to incur additional staffing costs").

2. Shareholders with Special Interests

The petitioners next argue the Commission acted arbitrarily and capriciously by "entirely fail[ing] to consider an important aspect of the problem," *Motor Vehicle Mfrs. Ass'n*, 463 U.S. at 43, 103 S. Ct. 2856, to wit, how union and state pension funds might use Rule 14a-11. Commenters expressed concern that these employee benefit funds would impose costs upon companies by using Rule 14a-11 as leverage to gain concessions, such as additional benefits for unionized employees, unrelated to shareholder value. The Commission insists it did consider this problem, albeit not *in haec verba*, along the way to its conclusion that "the totality of the evidence and economic theory" both indicate the rule "has the potential of creating the benefit of improved board performance and enhanced shareholder value." 75 Fed. Reg. at 56,761/1. Specifically, the Commission recognized "companies could be negatively affected if shareholders use the new rules to promote their narrow interests at the expense of other shareholders," *id.* at 56,772/3, but reasoned these potential costs "may be limited" because the ownership and holding requirements would "allow the use of the rule by only holders who demonstrated a significant, long-term commitment to the company," *id.* at 56,766/3, and who would therefore be less likely to act in a way that would diminish shareholder value. The Commission also noted costs may be limited because other shareholders may be alerted, through the disclosure requirements, "to the narrow interests of the nominating shareholder." *Id.*

The petitioners also contend the Commission failed to respond to the costs companies would incur even when a shareholder nominee is not ultimately elected. These costs may be incurred either by a board succumbing to the demands, unrelated to increasing value, of a special interest shareholder threatening to nominate a director, or by opposing and defeating such nominee(s). The Commission did not completely ignore these potential costs, but neither did it adequately address them.

Notwithstanding the ownership and holding requirements, there is good reason to believe institutional investors with special interests will be able to use the rule and, as more than one commenter noted, "public and union pension funds" are the institutional investors "most likely to make use of proxy access." Letter from Jonathan D. Urick, Analyst, Council of Institutional Investors, to SEC 2 (January 14, 2010), *available at* http://www.cii.org/UserFiles/file/resource%20center/correspondence/2010/1-14-10%20Proxy%20Access%20Comment%20Letter.pdf. Nonetheless, the Commission failed to respond to comments arguing that investors with a special interest, such as unions and state and local governments whose interests in jobs may well be greater than their interest in share value, can be expected to pursue self-interested objectives rather than the goal of maximizing shareholder value, and will likely cause companies to incur costs even when their nominee is unlikely to be elected. *See, e.g.*, Detailed Comments of Business Roundtable on the Proposed Election Contest Rules and the Proposed Amendment to the Shareholder Proposal Rules 102 (August 17, 2009), *available at* http://businessroundtable.org/uploads/hearings-letters/

downloads/BRT_Comment_Letter_to_SEC_on_ File_No_S7-10-09.pdf ("'state governments and labor unions . . . often appear to be driven by concerns other than a desire to increase the economic performance of the companies in which they invest'" (quoting Leo E. Strine, Jr., *Toward a True Corporate Republic: A Traditionalist Response to Bebchuk's Solution for Improving Corporate America*, 119 Harv. L. Rev. 1759, 1765 (2006))). By ducking serious evaluation of the costs that could be imposed upon companies from use of the rule by shareholders representing special interests, particularly union and government pension funds, we think the Commission acted arbitrarily.

3. Frequency of Election Contests

In the Proposing Release, the Commission estimated 269 companies per year, comprising 208 companies reporting under the Exchange Act and 61 registered investment companies, would receive nominations pursuant to Rule 14a-11. 74 Fed. Reg. at 29,064/1. In the Adopting Release, however, the Commission reduced that estimate to 51, comprising only 45 reporting companies and 6 investment companies, in view of "the additional eligibility requirements" the Commission adopted in the final version of Rule 14a-11. 75 Fed. Reg. at 56,743/3-56,744/1. (As originally proposed, Rule 14a-11 would have required a nominating shareholder to have held the securities for only one year rather than the three years required in the final rule. *See id.* at 56,755/1.) In revising its estimate, the Commission also newly relied upon "[t]he number of contested elections and board-related shareholder proposals" in a recent year, which it believed was "a better indicator of how many shareholders might submit a nomination" than were the data upon which it had based its estimate in the Proposing Release. *Id.* at 56,743/3.

The petitioners argue the Commission's revised estimate unreasonably departs from the estimate used in the Proposing Release, conflicts with its assertion the rule facilitates elections contests, and undermines its reliance upon frequent use of Rule 14a-11 to estimate the amount by which shareholders will benefit from "direct printing and mailing cost savings," *id.* at 56,756 & n. 872. The petitioners also contend the estimate is inconsistent with the Commission's prediction shareholders will initiate 147 proposals per year under Rule 14a-8, a rule not challenged here. *See id.* at 56,677/2.

The Commission was not unreasonable in predicting investors will use Rule 14a-11 less frequently than traditional proxy contests have been used in the past. As Commission counsel pointed out at oral argument, there would still be some traditional proxy contests; the total number of efforts by shareholders to nominate and elect directors will surely be greater when shareholders have two paths rather than one open to them. In any event, the final estimated frequency (51) with which shareholders will use Rule 14a-11 does not clearly conflict with the higher estimate in the Proposing Release (269), or the estimate of proposals under Rule 14a-8 (147), both of which were based upon looser eligibility standards.

In weighing the rule's costs and benefits, however, the Commission arbitrarily ignored the effect of the final rule upon the total number of election contests. That is, the Adopting Release does not address whether and to what extent Rule 14a-11 will take the place of traditional proxy contests. *Cf.* 75 Fed. Reg. at 56,772/2. Without this crucial datum, the Commission has no way of knowing whether the rule will facilitate enough election contests to be of net benefit. *See id.* at 56,761/1 (anticipating "beneficial effects" because [the] rule will "mak[e] election contests a more plausible avenue for shareholders to participate in the governance of their company").

We also agree with the petitioners that the Commission's discussion of the estimated frequency of nominations under Rule 14a-11 is internally inconsistent and therefore arbitrary. In discussing its benefits, the Commission predicted nominating shareholders would realize "[d]irect cost savings" from not having to print or mail their own proxy materials. *Id.* at 56,756/2. These savings would "remove a disincentive for shareholders to submit their own director nominations" and otherwise facilitate election contests. *Id.* The Commission then cited comment letters predicting the number of elections contested under Rule 14a-11 would be quite high. *See id.* at 56,756/3 n. 872. One of the comments reported, based upon the proposed rule and a survey of directors, that approximately 15 percent of all companies with shares listed on exchanges, that is, "hundreds" of public companies, expected a shareholder or group of shareholders to nominate a director using the new rule. Letter from Kenneth L. Altman, President, The Altman Group, Inc., to SEC 3 (January 19, 2010), *available at* http://www.sec.gov/comments/s7-10-09/s71009-605.pdf. Thus, the Commission anticipated frequent use of Rule 14a-11 when estimating benefits, but assumed infrequent use when estimating costs. *See, e.g., supra* at 1150 (SEC asserted solicitation and campaign costs would be minimized because of limited use of the rule).

...

III. CONCLUSION

For the foregoing reasons, we hold the Commission was arbitrary and capricious in promulgating Rule 14a-11. Accordingly, we have no occasion to address the petitioners' First Amendment challenge to the rule. The petition is granted and the rule is hereby

Vacated.

NOTES

1. The rule struck down by the court in *Business Roundtable* was contained in a release that consisted of 453 pages, with 78 devoted to cost-benefit analysis. See Exchange Act Release No. 62764 (Aug. 25, 2010), available at http://www.sec.gov/rules/final/2010/33-9136.pdf. Up to that point, the release likely contained the most detailed cost-benefit analysis conducted by the SEC. Yet the rule was still struck down for an inadequate analysis. What does that suggest about the role of cost-benefit analysis in the judicial review of rules?

2. The decision has been criticized. See J. Robert Brown, Jr., Shareholder Access and Uneconomic Economic Analysis: Business Roundtable v. SEC, 88 Denv. U. L. Rev. Online (2011). Much of the criticism has taken issue with the lack of deference to the SEC in the adoption of the rule. Do you agree?

3. What are some practical implications of this decision? In theory, the SEC could simply re-propose the rule, correct the deficiencies in the cost-benefit analysis, and adopt the requirement. Yet the SEC has not done so.

4. In a cost-benefit analysis, must everything be quantified? See ICI v. CFTC, 720 F.3d 370, 379 (D.C. Cir. 2013) ("The appellants further complain that CFTC failed to put a precise number on the benefit of data collection in preventing future financial crises. But the law does not require agencies to measure the immeasurable. CFTC's discussion of unquantifiable benefits fulfills its statutory obligation to consider and evaluate potential costs and benefits."). But to the extent costs or benefits cannot be quantified, can a cost-benefit analysis really be undertaken with any degree of certainty?

5. One consequence of the increased focus on cost-benefit analysis has been a dramatic increase in the number of nonlawyers at the SEC, particularly through the addition of a large number of economists in the Division of Economic and Risk Analysis, the office the conducts the agency's cost-benefit analysis. Consider the consequences of this reallocation.

6. Congress has considered legislation that would impose the requirement of cost-benefit analysis on all independent agencies. See Independent Agency Regulatory Analysis Act of 2012, S. 3468, 112th Cong. (2012). To the extent the legislation merely brings in independent agencies without the executive orders requiring cost-benefit analysis, is legislation necessary? Could the President add them to the executive order? See Executive Order 13579, 76 Fed. Reg. 41587 (July 11, 2011).

7. Compare §3-105(b) of the revised Model State APA, under which agencies must issue a regulatory analysis of a proposed rule that "must contain . . . a comparison of the probable costs and benefits of the proposed rule to the probable costs and benefits of inaction." See Rios v. Washington Dep't of Labor, 39 P.3d 961 (Wash. 2002) (explaining "feasibility" in the context of Washington law); Patient Advocates of Tex. v. Tex. Worker's Comp. Comm'n, 80 S.W.3d 66 (Tex. App. 2002).

F PUBLICATION AND ESTOPPEL

FEDERAL CROP INSURANCE CORP. v. MERRILL

332 U.S. 380 (1947)

MR. JUSTICE FRANKFURTER delivered the opinion of the Court.

. . . The relevant facts may be briefly stated. Petitioner (hereinafter called the Corporation) is a wholly Government-owned enterprise, created by the Federal

Crop Insurance Act, as an "agency of and within the Department of Agriculture." To carry out the purposes of the Act, the Corporation, "Commencing with the wheat . . . crops planted for harvest in 1945" is empowered "to insure, upon such terms and conditions not inconsistent with the provisions of this title as it may determine, producers of wheat . . . against loss in yields due to unavoidable causes, including drought. . . ." In pursuance of its authority, the Corporation on February 5, 1945, promulgated its Wheat Crop Insurance Regulations, which were duly published in the Federal Register on February 7, 1945. . . .

On March 26, 1945, respondents applied locally for insurance under the Federal Crop Insurance Act to cover wheat farming operations in Bonneville County, Idaho. Respondents informed the Bonneville County Agricultural Conservation Committee, acting as agent for the Corporation, that they were planting 460 acres of spring wheat and that on 400 of these acres they were reseeding on winter wheat acreage. The Committee advised respondents that the entire crop was insurable, and recommended to the Corporation's Denver Branch Office acceptance of the application. (The formal application itself did not disclose that any part of the insured crop was reseeded.) On May 28, 1945, the Corporation accepted the application.

In July, 1945, most of the respondents' crop was destroyed by drought. Upon being notified, the Corporation, after discovering that the destroyed acreage had been reseeded, refused to pay the loss, and this litigation was appropriately begun in one of the lower courts of Idaho. The trial court rejected the Corporation's contention, presented by a demurrer to the complaint, that the Wheat Crop Insurance Regulations barred recovery as a matter of law. Evidence was thereupon permitted to go to the jury to the effect that the respondents had no actual knowledge of the Regulations, insofar as they precluded insurance for reseeded wheat, and that they had in fact been misled by petitioner's agent into believing that spring wheat reseeded on winter wheat acreage was insurable by the Corporation. The jury returned a verdict for the loss on all the 460 acres and the Supreme Court of Idaho affirmed the resulting judgment. . . . That court in effect adopted the theory of the trial judge, that since the knowledge of the agent of a private insurance company, under the circumstances of this case, would be attributed to, and thereby bind, a private insurance company, the Corporation is equally bound.

The case no doubt presents phases of hardship. We take for granted that, on the basis of what they were told by the Corporation's local agent, the respondents reasonably believed that their entire crop was covered by petitioner's insurance. And so we assume that recovery could be had against a private insurance company. But the Corporation is not a private insurance company. It is too late in the day to urge that the Government is just another private litigant, for purposes of charging it with liability, whenever it takes over a business theretofore conducted by private enterprise or engages in competition with private ventures. Government is not partly public or partly private, depending upon the governmental pedigree of the type of a particular activity or the manner in which the Government conducts it. The Government may carry on its operations through conventional executive agencies or through corporate forms especially created for defined ends. . . . Whatever the form in which the Government functions, anyone entering into an arrangement with the Government takes the risk of having accurately ascertained that he who purports to act for the Government stays within the bounds of his authority. The scope of this authority may be explicitly defined by Congress or be limited by delegated legislation, properly exercised through the rulemaking power. And this is so even though, as here, the agent himself may have been unaware of the limitations upon his authority. . . .

If the Federal Crop Insurance Act had by explicit language prohibited the insurance of spring wheat which is reseeded on winter wheat acreage, the ignorance of such a restriction, either by the respondents or the Corporation's agent, would be immaterial and recovery could not be had against the Corporation for loss of such reseeded wheat. Congress could hardly define the multitudinous details appropriate for the business of crop insurance when the Government entered it. Inevitably "the terms and conditions" upon which valid governmental insurance can be had must be defined by the agency acting for the Government. And so Congress has legislated in this instance, as in modern regulatory enactments it so often does, by conferring the rulemaking power upon the agency created for carrying out its policy. See §516(b), 52 Stat. 72, 77, 7 U.S.C. §1516(b). Just as everyone is charged with knowledge of the United States Statutes at Large, Congress has provided that the appearance of rules and regulations in the Federal Register gives legal notice of their contents. 49 Stat. 502, 44 U.S.C. §307.

Accordingly, the Wheat Crop Insurance Regulations were binding on all who sought to come within the Federal Crop Insurance Act, regardless of actual knowledge of what is in the Regulations or of the hardship resulting from innocent ignorance. The oft-quoted observation in Rock Island, Arkansas & Louisiana R. Co. v. United States, 254 U.S. 141, 143, that "Men must turn square corners when they deal with Government," does not reflect a callous outlook. It merely expresses the duty of all courts to observe the conditions defined by Congress for charging the public treasury. The "terms and conditions" defined by the Corporation, under authority of Congress, for creating liability on the part of the Government preclude recovery for the loss of the reseeded wheat no matter with what good reason the respondents thought they had obtained insurance from the Government. . . .

The judgment is reversed and the cause remanded for further proceedings not inconsistent with this opinion.

Reversed.

NOTES

1. Rules publication is a sine qua non of a fair administrative law system. As already seen, substantive rules have the same legal effect as statutes. They have the full force of law, affecting legal rights and obligations in the same manner as laws enacted by the legislature. The *Merrill* decision is based on this principle.

The FCIC regulations are treated as having statutory effect, which means that, for purposes of the case, the Court should treat the terms of the regulations as though enacted by Congress. If Congress had, by statutory provision, prohibited insurance of the crop, no one could doubt that the prohibition would bar recovery. Since the FCIC regulations had statutory effect, the case must be treated *as if* a statute contained the prohibition. In such a case, the wheat farmers' ignorance was irrelevant.

2. Such a result is bearable only if there is a system of rules publication. To quote an English observer: "It would be intolerable if it could be said that obscure clerks in Whitehall poured forth streams of departmental legislation which nobody had any means of knowing. This would be the method attributed to Caligula of writing his laws in very small characters and hanging them up on high pillars 'the more effectively to ensnare the people.'" Carr, in Committee on Ministers' Powers, Minutes of Evidence 208 (1932).

3. A federal system of rules publication was established by the Federal Register Act of 1935. According to Judge Friendly, "The FRA was passed to mitigate the hardship of the principle *ignorantia legis neminem excusat* in an age when much 'law' takes the form of executive or administrative action not to be found in the statute books." United States v. Aarons, 310 F.2d 341, 346 (2d Cir. 1962).

Under the 1935 Act, all federal rules, regulations, orders, and other documents of "general applicability and legal effect" must be published in the Federal Register. The Register is published every weekday. The daily issues are ultimately bound and indexed in volumes that occupy a shelf each year (the Register for 1992 contained 62,920 pages). The federal publication system contains, in addition to the Federal Register, the Code of Federal Regulations. The Code is divided into 50 subject matter titles, and is revised annually. In 1993, these titles were grouped in 198 paperback volumes. The code is a compilation, in logical order, of federal rules and regulations, arranged on an agency-by-agency basis. The Federal Register Act requirement of rules publication is enforced by the Act's provision that no document required to be published "shall be valid as against any person who has not had actual knowledge" unless it has been filed for publication. Publication in the Register is a mandatory requirement for legal effectiveness; failure to publish renders a regulation unenforceable, except against a person who has actual knowledge. In the latter case, the regulation is binding even though it was not published. Hatcher v. United States, 733 F. Supp. 218 (M.D. Pa. 1990).

4. As a practical matter, who reads the Federal Register? See Daryl J. Levinson, Empire-Building Government in Constitutional Law, 118 Harv. L. Rev. 915, 935 n.71 (2005) ("The 2411 pages of the Federal Register in 1936 had multiplied to 75,795 by the end of 2003."). Certainly not the public at large. This may begin to change. Section 206 of the E-Government Act of 2002 (44 U.S.C. §3501) requires agencies, to the extent practicable, to publish on the Internet "all information about that agency required to be published in the Federal Register under paragraphs (1) and (2) of section 552(a)" and an electronic docket for rulemaking that includes comment letters and other materials submitted during the comment process. With the material electronically available, nonindustry experts will have greater access to and probable awareness of these proposals.

5. *State publication requirements.* Virtually all states (47) have publications similar to the Code of Federal Regulations. See www.administrativerules.org, Administrative Codes & Registers, A Section of the National Association for Secretaries of State.

6. Note that, in the *Merrill* case, the Idaho wheat farmers had acted on the basis of advice received from agency officials. They had informed the local agent of the FCIC of the nature of their crop and were advised that the entire crop was insurable. They had acted in reliance on this advice but were not protected by such reliance when their crop was destroyed. Why should the government insurance agency be immune when a private insurance company would be estopped from denying that the *apparent* authority and the *real* authority of its agent were not the same? Does the *Merrill* opinion give an adequate answer to this question? Is it enough to say that "Men must turn square corners when they deal with the Government" (i.e., it was up to the farmers to determine whether the FCIC agent's assurance that their crop was insurable was authorized by the applicable statutes and regulations)? Compare the following statement from Justice Jackson's dissenting opinion in the *Merrill* case: "It is very well to say that those who deal with the Government should turn square corners. But there is no reason why the square corners should constitute a one-way street." 332 U.S. at 387-388.

OFFICE OF PERSONNEL MANAGEMENT v. RICHMOND

496 U.S. 414 (1990)

JUSTICE KENNEDY delivered the opinion of the Court.

This case presents the question whether erroneous oral and written advice given by a Government employee to a benefit claimant may give rise to estoppel against the Government, and so entitle the claimant to a monetary payment not otherwise permitted by law. We hold that payments of money from the Federal Treasury are limited to those authorized by statute, and we reverse the contrary holding of the Court of Appeals.

I

Not wishing to exceed a statutory limit on earnings that would disqualify him from a disability annuity, respondent Charles Richmond sought advice from a federal employee and received erroneous information. As a result he earned more than permitted by the eligibility requirements of the relevant statute and lost six months of benefits. Respondent now claims that the erroneous and unauthorized advice should give rise to equitable estoppel against the Government, and that we should order payment of the benefits contrary to the statutory terms. Even on the assumption that much equity subsists in respondent's claim, we cannot agree with him or the Court of Appeals that we have authority to order the payment he seeks.

Respondent was a welder at the Navy Public Works Center in San Diego, California. He left this position in 1981 after petitioner, the Officer of Personnel Management (OPM) approved his application for a disability retirement. OPM determined that respondent's impaired eyesight prevented him from performing his job and made him eligible for a disability annuity under 5 U.S.C. §8837(a). Section 8337(a) provides this benefit for disabled federal employees who have completed five years of service. The statute directs, however, that the entitlement to disability payments will end if the retired employee is "restored to an earning capacity fairly comparable to the current rate of pay of the position occupied at the time of retirement." 5 U.S.C. §8337(d).

The statutory rules for restoration of earning capacity are central to this case. Prior to 1982, an individual was deemed restored to earning capacity, and so rendered ineligible for a disability annuity, if "in each of *2 succeeding calendar years* the income of the annuitant from wages or self-employment . . . equals at least 80 percent of the current rate of pay of the position occupied immediately before retirement." 5 U.S.C. §8337(d) (1976 ed.) (emphasis added). The provision was amended in 1982 by the Omnibus Budget Reconciliation Act, Pub. L. 97-253, 96 Stat. 792, to change the measuring period of restoration of earning capacity from two years to one: "Earning capacity is deemed restored if *in any calendar year* the income of the annuitant from wages or self-employment or both equals at least 80 percent of the current rate of pay of the position occupied immediately before retirement." 5 U.S.C. §8337(d) (emphasis added).

After taking disability retirement for his vision impairment, respondent undertook part-time employment as a school bus driver. From 1982 to 1985, respondent earned an average of $12,494 in this job, leaving him under the 80% limit for entitlement to continued annuity payments. In 1986, however, he had an opportunity to earn extra money by working overtime. Respondent asked an Employee Relations Specialist at the Navy Public Works Center's Civilian Personnel Department for information about how much he could earn without exceeding the 80% eligibility limit. Relying upon the terms of the repealed pre-1982 statute, under which respondent could retain the annuity unless his income exceeded the 80% limit in *two* consecutive years, the specialist gave respondent incorrect advice. The specialist also gave respondent a copy of Attachment 4 to Federal Personnel Manual Letter 831-64, published by petitioner OPM, which also stated the former 2-year eligibility rule. The OPM form was correct when written in 1981; but when given to respondent, the form was out of date and therefore inaccurate. Respondent returned to the Navy in January 1987, and again was advised in error that eligibility would be determined under the old 2-year rule.

After receiving the erroneous information, respondent concluded that he could take on the extra work as a school bus driver in 1986 while still receiving full disability benefits for impaired vision so long as he kept his income for the previous and following years below the statutory level. He earned $19,936 during 1986, exceeding the statutory eligibility limit. OPM discontinued respondent's disability annuity on June 30, 1987. The annuity was restored on January 1, 1988, since respondent did not earn more than allowed by the statute in 1987. Respondent thus lost his disability payments for a 6-month period, for a total amount of $3,993. . . .

A divided panel of the Court of Appeals [accepted] respondent's contention that the misinformation from Navy personnel estopped the Government, and that the estoppel required payment of disability benefits despite the statutory provision to the contrary. . . .

The Court of Appeals majority decided that "[b]ased on the Supreme Court's acknowledgment that the estoppel against the government is not foreclosed and based on court of appeals rulings applying estoppel against the government, our view is that estoppel is properly applied against the government in the present case." The Court reasoned that the provision of the out-of-date OPM form was "affirmative misconduct" that should estop the Government from denying respondent benefits in accordance with the statute. The facts of this case, it held, are "sufficiently unusual and extreme that no concern is warranted about exposing the public treasury to estoppel in broad or numerous categories of cases." . . .

II

From our earliest cases, we have recognized that equitable estoppel will not lie against the Government as against private litigants. . . .

The principles of these and many other cases were reiterated in Federal Crop Insurance Corp. v. Merrill, 332 U.S. 380 (1947), the leading case in our modern line of estoppel decisions. In *Merrill*, a farmer applied for insurance under the Federal Crop Insurance Act to cover his wheat farming operations. An agent of the Federal Crop Insurance Corporation advised the farmer that his entire crop qualified for insurance, and the farmer obtained insurance through the Corporation. After the crop was lost, it was discovered that the agent's advice had been in error, and that part of the farmer's crop was reseeded wheat, not eligible for federal insurance under the applicable regulation. While we recognized the serious hardship caused by the agent's misinformation, we nonetheless rejected the argument that his representations estopped the Government to deny insurance benefits. We recognized that "not even the temptations of a hard case" will provide a basis for ordering recovery contrary to the terms of the regulation, for to do so would disregard "the duty of all courts to observe the conditions defined by Congress for charging the public treasury." Id., at 385-386.

Despite the clarity of these earlier decisions, dicta in our more recent cases have suggested the possibility that there might be some situation in which estoppel against the Government could be appropriate. The genesis of this idea appears to be an observation found at the end of our opinion in Montana v. Kennedy, 366 U.S. 308. In that case, the petitioner brought a declaratory judgment action seeking to establish his American citizenship. After discussing the petitioner's two statutory claims at length, we rejected the final argument that a consular official's erroneous advice to petitioner's mother that she could not return to the United States while pregnant prevented petitioner from having been born in the United States and thus deprived him of United States citizenship. Our decision was limited to the observation that in light of the fact that no legal obstacle prevented petitioner's mother from returning to the United States,

> [W]hat may have been only the consular official's well-meant advice — "I am sorry, Mrs., you cannot [return to the United States] in that condition" — falls far short of misconduct such as might prevent the United States from relying on petitioner's foreign birth. In this situation, we need not stop to inquire whether, as some lower courts have held, there may be circumstances in which the United States is estopped to deny citizenship because of the conduct of its officials.

Id. at 314-315.

The proposition about which we did not "stop to inquire" in *Kennedy* has since taken on something of a life of its own. Our own opinions have continued to mention the possibility, in the course of rejecting estoppel arguments, that some type of "affirmative misconduct" might give rise to estoppel against the Government. . . .

The language in our decisions has spawned numerous claims for equitable estoppel in the lower courts. . . . [C]ourts of appeals have taken our statements as an invitation to search for an appropriate case in which to apply estoppel against the Government, yet we have reversed every finding of estoppel that we have reviewed. . . .

The Solicitor General proposes to remedy the present confusion in this area of the law with a sweeping rule. As it has in the past, the Government asks us to adopt "a flat rule that estoppel may not in any circumstances run against the Government." . . . The Government bases its broad rule first upon the doctrine of sovereign immunity. Noting that the "United States, as sovereign, is immune from suit save as it consents to be sued," . . . the Government asserts that the courts are without jurisdiction to entertain a suit to compel the Government to act contrary to a statute, no matter what the context or circumstances. The Government advances as a second basis for this rule the doctrine of separation of powers. The Government contends that to recognize estoppel based on the misrepresentations of Executive Branch officials would give those misrepresentations the force of law, and thereby invade the legislative province reserved to Congress. This rationale, too, supports the Government's contention that estoppel may never justify an order requiring executive action contrary to a relevant statute, no matter what statute or what facts are involved.

We have recognized before that the "arguments the Government advances for the rule are substantial." . . . And we agree that this case should be decided under a clearer form of analysis than "we will know an estoppel when we see one." . . . But it remains true that we need not embrace a rule that no estoppel will lie against the Government in any case in order to decide this case. We leave for another day whether an estoppel claim could ever succeed against the

Government. A narrower ground of decision is sufficient to address the type of suit presented here, a claim for payment of money from the Public Treasury contrary to a statutory appropriation.

III

The Appropriations Clause of the Constitution, Art. I, §9, cl. 7, provides that "No Money shall be drawn from the Treasury, but in Consequence of Appropriations made by Law." For the particular type of claim at issue here, a claim for money from the Federal Treasury, the Clause provides an explicit rule of decision. Money may be paid out only through an appropriation made by law; in other words, the payment of money from the Treasury must be authorized by a statute.... The benefits respondent claims were not "provided by" the relevant provision of the subchapter; rather, they were specifically denied. It follows that Congress has appropriated no money for the payment of the benefits respondent seeks, and the Constitution prohibits that any money "be drawn from the Treasury" to pay them.

Our cases underscore the straight-forward and explicit command of the Appropriations Clause. "It means simply that no money can be paid out of the Treasury unless it has been appropriated by an act of Congress." ...

We have not had occasion in past cases presenting claims of estoppel against the Government to discuss the Appropriations Clause, for reasons that are apparent.... [W]e decline today to accept the Solicitor General's argument for an across-the-board no-estoppel rule. But this makes it all the more important to state the law and to settle the matter of estoppel as a basis for money claims against the Government....

Extended to its logical conclusion, operation of estoppel against the Government in the context of payment of money from the Treasury could in fact render the Appropriations Clause a nullity. If agents of the Executive were able, by their unauthorized oral or written statements to citizens, to obligate the Treasury for the payment of funds, the control over public funds that the Clause reposes in Congress in effect could be transferred to the Executive. If, for example, the President or Executive Branch officials were displeased with a new restriction on benefits imposed by Congress to ease burdens on the fisc (such as the restriction imposed by the statutory change in this case) and sought to evade them, agency officials could advise citizens that the restrictions were inapplicable. Estoppel would give this advice the practical force of law, in violation of the Constitution.

It may be argued that a rule against estoppel could have the opposite result, that the Executive might frustrate congressional intent to appropriate benefits by instructing its agents to give claimants erroneous advice that would deprive them of the benefits. But Congress may always exercise its power to expand recoveries for those who rely on mistaken advice should it choose to do so. In numerous other contexts where Congress has been concerned at the possibility of significant detrimental reliance on the erroneous advice of Government agents, it has provided appropriate legislative relief....

One example is of particular relevance. In Schweiker v. Hansen, 450 U.S. 785 (1981), we rejected an estoppel claim made by a Social Security claimant who failed to file a timely written application for benefits as required by the relevant statute. Congress then addressed such situations in the Budget Reconciliation Act of 1989, by providing that for claims to old age, survivors, and disability insurance, and for supplemental security income,

> In any case in which it is determined to the satisfaction of the Secretary that an individual failed as of any date to apply for monthly insurance benefits under this title by reason of misinformation provided to such individual by any officer or employee of the Social Security Administration relating to such individual's eligibility for benefits under this title, such individual shall be deemed to have applied for such benefits on the later of [the date on which the misinformation was given or the date upon which the applicant became eligible for benefits apart from the application requirement].

Pub. L. 101-239, §10302, 103 Stat. 2481. The equities are the same whether executive officials' erroneous advice has the effect of frustrating congressional intent to withhold funds or to pay them. In the absence of estoppel for money claims, Congress has ready means to see that payments are made to those who rely on erroneous Government advice. Judicial adoption of estoppel based on agency misinformation would, on the other hand, vest authority in these agents that Congress would be powerless to constrain. . . .

Respondent [argues] that estoppel against the Government would have beneficial effects. But we are unwilling to "tamper with these established principles because it might be thought that they should be responsive to a particular conception of enlightened governmental policy." . . . And respondent's attempts to justify estoppel on grounds of public policy are suspect on their own terms. Even short of collusion by individual officers or improper Executive attempts to frustrate legislative policy, acceptance of estoppel claims for Government funds could have pernicious effects. It ignores reality to expect that the Government will be able to "secure perfect performance from its hundreds of thousands of employees scattered throughout the continent." . . . To open the door to estoppel claims would only invite endless litigation over both real and imagined claims of misinformation by disgruntled citizens, imposing an unpredictable drain on the public fisc. Even if most claims were rejected in the end, the burden of defending such estoppel claims would itself be substantial.

Also questionable is the suggestion that if the Government is not bound by its agents' statements, then citizens will not trust them, and will instead seek private advice from lawyers, accountants, and others, creating wasteful expenses. Although mistakes occur, we may assume with confidence that Government agents attempt conscientious performance of their duties, and in most cases provide free and valuable information to those who seek advice about Government programs. A rule of estoppel might create not more reliable advice, but less advice. . . . The natural consequence of a rule that made the Government liable for the statements of its agents would be a decision to cut back and impose strict controls upon Government provision of information in order to limit liability.

Not only would valuable informational programs be lost to the public, but the greatest impact of this loss would fall on those of limited means, who can least afford the alternative of private advice. . . . The inevitable fact of occasional individual hardship cannot undermine the interest of the citizenry as a whole in the ready availability of Government information. The rationale of the Appropriations Clause is that if individual hardships are to be remedied by payment of Government funds, it must be at the instance of Congress.

Respondent points to no authority in precedent or history for the type of claim he advances today. Whether there are any extreme circumstances that might support estoppel in a case not involving payment from the Treasury is a matter we need not address. As for monetary claims, it is enough to say that this Court has never upheld an assertion of estoppel against the Government by a claimant seeking public funds. In this context there can be no estoppel, for courts cannot estop the Constitution. The judgment of the Court of Appeals is

Reversed.

JUSTICE STEVENS, concurring in the judgment.

Although I join the Court's judgment, I cannot accept its reasoning. The Appropriations Clause of the Constitution has nothing to do with this case. Payments of pension benefits to retired and disabled federal servants are made "in Consequence of Appropriations made by Law" even if in particular cases they are the product of a mistaken interpretation of a statute or regulation. The Constitution contemplates appropriations that cover programs — not individual appropriations for individual payments. The Court's creative reliance on constitutional text is nothing but a red herring.

The dispute in this case is not about whether an appropriation has been made; it is instead about what rules govern administration of an appropriation that has been made. Once the issue is appropriately framed, it quickly becomes obvious that the Court's resolution of it is untenable. Three hypothetical changes in the facts of this case will illustrate the error in the Court's approach. Assume, first, that the forfeiture involved a permanent and total loss of pension benefits rather than a 6-month hiatus. Suppose also that respondent was a disabled serviceman, totally incapable of productive work, who was promised that his benefits would be unaffected if he enlisted in the reserve forces to show his continuing commitment to his country. Finally, assume that respondent was activated briefly for the sole purpose of enhancing his earnings, thereby depriving him of his pension permanently. Would the Court apply the harsh rule against estoppel that it announces today? I think not. Unless it found in the statute some unambiguous abrogation of estoppel principles, the Court would apply them to nullify the forfeiture. In doing so, the Court would construe the statute in a way consistent with congressional intent, and would ensure that the Executive administered the funds appropriated in a manner consistent with the terms of the appropriation.

This case, however, does not involve such extreme facts. Respondent's loss of benefits was serious but temporary, and, even if we assume that respondent was not adequately compensated for the stress of his increased workload, his additional earnings certainly mitigated the shortfall in benefits. I agree . . . that there are strong equities favoring respondent's position, but I am persuaded that unless the 5-to-4 decision in Federal Crop Ins. Corp v. Merrill, 332 U.S. 380 (1947), is repudiated by Congress or this Court, this kind of maladministration must be tolerated. . . . Accordingly, I concur in the Court's judgment but not its opinion.

[JUSTICES MARSHALL and BRENNAN dissented.]

NOTES

1. Note that the Court declined to adopt the government's suggestion of a categorical no-estoppel rule. However, didn't the opinion go almost that far in its actual holding? If the blatant misinformation given to Richmond was not enough to work an estoppel, can there ever be "some situation in which estoppel against the Government could be appropriate"?

2. Is Justice Stevens correct in his assertion that "[t]he Appropriations Clause of the Constitution has nothing to do with this case" and the Court's reliance on it "is nothing but a red herring"?

3. The *Merrill-Richmond* result leads to harsh decisions, since the individual has acted in reliance on the agency advice. For typical cases, see Nelson v. Secretary of Agriculture, 133 F.2d 453 (7th Cir. 1943) (suspension of broker from trading for nonregistration, even though he had been misled by agency pronouncements and he had registered as soon as he discovered his obligation); SEC v. Torr, 22 F. Supp. 602 (S.D.N.Y. 1938) (broker subjected to SEC disciplinary proceedings though he had been told by an SEC representative what he contemplated doing was not violation of the law). According to an FCIC case, "Something is wrong when the citizen can recover for a dented fender caused by a postal employee at the wheel of a government truck and one cannot when he is boobytrapped by an employee of Federal Crop Insurance." McFarlin v. FCIC, 438 F.2d 1237 (9th Cir. 1971).

4. Compare the approach of the court in Brandt v. Hickel, 427 F.2d 53 (9th Cir. 1970). Appellants had submitted a noncompetitive oil and gas lease offer to the Bureau of Land Management. The latter erroneously held the form of the offer defective and issued a decision providing that appellants "are allowed the right to substitute within thirty days new offer forms . . . without losing their priority." Appellants did submit an amended offer form, instead of appealing the decision. The Secretary of the Interior ruled, however, that priority went to an offer that had been submitted by another party in the interim. The Secretary decided that he could not be bound by the promise that loss of priority would not result, since the promise was unauthorized by statute or regulation. The court disagreed, concluding that estoppel should be invoked where the erroneous advice was in the form of a crucial misstatement in an official decision. Administrative regularity must yield to basic notions of fairness: "To say to these appellants, 'The joke is on you. You shouldn't have trusted us,' is hardly worthy of our great government." The approach of this case has been followed in the Ninth Circuit. United States v. Wharton, 514 F.2d 406 (9th Cir. 1975). Can the Ninth

Circuit follow this approach after the *Richmond* decision? Compare Gilmore v. Lujan, 947 F.2d 1409, 1412 (9th Cir. 1991), *supra* p. 1, on the estoppel issue: "For BLM to be estopped from enforcing its own regulations, however, appellant must demonstrate affirmative misconduct on the part of the government which goes beyond a mere failure to inform or assist.... Gilmore has made no such showing here." Do fraud and negligent misrepresentation constitute "affirmative misconduct"? See Padalino v. Standard Fire Insurance Co., 616 F. Supp. 2d 538, 548 (E.D. Pa. 2008) ("But neither *Heckler* nor *Merrill* dealt with reasonable reliance in the context of fraud or negligent misrepresentation....").

5. *Good faith reliance.* Decisions repudiating the no-estoppel rule still constitute the rare, though growing, exception. To deal with the unfairness of the *Merrill*-type case, proposals for corrective legislation have been put forward. Over 35 years ago, a task force on administrative procedure recommended a so-called good faith reliance statute in the following terms:

> No sanction shall be imposed by any agency for any act done or omitted in good faith by any person in conformity with, or in reliance upon, any rule, or any advisory letter, opinion, or other written statement of the agency addressed in writing to such person and obtained by him without fraud or material misrepresentation, notwithstanding the fact that, after such act or omission has taken place, such rule, or such letter, opinion, or other written statement is modified, amended, rescinded, revoked, or held invalid by the agency for any reason.

Commission on Organization of the Executive Branch of the Government, Task Force Report on Legal Services and Procedure 375 (1955).

For another attempt to draft a good faith reliance statute, see Asimow, Advice to the Public from Federal Administrative Agencies 41 (1973).

6. *Declaratory orders.* The Federal Administrative Procedure Act, 60 Stat. 239 (1946), 5 U.S.C. §554, deals with the problem of making agency advice reliable by providing for an administrative counterpart of the declaratory judgment:

> (a) This section applies, according to the provisions thereof, in every case of adjudication required by statute to be determined on the record after opportunity for an agency hearing....
>
> (e) The agency, with like effect as in the case of other orders, and in its sound discretion, may issue a declaratory order to terminate a controversy or remove uncertainty.

The purpose of this provision is to permit agencies to issue binding advance decisions. Note that declaratory orders are to have "like effect as in the case of other orders." This means they are as binding as decisions made in contested cases. They are also subject to judicial review on the same basis as other orders. Weinberger v. Hynson, Westcott & Dunning, 412 U.S. 609 (1973).

7. Note also the limitations on the APA declaratory order provision:

> (a) Declaratory orders are authorized only with regard to matters that are required by statute to be determined on the record after opportunity for an agency hearing. This excludes cases where advisory rulings are sought where no statutory hearing procedure is provided for (e.g., the SEC is not authorized to issue declaratory orders on whether particular securities must be registered under the Securities Act).

(b) The agency is not required to issue declaratory orders on request; it has discretion to refuse to issue any declaratory order. Yale Broadcasting Co. v. FCC, 478 F.2d 594 (D.C. Cir.), cert. denied, 414 U.S. 914 (1973).

However, agency refusals to issue declaratory orders are subject to judicial review. The APA provides for the issuance of declaratory orders to be in the "sound discretion" of the agency. This means that agencies may not abuse that discretion. Judicial review is available to ensure against abuse of discretion in agency refusals to issue declaratory orders. Intercity Transp. Co. v. United States, 737 F.2d 103 (D.C. Cir. 1984). Would either a good faith reliance statute or the APA declaratory order provision have helped the wheat farmers in the *Merrill* case or the disabled retiree in *Richmond*?

G RULEMAKING PROCEDURE

Federal Administrative Procedure Act

5 U.S.C. §553 (1946)

§553. Rule Making

(a) This section applies, according to the provisions thereof, except to the extent that there is involved —

(1) a military or foreign affairs function of the United States; or

(2) a matter relating to agency management or personnel or to public property, loans, grants, benefits, or contracts.

(b) General notice of proposed rule making shall be published in the Federal Register, unless persons subject thereto are named and either personally served or otherwise have actual notice thereof in accordance with law. The notice shall include —

(1) a statement of the time, place, and nature of public rule making proceedings;

(2) reference to the legal authority under which the rule is proposed; and

(3) either the terms or substance of the proposed rule or a description of the subjects and issues involved.

Except when notice or hearing is required by statute, this subsection does not apply —

(A) to interpretive rules, general statements of policy, or rules of agency organization, procedure, or practice; or

(B) when the agency for good cause finds (and incorporates the finding and a brief statement of reasons therefor in the rules issued) that notice and public procedure thereon are impracticable, unnecessary, or contrary to the public interest.

> **(c)** After notice required by this section, the agency shall give interested persons an opportunity to participate in the rule making through submission of written data, views, or arguments with or without opportunity for oral presentation. After consideration of the relevant matter presented, the agency shall incorporate in the rules adopted a concise general statement of their basis and purpose. When rules are required by statute to be made on the record after opportunity for an agency hearing, sections 556 and 557 of this title apply instead of this subsection.
>
> **(d)** The required publication or service of a substantive rule shall be made not less than 30 days before its effective date, except—
>
> **(1)** a substantive rule which grants or recognizes an exemption or relieves a restriction;
>
> **(2)** interpretative rules and statements of policy; or
>
> **(3)** as otherwise provided by the agency for good cause found and published with the rule.
>
> **(e)** Each agency shall give an interested person the right to petition for the issuance, amendment, or repeal of a rule.

NOTES

1. In 1996, Congress amended the Administrative Procedure Act to require that no "major rule" can take effect until 60 days after the federal agency submits to the House of Representatives, the Senate, and the Comptroller General a copy of the rule, a concise general statement about the rule (including whether it is a major rule), and the effective date of the rule. The agency also must make several other documents available to Congress and the Comptroller, including cost-benefit analysis information. See Pub. L. No. 104-121, 110 Stat. 868 (amendment to APA adding Chapter 8 entitled *Congressional Review of Agency Rulemaking*). The law defines "major rule" as "any rule that the Administrator of the Office of Information and Regulatory Affairs of the Office of Management and Budget finds . . . is likely to result in [:] . . . an annual effect on the economy of $100,000,000 or more; a major increase in costs prices . . . ; or significant adverse effects on competition, employment, investment, productivity, innovation, or on the ability of [U.S.]-based enterprises to compete with foreign-based enterprises in domestic and export markets." 5 U.S.C. §801. The 60-day period runs from the later of the date a report is submitted to Congress about the rule or publication in Federal Register. This presumably extends the minimum time period before a rule can become effective in §553(d).

2. As a general proposition, agencies engaged in rulemaking are no more subject to procedural requirements than the legislature is when enacting a statute. The Federal APA, however, provides a general requirement of antecedent publicity before agencies may engage in substantive rulemaking. "In the not-so-distant past, a government agency in the Soviet Union could impose controls on the production of commodities without bothering to involve the public in the decisionmaking process. By contrast, a government agency in the United States must usually give notice to, and accept comments from, the public before undertaking to place manacles on the invisible hand." Riverbend Farms v. Madigan, 958 F.2d 1479, 1482 (9th Cir. 1992).

3. It has been asserted that the procedure prescribed by §553 of the APA "is one of the greatest inventions of modern government." Davis, Administrative Law Text 142 (3d ed. 1972). This appears to be an overstatement, particularly when one bears in mind that a similar system of antecedent publicity was set up under the British Rules Publication Act, 1893. Yet it cannot be denied that the §553 requirements mark a substantial step forward in rulemaking procedure.

4. Rulemaking under §553 is often called "notice-and-comment rulemaking." The following is a summary of the section's requirements:

> The Administrative Procedure Act ensures that the massive federal bureaucracy remains tethered to those it governs — or so the theory goes. When an agency decides to issue a rule, it must first publish a notice of proposed rulemaking in the *Federal Register*, which is the guide for those members of the public — usually special interest groups — who want to participate in the rulemaking process. The notice must contain "(1) a statement of the time, place, and nature of public rule making proceedings; (2) reference to the legal authority under which the rule is proposed; and (3) either the terms or substance of the proposed rule or a description of the subjects and issues involved." 5 U.S.C. §553(b). Although the APA mandates no minimum comment period, some window of time, usually thirty days or more, is then allowed for interested parties to comment. . . . The public may comment "through submission of written data, views, or arguments with or without opportunity for oral presentation." 5 U.S.C. §553(c). After "consideration of the relevant matter presented," the agency publishes the final rule, accompanied by a "concise general statement of [its] basis and purpose," in the *Register.*

Riverbend Farms v. Madigan, 958 F.2d 1479, 1483-1484 (9th Cir. 1992).

5. Section 553 does not mandate anything like a formal hearing prior to rulemaking. All that it requires is that the agency publish notice of proposed rulemaking in the Federal Register and give interested persons an "opportunity" to participate in the rulemaking.

The APA language confers discretion on the agency to designate the procedure for public participation. The cases emphasize that the APA requires only an "opportunity" to submit written materials and not an oral hearing, adversary or otherwise. The form and extent of public participation are left entirely to the agency. The APA is satisfied if the agency states in its notice of proposed rulemaking in the Register that written data, views, and arguments may be sent by interested persons to a given agency address.

6. It is also up to the agency to determine what "consideration" shall be given to materials presented in response to notices of proposed rulemaking. Courts have sometimes construed the provision as requiring agencies to take into account alternatives presented by commentators. See Chamber of Commerce v. SEC, 412 F.3d 133, 145 (D.C. Cir. 2005) ("In sum, the disclosure alternative was neither frivolous nor out of bounds and the Commission therefore had an obligation to consider it."). What kind of burden does this impose on the agency? Must it consider and explain all significant alternatives or concerns raised by commentators? Section 553 does not require consideration exclusively on any "record." Even if the agency permits an oral presentation, it "may act not only on the basis of the comments received in response to its notice of rule making, but also upon the basis of information available in its own files, and upon the knowledge and expertise of the agency." California Citizens Band Ass'n v. United States, 375 F.2d 43, 54 (9th Cir.), cert. denied, 389 U.S. 844 (1967).

7. Section 553 provides for *deferred effectiveness* of agency rules: "In addition to the time required for the notice and comment procedures to run their course, an additional thirty days ordinarily must pass between the time the final rule is published and the time it takes effect." *Riverbend Farms* at 1484, *supra* note 4. Substantive rules are not to become effective until at least 30 days after publication. Note, however, that the 30-day limit has nothing to do with the APA requirement of notice-and-comment rulemaking. The APA does not require the notice of proposed rulemaking to be published a certain number of days before the rules are promulgated. Hence, "the gestation period from initial notice to final rule can be a couple of months, and often much longer depending on the time the agency allows for comments and the time it takes to digest those comments." Id.

8. Agencies possess discretion on the amount of time to be given between the notice and the rules promulgation. But here, as in other cases, discretion must be exercised reasonably, and the courts may intervene when there has been an abuse of discretion. A 30-day period for comment after the notice of proposed rulemaking has been held not unreasonable. Conference of Bank Supervisors v. OTS, 792 F. Supp. 837 (D.D.C. 1992). See also Petry v. Block, 737 F.2d 1193, 1200 (D.C. Cir. 1984) (30-day comment period shortest time period sufficient to meaningfully review and provide informed comment). Yet reasonableness in this respect depends upon the factual circumstances. In a case involving complicated regulations not detailed in the notice, a 60-day comment period was ruled inadequate. Estate of Smith v. Bowen, 656 F. Supp. 1093 (D. Colo. 1987).

9. Note that the notice-and-comment requirements of §553 apply only to substantive/legislative rules; there is an express exemption for procedural and interpretive rules. In addition, there is an escape clause permitting agencies to dispense with the APA requirements where they make specific findings that notice and public procedure are "impracticable, unnecessary, or contrary to the public interest." However, where agency regulations required notice and comment procedures for nonsubstantive/nonlegislative rules, such procedures were required for interpretive or procedural rules. Benten v. Kessler, 799 F. Supp. 281 (E.D.N.Y. 1992).

10. What happens when a court strikes down an agency regulation for violating the procedural requirements of §553? The general answer is that the regulation is deemed invalid and the previous regulatory regime reinstated. See Paulsen v. Daniels, 413 F.3d 999 (9th Cir. 2005) (later superseded by statute). Courts have sometimes allowed the rule to remain in place where equity demands. In what circumstances will this occur? See, e.g., *EPIC, supra* p. 311.

11. Is there any room to argue that the failure to meet these requirements can sometimes constitute harmless error? In fact, agencies are required to so argue. See 5 U.S.C. §706. But exactly what kind of procedural error is "harmless"? In U.S. Telecom Ass'n v. FCC, 400 F.3d 29 (D.C. Cir. 2005), the court concluded that a position taken by the FCC was a legislative rather than an interpretative rule and therefore subject to the requirements of §553. The agency had, however, met all of the requirements, including publication in the Federal Register. The only requirement of §553 not met was the labeling of the proposal as a "Petition for Declaratory Ruling" rather than as a "Notice of Proposed Rulemaking." The court found that this failure was "harmless." Compare, however, Paulsen v. Daniels, 413 F.3d 999 (9th Cir. 2005). There, the Bureau of Prisons issued interim regulations that became effective immediately. The Bureau provided an opportunity for comment before the rules became final. In rejecting the agency's argument that the failure to meet the procedural requirements of §553 was harmless, the court opined: "It is antithetical to the structure and purpose of the APA for an agency to implement a rule first, and then seek comment later." Id. at 1005. How can you reconcile these two cases? When is it appropriate for a court to find that the failure to follow the procedures in §553 is harmless?

12. What about changes from the proposed and final rule? Do these trigger any procedural requirements? Often, particularly as a result of the comment process, an agency will make changes in the final rule. Do these changes require separate notice and comment? If that were the case, the rulemaking process could become interminable. In addition, an agency might then have an incentive not to make needed changes in the final rule. What should the standard be? Go back to the original purpose of the notice requirement. As one court has stated:

> There is no question that an agency may promulgate a final rule that differs in some particulars from its proposal. Otherwise the agency "can learn from the comments on its proposals only at the peril of starting a new procedural round of commentary." An agency, however, does not have carte blanche to establish a rule contrary to its original proposal simply because it receives suggestions to alter it during the comment period. An interested party must have been alerted by the notice to the possibility of the changes eventually adopted from the comments. Although an agency, in its notice of proposed rulemaking, need not identify precisely every potential regulatory change, the notice must be sufficiently descriptive to provide interested parties with a fair opportunity to comment and to participate in the rulemaking.

Chocolate Mfrs. Ass'n v. Block, 755 F.2d 1098, 1103-1104 (4th Cir. 1985) (citations omitted).

The D.C. Circuit has employed the "logical outgrowth" test. This test requires that interested parties could have anticipated that a change to the final rule was possible and had an opportunity to comment on the subject. See International Union, UMW v. MSHA, 407 F.3d 1250, 1259 (D.C. Cir. 2005) (in adopting rules on coal mine ventilation, agency disavowed in proposed rule any intent to adopt a cap on air velocity; subsequent decision to adopt a cap in the final rule was not a "logical outgrowth"); Environmental Integrity Project v. EPA, 425 F.3d 992, 998 (D.C. Cir. 2005) (agency adoption of rule opposite of one proposed does not constitute a "logical outgrowth"); CSX Transp. v. Surface Transp. Bd., 584 F.3d 1076, 1082 (D.C. Cir. 2009) (mere mention of the existence of four-year data pool not enough notice for "logical outgrowth" that agency would switch from reliance on one-year data in final rule). The U.S. Supreme Court endorsed the "logical outgrowth" test, applying it in Long Island Care at Home v. Coke, 551 U.S. 158 (2007). According to the Court,

> [t]he Administrative Procedure Act requires an agency conducting notice-and-comment rulemaking to publish in its notice of proposed rulemaking "either the terms or substance of the proposed rule or a description of the subjects and issues involved." 5 U.S.C. §553(b)(3). The Courts of Appeals have generally interpreted this to mean that the final rule the agency adopts must be "a 'logical outgrowth' of the rule proposed." The object, in short, is one of fair notice. . . . Since the proposed rule was simply a proposal, its presence meant that the Department was *considering* the matter; after that consideration the Department might choose to adopt the proposal or to withdraw it. . . . We do not understand why such a possibility was not reasonably foreseeable.

Id. at 174-175 (citations omitted).

13. APA notice-and-comment procedures may be skipped when an agency for "good cause" finds that procedures are "impracticable, unnecessary, or contrary to the public interest." This exception has been used liberally to suspend procedures in the context of 9/11 and the war on terror. See, e.g., Jifry v. FAA, 370 F.3d 1174 (D.C. Cir. 2004) (suspending notice and comment procedures post-9/11 for rules amending requirements for pilot "airman certificates"). According to one commentator, the "good cause" exception contains an "adjustable parameter that, in cases like *Jifry* has been dialed down to the point where it has temporarily become as capacious as administrators 'deem necessary.' It has, in other words, temporarily become a legal grey hole." Adrian Vermeule, Our Schmittian Administrative Law, 122 Harv. L. Rev. 1095, 1125 (2009). The D.C. Circuit clarified requirements for the "good cause" exception. In Mack Trucks, Inc. v. EPA, 682 F.3d 87 (D.C. Cir. 2012), the D.C. Circuit found EPA's good cause claim regarding avoiding notice and comment procedures for an interim rule to prevent a particular manufacturer's noncompliance was invalid. The court first found that it owed the agency no particular deference with respect to a good cause claim. Nor was it important to the court that the rule was merely "interim." The court noted that "impracticability" allows an agency to address situations of immediate danger, not avoid application of a rule to a lone manufacturer slow in complying. The court found that "unnecessary" means matters that are essentially "ministerial," of no real consequence to industry or the public. The court found "public interest" to be met "only in that rare circumstance when ordinary procedures — generally presumed to serve the public interest — would in fact harm that interest." Id. at 95. The court explained that the good cause exception is "to be narrowly construed and only reluctantly countenanced." Id. at 93.

14. State administrative procedure acts may vary somewhat from the structure of the Federal APA, though most are patterned after it. States also have more consistently modified or amended their respective APAs in order to improve them or to take into account societal changes, such as the expansion of electronic modes of seeking and disseminating information. Here is the rulemaking procedure section of the Florida APA, for example:

> **(3)** Adoption Procedures.—
>
> **(a)** *Notices.*—
>
> **1.** Prior to the adoption, amendment, or repeal of any rule other than an emergency rule, an agency, upon approval of the agency head, shall give notice of its intended action, setting forth a short, plain explanation of the purpose and effect of the proposed action; the full text of the proposed rule or amendment and a summary thereof; a reference to the grant of rulemaking authority pursuant to which the rule is adopted; and a reference to the section or subsection of the Florida Statutes or the Laws of Florida being implemented or interpreted. The notice must include a summary of the agency's statement of the estimated regulatory costs, if one has been prepared . . . ; a statement that any person who wishes to provide the agency with information regarding the statement of estimated regulatory costs, or to provide a proposal for a lower cost regulatory alternative . . . must do so in writing within 21 days after publication of the notice. . . . The notice must state the procedure for requesting a public hearing on the proposed rule. . . .
>
> **2.** The notice shall be published in the Florida Administrative Register not less than 28 days prior to the intended action. The proposed rule shall be available for inspection and copying by the public at the time of the publication of notice.
>
> **3.** The notice shall be mailed to all persons named in the proposed rule and to all persons who, at least 14 days prior to such mailing, have made requests of the agency for advance notice of its proceedings. The agency shall also give such notice as is prescribed by rule to those particular classes of persons to whom the intended action is directed.
>
> **4.** The adopting agency shall file with the committee, at least 21 days prior to the proposed adoption date, a copy of each rule it proposes to adopt; a copy of any material incorporated by reference in the rule; a detailed written statement of the facts and circumstances justifying the proposed rule; a copy of any statement of estimated regulatory costs that has been prepared . . . ; a statement of the extent to which the proposed rule relates to federal standards or rules on the same subject; and the notice required by subparagraph 1.

Florida Administrative Procedure Act, Fla. Stat. §120.54 (2020). Florida amended its APA again in 2009 to provide, inter alia, for electronic website posting requirements for agency rules. See Larry Sellers, Florida Amends APA — Again, 34 Admin. & Reg. L. News No. 4, p. 30 (Summer 2009). See also John Gedid, Administrative Procedure for the Twenty-First Century: An Introduction to the 2010 Model State Administrative Procedure Act, 44 St. Mary's L.J. 241, 275-277 (2012) (citations omitted):

> G. Rulemaking
>
> The 2010 MSAPA has numerous new provisions that improve public notice and participation in rule making agency input from the public during rulemaking, and judicial review. Some new provisions in Article 3 regarding rulemaking include a definition of the agency record in rulemaking, advance notice of contemplated rulemaking, negotiated rulemaking, and a special, simplified procedure for direct final rules, which are expected to be noncontroversial. Most of these innovations are the result of experimentation by the states and federal government with different rulemaking procedures that turned out successfully. The 2010 MSAPA defines a rule as a "statement of general applicability that implements . . . law or policy . . . and has the force of law." Another important new provision in Article 3 is the express recognition and inclusion of agency procedure for use of guidance documents. The Act defines guidance documents as generally applicable records that express an agency's legal interpretation or explain the way in which the agency will exercise its discretion, but do not invoke the force of law. The new guidance document definition and procedure clarify the relationship between agency rules as contrasted with interpretive and policy statements. The 2010 MSAPA does not require agencies to use notice and comment procedure for the promulgation of guidance documents. However, the section limits agency use of guidance documents: if an agency seeks to rely on a guidance document in a proceeding, it must give an affected party an opportunity to address the legality or wisdom of the agency position. Similarly, if an agency proposes to act at variance with a guidance document, it must give a reasonable explanation for the variance. If an affected party relied on the guidance document, the agency must explain why its interest outweighs the party's interest. The agency must also maintain an index of all guidance documents and make that index available to the public. This provision should eliminate agencies' abuse of their broad promulgating discretion to create unknown or secret law to control the outcome of proceedings.

VERMONT YANKEE NUCLEAR POWER CORP. v. NATURAL RESOURCES DEFENSE COUNCIL

435 U.S. 519 (1978)

Mr. Justice Rehnquist delivered the opinion of the Court.

In 1946, Congress enacted the Administrative Procedure Act, which as we have noted elsewhere was not only "a new, basic and comprehensive regulation of procedures in many agencies," . . . but was also a legislative enactment which settled "long-continued and hard-fought contention, and enacts a formula upon which opposing social and political forces have come to rest." . . . Section [553] of the Act, dealing with rulemaking, requires that ". . . notice of proposed rulemaking shall be published in the Federal Register . . . ," describes the contents of that notice, and goes on to require in subsection (c) that after the notice the agency "shall give interested persons an opportunity to participate in the rulemaking through submission of written data, views, or arguments with or without opportunity for oral presentation. After consideration of the relevant matter presented, the agency shall incorporate in the rules adopted a concise general statement of their basis and purpose." 5 U.S.C. §553. Interpreting this provision of the Act in . . . United States v. Florida East Coast Railroad Co., 410 U.S. 224 (1973), we held that generally speaking this section of the Act established the maximum procedural requirements which Congress was willing to have the courts impose upon agencies in conducting rulemaking procedures. Agencies are free to grant additional procedural rights in the exercise of their discretion, but reviewing courts are generally not free to impose them if the agencies have not chosen to grant them. This is not to say necessarily that there are no circumstances which would ever justify a court in overturning agency action because of a failure to employ procedures beyond those required by the statute. But such circumstances, if they exist, are extremely rare.

Even apart from the Administrative Procedure Act this Court has for more than four decades emphasized that the formulation of procedures was basically to be left within the discretion of the agencies to which Congress had confided the responsibility for substantive judgments. . . .

It is in the light of this background of statutory and decisional law that we granted certiorari to review two judgments of the Court of Appeals for the District of Columbia Circuit because of our concern that they had seriously misread or misapplied this statutory and decisional law cautioning reviewing courts against engrafting their own notions of proper procedures upon agencies entrusted with substantive functions by Congress. We conclude that the Court of Appeals has done just that in these cases, and we therefore remand them to it for further proceedings. . . .

I

A

Under the Atomic Energy Act of 1954, 42 U.S.C. §2011 et seq., the Atomic Energy Commission was given broad regulatory authority over the development of nuclear energy. Under the terms of the Act, a utility seeking to construct and operate a nuclear power plant must obtain a separate permit or license at both the construction and the operation stage of the project. See 42 U.S.C. §§2133, 2232, 2235, 2239. In order to obtain the construction permit, the utility must file a preliminary safety analysis report, an environmental report, and certain information regarding the antitrust implications of the proposed project. See 10 CFR §§2.101, 50.30(f), 50.33(a), 50.34(a). This application then undergoes exhaustive review by the Commission's staff and by the Advisory Committee on Reactor Safeguards (ACRS), a group of distinguished experts in the field of atomic energy. Both groups submit to the Commission their own evaluation, which then becomes part of the record of the utility's application. See 42 U.S.C. §2039, 2232(b). The Commission staff also undertakes the review required by the National Environmental Policy Act of 1969 (NEPA), 42 U.S.C. §4321 et seq., and prepares a draft environmental impact statement, which, after being circulated for comment, 10 CFR §§51.22-51.26, is revised and becomes a final environmental impact statement. 10 CFR §51.26. Thereupon the three member Atomic Safety and Licensing Board conducts a public adjudicatory hearing, 42 U.S.C. §2241, and reaches a decision which can be appealed to the Atomic Safety and Licensing Appeal Board, and currently, in the Commission's discretion, to the Commission itself. 10 CFR §§2.714, 2.721, 2.786, 2.787. The final agency decision may be appealed to the courts of appeals. 42 U.S.C. §2239; 28 U.S.C. §2342. The same sort of process occurs when the utility applies for a license to operate the plant, 10 CFR §50.34(b), except that a hearing need only be held in contested cases and may be limited to the matters in controversy. . . .

[This case arises] from two separate decisions of the Court of Appeals for the District of Columbia Circuit. In the first, the court remanded a decision of the Commission to grant a license to petitioner Vermont Yankee Nuclear Power Corporation to operate a nuclear power plant. In the second, the court remanded a decision of that same agency to grant a permit to petitioner Consumers Power Company to construct two pressurized water nuclear reactors to generate electricity and steam. [Only the first decision is discussed in the extracts that follow.]

B

In December 1967, after the mandatory adjudicatory hearing and necessary review, the Commission granted petitioner Vermont Yankee a permit to build a nuclear power plant in Vernon, Vt. See 4 A.E.C. 36 (1967). Thereafter, Vermont Yankee applied for an operating license. Respondent Natural Resources Defense Council (NRDC) objected to the granting of a license, however, and therefore a hearing on the application commenced on August 10, 1971. Excluded from consideration at the hearings, over NRDC's objection, was the issue of the environmental effects of operations to reprocess fuel or dispose of wastes resulting from the reprocessing operations. This ruling was affirmed by the Appeal Board in June 1972.

In November 1972, however, the Commission, making specific reference to the Appeal Board's decision with respect to the Vermont Yankee license, instituted rulemaking proceedings "that would specifically deal with the question of consideration of environmental effects associated with the uranium fuel cycle in the individual cost-benefit analyses for light water cooled nuclear power reactors." App. 352. The notice of proposed rulemaking offered two alternatives, both predicated on a report prepared by the Commission's staff entitled "Environmental Survey of the Nuclear Fuel Cycle." The first would have required no quantitative evaluation of the environmental hazards of fuel reprocessing or disposal because the Environmental Survey had found them to be slight. The second would have specified numerical values for the environmental impact of this part of the fuel cycle, which values would then be incorporated into a table, along with the other relevant factors, to determine the overall cost-benefit balance for each operating license. See App. 356-357.

Much of the controversy in this case revolves around the procedures used in the rulemaking hearings which commenced in February 1973. In a supplemental notice of hearing the Commission indicated that while discovery or cross-examination would not be utilized, the Environmental Survey would be available to the public before the hearing along with the extensive background documents cited therein. All participants would be given a reasonable opportunity to present their position and could be represented by counsel if they so desired. Written and, time permitting, oral statements would be received and incorporated into the record. All persons giving oral statements would be subject to questioning by the Commission. At the conclusion of the hearing, a transcript would be made available to the public and the record would remain open for thirty days to allow the filing of supplemental written statements. See generally App. 361-363. More than forty individuals and organizations representing a wide variety of interests submitted written comments. On January 17, 1973, the Licensing Board held a planning session to schedule the appearance of witnesses and to discuss methods for compiling a record. The hearing was held on February 1 and 2, with participation from a number of groups, including the Commission's staff, the United States Environmental Protection Agency, a manufacturer of reactor equipment, a trade association from the nuclear industry, a group of electric utility companies, and a group called Consolidated National Intervenors who represented seventy-nine groups and individuals including respondent NRDC.

After the hearing, the Commission's staff filed a supplemental document for the purpose of clarifying and revising the Environmental Survey. Then, the Licensing Board forwarded its report to the Commission without rendering any decision. The Licensing Board identified as the principal procedural question the propriety of declining to use full formal adjudicatory procedures. The major substantive issue was the technical adequacy of the Environmental Survey.

In April 1974, the Commission issued a rule which adopted the second of the two proposed alternatives described above. The Commission also approved the procedures used at the hearing, and indicated that the record, including the Environmental Survey, provided an "adequate data base for the regulation adopted." . . .

Respondents appealed from both the Commission's adoption of the rule and its decision to grant Vermont Yankee's license to the Court of Appeals for the District of Columbia Circuit. . . .

D

With respect to the challenge of Vermont Yankee's license, the court . . . examined the rulemaking proceedings and, despite the fact that it appeared the agency employed all the procedures required by §553 and more, the court determined the proceedings to be inadequate and overturned the rule....

II

...

B

... Vermont Yankee argues that the court invalidated the rule because of the inadequacy of the procedures employed in the proceedings.... Respondent NRDC, on the other hand, labeling petitioner's view of the decision a "straw man," argues to this Court that the court merely held that the record was inadequate to enable the reviewing court to determine whether the agency had fulfilled its statutory obligation....

After a thorough examination of the opinion itself, we conclude that while the matter is not entirely free from doubt, the majority of the Court of Appeals struck down the rule because of the perceived inadequacies of the procedures employed in the rulemaking proceedings. The court first determined the intervenor's primary argument to be "that the decision to preclude 'discovery or cross-examination' denied them a meaningful opportunity to participate in the proceedings as guaranteed by due process." 547 F.2d at 643. The court then went on to frame the issue for decision thusly: "Thus, we are called upon to decide whether the procedures provided by the agency were sufficient to ventilate the issues." [547 F.2d, at 643 (footnotes omitted).] The court conceded that absent extraordinary circumstances it is improper for a reviewing court to prescribe the procedural format an agency must follow, but it likewise clearly thought it entirely appropriate to "scrutinize the record as a whole to insure that genuine opportunities to participate in a meaningful way were provided...." 547 F.2d at 644. The court also refrained from actually ordering the agency to follow any specific procedures, 547 F.2d at 653-654, but there is little doubt in our minds that the ineluctable mandate of the court's decision is that the procedures afforded during the hearings were inadequate. This conclusion is particularly buttressed by the fact that after the court examined the record, particularly the testimony of Dr. Pittman, and declared it insufficient, the court proceeded to discuss at some length the necessity for further procedural devices or a more "sensitive" application of those devices employed during the proceedings....

In prior opinions we have intimated that even in a rulemaking proceeding when an agency is making a "quasi-judicial" determination by which a very small number of persons are "'exceptionally affected, in each case upon individual grounds,'" in some circumstances additional procedures may be required in order to afford the aggrieved individuals due process. United States v. Florida East Coast R. Co., 410 U.S. 224, 242-245, quoting from Bi-Metallic Investment Co. v. State Board of Equalization, 239 U.S. 441, 446 (1915). It might also be true, although we do not think the issue is presented in this case and accordingly do not decide it, that a totally unjustified departure from well settled agency procedures of long standing might require judicial correction.

But this much is absolutely clear. Absent constitutional constraints or extremely compelling circumstances "the administrative agencies 'should be free to fashion their own rules of procedure and to pursue methods of inquiry capable of permitting them to discharge their multitudinous duties.'" Federal Communications Commn. v. Schreiber, 381 U.S. 279, 290 (1965). . . . Indeed, our cases could hardly be more explicit in this regard. The Court has, as we noted in FCC v. Schreiber, *supra*, at 290, and n.17, upheld this principle in a variety of applications, including that case where the District Court, instead of inquiring into the validity of the FCC's exercise of its rulemaking authority, devised procedures to be followed by the agency on the basis of its conception of how the public and private interest involved could best be served. Examining §4(j) of the Communications Act of 1934, the Court unanimously held that the Court of Appeals erred in upholding that action. And the basic reason for this decision was the Court of Appeals' serious departure from the very basic tenet of administrative law that agencies should be free to fashion their own rules of procedure.

We have continually repeated this theme through the years. . . .

Respondent NRDC argues that §553 of the Administrative Procedure Act merely establishes lower procedural bounds and that a court may routinely require more than the minimum when an agency's proposed rule addresses complex or technical factual issues or "Issues of Great Public Import." NRDC Brief, p. 49. We have, however, previously shown that our decisions reject this view. . . .

. . . In short, all of this leaves little doubt that Congress intended that the discretion of the *agencies* and not that of the courts be exercised in determining when extra procedural devices should be employed.

There are compelling reasons for construing §553 in this manner. In the first place, if courts continually review agency proceedings to determine whether the agency employed procedures which were, in the Court's opinion, perfectly tailored to reach what the court perceives to be the "best" or "correct" result, judicial review would be totally unpredictable. And the agencies, operating under this vague injunction to employ the "best" procedures and facing the threat of reversal if they did not, would undoubtedly adopt full adjudicatory procedures in every instance. Not only would this totally disrupt the statutory scheme, through which Congress enacted "a formula upon which opposing social and political forces have come to rest," . . . but all the inherent advantages of informal rulemaking would be totally lost.

Secondly, it is obvious that the court in this case reviewed the agency's choice of procedures on the basis of the record actually produced at the hearing, 547 F.2d at 644, and not on the basis of the information available to the agency when it made the decision to structure the proceedings in a certain way. This sort of Monday morning quarterbacking not only encourages but almost compels the agency to conduct all rulemaking proceedings with the full panoply of procedural devices normally associated only with adjudicatory hearings.

Finally, and perhaps most importantly, this sort of review fundamentally misconceives the nature of the standard for judicial review of an agency rule. The court below uncritically assumed that additional procedures will automatically result in a more adequate record because it will give interested parties more of an opportunity to participate and contribute to the proceedings. But informal rulemaking need not be based solely on the transcript of a hearing held before an agency. Indeed, the agency need not even hold a formal hearing. See 5 U.S.C. §553(c). Thus, the adequacy of the "record" in this type of proceeding is not correlated directly to the type of procedural devices employed, but rather turns on whether the agency has followed the statutory mandate of the Administrative Procedure Act or other relevant statutes. If the agency is compelled to support the rule which it ultimately adopts with the type of record produced only after a full adjudicatory hearing, it simply will have no choice but to conduct a full adjudicatory hearing prior to promulgating every rule. In sum, this sort of unwarranted judicial examination of perceived procedural shortcomings of a rulemaking proceeding can do nothing but seriously interfere with that process prescribed by Congress.

Respondent NRDC also argues that the fact that the Commission's inquiry was undertaken in the context of NEPA [National Environmental Policy Act] somehow permits a court to require procedures beyond those specified in §553 when investigating factual issues through rulemaking. The Court of Appeals was apparently also of this view, indicating that agencies may be required to "develop new procedures to accomplish the innovative task of implementing NEPA through rulemaking." 178 U.S. App. D.C. at 356, 547 F.2d at 653. But we search in vain for something in NEPA which would mandate such a result. We have before observed that "NEPA does not repeal by implication any other statute." . . . In fact, just two Terms ago, we emphasized that the only procedural requirements imposed by NEPA are those stated in the plain language of the Act. . . . Thus, it is clear NEPA cannot serve as the basis for a substantial revision of the carefully constructed procedural specifications of the APA.

In short, nothing in the APA, NEPA, the circumstances of this case, the nature of the issues being considered, past agency practice, or the statutory mandate under which the Commission operates permitted the court to review and overturn the rulemaking proceeding on the basis of the procedural devices employed (or not employed) by the Commission so long as the Commission employed at least the statutory minima, a matter about which there is no doubt in this case.

There remains, of course, the question of whether the challenged rule finds sufficient justification in the administrative proceedings that it should be upheld by the reviewing court. Judge Tamm, concurring in the result reached by the majority of the Court of Appeals, thought that it did not. There are also intimations in the majority opinion which suggest that the judges who joined it likewise may have thought the administrative proceedings an insufficient basis upon which to predicate the rule in question. We accordingly remand so that the Court of Appeals may review the rule as the Administrative Procedure Act provides. . . . The court should engage in this kind of review and not stray beyond the judicial province to explore the procedural format or to impose upon the agency its own notion of which procedures are "best" or most likely to further some vague, undefined public good. . . .

Reversed and remanded.

NOTES

1. The *Vermont Yankee* problem arises out of the trend toward rulemaking as a regulatory technique. The trend has been particularly apparent in the newer fields of environmental and nuclear regulation, which involve complex scientific and technical issues involving mathematical or experimental data. The factual issues in those fields have been deemed inappropriate for trial procedures. Instead, rulemaking has been expanded into these fact-intensive areas, with the issues resolved in the generic-type proceedings appropriate to the more traditional legislative-type rulemaking.

Some courts have, however, been unwilling to allow the agencies to limit themselves, in such cases, to the informal procedural requirements imposed by §553 of the APA, asserting that proceedings such as those involving nuclear regulation involve factual components of such relative importance that a greater assurance of accuracy is required than that accompanying notice-and-comment procedures. The lower court in *Vermont Yankee*, in particular, handed down a series of decisions holding that, in these rulemaking cases involving complicated scientific issues, procedures in excess of the bare minimum prescribed by the APA may be required.

Has *Vermont Yankee* aborted this line of cases? Does it mean that, if agencies are to be required to follow stricter procedures than those demanded by the APA, such requirements can be imposed only by Congress?

2. Should the APA be amended to require more than notice-and-comment procedures in rulemaking? See Chrysler Corp. v. Brown, 441 U.S. 281 (1979), where the Court referred to *Vermont Yankee* as holding that courts may not normally impose procedural requirements on an agency beyond those specified in the APA because courts upset the balance set by the APA when they impose procedures not required by that statute. "By the same token, courts are charged with maintaining the balance: ensuring that agencies comply with the 'outline of minimum essential rights and procedures' set out in the APA." Id. at 313. In *Chrysler*, the agency did not follow the notice-and-comment rulemaking procedures mandated by the APA. Without more, that would bar its regulations from having statutory effect. "Certainly regulations subject to the APA cannot be afforded the 'force and effect of law' if not promulgated pursuant to the statutory procedural minimum found in that Act." Id.

3. Given the decision in *Vermont Yankee* and the failure of Congress to amend the procedures in §553, doesn't this mean that rules will sometimes be adopted without adequate consideration of all of the necessary facts and issues? The answer is, not quite. This issue will resurface in Chapter 7. Suffice it to say at this point that an agency's decision to follow the procedures set forth in §553 and only those procedures does not guarantee that it will produce a record that will allow the rule to withstand judicial review.

4. What if an agency issues an interpretive rule that changes the meaning of a legislative rule? Must it use notice and comment rulemaking to eliminate or change the interpretation? At issue in Perez v. Mortgage Bankers Ass'n, 575 U.S. 92 (2015), was the Department of Labor's conflicting interpretations of its regulations. In 2006, the Department of Labor opined that mortgage-loan officers were exempt from the overtime requirement of the Fair Labor Standards Act of 1938 (FLSA). The Mortgage Bankers Association (MBA) argued that the Department of Labor's 2010 Administrative Interpretation stating that mortgage bankers were *not* exempt from the overtime requirement, and thus entitled to overtime pay, was procedurally invalid because it was not issued through notice-and-comment rulemaking.

The MBA's argument was based on the doctrine announced in Paralyzed Veterans of Am. v. D.C. Arena L.P., 117 F.3d 579 (D.C. Cir. 1997). "Under the *Paralyzed Veterans* doctrine, if 'an agency has given its regulation a definitive interpretation, and later significantly revises that interpretation, the agency has in effect amended its rule, something it may not accomplish' under the APA 'without notice and comment.'" 575 U.S. at 99.

In *Perez*, the Supreme Court ruled that the *Paralyzed Veterans* doctrine was inconsistent with the APA. The Court clarified that while it is true an agency must follow the same procedures when amending a rule as it followed when it issued the rule, the *Paralyzed Veterans* doctrine overlooks the APA's exception to notice-and-comment rulemaking for interpretive rules. Justice Sotomayor wrote, "So, the D.C. Circuit correctly read §2 of the APA to mandate that agencies use the same procedures when they amend or repeal a rule as they used to issue the rule in the first instance. . . . Where the court went wrong was in failing to apply that accurate understanding of §2 to the exemption for interpretive rules contained in §4: Because an agency is not required to use notice-and-comment procedures to issue an initial interpretive rule, it is also not required to use those procedures when it amends or repeals that interpretive rule." 575 U.S. at 101.

As was noted in *Vermont Yankee* and *Chrysler*, the *Paralyzed Veterans* doctrine was held invalid because it put forth a court-imposed procedural requirement that was stricter than that promulgated by Congress.

UNITED STATES v. FLORIDA EAST COAST RAILWAY

410 U.S. 224 (1973)

MR. JUSTICE REHNQUIST delivered the opinion of the Court.

Appellees, two railroad companies, brought this action in the District Court for the Middle District of Florida to set aside the incentive per diem rates established by appellant Interstate Commerce Commission in a rulemaking proceeding. Incentive Per Diem Charges — 1968, Ex parte No. 252 (Sub-No. 1), 337 I.C.C. 217 (1970). They challenged the order of the Commission on both substantive and procedural grounds. The District Court sustained appellees' position that the Commission had failed to comply with the applicable provisions of the Administrative Procedure Act, 5 U.S.C. §§551 et seq., and therefore set aside the order without dealing with the railways' other contentions. The District Court held that the language of §1(14)(a)[1] of the Interstate Commerce Act, 49 U.S.C. §1(14)(a), required the Commission in a proceeding such as this to act in accordance with the Administrative Procedure Act, 5 U.S.C. §556(d), and that the Commission's determination to receive submissions from the appellees only in written form was a violation of that section because the appellees were "prejudiced" by that determination within the meaning of that section. . . .

I. BACKGROUND OF CHRONIC FREIGHT CAR SHORTAGES

This case arises from the factual background of a chronic freight car shortage on the Nation's railroads. . . .

The Commission in 1966 commenced an investigation, Ex parte No. 252, Incentive Per Diem Charges, "to determine whether information presently available warranted the establishment of an incentive element increase, on an interim basis, to apply pending further study and investigation." 332 I.C.C. 11, 12 (1967). Statements of position were received from the Commission staff and a number of railroads. Hearings were conducted at which witnesses were examined. In October 1967, the Commission rendered a decision discontinuing the earlier proceeding, but announcing a program of further investigation into the general subject.

In December 1967, the Commission initiated the rulemaking procedure giving rise to the order that appellees here challenge. It directed Class I and Class II line-haul railroads to compile and report detailed information with respect to

---

1. Section 1(14)(a) provides:

> The Commission may, after hearing, on a complaint or upon its own initiative without complaint, establish reasonable rules, regulations, and practices with respect to car service by common carriers by railroad subject to this chapter, including the compensation to be paid and other terms of any contract, agreement, or arrangement for the use of any locomotive, car, or other vehicle not owned by the carrier using it (and whether or not owned by another carrier), and the penalties or other sanctions for nonobservance of such rules, regulations, or practices. In fixing such compensation to be paid for the use of any type of freight car, the Commission shall give consideration to the national level of ownership of such type of freight car and to other factors affecting the adequacy of the national freight car supply, and shall, on the basis of such consideration, determine whether compensation should be computed solely on the basis of elements of ownership expense involved in owning and maintaining such type of freight car, including a fair return on value, or whether such compensation should be increased by such incentive element or elements of compensation as in the Commission's judgment will provide just and reasonable compensation to freight car owners, contribute to sound car service practices (including efficient utilization and distribution of cars), and encourage the acquisition and maintenance of a car supply adequate to meet the needs of commerce and the national defense. The Commission shall not make any incentive element applicable to any type of freight car the supply of which the Commission finds to be adequate and may exempt from the compensation to be paid by any group of carriers such incentive element or elements if the Commission finds it to be in the national interest.

freight car demand and supply at numerous sample stations for selected days of the week during 12 four-week periods, beginning January 29, 1968.

Some of the affected railroads voiced questions about the proposed study or requested modification in the study procedures outlined by the Commission in its notice of proposed rulemaking. In response to petitions setting forth these carriers' views, the Commission staff held an informal conference in April 1968, at which the objections and proposed modifications were discussed. Twenty railroads, including appellee Seaboard, were represented at this conference, at which the Commission's staff sought to answer questions about reporting methods to accommodate individual circumstances of particular railroads. The conference adjourned on a note that undoubtedly left the impression that hearings would be held at some future date. A detailed report of the conference was sent to all parties to the proceeding before the Commission.

The results of the information thus collected were analyzed and presented to Congress by the Commission during a hearing before the Subcommittee on Surface Transportation of the Senate Committee on Commerce in May 1969. Members of the Subcommittee expressed dissatisfaction with the Commission's slow pace in exercising the authority that had been conferred upon it by the 1966 Amendments to the Interstate Commerce Act. . . .

The Commission, now apparently imbued with a new sense of mission, issued in December 1969 an interim report announcing its tentative decision to adopt incentive per diem charges on standard boxcars based on the information compiled by the railroads. The substantive decision reached by the Commission was that so-called "incentive" per diem charges should be paid by any railroad using on its lines a standard boxcar owned by another railroad. Before the enactment of the 1966 amendment to the Interstate Commerce Act, it was generally thought that the Commission's authority to fix per diem payments for freight car use was limited to setting an amount that reflected fair return on investment for the owning railroad, without any regard being had for the desirability of prompt return to the owning line or for the encouragement of additional purchases of freight cars by the railroads as a method of investing capital. The Commission concluded, however, that in view of the 1966 amendment it could impose additional "incentive" per diem charges to spur prompt return of existing cars and to make acquisition of new cars financially attractive to the railroads. It did so by means of a proposed schedule that established such charges on an across-the-board basis for all common carriers by railroads subject to the Interstate Commerce Act. Embodied in the report was a proposed rule adopting the Commission's tentative conclusions and a notice to the railroads to file statements of position within 60 days, couched in the following language.

That verified statements of facts, briefs, and statements of position respecting the tentative conclusions reached in the said interim report, the rules and regulations proposed in the appendix to this order, and any other pertinent matter, are hereby invited to be submitted pursuant to the filing schedule set forth below by an interested person whether or not such person is already a party to this proceeding. . . .

That any party requesting oral hearing shall set forth with specificity the need therefor and the evidence to be adduced. [337 I.C.C. 183, 213.]

Both appellee railroads filed statements objecting to the Commission's proposal and requesting an oral hearing, as did numerous other railroads. In April 1970, the Commission, without having held further "hearings," issued a supplemental report making some modifications in the tentative conclusions earlier reached, but overruling in toto the requests of appellees Seaboard and Florida East Coast.

The District Court held that in so doing the Commission violated §556(d) of the Administrative Procedure Act, and it was on this basis that it set aside the order of the Commission.

II. APPLICABILITY OF ADMINISTRATIVE PROCEDURE ACT

In United States v. Allegheny-Ludlum Steel Corp., [406 U.S. 742 (1972),] we held that the language of §1(14)(a) of the Interstate Commerce Act authorizing the Commission to act "after hearing" was not the equivalent of a requirement that a rule be made "on the record after opportunity for an agency hearing" as the latter term is used in §553(c) of the Administrative Procedure Act. Since the 1966 amendment to §1(14)(a), under which the Commission was here proceeding, does not by its terms add to the hearing requirement contained in the earlier language, the same result should obtain here unless that amendment contains language that is tantamount to such a requirement. Appellees contend that such language is found in the provisions of that Act requiring that:

> [T]he Commission shall give consideration to the national level of ownership of such type of freight car and to other factors affecting the adequacy of the national freight car supply, and shall, on the basis of such consideration, determine whether compensation should be computed....

While this language is undoubtedly a mandate to the Commission to consider the factors there set forth in reaching any conclusion as to imposition of per diem incentive charges, it adds to the hearing requirements of the section neither expressly nor by implication. We know of no reason to think that an administrative agency in reaching a decision cannot accord consideration to factors such as those set forth in the 1966 amendment by means other than a trial-type hearing or the presentation of oral argument by the affected parties. Congress by that amendment specified necessary components of the ultimate decision, but it did not specify the method by which the Commission should acquire information about those components.

Both of the district courts that reviewed this order of the Commission concluded that its proceedings were governed by the stricter requirements of §§556 and 557 of the Administrative Procedure Act, rather than by the provisions of §553 alone. The conclusion of the District Court for the Middle District of Florida, which we here review, was based on the assumption that the language in §1(14)(a) of the Interstate Commerce Act requiring rulemaking under that section to be done "after hearing" was the equivalent of a statutory requirement that the rule "be made on the record after opportunity for an agency hearing." Such an assumption is inconsistent with our decision in *Allegheny-Ludlum, supra.*

The District Court for the Eastern District of New York reached the same conclusion by a somewhat different line of reasoning. That court felt that because §1(14)(a) of the Interstate Commerce Act had required a "hearing," and because that section was originally enacted in 1917, Congress was probably thinking in terms of a "hearing" such as that described in the opinion of this Court in the roughly contemporaneous case of ICC v. Louisville & Nashville R. Co., 227 U.S. 88, 93 (1913). The ingredients of the "hearing" were there said that to be that "[a]ll parties must be fully apprised of the evidence submitted or to be considered, and must be given opportunity to cross-examine witnesses, to inspect documents and to offer evidence in explanation or rebuttal." Combining this view of congressional understanding of the term "hearing" with comments by the Chairman of the Commission at the time of the adoption of the 1966 legislation regarding the necessity for "hearings," that court concluded that Congress had, in effect, required that these proceedings be "on the record after opportunity for an agency hearing" within the meaning of §553(c) of the Administrative Procedure Act.

Insofar as this conclusion is grounded on the belief that the language "after hearing" of §1(14)(a), without more, would trigger the applicability of §§556 and 557, it, too, is contrary to our decision in *Allegheny-Ludlum, supra.* The District Court observed that it was "rather hard to believe that the last sentence of §553(c) was directed only to the few legislative sports where the words 'on the record' or their equivalent had found their way into the statute book." 318 F. Supp. at 496. This is, however, the language which Congress used, and since there are statutes on the books that do use these very words, see, e.g., the Fulbright Amendment to the Walsh-Healey Act, 41 U.S.C. §43a, and 21 U.S.C. §371(e)(3), the regulations provision of the Food and Drug Act, adherence to that language cannot be said to render the provision nugatory or ineffectual. We recognized in *Allegheny-Ludlum* that the actual words "on the record" and "after . . . hearing" used in §553 were not words of art, and that other statutory language having the same meaning could trigger the provisions of §§556 and 557 in rulemaking proceedings. But we adhere to our conclusion, expressed in that case, that the phrase "after hearing" in §1(14)(a) of the Interstate Commerce Act does not have such an effect.

III. "HEARING" REQUIREMENT OF §1(14)(A) OF THE INTERSTATE COMMERCE ACT

Inextricably intertwined with the hearing requirement of the Administrative Procedure Act in this case is the meaning to be given to the language "after hearing" in §1(14)(a) of the Interstate Commerce Act. Appellees, both here and in the court below, contend that the Commission procedure here fell short of that mandated by the "hearing" requirement of §1(14)(a), even though it may have satisfied §553 of the Administrative Procedure Act. The Administrative Procedure

Act states that none of its provisions "limit or repeal additional requirements imposed by statute or otherwise recognized by law." 5 U.S.C. §559. Thus, even though the Commission was not required to comply with §§556 and 557 of that Act, it was required to accord the "hearing" specified in §1(14)(a) of the Interstate Commerce Act. Though the District Court did not pass on this contention, it is so closely related to the claim based on the Administrative Procedure Act that we proceed to decide it now.

If we were to agree with the reasoning of the District Court for the Eastern District of New York with respect to the type of hearing required by the Interstate Commerce Act, the Commission's action might well violate those requirements, even though it was consistent with the requirements of the Administrative Procedure Act.

The term "hearing" in its legal context undoubtedly has a host of meanings. Its meaning undoubtedly will vary, depending on whether it is used in the context of a rulemaking-type proceeding or in the context of a proceeding devoted to the adjudication of particular disputed facts. It is by no means apparent what the drafters of the Esch Car Service Act of 1917, 40 Stat. 101, which became the first part of §1(14)(a) of the Interstate Commerce Act, meant by the term. Such an intent would surely be an ephemeral one if, indeed, Congress in 1917 had in mind anything more specific than the language it actually used, for none of the parties refer to any legislative history that would shed light on the intended meaning of the words "after hearing." What is apparent, though, is that the term was used in granting authority to the Commission to make rules and regulations of a prospective nature. . . .

Under these circumstances, confronted with a grant of substantive authority made after the Administrative Procedure Act was enacted, we think that reference to that Act, in which Congress devoted itself exclusively to questions such as the nature and scope of hearings, is a satisfactory basis for determining what is meant by the term "hearing" used in another statute. Turning to that Act, we are convinced that the term "hearing" as used therein does not necessarily embrace either the right to present evidence orally and to cross-examine opposing witnesses, or the right to present oral argument to the agency's decisionmaker.

Section 553 excepts from its requirements rulemaking devoted to "interpretive rules, general statements of policy, or rules of agency organization, procedure, or practice," and rulemaking "when the agency for good cause finds . . . that notice and public procedure thereon are impracticable, unnecessary, or contrary to the public interest." This exception does not apply, however, "when notice or hearing is required by statute"; in those cases, even though interpretive rulemaking be involved, the requirements of §553 apply. But since these requirements themselves do not mandate any oral presentation it cannot be doubted that a statute that requires a "hearing" prior to rulemaking may in some circumstances be satisfied by procedures that meet only the standards of §553. . . .

Similarly, even where the statute requires that the rulemaking procedure take place "on the record after opportunity for an agency hearing," thus triggering the applicability of §556, subsection (d) provides that the agency may proceed by the submission of all or part of the evidence in written form if a party will not be "prejudiced thereby." Again, the Act makes it plain that a specific statutory mandate that the proceedings take place on the record after hearing may be satisfied in some circumstances by evidentiary submission in written form only.

We think this treatment of the term "hearing" in the Administrative Procedure Act affords a sufficient basis for concluding that the requirement of a "hearing" contained in §1(14)(a), in a situation where the Commission was acting under the 1966 statutory rulemaking authority that Congress had conferred upon it, did not by its own force require the Commission either to hear oral testimony, to permit cross-examination of Commission witnesses, or to hear oral argument. Here, the Commission promulgated a tentative draft of an order, and accorded all interested parties 60 days in which to file statements of position, submissions of evidence, and other relevant observations. The parties had fair notice of exactly what the Commission proposed to do, and were given an opportunity to comment, to object, or to make some other form of written submission. The final order of the Commission indicates that it gave consideration to the statements of the two appellees here.

Given the "open-ended" nature of the proceedings, and the Commission's announced willingness to consider proposals for modification after operating experience had been acquired, we think the hearing requirement of §1(14)(a) of the Act was met.

Appellee railroads cite a number of our previous decisions dealing in some manner with the right to a hearing in an administrative proceeding. Although appellees have asserted no claim of constitutional deprivation in this proceeding, some of the cases they rely upon expressly speak in constitutional terms, while others are less than clear as to whether they depend upon the Due Process Clause of the Fifth and Fourteenth Amendments to the Constitution, or upon generalized principles of administrative law formulated prior to the adoption of the Administrative Procedure Act. . . .

The basic distinction between rulemaking and adjudication is illustrated by this Court's treatment of two related cases under the Due Process Clause of the Fourteenth Amendment. In Londoner v. Denver, cited in oral argument by appellees, 210 U.S. 373 (1908), the Court held that due process had not been accorded a landowner who objected to the amount assessed against his land as its share of the benefit resulting from the paving of a street. Local procedure had accorded him the right to file a written complaint and objection, but not to be heard orally. This Court held that due process of law required that he "have the right to support his allegations by argument however brief, and, if need be, by proof, however informal." Id., at 386. But in the later case of Bi-Metallic Investment Co. v. State Board of Equalization, 239 U.S. 441 (1915), the Court held that no hearing at all was constitutionally required prior to a decision by state tax officers in Colorado to increase the valuation of all taxable property in Denver by a substantial percentage. The Court distinguished *Londoner* by stating that there a small number of persons "were exceptionally affected, in each case upon individual grounds." Id., at 446.

Later decisions have continued to observe the distinction adverted to in *Bi-Metallic Investment Co., supra.* In Ohio Bell Telephone Co. v. Public Utilities Commn., 301 U.S. 292, 304-305 (1937), the Court noted the fact that the administrative proceeding there involved was designed to require the utility to refund previously collected rate charges. The Court held that in such a proceeding the agency could not, consistently with due process, act on the basis of undisclosed evidence that was never made a part of the record before the agency. . . . FCC v. WJR, 387 U.S. 265 (1949), established that there was no across-the-board constitutional right to oral argument in any administrative proceeding regardless of its nature. While the line dividing them may not always be a bright one, these decisions represent a recognized distinction in administrative law between proceedings for the purpose of promulgating policy-type rules or standards, on the one hand, and proceedings designed to adjudicate disputed facts in particular cases on the other.

Here, the incentive payments proposed by the Commission in its tentative order, and later adopted in its final order, were applicable across the board to all of the common carriers by railroad subject to the Interstate Commerce Act. No effort was made to single out any particular railroad for special consideration based on its own peculiar circumstances. Indeed, one of the objections of appellee Florida East Coast was that it and other terminating carriers should have been treated differently from the generality of the railroads. But the fact that the order may in its effects have been thought more disadvantageous by some railroads than by others does not change its generalized nature. Though the Commission obviously relied on factual inferences as a basis for its order, the source of these factual inferences was apparent to anyone who read the order of December 1969. The factual inferences were used in the formulation of a basically legislative-type judgment, for prospective application only, rather than in adjudicating a particular set of disputed facts.

The Commission's procedure satisfied both the provisions of §1(14)(a) of the Interstate Commerce Act and of the Administrative Procedure Act, and were not inconsistent with prior decisions of this Court. We, therefore, reverse the judgment of the District Court, and remand the case so that it may consider those contentions of the parties that are not disposed of by this opinion.

NOTES

1. Section 553 of the APA recognizes two types of rulemaking: informal and formal. Informal rulemaking is the normal notice-and-comment type already discussed. But §553 also recognizes the existence of formal rulemaking, where rules must be preceded by a trial-type hearing. It provides,

> When rules are required by statute to be made on the record after opportunity for an agency hearing, sections 556 and 557 of this title apply instead of this subsection.

Sections 556 and 557 are the sections that govern formal adjudicatory proceedings. Formal rulemaking must follow the essentials of the APA procedural requirements governing adjudicatory proceedings. The APA here calls for most of the procedural formalities required in adjudications, including the right to submit evidence and to cross-examine.

2. As the *Florida East Coast* decision indicates, an agency is held to formal rulemaking under the APA only when another statute requires a trial-type hearing before rules are issued. A statute requiring the agency to act "after hearing" is not enough to trigger the formal rulemaking requirement. Such statutory language is not the equivalent of a requirement that the rule be made "on the record after opportunity for an agency hearing." For another case so holding, see National Rifle Ass'n v. Brady, 914 F.2d 475 (4th Cir. 1990).

What if the statute says that a "public hearing" is required? Does the word "public" suggest an oral hearing rather than just written comment? Still, "public hearing" may not be quite as conclusive as "on the record after opportunity for an agency hearing." In Seacoast Anti-Pollution League v. Costle, 572 F.2d 872 (1st Cir. 1978), the court held that the words "on the record" need not be used to trigger a full adjudicatory hearing under the APA. The court then proceeded to find that Congress must have intended a full adjudicatory hearing by the words "public hearing" in the Federal Water Pollution Control Act because otherwise the basis for pollution discharge limits would be unclear. However, in 2006 the First Circuit reconsidered its holding in *Seacoast* when it decided that the agency, not the courts, should make the call regarding whether a hearing is required consistent with Supreme Court precedent on deference to agencies. In Dominion Energy Brayton Point v. Johnson, 443 F.3d 12 (1st Cir. 2006), the court found that where statutory language regarding a hearing requirement is ambiguous, the court should defer to the agency decision as required by Supreme Court precedent. In *Dominion Energy*, the court found the "public hearing" requirement in the Clean Water Act to be ambiguous and that since, consistent with the *Seacoast* court's finding, the statutory language was unclear, the agency determination should be upheld. As a result, in *Dominion Energy* the court upheld the agency decision that "public hearing" does not mean that a hearing on the record is required. Of course, if you were to ask a layperson what is meant by "public hearing," the person would probably say it means an oral (adjudicatory-type) hearing. Nonetheless, if Congress wanted oral hearings as opposed to simply written commentary, it could so specify by amending the relevant laws to say "on the record after opportunity for an agency hearing."

3. According to Judge Friendly, only a few federal statutes expressly require rules to be made "on the record" after hearing. He calls them "the few legislative sports where the words 'on the record' . . . had found their way into the statute book." Long Island R.R. v. United States, 318 F. Supp. 490, 496 (E.D.N.Y. 1970). Fifteen such statutes are listed in Hamilton, Procedures for the Adoption of Rules of General Applicability: The Need for Procedural Innovation in Administrative Rulemaking, 60 Cal. L. Rev. 1276 (1972). The best known of the statutes requiring trial-type hearings in rulemaking is the Food, Drug, and Cosmetic Act of 1938. Under it, before regulations fixing food standards may be issued, the Food and Drug Administration must hold a public hearing at which any person may be heard. The regulations must be based "only on substantial evidence of record at the hearing," and the order promulgating them must include findings of fact, based on the record, similar to those required in adjudicatory decisions. In addition, statutory review proceedings are authorized, patterned after those normally provided for review of orders that are judicial in nature. On review the agency findings of fact "if supported by substantial evidence, shall be conclusive." The scope of review is similar to that available in the case of administrative adjudications.

"There is substantial . . . literature that documents the extraordinary inefficiency of adopting general rules through use of adjudicatory procedures. The Food and Drug Administration, for instance, once spent over a decade conducting an oral evidentiary hearing to try to answer the question: What is peanut butter?" Administrative Conference, The Federal Administrative Judiciary (Draft) 145 (1992).

Trial-type procedures, with a requirement of basis on the record, are out of place in rulemaking. They imprison a legislative process within a formal straitjacket designed for an entirely different type of process. Proceedings under the Food, Drug, and Cosmetic Act are so cumbersome (e.g., the peanut butter standards case produced a record of 7,736 pages, and one on special dietary foods a transcript of over 35,000 pages) that they substantially impair FDA ability to provide new regulations that may be needed to protect the public. For a criticism of trial-type rulemaking, see Hamilton, *supra* at 1312-1313 ("In practice . . . the principal effect of imposing rulemaking on a record has often been the dilution of the regulatory process rather than the protection of persons from arbitrary action."); Hamilton, Rulemaking on a Record by the Food and Drug Administration, 50 Tex. L. Rev. 1132 (1972), where the peanut butter and dietary foods proceedings are described in detail. See also National Nutritional Foods Ass'n v. FDA, 491 F.2d 1141, 1142 (2d Cir. 1974), where the court states that the dietary foods regulations, effective December 31, 1974, began with a notice of rulemaking in 1962 followed by a notice of public hearing in 1968; the hearings lasted for almost two years.

4. Despite the burden on rulemaking, affected interests continued to fight for more than notice-and-comment requirements in statutes delegating rulemaking power. They succeeded in imposing trial-type hearing requirements prior to rulemaking under at least one other statute. Fair Labelling and Packaging Act of 1966, 15 U.S.C. §1455. Compare Child Protection and Toy Safety Act of 1969, 15 U.S.C. §1262(e)(1); Poison Prevention Packaging Act of 1970, 15 U.S.C. §1474(a) (agency given option to proceed through formal on-the-record or informal §553 APA rulemaking).

Other statutes adopt an approach in between the notice-and-comment requirements of §553 and the requirement of a trial-type hearing. For examples, see the Consumer Product Safety Act of 1972, 15 U.S.C. §2056; Coal Mine Health and Safety Act of 1969, 30 U.S.C. §811; Occupational Safety and Health Act of 1970, 29 U.S.C. §655. These are discussed in Hamilton, Rulemaking on a Record by the Food and Drug Administration, 50 Tex. L. Rev. 1132 (1972), note 3 *supra*.

H RULEMAKING AND DUE PROCESS

BI-METALLIC INVESTMENT CO. v. STATE BOARD OF EQUALIZATION

239 U.S. 441 (1915)

MR. JUSTICE HOLMES delivered the opinion of the court.

This is a suit to enjoin the State Board of Equalization and the Colorado Tax Commission from putting in force and the defendant Pitcher, as assessor of Denver, from obeying, an order of the boards, increasing the valuation of all taxable property in Denver 40 percent. The order was sustained and the suit directed to be dismissed by the supreme court of the state. . . . The plaintiff is the owner of real estate in Denver, and brings the case here on the ground that it was given no opportunity to be heard, and that therefore its property will be taken without due process of law, contrary to the 14th Amendment of the Constitution of the United States. That is the only question with which we have to deal. . . .

For the purposes of decision we assume that the constitutional question is presented in the baldest way — that neither the plaintiff nor the assessor of Denver, who presents a brief on the plaintiff's side, nor any representative of the city and county, was given an opportunity to be heard, other than such as they may have had by reason of the fact that the time of meeting of the boards is fixed by law. On this assumption it is obvious that injustice may be suffered if some property in the county already has been valued at its full worth. But if certain property has been valued at a rate different from that generally prevailing in the county, the owner has had his opportunity to protest and appeal as usual in our system of taxation, Hagar v. Reclamation Dist., 111 U.S. 701, 709, so that it must be assumed that the property owners in the county all stand alike. The question, then, is whether all individuals have a constitutional right to be heard before a matter can be decided in which all are equally concerned — here, for instance, before a superior board decides that the local taxing officers have adopted a system of undervaluation throughout a county, as notoriously often has been the case. The answer of this court in the State R. Tax Cases, 92 U.S. 575, at least, as to any further notice, was that it was hard to believe that the proposition was seriously made.

Where a rule of conduct applies to more than a few people, it is impracticable that everyone should have a direct voice in its adoption. The Constitution does not require all public acts to be done in town meeting or an assembly of the whole. General statutes within the state power are passed that affect the person or property of individuals, sometimes to the point of ruin, without giving them a chance to be heard. Their rights are protected in the only way that they can be in a complex society, by their power, immediate or remote, over those who make the rule. If the result in this case had been reached, as it might have been by the state's doubling the rate of taxation, no one would suggest that the

14th Amendment was violated unless every person affected had been allowed an opportunity to raise his voice against it before the body entrusted by the state Constitution with the power. In considering this case in this court we must assume that the proper state machinery had been used, and the question is whether, if the state Constitution had declared that Denver had been undervalued as compared with the rest of the state, and had decreed that for the current year the valuation should be 40 percent higher, the objection now urged could prevail. It appears to us that to put the question is to answer it. There must be a limit to individual argument in such matters if government is to go on. In Londoner v. Denver, 210 U.S. 373, 385, a local board had to determine "whether, in what amount, and upon whom" a tax for paving a street should be levied for special benefits. A relatively small number of persons was concerned, who were exceptionally affected, in each case upon individual grounds, and it was held that they had a right to a hearing. But that decision is far from reaching a general determination dealing only with the principle upon which all the assessments in a county had been laid.

Judgment affirmed.

NOTES

1. The traditional line in determining whether or not there is a due process right to be heard is that between Bi-Metallic Co. v. Colorado and Londoner v. Denver, 210 U.S. 373 (1908), referred to by Justice Holmes at the end of the *Bi-Metallic* opinion. The statute in *Londoner* authorized the Denver Board of Public Works, on petition of a majority of the owners of property fronting on a street, to order the paving of the street. On completion, the board was directed to apportion the cost of the paving among the abutting owners in proportion to the benefits received by them from the improvement. The landowners in *Londoner* claimed that the assessment on their lands violated due process because it had been made without opportunity for a hearing. The landowners had been given notice of the assessments and opportunity to file written objections, but no right to be heard orally. On these facts, the Court held that there had been a denial of due process:

> . . . But where the legislature of a state, instead of fixing the tax itself, commits to some subordinate body the duty of determining whether, in what amount, and upon whom it shall be levied, and of making its assessment and apportionment, due process of law requires that, at some stage of the proceedings, before the tax becomes irrevocably fixed, the taxpayer shall have an opportunity to be heard, of which he must have notice, either personal, by publication, or by a law fixing the time and place of the hearing. . . . If it is enough that, under such circumstances, an opportunity is given to submit in writing all objections to and complaints of the tax to the board, then there was a hearing afforded in the case at bar. But we think that something more than that, even in proceedings for taxation, is required by due process of law. Many requirements essential in strictly judicial proceedings may be dispensed

> with in proceedings of this nature. But even here a hearing, in its very essence, demands that he who is entitled to it shall have the right to support his allegations by argument, however brief; and, if need be, by proof, however informal.

Id. at 385-386.

Referring to the *Bi-Metallic* and *Londoner* cases, a commentator writes, "Although neither case specifically uses the terms *adjudicative* and *legislative*, those are the conventional labels used to describe the dichotomy" upon which procedural due process is based. G. O. Robinson, American Bureaucracy: Public Choice and Public Law 113 (1991). Hence, as Chief Justice Rehnquist tells us, the right to be heard turns upon "our longstanding characterization of the distinction between 'judicial' and 'legislative' proceedings." New Orleans Public Service v. Council of New Orleans, 491 U.S. 350, 373 (1989).

2. Compare the analysis of the *Bi-Metallic* and *Londoner* cases in the opinion in United States v. Florida East Coast Ry., *supra* p. 354. According to Justice Rehnquist, the decisions in *Bi-Metallic* and *Londoner* illustrate the "basic distinction between rulemaking and adjudication." The dividing line, so far as the due process right to be heard is concerned, is "a recognized distinction in administrative law between proceedings for the purpose of promulgating policy-type rules or standards, on the one hand, and proceedings designed to adjudicate disputed facts in particular cases on the other." *Supra* p. 371. See Alaska Airlines v. CAB, 545 F.2d 194, 200 (D.C. Cir. 1976): "In United States v. Florida East Coast R. Co.... the Supreme Court approved this [i.e., the *Bi-Metallic–Londoner*] distinction." For a similar approach by a state court, see Heir v. Degnan, 411 A.2d 194 (N.J. 1980).

3. Compare the following comment on the *Bi-Metallic* and *Florida East Coast* opinions in Nathanson, Probing the Mind of the Administrator: Hearing Variations and Standards of Judicial Review Under the Administrative Procedure Act and Other Federal Statutes, 75 Colum. L. Rev. 721, 724-727 (1975):

> In retrospect, the Justice's analogy to the state's doubling of the rate of taxation seems to have been remarkably ill-chosen. If the state had doubled the rate of taxation only for Denver, a serious constitutional question would certainly have been presented. Of course, the state was not doubling the rate of state taxation; rather, it was equalizing Denver's tax burden relative to the rest of the state. Presumably, the only justification for such an action was the assumed fact that the assessment for Denver had been based upon a more generous standard of valuation than that applied for property in other parts of the state or, at least, upon a standard different from that prescribed by law. Apparently, it was this assumed fact which the taxpayers of Denver wanted to challenge at a hearing before the Board of Equalization or, failing that, before the court on judicial review. On its face, such a challenge seems to present a factual issue eminently suitable for resolution either in judicial or quasi-judicial proceedings by examination of the data, or examination of witnesses familiar with the data, or both. Certainly, this issue was significantly different from those which the legislature considers when it decides whether to increase the general rate of taxation. Nevertheless, the general language of *Bi-Metallic* has been quoted repeatedly in subsequent cases as explaining why a hearing may be dispensed with when administrative action, essentially legislative in nature, affects a large number of people.

> One of the most recent and significant examples of this use of *Bi-Metallic* is Justice Rehnquist's opinion in United States v. Florida East Coast Railway. . . . Justice Rehnquist undertook to examine more fully the "basic distinction between rulemaking and adjudication," particularly as illustrated by the Court's treatment of two related cases under the due process clause — Londoner v. Denver and *Bi-Metallic.* The distinction drawn by Justice Rehnquist — essentially that adumbrated by Justice Holmes in *Bi-Metallic* — was between the general increase in the valuation of all taxable property in Denver, and the street paving assessment in *Londoner* which applied to a small number of people who "were exceptionally affected, in each case upon individual grounds."

Is Professor Nathanson being fair to either Justice Holmes or Justice Rehnquist? Is Professor Nathanson correct in stating that a trial-type proceeding would be appropriate to resolve the *Bi-Metallic* factual issue? Would evidence and arguments relating to plaintiff's particular property be relevant to the agency's decision whether or not to increase the valuation of *all* property in Denver?

Compare the situation in the *Londoner* case, where a trial would be appropriate for presentation of evidence and argument concerning plaintiff's individual fact pattern in relation to those of his neighbors.

4. See K. C. Davis, Administrative Law: Cases-Text-Problems 266 (1973):

> In 1942 a proposal was made that, for purposes of determining what findings should be made on the record (i.e., through a trial-type hearing), two types of facts should be recognized — adjudicative facts and legislative facts. Davis, An Approach to Problems of Evidence in the Administrative Process, 55 Harv. L. Rev. 364, 402 (1942). Adjudicative facts are the facts about the parties and their activities, businesses, and properties. Adjudicative facts usually answer the questions of who did what, where, how, why, with what motive or intent; adjudicative facts are roughly the kind of facts that go to a jury in a jury case. Legislative facts do not usually concern the immediate parties but are general facts which help the tribunal decide questions of law and policy and discretion. The terminology has been adopted by federal courts in several dozen opinions, by state courts in a good many opinions, and recently been carried into Supreme Court law through the Court's adoption during 1972 of the Federal Rules of Evidence.

Does the legislative-adjudicative facts distinction explain the difference in result in the *Londoner* and *Bi-Metallic* cases? Does it add anything to the traditional rulemaking-adjudication distinction followed in the *Bi-Metallic* and *Florida East Coast* cases?

IN RE APPEAL OF STRATTON CORP.

600 A.2d 297 (Vt. 1991)

DOOLEY, JUSTICE.

Appellant, the Stratton Corporation (Stratton), appeals the Windham Superior Court's dismissal of its challenge to a proposed rule of the Vermont Water

Resources Board reclassifying a portion of Kidder Brook. We conclude that dismissal was proper and affirm.

On March 3, 1989, appellees William and Elizabeth Uptegrove and the Stratton Area Citizens Committee filed a petition with the Board, seeking reclassification of Kidder Brook, an upland stream located in the towns of Jamaica and Stratton, from Class B to Class A. On May 16, 1989, the Board initiated rulemaking proceedings, as required by the Vermont Water Pollution Control Act, 10 V.S.A. §§1250-1254. In accordance with the procedures for rulemaking set forth in the Vermont Administration Procedures Act at 3 V.S.A. §§836-843, the Board published a proposed rule to reclassify the brook, held a public hearing on June 27, 1989, and set a July 6, 1989, deadline for public comment.

At the June 27 hearing, Stratton asserted that the Due Process Clause of the United States Constitution required the Board to conduct formal, trial-like proceedings rather than an informal rulemaking procedure. Stratton based this assertion on property rights in the land adjoining the brook and its plans for future development of the area. The Board rejected Stratton's due process argument and proceeded to hear testimony from proponents and opponents of reclassification, including representatives of Stratton. The Board extended the public comment period to July 20th to allow Stratton time to file additional written materials. On July 19, 1989, Stratton filed testimony of its consulting engineer detailing its permits and land development plans which would be threatened by the reclassification.

In all, Stratton presented approximately 125 pages of written testimony and supporting materials. It stated that it owned property on both sides of Kidder Brook and that it held six Act 250 land use permits involving these properties. According to Stratton, these permits would be subject to revocation or modification if the proposed reclassification were adopted. Further, Stratton had long-term plans for development in the Kidder Brook area. It was about to request an Act 250 permit to construct 498 homes and an 18-hole golf course in the area. Stratton claimed that these plans could be significantly affected or prevented by the reclassification.

On July 27th, the Board voted unanimously to proceed with adoption of the proposed rule to reclassify, and subsequently issued a written explanation and a denial of Stratton's request to reopen the proceedings. In response to Stratton's due process claim, the Board stated that it was "simply not convinced that reclassification of Kidder Brook to Class A [would] substantially affect any existing permit or development on lands owned by the Stratton Corporation." In support of this conclusion, the Board noted that Stratton's testimony, with one exception, showed only "generalized uneasiness" about the effect of the reclassification. The exception involved a contingency plan to build an on-site sewage disposal facility if its proposal to transfer waste water to another area were not approved. The Board found this contingency need to be speculative. Overall, the Board found that "there [was] no material issue of fact in dispute among the parties to this proceeding."

Stratton appealed the reclassification in the Windham Superior Court, alleging that the Board's actions were arbitrary, unreasonable, and "contrary to law." In subsequent filings, as well as in its brief to this Court, Stratton clarified that its only claim on appeal was that the Board should have conducted "a trial-type hearing to adjudicate disputed facts" raised by the petition. . . .

Stratton argues that the Board's proceeding was not rulemaking because of limits imposed by the Due Process Clause of the Fourteenth Amendment, and that it had a right to appeal from what was actually adjudication. . . .

In evaluating the merits, we turn first to the statutory scheme around which this dispute revolves. . . .

> Section 1253(c) provides that the Board may on its own motion, and it shall upon petition by a state agency, a municipality or by thirty or more persons in interest alleging that it or they suffer injustice or inequity as a result of the classification of any waters, initiate a *rulemaking proceeding* to reclassify all or any portion of the affected waters in the public interest. In the course of this proceeding, the board shall comply with the provisions of [the Vermont Administrative Procedure Act], and hold a public hearing convenient to the waters in question. If the board finds that the established classification is contrary to the public interest and that reclassification is in the public interest, it shall file a final proposal of reclassification in accordance with 3 V.S.A. §841. If the board finds that it is in the public interest to change the classification of any pond, lake or reservoir designated as Class A waters . . . , it shall so advise and consult with the department of health and shall provide in its *reclassification rule* a reasonable period of time before the *rule* becomes effective. (Emphasis added.)

Subsection (f) provides that when the Board is considering reclassification to class A, "[n]otwithstanding the provisions of subsection (c)" the Board need only determine whether the reclassification is in the public interest. Subsection (e) sets forth ten factors for consideration in determining the public interest.

The statutory language makes clear that the Legislature intended that the reclassification process be "a rulemaking proceeding" and labeled a resulting reclassification decision a "rule." . . . On its face, the statute declines to treat reclassification as a "contested case," subject to the formal, adjudicative provisions of the Vermont Administrative Procedure Act, 3 V.S.A. §§809-813. The question before us is whether this choice denies Stratton due process of law.

Due process requirements apply to the procedures that must be used in reaching agency determinations only if they are adjudicative, rather than rulemaking or legislative, in nature. Bi-Metallic Investment Co. v. State Bd. of Equalization, 239 U.S. 441, 446 (1915). In *Bi-Metallic*, the Court distinguished between an adjudication based on the particular facts concerning specific parties, and a legislative or rulemaking decision, which is made on the basis of general facts, and has a broad, prospective effect. Id. Only the former triggers procedural due process concerns. Id.

In his recent treatise, Professor Koch articulated three factors for assessing whether an agency action is rulemaking or adjudication: (1) whether the inquiry is of a generalized nature, rather than having "a specific, individualized focus";

(2) whether the inquiry "focuses on resolving some sort of the policy-type question and not merely resolution of factual disputes"; and (3) whether the result is of "prospective applicability and future effect." 1 C. Koch, Administrative Law & Practice §2.3, at 61-62 (1985). A review of these factors supports our conclusion that reclassification is a rulemaking decision.

First, the reclassification inquiry involves examination of generalized issues beyond the scope of the immediate parties, see 10 V.S.A. §1253(e), rather than issues of fact focused primarily on the rights and duties of these parties.... The ten criteria the Board must consider in determining the appropriate classification of the waters relate to the interests of all citizens of the state, not only landowners adjacent to the waters. See 10 V.S.A. §1253(e). As the New York Court of Appeals instructed:

> A judicial type of hearing would, of course, be appropriate when *punishing individual violations*, while it would be manifestly inappropriate in connection with the *adoption* of a water classification *affecting many municipalities, individuals and industries.* (Emphasis in original.)

Town of Waterford v. Water Pollution Control Board, 5 N.Y.2d 171, 184, 156 N.E.2d 427, 433, 281 N.Y.S.2d 785, 794 (1959)....

In considering this first factor, Professor Koch notes, the "result of rulemaking has no direct force of its own, except to set some norm which affects a subsequent decision." 1 C. Koch, Administrative Law & Practice §2.3, at 61 (1985). This is exactly the effect of the Board's classification. It determines the quality standards to which the water must be managed, but leaves actual management to the Secretary of Natural Resources.

Second, the Board's determination involves a policy question concerning the level of quality of a public waterway in the public interest, rather than resolutions of a discrete factual dispute. In many states, classification is done by the legislature and not the executive branch.... Classification also involves technical expertise and judgment.... Scientific, economic and technical factors pertaining to an overall usage plan are generally not adjudicative facts conducive to resolution in a trial-type hearing....

Finally, the reclassification decision is a rule of prospective applicability. Although it may well affect future land uses, it does not address past conduct. As the Board found, its impact on development of surrounding lands is speculative. The Board also found that reclassification did not directly affect any existing permits, including Act 250 permits. Stratton has not demonstrated those findings were wrong.

Stratton emphasizes that it is the principal land owner affected, and that reclassification will greatly impact its development plans. This alone does not turn the Board's action into a "contested case." As Justice Holmes observed, general rules "are passed that affect the person or property of individuals, sometimes to the point of ruin, without giving them a chance to be heard. Their rights are protected in the only way that they can be in a complex society, by their power, immediate or remote, over those who make the rule." *Bi-Metallic*, 239 U.S.

at 445. The classification decision affects the public generally. Stratton's interest may be different from that of other members of the public, but it has no right to turn a public issue into a private contest. See Hercules, Inc. v. EPA, 598 F.2d at 118 (the fact that plaintiff is the only producer of a chemical subject to an EPA water quality standard does not give it a right to an adjudicatory hearing on the standard); Anaconda Co. v. Ruckelshaus, 482 F.2d 1301, 1306 (10th Cir. 1973) (the fact that plaintiff alone is involved with emission standard is not conclusive since "there are many other interested parties and groups who are affected and are entitled to be heard"). Nor does Stratton have the right to redirect the focus from the public interest factors specified by the Legislature to how reclassification will affect its private development plans.

We have no difficulty concluding that a reclassification determination under 10 V.S.A. §1253 is a policy-based rule of general applicability, and not an adjudication of particular parties' rights. . . . The Legislature is free, if it chooses, to require that reclassification decisions be made pursuant to more formal, trial-type procedures. . . . Nothing in the federal constitution, however, compels it to do so. . . . We conclude that even if we view the record and the evidence before the Board in the light most favorable to Stratton, it could not prevail on its due process arguments as a matter of law. . . . The superior court did not err in dismissing the action.

Affirmed.

NOTES

1. Would it make any difference if Stratton were the only landholder affected by the reclassification? See Anaconda Co. v. Ruckelshaus, 482 F.2d 1301 (10th Cir. 1973), cited in the *Stratton* opinion. In *Anaconda*, the EPA issued a rule limiting sulfur oxide emissions in a Montana county within which the plaintiff copper company operated the only smelter. The rule was dependent on bitterly contested factual issues applicable alone to plaintiff's smelter — the only one coming within the rule. The court ruled that this was only rulemaking and that no adversary hearing had to be given before the rule was issued, despite the fact that the rule was particular in applicability and turned on contested adjudicative facts.

The *Anaconda* opinion dealt with the procedural due process claim as follows:

> Our final question is whether there was sufficient substance to Anaconda's contention so that it would appear that it has been deprived of procedural due process by EPA's refusal to grant a trial type adjudicatory hearing. . . . The trial court saw as a result of denial of an adjudicatory hearing a violation of procedural due process together with a violation of the Clean Air Act and the Administrative Procedure Act. We must disagree. The Administrative Procedure Act requires that there be an adjudicatory hearing only if the agency statute specifies that the particular rulemaking hearings be "on the record after opportunity for an agency hearing." No such

> requirement is set forth in the Clean Air Act. . . . The fact that Anaconda alone is involved is not conclusive on the question as to whether the hearing should be adjudicatory, for there are many other interested parties and groups who are affected and are entitled to be heard. So the guidelines enunciated by Mr. Justice Holmes in Bi-Metallic Investment Co. v. State Board of Equalization, 239 U.S. 441 (1915), are not applicable.
>
> We have also examined the early decision in Londoner v. Denver, 210 U.S. 373, 386 (1908), and nothing therein imposes the adjudicatory requirement. . . . From our examination of the Act and the related case law and statutes, it would appear that the congressional requirement of a public hearing has been satisfied. Notice has been given and the proposed regulation has been issued. Anaconda appeared at that hearing and submitted material and was given an opportunity to submit more material and information for a period of seventy-five days following the public hearing. We perceive no violation of Anaconda's right to procedural due process. . . . Unending procedure could be produced by an adjudicatory hearing. This could bring about unending delay, which would not only impede but completely stifle congressional policy. We do not, of course, condemn the trial court's concern for the rights of Anaconda. Those rights are important and the court should be sensitive to them, but those rights are not of such magnitude as to overcome congressional policy and the rights of the remainder of the community.

Id. at 1306-1307.

Would a trial-type proceeding have been appropriate before the EPA action? Would the type of evidence presented by Anaconda be different if this rulemaking hearing were instead an EPA proceeding to show cause why a cease and desist order should not be issued against excessive sulfur oxide emissions? What about if it were in a court proceeding to abate them as a nuisance?

2. Compare the discussion in the Schwartz article at the beginning of this chapter, *supra* p. 271, on the difference between legislative and judicial functions. As explained there, two principal tests have been urged:

(a) the Holmes *time* test, under which a legislative act is *future* in effect, while a judicial decision is based upon *present* or *past* facts, and

(b) the Dickinson *applicability* test, under which a legislative act is *general* in applicability, while a judicial decision is *particular* in applicability.

As indicated in the Schwartz article, *supra* p. 273, the Federal APA follows the Holmes test in its definition of "rule." *Stratton* and *Anaconda* follow essentially the same approach.

ASSOCIATION OF NATIONAL ADVERTISERS v. FTC

627 F.2d 1151 (D.C. Cir. 1979)

Tamm, J.

Plaintiffs, appellees here, brought an action in the United States District Court for the District of Columbia to prohibit Michael Pertschuk, Chairman of the Federal Trade Commission (Commission), from participating in a pending rulemaking proceeding concerning children's advertising. The district court, citing this court's decision in Cinderella Career & Finishing Schools, Inc. v. FTC, 425 F.2d 583 (D.C. Cir. 1970), found that Chairman Pertschuk had prejudged issues involved in the rulemaking and ordered him disqualified. We hold that the *Cinderella* standard is not applicable to the Commission's rulemaking proceeding. An agency member may be disqualified from such a proceeding only when there is a clear and convincing showing that he has an unalterably closed mind on matters critical to the disposition of the rulemaking. Because we find that the appellees have failed to demonstrate the requisite prejudgment, the order of the district court is reversed.

I

On April 27, 1978, the Commission issued a Notice of Proposed Rulemaking that suggested restrictions regarding television advertising directed toward children.[1]

On May 8, 1978, the Association of National Advertisers, Inc. (ANA) . . . petitioned Chairman Pertschuk to recuse himself from participation in the children's advertising inquiry. The petition charged that Pertschuk had made public statements concerning regulation of children's advertising that demonstrated prejudgment of specific factual issues sufficient to preclude his ability to serve as an impartial arbiter. . . . The charges were based on a speech Pertschuk delivered to the Action for Children's Television (ACT) Research Conference in November 1977, on several newspaper and magazine articles quoting Chairman Pertschuk's views on children's television, on the transcript of a televised interview, and on a press release issued by the Commission during the summer of 1977.

On July 13, 1978, Chairman Pertschuk declined to recuse himself from the proceeding. . . .

In August 1978, ANA . . . petitioned the district court to declare that Chairman Pertschuk should be disqualified from participating in the children's television proceeding. . . .

On November 3, 1978, the district court ruled on cross-motions for summary judgment. The court, relying on *Cinderella*, found that Chairman Pertschuk "has prejudged and has given the appearance of having prejudged issues of fact involved in a fair determination of the Children's Advertising rulemaking proceeding." Accordingly, the court granted the plaintiff's motion for summary

1. The proposed rule would

(a) Ban all televised advertising for any product which is directed to, or seen by, audiences composed of a significant proportion of children who are too young to understand the selling purpose of or otherwise comprehend or evaluate the advertising;

(b) Ban televised advertising for sugared food products directed to, or seen by, audiences composed of a significant proportion of older children, the consumption of which products poses the most serious dental health risks;

(c) Require televised advertising for sugared food products not included in Paragraph (b), which is directed to, or seen by, audiences composed of a significant proportion of older children, to be balanced by nutritional and/or health disclosures funded by advertisers. . . .

judgment and ordered Pertschuk enjoined from further participation. This appeal followed....

III

... We are, therefore, called upon to resolve two questions: (1) What is the appropriate standard by which to decide prejudgment in the context of a section 18 [of the FTC Act] proceeding? (2) Has Chairman Pertschuk made statements that demonstrate prejudgment under that standard?

A

Before we examine either the structure of section 18 or the content of Pertschuk's statements, we review our decision in Cinderella Career & Finishing Schools, Inc. v. FTC. In *Cinderella*, we held that the standard for disqualifying an administrator in an adjudicatory proceeding because of prejudgment is whether "a disinterested observer may conclude that [the decisionmaker] has in some measure adjudged the facts as well as the law of a particular case in advance of hearing it." 425 F.2d at 591.... This standard guarantees that the adjudicative hearing of a person facing administrative prosecution for past behavior is before a decisionmaker who has not prejudged facts concerning the events under review....

B

The district court in the case now before us held that "the standard of conduct delineated in *Cinderella*" governs agency decisionmakers participating in a section 18 proceeding. Section 18 authorizes the Commission to promulgate rules designed to "define with specificity acts or practices which are unfair or deceptive." Basically, it allows the Commission to enforce the broad command of section 5 of the FTC Act, which declares "unfair or deceptive acts or practices in or affecting commerce ... unlawful." The district court ruled that a section 18 proceeding, notwithstanding the appellation rulemaking, "is neither wholly legislative nor wholly adjudicative." According to the district court, the "adjudicative aspects" of the proceeding render *Cinderella* applicable....

The appellees urge us to uphold the district court's analysis of section 18. They emphasize two allegedly "adjudicatory aspects" of a section 18 proceeding: (1) interested persons are entitled to limited cross-examination of those who testify to disputed issues of material fact, see 15 U.S.C. §57a(c)(1)(B) (1976), and (2) a reviewing court must set aside any rule not supported by substantial evidence in the rulemaking record taken as a whole, see 15 U.S.C. §57a(e)(3)(A) (1976).

The district court's characterization of section 18 rulemaking as a "hybrid" or quasi-adjudicative proceeding, A. at 106, ignores the clear scheme of the APA. Administrative action pursuant to the APA is either adjudication or rulemaking. The two processes differ fundamentally in purpose and focus....

... Congress has, in the Magnuson-Moss Warranty–Federal Trade Commission Improvement (Magnuson-Moss) Act §202(a), 15 U.S.C. §57a (1976), and elsewhere, enacted specific statutory rulemaking provisions that require more procedures than those of section 553 but less than the full procedures required under sections 556 and 557. The presence of procedures not mandated by section 553, however, does not, as the appellees urge, convert rulemaking into quasi-adjudication. The appellees err by focusing on the details of administrative process rather than the nature of administrative action....

D

Our conclusion that neither the procedures nor the factual predicate of section 18 rulemaking converts it into adjudication is supported by United States v. Florida East Coast Railway, 410 U.S. 224 (1973). In that case, the Supreme Court held, over the protests of two dissenting Justices, that an Interstate Commerce Commission ratemaking proceeding was rulemaking. The dissent maintained that the rate order was "adjudicatory in the sense that [it] determine[d] the measure of financial responsibility of one road for its use of the rolling stock of another road." Id. at 252 (Douglas, J., joined by Stewart, J., dissenting). The dissent emphasized that the agency decision was based on "evidential facts," id. at 254, and that it could "have devastating effects on a particular [railroad] line," id. at 256. Nevertheless, the Court found that the proceeding was rulemaking because the agency final order was applicable to all common carriers rather than any particular railroad. The Court explained that the agency had predicated its decision on "factual inferences ... used in the formulation of a basically legislative-type judgment, for prospective application only, rather than in adjudicating a particular set of facts." Id. at 246.

The same analysis applies to section 18 rulemaking. A section 18 proceeding is directed to all members of an affected industry and is based on legislative fact. Even when evidentiary procedures are employed in the formulation of specific fact, the product of those procedures is "used in the formulation of a basically legislative-type judgment." Id. Although we recognize that the line between rulemaking and adjudication "may not always be a bright one," id. at 245, we have no doubt that section 18 proceedings fall clearly on the rulemaking side of the "recognized distinction in administrative law between proceedings for the purpose of promulgating policy-type rules ... on one hand, and proceedings designed to adjudicate disputed facts in particular cases on the other." Id. Accordingly, we now decide the standard of disqualification applicable in a section 18 rulemaking proceeding.

IV

A

Had Congress amended section 5 of the FTC Act to declare certain types of children's advertising unfair or deceptive, we would barely pause to consider a due process challenge. No court to our knowledge has imposed procedural requirements upon a legislature before it may act. Indeed, any suggestion that congress-men may not prejudge factual and policy issues is fanciful. A legislator must have the ability to exchange views with constituents and to suggest public policy that is dependent upon factual assumptions. Individual interests impinged upon by the legislative process are protected, as Justice Holmes wrote, "in the only way that they can be in a complex society, by [the individual's] power, immediate or remote, over those who make the rule." Bi-Metallic Investment Co. v. State Board of Equalization, 239 U.S. 441, 445 (1915).

Congress chose, however, to delegate its power to proscribe unfair or deceptive acts or practices to the Commission because "there were too many unfair practices for it to define." S. Rep. No. 597, 63d Cong., 2d Sess. 13 (1914). In determining the due process standards applicable in a section 18 proceeding, we are guided by its nature as rulemaking. When a proceeding is classified as rulemaking, due process ordinarily does not demand procedures more rigorous than those provided by Congress. See Vermont Yankee Nuclear Power Corp. v. NRDC, 435 U.S. 519, 524 and n.1, 542 and n.16 (1978). Congress is under no requirement to hold an evidentiary hearing prior to its adoption of legislation, and "Congress need not make that requirement when it delegates the task to an administrative agency." ...

B

We never intended the *Cinderella* rule to apply to a rulemaking procedure such as the one under review....

The legitimate functions of a policymaker, unlike an adjudicator, demand interchange and discussion about important issues. We must not impose judicial roles upon administrators when they perform functions very different from those of judges....

The *Cinderella* view of a neutral and detached adjudicator is simply an inapposite role model for an administrator who must translate broad statutory commands into concrete social policies. If an agency official is to be effective he must engage in debate and discussion about the policy matters before him. As this court has recognized before, "informal contacts between agencies and the public are the 'bread and butter' of the process of administration." ...

Accordingly, a Commissioner should be disqualified only when there has been a clear and convincing showing that the agency member has an unalterably closed mind on matters critical to the disposition of the proceeding....

VI

The appellees have a right to a fair and open proceeding; that right includes access to an impartial decisionmaker. Impartial, however, does not mean uninformed, unthinking, or inarticulate. The requirements of due process clearly recognize the necessity for rulemakers to formulate policy in a manner similar to legislative action. The standard enunciated today will protect the purposes of a section 18 proceeding, and, in so doing, will guarantee the appellees a fair hearing.

We would eviscerate the proper evolution of policymaking were we to disqualify every administrator who has opinions on the correct course of his agency's future action. . . . The importance and legitimacy of rulemaking procedures are too well established to deny administrators such a fundamental tool.

Finally, we eschew formulation of a disqualification standard that impinges upon the political process. . . . We are concerned that implementation of the *Cinderella* standard in the rulemaking context would plunge courts into the midst of political battles concerning the proper formulation of administrative policy. We serve as guarantors of statutory and constitutional rights, but not as arbiters of the political process. Accordingly, we will not order the disqualification of a rulemaker absent the most compelling proof that he is unable to carry out his duties in a constitutionally permissible manner.

Reversed.

NOTES

1. The court also held that the FTC chairman's statements did not demonstrate disqualifying legal bias. See *infra* Chapter 6, Section F.

2. Different views on the question of rulemaking procedural requirements were taken in two other D.C. Circuit cases. The first was Home Box Office, Inc. v. FCC, 567 F.2d 9 (D.C. Cir. 1977), where it was held that ex parte contacts invalidated FCC rules regulating pay-cable television. A number of participants before the commission sought out individual commissioners or staff members for the purpose of discussing ex parte and in confidence the merits of the proposed rules. Even though only informal rulemaking was involved, it was intolerable that there was one administrative record for the public and another for the commission and those "in the know." The public record must reflect what representations were made to an agency so that relevant information supporting or refuting those representations may be brought to the attention of reviewing courts. Secrecy is inconsistent with "fundamental notions of fairness implicit in due process and the ideal of reasoned decisionmaking . . . [that] undergirds all of our administrative law." Id. at 56. Once a notice of proposed rulemaking has been issued, agency personnel should refuse to discuss matters relating to the rules with any private party.

A contrary result was reached in Action for Children's Television v. FCC, 564 F.2d 458 (D.C. Cir. 1977). The court there refused to invalidate FCC action in informal rulemaking proceedings in which the commission had received industry proposals for self-regulation on the matters concerned "behind the closed doors" of the commission chairman in a private meeting with industry officials. The court refused to follow *Home Box Office*, which, it said, "painted a new perspective on ex parte contacts with a rather broad jurisprudential brush." Id. at 474. *Home Box Office* imposed a "novel requirement" that would prohibit or require publication of and opportunity for comment on all ex parte contacts, no matter how minor, during the notice-and-comment stage of rulemaking. This broad prescription was said to constitute a clear departure from established law when applied to informal rulemaking. The governing rule, in the view of this panel of the D.C. court, is that ex parte contacts do not per se vitiate agency informal rulemaking.

Which reaches the more desirable result—*Home Box Office* or *Action for Children's Television*? For a more recent case following the *Action for Children's Television* approach, see Orangetown v. Ruckelshaus, 740 F.2d 185 (2d Cir. 1984).

Even if desirable, is the *Home Box Office* holding consistent with the *Vermont Yankee* decision, *supra* p. 356?

3. On the general subject see the remarks of Judge McGowan before the Association of American Law Schools, January 4, 1981:

> I think it likely that ambivalence will continue to pervade the ex parte contact problem until we face up to the question of whether legislation by informal rulemaking under delegated authority is, in terms of process, to be assimilated to lawmaking by the Congress itself, or to the adversary trial carried on in the sanitized and insulated atmosphere of the courthouse. Anyone with experience of both knows that a courtroom differs markedly in style and tone from a legislative chamber. The customs, the traditions, the mores, if you please, of the process of persuasion, are emphatically not the same. What is acceptable in the one is alien to the other.

See also Rodriguez, Whither the Neutral Agency? Rethinking Bias in Regulatory Administration, 69 Buffalo L. Rev. 375 (2021).

4. What if an agency rulemaking is tainted by pressure from Congress or a congressional committee? See Strickland v. Commissioner, 48 F.3d 12 (1st Cir. 1995); Radio Association v. Dep't of Transportation, 47 F.3d 794 (6th Cir. 1995).

Additional Procedures: Reg-Flex

§604. Final Regulatory Flexibility Analysis

(a) When an agency promulgates a final rule under section 553 of this title [5 U.S.C.S. §553], after being required by that section or any other law to publish a general notice of proposed rulemaking, or promulgates a final interpretative rule involving the internal revenue laws of the United States as described in section 603(a) [5 U.S.C.S. §603(a)], the agency shall prepare a final regulatory flexibility analysis. Each final regulatory flexibility analysis shall contain—

(1) a succinct statement of the need for, and objectives of, the rule;

(2) a summary of the significant issues raised by the public comments in response to the initial regulatory flexibility analysis, a summary of the assessment of the agency of such issues, and a statement of any changes made in the proposed rule as a result of such comments;

(3) the response of the agency to any comments filed by the Chief Counsel for Advocacy of the Small Business Administration in response to the proposed rule, and a detailed statement of any change made to the proposed rule in the final rule as a result of the comments;

(4) a description of and an estimate of the number of small entities to which the rule will apply or an explanation of why no such estimate is available;

(5) a description of the projected reporting, recordkeeping and other compliance requirements of the rule, including an estimate of the classes of small entities which will be subject to the requirement and the type of professional skills necessary for preparation of the report or record;

(6) a description of the steps the agency has taken to minimize the significant economic impact on small entities consistent with the stated objectives of applicable statutes, including a statement of the factual, policy, and legal reasons for selecting the alternative adopted in the final rule and why each one of the other significant alternatives to the rule considered by the agency which affect the impact on small entities was rejected; and for a covered agency, as defined in section 609(d)(2), a description of the steps the agency has taken to minimize any additional cost of credit for small entities.

U.S. TELECOM ASS'N v. FCC

400 F.3d 29 (D.C. Cir. 2005)

[The FCC had issued an order containing conditions under which wireline telecommunications carriers must transfer telephone numbers to wireless carriers (the "*Intermodal Order*"). Although contending that the order was interpretive and therefore not subject to the notice-and-comment requirements of §553, the agency nonetheless published it in draft form and invited comments. The D.C. Circuit found that the order was a legislative rule subject to the notice-and-comment requirements in the APA. By publishing the draft and asking for comments, however, the agency had met these requirements. The FCC had not, however, conducted a regulatory-flexibility analysis under §604.]

GARLAND, Circuit Judge . . .

IV

The Regulatory Flexibility Act [RFA] also imposes procedural requirements on agency rulemaking, in particular the preparation of a "final regulatory flexibility analysis" regarding the effect of the rule on small businesses. See 5 U.S.C. §604. . . . That requirement applies "when an agency promulgates a final rule under section 553 of this title, after being required by that section or any other law to publish a general notice of proposed rulemaking." Id. Because we have concluded that the FCC was required by section 553 to publish such a notice, the RFA's requirements are applicable to the *Intermodal Order.*

By contrast to the notice-and-comment requirements, there is no dispute that the FCC utterly failed to follow the RFA when it issued the *Intermodal Order.* Nor is there an argument that the Commission's failure was harmless, as it is impossible to determine whether a final regulatory flexibility analysis which must include an explanation for the rejection of alternatives designed to minimize significant economic impact on small entities, see id. §604(a)(3) [now §604(a)(4)], would have affected the final order when it was never prepared in the first place. See *Sprint Corp.*, 315 F.3d at 377 (holding that the wholesale failure to afford proper notice and comment was not harmless because "the effect of the Commission's procedural errors is uncertain").

The RFA outlines the remedies available for its violation as follows: In granting any relief in an action under this section, the court shall order the agency to take corrective action . . . including, but not limited to —

(A) remanding the rule to the agency, and
(B) deferring the enforcement of the rule against small entities unless the court finds that continued enforcement of the rule is in the public interest.

Id. §611(a)(4). A combination of the two specified remedies — remand coupled with a stay of enforcement against small entities — is appropriate here.

The petitioners contend that the order will have a serious impact on small rural carriers, which will have to impose the initial cost of implementation and the continuing cost of transporting calls to ported numbers on a narrow base of rural subscribers. Those costs, the petitioners argue, "bring[] no benefit to the vast majority of rural subscribers that are unwilling to give up their wireline service, yet must bear the cost burden nonetheless." . . . The petitioners do not seek to undo any porting of numbers that has already occurred; they ask only to stay the mandatory obligation to accede to new porting requests. . . .

The FCC does not contest the petitioners' argument, and it gives no reasons why continued enforcement of the order with respect to small entities pending a final regulatory flexibility analysis would be in the public interest. Rather, it stands on its contention that no regulatory flexibility analysis was required at all. See FCC Br. at 30. Under these circumstances, we have no basis for finding that continued enforcement against statutorily defined small entities during the remand would be in the public interest.

Accordingly, we remand the *Intermodal Order* to the FCC for the Commission to prepare the required final regulatory flexibility analysis. We stay future enforcement of the *Intermodal Order* only as applied to carriers that qualify as small entities under the RFA. The stay will remain in effect until the FCC completes its final regulatory flexibility analysis and publishes it in accordance with 5 U.S.C. §604(b). Of course, nothing in this disposition prevents small carriers from voluntarily adhering to the *Intermodal Order*'s number portability requirements during that period.

V

For the foregoing reasons, we deny the petitions with respect to the APA claim, and grant the petitions with respect to the RFA claim. We remand the *Intermodal Order* to the FCC for the purpose of preparing a final regulatory flexibility analysis, and we stay future enforcement of the order against carriers that are "small entities" under the RFA until the FCC prepares and publishes that analysis.

So ordered.

NOTES

1. What is the purpose of Reg-Flex? Why do you think Congress required it?

2. How burdensome is this requirement for an agency? In Little Bay Lobster Co. v. Evans, 352 F.3d 462 (1st Cir. 2003), the National Marine Fisheries Service issued final rules imposing stringent limits on lobster fishing in certain areas. The rule has a significant impact on small businesses. "The regime at issue in this case unquestionably affects a substantial number of small businesses; most, if not all, of the affected fishing is done by such entities." Id. at 470. Moreover, the agency conducted only a cursory analysis of the impact on small businesses under Reg-Flex. "Admittedly the final statement did little more than acknowledge that 'several commentators' had objected to the change in the boundary line and responded by referring to the 'current consensus' in support of the new regime as a whole. . . ." Id. at 471. As the court concluded: "The agency's obligation is simply to make a reasonable good faith effort to address comments and alternatives. And, where the agency has addressed a range of comments and considered a set of alternatives to the proposal adopted, the burden is upon the critic to show why a brief response on one set of comments or the failure to analyze one element as a separate alternative condemns the effort." Id. (Citations omitted.) What does the reasoning of this case tell you about the importance of Reg-Flex?

I RULEMAKING BY ADJUDICATION

NLRB v. WYMAN-GORDON CO.

394 U.S. 759 (1969)

MR. JUSTICE FORTAS announced the judgment of the Court and delivered an opinion in which THE CHIEF JUSTICE, MR. JUSTICE STEWART, and MR. JUSTICE WHITE join.

On the petition of the International Brotherhood of Boilermakers and pursuant to its powers under §9 of the National Labor Relations Act, 29 U.S.C. §159, the National Labor Relations Board ordered an election among the production and maintenance employees of the respondent company. At the election, the employees were to select one of two labor unions as their exclusive bargaining representative, or to choose not to be represented by a union at all. In connection with the election, the Board ordered the respondent to furnish a list of the names and addresses of its employees who could vote in the election, so that the unions could use the list for election purposes. The respondent refused to comply with the order, and the election was held without the list. Both unions were defeated in the election.

The Board upheld the unions' objections to the election because the respondent had not furnished the list, and the Board ordered a new election. The respondent again refused to obey a Board order to supply a list of employees, and the Board issued a subpoena ordering the respondent to provide the list or else produce its personnel and payroll records showing the employees' names and addresses. The Board filed an action in the United States District Court for the District of Massachusetts seeking to have its subpoena enforced or to have a mandatory injunction issued to compel the respondent to comply with its order.

The District Court held the Board's order valid and directed the respondent to comply. 270 F. Supp. 280 (1967). The United States Court of Appeals for the First Circuit reversed. 397 F.2d 394 (1968). The Court of Appeals thought that the order in this case was invalid because it was based on a rule laid down in an earlier decision by the Board, Excelsior Underwear Inc., 156 N.L.R.B. 1236 (1966), and the *Excelsior* rule had not been promulgated in accordance with the requirements that the Administrative Procedure Act prescribes for rule making, 5 U.S.C. §533. We granted certiorari to resolve a conflict among the circuits concerning the validity and effect of the *Excelsior* rule. 393 U.S. 932 (1968).

I

The *Excelsior* case involved union objections to the certification of the results of elections that the unions had lost at two companies. The companies had denied the unions a list of the names and addresses of employees eligible to vote. In the course of the proceedings, the Board "invited certain interested parties" to file briefs and to participate in oral argument of the issue whether the Board should require the employer to furnish lists of employees. 156 N.L.R.B., at 1238. Various employer groups and trade unions did so, as amici curiae. After these proceedings, the Board issued its decision in *Excelsior.* It purported to establish the general rule that such a list must be provided, but it declined to apply its new rule to the companies involved in the *Excelsior* case. Instead, it held that the rule would apply "only in those elections that are directed, or consented to, subsequent to 30 days from the date of [the] Decision." Id. at 1240, n.5.

Specifically, the Board purported to establish

> a requirement that will be applied in all election cases. That is, within 7 days after the Regional Director has approved a consent-election agreement entered into by

> the parties . . . , or after the Regional Director or the Board has directed an election . . . , the employer must file with the Regional Director an election eligibility list, containing the names and addresses of all the eligible voters. The Regional Director, in turn, shall make this information available to all parties in the case. Failure to comply with this requirement shall be grounds for setting aside the election whenever proper objections are filed.

Id. at 1239-1240.

Section 6 of the National Labor Relations Act empowers the Board "to make . . . , in the manner prescribed by the Administrative Procedure Act, such rules and regulations as may be necessary to carry out the provisions of this Act." 29 U.S.C. §156. The Administrative Procedure Act contains specific provisions governing agency rule making, which it defines as "an agency statement of general or particular applicability and future effect," 5 U.S.C. §551(4). The Act requires, among other things, publication in the Federal Register of notice of proposed rule making and of hearing; opportunity to be heard; a statement in the rule of its basis and purposes; and publication in the Federal Register of the rule as adopted. See 5 U.S.C. §553. The Board asks us to hold that it has discretion to promulgate new rules in adjudicatory proceedings, without complying with the requirements of the Administrative Procedure Act.

The rulemaking provisions of that Act, which the Board would avoid, were designed to assure fairness and mature consideration of rules of general application. . . . They may not be avoided by the process of making rules in the course of adjudicatory proceedings. There is no warrant in law for the Board to replace the statutory scheme with a rulemaking procedure of its own invention. Apart from the fact that the device fashioned by the Board does not comply with statutory command, it obviously falls short of the substance of the requirements of the Administrative Procedure Act. The "rule" created in *Excelsior* was not published in the Federal Register, which is the statutory and accepted means of giving notice of a rule as adopted; only selected organizations were given notice of the "hearing," whereas notice in the Federal Register would have been general in character; under the Administrative Procedure Act, the terms or substance of the rule would have to be stated in the notice of hearing, and all interested parties would have an opportunity to participate in the rule making.

The Solicitor General does not deny that the Board ignored the rulemaking provisions of the Administrative Procedure Act. But he appears to argue that *Excelsior's* command is a valid substantive regulation, binding upon this respondent as such, because the Board promulgated it in the *Excelsior* proceeding, in which the requirements for valid adjudication had been met. This argument misses the point. There is no question that, in an adjudicatory hearing, the Board could validly decide the issue whether the employer must furnish a list of employees to the union. But that is not what the Board did in *Excelsior*. The Board did not even apply the rule it made to the parties in the adjudicatory proceeding, the only entities that could properly be subject to the order in that case. Instead, the Board purported to make a rule: i.e., to exercise its quasi-legislative power.

Adjudicated cases may and do, of course, serve as vehicles for the formulation of agency policies, which are applied and announced therein. See Friendly, The Federal Administrative Agencies 36-52 (1962). They generally provide a guide to action that the agency may be expected to take in future cases. Subject to the qualified role of stare decisis in the administrative process, they may serve as precedents. But this is far from saying, as the Solicitor General suggests, that commands, decisions, or policies announced in adjudication are "rules" in the sense that they must, without more, be obeyed by the affected public.

In the present case, however, the respondent itself was specifically directed by the Board to submit a list of the names and addresses of its employees for use by the unions in connection with the election. This direction, which was part of the order directing that an election be held, is unquestionably valid.... Even though the direction to furnish the list was followed by citation to "Excelsior Underwear Inc., 156 N.L.R.B. No. 111," it is an order in the present case that the respondent was required to obey. Absent this direction by the Board, the respondent was under no compulsion to furnish the list because no statute and no validly adopted rule required it to do so.

Because the Board in an adjudicatory proceeding directed the respondent itself to furnish the list, the decision of the Court of Appeals for the First Circuit must be reversed.

II

The respondent also argues that it need not obey the Board's order because the requirement of disclosure of employees' names and addresses is substantively invalid. This argument lacks merit. The objections that the respondent raises to the requirement of disclosure were clearly and correctly answered by the Board in its *Excelsior* decision. All of the United States Courts of Appeals that have passed on the question have upheld the substantive validity of the disclosure requirement, and the court below strongly intimated a view that the requirement was substantively a proper one, 397 F.2d, at 396.

We have held in a number of cases that Congress granted the Board a wide discretion to ensure the fair and free choice of bargaining representatives.... The disclosure requirement furthers this objective by encouraging an informed employee electorate and by allowing unions the right of access to employees that management already possesses. It is for the Board and not for this Court to weigh against this interest the asserted interest of employees in avoiding the problems that union solicitation may present....

The judgment of the Court of Appeals is reversed, and the case is remanded to that court with directions to enforce the Board's order against the respondent.

It is so ordered.

MR. JUSTICE BLACK, with whom MR. JUSTICE BRENNAN and MR. JUSTICE MARSHALL join, concurring in the result.

I agree with ... the prevailing opinion of Mr. Justice Fortas, holding that the *Excelsior* requirement that an employer supply the union with the names and addresses of its employees prior to an election is valid on its merits and can be enforced by a subpoena. But I cannot subscribe to the criticism in that opinion of the procedure followed by the Board in adopting that requirement in the *Excelsior* case, 156 N.L.R.B. 1236 (1966). Nor can I accept the novel theory by which the opinion manages to uphold enforcement of the *Excelsior* practice in spite of what it considers to be statutory violations present in the procedure by which the requirement was adopted. Although the opinion is apparently intended to rebuke the Board and encourage it to follow the plurality's conception of proper administrative practice, the result instead is to free the Board from all judicial control whatsoever regarding compliance with procedures specifically required by applicable federal statutes such as the National Labor Relations Act, 29 U.S.C. §151 et seq., and the Administrative Procedure Act, 5 U.S.C. §551 et seq. Apparently, under the prevailing opinion, courts must enforce any requirement announced in a purported "adjudication" even if it clearly was not adopted as an incident to the decision of a case before the agency, and must enforce "rules" adopted in a purported "rule making" even if the agency materially violated the specific requirements that Congress had directed for such proceedings in the Administrative Procedure Act. I for one would not give judicial sanction to any such illegal agency action.

In the present case, however, I am convinced that the *Excelsior* practice was adopted by the Board as a legitimate incident to the adjudication of a specific case before it, and for that reason I would hold that the Board properly followed the procedures applicable to "adjudication" rather than "rule making." Since my reasons for joining in reversal of the Court of Appeals differ so substantially from those set forth in the prevailing opinion, I will spell them out at some length.

Most administrative agencies, like the Labor Board here, are granted two functions by the legislation creating them: (1) the power under certain conditions to make rules having the effect of laws, that is, generally speaking, quasi-legislative power; and (2) the power to hear and adjudicate particular controversies, that is, quasi-judicial power. The line between these two functions is not always a clear one and in fact the two functions merge at many points. For example, in exercising its quasi-judicial function an agency must frequently decide controversies on the basis of new doctrines, not theretofore applied to a specific problem, though drawn to be sure from broader principles reflecting the purposes of the statutes involved and from the rules invoked in dealing with related problems. If the agency decision reached under the adjudicatory power becomes a precedent, it guides future conduct in much the same way as though it were a new rule promulgated under the rule-making power, and both an adjudicatory order and a formal "rule" are alike subject to judicial review. Congress gave the Labor Board both of these separate but almost inseparably related powers. No language in the National Labor Relations Act requires that the grant or the exercise of one power was intended to exclude the Board's use of the other.

Nor does any language in the Administrative Procedure Act require such a conclusion. The Act does specify the procedure by which the rule-making power is to be exercised, requiring publication of notice for the benefit of interested parties and provision of an opportunity for them to be heard, and, after establishment of a rule as provided in the Act, it is then to be published in the Federal Register. Congress had a laudable purpose in prescribing these requirements, and it was evidently contemplated that administrative agencies like the Labor Board would follow them when setting out to announce a new rule of law to govern parties in the future. In this same statute, however, Congress also conferred on the affected administrative agencies the power to proceed by adjudication, and Congress specified a distinct procedure by which this adjudicatory power is to be exercised. The Act defines "adjudication" as "agency process for the formulation of an order," and "order" is defined as "the whole or a part of a final disposition, whether affirmative, negative, injunctive, or declaratory in form, of an agency in a matter other than rule making but including licensing." 5 U.S.C. §§551(7), (6). Thus, although it is true that the adjudicatory approach frees an administrative agency from the procedural requirements specified for rule making, the Act permits this to be done whenever the action involved can satisfy the definition of "adjudication" and then imposes separate procedural requirements that must be met in adjudication. Under these circumstances, so long as the matter involved can be dealt with in a way satisfying the definition of either "rule making" or "adjudication" under the Administrative Procedure Act, that Act, along with the Labor Relations Act, should be read as conferring upon the Board the authority to decide, within its informed discretion, whether to proceed by rule making or adjudication. Our decision in SEC v. Chenery Corp., 332 U.S. 194 (1947), though it did not involve the Labor Board or the Administrative Procedure Act, is nonetheless equally applicable here. As we explained in that case, "the choice made between proceeding by general rule or by individual, ad hoc litigation is one that lies primarily in the informed discretion of the administrative agency." Id., at 203.

In the present case there is no dispute that all the procedural safeguards required for "adjudication" were fully satisfied in connection with the Board's *Excelsior* decision, and it seems plain to me that that decision did constitute "adjudication" within the meaning of the Administrative Procedure Act, even though the requirement was to be prospectively applied. See Great Northern R. Co. v. Sunburst Co., 287 U.S. 358 (1932). The Board did not abstractly decide out of the blue to announce a brand new rule of law to govern labor activities in the future, but rather established the procedure as a direct consequence of the proper exercise of its adjudicatory powers. Sections 9(c) (1) and (2) of the Labor Relations Act empower the Board to conduct investigations, hold hearings, and supervise elections to determine the exclusive bargaining representative that the employees wish to represent them. This is a key provision of the plan Congress adopted to settle labor quarrels that might interrupt the free flow of commerce. A controversy arose between the Excelsior Company and its employees as to the bargaining agent the employees desired to act for them. The Board's power to provide the procedures for the election was invoked, an election was held, and the losing unions sought to have that election set aside. Undoubtedly the Board proceeding for determination of whether to confirm or set aside that election was "agency process for the formulation of an order" and thus was "adjudication" within the meaning of the Administrative Procedure Act.

The prevailing opinion seems to hold that the *Excelsior* requirement cannot be considered the result of adjudication because the Board did not apply it to the parties in the *Excelsior* case itself, but rather announced that it would be applied only to elections called thirty days after the date of the *Excelsior* decision. But the *Excelsior* order was nonetheless an inseparable part of the adjudicatory process. The principal issue before the Board in the *Excelsior* case was whether the election should be set aside on the ground, urged by the unions, that the employer had refused to make the employee lists available to them. See 156 N.L.R.B. at 1236-1238. The Board decided that the election involved there should not be set aside and thus rejected the contention of the unions. In doing so, the Board chose to explain the reasons for its rejection of their claim, and it is this explanation, the Board's written opinion, which is the source of the *Excelsior* requirement. The Board's opinion should not be regarded as any less an appropriate part of the adjudicatory process merely because the reason it gave for rejecting the unions' position was not that the Board disagreed with them as to the merits of the disclosure procedure but rather, see 156 N.L.R.B. at 1239, 1240, n.5, that while fully agreeing that disclosure should be required, the Board did not feel that it should upset the Excelsior Company's justified reliance on previous refusals to compel disclosure by setting aside this particular election.

Apart from the fact that the decisions whether to accept a "new" requirement urged by one party and, if so, whether to apply it retroactively to the other party are inherent parts of the adjudicatory process, I think the opposing theory accepted by the Court of Appeals and by the prevailing opinion today is a highly impractical one. In effect, it would require an agency like the Labor Board to proceed by adjudication only when it could decide, *prior* to adjudicating a particular case, that any new practice to be adopted would be applied retroactively. Obviously, this decision cannot properly be made until all the issues relevant to adoption of the practice are fully considered in connection with the final decision of that case. If the Board were to decide, after careful evaluation of all the arguments presented to it in the adjudicatory proceeding, that it might be fairer to apply the practice only prospectively, it would be faced with the unpleasant choice of either starting all over again to evaluate the merits of the question, this time in a "rule-making" proceeding, or overriding the considerations of fairness and applying its order retroactively anyway, in order to preserve the validity of the new practice and avoid duplication of effort. I see no good reason to impose any such inflexible requirement on the administrative agencies.

For all of the foregoing reasons I would hold that the Board acted well within its discretion in choosing to proceed as it did, and I would reverse the judgment of the Court of Appeals on this basis.

MR. JUSTICE DOUGLAS, dissenting. . . .

I am willing to assume that, if the Board decided to treat each case on its special facts and perform its adjudicatory function in the conventional way, we should have no difficulty in affirming its action. The difficulty is that it chose a different course in the *Excelsior* case and, having done so, it should be bound to follow the procedures prescribed in the Act as my Brother Harlan has outlined them. When we hold otherwise, we let the Board "have its cake and eat it too." . . .

. . . A rule like the one in *Excelsior* is designed to fit all cases at all times. It is not particularized to special facts. It is a statement of far-reaching policy covering all future representation elections.

It should therefore have been put down for the public hearing prescribed by the Act.

The rule-making procedure performs important functions. It gives notice to an entire segment of society of those controls or regimentation that is forthcoming. It gives an opportunity to persons affected to be heard. Recently the proposed Rules of the Federal Highway Administration governing the location and design of freeways, 33 Fed. Reg. 15663, were put down for a hearing; and the Governor of every State appeared or sent an emissary. The result was a revision of the Rules before they were promulgated. 34 Fed. Reg. 727.

This is not an uncommon experience. Agencies discover that they are not always repositories of ultimate wisdom; they learn from the suggestions of outsiders and often benefit from that advice. See Friendly, The Federal Administrative Agencies 45 (1962).

This is a healthy process that helps make a society viable. The multiplication of agencies and their growing power make them more and more remote from the people affected by what they do and make more likely the arbitrary exercise of their powers. Public airing of problems through rule making makes the bureaucracy more responsive to public needs and is an important brake on the growth of absolutism in the regime that now governs all of us. . . .

Rule making is no cure-all; but it does force important issues into full public display and in that sense makes for more responsible administrative action. I would hold the agencies governed by the rule-making procedure strictly to its requirements and not allow them to play fast and loose as the National Labor Relations Board apparently likes to do. . . .

MR. JUSTICE HARLAN, dissenting.

The language of the Administrative Procedure Act does not support the Government's claim that an agency is "adjudicating" when it announces a rule which it refuses to apply in the dispute before it. The Act makes it clear that an agency "adjudicates" only when its procedures result in the "formulation of an *order*." 5 U.S.C. §551(7). (Emphasis supplied.) An "order" is defined to include "the whole or a *part* of a final disposition . . . of an agency *in a matter other than rule making*. . . ." 5 U.S.C. §551(6). (Emphasis supplied.) This definition makes it apparent that an agency is not adjudicating when it is making a rule, which the Act defines as "an agency statement of general or particular applicability and *future effect*. . . ." 5 U.S.C. §551(4). (Emphasis supplied.) Since the Labor Board's *Excelsior* rule was to be effective only thirty days after its promulgation, it clearly falls within the rule-making requirements of the Act.

Nor can I agree that the natural interpretation of the statute should be rejected because it requires the agency to choose between giving its rules immediate effect or initiating a separate rule-making proceeding. An agency chooses to apply a rule prospectively only because it represents such a departure from pre-existing understandings that it would be unfair to impose the rule upon the parties in pending matters. But it is precisely in these situations, in which established patterns of conduct are revolutionized, that rule-making procedures perform the vital functions that my Brother Douglas describes so well in a dissenting opinion with which I basically agree.

Given the fact that the Labor Board has promulgated a rule in violation of the governing statute, I believe that there is no alternative but to affirm the judgment of the Court of Appeals in this case. If, as the plurality opinion suggests, the NLRB may properly enforce an invalid rule in subsequent adjudications, the rule-making provisions of the Administrative Procedure Act are completely trivialized. Under today's prevailing approach, the agency may evade the commands of the Act whenever it desires and yet coerce the regulated industry into compliance. It is no answer to say that "respondent was under no compulsion to furnish the list because no statute and no validly adopted rule required it to do so," when the Labor Board was threatening to issue a subpoena which the courts would enforce. In what other way would the administrative agency compel obedience to its invalid rule?

One cannot always have the best of both worlds. Either the rule-making provisions are to be enforced or they are not. Before the Board may be permitted to adopt a rule that so significantly alters pre-existing labor-management understandings, it must be required to conduct a satisfactory rulemaking proceeding, so that it will have the benefit of wide-ranging argument before it enacts its proposed solution to an important problem. . . .

NOTES

1. In exercising adjudicatory power, an agency, like a court, must sometimes decide cases on the basis of new doctrines not theretofore applied to the specific problem. As Justice Black states in his concurring opinion in *Wyman-Gordon*, if the agency decision becomes a precedent, it guides future conduct in much the same way as though it were a new rule promulgated under rulemaking power. There is retroactive effect in lawmaking by adjudication that may involve unfairness to the parties. A court, which has only the power to decide contested cases, may find it difficult to avoid such unfairness. But the agency has another instrument at its disposal: it can lay down the new law by rulemaking and so give fair notice of it in advance. Should it be legally required to do so? Would the answer be the same if the statute is not interpreted to require rulemaking?

The leading federal decision is SEC v. Chenery Corp., 332 U.S. 194 (1947), usually known as the second *Chenery* case. *Chenery II* established that an agency is not barred from applying a new principle in an adjudicatory proceeding simply because it had the power to announce that principle in advance by using its power of rulemaking. In *Chenery II* the Court upheld the refusal of the SEC to approve a corporation's reorganization on terms that would allow a profit to corporate directors and officers who had bought its stock with inside knowledge. The SEC had power to approve schemes that were "fair and equitable," and previously it had made no objection to "inside" dealings in such circumstances. Though pressed with the argument that the SEC should not be allowed to "legislate retrospectively" in this way, the majority held that to tie the commission's hands would "stultify the administrative process." Id. at 202. But there were powerful dissenters. In exceptionally strong language Justice Jackson accused the majority of encouraging "conscious lawlessness," and Justice Frankfurter agreed with him. Id. at 217.

A more recent case following the second *Chenery* rule is NLRB v. Bell Aerospace Co., 416 U.S. 267 (1974). The lower court there had refused to enforce an NLRB bargaining order on the ground that the board had made such a significant change in its previous definition of types of workers protected by the National Labor Relations Act that rulemaking rather than adjudication was required. The Supreme Court reversed, unanimously reaffirming that even in cases involving marked policy departures, agencies are not precluded from announcing new principles in an adjudicative proceeding; the choice between rulemaking and adjudication still lies within the agency's discretion. The board can decide to proceed with caution, developing its standards in a case-by-case manner rather than through a generalized rule.

The second *Chenery* rule, as confirmed in *Bell Aerospace*, is a "maxim of administrative law [that] permits an agency to develop a body of regulatory law and policy either through case-by-case decisionmaking (a quasi-adjudicative process) or through rulemaking (a quasi-legislative process)." American Tel. & Tel. Co. v. FCC, 978 F.2d 727, 731 (D.C. Cir. 1992).

2. According to Justice Scalia, *Wyman-Gordon* stands for the proposition "that adjudication could *not* be purely prospective, since otherwise it would constitute rulemaking." Bowen v. Georgetown University Hospital, 488 U.S. 204, 221 (1988) (Scalia, J., concurring).

Is this a correct characterization of the *Wyman-Gordon* holding? Consider the court's conclusion in The Central Tex. Tel. Coop. v. FCC, 402 F.3d 205 (D.C. Cir. 2005), that orders may be used to "establish broad legal principles." Id. at 210. In that case, the court chided the FCC for not arguing that a position issued in a declaratory ruling was an order rather than a rule. The agency had received a petition for declaratory relief, published the petition in the Federal Register and invited comments, ultimately receiving over 100. The FCC chose to defend its failure to meet all of the procedural requirements for substantive rulemaking by arguing that the ultimate position was interpretive. As the court noted: "Although the Commission used the Federal Register to notify interested parties of [the party's] petition, and to solicit comments on the issues the petition raised, the Federal Register announcement did not suggest that the proceeding would be anything other than an adjudication." Id.

3. If the *Excelsior* requirement had been promulgated as an NLRB regulation, would the Court have reached the same result? See American Tel. & Tel. Co. v. FCC, 978 F.2d 727, 733 (D.C. Cir. 1992) ("an agency would be required to apply a rule in an adjudication until it had revoked the rule in a new rulemaking"). Did the *Excelsior* prospective ruling have the binding character that is the essential element of a rule or regulation?

In a post-*Chenery* case, Judge Friendly referred to what he termed "the Supreme Court's rather pointed hint" in the *Chenery* opinion "that since an administrative agency has 'the ability to make new law prospectively through exercise of its rulemaking powers, it has less reason [than a court] to rely upon ad hoc adjudication to formulate new standards of conduct' and that the 'function of filling in the interstices' of regulatory statutes 'should be performed, as much as possible, through this quasi-legislative promulgation of rules to be applied in the future.'" NLRB v. Majestic Weaving Co., 355 F.2d 854, 860 (2d Cir. 1966).

4. According to Administrative Conference, The Federal Administrative Judiciary (Draft) 144 (1992):

> Rulemaking can be expected to yield higher-quality rules than adjudication. When an agency announces a "rule" in the process of adjudicating a specific dispute, it has before it only the parties to the particular dispute and the evidence those parties tender. Traditionally, that evidence focuses on the specific, historical facts related to those parties and their relationship. The factual pattern on which the agency predicates its rule may be widely generalizable or entirely idiosyncratic. The agency has no way of knowing whether the fact pattern before it applies to 100 percent, 50 percent, 10 percent, or 1 percent of superficially analogous relationships or incidents. Other common patterns may suggest entirely different rules. Moreover, the process of making a general rule of conduct should not be based primarily on resolution of specific historical facts. The primary purpose of rules is to effect future conduct or to resolve issues of legislative fact. Thus, rules should be based on evidence relevant to that goal. An agency contemplating announcement of a rule should search for answers to questions like: how can we channel the future conduct of regulatees or beneficiaries in ways that will further our statutory mission? or, what is the general relationship between exposure to a particular toxic substance and various adverse health effects? An adjudication rarely yields significant, high quality evidence relevant to those questions.

Compare Arizona Dep't of Revenue v. Transamerica Title, 604 P.2d 1139, 1143 (Ariz. Ct. App. 1979): "[A]n agency's formal promulgation of rules and regulations of general application is usually to be favored over the generation of policy in a piecemeal fashion through individual adjudicatory orders."

Consider the following excerpt from the Florida Administrative Procedure Act:

> 120.54 RULEMAKING.—
>
> **(1)** GENERAL PROVISIONS APPLICABLE TO ALL RULES OTHER THAN EMERGENCY RULES.—

> **(a)** Rulemaking is not a matter of agency discretion. Each agency statement defined as a rule by s. 120.52 shall be adopted by the rulemaking procedure provided by this section as soon as feasible and practicable.
>
> **1.** Rulemaking shall be presumed feasible unless the agency proves that:
>
> a. The agency has not had sufficient time to acquire the knowledge and experience reasonably necessary to address a statement by rulemaking; or
>
> b. Related matters are not sufficiently resolved to enable the agency to address a statement by rulemaking.
>
> **2.** Rulemaking shall be presumed practicable to the extent necessary to provide fair notice to affected persons of relevant agency procedures and applicable principles, criteria, or standards for agency decisions unless the agency proves that:
>
> a. Detail or precision in the establishment of principles, criteria, or standards for agency decisions is not reasonable under the circumstances; or
>
> b. The particular questions addressed are of such a narrow scope that more specific resolution of the matter is impractical outside of an adjudication to determine the substantial interests of a party based on individual circumstances.

Fla. Stat. §120.54 (2020). If rulemaking is better than creating rules in adjudication, why not take the decision out of the agency's hands, as the Florida statute seems to do? Are there any arguments for allowing agencies to retain discretion in this area?

J RULEMAKING AND THE INTERNET

Section 206 of the E-Government Act of 2002

44 U.S.C. §3501

> **(a)** Purposes.—The purposes of this section are to—
>
> **(1)** improve performance in the development and issuance of agency regulations by using information technology to increase access, accountability, and transparency; and
>
> **(2)** enhance public participation in Government by electronic means, consistent with requirements under subchapter II of chapter 5 of title 5, United States Code (commonly referred to as the "Administrative Procedures Act").

(b) Information Provided by Agencies Online. — To the extent practicable as determined by the agency in consultation with the Director, each agency (as defined under section 551 of title 5, United States Code) shall ensure that a publicly accessible Federal Government website includes all information about that agency required to be published in the Federal Register under paragraphs (1) and (2) of section 552(a) of title 5, United States Code.

(c) Submissions by Electronic Means. — To the extent practicable, agencies shall accept submissions under section 553(c) of title 5, United States Code, by electronic means.

(d) Electronic Docketing. —

(1) In general. — To the extent practicable, as determined by the agency in consultation with the Director, agencies shall ensure that a publicly accessible Federal Government website contains electronic dockets for rulemakings under section 553 of title 5, United States Code.

(2) Information available. — Agency electronic dockets shall make publicly available online to the extent practicable, as determined by the agency in consultation with the Director —

(A) all submissions under section 553(c) of title 5, United States Code; and

(B) other materials that by agency rule or practice are included in the rulemaking docket under section 553(c) of title 5, United States Code, whether or not submitted electronically.

(e) Time Limitation. — Agencies shall implement the requirements of this section consistent with a timetable established by the Director and reported to Congress in the first annual report under section 3606 of title 44 (as added by this Act).

Lauren Moxley

E-RULEMAKING AND DEMOCRACY

68 Admin. L. Rev. 661, 665-672 (2016)

. . .

I. NOTICE AND COMMENT RULEMAKING: BEFORE THE INTERNET

The public has had the opportunity to comment on proposed federal regulations since the innovation of notice-and-comment rulemaking under the

Administrative Procedure Act (APA) in 1946.[12] The APA was Congress's response to the tremendous growth of the regulatory state during the New Deal era.[13] Its strictures were designed to broker a compromise between critics of the regulatory state, who were skeptical of the administrative apparatus's conformity with the Constitution, and supporters of the regulatory state, who advocated for agencies' technical expertise as a necessary response to the problems of an increasingly complex society.[14]

Notice-and-comment rulemaking was the APA's single most significant invention.[15] Before the APA, congressionally created regulatory agencies were able to issue "rules" in the form of decisions resulting from adjudication between regulated parties, which would bind future regulated parties.[16] Congress's decision to give agencies rulemaking authority through notice-and-comment processes was thus a novel democratic guarantee. Congress required regulatory agencies to give all "interested persons an opportunity to participate in the rule making through submission of written data, views, or arguments," and to consider "the relevant matter presented."[17] Congress also required agencies to incorporate a response to the public's comments in a concise statement along with the final regulation.[18] Over time, federal courts gave teeth to the APA's statutory language, requiring agencies to explain their decisionmaking process by teasing out and summarizing major policy issues raised in the comments and explaining the agency's course of action in light of its statutory obligations.[19]

The growth of the regulatory state during the New Deal meant that unelected administrative rulemakers were exercising significant and growing lawmaking authority — an authority derived from a constitutionally uneasy blend of legislative, adjudicative, and executive powers. By allowing the public to weigh in on proposed regulations, Congress's innovation of notice-and-comment rulemaking thus introduced two distinct democratic checks on the federal regulatory state.

---

12. *See generally*, Administrative Procedure Act (APA), 5 U.S.C. §§551-59 (2012) (establishing administrative procedures for agencies).

13. *See* James M. Landis, The Administrative Process 1 (1938).

14. *See* Martin Shapiro, *APA: Past, Present, Future*, 72 Va. L. Rev. 447, 452-54 (1986); *see also* Cass R. Sunstein, *Constitutionalism after the New Deal*, 101 Harv. L. Rev. 421, 448 (1987); McNollgast, *The Political Origins of the Administrative Procedure Act*, 15 J.L. Econ. & Org. 180 (1999).

15. *See* 5 U.S.C. §553 (2012); *see also* Stephen G. Breyer et al., Administrative Law and Regulatory Policy: Problems, Text, and Cases, 519 (7th ed. 2011); Kenneth Culp Davis, Discretionary Justice: A Preliminary Inquiry 65 (1969) (calling informal rulemaking "one of the greatest inventions of modern government").

16. *See* Cary Coglianese, *E-Rulemaking: Information Technology and Regulatory Policy, New Directions in Digital Government Research* 5 (2004) [hereinafter Regulatory Policy Program Report], http://www.ksg.harvard.edu/press/E-Rulemaking_Report.pdf.

17. *See* 5 U.S.C. §553(c).

18. *Id.*

19. *See Indep. U.S. Tanker Owners Comm. v. Dole*, 809 F.2d 847, 852 (D.C. Cir. 1987) ("At the least, such a statement should indicate the major issues of policy that were raised in the proceedings and explain why the agency decided to respond to these issues as it did, particularly in light of the statutory objectives that the rule must serve."); *United States v. Nova Scotia Food Prods. Corp.*, 568 F.2d 240, 252 (2d Cir. 1977) ("To suppress meaningful comment by failure to disclose the basic data relied upon is akin to rejecting comment altogether. For unless there is common ground, the comments are unlikely to be of a quality that might impress a careful agency.").

First, it provided a democratic check on unelected technocrats who were otherwise only indirectly accountable to the American people.[20] Second, requiring public comments on proposed regulations enhanced the information available to regulators.[21] By harnessing the tremendous information power of the American people, notice-and-comment rulemaking prevented regulators from making costly mistakes and improved the quality of regulations by exposing rulemakers to a diversity of information held by industry insiders as well as members of the general public.[22]

In practice, however, the APA's democratic promises fell short. Until the early 1990s, only Beltway insiders made use of the APA's procedural constraints on the administrative state. Before the Internet, members of the public could access proposed and final regulations only by viewing paper copies of the Federal Register and Code of Federal Regulations available at select libraries.[23] And rulemaking "dockets" — an umbrella term encompassing all materials related to a rulemaking, including proposed and final rules, public comments, and scientific and technical findings — sat in file cabinets in vast, disorganized docketing rooms in Washington D.C.[24] Because of the physical impediments to accessing necessary materials, before the Internet, informed participation required physical travel to a labyrinth docketing room in Washington D.C.[25] It is unsurprising, then, that little empirical research is available on public participation in notice-and-comment rulemaking for the first five decades of the APA.[26] Three studies analyzing participation across multiple agencies in 1989, 1992-1994, and 1996, found that the median number of comments submitted for each rule was twenty-five, twelve, and thirty-three, respectively.[27] In a study of fourteen rulemakings from 1996, the greatest number of comments submitted on a single rulemaking was 2,250.[28]

Nearly half a century after the APA's enactment, two changes transformed notice-and-comment's potential from theory to reality: (1) the growing prevalence of notice-and-comment rulemaking as the basis for regulatory activity and (2) the Internet.[29] In large part due to increasingly stringent judicial review, agencies largely shifted from "formal" adjudicatory procedures to "informal" notice-and-comment rulemaking processes.[30] As agencies responded to legal incentives

---

20. *See* 5 U.S.C. §553(c); *see also* Cornelius M. Kerwin & Scott R. Furlong, Rulemaking: How Government Agencies Write Law and Make Policy 167 (4th ed. 2010).

21. *See* 5 U.S.C. §553(c).

22. *See* Sunstein, [Democratizing Regulation, Digitally, Democracy J. (Fall 2014).]

23. *See* Kerwin & Furlong, *supra* note 20, at 10-22.

24. *See* Regulatory Policy Program Report, *supra* note 16, at 10.

25. *Id.* at 10-11; *see also* Breyer et al., *supra* note 15, at 570; [Cynthia Farina, Achieving the Potential: The Future of Federal E-Rule Making 21-22 (2008).]

26. *See* Kerwin & Furlong, *supra* note 20, at 189.

27. *See* Gary Coglianese, *Citizen Participation in Rulemaking: Past, Present, and Future*, 55 Duke L.J. 943, 950 (2006).

28. *See id.*

29. *See* Regulatory Policy Program Report, *supra* note 16, at 5; *see also* Stuart W. Shulman et al., *Electronic Rulemaking: A Public Participation Research Agenda for the Social Sciences*, 126 Soc. Sci. Comput. Rev. 162, 172-73 (2003).

30. *See* Regulatory Policy Program Report, *supra* note 16, at 5.

to utilize notice-and-comment rulemaking, the Internet and the proliferation of personal computers made accessing notices of proposed rulemaking and submitting comments a viable option for the general public. The vast technological advances of the 1980s and 1990s thus breathed new meaning into the democratic accountability and information-enhancing promises motivating the original enactment in the APA. By the mid-1990s, a few early-moving agencies began to remedy democratic deficits in paper-based notice-and-comment rulemaking by experimenting with e-rulemaking by moving regulatory materials and public comments to online forums.

II. E-RULEMAKING: TWO DEMOCRATIC PROMISES MADE POSSIBLE

A. The Innovation and Evolution of E-Rulemaking

The federal government's interest in e-rulemaking is "almost as old as the Internet."[31] In the early 1990s, three agencies — the FCC, the Department of Transportation (DOT), and the Nuclear Regulatory Commission (NRC) — capitalized on the Clinton Administration's identification of a universal demand for "earlier and more frequent" opportunities for participation in the rulemaking process by digitizing rulemaking materials and making them available to the public online.[32] By the mid-1990s, the American people could access the Federal Register and the Code of Federal Regulations online.[33] As agencies increased their utilization of digital technologies, e-rulemaking gained legal legitimacy.[34]

By the turn of the 21st century, the government turned its attention to streamlining individual agency e-rulemaking efforts. In 2002, the Bush Administration enacted the E-Rulemaking Initiative in an effort to simplify cumbersome paper-based rulemaking processes and to digitize materials in a government-wide, centralized online rulemaking management system.[35] To implement its centralized system, the Office of Management and Budget (OMB) prohibited executive agencies from operating "duplicative or ancillary" electronic tools (e-tools) related to rulemaking, reasoning that creating and operating separate systems would waste resources.[36]

---

31. *See* Achieving the Potential, *supra* note [25], at 21 ("The roots of federal *e-rulemaking* stretch back almost as far as creation of the World Wide Web."); *Improving Regulatory Systems*, Nat'l Pub. Radio Library (1993), http://govinfo.library.unt.edu/npr/library/reports/reg04.html (emphasizing the need to develop information technology in order to improve public awareness and participation in the regulatory process).

32. *See* Achieving the Potential, *supra* note [25], at 3, 21-22; Cynthia R. Farina et al., *Rulemaking* 2.0, 65 U. Miami L. Rev. 395, 447 (2011) ("The true potential of Rulemaking 2.0 is unknowable at this point because *e-rulemaking* has not tried systematically to address the barriers of stakeholder unawareness, process ignorance, and rulemaking information overload.").

33. *See* Regulatory Policy Program Report, *supra* note 16, at 13.

34. In 1995, for example, the Administrative Conference of the United States concluded that administering rulemaking online comported with the APA's basic requirements. *See* Kerwin & Furlong, *supra* note 20, at 189.

35. *See* Mark Forman, *E-Government Strategy*, E-Government Task Force, 27 (Feb. 27, 2002), http://photos.state.gov/libraries/bahrain/231771/PDFs/egov_strategy.pdf.

36. *See* Achieving the Potential, *supra* note [25], at 12.

The decision to create a centralized rulemaking web portal was ultimately realized in Regulations.gov.[37] In January 2003, Regulations.gov allowed the public to access and comment on executive agencies' proposed regulations.[38] In September 2005, Regulations.gov was updated to include the Federal Docket Management System (FDMS), an electronic document management database that contains electronic versions of rulemaking materials and simple search mechanisms.[39] FDMS improved management capabilities from the agencies' end.[40] The OMB further revised Regulations.gov in 2007, introducing an RSS feed, a fast indexed-based commercial search engine with a full-text search capability.[41] By 2008, all executive agencies had adopted FDMS and eliminated alternative docket and commenting systems.[42]

B. E-Rulemaking in Executive Agencies

The Obama Administration's emphasis on open government made way for a natural expansion of the Bush Administration's advances in e-rulemaking. The Obama Administration's Executive Order 13,563,[43] a "kind of mini-constitution for the regulatory state,"[44] marks the federal government's most significant commitment to e-rulemaking to date. Issued in January 2011, Executive Order 13,563 requires agencies to base regulations "on the open exchange of information and perspectives among State, local, and tribal officials, experts in relevant disciplines, affected stakeholders in the private sector, and the public as a whole."[45] To promote such an open exchange of information, it directs executive agencies to take three steps to the extent feasible and permitted by law. First, it requires executive agencies to afford the public with a "meaningful opportunity to comment through the Internet on any proposed regulation, with a comment period that should generally be at least 60 days."[46] Second, it obligates executive agencies to use Regulations.gov in order to provide timely access to the rulemaking docket — which includes relevant scientific and technical findings such as the

---

37. *See, e.g., Presidential Initiatives: E-Rulemaking,* White House Archives [hereinafter *Presidential Initiatives*], http://georgewbush-whitehouse.archives.gov/omb/egov/c-3-1-er.html.

38. *See id.* ("With the emergence of the Internet, citizens are going online to exercise this right more than ever before. In January 2003, the interagency eRulemaking Program developed Regulations.gov... to provide citizens with a central place to learn about all proposed regulations and to have their comments shape the rulemaking process at Federal agencies. Regulations.gov removes logistical and institutional barriers that previously made it difficult, if not impossible, for a citizen to navigate the vastness of Federal regulatory activities.").

39. *See* Achieving the Potential, *supra* note [25], at 3, 23-24.

40. *See Presidential Initiatives, supra* note 37 (noting that the Federal Docket Management System (FDMS) provides "secure login, e-Authentication single sign-on, role-based access control, e-mail notification, configurable workflow management, electronic records management... and a system integrated with the digitization and ingestion of paper documents").

41. *Id.*

42. *See* Achieving the Potential, *supra* note [25], at 12.

43. *See* Exec. Order No. 13,563, 76 Fed. Reg. 3,821 (Jan. 18, 2011).

44. *See, e.g.,* Cass R. Sunstein, *The Real World of Cost-Benefit Analysis: Thirty-Six Questions (and Almost as Many Answers),* 114 Colum. L. Rev. 167, 170 (2014).

45. *See* Exec. Order No. 13,563, *supra* note 43, at 3,821.

46. *Id.*

analysis of costs and benefits — in an open format that can be easily searched and downloaded.[47] Third, it requires agencies to provide "an opportunity for public comment on all pertinent parts of the rulemaking docket, including relevant scientific and technical findings."[48] In an effort to extend participation to members of the public likely affected and with relevant expertise, Executive Order 13,563 also instructed agencies to "seek out the views of those who are likely to be affected, including those who are likely to benefit from and those who are potentially subject to such rulemaking."[49]

Executive Order 13,563 reinforced Regulations.gov as the focal point for the public participation in the notice-and-comment process. Today, Regulations.gov provides all executive agencies with access to rulemaking materials, including relevant scientific and technical findings, along with a simple form to submit comments on proposed regulations.[50] Members of the public can browse an education section describing the regulatory process and the role of public comments in informing regulatory decisions, access a particular rulemaking or regulatory activity by using one of the many search functions available on the homepage, and download XML data sets to conduct their own data analysis.[51] FDMS remains the primary interface point for executive agencies.[52] It has eliminated the need for paper records, though comments submitted via email, fax, or mail must be inputted or digitized.[53]

Importantly, Executive Order 13,563 requires executive agencies engaging in e-rulemaking to conduct a cost-benefit analysis. The Order notes that "our regulatory system must protect public health, welfare, safety, and our environment while promoting economic growth, innovation, competitiveness, and job creation."[54] Therefore, the regulatory system must be "based on the best available science," "allow for public participation and an open exchange of ideas," and "promote productivity and reduce uncertainty."[55] To achieve this, the regulatory system must "take into account benefits and costs, both quantitative and qualitative," and use the "best, most innovative, and least burdensome tools for achieving regulatory ends."[56] Accordingly, Executive Order 13,563 requires executive agencies to conduct cost-benefit analysis by:

> (1) propos[ing] or adopt[ing] a regulation only upon a reasoned determination that its benefits justify its costs (recognizing that some benefits and costs are difficult to quantify); (2) tailor[ing] its regulations to impose the least burden on society, consistent with obtaining regulatory objectives, taking into account, among other things, and to the extent practicable, the costs of cumulative regulations; (3) select[ing], in

47. *Id.*
48. *Id.*
49. *Id.*
50. *See* Regulations.gov, http://www.regulations.gov (last visited Oct. 18, 2016).
51. *Id.*
52. Achieving the Potential, *supra* note [25], at 12.
53. *Id.* at 12-13.
54. Exec. Order No. 13,563, *supra* note 43, at 3,821.
55. *Id.*
56. *Id.*

> choosing among alternative regulatory approaches, those approaches that maximize net benefits (including potential economic, environmental, public health and safety, and other advantages; distributive impacts; and equity); (4) to the extent feasible, specify[ing] performance objectives, rather than specifying the behavior or manner of compliance that regulated entities must adopt; and (5) identify[ing] and assess[ing] available alternatives to direct regulation, including providing economic incentives to encourage the desired behavior, such as user fees or marketable permits, or providing information upon which choices can be made by the public.[57]

In applying these principles, the Order directs each agency "to use the best available techniques to quantify anticipated present and future benefits and costs as accurately as possible."[58] Moreover, "where appropriate and permitted by law, each agency may consider (and discuss qualitatively) values that are difficult or impossible to quantify, including equity, human dignity, fairness, and distributive impacts."[59]

C. E-Rulemaking in Independent Agencies

In July 2011, President Obama issued Executive Order 13,579, which provides that independent agencies *should* follow Executive Order 13,563.[60] Under Executive Order 13,579, independent agencies are encouraged but not required to use Regulations.gov and FDMS to provide access to the rulemaking docket and to provide opportunity for public comment. Acknowledging the epistemic potential of e-rulemaking, Executive Order 13,579 provides that regulatory "decisions are informed and improved by allowing interested members of the public to have a meaningful opportunity to participate in rulemaking."[61] Notably, Executive Order 13,579 also makes cost-benefit analysis optional, providing that regulatory decisions "*should* be made only after consideration of their costs and benefits."[62]

Although 160 agencies use FDMS and Regulations.gov, a small number of independent agencies have continued to use their own electronic docketing and online commenting systems as permitted by law.[63] The FCC is one of the few that has not integrated with the federal FDMS system accessible through Regulations.gov. Instead, the FCC manages its own e-rulemaking system, the Electronic Comment Filing System (ECFS).[64] . . .

■ ■ ■

57. *Id.*

58. *Id.*

59. *Id.*

60. Exec. Order No. 13,579, 76 Fed. Reg. 41,587 (July 11, 2011).

61. *Id.*

62. *Id.* (emphasis added).

63. *See generally* Regulations.gov Exchange, White House, *https://www.whitehouse.gov/open/innovations/regulations-gov-exchange* (last visited Oct. 17, 2016).

64. *See Welcome to the New Electronic Comment Filing System*, FCC (last visited Oct. 17, 2016, 5:25 PM), https://www.fcc.gov/ecfs/.

E-rulemaking is highly efficient, but that does not mean the Internet is without its issues. Among today's challenges for administrative agencies in the Internet era is how to deal effectively with rulemaking comments submitted by bots and trolls, or simply to deal with the geometric increase in the number of comments that technology facilitates. For more on these challenges, see Savitz, Public Comments Run Amok: Reforming the Notice and Comment Process to Help Reduce the Negative Effects of Mass and Fake Comments, 69 Buffalo L. Rev. 759 (2021); Weaver, Rulemaking in an Internet Era: Dealing with Bots, Trolls, & "Form Letters", 27 Geo. Mason L. Rev. 553 (2020); Livermore, Eidelman & Grom, Computationally Assisted Regulatory Participation, 93 Notre Dame L. Rev. 977 (2018); Duguay, Views or Votes: The Challenge of Mass Comments in Rulemaking, 26 Geo. Mason L. Rev. 625 (2018).

John L. Gedid

ADMINISTRATIVE PROCEDURE FOR THE TWENTY-FIRST CENTURY: INTRODUCTION TO THE 2010 MODEL STATE ADMINISTRATIVE PROCEDURE ACT

44 St. Mary's L.J. 241, 277-278 (2012)

I. ELECTRONIC PROCEDURE

The 2010 MSAPA also includes entirely new material on electronic procedure. These provisions draw upon developments — the advent of personal computing and the Internet — that have occurred since earlier versions of the MSAPA and deal with technology that did not exist at the time of the last revision of the Act. The 1961 MSAPA had one section on publication, public access, and availability of rules and orders. On the other hand, the 2010 MSAPA contains an innovative, new article involving electronic provisions. Although the article provides more detail than the 1961 MSAPA, it is justified by the unforeseen developments in electronics that have occurred in the past forty years. The drafters explain that "the development of the Internet and the widespread use of electronic media have made public access to agency law and policy much easier. The arrival of the Internet and electronic information transfer . . . has revolutionized communication. It has made available rapid, efficient[,] and low cost communication and information transfer." Consistent with those changes, the stated objective of Article 2 is to "provide easy public access to agency law and policy." The provisions in Article 2 require publication of all notices, rules, guidance documents, and orders on an agency website. Many state and federal agencies have successfully used these types of electronic provisions. (citations omitted).

CHAPTER 4 PROBLEM

Flight-Tex, a wholly owned subsidiary of Tele-Tex Corporation, manufactures flight simulation hardware and software. A significant portion of the subsidiary's sales come from Taiwan and India, in addition to the United States.

Congress created the Transportation Security Administration (TSA) when it adopted the Transportation Security Act. Among other things, the Act charges the TSA with the obligation to "develop policies, strategies, and plans for dealing with threats to transportation security." The Act also states that agency rules must be made after the opportunity for a "public hearing."

A month ago, the TSA announced the following in the Federal Register:

NOTICE OF RULEMAKING

The TSA is Considering Implementing the Following Rule:

The sale of flight simulation equipment by any entity with facilities in the United States shall be prohibited to purchasers in the Middle East.

The statement requested comments on the regulation and established a 15-day comment period, but announced that the rule would be effective immediately. The statement further provided that it was an "interpretation" of the statute but that in the event the statement was later found to be a substantive/legislative rule, the need to protect the United States from possible terrorist attacks constituted "good cause" and excused the TSA from the need to comply with any procedural requirements contained in §553.

Concerned about the impact of the proposition on the company's revenues, Tele-Tex and Flight-Tex submitted written comments based on the notice of rulemaking but complained bitterly about the brief period for comment. Both company and subsidiary requested a chance for oral testimony on the rule. Last week, TSA published a final rule that banned flight simulation software sales to "purchasers located outside the United States." You have been asked by the general counsel of Tele-Tex to discuss the possible challenges that could be made to the final rule, and the likelihood of success. The general counsel has also asked for your opinion about the likelihood that a court might be persuaded to require public hearings by TSA prior to rule promulgation due to the importance of the matter. You placed a call to the agency and talked to an agency official who said that the agency's view is that the words "public hearing" in the statute mean that only written submissions are required, but that in the case of worldwide sales bans, the agency typically does conduct oral hearings, inviting those most affected by the rule to give testimony.

Right to Be Heard

Administrative law is dominated by thinking about the procedures to be applied in any given case. Indeed, "[p]rocedure, not substance, is what most distinguishes our [system] from others." Riverbend Farms v. Madigan, 958 F.2d 1479 (9th Cir. 1992). The right to be heard goes back beyond the very origins of law. In our own system, the law of administrative procedure starts with the constitutional requirement that no person may be deprived of "life, liberty, or property without due process of law." U.S. Const. amends. V, XIV. Due process in its application to administrative law is essentially a requirement of notice and hearing. As Justice Douglas put it some years ago, "[n]otice and opportunity to be heard are fundamental to due process of law." Joint Anti-Fascist Refugee Comm. v. McGrath, 341 U.S. 123, 178 (1951). The notion that persons subject to governmental action should be heard prior to feeling any negative effects is so basic to fundamental justice that many statutes provide for some type of hearing, making constitutional appeals fairly rare. However, recently, as government policymakers have stressed remaking government to favor efficiency over bureaucracy and delay, the concept of being heard has received considerable attention. To what extent can governmental efficiency be reconciled with an individual's right to be heard prior to governmental action? In this chapter, we shall deal with the questions of when due process requires a hearing before agency action and the kind of hearing that due process demands.

A PRIVILEGES

SMITH v. LIQUOR CONTROL COMMISSION

169 N.W.2d 803 (Iowa 1969), app. dismissed, 400 U.S. 885 (1970)

GARFIELD, C.J.

Plaintiff Iris Smith brought certiorari in the district court to review, as in excess of jurisdiction and illegal, orders of Iowa Liquor Control Commission (herein called "commission") confirming the revocation by operation of law of her class "B" state beer permit and cancelling her class "C" Iowa Liquor Control license. Following trial the cancellation of the liquor license was annulled but the order confirming revocation of the state beer permit was sustained. (See rule 316 Rules of Civil Procedure.) Plaintiff has appealed from so much of the court order as sustained the commission's action as to the beer permit. . . .

The trial court reasoned that the statutes under which the beer permit was, in effect, revoked do not require prior notice to the permittee or opportunity to be heard; the right of a state legislature to provide for revocation of permits for the sale of beer without notice or hearing is well established; the commission's return to the writ of certiorari shows it had before it a copy of the record entry of the sentence of Elsie Watts, reports of its investigating officer, a copy of the statement of Steve Johnson, the minor to whom Elsie sold the beer in plaintiff's tavern, with a photocopy of his draft registration card which he exhibited to Elsie showing his then age as eighteen.

The court concluded it cannot be said the commission acted capriciously or arbitrarily (as plaintiff's petition for the writ alleged), with such records before it, in ordering revocation of the permit and the claim the commission denied plaintiff due process of law in so doing without notice or hearing is disposed of by our decision in Walker v. City of Clinton, 244 Iowa 1099, 1102-1105, 59 N.W.2d 785, 787-788. . . .

The errors relied on for reversal are in substance: . . . The commission's order violated plaintiff's constitutional right to due process of law in that it was made without notice to plaintiff or hearing date set.

. . . Plaintiff's brief concedes we have consistently held revocation of beer permits without notice or opportunity for hearing does not violate the permittee's constitutional right to due process of law. In Walker v. City of Clinton, 244 Iowa 1099, 1102-1103, 59 N.W.2d 785, 787, the city council revoked a beer permit issued by it without notice or hearing. In reversing the trial court's annulment of the revocation on certiorari we held:

> The right of a legislature to provide, without notice or hearing, for revocation of licenses, or permits, for the sale of beer is so well established that it seems hardly debatable. Constitutional questions of due process and taking of property without compensation have been repeatedly answered by the statement that a license to . . . sell . . . beer, . . . is a privilege granted by the state and is in no sense a property right. Such a license does not constitute a contract with the state or with the municipality or other governing body which the state empowers to issue it. When the licensee takes this privilege he does so subject to the provisions of the statutes under which it is granted; and if these statutes say or fairly imply that he is entitled to no notice or hearing before revocation, he cannot be heard to complain if he is given none.

Pertinent authorities are reviewed in some detail. The *Walker* decision is followed under similar facts in Michael v. Town of Logan, 247 Iowa 574, 577-579, 73 N.W.2d 714, 716-717.

Anno. 35 A.L.R.2d 1067, 1070, following the report of Green Mountain Post No. 1, American Legion v. Liquor Control Board, 117 Vt. 405, 94 A.2d 230, 35 A.L.R.2d 1060, cites numerous precedents from different jurisdictions, including our *Walker* case, for each of these propositions: "The numerical weight of authority is to the effect that, as a matter of constitutional law, a liquor or beer license can be revoked without notice and hearing" and "In particular, it has been held that due process is not violated by revocation without notice and hearing."

Central States Theatre Corp. v. Sar, 245 Iowa 1254, 1263, 66 N.W.2d 450, 455, holds it is a violation of due process to grant unlimited discretion to an administrative board to deny a license to a legitimate business without setting up reasonable standards for the board to follow. In distinguishing that case from Walker v. City of Clinton, supra, and cases cited therein, the *Central States* opinion says they "are based upon the rule that when a business is inherently illegal a permit to operate may be granted or refused at the will of the licensing body, is a privilege rather than a property right, and may be revoked without notice or hearing." . . .

Affirmed.

NOTES

1. The decision to revoke the beer permit was plainly adjudicatory in nature. Why, then, wasn't the licensee entitled to notice and hearing? The all too easy answer of the Iowa court illustrates the most important exception to the due process right to be heard: due process protects only *life, liberty, or property*. "Due process of law is not applicable unless one is being deprived of something to which he has a right." Bailey v. Richardson, 182 F.2d 46 (D.C. Cir. 1950), aff'd by equally divided Court, 341 U.S. 918 (1951). If the individual is being given something by government to which he has no preexisting "right," he is being given a mere "privilege." Grant of a privilege creates no vested right. As the Iowa court put it in an earlier case, the privilege "may be withdrawn at will and is not entitled to protection under the due process clause." Gilchrist v. Bierring, 14 N.W.2d 724, 730 (Iowa 1944).

2. Under the privilege concept, since government can completely withdraw the privilege, it may impose conditions on it, as the power to exclude altogether includes the lesser power to condition. The next logical step is the approach of the Iowa court, quoted in the *Smith* opinion, that the individual is entitled to only those procedures laid down in the relevant statute: "When the licensee takes this privilege he does so subject to the provisions of the statutes under which it is granted; and if these statutes fairly say or imply that he is entitled to no notice or hearing before revocation, he cannot be heard to complain if he is given none." *Smith*, 169 N.W.2d at 807. How far can the privilege concept be pushed, even if we follow the traditional view that a privilege must be taken under the conditions laid down by the statute? What if the statute conditions grant the privilege on racial or religious factors? See Cafeteria Workers Union v. McElroy, 367 U.S. 886 (1961). Mrs. Brawner had worked for six years as a cook in a privately operated cafeteria on a naval base. Her authority to enter the premises had been withdrawn by the base commander on the ground that she had failed to meet the security requirements of the installation. The Court held that due process did not require a hearing, because she had no "right" to enter the base; access to a military installation was a privilege that could be summarily denied. The Court did, however, recognize that there were constitutional restraints even in such a case: "We may assume that Rachel Brawner could not constitutionally have been excluded . . . if the announced grounds for her exclusion had been patently arbitrary or discriminatory — that she could not have been kept out because she was a Democrat or a Methodist." Id. at 898. But it did not follow that she was entitled to a hearing when the reason given for her exclusion was "entirely rational."

The dividing line drawn by the *Cafeteria Workers* opinion is that between substantive and procedural due process. Even the holder of a privilege is protected by the substantive due process guaranty against arbitrary or discriminatory action. It is only procedural due process that does not protect the privilege.

Compare the following from the dissenting *Cafeteria Workers* opinion of Justice Brennan:

> I assume for present purposes that separation as a "security risk," if the charge is properly established, is not unconstitutional. But the Court goes beyond that. It holds that the mere assertion by government that exclusion is for a valid reason forecloses further inquiry. That is, unless the government official is foolish enough to admit what he is doing — and few will be so foolish after today's decision — he may employ "security requirements" as a blind behind which to dismiss at will for the most discriminatory of causes.
>
> Such a result in effect nullifies the substantive right — not to be arbitrarily injured by Government — which the Court purports to recognize. What sort of right is it which enjoys absolutely no procedural protection?

Id. at 900.

3. *Licenses.* The privilege concept was most widely used in the field of occupational and business licensing. A professional license, such as that to practice law, has always been considered a "right" that may not be taken away summarily. The same is true of other professional licenses, including those of doctors, dentists, chiropractors, and architects, as well as most occupational and business licenses. As the Iowa court once put it, "where the state confers a license to engage in a profession, trade or occupation, not inherently inimical to the public welfare, such license becomes a valuable personal right which cannot be denied or abridged in any manner except after due notice and a fair and impartial hearing." Gilchrist v. Bierring, 14 N.W.2d 724, 912 (Iowa 1944). The court that made this statement distinguished licenses, such as liquor licenses, on the ground that they conferred no rights. The reasoning to support this result was that expressed in Smith v. Liquor Control Comm'n. Licenses to engage in occupations at the opposite end of the scale of social respectability from the learned professions, such as licenses to sell liquor or cigarettes, to operate billiard parlors, dance halls, and the like, were labeled as mere privileges — which meant that they were not protected by procedural due process. Unless a statute provided otherwise, there was no right to be heard before they were suspended or revoked.

4. *Immigration.* Licensing is primarily a state function and the license cases using the privilege concept are state cases. There are, however, also federal privilege cases. Among the most striking are the immigration cases. The leading case is Knauff v. Shaughnessy, 338 U.S. 537 (1950). The question there was whether the United States could exclude the noncitizen wife of a World War II veteran, without hearing, solely on a finding by the Attorney General that her admission would be prejudicial to the interest of the United States. The case presented primarily a question of statutory interpretation — had Congress authorized summary administrative action in a case like this? A bare plurality of the Court held that the relevant statutes allowed action without a hearing. The dissenting Justices felt that the legislative language was not strong enough to deprive this noncitizen of the hearing to which noncitizens seeking admission are normally entitled by statute. But, on the question of the authority of Congress to authorize exclusion without a hearing, the entire Court was in agreement. The reason was the privilege concept. In the words of the *Knauff* Court,

> an alien who seeks admission to this country may not do so under any claim of right. Admission of aliens to the United States is a privilege granted by the sovereign United States Government. Such privilege is granted to an alien only upon such terms as the United States shall prescribe. It must be exercised in accordance with the procedure which the United States provides.

Id. at 542.

Compare the deportation case, where, since the Japanese Immigrant Case, 189 U.S. 86 (1903), it has been established that there is a due process right to be heard. The traditional justification is that a noncitizen who has entered this country has acquired a "right" in remaining, of which he cannot be deprived without a hearing.

5. *Government employment and contracts.* Among the most important privilege cases have been those concerning government employees and government contracts. Government employment and government contracts were regarded as analogous to private employment and private contracts. The public employee was not treated as one vested with "rights" that the courts will enforce. "The petitioner may have a constitutional right to talk politics," reads the famous Holmes statement, "but he has no constitutional right to be a policeman." McAuliffe v. Mayor of New Bedford, 155 Mass. 216, 220 (1892). The same was true of the government contractor. No one has a "right," in the sense of a legal right, to do business with the government.

The result was that neither the public employee nor the government contractor was protected by procedural due process. As the opinion in the *Cafeteria Workers* case, note 2 *supra*, put it, "the Court has consistently recognized that an interest closely analogous to Rachel Brawner's, the interest of a government employee in retaining his job, can be summarily denied. It has become a settled principle that government employment, in the absence of legislation, can be revoked at the will of the appointing officer." 367 U.S. at 896. Similarly, agency decisions could be made in contract debarment cases without giving the government contractor any procedural rights other than those provided for in the relevant statute.

6. *Government largess.* The privilege concept has had its broadest potential in the burgeoning field of social welfare. The traditional approach has been that no person has any "right" to the largess dispensed by government. Such largess was characterized as a mere "gratuity" or "privilege," which could be withheld, granted, or revoked at the pleasure of the donor. This has been true regardless of the nature of the largess dispensed in the particular case — whether it was a pension, welfare aid, veterans' disability benefit, or any other benefit to which the individual had no preexisting "right." In Justice Brandeis' words, "Pensions, compensation, allowances, and privileges are gratuities. They involve no agreement of parties; and the grant of them creates no vested right. The benefits conferred by gratuities may be redistributed or withdrawn at any time in the discretion of Congress." Lynch v. United States, 292 U.S. 571, 577 (1934). Those dependent on public largess were placed in a subordinate status. In 1966, for example, a federal court could dismiss a suit by a welfare recipient on the simple ground that there was no "right" to welfare. Smith v. Board of Comm'rs, 259 F. Supp. 423 (D.D.C. 1966), aff'd, 380 F.2d 632 (D.C. Cir. 1967). At the beginning of 1967, only that one action by welfare claimants had been finally decided in the federal courts.

7. Note also the practical implications of the privilege concept in the evolving society. The expanding area of present-day administrative law is in the field of social welfare. Government has assumed benefactory functions in a geometric progression, becoming a gigantic fount that pours out largess on which an ever-increasing number of people depend. If this entire public largess involves mere privileges, it means that an ever-larger area of administrative power is insulated from the safeguards of procedural due process. Those dependent on public largess become only clients, in a subordinate legal status. Yet it is precisely those who depend on public benefactions who are most in need of protection. Unlike regulated business entities, they have neither the resources nor the ability to protect themselves against arbitrary administrative action. Under the traditional approach, the joyless reaches of the welfare state will be littered with dependents left outside the pale of legal protection.

Does the distinction between "rights" and "privileges" have a legitimate place in present-day administrative law?

Over a half-century ago, Justice Frankfurter pointed out that to describe something as a "privilege" does not meet the problem of due process. Garner v. Board of Public Works, 341 U.S. 716, 725 (1951) (concurring). It does not follow that, because the law does not guarantee a "right" to public employment or a particular benefit, the agency administering the relevant statute should be permitted to resort to any scheme for depriving people of their government positions or benefits. If summarily taking away a "right" is unjust, the same is true of the taking away of a "privilege."

The argument the other way rests on the notion that a "privilege" is something that government need not permit or is under no legal obligation to grant. Thus, the police power plainly includes the power to prohibit the sale of liquor or cigarettes. Similarly, without statutory provisions, there is no legal requirement that government provide any welfare, old age, or comparable benefits. But that has nothing to do with the due process issue. "The fact that the State has a right to regulate, and arguably completely prohibit, the conduct in question here does not relieve it of its duty to regulate fairly." Avard v. Dupuis, 376 F. Supp. 479, 482 (D.N.H. 1974). The legislature may prohibit the sale of liquor; yet, what does that have to do with the question of whether, where the legislature has permitted liquor to be sold under a licensing scheme, the legislative delegate that administers the scheme should be permitted to act without observing the fundamentals of fair play? The tag used to characterize the administrative function should not be determinative. To say that there is no "right" to something like a government contract should not mean that an agency may act arbitrarily (substantively or procedurally) against a person. If it violates due process to take away the doctor's license summarily, the same should be true when the liquor license is revoked summarily.

B ENTITLEMENTS

1. The Due Process Revolution

GOLDBERG v. KELLY

397 U.S. 254 (1970)

MR. JUSTICE BRENNAN delivered the opinion of the Court.

The question for decision is whether a State which terminates public assistance payments to a particular recipient without affording him the opportunity for an evidentiary hearing prior to termination denies the recipient procedural due process in violation of the Due Process Clause of the Fourteenth Amendment.

This action was brought in the District Court for the Southern District of New York by residents of New York City receiving financial aid under the federally assisted program of Aid to Families with Dependent Children (AFDC) or under New York State's general Home Relief program. Their complaint alleged that the New York State and New York City officials administering these programs terminated, or were about to terminate, such aid without prior notice and hearing, thereby denying them due process of law. At the time the suits were filed there was no requirement of prior notice or hearing of any kind before termination of financial aid. However, the State and city adopted procedures for notice and hearing after the suits were brought, and the plaintiffs, appellees here, then challenged the constitutional adequacy of those procedures. . . .

[T]he New York City Department of Social Services promulgated Procedure No. 68-18. A caseworker who has doubts about the recipient's continued eligibility must first discuss them with the recipient. If the caseworker concludes that the recipient is no longer eligible, he recommends termination of aid to a unit supervisor. If the latter concurs, he sends the recipient a letter stating the reasons for proposing to terminate aid and notifying him that within seven days he may request that a higher official review the record, and may support the request with a written statement prepared personally or with the aid of an attorney or other person. If the reviewing official affirms the determination of ineligibility, aid is stopped immediately and the recipient is informed by letter or the reasons for the action. Appellees' challenge to this procedure emphasized the absence of any provisions for the personal appearance of the recipient before the reviewing official, for oral presentation of evidence, and for confrontation and cross-examination of adverse witnesses. However, the letter does inform the recipient that he may request a post-termination "fair hearing." This is a proceeding before an independent state hearing officer at which the recipient may appear personally, offer oral evidence, confront and cross-examine the witnesses against him, and have a record made of the hearing. If the recipient prevails at the "fair hearing" he is paid full funds erroneously withheld. . . . A recipient whose aid is not restored by a "fair hearing" decision may have judicial review. . . .

I

The constitutional issue to be decided, therefore, is the narrow one whether the Due Process Clause requires that the recipient be afforded an evidentiary hearing *before* the termination of benefits. The District Court held that only a pre-termination evidentiary hearing would satisfy the constitutional command, and rejected the argument of the state and city officials that the combination of the post-termination "fair hearing" with the informal pre-termination review disposed of all due process claims. The Court said: "While post-termination review is relevant, there is one overpowering fact which controls here. By hypothesis, a welfare recipient is destitute, without funds or assets. . . . Suffice it to say that to cut off a welfare recipient in the face of . . . 'brutal need' without a prior hearing of some sort is unconscionable, unless overwhelming considerations justify it." Kelly v. Wyman, 294 F. Supp. 893, 899, 900 (1968). The Court rejected the argument that the need to protect the public's tax revenues supplied the requisite "overwhelming consideration."

> Against the justified desire to protect public funds must be weighed the individual's overpowering need in this unique situation not to be wrongfully deprived of assistance. . . . While the problem of additional expense must be kept in mind, it does not justify denying a hearing meeting the ordinary standards of due process. Under all the circumstances, we hold that due process requires an adequate hearing before termination of welfare benefits and the fact that there is a later constitutionally fair proceeding does not alter the result. . . .

Appellant does not contend that procedural due process is not applicable to the termination of welfare benefits. Such benefits are a matter of statutory entitlement for persons qualified to receive them.[1] Their termination involves state action that adjudicates important rights. The constitutional challenge cannot be answered by an argument that public assistance benefits are "a 'privilege' and not a 'right.'" Shapiro v. Thompson, 394 U.S. 618, 627, n.6 (1969). Relevant constitutional restraints apply as much to the withdrawal of public assistance benefits as to disqualification for unemployment compensation, Sherbert v. Verner, 374 U.S. 398 (1963); or to denial of a tax exemption, Speiser v. Randall, 357 U.S. 513 (1958); or to discharge from public employment, Slochower v. Board of Higher Education, 350 U.S. 551 (1956). The extent to which procedural due process must be afforded the recipient is influenced by the extent to which he may be "condemned to suffer grievous loss." . . .

It is true, of course, that some governmental benefits may be administratively terminated without affording the recipient a pre-termination evidentiary hearing. But we agree with the District Court that when welfare is discontinued, only a pre-termination evidentiary hearing provides the recipient with procedural due process. . . . For qualified recipients, welfare provides the means to obtain essential food, clothing, housing, and medical care. . . . Thus the crucial factor in this context — a factor not present in the case of the blacklisted government contractor, the discharged government employee, the taxpayer denied a tax exemption, or virtually anyone else whose governmental largesse is ended — is that termination of aid pending resolution of a controversy over eligibility may deprive an *eligible* recipient of the very means by which to live while he waits. Since he lacks independent resources, his situation becomes immediately desperate. His need to concentrate upon finding the means for daily subsistence, in turn, adversely affects his ability to seek redress from the welfare bureaucracy.

Moreover, important governmental interests are promoted by affording recipients a pre-termination evidentiary hearing. From its founding, the Nation's basic commitment has been to foster the dignity and wellbeing of all persons within its borders. We have come to recognize that forces not within the control of the poor contribute to their poverty. This perception, against the background of our traditions, has significantly influenced the development of the contemporary public assistance system. Welfare, by meeting the basic demands

---

1. It may be realistic today to regard welfare entitlements as more like "property" than a "gratuity." Much of the existing wealth in this country takes the form of rights which do not fall within traditional common-law concepts of property. It has been aptly noted that

> [s]ociety today is built around entitlement. The automobile dealer has his franchise, the doctor and lawyer their professional licenses, the worker his union membership contract and pension rights, the executive his contract and stock options; all are devices to aid security and independence. Many of the most important of these entitlements now flow from government: subsidies to farmers and businessmen, routes for airlines and channels for television stations; long term contracts for defense, space, and education; social security pensions for individuals. Such sources of security, whether private or public, are no longer regarded as luxuries or gratuities; to the recipients they are essentials, fully deserved, and in no sense a form of charity. It is only the poor whose entitlements, although recognized by public policy, have not been effectively enforced.

Reich, Individual Rights and Social Welfare: The Emerging Legal Issues, 74 Yale L.J. 1245, 1255 (1965). See also Reich, The New Property, 73 Yale L.J. 733 (1964).

of subsistence, can help bring within the reach of the poor the same opportunities that are available to others to participate meaningfully in the life of the community. At the same time, welfare guards against the society malaise that may flow from a widespread sense of unjustified frustration and insecurity. Public assistance, then, is not mere charity, but a means to "promote the general Welfare, and secure the Blessings of Liberty to ourselves and our Posterity." The same governmental interests which counsel the provision of welfare, counsel as well its uninterrupted provision to those eligible to receive it; pre-termination evidentiary hearings are indispensable to that end.

Appellant does not challenge the force of these considerations but argues that they are outweighed by countervailing governmental interests in conserving fiscal and administrative resources. These interests, the argument goes, justify the delay of any evidentiary hearing until after discontinuance of the grants. Summary adjudication protects the public fisc by stopping payments promptly upon discovery of reason to believe that a recipient is no longer eligible. Since most terminations are accepted without challenge, summary adjudication also conserves both the fisc and administrative time and energy by reducing the number of evidentiary hearings actually held.

We agree with the District Court, however, that these governmental interests are not overriding in the welfare context. The requirement of a prior hearing doubtless involves some greater expense, and the benefits paid to ineligible recipients pending decision at the hearing probably cannot be recouped, since these recipients are likely to be judgment-proof. But the State is not without weapons to minimize these increased costs. Much of the drain on fiscal and administrative resources can be reduced by developing procedures for prompt pre-termination hearings and by skillful use of personnel and facilities. Indeed, the very provision for a post-termination evidentiary hearing in New York's Home Relief program is itself cogent evidence that the State recognizes the primacy of the public interest in correct eligibility determinations and therefore in the provision of procedural safeguards. Thus, the interest of the eligible recipient in uninterrupted receipt of public assistance, coupled with the State's interest that his payments not be erroneously terminated, clearly outweighs the State's competing concern to prevent any increase in its fiscal and administrative burdens. As the District Court correctly concluded, "[t]he stakes are simply too high for the welfare recipient, and the possibility for honest error or irritable misjudgment too great, to allow termination of aid without giving the recipient a chance, if he so desires, to be fully informed of the case against him so that he may contest its basis and produce evidence in rebuttal." 294 F. Supp. at 904-905.

II

We also agree with the District Court, however, that the pre-termination hearing need not take the form of a judicial or quasi-judicial trial. We bear in mind that the statutory "fair hearing" will provide the recipient with a full administrative review. Accordingly, the pre-termination hearing has one function only: to produce an initial determination of the validity of the welfare department's grounds for discontinuance of payments in order to protect a recipient against an erroneous termination of his benefits. . . . Thus, a complete record and a comprehensive opinion, which would serve primarily to facilitate judicial review and to guide future decisions, need not be provided at the pre-termination stage. We recognize, too, that both welfare authorities and recipients have an interest in relatively speedy resolution of questions of eligibility, that they are used to dealing with one another informally, and that some welfare departments have very burdensome caseloads. These considerations justify the limitation of the pre-termination hearing to minimum procedural safeguards, adapted to the particular characteristics of welfare recipients, and to the limited nature of the controversies to be resolved. We wish to add that we, no less than the dissenters, recognize the importance of not imposing upon the States or the Federal Government in this developing field of law any procedural requirements beyond those demanded by rudimentary due process.

"The fundamental requisite of due process of law is the opportunity to be heard." Grannis v. Ordean, 234 U.S. 385, 394 (1914). The hearing must be "at a meaningful time and in a meaningful manner." Armstrong v. Manzo, 380 U.S. 545, 552 (1965). In the present context these principles require that a recipient have timely and adequate notice detailing the reasons for a proposed termination, and an effective opportunity to defend by confronting any adverse witnesses and by presenting his own arguments and evidence orally. These rights are important in cases such as those before us, where recipients have challenged proposed terminations as resting on incorrect or misleading factual premises or on misapplication of rules or policies to the facts of particular cases.

We are not prepared to say that the seven-days notice currently provided by New York City is constitutionally insufficient per se, although there may be cases where fairness would require that a longer time be given. Nor do we see any constitutional deficiency in the content or form of the notice. New York employs both a letter and a personal conference with a caseworker to inform a recipient of the precise questions raised about his continued eligibility. Evidently the recipient is told the legal and factual bases for the Department's doubts. This combination is probably the most effective method of communicating with recipients.

The city's procedures presently do not permit recipients to appear personally with or without counsel before the official who finally determines continued eligibility. Thus a recipient is not permitted to present evidence to that official orally, or to confront or cross-examine adverse witnesses. These omissions are fatal to the constitutional adequacy of the procedures.

The opportunity to be heard must be tailored to the capacities and circumstances of those who are to be heard. It is not enough that a welfare recipient may present his position to the decision maker in writing or secondhand through his caseworker. Written submissions are an unrealistic option for most recipients, who lack the educational attainment necessary to write effectively and who cannot obtain professional assistance. Moreover, written submissions do not afford the flexibility of oral presentations; they do not permit the recipient to mold his argument to the issues the decision maker appears to regard as important. Particularly where credibility and veracity are at issue, as they must be in many termination proceedings, written submissions are a wholly unsatisfactory basis for decision. The secondhand presentation to the decision maker by the caseworker has its own deficiencies; since the caseworker usually gathers the facts upon which the charge of ineligibility rests, the presentation of the recipient's side of the controversy cannot safely be left to him. Therefore a recipient must be allowed to state his position orally. Informal procedures will suffice; in this context due process does not require a particular order of proof or mode of offering evidence. . . .

In almost every setting where important decisions turn on questions of fact, due process requires an opportunity to confront and cross-examine adverse witnesses. . . .

"The right to be heard would be, in many cases, of little avail if it did not comprehend the right to be heard by counsel." Powell v. Alabama, 287 U.S. 45, 68-69 (1932). We do not say that counsel must be provided at the pre-termination hearing, but only that the recipient must be allowed to retain an attorney if he so desires. Counsel can help delineate the issues, present the factual contentions in an orderly manner, conduct cross-examinations, and generally safeguard the interests of the recipient. We do not anticipate that this assistance will unduly prolong or otherwise encumber the hearing. . . .

Finally, the decision maker's conclusion as to a recipient's eligibility must rest solely on the legal rules and evidence adduced at the hearing.

. . . To demonstrate compliance with this elementary requirement, the decision maker should state the reasons for his determination and indicate the evidence he relied on, . . . though his statement need not amount to a full opinion or even formal findings of fact and conclusions of law. And, of course, an impartial decision maker is essential. . . . We agree with the District Court that prior involvement in some aspects of a case will not necessarily bar a welfare official from acting as a decision maker. He should not, however, have participated in making the determination under review.

Affirmed.

William J. Brennan, Jr.

REASON, PASSION AND "THE PROGRESS OF THE LAW"*

10 Cardozo L. Rev. 3, 19-22 (1988)

[Goldberg v. Kelly] required the Court to confront an issue that the Framers could not have specifically foreseen: the requirements of due process in a bureaucratized society. Some have characterized *Goldberg* as an effort to make the welfare system more rational. They see the Court's insistence that certain trial-type procedures be used in pretermination hearings as a spur to greater formality in welfare administration. From this perspective, *Goldberg* appears as a triumph

* Reprinted with permission. Cardozo Law Review © 1988.

of the model of reason, holding the welfare system to a demanding standard of rationality that only an even more advanced bureaucracy could satisfy.

I certainly have no regrets about the extent to which *Goldberg* may have made the welfare system more rational. I want to suggest, however, that *Goldberg* can be seen in another way. I believe that the decision can be seen as an expression of the importance of passion in governmental conduct, in the sense of attention to the concrete human realities at stake. From this perspective, *Goldberg* can be seen as injecting passion into a system whose abstract rationality had led it astray.

Examining the record in *Goldberg*, one could say that New York's welfare termination procedure provided considerable protection against arbitrary decisions. The state required that, where officials proposed discontinuing benefits, notice describing the reason for this proposal was to be given to the recipient at least seven days in advance. The recipient was permitted to submit a written statement stating why public assistance should not be terminated, and could request that the initial recommendation be reviewed by a higher official. Once this higher official decided that aid should be discontinued, it was. The recipient was then entitled to a hearing before an independent state officer at which the appellant was able to present oral evidence, confront and cross-examine adverse witnesses, and have a record made of the hearing. A recipient whose aid was not restored was then entitled to judicial review. Those who prevailed were entitled to a refund of all money improperly withheld.

In many respects, the New York system for managing welfare terminations was a model of rationality. One who saw the due process clause as a mandate that the state govern according to reason could maintain that the welfare system was constitutionally adequate, for all were subject to rules that were impersonally applied. A significant issue in *Goldberg* therefore was whether progress in the rationality of government always means progress in the law of due process.

The Court said that it does not. The Court did so because it realized that the state's procedures lacked one vital element: appreciation of the drastic consequences of terminating a recipient's only means of subsistence. Provision of a hearing only *after* benefits were terminated was profoundly inappropriate for a person dependent upon the government for the very resources with which to live. As we observed, the situation of such a person "becomes immediately desperate. His need to concentrate upon finding the means for daily subsistence, in turn, adversely affects his ability to seek redress from the welfare bureaucracy." The brief for the recipient told the human stories that the state's administrative regime seemed unable to hear:

> After termination, Angela Valez and her four young children were evicted for nonpayment of rent and all forced to live in one small room of a relative's already crowded apartment. The children had little to eat during the four months it took for the Department to correct its error. Esther Lett and her four children at once began to live on the handouts of impoverished neighbors; within two weeks all five required hospital treatment because of the inadequacy of their diet. Soon after, Esther Lett fainted in a welfare center while seeking an emergency food payment of $15 to feed herself and her children for three days. Pearl Frye and her 8 children

> "had gone hungry," living on peanut butter and jelly sandwiches and rice supplied by friends who were also dependent on public assistance. Juan DeJesus found himself homeless, living in temporary shelter provided by a friend. . . .

The standard rules for reviewing claims of unfair denials of government benefits may have been predictably applied in *Goldberg*, and those rules surely limited the discretion of officials at each stage of the proceedings. Such a product of formal reason, however, did not comport with due process. It did not do so because it lacked that dimension of passion, of empathy, necessary for a full understanding of the human beings affected by those procedures. As the Framers proclaimed by their rejection of Parliamentary sovereignty, merely following the rules is not enough to satisfy the demands of due process.

Goldberg thus demonstrated that the due process clause is not simply the blueprint for an empire of reason. It built upon Cardozo's insights by declaring that sterile rationality is no more appropriate for our administrative officials than for our judges. Whether the government treats its citizens with dignity is a question whose answer must lie in the intricate texture of daily life. Neither a judge nor an administrator who operates on the basis of reason alone can fully grasp that answer, for each is cut off from the wellspring from which concepts such as dignity, decency, and fairness flow. In *Goldberg*, the application of standard rules to all recipients was simply blind to the brute fact of dependence. A government insensitive to such a reality cannot be said to treat individuals with the respect that due process demands — not because its officials do not reason, but because they cannot understand. . . .

NOTES

1. Goldberg v. Kelly marked a watershed in the law of administrative procedure. In his just-quoted Cardozo lecture, Justice Brennan himself characterized *Goldberg* "as the opening shot in a modern 'due process revolution.'" Id. at 19. Not long after it was decided, Judge Friendly asserted that, under it, "we have witnessed a greater expansion of procedural due process . . . than in the entire period since ratification of the Constitution." Friendly, Some Kind of Hearing, 123 U. Pa. L. Rev. 1267, 1273 (1975).

2. Note the statement by the Court that the required hearing "need not take the form of a judicial or quasi-judicial trial." 397 U.S. at 266. Is this statement consistent with the detailed hearing requirements listed by the Court?

What are the essential rights safeguarded in a judicial-type trial? They may be summarized as including the right to:

- **(a)** notice, including an adequate formulation of the subjects and issues involved in the case;
- **(b)** present evidence (both testimonial, typically under oath, and documentary) and argument;

(c) rebut adverse evidence, through cross-examination and other appropriate means;
(d) appear with counsel;
(e) have the decision based only upon evidence introduced into the record of the hearing; and
(f) have a complete record, which consists of a transcript of the testimony and arguments, together with the documentary evidence and all other papers filed in the proceeding.

The details of these rights will be covered in the next chapter. They are listed here for comparison with the hearing requirements stated in Goldberg v. Kelly.

Compare Friendly, Some Kind of Hearing, 123 U. Pa. L. Rev. 1267, 1299 (1975): "Goldberg v. Kelly is the lodestar in this area, but it sheds an uncertain light. After the usual litany that the required hearing 'need not take the form of a judicial or quasi-judicial trial,' Mr. Justice Brennan proceeded to demand almost all the elements of one."

In a footnote, Judge Friendly notes as the two omissions to the Brennan recitation a verbatim transcript and testimony under oath. He disagrees with the comment of one observer that the former has "no significance," citing Davis, Administrative Law Text, 169-170 (3d ed. 1972).

Professor Davis asks, id. at 170, "Do not the items the Court required add up to the opposite of its statement that the hearing 'need not take the form of a judicial or quasi-judicial trial'? What can be the meaning of 'trial' if it is not essentially the sum of the items the Court required?"

3. It should be noted that though, as seen, Goldberg v. Kelly does not demand a formal record, the omission from the Court's list of hearing requirements has little practical significance. In a hearing run by attorneys on both sides, the procedure inevitably approaches that of the courtroom. Goldberg v. Kelly stated as an "elementary requirement" that the decision "must rest solely on the legal rules and evidence adduced at the hearing." The normal way to meet this requirement is to have a verbatim transcript of the evidence and arguments at the hearing, so that the decisionmaker can more readily rest the decision solely on the record and a reviewing court can see that he has done so. At any rate, welfare agencies uniformly have had verbatim transcripts made of hearings held by them in compliance with Goldberg v. Kelly. This has been true even in California, despite McCullough v. Terzian, 470 P.2d 4 (Cal. 1970), which held expressly that there need not be a record in welfare pretermination hearings.

BROOKPARK ENTERTAINMENT, INC. v. TAFT

951 F.2d 710 (6th Cir. 1991)

RALPH B. GUY, JR., Circuit Judge.

The plaintiff, a nightclub, challenges the constitutionality of an Ohio statute allowing for the revocation of its liquor license by popular referendum. The district court dismissed the action, finding that the . . . plaintiff's constitutional challenges were meritless. . . . We hold that the challenged Ohio statute is facially unconstitutional under the Due Process Clause of the Fourteenth Amendment. Therefore, we remand the case to the district court with instructions to enter a judgment for the plaintiff.

I

The facts are essentially undisputed. The plaintiff, Brookpark Entertainment, Inc., operates the Crazy Horse Saloon in Cleveland. Brookpark sells alcoholic beverages under a series of permits issued by the Ohio Department of Liquor Control.

The Department suspended Brookpark's liquor permits during the summer of 1989. On November 16, 1989, the Department found that Brookpark had violated Ohio liquor control laws by selling liquor during the suspension. . . . The Department imposed no penalty for the violation.

The Department's decision not to penalize Brookpark for the violation did not end Brookpark's problems. Under Ohio law, the voters living in the same precinct as a liquor establishment can revoke the establishment's license by referendum within one year of a finding of any liquor law violation. . . . During the summer of 1990, Dale Miller, a Cleveland city council member, and several other citizens began circulating petitions to put Brookpark's liquor license on the ballot. . . . The Board of Elections validated the petitions and certified this question for the November 6, 1990, ballot: "Shall the sale of spirituous liquor, mixed beverages, wine and beer by Brookpark Entertainment, Inc., dba Crazy Horse Saloon at 16600 Brookpark Rd., Cleveland, Ohio 44135 be permitted in this precinct?"

Brookpark filed this action on October 23, 1990, alleging that the Ohio "particular premises" local option law is facially unconstitutional. . . .

Brookpark first argues that the Ohio "particular premises" local option statute violates the Due Process Clause of the Fourteenth Amendment. We agree.

The district court stated, and the defendants argue on appeal, that an Ohio liquor license is not property within the meaning of the Due Process Clause. "The due process clause only protects those interests to which one has a 'legitimate claim of entitlement.' This has been defined to include 'any significant property interests, including statutory entitlements.'" . . . "Government licenses are . . . a form of property insofar as they constitute an entitlement to engage in a valuable activity." . . . An individual having "present enjoyment of the benefit and a claim of entitlement to its continuation under state law [has] a property interest which [is] protected by the due process clause."

To decide whether a liquor license is property under the Due Process Clause, we must examine both Ohio law and federal constitutional law. "Although the underlying substantive interest is created by 'an independent source such as state law,' federal constitutional law determines whether that interest rises to the level of a 'legitimate claim of entitlement' protected by the Due Process

Clause." Memphis Light, Gas & Water Div. v. Craft, 436 U.S. 1, 9 (1978). The license may rise to the level of property under the Due Process Clause even though Ohio chooses not to call it property. "[W]e must look behind labels, and decide whether the plaintiff's license was 'property' in a functional sense." Reed v. Village of Shorewood, 704 F.2d 943, 948 (7th Cir. 1983). In short, we look to Ohio law to determine the *nature* of the interest, not the *label* to apply to it.

We therefore begin our inquiry by examining the interests that attach to an Ohio liquor license. We recently examined Ohio liquor licenses to determine whether they are property for the purposes of federal tax and bankruptcy law. In re Terwilliger's Catering Plus, Inc., 911 F.2d 1168 (6th Cir. 1990). In concluding that Ohio liquor licenses are property, we stated:

> Ohio allows a liquor license to be transferred, sold, inherited, and renewed. . . . It is undeniable that a liquor license has pecuniary value to its holder since the license enables the holder to sell alcoholic beverages and can be sold for value. Since the state has vested the owner of a liquor license with these beneficial interests, a liquor license with these beneficial interests, a liquor license constitutes "property" or "rights to property" within the meaning of federal tax lien law.

Id., 911 F.2d at 1171.

In addition to the rights to transfer, sell, bequeath, and renew, a holder of an Ohio liquor license also has the right to a hearing before revocation and the right to appeal any adverse determination of the Department. Ohio Rev. Code §§4301.27, 4301.28. In *Reed*, the Seventh Circuit held that an Illinois liquor license was property within the meaning of the Due Process Clause even though it could not be sold or bequeathed. 704 F.2d at 948. The court found that the Illinois license was property because the holder had a right of renewal and the license could be securely held for its term unless there was cause for revocation. Id. While the Ohio revocation provision does not state that a license can be revoked only for cause, the notice, hearing, and appeal provisions would be pointless unless the legislature intended there to be some reason for revocation. Since an Ohio license can be sold and bequeathed, it has even more of the attributes of property than the Illinois license at issue in *Reed*.

The defendants rely on a series of Ohio cases to support their contention that a liquor license is not property. In State ex rel. Zugravu v. O'Brien, 130 Ohio St. 23, 196 N.E. 664 (1935), the Ohio Supreme Court concluded that a liquor licensee had no property interests because the legislature could terminate the license. Id. 196 N.E. at 666. . . . The Ohio Court of Appeals has also held that a liquor license is not a property interest. Scioto Trails Co. v. Ohio Dept. of Liquor Control, 11 Ohio App. 3d 75, 462 N.E.2d 1386 (1983). The *Scioto Trails* court cited *Zugravu* for the proposition that no property interest attaches because the license is revocable. Id., 462 N.E.2d at 1389. . . .

The Ohio cases cited by the defendants do not alter our conclusion that a liquor license is property. First, we emphasize that we do not rely on the labels that a state gives to the interests it has created. In deciding that Ohio liquor licenses were property for tax and bankruptcy purposes, we stated:

> Although it is true that the state has the right to decide what property interests it wishes to create, it cannot thwart the operation of the Tax Code by classifying the interests it has created as something other than property rights. . . . While several Ohio courts have refused to label the rights granted to the [liquor] licensee as "property rights," the state nonetheless has chosen to grant the licensee rights tantamount to property rights in all but name.

Terwilliger's, 911 F.2d at 1171-72.

As in *Terwilliger's* we do not find persuasive the labeling applied by the Ohio courts. . . . *Zugravu* [and] *Scioto Trails* . . . hold that the license is not property because the legislature can revoke it. According to this argument, the holder cannot complain about the state-provided deprivation procedures, however unreasonable and arbitrary, because those procedures are part of the interest that the holder knowingly obtained. While this argument has some superficial appeal, the Supreme Court has explicitly rejected it.

[I]t is settled that the "bitter with the sweet" approach misconceives the constitutional guarantee. . . . The point is straightforward: the Due Process Clause provides that certain substantive rights — life, liberty, and property — cannot be deprived except pursuant to constitutionally adequate procedures. The categories of substance and procedure are distinct. Were the rules otherwise, the Clause would be reduced to a mere tautology. *"Property" cannot be defined by the procedures provided for its deprivation any more than can life or liberty. The right to due process "is conferred, not by legislative grace, but by constitutional guarantee.* While the legislature may elect not to confer a property interest in [public] employment, it may not constitutionally authorize the deprivation of such an interest, once conferred, without appropriate procedural safeguards." Cleveland Bd. of Educ. v. Loudermill, 470 U.S. 532, 541 (1985).

An Ohio liquor licensee holds a substantial and valuable interest and has a claim to its continuation under state law. Accordingly, we hold that a holder of an Ohio liquor license has a property interest protected under the Due Process Clause. Therefore, the state must accord a liquor licensee due process before revoking the license. [The court held that the license could not be revoked by referendum, but only after the notice and hearing required by due process.]

Accordingly, we reverse the district court's dismissal and remand the case with instructions to enter a declaratory judgment that the challenged provisions of the Ohio liquor control law facially violate the Due Process Clause. We further instruct the district court to grant Brookpark appropriate injunctive relief and other relief as necessary. . . .

NOTES

1. What about the other pre–Goldberg v. Kelly privilege cases? Is the government employee now protected by procedural due process? See Cleveland Bd. of Education v. Loudermill, 470 U.S. 532 (1985). Is the same true of the government contractor? See W. G. Cosby Transfer Corp. v. Froehlke, 480 F.2d 498 (4th Cir. 1973).

2. The big exception to Goldberg v. Kelly is the case of the entering immigrant. See Landon v. Plasencia, 459 U.S. 21 (1982). It arose out of an order, following an exclusion hearing, that denied the respondent, a permanent resident immigrant, admission to the United States when she attempted to return from a brief visit abroad. The court of appeals held that a meaningful departure from the country did not occur and therefore the respondent was entitled to a deportation hearing. The Supreme Court disagreed, holding that only an exclusion proceeding was involved. The Immigration and Naturalization Service (now ICE) could determine whether the respondent was attempting to "enter" the United States and whether she was excludable. In her opinion, Justice O'Connor stated, "This Court has long held that an alien seeking initial admission to the United States acquires a privilege and has no constitutional rights regarding his application." Id. at 32. On the other hand, once an alien gains admission, his constitutional status changes. He then "is entitled to a fair hearing when threatened with deportation." Id.

Henry J. Friendly

SOME KIND OF HEARING*

123 U. Pa. L. Rev. 1267, 1275-1277 (1975)

Good sense would suggest that there must be some floor below which no hearing of any sort is required. One wonders whether even the most outspoken of the Justices would require one on the complaint of an AFDC recipient, recounted by Professor Bernard Schwartz, that "I didn't receive one housedress, underwears. . . . They gave me two underwears for $14.10 . . . it should have been $17.60 instead of $14.10."[1]

Although the value of even small benefits should not be deprecated, given the precarious financial condition of the recipients of AFDC, the cost of providing an evidentiary hearing in such a case must so far outweigh the likelihood or the value of more accurate determinations that final reliance should be placed

* Reprinted by permission. University of Pennsylvania Law Review © 1975.

1. Schwartz & Wade, [Legal Control of Government (1972)] at 123. The quoted remarks were made by an AFDC recipient who was complaining that the special welfare grant she had received was less than the full grant for which she had applied. See also Baum, Mass Administrative Justice: AFDC Fair Hearings 52-53 (paper presented at ABA Section of Administrative Law, Center for Administrative Justice, Conference June 4-6, 1973). . . .

The lengthy procedures now required with respect to reductions in, or denials of, special benefits to AFDC recipients are principally the result of federal regulations and state "fair hearing" statutes. See, e.g., 45 C.F.R. §205.10 (1973); 18 N.Y.C.R.R. §358.16 (1974) (prescribing details of fair hearing in New York). See also id. §§358.4(a)-(c) (1974) (hearing protection for recipients of food stamps, cash assistance benefits, and social services). However, given the expressed dissatisfaction of state officials with federal hearing requirements, see Baum, supra at 25, 32-38 and the recent loosening of the federal regulations, see Developments in Welfare Law — 1973, 59 Cornell L. Rev. 859, 936-39 (1974), it is quite possible that state "fair hearing" statutes and regulations will be limited, thereby provoking a constitutional battle.

on the informed good faith of program administrators. Until recently one would have thought there was also a floor with respect to school discipline, but Goss v. Lopez [*infra* p. 424] seems to permit dispensing with a "rudimentary hearing" only in the case of "[s]tudents whose presence poses a continuing danger to persons or property or an ongoing threat of disrupting the academic process. . . ."

It should be realized that procedural requirements entail the expenditure of limited resources, that at some point the benefit to individuals from an additional safeguard is substantially outweighed by the cost of providing such protection, and that the expense of protecting those likely to be found undeserving will probably come out of the pockets of the deserving.[2] This is particularly true in an area such as public housing where the number of qualified applicants greatly exceeds the available space, so that, from an overall standpoint, the erroneous rejection or even the eviction of one family may mean only that an equally deserving one will benefit. However, particularly in the light of Goss v. Lopez, it seems impossible at the moment to predict at what level, if any, the Court will set the floor below which no hearing is needed.

2. Flexible Due Process

GOSS v. LOPEZ

419 U.S. 565 (1975)

MR. JUSTICE WHITE delivered the opinion of the Court.

This appeal by various administrators of the Columbus, Ohio, Public School System ("CPSS") challenges the judgment of a three-judge federal court, declaring that appellees — various high school students in the CPSS — were denied due process of law contrary to the command of the Fourteenth Amendment in that they were temporarily suspended from their high schools without a hearing either prior to suspension or within a reasonable time thereafter, and enjoining the administrators to remove all references to such suspensions from the students' records.

2. . . . . Some of the potential dimensions of the problem are reflected by the fact that in 1972 more than thirteen million persons received maintenance assistance under the federal government's various categorical assistance programs, at a cost of about $10.5 billion. By far the most significant category was Aid to Families with Dependent Children (AFDC) which numbered about 10.5 million persons as recipients and cost approximately $6.5 billion. Baum, supra note 1, at 1. Balanced against the assistance claimant's interest in receiving a full and fair hearing with respect to any proposed action affecting his aid is the legitimate interest of the states and federal government in expunging unqualified recipients from the welfare roles. For example, in 1971 the state of Michigan paid out about $450,000 to recipients awaiting negative action hearings and the initial decision was reversed in only 8 percent of a recent sample of such cases. Id. 32.

I

. . . The proof below established that the suspension in question arose out of a period of widespread student unrest in the CPSS during February and March of 1971. Six of the named plaintiffs, Rudolph Sutton, Tyrone Washington, Susan Cooper, Deborah Fox, Clarence Byars and Bruce Harris, were students at the Marion-Franklin High School and were each suspended for ten days on account of disruptive or disobedient conduct committed in the presence of the school administrator who ordered the suspension. One of these, Tyrone Washington, was among a group of students demonstrating in the school auditorium while a class was being conducted there. He was ordered by the school principal to leave, refused to do so and was suspended. Rudolph Sutton, in the presence of the principal, physically attacked a police officer who was attempting to remove Tyrone Washington from the auditorium. He was immediately suspended. The other four Marion-Franklin students were suspended for similar conduct. None was given a hearing to determine the operative facts underlying the suspension, but each, together with his or her parents, was offered the opportunity to attend a conference, subsequent to the effective date of the suspension, to discuss the student's future. . . .

On the basis of this evidence, the three-judge court declared that plaintiffs were denied due process of law because they were "suspended without hearing prior to suspension or within a reasonable time thereafter," and that §3313.66 Ohio Rev. Code and regulations issued pursuant thereto were unconstitutional in permitting such suspensions. It was ordered that all references to plaintiffs' suspensions be removed from school files. . . .

The defendant school administrators have appealed the three-judge court's decision. Because the order below granted plaintiffs' request for an injunction — ordering defendants to expunge their records — this Court has jurisdiction of the appeal pursuant to 28 U.S.C. §1253. We affirm.

II

At the outset, appellants contend that because there is no constitutional right to an education at public expense, the Due Process Clause does not protect against expulsions from the public school system. This position misconceives the nature of the issue and is refuted by prior decisions. The Fourteenth Amendment forbids the State to deprive any person of life, liberty or property without due process of law. Protected interests in property are normally "not created by the Constitution. Rather, they are created and their dimensions are defined" by an independent source such as state statutes or rules entitling the citizen to certain benefits. Board of Regents v. Roth, 408 U.S. 564, 577. . . .

Here, on the basis of state law, appellees plainly had legitimate claims of entitlement to a public education. Ohio Rev. Code §§3313.48 and 3313.64 direct local authorities to provide a free education to all residents between six and twenty-one years of age, and a compulsory attendance law requires attendance for a school year of not less than thirty-two weeks. Ohio Rev. Code §3321.04. It is true that §3313.66 of the code permits school principals to suspend students for up to two weeks; but suspensions may not be imposed without any grounds whatsoever. All of the schools had their own rules specifying the grounds for expulsion or suspension. Having chosen to extend the right to an education to people of appellees' class generally, Ohio may not withdraw that right on grounds of misconduct absent fundamentally fair procedures to determine whether the misconduct has occurred. . . .

. . . The authority possessed by the State to prescribe and enforce standards of conduct in its schools, although concededly very broad, must be exercised consistently with constitutional safeguards. Among other things, the State is constrained to recognize a student's legitimate entitlement to a public education as a property interest which is protected by the Due Process Clause and which may not be taken away for misconduct without adherence to the minimum procedures required by that clause.

The Due Process Clause also forbids arbitrary deprivations of liberty. "Where a person's good name, reputation, honor, or integrity is at stake because of what the government is doing to him," the minimal requirements of the clause must be satisfied. . . . School authorities here suspended appellees from school for periods of up to ten days based on charges of misconduct. If sustained and recorded, those charges could seriously damage the students' standing with their fellow pupils and their teachers as well as interfere with later opportunities for higher education and employment. It is apparent that the claimed right of the State to determine unilaterally and without process whether that misconduct has occurred immediately collides with the requirements of the Constitution.

Appellants proceed to argue that even if there is a right to a public education protected by the Due Process Clause generally, the clause comes into play only when the State subjects a student to a "severe detriment or grievous loss." The loss of ten days, it is said, is neither severe nor grievous and the Due Process Clause is therefore of no relevance. Appellee's argument is again refuted by our prior decisions; for in determining "whether due process requirements apply in the first place, we must look not to the 'weight' but to the *nature* of the interest at stake." Board of Regents v. Roth, [408 U.S. 564 (1972)]. . . .

A short suspension is of course a far milder deprivation than expulsion. But, "education is perhaps the most important function of state and local governments." Brown v. Board of Education, 347 U.S. 483, 493 (1954), and the total exclusion from the educational process for more than a trivial period, and certainly if the suspension is for ten days, is a serious event in the life of the suspended child. Neither the property interest in educational benefits temporarily denied nor the liberty interest in reputation, which is also implicated, is so insubstantial that suspensions may constitutionally be imposed by any procedure the school chooses, no matter how arbitrary.

III

"Once it is determined that due process applies, the question remains what process is due." . . .

. . . At the very minimum . . . students facing suspension and the consequent interference with a protected property interest must be given *some* kind of notice and afforded *some* kind of hearing. "Parties whose rights are to be affected are entitled to be heard; and in order that they may enjoy that right they must first be notified." Baldwin v. Hale, 68 U.S. 223, 233 (1863).

It also appears from our cases that the timing and content of the notice and the nature of the hearing will depend on appropriate accommodation of the competing interests involved. . . . The student's interest is to avoid unfair or mistaken exclusion from the educational process, with all of its unfortunate consequences. The Due Process Clause will not shield him from suspensions properly imposed, but it disserves both his interest and the interest of the State if his suspension is in fact unwarranted. The concern would be mostly academic if the disciplinary process were a totally accurate, unerring process, never mistaken and never unfair. Unfortunately, that is not the case, and no one suggests that it is. Disciplinarians, although proceeding in utmost good faith, frequently act on the reports and advice of others; and the controlling facts and the nature of the conduct under challenge are often disputed. The risk of error is not at all trivial, and it should be guarded against if that may be done without prohibitive cost or interference with the educational process.

The difficulty is that our schools are vast and complex. Some modicum of discipline and order is essential if the educational function is to be performed. Events calling for discipline are frequent occurrences and sometimes require immediate, effective action. Suspension is considered not only to be a necessary tool to maintain order but a valuable education device. The prospect of imposing elaborate hearing requirements in every suspension case is viewed with great concern, and many school authorities may well prefer the untrammeled power to act unilaterally, unhampered by rules about notice and hearing. But it would be a strange disciplinary system in an educational institution if no communication was sought by the disciplinarian with the student in an effort to inform him of his defalcation and to let him tell his side of the story in order to make sure that an injustice is not done. . . .

We do not believe that school authorities must be totally free from notice and hearing requirements if their schools are to operate with acceptable efficiency. Students facing temporary suspension have interests qualifying for protection of the Due Process Clause, and due process requires, in connection with a suspension of ten days or less, that the student be given oral or written notice of the charges against him and, if he denies them, an explanation of the evidence the authorities have and an opportunity to present his side of the story. The clause requires at least these rudimentary precautions against unfair or mistaken findings of misconduct and arbitrary exclusion from school.

There need be no delay between the time "notice" is given and the time of the hearing. In the great majority of cases the disciplinarian may informally discuss the alleged misconduct with the student minutes after it has occurred. We hold only that, in being given an opportunity to explain his version of the facts at this discussion, the student first be told what he is accused of doing and what the basis of the accusation is. . . . Since the hearing may occur almost immediately following the misconduct, it follows that as a general rule notice and hearing should precede removal of the student from school. We agree with the District Court, however, that there are recurring situations in which prior notice and hearing cannot be insisted upon. Students whose presence poses a continuing danger to persons or property or an ongoing threat of disrupting the academic process may be immediately removed from school. In such cases, the necessary notice and rudimentary hearing should follow as soon as practicable, as the District Court indicated.

In holding as we do, we do not believe that we have imposed procedures on school disciplinarians which are inappropriate in a classroom setting. Instead we have imposed requirements which are, if anything, less than a fair-minded school principal would impose upon himself in order to avoid unfair suspensions. . . .

We stop short of construing the Due Process Clause to require, countrywide, that hearings in connection with short suspensions must afford the student the opportunity to secure counsel, to confront and cross-examine witnesses supporting the charge or to call his own witnesses to verify his version of the incident. Brief disciplinary suspensions are almost countless. To impose in each such case even truncated trial-type procedures might well overwhelm administrative facilities in many places and, by diverting resources, cost more than it would save in educational effectiveness. Moreover, further formalizing the suspension process and escalating its formality and adversary nature may not only make it too costly as a regular disciplinary tool but also destroy its effectiveness as part of the teaching process.

On the other hand, requiring effective notice and informal hearing permitting the student to give his version of the events will provide a meaningful hedge against erroneous action. At least the disciplinarian will be alerted to the existence of disputes about facts and arguments about cause and effect. He may then determine himself to summon the accuser, permit cross-examination and allow the student to present his own witnesses. In more difficult cases, he may permit counsel. In any event, his discretion will be more informed and we think the risk of error substantially reduced.

Requiring that there be at least an informal give-and-take between student and disciplinarian, preferably prior to the suspension, will add little to the fact-finding function where the disciplinarian has himself witnessed the conduct forming the basis for the charge. But things are not always as they seem to be, and the student will at least have the opportunity to characterize his conduct and put it in what he deems the proper context.

We should also make it clear that we have addressed ourselves solely to the short suspension, not exceeding ten days. Longer suspensions or expulsions for the remainder of the school term, or permanently, may require more formal procedures. Nor do we put aside the possibility that in unusual situations, although involving only a short suspension, something more than the rudimentary procedures will be required.

IV

The District Court found each of the suspensions involved here to have occurred without a hearing, either before or after the suspension, and that each suspension was therefore invalid and the statute unconstitutional insofar as it permits such suspensions without notice or hearing. Accordingly, the judgment is affirmed.

MR. JUSTICE POWELL, with whom THE CHIEF JUSTICE, MR. JUSTICE BLACKMUN, and MR. JUSTICE REHNQUIST join, dissenting.

The Court today invalidates an Ohio statute that permits student suspensions from school without a hearing "for not more than ten days." The decision unnecessarily opens avenues for judicial intervention in the operation of our public schools that may affect adversely the quality of education. The Court holds for the first time that the federal courts, rather than educational officials and state legislatures, have the authority to determine the rules applicable to routine classroom discipline of children and teenagers in the public schools. It justifies this unprecedented intrusion into the process of elementary and secondary education by identifying a new constitutional right: the right of a student not to be suspended for as much as a single day without notice and a due process hearing either before or promptly following the suspension. . . .

No one can foresee the ultimate frontiers of the new "thicket" the Court now enters. Today's ruling appears to sweep within the protected interest in education a multitude of discretionary decisions in the educational process. Teachers and other school authorities are required to make decisions that may have serious consequences for the pupil. . . .

It hardly need be said that if a student, as a result of a day's suspension, suffers "a blow" to his "self-esteem," "feels powerless," views "teachers with resentment," or feels "stigmatized by his teachers," identical psychological harms will flow from many other routine and necessary school decisions. The student who is given a failing grade, who is not promoted, who is excluded from certain extracurricular activities, who is assigned to a school reserved for children of less than average ability, or who is placed in the "vocational" rather than the "college preparatory" track, is unlikely to suffer any less psychological injury than if he were suspended for a day for a relatively minor infraction.

If, as seems apparent, the Court will now require due process procedures whenever such routine school decisions are challenged, the impact upon public education will be serious indeed. The discretion and judgment of federal courts across the land often will be substituted for that of the fifty state legislatures, the 14,000 school boards and the 2,000,000 teachers who heretofore have been responsible for the administration of the American public school system. If the Court perceives a rational and analytically sound distinction between the discretionary decision by school authorities to suspend a pupil for a brief period, and the types of discretionary school decisions described above, it would be prudent to articulate it in today's opinion. Otherwise, the federal courts should prepare themselves for a vast new role in society.

Not so long ago, state deprivations of the most significant forms of state largesse were not thought to require due process protection on the ground that the deprivation resulted only in the loss of a state provided "benefit." . . . In recent years the Court, wisely in my view, has rejected the "wooden distinction between 'rights' and 'privileges,'" Board of Regents v. Roth, [408 U.S. 564 (1972),] and looked instead to the significance of the state created or enforced right and to the substantiality of the alleged deprivation. Today's opinion appears to abandon this reasonable approach by holding in effect that government infringement of any interest to which a person is entitled, no matter what the interest or how inconsequential the infringement, requires *constitutional* protection. As it is difficult to think of any less consequential infringement than suspension of a junior high school student for a single day, it is equally difficult to perceive any principled limit to the new reach of procedural due process.

NOTES

1. Note Justice Powell's assertion that the *Goss* holding applies to the "student who is given a failing grade, who is not promoted . . . or who is placed in the 'vocational' rather than the 'college preparatory' track." Does *Goss* apply to academic, as well as disciplinary, determinations? See Board of Curators of University of Missouri v. Horowitz, 435 U.S. 78 (1978).

2. Compare Ingraham v. Wright, 430 U.S. 651 (1977). The question at issue was whether imposition of disciplinary corporal punishment in public school was consonant with the requirements of due process. The Court found that corporal punishment implicated a constitutionally protected liberty interest. It did not, however, conclude from this that notice and hearing were required by due process prior to imposition of the disciplinary penalty. In this case, said the Court, traditional common law remedies were fully adequate to afford due process.

3. Is *Ingraham* consistent with Goss v. Lopez? According to the *Ingraham* opinion, the two cases are different: "Unlike Goss v. Lopez . . . , this case does not involve the state-created property interest in public education. The purpose of corporal punishment is to correct a child's behavior without interrupting his education."

4. *Flexible due process.* The *Goss* case suggests strongly for the first time after *Goldberg* that due process requirements might be viewed flexibly, based on circumstances at hand. Judge Friendly cites as an example of how the flexible due process approach would work cases involving counsel in school discipline cases governed by Goss v. Lopez, *supra*:

> One possible application . . . in the school situation might be allowing the school officials to appoint a staff member to assist the student in the preparation of his

> defense in lieu of retaining counsel. Similarly, courts may distinguish between the right to retain counsel at different levels of the educational process (e.g., secondary school v. college) based on a difference in the perceived effect on the overall educational process of the presence of such counsel in disciplinary proceedings. Goss v. Lopez would not seem to proscribe such experimentation and differentiation since although intimating in dictum that "more formal procedures" might be required in cases of longer suspension or expulsion, the holding — in the context of a "short suspension" — left it to the informed discretion of the school administrator to determine whether counsel should be permitted in a particular case.

Friendly, *supra* p. 431, at 1289.

Under Judge Friendly's approach, due process requirements depend on incremental analysis — i.e., gains versus losses for each additional procedure required. Full judicialization may be demanded in cases with the most serious consequences, such as welfare termination or school expulsion. In other cases, due process may demand less judicialization. Since there are alternatives less burdensome than fully judicialized hearings, the law should choose the less burdensome alternatives where the incremental gain in the more burdensome procedure would be outweighed by the marginal cost, e.g., in time and expense. Goldberg v. Kelly, *supra* p. 419, used such an incremental approach. The opinion there stated that "[t]he extent to which procedural due process must be afforded the recipient is influenced by the extent to which he may be 'condemned to suffer grievous loss' . . . and depends upon whether the recipient's interest in avoiding that loss outweighs the governmental interest in summary adjudication." Compare the similar approach in Mathews v. Eldridge, *infra* p. 440.

What has been said comes down to the principle that, even where due process imposes a right to be heard, it does not necessarily demand all the essentials of a judicial trial in every case.

5. The drastic consequences involved in the cutting off of welfare led Goldberg v. Kelly to demand all but full judicialization for welfare termination hearings. In Goss v. Lopez, on the other hand, where school suspensions were ruled subject to due process procedural requirements, the Court stated only that students facing suspension "must be given some kind of notice and afforded some kind of hearing." The *Goss* opinion stated expressly that it stopped "short of construing the due process clause to require, countrywide, that hearings in connection with short suspensions must afford the student the opportunity to secure counsel, to confront and cross-examine witnesses . . . or to call his own witnesses. . . ." *Goss*, 419 U.S. at 583. Because the impact of a short suspension on the student was slight as compared with the undesirable consequences of subjecting routine school discipline to the formalities of trial-type procedures, an informal hearing was all that was required. In what the *Goss* opinion called the "informal give-and-take between student and disciplinarian," it was up to the latter whether to summon the accuser, permit cross-examination, allow the student to present witnesses, or permit counsel. Id. at 584. Though both welfare terminations and short student suspensions adversely affect individual entitlements and are consequently subject to due process requirements, the detailed procedures demanded are not the same in both cases.

See Ingraham v. Wright, 430 U.S. 651 (1977), discussed in *supra* notes 2 and 3, where the Court held that due process did not require notice and hearing prior to imposition of corporal punishment in public schools. The *Ingraham* opinion went on to say that "even if the need for advance procedural safeguards were clear, the question would remain whether the incremental benefit could justify the cost." Id. at 680. Prior hearing as a universal constitutional requirement in corporal punishment cases would unduly burden school discipline. "At some point the benefit of an additional safeguard to the individual affected . . . and to society in terms of increased assurance that the action is just, may be outweighed by the cost.' . . . We think that point has been reached in this case." Id. at 682.

MATHEWS v. ELDRIDGE

424 U.S. 319 (1976)

MR. JUSTICE POWELL delivered the opinion of the Court.

The issue in this case is whether the Due Process Clause of the Fifth Amendment requires that prior to the termination of Social Security disability benefit payments the recipient be afforded an opportunity for an evidentiary hearing.

I

Cash benefits are provided to workers during periods in which they are completely disabled under the disability insurance benefits program created by the 1956 amendments to Title II of the Social Security Act. 70 Stat. 815, 42 U.S.C. §423. Respondent Eldridge was first awarded benefits in June 1968. In March 1972, he received a questionnaire from the state agency charged with monitoring his medical condition. Eldridge completed the questionnaire, indicating that his condition had not improved and identifying the medical sources, including physicians, from whom he had received treatment recently. The state agency then obtained reports from his physician and a psychiatric consultant. After considering these reports and other information in his file the agency informed Eldridge by letter that it had made a tentative determination that his disability had ceased in May 1972. The letter included a statement of reasons for the proposed termination of benefits, and advised Eldridge that he might request reasonable time in which to obtain and submit additional information pertaining to his condition.

In his written response, Eldridge disputed one characterization of his medical condition and indicated that the agency already had enough evidence to establish his disability. The state agency then made its final determination that he had ceased to be disabled in May 1972. This determination was accepted by the Social Security Administration (SSA), which notified Eldridge in July that his benefits would terminate after that month. The notification also advised him of his right to seek reconsideration by the state agency of this initial determination within six months.

Instead of requesting reconsideration Eldridge commenced this action challenging the constitutional validity of the administrative procedures established by the Secretary of Health, Education, and Welfare for assessing whether there exists a continuing disability.... In support of his contention that due process requires a pretermination hearing, Eldridge relied exclusively upon this Court's decision in Goldberg v. Kelly, 397 U.S. 254 (1970), which established a right to an "evidentiary hearing" prior to termination of welfare benefits. The Secretary contended that *Goldberg* was not controlling since eligibility for disability benefits, unlike eligibility for welfare benefits, is not based on financial need and since issues of credibility and veracity do not play a significant role in the disability entitlement decision, which turns primarily on medical evidence.

The District Court concluded that the administrative procedures pursuant to which the Secretary had terminated Eldridge's benefits abridged his right to procedural due process. The court viewed the interest of the disability recipient in uninterrupted benefits as indistinguishable from that of the welfare recipient in *Goldberg*. It further noted that decisions subsequent to *Goldberg* demonstrated that the due process requirement of pretermination hearings is not limited to situations involving the deprivation of vital necessities.... Reasoning that disability determinations may involve subjective judgments based on conflicting medical and nonmedical evidence, the District Court held that prior to termination of benefits Eldridge must be afforded an evidentiary hearing of the type required for welfare beneficiaries under Title IV of the Social Security Act. Id., at 528. Relying entirely upon the District Court's opinion, the Court of Appeals for the Fourth Circuit affirmed the injunction barring termination of Eldridge's benefits prior to an evidentiary hearing. 493 F.2d 1230 (1974). We reverse....

III

A

Procedural due process imposes constraints on governmental decisions which deprive individuals of "liberty" or "property" interests within the meaning of the Due Process Clause of the Fifth or Fourteenth Amendments. The Secretary does not contend that procedural due process is inapplicable to terminations of social security disability benefits. He recognizes, as has been implicit in our prior decisions ... that the interest of an individual in continued receipt of these benefits is a statutorily created "property" interest protected by the Fifth Amendment.... Rather, the Secretary contends that the existing administrative procedures, detailed below, provide all the process that is constitutionally due before a recipient can be deprived of that interest.

This court consistently has held that some form of hearing is required before an individual is finally deprived of a property interest. . . . The "right to be heard before being condemned to suffer grievous loss of any kind, even though it may not involve the stigma and hardships of criminal conviction, is a principle basic to our society." . . . The fundamental requirement of due process is the opportunity to be heard "at a meaningful time and in a meaningful manner." . . . Eldridge agrees that the review procedures available to a claimant before the initial determination of ineligibility becomes final would be adequate if disability benefits were not terminated until after the evidentiary hearing stage of the administrative process. The dispute centers upon what process is due prior to the initial termination of benefits, pending review.

In recent years this Court increasingly has had occasion to consider the extent to which due process requires an evidentiary hearing prior to the deprivation of some type of property interest even if such a hearing is provided thereafter. In only one case, Goldberg v. Kelly, 397 U.S. 254, 266-271 (1970), has the Court held that a hearing closely approximating a judicial trial is necessary. In other cases requiring some type of pretermination hearing as a matter of constitutional right the Court has spoken sparingly about the requisite procedures. Sniadach v. Family Finance Corp., 395 U.S. 337 (1969), involving garnishment of wages, was entirely silent on the matter. In Fuentes v. Shevin, 407 U.S. 67, 96-97 (1972), the Court said only that in a replevin suit between two private parties the initial determination required something more than an ex parte proceeding before a court clerk. Similarly, Bell v. Burson, 402 U.S. 535, 540 (1971), held, in the context of the revocation of a state-granted driver's license, that due process required only that the prerevocation hearing involve a probable-cause determination as to the fault of the licensee, noting that the hearing "need not take the form of a full adjudication of the question of liability." See also North Georgia Finishing, Inc. v. DiChem, Inc., 419 U.S. 601, 607 (1975). More recently, in Arnett v. Kennedy, 416 U.S. 134 (1974), we sustained the validity of procedures by which a federal employee could be dismissed for cause. They included notice of the action sought, a copy of the charge, reasonable time for filing a written response, and an opportunity for an oral appearance. Following dismissal, an evidentiary hearing was provided. Id. at 142-146.

These decisions underscore the truism that "'[d]ue process,' unlike some legal rules, is not a technical conception with a fixed content unrelated to time, place and circumstances." Cafeteria & Restaurant Workers Local 473 v. McElroy, 367 U.S. 886, 895 (1961). "[D]ue process is flexible and calls for such procedural protections as the particular situation demands." Morrissey v. Brewer, 408 U.S. 471, 481 (1972). Accordingly, resolution of the issue whether the administrative procedures provided here are constitutionally sufficient requires analysis of the governmental and private interests that are affected. Arnett v. Kennedy, 416 U.S., at 167-168 (Powell, J., concurring); Goldberg v. Kelly, 397 U.S., at 263-266; Cafeteria & Restaurant Workers Local 473 v. McElroy, 367 U.S., at 895. More precisely, our prior decisions indicate that identification of the specific dictates of due process generally requires consideration of three distinct factors: first, the private interest that will be affected by the official action; second, the risk of an erroneous deprivation of such interest through the procedures used, and the probable value, if any, of additional or substitute procedural safeguards; and finally, the government's interest, including the function involved and the fiscal and administrative burdens that the additional or substitute procedural requirement would entail. See, e.g., Goldberg v. Kelly, 397 U.S., at 263-271.

We turn first to a description of the procedures for the termination of Social Security disability benefits, and thereafter consider the factors bearing upon the constitutional adequacy of these procedures.

B

The disability insurance program is administered jointly by state and federal agencies. State agencies make the initial determination whether a disability exists, when it began, and when it ceased. 42 U.S.C. §421. The standards applied and the procedures followed are prescribed by the Secretary, see §421(b), who has delegated his responsibilities and powers under the Act to the SSA. See 40 Fed. Reg. 4473 (1975).

. . . The principal reasons for benefits termination are that the worker is no longer disabled or has returned to work. As Eldridge's benefits were terminated because he was determined to be no longer disabled, we consider only the sufficiency of the procedures involved in such cases.

The continuing eligibility investigation is made by a state agency acting through a "team" consisting of a physician and a nonmedical person trained in disability evaluation. The agency periodically communicates with the disabled worker, usually by mail — in which case he is sent a detailed questionnaire — or by telephone, and requests information concerning his present condition, including current medical restrictions and sources of treatment, and any additional information that he considers relevant to his continued entitlement to benefits. SSA Claims Manual (CM) §6705.1; Disability Insurance State Manual (DISM) §353.3.

Information regarding the recipient's current condition is also obtained from his sources of medical treatment. DISM §353.4. If there is a conflict between the information provided by the beneficiary and that obtained from medical sources such as his physician, or between two sources of treatment, the agency may arrange for an examination by an independent consulting physician. Ibid. Whenever the agency's tentative assessment of the beneficiary's condition differs from his own assessment, the beneficiary is informed that benefits may be terminated, provided a summary of the evidence upon which the proposed determination to terminate is based, and afforded an opportunity to review the medical reports and other evidence in his case file. He also may respond in writing and submit additional evidence. Id., §353.6.

The state agency then makes its final determination, which is reviewed by an examiner in the SSA Bureau of Disability Insurance. 42 U.S.C. §421©; CM §§6701(b), (c). If, as is usually the case, the SSA accepts the agency determination it notifies the recipient in writing, informing him of the reasons for the decision, and of his right to seek de novo reconsideration by the state agency. 20 C.F.R. §§404.907, 404.909. Upon acceptance by the SSA, benefits are terminated effective two months after the month in which medical recovery is found to have occurred. 42 U.S.C. (Supp. III) §423(a).

If the recipient seeks reconsideration by the state agency and the determination is adverse, the SSA reviews the reconsideration determination and notifies the recipient of the decision. He then has a right to an evidentiary hearing before an SSA administrative law judge. 20 C.F.R. §§404.917, 404.927. The hearing is nonadversary, and the SSA is not represented by counsel. As at all prior and subsequent stages of the administrative process, however, the claimant may be represented by counsel or other spokesmen. §404.934. If this hearing results in an adverse decision, the claimant is entitled to request discretionary review by the SSA Appeals Council, §404.945, and finally may obtain judicial review. 42 U.S.C. §405(g); 20 C.F.R. §404.951.

Should it be determined at any point after termination of benefits, that the claimant's disability extended beyond the date of cessation initially established, the worker is entitled to retroactive payments. 42 U.S.C. §404. Cf. id., §423(b); 20 C.F.R. §§404.501, 404.503, 404.504. If, on the other hand, a beneficiary receives any payments to which he is later determined not to be entitled, the statute authorizes the Secretary to attempt to recoup these funds in specified circumstances. 42 U.S.C. §404.

C

Despite the elaborate character of the administrative procedures provided by the Secretary, the courts below held them to be constitutionally inadequate, concluding that due process requires an evidentiary hearing prior to termination. In light of the private and governmental interests at stake here and the nature of the existing procedures, we think this was error.

Since a recipient whose benefits are terminated is awarded full retroactive relief if he ultimately prevails, his sole interest is in the uninterrupted receipt of this source of income pending final administrative decision on his claim. His potential injury is thus similar in nature to that of the welfare recipient in *Goldberg*, see 397 U.S., at 263-264, the nonprobationary federal employee in *Arnett*, see 416 U.S., at 146, and the wage earner in *Sniadach*. See 395 U.S., at 341-342.

Only in *Goldberg* has the Court held that due process requires an evidentiary hearing prior to a temporary deprivation. It was emphasized there that welfare assistance is given to persons on the very margin of subsistence: "The crucial factor in this context — a factor not present in the case of . . . virtually anyone else whose governmental entitlements are ended — is that termination of aid pending resolution of a controversy over eligibility may deprive an *eligible* recipient of the very means by which to live while he waits." 397 U.S., at 264 (emphasis in original). Eligibility for disability benefits, in contrast, is not based upon financial need. Indeed, it is wholly unrelated to the worker's income or support from many other sources, such as earnings of other family members, workmen's compensation awards, tort claims awards, savings, private insurance, public or private pensions, veterans' benefits, food stamps, public assistance, or the "many other important programs both public and private, which contain provisions for disability payments affecting a substantial portion of the work force. . . ." Richardson v. Belcher, 404 U.S., at 85-87 (Douglas, J., dissenting). . . .

As *Goldberg* illustrates, the degree of potential deprivation that may be created by a particular decision is a factor to be considered in assessing the validity of any administrative decisionmaking process. . . . The potential deprivation here is generally likely to be less than in *Goldberg*, although the degree of difference can be overstated. As the District Court emphasized, to remain eligible for benefits a recipient must be "unable to engage in substantial gainful activity." 42 U.S.C. §423; 361 F. Supp., at 523. Thus, in contrast to the discharged federal employee in *Arnett*, there is little possibility that the terminated recipient will be able to find even temporary employment to ameliorate the interim loss.

As we recognized last Term in Fusari v. Steinberg, 419 U.S. 379, 389 (1975), "the possible length of wrongful deprivation of . . . benefits [also] is an important factor in assessing the impact of official action on private interests." The Secretary concedes that the delay between a request for a hearing before an Administrative Law Judge and a decision on the claim is currently between ten and eleven months. Since a terminated recipient must first obtain a reconsideration decision as a prerequisite to invoking his right to an evidentiary hearing, the delay between the actual cut-off of benefits and final decision after a hearing exceeds one year.

In view of the torpidity of this administrative review process, cf. id., at 383-384, 386, and the typically modest resources of the family unit of the physically disabled worker, the hardship imposed upon the erroneously terminated disability recipient may be significant. Still, the disabled worker's need is likely to be less than that of a welfare recipient. In addition to the possibility of access to private resources, other forms of government assistance will become available where the termination of disability benefits places a worker or his family below the subsistence level. See Arnett v. Kennedy, supra, at 169 (Powell, J., concurring), id., at 201-202 (White, J., concurring in part and dissenting in part). In view of these potential sources of temporary income, there is less reason here than in *Goldberg* to depart from the ordinary principle, established by our decisions, that something less than an evidentiary hearing is sufficient prior to adverse administrative action.

D

An additional factor to be considered here is the fairness and reliability of the existing pretermination procedures, and the probable value, if any, of additional procedural safeguards. Central to the evaluation of any administrative process is the nature of the relevant inquiry . . . . In order to remain eligible for benefits the disabled worker must demonstrate by means of "medically acceptable clinical and diagnostic techniques," 42 U.S.C. §423(d)(3), that he is unable "to engage in any substantial gainful activity by reason of any *medically determinable* physical or mental impairment. . . ." §423(a)(1)(A) (emphasis supplied). In short, a medical assessment of the worker's physical or mental condition is required. This is a more sharply focused and easily documented decision than the typical determination of welfare entitlement. In the latter case, a wide variety of information may be deemed relevant, and issues of witness credibility and veracity often are critical to the decisionmaking process. *Goldberg* noted that in such circumstances "written submissions are a wholly unsatisfactory basis for decision." 397 U.S., at 269.

By contrast, the decision whether to discontinue disability benefits will turn, in most cases, upon, "routine, standard, and unbiased medical reports by physician specialists," Richardson v. Perales, 402 U.S., at 404, concerning a subject whom they have personally examined. In *Richardson* the Court recognized the "reliability and probative worth of written medical reports," emphasizing that while there may be "professional disagreement with the medical conclusions" the "specter of questionable credibility and veracity is not present." Id., at 405, 407. To be sure, credibility and veracity may be a factor in the ultimate disability assessment in some cases. But procedural due process rules are shaped by the risk of error inherent in the truth-finding process as applied to the generality of cases, not the rare exceptions. The potential value of an evidentiary hearing, or even oral presentation to the decisionmaker, is substantially less in this context than in *Goldberg.*

The decision in *Goldberg* also was based on the Court's conclusion that written submissions were an inadequate substitute for oral presentation because they did not provide an effective means for the recipient to communicate his case to the decisionmaker. Written submissions were viewed as an unrealistic option, for most recipients lacked the "educational attainment necessary to write effectively" and could not afford professional assistance. In addition, such submissions would not provide the "flexibility of oral presentations" or "permit the recipient to mold his argument to the issues the decisionmaker appears to regard as important." 397 U.S., at 269. In the context of the disability-benefits-entitlement assessment the administrative procedures under review here fully answer these objections.

The detailed questionnaire which the state agency periodically sends the recipient identifies with particularity the information relevant to the entitlement decision, and the recipient is invited to obtain assistance from the local SSA office in completing the questionnaire. More important, the information critical to the entitlement decision usually is derived from medical sources, such as the treating physician. Such sources are likely to be able to communicate more effectively through written documents than are welfare recipients or the lay witnesses supporting their cause. The conclusions of physicians often are supported by X-rays and the results of clinical or laboratory tests, information typically more amenable to written than to oral presentation. . . .

A further safeguard against mistake is the policy of allowing the disability recipient or his representative full access to all information relied upon by the state agency. In addition, prior to the cut-off of benefits the agency informs the recipient of its tentative assessment, the reasons therefor, and provides a summary of the evidence that it considers most relevant. Opportunity is then afforded the recipient to submit additional evidence or arguments, enabling him to challenge directly the accuracy of information in his file as well as the correctness of the agency's tentative conclusions. These procedures, again as contrasted with those before the Court in *Goldberg*, enable the recipient to "mold" his argument to respond to the precise issues which the decisionmaker regards as crucial.

Despite these carefully structured procedures, amici point to the significant reversal rate for appealed cases as clear evidence that the current process is inadequate. Depending upon the base selected and the line of analysis followed, the relevant reversal rates urged by the contending parties vary from a high of 58.6 percent for appealed reconsideration decisions to an overall reversal rate of only 3.3 percent. Bare statistics rarely provide a satisfactory measure of the fairness of a decisionmaking process. Their adequacy is especially suspect here since the administrative review system is operated on an open-file basis. A recipient may always submit new evidence, and such submissions may result in additional medical examinations. Such fresh examinations are held in approximately 30 percent to 40 percent of the appealed cases, either at the reconsideration or evidentiary hearing stage of the administrative process. . . . In this context, the value of reversal rate statistics as one means of evaluating the adequacy of the pre-termination process is diminished. Thus, although we view such information as relevant, it is certainly not controlling in this case.

E

In striking the appropriate due process balance the final factor to be assessed is the public interest. This includes the administrative burden and other societal costs that would be associated with requiring, as a matter of constitutional right, an evidentiary hearing upon demand in all cases prior to the termination of disability benefits. The most visible burden would be the incremental cost resulting from the increased number of hearings and the expense of providing benefits to ineligible recipients pending decision. No one can predict the extent of the increase, but the fact that full benefits would continue until after such hearings would assure the exhaustion in most cases of this attractive option. Nor would the theoretical right of the Secretary to recover undeserved benefits result, as a practical matter, in any substantial offset to the added outlay of public funds. The parties submit widely varying estimates of the probable additional financial cost. We only need say that experience with the constitutionalizing of government procedures suggests that the ultimate additional cost in terms of money and administrative burden would not be insubstantial.

Financial cost alone is not a controlling weight in determining whether due process requires a particular procedural safeguard prior to some administrative decision. But the Government's interest, and hence that of the public, in conserving scarce fiscal and administrative resources, is a factor that must be weighed. At some point the benefit of an additional safeguard to the individual affected by the administrative action and to society in terms of increased assurance that the action is just, may be outweighed by the cost. Significantly, the cost of protecting those whom the preliminary administrative process has identified as likely to be found undeserving may in the end come out of the pockets of the deserving since resources available for any particular program of social welfare are not unlimited. . . .

But more is implicated in cases of this type than ad hoc weighing of fiscal and administrative burdens against the interests of a particular category of claimants. The ultimate balance involves a determination as to when, under our constitutional system, judicial-type procedures must be imposed upon administrative action to assure fairness. We reiterate the wise admonishment of Mr. Justice Frankfurter that differences in the origin and function of administrative agencies "preclude wholesale transplantation of the rules of procedure, trial, and review which have evolved from the history and experience of the courts." FCC v. Pottsville Broadcasting Co., 309 U.S. 134, 143 (1940). The judicial model of an evidentiary hearing is neither a required, nor even the most effective, method of decision making in all circumstances. The essence of due process is the requirement that "a person in jeopardy of serious loss [be given] notice of the case against him and opportunity to meet it." Joint Anti-Fascist Refugee Committee v. McGrath, 341 U.S., at 171-172 (Frankfurter, J., concurring.) All that is necessary is that the procedures be tailored, in light of the decision to be made, to "the capacities and circumstances of those who are to be heard," Goldberg v. Kelly, 397 U.S., at 268-269 (footnote omitted), to insure that they are given a meaningful opportunity to present their case. In assessing what process is due in this case, substantial weight must be given to the good-faith judgments of the individuals charged by Congress with the administration of the social welfare system that the procedures they have provided assure fair consideration of the entitlement claims of individuals. See Arnett v. Kennedy, 416 U.S., at 202 (White, J., concurring and dissenting in part). This is especially so where, as here, the prescribed procedures not only provide the claimant with an effective process for asserting his claim prior to any administrative action, but also assure a right to an evidentiary hearing, as well as to subsequent judicial review, before the denial of his claim becomes final. Cf. Boddie v. Connecticut, 401 U.S., 371, 378 (1971).

We conclude that an evidentiary hearing is not required prior to the termination of disability benefits and that the present administrative procedures fully comport with due process.

The judgment of the Court of Appeals is reversed.

[JUSTICES BRENNAN and MARSHALL dissented. JUSTICE STEVENS took no part in the case.]

NOTES

1. See J. Mashaw, Due Process in the Administrative State 102-103 (1985):

> [Under Mathews v. Eldridge,] instrumental rationality is recognized as the goal of administrative decision-making. Procedure is to be evaluated in terms of its competence, in particular, its propensity to prevent error. The necessary trade-offs between individual protection from erroneous deprivations and the accomplishment of collective ends through governmental action are to be considered explicitly. Due process adjudication henceforth should proceed not as a battle of obscure and competing precedents, analogies, and abstract legal characterizations, but by attention to the costs and benefits of organizing administrative decision-making in one form or another.

2. A commentator asserts that the Court's application of Mathews v. Eldridge has been "erratic, even incoherent." Robinson, American Bureaucracy: Public Choice and Public Law 121 (1991). Is this valid? Compare O'Connor, J., dissenting, in Zinermon v. Burch, 494 U.S. 113, 148-149 (1990): the Mathews v. Eldridge "test reflects a carefully crafted accommodation of conflicting interests weighed in light of what fundamental fairness requires."

3. Before Mathews v. Eldridge, the federal courts had held that the Goldberg v. Kelly requirement of a pretermination hearing applied to cases involving monetary benefits, comparable to welfare payments:

Unemployment compensation. California Human Resources Dep't v. Java, 402 U.S. 121 (1971) (though the Court avoided the due process issue by holding that the hearing was required by the governing federal statute, Justice Douglas, concurring, declared, "here, as in *Goldberg*, the requirements of procedural due process protect the payment of benefits owing the displaced employees").

Medicare payments. Martinez v. Richardson, 472 F.2d 1121 (10th Cir. 1973).

Veterans pension benefits. Plato v. Roudebush, 397 F. Supp. 1295 (D. Md. 1975).

Are all these cases overruled by Mathews v. Eldridge? In cases other than welfare cases where only monetary entitlements are at stake, will the Mathews v. Eldridge balance ever tilt against the government?

4. Under Goss v. Lopez, *supra* p. 432, school pupils must be afforded presuspension hearings, even where the suspensions are for shorter than ten days. Presumably this means that due process requires hearings before even very brief suspensions. Is such a requirement for a pupil suspended for a few days — or even a few hours — consistent with Mathews v. Eldridge?

Justice Powell emphasizes that "the degree of potential deprivation that may be created by a particular decision is a factor to be considered in assessing the validity of any administrative decision-making process." 424 U.S. at 341. If that is the case, who suffers the greater deprivation, the pupil subject to a short suspension or the disabled worker whose disability payments are ended?

5. If a post-termination hearing is enough in disability cases, is the same true in all other monetary benefit cases other than welfare cases? See Robbins v. Railroad Retirement Bd., 594 F.2d 448 (5th Cir. 1979) (pretermination hearing not required by due process in unemployment benefits case; enough if fair post-termination procedures provided). Why should the Goldberg v. Kelly welfare case now be treated differently since, as Justice Powell recognizes, even with regard to the degree of deprivation the difference between welfare and disability termination can be overstated? According to Curlott v. Campbell, 598 F.2d 1175, 1181 (9th Cir. 1979), Goldberg v. Kelly is "unique and exceptional because welfare benefits provide the means by which welfare recipients live."

See Redish & Marshall, Adjudicatory Independence and the Values of Procedural Due Process, 95 Yale L.J. 455, 472 (1986):

> The development of the *Mathews* balancing test gave rise to a structure within which an individual can possess an undisputed property interest — and thus, a clear right to due process — but have no right to any procedures at all. In other words, balancing can lead to the anomalous result that an individual will have a clear due process right to no process.

Do you agree? See City of Los Angeles v. David, 538 U.S. 715 (2003) (although due process is invoked, there is no right to a prompt hearing when a delay causes a purely monetary harm).

REAMS v. IRVIN

561 F.3d 1258 (11th Cir. 2009)

BIRCH, Circuit Judge:

Edna Reams ("Reams") appeals the district court's grant of summary judgment on qualified immunity grounds in favor of Tommy Irvin, Commissioner of the Georgia Department of Agriculture ("GDA"); Melissa Dennis, Director of the Equine Division of the GDA; and Laura Fokes, an equine inspector employed by the state of Georgia (collectively, "Appellees"), in this 42 U.S.C. §1983 civil rights action arising out of Appellees' impoundment of forty-nine of Reams' equine[s]. On appeal, Reams argues that Appellees were not entitled to qualified immunity because their failure to provide her with (1) an opportunity to be heard prior to seizing her equines, (2) adequate notice of her right to and the procedures for requesting a hearing, and (3) adequate post-deprivation process, violated her clearly established due process rights. For the reasons that follow, we AFFIRM.

I. BACKGROUND

On 3 January 2006, Fokes obtained a warrant from the Macon County Magistrate Court to inspect Reams' family farm, located in Andersonville, Georgia, to determine whether the equines Reams kept on her land were being provided inadequate food and water in violation of the Georgia Humane Care for Equines Act, O.C.G.A. §4-13-1 (2008) ("the Act"). On 5 January 2006, Fokes and Dennis, along with Henry Loper, a doctor of veterinary medicine ("DVM") and federal Veterinary Medical Officer ("VMO") employed by the United States Department of Agriculture as a field veterinarian, arrived at Reams' farm to execute the warrant. Dr. Loper determined that forty-six horses and three donkeys were not being provided with adequate food and water. As a result of Dr. Loper's assessment, GDA officials impounded those forty-nine equines. Reams, who was in Kansas when GDA officials executed the warrant, was not advised of her right to challenge the impoundment.

During a 26 January 2006 conference with Dennis and Fokes, Reams contested the impoundment and requested a hearing. Appellees did not at that time advise Reams of her right to file a petition with the GDA pursuant to O.C.G.A. §2-2-9.1(d). . . . Irvin subsequently issued an administrative order, citing Reams with failure to provide adequate food, water, and/or humane care to the impounded equines, directing her to reduce her herd to thirty equines, and assessing a fine of $74,000. It was not until she received the administrative order that Reams was explicitly notified of her right to a hearing. On 28 February 2006, Reams filed a Petition for Agency Review with the GDA challenging the administrative order, including the impoundment of her horses. After the GDA informed Reams that it would sell her equines if she refused to sign [a] consent order, Reams filed an emergency petition in Fulton County Superior Court to stay the sale of her equines pending the administrative review. On 23 March 2006, the court issued an order staying the sale of Reams' horses and authorizing Reams to retrieve her horses from the impound facility, so long as she provided a written assurance of adequate care and posted a $47,360 bond for the impoundment costs. The order also permitted GDA officials to access Reams' property until the conclusion of her administrative appeal in order to inspect the previously seized equines. At her own expense, Reams retrieved her equines, whose condition, she alleged, had worsened during their impoundment.

While her administrative action was still pending, Reams filed the instant §1983 complaint in the United States District Court for the Northern District of Georgia. On 31 July 2006, she filed a motion with the GDA to stay the administrative proceedings pending the determination of her constitutional claims in federal court. . . .

In July 2007, Appellees moved for summary judgment on Reams' §1983 complaint, arguing that (1) Reams failed to show that she was denied procedural due process because a pre-deprivation hearing was impracticable, and (2) O.C.G.A. §2-2-9.1(d), which allows an owner of equines to contest an impoundment or an administrative order of the GDA disposing of impounded property, provided constitutionally adequate post-deprivation process.

The district court granted the motion, finding that Reams failed to demonstrate a constitutional violation and therefore, appellees were entitled to qualified immunity . . . . Reams now appeals.

II. DISCUSSION

On appeal, Reams argues that the district court erred in finding that: (1) a pre-deprivation hearing was not required; (2) statutory notice of a hearing right was sufficient; and (3) the post-deprivation process was adequate to satisfy due process. She asserts that because she demonstrated that GDA officials violated her clearly established due process rights, the district court erred in concluding that they were entitled to qualified immunity.

A. Right to Pre-Deprivation Hearing

"The fundamental requirement of due process is the opportunity to be heard 'at a meaningful time and in a meaningful manner.'" Mathews v. Eldridge, 424 U.S. 319, 333, 96 S. Ct. 893, 902, 47 L. Ed. 2d 18 (1976) . . . ("Due process entitles an individual to notice and some form of hearing before state action may finally deprive him or her of a property interest."). In this case, Reams contends that a hearing prior to the impoundment of her equines was required to satisfy due process. We disagree.

Although the Due Process Clause generally requires notice and an opportunity to be heard *before* the government seizes one's property, see, e.g., Quik Cash Pawn & Jewelry, Inc. v. Sheriff of Broward County, 279 F.3d 1316, 1322 (11th Cir. 2002), the Supreme Court has "rejected the proposition that 'at a meaningful time and in a meaningful manner' *always* requires the State to provide a hearing prior to the initial deprivation of property." Parratt v. Taylor, 451 U.S. 527, 540-41, 101 S. Ct. 1908, 1915-16, 68 L. Ed. 2d 420 (1981) (noting that its rejection of such a rule "is based in part on the impracticability in some cases of providing any preseizure hearing under a state-authorized procedure, and the assumption that at some time a full and meaningful hearing will be available"), overruled on other grounds by Daniels v. Williams, 474 U.S. 327, 106 S. Ct. 662, 88 L. Ed. 2d 662 (1986). Rather, because "due process is a flexible concept that varies with the particular circumstances of each case," we must apply the balancing test articulated in Mathews v. Eldridge, 424 U.S. 319, 96 S. Ct. 893, 47 L. Ed. 2d 18, to determine whether pre-deprivation process was required in this case. *Grayden*, 345 F.3d at 1232-33; see also Bailey v. Bd. of County Com'rs of Alachua County, Fla., 956 F.2d 1112, 1123 n.12 (11th Cir. 1992) ("The need for some form of pre-deprivation hearing is determined from balancing the competing interests at stake."). Under *Mathews*, the specific dictates of due process in any given case are determined by considering: (1) the private interest that will be affected by the official action; (2) the risk of an erroneous deprivation of such interest through the procedures used and the probable value, if any, of additional or substitute procedural safeguards; and (3) the government's interest, "including the function involved and the fiscal and administrative burdens that the additional or substitute procedural requirement would entail." 424 U.S. at 335, 96 S. Ct. at 903.

While Reams' interest in maintaining her property rights to the impounded equines was not insubstantial, see, e.g., Porter v. DiBlasio, 93 F.3d 301, 306 (7th

Cir. 1996) ("[T]here can be no dispute that an animal owner has a substantial interest in maintaining his rights in a seized animal. Such is especially the case with potential income-generating animals such as horses."), given the standards and procedures for inspection and impoundment prescribed by the Act, and the fact that the state largely complied with these procedures, we find that the risk of an erroneous deprivation in this case was relatively low. See *Grayden*, 345 F.3d at 1234-35 (standards and procedures for inspection and condemnation under city code, which authorized enforcement officer to enter and inspect building to determine its condition, provided protection against risk of erroneous deprivation); cf. Siebert v. Severino, 256 F.3d 648, 660 (7th Cir. 2001) (risk of erroneous deprivation of interest in horses was great where state used volunteer investigator "who apparently lacked sufficient knowledge about horses to determine whether appropriate care was given"). Insofar as the decision to impound Reams' equines was based upon an examination of the equines and an assessment of their condition by a veterinarian, we find that an evidentiary hearing prior to impoundment was of limited potential value and thus agree with the district court that a post-deprivation, versus a pre-deprivation, hearing was "unlikely to spawn significant factual errors." . . . Moreover, as demonstrated by the GDA's immediate seizure of Reams' equines, requiring additional procedural safeguards in the form of a hearing prior to impoundment would run the risk of causing further harm to animals who are being deprived of adequate food and water. Cf. *Siebert*, 256 F.3d at 660.

Finally, the state's interest in preventing the inhumane treatment of animals is undeniably substantial and would be significantly compromised if the state were to require a hearing before impounding malnourished equines. Based on the foregoing, we conclude that a balancing of the competing interests in this case demonstrates that a pre-deprivation hearing was not mandated by the Due Process Clause.

B. Adequacy of Notice

We also reject Reams' contention that she was entitled to personal notice of her right to challenge the impoundment. To be constitutionally adequate, "notice must be 'reasonably calculated, under all the circumstances, to apprise interested parties of the pendency of the action and afford them an opportunity to present their objections.'" *Grayden*, 345 F.3d at 1242 (quoting Mullane v. Cen. Hanover Bank & Trust Co., 339 U.S. 306, 314, 70 S. Ct. 652, 657, 94 L. Ed. 865 (1950)). "For one hundred years, the Supreme Court has declared that a publicly available statute may be sufficient to provide [constitutionally adequate] notice because individuals are presumptively charged with knowledge of such a statute." Id. at 1239. Thus, where remedial procedures are "established by published, generally available state statutes and case law," law enforcement officials need not take additional steps to inform a property owner of her remedies. City of West Covina v. Perkins, 525 U.S. 234, 241, 119 S. Ct. 678, 681, 142 L. Ed. 2d 636 (1999). Cf. *Memphis Light*, 436 U.S. at 19, 98 S. Ct. at 1565 (where administrative procedures for resolving accounting disputes were not described in any publicly available document, due process required utility company to inform customers of those procedures "or some specified avenue of relief").

In *Grayden*, we held that statutory notice of state remedies in connection with a condemnation order that gave the tenants only thirty-six hours to vacate their homes was constitutionally inadequate because it was not "reasonably calculated to inform the tenants . . . of their right to choose between acquiescing in or contesting [the] condemnation order." 345 F.3d at 1243. In so holding, we emphasized the "extremely important" fact that the tenants were facing eviction and had only thirty-six hours to vacate their homes, during which time "they had to complete a multitude of tasks, which ranged from securing alternate shelter to collecting their personal belongings to making accommodations for work or school." Id.

. . .

Under the circumstances of this case, we find that statutory notice of the right to contest the impoundment was reasonably calculated to provide Reams with contemporaneous notice of her right to, and the procedures for requesting, a hearing, and was thus constitutionally sufficient. Pursuant to O.C.G.A. §2-2-9.1(d), Reams had thirty days from the time of the impoundment to request a hearing. [T]his was ample time for Reams to consult publicly available documents, discover her right to a hearing, and exercise that right.

C. Adequacy of Post-Deprivation Remedies

Reams contends that, even if she was not entitled to pre-deprivation notice and a hearing, the process she did receive was constitutionally inadequate because: (1) she had to wait seven months before she was afforded an initial hearing, and (2) the settlement conference in which she participated with GDA officials "was not meaningful in a constitutional sense as it did not offer [her] the right to subpoena evidence or witnesses, directly or cross-examine witnesses, or present her case to an unbiased decision-maker."

The Humane Care for Equines Act affords equine owners an opportunity for a hearing to contest any impoundment. It provides:

> Any . . . equine owner . . . aggrieved or adversely affected by any order or action of the Commissioner to include . . . impoundment . . . upon petition within 30 days after the issuance of such order or the taking of such action, shall have a right to a hearing before a hearing officer appointed or designated for such purpose by the Commissioner. The decision of the hearing officer shall constitute an initial decision of the Department of Agriculture, and any party to the hearing . . . shall have the right to final agency review before the Commissioner.

O.C.G.A. §2-2-9.1(d). Even assuming, *arguendo*, that the process Reams received under the Act was inadequate "from a timeliness standpoint" and not "truly meaningful," her §1983 due process claim is nevertheless incognizable. It is well-settled that a constitutional violation is actionable under §1983 "only when the state refuses to provide a process sufficient to remedy the procedural deprivation." McKinney v. Pate, 20 F.3d 1550, 1557 (11th Cir. 1994) (en banc) . . . ; *Cotton*, 216 F.3d at 1331 ("It is the state's failure to provide adequate procedures to remedy the otherwise procedurally flawed deprivation of a protected interest that gives rise to a federal procedural due process claim."). In *Cotton*, we observed that

> [t]his rule (that a section 1983 claim is not stated unless inadequate state procedures exist to remedy an alleged procedural deprivation) recognizes that the state must have the opportunity to remedy the procedural failings of its subdivisions and agencies in the appropriate fora-agencies, review boards, and state courts before being subjected to a claim alleging a procedural due process violation.

Cotton, 216 F.3d at 1331 (quotation marks omitted); see Horton v. Bd. of Co. Com'rs of Flagler Co., 202 F.3d 1297, 1300 (11th Cir. 2000) (no federal procedural due process violation under *McKinney* if state courts "generally would provide an adequate remedy for the procedural deprivation the federal court plaintiff claims to have suffered").

The question is thus whether the state provided Reams with the means to present her allegations, demonstrate that the impoundment was wrongful, and receive redress from that deprivation. See Narey v. Dean, 32 F.3d 1521, 1527 (11th Cir. 1994). We find that it did. In addition to administrative review, an equine owner like Reams who is adversely affected by an order or action of the Commissioner may, pursuant to O.C.G.A. §2-2-9.1(n), seek judicial review of the Commissioner's final decision in accordance with the Georgia Administrative Procedures Act ("APA"). That Act provides:

> Any person who has exhausted all administrative remedies available within the agency and who is aggrieved by a final decision in a contested case is entitled to judicial review under this chapter. . . . A preliminary, procedural, or intermediate agency action or ruling is immediately reviewable if review of the final agency decision would not provide an adequate remedy.

O.C.G.A. §50-13-19(a). On review, the superior court "may reverse or modify the [agency's] decision if substantial rights of the appellant have been prejudiced because the administrative findings, inferences, conclusions, or decisions are . . . [i]n violation of constitutional or statutory provisions." Id. §50-13-19(h). Because "[i]nherent in [the] power to review is the power to remedy deficiencies and to cure violations of due process," *McKinney*, 20 F.3d at 1563, the review available in this case "more than satisfies [the] requirement" that the state provide a remedy that is adequate to correct the alleged procedural due process violation. *Narey*, 32 F.3d at 1527 (quotation marks and citation omitted); *Cotton*, 216 F.3d at 1331 ("[C]ertiorari [to the state courts] is generally an adequate state remedy."). Accordingly, we agree with the district court that "[t]he judicial safety valve provided by the Georgia [APA] foreclose[d] any constitutional challenge to the procedural adequacy of the hearing-and-appeal procedure set forth in the Humane Care for Equines Act." Inasmuch as Reams failed to establish a constitutional violation, appellees were entitled to qualified immunity. See *McKinney*, 20 F.3d at 1557 (due process violation not complete "unless and until [a] State fails to provide due process" (citation and quotation marks omitted)).

III. CONCLUSION

[B]ecause we conclude that available state remedies were adequate to cure any erroneous deprivation of Reams' protected interest in her equines, Reams has failed to establish that her procedural due process rights were violated. Accordingly, the district court did not err in finding that Appellees were entitled to qualified immunity.

AFFIRMED.

TURNER v. ROGERS

564 U.S. 431 (2011)

JUSTICE BREYER delivered the opinion of the Court:

South Carolina's Family Court enforces its child support orders by threatening with incarceration for civil contempt those who are (1) subject to a child support order, (2) able to comply with that order, but (3) fail to do so. We must decide whether the Fourteenth Amendment's Due Process Clause requires the State to provide counsel (at a civil contempt hearing) to an indigent person potentially faced with such incarceration. We conclude that where as here the custodial parent (entitled to receive the support) is unrepresented by counsel, the State need not provide counsel to the noncustodial parent (required to provide the support). But we attach an important caveat, namely, that the State must nonetheless have in place alternative procedures that assure a fundamentally fair determination of the critical incarceration-related question, whether the supporting parent is able to comply with the support order.

I

A

South Carolina family courts enforce their child support orders in part through civil contempt proceedings. Each month the family court clerk reviews outstanding child support orders, identifies those in which the supporting parent has fallen more than five days behind, and sends that parent an order to "show cause" why he should not be held in contempt. If he fails to make the required showing, the court may hold him in civil contempt. And it may require that he be imprisoned unless and until he purges himself of contempt by making the required child support payments (but not for more than one year regardless).

B

In June 2003 a South Carolina family court entered an order, which (as amended) required petitioner, Michael Turner, to pay $51.73 per week to respondent, Rebecca Rogers, to help support their child. Over the next three years, Turner repeatedly failed to pay the amount due and was held in contempt on five occasions. The first four times he was sentenced to 90 days' imprisonment, but he ultimately paid the amount due (twice without being jailed, twice after spending two or three days in custody). The fifth time he did not pay but completed a 6-month sentence.

After his release in 2006 Turner remained in arrears. On March 27, 2006, the clerk issued a new "show cause" order. And after an initial postponement due to Turner's failure to appear, Turner's civil contempt hearing took place on January 3, 2008. Turner and Rogers were present, each without representation by counsel.

The hearing was brief. The court clerk said that Turner was $5,728.76 behind in his payments. The judge asked Turner if there was "anything you want to say." Turner replied,

> Well, when I first got out, I got back on dope. I done meth, smoked pot and everything else, and I paid a little bit here and there. And, when I finally did get to working, I broke my back, back in September. I filed for disability and SSI. And, I didn't get straightened out off the dope until I broke my back and laid up for two months. And, now I'm off the dope and everything. I just hope that you give me a chance. I don't know what else to say. I mean, I know I done wrong, and I should have been paying and helping her, and I'm sorry. I mean, dope had a hold to me.

The judge then said, "[o]kay," and asked Rogers if she had anything to say. After a brief discussion of federal benefits, the judge stated,

> If there's nothing else, this will be the Order of the Court. I find the Defendant in willful contempt. I'm [going to] sentence him to twelve months in the Oconee County Detention Center. He may purge himself of the contempt and avoid the sentence by having a zero balance on or before his release. I've also placed a lien on any SSI or other benefits.

The judge added that Turner would not receive good-time or work credits, but "[i]f you've got a job, I'll make you eligible for work release." When Turner asked why he could not receive good-time or work credits, the judge said, "[b]ecause that's my ruling."

. . . [T]he judge [did not] ask any followup questions or otherwise address the ability-to-pay issue. After the hearing, the judge filled out a prewritten form titled "Order for Contempt of Court," which included the statement:

> Defendant (was) (was not) gainfully employed and/or (had) (did not have) the ability to make these support payments when due.

But the judge left this statement as is without indicating whether Turner was able to make support payments.

C

While serving his 12-month sentence, Turner, with the help of pro bono counsel, appealed. He claimed that the Federal Constitution entitled him to counsel at his contempt hearing. The South Carolina Supreme Court decided Turner's appeal after he had completed his sentence. And it rejected his "right to counsel" claim.

The court pointed out that civil contempt differs significantly from criminal contempt. The former does not require all the "constitutional safeguards" applicable in criminal proceedings. 387 S.C., at 145. And the right to government-paid counsel, the Supreme Court held, was one of the "safeguards" not required.

Turner sought certiorari. In light of differences among state courts (and some federal courts) on the applicability of a "right to counsel" in civil contempt proceedings enforcing child support orders, we granted the writ.

III

A

We must decide whether the Due Process Clause grants an indigent defendant, such as Turner, a right to state-appointed counsel at a civil contempt proceeding, which may lead to his incarceration. This Court's precedents provide no definitive answer to that question. This Court has long held that the Sixth Amendment grants an indigent defendant the right to state-appointed counsel in a criminal case. Gideon v. Wainwright, 372 U.S. 335 (1963). And we have held that this same rule applies to criminal contempt proceedings (other than summary proceedings). United States v. Dixon, 509 U.S. 688, 696 (1993); Cooke v. United States, 267 U.S. 517, 537 (1925).

But the Sixth Amendment does not govern civil cases. Civil contempt differs from criminal contempt in that it seeks only to "coerc[e] the defendant to do" what a court had previously ordered him to do. Gompers v. Bucks Stove & Range Co., 221 U.S. 418, 442 (1911). A court may not impose punishment "in a civil contempt proceeding when it is clearly established that the alleged contemnor is unable to comply with the terms of the order." Hicks v. Feiock, 485 U.S. 624, 638, n. 9 (1988). And once a civil contemnor complies with the underlying order, he is purged of the contempt and is free. 485 U.S., at 633 (he "carr[ies] the keys of [his] prison in [his] own pockets" (internal quotation marks omitted)).

Consequently, the Court has made clear (in a case not involving the right to counsel) that, where civil contempt is at issue, the Fourteenth Amendment's Due Process Clause allows a State to provide fewer procedural protections than in a criminal case. 485 U.S., at 637-641 (State may place the burden of proving inability to pay on the defendant).

This Court has decided only a handful of cases that more directly concern a right to counsel in civil matters. And the application of those decisions to the present case is not clear. On the one hand, the Court has held that the Fourteenth Amendment requires the State to pay for representation by counsel in a civil "juvenile delinquency" proceeding (which could lead to incarceration). In re Gault, 387 U.S. 1, 35-42 (1967). Moreover, in Vitek v. Jones, 445 U.S. 480, 496-497 (1980), a plurality of four Members of this Court would have held that the Fourteenth Amendment requires representation by counsel in a proceeding to transfer a prison inmate to a state hospital for the mentally ill. Further, in Lassiter v. Department of Social Servs. of Durham Cty., 452 U.S. 18 (1981), a case that focused upon civil proceedings leading to loss of parental rights, the Court wrote that the

> pre-eminent generalization that emerges from this Court's precedents on an indigent's right to appointed counsel is that such a right has been recognized to exist only where the litigant may lose his physical liberty if he loses the litigation.

452 U.S., at 25. And the Court then drew from these precedents "the presumption that an indigent litigant has a right to appointed counsel only when, if he loses, he may be deprived of his physical liberty." 452 U.S., at 26-27.

On the other hand, the Court has held that a criminal offender facing revocation of probation and imprisonment does not ordinarily have a right to counsel at a probation revocation hearing. Gagnon v. Scarpelli, 411 U.S. 778 (1973); see also Middendorf v. Henry, 425 U.S. 25 (1976) (no due process right to counsel in summary court-martial proceedings). And, at the same time, *Gault, Vitek* and *Lassiter* are readily distinguishable. The civil juvenile delinquency proceeding at issue in *Gault* was "little different" from, and "comparable in seriousness" to, a criminal prosecution. 387 U.S., at 28, 36. In *Vitek*, the controlling opinion found no right to counsel. 445 U.S., at 499-500 (Powell, J., concurring in part) (assistance of mental health professionals sufficient). And the Court's statements in *Lassiter* constitute part of its rationale for denying a right to counsel in that case. We believe those statements are best read as pointing out that the Court previously had found a right to counsel "only" in cases involving incarceration, not that a right to counsel exists in all such cases (a position that would have been difficult to reconcile with *Gagnon*).

B

Civil contempt proceedings in child support cases constitute one part of a highly complex system designed to assure a noncustodial parent's regular payment of funds typically necessary for the support of his children. Often the family receives welfare support from a state-administered federal program, and the State then seeks reimbursement from the noncustodial parent. See 42 U.S.C. §§608(a)(3) (2006 ed., Supp. III), 656(a)(1) (2006 ed.); S.C. Code Ann. §§43-5-65(a)(1), (2) (2010 Cum. Supp.). Other times the custodial parent (often the mother, but sometimes the father, a grandparent, or another person with custody) does not receive government benefits and is entitled to receive the support payments herself.

The Federal Government has created an elaborate procedural mechanism designed to help both the government and custodial parents to secure the payments to which they are entitled. These systems often rely upon wage withholding, expedited procedures for modifying and enforcing child support orders, and automated data processing. 42 U.S.C. §§666(a), (b), 654(24). But sometimes States will use contempt orders to ensure that the custodial parent receives support payments or the government receives reimbursement.

We here consider an indigent's right to paid counsel at such a contempt proceeding. It is a civil proceeding. And we consequently determine the "specific dictates of due process" by examining the "distinct factors" that this Court has previously found useful in deciding what specific safeguards the Constitution's Due Process Clause requires in order to make a civil proceeding fundamentally fair. Mathews v. Eldridge, 424 U.S. 319, 335 (1976) (considering fairness of an administrative proceeding). As relevant here those factors include (1) the nature of "the private interest that will be affected," (2) the comparative "risk" of an "erroneous deprivation" of that interest with and without "additional or substitute procedural safeguards," and (3) the nature and magnitude of any countervailing interest in not providing "additional or substitute procedural requirement[s]. See also *Lassiter*, 452 U.S., at 27-31 (applying the Mathews framework).

The "private interest that will be affected" argues strongly for the right to counsel that Turner advocates. That interest consists of an indigent defendant's loss of personal liberty through imprisonment. The interest in securing that freedom, the freedom "from bodily restraint," lies "at the core of the liberty protected by the Due Process Clause." Foucha v. Louisiana, 504 U.S. 71, 80 (1992). And we have made clear that its threatened loss through legal proceedings demands "due process protection." Addington v. Texas, 441 U.S. 418, 425 (1979).

Given the importance of the interest at stake, it is obviously important to assure accurate decisionmaking in respect to the key "ability to pay" question. Moreover, the fact that ability to comply marks a dividing line between civil and criminal contempt, *Hicks*, 485 U.S., at 635, n. 7, reinforces the need for accuracy. That is because an incorrect decision (wrongly classifying the contempt proceeding as civil) can increase the risk of wrongful incarceration by depriving the defendant of the procedural protections (including counsel) that the Constitution would demand in a criminal proceeding.

On the other hand, the Due Process Clause does not always require the provision of counsel in civil proceedings where incarceration is threatened. See *Gagnon*, 411 U.S. 778. And in determining whether the Clause requires a right to counsel here, we must take account of opposing interests, as well as consider the probable value of "additional or substitute procedural safeguards." *Mathews*, supra, at 335.

Doing so, we find three related considerations that, when taken together, argue strongly against the Due Process Clause requiring the State to provide indigents with counsel in every proceeding of the kind before us.

First, the critical question likely at issue in these cases concerns, as we have said, the defendant's ability to pay. That question is often closely related to the question of the defendant's indigence. But when the right procedures are in place, indigence can be a question that in many — but not all — cases is sufficiently straightforward to warrant determination prior to providing a defendant with counsel, even in a criminal case. Federal law, for example, requires a criminal defendant to provide information showing that he is indigent, and therefore entitled to state-funded counsel, before he can receive that assistance. See 18 U.S.C. §3006A(b).

Second, sometimes, as here, the person opposing the defendant at the hearing is not the government represented by counsel but the custodial parent unrepresented by counsel.

A requirement that the State provide counsel to the noncustodial parent in these cases could create an asymmetry of representation that would "alter significantly the nature of the proceeding." *Gagnon*, supra, at 787. Doing so could mean a degree of formality or delay that would unduly slow payment to those immediately in need. And, perhaps more important for present purposes, doing so could make the proceedings less fair overall, increasing the risk of a decision that would erroneously deprive a family of the support it is entitled to receive. The needs of such families play an important role in our analysis.

Third, as the Solicitor General points out, there is available a set of "substitute procedural safeguards," *Mathews*, 424 U.S., at 335, which, if employed together, can significantly reduce the risk of an erroneous deprivation of liberty. They can do so, moreover, without incurring some of the drawbacks inherent in recognizing an automatic right to counsel. Those safeguards include (1) notice to the defendant that his "ability to pay" is a critical issue in the contempt proceeding; (2) the use of a form (or the equivalent) to elicit relevant financial information; (3) an opportunity at the hearing for the defendant to respond to statements and questions about his financial status, (e.g., those triggered by his responses on the form); and (4) an express finding by the court that the defendant has the ability to pay. In presenting these alternatives, the Government draws upon considerable experience in helping to manage statutorily mandated federal-state efforts to enforce child support orders. It does not claim that they are the only possible alternatives, and this Court's cases suggest, for example, that sometimes assistance other than purely legal assistance (here, say, that of a neutral social worker) can prove constitutionally sufficient. But the Government does claim that these alternatives can assure the "fundamental fairness" of the proceeding even where the State does not pay for counsel for an indigent defendant.

While recognizing the strength of Turner's arguments, we ultimately believe that the three considerations we have just discussed must carry the day. In our view, a categorical right to counsel in proceedings of the kind before us would carry with it disadvantages (in the form of unfairness and delay) that, in terms of ultimate fairness, would deprive it of significant superiority over the alternatives that we have mentioned. We consequently hold that the Due Process Clause does not automatically require the provision of counsel at civil contempt proceedings to an indigent individual who is subject to a child support order, even if that individual faces incarceration (for up to a year). In particular, that Clause does not require the provision of counsel where the opposing parent or other custodian (to whom support funds are owed) is not represented by counsel and the State provides alternative procedural safeguards equivalent to those we have mentioned (adequate notice of the importance of ability to pay, fair opportunity to present, and to dispute, relevant information, and court findings).

We do not address civil contempt proceedings where the underlying child support payment is owed to the State, for example, for reimbursement of welfare funds paid to the parent with custody. Those proceedings more closely resemble debt-collection proceedings. The government is likely to have counsel or some other competent representative. And this kind of proceeding is not before us. Neither do we address what due process requires in an unusually complex case where a defendant "can fairly be represented only by a trained advocate." *Gagnon*, 411 U.S., at 788.

IV

The record indicates that Turner received neither counsel nor the benefit of alternative procedures like those we have described. He did not receive clear notice that his ability to pay would constitute the critical question in his civil contempt proceeding. No one provided him with a form (or the equivalent) designed to elicit information about his financial circumstances. The court did not find that Turner was able to pay his arrearage, but instead left the relevant "finding" section of the contempt order blank. The court nonetheless found Turner in contempt and ordered him incarcerated. Under these circumstances Turner's incarceration violated the Due Process Clause.

We vacate the judgment of the South Carolina Supreme Court and remand the case for further proceedings not inconsistent with this opinion.

It is so ordered.

NOTES

1. Does the Court really do the kind of balancing envisioned in *Mathews*? For example, in weighing the disadvantages of a right to counsel, isn't the Court simply making a straightforward policy decision? Is there really any balancing taking place? See Tom Pryor, A More Perfect Union? Democracy in the Age of Ballot Initiatives: Turner v. Rogers, the Right to Counsel, and the Deficiencies of Mathews v. Eldridge, 97 Minn. L. Rev. 1854 (2013) (maintaining that the Court failed to properly apply the *Mathews* criteria in *Turner*). Do you agree with the Court's statement that forms and inquiries from a judge can adequately substitute for representation by counsel? Can't the same arguments be made in virtually every civil case involving right to counsel? Why wouldn't the same be true at least in some criminal cases?

2. Do you think the *Turner* decision definitively ends the question of right to counsel in civil cases? See Jacob R. Fiddelman, Protecting the Liberty of Indigent Civil Contemnors in the Absence of a Right to Appointed Counsel, 46 Colum. J.L. & Soc. Probs. 431, 432 (2013) ("The Court's unanimous rejection of this proposition in Turner v. Rogers was arguably the last gasp of the Civil Gideon movement as a matter of federal constitutional law."); but see John Pollock, The Case Against Case-by-Case: Courts Identifying Categorical Rights to Counsel in Basic Human Needs Civil Cases, 61 Drake L. Rev. 763, 765-766 (2013) ("Fortunately, as I wrote in an online symposium occurring the week the *Turner* decision was released, the state courts have been vigilant for decades in protecting the rights of indigent civil litigants through the use of state constitutions or by distinguishing *Lassiter*. Thus, *Turner* will not be the last word on the constitutional right to counsel in civil cases any more than *Lassiter* has been."); Hon. David J. Dreyer, Déjà vu All Over Again: Turner v. Rogers and the Civil Right to Counsel, 61 Drake L. Rev. 639, 653 (2013) ("The supposedly good news from *Turner* is that the Court specifically and deliberately did not address civil contempt cases in which the petitioner is represented, when the State is a party, or unusually complex cases needing a trained advocate. Arguably, a door might be open for a trial court to appoint counsel in such situations. However, the bad news from *Turner* is the same — the Court likewise failed to address whether due process must require appointed counsel in those circumstances.").

3. In Hamdi v. Rumsfeld, 542 U.S. 507 (2004), the Supreme Court used the now-ubiquitous Mathews v. Eldridge balancing test to determine whether a U.S.-born person who was captured during combat in Afghanistan, and was classified as an enemy combatant, could challenge the classification under due process principles. The Court answered yes, and determined that a person in Hamdi's position be afforded notice of the factual basis for classification and an opportunity to rebut the government's assertions before a neutral decisionmaker. Does the Supreme Court's use of Mathews v. Eldridge to decide the *Hamdi* case turn *Mathews* into an omnibus test for due process? Will *Mathews* now be used as the test in all due process cases, no matter the context? See United States v. Warsame, 547 F. Supp. 2d 982 (D. Minn. 2008) (analyzing application of *Mathews* test to criminal proceedings under Foreign Intelligence Surveillance Act (FISA)); United States v. Abuhamra, 389 F.3d 309 (7th Cir. 2005) (citing to *Hamdi* in applying *Mathews* test to determine due process in the context of a post-verdict bail determination).

4. Can there ever be a situation under *Mathews* when no process is due if the government interest in *Hamdi*, arising out of a wartime battlefield scenario, is not enough to foreclose some process?

What do you think of the following comment in light of the Court's decision in *Hamdi* to use a *Mathews* due process analysis to resolve the case?

> [W]e are faced with a governmental system that has greatly overvalued, and hence overemphasized, the kind of decisions that can be made by means of the judicial process — and decisions of logic. The embracing of the judicial model has been to the detriment of the kind of decisions made by individuals possessing administrative discretion derived from a popular or political mandate — decisions of will. This change has come about in part because there has been a failure of confidence in the quality of government administrators and their administrative decisions. More fundamentally, there has developed a distrust of the political process as a means of making the important decisions affecting our society and our very lives. Reacting against the output of the administrative state, we have been led to believe that the judicial process and its procedures, and their promise of insulation from at least some types of political pressure, are the answer to this crisis of confidence. . . .
>
> Overproceduralization is the aspect of judicialization most readily perceived as an evil in the political system. It has long been a whipping boy; politicians, writers, and the man on the street traditionally have inveighed against bureaucrats, tangles of red tape, and governmental delay and waste. The causes of this phenomenon are not, however, to be found in the penchant of "pointy-headed" bureaucrats for thwarting the public in a Kafkaesque world. I would argue that its primary cause is

an attempt by government to do too much. This overreaching in terms of the overall scope of governmental functions inevitably leads to specific overloads in the system. There is, first, over-extension of the individual agencies charged with the expansive functions. When agencies attempt to accomplish impossible tasks or tasks beyond the political or financial resources available to them, their institutional structures are subjected to enormous strain. The most basic defense mechanism such an organization has is to insulate itself from controversial substantive decisions with layers of procedure, quasi-judicial appeal boards, and highly complex regulatory codes.

The expansion of government programs into more and more substantive areas has also resulted in an understanding of due process alien to the framers of either the fifth or the fourteenth amendments, and this in turn produces overproceduralization. Since Goldberg v. Kelly we have embraced an increasingly abstract conception of due process. The right to a more or less formalized hearing has come to be held as an article of faith. This is not a necessary implication of the Constitution's mandate of due process. It has become a legal and judicial dogma that fundamental fairness to participants can only be achieved through the use of hearings with guaranteed procedural steps. While there is an overwhelmingly convincing historical and moral argument for this view in the area where the state seeks to impose criminal sanctions, the proposition is subject to serious question when grants of government benefits are involved. The contemporary movement of the law away from the traditional dichotomy between rights and privileges has had the effect of ossifying administrative structures. It causes these structures to be progressively less responsive to the needs which they were created to address. As in the development of the ancient forms of action in the common law, turning procedures into due process rights turns government programs into ritual acts increasingly unrelated to real human needs.

Smith, Judicialization: The Twilight of Administrative Law,* 1985 Duke L.J. 427, 446, 459-460.

3. The Narrowing Scope of Property and Liberty Interests

a. Property Interests

CUSHMAN v. SHINSEKI

576 F.3d 1290 (Fed. Cir. 2009)

PROST, Circuit Judge.

This case involves an alleged violation of a veteran's right to due process under the Fifth Amendment to the United States Constitution, where the

* Reprinted with permission.

medical record on which his service-connected disability claim was evaluated contained an improperly altered document. . . .

Philip Cushman served in a United States Marine Corps combat infantry battalion in Vietnam during the Vietnam War. While he was fortifying a bunker in Vietnam, a heavy sandbag fell on Mr. Cushman's back and damaged his spine. He was honorably discharged in January of 1970. Mr. Cushman underwent four spinal surgeries to treat his injury and has received continuous pain medication. . . .

In October of 1976, Mr. Cushman went to the Portland DVA Outpatient Clinic to have his condition reassessed. Records from that visit diagnosed him as having a postoperative ruptured intervertebral disc, with radiculopathy and degenerative joint disease affecting his lumbar and lumbosacral spine. In November of 1976 . . . he returned to the DVA Outpatient Clinic for another assessment. This assessment, dated November 15, 1976, was the last entry in Mr. Cushman's medical record before his files were sent to the Portland Regional Office. The last comment in the record stated, "Is worse + must stop present type of work."

Mr. Cushman filed a request with the DVA for a total disability based upon individual unemployability ("TDIU") rating in May of 1977. With his request, Mr. Cushman included a letter from his former employer explaining that Mr. Cushman could not continue to work at the flooring store because he was always lying on his back to do paperwork. . . .

[After two hearings and various appeals denying his request for total disability, Mr. Cushman discovered that his initial record from the DVA had been altered.] The medical record before the Regional Office and Board . . . differed from the medical record on file at the DVA Outpatient Clinic. Namely, one of the doctor's entries had been altered to change the language "Is worse + must stop present type of work" to instead read, "Is worse + must stop present type of work, *or at least [] bend [] stoop lift*" (emphasis added, brackets indicate illegible or stray marks). The altered record also contained the additional entry, "says he is applying for reevaluation of back condition," which does not appear in the official record on file with the Outpatient Clinic. The alterations appeared in the last, i.e., most recent, doctor's notes documenting Mr. Cushman's condition.

Upon learning of the nonconforming records, Mr. Cushman challenged the Regional Office's 1977 decision, and the Board's 1980 and 1982 decisions as containing clear and unmistakable error ("CUE"). He argued that those decisions were based on medical records that were improperly altered to understate his disability. In February of 1999, the Board denied his claim on grounds that the 1977 decision was subsumed by the 1980 and 1982 decisions by the Board. The Board did not address Mr. Cushman's argument that the 1980 and 1982 decisions imported the same CUE. . . .

In October of 2003, Mr. Cushman moved the Board to reverse its 1980 and 1982 decisions. Mr. Cushman argued that consideration of the improperly altered medical record constituted CUE. He also argued that the Board incorrectly interpreted the governing regulations and failed to construe the term "substantially gainful employment." In August of 2005, the Board ruled that the 1980 and 1982 decisions did not contain CUE because the decisions gave no indication that the

Board relied specifically on the altered document. It was therefore not possible to prove that consideration of the altered document was outcome determinative, as required by the CUE standard.... [M]r. Cushman appealed the Board's August 2005 decision to the Veterans Court, challenging the Board's statutory interpretation and making CUE and due process arguments related to the consideration of his nonconforming medical records. In February of 2008, a single-judge panel of the Veterans Court affirmed the Board. Mr. Cushman moved for reconsideration by a full panel. The motion was denied in May of 2008 and judgment was entered in June. In July, Mr. Cushman timely appealed the case to this court.

III. DUE PROCESS

Mr. Cushman asserts that he was denied a full and fair hearing on the factual issues of his claim due to the presence of the altered medical record. Mr. Cushman therefore raises a genuine issue of procedural due process under the Fifth Amendment to the Constitution.... We find that this court has jurisdiction to resolve the due process issue in deciding his claim.

In order to allege that the denial of his claim involved a violation of his due process rights, Mr. Cushman must first prove that as a veteran alleging a service-connected disability, he has a constitutional right to a fundamentally fair adjudication of his claim. The right to due process of applicants for veterans' benefits is an issue of first impression for this court.

The Due Process Clause of the Fifth Amendment guarantees that an individual will not be deprived of life, liberty, or property without due process of law. U.S. Const. amend. V. Due process of law has been interpreted to include notice and a fair opportunity to be heard.... To raise a due process question, the claimant must demonstrate a property interest entitled to such protections....

It is well established that disability benefits are a protected property interest and may not be discontinued without due process of law.... The Supreme Court has not, however, resolved the specific question of whether applicants for benefits, who have not yet been adjudicated as entitled to them, possess a property interest in those benefits....

The Supreme Court has, however, offered guidance relevant to our resolution of this question by explaining, "'[t]o have a property interest in a benefit, a person clearly must have more than an abstract need or desire' and 'more than a unilateral expectation of it. He must, instead, have a legitimate claim of entitlement to it.'" Town of Castle Rock, Colo. v. Gonzales, 545 U.S. 748, 756 (2005) (quoting Bd. of Regents of State Colls. v. Roth, 408 U.S. 564, 577 (1972)). The Court has also clarified that "a benefit is not a protected entitlement if government officials may grant or deny it in their discretion." *Id.* at 756 (citing Ky. Dep't of Corr. v. Thompson, 490 U.S. 454, 462-63 (1989)).

In Richardson v. Perales, the Supreme Court strongly implied that certain due process protections are applicable to the adjudicative administrative proceedings associated with social security disability claim hearings. 402 U.S. 389, 401-02 (1971). The Court has also noted "that the benefits at stake in DVA proceedings, which are not granted on the basis of need, are more akin to the Social Security benefits involved in *Eldridge* than they are to the welfare payments" at issue in *Goldberg*.[1] We believe the protected property interests implicated in social security proceedings provide a helpful analogy in assessing the property interests of veteran applicants for service-connected disability benefits.

Like the statutorily created right of an eligible recipient to social security benefits, entitlement to veteran's benefits arises from a source that is independent from the DVA proceedings themselves. 38 U.S.C. §1110 (2000) (providing for wartime disability compensation); *id.* §1121 (providing for wartime death compensation for designated heirs and dependents); *id.* §1131 (providing for peacetime disability compensation); *id.* §1141 (providing for peacetime death compensation for designated heirs and dependents). These statutes provide an absolute right of benefits to qualified individuals.

Although the due process question is one of first impression for this court, the Ninth Circuit has previously held that "both applicants for and recipients of [service-connected death and disability] benefits possess a constitutionally protected property interest in those benefits." Nat'l Ass'n of Radiation Survivors v. Derwinski, 994 F.2d 583, 588 n.7 (9th Cir. 1992). Additionally, seven of our sister circuits have addressed similar questions concerning statutorily mandated benefits. "Every regional circuit to address the question . . . has concluded that applicants for benefits, no less than benefits recipients, may possess a property interest in the receipt of public welfare entitlements." Kapps v. Wing, 404 F.3d 105, 115 (2d Cir. 2005) [citations to other circuit decisions omitted].

In response, the government cites three cases in which circuit courts found that an individual did not obtain a protected property interest merely by applying for benefits. See Banks v. Block, 700 F.2d 292 (6th Cir. 1983) (declining to find a property interest in food stamp benefits after expiration of the eligibility period); Holman v. Block, 823 F.2d 56 (4th Cir. 1987) (same); De Journett v. Block, 799 F.2d 430 (8th Cir. 1986) (finding that an applicant had no protected property interest in a discretionary loan). The cited cases, however, are distinguishable from the present case. *Banks* and *Holman* deal with the rights of an applicant who is no longer eligible for benefits. *De Journett* deals with the denial of a discretionary benefit. As cited above, the respective circuits of these three cases have found that due process attaches in the context of nondiscretionary benefits.

Veteran's disability benefits are nondiscretionary, statutorily mandated benefits. A veteran is entitled to disability benefits upon a showing that he meets the eligibility requirements set forth in the governing statutes and regulations. We

---

1. The Court has also commented that recipients in *Goldberg*, who had not yet shown that they were within the statutory terms of eligibility, "had a right to a hearing at which they might attempt to do so." *Roth*, 408 U.S. at 577 (commenting on Goldberg v. Kelly, 397 U.S. 254 (1970)). The right to a hearing necessarily implies the right to a fair hearing. *See, e.g., Mullane*, 339 U.S. at 315 ("[P]rocess which is a mere gesture is not due process."). As such, *Roth* suggests that at least some due process protections attach to procedures for determining eligibility for benefits even outside of the social security context.

conclude that such entitlement to benefits is a property interest protected by the Due Process Clause of the Fifth Amendment to the United States Constitution.

TOWN OF CASTLE ROCK v. GONZALES

545 U.S. 748 (2005)

[This case has what Justice Scalia in the beginning of the opinion states are "horrible" facts, and they are. Plaintiff in this case, Gonzales, had obtained a restraining order against her husband. The order required that the husband stay at least 100 yards away from the family home. The husband disobeyed the order and kidnapped then murdered their three children. Gonzales sued the Town of Castle Rock, arguing that the police department failed to treat the enforcement of the restraining order as a mandatory requirement, denying her due process.]

JUSTICE SCALIA delivered the opinion of the Court.

. . .

Our cases recognize that a benefit is not a protected entitlement if government officials may grant or deny it in their discretion. See, e.g., Kentucky Dep't of Corrections v. Thompson, 490 U.S. 454, 462-463 (1989). The Court of Appeals in this case determined that Colorado law created an entitlement to enforcement of the restraining order because the "court-issued restraining order . . . specifically dictated that its terms must be enforced" and a "state statute command[ed]" enforcement of the order when certain objective conditions were met (probable cause to believe that the order had been violated and that the object of the order had received notice of its existence).

. . .

The critical language in the restraining order came not from any part of the order itself (which was signed by the state-court trial judge and directed to the restrained party, respondent's husband), but from the preprinted notice to law-enforcement personnel that appeared on the back of the order. That notice effectively restated the statutory provision describing "peace officers' duties" related to the crime of violation of a restraining order. At the time of the conduct at issue in this case, that provision read as follows:

> "(a) Whenever a restraining order is issued, the protected person shall be provided with a copy of such order. *A peace officer shall use every reasonable means to enforce a restraining order.*
>
> "(b) *A peace officer shall arrest, or, if an arrest would be impractical under the circumstances, seek a warrant for the arrest of a restrained person* when the peace officer has information amounting to probable cause that:
>
> "(I) The restrained person has violated or attempted to violate any provision of a restraining order; and
>
> "(II) The restrained person has been properly served with a copy of the restraining order or the restrained person has received actual notice of the existence and substance of such order.

> "(c) In making the probable cause determination described in paragraph (b) of this subsection (3), a peace officer shall assume that the information received from the registry is accurate. *A peace officer shall enforce a valid restraining order whether or not there is a record of the restraining order in the registry.*" Colo. Rev. Stat. §18-6-803.5(3) (Lexis 1999) (emphases added).

We do not believe that these provisions of Colorado law truly made enforcement of restraining orders *mandatory.* A well established tradition of police discretion has long coexisted with apparently mandatory arrest statutes. . . ." In each and every state there are long-standing statutes that, by their terms, seem to preclude nonenforcement by the police. . . . However, for a number of reasons, including their legislative history, insufficient resources, and sheer physical impossibility, it has been recognized that such statutes cannot be interpreted literally. . . . [T]hey clearly do not mean that a police officer may not lawfully decline to make an arrest. As to third parties in these states, the full-enforcement statutes simply have no effect, and their significance is further diminished." 1 ABA Standards for Criminal Justice 1-4.5, commentary, pp. 1-124 to 1-125 (2d ed. 1980) (footnotes omitted).

. . .

The deep-rooted nature of law-enforcement discretion, even in the presence of seemingly mandatory legislative commands, is illustrated by Chicago v. Morales, 527 U.S. 41 (1999), which involved an ordinance that said a police officer "'shall order'" persons to disperse in certain circumstances, *id.*, at 47, n. 2. This Court rejected out of hand the possibility that "the mandatory language of the ordinance . . . afford[ed] the police *no* discretion." *Id.*, at 62, n. 32. It is, the Court proclaimed, simply "common sense that *all* police officers must use some discretion in deciding when and where to enforce city ordinances." *Ibid.* (emphasis added).

Against that backdrop, a true mandate of police action would require some stronger indication from the Colorado Legislature than "shall use every reasonable means to enforce a restraining order" (or even "shall arrest . . . or . . . seek a warrant"), §§18-6-803.5(3)(a), (b). That language is not perceptibly more mandatory than the Colorado statute which has long told municipal chiefs of police that they "shall pursue and arrest any person fleeing from justice in any part of the state" and that they "shall apprehend any person in the act of committing any offense . . . and, forthwith and without any warrant, bring such person before a . . . competent authority for examination and trial." Colo. Rev. Stat. §31-4-112 (Lexis 2004). It is hard to imagine that a Colorado peace officer would not have some discretion to determine that — despite probable cause to believe a restraining order has been violated — the circumstances of the violation or the competing duties of that officer or his agency counsel decisively against enforcement in a particular instance. The practical necessity for discretion is particularly apparent in a case such as this one, where the suspected violator is not actually present and his whereabouts are unknown. Cf. Donaldson v. Seattle, 65 Wash. App. 661, 671-672, 831 P.2d 1098, 1104 (1992) ("There is a vast difference between a mandatory duty to arrest [a violator who is on the scene] and a mandatory duty to conduct a follow up investigation [to locate an absent violator]. . . . A mandatory duty to investigate would be completely open-ended as to priority, duration and intensity.").

. . .

The dissent, after suggesting various formulations of the entitlement in question, ultimately contends that the obligations under the statute were quite precise: either make an arrest or (if that is impractical) seek an arrest warrant. . . . The problem with this is that the seeking of an arrest warrant would be an entitlement to nothing but procedure — which we have held inadequate even to support standing, see Lujan v. Defenders of Wildlife, 504 U.S. 555 (1992); much less can it be the basis for a property interest. . . . After the warrant is sought, it remains within the discretion of a judge whether to grant it, and after it is granted, it remains within the discretion of the police whether and when to execute it. Respondent would have been assured nothing but the seeking of a warrant. This is not the sort of "entitlement" out of which a property interest is created.

. . .

[Moreover,] it is by no means clear that an individual entitlement to enforcement of a restraining order could constitute a "property" interest for purposes of the Due Process Clause. Such a right would not, of course, resemble any traditional conception of property. Although that alone does not disqualify it from due process protection, as *Roth* and its progeny show, the right to have a restraining order enforced does not "have some ascertainable monetary value," as even our "*Roth*-type property-as-entitlement" cases have implicitly required. Merrill, The Landscape of Constitutional Property, 86 Va. L. Rev. 885, 964 (2000).[12] Perhaps most radically, the alleged property interest here arises *incidentally*, not out of some new species of government benefit or service, but out of a function that government actors have always performed — to wit, arresting people who they have probable cause to believe have committed a criminal offense. . . .

The indirect nature of a benefit was fatal to the due process claim of the nursing-home residents in O'Bannon v. Town Court Nursing Center, 447 U.S. 773 (1980). We held that, while the withdrawal of "direct benefits" (financial payments under Medicaid for certain medical services) triggered due process protections, *id.*, at 786-787, the same was not true for the "indirect benefit[s]" conferred on Medicaid patients when the Government enforced "minimum standards of care"

---

12. The dissent suggests that the interest in having a restraining order enforced does have an ascertainable monetary value, because one may "contract with a private security firm . . . to provide protection" for one's family. . . . Respondent probably could have hired a private firm to guard her house, to prevent her husband from coming onto the property, and perhaps even to search for her husband after she discovered that her children were missing. Her alleged entitlement here, however, does not consist in an abstract right to "protection," but (according to the dissent) in enforcement of her restraining order through the arrest of her husband, or the seeking of a warrant for his arrest, after she gave the police probable cause to believe the restraining order had been violated. A private person would not have the power to arrest under those circumstances because the crime would not have occurred in his presence. Colo. Rev. Stat. §16-3-201 (Lexis 1999). And, needless to say, a private person would not have the power to obtain an arrest warrant.

for nursing-home facilities, *id.*, at 787. "[A]n indirect and incidental result of the Government's enforcement action . . . does not amount to a deprivation of any interest in life, liberty, or property." *Ibid.* In this case, as in *O'Bannon*, "[t]he simple distinction between government action that directly affects a citizen's legal rights . . . and action that is directed against a third party and affects the citizen only indirectly or incidentally, provides a sufficient answer to" respondent's reliance on cases that found government-provided services to be entitlements. *Id.*, at 788. . . .

NOTES

1. On August 26, 1996, President Clinton signed into law the Personal Responsibility and Work Opportunity Reconciliation Act of 1996 (PRWORA, also known as the Welfare Reform Act). It eliminated the guarantee of federal dollars to poor families and substituted them with block grants, called Temporary Assistance to Needy Families (TANF). These block grants provide lump-sum payments to states, which now determine the eligibility and benefit levels for families. States are required to meet stringent work requirements and five-year lifetime limits on assistance. By placing welfare in states' hands and having stringent requirements, Congress has purported to take away individual entitlement to welfare. In the past, the U.S. Supreme Court has interpreted the entitlement to welfare as a property interest, constitutionally protected by the Due Process Clause of the Fourteenth Amendment. Therefore, individuals would typically receive notice and a hearing before losing benefits. Goldberg v. Kelly, 397 U.S. 254, 266 (1970). Section 401(b) of the PRWORA, which establishes TANF, states, "This part shall not be interpreted to entitle any individual or family to assistance under any state program funded under this part." Pub. L. No. 104-193, §401(b) (1996) (codified at 42 U.S.C. §601(b) (1997)). Since the legislation expressly forbids interpreting the grant of welfare funds as creating an entitlement, can a court find a property interest in welfare funding for the purpose of finding a property interest protected by the Due Process Clause? See Chase, Note, Maintaining Procedural Protections for Welfare Recipients: Defining Property for the Due Process Clause, 23 N.Y.U. Rev. L. & Soc. Change 571, 580 (1997) ("While the legislative statements of non-entitlement are evidence that there is no protected interest, it is unlikely that a court's entitlement analysis would end there. If the applicable law creates a legitimate expectation of receiving benefits, governments cannot avoid compliance with the Due Process Clause by simply stating that no entitlement exists. A court would, therefore, delve further into the Personal Responsibility Act . . . and see if recipients have legitimate reasons to expect that they are entitled to the benefits. If the . . . federal regulations mandate that every person fitting certain eligibility requirements is to be provided with assistance, it is likely the court would hold that there is an entitlement, notwithstanding the disclaimers to the contrary." (footnotes omitted)).

2. Even if substantive property interests can be defeated by statutory language of discretion or no entitlement, can a welfare plaintiff argue that a property interest in a hearing exists because of statutory language providing for certain procedures with respect to reinstating a particular benefit? See Shvarstman v. Apfel, 138 F.3d 1196 (7th Cir. 1998), holding that a property interest under the Food Stamp Act is not created by recertification procedures in statutes and regulations because such a decision would effectively eliminate the distinction between property and the procedures that are constitutionally required to protect property. Would a standards-based approach requiring that certain procedures be followed in any case of benefits deprivation by the government be a superior approach to due process? See Shapiro & Levy, Government Benefits and the Rule of Law: Toward a Standards-Based Theory of Due Process, 57 Admin. L. Rev. 107 (2005). If the trend in welfare benefits administration is to push it from federal to local government, what are the constitutional implications? Given that localities are not generally bound by administrative procedure acts, will the DPC take on heightened importance? See Christine N. Cimini, Principles of Non-Arbitrariness: Lawlessness in the Administration of Welfare, 57 Rutgers L. Rev. 451 (2005).

b. Liberty Interests

HEDRICH v. BOARD OF REGENTS

274 F.3d 1174 (7th Cir. 2001)

Diane P. Wood, Circuit Judge:

Mary Anne Hedrich was an assistant professor in the Department of Health, Physical Education, Recreation and Coaching at the University of Wisconsin at Whitewater (the University). She was unsuccessful in her effort to be awarded tenure, however, and she eventually filed this suit alleging violations of state and federal law. The district court ultimately dismissed all of her theories either under Rule 12(b)(6) or on summary judgment. . . .

II

Hedrich was hired by the University in 1990 as a tenure-track faculty member of the Department of Health, Physical Education, Recreation and Coaching (the Department). When she joined the Department, the majority of the tenured faculty was female, but it also included some men, including Dr. Steven Albrechtsen. Years earlier, Albrechtsen had filed a sex discrimination claim against the University after it failed to promote him. Hedrich and Albrechtsen became friends.

In the late fall of 1995, Hedrich came up for tenure. . . . The tenured faculty in the Department met December 4, 8, and 18 of 1995 to review Hedrich's tenure file, which included materials related to her teaching (peer and student evaluations), her scholarship (research, publications, presentations at professional associations), and her service and committee work for the University. Hedrich made an oral presentation to the committee on December 4, 1995. The committee ultimately rated Hedrich above average in teaching and service, but it gave her a below average rating for scholarly activity. Hedrich had submitted four manuscripts to national peer-reviewed journals for consideration, but none had yet been accepted for publication. At the time of the review, Hedrich had no publications to her credit despite the fact that Barnett had told her in two previous performance reviews that this would be a critical factor in her tenure decision. The committee voted 7 to 1 to deny Hedrich tenure. Only Albrechtsen voted in Hedrich's favor. . . .

Hedrich received notice of the faculty committee's decision on January 16, 1996. On January 25, 1996, she received a letter from Provost Schellenkamp telling her that the 1996-97 academic year would be her last. Hedrich immediately sought an explanation from [the Department Chairman] for the decision and he cited her low rating for scholarly activity. Hedrich requested reconsideration by the faculty, but after two meetings the faculty reconfirmed its decision. [Hedrich then filed a series of internal appeals within the University, which ultimately failed to overturn the Department's recommendation on her tenure.]

Hedrich began looking for alternative academic employment in the spring of 1997. She applied for two positions that year. She applied for one position in the spring of 1998 and two that fall. Finally, she applied for two positions in 1999. All her applications were without success. Hedrich ultimately took a position as a staff nurse in Pewaukee, Wisconsin.

On September 1, 1998, Hedrich filed a complaint with the Wisconsin Personnel Commission (WPC) alleging gender, age, and sexual orientation discrimination. The WPC dismissed her complaint as not timely. It concluded that Hedrich did not file her charge until more than 300 days after any reasonable person would have known that her tenure application had been denied. Later in September of 1998, Hedrich filed the same charges with the EEOC. The EEOC also dismissed her complaint as untimely.

Hedrich then filed suit in Wisconsin state court. The defendants removed the case to federal court. Hedrich's complaint alleged several violations of law[, among them] that defendants deprived her of her "constitutionally protected liberty interest in her good name and reputation without due process of law." . . . Defendants filed motions to dismiss on the pleadings and on summary judgment; they succeeded in their effort to win summary judgment. Hedrich now appeals. . . .

III

C. Liberty Interest

Hedrich . . . contends that the defendants' actions in denying her tenure deprived her of her liberty interest in pursuing her chosen career, in violation of her due process rights. As we explained recently, if the character and circumstances of a public employer's . . . conduct or statements are such as to have destroyed an employee's freedom to take advantage of other employment opportunities, the employee can bring suit based on the deprivation of his freedom to pursue the occupation of his choice. . . .

In order to reach a jury on her liberty interest claim, Hedrich first had to present evidence that the defendants engaged in conduct that was so stigmatizing that it crossed the line from mere defamation, which is not actionable under the Constitution, see Paul v. Davis, 424 U.S. 693, 701 (1976), over to an infringement of a liberty interest. The denial of tenure or employment is not, by itself, stigmatizing conduct in the legal sense of the term. Wooten v. Clifton Forge School Bd., 655 F.2d 552, 555 (4th Cir. 1981) (no liberty interest claim arises merely from denial of tenure). As we explained in Lawson v. Sheriff of Tippecanoe County, 725 F.2d 1136, 1138-39 (7th Cir. 1984), a termination is only stigmatizing if it is accompanied by a publicly announced reason that impugns "[the employee's] moral character," *id.* at 1138, or implies "dishonesty or other job-related moral turpitude," *id.* at 1139. See also Board of Regents of State Colleges v. Roth, 408 U.S. 564, 573 (1972).

Hedrich urges that she was stigmatized by the defendants' statements that she did not meet [the University's] standards of scholarship. This inference can be drawn, however, from practically every denial of tenure or termination. Labeling an employee as incompetent or otherwise unable to meet an employer's expectations does not infringe the employee's liberty. Head v. Chicago Sch. Reform Bd. of Trustees, 225 F.3d 794, 801 (7th Cir. 2000). Alternatively, Hedrich contends that she was stigmatized by the defendants' claims that she did not submit the relevant documentation for consideration by the faculty. This, she argues, portrays her to be a dolt. The district court found that no properly presented evidence could support the proposition that the defendants' statements were false. See Strasburger v. Board of Education, 143 F.3d 351, 356 (7th Cir. 1998). Even assuming that Hedrich did present such evidence, however, these statements do not suggest the kind of moral turpitude or dishonesty that would give rise to a liberty interest claim.

If Hedrich could identify stigmatizing statements made by her employer, she would then have to provide evidence that these were made public and that as a result it was virtually impossible for [her] to find new employment in [her] chosen field. *Head*, 225 F.3d at 801. Hedrich cannot satisfy either of these requirements. The only evidence she points to is the fact that over three years she applied for seven academic jobs and was not hired. From this she believes that a reasonable jury could infer that the defendants were publicly defaming her and that it was virtually impossible for her to find an academic position. Anyone familiar with the academic job market knows that failing to receive a tenure track position after only seven applications is commonplace, even under the best of circumstances. There is also no question that once a person has been denied tenure, finding another academic position is considerably more difficult; failing on seven attempts in that case is not surprising. Nonetheless, Hedrich's evidence could not be construed by a trier of fact to show that the consequences of her tenure denial have been any more severe than any other professional's failure to receive a desired promotion. Hedrich's liberty interest claim was properly denied.

IV

We recognize that the denial of tenure is a serious matter for someone who is trying to pursue an academic career. It is possible — though we express no opinion on the point — that Hedrich's tenure application could have been handled better. The University may have lost a quality faculty member. But on the record before us, no reasonable jury could conclude that Hedrich's denial of tenure violated her rights under federal law. We therefore affirm.

MARION v. COLUMBIA CORRECTIONAL INSTITUTION

559 F.3d 693 (7th Cir. 2009)

RIPPLE, Circuit Judge.

War Marion, an inmate in the Wisconsin prison system, brought this action . . . alleging that prison officials had denied him . . . due process of law during a disciplinary hearing that resulted in 240 days of disciplinary segregation. The district court screened the complaint, and dismissed it for failure to state a claim upon which relief may be granted. After Mr. Marion appealed that dismissal, we instructed the parties to address whether his 240-day segregation was an "atypical and significant hardship" and therefore implicates a liberty interest, as that term has been explained in Wilkinson v. Austin, 545 U.S. 209 (2005), and Sandin v. Conner, 515 U.S. 472 (1995). In harmony with the relevant cases of this circuit, as well as those of our sister circuits, we hold that the 240 days of segregation in this case was sufficiently long to implicate a cognizable liberty interest if the conditions of confinement during that period were sufficiently severe. Mr. Marion therefore should have been allowed to develop a factual record of the conditions of his confinement during his period of segregation. Accordingly, we reverse the dismissal of this action and remand this case for further proceedings consistent with this opinion.

I. BACKGROUND

A

Mr. Marion alleges the following facts; we must assume them to be true for purposes of this appeal. . . .

Mr. Marion and his cellmate, Clifford Snipes, were in their cell at the Columbia Correctional Institution in Wisconsin when the prison's psychologist, Dr. Andrea Nelson, delivered puzzles to them. Snipes began arguing with Mr. Marion because Mr. Marion received more puzzles than Snipes. Snipes then charged at him; Mr. Marion responded by clenching his fists. When Dr. Nelson returned to the cell, she saw Mr. Marion's response and went to alert corrections officers. Correctional officers came to the cell to separate Mr. Marion and Snipes; Mr. Marion was placed in segregation.

Prison officials then began formal disciplinary proceedings, which, Mr. Marion alleges, lacked adequate procedural protection. First, prison officials issued Mr. Marion a conduct report containing false accusations of misconduct. The prison then scheduled a hearing to allow him to contest the report, but refused his request for two (of four) witnesses, specifically, Dr. Nelson and the captain who investigated the incident. Next, prison officials appointed a prison advocate for Mr. Marion, but the advocate failed to assist him. Finally, prison staff kept Mr. Marion away from the hearing and later signed a false statement that he had refused to attend. At the conclusion of the hearing, Mr. Marion was disciplined with 240 days — approximately eight months — of segregation. Because Mr. Marion already was serving a term of 180 days of segregation at the less restrictive "D.S.2" level, he was moved to the more restrictive "D.S.1" segregation unit. Mr. Marion claims that he was required to serve a total of 420 days in D.S.1 segregation.

. . .

II. DISCUSSION

B

We begin our evaluation of these arguments with an examination of the Supreme Court's decisions in *Sandin* and *Wilkinson*. In *Sandin*, 515 U.S. 472, the Supreme Court addressed whether a prisoner's sentence of thirty days of segregated confinement triggered due process considerations. It first observed that the Court previously had not addressed "whether disciplinary confinement of inmates itself implicates constitutional liberty interests." *Id.* at 486. The Court then held that a prisoner's sentence of thirty days of segregated confinement "did not present the type of atypical, significant deprivation in which a State might conceivably create a liberty interest." *Id.* It further concluded that the prisoner's confinement "did not exceed similar, but totally discretionary, confinement in either duration or degree of restriction," nor did it affect the length of his sentence. *Id.* at 486-87.

The Supreme Court revisited the issue of prison segregation and due process rights in *Wilkinson*. In that case, prisoners were transferred to a maximum-security prison and placed in segregated confinement for an indefinite duration. *Wilkinson*, 545 U.S. at 214, 216-17. The prisoners were denied virtually all sensory and environmental stimuli, permitted little human contact and disqualified from parole eligibility. *Id.* at 214-15. The Court concluded that although "any of these conditions standing alone might not be sufficient to create a liberty interest, taken together they impose an atypical and significant hardship within the correctional context." *Id.* at 224.

The Supreme Court's decisions in *Sandin* and *Wilkinson* establish that disciplinary segregation *can* trigger due process protections depending on the duration and conditions of segregation. *See Wilkinson*, 545 U.S. at 224; *Sandin*, 515 U.S. at 486. Although the defendants contend that a prisoner's due process protections are triggered only by indefinite segregation and parole disqualification, we have declined to read *Wilkinson*'s holding as being limited to its specific facts. *See Westefer*, 422 F.3d at 590 ("Illinois' contention that the liberty interest identified in *Wilkinson* turned exclusively on the absence of parole constitutes, [in] our view, far too crabbed a reading of the decision."). The Supreme Court's decisions are helpful in setting out the durational parameters of a prison-segregation due process analysis. There nevertheless remains a significant area in which the presence of a cognizable liberty interest is not self-evident from a reading of these cases. In these situations, we must make the necessary determination by analyzing the combined import of the duration of the segregative confinement *and* the conditions endured by the prisoner during that period.

The defendants correctly note that, in some cases, we have described an inmate's liberty interest in avoiding segregation as very limited or even nonexistent. For example, in Townsend v. Fuchs, 522 F.3d 765 (7th Cir. 2008), which involved a prisoner segregation term of fifty-nine days, we concluded that "inmates have no liberty interest in avoiding transfer to discretionary segregation — that is, segregation imposed for administrative, protective, or investigative purposes." *Townsend*, 522 F.3d at 766, 771. However, those cases, like *Sandin*, all involve relatively short periods of segregation. . . . In a number of other cases, we have explained that a liberty interest *may* arise if the length of segregated confinement is substantial and the record reveals that the conditions of confinement are unusually harsh. . . .

Mr. Marion's term of 240 days' segregation is significantly longer than terms of segregation imposed in cases where we have affirmed dismissal without requiring a factual inquiry into the conditions of confinement. *See* Townsend v. Fuchs, 522 F.3d 765, 766 (7th Cir. 2008); Holly v. Woolfolk, 415 F.3d 678, 679 (7th Cir. 2005); Hoskins v. Lenear, 395 F.3d 372, 374-75 (7th Cir. 2005). Indeed, a term of 240 days of segregation is more akin to the confinements for which we have ordered remands for further inquiry into the conditions of confinement. Following [those] cases, it is clear that a term of segregation as lengthy as Mr. Marion's requires scrutiny of the actual conditions of segregation.

Our decision that Mr. Marion's complaint states a claim is consistent with the decisions of our sister circuits. Indeed, other courts of appeals have held that periods of confinement that approach or exceed one year may trigger a cognizable liberty interest without any reference to conditions.[4] Accordingly, the

4. *See* Iqbal v. Hasty, 490 F.3d 143, 161 (2d Cir. 2007), cert. granted sub nom. Ashcroft v. Iqbal, 128 S. Ct. 2931, 171 L. Ed. 2d 863 (2008) (explaining that a segregated confinement of 305 days or more necessarily triggers due process protections, and segregation lasting 101 to 305 days may trigger due process protections, depending on the conditions of segregation); Trujillo v. Williams, 465 F.3d 1210, 1225 (10th Cir. 2006) (reversing dismissal of claim involving 750 days' segregation, stating that when a "prisoner is subjected to a lengthy period of segregation, the duration of that confinement may itself be atypical and significant"); Williams v. Fountain, 77 F.3d 372, 374 (11th Cir. 1996) (holding that one year of solitary confinement was sufficient to state a claim); *but see* Smith v. Mensinger, 293 F.3d 641, 654 (3d Cir. 2002) (holding that seven months' segregation, alone, does not implicate a liberty interest).

approach of other circuits suggests that Mr. Marion's claim of confinement in segregation for 240 days may implicate a liberty interest, and therefore, further fact-finding is necessary.

The defendants maintain that, as a matter of law, Mr. Marion cannot state a claim under the Due Process Clause because the conditions of his confinement are not harsher than the conditions found in the most restrictive prison in Wisconsin. . . . The defendants' argument is decidedly premature at the pleading stage. Mr. Marion has complied with Federal Rule of Civil Procedure 8 and has put the defendants on reasonable notice of his allegation that he was denied due process of law when he was punished with 240 days of segregation in D.S.1. Moreover, . . . the Supreme Court has stated that whether an inmate has a protected liberty interest must be determined from the *actual* conditions of confinement and not simply from a review of state regulations. *See Wilkinson*, 545 U.S. at 223 ("After *Sandin*, it is clear that the touchstone of the inquiry into the existence of a protected, state-created liberty interest in avoiding restrictive conditions of confinement is not the language of regulations regarding those conditions but the nature of those conditions themselves 'in relation to the ordinary incidents of prison life.'" (quoting *Sandin*, 515 U.S. at 484)). As *Wilkinson* and the decisions from our sister circuits also emphasize, we must take into consideration all of the circumstances of a prisoner's confinement in order to ascertain whether a liberty interest is implicated. Without a factual record, we cannot determine whether the actual conditions of Mr. Marion's lengthy segregation are harsher than the conditions found in the most restrictive prison in Wisconsin. We therefore must reverse the dismissal of Mr. Marion's due process claim and remand this case to the district court for further proceedings.

CONCLUSION

Accordingly, we reverse the judgment of the district court and remand the case for further proceedings consistent with this opinion.

NOTES

1. Is the *Hedrich* case consistent with Goss v. Lopez in its characterization of liberty interests? Does the court in *Hedrich* talk about liberty interests in a different way than the Supreme Court does in *Goss*? The *Goss* Court seemed to suggest that a reputational interest is cognizable as a liberty interest if some other, more tangible interest, such as a property interest, is implicated. In *Goss*, of course, there was both a property interest and a liberty interest. Is that true in *Hedrich*? The *Hedrich* court seems to be looking for an extraordinary level of stigma in order to find a cognizable liberty interest — what has been termed a "stigma plus" standard. Did the *Goss* Court speak about stigma in a different way?

2. Some have suggested that the due process "liberty interest" standard for prison deprivations is different from the "liberty interest" standard outside prison. Such a suggestion makes some sense since those in prison have already been deprived of liberty pursuant to some formalized process. Look carefully at *Hedrich* and *Marion*, though. Are they in some ways similar? In the end, how does the court in each case determine whether a cognizable liberty interest is at stake?

C EXCEPTIONS TO DUE PROCESS REQUIREMENTS

1. Pure Administrative Process/No Facts to Be Found

HOLLINRAKE v. IOWA LAW ENFORCEMENT ACADEMY

452 N.W.2d 598 (Iowa 1990)

LARSON, Justice.

Edward J. Hollinrake, who was denied certification as a peace officer by the Iowa Law Enforcement Academy (academy) because his eyesight did not meet its minimum standards, sought judicial review in district court. The district court dismissed his petition, and he appealed. We affirm. . . .

Essentially, the record shows that Hollinrake's distance vision in his left eye does not meet the standards of 501 Iowa Administrative Code 2.1(9), which requires uncorrected vision of "not less than 20/100 in both eyes, corrected to 20/20." The academy determined that Hollinrake did not meet the vision criteria of the rule and therefore could not be certified. In making this determination, the academy interpreted rule 2.1(9) to require 20/20 corrected vision in each eye. . . .

III. THE RIGHT TO A HEARING

Hollinrake's certification was denied without a hearing, and he contends this was error. As he points out, Iowa Code §17A.18(1) provides that, when the granting of a license is required, by the constitution or a statute, to be preceded by notice and an opportunity for an evidentiary hearing, the provisions of chapter 17A regarding contested cases apply. This would ordinarily involve a hearing. Iowa Code chapter 80B, the Law Enforcement academy statute, does not provide for advance notice and hearing except in the case of a *revocation* of an officer's certification. See Iowa Code §80B.132(9). The question thus becomes whether some other statute, or our constitution, requires a hearing in such a case. Under Iowa Code §17A.2(2), a hearing is required if the action involves the determination of disputed facts of particular applicability under the circumstances, commonly referred to as "adjudicative facts." . . .

In this case, there are no disputed adjudicative facts. The only evidence on which the academy denied Hollinrake's certification, the results of his eye examination, was presented by Hollinrake himself. Certification was denied on the ground that Hollinrake lacked the minimum visual acuity required by the rules.

If a certification decision turns on circumstances peculiar to the applicant, an evidentiary hearing may be required under the constitution. See B. Schwartz, Administrative Law §84, at 238-239 (1976). Thus, Hollinrake should be afforded a hearing if, for example, the denial of his license was premised on misconduct or character defects or if he disagreed with the factual basis for the decision. Id. In the instant case, Hollinrake had no such claims. The sole deficiency in his application related to a "generalized legislative fact" — a standardized vision requirement. . . .

When a decision is based solely on legislative facts, due process does not require a hearing:

> In general, procedural due process demands that whenever a state agency determines the legal rights, privileges, or duties of a specific party based upon that party's particular facts and circumstances, the state agency is bound to provide an opportunity for an evidentiary hearing. Stated differently, a state must *usually* provide an individual with an opportunity for a hearing of some sort when it takes action of *particular applicability*, defining a person's rights, on the basis of adjudicative facts. As noted earlier, adjudicative facts are individualized facts concerning the circumstances of the specific party — the facts of the particular case. "Adjudicative facts are the facts about the parties and their activities, businesses, and properties. . . . [T]hey usually answer the questions of who did what, where, when, how, why, with what motive or intent; adjudicative facts are the kind of facts that go to a jury in a jury case." . . . "Legislative facts do not relate to particular parties; they are generalized facts which apply more broadly and may, as Justice Holmes once phrased it, serve as a ground for laying down a rule of law." . . .
>
> The rationale for this rule is explained: The whole function of the required *evidentiary* hearing is . . . to find adjudicatory facts in the best way available — through the mechanism of an oral adversary hearing. When there are *no* relevant adjudicative facts to dispute, therefore, there is no more need for a hearing as a matter of due process than there is a matter of statutory requirement. Obviously, neither the Constitution nor a statute should be read to require a wholly useless act. . . .
>
> A hearing is not required by constitution in an agency adjudication when there is no material issue of fact that is disputed by the parties. . . .

Under the circumstances of this case, Hollinrake was not entitled to a hearing on either constitutional or statutory grounds. . . .

NOTES

1. *Pure administrative process.* Other cases where there is no right to be heard even though they fall on the adjudicatory side of the *Bi-Metallic–Londoner* line involve what has been called the "pure administrative process." These are the cases where decisions are made on the basis of observation by technical experts or objective tests. There are three principal categories of such decisions: those made on the basis of (a) inspections; (b) tests; and (c) elections.

(a) Consider administrative decisions such as those involving the grading of grain. Would it make sense to have such decisions based on the record of a trial-type hearing? The surest way to grade grain is for the skilled inspector to test samples of it. The same is true of the countless other cases where decisions are based on inspections — those involving inspections of other agricultural commodities, ships, planes, locomotives, and the like, to determine their quality or safety. Determinations of this type run into the many millions each year and are based on the observations of the qualified administrators rather than any formal procedure.

(b) Compare the agency decision that evaluates the skill or competence of an individual. How should the agency decide whether a license applicant is qualified to drive an automobile or practice law? By evidence developed in a trial-type proceeding?

(c) A third case is the decision in a labor representation proceeding, where an agency decision to certify the union turns on whether the majority of employees in the bargaining unit desire to be represented by the union. What is the rational method of decision in such a case?

2. Does the *Hollinrake* case come within this exception? Into which category does it fit? Compare Connecticut Light & Power v. Norwalk, 425 A.2d 576 (Conn. 1979) (decision on effectiveness of new equipment in reducing air pollution depends on inspection, examination, or testing; hence, no right to be heard before decision), and Union of Concerned Scientists v. NRC, 735 F.2d 1437 (D.C. Cir. 1984) (evaluation of emergency preparedness exercises is not a determination resting solely on test or inspection).

3. *Mathematical application.* In *Londoner*, the agency was directed to apportion the cost of the street paving among the abutting property owners in proportion to the benefits received by them from the improvement. Statutes providing for assessments for the cost of improvements sometimes provide for the assessments to be made on the basis of the so-called foot-frontage rule, under which the abutting owner's share of the cost is measured by his property's frontage on the street that has been benefitted.

Despite *Londoner*, when the assessment is to be made on the basis of the foot-frontage rule alone, does the abutting property owner have a due process right to be heard prior to the assessment?

When the decision is based on mechanical application of a mathematical rule or formula, there is no due process right to be heard even though the decision is adjudicatory within the *Bi-Metallic–Londoner* dividing line. See

Pullman Co. v. Knott, 235 U.S. 23 (1914), which rejected a claim that due process demanded a hearing before companies could be ordered to pay a tax on gross receipts derived from business done in the taxing state. The statute required the companies to make a report listing their gross receipts from business done and fixed a percentage ($1.50 per $100) to be paid. According to Justice Holmes, "If the companies do as required there is nothing to be heard about. They fix the amount and the statute establishes the proportion to be paid over." Id. at 26.

4. May cases involving medical questions be decided by doctors who have physically examined the individuals involved? In Britain, as in this country, there are administrative tribunals that decide medical questions, such as those arising under claims for disability benefits under the British equivalent of the Social Security Act. The British tribunals are called Medical Boards and Medical Appeal Tribunals. Fully qualified doctors serve on these tribunals, and their decisions are based on their personal examinations of the claimants as part of the proceedings before the tribunals. In this country, we do things differently. Under the Social Security Act, decisions on disability are made by lawyers, not doctors; the examining doctors are only witnesses, not deciders. See the procedure described in Richardson v. Perales, *infra* p. 565. Yet it is only by an act of faith that the lawyer is considered better qualified than a doctor to determine whether a Social Security claimant is disabled by a manual impediment from carrying on his trade as a carpenter. Would the British system of decision of medical issues by doctors be constitutional in this country? See White v. Industrial Accident Comm'n, 362 P.2d 302 (Or. 1961) (medical board of three doctors may be given power to decide disability questions). But see Mortensen v. Board of Trustees, 473 P.2d 866 (Haw. 1970):

> We disagree with this decision of the Oregon court. . . . Where an ascertainment of the truth is more likely through the use of a trial-type hearing, it should be used at some point in the administrative process. Real expertise will not be hindered but strengthened by its exposure to the fire of cross-examination, rebuttal evidence, and argument. An examination or inspection by an expert is simply no substitute for a trial-type hearing except, perhaps, in certain limited circumstances.

Id. at 871-872.

Is "ascertainment of the truth more likely" on this type of medical question "through the use of a trial-type hearing"?

5. Compare the response of one American agency to the problem of evaluating scientific evidence:

> The development of effective decision making techniques for the evaluation of scientific studies has been one of the most elusive problems for the administrative process. The implementation of health and safety laws often requires an evaluation of the scientific reliability of laboratory animal, clinical, or epidemiological test data, a determination of risks and benefits based upon those data and other factors, and a final "regulatory conclusion" in which the relevant law is applied in light of the previous conclusions. For example, health and safety agencies commonly are required to determine whether a particular chemical is carcinogenic or otherwise harmful as a prerequisite to reaching a regulatory conclusion.

The quality and legitimacy of these agency decisions can be improved by counseling with eminent scientific experts outside of the agency. Some scientists and others have supported the idea of a "science court" or an institution to which administrative agencies could refer scientific disputes for resolution by expert scientists. In response, agencies have developed several methods of obtaining scientific input, including the use of advisory committees. Science advisory committees are the most common method used to obtain such assistance before an agency reaches a decision. In addition, the Food and Drug Administration (FDA) has created and used twice a unique procedure, the Public Board of Inquiry (PBOI), to obtain independent scientific review of particular regulatory decisions. The PBOI combines the elements of a "scientific hearing" with the more typical "adversarial hearing" approach for the evaluation of scientific evidence.

The PBOI is one of three alternative informal methods of proceeding that FDA offers applicants in lieu of the formal adjudication by an administrative law judge (ALJ) that would otherwise be held to review certain decisions concerning the approval of food additives and new drugs. The other two alternatives are a hearing before an advisory committee or an informal hearing before the Commissioner of FDA. The PBOI consists of a panel of three scientists appointed by the Commissioner. Two of the three scientists are selected from recommendations of the parties. The Board obtains scientific "testimony" within an informal quasi-adjudicative hearing framework, in which the advocacy role of lawyers is minimized in favor of a "scientific forum" approached — although the Board's decision is an "initial decision" and has the same legal status as an initial decision of an ALJ.

FDA's two PBOI hearings occurred in 1980 and 1983. In the first, a PBOI was convened to determine whether Aspartame, now a widely used artificial sweetener, should be approved as a food additive. In the 1983 proceeding, a PBOI was convened to determine whether Depo Provera, a drug approved in other countries as a contraceptive, should be approved for that use in the United States.

Some analysts contend that FDA's experiences confirm the validity of the "science court" idea for the evaluation of scientific evidence. They argue that techniques like the PBOI are more effective for obtaining scientific advice than traditional adversarial hearings because a PBOI provides the presiding scientists with the flexibility to operate according to procedures that are customary to scientific inquiry. . . .

50 Fed. Reg. 52893 (Dec. 27, 1985).

2. Waiver

NATIONAL INDEPENDENT COAL OPERATORS' ASS'N v. KLEPPE

423 U.S. 388 (1976)

Mr. Chief Justice Burger delivered the opinion of the Court.

This case presents the question whether the Federal Coal Mine Health and Safety Act of 1969, 83 Stat. 742, 30 U.S.C. §801 et seq., requires the Secretary of the

Interior to prepare a decision with formal findings of fact before assessing a civil penalty against a mine operator absent a request by the mine operator for an administrative hearing. . . .

The statute, §109(a)(3), 30 U.S.C. §819(a)(3), is part of the enforcement scheme of the Federal Coal Mine Health and Safety Act of 1969. The Act prescribes health and safety standards for the protection of coal miners, Titles II and III, 30 U.S.C. §§841, 861 et seq.; it requires coal mine operators and miners to comply with the standards. . . .

As part of the enforcement scheme, the Act requires the Secretary to assess and collect civil penalties. Section 109(a)(1), 30 U.S.C. §819(a)(1), subjects mine operators to civil penalties not exceeding $10,000 for each violation of a mandatory standard or other provisions of the Act. . . .

The provision in question, §109(a)(3), authorizes the Secretary to assess a civil penalty only after the operator charged with a violation "has been given an opportunity for a public hearing and the Secretary has determined, by decision incorporating his findings of fact therein, that a violation did occur, and the amount of the penalty which is warranted. . . ." Hearings under this section are to be considered with other proceedings when appropriate. They must be of record and subject to provisions of the Administrative Procedure Act, 5 U.S.C. §554. If the operator does not pay the penalty assessed, the Secretary is required pursuant to §109(a)(4), 30 U.S.C. §819(a)(4), to petition for judicial enforcement of the assessment in the district court for the district in which the mine is located. At that stage the court must resolve the issues relevant to the amount of the penalty in a de novo proceeding with a jury trial if requested. . . .

We are concerned in this case with the regulations the Secretary has adopted to govern only one part of this statutory scheme: the assessment of penalties under §109(a)(3). . . . These regulations provide that assessment officers assess a penalty based on a notice of violation issued by mine inspectors and a penalty schedule graduated according to the seriousness of the violation. . . .

The regulations also provide that the operators are to be advised when they receive original or reissued proposed orders that they have fifteen working days from the receipt of the order to "protest the proposed assessment, either partly or in its entirety." If the operator fails to make a timely protest and request adjudication, he is "deemed to have waived his right to protest including his right of formal adjudication and opportunity for hearing. . . ." The proposed assessment order then becomes the "final assessment of the Secretary." 30 C.F.R. §100.4(d-h) (1972).

In any case in which an operator makes a timely request for a formal hearing, by so indicating in his protest, or in response to a reissued or amended proposed assessment order, the assessment officer is required to forward the matter to the Office of the Solicitor, Department of the Interior; a petition to assess a penalty can then be filed by the Solicitor with the Department's Office of Hearings and Appeals. 30 C.F.R. §100.4(i)(1) (1972), 43 C.F.R. §4.540(a) (1972). The petition is served on the operator, who then has an opportunity to answer and secure a public hearing. 30 C.F.R. §100.4(i)(2) (1972). A hearing de novo is conducted and the examiner is free to assess a different penalty. 30 C.F.R. §100.4.(i)(4) (1972). The Bureau of Mines, represented by the Office of the Solicitor, has the burden of proving the penalty by a preponderance of the evidence. 43 C.F.R. §4.587 (1972). The regulations provide that the hearing examiner consider the statutory criteria. 43 C.F.R. §4.546 (1972). The decision is subject to review by the Secretary's delegate, the Board of Mine Operations Appeals. . . .

Under the Act, a mine operator plainly has a right to notice of violations and proposed penalties; it is equally clear that an operator has a right to be heard, if a hearing is requested. In this Court the mine operators continue to urge that the Secretary may not assess a civil penalty without making formal "findings of fact" even though no hearing was requested as to the violation charged and the proposed order. Section 109(a)(3) provides that:

> [a] civil penalty shall be assessed by the Secretary only after the person charged with a violation under this Act has been given an opportunity for a public hearing and the Secretary has determined, by a decision incorporating his findings of fact therein, that a violation did occur, and the amount of the penalty which is warranted. . . .

The operators argue that a penalty assessment itself is an adjudicatory function and hence the Secretary must make a formal "decision incorporating findings of fact" even when the operator has not requested a hearing on the violation issue. In short, what they argue for is the same type of formal findings of fact that are the usual product of the adversary hearing to which they have an absolute right, but which was waived by failure to make a request.

Section 109(a)(3) provides the mine operators with no more than "an opportunity" for a hearing. The word "opportunity" would be meaningless if the statute contemplated formal adjudicated findings whether or not a requested evidentiary hearing is held. Absent a request, the Secretary has a sufficient factual predicate for the assessment of a penalty based on the reports of the trained and experienced inspectors who find violations; when the assessment officers fix penalties as the Secretary's "authorized representatives," the operators may still have review of the penalty in the district court. . . .

We therefore agree with the Court of Appeals that language of the statute, especially when read in light of its legislative history, requires the Secretary to make formal findings of fact specified in §109(a)(3) only when the mine operator requests a hearing. The requirement for a formal hearing under §109(a)(3) is keyed to a request, and the requirement for formal findings is keyed to the same request. . . .

We conclude, as did the Court of Appeals, that the Federal Coal Mine Health and Safety Act of 1969 does not mandate a formal decision with findings as a predicate for a penalty assessment order unless the mine operator exercises his statutory right to request a hearing on the factual issues relating to the penalty, and the judgment of the Court of Appeals is therefore affirmed.

NOTES

1. In 1955 the Lord Chancellor appointed the Committee on Administrative Tribunals and Enquiries (usually known as the Franks Committee, after its chairman, Lord Franks) to conduct a comprehensive investigation of British administrative law. Bernard Schwartz was invited to give evidence before the Franks Committee in November 1956. During the session, after American administrative procedure, with the right to a full trial-type hearing discussed in this chapter, had been described, the following exchange took place with the question being asked by a barrister member of the Franks Committee:

> Does that in any way tend to gum up the administrative works?—Let me put it this way: when we use the term "hearing" we mean a full hearing with witnesses and evidence, documentary and oral.... It does not gum up the works for two reasons, first, with us much more than in this country the tradition of oral argument is different, there is always a power in the tribunal to cut argument short, and even in our highest courts the arguments are very short by English standards. When you allow it you allow it to a limited extent, a half-hour or an hour, whatever the case may be. Secondly, and much more important, is the fact that in our experience the rights which individuals have are not insisted upon in every case. If they were to insist upon their full rights in every case, administration would become impossible, there is no doubt of this whatsoever, because some of our important agencies each render well over a million decisions each year. If you had more than a very small percentage of hearings in the first place and then appeals from the initial decision and then the oral argument, these agencies would be spending all their time just hearing these cases and they would not be able to get any of their administrative tasks done. It does not happen in that way for various reasons, in part the question of expense, in part the fact that there is no point really at issue and therefore no point in going through the formality of a hearing. I have seen the figures in some agencies, and in none of them are full rights insisted upon in more than 5 percent of the cases. That is what makes the thing workable.

Committee on Administrative Tribunals and Enquiries, Minutes of Evidence 1034 (1956).

It is consequently not strictly accurate to speak of the due process right to be heard. More accurately, as Chief Justice Burger points out, it is the right to an *opportunity* to be heard. Like other constitutional rights, the right to be heard can be waived. Formal adjudicatory procedure is not required when the mine operator chooses not to request a hearing on the proposed penalty. Compare Reno v. Flores, 507 U.S. 292 (1993) (automatic hearing in every case not required; due process satisfied by *right* to a hearing, which may be waived).

As Schwartz indicated in his Franks Committee testimony, it is widespread waiver of the right to be heard that makes the administrative process workable in practice. The vast bulk of agency decisions are made without resort to formal proceedings because the right is waived most of the time. Hearings are actually held in less than 5 percent of the cases disposed of by federal regulatory agencies. In nonregulatory agencies, the percentage of hearings is even smaller.

During the 1992 fiscal year, the Department of Health and Human Services handled over 100 million claims under the Social Security Act; in that period, only some 250,000 agency hearings were held.

2. Should a hearing be required when no disputed issues are raised? See Altenheim German Home v. Tarnock, 902 F.2d 582 (7th Cir. 1990). "In such situations," said the lower court in *Coal Operators*, "the rationale is that Congress does not intend administrative agencies to perform meaningless tasks." Nat'l Indep. Coal Operators' Ass'n v. Morton, 494 F.2d 987 (D.C. Cir. 1974).

In Costle v. Pacific Legal Foundation, 445 U.S. 198 (1980), the EPA had extended the permit of a sewage plant owned by Los Angeles. Respondent's post-determination request for an adjudicatory hearing was denied on the ground that it did not set forth material issues of fact relevant to the question whether the permit should be extended. The court of appeals held that the EPA had failed to provide the "opportunity for public hearing" as required by statute. The court concluded that the EPA was required to justify failure to hold a hearing on a permit action by proof that the material facts supporting the action "are not subject to dispute."

The Supreme Court held that the lower court had erred in this conclusion. The courts may not require the agency to justify failure to hold a hearing by proof that the material facts supporting its actions "are not subject to dispute." On the contrary, the Court specifically approved the EPA's rules that require an applicant who seeks a hearing to meet a threshold burden of tendering evidence showing the need for a hearing. The EPA did not err in failing to hold an adjudicatory hearing on the issues raised in respondent's request because the request did not set forth material issues of fact pertinent to the question whether the permit's expiration date should be extended.

3. Postponed Hearings and Emergency Cases

HASKELL v. DEPARTMENT OF AGRICULTURE

930 F.2d 816 (10th Cir. 1991)

LOGAN, Circuit Judge.

Appellant William C. Haskell, Jr. (Haskell) sought review of an administrative decision of the appellee United States Department of Agriculture (Secretary) permanently disqualifying his store, Haskell Brothers Grocery, from participation in the food stamp program. 7 C.F.R. §178.6(a). Haskell's store was charged with thirteen separate violations of Food and Nutrition Service (FNS) regulations including trafficking in food stamps for cash and marijuana and exchanging food stamps for ineligible items. . . . These violations resulted in a decision by the Secretary to disqualify the store permanently from participation in the food stamp program.

Upon review of the Secretary's decision, the district court granted the Secretary's motion for summary judgment and denied Haskell's cross motion for summary judgment and motion to suppress. . . .

Haskell . . . argues that the district court erred in concluding that he was afforded adequate procedural due process during the administrative proceedings. The district court, assuming that Haskell possessed a property interest in the privilege of continued participation in the food stamp program, determined that he had received adequate notice, opportunity to be heard via the submission of information to the review officer, and opportunity to reply to the charge letter. . . . Although Haskell was not afforded an evidentiary hearing at the administrative level, he sought and received de novo review of the administrative decision from the district court. When such an opportunity for judicial review exists, the lack of an evidentiary hearing at the administrative level is not a denial of due process. . . . "[O]nce a participant seeks review de novo, the adequacy of the administrative process as an abstract matter is no longer important. . . . The adequacy of the prior process is no more important than the 'process' that precedes an agency's decision to commence a proceeding or suit. . . ." The judgment of the United States District Court for the District of Kansas is affirmed.

NOTES

1. "The demands of due process do not require a hearing, at the initial stage or at any particular point or at more than one point in an administrative proceeding so long as the requisite hearing is held before the final order becomes effective." Opp Cotton Mills v. Administrator, 312 U.S. 126, 152-153 (1941). This means that, even where there is a due process right to be heard, the hearing need not be held at any particular stage of the proceeding. As Justice White put it, "In passing upon claims to a hearing . . . , the usual rule of this Court had been that a full hearing at some time suffices." Arnett v. Kennedy, 416 U.S. 134, 187 (1974) (concurring).

In the normal hearing case, of course, the opportunity to be heard is afforded before the agency makes a decision or takes other action. But the hearing need not be given at that stage. The opportunity to be heard may be given by the agency after it acts; where only property rights are involved, mere postponement of the opportunity to be heard is not a denial of due process.

2. *Provisional action.* An example of provisional administrative action is provided under the Occupational Safety and Health Act of 1970, 29 U.S.C. §659. It empowers the Secretary of Labor to issue citations with proposed penalties. If the employer fails to contest the citation, it becomes final. However, if he does contest it, the Occupational Safety and Health Review Commission is required to conduct a hearing and then issue an order either affirming, modifying, or vacating the secretary's citation or proposed penalty. See McLean Trucking Co. v. Occupational Safety and Health Review Comm'n, 503 F.2d 8 (4th Cir. 1974) (contention rejected that procedural due process was denied by permitting secretary to issue citations with proposed penalties without giving employers opportunity to be heard). Compare the similar procedure in National Independent Coal Operators' Ass'n v. Kleppe, *supra* p. 483.

3. *Judicial review.* The required hearing may even be given at the stage of judicial review. Compare the statement of Justice Douglas in Bowles v. Willingham, 321 U.S. 503, 520 (1944), in answer to a due process claim based on lack of opportunity to be heard before an agency order: "Here Congress has provided for judicial review of the Administrator's action. To be sure, that review comes after the order had been promulgated. . . . But . . . that review satisfies the requirements of due process."

Does Douglas mean that, even if there is no opportunity to be heard before the agency, the existence of judicial review satisfies the requirements of procedural due process? What does such a rule do to the right to be heard as a constitutional requirement, in view of the widespread availability of judicial review in our system?

Compare the statement of the Court in Goss v. Lopez, 419 U.S. 565 (1975), answering a claim that the absence of the opportunity to be heard before an agency was cured by a statutory provision for judicial review:

> Appellants point to the fact that some process is provided under Ohio law by way of judicial review. Ohio Rev. Code §2501.06. Appellants do not cite any case in which this general administrative review statute had been used to appeal from a disciplinary decision by a school official. If it be assumed that it could be so used, it is for two reasons insufficient to save inadequate procedures at the school level. First, although new proof may be offered in a §2501.06 proceeding, Shaker Coventry Corp. v. Shaker Heights, Ohio Com. Pl., 176 N.E.2d 332, the proceeding is not de novo. In re Locke, 33 Ohio App. 2d 177, 294 N.E.2d 230. Thus the decision by the school — even if made upon inadequate procedures — is entitled to weight in the court proceeding. Second, without a demonstration to the contrary, we must assume that delay will attend any §2501.06 proceeding, that the suspension will not be stayed pending hearing, and that the student meanwhile will irreparably lose his educational benefits.

Id. at 581.

Judicial review should serve as a substitute for an agency hearing only where it is broad enough to allow the private party to present his case adequately, with full opportunity to submit evidence and arguments. In addition, the court must be able to decide the merits of the case on its own independent judgment; where due process requires a hearing, it must be on the merits of the controversy. Such a full hearing on review is available only in a trial *de novo* in the reviewing court. A trial *de novo* on review is rare but, when it is given, it can, as *Haskell* shows, take the place of the administrative hearing that may be required by due process.

4. Note that in National Independent Coal Operators' Ass'n v. Kleppe, *supra* p. 483, the statute provided for judicial enforcement of a penalty assessed by the secretary in a *de novo* proceeding in the district court.

Would such a provision permit Congress to authorize summary assessment of the penalty by the secretary? See Mohawk Co. v. Occupational Safety & Health Review Comm'n, 549 F.2d 859 (2d Cir. 1977).

LIBERTAS CLASSICAL ASS'N v. WHITMER

498 F. Supp. 3d 961 (W.D. Mich. 2020)

OPINION AND ORDER DENYING PLAINTIFF'S MOTIONS FOR PRELIMINARY INJUNCTION AND ORDER OF ABSTENTION

I.

[T]he Ottawa County [Michigan] Department of Public Health contacted Libertas about the COVID-19 measures. During the first week of school in early September, Defendant Marcia Mansaray spoke with Robert Davis, the headmaster at Libertas. Mansaray informed Davis that an anonymous person alleged that students at Libertas were not wearing face coverings. After Ottawa County received a second anonymous tip, Mansaray sent an email to Davis sometime around September 22. Mansaray informed Davis about the requirement for face coverings. Mansaray concluded the email with a request and a warning. She requested "cooperation and enforcement of these requirements." She warned that if additional complaints were made, there might be "enforcement from state or local officials." She further warned that that "one or more positive cases of COVID-19 in the school building will necessitate that the school follow these requirements."

[D]irector Robert Gordon of the Michigan Department of Health and Human Services quickly issued Emergency Orders using provisions of Michigan's Public Health Code to enact restrictions designed to slow the spread of COVID-19.... On October 6, Gordon issued an order requiring local health departments to notify schools of confirmed COVID-19 cases and also required schools to post the notice on their website. On October 9, Gordon rescinded the October 5 Emergency Order and replaced it with a different order that generally regulated the size of gatherings and required the use of face coverings in different situations. Gordon primarily relied on Michigan Compiled Laws §333.2251 and §333.2253 as authority for his Emergency Orders....

Relevant to this dispute, the mandates for [these] emergency orders are functionally the same. The sizes of indoor gatherings are limited, people must socially distance, and the people gathering must wear masks. School classrooms are probably exempt from the social distance requirements and the occupancy limitations, but not from the requirement for face coverings. The orders do include exceptions for face covering. The orders also contain an exception for worship.

In early October, Ottawa County sent . . . Desist Order[s] to Libertas. . . . Ottawa County alleged Libertas was in violation of limitations on the size of indoor gatherings, the requirement that the individuals wear face coverings, and the social distancing requirements. Ottawa County ordered Libertas to "immediately cease all operations that are not in compliance with current Emergency Order. . . .

Counsel for Ottawa County and counsel for Libertas exchanged emails over the next few days.

On Sunday, October 18, 2020, Libertas filed its complaint in this Court. On October 21, 2020, the County issued [another] Cease and Desist Order. . . . The order determined that Libertas failed to report the infections of . . . teacher[s] to the County as required by Michigan Administrative Rule 325.173(9)(a) and (b). The order determined that Libertas failed to identify the students, classes, and contacts with staff that were necessary for contact tracing, which violated Rule 325.174(2)(a)-(f). The order made other determinations as well. The County then required Libertas to do the following:

> A. Libertas must notify the parents of all students attending Libertas School and Libertas staff using the attached letter, that there is an outbreak of COVID-19 associated with Libertas School and also provide a copy of this Cease and Desist Order and must publish the Public Notice on its website as required by Director Gordon's October 6, 2020 Emergency Order;
>
> B. Libertas must provide to OCDPH the names and contact information of all known cases of COVID-19 among students and staff associated with Libertas School;
>
> C. Libertas must provide OCDPH a list of names and contact information for students, teachers, staff and volunteers that meet the definition provided above of a "close contact" for [Teacher 2] and [Teacher 1] including the class list for their classroom(s) and a listing of any in-person school assemblies or school events held during their attendance at school during the period of October 8 to the present; and
>
> D. Failure to comply with this order will leave ODCPH without the necessary information to complete a full investigation therefore we must assume that all students and staff are close contacts. All close contacts must remain in quarantine for a period of 14 days from Thursday October 22 through Thursday November 5, 2020, therefore, unless there is full compliance with A, B, and C above, Libertas is ordered to cease and desist all in person activities as of 12:01 p.m. on Thursday, October 22, 2020. . . . On October 22, 2020, the County filed a statement indicating that it intended to seek an injunction to enforce face coverings and social distancing at Libertas. Around 9:00 p.m., the County posted closure notices at the school. Libertas remains closed.

. . .

II.

. . . Libertas asserts that the October 9 Emergency Order violates the right to procedural due process found in the Michigan and the federal constitutions. Libertas argues that the County threatened to close the school if it did not comply with the requirements of the October 9 order. Libertas reasons that, before any person can be deprived of a right or liberty interest, that person is entitled to a hearing to challenge the order. Ordinarily, due process demands some sort of hearing before the deprivation of a liberty or property interest. *Hodel v. Virginia*

Mining & Reclamation Ass'n, Inc., 452 U.S. 264, 299, 101 S. Ct. 2352, 69 L. Ed. 2d 1 (1981). However, "summary administrative action may be justified in emergency situations." *Id.* at 300 (collecting cases). Our Supreme Court has held that [p]rotection of health and safety of the public is a paramount government interest which justifies summary administrative action. Indeed, deprivation of property to protect the public health and safety is "[o]ne of the oldest examples" of permissible summary action. Moreover, the administrative action provided through immediate cessation orders responds to situations in which swift action is necessary to protect public health and safety. *Id.* at 300-01 (internal citations omitted). Multiple district courts have cited this portion of *Hodel* to deny preliminary injunction challenges to COVID-19 related procedural due process claims. *See, e.g., Page v. Cuomo*, 478 F. Supp. 3d 355 (N.D.N.Y Aug. 11, 2020); *Carmichael v. Ige*, 470 F. Supp. 3d 1133 (D. Haw. July 2, 2020) (14 day travel quarantine); World Gym, Inc. v. Baker, 474 F. Supp. 3d 426 (D. Mass. July 24, 2020) (shut down order); *Benner v. Wolf*, 461 F. Supp. 3d 154 (M.D. Pa. 2020); *910 E. Main LLC v. Edwards*, 481 F. Supp. 3d 607 (W.D. La. Aug. 21, 2020).

Libertas has not demonstrated a likelihood of success on the merits for a procedural due process challenge to the . . . cease and desist orders. Under the sort of emergency situation presented by COVID-19, courts have found that a pre-deprivation hearing is not required. The two orders required information be provided, indicated a rather short time to comply, and outlined possible consequences. Libertas cannot claim that it was not on notice of the possibility that it might be shut down. Libertas has not asserted the lack of or the inadequacy of post-deprivation proceedings.

NOTES

1. See Fuentes v. Shevin, 407 U.S. 67 (1972):

> There are "extraordinary situations" that justify postponing notice and opportunity for a hearing. . . . These situations, however, must be truly unusual. Only in a few limited situations has this Court allowed outright seizure without opportunity for a prior hearing. First, in each case, the seizure has been directly necessary to secure an important governmental or general public interest. Second, there has been a special need for very prompt action. Third, the State has kept strict control over its monopoly of legitimate force: the person initiating the seizure has been a government official responsible for determining, under the standards of a narrowly drawn statute, that it was necessary and justified in the particular instance. Thus, the Court has allowed summary seizure of property to collect the internal revenue of the United States, to meet the needs of a national war effort, to protect against the economic disaster of a bank failure, and to protect the public from misbranded drugs and contaminated food.

Id. at 90-92.

2. The classic case is North American Cold Storage Co. v. Chicago, 211 U.S. 306 (1908). At issue was a municipal ordinance that provided for the summary seizure and destruction of food in cold storage that was unfit for human consumption. The owner of allegedly putrid poultry claimed that due process was denied because it was not given an opportunity to be heard prior to seizure and destruction. Held, due process was not denied where an emergency existed that would require speedy action to protect the public from contaminated food.

When the contaminated food or misbranded drugs are about to be sold, the luxury of a hearing simply cannot be afforded. In the emergency case, the emergency itself is complete justification for summary action. The right to be heard must give way to the need for immediate protection of the public. See Cowell v. NTSB, 612 F.2d 505 (10th Cir. 1980) (emergency revocation of airman certificate).

3. Is the emergency exception limited to cases involving danger to public health or safety? See Louisiana State Bar Ass'n v. Ehmig, 277 So. 2d 137 (La. 1973):

> Although it has been recognized that emergency or temporary action can be used to suspend or curtail certain rights pending a hearing on the matter, this type of action is to be allowed only where the public health and safety are involved. . . . We find that such emergency action is not appropriate in the case of an attorney who has been convicted of a crime; the public health and safety are not involved to the extent necessary to justify a suspension of his license without a prior hearing.

Id. at 140.

And see Parrish v. Daly, 350 F. Supp. 735 (S.D. Ind. 1972), citing Phillips v. Commissioner, 283 U.S. 589 (1931), and Fuentes v. Shevin, note 1 *supra*.

> In his memorandum in support of the petition for a temporary restraining order, the plaintiff argues that it is unjust and improper for the Internal Revenue Service to seize his property for payment of taxes without any prior hearing, and that he is therefore deprived the due process of law as guaranteed by the Constitution of the United States. Nevertheless, the Supreme Court of the United States has long ago established that, in view of the necessity of the collection of the revenues to sustain the Government, and in view of the protection of the right to a post-seizure adjudication, the taxing authorities may lawfully seize a citizen's property in payment of taxes, prior to the opportunity for any adjudication of his liability.

Id. at 737.

Even if the Louisiana court was wrong in its assertion that the emergency exception must be limited to cases where health and safety are involved, is summary action in tax cases justified? See Freedman, Summary Action by Administrative Agencies, 40 U. Chi. L. Rev. 1, 13-14 (1972), for a critique of the tax cases.

The Supreme Court, however, went out of its way in G. M. Leasing Corp. v. United States, 429 U.S. 338 (1977), to reaffirm the cases sustaining the governmental power to collect taxes by summary administrative proceedings; as long as there was adequate opportunity for a post-seizure determination of the taxpayer's rights, the requirements of due process were met. The Court restated the traditional rationale for the tax cases — "that the very existence of government depends upon the prompt collection of the revenues." Id. at 352, n. 18.

4. Explaining the emergency cases such as North American Cold Storage Co. v. Chicago, Justice White states, "Where the Court has rejected the need for a hearing prior to the initial 'taking,' a principal rationale has been that a hearing would be provided before the taking became final." Arnett v. Kennedy, 416 U.S. 134, 178 (1974) (concurring).

Both the *Libertas* and *North American Cold Storage* opinions stressed that there was a right to a hearing after the summary agency action — in *Libertas*, noting that the school had not objected to post-deprivation process, and in *North American Cold Storage*, and in the courts, in a tort action against the officers who seized the poultry.

Why, then, a separate category of "emergency" cases? Why aren't cases such as *Libertas* and *North American Cold Storage* merely illustrative of the principle that a hearing need not be given at any particular stage of the proceeding?

The Court in *Goss, supra* p. 432, stresses the immediate impact of the agency decision, which would not be stayed pending the later hearing. In the nonemergency case, the postponed hearing satisfies due process only if the individual is not injured in the interim. Pending the hearing, there should be provision for a stay of the agency act. But see Mathews v. Eldridge, *supra* p. 440. In the emergency cases, adverse effect may occur immediately. Emergency permits instant destruction of the infected poultry and school closure; any hearing comes after these drastic acts have taken place.

CHAPTER 5 PROBLEM

Tele-Tex Arms, Inc. ("Tele-Tex") is a gun shop, shooting range, and ice cream shop located in New York, owned and operated by Juliet Capulet. Tele-Tex's license was issued by the New York City Police Department ("NYPD") License Division (the "License Division" or the "Division"). The license is conditioned upon compliance with regulations under the Rules of the City of New York ("Rules") that require gun dealers to adhere to certain security restrictions and provide that the licensee's "premises and firearms [] shall be subject to inspection at all times by members of the Police Department." If a gun dealer fails to comply with the Rules, the Division may suspend or revoke the dealer's license "for good cause by the issuance of a Notice of Determination Letter to the licensee, which shall state in brief the grounds for the suspension or revocation and notify the licensee of the opportunity for a hearing." In the wake of the September 11, 2001 terrorist attacks, the NYPD was tasked with providing "enhanced security to sensitive locations within its boundaries," known as "Alpha posts." Tele-Tex was an Alpha post.

One year ago, Captain M. Montague, an NYPD officer, entered Tele-Tex under the Alpha post program and searched the premises. The search revealed the security at Tele-Tex to be "grossly inadequate." Security issues included an unwatched counter area, a large hole in Tele-Tex's backyard fence, and two unlocked safes. The next day, the License Division advised Juliet Capulet by letter only that, "as a result of failure to provide adequate security for Tele-Tex," her dealer's license was suspended. The letter directed Capulet to surrender all firearms "pending the conclusion of the [License Division's] investigation," which would determine whether Tele-Tex's license would be "continued, suspended, or revoked." The letter told Capulet that Sergeant C. Paris was assigned to her case and provided Paris's contact number, but did not notify Capulet of the opportunity for a hearing. Later, officers from the NYPD seized approximately 300 weapons from Tele-Tex, many of which, according to Capulet, had already been sold to customers who later demanded a refund. When Capulet asked if she could have some time to retain an attorney to represent her before the seizure, Sergeant Paris told her no. "Attorneys are not allowed to be involved in these matters due to security concerns in delaying seizure of weapons." He added, "Anyway an attorney really cannot help you. Since 9/11, no one has really questioned us on security issues related to gun shops."

Soon after, Capulet sent a letter to the License Division, informing the Division of planned security improvements at Tele-Tex. The letter included assurances by Capulet that she would "restore the fences in the backyard area," install video surveillance in the store, renovate Tele-Tex's counter area, and build a "large concrete room where her gun safes are housed." To date, Capulet has received no notice either of a reinspection by the Division or a hearing. Several months later, Capulet received a second letter from the License Division that suspended Tele-Tex's shooting range license pending investigation of the initial incident report. The letter failed to acknowledge Capulet's letter to the Division or inform Capulet of her right to a hearing.

Juliet Capulet and Tele-Tex want to file a suit against the City. According to Capulet, the NYPD License Division's actions have resulted in the loss of several months' sales and profits. Capulet believes that she has been denied due process rights to notice of violations, the right to a pre-seizure and/or post-seizure hearing, the denial of counsel, and damages as a result of the weapons seizures. Please advise Capulet and Tele-Tex about the viability of any due process arguments.

CHAPTER 6

Evidentiary Hearings* and Decisions

Kenneth F. Warren

ADMINISTRATIVE LAW IN THE POLITICAL SYSTEM**

178-179 (6th ed. 2020)

[W]hen an agency is required by statute to hold a full hearing under specified conditions, the APA outlines how the hearing should be conducted. Section 554 of the act, "Adjudications," sets forth steps and features to be included in formal order making (that is, in a fair hearing). Each year, federal agencies conduct literally millions of hearings, with the Social Security Administration alone conducting well over one million disability disputes, although well over 90 percent are not elaborate formal hearings. If state agencies are included, we can say that public agencies conduct many millions of cases each year. The agency hearing, even a formal hearing, is not expected to be a copy of a formal trial, but hearings should reflect basic court procedures. One fundamental reason for this is that the courts have found that it is easier to review legal points and procedures if the agency hearing process closely resembles actual court proceedings. Judges have found it difficult to review the fairness of hearing procedures when hearings have been "too informal." . . .

In an attempt to achieve due process in agency hearings, the major provisions of the APA require agencies to (1) provide appropriate persons proper notice as to the "time, place, and nature of the hearing," "the legal authority and jurisdiction under which the hearing is to be held," and "the matters of fact and law asserted"; (2) take into consideration "the convenience and necessity of the parties or their representatives" when scheduling the time and place of the hearing; (3) afford all concerned parties (normally limited to litigants in the dispute) the opportunity to submit and consider all relevant facts, arguments, and

* According to Matthews v. Eldridge, 424 U.S. 319 (1976), "the term 'evidentiary hearing' refers to a hearing generally of the type required in Goldberg [v. Kelly, supra p. 419]."

** Reprinted with permission. © Routledge (Taylor & Francis).

proposed settlements or adjustments as time and public interest may permit; and (4) forbid agency employees who have acted as investigators or prosecutors in a case to participate in a hearing decision, except as counsel or a witness in the public proceeding. In addition to these provisions, sections subsequent to 554 strengthen the effort to achieve a fair hearing by legally obligating agencies to (1) allow persons in hearings to be represented by counsel; (2) conclude hearing business "within a reasonable time"; (3) promptly inform interested parties as to the action taken intended and, in the case of denied requests, the reason why the request was denied; (4) arrive at decisions, rules, or orders in light of the "whole record" or part of the record that is based on "substantial evidence"; (5) provide unbiased and quasi-independent administrative law judges (formerly known as hearing examiners), who can reach decisions fairly and impartially; (6) permit persons to dispute and challenge agency evidence and opinions by providing adequate time and opportunity for persons to present conflicting data, conduct cross-examination, and so on "as may be required for a full and true disclosure of the facts"; (7) keep a complete transcript of the hearing proceedings to constitute the "exclusive record," or reviewable basis for decision; (8) state and substantiate in the record all findings and conclusions; (9) provide for within-agency appeal; and (10) permit and prepare for judicial review of agency actions.

In this chapter, we look at the trial-type administrative hearings required by due process, statute, or regulation, and explore the forms those hearings may take. Though formal administrative hearings share many characteristics with court trials, they are characterized by greater procedural flexibility than found in judicial proceedings. This chapter will address the procedures that agency adjudications must follow, beginning with parties, and proceeding through the process from notice to final decision.

A PARTIES IN INTEREST AND INTERVENTION

APA Section 554(c)

The agency shall give all interested parties opportunity for — the submission and consideration of facts, arguments, offers of settlement, or proposals of adjustment when time, the nature of the proceeding, and the public interest permit; and to the extent that the parties are unable so to determine a controversy by consent, hearing and decision on notice and in accordance with sections 556 and 557 of this title.

5 U.S.C. §554(c)

OFFICE OF COMMUNICATION OF THE UNITED CHURCH OF CHRIST v. FCC

359 F.2d 994 (D.C. Cir. 1966)

BURGER, J.

This is an appeal from a decision of the Federal Communications Commission granting to the Intervenor a one-year renewal of its license to operate television station WLBT in Jackson, Mississippi. Appellants filed with the Commission a timely petition to intervene to present evidence and arguments opposing the renewal application. The Commission dismissed Appellants' petition and, without a hearing, took the unusual step of granting a restricted and conditional renewal of the license. . . .

The questions presented are (a) whether Appellants, or any of them, have standing before the Federal Communications Commission as parties in interest under Section 309(d) of the Federal Communications Act to contest the renewal of a broadcast license; and (b) whether the Commission was required by Section 309(e) to conduct an evidentiary hearing on the claims of the Appellants prior to acting on renewal of the license.

Because the question whether representatives of the listening public have standing to intervene in a license renewal proceeding is one of first impression, we have given particularly close attention to the background of these issues and to the Commission's reasons for denying standing to Appellants.

BACKGROUND

The complaints against Intervenor embrace charges of discrimination on racial and religious grounds and of excessive commercials. As the Commission's order indicates, the first complaints go back to 1955 when it was claimed that WLBT had deliberately cut off a network program about race relations problems on which the General Counsel of the NAACP was appearing and had flashed on the viewer's screens a "Sorry, Cable Trouble" sign. In 1957 another complaint was made to the Commission that WLBT had presented a program urging the maintenance of racial segregation and had refused requests for time to present the opposing viewpoint. Since then numerous other complaints have been made. . . .

To block license renewal, Appellants filed a petition in the Commission urging denial of WLBT's application and asking to intervene in their own behalf and as representatives of "all other television viewers in the State of Mississippi." The petition stated that the Office of Communication of the United Church of Christ is an instrumentality of the United Church of Christ, a national denomination with substantial membership within WLBT's prime service area. It listed Appellants Henry and Smith as individual residents of Mississippi, and asserted that both owned television sets and that one lived within the prime service area of WLBT; both are described as leaders in Mississippi civic and civil rights groups.

Dr. Henry is president of the Mississippi NAACP; both have been politically active. . . .

The petition claimed that WLBT failed to serve the general public because it provided a disproportionate amount of commercials and entertainment and did not give a fair and balanced presentation of controversial issues, especially those concerning Negroes. . . .

Appellants claim standing before the Commission on the grounds that:

(1) They are individuals and organizations who were denied a reasonable opportunity to answer their critics, a violation of the Fairness Doctrine.

(2) These individuals and organizations represent the nearly one half of WLBT's potential listening audience who were denied an opportunity to have their side of controversial issues presented, equally a violation of the Fairness Doctrine, and who were more generally ignored and discriminated against in WLBT's programs. . . .

The Commission denied the petition to intervene on the ground that standing is predicated upon the invasion of a legally protected interest or an injury which is direct and substantial and that "petitioners . . . can assert no greater interest or claim of injury than members of the general public." . . .

STANDING OF APPELLANTS[1]

The Commission's denial of standing to Appellants was based on the theory that, absent a potential direct, substantial injury or adverse effect from the administrative action under consideration, a petitioner has no standing before the Commission and that the only types of effects sufficient to support standing are economic injury and electrical interference. It asserted its traditional position that members of the listening public do not suffer any injury peculiar to them and that allowing them standing would pose great administrative burdens.

Up to this time, the courts have granted standing to intervene only to those alleging electrical interference, NBC v. FCC (KOA), 76 U.S. App. D.C. 238, 132 F.2d 545 (1942), aff'd, 319 U.S. 239 (1943), or alleging some economic injury, e.g., FCC v. Sanders Bros. Radio Station, 309 U.S. 470 (1940). It is interesting to note, however, that the Commission's traditionally narrow view of standing initially led it to deny standing to the very categories it now asserts are the only ones entitled thereto. In *Sanders* the Commission argued that economic injury was not a basis for standing, and in *KOA* that electrical interference was insufficient. This history indicates that neither administrative nor judicial concepts of standing have been static.

What the Commission apparently fails to see in the present case is that the courts have resolved questions of standing as they arose and have at no time manifested an intent to make economic interest and electrical interference the

1. All parties seem to consider that the same standards are applicable to determining standing before the Commission and standing to appeal a Commission order to this court. . . . We have, therefore, used the cases dealing with standing in the two tribunals interchangeably.

exclusive grounds for standing. *Sanders*, for instance, granted standing to those economically injured on the theory that such persons might well be the only ones sufficiently interested to contest a Commission action. 309 U.S. 470, 477. In *KOA* we noted the anomalous result that, if standing were restricted to those with an economic interest, educational and nonprofit radio stations, a prime source of public-interest broadcasting, would be defaulted. Because such a rule would hardly promote the statutory goal of public-interest broadcasting, we concluded that nonprofit stations must be heard without a showing of economic injury and held that all broadcast licensees could have standing by showing injury other than financial (there, electrical interference). Our statement that *Sanders* did not limit standing to those suffering direct economic injury was not disturbed by the Supreme Court when it affirmed *KOA*. 319 U.S. 239 (1943). . . .

We see no reason to believe, therefore, that Congress through its committees had any thought that electrical interference and economic injury were to be the exclusive grounds for standing or that it intended to limit participation of the listening public to writing letters to the Complaints Division of the Commission. Instead, the Congressional reports seem to recognize that the issue of standing was to be left to the courts.

The Commission's rigid adherence to a requirement of direct economic injury in the commercial sense operates to give standing to an electronics manufacturer who competes with the owner of a radio-television station only in the sale of appliances, while it denies standing to spokesmen for the listeners, who are most directly concerned with and intimately affected by the performance of a licensee. Since the concept of standing is a practical and functional one designed to insure that only those with a genuine and legitimate interest can participate in a proceeding, we can see no reason to exclude those with such an obvious and acute concern as the listening audience. This much seems essential to insure that the holders of broadcasting licenses be responsive to the needs of the audience, without which the broadcaster could not exist.

There is nothing unusual or novel in granting the consuming public standing to challenge administrative actions. In Associated Industries of New York State, Inc. v. Ickes, 134 F.2d 694 (2d Cir. 1943), vacated as moot, 320 U.S. 707 (1943), coal consumers were found to have standing to review a minimum price order. In United States v. Public Utilities Commission, 80 U.S. App. D.C. 227, 151 F.2d 609 (1945), we held that a consumer of electricity was affected by the rates charged and could appeal an order setting them. Similarly in Bebchick v. Public Utilities Commission, 109 U.S. App. D.C. 298, 287 F.2d 337 (1961), we had no difficulty in concluding that a public transit rider had standing to appeal a rate increase. A direct economic injury, even if small as to each user, is involved in the rate cases, but standing has also been granted to a passenger to contest the legality of Interstate Commerce Commission rules allowing racial segregation in railroad dining cars. Henderson v. United States, 339 U.S. 816 (1950). Moreover, in Reade v. Ewing, 205 F.2d 630 (2d Cir. 1953), a consumer of oleomargarine was held to have standing to challenge orders affecting the ingredients thereof.

These "consumer" cases were not decided under the Federal Communications Act, but all of them have in common with the case under review the interpretation of language granting standing to persons "affected" or "aggrieved." The Commission fails to suggest how we are to distinguish these cases from those involving standing of broadcast "consumers" to oppose license renewals in the Federal Communications Commission. The total number of potential individual suitors who are consumers of oleomargarine or public transit passengers would seem to be greater than the number of responsible representatives of the listening public who are potential intervenors in a proceeding affecting a single broadcast reception area. Furthermore, assuming we look only to the commercial economic aspects and ignore vital public interest, we can-not believe that the economic stake of the consumers of electricity or public transit riders is more significant than that of listeners who collectively have a huge aggregate investment in receiving equipment....

Nor does the fact that the Commission itself is directed by Congress to protect the public interest constitute adequate reason to preclude the listening public from assisting in that task....

The theory that the Commission can always effectively represent the listener interests in a renewal proceeding without the aid and participation of legitimate listener representatives fulfilling the role of private attorneys general is one of those assumptions we collectively try to work with so long as they are reasonably adequate. When it becomes clear, as it does to us now, that it is no longer a valid assumption which stands up under the realities of actual experience, neither we nor the Commission can continue to rely on it. The gradual expansion and evolution of concepts of standing in administrative law attests that experience rather than logic or fixed rules has been accepted as the guide.

The Commission's attitude in this case is ambivalent in the precise sense of that term. While attracted by the potential contribution of widespread public interest and participation in improving the quality of broadcasting, the Commission rejects effective public participation by invoking the oft-expressed fear that a "host of parties" will descend upon it and render its dockets "clogged" and "unworkable." The Commission resolves this ambivalence for itself by contending that in this renewal proceeding the viewpoint of the public was adequately represented since it fully considered the claims presented by Appellants even though denying them standing. It also points to the general procedures for public participation that are already available, such as the filing of complaints with the Commission, the practice of having local hearings, and the ability of people who are not parties in interest to appear at hearings as witnesses. In light of the Commission's procedure in this case and its stated willingness to hear witnesses having complaints, it is difficult to see how a grant of formal standing would pose undue or insoluble problems for the Commission.

We cannot believe that the Congressional mandate of public participation which the Commission says it seeks to fulfill was meant to be limited to writing letters to the Commission, to inspection of records, to the Commission's grace in considering listener claims, or to mere nonparticipating appearance at hearings.

We cannot fail to note that the long history of complaints against WLBT beginning in 1955 had left the Commission virtually unmoved in the subsequent renewal proceedings, and it seems not unlikely that the 1964 renewal application might well have been routinely granted except for the determined and sustained efforts of Appellants at no small expense to themselves. Such beneficial contribution as these Appellants, or some of them, can make must not be left to the grace of the Commission.

Public participation is especially important in a renewal proceeding, since the public will have been exposed for at least three years to the licensee's performance, as cannot be the case when the Commission considers an initial grant, unless the applicant has a prior record as a licensee. In a renewal proceeding, furthermore, public spokesmen, such as Appellants here, may be the only objectors. In a community served by only one outlet, the public interest focus is perhaps sharper and the need for airing complaints often greater than where, for example, several channels exist. Yet if there is only one outlet, there are no rivals at hand to assert the public interest, and reliance on opposing applicants to challenge the existing licensee for the channel would be fortuitous at best. Even when there are multiple competing stations in a locality, various factors may operate to inhibit the other broadcasters from opposing a renewal application. An imperfect rival may be thought a desirable rival, or there may be a "gentleman's agreement" of deference to a fellow broadcaster in the hope he will reciprocate on a propitious occasion.

Thus we are brought around by analogy to the Supreme Court's reasoning in *Sanders*; unless the listeners — the broadcast consumers — can be heard, there may be no one to bring programming deficiencies or offensive over commercialization to the attention of the Commission in an effective manner. By process of elimination those "consumers" willing to shoulder the burdensome and costly processes of intervention in a Commission proceeding are likely to be the only ones "having a sufficient interest" to challenge a renewal application. The late Edmond Cahn addressed himself to this problem in its broadest aspects when he said, "Some consumers need bread; others need Shakespeare; others need their rightful place in the national society — what they all need is processors of law who will consider the people's needs more significant than administrative convenience." Law in the Consumer Perspective, 112 U. Pa. L. Rev. 1, 13 (1963). . . .

We recognize [that] . . . regulatory agencies, the Federal Communications Commission in particular, would ill serve the public interest if the courts imposed such heavy burdens on them as to overtax their capacities. The competing consideration is that experience demonstrates consumers are generally among the best vindicators of the public interest. In order to safeguard the public interest in broadcasting, therefore, we hold that some "audience participation" must be allowed in license renewal proceedings. We recognize this will create problems for the Commission but it does not necessarily follow that "hosts" of protestors must be granted standing to challenge a renewal application or that the Commission need allow the administrative processes to be obstructed or overwhelmed by captious or purely obstructive protests. The

Commission can avoid such results by developing appropriate regulations by statutory rulemaking. Although it denied Appellants standing, it employed ad hoc criteria in determining that these Appellants were responsible spokesmen for representative groups having significant roots in the listening community. These criteria can afford a basis for developing formalized standards to regulate and limit public intervention to spokesmen who can be helpful. A petition for such intervention must "contain specific allegations of fact sufficient to show that the petitioner is a party in interest and that a grant of the application would be prima facie inconsistent" with the public interest. 74 Stat. 891 (1960), 47 U.S.C. §309(d)(1) (1964).

The responsible and representative groups eligible to intervene cannot here be enumerated or categorized specifically; such community organizations as civic associations, professional societies, unions, churches, and educational institutions or associations might well be helpful to the Commission. These groups are found in every community; they usually concern themselves with a wide range of community problems and tend to be representatives of broad as distinguished from narrow interests, public as distinguished from private or commercial interests.

The Commission should be accorded broad discretion in establishing and applying rules for such public participation, including rules for determining which community representatives are to be allowed to participate and how many are reasonably required to give the Commission the assistance it needs in vindicating the public interest. The usefulness of any particular petitioner for intervention must be judged in relation to other petitioners and the nature of the claims it asserts as basis for standing. Moreover it is no novelty in the administrative process to require consolidation of petitions and briefs to avoid multiplicity of parties and duplication of effort.

The fears of regulatory agencies that their processes will be inundated by expansion of standing criteria are rarely borne out. Always a restraining factor is the expense of participation in the administrative process, an economic reality which will operate to limit the number of those who will seek participation; legal and related expenses of administrative proceedings are such that even those with large economic interests find the costs burdensome. Moreover, the listening public seeking intervention in a license renewal proceeding cannot attract lawyers to represent their cause by the prospect of lucrative contingent fees, as can be done, for example, in rate cases.

We are aware that there may be efforts to exploit the enlargement of intervention, including spurious petitions from private interests not concerned with the quality of broadcast programming, since such private interests may sometimes cloak themselves with a semblance of public interest advocates. But this problem, as we have noted, can be dealt with by the Commission under its inherent powers and by rulemaking.

In line with this analysis, we do not now hold that all of the Appellants have standing to challenge WLBT's renewal. We do not reach that question. As to these Appellants we limit ourselves to holding that the Commission must allow standing to one or more of them as responsible representatives to assert and prove the claims they have urged in their petition.

It is difficult to anticipate the range of claims which may be raised or sought to be raised by future petitioners asserting representation of the public interest. It is neither possible nor desirable for us to try to chart the precise scope or patterns for the future. The need sought to be met is to provide a means for reflection of listener appraisal of a licensee's performance as the performance meets or fails to meet the licensee's statutory obligation to operate the facility in the public interest. The matter now before us is one in which the alleged conduct adverse to the public interest rests primarily on claims of racial discrimination, some elements of religious discrimination, oppressive over-commercialization by advertising announcements, and violation of the Fairness Doctrine. Future cases may involve other areas of conduct and programming adverse to the public interest; at this point we can only emphasize that intervention on behalf of the public is not allowed to press private interests but only to vindicate the broad public interest relating to a licensee's performance of the public trust inherent in every license. . . .

NOTES

1. The *Office of Communication* opinion was a landmark in the movement to broaden the right of a potentially affected party to participate in agency proceedings. Such broadening of intervention has been one of the foundations of the law of environmental and consumer protection, as well as other areas of public interest law. If public interest claims are to be adequately considered in today's legal system, the concept of who is permitted to vindicate the public interest must be accordingly expanded.

2. As Judge Burger points out in his *Office of Communication* opinion, the question of who has a right to be heard before the agency is closely related to the question of who has standing to seek judicial review of agency action (see Chapter 7, Section D). As a general proposition, one who has the right to be heard before the agency should have standing to seek review, and vice versa. The test in either case is that of *adverse effect*; existence of such an effect that is not too remote should give the individual the right to appear both at the administrative and judicial levels. See ECEE, Inc. v. FERC, 645 F.2d 339 (5th Cir. 1981) (standing to intervene before agency not governed by Article III limitations).

3. The need to broaden participation in the hearing process has led the courts to adopt an increasingly generous answer to the question of who has a right to appear before an agency. There has been a progressive expansion of the concept of "party in interest" from named parties to competitors, and then to the consuming public. The trend, however, has not been uniform. For example, in Envirocare v. Nuclear Regulatory Commission, 194 F.3d 72 (D.C. Cir. 1999), the U.S. Court of Appeals for the D.C. Circuit upheld the decision of the NRC to exclude Envirocare from licensing proceedings involving two separate radioactive waste disposal companies. Envirocare sought to become involved because amendment of the separate licenses would give the two companies status as a "general commercial facility" similar to Envirocare, but without requiring the companies to meet the same regulatory standards required of Envirocare.

Economic injury can also give rise to the right to intervene. Under FCC v. Sanders Bros. Radio Station, 309 U.S. 470 (1940), the operator of a radio station has a right to be heard before the FCC grants a license to operate another station in the community, even though there is no possibility of electrical interference. The existing licensee suffers direct economic injury in its competition with the new station for advertising revenue. However, as mentioned, there are some limits to economic injury as a basis for the right to intervene in agency proceedings. See, e.g., Kerm, Inc. v. FCC, 353 F.3d 57 (D.C. Cir. 2004) (no right to intervene where a competitor made only vague allegations of injury).

4. The right of consumers to intervene has been more difficult, primarily because the law started with the theory of the agency as the vindicator of the public interest. This theory assumed that there are only two necessary parties in these cases — the agency and the company being regulated — and that the agency must be relied on to protect the consuming public. As Judge Burger's opinion shows, the courts have now come to recognize that the theory of the agency as protector of the consumer is not always consistent with reality.

Interests of a noneconomic nature that are widely shared, including those involving aesthetics and ecology, may be vindicated by participation in the agency proceeding. See Palisades Citizens Ass'n v. CAB, 420 F.2d 188 (D.C. Cir. 1969). In addition to the provisions of APA §554(c) permitting intervention in formal adjudications, APA §555(b) permits an interested person to "appear before an agency or its responsible employees for the presentation, adjustment, or determination of an issue, request, or controversy in a proceeding." While §554(c) applies only to agency adjudications, APA §555(b) applies to "all forms of agency action." Such participation is granted only at agency discretion, though, and agencies have "authority to shape the manner in which intervenors will participate." See, e.g., Animal Legal Def. Fund, Inc. v. Vilsack, 237 F. Supp. 3d 15 (D.D.C. 2017).

SARASOTA COUNTY PUBLIC HOSPITAL v. DEPARTMENT OF HEALTH

553 So. 2d 189 (Fla. Dist. Ct. App. 1989)

HALL, Judge.

Sarasota County Public Hospital Board d/b/a Memorial Hospital appeals the final order of the Department of Health and Rehabilitative Services dismissing . . . its petition for a formal administrative hearing to comparatively review its certificate of need application with that of HCA Doctors Hospital of Sarasota. We reverse.

In March of 1988 both Memorial Hospital and Doctors Hospital filed certificate of need applications to construct acute care hospitals providing similar services within close proximity to each other in the city of Sarasota. Neither application proposed the addition of beds above licensed capacity. Rather, Doctors Hospital proposed to construct a completely new replacement of its existing physical plant at a different location. . . . Memorial Hospital proposed to construct a satellite hospital by transferring beds from its main physical plant. HRS received both applications in the same reviewing cycle but it did not comparatively review the applications. . . .

HRS issued notices of intent to approve Doctors' application and to deny Memorial's application. Memorial contested HRS's decisions in a petition for a formal administrative hearing in which it sought comparative review of the two applications . . . on the basis that both proposed the construction of comparable facilities providing the same range of services and both intended to serve the growing population of eastern Sarasota County.

Doctors moved to dismiss Memorial's petition. . . .

After conducting a hearing on Doctor's motion to dismiss, the hearing officer issued an order in which he recommended that the motion be granted. . . .

HRS adopted the hearing officer's recommended order in its final order dismissing Memorial's challenge to Doctors' application. . . . Robert May, the certificate of need review consultant who prepared the state agency action reports on both Doctors' and Memorial's applications, testified . . . :

> The proposed facility satellite would not only be expensive to construct and equip ($28 million) but its establishment could be a duplication of health care services. Doctor's [sic] Memorial [sic] Hospital, is being reviewed in the same batching cycle for the relocation of its facility based on physical plant deficiencies and age of the facility. If the department approved this relocation, Doctor's [sic] Memorial [sic] Hospital, would be within 2.1 miles of the proposed satellite facility.

It seems to us that May's concern with duplication of services by two hospitals being within 2.1 miles of each other can only be based on a concern that the area to be serviced by both projects could not support both, i.e., could not support the number of beds in both projects. In other words, Mr. May was, at least in part, determining the need for health care in eastern Sarasota County in accordance with a quantitative standard. A determination made in this manner indicates that the applications are mutually exclusive and, under Bio-Medical Applications v. Dept. of Health, 370 So. 2d 19 (Fla. 2d DCA 1979), they must be comparatively reviewed.

In *Bio-Medical*, Bio-Medical Applications of Clearwater, Inc. which had filed an application for a certificate of need and capital expenditure approval to construct a kidney dialysis center in Clearwater, sought to consolidate the review proceedings on its application with those on Kidneycare's, which was a nearly identical application. This court applied the ruling of Ashbacker Radio Corp. v. F.C.C., 318 U.S. 327 (1945), that the grant of one of two bona fide and mutually exclusive applications for administrative approval without a hearing on both deprives the loser of the hearing to which he is entitled and held that a material error in procedure had occurred. . . . This court stated that the basis for the *Ashbacker* ruling is the fundamental doctrine of fair play "which administrative agencies must diligently respect and courts must ever be alert to enforce."

This fundamental doctrine of fair play is particularly applicable to the instant case because there was some comparison of Doctors' application during the review of Memorial's application and fairness dictates that Memorial is entitled to an opportunity to be heard at the same time as Doctors: "Only in that way can each party be given a fair opportunity to persuade the agency that its proposal would serve the public interest better than that of its competitor."

As in *Bio-Medical*, we find that a material error in procedure occurred in this case and we therefore remand it, pursuant to the dictates of section 120.68(8), Florida Statutes (1987), with directions that Memorial's petition for a formal administrative hearing to comparatively review the parties certificate of need application be granted.

NOTES

1. *Sarasota Hospital* involves the application of the *Ashbacker* Doctrine, laid down in Ashbacker Radio Corp. v. FCC, 326 U.S. 327 (1945), which provides important procedural protections in licensing and other cases:

> *Ashbacker* involved competing applications for the same radio frequency. Because of the interference which would result if two applicants received a license for the same radio frequency, only one license could be granted. The FCC granted a license to one applicant and then scheduled a hearing for the other applicant. The Supreme Court recognized that because the applications were mutually exclusive in that only one license could be granted, the approval of one without a hearing to both deprived the loser of a hearing to which he was entitled under the governing statute. The Court therefore required a hearing on each competing application before a license could be granted.

Charter Medical v. HCA Health Services, 542 N.E.2d 82, 84 (Ill. App. Ct. 1989).

2. A federal case referred to "the towering shadow of *Ashbacker* . . . and its progeny, perhaps the most important series of cases in American administrative law." Citizens Communications Center v. FCC, 447 F.2d 1201, 1210-1211 (D.C. Cir. 1971). Though this characterization is exaggerated, the *Ashbacker* Doctrine has been widely applied in cases where license applications are mutually exclusive. In broadcasting, of course, the doctrine is virtually compelled by the physical nature of the medium; electrical interference makes it impossible to grant more than one license on the same frequency.

According to Reuters Ltd. v. FCC, 781 F.2d 946, 951 (D.C. Cir. 1986), "*Ashbacker*'s teaching applies not to prospective applicants but *only to parties whose applications have been declared mutually exclusive.*" This is a foundational requirement for the procedural protections provided by *Ashbacker.*

3. Should the *Ashbacker* Doctrine be limited to cases of physical mutual exclusiveness? How does *Sarasota Hospital* answer this question? According to Judge Friendly, *Ashbacker* "laid down a general principle that an administrative agency was not to grant one application for a license without some appropriate consideration of another bona fide and timely filed application to render the same service." Railway Express Agency v. United States, 205 F. Supp. 831, 834 (S.D.N.Y. 1962). What is the "appropriate consideration" referred to by Friendly?

Compare the New York court with that of New Mexico in In re Applications of Mission Petroleum Carriers, Inc., 827 P.2d 1291, 1293 (N.M. 1992): "Although comparative review is usually only necessary when there is mutual exclusivity, see Bernard Schwartz, Administrative Law §6.2 (1984) . . . , here, each application may have prejudiced the other . . . and so a comparative review should have been provided to afford a fair review."

Where *Ashbacker* applies to two mutually exclusive applications, one may not be granted without a hearing involving both. The result is what *Sarasota Hospital* terms "comparative review" — usually called a comparative hearing, which consolidates the competing applications into one case with one hearing in which the applicants are heard on a comparative basis. The typical comparative hearing has involved all the applicants competing for a given broadcast frequency.

B NOTICE AND PLEADINGS

COMMENTS

1. See Goldberg v. Kelly, 397 U.S. 254, 267-268 (1970):

> "The fundamental requisite of due process of law is the opportunity to be heard." . . . The hearing must be "at a meaningful time and in a meaningful manner." . . . In the present context those principles require that a recipient have timely and adequate notice detailing the reasons for proposed termination. . . . We are not prepared to say that the seven-days notice currently provided by New York City is constitutionally insufficient per se, although there may be cases where fairness would require that a longer time be given. Nor do we see any constitutional deficiency in the content or form of the notice. New York employs both a letter and a personal conference with a caseworker to inform a recipient of the precise questions raised about his continued eligibility. Evidently the recipient is told the legal and factual bases for the Department's doubts.

Compare the above with the Federal Administrative Procedure Act, 5 U.S.C. §554:

(b) Persons entitled to notice of an agency hearing shall be timely informed of—

> **(1)** the time, place, and nature of the hearing;
> **(2)** the legal authority and jurisdiction under which the hearing is to be held; and
> **(3)** the matters of fact and law asserted.

2. The right to be heard includes the right to notice: "Due process requires notice that gives an agency's reason for its action in sufficient detail that the affected party can prepare a responsive defense." Barnes v. Healy, 980 F.2d 572, 579 (9th Cir. 1992). As the APA provision indicates, the notice must contain the time of the hearing. An implied requirement is that the notice be "timely." The notice must give sufficient time to enable the individual to prepare a case. There is no mechanical rule governing adequacy of time; the standard is one of reasonableness, and its application depends on the facts of the particular case. The Goldberg v. Kelly extract indicates that seven days' notice in welfare termination cases would normally be adequate, though there may be cases where fairness would require that a longer time be given. State statutes may fix a minimum time requirement for notice.

The Federal APA states that the notice must state the agency's jurisdiction. Administrative jurisdiction does not, however, depend on the technicalities of personal service, such as those still governing the jurisdiction of most courts. Unless a statute requires it, the agency is not legally required to serve the notice personally. Agencies may use service through the mails, and agency rules generally provide for service by registered mail. A court has held that service by ordinary mail was adequate where the individual could not show harm in the agency's failure to use registered mail. Olin Industries v. NLRB, 192 F.2d 799 (5th Cir. 1951), cert. denied, 343 U.S. 919 (1952).

The notice of hearing is the administrative equivalent of the complaint in a civil case; in many agencies, the notice instituting a proceeding is called a complaint. What, if any, further pleadings there will be is up to the agency concerned. Agencies commonly provide, in their rules of procedure, for the filing of an answer within a stated period of time.

3. The common-law technicalities are wholly absent from the law governing pleadings in administrative proceedings. "Due process does not require that notices of administrative proceedings 'be drafted with the certainty of a criminal pleading,' as long as the notice is sufficient for persons whose rights may be affected to understand the substance and nature of the grounds upon which they are called to answer." Langlitz v. Board of Registration of Chiropractors, 486 N.E.2d 48, 51 (Mass. 1985). The test is one of fair notice. "Thus, the test is one of fairness under the circumstances of each case—whether the [individual] knew what conduct was in issue and had a fair opportunity to present his defense." Soule Glass & Glazing Co. v. NLRB, 652 F.2d 1055, 1074 (1st Cir. 1981). If the fairness test is met, possible technical deficiencies are irrelevant. With regard to pleading, as with other aspects of administrative procedure, the yardstick is fundamental fairness; and it is the actuality, not the appearance, of fairness that controls.

YELLOW FREIGHT SYSTEM v. MARTIN

954 F.2d 353 (6th Cir. 1992)

BOYCE F. MARTIN, JR., Circuit Judge.

This case requires us to balance the need for expeditious resolution of employment discharge cases and the employer's right to a full and fair adjudicative process. In this case, Yellow Freight System, Inc., challenges the Secretary of Labor's decision that Yellow Freight violated 49 U.S.C. App. §2305(a), which is part of the Surface Transportation Assistance Act of 1982. In this opinion, 49 U.S.C. App. §2305(a) and U.S.C. App. §2305(b) will be referred to as §405(a) and §405(b), respectively, which are the section numbers used by Congress in the original act. In support of their challenge, Yellow Freight argues (1) the Secretary incorrectly interpreted §405(a), and (2) the Secretary violated its due process rights by refusing to reopen the administrative hearing. For the following reasons, we refuse to enforce the Secretary's decision.

Yellow Freight is a large interstate trucking company with several hundred terminals nationwide. Yellow Freight hired Thomas E. Moyer, the complainant, as a truck driver in 1978. On February 29, 1988, Yellow Freight dispatched Moyer from its Ritchfield, Ohio, terminal to pick up a truck. While returning to the terminal, Moyer's truck suffered a mechanical breakdown. Moyer contacted a Yellow Freight dispatcher who instructed him to go to the nearest telephone and presumably, inform the company's mechanics of his situation.

As Moyer descended from the truck, he aggravated a preexisting medical condition. Moyer contacted the dispatcher who once again told Moyer to go to a telephone, call the mechanics, and return to the truck to await help. Another Yellow Freight driver stopped to assist Moyer and eventually drove him to the terminal. At the terminal, Moyer told the dispatcher that he was ill and needed to go to a hospital. The dispatcher insisted that Moyer inform company mechanics of the breakdown and report the location of the truck. Eventually an ambulance arrived and medical personnel transported Moyer to the hospital.

After the incident, Yellow Freight placed Moyer on a four-day suspension for returning to the terminal and leaving the truck unattended and for failing to follow company procedure for drivers experiencing mechanical breakdowns. Between June and October 1988, Yellow Freight issued Moyer four warning letters for being unavailable for dispatch without an excuse. The final warning concerned Moyer's absence on October 5, 1988. On that date Moyer testified at a grievance proceeding for Robert E. Lee, a fellow employee. In this proceeding, Lee challenged Yellow Freight's decision to fire him following his receipt of a letter from Yellow Freight that allegedly gave him 72 hours to appear at the terminal. Moyer testified that Lee had a back injury and was unable to respond to the company's demand. After issuing this letter concerning Moyer's October 5 absence, Yellow Freight terminated Moyer on November 9, 1988.

On November 14, 1988, Moyer filed a complaint with the Secretary of Labor alleging that Yellow Freight had violated §405 of the Surface Transportation

Assistance Act by discharging him in retaliation for his refusal to drive a truck while he was ill on February 29, 1988. In a letter dated November 30, 1988, the Department of Labor's Occupational Safety and Health Administration notified Yellow Freight of the complaint, and requested the following information:

> [A] full and complete written account of the facts and a statement of your position in respect to the allegation that Mr. Moyer was discharged on November 9, 1988 in reprisal for not operating his commercial vehicle because of illness.

Subsequently, in a letter dated March 17, 1989, OSHA's regional administrator informed Yellow Freight of his findings. He stated:

> The U.S. Department of Labor has completed its investigation of the complaint of Thomas E. Moyer, a former employee, who alleged that your company discriminated against him in violation of section 405(b) of the Surface Transportation Assistance Act of 1982 (49 U.S.C. 2310 et seq.). As set forth in the enclosed Findings, I have determined that Mr. Moyer's complaint has no merit.

Moyer objected to OSHA's findings and requested an administrative hearing. After an evidentiary hearing, an administrative law judge recommended the Secretary find no violation of §405(b) because on February 29, 1988, Moyer was not engaged in any activity protected by that provision. The administrative law judge noted that although Moyer testified that he believed his discharge may have also resulted from his testimony in the Lee grievance proceeding, there [was] insufficient evidence on the nature of the Lee proceeding to find a violation of another provision, §405(a).

After reviewing the record, the Secretary agreed with the administrative law judge that Yellow Freight's discharge of Moyer did not violate §405(b). The Secretary, however, contrary to the finding of the administrative law judge, concluded Moyer's discharge violated §405(a). The Secretary found that Yellow Freight discharged Moyer in retaliation for his testimony at Lee's grievance hearing, and that the nature of Lee's hearing rendered Moyer's testimony protected under §405(a)....

The Secretary ordered Yellow Freight to reinstate Moyer, and remanded the case to the administrative law judge for a determination of the appropriate relief.

... Yellow Freight filed a petition with this court alleging a violation of due process and requesting a review of the Secretary's Decision and Order of Remand.... [The court held that the Secretary correctly interpreted §405(a).]

Next, we face a more difficult issue raised by Yellow Freight: whether the Secretary deprived Yellow Freight of due process by finding a violation of §405(a) and refusing to reopen the administrative hearing to allow evidence on the §405(a) issue. Yellow Freight alleges the Secretary found the company guilty of violating §405(a) without giving it prior notice of a §405(a) charge and a corresponding opportunity to respond to the charge.

The fundamental elements of procedural due process are notice and an opportunity to be heard.... Congress incorporated these notions of due process in the Administrative Procedure Act. Under the Act, "[p]ersons entitled to notice of any agency hearing shall be timely informed of . . . the matters of fact and law asserted." 5 U.S.C. §554(b). To satisfy the requirements of due process, an administrative agency must give the party charged a clear statement of the theory on which the agency will proceed with the case. . . . Additionally, "an agency may not change theories in midstream without giving respondents reasonable notice of the change." . . .

NLRB v. Homemaker Shops, Inc., 724 F.2d 535 (6th Cir. 1984) is illustrative of these principles. In *Homemaker Shops*, the complaint alleged only that the employer had unlawfully *assisted* the union. Id. at 542. During an evidentiary hearing, the Board's attorney reiterated the same allegation. Under these circumstances, we held that the Board could not find the company guilty of the distinct charge of unlawfully *dominating* the union. We stated:

> The fundamental fairness inherent in administrative due process cannot permit the [government] to plead a certain charge, insist at hearing that only that charge is being litigated, and then raise a related, but more onerous charge only after the hearing record is closed.

Id. at 544. . . .

On the record before us, we conclude that prior to the administrative hearing, the Secretary failed to give Yellow Freight adequate notice of a §405(a) issue. The letter from OSHA notifying the company of Moyer's complaint referred only to Yellow Freight's discharge of Moyer in retaliation for not operating his vehicle because of illness, which is a §405(b) issue. Moyer's written complaint does not give any indication that he was complaining that Yellow Freight fired him for testifying in a safety-related hearing. OSHA's letter to Yellow Freight conveying OSHA's findings after the preliminary investigation also characterized Moyer's complaint in terms of §405(b). Finally, Moyer's objections to these findings set forth only a §405(b) issue. Thus, prior to the administrative hearing neither the Department of Labor nor Moyer had given Yellow Freight notice of a possible §405(a) issue.

Notwithstanding the possible lack of notice prior to the administrative hearing, due process is not offended if an agency decides an issue the parties fairly and fully litigated at a hearing. When parties fully litigate an issue they obviously have notice of the issue and have been given an opportunity to respond. This satisfies the requirement of administrative due process. "[T]he test is one of fairness under the circumstances of each case — whether the employer knew what conduct was in issue and had an opportunity to present his defense." . . . Focusing on this theme, the Secretary contends that Yellow Freight impliedly consented to litigate a §405(a) issue. The Secretary argues that at the hearing Moyer "clearly" raised a §405(a) issue by introducing evidence that established the company discharged him for testifying at a safety-related grievance proceeding. The Secretary argues that when Yellow Freight failed to object to the introduction of this evidence . . . the company impliedly consented to litigate the §405(a) issue.

The general rule is when issues not raised in pleadings are raised by the express or implied consent of the parties, the court may treat the issues in all respects as if the parties had raised them in the pleadings. Fed. R. Civ. P 15(b); 29 C.F.R. §18.43(c). Thus, if an issue is tried fully by the parties, a court or agency may base its decision on that issue and may deem the pleadings amended accordingly, even though the parties did not set forth the theory in the pleadings. . . ." This rule is designed to allow parties . . . to get to the heart of the matter and not have relevant issues obscured by pleading niceties. It was not designed to allow parties to change theories in mid-stream." . . .

In this case, we do not believe that Moyer clearly raised the issue of a §405(a) violation or that Yellow Freight did or should have understood that some of the evidence was directed at a §405(a) issue. Hence, we do not believe Yellow Freight impliedly consented to litigate the issue. . . .

In summation, the Secretary found Yellow Freight guilty of violating §405(a) without giving the company prior notice of a possible §405(a) issue. Yellow Freight did not impliedly consent to try the §405(a) issue during the administrative hearing and did not, in fact, try the issue; therefore, the Secretary did not give Yellow Freight an opportunity to respond before finding a violation of §405(a). Taking these factors into consideration, we find the Secretary's actions violated Yellow Freight's due process rights.

Finding that the Secretary violated Yellow Freight's due process rights, we refuse to enforce the Secretary's order. On remand, the Secretary can re-examine the §405(a) issue after giving Yellow Freight proper notice and a full and fair opportunity to respond.

NOTES

1. The Federal APA provision already quoted requires the agency notice to inform the individual of "the matters of fact and law asserted." Specification of the issues is one of the basic elements of fair procedure. The notice instituting the proceeding must not only tell when and where the hearing will be held; it must also apprise the individual of the issues involved. "Basic notions of fundamental fairness also dictate that a person . . . must be adequately informed in advance of the questions to be address at the hearing so that the person can be prepared to present evidence and arguments on those questions." Robertson v. Cass County Social Services, 492 N.W.2d 599, 602 (N.D. 1992). Note, however, that despite the *Martin* case, a party may be deemed to have received proper notice despite the notice's failure to mention a specific statutory provision if a complaint sufficiently describes facts and issues involving such a provision. See Yellow Freight System v. Reich, 27 F.3d 1133 (6th Cir. 1994).

2. In Wolfenbarger v. Hennessee, 520 P.2d 809 (Okla. 1974), the following notice was sent to appellant:

> THE CITY OF LAWTON, OKLAHOMA TO:
> *John and Rosemary Wolfenbarger dba Honest John's Pawn Shop*
> Licensee

> You are hereby notified that pursuant to the terms of the Ordinances of the City of Lawton, Oklahoma, pertaining to the licensing and regulating of Pawnbrokers and Secondhand Dealers within the City of Lawton, Oklahoma, the Mayor and City Council of said city will hold a public hearing in the Council Chambers at the City Hall in Lawton, Oklahoma at 10:30 A.M. on Tuesday, November 2, 1971, to determine whether or not the Pawnbrokers and Secondhand Dealers license previously issued to you pursuant to the terms of said Ordinances should be revoked because of violations of the Ordinances of said City governing the operation of Pawnbrokers and Secondhand Dealers. At said time and place you may appear and show cause, if any you have, why said license should not be revoked.
>
> Dated this 26th day of October, 1971.
>
> City Council of the City of Lawton, Oklahoma.

The revocation of appellant's license was annulled: "In a proceeding for revocation of a license the complainant must definitely set forth the nature of the charge and be sufficiently explicit to advise a person charged of the particular kind of misconduct which it is proposed to prove against him." The notice here failed to give the licensee fair notice of the acts or omissions with which he was charged so that he might prepare his defense.

3. The test is one of reasonableness in relation to the facts. The individual must be given such notice of the issues involved at the hearing as will reasonably enable her to prepare her case.

See Fruitvale Canning Co., 3 Pike & Fischer Admin. L. 2d 227 (FTC 1953):

> Common justice would indicate that a complaint in the "bare bones" language of the statute is insufficient, particularly in a case involving violations of the broad terms of the Federal Trade Commission Act.... [F]airness would again indicate the respondents in this type of complaint are entitled to have spelled out in the complaint such illustrative examples as will clearly indicate the challenged practices.

The cases emphasize the "notice-giving function," rather than technical formalities. The test in determining the adequacy of an agency notice is whether it reasonably informs the individual of the matters to be dealt with at the hearing: Does it tell him enough to enable him to prepare his case? If it does, it is irrelevant that the technical requirements to make out a "cause of action" are not present:

> Since the basic element to be satisfied is the opportunity to prepare one's case, the actual content of the notice is not dispositive. The question is whether the complaining party had sufficient notice and information to understand the nature of the proceedings. That is, unlike a formal complaint in a civil action, defects in administrative notice may be cured by other evidence that the parties knew what the proceedings would entail.

North State Telephone Co. v. Alaska Public Utilities Comm'n, 522 P.2d 711, 714 (Alaska 1974). Further, the specific requirements for the notice vary depending on the type of proceeding. According to Hess & Clark v. FDA, 495 F.2d 975, 984 (D.C. Cir. 1974),

> [A] notice that may be "adequate" for the purpose of scheduling a hearing is not necessarily adequate for the purpose of beginning a summary judgment procedure. . . . Of course, administrative agencies are not bound by the same details of procedure as the courts. But the agencies are governed by the same basic requirements of fairness and notice, and these include specificity of notice and opportunity to respond if what is instituted is intended to be a procedure for summary disposition without hearing. If the Commissioner of FDA is relying on his Notice as a device for invoking a summary judgment procedure that avoids the statute's general requirement of a hearing, he must include in such notice references to the "facts" that he deems to be established in order that there may be meaningful opportunity to controvert the alleged facts and present a material issue for hearing. This includes, at a minimum, presentation of the prima facie case . . . as a predicate for withholding the hearing required in general for revocation of an approved application.

4. In a judicial court proceeding, if a complaint does not contain enough detail, further clarity can be secured through a bill of particulars. Agencies, however, have been reluctant to furnish bills of particulars, and their denials have been sustained by the courts. The judicial hands-off policy is based on the differences between the typical administrative and judicial proceeding. Denial of a bill of particulars, states an oft-cited remark of Judge Learned Hand, "is important only when a party must meet his adversary's case without opportunity to prepare; it is of slight value in a trial by hearings at intervals." NLRB v. Remington Rand, Inc., 94 F.2d 862, 873 (2d Cir.), cert. denied, 304 U.S. 576 (1938). The justification is that the individual receives the particulars needed to flesh out a skeleton complaint from the evidence presented at the hearing. The agency proceeding, unlike the typical court case, need not proceed continuously from beginning to end. It may instead be a "trial at intervals," with recesses after the presentation of each party's case. The individual who is surprised by the particulars learned through evidence presented at the hearing has time to prepare to meet them during the recess before he presents his case.

5. An important aspect of modern judicial procedure is the pretrial conference. The Federal APA expressly authorizes such "conferences for the settlement or simplification of the issues by consent of the parties." 5 U.S.C. §556(c). The major federal agencies provide expressly in their procedure rules for prehearing conferences, and these play an increasingly important part in agency practice.

Compare Recommendation 70-4 of the Administrative Conference, 1 C.F.R. §305.70-4 (1986), recommending that at least one prehearing conference should be held in proceedings where the issues are complex or it appears likely there will be long hearings.

6. Discovery occupies a significant place in pretrial procedure in the courts. One state requires prehearing discovery in agency proceedings as an element of fair procedure. Cal. Gov't Code §11507.6 codifying the rule laid down in Shively v. Stewart, 421 P.2d 65 (Cal. 1966). For a comparable case in another state, see Matter of Miller, 542 P.2d 1182 (N.M. Ct. App. 1975). There is no similar federal requirement. Discovery does not have the important role in agency proceedings that it does in the federal courts. Only a handful of federal agencies have adopted discovery rules patterned on those in the Federal Rules of Civil Procedure. This is true despite a strong recommendation by the Administrative Conference that agencies adopt a comprehensive discovery system. Recommendation 70-4, 1 C.F.R. §305.70-4 (1981).

C NATURE OF HEARING

JOHNSON NEWSPAPER CORP. v. MELINO

564 N.E.2d 1046 (N.Y. 1990)

HANCOCK, Judge.

In this CPLR article 78 proceeding petitioner, the publisher of a Watertown newspaper seeks an order compelling public access to a disciplinary hearing involving a dentist, a licensed professional supervised by the Board of Regents under article 130 of the Education Law. Supreme Court dismissed the proceeding and the Appellate Division affirmed. Petitioner's appeal presents two questions:

(1) whether there is a public right of access to such a professional disciplinary hearing under the Federal or State Constitution; and
(2) if not, whether there is a common-law right of access to the proceedings grounded in the public policy of this State.
(3) For reasons which will appear, we answer both questions in the negative and, therefore, affirm.

I

Professional disciplinary proceedings under Education Law §6510 generally involve a three-part process. At the first stage, the Education Department's Office of Professional Discipline (OPD) conducts an adversarial hearing on the charges of misconduct (Education Law §6510[3][c]). Thereafter, the hearing panel prepares a written report, which includes a recommendation of guilty or not guilty, and, if necessary, a penalty recommendation (§6510[3][d]). The Regents' review committee reviews the report and the hearing transcript, and prepares a written report of its own (§6510[4][b]). The two reports and the hearing transcript are then forwarded to the Board of Regents which renders a final decision (§6510[4][c]). It is the petitioner's claimed right of access to the OPD hearing that is at issue on this appeal.

Petitioner Johnson Newspaper Corporation is the publisher of the Watertown Daily Times. In 1988, petitioner sought access to the disciplinary hearing involving a dentist who was charged with misconduct. The OPD refused this request, stating that it was the policy of the Board of Regents to conduct closed professional disciplinary hearings unless the accused professional specifically requested an open hearing. Petitioner thereafter commenced this article 78 proceeding seeking a judgment enjoining enforcement of this policy and declaring professional disciplinary hearings presumptively open to the press and public. . . .

II

In addressing petitioner's argument that there is a constitutionally based public right of access to a professional disciplinary hearing (U.S. Const. 1st Amend.), the Appellate Division applied what it described as the Supreme Court's two-tiered test. The test, the court stated quoting Press-Enterprise Co. v. Superior Ct., 478 U.S. 1, "includes 'whether the place and process have historically been open to the press and general public' and 'whether public access plays a significant positive role in the functioning of the particular process in question.'" The Appellate Division concluded that there is no First Amendment right of access inasmuch as there is "no historical basis for open professional disciplinary hearings" and no showing that "the public played a significant role in the licensing or policing of professionals." Petitioner's primary contention here is that the first step in the Appellate Division's analysis — whether there exists an historical tradition of openness — is no longer a valid criterion of whether access is protected by the First Amendment. We disagree and conclude that the test as applied by the Appellate Division remains valid.

The two most recent Supreme Court opinions dealing with the First Amendment right of access are Press-Enterprise Co. v. Superior Ct. of Cal. (*Press-Enterprise I*), 464 U.S. 501 [upholding First Amendment right of access for voir dire proceeding in a criminal trial] and Press-Enterprise Co. v. Superior Ct. (*Press-Enterprise II*), 478 U.S. 1 [First Amendment right of access for preliminary hearing in criminal case]. There is no basis in either opinion for concluding that the Supreme Court no longer relies on the historical tradition of access as a significant consideration in determining whether a particular proceeding should receive First Amendment protection....

Here, because there is no suggestion that professional disciplinary hearings have any tradition of being open to the public and no showing that the public access plays "a significant positive role" in the functioning of the proceedings ... we conclude that the Appellate Division properly held that there is no First Amendment right of access. Petitioner argues, nevertheless, that irrespective of the existence of a First Amendment right, we should hold that there is a right of access under the broader protections afforded by our State Constitution (N.Y. Const., art. I, §8). Although our Court has in some cases found our State Constitution to be more protective of expressional freedoms than the Federal Constitution ... there is no such precedent with respect to the right of access. Petitioner has cited no authority and makes no persuasive argument for the proposition that our State Constitution affords a protected right of access to disciplinary hearings, and we decline to so hold.

III

Petitioner argues that, notwithstanding the absence of a Federal or State constitutional right, a presumptive right of access to professional disciplinary hearings exists in the common law of this State. It relies principally on Matter of Herald Co. v. Weisenberg, 59 N.Y.2d 378 where the Court held that unemployment compensation hearings should be presumptively open. There, the Court discerned no basis "for setting aside the strong public policy in this State of public access to judicial and administrative proceedings" . . . and noted specifically that there is nothing in the statutes or departmental regulations governing unemployment compensation hearings suggesting that they could be closed. The Court reasoned: "That section 537 concerns only disclosure of information acquired through the reporting requirements of article 18, and not closure of hearings, is emphasized by the language of the provisions dealing with hearings. Section 622 and the regulation promulgated thereunder (12 N.Y.C.R.R. 461.4) set forth in some detail the procedures and rules to be followed at such hearings, yet neither mentions closure. In light of the failure of either the Legislature or the commissioner to provide for closing unemployment compensation hearings, it would be inappropriate to read into section 537 a blanket order of closure. Moreover, this conclusion is consistent with the position of the Department of Labor on this appeal that it had no objection to the presence of the press at the hearing, as well as with the long-standing position of the Attorney-General (1959 Opns. Atty. Gen. 80)." (Id. at 382-383.)

The rationale of *Weisenberg*, we believe, leads to the conclusion that professional disciplinary hearings held pursuant to Education Law §7510 are not presumptively open. In *Weisenberg*, not only was there nothing in the statute or regulations indicative of a policy of confidentiality, but the posture of the Commissioner of Labor and the long-standing position of the Attorney General (1959 Opns. Atty. Gen. 80) were supportive of a policy of public access to such hearings. Here, by contrast, the applicable statute (see Education Law §6510[8]) manifests a governmental policy of preserving the confidentiality of information pertaining to disciplinary proceedings until a determination has been reached. The same policy of confidentiality is reflected in analogous statutes pertaining to disciplinary proceedings in the legal profession (see Judiciary Law §90[10]), the medical profession (see Public Health Law §230[10], [11][a]; Education Law §6510-a), and to disciplinary hearings conducted by the State Commission on Judicial Conduct (see Judiciary Law §44[4]).

Moreover, in the case of professional disciplinary hearings conducted under article 130 of the Education Law, as distinguished from unemployment compensation hearings held under article 18 of the Labor Law . . . , the established policy of the Board of Regents has been to keep the proceedings private until final determination unless the respondent requests otherwise. And the difference in the policy considerations underlying professional disciplinary hearings and unemployment compensation hearings is displayed in the contrasting conclusions reached by the Attorney-General to the effect that unemployment compensation hearings should be open . . . while in professional disciplinary proceedings predecisional materials may be withheld under the Freedom of Information Law. . . .

We conclude that our statutes and case law reflect a policy of keeping disciplinary proceedings involving licensed professionals confidential until they are finally determined. The policy serves the purpose of safeguarding information that a potential complainant may regard as private or confidential and thereby removes a possible disincentive to the filing of complaints of professional misconduct. . . . The State's policy also evinces a sensitivity to the possibility of irreparable harm to a professional's reputation resulting from unfounded accusations — possibility which is enhanced by the more relaxed nature of the procedures and evidentiary rules followed in disciplinary proceedings in which hearsay evidence may be received. Indeed, our Court has recognized that professional reputation "once lost, is not easily restored." . . .

The order of the Appellate Division should, accordingly, be affirmed, with costs.

NOTES

1. Compare FCC v. Schreiber, 381 U.S. 279 (1965). At issue there was the power of an agency to order public proceedings. The FCC, in an investigatory proceeding on television programming, sought information from respondent. He refused unless assured it would be kept confidential. The request for confidential treatment was denied under an FCC order requiring the proceeding to be public, though the presiding officer might order nonpublic sessions where the public interest, the proper dispatch of business, and the ends of justice would be served. The Court upheld the FCC action, saying that the requirement of public proceedings accords with the general policy favoring disclosure of agency proceedings. Likewise, in Detroit Free Press v. Ashcroft, 303 F.3d 681 (6th Cir. 2002), the court found that even after the September 11, 2001, terrorist attacks, the executive branch could not simply close all deportation proceedings that it unilaterally deemed to be "special interest" cases. Id. at 683. According to the court:

> Today, the Executive Branch seeks to take [the First Amendment free press] safeguard away from the public by placing its actions beyond public scrutiny. Against non-citizens, it seeks the power to secretly deport a class if it unilaterally calls them "special interest" cases. The Executive Branch seeks to uproot people's lives, outside the public eye, and behind a closed door. Democracies die behind closed doors. The First Amendment, through a free press, protects the people's right to know that their government acts fairly, lawfully, and accurately in deportation proceedings. When government begins closing doors, it selectively controls information rightfully belonging to the people. Selective information is misinformation. The Framers of the First Amendment "did not trust any government to separate the true from the false for us." Kleindienst v. Mandel, 408 U.S. 753, 773, 33 L. Ed. 2d 683, 92 S. Ct. 2576 (1972) (quoting Thomas v. Collins, 323 U.S. 516, 545, 89 L. Ed. 430, 65 S. Ct. 315 (Jackson, J., concurring)). They protected the people against secret government.

Id. The court upheld a district court injunction finding the government blanket practice of closing these hearings unconstitutional. Id. The court stated,

> [w]hile we sympathize and share the Government's fear that dangerous information might be disclosed in some of these hearings, we feel that the ordinary process

> of determining whether closure is warranted on a case-by-case basis sufficiently addresses their concerns. Using this stricter standard does not mean that information helpful to terrorists will be disclosed, only that the Government must be more targeted and precise in its approach.

Id. at 692-693.

2. As a general proposition, there is a strong policy favoring public trials, which applies to agencies as well as courts. When due process requires a hearing it normally requires a public hearing. The New York court had previously so held in Herald Co. v. Weisenberg, 452 N.E.2d 1190 (N.Y. 1983), discussed in the *Johnson Newspaper* opinion. The case arose out of an action by a newspaper to vacate an order of an administrative law judge closing an unemployment insurance hearing to the public. The court held that such an agency hearing must follow "the strong public policy in this State of public access to judicial and administrative proceedings." That means that the hearing is presumed to be open and may not be closed to the public unless a compelling reason for closure is demonstrated and only after the affected members of the news media are given an opportunity to be heard. Was such a compelling reason demonstrated in *Johnson Newspaper*? Compare United States v. Miami University, 294 F.3d 797 (6th Cir. 2002) (university disciplinary hearings not open to the public); WBZ-TV4 v. Executive Office of Labor, 610 N.E.2d 923 (Mass. 1993) (employment agency's license application hearing not open to public).

3. "In fixing the time and place for hearings, due regard shall be had for the convenience of the parties or their representatives." Federal Administrative Procedure Act, 5 U.S.C. §554(b). The APA requires agencies, in fixing the time and place of hearings, to have due regard for the convenience of counsel, as well as the parties. The kind of case contemplated is illustrated by a state case where a hearing was scheduled for the convenience of agency members on a Saturday, despite the fact that petitioner's counsel was a practicing member of the Jewish faith; fundamental fairness was found to be lacking when the agency refused to reschedule the hearing for another day. Romeo v. Union Free School Dist., 368 N.Y.S.2d 726 (Sup. Ct. 1975).

D COUNSEL

COMMENTS

1. See Goldberg v. Kelly, 397 U.S. 254, 270-271 (1970):

> The right to be heard would be, in many cases, of little avail if it did not comprehend the right to be heard by counsel. . . . We do not say that counsel must be provided at the pre-termination hearing, but only that the recipient must be allowed to retain an attorney if he so desires. Counsel can help delineate the issues, present the factual

contentions in an orderly manner, conduct cross-examination and generally safeguard the interests of the recipient. We do not anticipate that this assistance will unduly pro-long or otherwise encumber the hearing.

> **Federal Administrative Procedure Act**
>
> **5 U.S.C. §555(b)**
>
> A person compelled to appear in person before an agency or representative thereof is entitled to be accompanied, represented, and advised by counsel or, if permitted by the agency, by other qualified representative. A party is entitled to appear in person or by or with counsel or other duly qualified representative in an agency proceeding.

2. The right to counsel has rarely been challenged in adjudicatory proceedings. So far as is known, there are no cases involving such challenges in independent regulatory agencies. An unrestricted right to counsel as so ringingly asserted in Goldberg v. Kelly may, however, pose problems in nonregulatory agencies, such as the welfare agency in *Goldberg.*

The difficulty in this respect was stated some years ago:

> To be sure, counsel can often perform useful functions even in welfare cases or other instances of mass justice; they may bring out facts ignored by or unknown to the authorities, or help to work out satisfactory compromises. But this is only one side of the coin. Under our adversary system the role of counsel is not to make sure the truth is ascertained but to advance his client's cause by any ethical means. Within the limits of professional propriety, causing delay and sowing confusion not only are his right but may be his duty. The appearance of counsel for the citizen is likely to lead the government to provide one — or at least to cause the government's representative to act like one. The result may be to turn what might have been a short conference leading to an amicable result into a protracted controversy.

Friendly, Some Kind of Hearing, 123 U. Pa. L. Rev. 1267, 1287-1288 (1975).

Compare Wolff v. McDonnell, 418 U.S. 539, 570 (1974), involving loss of good-time credits by prisoners for serious misconduct, where the Court held that the procedure for determining whether such misconduct had occurred must observe "minimum" due process requirements, but refused to recognize a right to counsel:

> . . . The insertion of counsel into the disciplinary proceedings inevitably give the proceedings a more adversary cast and tend to reduce their utility as a means to further correctional goals. There would also be delay and very practical problems in providing counsel in sufficient numbers at the time and place where hearings are to be held. At this stage of the development of these procedures we are not prepared to hold that inmates have a right to either retained or appointed counsel in disciplinary proceedings.

> Where an illiterate inmate is involved, however, or where the complexity of the issue makes it unlikely that the inmate will be able to collect and present the evidence necessary for an adequate comprehension of the case, he should be free to seek the aid of a fellow inmate, or if that is forbidden, to have adequate substitute aid in the form of help from the staff or from a sufficiently competent inmate designated by the staff.

According to Judge Friendly, *supra*, "[t]his is a sensible compromise, which may be emulated, mutatis mutandis, in other contexts, such as student or employee discipline, where the disadvantages of the presence of counsel may outweigh the benefits."

3. Note that the Goldberg v. Kelly extract, *supra* p. 523, speaks only of a right to retain counsel. The Court stressed that it did not say that counsel must be provided at the hearing, but only that the individual must be allowed to retain an attorney. The cases thus far reject the extension of Gideon v. Wainwright, 372 U.S. 335 (1963), to administrative law, by refusing to require appointed counsel for indigents in administrative proceedings. Illustrative cases include Ferguson v. Gathright, 485 F.2d 504 (4th Cir. 1973), cert. denied, 415 U.S. 933 (1974) (driver's license revocation); Tyson v. New York City Housing Authority, 369 F. Supp. 513 (S.D.N.Y. 1974) (public housing eviction); Brown v. Lavine, 333 N.E.2d 374 (N.Y. 1975) (welfare).

Immigration advocates have long argued for the right to government-appointed counsel in removal (deportation) hearings, however, noting that the stakes in these proceedings are more analogous to criminal trials than to administrative hearings and that the complexity of immigration advocacy demands significant expertise. See J.E. F.M. v. Lynch, 837 F.3d 1029 (9th Cir. 2016). In August 2017, the American Bar Association added its voice with adopted Resolution 115, recommending "the appointment of counsel at federal government expense to represent all indigent persons in removal proceedings."

4. Related to the question of the right to counsel before agencies is that of who may be qualified to appear as counsel before agencies. Federal agencies have power to regulate the qualifications of counsel who appear before them under Goldsmith v. Board of Tax Appeals, 270 U.S. 117 (1926), which held that the power to prescribe rules of procedure includes authority to control practice. Agency power over practice is, however, limited by 5 U.S.C. §500, which provides that any member of the bar in good standing may represent others before any federal agency (except the Patent Office).

According to Herman v. Dulles, 205 F.2d 715, 717 (D.C. Cir. 1953), "the existing powers of the agencies to control practice before them are not changed by the Administrative Procedure Act." Thus, the APA does not affect the authority of federal agencies to allow individuals who are not members of the bar to practice before them. In the states, the power to control the practice of law is generally vested in the courts, which may act to proscribe practice by laymen in agency hearings as well as in courts. See, e.g., Unauthorized Practice Comm'n v. Cortez, 692 S.W.2d 47 (Tex. 1985). Comparable power does not exist in the federal courts. Under the *Goldsmith* case, the federal agencies themselves possess power to control practice before them, and this includes the power to permit nonlawyers to act as counsel. Representation by nonlawyers has been widespread in federal agencies, notably in tax, veterans' affairs, and Social Security cases, as well as in some of the major regulatory agencies. The APA states that it "does not grant or deny a person who is not a lawyer the right to appear for or represent others before an agency or in an agency proceeding." 5 U.S.C. §555(b). Under this provision the APA does not have any effect on the question of lay practice.

E FROM EXAMINERS TO ADMINISTRATIVE LAW JUDGES

GUERRERO v. NEW JERSEY

643 F.2d 148 (3d Cir. 1981)

PER CURIAM. . . . Appellant, Dr. Floro A. Guerrero, was found guilty of gross medical malpractice by the New Jersey Board of Medical Examiners in violation of N.J. Stat. Ann. §45: 9-16 (West) (Supp. 1980). The only issue before us is whether the New Jersey administrative procedure, as codified in N.J. Stat. Ann. §52: 14B-10(c) (West) (Supp. 1980), providing for the hearing of cases in first instance by administrative law judges rather than the ultimate deciding agency, denies appellant due process or equal protection of the law. Because we find no constitutional infirmity in the New Jersey statutory scheme, we affirm the judgment of the district court.

Appellant's case was heard by an administrative law judge who then filed a written decision with the New Jersey State Board of Medical Examiners containing findings of fact and conclusions of law. Appellant's counsel filed written exceptions to the ALJ's factual findings and legal conclusions, appending excerpts from the hearing transcript. The Board then adopted the ALJ's decision "in its entirety and without modification" although it did in fact modify the recommended sanction. The essence of appellant's due process claim is that the Board's failure to take evidence and hear testimony itself deprived him of a meaningful right to be heard.

It has been settled since Morgan v. United States, 298 U.S. 468 (1936), that in administrative adjudications, deciding officers need not actually hear the witnesses' testimony. Although the Court stated that "the one who decides must actually hear," it clarified its statement by indicating that it was permissible for a decision to be based solely on a considered review of the evidence and legal arguments. The Court held that "[e]vidence may be taken by an examiner. Evidence thus taken may be sifted and analyzed by competent subordinates. . . . [T]he officers who make the determination must consider and appraise the evidence which justifies them." *Morgan*, 298 U.S. at 481-482.

This court has adhered to the principle that administrative officers charged with a decision need not personally hear testimony but may instead rely on a written record. In National Labor Relations Board v. Stocker Mfg. Co., 185 F.2d 451 (3d Cir. 1950), this court, relying on *Morgan* and National Labor Relations Board v. Mackay Radio & Telegraph Co., 304 U.S. 333, (1938) (in which the Court held that the NLRB could act solely upon transcribed records and oral arguments without the benefit of a report by the trial examiner who heard the testimony), held that:

> The doctrine of these cases clearly permits the Board to make its findings and predicate its orders upon the written record without hearing the witnesses testify or availing itself of findings and recommendations prepared by the officer who heard and observed the witnesses testify. Under the *Mackay* case, due process permits dispensing with the hearing examiner's report altogether. The *Morgan* opinion says that the officer who actually decides the controversy may do so on the basis of evidence taken by an examiner and thereafter sifted and analyzed by some other subordinate. Due process in administrative proceedings of the type now under consideration does not require that the testimony be evaluated by an officer who heard and observed the witnesses. 185 F.2d at 451.

Other circuits are in accord. . . .

Appellant contends that because of the severity of the penalty involved — revocation of his professional license — his case is distinguishable from the type of administrative proceeding contemplated by the *Morgan* line of cases. He believes that the vital interest at stake compels the Board of Medical Examiners actually to hear witnesses' testimony. We do not agree. . . . We do not believe that it is inconsistent with due process for the Board to make its decision on the basis of an ALJ's report containing findings of fact and conclusions of law, written exceptions thereto, and oral argument.

We hold that the procedure for administrative adjudications established by N.J. Stat. Ann. §52:14B-10(c) (West) (Supp. 1980) does not violate appellant's right to due process of law. . . . Accordingly, the judgment of the district court will be affirmed.

NOTES

1. When the APA applies, the agency hearing must be presided over by the agency head (or one or more of the commissioners or board members, if it is a multihead agency) or an administrative law judge. In practice, as already pointed out, agency heads almost never preside at hearings, so that the APA provision essentially requires administrative law judges to preside at agency hearings. What about the appointment, and removal, of these ALJs, though? At the end of its 2017-2018 term, the U.S. Supreme Court resolved what had become a Circuit split over the methods agencies employ to appoint ALJs. See Lucia v. SEC, ___U.S.___, 138 S. Ct. 2044 (2018), *supra* Chapter 1. Until the decision in *Lucia*, SEC ALJs were selected through a "merit-selection" process run by the Office of Personnel Management. In *Lucia* the Court held that the ALJs had been appointed in a manner inconsistent with article II, §2, cl. 2, the Appointments Clause of the U.S. Constitution. For many agencies, Lucia raises questions about their method of appointing ALJs, including the merit selection process and, potentially, the good cause requirement for removal. Some of the initial impact of the decision indicates a great deal of agency uncertainty as to *Lucia*'s impact. That the decision based the unconstitutionality of the appointments on inadequate agency procedure rather than a fundamental separation of powers problem, narrows the potential impact of the case from what would otherwise have been a significant erosion of the independence of agencies.

2. The obvious solution to the problem of presiding at hearings is delegation. See Ramspeck v. Federal Trial Examiners Conference, 345 U.S. 128, 130-131 (1953):

> Many of the regulatory powers which Congress has assigned federal administrative agencies can be exercised only after notice and hearing required by the Constitution or by statute. These agencies have such a volume of business, including cases in which a hearing is required, that the agency heads, the members of boards or commissions, can rarely preside over hearings in which evidence is required. The agencies met this problem long before the Administrative Procedure Act by designating hearing or trial examiners to preside over hearings for the reception of evidence. Such an examiner generally made a report to the agency setting forth proposed findings of fact and recommended action. The parties could address to the agency exceptions to the findings, and, after receiving briefs and hearing oral argument, the agency heads would make the final decision.

In his dissent in *Ramspeck*, Justice Black stated, "The Administrative Procedure Act was designed to give trial examiners in the various administrative agencies a new status of freedom from agency control. Henceforth they were to be 'very nearly the equivalent of judges even though operating within the Federal system of administrative justice.'"

3. The APA set up within each agency a corps of independent hearing examiners who were to be the administrative counterparts of trial judges. The examiner was, it is true, left within the agency for housekeeping purposes. But his appointment, compensation, and tenure were largely removed from agency control and vested in the Civil Service Commission. In 1978, Congress confirmed the change in title by a statute providing that "hearing examiner" in the relevant APA sections should be changed to "administrative law judge." This change has significantly elevated the status of hearing officers.

ADMINISTRATIVE CONFERENCE OF THE UNITED STATES, FEDERAL ADMINISTRATIVE LAW JUDGE HEARINGS

7-10 (1980)

The ALJ [administrative law judge] is the central figure in formal administrative adjudication. . . .

The position of administrative law judge (formerly called "hearing examiner") did not even exist until the Administrative Procedure Act (APA) was enacted in 1946. Prior to the APA, there were no reliable safeguards to ensure the objectivity and judicial capability of presiding officers in formal administrative proceedings.

1. THE ALJ'S ROLE UNDER THE ADMINISTRATIVE PROCEDURE ACT

Despite the wide variety of types of cases heard by ALJs throughout the government, the functions of the ALJ are substantially the same in most cases. The ALJ normally has the following duties, grounded in his powers specified in the APA:

— Administer oaths and affirmations.
— Issue subpoenas authorized by law.
— Rule upon offers of proof and receive relevant evidence.
— Take or cause the taking of depositions.
— Hold conferences for the settlement or simplification of the issues by consent of the parties.
— Dispose of procedural requests or similar matters.
— Question witnesses as necessary or desirable.
— Consider the facts in the record, arguments or contentions made, or questions resolved.
— Determine credibility of witnesses and make findings of fact and conclusions of law.
— Make decisions on the basis of reliable, probative, and substantial evidence on the record.
— Take any other action authorized by agency rule that is consistent with the provisions of the APA.

Not only does the APA specify the authority of ALJs as presiding officers, it also attempts to insure their impartiality and independence. A chief effect of the Act was to lodge in the Civil Service Commission (now the Office of Personnel Management, Pub. L. 95-454, 1978) exclusive authority for the initial examination and certification for selection of ALJs, the determination of applicable pay scales, and action on agency initiatives to terminate appointments of ALJs. The Act requires that the ALJ'S functions (as well as those of other agency decision makers) be conducted in an impartial manner. Moreover, if a disqualification petition is filed against an ALJ in any case, the agency must determine that issue on the record, and as part of the decision in that case. The Act also prescribes that an ALJ may not be responsible to, or subject to supervision by, anyone performing investigative or prosecutorial functions for an agency. This "separation of functions" requirement is designed to prevent the investigative or prosecutorial arm of an agency from controlling a hearing or influencing the ALJ. Finally, to insure that the ALJ is well insulated from improper agency pressure and controls, the APA contains two other provisions designed to make the ALJ at least semi-independent of the employing agency: ALJs are to be assigned to their cases in rotation so far as practicable; and they may not perform duties inconsistent with their role as ALJs. They receive their pay as prescribed by the Office of Personnel Management (OPM) independently of agency recommendation or ratings, and are removable by the agency only after good cause is established before the Merit System Protection Board after opportunity for hearing. . . .

NOTES

1. When the APA applies, the agency hearing must be presided over by the agency head (or one or more of the commissioners or board members, if it is a multihead agency) or an administrative law judge. In practice, as already pointed out, agency heads almost never preside at hearings, so that the APA provision essentially requires administrative law judges to preside at agency hearings. What about the appointment, and removal, of these ALJs, though? See the discussion of Lucia v. SEC, ___U.S. ___, 138 S. Ct. 2044(2018), *supra* Note 1, p. 525.

2. *Non-APA hearing officers.* There are, however, still federal hearings that are presided over by non-APA hearing officers. The APA states that its provision requiring hearings by agency heads or administrative law judges "does not supersede the conduct of specified classes or proceedings . . . by or before boards or other employees specifically provided for by or designed under statute." The most important use of this saving clause has been in immigration matters.

3. "Some critics of the federal agency adjudicatory system have proposed a major structural change in which all ALJs are employed by a single entity, the ALJ Corps. Such a restructuring would have the potential advantage of increasing the degree of independence of ALJs still further. To the extent that even statutorily independent ALJs develop some degree of dependence on the agency at which they preside, or some identification with the interests of that agency, this structural removal of ALJs from the agency could reduce the potential bias or public perception of bias in agency adjudicatory decision-making. The Corps would assign ALJs to adjudications at different agencies based on its periodic assessments of changing relative workloads." Administrative Conference, The Federal Administrative Judiciary (Draft) 169 (1992).

4. *State hearing officers.* State Administrative Procedure Acts do not generally contain provisions for independent hearing officers comparable to those in the Federal APA. The situation under these acts is the same as it was in federal agencies before the APA. It is illustrated by Diles v. Woolsey, 468 F.2d 614 (8th Cir. 1972). The court there held that a referee, who was dismissed after more than 15 years' service because he had become persona non grata to the members of the Arkansas Workmen's Compensation Commission, was not dismissed for any constitutionally impermissible reason. Compare Matthew v. Juras, 519 P.2d 402 (Or. Ct. App. 1974) (fact that hearing officer employee of agency not violative of due process).

5. The most important exception to the state pattern of hearing officer dependence is the system set up by the California Administrative Procedure Act, Cal. Gov't Code §§11370.3, 11502. It provides for a staff of independent hearing officers (now called administrative law judges) appointed and maintained by the Office of Administrative Hearings. The office appoints, from those admitted to practice law, as many hearing officers as necessary to fill the needs of state agencies, for a term of at least five years. All hearings of state agencies required to be conducted under the California APA are to be conducted by OAH hearing officers.

The California APA establishes a central pool of independent hearing officers who are assigned to different agencies as they are needed. In this respect it goes further than the Federal APA, for under the latter statute administrative law judges work within the agencies in which they are appointed and are members of the agency's staff for housekeeping purposes. At least 11 other states have set up hearing officer systems comparable to that in California. See Hackensack v. Winner, 410 A.2d 1146 (N.J. 1980). Note that, following the federal model, these states have changed the hearing officer title to administrative law judge. Other states have also followed the federal title change (though in many of them the change has been in name only). The ultimate result may be an ever-growing federal and state administrative judiciary that will dwarf the traditional judiciary in the courts.

F BIAS

CAPERTON v. A. T. MASSEY COAL CO.

556 U.S. 868 (2009)

JUSTICE KENNEDY delivered the opinion of the Court.

In this case the Supreme Court of Appeals of West Virginia reversed a trial court judgment, which had entered a jury verdict of $50 million. Five justices heard the case, and the vote to reverse was 3 to 2. The question presented is whether the Due Process Clause of the Fourteenth Amendment was violated when one of the justices in the majority denied a recusal motion. The basis for the motion was that the justice had received campaign contributions in an extraordinary amount from, and through the efforts of, the board chairman and principal officer of the corporation found liable for the damages.

Under our precedents there are objective standards that require recusal when "the probability of actual bias on the part of the judge or decisionmaker is too high to be constitutionally tolerable." Withrow v. Larkin, 421 U.S. 35, 47 (1975). Applying those precedents, we find that, in all the circumstances of this case, due process requires recusal.

I

In August 2002 a West Virginia jury returned a verdict that found respondents A. T. Massey Coal Co. and its affiliates (hereinafter Massey) liable for fraudulent misrepresentation, concealment, and tortious interference with existing contractual relations. The jury awarded petitioners Hugh Caperton, Harman Development Corp., Harman Mining Corp., and Sovereign Coal Sales (hereinafter Caperton) the sum of $50 million in compensatory and punitive damages. In June 2004 the state trial court denied Massey's post-trial motions challenging the verdict and the damages award, finding that Massey "intentionally acted in utter disregard of [Caperton's] rights and ultimately destroyed [Caperton's] businesses because, after conducting cost-benefit analyses, [Massey] concluded it was in its financial interest to do so." In March 2005 the trial court denied Massey's motion for judgment as a matter of law.

Don Blankenship is Massey's chairman, chief executive officer, and president. After the verdict but before the appeal, West Virginia held its 2004 judicial elections. Knowing the Supreme Court of Appeals of West Virginia would consider the appeal in the case, Blankenship decided to support an attorney who sought to replace Justice McGraw. Justice McGraw was a candidate for reelection to that court. The attorney who sought to replace him was Brent Benjamin.

In addition to contributing the $1,000 statutory maximum to Benjamin's campaign committee, Blankenship donated almost $2.5 million to "And For The Sake Of The Kids," a political organization formed under 26 U.S.C. §527. The §527 organization opposed McGraw and supported Benjamin. Blankenship's donations accounted for more than two-thirds of the total funds it raised. This was not all. Blankenship spent, in addition, just over $500,000 on independent expenditures — for direct mailings and letters soliciting donations as well as television and newspaper advertisements — "to support . . . Brent Benjamin."

To provide some perspective, Blankenship's $3 million in contributions were more than the total amount spent by all other Benjamin supporters and three times the amount spent by Benjamin's own committee. Caperton contends that Blankenship spent $1 million more than the total amount spent by the campaign committees of both candidates combined.

Benjamin won. He received 382,036 votes (53.3%), and McGraw received 334,301 votes (46.7%).

In October 2005, before Massey filed its petition for appeal in West Virginia's highest court, Caperton moved to disqualify now-Justice Benjamin under the Due Process Clause and the West Virginia Code of Judicial Conduct, based on the conflict caused by Blankenship's campaign involvement. Justice Benjamin denied the motion in April 2006. He indicated that he "carefully considered the bases and accompanying exhibits proffered by the movants." But he found "no objective information . . . to show that this Justice has a bias for or against any litigant, that this Justice has prejudged the matters which comprise this litigation, or that this Justice will be anything but fair and impartial." In December 2006 Massey filed its petition for appeal to challenge the adverse jury verdict. The West Virginia Supreme Court of Appeals granted review.

In November 2007 that court reversed the $50 million verdict against Massey. The majority opinion, authored by then-Chief Justice Davis and joined by Justices Benjamin and Maynard, found that "Massey's conduct warranted the type of judgment rendered in this case." It reversed, nevertheless, based on two independent grounds — first, that a forum-selection clause contained in a contract to which Massey was not a party barred the suit in West Virginia, and, second, that res judicata barred the suit due to an out-of-state judgment to which Massey was not a party. Justice Starcher dissented, stating that the "majority's opinion is morally and legally wrong." Justice Albright also dissented, accusing the majority of "misapplying the law and introducing sweeping 'new law' into our jurisprudence that may well come back to haunt us."

Caperton sought rehearing, and the parties moved for disqualification of three of the five justices who decided the appeal. Photos had surfaced of Justice Maynard vacationing with Blankenship in the French Riviera while the case was pending. Justice Maynard granted Caperton's recusal motion. On the other side Justice Starcher granted Massey's recusal motion, apparently based on his public criticism of Blankenship's role in the 2004 elections. In his recusal memorandum Justice Starcher urged Justice Benjamin to recuse himself as well. He noted that "Blankenship's bestowal of his personal wealth, political tactics, and 'friendship' have created a cancer in the affairs of this Court." Justice Benjamin declined Justice Starcher's suggestion and denied Caperton's recusal motion.

The court granted rehearing. Justice Benjamin, now in the capacity of acting chief justice, selected Judges Cookman and Fox to replace the recused justices. Caperton moved a third time for disqualification, arguing that Justice Benjamin had failed to apply the correct standard under West Virginia law — *i.e.*, whether "a reasonable and prudent person, knowing these objective facts, would harbor doubts about Justice Benjamin's ability to be fair and impartial." Caperton also included the results of a public opinion poll, which indicated that over 67% of West Virginians doubted Justice Benjamin would be fair and impartial. Justice Benjamin again refused to withdraw, noting that the "push poll" was "neither credible nor sufficiently reliable to serve as the basis for an elected judge's disqualification."

In April 2008 a divided court again reversed the jury verdict, and again it was a 3-to-2 decision. Justice Davis filed a modified version of her prior opinion, repeating the two earlier holdings. She was joined by Justice Benjamin and Judge Fox. Justice Albright, joined by Judge Cookman, dissented: "Not only is the majority opinion unsupported by the facts and existing case law, but it is also fundamentally unfair. Sadly, justice was neither honored nor served by the majority."

We granted certiorari.

II

It is axiomatic that "[a] fair trial in a fair tribunal is a basic requirement of due process." *Murchison, supra*, at 136. As the Court has recognized, however, "most matters relating to judicial disqualification [do] not rise to a constitutional level." FTC v. Cement Institute, 333 U.S. 683, 702 (1948). The early and leading case on the subject is Tumey v. Ohio, 273 U.S. 510 (1927). There, the Court stated that "matters of kinship, personal bias, state policy, remoteness of interest, would seem generally to be matters merely of legislative discretion." *Id.*, at 523.

The *Tumey* Court concluded that the Due Process Clause incorporated the common-law rule that a judge must recuse himself when he has "a direct, personal, substantial, pecuniary interest" in a case. This rule reflects the maxim that "[n]o man is allowed to be a judge in his own cause; because his interest would certainly bias his judgment, and, not improbably, corrupt his integrity." The Federalist No. 10, p 59 (J. Cooke ed. 1961) (J. Madison); see Frank, Disqualification of Judges, 56 Yale L.J. 605, 611-612 (1947). Under this rule, "disqualification for bias or prejudice was not permitted"; those matters were left to statutes and judicial codes. Personal bias or prejudice "alone would not be sufficient basis for imposing a constitutional requirement under the Due Process Clause."

As new problems have emerged that were not discussed at common law, however, the Court has identified additional instances which, as an objective matter, require recusal. These are circumstances "in which experience teaches that the probability of actual bias on the part of the judge or decisionmaker is too high to be constitutionally tolerable." *Withrow*, 421 U.S., at 47. To place the present case in proper context, two instances where the Court has required recusal merit further discussion.

A

The first involved the emergence of local tribunals where a judge had a financial interest in the outcome of a case, although the interest was less than what would have been considered personal or direct at common law. This was the problem addressed in *Tumey.* There, the mayor of a village had the authority to sit as a judge (with no jury) to try those accused of violating a state law prohibiting the possession of alcoholic beverages. Inherent in this structure were two potential conflicts. First, the mayor received a salary supplement for performing judicial duties, and the funds for that compensation derived from the fines assessed in a case. No fines were assessed upon acquittal. The mayor-judge thus received a salary supplement only if he convicted the defendant. Second, sums from the criminal fines were deposited to the village's general treasury fund for village improvements and repairs. The Court held that the Due Process Clause required disqualification "both because of [the mayor-judge's] direct pecuniary interest in the outcome, and because of his official motive to convict and to graduate the fine to help the financial needs of the village." It so held despite observing that "[t]here are doubtless mayors who would not allow such a consideration as $12 costs in each case to affect their judgment in it. The Court articulated the controlling principle:

"Every procedure which would offer a possible temptation to the average man as a judge to forget the burden of proof required to convict the defendant, or which might lead him not to hold the balance nice, clear and true between the State and the accused, denies the latter due process of law."

The Court was thus concerned with more than the traditional common-law prohibition on direct pecuniary interest. It was also concerned with a more general concept of interests that tempt adjudicators to disregard neutrality. This concern with conflicts resulting from financial incentives was elaborated in Ward v. Monroeville, 409 U.S. 57 (1972), which invalidated a conviction in another mayor's court. In *Monroeville*, unlike in *Tumey*, the mayor received no money; instead, the fines the mayor assessed went to the town's general fund. The Court held that "[t]he fact that the mayor [in *Tumey*] shared directly in the fees and costs did not define the limits of the principle." 409 U.S., at 60. The principle, instead, turned on the "'possible temptation'" the mayor might face; the mayor's "executive responsibilities for village finances may make him partisan to maintain the high level of contribution [to those finances] from the mayor's court." Ibid. As the Court reiterated in another case that Term, "the [judge's] financial stake need not be as direct or positive as it appeared to be in *Tumey.* Gibson v. Berryhill, 411 U.S. 564, 579 (1973). (an administrative board composed of optometrists had a pecuniary interest of "sufficient substance" so that it could not preside over a hearing against competing optometrists).

The Court in *Lavoie* further clarified the reach of the Due Process Clause regarding a judge's financial interest in a case. There, a justice had cast the deciding vote on the Alabama Supreme Court to uphold a punitive damages award against an insurance company for bad-faith refusal to pay a claim. At the time of his vote, the justice was the lead plaintiff in a nearly identical lawsuit pending in Alabama's lower courts. His deciding vote, this Court surmised, "undoubtedly 'raised the stakes'" for the insurance defendant in the justice's suit. 475 U.S., at 823-824. The Court stressed that it was "not required to decide whether in fact [the justice] was influenced." *Id.* The proper constitutional inquiry is "whether sitting on the case then before the Supreme Court of Alabama 'would offer a possible temptation to the average . . . judge to . . . lead him not to hold the balance nice, clear and true.'" *Ibid.* The Court underscored that "what degree or kind of interest is sufficient to disqualify a judge from sitting 'cannot be defined with precision.'" In the Court's view, however, it was important that the test have an objective component.

The *Lavoie* Court proceeded to distinguish the state-court justice's particular interest in the case, which required recusal, from interests that were not a constitutional concern. For instance, "while [the other] justices might conceivably have had a slight pecuniary interest" due to their potential membership in a class-action suit against their own insurance companies, that interest is "'too remote and insubstantial to violate the constitutional constraints.'" 475 U.S., at 825-826. . . . [Ed. Note: The second circumstance, criminal contempt, is omitted.]

III

Based on the principles described in these cases we turn to the issue before us. This problem arises in the context of judicial elections, a framework not presented in the precedents we have reviewed and discussed. Caperton contends that Blankenship's pivotal role in getting Justice Benjamin elected created a constitutionally intolerable probability of actual bias. Though not a bribe . . . , Justice Benjamin would nevertheless feel a debt of gratitude to Blankenship for his extraordinary efforts to get him elected. That temptation, Caperton claims, is as strong and inherent in human nature as was the conflict the Court confronted in *Tumey* and *Monroeville* when a mayor-judge (or the city) benefited financially from a defendant's conviction. . . .

Justice Benjamin was careful to address the recusal motions and explain his reasons why, on his view of the controlling standard, disqualification was not in order. In four separate opinions issued during the course of the appeal, he explained why no actual bias had been established. He found no basis for recusal because Caperton failed to provide "objective evidence" or "objective information," but merely "subjective belief" of bias. Nor could anyone "point to any actual conduct or activity on [his] part which could be termed 'improper.'" In other words, based on the facts presented by Caperton, Justice Benjamin conducted a probing search into his actual motives and inclinations; and he found none to be improper. We do not question his subjective findings of impartiality and propriety. Nor do we determine whether there was actual bias.

Following accepted principles of our legal tradition respecting the proper performance of judicial functions, judges often inquire into their subjective motives and purposes in the ordinary course of deciding a case. This does not mean the inquiry is a simple one. "The work of deciding cases goes on every day in hundreds of courts throughout the land. Any judge, one might suppose, would find it easy to describe the process which he had followed a thousand times and more. Nothing could be farther from the truth." B. Cardozo, The Nature of the Judicial Process 9 (1921). The judge inquires into reasons that seem to be leading to a particular result. Precedent and *stare decisis* and the text and purpose of the law and the Constitution; logic and scholarship and experience and common sense; and fairness and disinterest and neutrality are among the factors at work. To bring coherence to the process, and to seek respect for the resulting judgment, judges often explain the reasons for their conclusions and rulings. There are instances when the introspection that often attends this process may reveal that what the judge had assumed to be a proper, controlling factor is not the real one at work. If the judge discovers that some personal bias or improper consideration seems to be the actuating cause of the decision or to be an influence so difficult to dispel that there is a real possibility of undermining neutrality, the judge may think it necessary to consider withdrawing from the case.

The difficulties of inquiring into actual bias, and the fact that the inquiry is often a private one, simply underscore the need for objective rules. Otherwise there may be no adequate protection against a judge who simply misreads or misapprehends the real motives at work in deciding the case. The judge's own inquiry into actual bias, then, is not one that the law can easily superintend or review, though actual bias, if disclosed, no doubt would be grounds for appropriate relief. In lieu of exclusive reliance on that personal inquiry, or on appellate review of the judge's determination respecting actual bias, the Due Process

Clause has been implemented by objective standards that do not require proof of actual bias. In defining these standards the Court has asked whether, "under a realistic appraisal of psychological tendencies and human weakness," the interest "poses such a risk of actual bias or prejudgment that the practice must be forbidden if the guarantee of due process is to be adequately implemented."

We turn to the influence at issue in this case. Not every campaign contribution by a litigant or attorney creates a probability of bias that requires a judge's recusal, but this is an exceptional case. We conclude that there is a serious risk of actual bias — based on objective and reasonable perceptions — when a person with a personal stake in a particular case had a significant and disproportionate influence in placing the judge on the case by raising funds or directing the judge's election campaign when the case was pending or imminent. The inquiry centers on the contribution's relative size in comparison to the total amount of money contributed to the campaign, the total amount spent in the election, and the apparent effect such contribution had on the outcome of the election.

Applying this principle, we conclude that Blankenship's campaign efforts had a significant and disproportionate influence in placing Justice Benjamin on the case. Blankenship contributed some $3 million to unseat the incumbent and replace him with Benjamin. His contributions eclipsed the total amount spent by all other Benjamin supporters and exceeded by 300% the amount spent by Benjamin's campaign committee. Caperton claims Blankenship spent $1 million more than the total amount spent by the campaign committees of both candidates combined. Massey responds that Blankenship's support, while significant, did not cause Benjamin's victory. In the end the people of West Virginia elected him, and they did so based on many reasons other than Blankenship's efforts. Massey points out that every major state newspaper, but one, endorsed Benjamin. It also contends that then-Justice McGraw cost himself the election by giving a speech during the campaign, a speech the opposition seized upon for its own advantage.

Justice Benjamin raised similar arguments. He asserted that "the outcome of the 2004 election was due primarily to [his own] campaign's message," as well as McGraw's "devastat[ing]" speech in which he "made a number of controversial claims which became a matter of statewide discussion in the media, on the internet, and elsewhere." Whether Blankenship's campaign contributions were a necessary and sufficient cause of Benjamin's victory is not the proper inquiry. Much like determining whether a judge is actually biased, proving what ultimately drives the electorate to choose a particular candidate is a difficult endeavor, not likely to lend itself to a certain conclusion. This is particularly true where, as here, there is no procedure for judicial factfinding and the sole trier of fact is the one accused of bias. Due process requires an objective inquiry into whether the contributor's influence on the election under all the circumstances "would offer a possible temptation to the average . . . judge to . . . lead him not to hold the balance nice, clear and true." *Tumey, supra*, at 532. In an election decided by fewer than 50,000 votes (382,036 to 334,301), Blankenship's campaign contributions — in comparison to the total amount contributed to the campaign, as well as the total amount spent in the election — had a significant and disproportionate influence on the electoral outcome. And the risk that Blankenship's influence engendered actual bias is sufficiently substantial that it "must be forbidden if the guarantee of due process is to be adequately implemented."

The temporal relationship between the campaign contributions, the justice's election, and the pendency of the case is also critical. It was reasonably foreseeable, when the campaign contributions were made, that the pending case would be before the newly elected justice. The $50 million adverse jury verdict had been entered before the election, and the Supreme Court of Appeals was the next step once the state trial court dealt with post-trial motions. So it became at once apparent that, absent recusal, Justice Benjamin would review a judgment that cost his biggest donor's company $50 million. Although there is no allegation of a *quid pro quo* agreement, the fact remains that Blankenship's extraordinary contributions were made at a time when he had a vested stake in the outcome. Just as no man is allowed to be a judge in his own cause, similar fears of bias can arise when — without the consent of the other parties — a man chooses the judge in his own cause. And applying this principle to the judicial election process, there was here a serious, objective risk of actual bias that required Justice Benjamin's recusal.

Justice Benjamin did undertake an extensive search for actual bias. But, as we have indicated, that is just one step in the judicial process; objective standards may also require recusal whether or not actual bias exists or can be proved. Due process "may sometimes bar trial by judges who have no actual bias and who would do their very best to weigh the scales of justice equally between contending parties." *Murchison*, 349 U.S., at 136. The failure to consider objective standards requiring recusal is not consistent with the imperatives of due process. We find that Blankenship's significant and disproportionate influence — coupled with the temporal relationship between the election and the pending case — "'offer a possible temptation to the average . . . judge to . . . lead him not to hold the balance nice, clear and true.'" *Lavoie*, 475 U.S., at 825 (quoting *Monroeville*, 409 U.S., at 60, in turn quoting *Tumey*, 273 U.S., at 532). On these extreme facts the probability of actual bias rises to an unconstitutional level.

IV

Our decision today addresses an extraordinary situation where the Constitution requires recusal. Massey and its *amici* predict that various adverse consequences will follow from recognizing a constitutional violation here — ranging from a flood of recusal motions to unnecessary interference with judicial elections. We disagree. The facts now before us are extreme by any measure. The parties point to no other instance involving judicial campaign contributions that presents a potential for bias comparable to the circumstances in this case.

It is true that extreme cases often test the bounds of established legal principles, and sometimes no administrable standard may be available to address the perceived wrong. But it is also true that extreme cases are more likely to cross constitutional limits, requiring this Court's intervention and formulation of objective standards. This is particularly true when due process is violated.

This Court's recusal cases are illustrative. In each case the Court dealt with extreme facts that created an unconstitutional probability of bias that "'cannot be defined with precision.'" Yet the Court articulated an objective standard to protect the parties' basic right to a fair trial in a fair tribunal. The Court was careful to distinguish the extreme facts of the cases before it from those interests that would not rise to a constitutional level. In this case we do nothing more than what the Court has done before. . . . As such, it is worth noting the effects, or lack thereof, of the Court's prior decisions. Even though the standards announced in those cases raised questions similar to those that might be asked after our decision today, the Court was not flooded with *Monroeville* or *Murchison* motions. That is perhaps due in part to the extreme facts those standards sought to address. Courts proved quite capable of applying the standards to less extreme situations.

One must also take into account the judicial reforms the States have implemented to eliminate even the appearance of partiality. Almost every State — West Virginia included — has adopted the American Bar Association's objective standard: "A judge shall avoid impropriety and the appearance of impropriety." ABA Annotated Model Code of Judicial Conduct, Canon 2 (2004); see Brief for American Bar Association as *Amicus Curiae* 14, and n 29. The ABA Model Code's test for appearance of impropriety is "whether the conduct would create in reasonable minds a perception that the judge's ability to carry out judicial responsibilities with integrity, impartiality and competence is impaired." Canon 2A, Commentary; see also W. Va. Code of Judicial Conduct, Canon 2A, and Commentary (2009) (same).

The West Virginia Code of Judicial Conduct also requires a judge to "disqualify himself or herself in a proceeding in which the judge's impartiality might reasonably be questioned." Canon 3E(1); see also 28 U.S.C. §455(a) ("Any justice, judge, or magistrate judge of the United States shall disqualify himself in any proceeding in which his impartiality might reasonably be questioned"). Under Canon 3E(1), "'[t]he question of disqualification focuses on whether an objective assessment of the judge's conduct produces a reasonable question about impartiality, not on the judge's subjective perception of the ability to act fairly.'" Indeed, some States require recusal based on campaign contributions similar to those in this case.

These codes of conduct serve to maintain the integrity of the judiciary and the rule of law. The Conference of the Chief Justices has underscored that the codes are "[t]he principal safeguard against judicial campaign abuses" that threaten to imperil "public confidence in the fairness and integrity of the nation's elected judges." . . .

States may choose to "adopt recusal standards more rigorous than due process requires."

"The Due Process Clause demarks only the outer boundaries of judicial disqualifications. Congress and the states, of course, remain free to impose more rigorous standards for judicial disqualification than those we find mandated here today." *Lavoie*, 475 U.S., at 828. Because the codes of judicial conduct provide more protection than due process requires, most disputes over disqualification will be resolved without resort to the Constitution. Application of the constitutional standard implicated in this case will thus be confined to rare instances.

The judgment of the Supreme Court of Appeals of West Virginia is reversed, and the case is remanded for further proceedings not inconsistent with this opinion.

It is so ordered.

CHIEF JUSTICE ROBERTS, with whom JUSTICE SCALIA, JUSTICE THOMAS, and JUSTICE ALITO join, dissenting.

I, of course, share the majority's sincere concerns about the need to maintain a fair, independent, and impartial judiciary — and one that appears to be such. But I fear that the Court's decision will undermine rather than promote these values. Until today, we have recognized exactly two situations in which the Federal Due Process Clause requires disqualification of a judge: when the judge has a financial interest in the outcome of the case, and when the judge is trying a defendant for certain criminal contempts. Vaguer notions of bias or the appearance of bias were never a basis for disqualification, either at common law or under our constitutional precedents. Those issues were instead addressed by legislation or court rules.

Today, however, the Court enlists the Due Process Clause to overturn a judge's failure to recuse because of a "probability of bias." Unlike the established grounds for disqualification, a "probability of bias" cannot be defined in any limited way. The Court's new "rule" provides no guidance to judges and litigants about when recusal will be constitutionally required. This will inevitably lead to an increase in allegations that judges are biased, however groundless those charges may be. The end result will do far more to erode public confidence in judicial impartiality than an isolated failure to recuse in a particular case.

I

There is a "presumption of honesty and integrity in those serving as adjudicators." All judges take an oath to uphold the Constitution and apply the law impartially, and we trust that they will live up to this promise. See Republican Party of Minn. v. White, 536 U.S. 765, 796 (2002) (Kennedy, J., concurring) ("We should not, even by inadvertence, 'impute to judges a lack of firmness, wisdom, or honor'" (quoting Bridges v. California, 314 U.S. 252, 273 (1941))). We have thus identified only *two* situations in which the Due Process Clause requires disqualification of a judge: when the judge has a financial interest in the outcome of the case, and when the judge is presiding over certain types of criminal contempt proceedings.

It is well established that a judge may not preside over a case in which he has a "direct, personal, substantial, pecuniary interest." Tumey v. Ohio, 273 U.S.

510, 523 (1927). This principle is relatively straightforward, and largely tracks the longstanding common-law rule regarding judicial recusal. For example, a defendant's due process rights are violated when he is tried before a judge who is "paid for his service only when he convicts the defendant." . . .

Our decisions in this area have also emphasized when the Due Process Clause does *not* require recusal:

> "All questions of judicial qualification may not involve constitutional validity. Thus matters of kinship, personal bias, state policy, remoteness of interest, would seem generally to be matters merely of legislative discretion." *Tumey, supra,* at 523.

[I]n any given case, there are a number of factors that could give rise to a "probability" or "appearance" of bias: friendship with a party or lawyer, prior employment experience, membership in clubs or associations, prior speeches and writings, religious affiliation, and countless other considerations. We have never held that the Due Process Clause requires recusal for any of these reasons, even though they could be viewed as presenting a "probability of bias." Many state *statutes* require recusal based on a probability or appearance of bias, but "that alone would not be sufficient basis for imposing a *constitutional* requirement under the Due Process Clause." *Lavoie, supra,* at 820. (emphasis added). States are, of course, free to adopt broader recusal rules than the Constitution requires — and every State has — but these developments are not continuously incorporated into the [federal] Due Process Clause. . . .

NOTES

1. See Goldberg v. Kelly, 397 U.S. 254, 271 (1970): "[O]f course, an impartial decision maker is essential." See also Withrow v. Larkin, 421 U.S. 35, 46-47 (1975): "[C]oncededly, a 'fair trial in a fair tribunal is a basic requirement of due process.' . . . Not only is a biased decision maker constitutionally unacceptable but 'our system of law has always endeavored to prevent even the probability of unfairness.'"

2. The "requirement of neutrality in adjudicative proceedings safeguards the two central concerns of procedural due process, the prevention of unjustified or mistaken deprivations and the promotion of participation and dialogue by affected individuals in the decision-making process." It ensures "that no person will be deprived of his interests in the absence of a proceeding in which he may present his case with assurance that the arbiter is not predisposed to find against him." Marshall v. Jerrico, Inc., 446 U.S. 238 (1980).

3. The meaning of "bias" in law is narrower than "bias" in the dictionary. It is legal bias — i.e., bias that requires an adjudicator to disqualify himself — that we are addressing here. Generally, the rules governing legal bias apply equally in courts and agencies; hence some of the cases used in our discussion are cases involving courts.

4. The most obvious type of legal bias is financial interest, usually referred to simply as interest. This type of bias is not limited to direct personal pecuniary gain, but can also exist when the adjudicating agency stands to benefit substantially from a particular outcome. The leading case is Tumey v. Ohio, 273 U.S. 510 (1927), which arose out of a conviction in a mayor's court for traffic offenses. The mayor shared in the fees and costs levied against convicted violators. This gave him a direct pecuniary interest that rendered his decision voidable. A system in which the judge is paid when he convicts cannot be regarded as due process.

Compare Ward v. Monroeville, 409 U.S. 57 (1972), also involving traffic convictions in a mayor's court where the mayor was responsible for village finances, which through fines, forfeitures, costs, and fees provided a major part of the village's income. See also Esso Standard Oil Co. (P.R.) v. Mujica Cotto, 389 F.3d 212 (1st Cir. 2004); United Church of the Medical Ctr. v. Medical Ctr. Comm'n, 689 F.2d 693 (7th Cir. 1982). Do you think the bias in *Caperton* is the same as the bias in either *Tumey* or *Monroeville*? How is *Caperton* the same and different from those two cases? Did Judge Benjamin have a "direct" financial interest in the outcome of the case?

5. What about bias by administrative law judges? Should the same rules be applied to them? See Barnett, Resolving the ALJ Quandary, 66 Vand. L. Rev. 797 (2013). What about allegations of bias during the rulemaking process? See Association of National Advertisers v. FTC, *supra* p. 382.

1616 SECOND AVE. v. STATE LIQUOR AUTHORITY

550 N.E.2d 910 (N.Y. 1990)

Chief Judge WACHTLER.

The issue on this appeal is whether public statements made by the Chairman of the State Liquor Authority (SLA) concerning charges then pending in an SLA proceeding against a licensee, disqualified the Chairman from participating in administrative review of that proceeding. We conclude that, because the Chairman's statements to a legislative oversight committee indicated prejudgment of facts in issue in an adjudicatory proceeding, his failure to disqualify himself from that proceeding deprived the licensee of due process of law under the Federal Constitution.

I

Petitioner 1616 Second Avenue Restaurant, Inc., operates a Manhattan restaurant known as Dorrian's Red Hand. Since 1962, Dorrian's has sold alcoholic beverages for on-premise consumption pursuant to a license issued by respondent SLA. In August 1986, attention was focused on Dorrian's because of its connection with the highly publicized "preppie murder" case: the young victim and the accused killer, Robert Chambers, had been in Dorrian's on August 26, shortly before the crime. As a result, the SLA and the New York City Police Department's Social Club Task Force began to closely monitor Dorrian's for violations of the Alcoholic Beverage Control Law, especially those involving underage drinkers.

On February 10, 1987, Dorrian's was charged by the SLA with violating section 65 (1) of the Alcoholic Beverage Control Law by allegedly selling or giving away alcoholic beverages to four underage patrons on November 14-16, 1986. Two of the charges were sustained following a hearing before an Administrative Law Judge commenced on April 15, 1987. The findings were controverted by petitioner and the matter was referred to the five Commissioners of the SLA, including its Chairman, respondent Thomas Duffy, for factual review and for determination of an appropriate penalty (see, 9 N.Y.C.R.R. 54.4[g]; 54.6[a]).

In the interim between the filing of the charges and the commencement of the hearing, Chairman Duffy had been called upon to testify before a committee of the New York State Senate that oversees SLA operations. The questioning covered a wide range of topics, but for a time focused on the issue of underage drinking and the charges against Dorrian's. Duffy's public discussion of the charges prompted petitioner to request that Duffy recuse himself from consideration of the charges against Dorrian's on the ground that he had prejudged the matter. Chairman Duffy declined to do so and, with his participation, the commissioners adopted the findings of the Administrative Law Judge and imposed a 10-day suspension, a 10-day deferred suspension and a $1,000 bond claim.

Petitioner then commenced this article 78 proceeding seeking to annul the SLA's determination. Upon transfer from Supreme Court pursuant to CPLR 7804(g), the Appellate Division confirmed the determination without comment. We granted leave to consider whether the Chairman's public statements disqualified him from participating in the SLA proceeding. Concluding that they did, we now reverse.

II

Before examining the substance of the Chairman's statements, we turn to the governing principles.

It is beyond dispute that an impartial decision maker is a core guarantee of due process, fully applicable to adjudicatory proceedings before administrative agencies. . . . No single standard determines whether an administrative decision maker should disqualify himself from a proceeding for lack of impartiality. Many concepts are embraced under the heading of bias, including advance knowledge of facts, personal interest, animosity, favoritism and prejudgment. Not all require disqualification in all circumstances. Disqualification is more likely to be required where an administrator has a preconceived view of facts at issue in a specific case as opposed to prejudgment of general questions of law or policy.

For example, administrative officials are expected to be familiar with the subjects of their regulations and to be committed to the goals for which their agency was created. Thus a predisposition on questions of law or policy and advance knowledge of general conditions in the regulated field are common, and it is expected that they will influence an administrator engaged in a legislative role such as rule making.... Similarly, mere familiarity with the facts of a pending proceeding or taking a public position on a policy issue related to the proceeding have been held insufficient to require disqualification....

On the other hand, disqualification may be required for prejudgment of specific facts at issue in an adjudicatory proceeding.... It has been noted, moreover, that public statements that indicate prejudgment are especially problematic. While conscientious officials are presumably able to put aside privately held judgments, public statements touching on the facts of a proceeding create special problems. Such statements "may have the effect of entrenching [the official] in a position which he has publicly stated, making it difficult, if not impossible, for him to reach a different conclusion in the event he deems it necessary to do so after consideration of the record." ...

Thus, where, as in this case, an administrative official has made public comments concerning a specific dispute that is to come before him in his adjudicatory capacity, he will be disqualified on the ground of prejudgment if "'a disinterested observer may conclude that [he] has in some measure adjudged the facts as well as the law of a particular case in advance of hearing it.'" ...

III

Under this standard, Chairman Duffy was disqualified from participating in the SLA proceeding against petitioner. During his testimony before the Senate committee overseeing SLA operations, the committee chairman brought up the issue of underage drinking, introducing it as follows:

> *Senator Goodman:* One case in particular that I'd like to use to exemplify the problem has become rather notorious. It's the case of a bar called Dorian's [sic] at number 1616 Second Avenue in New York City....
>
> It's my impression that, despite the issuance of four summons by the police task force and your intervention on several occasions, that absolutely nothing of any use has occurred in preventing the sale to under age people.

After noting that charges were pending before the SLA on the matter, the Chairman responded:

> *Chairman Duffy:* The summonses were served. It turns out that three of the people who were drinking and under age in that premises live outside the state of New York. One lives in Europe, and two are college students who don't live here. We have one who is a person who lives in New York, and the summonses have been dismissed in Criminal Court, I think for lack of prosecution and what I am trying to do at the State Liquor Authority is to bring to bear on these kind of charges some innovative ways of establishing guilt by substantial evidence.
>
> For example, I'm not satisfied to say that in the Dorian case, we will dismiss our proceedings against that establishment because we can't bring in the people who are outside the state. What I'm trying to do, and the reason that we're taking our time to do this is, I'm trying to come up with alternate ways to establish by a substantial evidence that in fact there was an under-age person who consumed and was served alcoholic beverages at that location....

> [A]s far as Dorian's is concerned, I think that I'm doing a great job in the Dorian's matter because I am going to bring Dorian's to justice without begging off and saying, Well, they're outside the state and I can't proceed, and I want to make a record in Dorian's case and, if I can make a record that's going to establish that they sold drinks to minors — and that's what we need, a record — there are people that complain. They [know] that these people are less than 21, and I simply can't do it on somebody's conjecture that this person is less than 21. I've got to have a record.
>
> I'm in the process of compiling that record and we're going to be in the process of being able to report to you the results of hearings and board votes with respect to that.

Viewed as a whole, this testimony could only be regarded by a disinterested observer as evidencing Chairman Duffy's belief that petitioner had in fact violated the law regarding the sale of alcohol to minors and his commitment to establishing that fact in the SLA proceeding. His remarks contain no hint that the charges might turn out to be unfounded. From all that appears, the only question in the Chairman's mind was not whether petitioner was guilty, but whether the SLA would be hamstrung in their efforts to establish guilt because some of the witnesses lived out of state. . . .

But whether or not he had actually prejudged the matter, his statements nonetheless gave the impression that he had, and that impression lent an impermissible air of unfairness to the proceeding. More importantly, those statements and the message they conveyed to a "disinterested observer" established the Chairman's public position on the issue. Whether or not he believed petitioner to be guilty when he made the statements, his public alignment with that position, especially in front of the Senate committee that oversees his agency's operations, might have made it more difficult to reach a contrary conclusion in the adjudicatory proceeding. In effect, to find petitioner innocent would require a public confession of error by the Chairman. That is an impermissible burden to place on petitioner. . . .

Inasmuch as the findings of the Administrative Law Judge are not compromised by the Chairman's apparent prejudgment, the proper remedy is reconsideration of those findings, without the participation of the Chairman, by the remainder of the SLA Commissioners.

Accordingly, the judgment of the Appellate Division should be reversed and the petition granted to the extent of annulling the determination and remitting to the State Liquor Authority for further proceedings in accordance with this opinion.

NOTES

1. A second type of legal bias that is expressly mentioned in the Federal APA is personal bias or prejudice. It is illustrated by United States v. Eduardo-Franco, 885 F.2d 1002 (2d Cir. 1989). It involved a drug prosecution against four Colombian nationals. The judge made the following remarks about Colombians: "They don't have too much regard for Judges. They only killed 32 Chief Judges in that nation. Their regard for the judicial system, the men who run their laws, I'm glad I'm in America." These remarks were held to be an indication of extrajudicial bias that demonstrated that defendants could not receive a fair trial. But compare Neoplan v. Industrial Claims Appeal Office, 778 P.2d 312 (Colo. Ct. App. 1989) (fact that hearing officer called petitioner's attorney "smart ass" and "nasty little fellow" some years earlier did not demonstrate personal bias).

2. Application of the rule against personal bias presents greater difficulty in agencies than in courts because agencies are usually set up to promote affirmative policies, such as furthering the rights of workers to organize and bargain collectively. In giving effect to the basic legislative policies underlying its creation, the agency cannot be expected to act with that "cold neutrality of an impartial judge" of which Burke speaks. In this sense, an agency established to protect the rights of labor is bound to be pro-labor or anti-employer. But that alone would not make out the case of personal bias or prejudice needed to disqualify.

3. If freedom from bias is taken in the broad dictionary sense of absence of preconceptions, no one can ever have a fair trial. The judicial mind is no blank piece of paper; the judge or administrative adjudicator starts with inevitable preconceptions. In this sense there is prejudgment in every case. But does such prejudgment constitute legal bias? The easiest legal bias case is that of general prejudgment. Thus, may a member of the FCC known for his vigorous policy against concentration of ownership in broadcasting sit in cases involving the policy? See Chronicle Broadcasting Co., 26 Pike & Fischer Admin. L. 2d 270 (FCC 1969). What about a member of a rate-fixing agency who is elected on a campaign pledge to change railroad rates or is appointed by a governor who had been elected on a platform to reduce telephone rates? See Southern Pacific Co. v. Board of Railroad Commr's, 78 F. 236 (N.D. Cal. 1896); Georgia Continental Telephone Co. v. Public Service Comm'n, 8 F. Supp. 434 (N.D. Ga. 1934). But see Field, J., dissenting in Spring Valley Water Works v. Schottler, 110 U.S. 347, 364 (1884) (elective agency cannot be impartial; bound to be biased in favor of lower rates).

See also Rombough v. FAA, 594 F.2d 893 (2d Cir. 1979), upholding the FAA's refusal to disqualify the Federal Air Surgeon from participating in the decision on pilots' petitions for exemption from the FAA's age-60 rule, because he had warned petitioners and others of what the agency's consistent position regarding such petitions had been. It is not improper for agency officials to form views that may influence their decisions.

Federal Administrative Procedure Act

5 U.S.C. §556(b)

The functions of presiding employees and of employees participating in decisions in accordance with section 557 of this title shall be conducted in an impartial manner. A presiding or participating employee may at any time disqualify himself. On the filing in good faith of a timely and sufficient

> affidavit of personal bias or other disqualification of a presiding or participating employee, the agency shall determine the matter as a part of the record and decision in the case.

4. In the federal courts, a district judge may not decide the truth of the facts alleged in an affidavit to disqualify him for bias. Berger v. United States, 255 U.S. 22 (1921). Should the same be true of an administrative law judge against whom an affidavit is filed under §556(b)?

5. How is an agency member disqualified? In American Cyanamid Co. v. FTC, 363 F.2d 757 (6th Cir. 1966), the FTC refused to rule on a motion to disqualify its chairman, stating that "[u]nder the Commission's practice, disqualification is treated as a matter primarily for determination by the individual member concerned." American Cyanamid Co., 60 F.T.C. 1881 (1962). Was the FTC correct in leaving disqualification to the discretion of the agency member concerned? On September 15, 1981, the FTC added the following to its rules of practice:

> **(1)** Whenever any participant in a proceeding shall deem a commissioner for any reason to be disqualified from participation in that proceeding, such participant may file with the secretary a motion to the commission to disqualify the commissioner, such motion to be supported by affidavits and other information setting forth with particularity the alleged grounds for disqualification. . . .
>
> **(3)(i)** Such motion shall be addressed in the first instance by the commissioner whose disqualification is sought.
>
> **(ii)** In the event such commissioner declines to excuse himself or herself from further participation in the proceeding, the commission shall determine the motion without the participation of such commissioner.

Note that the decision on disqualification at the agency level is not the last word. The disqualification of agency members as well as that of administrative law judges is a matter to be considered on judicial review. Participation by an agency member who should have stepped down is a ground for reversal on review.

ROSA v. BOWEN

677 F. Supp. 782 (D.N.J. 1988)

SAROKIN, District Judge.

On December 5, 1985, this court remanded plaintiff's social security disability case to the Secretary of the Department of Health and Human Services ("the Secretary") for further administrative proceedings. The Appeals Council of the Department of Health and Human Services, in turn, vacated its prior denial of plaintiff's request for review and remanded the case to an administrative law judge ("ALJ") for a hearing. That hearing was an offense to the Social Security Act. The court therefore vacates the Secretary's decision a second time and remands the case for a fair hearing.

BACKGROUND

Plaintiff is a fifty-year-old woman who was born in Puerto Rico and moved to New Jersey in 1958. Until August 12, 1982, she held a steady job. At that time, however, she entered the hospital with rectal bleeding, abdominal cramps, and weakness. She was diagnosed as suffering from ulcerative colitis and uncontrolled diabetes mellitus. Since her hospitalization in 1982, plaintiff has not returned to work.

She filed for disability insurance benefits and supplemental security income on December 20, 1982. The Secretary denied her application, but this court remanded the case for further administrative action on December 5, 1985. The Appeals Council of the Department of Health and Human Services, which had earlier denied plaintiff's request for review, then vacated that denial and remanded the case to an ALJ for a hearing.

The ALJ convened the hearing on the morning of September 5, 1986. Plaintiff was represented by an attorney at that hearing, and also had a Spanish language interpreter. The hearing lasted slightly less than one hour.

On October 27, 1986, the ALJ issued a recommended decision in which he found plaintiff not disabled and recommended that she be denied disability insurance benefits as well as supplemental security income. The Appeals Council adopted the findings and conclusions of the ALJ in a decision dated January 30, 1987.

On her appeal from the adverse decision of the Secretary, plaintiff contends that the Secretary's decision was not supported by substantial evidence as 42 U.S.C. §405(g) requires. Defendant, in response, argues that his decision was in fact so supported. Plaintiff, however, also argues that defendant denied her due process and her statutory right to a hearing. Because the transcript so vividly demonstrates an abject violation of plaintiff's statutory rights, the court does not reach the merits of plaintiff's disability claim.

DISCUSSION

Although a district court's most frequent task in disability cases is to determine whether the Secretary's decisions are supported by substantial evidence, *see* 42 U.S.C. §405(g), a court may also ascertain whether a claimant was accorded a full or fair hearing. . . .

When the Secretary fails or refuses to provide a disability claimant with the fair procedures to which the claimant is entitled, a court may remand the case to the Secretary with instructions to afford the claimant fair treatment. In the case before the court, plaintiff's entitlement to a fair hearing flowed from the Social Security Act itself, 42 U.S.C. §405(b)(1), which provides that "[u]pon request by any . . . individual [applying for disability benefits] . . . , [the Secretary] shall give such applicant reasonable notice, an opportunity for a hearing with respect to such decision, and, if a hearing is held, shall, on the basis of evidence adduced at the hearing, affirm, modify, or reverse his findings of fact and such decision."

The hearing that the Secretary actually provided for the plaintiff was shameful in its atmosphere of alternating indifference, personal musings, impatience and condescension. The court is confident that the hearing was not the sort of procedure which Congress intended in enacting 42 U.S.C. §405(b)(1).

As the transcript of the hearing speaks largely for itself, the court here recounts only the most offensive and egregious improprieties:

The ALJ's most pressing concern at the hearing was expedience. His denials of all of the claimant's attorney's procedural requests were not merely perfunctory; they were impatient and irritated. Plaintiff's attorney began the hearing by requesting a subpoena for plaintiff's treating physician. The ALJ ruled that "the motion is denied as usual, you know." The lawyer then asked for permission to make an opening statement. The ALJ refused the request, asking rhetorically, "what are you going to say that won't come out in the hearing? . . . I'd prefer you to have a closing statement after we're fully aware of all of the facts, and you can put that in writing."

Later in the hearing, the attorney again requested a subpoena for a physician. The ALJ denied the request on the grounds that "we'd never get them if we started bringing them in. There won't be anybody to do the examinations — they'd all quit on us. You know that. . . . It would destroy the system." Still later, plaintiff testified that she received some money from her former employer in 1984 upon her official termination, even though she had not reported for work since 1982. The following colloquy ensued:

ALJ: That's a bunch of nonsense, a bunch of nonsense. . . . [B]ring in a guy from Victory [her former employer] to testify as to why she got this money. . . .

Attorney: May I — may I request a subpoena for that purpose?

ALJ: Oh, no. See if you can get them to consent. I don't believe her. I don't believe her at all.

Attorney: I have no way to compel anybody from Victory to come over here. . . .

ALJ: No, I'm not going to issue a subpoena because this case is ending today. You know what I mean?

Nor did the ALJ confine his impatience to his rulings on the claimant's procedural requests. He continually harassed the claimant's attorney and ordered him to accelerate his presentation of the case. After one transcript page of testimony about the claimant's background, the ALJ interrupted: "All right, go ahead Joel, ask her about her problem." After another page of testimony, the judge interjected with annoyance: "Lead her. Lead her." Then, after seventeen transcript pages of generally irrelevant dialogue between the ALJ, the claimant, and her attorney, the ALJ ordered plaintiff's attorney to finish the case in ten minutes. When the attorney took exception to that order, the ALJ said: "Take exception all you want. We start the next case at a quarter to ten.". Four pages later, the judge further restricted the attorney's allotted time: "All right, now Joel, come on.

You've got one minute and then we're going to move on to your next case." The attorney noted his exception to that order, and the ALJ's response can only be described as jeering: "Come on, you got one last question. Make it a good one." When the attorney attempted to dispute the ALJ's time limitation, the judge revealed the true motivation for his hurry: "Joel, we got three cases together this morning. Don't you want to go to lunch at all?"

During the few moments that the ALJ actually devoted to the substance of the hearing, his focus was wholly improper. He measured the gravity of plaintiff's condition against his own mother's illnesses. He gave extensive advice to the plaintiff about the proper medication for, and diagnosis of, her illnesses. He even offered his opinion as to whether a person suffers more from diarrhea than from constipation.

Most importantly, the ALJ demonstrated genuine contempt for the statute he was administering. After hearing plaintiff testify for a few minutes, the ALJ became convinced that plaintiff was not entitled to benefits for the first year or two of her claimed period of disability. He used this conclusion to attempt to turn the hearing into a cheap bargaining session, in which the ALJ would agree to make a finding of disability in exchange for plaintiff's choosing a later disability onset date and ending the hearing:

> **ALJ:** I'm not going to pay her back to '82. That you could forget. . . . You got to amend your onset date here. . . .
>
> **ALJ:** Well, change the onset date, and stop this. I'm not going to go beyond this anyway. Pick a date in '85, and I'll, I'll be very favorably to, to end this thing. . . .
>
> **ALJ:** What's your new onset date? Pick a date in the middle of '85 and you can go home. Well you can't go home, but you can send her home. Now how many times — that's an offer you can't refuse.

This court can do nothing to highlight the wrongfulness and offensiveness of the ALJ's behavior; his conduct speaks for itself. Courts have, on other occasions, reprimanded administrators for excessive preoccupation with expedience. . . .

Courts have also emphasized that it is the duty of an administrative law judge to develop an administrative record fully and fairly, even where a claimant is represented by counsel. . . .

Even where no one error, standing alone, would suffice to set aside an administrator's determination, a large number of errors can have the combined effect of rendering a hearing unfair and inadequate. . . .

The court has no difficulty in concluding that the ALJ's errors combined to create an unfair hearing in this case. This court has previously criticized this agency's heartlessness in the repeated and unfounded rejection of a multitude of clearly valid claims. However, even in those cases, the unjust results followed seemingly adequate procedures. In this matter there was not even the pretense of a full and fair hearing. Once we forsake fairness and due process because of the pressure of heavy caseloads, then our system of justice will end. Although administrative hearings are not formal trials, nor should they be so informal or limited that their fairness is destroyed.

The hearing conducted in this matter fell far below the standards of the Social Security Act, 42 U.S.C. §405(b)(1). Accordingly, the court vacates the decision of the Secretary and remands the case for a full and fair hearing.

NOTES

1. Can personal bias be shown from conduct during the hearing? See NLRB v. Phelps, 136 F.2d 562 (5th Cir. 1943), where the examiner took over the prosecution, personally issuing a show cause order converting the proceeding into one against a corporation not named as respondent. However, as the *Rosa* case shows, evidence of bias must be particularly strong. A more common result of a bias challenge based on hearing conduct is found in St. Anthony Hospital v. Department of Health and Human Services, 309 F.3d 680 (10th Cir. 2002). But compare Nuclear Information and Resource Service v. NRC, 509 F.3d 562 (D.C. Cir. 2007) (Commissioner's derogatory statements about a party in another proceeding not enough for disqualification where comments were more indicative of a "personal style" than required bias).

2. *Rule of necessity.* The great exception to the rule that an adjudicator tainted with legal bias must disqualify himself is the rule of necessity. "From the very necessity of the case has grown the rule that disqualification will not be permitted to destroy the only tribunal with power in the premises." Brinkley v. Hassig, 83 F.2d 351, 357 (10th Cir. 1936). When the disqualification removes the only tribunal that has jurisdiction over the case, that tribunal may continue to sit; in such a case the right of the individual gives way to the public interest in having the law enforced.

In February 1976, 44 federal judges brought suit in the federal district court for damages to compensate for the effects of inflation since 1969 on federal judicial salaries, which, the judges contended, had led to the practical nullification of the constitutional prohibition against the diminishing of judicial salaries. The judges contended that Congress had violated the judges' constitutional right to "compensation" by failing to offset adequately the impact of inflation on their salaries. Atkins v. United States, 556 F.2d 1028 (Ct. Cl. 1977), cert. denied, 434 U.S. 1009 (1978). How can such a case be decided by the federal courts? Doesn't every federal judge have a disqualifying financial interest? See United States v. Will, 449 U.S. 200 (1980). It arose out of an action by federal judges similar to that referred to in note 1. The Supreme Court candidly recognized that each of the justices had a direct financial interest. But, said the Court, it could not renounce jurisdiction of the case. If all the justices were to disqualify themselves, there would be no forum available to decide the case. "It was precisely considerations of this kind that gave rise to the Rule of Necessity, a well-settled principle at common law that . . . 'although a judge had better not, if it can be avoided, take part in the decision of a case in which he has any personal interest, yet he not only may but must do so if the case cannot be heard otherwise.'"

For a more recent example, see Ignacio v. Judges of U.S. Court of Appeals for Ninth Circuit, 453 F.3d 1160 (9th Cir. 2006). There, an individual named all Ninth Circuit judges as parties to his federal action, making it impossible for the court to name a panel of judges who were not a party to the suit. The court applied the Rule of Necessity to hold that recusal was not required.

G COMBINATION OF FUNCTIONS

WITHROW v. LARKIN

421 U.S. 35 (1975)

MR. JUSTICE WHITE delivered the opinion of the Court.

The statutes of the State of Wisconsin forbid the practice of medicine without a license from an examining board composed of practicing physicians. The statutes also define and forbid various acts of professional misconduct, proscribe fee splitting, and make illegal the practice of medicine under any name other than the name under which a license has issued if the public would be misled, such practice would constitute unfair competition with another physician, or other detriment to the profession would result. To enforce these provisions, the examining board is empowered under Wis. Stat. Ann. §§448.17 and 448.18 to warn and reprimand, temporarily to suspend the license, and

> to institute criminal action or action to revoke license when it finds cause therefor under any criminal or revocation statute. . . .

When an investigative proceeding before the board was commenced against him, appellee brought this suit against appellants, the individual members of the Examining Board, seeking an injunction against the enforcement of the statutes. The District Court issued a preliminary injunction, the appellants appealed, and we noted probable jurisdiction, 417 U.S. 943 (1974).

I

Appellee, a resident of Michigan and licensed to practice medicine there, obtained a Wisconsin license in August 1971 under a reciprocity agreement between Michigan and Wisconsin governing medical licensing. His practice in Wisconsin consisted of performing abortions at an office in Milwaukee. On June 20, 1973, the Board sent to appellee a notice that it would hold an investigative hearing on July 12, 1973, under Wis. Stat. Ann. §448.17 to determine whether he had engaged in certain proscribed acts. The hearing would be closed to the public, although appellee and his attorney could attend. They would not, however, be permitted to cross-examine witnesses. Based upon the evidence presented at the hearing, the Board would decide "whether to warn or reprimand if it finds such practice and whether to institute criminal action or action to revoke license if probable cause therefor exists under criminal or revocation statutes." App. 14.

On July 6, 1973, appellee filed his complaint in this action under 42 U.S.C. §1983 seeking preliminary and permanent injunctive relief and a temporary restraining order preventing the Board from investigating him and from conducting the investigative hearing. . . .

On November 19, 1973, the three-judge District Court found . . . that §448.18(7) was unconstitutional as a violation of due process guarantees and enjoined the Board from enforcing it. Its holding was that:

> for the board temporarily to suspend Dr. Larkin's license at its own contested hearing on charges evolving from its own investigation would constitute a denial to him of his rights to procedural due process. Insofar as §448.18(7) authorizes a procedure wherein a physician stands to lose his liberty or property, absent the intervention of an independent, neutral and detached decision-maker, we concluded that it was unconstitutional and unenforceable.

368 F. Supp. at 797.

II

The District Court framed the constitutional issue which it addressed as being whether "for the Board temporarily to suspend Dr. Larkin's license at its own contested hearing on charges evolving from its own investigation would constitute a denial to him of his rights to procedural due process." 368 F. Supp. at 797. The question was initially answered affirmatively, and in its amended judgment the court asserted that there was a high probability that appellee would prevail on the question. Its opinion stated that the "state medical examining board did not qualify as [an independent] decisionmaker [and could not] properly rule with regard to the merits of the same charge it investigated and, as in this case, presented to the district attorney." Id. at 798. We disagree. On the present record, it is quite unlikely that appellee would ultimately prevail on the merits of the due process issue presented to the District Court, and it was an abuse of discretion to issue the preliminary injunction.

Concededly, a "fair trial in a fair tribunal is a basic requirement of due process." In re Murchison, 349 U.S. 133, 136 (1955). This applies to administrative agencies which adjudicate as well as to courts. Gibson v. Berryhill, 411 U.S. 564, 579 (1973). Not only is a biased decisionmaker constitutionally unacceptable but "our system of law has always endeavored to prevent even the probability of unfairness." *Murchison, supra*; cf. Tumey v. Ohio, 273 U.S. 510, 532 (1927). In pursuit of this end, various situations have been identified in which experience teaches that the probability of actual bias on the part of the judge or decisionmaker is too high to be constitutionally tolerable. Among these cases are those in which the adjudicator has a pecuniary interest in the outcome and in which he has been the target of personal abuse or criticism from the party before him.

The contention that the combination of investigative and adjudicative functions necessarily creates an unconstitutional risk of bias in administrative adjudication has a much more difficult burden of persuasion to carry. It must overcome a presumption of honesty and integrity in those serving as adjudicators; and it must convince that, under a realistic appraisal of psychological tendencies and human weakness, conferring investigative and adjudicative powers on the same individuals poses such a risk of actual bias or prejudgment that the practice must be forbidden if the guarantee of due process is to be adequately implemented.

Very similar claims have been squarely rejected in prior decisions of this court. [The Court here discussed FTC v. Cement Inst., 333 U.S. 683 (1948).]

More recently we have sustained against due process objection a system in which a Social Security examiner has responsibility for developing the facts and making a decision as to disability claims, and observed that the challenge to this combination of functions "assumes too much and would bring down too many procedures designed, and working well, for a government structure of great and growing complexity." Richardson v. Perales, 402 U.S. 289, 410 (1971).

That is not to say that there is nothing to the argument that those who have investigated should not then adjudicate. The issue is substantial, it is not new, and legislators and others concerned with the operations of administrative agencies have given much attention to whether and to what extent distinctive administrative functions should be performed by the same persons. No single answer has been reached. Indeed, the growth, variety, and complexity of the administrative processes have made any one solution highly unlikely. Within the Federal Government itself, Congress has addressed the issue in several different ways, providing for varying degrees of separation from complete separation of functions to virtually none at all. For the generality of agencies, Congress has been content with §5 of the Administrative Procedure Act, 5 U.S.C. §554(d), which provides that no employee engaged in investigating or prosecuting may also participate or advise in the adjudicating function, but which also expressly exempts from this prohibition "the agency or a member or members of the body comprising the agency."

It is not surprising, therefore, to find that "[t]he case law, both federal and state, generally rejects the idea that the combination [of] judging [and] investigating functions is a denial of due process, . . ." 2 K. Davis, Administrative Law Treatise, §13.02 (1958), at 175. Similarly, our cases, although they reflect the substance of the problem, offer no support for the bald proposition applied in this case by the District Court that agency members who participate in an investigation are disqualified from adjudicating. The incredible variety of administrative mechanisms in this country will not yield to any single organizing principle.

Appellee relies heavily on In re Murchison, *supra*, in which a state judge, empowered under state law to sit as a "one-man grand jury" and to compel witnesses to testify before him in secret about possible crimes, charged two such witnesses with criminal contempt, one for perjury and the other for refusing to answer certain questions, and then himself tried and convicted them. This Court found the procedure to be a denial of due process of law not only because the judge in effect became part of the prosecution and assumed an adversary position, but also because as a judge, passing on guilt or innocence, he very likely relied on "his own personal knowledge and impression of what had occurred in the grand jury room," an impression that "could not be tested by adequate cross-examination." Id., 349 U.S., at 138.

Plainly enough, *Murchison* has not been understood to stand for the broad rule that the members of an administrative agency may not investigate the facts, institute proceedings, and then make the necessary adjudications. The court did not purport to question the *Cement Institute* case, *supra*, or the Administrative Procedure Act and did not lay down any general principle that a judge before whom an alleged contempt is committed may not bring and preside over the ensuing contempt proceedings. The accepted rule is to the contrary. . . .

Nor is there anything in this case that comes within the strictures of *Murchison.*[1] When the Board instituted its investigative procedures, it stated only that it would investigate whether proscribed conduct had occurred. Later in noticing the adversary hearing, it asserted only that it would determine if violations had been committed which would warrant suspension of appellee's license. Without doubt, the Board then anticipated that the proceeding would eventuate in an adjudication of the issue; but there was no more evidence of bias or the risk of bias or prejudgment than inhered in the very fact that the Board had investigated and would now adjudicate. Of course, we should be alert to the possibilities of bias that may lurk in the way particular procedures actually work in practice. The processes utilized by the Board, however, do not in themselves contain an unacceptable risk of bias. The investigative proceeding had been closed to the public, but appellee and his counsel were permitted to be present throughout; counsel actually attended the hearings and knew the facts presented to the Board. No specific foundation has been presented for suspecting that the Board had been prejudiced by its investigation or would be disabled from hearing and deciding on the basis of the evidence to be presented at the contested hearing. The mere exposure to evidence presented in nonadversary investigative procedures is insufficient in itself to impugn the fairness of the board members at a later adversary hearing. Without a showing to the contrary, state administrators "are assumed to be men of conscience and intellectual discipline, capable of judging a particular controversy fairly on the basis of its own circumstances." United States v. Morgan, 313 U.S. 409, 421 (1941).

We are of the view, therefore, that the District Court was in error when it entered the restraining order against the Board's contested hearing and when it granted the preliminary injunction based on the untenable view that it would be unconstitutional for the Board to suspend appellee's license "at its own contested hearing on charges evolving from its own investigation. . . ." The contested hearing should have been permitted to proceed.

---

1. It is asserted by appellants, Brief of Appellants 25 n.9, and not denied by appellee that an agency employee performed the actual investigation and gathering of evidence in this case and that an assistant attorney general then presented the evidence to the Board at the investigative hearings. While not essential to our decision upholding the constitutionality of the Board's sequence of functions, these facts, if true, show that the Board had organized itself internally to minimize the risks arising from combining investigation and adjudication, including the possibility of Board members relying at later suspension hearings upon evidence not then fully subject to effective confrontation.

III

Nor do we think the situation substantially different because the Board . . . proceeded to make and issue formal findings of fact and conclusions of law asserting that there was probably cause to believe that appellee had engaged in various acts prohibited by the Wisconsin statutes. . . . Although the District Court did not emphasize this aspect of the case before it, appellee stresses it in attempting to show prejudice and prejudgment. We are not persuaded.

Judges repeatedly issue arrest warrants on the basis that there is probable cause to believe that a crime has been committed and that the person named in the warrant has committed it. Judges also preside at preliminary hearings where they must decide whether the evidence is sufficient to hold a defendant for trial. Neither of these pretrial involvements has been thought to raise any constitutional barrier against the judge presiding over the criminal trial and, if the trial is without a jury, against making the necessary determination of guilt or innocence. Nor has it been thought that a judge is disqualified from presiding over injunction proceedings because he has initially assessed the facts in issuing or denying a temporary restraining order or a preliminary injunction. It is also very typical for the members of administrative agencies to receive the results of investigations, to approve the filing of charges or formal complaints instituting enforcement proceedings, and then to participate in the ensuing hearings. This mode of procedure does not violate the Administrative Procedure Act, and it does not violate due process of law. We should also remember that it is not contrary to due process to allow judges and administrators who have had their initial decisions reversed on appeal to confront and decide the same questions a second time around. . . .

Here, the Board stayed within the accepted bounds of due process. Having investigated, it issued findings and conclusions asserting the commission of certain acts and ultimately concluding that there was probable cause to believe that appellee had violated the statutes.

The risk of bias or prejudgment in this sequence of functions has not been considered to be intolerably high or to raise a sufficiently great possibility that the adjudicators would be so psychologically wedded to their complaints that they would consciously or unconsciously avoid the appearance of having erred or changed position. Indeed, just as there is no logical inconsistency between a finding of probable cause and an acquittal in a criminal proceeding, there is no incompatibility between the agency filing a complaint based on probable cause and a subsequent decision, when all the evidence is in, that there has been no violation of the statute. Here, if the Board now proceeded after an adversary hearing to determine that appellee's license to practice should not be temporarily suspended, it would not implicitly be admitting error in its prior finding of probable cause. Its position most probably would merely reflect the benefit of a more complete view of the evidence afforded by an adversary hearing.

The initial charge or determination of probable cause and the ultimate adjudication have different bases and purposes. The fact that the same agency makes them in tandem and that they relate to the same issues does not result in a procedural due process violation. Clearly, if the initial view of the facts based on the evidence derived from nonadversarial processes as a practical or legal matter foreclosed fair and effective consideration at a subsequent adversary hearing leading to ultimate decision, a substantial due process question would be raised. But in our view, that is not this case. . . .

The judgment of the District Court is reversed and the case is remanded to that court for further proceedings consistent with this opinion.

BEER GARDEN v. STATE LIQUOR AUTHORITY

590 N.E.2d 1193 (N.Y. 1992)

KAYE, Judge.

These appeals raise two administrative law questions: the validity of a regulation of the State Liquor Authority (the SLA) and the propriety of an SLA Commissioner's participation in final agency decisions against petitioner licensees. As to both questions we agree with the licensees: the regulation is invalid as applied because it conflicts with the authorizing legislation, and the Commissioner (who was SLA Counsel when the charges against the licensees were filed and heard) should have recused herself from the final agency determinations. [Only the second question is discussed here.]

In 1986, the SLA issued petitioner Beer Garden, Inc., a New York City nightclub, a license for the on-premise sale of alcoholic beverages. Three SLA notices are the focus of Beer Garden's appeal. *First*, in December 1988, a proceeding to cancel or revoke Beer Garden's license was initiated by a Notice of Pleading and Hearing charging that the "occurrence of noise, disturbance, misconduct or disorder in the licensed premises, in areas in front of or adjacent to the licensed premises, or in the parking lot of the licensed premises has resulted in the licensed premises becoming a focal point for police attention; all cause for revocation, cancellation or suspension of the license in accordance with Rule 36.-1(q) of the Rules of the State Liquor Authority."

Second, in March 1989, the SLA served Beer Garden with notice of a proceeding to suspend its license, charging that the licensee had two months earlier sold alcoholic beverages to a minor in violation of Alcoholic Beverage Control Law §65(1). The notice specified a 30-day suspension as the maximum possible penalty. *Third*, a Notice of Interview was served on Beer Garden in October 1989, informing the licensee that based on the same "focal point" allegation made in the first notice, an interview would be scheduled in connection with renewal of its license for 1989-1992.

All three notices were issued over the stamped signature of "Sharon L. Tillman, Counsel to the Authority." The first two notices advised Beer Garden that failure to appear and plead would be deemed "no contest" of the charges; all three notices stated that Beer Garden could be represented by counsel and, at any hearing or interview, could introduce evidence in its own behalf.

Under SLA regulations, the Administrative Law Judge is authorized to make findings as to whether the evidence sustained the charges, and may also recommend a penalty. Between November 1989 and April 1990, the ALJ conducted hearings on the revocation and suspension proceedings. . . . In March 1990, the ALJ found the charges sustained factually and, without recommendation as to penalty, he referred the matter to the Commissioner for final determination. . . .

On June 30, 1990, Tillman left her position as Counsel to become an SLA Commissioner.

On August 1, 1990, the Commissioners voted to . . . adopt the ALJ's findings, and sustain the charges, imposing a penalty of revocation and $1,000 bond forfeiture. . . . Three of the five Commissioners, including Commissioner Tillman, concurred in the dispositions. . . .

The matter was reconsidered one week later at the request of Beer Garden's attorney, who had been unable to attend the earlier session, and at that time he asked that Commissioner Tillman recuse herself based on her role as SLA Counsel during the hearing process. She refused. Upon reconsideration, the three Commissioners adhered to their original determination. . . . Beer Garden then commenced the present CPLR article 78 proceeding. . . .

Commissioner Tillman was the attorney for the SLA during the entire period the matter against Beer Garden was pending before the ALJ, and the charges bore her signature. The challenge here is not to the dual investigatory/adjudicatory role of the agency. Rather it concerns an individual's participation, as advocate for the agency's position, in the very matter over which she is later required to pass impartial judgment (compare, Withrow v. Larkin, 421 U.S. 35).

Judiciary Law §14 provides that no Judge shall "sit as such in, or take any part in the decision of, an action, claim, matter, motion or proceeding to which he [or she] is a party, or in which he [or she] has been attorney or counsel." While we recognize that this provision pertains only to courts of record, the common-law rule of disqualification embodied by the statute has been applied to administrative tribunals exercising quasi-judicial functions. . . .

The SLA urges that Tillman did not actively participate in the hearing before the ALJ and had no actual knowledge of the facts of the present case. Mere "appearance of impropriety," the SLA maintains, will not suffice to mandate recusal where no actual bias is shown, citing this Court's recent decision in Matter of 1616 Second Ave. Rest. v. New York State Liq. Auth., 75 N.Y.2d 158.

In the present circumstances, we disagree. In *1616 Second Avenue*, the Court was concerned with whether public statements made by the Chairman of the SLA relating to charges then pending in an SLA proceeding against a licensee disqualified the Chairman from participating in the administrative review of that proceeding. . . . Those circumstances necessarily required the Court to examine the statements and determine whether the comments gave the impression that the Chairman had pre-judged the facts. The present case involves a different concern for propriety: whether one who has appeared, even if it be in form only, as counsel in the prosecution of legal charges can later adjudicate that very dispute.

"'Next in importance to the duty of rendering a righteous judgment, is that of doing it in such a manner as will beget no suspicion of the fairness and integrity of the judge.' So vital is deemed the observance of this principle that it has been held that a judge disqualified under a statute cannot act even with the consent of the parties interested, because the law was not designed merely for the protection of the parties to the suit, but for the general interests of justice." ...

Courts of this State, while finding no actual fault in the conduct of the hearing, have held "as a matter of propriety" that administrative officers should recuse themselves in situations where prior involvement creates an appearance of partiality.... Fundamental fairness requires "at least that one who participates in a case on behalf of any party, whether actively or merely formally by being on pleadings or briefs, take no part in the decision of that case by any tribunal on which [that person] may thereafter sit." ...

Tillman's role as Beer Garden's "prosecutor" in this case was inherently incompatible with her subsequent participation as its Judge.... That circumstance and fundamental fairness require that she recuse herself from any reconsideration of the surviving charge.

Accordingly ..., the order of the Appellate Division should be modified, with costs to petitioner, by remitting the matter to the Supreme Court with directions to remand to the State Liquor Authority for further proceedings in accordance with this opinion.

NOTES

1. Why does the New York court reach a different result from that in Withrow v. Larkin?

2. See Vali Convalescent Inst. v. Industrial Commission, 649 P.2d 33, 37 (Utah 1982): "[T]he practice of an agency acting as prosecutor and judge is not unconstitutional, at least if those functions . . . are kept separate within the agency." Note that the *Withrow* decision deals only with the combination of functions within the same agency. It does not reach the question of whether the same agency officials may exercise prosecutorial and judicial functions. See also Appeal of Feldman, 346 A.2d 895 (Pa. Cmwlth. Ct. 1975) (where the same agency attorney both litigated the school employee dismissal case and assisted in preparation of the decision).

Compare Cardine, J., dissenting, in State Transp. Comm'n v. Ford, 844 P.2d 496, 499 (Wyo. 1992):

> This must indeed have been a strange administrative agency hearing. There was a prosecutor from the attorney general's office, a hearing officer from the attorney general's office, a presiding officer from the commission, and the commission which was the fact finding and decision-making body....
>
> The hearing, likened to a jury trial, was that the prosecutor was an attorney general; the presiding judge was an attorney general; the jury was the commission. The essence of the court's decision is that as long as the members of the commission

do not also come from the office of the attorney general, the hearing satisfies due process and all other constitutional guarantees to a fair hearing. With this I cannot agree.

I discern the issue to be . . . whether both the prosecutor and hearing officer can be the same person, i.e., from the same state agency. I would hold they cannot be the same. . . . Had appellant . . . been unable to show that the hearing officer was partial, biased, or prejudiced, I still would not allow a hearing in which the attorney general acted as both prosecutor and judge. This for the same reason that we do not allow the prosecutor and judge in our court system to be the same person or even from the same branch of government.

Federal Administrative Procedure Act

5 U.S.C. §554

(d) The employee who presides at the reception of evidence pursuant to section 556 of this title shall make the recommended decision or initial decision required by section 557 of this title, unless he becomes unavailable to the agency. Except to the extent required for the disposition of ex parte matters as authorized by law, such an employee may not—

1. consult a person or party on a fact in issue, unless on notice and opportunity for all parties to participate; or

2. be responsible to or subject to the supervision or direction of an employee or agent engaged in the performance of investigative or prosecuting functions for an agency. An employee or agent engaged in the performance of investigative or prosecuting functions for an agency in a case may not, in that or a factually related case, participate or advise in the decision, recommended decision, or agency review pursuant to section 557 of this title, except as witness or counsel in public proceedings. This subsection does not apply—

(A) in determining applications for initial licenses;

(B) to proceedings involving the validity or application of rates, facilities, or practices of public utilities or carriers; or

(C) to the agency or a member or members of the body comprising the agency.

3. Note the Court's determination in Withrow v. Larkin that the combination of investigating and judging functions does not violate due process guarantees.

4. The provisions of the APA §554(d), provide for internal separation of functions, along the lines proposed by the Attorney General's Committee. They separate those who investigate and prosecute from those who hear and decide (at least at the initial level). As already seen, hearings under the APA are conducted by independent administrative law judges. Section 554(d) insulates them from unauthorized contacts. Some of the APA wording is ambiguous. Thus, the prohibition is against consultation of "a person or party." Does this language preclude contacts with agency personnel where the agency was not a party? The bar also extends only to consultation "on a fact in issue." Would this exclude consultation on issues of law and policy? What do you think of FERC's attempt (*infra*) to address these issues directly?

Despite the APA provisions problems may arise because both prosecutors and hearing officers work in the same agency. See, e.g., Brown v. United States, 377 F. Supp. 530 (N.D. Tex. 1974), where the hearing examiner flew from Washington to Dallas (where the hearing was held) with the attorney who prosecuted the case; they discussed the case on the way down, stayed at the same hotel and again discussed the case on the way back to the airport. For a similar state case, see Wells v. De Norte School Dist., 753 P.2d 770 (Colo. Ct. App. 1987) (hearing officer had lunch at table with agency counsel and witness).

5. Section 554(d) also cuts off those engaged in investigating or prosecuting from the decision process. For an illustrative case, see Columbia Research Corp. v. Schaffer, 256 F.2d 677 (2d Cir. 1958), a fraud order case where the decision was made by the agency's general counsel and the prosecution conducted by the assistant general counsel. Held, the APA was violated where the subordinate was prosecutor and his superior was judge, as much as it would be in the reverse situation where the adjudicator was subordinate to the prosecutor.

6. Note the exceptions contained in §554(d). The most important of them is the exception of the agency heads themselves. Under it an agency head may not be disqualified merely because he supervised the investigation or prosecution of the case. The FTC's practice of reviewing the recommendations of its investigative employees and then making the decision to initiate a complaint falls within the exception. FTC v. Cinderella Career and Finishing Schools, 404 F.2d 1308 (D.C. Cir. 1968). Compare United States v. Litton Industries, 462 F.2d 14 (9th Cir. 1972) (agency heads may conduct simultaneous investigative and adjudicatory proceedings against same corporation).

According to former Justice William J. Brennan, the APA provision on the combination of functions,

> embodies the theory of internal separation, leaving the functions with the agency but providing safeguards to assure the insulation from one another and to further the independence of personnel engaged in judging. . . . The federal statute has not, however, escaped criticism; it has been said that it deals only partially with the problem of separation. "Ultimate decision still rests with the agency, which also exercises general supervision over investigation and prosecution." Schwartz, supra, p. 104.

In re Larsen, 86 A.2d 430, 436 (N.J. Super. 1952) (concurring).

7. Note that the APA separation of functions provision is part of the section dealing with adjudications. This means that it does not apply at all to rulemaking. See United Steelworkers v. Marshall, 647 F.2d 1189 (D.C. Cir. 1980).

In 2002, the Federal Energy Regulatory Commission (FERC) announced a comprehensive policy with respect to separation of functions and ex parte contacts to help bring clarity to application of APA requirements to the agency's complex operations. The new guidelines have proved controversial, however, as the U.S. Court of Appeals for the D.C. Circuit struck down a provision involving communications between "market monitors" and agency staff as a violation of the APA. See Electric Power Supply Ass'n v. FERC, 391 F.3d 1255 (D.C. Cir. 2004).

H EVIDENCE

COMMENTS

By their own terms, the Federal Rules of Evidence apply only in courts and, even then, only in some proceedings. FRE Rule 1101. In the absence of a mandate to follow the technical mandates set out in the federal evidence rules, agency proceedings generally apply a more flexible, less strict, determination of evidentiary admissibility.

> **Federal Administrative Procedure Act**
>
> 5 U.S.C. §556(d)
>
> Any oral or documentary evidence may be received; but the agency as a matter of policy shall provide for the exclusion of irrelevant, immaterial, or unduly repetitious evidence. A sanction may not be imposed or rule or order issued except on consideration of the whole record or those parts thereof cited by a party and supported by and in accordance with the reliable, probative, and substantial evidence.... A party is entitled to present his case or defense by oral or documentary evidence, to submit rebuttal evidence, and to conduct such cross-examination as may be required for a full and true disclosure of the facts.

1. See the remarks of Field, J., sitting as circuit justice, in In re Pacific Railway Comm'n, 32 F. 241 (N.D. Cal. 1887), a case involving respondent railway commissioners:

> The conclusion we have thus reached disposes of the petition of the railway commissioners, and renders it unnecessary . . . to make any comment upon the extraordinary position taken by them according to the statement of the respondent, to which we have referred, that they did not regard themselves bound in their examination by the ordinary rules of evidence, but would receive hearsay . . . surmises, and information of every character that might be called to their attention.

See also Oceanic Fisheries v. Alaska Industrial Bd., 109 F. Supp. 103 (D. Alaska 1953):

> The notion that hearsay should be admitted and given its natural probative effect is no longer novel. It is one of the principal distinguishing features of administrative procedure. The desire to escape from the rigidity of common law rules of evidence, often highly technical, with the expense, inconvenience and delay entailed in adhering thereto and the inability of the courts to expeditiously dispose of controversies arising under regulatory statutes, led to the creation of a multitude of administrative tribunals which are rapidly preempting a field once considered to be the exclusive domain of the courts. Whatever may be their shortcomings, it does not appear that the liberalization of the rules of evidence is one of them.

Which states the better view, the statement of Justice Field or that of the district judge in *Oceanic Fisheries*?

Compare Opp. Cotton Mills v. Administrator, 312 U.S. 126, 155 (1941): "[I]t has long been settled that the technical rules for the exclusion of evidence applicable in jury trials do not apply to proceedings before federal administrative agencies in the absence of a statutory requirement that such rules are to be observed."

What does the rule that agencies are not bound by the rules of evidence mean in practice? Simply this: that "relevant evidence not admissible in court, including hearsay, is admissible at an administrative hearing." Tyra v. Secretary of HHS, 896 F.2d 1024, 1030 (6th Cir. 1990). See also Peabody Coal Co. v. McCandless, 255 F.3d 465 (7th Cir. 2001) (holding that agencies need not follow rules of evidence relating to expert testimony set out by the U.S. Supreme Court in *Daubert* and *Kumho Tire*).

See Willapoint Oysters v. Ewing, 174 F.2d 676 (9th Cir.), cert. denied, 338 U.S. 860 (1949):

> The common law exclusionary rules of evidence are not based in Constitutional interdictions and are not applicable to administrative proceedings, even of judicial character, in the absence of statutory requirement. Neither [the instant enabling statute] nor . . . the Administrative Procedure Act . . . so require, either expressly or by implication from the language used. To the contrary, the latter Act enjoins that: ". . . Any oral or documentary evidence may be received. . . ." Thus the receipt of such evidence, over objection . . . is not such a grievous error as to require reversal.

"Administrative proceedings are governed by the APA, not the Federal Rules of Evidence. . . . If hearsay evidence satisfies the APA standard, agencies may consider it." Anderson v. United States, 799 F. Supp. 1198 (Ct. Int'l Trade 1992).

2. See 29 U.S.C. §160(b):

> Any such [NLRB unfair labor practice] proceeding shall, so far as practicable, be conducted in accordance with the rules of evidence applicable in the district courts of the United States under the rules of civil procedure for the district courts of the United States.

What is the effect of this Taft-Hartley Act provision? See Walter N. Yoder & Sons v. NLRB, 754 F.2d 531 (4th Cir. 1985). According to Justice Scalia, dissenting, in NLRB v. Curtin Matheson Scientific, 494 U.S. 775 (1990), it makes NLRB procedure "even somewhat more judicialized than ordinary formal adjudication." How does the Taft-Hartley provision compare with Revised Model State APA §10? The pertinent parts of that section read as follows:

> The rules of evidence as applied in [nonjury] civil cases in the [District Courts of this State] shall be followed.

3. Some agencies direct that the federal rules of evidence be followed in proceedings.

Should other agencies be required to follow the rules of evidence? See Woolsey v. NSTB, 993 F.2d 516 (5th Cir. 1993): "In 1986, the Administrative Conference of the United States adopted recommendations which stated that it would be improper to *require* agencies to apply the Federal Rules of Evidence."

WAGSTAFF v. DEPARTMENT OF EMPLOYMENT SECURITY

826 P.2d 1069 (Utah Ct. App. 1992)

ORME, Judge.

Petitioner, a former Air Force employee charged for drug use, challenges a decision of the Board of Review of the Industrial Commission denying him unemployment compensation benefits....

FACTS

Petitioner, Dennis L. Wagstaff, began working at Hill Air Force Base (HAFB) as a store checker in 1978. After receiving several promotions and a "secret" security clearance, Wagstaff became a jet aircraft hydraulic mechanic....

In July 1989, the Air Force Office of Special Investigations (OSI) received information that civilian maintenance personnel at HAFB were using illegal drugs both on and off the base. OSI immediately initiated an investigation into the alleged drug use....

Although the OSI investigation did not turn up any tangible evidence concerning Wagstaff, according to an OSI report several of Wagstaff's coworkers implicated him in the illegal use of drugs. Consequently, in October 1989, OSI called Wagstaff in for questioning. Under OSI examination, Wagstaff admitted using drugs on one occasion while employed at the base. According to Wagstaff, in June or July, 1989, during a lunch break, he went with several of his co-workers to a park in Clearfield where someone produced a small bag of cocaine, which they all snorted. Wagstaff maintained, however, that aside from that one incident, and trying marijuana in high school some twenty years earlier, he had never used drugs....

Based on Wagstaff's admission concerning the incident in the park, and apparently on implications of other illegal drug use contained in the OSI report, the Air Force terminated Wagstaff's employment in January 1990. After his removal, Wagstaff applied for unemployment benefits through the Department of Employment Security. Because the Department found the Air Force terminated Wagstaff for just cause, it denied his claim for benefits. Wagstaff challenged the initial decision and requested a formal hearing.

At the formal hearing before an administrative law judge, Wagstaff admitted participating in the lunchtime cocaine incident at the park, but denied any other illegal drug use, and claimed that the park incident was a one-time indiscretion. To support its argument that Wagstaff's use of cocaine at the park was not a one-time affair, the Air Force introduced the OSI report through the testimony of one of several OSI investigators who participated in the report's preparation. The Air Force failed, however, to produce at the hearing the two co-workers who had implicated Wagstaff in other incidents of alleged drug use.

Because the administrative law judge found that the Air Force did not adequately establish the culpability element of a "just cause" discharge, he reversed the Department's initial decision. . . .

The Industrial Commission's board of Review, by a 2-1 vote, reversed the administrative law judge. Wagstaff now appeals that decision, claiming that (1) the Board erroneously considered inadmissible hearing evidence when reaching its decision. . . .

At Wagstaff's evidentiary hearing before the Department's administrative law judge, the Air Force introduced the OSI report, which included statements by several of Wagstaff's former co-workers implicating him in other illegal drug use. The Board acknowledged in its opinion, with our emphasis, that "[b]ecause the Air Force did not call as witnesses the former fellow workers of the claimant who had identified him as using drugs on and off base, much of the OSI report is *hearsay evidence* as it relates to Mr. Wagstaff's claim for unemployment benefits." However, because hearsay evidence is admissible in administrative proceedings . . . admission of the OSI report during Wagstaff's hearing was not improper. Although there was nothing wrong with *admission* of this hearsay evidence, "findings of fact cannot be based *exclusively* on hearsay evidence. They must be supported by a residuum of legal evidence competent in a court of law."[1] . . .

In this case, part of the OSI report admitted at the hearing dealt with Wagstaff's lunchtime drug incident with his co-workers at the park. The report contained Wagstaff's own admission, which is not hearsay, see Utah R. Evid. 801(d)(2), as well as his co-workers' statements concerning the incident. Given Wagstaff's admissions, in the report and at the administrative hearing, there was ample

1. Although the residuum rule imposes inconsistent standards on administrative agencies in admitting evidence and making findings, and therefore its use is in decline in many states, "this Court has reaffirmed Utah's position that the residuum rule applies to administrative proceedings." Mayes v. Department of Employment Sec., 754 P.2d 989, 992 (Utah Ct. App. 1988); Williams v. Schwendiman, 740 P.2d 1354, 1356 (Utah Ct. App. 1987).

non-hearsay evidence to support the finding that Wagstaff had used cocaine during his lunch break on one occasion in June or July of 1989.

However, at the same time that he admitted the single instance of cocaine use, Wagstaff denied any other illegal drug use while he was employed at HAFB. Aside from the OSI report, no other evidence was presented at the hearing to refute Wagstaff's exculpatory testimony or implicate him in illegal drug use except on that one occasion. Thus, the only evidentiary support for any other illegal drug use by Wagstaff was the hearsay statements of his co-workers contained in the OSI report. Consequently, a finding, or even an inference, that Wagstaff was involved in more than one instance of illegal drug use would be unsupported by a residuum of competent legal evidence. Accordingly, any consideration of the OSI report by the Board was improper, and we approach our review from the perspective that the "just cause" nature of Wagstaff's termination must be evaluated solely with reference to the single admitted instance of drug use....

NOTES

1. The so-called legal residuum rule originated in Carroll v. Knickerbocker Ice Co., 113 N.E. 507, 509 (N.Y. 1916), where the court reversed an agency decision based wholly on hearsay: "[W]hile the Commission's inquiry is not limited by the common law or statutory rules of evidence or by technical or formal rules of procedure, and it may, in its discretion, accept any evidence that is offered, still in the end there must be a residuum of legal evidence to support the claim before an award can be made."

How much is a residuum? Not very much, according to a later New York decision. The required residuum need not be enough to establish the facts found independently of the hearsay or other incompetent evidence. It is sufficient if it lends any support by way of corroboration, even through wholly circumstantial evidence. Altschuller v. Bressler, 46 N.E.2d 886 (N.Y. 1943).

See 2 Larson, The Law of Workmen's Compensation §79.30 (1975), criticizing the legal residuum rule:

> One cannot help wondering, however, whether the legislatures really meant to produce a hybrid situation in which commissions could freely hear all the incompetent evidence they pleased, but could make no legal use of it — especially since the avowed object of the provision, that of escaping the bickerings which had so long discredited the rules of evidence in common-law trials, would thereby be thwarted; for the same old quarrels would be staged, the only difference being that they would be fought in the name of probative-value-to-support-awards rather than in the name of admissibility.

Is this a fair criticism of the residuum rule?

2. Despite criticism, the legal residuum rule is followed in many states that have cases on the matter. See Kenneth F. Warren, Administrative Law in the

Political System 193 (6th ed. 2020); Elliot B. Glicksman, The Modern Hearsay Rule Should Find Administrative Law Application, 1999 Nebraska L. Rev. 135-146.

RICHARDSON v. PERALES

402 U.S. 389 (1971)

MR. JUSTICE BLACKMUN delivered the opinion of the Court.

In 1966 Pedro Perales, a San Antonio truck driver, then age 34, height 5′11″, weight about 220 pounds, filed a claim for disability insurance benefits under the Social Security Act. . . .

The issue here is whether physicians' written reports of medical examinations they have made of a disability claimant may constitute "substantial evidence" supportive of a finding of nondisability . . . when the claimant objects to the admissibility of those reports and when the only live testimony is presented by his side and is contrary to the reports.

I

In his claim Perales asserted that on September 29, 1965, he became disabled as a result of an injury to his back sustained in lifting an object at work. . . .

In April 1966 Perales consulted Dr. Max Morales, Jr., a general practitioner of San Antonio. Dr. Morales hospitalized the patient from April 15 to May 2. His final discharge diagnosis was "Back sprain, lumbo-sacral spine."

Perales then filed his claim. As required by §221 of the Act, 42 U.S.C. §421, the claim was referred to the state agency for determination. The agency obtained the hospital records and a report from Dr. Morales. The report set forth no physical findings or laboratory studies, but the doctor again gave as his diagnosis "Back sprain — lumbo-sacral spine," this time "moderately severe," with "Ruptured disk not ruled out." The agency arranged for a medical examination, at no cost to the patient, by Dr. John H. Langston, an orthopedic surgeon. This was done May 25.

Dr. Langston's ensuing report to the Division of Disability Determination was devastating from the claimant's standpoint. . . .

The state agency denied the claim. Perales requested reconsideration. . . .

The state agency then arranged for an examination by Dr. James M. Bailey, a board-certified psychiatrist with a subspecialty in neurology. Dr. Bailey's report to the agency on August 30, 1966, concluded with the following diagnosis:

> Paranoid personality, manifested by hostility, feelings of persecution and long history of strained inter-personal relationships.
>
> I do not feel that this patient has a separate psychiatric illness at this time. It appears that his personality is conducive to anger, frustrations, etc.

The agency again reviewed the file. The Bureau of Disability Insurance of the Social Security Administration made its independent review. The report and opinion of Dr. Morales, as the claimant's attending physician, was considered, as were those of the other examining physicians. The claim was again denied.

Perales requested a hearing before a hearing examiner. The agency then referred the claimant to Dr. Langston and to Dr. Richard H. Mattson for electromyography studies. Dr. Mattson's notes referred to "some chronic or past disturbance of function in the nerve supply" to the left and right anterior tibialis muscles and right extensor digitorium brevis muscles that was "strongly suggestive of lack of maximal effort" and was "the kind of finding that is typically associated with a functional or psychogenic component to weakness." There was no evidence of "any active process effecting [sic] the nerves at present." Dr. Langston advised the agency that Dr. Mattson's finding of "very poor effort" verified what Dr. Langston had found on the earlier physical examination.

The requested hearing was set for January 12, 1967, in San Antonio. Written notice thereof was given the claimant with a copy to his attorney. The notice contained a definition of disability, advised the claimant that he should bring all medical and other evidence not already presented, afforded him an opportunity to examine all documentary evidence on file prior to the hearing, and told him that he might bring his own physician or other witnesses and be represented at the hearing by a lawyer.

The hearing took place at the time designated. A supplemental hearing was held March 31. The claimant appeared at the first hearing with his attorney and with Dr. Morales. The attorney formally objected to the introduction of the several reports of Drs. Langston, Bailey, Mattson, and Lambert, and of the hospital records. Various grounds of objection were asserted, including hearsay, absence of an opportunity for cross-examination, absence of proof the physicians were licensed to practice in Texas, failure to demonstrate that the hospital records were proved under the Business Records Act, and the conclusory nature of the reports. These objections were overruled and the reports and hospital records were introduced. The reports of Dr. Morales and of Dr. Munslow were then submitted by the claimant's counsel and admitted.

At the two hearings oral testimony was submitted by claimant Perales, by Dr. Morales, by a former fellow employee of the claimant, by a vocational expert, and by Dr. Lewis A. Leavitt, a physician board-certified in physical medicine and rehabilitation, and chief of, and professor in, the Department of Physical Medicine at Baylor University College of Medicine. Dr. Leavitt was called by the hearing examiner as an independent "medical adviser," that is, as an expert who does not examine the claimant but who hears and reviews the medical evidence and who may offer an opinion. The adviser is paid a fee by the government. The claimant, through his counsel, objected to any testimony by Dr. Leavitt not based upon examination or upon a hypothetical. Dr. Leavitt testified over this objection and was cross-examined by the claimant's attorney. He stated that the consensus of the various medical reports was that Perales had a mild low-back syndrome of musculo-ligamentous origin.

The hearing examiner, in reliance upon the several medical reports and the testimony of Dr. Leavitt, observed in his written decision, "There is objective medical evidence of impairment which the heavy preponderance of the evidence indicates to be of mild severity. . . . Taken altogether, the Hearing Examiner is of the conclusion that the claimant has not met the burden of proof." . . . The hearing examiner's decision, then, was that the claimant was not entitled to a period of disability or to disability insurance benefits. . . .

The claimant then made a request for review by the Appeals Council. . . . The Appeals Council ruled that the decision of the hearing examiner was correct.

Upon this adverse ruling the claimant instituted the present action for review. . . . On appeal the Fifth Circuit held that the hearsay evidence in the case was admissible under the act; that, specifically, the written reports of the physicians were admissible in the administrative hearing; that Dr. Leavitt's testimony also was admissible; but that all this evidence together did not constitute substantial evidence when it was objected to and when it was contradicted by evidence from the only live witnesses. Cohen v. Perales, 412 F.2d 44 (5th Cir. 1969).

On rehearing, the Court of Appeals observed that it did not mean by its opinion that uncorroborated hearsay could never be substantial evidence supportive of a hearing examiner's decision adverse to a claimant. It emphasized that its ruling that uncorroborated hearsay could not constitute substantial evidence was applicable only when the claimant had objected and when the hearsay was directly contradicted by the testimony of live medical witnesses and by the claimant in person. Cohen v. Perales, 416 F.2d 1250 (5th Cir. 1969). Certiorari was granted in order to review and resolve this important procedural due process issue. 397 U.S. 1035 (1970).

II

We therefore are presented with the not uncommon situation of conflicting medical evidence. . . .

The issue revolves, however, around a system which produces a mass of medical evidence in report form. May material of that kind ever be "substantial evidence" when it stands alone and is opposed by live medical evidence and the client's own contrary personal testimony? The courts below have held that it may not.

III

The Social Security Act has been with us since 1935. Act of August 14, 1935, 49 Stat. 620. It affects nearly all of us. The system's administrative structure and procedures, with essential determinations numbering into the millions, are of a size and extent difficult to comprehend. But, as the Government's brief here accurately pronounces, "Such a system must be fair — and it must work." Congress has provided that the Secretary:

> . . . shall have full power and authority to make rules and regulations and to establish procedures . . . necessary or appropriate to carry out such provisions, and shall adopt reasonable and proper rules and regulations to regulate and provide for the

> nature and extent of the proofs and evidence and the method of taking and furnishing the same in order to establish the right to benefits hereunder.

§205(a); 42 U.S.C. §405(a). Section 205(b) directs the Secretary to make findings and decisions; on request to give reasonable notice and opportunity for a hearing; and in the course of any hearing to receive evidence. It then provides:

> Evidence may be received at any hearing before the Secretary even though inadmissible under rules of evidence applicable to court procedure.

In carrying out these statutory duties the Secretary has adopted regulations that state, among other things:

> The hearing examiner shall inquire fully into the matters at issue and shall receive in evidence the testimony of witnesses and any documents which are relevant and material to such matters.... The ... procedure at the hearing generally ... shall be in the discretion of the hearing examiner and of such nature as to afford the parties a reasonable opportunity for a fair hearing.

20 C.F.R. §404.927.

From this it is apparent that (a) the Congress granted the Secretary the power by regulation to establish hearing procedures; (b) strict rules of evidence, applicable in the courtroom, are not to operate at social security hearings so as to bar the admission of evidence otherwise pertinent; and (c) the conduct of the hearing rests generally in the examiner's discretion. There emerges an emphasis upon the informal rather than the formal. This, we think, is as it should be, for this administrative procedure, and these hearings, should be understandable to the layman claimant, should not necessarily be stiff and comfortable only for the trained attorney, and should be liberal and not strict in tone and operation. This is the obvious intent of Congress so long as the procedures are fundamentally fair.

IV

With this background and this atmosphere in mind, we turn to the statutory standard of "substantial evidence" prescribed by §205(g). The Court had considered this very concept in other, yet similar, contexts. The National Labor Relations Act, §10(e), in its original form, provided that the NLRB's findings of fact "if supported by evidence, shall be conclusive." 49 Stat. 449, 454. The Court said this meant "supported by substantial evidence" and that this was "more than a mere scintilla. It means such relevant evidence as a reasonable mind might accept as adequate to support a conclusion." Consolidated Edison Co. v. NLRB, 305 U.S. 197, 229 (1938). The Court has adhered to that definition in varying statutory situations....

V

The question, then, is as to what procedural due process requires with respect to examining physicians' reports in a social security disability claim hearing. We conclude that a written report by a licensed physician who has examined the claimant and who sets forth in his report his medical findings in his area of competence may be received as evidence in a disability hearing and, despite its hearsay character and an absence of cross-examination, and despite the presence of opposing direct medical testimony and testimony by the claimant himself, may constitute substantial evidence supportive of a finding by the hearing examiner adverse to the claimant, when the claimant has not exercised his right to subpoena the reporting physician and thereby provide himself with the opportunity for cross-examination of the physician.

We are prompted to this conclusion by a number of factors that, we feel, assure underlying reliability and probative value:

1. The identity of the five reporting physicians is significant. Each report presented here was prepared by a practicing physician who had examined the claimant. A majority (Drs. Langston, Bailey, and Mattson) were called into the case by the state agency. Although each received a fee, that fee is recompense for his time and professional assignment. We cannot, and do not, ascribe bias to the work of these independent physicians, or any interest on their part in the outcome of the administrative proceeding beyond the professional curiosity a dedicated medical man possesses.

2. The vast workings of the social security administrative system make for reliability and impartiality in the consultant reports. We bear in mind that the agency operates essentially, and is intended so to do, as an adjudicator and not as an advocate or adversary. This is the congressional plan. We do not presume on this record to say that it works unfairly.[1]

3. One familiar with medical reports and the routine of the medical examination, general or specific, will recognize their elements of detail and of value. The particular reports of the physicians who examined claimant Perales were based on personal consultation and personal examination and rested on accepted medical procedures and tests. . . .

These are routine, standard, and unbiased medical reports by physician specialists concerning a subject whom they had seen. That the reports were adverse to Perales' claim is not in itself bias or an indication of nonprobative character.

4. The reports present the impressive range of examination to which Perales was subjected. A specialist in neurosurgery, one in neurology, one in psychiatry, one in orthopedics, and one in physical medicine and rehabilitation add up to definitive opinion in five medical specialties, all somewhat related, but different in their emphases. It is fair to say that the claimant received professional examination and opinion on a scale beyond the reach of most persons and that this case reveals a patient and careful endeavor by the state agency and the examiner to ascertain the truth.

---

1. We are advised by the Government's brief, page 18, notes 7 and 8, that in fiscal year 1968, 515,938 disability claims were processed; that, of these, 343,628 (66.601%) were allowed prior to the hearing stage; that approximately one-third of the claims that went to hearing were allowed; and that 320,164 consultant examinations were obtained.

5. So far as we can detect, there is no inconsistency whatsoever in the reports of the five specialists. Yet each result was reached by independent examination in the writer's field of specialized training.

6. Although the claimant complains of the lack of opportunity to cross-examine the reporting physicians, he did not take advantage of the opportunity afforded him under 20 C.F.R. §404.926 to request subpoenas for the physicians. The five-day period specified by the regulation for the issuance of the subpoenas surely afforded no real obstacle to this, for he was notified that the documentary evidence on file was available for examination before the hearing and, further, a supplemental hearing could be requested. In fact, in this very case there was a supplemental hearing more than two and a half months after the initial hearing. This inaction on the claimant's part supports the Court of Appeals' view, 412 F.2d, at 50-51, that the claimant as a consequence is to be precluded from now complaining that he was denied the rights of confrontation and cross-examination.

7. Courts have recognized the reliability and probative worth of written medical reports even in formal trials and, while acknowledging their hearsay character, have admitted them as an exception to the hearsay rule. . . .

8. Past treatment by reviewing courts of written medical reports in social security disability cases is revealing. . . . The courts have reviewed administrative determinations, and upheld many adverse ones, where the only supporting evidence has been reports of this kind, buttressed sometimes, but often not, by testimony of a medical adviser such as Dr. Leavitt. . . .

9. There is an additional and pragmatic factor which, although not controlling, deserves mention. This is what Chief Judge Brown has described as "the sheer magnitude of that administrative burden," and the resulting necessity for written reports without "elaboration through the traditional facility of oral testimony." Page v. Cellebrezze, 311 F.2d 757, 760 (5th Cir. 1963). With over 20,000 disability claim hearings annually, the cost of providing live medical testimony at those hearings, where need has not been demonstrated by a request for a subpoena, over and above the cost of the examinations requested by hearing examiners, would be a substantial drain on the trust fund and on the energy of physicians already in short supply.

VI

Perales relies heavily on the Court's holding and statements in Goldberg v. Kelly [*supra* p. 419], particularly the comment that due process requires notice "and an effective opportunity to defend by confronting any adverse witness. . . ." *Kelly*, however, had to do with termination of AFDC benefits without prior notice. It also concerned a situation, the Court said, "where credibility and veracity are at issue, as they must be in many termination proceedings."

The Perales proceeding is not the same. We are not concerned with termination of disability benefits once granted. Neither are we concerned with a change of status without notice. Notice was given to claimant Perales. The physicians' reports were on file and available for inspection by the claimant and his counsel.

And the authors of those reports were known and were subject to subpoena and to the very cross-examination which the claimant asserts he had not enjoyed. Further, the spectre of questionable credibility and veracity is not present; there is professional disagreement with the medical conclusions, to be sure, but there is no attack here upon the doctors' credibility or veracity. *Kelly* affords little comfort to the claimant.

Perales also . . . would describe the medical reports in question as "mere uncorroborated hearsay" and would relate this to Mr. Chief Justice Hughes' sentence in Consolidated Edison Co. v. NLRB, 305 U.S. 197, 230: "Mere uncorroborated hearsay or rumor does not constitute substantial evidence."

Although the reports are hearsay in the technical sense, because their content is not produced live before the hearing examiner, we feel that the claimant and the Court of Appeals read too much into the single sentence from *Consolidated Edison.* The contrast the Chief Justice was drawing, at the very page cited, was not with material that would be deemed formally inadmissible in judicial proceedings but with material "without a basis in evidence having rational probative force." This was not a blanket rejection by the Court of administrative reliance on hearsay irrespective of reliability and probative value. The opposite was the case.

The claimant, the District Court and the Court of Appeals also criticize the use of Dr. Leavitt as a medical adviser. . . . Inasmuch as medical advisers are used in approximately 13% of disability claim hearings, comment as to this practice is indicated. We see nothing "reprehensible" in the practice, as the claimant would describe it. The trial examiner is a layman; the medical adviser is a board-certified specialist. He is used primarily in complex cases for explanation of medical problems in terms understandable to the layman-examiner. He is a neutral adviser. . . . We see nothing unconstitutional or improper in the medical adviser concept and in the presence of Dr. Leavitt in this administrative hearing.

Finally, the claimant complains of the system of processing disability claims. He suggests, and is joined in this by the briefs of amici, that the Administrative Procedure Act, rather than the Social Security Act, governs the processing of claims and specifically provides for cross-examination, 5 U.S.C. §556(d). . . .

We need not decide whether the APA has general application to social security disability claims, for the social security administrative procedure does not vary from that prescribed by the APA. Indeed, the latter is modeled upon the Social Security Act. . . . The cited §556(d) provides that any documentary evidence "may be received" subject to the exclusion of the irrelevant, the immaterial, and the unduly repetitious. It further provides that a

> party is entitled to present his case or defense by oral or documentary evidence . . . and to conduct such cross-examination as may be required for a full and true disclosure of the facts [and in] determining claims for money or benefits an agency may, where a party will not be prejudiced thereby, adopt procedures for the submission of all or part of the evidence in written form.

These provisions conform, and are consistent with, rather than differ from or supersede, the authority given the Secretary by the Social Security Act's §205(a) and (b) "to establish procedures," and

> to regulate and provide for the nature and extent of the proofs and evidence and the method of taking and furnishing the same in order to establish the right to benefits, [and to receive evidence] even though inadmissible under rules of evidence applicable to court procedure.

Hearsay, under either Act, is thus admissible up to the point of relevancy.

The matter comes down to the question of the procedure's integrity and fundamental fairness. We see nothing that works in derogation of that integrity and of that fairness in the admission of consultants' reports, subject as they are to being material and to the use of the subpoena and consequent cross-examination. This precisely fits the statutorily prescribed "cross-examination as may be required for a full and true disclosure of the facts." That is the standard. It is clear and workable and does not fall short of procedural due process. . . .

We therefore reverse and remand for further proceedings. We intimate no view as to the merits. It is for the district court now to determine whether the Secretary's findings, in the light of all material proffered and admissible, are supported by "substantial evidence" within the command of §205(g).

It is so ordered.

[JUSTICE DOUGLAS dissented, in an opinion concurred in by JUSTICES BLACK and BRENNAN.]

NOTES

1. Is the *Perales* decision, as has been claimed by some commentators, a flat rejection of the legal residuum rule? Compare the earlier statement in Consolidated Edison Co. v. NLRB, 305 U.S. 197, 230 (1938), where the Court, after recognizing that an agency might admit incompetent evidence, interposed the famous caveat, "this assurance of a desirable flexibility in administrative procedure does not go so far as to justify orders without a basis in evidence having rational probative force. Mere uncorroborated hearsay or rumor does not constitute substantial evidence." See also Jacobowitz v. United States, 424 F.2d 555, 561 (Ct. Cl. 1970): "Even though uncorroborated hearsay may have some probative value, it may lack sufficient probative force, standing alone, to constitute substantial evidence that will support a decision of an administrative agency." But compare Schaefer v. United States, 633 F.2d 945, 952 (Ct. Cl. 1980): "[H]earsay evidence can therefore be 'substantial evidence' if it has sufficient probative force such that a reasonable man might accept it as adequate to support the conclusion reached by the agency." Consistent with *Perales*, federal courts have largely rejected the residuum rule. See Kenneth F. Warren, Administrative Law in the Political System 193 (6th ed. 2020).

2. The lower court in *Perales* had relied on the residuum rule as stated in the *Consolidated Edison* case. Is the *Perales* opinion's distinction of *Consolidated Edison* convincing?

3. Is the *Perales* decision consistent with the APA requirement that agency orders must be "supported by and in accordance with the reliable, probative, and substantial evidence"? How can supporting evidence be "reliable" and "probative" if it is wholly incompetent? See Echostar Communications Corp. v. FCC, 292 F.3d 749, 753 (D.C. Cir. 2002) (hearsay evidence may be reliable and trustworthy if both given under oath and undisputed).

Compare the *Perales* Court's treatment of the "three-hat" hearing officer. Both that aspect of *Perales* and the holding on evidence are strongly influenced by the need to make the Social Security Administration (SSA) system of mass justice workable. (Note that, by 1992, the number of SSA disability hearings had increased, from the 20,000 mentioned by the Court, to over 250,000 annually.) The Court stressed the magnitude of the administrative burden and the resulting necessity for written reports. The cost of providing live medical testimony would be too great a drain on the funds available to the SSA. Where the same problem does not exist, might reliance on uncorroborated hearsay alone lead to a different judicial reception? Compare School Bd. v. Department of Health, Education, and Welfare, 525 F.2d 900, 906 (5th Cir. 1976), by the same lower court as in the *Perales* case:

> Based on the Supreme Court's approach in *Perales*, we must reject any per se rule that hearsay cannot constitute substantial evidence. Rather, we must look to those factors which "assure underlying reliability and probative value," 402 U.S. at 402, to determine whether the hearsay in the present case constitutes substantial evidence.
>
> After considering the administrative record in depth, we agree with the School Board that certain portions of the record consist of nothing more than rumor and opinion on the part of unidentified out-of-court declarants. Such evidence is to be given little weight, and would not constitute substantial evidence in the present record.... However, other hearsay evidence in the record carries special indicia of probativeness and trustworthiness, and, when considered in light of facts unique to this case, leads to a conclusion that substantial evidence supports the hearing examiner's findings.

4. Note the *Perales* opinion's emphasis on the claimant's right to subpoena the examining physicians as witnesses. Is the *Perales* decision applicable in situations where the right to subpoena and cross examine have been denied? See Demenech v. Department of Health and Human Services, 913 F.2d 882 (11th Cir. 1990) (no); Lopez v. Chater, Commissioner of Social Security, 8 F. Supp. 152 (D.P.R. 1998) (yes). Should the failure to subpoena the declarant of hearsay amount to a waiver of the right later to object to the sufficiency of the evidence?

See Note, 85 Harv. L. Rev. 326, 332-33 (1971), which asserts that the *Perales* "Court relied upon the claimant's theoretical right to subpoena witnesses without asking whether that right was effectively available to most claimants. In fact, it may not be; most claimants are not represented by counsel and neither the notice of hearing nor the booklet given to applicants for benefits informs them of the right."

5. What about where an agency determines a constitutional right? Should an administrative agency apply formal rules of evidence, or at least apply the residuum rule, if a constitutional issue is implicated? See Waters v. Churchill, 511 U.S. 661 (1994) (formal rules of evidence not required, but evidence must be reliable).

I BURDEN OF PROOF

DIRECTOR, OFFICE OF WORKERS' COMPENSATION PROGRAMS v. GREENWICH COLLIERIES

512 U.S. 267 (1994)

JUSTICE O'CONNOR delivered the opinion of the Court.

In adjudicating benefits claims under the Black Lung Benefits Act (BLBA), 83 Stat. 792, as amended, 30 U.S.C. §901 et seq. (1998 ed. and Supp. IV), and the Longshore and Harbor Workers' Compensation Act (LHWCA), 44 Stat. 1424, as amended, 33 U.S.C. §901 et seq., the Department of Labor applies what it calls the "true doubt" rule. This rule essentially shifts the burden of persuasion to the party opposing the benefits claim — when the evidence is evenly balanced, the benefits claimant wins. This litigation presents the question whether the rule is consistent with §7(c) of the Administrative Procedure Act (APA), which states that "except as otherwise provided by statute, the proponent of a rule or order has the burden of proof." 5 U.S.C. §556(d).

I

We review two separate decisions of the Court of Appeals for the Third Circuit. In one, Andrew Ondecko applied for disability benefits under the BLBA after working as a coal miner for 31 years. The Administrative Law Judge (ALJ) determined that Ondecko had pneumoconiosis (or black lung disease), that he was totally disabled by the disease, and that the disease resulted from coal mine employment. In resolving the first two issues, the ALJ relied on the true doubt rule. In resolving the third, she relied on the rebuttable presumption that a miner with pneumoconiosis who worked in the mines for at least 10 years developed the disease because of his employment. The Department's Benefits Review Board affirmed, concluding that the ALJ had considered all the evidence, had found each side's evidence to be equally probative, and had properly resolved the dispute in Ondecko's favor under the true doubt rule. The Court of Appeals vacated the Board's decision, holding that the true doubt rule is inconsistent with the Department's own regulations under the BLBA, §718.403, as well as with Mullins

Coal Co. of Va. v. Director, Office of Workers' Compensation Programs, 484 U.S. 135 (1987).

In the other case, Michael Santoro suffered a work-related back and neck injury while employed by respondent Maher Terminals. Within a few months Santoro was diagnosed with nerve cancer, and he died shortly thereafter. His widow filed a claim under the LHWCA alleging that the work injury had rendered her husband disabled and caused his death. After reviewing the evidence for both sides, the ALJ found it equally probative and, relying on the true doubt rule, awarded benefits to the claimant. The Board affirmed, finding no error in the ALJ's analysis or his application of the true doubt rule. The Court of Appeals reversed, holding that the true doubt rule is inconsistent with §7(c) of the APA. 992 F.2d 1277 (1993). In so holding, the court expressly disagreed with Freeman United Coal Mining Co. v. Office of Workers' Compensation Program, 988 F.2d 706 (CA7 1993). We granted certiorari to resolve the conflict. 510 U.S. 1068 (1994).

II

As a threshold matter, we must decide whether §7(c)'s burden of proof provision applies to adjudications under the LHWCA and the BLBA. Section 7(c) of the APA applies "except as otherwise provided by statute," and the Department argues that the statutes at issue here make clear that §7(c) does not apply. We disagree.

The Department points out that in conducting investigations or hearings pursuant to the LHWCA, the "Board shall not be bound by common law or statutory rules of evidence or by technical or formal rules of procedure, except as provided by this chapter." 33 U.S.C. §923(a). But the assignment of the burden of proof is a rule of substantive law, so it is unclear whether this exception even applies. More importantly, §923 by its terms applies "except as provided by this chapter," and the chapter provides that §7(c) does indeed apply to the LHWCA. We do not lightly presume exemptions to the APA, Brownell v. Tom We Shung, 352 U.S. 180, 185 (1956), and we do not think §554(c)(2). We do not lightly presume exemption.

The Department's argument under the BLBA fares no better. The BLBA also incorporates the APA (by incorporating parts of the LHWCA), but it does so "except as otherwise provided . . . by regulations of the Secretary." The Department argues that the following BLBA regulation so provides: "In enacting [the BLBA], Congress intended that claimants be given the benefit of all reasonable doubt as to the existence of total or partial disability or death due to pneumoconiosis." But we do not think this regulation can fairly be read as authorizing the true doubt rule and rejecting the APA's burden of proof provision. Not only does the regulation fail to mention the true doubt rule or §7(c), it does not even mention the concept of burden shifting or burdens of proof. Accordingly — and assuming, arguendo, that the Department has the authority to displace §7(c) through regulation — this ambiguous regulation does not overcome the presumption that these adjudications under the BLBA are subject to §7(c)'s burden of proof provision.

III

We turn now to the meaning of "burden of proof" as used in §7(c). Respondents contend that the Court of Appeals was correct in reading "burden of proof" to include the burden of persuasion. The Department disagrees, contending that "burden of proof" imposes only the burden of production (i.e., the burden of going forward with evidence). The cases turn on this dispute, for if respondents are correct, the true doubt rule must fall: because the true doubt rule places the burden of persuasion on the party opposing the benefits award, it would violate §7(c)'s requirement that the burden of persuasion rest with the party seeking the award.

A

Because the term "burden of proof" is nowhere defined in the APA, our task is to construe it in accord with its ordinary or natural meaning. It is easier to state this task than to accomplish it, for the meaning of words may change over time, and many words have several meanings even at a fixed point in time. Here we must seek to ascertain the ordinary meaning of "burden of proof" in 1946, the year the APA was enacted.

For many years the term "burden of proof" was ambiguous because the term was used to describe two distinct concepts. Burden of proof was frequently used to refer to what we now call the burden of persuasion — the notion that if the evidence is evenly balanced, the party that bears the burden of persuasion must lose. But it was also used to refer to what we now call the burden of production — a party's obligation to come forward with evidence to support its claim. See J. Thayer, Evidence at the Common Law 355-384 (1898) (detailing various uses of the term "burden of proof" among 19th-century English and American courts). . . .

This Court tried to eliminate the ambiguity in the term "burden of proof" when it adopted the Massachusetts approach. Hill v. Smith, 260 U.S. 592 (1923). Justice Holmes wrote for a unanimous Court that "it will not be necessary to repeat the distinction, familiar in Massachusetts since the time of Chief Justice Shaw, and elaborated in the opinion below, between the burden of proof and the necessity of producing evidence to meet that already produced. The distinction is now very generally accepted, although often blurred by careless speech." Id. at 594.

In the two decades after *Hill*, our opinions consistently distinguished between burden of proof, which we defined as burden of persuasion, and an alternative concept, which we increasingly referred to as the burden of production or the burden of going forward with the evidence. . . . During this period the Courts of Appeals also limited the meaning of burden of proof to burden of persuasion, and explicitly distinguished this concept from the burden of production.

. . .

We interpret Congress' use of the term "burden of proof" in light of this history, and presume Congress intended the phrase to have the meaning generally accepted in the legal community at the time of enactment. These principles lead us to conclude that the drafters of the APA used the term "burden of proof" to mean the burden of persuasion. As we have explained, though the term had once been ambiguous, that ambiguity had largely been eliminated by the early 20th century. After *Hill*, courts and commentators almost unanimously agreed that the definition was settled. And Congress indicated that it shared this settled understanding, when in the Communications Act of 1934 it explicitly distinguished between the burden of proof and the burden of production. 47 U.S.C. §§309(e) and 312(d) (a party has both the "burden of proceeding with the introduction of evidence and the burden of proof"). Accordingly, we conclude that as of 1946 the ordinary meaning of burden of proof was burden of persuasion, and we understand the APA's unadorned reference to "burden of proof" to refer to the burden of persuasion.

B

We recognize that we have previously asserted the contrary conclusion as to the meaning of burden of proof in §7(c) of the APA. In NLRB v. Transportation Management Corp., 462 U.S. 393 (1983), we reviewed the National Labor Relations Board's (NLRB's) conclusion that the employer had discharged the employee because of the employee's protected union activity. In such cases the NLRB employed a burden shifting formula typical in dual motive cases: The employee had the burden of persuading the NLRB that antiunion animus contributed to the employer's firing decision; the burden then shifted to the employer to establish as an affirmative defense that it would have fired the employee for permissible reasons even if the employee had not been involved in union activity. The employer claimed that the NLRB's burden shifting formula was inconsistent with the National Labor Relations Act (NLRA), but we upheld it as a reasonable construction of the NLRA. . . .

The central issue in *Transportation Management* was whether the NLRB's burden shifting approach was consistent with the NLRA. The parties and the amici in *Transportation Management* treated the APA argument as an afterthought, devoting only one or two sentences to the question. None of the briefs in the case attempted to explain the ordinary meaning of the term. *Transportation Management*'s cursory answer to an ancillary and largely unbriefed question does not warrant the same level of deference we typically give our precedents.

Moreover, *Transportation Management* reached its conclusion without referring to Steadman v. SEC, 450 U.S. 91 (1981), our principal decision interpreting the meaning of §7(c). In *Steadman* we considered what standard of proof §7(c) required, and we held that the proponent of a rule or order under §7(c) had to meet its burden by a preponderance of the evidence, not by clear and convincing evidence. Though we did not explicitly state that §7(c) imposes the burden of persuasion on the party seeking the rule or order, our reasoning strongly implied that this must be so. We assumed that burden of proof meant burden of persuasion when we said that we had to decide "the degree of proof which must be adduced by the proponent of a rule or order to carry its burden of persuasion in an administrative proceeding." 450 U.S. at 95. . . . More important, our holding that the party with the burden of proof must prove its case by a preponderance only makes sense if the burden of proof means the burden of persuasion. A standard of proof, such as preponderance of the evidence, can apply only to a burden of persuasion, not to a burden of production.

We do not slight the importance of adhering to precedent, particularly in a case involving statutory interpretation. But here our precedents are in tension, and we think our approach in *Steadman* makes more sense than does the *Transportation Management* footnote. And although we reject *Transportation Management*'s reading of §7(c), the holding in that case remains intact. The NLRB's approach in *Transportation Management* is consistent with §7(c) because the NLRB first required the employee to persuade it that antiunion sentiment contributed to the employer's decision. Only then did the NLRB place the burden of persuasion on the employer as to its affirmative defense.

C

In addition to the *Transportation Management* footnote, the Department relies on the Senate and House Judiciary Committee Reports on the APA to support its claim that burden of proof means only burden of production. . . .

The Department argues that this legislative history indicates congressional intent to impose a burden of production on the proponent. But even if that is so, it does not mean that §7(c) is concerned only with imposing a burden of production. That Congress intended to impose a burden of production does not mean that Congress did not also intend to impose a burden of persuasion.

Moreover, these passages are subject to a natural interpretation compatible with congressional intent to impose a burden of persuasion on the party seeking an order. The primary purpose of these passages is not to define or allocate the burden of proof. The quoted passages are primarily concerned with the burden placed on the opponent in administrative hearings ("other parties . . . have a burden to maintain"), particularly where the opponent is the Government. The Committee appeared concerned with those cases in which the "proponent" seeks a license or other privilege from the Government, and in such cases did not want to allow the agency "to stand mute and arbitrarily disbelieve credible evidence." The Reports make clear that once the licensee establishes a prima facie case, the burden shifts to the Government to rebut it. This is perfectly compatible with a rule placing the burden of persuasion on the applicant, because when the party with the burden of persuasion establishes a prima facie case supported by "credible and credited evidence," it must either be rebutted or accepted as true.

The legislative history the Department relies on is imprecise and only marginally relevant. Congress chose to use the term "burden of proof" in the text of the statute, and given the substantial evidence that the ordinary meaning of burden of proof was burden of persuasion, this legislative history cannot carry the day.

D

In part due to Congress' recognition that claims such as those involved here would be difficult to prove, claimants in adjudications under these statutes benefit from certain statutory presumptions easing their burden. Similarly, the Department's solicitude for benefits claimants is reflected in the regulations adopting additional presumptions. But with the true doubt rule the Department attempts to go one step further. In so doing, it runs afoul of the APA, a statute designed "to introduce greater uniformity of procedure and standardization of administrative practice among the diverse agencies whose customs had departed widely from each other." Wong Yang Sung v. McGrath, 339 U.S. 33, 41 (1950). That concern is directly implicated here, for under the Department's reading each agency would be free to decide who shall bear the burden of persuasion. Accordingly, the Department cannot allocate the burden of persuasion in a manner that conflicts with the APA.

IV

Under the Department's true doubt rule, when the evidence is evenly balanced the claimant wins. Under the Department's reading each agency would be free to decide who shall bear the burden of persuasion hold that the true doubt rule violates §7(c) of the APA.

Because we decide these cases on the basis of §7(c), we need not address the Court of Appeals' holding in *Greenwich Collieries* that the true doubt rule conflicts with §718.403 or with *Mullins Coal, supra.*

Affirmed.

NOTES

1. A leading case on the standard of proof under the APA is Steadman v. SEC, 450 U.S. 91 (1981), discussed in the *Greenwich Collieries* opinion. The SEC had issued an order, after a lengthy evidentiary hearing, barring petitioner from associating with an investment adviser or dealer in securities. The order was based upon a finding that petitioner had violated various antifraud provisions of the federal securities laws. Petitioner challenged the commission's use of the preponderance of the evidence standard of proof in determining whether he had violated the statutes. He contended that, because of the potentially severe sanctions that the commission was empowered to impose, the commission was required to weigh the evidence against a clear and convincing standard of proof. The Supreme Court rejected this contention. In a proceeding subject to the APA, Congress had spoken in that statute. The Court interpreted §556(d) of the APA as establishing a standard of proof and held that the standard adopted was "the traditional preponderance-of-the-evidence standard." Where Congress has thus spoken, the Court should defer. Deference to congressionally prescribed standards of proof and rules of evidence in agency proceedings is as appropriate as it is in judicial proceedings.

2. It is easy to overlook the practical importance of the burden of proof. All too often, determining where the burden of proof lies determines who prevails in the case. The normal rule is that, in an agency, as in a court, the moving party has the burden of proof. The Federal APA codifies this rule in its provision that, "except as otherwise provided by statute, the proponent of a rule or order has the burden of proof." 5 U.S.C. §556(d). See, e.g., Schaffer v. West, 546 U.S. 49 (2005) (where statute is silent about burden of proof, burden of proof is on plaintiff (moving party)).

3. Compare the special burden of proof rule in the Social Security disability case. A claimant may have the burden of going forward, but the ultimate burden of proof is on the agency. Thus, a claimant is entitled to disability benefits when he presents probative evidence of disability, where the agency has not met the burden of persuasion to the contrary. Similarly, if a claimant shows he is not able to perform the work in which he was engaged, the burden shifts to the agency to prove that there is other available work that claimant can perform. Kirkland v. Weinberger, 480 F.2d 46 (5th Cir. 1973); Stark v. Weinberger, 497 F.2d 1092 (7th Cir. 1974).

J ILLEGALLY OBTAINED EVIDENCE

POWELL v. SECRETARY OF STATE

614 A.2d 1303 (Me. 1992)

CLIFFORD, Justice.

The Secretary of State appeals from an order of the Superior Court (Kennebec County, Alexander, J.) vacating the decision of a hearing examiner upholding the administrative license suspension of Kershaw Powell. Powell's license had been suspended for operating a motor vehicle while having 0.08 percent or more by weight of alcohol in his blood. . . . The Superior Court determined that the exclusionary rule associated with the fourth amendment to the United States Constitution applies to administrative license suspension hearings and that the hearing examiner should have considered whether the evidence presented in the administrative proceeding was obtained in violation of Powell's constitutional rights. Because the constitutionality of Powell's stop is not an issue that the applicable statute requires or even allows the hearing examiner to decide, and because we are unpersuaded by Powell's contention that the federal fourth amendment exclusionary rule must be applied in administrative license suspension hearings, we vacate the Superior Court judgment and remand for entry of a judgment affirming the decision of the Secretary of State. . . . Powell was the operator of a vehicle that turned around before reaching a roadblock set up to detect persons operating motor vehicles while under the influence of alcohol. Powell was pursued and stopped, and subsequently arrested for operating under the influence. . . . The District Court suppressed all evidence obtained following the stop on the ground that the arresting officer lacked a reasonable and articulable suspicion of criminal activity to justify the stop of Powell's vehicle. . . .

Pursuant to 29 M.R.S.A. §§1311-A(2), (3), Powell's license to operate a motor vehicle was suspended by the Secretary of State based on the arresting officer's report and the results of the blood-alcohol test administered to Powell. Pursuant to 29 M.S.R.A. §§1311-A(7), (8) (Pamph. 1991), Powell invoked his right to a hearing on the administrative license suspension. Powell, who was represented at the hearing, contested only the issue of probable cause . . . and argued that the decision of the District Court to suppress all evidence flowing from the stop was binding on the administrative proceeding and that the exclusionary rule should apply. Relying on 29 M.S.R.A. §1311-A(8)(B), the hearing examiner ruled that his only statutory task was to determine whether there was probable cause to believe that Powell was operating with excessive alcohol in his blood. He further concluded that the reasonableness of the stop was a separate issue and was not before him. The hearing officer, after determining that neither the exclusionary rule nor principles of collateral estoppel applied to an administrative license suspension hearing, upheld Powell's suspension. Powell appealed to the Superior Court. . . .

The Superior Court vacated the decision of the hearing examiner, concluding that because the administrative license suspension was "quasi-criminal," Powell was entitled to have the exclusionary rule applied, and to have the admissibility of evidence tested according to general notions of "due process and fair play." The Secretary of State then appealed to this court. . . .

Even though the statute does not require an examination of the initial stop, Powell contends that the fourth amendment requires the application of the exclusionary rule in an administrative license suspension hearing. The exclusionary rule is a judicially created remedy designed to safeguard fourth amendment rights. . . . The prime purpose of the rule is to deter unlawful police conduct. . . . The remedy of exclusion for violation of the fourth amendment has generally been limited to criminal cases. "As with any remedial device, the application of the rule has been restricted to those areas where its remedial objectives are thought most efficaciously served." . . . In the complex and turbulent history of the [exclusionary] rule, the court never has applied it to exclude evidence from a civil proceeding, federal or state." United States v. Janis, 428 U.S. 433, 447 (1976). Neither the United States Supreme Court nor this court has directly addressed the applicability of fourth amendment protections and exclusionary rule remedies to administrative license suspension proceedings. The United States Supreme Court has applied the exclusionary rule to a proceeding involving property forfeiture, concluding that a civil forfeiture proceeding based on criminal conduct is "quasi-criminal" in nature. . . . The Supreme Court, however, held the rule to be inapplicable to a civil federal deportation proceeding. Immigration & Naturalization Serv. v. Lopez-Mendoza, 468 U.S. 1032, 1041-42 (1984).

The *Lopez-Mendoza* Court used the framework set forth in United States v. Janis for deciding in what types of proceedings application of the exclusionary rule is appropriate. Id. (citing *Janis*, 428 U.S. at 446-48). The Court employed a balancing test weighing the likely social benefits of excluding evidence flowing from an unlawful seizure against the likely costs and benefits of using such evidence in a civil proceeding. Id.

In applying such a test in the instant administrative license suspension proceeding, we conclude that the fourth amendment's exclusionary rule should not be applied. Because the evidence has already been excluded from the criminal proceeding, there is little additional deterrent effect on police conduct by preventing consideration of the evidence by the hearing examiner. The costs to society resulting from excluding the evidence, on the other hand, would be substantial. The purpose of administrative license suspensions is to protect the public.... Because of the great danger posed by persons operating motor vehicles while intoxicated, it is very much in the public interest that such persons be removed from our highways....

In addition, the application of fourth amendment principles would add an undue burden to license suspension hearings. Contrary to the conclusion of the Superior Court, a license suspension hearing is not a quasi-criminal proceeding, but rather a "reasonable regulatory measure to protect public safety." ... Requiring hearing examiners to apply the exclusionary rule would unnecessarily complicate and burden an administrative proceeding designed to focus on the single issue of whether a person was operating a vehicle with excessive alcohol in his blood. Powell's contention that the exclusionary rule of the fourth amendment should be applied to administrative license suspension hearings is unpersuasive....

The Superior Court, in vacating the decision of the hearing examiner, went beyond the fourth amendment analysis raised by Powell at the administrative hearing, and concluded that notions of fundamental fair play should operate to keep out illegally seized evidence from an administrative license suspension proceeding.... [O]ur review of the record discloses no violation of Powell's right to procedural due process. Powell received fair notice, a full hearing with the right to call his own witnesses and cross-examine others, and was informed of his right to appellate review.

The entry is:

Judgment vacated. Remanded to the Superior Court for entry of judgment affirming the decision of the Secretary of State.

NOTES

1. A leading Supreme Court decision on application of the exclusionary rule in administrative proceedings is INS v. Lopez-Mendoza, 468 U.S. 1032 (1984), cited in the *Powell* opinion. *Lopez-Mendoza* arose out of a deportation proceeding. The immigrant the government sought to deport objected to evidence introduced at the deportation hearing, contending that it should have been suppressed as the fruit of an unlawful arrest. The INS, precursor to the current Immigration and Customs Enforcement (ICE), held that the evidence was admissible because it was inappropriate to apply the exclusionary rule to deportation proceedings. The Supreme Court agreed. The Court followed a cost-benefit analysis (CBA) approach that weighed the benefits secured from the exclusionary rule against the costs of applying the rule in a deportation case. The deterrent value of the exclusionary rule was seen to be its primary benefit. The Court found the benefit to be significantly reduced in the deportation case. It then concluded that "the social costs of applying the exclusionary rule in deportation proceedings are both unusual and significant." In the *Lopez-Mendoza* calculus, these costs, particularly in terms of delay and the increased burden on the agency, outweighed the benefits.

2. In making a determination whether to exclude evidence obtained illegally, should a court do more than ask whether a right guaranteed by the Constitution has been violated in the given case? Under *Lopez-Mendoza* and *Powell*, an affirmative answer is not enough to lead to a decision in favor of the individual. Instead, a balancing is required to determine whether the right to be free from the constitutional violation is itself guaranteed in the particular proceeding. If the balance tilts against the right in the given case, the government action will be upheld even though there has been a constitutional violation.

3. Should a balancing be applied to the denial of procedural rights in an administrative hearing — even where the right is so fundamental as that embodied in the exclusionary rule? See Schwartz, Cost-Benefit Analysis in Administrative Law: Does It Make Priceless Procedural Rights Worthless?, 37 Admin. L. Rev. 1 (1985). Do you agree with the implication of this title?

Compare L. Tribe, Constitutional Choices, viii (1985):

> [C]onstitutional choices, whatever else their character, must be made and assessed as fundamental choices of principle, not as instrumental calculations of utility or as pseudo-scientific calibrations of social cost against social benefit — calculations and calibrations whose essence is to deny the decision maker's personal responsibility for choosing. The point deserves particular emphasis at a time when the Supreme Court, long our nation's principal expositor of the Constitution, is coming increasingly to resemble a judicial Office of Management and Budget, straining constitutional discourse through a managerial sieve in which the "costs" (usually tangible and visible) are supposedly "balanced" against the "benefits" (usually ephemeral and diffuse) of treating constitutional premises seriously.

See also Titone, J., dissenting, Boyd v. Constantine, 613 N.E.2d 511 (N.Y. 1993), asserting that the balancing approach to the exclusionary rule is

> jurisprudentially flawed because it drastically limits the class of administrative proceedings in which the exclusionary rule will apply in the future and reduces the general rule of suppression . . . to a minor footnote in the exclusionary rule's history, having little practical significance. Indeed, the outcome in this case highlights pitfalls of the amorphous "balancing" approach, which requires the Court to measure

the potential deterrent effect that a particular application of the exclusionary rule might have and then weight the societal value of that application against the loss to society that inevitably results from the suppression of otherwise reliable evidence. Applied in certain marginal cases, this "balancing" approach can serve to weed out instances in which the deterrent value of the exclusionary rule is too insignificant to warrant the consequent impairment of the truth-finding process. . . . On the other hand, if applied as the sole guiding principle, the "balancing" approach, which has no real objective criteria, can lead to result-oriented decision-making and, ultimately, to the devaluation of the exclusionary rule as an important component of our system of constitutional enforcement.

The problem with a "balancing" approach is that there are no specific, uniformly applicable scales for measuring the relative weight to be assigned to the two factors that are being compared, i.e., the deterrent value of applying the exclusionary rule in the particular context and the loss to society arising from the suppression of otherwise probative evidence. The vocabulary of the "balancing" approach thus can be used to justify virtually any outcome, depending on the subjective beliefs that the individual decision-makers have about the merits of the exclusionary rule.

Furthermore, in most instances, the "balancing" approach is inherently weighted against application of the exclusionary rule, since it focuses on the facts in the individual situation before the Court rather than the broader societal concerns that led to the development of the suppression principle.

K DECISION PROCESS

Because most administrative agencies combine rulemaking with adjudicatory and enforcement functions, some insulation of the decision-making process is required to ensure the fairness and neutrality of decisions. The APA contains the following regarding the process of adjudicatory decision-making:

Federal Administrative Procedure Act

5 U.S.C. §557

(b) When the agency did not preside at the reception of the evidence, the presiding employee, or, in cases not subject to section 554(d) of this title, an employee qualified to preside at hearings pursuant to section 556 of this title, shall initially decide the case unless the agency requires, either in specific cases or by general rule, the entire record to be certified to it for decision. When the presiding employee makes an initial decision, that decision then becomes the decision of the agency without further proceedings unless there is an appeal to, or review on motion of, the agency within time provided by rule. On appeal from or review of the initial decision, the agency has all the powers which it would have in making the initial decision except as it may limit the issues on notice or by rule. When the agency makes the decision without having presided at the reception of the evidence, the presiding employee or an employee qualified to preside at hearings pursuant to section 556 of this title shall first recommend a decision, except that in rulemaking or determining applications for initial licenses —

(1) instead thereof the agency may issue a tentative decision or one of its responsible employees may recommend a decision; or

(2) this procedure may be omitted in a case in which the agency finds on the record that due and timely execution of its functions imperatively and unavoidably so requires.

(c) Before a recommended, initial, or tentative decision, or a decision on agency review of the decision of subordinate employees, the parties are entitled to a reasonable opportunity to submit for the consideration of the employees participating in the decisions —

(1) proposed findings and conclusions; or

(2) exceptions to the decisions or recommended decisions of subordinate employees or to tentative agency decisions; and

(3) supporting reasons for the exceptions or proposed findings or conclusions. The record shall show the ruling on each finding, conclusion, or exception presented. All decisions, including initial, recommended, and tentative decisions, are a part of the record.

NOTES

1. Prior to the guidance provided by the APA, agency decisions were usually treated as institutional decisions, involving the input of experts and others within the agency in a shared decision-making model unlike what we would expect to see today. During the 1930s and 1940s, the Supreme Court addressed these concerns about agency adjudicatory process in four cases referred to as the *Morgan* cases. These cases concerned rate setting for livestock agencies, a process treated as an agency adjudication entitled to due process. Because the Secretary of Agriculture made the final decision, the cases focused on the process by which he reached his conclusions and, especially, the input and advice the Secretary could receive. Not surprisingly given that the Secretary was responsible for dozens of regulatory schemes, his decision was based on consultation with subordinates, conferences with the examiners who actually heard the evidence, and review of memoranda. The first *Morgan* case, *Morgan I*, addressed the issue of the Secretary issuing the rate order without having personally heard or read any of the evidence presented at the hearing. Morgan v. United States, 298 U.S. 468 (1936). In an oft-quoted passage, the Court in *Morgan I* held that, "[t]he one who decides must hear," meaning that the agency order must issue from the individual who considered and appraised the evidence. *Morgan I* permitted the Secretary to delegate decision-making authority as long as such delegation was authorized by statute. This delegation was essential because no Secretary is likely to be able to hear all cases under their jurisdiction and has become the almost-universal method for meeting the mandate of *Morgan I*. *Morgan II* involved the propriety of the Secretary basing the decision on *ex parte* information that the industry didn't see until issuance of the order, a procedure that the Court held impermissibly infringed on the right to a hearing. Morgan v. United States, 304 U.S. 1 (1938). In the *Morgan* cases' final journey to the Supreme Court, *Morgan IV*, the Court drew a firm limit, though. The district court had authorized the industry to depose the Secretary and question him regarding the process by which he reached the conclusions of his order. United States v. Morgan, 313 U.S. 409 (1941). The Court cited *Morgan I*, noting that the proceeding resembled "a judicial proceeding," and held that the Secretary should never have been subjected to this examination. Such an examination of the mental processes of the Secretary, like a judge, would be destructive of "the integrity" of the decision-making process.

Developments in the law have rendered irrelevant many of the legal issues raised by the *Morgan* cases. Courts and statutes generally authorize broad power to delegate to agency decision makers. How else do provisions in the APA deal with the problems presented in the *Morgan* cases?

Note how §557(b) turns around *Morgan I*'s "the one who decides must hear" principle, by vesting the one who hears with the power to decide. APA hearings are presided over by administrative law judges to whom the APA gives hearing powers comparable to those of trial judges. But it also gives them substantial decision powers. Under §557(b) the administrative law judge is empowered to issue an initial decision that becomes *the* decision of the agency unless appealed. Section 557(b) permits the agency to retain full decision power by requiring (in specific cases or by general rule) that the record be certified directly to it for decision. In practice, however, virtually all the federal agencies provide in their rules for initial decisions by administrative law judges.

2. In the vast majority of federal agency cases, there is an initial decision by the administrative law judge who presided at the hearing. In cases where the agency requires the record to be certified to it for initial decision, §557 requires the administrative law judge to recommend a decision, with the latter taking the place of the pre-APA intermediate report. Can it be said that under §557 there is now a personal process of hearing and decision (at least at the initial decision level) similar to that in a trial court?

FCC v. ALLENTOWN BROADCASTING CORP.

349 U.S. 358 (1955)

MR. JUSTICE REED delivered the opinion of the Court.

This case involves the disposition of two applications for construction permits for standard broadcast stations. One application was filed by the Easton

Publishing Co. for Easton, Pennsylvania, and the other by the Allentown Broadcasting Corp. for Allentown, Pennsylvania. Both were for the same frequency, and, despite the fact that neither station would render service to the other community, simultaneous operation of the two stations would cause mutually destructive interference.

Hearings were . . . held in 1951 by an examiner whose initial decision recommended that the Allentown application be granted. Easton filed exceptions to that decision with the Commission, and after oral argument the Commission issued its final decision, disagreeing with its examiner and granting the station to Easton. . . .

In reaching its conclusion to set aside the Commission's order awarding the license to Easton, the Court of Appeals found that the Commission's reversal of its Hearing Examiner was erroneous. That court analyzed the evidence before the Commission as to Easton's uncertainty on affiliating with radio networks to secure their programs for its listeners, the reluctance, evasiveness and lack of candor of Easton's principal witnesses and the concentration of local communications media in the hands of the Easton applicant who was the publisher of the only local newspaper, the licensee of one of two FM radio stations and of the only television station. The court agreed with the Examiner and overruled the Commission. None of the above circumstances are in themselves a bar to the Commission's grant of license. Each involves appraisals of testimony that put into a record facts derived from various witnesses by interrogation. There was substantial evidence considering the whole record that had to be weighed, pro and con, as to types of programs, evasiveness of witnesses, and the desirability of allocating an additional license to an applicant who already controlled other means of communication.

The Court of Appeals' conclusion of error as to evasiveness relies largely on its understanding that the Examiner's findings based on demeanor of a witness are not to be overruled by a Board without a "'very substantial preponderance in the testimony as recorded,'" citing National Labor Relations Board v. Universal Camera Corp., 2 Cir., 190 F.2d 429, 430. We think this attitude goes too far. It seems to adopt for examiners of administrative agencies the "clearly erroneous" rule of the Fed. Rules Civ. Proc. 52(a), U.S.C.A., applicable to courts. In Universal Camera Corp. v. Labor Board, 340 U.S. 474, 492, we said, as to the Labor Management Relations Act hearings:

> Section 10(c) of the Labor Management Relations Act provides that "If upon the preponderance of the testimony taken the Board shall be of the opinion that any person named in the complaint has engaged in or is engaging in any such unfair labor practice, then the Board shall state its findings of fact. . . ." 61 Stat. 147, 29 U.S.C. (supp. III) §160(c), 29 U.S.C.A. §160(c). The responsibility for decision thus placed on the Board is wholly inconsistent with the notion that it has the power to reserve an examiner's findings only when they are "clearly erroneous." Such a limitation would make so drastic a departure from prior administrative practice that explicitness would be required.

That comment is here applicable. See also §8 of the Administrative Procedure Act, 60 Stat. 242, 5 U.S.C.A. §1007. . . . Reversed.

NOTES

1. Note the Court's reliance on §10(c) of the Labor Act. But §557(b) of the Federal APA is even clearer in supporting the result research. It provides expressly that "[o]n appeal from or review of the initial decision, the agency has all the powers which it would have in making the initial decision." This means that the agency on appeal from an initial decision has all the decision-making powers of a tribunal of first instance. See Glenroy Construction Co. v. NLRB, 527 F.2d 465 (7th Cir. 1975) (change of hearing officer title to administrative law judge held not to change *Allentown* rule).

2. Does this mean that the agency has unlimited latitude to disagree with the administrative law judge — the one person who heard the witness and observed their demeanor? See Bullion v. FDIC, 881 F.2d 1368 (5th Cir. 1989) (reviewing court's deference is to agency, not the ALJ). However, the cases require agencies to explain the grounds for rejection of the administrative law judge's initial decision or findings. See, e.g., Reyes v. Bowen, 845 F.2d 242 (10th Cir. 1988); Graziano v. Board of Education, 513 N.E.2d 282 (Ohio 1987).

Compare the following from the Report of the Attorney General's Committee on Administrative Procedure 51 (1941), on whose recommendations the APA was based:

> In general, the relationship upon appeal between the hearing commissioner and the agency ought to a considerable extent to be that of trial court to appellate court. Conclusions, interpretations, law, and policy should, of course, be open to full review. On the other hand, on matters which the hearing commissioner, having heard the evidence and seen the witnesses, is best qualified to decide, the agency should be reluctant to disturb his findings unless error is clearly shown.

3. The *Allentown* decision indicates that the intent of the Attorney General's Committee in this respect was not fully carried out by the APA. The agency is not limited to appellate power on appeals from administrative law judges' initial decisions.

Under the APA, initial decisions by administrative law judges become final (i.e., vested with the status of agency decisions) if not appealed to the agency. In the vast majority of cases, it was hoped, this would make for final decision by the one who heard, because the initial decision would tend to be accepted, just as are those of trial courts, by the parties in most cases. This intent has been frustrated by the APA provision not limiting the agency to appellate power on appeals from initial decisions, as interpreted in the *Allentown* case. Under *Allentown* the losing party at the initial decision stage has everything to gain by taking an appeal. As the agency is not restricted to appellate power, he has the same chance for a favorable decision on appeal that he had at the trial level; the agency may decide for him even though the findings below were not "clearly erroneous."

Compare the situation in the Immigration and Naturalization Service, as explained in Ortiz-Salas v. INS, 992 F.2d 105 (7th Cir. 1993):

Ortiz argues that he was entitled to plenary review by the Board [of Immigration Appeals] and he cites cases in which the Board indeed granted the appellant who was challenging denial of . . . relief plenary review of the immigration judge's ruling denying relief. . . . The government ripostes rather astonishingly that the Board has no fixed standard of review—sometimes it reviews the immigration judge for abuse of discretion, sometimes it reviews him de novo.

That won't do. It is an undue hardship to require the alien to guess at the standard of review that will be applied to his appeal, or, if he doesn't want to roll the dice, to argue his appeal in light of all possible standards of review. And it is irresponsible for the Board to fail to define its relationship to the immigration judges. . . . [O]ur complaint is not that the Board has had difficulty hammering out a position but that it seems not to have noticed that there is an issue. . . . The question on which the Board seems not to have made up its mind is whether the immigration judge is a sufficiently responsible officer to justify the Board's in effect delegating the making of the necessary discretionary judgment to him, subject only to the limited review implied by the abuse of discretion standard; or whether the Board should make the discretionary judgment itself, giving no particular weight to the immigration judge's determination. Agencies generally are free to substitute their judgment for that of their hearing officers . . . though there are exceptions, . . . not limited to the case . . . where the hearing officer has made determinations about the credibility of witnesses. . . . All we ask is that the Board of Immigration Appeals indicate what standard of review it means to use in these cases.

EADS v. SECRETARY OF HEALTH AND HUMAN SERVICES

983 F.2d 815 (7th Cir. 1993)

POSNER, Circuit Judge.

The district court affirmed the denial of social security disability benefits to Thomas Eads, who appeals. Eads suffers from poorly controlled diabetes, aggravated by extreme obesity. He claims that he cannot work because he must elevate his legs for several hours during every eight-hour period. The record before the administrative law judge contained no medical evidence directly supporting the claim, and the administrative law judge did not believe Eads's testimony. Ordinarily this would be the end of the case. But in support of a request that the Appeals Council of the Social Security Administration exercise its discretion to review the administrative law judge's decision, Eads submitted a letter from his doctor which stated for the first time that Eads cannot sit for more than half an hour at a time, but must "be supine periodically in order to keep his legs elevated." The Council nevertheless refused to review the administrative law judge's decision, and the district judge refused to consider the letter because it had not been before the administrative law judge. We must decide whether the district judge's action was correct. The question is a difficult one to which the courts, as we shall see, have given discrepant answers. The Social Security Administration asks us to clarify it. We shall try.

The Appeals Council has a certiorari-type jurisdiction over decisions by administrative law judges denying benefits. 20 C.F.R. §§404.967, 416.1467. (There are two social security disability benefits programs — Disability Insurance, for people who have qualified for social security benefits by paying social security taxes for the relevant period, and Supplemental Security Income, for people who have not.) But the pertinent regulations are the same for the two programs. . . . If the Council denies an application to review such a decision, the effect is to make the decision final, and therefore . . . judicially reviewable. . . . The claimant has exhausted his administrative remedies; the case is ripe for judicial review.

The analogy to certiorari is imperfect, however, because the claimant is permitted to submit new evidence to the Appeals Council in support of his application for review, provided that it is new and material. . . . Since the submission of the evidence precedes the Appeals Council's decision, and that decision, even when it denies review, is a precondition to judicial review, the new evidence is a part of the administrative record that goes to the district court in the judicial review proceeding, and then to this court if there is an appeal. It might seem therefore that the district judge and we would be free to consider the new evidence that was before the Appeals Council in deciding whether the decision denying benefits was supported by the record as a whole. And of course this is right when the Council has accepted the case for review and made a decision on the merits, based on all the evidence before it, which then becomes the decision reviewed in the courts. . . . It is wrong when the Council has refused to review the case. For then the decision reviewed in the courts is the decision of the administrative law judge. . . . The correctness of that decision depends on the evidence that was before him. . . . He cannot be faulted for having failed to weigh evidence never presented to him, such as the doctor's letter in this case, which added a potentially crucial detail to the medical records that had omitted it (that is, had omitted any mention of the fact, if it is a fact, that Eads has to elevate his legs periodically).

In the social security dispute-resolution system, as in a standard judicial system, there is provision for newly discovered evidence. Such evidence does not show that the trier of fact erred by failing to consider it — he could not have considered it, it wasn't submitted to him — but it may furnish a reason why justice requires that the trier of fact reexamine his decision in light of it. The vehicle for such reexamination in the federal court system is Rule 60(b) of the Federal Rules of Civil Procedure. The counterpart in the social security system is found in 20 C.F.R. §§404.987-404.989, 416.1487-416.1489, which authorize petitions to reopen. . . . No such petition has been filed in this case. There are, however, other routes for bringing in newly discovered evidence. One of course is to submit it to the Appeals Council, as was done here. If the Council refuses to consider it, that refusal is not itself a final, appealable order — the administrative law judge's decision is, having been made final and appealable by the refusal. But, as an interim order in the administrative proceeding, it is reviewable. Review is limited, because the decision to refuse to review the administrative law judge's decision is discretionary. . . . Eads does not, however, ask us to review the Appeals

Council's refusal to review the administrative law judge's decision, and anyway that refusal was not based on any contestable legal determinations. And finally, 42 U.S.C. §405(g)(6) authorizes the court to remand the case to the Social Security Administration for consideration of newly discovered evidence. Eads could have submitted the doctor's letter to the district court as a basis for requesting such a remand. He did not do that either.

He stakes his all on persuading us to reverse the denial of disability benefits on the ground that the administrative law judge's decision is erroneous when evaluated in the light of all the evidence in the case, including evidence that the administrative law judge could not have considered because it was never submitted to him. This we cannot properly do. It would change our role from that of a reviewing court to that of an administrative law judge, required to sift and weigh evidence in the first instance, rather than limited as we are to reviewing evidentiary determinations made by the front-line factfinder. . . . [W]e note that without the doctor's letter it is plain that the administrative law judge did not commit clear error in finding against Eads. There is no need to explain this conclusion in detail; it was adequately discussed by the district judge.

AFFIRMED.

NOTES

1. The *Eads* case illustrates one method of dealing with the *Allentown* problem — certiorari-type review, which vests the reviewing body with discretionary authority to grant or deny review. Normally, the party appealing from the ALJ is not permitted to submit new evidence at that stage. It is illustrated by the practice in the Civil Aeronautics Board, when that agency regulated civil aviation. Pursuant to a 1961 Presidential Reorganization Plan, the board provided for a certiorari-type review procedure. The losing party at the initial decision stage in a CAB case filed a petition for discretionary review with the board, which had complete discretion to grant or deny review. See National Aviation Trades Ass'n v. CAB, 420 F.2d 209 (D.C. Cir. 1969). Only about half of the CAB cases decided by administrative law judges were reviewed by the board. The SEC has also adopted a modified certiorari review procedure. 17 C.F.R. §201.17 (1986). For a discussion of certiorari review, see Gilliland, The Certiorari-Type Review, 26 Admin. L. Rev. 53 (1974).

2. Another method of dealing with *Allentown* has been followed in the FCC. Amendments to the Communications Act in 1962 authorized the FCC to set up a review board of three or more employees to perform the review functions of the Commission, with discretionary power in the Commission to grant or deny further review. The FCC set up a review board composed of four senior employees assigned to the board by the Commission. This board now hears the appeals from FCC administrative law judges' initial decisions. About half the judges' decisions are appealed to the board. The board sits in rotation panels of three; they decide after receiving exceptions and briefs and after hearing oral argument.

The review board has the *Allentown* power of full review; it has the same APA powers that the agency would have in making the initial decision.

3. Appeal to the review board is now the last appeal of right in the FCC. There is no longer any appeal of right to the Commission itself. Instead there is a certiorari-type review of review board decisions by the Commission that is initiated by the filing of an application for review. Such applications can be, and usually are, denied by the Commission by simple denials without any reasons.

L DECISIONS AND FINDINGS

ADAMS v. BOARD OF REVIEW OF INDUS. COMM'N

821 P.2d 1 (Utah Ct. App. 1991)

BENCH, Judge.

Petitioner Roberta Adams seeks review of the Industrial Commission's decision to deny her benefits under the Utah Occupational Disease Disability Law, Utah Code Ann. §§35-2-1 to-65 (1988). We vacate the Commission's order.

FACTS

Adams worked as a telemarketer for Unicorp. Her duties consisted primarily of dialing telephone numbers and talking on the telephone while sitting at a desk. . . . After working at Unicorp for approximately one year, Adams left Unicorp to seek medical attention for debilitating pain she claimed had developed gradually as a result of her employment. In general, Adams now claims that the repetitive motion of calling on a manual phone and holding the phone to her mouth and ear caused neck pain, neck stiffness, muscle spasm, pain in her right arm and shoulder, a "pins and needles" sensation and numbness in her right shoulder and arm, and fatigue.

When Adams informed her supervisor of her pain, he referred her to his chiropractor, Dr. Robert Pope, for treatment. Dr. Pope examined her and diagnosed her as having "cervicobrachial syndrome, carpal tunnel syndrome, myofascitis, and brachial neuralgia." . . . Dr. Pope also indicated that he believed there was a very high probability that Adams's condition resulted from her job duties. [Other doctors consulted by Adams made similar diagnoses.]

The Workers Compensation Fund (the Fund) required Adams to undergo an independent medical evaluation by Dr. Edward Spencer. Dr. Spencer . . . found that her major problem was psychological and did not require any additional medical or surgical treatment for her condition. . . . [Another Fund doctor] concluded that Adams was in need of psychiatric diagnosis and treatment.

As directed by the Fund, Adams was then examined by Dr. David L. McCann, a psychiatrist. . . . Dr. McCann concluded that Adams suffered from a personality disorder and did not have any physical impairment or other problems associated with her employment, but that her complaints were motivated by a desire to obtain compensation.

A hearing was then held where the foregoing conflicting diagnoses were presented to an administrative law judge (A.L.J.). The A.L.J. denied benefits. Adams appealed the A.L.J.'s decision to the Commission, which affirmed the decision and adopted the findings and conclusions of the A.L.J. as its own. Adams now seeks a review of the Commission's decision. . . .

ADEQUACY OF FINDINGS

An administrative agency must make findings of fact and conclusions of law that are adequately detailed so as to permit meaningful appellate review.

> In order for us to meaningfully review the findings of the Commission, the findings must be "sufficiently detailed and include enough subsidiary facts to disclose the steps by which the ultimate conclusion on each factual issue was reached." . . . [T]he failure of an agency to make adequate findings of fact in material issues renders its findings *"arbitrary and capricious"* unless the evidence is "clear, uncontroverted and capable of only one conclusion." . . .

The Utah Supreme Court has clearly described the detail required in administrative findings in order for findings to be deemed adequate.

> [An administrative agency] cannot discharge its statutory responsibilities without making findings of fact on all necessary ultimate issues under the governing statutory standards. It is also essential that [an administrative agency] make subsidiary findings in sufficient detail that the critical subordinate factual issues are highlighted and resolved in such a fashion as to demonstrate that there is a logical and legal basis for the ultimate conclusions. The importance of complete, accurate, and consistent findings of fact is essential to a proper determination by an administrative agency. To that end, findings should be sufficiently detailed to disclose the steps by which the ultimate factual conclusions, or conclusions of mixed fact and law, are reached. . . . *Without such findings, this Court cannot perform its duty of reviewing [an administrative agency's] order in accordance with established legal principles and of protecting the parties and the public from arbitrary and capricious administration action.*

Milne Truck Lines, Inc. v. Public Serv. Comm'n, 720 P.2d 1373, 1378 (Utah 1986) (emphasis added).

If agency findings reveal the steps taken by the agency in reaching its decision, the failure to disclose a specific subsidiary finding may or may not be fatal to the agency's decision. A finding may be implied if it is clear from the record, and therefore apparent upon review, that the finding was actually made as part of the tribunal's decision. . . . We may not merely assume, however, that an undisclosed finding was in fact made. The party wishing to defend an agency decision must carry its burden of showing that the undisclosed finding was actually made.

> For this Court to sustain an order, the findings must be sufficiently detailed to demonstrate that the Commission has properly arrived at the ultimate factual findings and has properly applied the governing rules of law to those findings. . . . It is not the prerogative of this Court to search the record to determine whether findings could have been made by the Commission to support its order, for to do so would be to usurp the function with which the Commission is charged. . . .

The findings made by the A.L.J. and adopted by the Commission in the present case are inadequate in that they do not disclose the steps taken by the Commission in reaching its decision to deny Adams benefits. The Commission's "findings" amount to the following single conclusory statement as to causation: "The preponderance of medical evidence in this case establishes that the applicant's various listed symptoms are not related to her work as a telemarketer at Unicorp."

Because the Commission concluded that Adams failed to prove causation, the Commission denied her benefits. The Commission correctly indicated in its adopted conclusions of law that causation is one of the ultimate factual conclusions that must be proven by a claimant. . . . However, the Commission's conclusion that Adams failed to prove causation, without supporting findings, is arbitrary. "Administrative bodies may not rely upon findings that contain only ultimate conclusions." . . . Given the numerous legal and factual questions regarding causation in this case, the Commission's solitary finding that Adams failed to prove causation does not give the parties any real indication as to the bases for its decision and the steps taken to reach it, nor does it give a reviewing court anything to review.

While the purported "Findings of Fact" written by the A.L.J. contain an informative summary of the evidence presented, such a rehearsal of contradictory evidence does not constitute findings of fact. In order for a finding to truly constitute a "finding of fact," it must indicate what the A.L.J. determines in fact occurred, not merely what the contradictory evidence indicates might have occurred. . . .

As is apparent in the recitation of the various diagnoses presented to the A.L.J., the doctors each had differing explanations for Adams's medical condition and whether it was caused by her employment. The evidence did not merely indicate two possible versions of a fact whereby we could conclude that the denial of benefits necessarily indicates that the Commission accepted one version over another. The evidence shows several possible configurations and degrees of injury and/or disease, if any, and the causes, if any, thereby creating a matrix of possible factual findings. A mere summary of the conflicting evidence in this case therefore does not give a clear indication of the A.L.J.'s or the Commission's view as to what in fact occurred. Since we cannot even determine why the Commission found there was no causation shown, we clearly cannot assume that the Commission actually made any of the possible subsidiary findings. The findings are therefore inadequate.

In order for this court to address the errors claimed by Adams, we must have findings that indicate respectively (1) the issues decided; (2) the legal interpretations and applications made; and (3) the subsidiary factual findings in support of the decision. A simple conclusion that Adams failed to prove medical causation does not contain any of the foregoing information.

At a minimum, there should have been a finding in the present case identifying the occupational disease or injury, if any, suffered by Adams. The Commission could not logically conclude that Adams's medical condition, if any, was not caused by her employment without first establishing what her medical condition was. This it failed to do. The Commission's findings of fact simply do not "resolve all issues of material fact necessary to justify the conclusions of law and judgment entered thereon." . . .

The Commission should have also given some explanation, factual or legal, as to how Adams failed to prove causation. An applicant with a pre-existing condition must prove both legal and medical causation. . . . The . . . findings do not make it clear whether it believed that Adams failed to prove medical or legal causation. Both issues were apparently involved in this matter. Inasmuch as our standard of review varies depending upon whether Adams failed to prove legal or medical causation, the Commission's failure to identify whether Adams failed to prove legal or medical causation prevents us from reviewing that conclusion.

When multiple conflicting versions of the facts create a matrix of possible factual findings, we are unable on appeal to assume that any given finding was in fact made. . . . Because of the matrix of factual possibilities in the present case, we are unable to conduct a meaningful review. We therefore hold that the Commission's denial of benefits based upon a solitary finding regarding the ultimate issue of causation fails "to disclose the steps by which the ultimate factual conclusions, or conclusions of mixed fact and law, are reached," id., and therefore renders the action arbitrary. . . ." The importance of complete, accurate, and consistent findings of fact is essential to a proper determination by an administrative agency." . . . The findings are an integral part of the logical process a tribunal must go through in reaching a decision. . . . Once an administrative agency attempts to state its findings, identify the applicable law, and articulate its logic, it may discover that critical facts are not properly before it, that the law is other than anticipated, or that its initial logic is flawed. In such situations, a result contrary to the initial conclusions of the body may be dictated. The process of articulation clearly enhances agency self-discipline and protects against arbitrary and capricious decisions. Without the safeguard of adequate findings, there is no guarantee that the agency followed a logical process in reaching its decision. If, on the other hand, the agency identifies the facts, law, and reasoning supporting its decision, it reveals its logical process and the parties can be assured that a logical process occurred, even if it is in some manner flawed.

If an agency's logical process is flawed, its shortcomings can be corrected on review, but only if the agency creates findings revealing the evidence upon which it relies, the law upon which it relies, and its interpretation of the law. Absent adequate findings, a petitioner wishing to challenge an agency's factual findings will not be able to marshal the evidence in support of the findings. . . . Nor will a petitioner be able to challenge the agency's undeclared interpretation of the law or its undisclosed logic....

If findings are inadequate, this court will be unable to effectively and efficiently perform its duty of review. "To enable this Court to determine whether an order is arbitrary and capricious, the Commission must make findings of fact that are sufficiently detailed to apprise the parties and the Court of the basis for the Commission's decision." ... While these disadvantages may not be reflected in the initial outcome of the hearing below, they directly affect the ultimate outcome of the matter on review....

RELIEF

As a general rule, the appropriate relief for an agency's failure to make adequate findings is to vacate the order complained of and to order the agency to "make more adequate findings in support of, and more fully articulate [the] reasons for, the determination ... made." ... The process of articulation may or may not cause the Commission to reach a different decision. Since we vacate the Commission's order denying benefits, it is free to deny benefits or grant benefits as may be dictated by its new findings of fact and conclusions of law.

CONCLUSION

We vacate the Commission's order denying Adams benefits and direct the Commission to produce adequate findings of fact and conclusions of law and enter a new order.

NOTES

Federal Administrative Procedure Act

5 U.S.C. §557(c)

(3) ... All decisions, including initial, recommended, and tentative decisions, are a part of the record and shall include a statement of—

(A) findings and conclusions, and the reasons or basis therefor, on all the material issues of fact, law, or discretion presented on the record and

(B) the appropriate rule, order, sanction, relief, or denial thereof.

1. "It is hornbook law that an agency must set forth clearly the basis of reaching its decision." Carolina Power Co. v. FERC, 716 F.2d 52, 55 (D.C. Cir. 1983). See Illinois v. United States, 371 F. Supp. 1136 (N.D. Ill. 1976):

> The Congressional policy in setting forth the requirements of 5 U.S.C. §557(c)(3)(A) that findings be set forth would seem at least fourfold:

1. to prevent arbitrary and capricious decisions in a manner violative of due process;
2. as an explanation to the parties involved as to the basis for the decision;
3. to give guidance to parties similarly situated; and
4. to provide a basis for judicial review by the courts.

Of these reasons the one most often mentioned by courts is the need for findings as a basis for effective judicial review. In Justice Cardozo's oft-quoted words, "We must know what a decision means before the duty becomes ours to say whether it is right or wrong." United States v. Chicago, Milwaukee, St. Paul, & Pacific Railroad, 294 U.S. 499, 511 (1935). An agency's "ipse dixit assertion frustrates judicial review." District 1199P v. NLRB, 864 F.2d 1096, 1104 (3d Cir. 1989). Findings, on the other hand, "enable meaningful judicial review." Appeal of Psychiatric Insts., 564 A.2d 818, 822 (N.H. 1989). Indeed, the findings requirement "is not a mere technicality but is an absolute necessity without which judicial review would be impossible." CF Industries v. PSC, 599 S.W.2d 536, 541 (Tenn. 1980). Compare Commercial Carriers v. Indus. Comm'n of Utah, 888 P.2d 707, 711 (Utah Ct. App. 1994) ("[T]he question addressed by the *Adams* court was not whether the findings were supported by substantial evidence, but rather whether the findings sufficiently disclosed the logical process employed to permit meaningful review.").

2. Findings are of two kinds: basic and ultimate. The distinction was explained in a federal case as follows: (1) from consideration of the evidence, a determination of facts of a basic or underlying nature must be reached; and (2) from these basic facts the ultimate facts, usually in the language of the statute, are to be inferred. Saginaw Broadcasting Co. v. FCC, 96 F.2d 554 (D.C. Cir.), cert. denied, 305 U.S. 613 (1938).

As *Adams* shows, it is not enough for an agency to make only ultimate findings. "Findings of ultimate facts expressed in the language of the statute are not enough in the absence of basic findings to support them." Blue Cross v. Bell, 607 P.2d 498, 505 (Kan. 1980). In Florida v. United States, 282 U.S. 194 (1931), the ICC had issued an order regulating intrastate rates for log shipments, supported by the finding that the previous rates had resulted in "unjust discrimination against interstate commerce." The Commission had made no findings as to the revenue derived from the new rates or the effect of the rates upon the income of the carrier, which would support the ultimate finding of discrimination. The Court reversed because of "the lack of the basic or essential findings required to support the Commission's order."

3. Where the basic facts are found, may the ultimate facts be implied? See Wichita Railroad v. Public Utilities Comm'n, 260 U.S. 48 (1922). The agency there was authorized to change electricity rates if it found they were "unjust, unreasonable, unjustly discriminatory or unduly preferential." An order raising rates was invalidated, even though all the basic, underlying facts were found, because there was no express finding that the previous rates had been "unjust" or "unreasonable" or "unjustly discriminatory" or "unduly preferential." The Court refused to accept the argument that lack of an express finding might be supplied by implication: "an express finding of unreasonableness by the Commission was indispensable."

M RECONSIDERATION

ICC v. BROTHERHOOD OF LOCOMOTIVE ENGINEERS

482 U.S. 270 (1987)

JUSTICE SCALIA delivered the opinion of the Court.

On September 15, 1980, Union Pacific Railroad Co. (UP) and Missouri Pacific Railroad Co. (MP) and their respective corporate parents filed a joint application with the Interstate Commerce Commission (ICC or Commission) seeking permission for UP to acquire control of MP. The same day, a similar but separate application was jointly filed by UP and the Western Pacific Railroad Co. (WP). In a consolidated proceeding, the control applications were opposed by a number of labor organizations, including respondents Brotherhood of Locomotive Engineers (BLE) and United Transportation Union (UTU), as well as several competing rail-roads, including petitioner Missouri-Kansas-Texas Railroad Co. (MKT) and the Denver and Rio Grande Western Railroad Co. (DRGW). MKT and DRGW, in addition to opposing the mergers, filed responsive applications seeking the right to conduct operations using the track of the new consolidated carrier in the event that the control applications were approved. MKT's request for trackage rights specified that "MKT, with its own employees, and at its sole cost and expense, shall operate its engines, cars and trains on and along Joint Track." DRGW's application indicated that it "may, at its option, elect to employ its own crews for the movement of its trains, locomotives and cars to points on or over the Joint Track."

On October 20, 1982, the ICC approved UP's control acquisitions and granted MKT's application for trackage rights over 200 miles of MP and UP track in four States and DRGW's application for rights over 619 miles of MP track between Pueblo and Kansas City. . . . The approved trackage rights were to become effective "immediately upon consummation of the consolidations." . . . Although numerous parties, including BLE, had petitioned for review of the Commission's October 20, 1982, order . . . no question concerning the crewing of MKT or DRGW trains was raised at that time. However, on April 4, 1983, BLE filed with the Commission a "Petition for Clarification," contending that the Commission had no jurisdiction to, and as a matter of consistent practice did not, inject itself into labor matters such as crew selection, and asking the Commission to declare that its October 20, 1982, order did not have the intent or effect of authorizing the tenant carriers to use their own crews on routes that they had not previously served. In a brief order served May 18, 1983, the Commission denied the petition, ruling that its prior decision "does not require clarification." The tenant railroads, it said, had proposed to use their own crews in their trackage rights application, and "our approval of the applications authorizes such operations."

Within the period prescribed by Commission rules for filing petitions for administrative review, . . . both BLE and UTU sought "reconsideration" of the Commission's denial. In addition to repeating BLE's earlier arguments, the unions contended that the tenant railroads' crewing procedures constituted a unilateral change in working conditions forbidden by the . . . Railway Labor Act, 45 U.S.C. §151 et seq. (RLA), and by collective-bargaining agreements, and that the Commission had made no findings that would justify exempting the trackage rights transaction from applicable labor laws. In a lengthy order served on October 25, 1983, responding in some detail to all of the major contentions, the Commission denied the petitions. . . .

On December 16, 1983, BLE petitioned for judicial review of the May 18, 1983, and October 25, 1983, orders. . . . We now conclude that the petitions for review must be dismissed.

I

. . . With certain exceptions not relevant here . . . , judicial review of final orders of the ICC is governed by the Hobbs Act, 28 U.S.C. §2341 et seq., which provides that any party aggrieved by a "final order" of the Commission "may, within 60 days after its entry, file a petition to review the order in the court of appeals wherein venue lies." §2344. . . . However, although the timeliness requirements of the Hobbs Act were satisfied, the order from which the unions have appealed is unreviewable.

The Commission's authority to reopen and reconsider its prior actions stems from 49 U.S.C. §10327(g), which provides:

> The Commission may, at any time on its own initiative because of material error, new evidence, or substantially changed circumstances —
>
> (A) reopen a proceeding;
>
> (B) grant rehearing, reargument, or reconsideration of an action of the Commission; and
>
> (C) change an action of the Commission.
>
> "An interested party may petition to reopen and reconsider an action of the Commission under this paragraph under regulations of the Commission."

When the Commission reopens a proceeding for any reason and, after reconsideration issues a new and final order setting forth the rights and obligations of the parties, that order — even if it merely reaffirms the rights and obligations set forth in the original order — is reviewable on its merits. . . . Where, however, the Commission *refuses* to reopen a proceeding, what is reviewable is merely the lawfulness of the refusal. Absent some provision of law requiring a reopening (which is not asserted to exist here), the basis for challenge must be that the refusal to reopen was "arbitrary, capricious, [or] an abuse of discretion." 5 U.S.C.

§706(2)(A). We have said that overturning the refusal to reopen requires "a showing of the clearest abuse of discretion," . . . and we have actually reversed the ICC only once, see Atchison, T. & S.F.R. Co. v. United States, 284 U.S. 248 (1932), in a decision that was "promptly restricted . . . to its special facts, . . . and . . . stands virtually alone." . . . More importantly for present purposes, all of our cases entertaining review of a refusal to reopen appear to have involved petitions alleging "new evidence" or "changed circumstances" that rendered the agency's original order inappropriate. . . . We know of no case in which we have reviewed the denial of a petition to reopen based upon no more than "material error" in the original agency decision. There is good reason for distinguishing between the two. If review of denial to reopen for new evidence or changed circumstances is unavailable, the petitioner will have been deprived of all opportunity for judicial consideration — even on a "clearest abuse of discretion" basis — of facts which, through no fault of his own, the original proceeding did not contain. By contrast, where no new data but only "material error" has been put forward as the basis for reopening, an appeal places before the courts precisely the same substance that could have been brought there by appeal from the original order -but asks them to review it on the strange, one-step-removed basis of whether the agency decision is not only unlawful, but *so* unlawful that the refusal to reconsider it is an abuse of discretion. Such an appeal serves no purpose whatever where a petition for reconsideration has been filed within a discretionary review period specifically provided by the agency (and within the period allotted for judicial review of the original order), since in that situation the petition tolls the period for judicial review of the original order, which can therefore be appealed to the courts *directly* after the petition for reconsideration is denied. And where the petition is filed *outside* that period (and outside the period for judicial review of the original order) judicial review would serve only the peculiar purpose of extending indefinitely the time within which *seriously* mistaken agency orders can be judicially overturned. That is to say, the Hobbs Act's 60-day limitation provision would effectively be subjected to a proviso that reads: "Provided, however, that if the agency error is so egregious that refusal to correct it would be an abuse of discretion, judicial review may be sought at any time."

For these reasons, we agree with the conclusion reached in an earlier case by the Court of Appeals that, where a party petitions an agency for reconsideration on the ground of "material error," i.e., on the same record that was before the agency when it rendered its original decision, "an order which merely denies rehearing of . . . [the prior] order is not itself reviewable." . . .

Even if our search for statutory authorization were limited to the text of the Hobbs Act, it seems to us not inventiveness but the most plebeian statutory construction to find implicit in the 60-day limit upon judicial review a prohibition against the agency's permitting, or a litigant's achieving, perpetual availability of review by the mere device of filing a suggestion that the agency has made a mistake and should consider the matter again. Substantial disregard of the Hobbs Act is effected . . . by . . . on-the-merits-review of an agency decision of law rendered 14 months before the petition for review was filed, *using the same standard of review that would have been applied had appeal been filed within the congressionally prescribed 60-day period.*

Statutory authority for preventing this untoward result need not be sought solely in the Hobbs Act, however. While the Hobbs Act specifies the form of proceeding for judicial review of ICC orders, it is the Administrative Procedure Act (APA) that codifies the nature and attributes of judicial review, including the traditional principle of its unavailability "to the extent that . . . agency action is committed to agency discretion by law." 5 U.S.C. §701(a)(2). We have recently had occasion to apply this limitation to the general grant of jurisdiction contained in 28 U.S.C. §1331, see Heckler v. Chaney, 470 U.S. 821 (1985); it applies to the general grant of jurisdiction of the Hobbs Act as well. In *Chaney* we found that the type of agency in question "has traditionally been 'committed to agency discretion,' and . . . that the Congress enacting the APA did not intend to alter that tradition." Id., at 832. As discussed above, we perceive that a similar tradition of non-reviewability exists with regard to refusals to reconsider for material error, by agencies as by lower courts; and we believe that to be another tradition that 5 U.S.C. §701(a)(2) was meant to preserve. We are confirmed in that view by the impossibility of devising an adequate standard of review for such agency action. One is driven either to apply the ordinary standards for reviewing errors of fact or law (in which event the time limitation of the Hobbs Act — or whatever other time limitation applies to the particular case — will be entirely frustrated); or else to adopt some "clearly erroneous" standard (which produces the strange result that only *really bad* mistakes escape the time limitation — whatever "really bad" might mean in this context where great deference is already accorded to agency action). . . . The vast majority of denials of reconsideration, however, are made *without statement of reasons*, since 5 U.S.C. §555(e) exempts from the normal APA requirement of "a brief statement of the grounds for denial" agency action that consists of "affirming a prior denial." One wonders how, in this more normal context [one] would go about determining [the] answer . . . to the question of reviewability — and if the answer permits review, what standard to apply. Under the proper analysis, the solution is clear: If the petition that was denied sought reopening on the basis of new evidence or changed circumstances review is available and abuse of discretion is the standard; otherwise, the agency's refusal to go back over ploughed ground is nonreviewable. . . .

The case is remanded to the Court of Appeals with instructions to dismiss the petitions for lack of jurisdiction.

Vacated and remanded.

NOTES

1. After the agency decision, a losing party may file a petition to reopen the proceeding or reconsider the decision. As Justice Scalia stresses, such a petition is addressed to the discretion of the agency concerned. As a matter committed to discretion, could the agency denial of a petition be reviewed for abuse of discretion?

2. What about constitutional claims? In 2020, the First Circuit joined six other circuit courts in holding that federal appellate courts have limited jurisdiction to review constitutional claims or errors arising in motions to reopen or reconsider. See Thompson v. Barr, 959 F.3d 476, 483 (1st Cir. 2020).

CHAPTER 6 PROBLEM

Tele-Tex is a solar power operator attempting to make alternative energy inroads into the deeply coal-committed state of West Dakota. The company claims that it has been dogged by the West Dakota Energy Commission (WDEC), the state agency that oversees utility and energy providers' compliance with state statutes and regulations. WDEC recently slapped Tele-Tex with a charge of failing to adequately permit a large solar power site located on the site of a former mine. The charge claims a violation of §8(a)(3) of the state energy compliance code, which requires that "the placement of all utility equipment must be in accordance with approved permits." Specifically, the WDEC alleges that the placement of 5 to 10 percent of the solar panels differs from the approved and permitted locations. As a remedy, the agency is demanding the dismantling of the entire solar array. Tele-Tex, in defense, argues that, while the location of some of the panels deviates slightly from the plan submitted for approval, it claims that the changes were minimal, that the placements are substantially compliant, and that the remedy requested by the agency is exaggerated and unjustified.

The case was assigned to Roger Jefe, a relatively new administrative law judge (ALJ) at WDEC. Before Jefe became an ALJ, he ran public relations for the region's top coal industry association, whose mission it was to keep the state alternative-energy-free. Over the years, Jefe had published articles in trade journals about the benefits of coal and the hidden dangers of solar and wind power. In one article, he wrote, "America is built on a bedrock of coal. The region is unlikely to survive if alternative energy (solar, wind) wins the battle to shut down coal. We all have an obligation to fight for our way of life." Since becoming an ALJ, Jefe has sided with an industry other than coal only once in 50 decisions. As a result of this background, Tele-Tex filed a Motion of Recusal asking Jefe to step down as the ALJ in the case. Shortly thereafter, local and national media picked up on the WDEC v. Tele-Tex story and began to run stories about the allegations involved in the case. A local environmental group, Clean Energy Power (CEP), filed a petition to intervene in the proceeding as a party in interest. Roger Jefe quickly dismissed the recusal motion and CEP's intervention petition.

The newspaper articles about the case revealed some extensive investigative reporting by local area journalists. Articles, for example, included interviews with executives at some of the nearby coal plants. In one story, coal employees quoted in the articles opined on the placement of Tele-Tex's solar panels as being "hugely different" from the placement that was approved. One coal company submitted affidavits from two supervisors quoted in the newspaper articles and also an affidavit of one of the local reporters who claimed to be able to verify the placement discrepancies. To corroborate this evidence, Jefe dispatched a WDEC staff person to follow up and fill in the holes in the media investigation of events. The staffer did so and wrote her findings up in a memo to Jefe. The staffer concluded that the placement discrepancies were significant.

Two months ago, Jefe sent a letter to Tele-Tex asking for any evidence it might have related to the dispute to be sent in the form of documents or witness statements. The ALJ indicated that he felt there was no need for a live hearing or any oral testimony or cross examination since very few facts seemed to be "disputed." Tele-Tex responded with several affidavits from installers and engineers indicating that the placement discrepancies were minimal.

A few days ago and without a hearing, Jefe released his decision on the matter. According to Jefe, in a one-page opinion, the "bulk of the evidence strongly suggests that the placement of Tele-Tex's solar panels differs significantly from the approved and permitted locations." The opinion further ordered dismantling of the solar arrays. In a footnote, Jefe explained that he was particularly swayed by the credibility and thoroughness of statements by the agency staffer and the local reporter who covered the case.

Assume you are an associate working for the attorneys hired by Tele-Tex. The partner on the case has asked you to write a memo detailing all of the possible procedural arguments based purely on administrative law (West Dakota state law follows the federal APA) that might be made on behalf of the company as well as discussing weaknesses in its position.

Judicial Review

Kenneth F. Warren

ADMINISTRATIVE LAW IN THE POLITICAL SYSTEM*

256-257, 260 (6th ed. 2020)

Historically, the courts have often expressed intolerance for administrative actions that undermine the principles of procedural due process. If constitutional democracy is to be preserved, agency administrators cannot be allowed to ignore laws designed to regulate their behavior or use their discretionary powers in a reckless or wanton manner. Our government employs many formal and informal controls to guard against administrative abuses while preserving minimally acceptable democratic accountability standards. Some argue that the judiciary provides the best institutional check against public administrators who act afoul. Yet the courts hear very few cases; take a relatively long time to act; are expensive, time consuming, and inconvenient; and are quite particular and frequently unpredictable about the kinds of cases they regard as reviewable. Nevertheless, they do have the power to overrule agency actions and always represent a threat to administrators who may contemplate violating procedural due process standards. . . .

It should be emphasized that it is exceedingly difficult to have a federal appellate court decision overridden, because the Supreme Court simply lacks the time to review many appellate court rulings. The Supreme Court may overrule a circuit court decision, and the circuit courts may set aside district court holdings: they often do. But it takes a constitutional amendment to overturn a Supreme Court decision on the Constitution. However, if the High Court overrules a congressional statute, Congress can void the court's decision by simply amending the statute or passing another statute, as long as the statutory changes are constitutional. Of the thousands of appellate and Supreme Court decisions involving constitutional questions that have been made over the years, virtually all have been allowed to stand by Congress. . . .

The number of civil cases filed in the district courts, where the vast majority of administrative law cases are heard, went from 59,284 in 1960, to 168,789 in 1980, to 292,076 in 2017 (latest statistics available), or up 493% from 1960. The number of federal judges has also increased dramatically in response to

---

* Reprinted with permission of Routledge (Taylor & Francis).

the increasing number of cases filed in federal court. In 1960 there were only 318 federal judges (nine Supreme Court justices, 68 circuit judges, and 241 district judges), while as of 2017, there were 851 federal judges (nine Supreme Court justices, 179 circuit judges, and 663 district judges), constituting a significant increase of 151%, yet one that is failing dismally to keep pace with the much sharper increase in caseloads, especially since the total number or Supreme Court, appellate, and district judges has remained identical since 2003.

NOTES

1. Justice White wrote decades ago. At least based upon workload, his views were prescient. In fact, the number of cert petitions has increased significantly. See Peter S. Menell & Ryan Vacca, Revisiting and Confronting the Federal Judiciary Capacity "Crisis": Charting a Path for Federal Judiciary Reform, 108 Calif. L. Rev. 789, 865 (2020) ("The number of petitions . . . steadily rose from one thousand in 1947 to a peak of more than ten thousand in 2005. It has since fallen back to around seven thousand per year."). What Justice White did not predict, however, was the decline in the relative number of petitions that would be granted. See Adam Feldman & Alexander Kappner, Finding Certainty in Cert: An Empirical Analysis of the Factors Involved in Supreme Court Certiorari Decisions from 2001-2015, 61 Vill. L. Rev. 795 (2016) ("During the 2013 Supreme Court term, for instance, 7,376 writs of certiorari (cert) were filed with the Supreme Court. The Court granted plenary review in only seventy-six or approximately 1% of these cases."). Some have characterized this "shrinking docket" phenomenon as a "paradox" given the concomitant increase in the number of cases terminating in federal courts of appeals. See Wyatt G. Sassman, How Circuits Can Fix Their Splits, 103 Marq. L. Rev. 1401, 1419-1420 (2020).

2. The Court does not have to explain the reasons for the denial of certiorari and does not disclose how Justices voted on the matter. Perhaps unsurprisingly, the nature of the Court's cert process has been described as a "black box." Carolyn Shapiro, The Law Clerk Proxy Wars: Secrecy, Accountability, and Ideology in the Supreme Court, 37 Fla. St. U. L. Rev. 101, 103 (2009). Should this system be changed? For a discussion of some of the problems with the current cert review process and one potential solution, see Daniel Epps & William Ortman, The Lottery Docket, 116 Mich. L. Rev. 705 (2018).

3. Many scholars have viewed the courts in the early days of the administrative state created during the Roosevelt administration not as guardians against a potentially abusive bureaucracy, but as agents bent on undoing reforms. See Daniel B. Rodriguez & Barry R. Weingast, Engineering the Modern Administrative State: Political Accommodation and Legal Strategy in the New Deal Era, 46 B.Y.U. L. Rev. 147, 178 (2020) (describing the "conventional wisdom" as emphasizing "the Supreme Court as distrusting of administrative agency power and just standing at the ready to strike down the efforts a collaboratively leftist president and Congress to expand regulatory power."). A more nuanced view holds that the courts of the New Deal era were merely one arm of government working to invent administrative law while protecting their interests, such as the constitutional requirements of due process. See id. at 215. How would you describe the role of the courts today? What should the role be?

4. In the context of agency review, courts must answer two questions, expressly or by implication, before the case can be disposed of on the merits: (1) Is review available? (2) What is the scope of the court's reviewing power? These are the questions to be dealt with in this chapter. In answering the first question, the reviewing judge should first look to the governing legislation. The examination will reveal one of three possibilities: "Judicial review of administrative action may be specifically provided for or specifically denied by the legislature, or the legislature may simply be silent on the subject." Lee v. Firemen's and Policemen's Civil Service Comm'n, 526 S.W.2d 553, 555 (Tex. Civ. App. 1975). Statutes that are silent with respect to judicial review may raise concerns over an excessive degree of agency discretion that can accompany a lack of judicial oversight. Although we will consider this issue later in the chapter, how might courts address this concern?

5. The typical review statute is patterned on §5 of the Federal Trade Commission Act of 1914. Under it,

> [a]ny person, partnership, or corporation required by an order of the Commission to cease and desist from using any method of competition or act or practice may obtain a review of such order in the court of appeals of the United States, within any circuit where the method of competition or the act or practice in question was used or where such person, partnership, or corporation resides or carries on business, by filing in the court, within sixty days from the date of the service of such order, a written petition praying that the order of the Commission be set aside.

15 U.S.C. §45(c). Note that the provision provides that the matter must be filed in the U.S. Court of Appeals. What is the consequence of sidestepping the federal district court? What does this suggest about the perceived role of the findings of the administrative agency?

6. What happens when Congress does not specifically identify the court that should hear any challenge? The D.C. Circuit has developed an analytical framework for dealing with the issue. In American Petroleum Institute v. SEC, 714 F.3d 1329 (D.C. Cir. 2013), the court reiterated that, while Congress was free to select the appropriate court, the normal default rule was to have the matter go first to the district court. In that case, the panel noted that the securities laws expressly provided jurisdiction in the U.S. Court of Appeals only for persons "adversely affected" by a rule under specifically enumerated provisions. Because the rule at issue was not adopted under one of the enumerated provisions, the court concluded that the matter had to be resolved first in the district court.

7. When Congress does assign jurisdiction to the court of appeals, parties typically have the option of bringing the matter to the D.C. Circuit. For example, in *American Petroleum Institute*, the court addressed §25 of the Securities Exchange Act of 1934. The Act gave jurisdiction to the circuit where the aggrieved party "resides or has his principal place of business" or "the District of Columbia Circuit. . . ." 15 U.S.C. §78y(a)(1). Because the D.C. Circuit is almost always one of the choices, it explains why the D.C. Circuit plays a critical role in determining administrative law, a role, given the volume of the cases, that may be greater than that played by the Supreme Court. Discuss this approach. Should one circuit have such a prominent role in the judicial review process? What is unique about the D.C. Circuit that affects this analysis? Some have suggested that D.C. Circuit decisions are entitled to "appropriate weight" because their universal jurisdiction over certain types of cases, especially those dealing with administrative law, affords them special expertise in the area. See Samuel L. Zimmerman, Understanding Confidentiality: Program Effectiveness and the Freedom of Information Act Exemption 4, 53 Wm. & Mary L. Rev. 1087, 1102 n. 105 (2012). Indeed, Richard Pierce has praised the D.C. Circuit for its establishment of key administrative law doctrines and its tendency to "set the table" for the Supreme Court. The Special Contributions of the D.C. Circuit to Administrative Law, 90 Geo. L.J. 779, 779-782 (2002). But these arguments assume that the D.C. Circuit *should* have the unique opportunity to tackle a disproportionate number of administrative law cases in the first place.

8. How far does the principle just stated extend? Should such a special "administrative court" to review agency acts be set up in other jurisdictions, in preference to the present system of review in the ordinary courts? See Garner v. Teamsters Local 776, 346 U.S. 485, 495 (1953), comparing "this country, where one system of law courts applies both [administrative law and private law]" with "the Continental practice which administers public law through a system of courts separate from that which deals with private law questions." What about specialized courts for particular types of cases? See Freytag v. Commissioner of Internal Revenue, 501 U.S. 868, 911 (1991) (Scalia, J., dissenting) ("Congress could . . . establish the Social Security Court — composed of judges serving 5-year terms [to review] denials of Social Security benefits. . . . The Tax Court is indistinguishable from my hypothetical Social Security Court."). What would be the consequences of this type of court? See Vanessa Casado Perez, Specialization Trend: Water Courts, 49 Env't L. 587, 591-592 (2019) ("Specialized courts are expected to make quicker decisions . . . and provide higher quality decisions . . . [but,] beyond the costs of setting up a new infrastructure[,] [s]pecialized courts present a higher risk of capture because they may have fewer players . . . who will always face a small number of judges.").

A JUDICIAL REVIEW AND STATUTORY SILENCE

STARK v. WICKARD

321 U.S. 288 (1944)

MR. JUSTICE REED delivered the opinion of the Court.

This class action was instituted in the United States District Court for the District of Columbia, to procure an injunction prohibiting the respondent

Secretary of Agriculture from carrying out certain provisions of his Order No. 4, effective August 1, 1941, dealing with the marketing of milk in the Greater Boston, Massachusetts, area. . . . The district court dismissed the suit for failure to state a claim upon which relief can be granted, and its judgment was affirmed by the Court of Appeals for the District of Columbia, 136 F.2d 786. . . .

The petitioners are producers of milk, who assert that by §§904.7(b)(5) and 904.9 of his Order, the Secretary is unlawfully diverting funds that belong to them. The courts below dismissed the action on the ground that the Act vests no legal cause of action in milk producers. . . .

The district court for the District of Columbia has a general equity jurisdiction authorizing it to hear the suit; but in order to recover, the petitioners must go further and show that the act of the Secretary amounts to an interference with some legal right of theirs. If so, the familiar principle that executive officers may be restrained from threatened wrongs in the ordinary courts in the absence of some exclusive alternative remedy will enable the petitioners to maintain their suit; but if the complaint does not rest upon a claim of which courts take cognizance, then it was properly dismissed. The petitioners place their reliance upon such rights as may be expressly or impliedly created by the Agricultural Marketing Agreement Act of 1937 and the Order issued thereunder.

. . .

The immediate object of the Act is to fix minimum prices for the sale of milk by producers to handlers. . . .

By Order No. 4, the Secretary of Agriculture did fix minimum prices for each class of milk and required each handler in the Boston area to pay not less than those minima to producers, 7 C.F.R. 1941 Supp., §904.4, less specified deductions. . . .

Were no administrative deductions necessary, the blended price per hundredweight of milk could readily be determined by dividing the total value of the milk used in the marketing area at the minimum prices for each classification by the number of hundredweight of raw milk used in the area. However, the Order requires several adjustments for purposes admittedly authorized by statute, so that the determination of the blended price as actually made is drawn from the total use value less a sum which the administrator is directed to retain to meet various incidental adjustments. In practice, each handler discharges his obligation to the producers of whom he bought milk by making two payments: one payment, the blended price, is apportioned from the values at the minimum price for the respective classes less administrative deductions and is made to the producer himself; the other payment is equal to these deductions and is made, in the language of the Order, "to the producer, through the market administrator," in order to enable the administrator to cover the differentials and deductions in question. It is the contention of the petitioners that by §904.7(b)(6) of the Order the Secretary has directed the administrator to deduct a sum for the purpose of meeting payments to cooperatives as required by §904.9, and that the Act does not authorize the Secretary to include in his order provision for payments of that kind or for deductions to meet them. . . .

These producer petitioners allege that they have delivered milk to handlers in the "Greater Boston," Massachusetts, marketing area under the provisions of the Order. They state that they are not members of a cooperative association entitled under the Order to the contested payments and that, as producers, many of them voted against the challenged amendment on the producers' referendum under §§8c(9) and 8c(19) of the Act. These allegations are admitted by the defense upon which dismissal was based, namely, that the petition fails to state a claim upon which relief could be granted. From the preceding summary of the theory and plan of the statutory regulation of minimum prices for milk affecting interstate commerce, it is clear that these petitioners have exercised the right granted them by the statute and Order to deliver their milk to "Greater Boston" handlers at the guaranteed minimum prices fixed by the Secretary of Agriculture in the Order. Sec. 904.4. Upon accepting that delivery the handler was required by the Order to pay to these producers their minimum prices in the manner set forth in §904.8. Simply stated, this section required the handler to pay directly to the producer the blended price as determined by the administrator and to pay to the producers through the administrator for use in meeting the deductions authorized by the order of the Secretary and approved by two-thirds of the producers, §8c(9)(B), the difference between the blended price and the minimum price. The Order directed the administrator to deduct from the funds coming into his hands from the producers' sale price the payments to cooperatives. §904.9.

It is this deduction which the producers challenge as beyond the Secretary's statutory power. The respondents answer that the petitioners have not such a legal interest in this expenditure or in the administrator's settlement fund as entitles them to challenge the action of the Secretary in directing the disbursement. The Government says that as the producers pay nothing into the settlement fund and receive nothing from it, they have no legally protected right which gives them standing to sue. There is, of course, no question but that the challenged deduction reduces pro tanto the amount actually received by the producers for their milk.

By the statute and Order, the Secretary has required all area handlers dealing in the milk of other producers to pay minimum prices as just described. §§904.1(6), 904.4; Act, §8c(14). The producer is not compelled by the Order to deliver (Act §8c(13)(B)) but neither can he be required to market elsewhere and if he finds a dealer in the area who will buy his product, the producer by delivery of milk comes within the scope of the Act and the Order. The Order fixing the minimum price obviously affects by direct Governmental action the producer's business relations with handlers. . . . In substance petitioners' allegation is that in effect the Order directed without statutory authority a deduction of a sum to pay the United States a sales tax on milk sold. The statute and Order create a right in the producer [petitioner] to avail himself of the protection of a minimum price afforded by Governmental action. Such a right created by statute is mandatory in character and obviously capable of judicial enforcement. . . .

The mere fact that Governmental action under legislation creates an opportunity to receive a minimum price does not settle the problem of whether or not the particular claim made here is enforceable by the District Court. The deduction for cooperatives may have detrimental effect on the price to producers and that detriment be *damnum absque injuria*. It is only when a complainant possesses something more than a general interest in the proper execution of the laws that he is in a position to secure judicial intervention. His interest must rise to the dignity of an interest personal to him and not possessed by the people generally. Such a claim is of that character which constitutionally permits adjudication by courts under their general powers.

We deem it clear that on the allegations of the complaint these producers have such a personal claim as justifies judicial consideration. . . .

However, even where a complainant possesses a claim to executive action beneficial to him, created by federal statute, it does not necessarily follow that actions of administrative officials, deemed by the owner of the right to place unlawful restrictions upon his claim, are cognizable in appropriate federal courts of first instance. . . .

Without considering whether or not Congress could create such a definite personal statutory right in an individual against a fund handled by a Federal agency, as we have here, and yet limit its enforceability to administrative determination, despite the existence of federal courts of general jurisdiction established under Article III of the Constitution, the Congressional grant of jurisdiction of this proceeding appears plain. There is no direct judicial review granted by this statute for these proceedings. The authority for a judicial examination of the validity of the Secretary's action is found in the existence of courts and the intent of Congress as deduced from the statutes and precedents as hereinafter considered.

The Act bears on its face the intent to submit many questions arising under its administration to judicial review. §§8a(6), 8c(15)(A) and (B). It specifically states that the remedies specifically provided in §8a are to be in addition to any remedies now existing at law or equity. §8a(8). This Court has heretofore construed the Act to grant handlers judicial relief in addition to the statutory review specifically provided by §8c(15). On complaint by the United States, the handler was permitted by way of defense to raise issues of a want of statutory authority to impose provisions on handlers which directly affect such handlers. . . .

With this recognition by Congress of the applicability of judicial review in this field, it is not to be lightly assumed that the silence of the statute bars from the courts an otherwise justiciable issue. . . . Here, there is no forum, other than the ordinary courts, to hear this complaint. When, as we have previously concluded in this opinion, definite personal rights are created by federal statute, similar in kind to those customarily treated in courts of law, the silence of Congress as to judicial review is, at any rate in the absence of an administrative remedy, not to be construed as a denial of authority to the aggrieved person to seek appropriate relief in the federal courts in the exercise of their general jurisdiction. When Congress passes an Act empowering administrative agencies to carry on governmental activities, the power of those agencies is circumscribed by the authority granted. This permits the courts to participate in law enforcement entrusted to administrative bodies only to the extent necessary to protect justiciable individual rights against administrative action fairly beyond the granted powers. The responsibility of determining the limits of statutory grants of authority in such instances is a judicial function entrusted to the courts by Congress by the statutes establishing courts and marking their jurisdiction.... This is very far from assuming that the courts are charged more than administrators or legislators with the protection of the rights of the people. Congress and the Executive supervise the acts of administrative agents. The powers of departments, boards and administrative agencies are subject to expansion, contraction or abolition at the will of the legislative and executive branches of the government. These branches have the resources and personnel to examine into the working of the various establishments to determine the necessary changes of function or management. But under Article III, Congress established courts to adjudicate cases and controversies as to claims of infringement of individual rights whether by unlawful action of private persons or by the exertion of unauthorized administrative power.

It is suggested that such a ruling puts the agency at the mercy of objectors, since any provisions of the Order may be attacked as unauthorized by each producer. To this objection there are adequate answers. The terms of the Order are largely matters of administrative discretion as to which there is no justiciable right or are clearly authorized by a valid act.... Technical details of the milk business are left to the Secretary and his aides. The expenses of litigation deter frivolous contentions. If numerous parallel cases are filed, the courts have ample authority to stay useless litigation until the determination of a test case.... Should some provisions of an order be held to exceed the statutory power of the Secretary, it is well within the power of a court of equity to so mold a decree as to preserve in the public interest the operation of the portion of the order which is not attacked pending amendment.

It hardly need be added that we have not considered the soundness of the allegations made by the petitioners in their complaint. The trial court is free to consider whether the statutory authority given the Secretary is a valid answer to the petitioners' contention. We merely determine the petitioners have shown a right to a judicial examination of their complaint. Reversed.

NOTES

1. Although it might be tempting to view *Stark* as a broad endorsement of judicial review where the relevant statute is silent on the subject, subsequent jurisprudence has not borne out such a reading. In 1984, the Court declined to extend its holding in *Stark* to dairy product consumers, who sought judicial review of milk market orders under the same 1937 Act. Block v. Community Nutrition Institute, 467 U.S. 340 (1984). The Court's rationale emphasized the difference between producers and consumers under the Act, indicating that the absence of a role for consumers in this complex statutory scheme suggests that permitting consumer suits would undermine Congress' intent. Id. at 351-352. The Ninth Circuit went one step further. In Pescosolido v. Block, that court held that the Act also precluded producers from seeking judicial review except when they satisfied the conditions that were present in *Stark*: (1) they claim a threat to "definite, personal rights"; (2) the agency acted outside of its delegated authority; and (3) handlers would not have standing to bring suit on the same issue. 765 F.2d 827, 832 (9th Cir. 1985); see also United Dairymen of Ariz. v. Veneman, 279 F.3d 1160, 1163, 1165 (9th Cir. 2002) (explaining and applying the decision in *Pescosolido*). However, the Eighth Circuit viewed *Community Nutrition Institute* and its interpretation of *Stark* more broadly, writing that the former requires "an examination of the over-all [*sic*] structure of the Act . . . to determine if judicial review is precluded." Minn. Milk Producers Ass'n v. Madigan, 956 F.2d 816, 818 (8th Cir. 1992). In your opinion, should *Stark* be read narrowly or broadly? Which view is more consistent with the text of the opinion?

2. What is the source of the approach to reviewability set out in *Stark*? See Abbott Laboratories v. Gardner, 387 U.S. 136, 140 (1967) ("[A] survey of our cases shows that judicial review of a final agency action by an aggrieved person will not be cut off unless there is persuasive reason to believe that such was the purpose of Congress."). To the extent it is a matter of congressional intent, is *Stark* merely setting out a rule of construction? See also Bowen v. Michigan Academy, 476 U.S. 667, 674 (1986) ("As a general matter, '[t]he mere fact that some acts are made reviewable should not suffice to support an implication of exclusion as to others. The right to review is too important to be excluded on such slender and indeterminate evidence of legislative intent.'").

3. Justice Frankfurter dissented in Stark v. Wickard. In an oft-quoted statement, he declared, "There is no such thing as a common law of judicial review in the federal courts." What does this statement mean? Assuming that this is an accurate description of the majority's holding, what are the implications of this approach?

4. To some degree, this case addresses the role of the courts in the administrative process. Are there alternatives to judicial review in the administrative context? As Justice Frankfurter noted in his dissent, the Secretary could not issue an order "fixing rates" unless approved by two-thirds of the producers. Producers, therefore, had a collective ability to block orders they opposed. Why was this not an adequate "remedy"?

B STATUTORY PRECLUSION

The Federal Administrative Procedure Act (APA), 5 U.S.C. §702, provides an explicit right of review for any person suffering "legal wrong" by an "agency action." The action must be expressly permitted in the statute or a "final agency action." See 5 U.S.C. §704. The APA, however, contains exceptions: judicial review is not permitted "to the extent that — (1) statutes preclude judicial review." 5 U.S.C. §701(a)(1).

DEPARTMENT OF ENVIRONMENTAL PROTECTION v. CIVIL SERVICE COMMISSION

579 N.E.2d 1385 (N.Y. 1991)

CHIEF JUDGE WACHTLER.

Respondent John Daly, an employee of the Department of Environmental Protection's Owl's Head Water Pollution Control Plant, was charged with threatening Jerome Gibbs, a fellow employee, and then punching him in the stomach and knocking him into a wall. Earlier in the day, Gibbs had allegedly been the subject of a racially motivated attack. According to Gibbs, Daly's threats were designed to keep Gibbs from pressing criminal charges against the two coemployees who had been involved in the earlier incident.

In July of 1986, the Department charged Daly with misconduct arising out of the incident. After a hearing at which both Daly and Gibbs testified, the Administrative Law Judge credited Gibbs' testimony and recommended that Daly be dismissed. The Commissioner of the Department adopted the findings of the Administrative Law Judge and terminated Daly's employment effective October 31, 1986.

Daly appealed the determination to the Civil Service Commission pursuant to Civil Service Law §76. The Commission reviewed the transcript of the administrative hearing and reversed the determination of guilt and penalty of dismissal, ordering Daly restored to his position with full back pay. The Department commenced this CPLR article 78 proceeding in August 1988, seeking a judgment reversing the determination of the Civil Service Commission and reinstating the determination of guilt and the penalty of dismissal. Supreme Court, New York County, transferred the matter to the Appellate Division, which confirmed the determination of the Civil Service Commission and dismissed the proceeding, with two Justices dissenting.

On this appeal, we must construe the language of section 76 of the Civil Service Law to determine whether there is any impediment to our review of the Civil Service Commission's determination. Section 76 permits certain aggrieved employees to appeal a determination in a disciplinary proceeding either to the Commission or to the courts through an article 78 proceeding. If the employee chooses to take an appeal to the Commission, as Daly did in this case, subdivision (3) provides that the Commission's decision "shall be final and conclusive, and not subject to further review in any court." We must decide, then, the extent to which this language affects our competence to review the determination at issue here. . . .

In Abbott Laboratories v. Gardner (387 U.S. 136, 140), the United States Supreme Court, applying a "clear and convincing evidence" test, held that "judicial review of a final agency action by an aggrieved person will not be cut off unless there is persuasive reason to believe that such was the purpose of Congress." . . . Our own cases state a similar rule (see, e.g., Matter of Dairylea Coop. v. Walkley, 38 N.Y.2d 6, 11).

The language contained in section 76 is clear and unambiguous in its intent to preclude judicial review of Commission decisions. The legislative history further supports this conclusion. In an April 28, 1941 letter to Governor Lehman, Senator Seymour Halpern, the sponsor of the 1941 bill which added this language to the Civil Service Law, wrote that "[the bill was] designed to make removals and disciplinary procedure a matter of administration and to keep such cases out of the courts."

Our consideration of this question does not end with the statutory language and its legislative history, however. "Even where judicial review is proscribed by statute, the courts have the power and the duty to make certain that the administrative official has not acted in excess of the grant of authority given . . . by statute or in disregard of the standard prescribed by the legislature."

. . .

[W]e emphasize that however explicit the statutory language, judicial review cannot be completely precluded. First, if a constitutional right is implicated, some sort of judicial review must be afforded the aggrieved party. We suggested as much in dictum in Long Is. Coll. Hosp. v. Catherwood (23 N.Y.2d 20, 36, n.3), in which we noted that "in the absence of some procedure for the review of a final agency action, a serious constitutional question might arise, for, as was recently observed, 'there must be some type of effective judicial review of final, substantive agency action which seriously affects personal or property rights'" (quoting Gardner v. Toilet Goods Assn., 387 U.S. 167, 177, per Fortas, J.).

Second, judicial review is mandated when the agency has acted illegally, unconstitutionally, or in excess of its jurisdiction. In Matter of Pan Am. World Airways v. New York State Human Rights Appeal Bd. (61 N.Y.2d 542, 548), for example, we stated that even if statutory language precluded review, "[s]ome standards to guide [the agency's] broad discretion are necessary if the statute is to be valid." Quoting from *Baer* . . . , we said that a court should step in if an agency acts in violation of the Constitution, statutes or its own regulations. . . .

[T]his is an extremely narrow standard of review. Once courts have determined that an agency has not acted in excess of its authority or in violation of the Constitution or of the laws of this State, judicial review is completed.

Given this limited standard, the substance of the Commission's determination in this case is unreviewable in the courts. Despite the fact that the Commission disregarded the credibility determinations of the Administrative Law Judge, there is no showing that this was unconstitutional, illegal, or outside the Commission's jurisdiction. . . .

Accordingly, the judgment of the Appellate Division should be affirmed, with costs.

NOTES

1. The court in this case acknowledged that the legislature had clearly intended to preclude judicial review. Despite this intent, courts retained at least a limited right to review agency decisions under the state constitution. As a subsequent court would note, "statutory preclusion of all judicial review of the decisions rendered by an administrative agency in every circumstance would constitute a grant of unlimited and potentially arbitrary power too great for the law to countenance." Matter of De Guzman v. State of N.Y. Civ. Serv. Comm'n, 129 A.D.3d 1189, 1190, 11 N.Y.S.3d 296 (2015); see also Michael Sebring, Restoring the Essential Safeguard: Why the *Abbott* Test for Preclusion of Judicial Review of Agency Action Is an Inadequate Method for Protecting Separation of Powers, 18 Geo. J. L. & Pub. Pol'y 181, 189 (Under full preclusion of judicial review, "[a]rbitrary and capricious agency actions cannot be challenged in court. There is no check on abuse of agency discretion. Would-be challengers are precluded from claiming that the agency acted outside the scope of its statutory authority. People who have had their constitutional rights violated by agency action are barred entirely from any judicial remedy."). Do you agree with this reasoning? Could there ever be instances where the legislature should have a right to preclude all judicial review?

2. Under the APA, review of final agency action is not permitted to the extent precluded by statute. Preclusion, however, must confront the "'strong presumption' favoring judicial review of administrative action." Mach Mining, LLC v. EEOC, 575 U.S. 480, 486 (2015). Is this presumption appropriate? What can be the consequences to a complex regulatory framework when the Court reads into it a right of review that was not contemplated by Congress? As a preliminary matter, the APA creates a presumption in favor of judicial review of agency action that can be rebutted "only if the relevant statute precludes judicial review, or if the action is committed to agency discretion by law." Bourdon v. United States Dep't of Homeland Security, 983 F.3d 473, 477-478 (mem) (11th Cir. 2020) (citations omitted) (internal quotations omitted). To determine whether a statute actually has preclusive effect, courts must then consider not just the language of the statute in question, but the overall structure of the statute itself. Id. at 478. Finally, the agency bears the burden of demonstrating that there is clear and convincing evidence that a particular statute precludes all judicial review. Id. When a statute precludes judicial review of only certain types of agency actions, a court may then need to determine whether the action at issue actually falls within those categories. See Am. Hospital Ass'n v. Azar, 964 F.3d 1230, 1237 (D.C. Cir. 2020). Even if the court concludes, at this stage, that judicial review is precluded, it may permit judicial review nonetheless if the agency acted outside of its statutory authority or in an unconstitutional manner, as suggested in Department of Environmental Protection v. Civil Service Commission. See also Alaka'I Na Keiki, Inc. v. Matayoshi, 277 P.3d 988, 1007 (Haw. 2012) (holding that even if "final and conclusive" language precluded judicial review, it would not apply in this instance in which petitioners alleged that the agency acted outside of its statutory authority).

3. Although "strong," the presumption favoring judicial review can be rebutted. Should the burden of rebutting the presumption depend upon the type of claim? What if, for example, the claim is constitutional? See Webster v. Doe, 486 U.S. 592, 603 (1988) ("where Congress intends to preclude judicial review of constitutional claims[,] its intent to do so must be clear"). The Court explicitly required that the government make this "heightened showing" "to avoid the 'serious constitutional question' that would arise if a federal statute were construed to deny any judicial forum for a colorable constitutional claim." Id. What are some of the consequences of this approach? See Mila Sohoni, Agency Adjudication and Judicial Nondelegation: An Article III Canon, 107 Nw. U. L. Rev. 1569, 1611 (2013) ("Courts go to extraordinary lengths to read statutory language that straightforwardly precludes review to permit review of constitutional claims (and sometimes nonconstitutional claims too), even in the face of quite reasonable accusations that judicial insistence on securing review is thwarting evident legislative intent. The tenacity with which courts search for pathways to judicial review reflects the importance of that review.").

4. What about nonconstitutional claims? Presumptions and rules of construction exist here as well. See Sackett v. EPA, 566 U.S. 120, 128 (2012) (noting that while APA creates a presumption of review, the presumption "may be overcome by inferences of intent drawn from the statutory scheme as a whole") (quoting Block v. Community Nutrition Institute, 467 U.S. 340, 345, 104 S. Ct. 2450, 81 L. Ed. 2d 270 (1984)). How is this approach different from the test applied in the case of the preclusion of constitutional claims?

5. Given this approach, how might a federal court construe the language at issue in the opinion by Chief Judge Wachtler in *Department of Environmental Protection*? The court in that case viewed language indicating that a decision "shall be final and conclusive, and not subject to further review in any court" as "clear and unambiguous." Would a federal court, for example, be likely to find that the language precluded review of constitutional claims? See Cuzzo Speed Techs., L.L.C. v. Lee, 136 S. Ct. 2131, 2141 (2016) (holding that a statute making certain agency decisions "final and unappealable" barred review of certain claims, but not necessarily constitutional claims); Rodrigue v. United States, 968 F.2d 1430, 1434 (1st Cir. 1992) (holding that a statute making agency decisions "final and conclusive" precluded judicial review of at least nonconstitutional claims in light of legislative history indicating that that such decisions were final and conclusive "for all purposes").

6. Nonetheless, assuming Congress uses unequivocal language, can judicial review be entirely eliminated, even for constitutional violations? Is there a due process right to judicial review? See Marshall, J., dissenting in Ortwein v. Schwabs, 410 U.S. 656, 666 (1973): "The extent to which the State may commit to administrative agencies the unreviewable authority to restrict pre-existing rights is one of the great questions of constitutional law about which courts and commentators have debated for generations." Compare the view expressed by

Justice Brandeis in an oft-quoted statement: "The supremacy of law demands that there shall be an opportunity to have some court decide . . . whether the proceeding in which the facts were adjudicated was conducted regularly." St. Joseph Stock Yards Co. v. United States, 298 U.S. 38, 84 (1936) (Brandeis, J., concurring). See also Bartlett v. Bowen, 816 F.2d 695, 703 (D.C. Cir. 1987):

> In our view, a statutory provision precluding *all* judicial review of constitutional issues removes from the courts an essential judicial function under our implied constitutional mandate of separation of powers, and deprives an individual of an independent forum for the adjudication of a claim of constitutional right. We have little doubt that such a "limitation on the jurisdiction of *both* state and federal courts to review the constitutionality of federal legislation . . . would be [an] unconstitutional" infringement of due process.

See also Luis Inaraja Vera, Delayed Judicial Review of Agency Action, 56 Harv. J. on Legis. 199, 241-242 (2019) (Judicial review is "a necessary structural element of our legal system" given that review is necessary to prevent arbitrary government action, which the Constitution prohibits. But, review is uncertain primarily because of the Supreme Court's failure to provide a "clear framework delineating Congress's power to restrict the jurisdiction of federal courts.").

7. What impact does judicial review have on agency behavior? In *Sackett*, "[t]he Government warn[ed] that the EPA [was] less likely to use [compliance] orders if they [were] subject to judicial review." 566 U.S. at 130. Justice Scalia, in writing for the majority, responded, "That may be true — but it will be true for all agency actions subjected to judicial review. The APA's presumption of judicial review is a repudiation of the principle that efficiency of regulation conquers all." Id. What does he mean by this observation? Is he correct?

C APA AND REVIEW OF DISCRETION

Express statutory denial is not the only exception to judicial review included in the APA. Section 701 also denies a right of review for matters that are "committed to agency discretion by law." 5 U.S.C. §701(a)(2).

HECKLER v. CHANEY

470 U.S. 821 (1985)

JUSTICE REHNQUIST delivered the opinion of the Court.

This case presents the question of the extent to which a decision of an administrative agency to exercise its "discretion" not to undertake certain enforcement actions is subject to judicial review under the Administrative Procedure Act, 5 U.S.C. §501 et seq. (APA). . . .

I

Respondents have been sentenced to death by lethal injection of drugs under the laws of the States of Oklahoma and Texas. Those States, and several others, have recently adopted this method for carrying out the capital sentence. Respondents first petitioned the [Food and Drug Administration] FDA, claiming that the drugs used by the States for this purpose, although approved by the FDA for the medical purposes stated on their labels, were not approved for use in human executions. They alleged that the drugs had not been tested for the purpose they were to be used, and that, given that the drugs would likely be administered by untrained personnel, it was also likely that the drugs would not induce the quick and painless death intended. They urged that use of these drugs for human execution was the "unapproved use of an approved drug" and constituted a violation of the [Food, Drug, and Cosmetic] Act's ["FDCA"] prohibitions against "misbranding." . . . Accordingly, respondents claimed that the FDA was required to approve the drugs as "safe and effective" for human execution before they could be distributed in interstate commerce. See 21 U.S.C. §355. They therefore requested the FDA to take various investigatory and enforcement actions to prevent these perceived violations; they requested the FDA to affix warnings to the labels of all the drugs stating that they were unapproved and unsafe for human execution, to send statements to the drug manufacturers and prison administrators stating that the drugs should not be so used, and to adopt procedures for seizing the drugs from state prisons and to recommend the prosecution of all those in the chain of distribution who knowingly distribute or purchase the drugs with intent to use them for human execution.

The FDA Commissioner responded, refusing to take the requested actions. The Commissioner first detailed his disagreement with respondents' understanding of the scope of FDA jurisdiction over the unapproved use of approved drugs for human execution, concluding that FDA jurisdiction in the area was generally unclear but in any event should not be exercised to interfere with this particular aspect of state criminal justice systems. He went on to state:

> Were FDA clearly to have jurisdiction in the area, moreover, we believe we would be authorized to decline to exercise it under our inherent discretion to decline to pursue certain enforcement matters. The unapproved use of approved drugs is an area in which the case law is far from uniform. Generally, enforcement proceedings in this area are initiated only when there is a serious danger to the public health or a blatant scheme to defraud. We cannot conclude that those dangers are present under State lethal injection laws, which are duly authorized statutory enactments in furtherance of proper State functions. . . .

Respondents then filed the instant suit in the United States District Court for the District of Columbia, claiming the same violations of the FDCA and asking that the FDA be required to take the same enforcement actions requested in the prior petition. Jurisdiction was grounded in the general federal-question jurisdiction statute, 28 U.S.C. §1331, and review of the agency action was sought under the judicial review provisions of the Administrative Procedure Act, 5 U.S.C. §§701-706. . . .

II

. . .

[T]his case turns on the important question of the extent to which determinations by the FDA *not to exercise* its enforcement authority over the use of drugs in interstate commerce may be judicially reviewed. That decision in turn involves the construction of two separate but necessarily interrelated statutes, the APA and the FDCA.

The APA's comprehensive provisions for judicial review of "agency actions" are contained in 5 U.S.C. §§701-706. Any person "adversely affected or aggrieved" by agency action, see §702, including a "failure to act," is entitled to "judicial review thereof," as long as the action is a "final agency action for which there is no other adequate remedy in a court," see §704. The standards to be applied on review are governed by the provisions of §706. But before any review at all may be had, a party must first clear the hurdle of §701(a). That section provides that the chapter on judicial review "applies, according to the provisions thereof, except to the extent that — (1) statutes preclude judicial review; or (2) agency action is committed to agency discretion by law." Petitioner urges that the decision of the FDA to refuse enforcement is an action "committed to agency discretion by law" under §701(a)(2).

This Court has not had occasion to interpret this second exception in §701(a) in any great detail. On its face, the section does not obviously lend itself to any particular construction; indeed, one might wonder what difference exists between §(a)(1) and §(a)(2). The former section seems easy in application; it requires construction of the substantive statute involved to determine whether Congress intended to preclude judicial review of certain decisions. . . . But one could read the language "committed to agency discretion *by law*" in §(a)(2) to require a similar inquiry. In addition, commentators have pointed out that construction of §(a)(2) is further complicated by the tension between a literal reading of §(a)(2), which exempts from judicial review those decisions committed to agency "discretion," and the primary scope of review prescribed by §706(2)(A) — whether the agency's action was "arbitrary, capricious, or an *abuse of discretion.*" How is it, they ask, that an action committed to agency discretion can be unreviewable and yet courts still can review agency actions for abuse of that discretion? . . . The APA's legislative history provides little help on this score. Mindful, however, of the common-sense principle of statutory construction that sections of a statute generally should be read "to give effect, if possible, to every clause . . . ," . . . we think there is a proper construction of §(a)(2) which satisfies each of these concerns.

This Court first discussed §(a)(2) in Citizens to Preserve Overton Park v. Volpe, 401 U.S. 402 (1971). That case dealt with the Secretary of Transportation's approval of the building of an interstate highway through a park in Memphis,

Tennessee. The relevant federal statute provided that the Secretary "shall not approve" any program or project using public parkland unless the Secretary first determined that no feasible alternatives were available. . . . Interested citizens challenged the Secretary's approval under the APA, arguing that he had not satisfied the substantive statute's requirements. This Court first addressed the "threshold question" of whether the agency's action was at all reviewable. After setting out the language of §701 (a), the Court stated:

> In this case, there is no indication that Congress sought to prohibit judicial review and there is most certainly no "showing of 'clear and convincing evidence' of a . . . legislative intent" to restrict access to judicial review. Abbott Laboratories v. Gardner, 387 U.S. 136, 141 (1967). . . .
>
> Similarly, the Secretary's decision here does not fall within the exception for action "committed to agency discretion." This is a very narrow exception. . . . The legislative history of the Administrative Procedure Act indicates that it is applicable in those rare instances where "statutes are drawn in such broad terms that in a given case there is no law to apply." S. Rep. No. 752, 79th Cong., 1st Sess., 26 (1945).

Overton Park, *supra*, at 410 (footnote omitted).

The above quote answers several of the questions raised by the language of §701(a), although it raises others. First, it clearly separates the exception provided by §701(a)(1) from the §701(a)(2) exception. The former applies when Congress has expressed an intent to preclude judicial review. The latter applies in different circumstances; even where congress has not affirmatively precluded review, review is not to be had if the statute is drawn so that a court would have no meaningful standard against which to judge the agency's exercise of discretion. In such a case, the statute ("law") can be taken to have "committed" the decision-making to the agency's judgment absolutely. This construction avoids conflict with the "abuse of discretion" standard of review in §706 — if no judicially manageable standards are available for judging how and when an agency should exercise its discretion then it is impossible to evaluate agency action for "abuse of discretion." In addition, this construction satisfies the principle of statutory construction mentioned earlier, by identifying a separate class of cases to which §701(a)(2) applies.

To this point our analysis does not differ significantly from that of the Court of Appeals. That court purported to apply the "no law to apply" standard of *Overton Park*. We disagree, however, with that court's insistence that the "narrow construction" of §(a)(2) required application of a presumption of reviewability even to an agency's decision not to undertake certain enforcement actions. Here we think the Court of Appeals broke with tradition, case law, and sound reasoning.

Overton Park did not involve an agency's refusal to take requested enforcement action. It involved an affirmative act of approval under a statute that set clear guidelines for determining when such approval should be given. Refusals to take enforcement steps generally involve precisely the opposite situation, and in that situation we think the presumption is that judicial review is not available. This Court has recognized on several occasions over many years that an agency's decision not to prosecute or enforce, whether through civil or criminal process, is a decision generally committed to an agency's absolute discretion.... This recognition of the existence of discretion is attributable in no small part to the general unsuitability for judicial review of agency decisions to refuse enforcement.

The reasons for this general unsuitability are many. First, an agency decision not to enforce often involves a complicated balancing of a number of factors which are peculiarly within its expertise. Thus, the agency must not only assess whether a violation has occurred, but whether agency resources are best spent on this violation or another, whether the agency is likely to succeed if it acts, whether the particular enforcement action requested best fits the agency's overall policies, and indeed, whether the agency has enough resources to undertake the action at all. An agency generally cannot act against each technical violation of the statute it is charged with enforcing. The agency is far better equipped than the courts to deal with the many variables involved in the proper ordering of its priorities. Similar concerns animate the principle of administrative law that courts generally will defer to an agency's construction of the statute it is charged with implementing, and to the procedures it adopts for implementing that statute....

In addition to these administrative concerns, we note that when an agency refuses to act it generally does not exercise its *coercive* power over an individual's liberty or property rights, and thus does not infringe upon areas that courts often are called upon to protect. Similarly, when an agency *does* act to enforce, that action itself provides a focus for judicial review, inasmuch as the agency must have exercised its power in some manner. The action at least can be reviewed to determine whether the agency exceeded its statutory powers.... Finally, we recognize that an agency's refusal to institute proceedings shares to some extent the characteristics of the decision of a prosecutor in the Executive Branch not to indict — a decision which has long been regarded as the special province of the Executive Branch, inasmuch as it is the executive who is charged by the Constitution to "take Care that the Laws be faithfully executed." U.S. Const., Art. II, §3.

We of course only list the above concerns to facilitate understanding of our conclusion that an agency's decision not to take enforcement action should be presumed immune from judicial review under §701(a)(2). For good reasons, such a decision has traditionally been "committed to agency discretion," and we believe that the Congress enacting the APA did not intend to alter that tradition.... In so stating, we emphasize that the decision is only presumptively unreviewable; the presumption may be rebutted where the substantive statute has provided guidelines for the agency to follow in exercising its enforcement powers. Thus, in establishing this presumption in the APA, Congress did not set agencies free to disregard legislative direction in the statutory scheme that the agency administers. Congress may limit an agency's exercise of enforcement power if it wishes, either by setting substantive priorities, or by otherwise circumscribing an agency's power to discriminate among issues or cases it will pursue.

III

[Ed. Note: At this point, the Court discusses whether any provision of the FDCA requires that the agency pursue enforcement action, thus removing such decisions from agency discretion. The Court finds no such provisions.]

We therefore conclude that the presumption that agency decisions not to institute proceedings are unreviewable under §701(a)(2) of the APA is not overcome by the enforcement provisions of the FDCA. The FDA's decision not to take the enforcement actions requested by respondents is therefore not subject to judicial review under the APA. The general exception to reviewability provided by §701(a)(2) for action "committed to agency discretion" remains a narrow one, see *Overton Park*, 401 U.S. 402 (1971), but within that exception are included agency refusals to institute investigative or enforcement proceedings, unless Congress has indicated otherwise. In so holding, we essentially leave to Congress, and not to the courts, the decision as to whether an agency's refusal to institute proceedings should be judicially reviewable. No colorable claim is made in this case that the agency's refusal to institute proceedings violated any constitutional rights of respondents, and we do not address the issue that would be raised in such a case. Cf. Johnson v. Robison, 415 U.S. 361, 366 (1974). Yick Wo v. Hopkins, 118 U.S. 356, 372-374 (1886). The fact that the drugs involved in this case are ultimately to be used in imposing the death penalty must not lead this Court or other courts to import profound differences of opinion over the meaning of the Eighth Amendment to the United States Constitution into the domain of administrative law. The judgment of the Court of Appeals is reversed.

NOTES

1. Justice Marshall, concurring in the judgment, asserted that the decision laid down the rule "that agency decisions not to take 'enforcement action' are unreviewable unless Congress has rather specifically indicated otherwise." Marshall stated,

> I write separately to argue for a different basis of decision: that refusals to enforce, like other agency actions, are reviewable in the absence of a "clear and convincing" congressional intent to the contrary, but that such refusals warrant deference when, as in this case, there is nothing to suggest that an agency with enforcement discretion has abused that discretion.

2. According to Trout Unlimited v. Pirzadeh, *Heckler* held, "[a]n agency's decision not to take enforcement action is presumptively unreviewable, but that presumption may be overcome if a meaningful legal standard constrains the agency's discretion." No. 20-35504, 2021 U.S. App. LEXIS 18064, at *45 (9th Cir. June 17, 2021). What are some other examples of areas where agencies may have unreviewable discretion? See id. at *27 (holding that the Clean Water Act precluded judicial review of certain decisions, like "declining to initiate notice and comment with respect to a particular geographical area or . . . declining to determine that discharge into an area will have an unacceptable adverse effect" because "[t]he statute grant[ed] unfettered discretion to the Administrator to make those decisions." (internal quotation marks omitted)).

3. What about efforts to challenge broad statutory mandates given to agencies? In Norton v. Southern Utah Wilderness Alliance, 542 U.S. 55 (2004), plaintiffs challenged the policies of the Bureau of Land Management (BLM) concerning the use of off-road vehicles in certain wilderness areas. In upholding the dismissal of the claim, the unanimous Court noted that challenges under the APA had to be "discrete" agency actions. The BLM was subject to a statutory mandate to manage wilderness areas "in a manner so as not to impair the suitability of such areas for preservation as wilderness." The provision, while mandatory, gave the agency "a great deal of discretion in deciding how to achieve it." As the opinion reasoned: "If courts were empowered to enter general orders compelling compliance with broad statutory mandates, they would necessarily be empowered, as well, to determine whether compliance was achieved — which would mean that it would ultimately become the task of the supervising court, rather than the agency, to work out compliance with the broad statutory mandate, injecting the judge into day-to-day agency management." Do you agree with this analysis?

4. What about a statute that gives the head of an agency the power, in his or her "discretion[,] to terminate any officer or employee" that the agency head "shall deem . . . necessary or advisable in the interests of the United States . . . "? Does the provision provide a meaningful standard of review, or does it leave the decision entirely to the discretion of the agency head, therefore making it unreviewable? The answer is in Webster v. Doe, 486 U.S. 592 (1988).

5. Statutes often contain what can only be characterized as "vague" standards. Take, for example, the EEOC's statutory obligation to engage in informal methods of "conciliation" before suing an employer for discrimination. Can a party subject the conciliation process to judicial review? See Mach Mining LLC v. EEOC, 575 U.S. 480, 488 (2015) ("[T]he statute provides the EEOC with wide latitude over the conciliation process, and that feature becomes significant when we turn to defining the proper scope of judicial review.").

6. The Supreme Court discussed Heckler v. Chaney in its 2020 decision in Department of Homeland Security v. Regents of the University of California, *supra* p. 713. In addressing the government's argument that the government action was unreviewable as committed to agency discretion by law, the Court wrote:

> The APA establishes a "basic presumption of judicial review [for] one 'suffering legal wrong because of agency action.'" That presumption can be rebutted by a showing that the relevant statute "preclude[s]" review, §701(a)(1), or that the "agency action is committed to agency discretion by law," §701(a)(2). The latter exception is at issue here. To "honor the presumption of review, we have read the exception in §701(a)(2) quite narrowly," confining it to those rare "administrative decision[s] traditionally left to agency discretion." This limited category of unreviewable actions includes an

agency's decision not to institute enforcement proceedings, and it is on that exception that the Government primarily relies.

In *Chaney* several death-row inmates petitioned the Food and Drug Administration (FDA) to take enforcement action against two States to prevent their use of certain drugs for lethal injection. The Court held that the FDA's denial of that petition was presumptively unreviewable in light of the well-established "tradition" that "an agency's decision not to prosecute or enforce" is "generally committed to an agency's absolute discretion." We identified a constellation of reasons that underpin this tradition. To start, a non-enforcement decision "often involves a complicated balancing of a number of factors which are peculiarly within [the agency's] expertise," such as "whether the particular enforcement action requested best fits the agency's overall policies." The decision also mirrors, "to some extent," a prosecutor's decision not to indict, which has "long been regarded as the special province of the Executive Branch." And, as a practical matter, "when an agency refuses to act" there is no action to "provide[ ] a focus for judicial review."

The Government contends that a general non-enforcement policy is equivalent to the individual non-enforcement decision at issue in *Chaney*. In each case, the Government argues, the agency must balance factors peculiarly within its expertise, and does so in a manner akin to a criminal prosecutor. Building on that premise, the Government argues that the rescission of a non-enforcement policy is no different — for purposes of reviewability — from the adoption of that policy. While the rescission may lead to increased enforcement, it does not, by itself, constitute a particular enforcement action. Applying this logic to the facts here, the Government submits that DACA is a non-enforcement policy and that its rescission is therefore unreviewable.

But we need not test this chain of reasoning because DACA is not simply a non-enforcement policy. For starters, the DACA Memorandum did not merely "refus[e] to institute proceedings" against a particular entity or even a particular class. Instead, it directed USCIS to "establish a clear and efficient process" for identifying individuals who met the enumerated criteria. Based on this directive, USCIS solicited applications from eligible aliens, instituted a standardized review process, and sent formal notices indicating whether the alien would receive the two-year forbearance. These proceedings are effectively "adjudicat[ions]." And the result of these adjudications — DHS's decision to "grant deferred action," is an "affirmative act of approval," the very opposite of a "refus[al] to act." In short, the DACA Memorandum does not announce a passive non-enforcement policy; it created a program for conferring affirmative immigration relief. The creation of that program — and its rescission — is an "action [that] provides a focus for judicial review."

The benefits attendant to deferred action provide further confirmation that DACA is more than simply a non-enforcement policy. As described above, by virtue of receiving deferred action, the 700,000 DACA recipients may request work authorization and are eligible for Social Security and Medicare. Unlike an agency's refusal to take requested enforcement action, access to these types of benefits is an interest "courts often are called upon to protect."

Because the DACA program is more than a non-enforcement policy, its rescission is subject to review under the APA.

Department of Homeland Security v. Regents of the University of California, ___U.S.___, 140 S. Ct. 1891, 1905-07 (June 18, 2020).

The government argues in *DACA* that, for the purpose of reviewability, rescission of the DACA non-enforcement policy is not different from adoption of that policy the first place. Although rescinding the policy would certainly lead to increased enforcement, they argue that the rescission is a simple non-enforcement and, thus, unreviewable. The Court majority, though, noted that DACA was more than a simple non-enforcement policy, analogizing it to an "adjudication." What facts supported the Court's determination that DACA was more than a non-enforcement policy? Did the situation here provide more of a "focus for judicial review," than does the usual determination of whether to pursue prosecution?

MASSACHUSETTS v. EPA

549 U.S. 497 (2007)

JUSTICE STEVENS delivered the opinion of the Court.

A well-documented rise in global temperatures has coincided with a significant increase in the concentration of carbon dioxide in the atmosphere. Respected scientists believe the two trends are related. For when carbon dioxide is released into the atmosphere, it acts like the ceiling of a greenhouse, trapping solar energy and retarding the escape of reflected heat. It is therefore a species — the most important species — of a "greenhouse gas."

Calling global warming "the most pressing environmental challenge of our time," a group of States, local governments, and private organizations, alleged in a petition for certiorari that the Environmental Protection Agency (EPA) has abdicated its responsibility under the Clean Air Act to regulate the emissions of four greenhouse gases, including carbon dioxide. Specifically, petitioners asked us to answer two questions concerning the meaning of §202(a)(1) of the Act: whether EPA has the statutory authority to regulate greenhouse gas emissions from new motor vehicles; and if so, whether its stated reasons for refusing to do so are consistent with the statute....

I

Section 202(a)(1) of the Clean Air Act . . . provides:

> "The [EPA] Administrator shall by regulation prescribe (and from time to time revise) in accordance with the provisions of this section, standards applicable to the emission of any air pollutant from any class or classes of new motor vehicles or new motor vehicle engines, which in his judgment cause, or contribute to, air pollution which may reasonably be anticipated to endanger public health or welfare. . . ."

The Act defines "air pollutant" to include "any air pollution agent or combination of such agents, including any physical, chemical, biological, radioactive . . . substance or matter which is emitted into or otherwise enters the ambient air." §7602(g). "Welfare" is also defined broadly: among other things, it includes "effects on . . . weather . . . and climate." §7602(h). . . .

On October 20, 1999, a group of 19 private organizations filed a rulemaking petition asking EPA to regulate "greenhouse gas emissions from new motor vehicles under §202 of the Clean Air Act." . . .

Fifteen months after the petition's submission, EPA requested public comment on "all the issues raised in [the] petition," adding a "particular" request for comments on "any scientific, technical, legal, economic or other aspect of these issues that may be relevant to EPA's consideration of this petition." . . . EPA received more than 50,000 comments over the next five months. . . .

On September 8, 2003, EPA entered an order denying the rulemaking petition. . . . The agency gave two reasons for its decision: (1) that contrary to the opinions of its former general counsels, the Clean Air Act does not authorize EPA to issue mandatory regulations to address global climate change, . . . and (2) that even if the agency had the authority to set greenhouse gas emission standards, it would be unwise to do so at this time. . . .

V

The scope of our review of the merits of the statutory issues is narrow. As we have repeated time and again, an agency has broad discretion to choose how best to marshal its limited resources and personnel to carry out its delegated responsibilities. See Chevron U.S.A. Inc. v. NRDC, 467 U.S. 837, 842-845 (1984). That discretion is at its height when the agency decides not to bring an enforcement action. Therefore, in Heckler v. Chaney, 470 U.S. 821 (1985), we held that an agency's refusal to initiate enforcement proceedings is not ordinarily subject to judicial review. Some debate remains, however, as to the rigor with which we review an agency's denial of a petition for rulemaking.

There are key differences between a denial of a petition for rulemaking and an agency's decision not to initiate an enforcement action. . . . In contrast to nonenforcement decisions, agency refusals to initiate rulemaking "are less frequent, more apt to involve legal as opposed to factual analysis, and subject to special formalities, including a public explanation." . . . They moreover arise out of denials of petitions for rulemaking which (at least in the circumstances here) the affected party had an undoubted procedural right to file in the first instance. Refusals to promulgate rules are thus susceptible to judicial review, though such review is "extremely limited" and "highly deferential." . . .

EPA concluded in its denial of the petition for rulemaking that it lacked authority under 42 U.S.C. §7521(a)(1) to regulate new vehicle emissions because carbon dioxide is not an "air pollutant" as that term is defined in §7602. In the alternative, it concluded that even if it possessed authority, it would decline to do so because regulation would conflict with other administration priorities. As discussed earlier, the Clean Air Act expressly permits review of such an action. §7607(b)(1). We therefore "may reverse any such action found to be . . . arbitrary, capricious, an abuse of discretion, or otherwise not in accordance with law." §7607(d)(9). . . .

NOTES

1. In finding the decision subject to review, the Court upheld what has been characterized as a "long-standing" rule of the D.C. Circuit that denial of rulemaking petitions is subject to review. See Jack M. Beerman, The Turn Toward Congress in Administrative Law, 89 B.U. L. Rev. 727 (2009). But shouldn't the decision turn on congressional intent and the specific language of the statute? In this case, the head of the agency could, "in his judgment," proceed with rulemaking. Doesn't this language suggest that the issue was entirely discretionary? See Am. Horse Prot. Ass'n, Inc. v. Lyng, 812 F.2d 1, 4-5 (D.C. Cir. 1987) (explaining why denials of petitions for rulemaking are subject to judicial review and that review of such decisions is highly deferential).

2. What if the agency had simply ignored the petition? See Sidney Shapiro, Rulemaking Inaction and the Failure of Administrative Law, 68 Duke L.J. 1805, 1820 (2019) ("An agency has an obligation under the APA to respond to a rulemaking petition within a reasonable amount of time, and this requirement is judicially enforceable. . . . But the factors [for identifying a reasonable delay] are not particularly helpful . . . because their comparative importance has never been established."). Is this case really an attempt to discern congressional intent or the Court's view of the best result? How much might this holding interfere with the regulatory agenda of an administration? See id. at 1818 (arguing that the highly deferential attitude of courts when reviewing an agency's denial of a rulemaking petition means that "[a]n agency is likely to prevail" in lawsuits challenging such denials).

3. What is the effect of the decision? Does it mean that the EPA must initiate rulemaking proceedings with respect to greenhouse gases?

4. In the aftermath of the decision in Massachusetts v. EPA, the EPA did propose and adopt rules addressing carbon-dioxide emissions, particularly in connection with automobiles. Consistent with the rule of unintended consequences, however, the Supreme Court subsequently held that because greenhouse gases were subject to the Clean Air Act, common law public nuisance claims against private power companies were preempted. See American Elec. Power Co. v. Conn, 564 U.S. 410 (2011).

D STANDING

APA §702. Right of Review

A person suffering legal wrong because of agency action, or adversely affected or aggrieved by agency action within the meaning of a relevant statute, is entitled to judicial review thereof. An action in a court of the

> United States seeking relief other than money damages and stating a claim that an agency or an officer or employee thereof acted or failed to act in an official capacity or under color of legal authority shall not be dismissed nor relief therein be denied on the ground that it is against the United States or that the United States is an indispensable party.

The law of standing in the administrative context has generated a number of complicated issues. The issue has a constitutional dimension. As the Supreme Court has noted:

> [A]t an irreducible minimum, Art. III requires the party who invokes the court's authority to "show that he personally has suffered some actual or threatened injury as a result of the putatively illegal conduct of the defendant," . . . and that the injury "fairly can be traced to the challenged action" and "is likely to be redressed by a favorable decision." . . .
>
> The requirement of "actual injury redressable by the court" . . . serves several of the "implicit policies embodied in Article III." . . . It tends to assure that the legal questions presented to the court will be resolved, not in the rarified atmosphere of a debating society, but in a concrete factual context conducive to a realistic appreciation of the consequences of judicial action. The "standing" requirement serves other purposes. Because it assures an actual factual setting in which the litigant asserts a claim of injury in fact, a court may decide the case with some confidence that its decision will not pave the way for lawsuits which have some, but not all, of the facts of the case actually decided by the court.

Valley Forge Christian College v. Americans United, 454 U.S. 464, 472 (1982). In addition, the Court has grafted onto the standing requirement a need to show that the relevant plaintiff falls within the "zone of interest," a vague standard that focuses on the particular statutory framework at issue.

Establishing injury in fact for purposes of Article III standing has, however, proved to be surprisingly difficult.

LUJAN v. DEFENDERS OF WILDLIFE

504 U.S. 555 (1992)

JUSTICE SCALIA delivered the opinion of the court. . . .

This case involves a challenge to a rule promulgated by the Secretary of the Interior interpreting §7 of the Endangered Species Act of 1973 (ESA), 87 Stat. 892, as amended, 16 U.S.C. §1536, in such fashion as to render it applicable only to actions within the United States or on the high seas. The preliminary issue, and the only one we reach, is whether respondents here, plaintiffs below, have standing to seek judicial review of the rule.

The ESA, 87 Stat. 884, as amended, 16 U.S.C. §1531 *et seq.*, seeks to protect species of animals against threats to their continuing existence caused by man. . . . The ESA instructs the Secretary of the Interior to promulgate by regulation a list of those species which are either endangered or threatened under enumerated criteria, and to define the critical habitat of these species. 16 U.S.C. §§1533, 1536. Section 7(a)(2) of the Act then provides, in pertinent part:

> "Each Federal agency shall, in consultation with and with the assistance of the Secretary [of the Interior], insure that any action authorized, funded, or carried out by such agency . . . is not likely to jeopardize the continued existence of any endangered species or threatened species or result in the destruction or adverse modification of habitat of such species which is determined by the Secretary, after consultation as appropriate with affected States, to be critical." 16 U.S.C. §1536(a)(2).

. . .

Over the years, our cases have established that the irreducible constitutional minimum of standing contains three elements: First, the plaintiff must have suffered an "injury in fact" — an invasion of a legally-protected interest which is (a) concrete and particularized, . . . and (b) "actual or imminent, not 'conjectural' or 'hypothetical.'" . . . Second, there must be a causal connection between the injury and the conduct complained of — the injury has to be "fairly . . . trace[able] to the challenged action of the defendant, and not . . . th[e] result [of] the independent action of some third party not before the court." . . . Third, it must be "likely," as opposed to merely "speculative," that the injury will be "redressed by a favorable decision." . . . The party invoking federal jurisdiction bears the burden of establishing these elements. . . . Since they are not mere pleading requirements but rather an indispensable part of the plaintiff's case, each element must be supported in the same way as any other matter on which the plaintiff bears the burden of proof, i.e., with the manner and degree of evidence required at the successive stages of the litigation. . . .

When the suit is one challenging the legality of government action or inaction, the nature and extent of facts that must be averred (at the summary judgment stage) or proved (at the trial stage) in order to establish standing depends considerably upon whether the plaintiff is himself an object of the action (or forgone action) at issue. If he is, there is ordinarily little question that the action or inaction has caused him injury, and that a judgment preventing or requiring the action will redress it. When, however, as in this case, a plaintiff's asserted injury arises from the government's allegedly unlawful regulation (or lack of regulation) of *someone else*, much more is needed. In that circumstance, causation and redressability ordinarily hinge on the response of the regulated (or regulable) third party to the government action or inaction — and perhaps on the response of others as well. The existence of one or more of the essential elements of standing "depends on the unfettered choices made by independent actors not before the courts and whose exercise of broad and legitimate discretion the courts cannot presume either to control or to predict" . . . and it becomes the burden of the plaintiff to adduce facts showing that those choices have been or will be made in such manner as to produce causation and permit redressability of injury.... Thus, when the plaintiff is not himself the object of the government action or inaction he challenges, standing is not precluded, but it is ordinarily "substantially more difficult" to establish....

A

Respondents' claim to injury is that the lack of consultation with respect to certain funded activities abroad "increas[es] the rate of extinction of endangered and threatened species." Of course, the desire to use or observe an animal species, even for purely aesthetic purposes, is undeniably a cognizable interest for purpose of standing.... "But the 'injury in fact' test requires more than an injury to a cognizable interest. It requires that the party seeking review be himself among the injured." ... To survive the Secretary's summary judgment motion, respondents had to submit affidavits or other evidence showing, through specific facts, not only that listed species were in fact being threatened by funded activities abroad, but also that one or more of respondents' members would thereby be "directly" affected apart from their "'special interest' in th[e] subject." ...

With respect to this aspect of the case, the Court of Appeals focused on the affidavits of two Defenders' members — Joyce Kelly and Amy Skilbred. Ms. Kelly stated that she traveled to Egypt in 1986 and "observed the traditional habitat of the endangered nile crocodile there and intend[s] to do so again, and hope[s] to observe the crocodile directly," and that she "will suffer harm in fact as a result of [the] American ... role ... in overseeing the rehabilitation of the Aswan High Dam on the Nile ... and [in] develop[ing] ... Egypt's ... Master Water Plan."

Ms. Skilbred averred that she traveled to Sri Lanka in 1981 and "observed th[e] habitat" of "endangered species such as the Asian elephant and the leopard" at what is now the site of the Mahaweli Project funded by the Agency for International Development (AID), although she "was unable to see any of the endangered species"; "this development project," she continued, "will seriously reduce endangered, threatened, and endemic species habitat including areas that I visited ... [, which] may severely shorten the future of these species"; that threat, she concluded, harmed her because she "intend[s] to return to Sri Lanka in the future and hope[s] to be more fortunate in spotting at least the endangered elephant and leopard."

When Ms. Skilbred was asked at a subsequent deposition if and when she had any plans to return to Sri Lanka, she reiterated that "I intend to go back to Sri Lanka," but confessed that she had no current plans: "I don't know [when]. There is a civil war going on right now. I don't know. Not next year, I will say. In the future."

We shall assume for the sake of argument that these affidavits contain facts showing that certain agency-funded projects threaten listed species — though that is questionable. They plainly contain no facts, however, showing how damage to the species will produce "imminent" injury to Mss. Kelly and Skilbred. That the women "had visited" the areas of the projects before the projects commenced proves nothing. As we have said in a related context, "'[p]ast exposure to illegal conduct does not in itself show a present case or controversy regarding injunctive relief . . . if unaccompanied by any continuing, present adverse effects.'" . . . And the affiants' profession of an "inten[t]" to return to the places they had visited before — where they will presumably, this time, be deprived of the opportunity to observe animals of the endangered species — is simply not enough. Such "some day" intentions — without any description of concrete plans, or indeed even any specification of *when* the some day will be — do not support a finding of the "actual or imminent" injury that our cases require.

Besides relying upon the Kelly and Skilbred affidavits, respondents propose a series of novel standing theories. The first, inelegantly styled "ecosystem nexus," proposes that any person who uses *any part* of a "contiguous ecosystem" adversely affected by a funded activity has standing even if the activity is located a great distance away. This approach, as the Court of Appeals correctly observed, is inconsistent with our opinion in *National Wildlife Federation*, which held that a plaintiff claiming injury from environmental damage must use the area affected by the challenged activity and not an area roughly "in the vicinity" of it. 497 U.S., at 887-889. . . .

B

Besides failing to show injury, respondents failed to demonstrate redressability. Instead of attacking the separate decisions to fund particular projects allegedly causing them harm, the respondents chose to challenge a more generalized level of government action (rules regarding consultation), the invalidation of which would affect all overseas projects. This programmatic approach has obvious practical advantages, but also obvious difficulties insofar as proof of causation or redressability is concerned. As we have said in another context, "suits challenging, not specifically identifiable Government violations of law, but the particular programs agencies establish to carry out their legal obligations . . . [are], even when premised on allegations of several instances of violations of law, . . . rarely if ever appropriate for federal court adjudication." . . .

The most obvious problem in the present case is redressability. Since the agencies funding the projects were not parties to the case, the District Court could accord relief only against the Secretary. He could be ordered to revise his regulation to require consultation for foreign projects. But this would not remedy respondents' alleged injury unless the funding agencies were bound by the Secretary's regulation, which is very much an open question. Whereas in other contexts the ESA is quite explicit as to the Secretary's controlling authority, . . . with respect to consultation the initiative, and hence arguably the initial responsibility for determining statutory necessity, lies with the agencies. . . .

The short of the matter is that redress of the only injury-in-fact respondents complain of requires action (termination of funding until consultation) by the individual funding agencies; and any relief the District Court could have provided in this suit against the Secretary was not likely to produce that action. . . .

A further impediment to redressability is the fact that the agencies generally supply only a fraction of the funding for a foreign project. AID [United States Agency for International Development], for example, has provided less than 10 percent of the funding for the Mahaweli Project. Respondents have produced nothing to indicate that the projects they have named will either be suspended, or do less harm to listed species, if that fraction is eliminated. As in *Simon*, 426 U.S., at 43-44, it is entirely conjectural whether the nonagency activity that affects respondents will be altered or affected by the agency activity they seek to achieve. There is no standing.

We hold that respondents lack standing to bring this action and that the Court of Appeals erred in denying the summary judgment motion filed by the United States. The opinion of the Court of Appeals is hereby reversed, and the cause remanded for proceedings consistent with this opinion.

It is so ordered.

NOTES

1. During the oral argument, Chief Justice Rehnquist strikingly stated his difficulty with petitioners' standing claim: "This is beginning to sound like the 'House That Jack Built.' We're talking about the secretary of the interior and World Bank contributions to something in Thailand. There seems to be so much distance." Was the Chief Justice's comment fair to petitioners' standing argument?

2. How far does *Lujan* go in using the "injury in fact" test to limit standing? The Court seemed to emphasize the indeterminate nature of the injury. As the Court noted: "Such 'some day' intentions — without any description of concrete plans, or indeed even any specification of *when* the same day will be — do not support a finding of the 'actual or imminent' injury that our cases require." In Bennett v. Spear, 520 U.S. 154 (1997), *infra* p. 635, in contrast, the Court found "injury in fact" even though the complained of behavior would result only in a reduction in the aggregate amount of available water. This alone did not necessarily mean a reduction in the amount of water to the irrigation districts bringing suit. Instead, that depended upon the water allocation practices adopted by the agency following the reduction. Nonetheless, the Court found sufficient injury to meet the Article III requirement of "injury in fact." "Given petitioners' allegation that the amount of available water will be reduced and that they will be adversely affected thereby, it is easy to presume specific facts under which petitioners will be injured — for example, the Bureau's distribution of the reduction pro rata among its customers." Are these two cases consistent?

3. To demonstrate injury in fact, plaintiffs must show something more than speculative injury. The Supreme Court has sometimes required that prospective injury at least be "certainly impending." In Clapper v. Amnesty International USA, 568 U.S. 398 (2013), plaintiffs, attorneys, and human rights, labor, legal, and media organizations, asserted that they incurred "injury" by a provision in the

Foreign Intelligence Surveillance Act (FISA) that authorized surveillance of non-U.S. persons reasonably believed to be located outside the United States. Plaintiffs alleged that their conversations could be the subject of surveillance under the provisions. The Court (by a 5-to-4 decision) held that the allegation of injury was "highly speculative" and relied on "a highly attenuated chain of possibilities . . . [and] does not satisfy the requirement that threatened injury must be certainly impending." For the injury to occur, the Government would, among other things, have to target the Plaintiffs' communications, rely on the challenged provision as the means of surveillance, obtain a court order approving the surveillance, and successfully capture the communications. Moreover, the fact that the Government could use other authority for the surveillance meant that even in the event surveillance occurred, the injury was not "fairly traceable" to the provision in the FISA at issue. What would plaintiffs have to do to successfully challenge this statute? Given this "highly attenuated chain," is the majority in fact dispatching the standard that harm need only be imminent? Alternatively, was the Court indicating that the degree of imminence required might vary with the facts of the case? See Ree v. Zappos.com, Inc., 888 F.3d 1020, 1026 (9th Cir. 2018) ("*Clapper's* standing analysis was 'especially rigorous' because the case arose in a sensitive national security context involving intelligence gathering and foreign affairs, and because the plaintiffs were asking the courts to declare actions of the executive and legislative branches unconstitutional.").

4. The Court continues to define the contours of the injury in fact requirement. In Spokeo v. Robins, the Court emphasized that the alleged injury must be *both* concrete *and* particularized. 136 S. Ct. 1540, 1548 (2016) ("Particularization is necessary to establish injury in fact, but it is not sufficient. An injury in fact must also be 'concrete.'"). *Spokeo* considered whether a consumer had standing to sue a company under the Fair Credit Reporting Act ("FCRA") on the ground that the company had disseminated incorrect information about him, thereby violating the statutory provisions of the FCRA requiring that such companies "'follow reasonable procedures to assure maximum possible accuracy of'" consumer reports. See id. at 1545-1546. The Court's task was to determine whether the "intangible harm" that Robins had suffered as a result of Spokeo's statutory violation "constitute[d] injury in fact." Id. at 1549. Although the Court recognized that "Congress is well positioned to identify intangible harms that meet minimum Article III requirements," it held that "Congress' role in identifying and elevating intangible harms does not mean that a plaintiff *automatically* satisfies the injury-in-fact requirement." Id. Rather, "Article III standing requires a concrete injury even in the context of a statutory violation." Id. This holding precludes "bare procedural violation[s]" alone from satisfying the injury in fact requirement, but still permits standing where a statutory violation creates a "risk of real harm" that is sufficient to satisfy the concreteness requirement. Id. at 1549-1550. Does *Spokeo* facilitate the analysis required to identify injury in fact, or does it "create[] more confusion?" See James Hannaway, Standing on Shaky Ground: How Circuit Courts Reconcile Legal Rights and Injuries in Fact After *Spokeo v. Robins*, 87 Geo. Wash. L. Rev. 706, 711 (2019). James Hannaway's analysis of 38 post-*Spokeo* circuit court decisions suggests the latter; relying on a variety of possible framework interpretations of *Spokeo* and a number of statutory interpretive tools, exactly half of the cases surveyed found injury in fact. Id. at 728, 730, 735.

5. What about the role of organizations in bringing actions on behalf of their members? They may do so although the injury still must meet the requirement that it be concrete and particularized. Sierra Club v. Morton, 405 U.S. 727, 734-736 (1972). Thus, in Summers v. Earth Island Institute, 555 U.S. 488 (2009), the Court found that a "group of organizations dedicated to protecting the environment" did not have standing to challenge regulations issued by the Forest Service where an affidavit executed by a member was "insufficient to satisfy the requirement of imminent injury. . . ." The dissent proposed what the majority described as "a hitherto unheard-of test for organizational standing" that would effectively recognize that some of the 70,000 members would suffer the requisite injury as a result of the regulations under challenge. What do you make of this approach? For a description of the tests currently used to assess whether an organization has standing to sue on behalf of its members, see Mark Hall & Christian Turner, The Nature of Standing, 29 Wm. & Mary Bill Rts. J. 67, 84-86 (2020).

It is not enough to meet the Article III requirements of an injury in fact to have standing. The Supreme Court added an additional interpretive gloss more closely tied to the purpose of the relevant statute. Sometimes described as "prudential" limitations on standing, sometimes attributed to the intent of Congress, parties seeking to bring actions under specific statutory frameworks also needed to fit within the statute's zone of interest.

BENNETT v. SPEAR

520 U.S. 154 (1997)

SCALIA, J., delivered the opinion for a unanimous Court.

This is a challenge to a biological opinion issued by the Fish and Wildlife Service in accordance with the Endangered Species Act of 1973 (ESA), 87 Stat. 884, as amended, 16 U.S.C. §1531 et seq., concerning the operation of the Klamath Irrigation Project by the Bureau of Reclamation, and the project's impact on two varieties of endangered fish. The question for decision is whether the petitioners, who have competing economic and other interests in Klamath Project water, have standing to seek judicial review of the biological opinion under the citizen-suit provision of the ESA, §1540(g)(1), and the Administrative Procedure Act (APA), 80 Stat. 392, as amended, 5 U.S.C. §701 et seq.

I

The ESA requires the Secretary of the Interior to promulgate regulations listing those species of animals that are "threatened" or "endangered" under specified criteria, and to designate their "critical habitat." 16 U.S.C. §1533. The ESA further requires each federal agency to "insure that any action authorized, funded, or carried out by such agency . . . is not likely to jeopardize the continued existence of any endangered species or threatened species or result in the destruction or adverse modification of habitat of such species which is determined by the Secretary . . . to be critical." §1536(a)(2). If an agency determines that action it proposes to take may adversely affect a listed species, it must engage in formal consultation with the Fish and Wildlife Service, as delegate of the Secretary, ibid.; 50 C.F.R. §402.14 (1995), after which the Service must provide the agency with a written statement (the Biological Opinion) explaining how the proposed action will affect the species or its habitat, 16 U.S.C. §1536(b)(3)(A). If the Service concludes that the proposed action will "jeopardize the continued existence of any [listed] species or result in the destruction or adverse modification of [critical habitat]," §1536(a)(2), the Biological Opinion must outline any "reasonable and prudent alternatives" that the Service believes will avoid that consequence, §1536(b)(3)(A). Additionally, if the Biological Opinion concludes that the agency action will not result in jeopardy or adverse habitat modification, or if it offers reasonable and prudent alternatives to avoid that consequence, the Service must provide the agency with a written statement (known as the "Incidental Take Statement") specifying the "impact of such incidental taking on the species," any "reasonable and prudent measures that the [Service] considers necessary or appropriate to minimize such impact," and setting forth "the terms and conditions . . . that must be complied with by the Federal agency . . . to implement [those measures]." §1536(b)(4).

The Klamath Project, one of the oldest federal reclamation schemes, is a series of lakes, rivers, dams and irrigation canals in northern California and southern Oregon. The project was undertaken by the Secretary of the Interior pursuant to the Reclamation Act of 1902, 32 Stat. 388, as amended, 43 U.S.C. §371 et seq., and the Act of Feb. 9, 1905, 33 Stat. 714, and is administered by the Bureau of Reclamation, which is under the Secretary's jurisdiction. In 1992, the Bureau notified the Service that operation of the project might affect the Lost River Sucker (*Deltistes luxatus*) and Shortnose Sucker (*Chasmistes brevirostris*), species of fish that were listed as endangered in 1988, see 53 Fed. Regs. 27,130-27,133 (1988). After formal consultation with the Bureau in accordance with 50 C.F.R. §402.14 (1995), the Service issued a Biological Opinion which concluded that the "'long-term operation of the Klamath Project was likely to jeopardize the continued existence of the Lost River and shortnose suckers.'" App. to Pet. for Cert. 3. The Biological Opinion identified "reasonable and prudent alternatives" the Service believed would avoid jeopardy, which included the maintenance of minimum water levels on Clear Lake and Gerber reservoirs. The Bureau later notified the Service that it intended to operate the project in compliance with the Biological Opinion.

Petitioners, two Oregon irrigation districts that receive Klamath Project water and the operators of two ranches within those districts, filed the present action against the director and regional director of the Service and the Secretary of the Interior. Neither the Bureau nor any of its officials is named as defendant.

The complaint asserts that the Bureau "has been following essentially the same procedures for storing and releasing water from Clear Lake and Gerber reservoirs throughout the twentieth century," id. at 36; that "there is no scientifically or commercially available evidence indicating that the populations of endangered suckers in Clear Lake and Gerber reservoirs have declined, are declining, or will decline as a result" of the Bureau's operation of the Klamath Project, id. at 37; that "there is no commercially or scientifically available evidence indicating that the restrictions on lake levels imposed in the Biological Opinion will have any beneficial effect on the . . . populations of suckers in Clear Lake and Gerber reservoirs," id. at 39; and that the Bureau nonetheless "will abide by the restrictions imposed by the Biological Opinion," id. at 32. . . .

The District Court dismissed the complaint for lack of jurisdiction. It concluded that petitioners did not have standing because their "recreational, aesthetic, and commercial interests . . . do not fall within the zone of interests sought to be protected by ESA." Id. at 28. The Court of Appeals for the Ninth Circuit affirmed. Bennett v. Plenert, 63 F.3d 915 (1995). It held that the "zone of interests" test limits the class of persons who may obtain judicial review not only under the APA, but also under the citizen-suit provision of the ESA, 16 U.S.C. §1540(g), and that "only plaintiffs who allege an interest in the preservation of endangered species fall within the zone of interests protected by the ESA," 63 F.3d at 919 (emphasis in original). We granted certiorari. 517 U.S. 1102 (1996).

In this Court, petitioners raise two questions: first, whether the prudential standing rule known as the "zone of interests" test applies to claims brought under the citizen-suit provision of the ESA; and second, if so, whether petitioners have standing under that test notwithstanding that the interests they seek to vindicate are economic rather than environmental.

II

We first turn to the question the Court of Appeals found dispositive: whether petitioners lack standing by virtue of the zone-of-interests test. Although petitioners contend that their claims lie both under the ESA and the APA, we look first at the ESA because it may permit petitioners to recover their litigation costs, see 16 U.S.C. §1540(g)(4), and because the APA by its terms independently authorizes review only when "there is no other adequate remedy in a court," 5 U.S.C. §704.

The "zone of interests" formulation was first employed in Association of Data Processing Service Organizations, Inc. v. Camp, 397 U.S. 150 (1970). There, certain data processors sought to invalidate a ruling by the Comptroller of the Currency authorizing national banks to sell data processing services on the ground that it violated, inter alia, §4 of the Bank Service Corporation Act of 1962, 76 Stat. 1132, which prohibited bank service corporations from engaging in "any activity other than the performance of bank services for banks." The Court of Appeals had held that the banks' data-processing competitors were without standing to challenge the alleged violation of §4. In reversing, we stated the applicable prudential standing requirement to be "whether the interest sought to be protected by the complainant is arguably within the zone of interests to be protected or regulated by the statute or constitutional guarantee in question." *Data Processing, supra,* at 153. Data Processing, and its companion case, Barlow v. Collins, 397 U.S. 159 (1970), applied the zone-of-interests test to suits under the APA, but later cases have applied it also in suits not involving review of federal administrative action, see Dennis v. Higgins, 498 U.S. 439, 449 (1991); Boston Stock Exchange v. State Tax Comm'n, 429 U.S. 318, 320-321, n.3 (1977); see also Note, A Defense of the "Zone of Interests" Standing Test, 1983 Duke L.J. 447, 455-456, and nn.40-49 (1983) (cataloging lower court decisions), and have specifically listed it among other prudential standing requirements of general application, see, e.g., *Allen, supra,* at 751; *Valley Forge, supra,* at 474-475. We have made clear, however, that the breadth of the zone of interests varies according to the provisions of law at issue, so that what comes within the zone of interests of a statute for purposes of obtaining judicial review of administrative action under the "'generous review provisions'" of the APA may not do so for other purposes, Clarke v. Securities Industry Assn., 479 U.S. 388, 400, n.16 (1987) (quoting *Data Processing,* supra, at 156).

Congress legislates against the background of our prudential standing doctrine, which applies unless it is expressly negated. See Block v. Community Nutrition Institute, 467 U.S. 340, 345-348 (1984). Cf. Associated Gen. Contractors of Cal., Inc. v. Carpenters, 459 U.S. 519, 532-533, and n.28 (1983). The first question in the present case is whether the ESA's citizen-suit provision . . . negates the zone-of-interests test (or, perhaps more accurately, expands the zone of interests). We think it does. The first operative portion of the provision says that "any person may commence a civil suit" — an authorization of remarkable breadth when compared with the language Congress ordinarily uses. Even in some other environmental statutes, Congress has used more restrictive formulations, such as "[any person] having an interest which is or may be adversely affected," 33 U.S.C. §1365(g) (Clean Water Act); see also 30 U.S.C. §1270(a) (Surface Mining Control and Reclamation Act) (same); "any person suffering legal wrong," 15 U.S.C. §797(b)(5) (Energy Supply and Environmental Coordination Act); or "any person having a valid legal interest which is or may be adversely affected . . . whenever such action constitutes a case or controversy," 42 U.S.C. §9124(a) (Ocean Thermal Energy Conversion Act). And in contexts other than the environment, Congress has often been even more restrictive. In statutes concerning unfair trade practices and other commercial matters, for example, it has authorized suit only by "any person injured in his business or property," 7 U.S.C. §2305(c); see also 15 U.S.C. §72 (same), or only by "competitors, customers, or subsequent purchasers," §298(b).

Our readiness to take the term "any person" at face value is greatly augmented by two interrelated considerations: that the overall subject matter of this legislation is the environment (a matter in which it is common to think all persons have an interest) and that the obvious purpose of the particular provision in question is to encourage enforcement by so-called "private attorneys general" — evidenced by its elimination of the usual amount-in-controversy and diversity-of-citizenship requirements, its provision for recovery of the costs of litigation (including even expert witness fees), and its reservation to the Government of a right of first refusal to pursue the action initially and a right to intervene later. Given these factors, we think the conclusion of expanded standing follows a fortiori from our decision in Trafficante v. Metropolitan Life Ins. Co., 409 U.S. 205 (1972), which held that standing was expanded to the full extent permitted under Article III by a provision of the Civil Rights Act of 1968 that authorized "any person who claims to have been injured by a discriminatory housing practice" to sue for violations of the Act. There also we relied on textual evidence of a statutory scheme to rely on private litigation to ensure compliance with the Act. See id. at 210-211. The statutory language here is even clearer, and the subject of the legislation makes the intent to permit enforcement by every man even more plausible.

It is true that the plaintiffs here are seeking to prevent application of environmental restrictions rather than to implement them. But the "any person" formulation applies to all the causes of action authorized by §1540(g) — not only to actions against private violators of environmental restrictions, and not only to actions against the Secretary asserting underenforcement under §1533, but also to actions against the Secretary asserting overenforcement under §1533. As we shall discuss below, the citizen-suit provision does favor environmentalists in that it covers all private violations of the Act but not all failures of the Secretary to meet his administrative responsibilities; but there is no textual basis for saying that its expansion of standing requirements applies to environmentalists alone. The Court of Appeals therefore erred in concluding that petitioners lacked standing under the zone-of-interests test to bring their claims under the ESA's citizen-suit provision. . . .

The Court of Appeals erred in affirming the District Court's dismissal of petitioners' claims for lack of jurisdiction. Petitioners' complaint alleges facts sufficient to meet the requirements of Article III standing, and none of their ESA claims is precluded by the zone-of-interests test. Petitioners' §1533 claim is reviewable under the ESA's citizen-suit provision, and petitioners' remaining claims are reviewable under the APA.

The judgment of the Court of Appeals is reversed, and the case is remanded for further proceedings consistent with this opinion.

It is so ordered.

NOTES

1. What is the basis for the "zone of interests" requirement for standing? Some courts described the approach as a prudential requirement. However, the Supreme Court has described that label as "misleading." Lexmark International, Inc. v. Static Control Components, Inc., 572 U.S. 118, 125 (2014). In Lexmark International, the Court noted that the zones of interest test turned on the intent of Congress and therefore required application of "traditional principles of statutory interpretation." Id. at 127. At the same time, the Court presumed that Congress, in specifying those persons entitled to judicial review, did so "against the background of the zone-of-interests limitation" and therefore that was the applicable standard unless "expressly negated." What do you make of this analysis? Is it an accurate description of congressional intent? See also Bank of America Corp. v. City of Miami, Florida, 137 S. Ct. 1296 (2017) (describing issue as "whether the statute grants the plaintiff the cause of action that he asserts"). What difference does it make whether the zone of interest is a prudential requirement or a matter of congressional intent?

2. Is the zone of interest test even necessary? See New Hampshire Bankers Ass'n v. Nelson, 302 A.2d 810, 811 (N.H. 1973) ("The defendant supports his lack-of-standing contention by arguing adoption of the federal bipartite standing test wherein the complainant must allege not only that he suffered 'injury in fact' but also that 'the interest sought to be protected by the complainant is arguably within the zone of interests to be protected or regulated by the statute. . . .' . . . The second part of this test has been severely criticized by those favoring the single injury in fact test that has been adopted by most State courts. . . . We hold that the legislature has indicated a preference for the single 'injury in fact' test in appeals under RSA ch. 541."). See also Carson v. Simon, 978 F.3d 1051, 1058 (8th Cir. 2020) (per curiam) ("Where constitutional standing is present, refusing to hear a case based on prudential standing 'is in some tension with . . . the principle that a federal court's obligation to hear and decide cases within its jurisdiction is virtually unflagging.'").

3. Just one term after *Bennett*, the U.S. Supreme Court arguably stretched "zone of interests" analysis even further in National Credit Union Administration (NCUA) v. First National Bank, 522 U.S. 479 (1998). There, the NCUA's interpretation of the Federal Credit Union Act (FCUA) to expand the definition of credit union was challenged by a group of banks and a banking association because of the banking competition implications of the ruling. A federal district court dismissed the suit on the grounds that the banks and banking association were not within the FCUA's "zone of interests" because, despite the banking entities claim of competitive injury, the FCUA was passed "to establish a place for credit unions within the country's financial market, and specifically not to protect the competitive interest of banks." The Supreme Court disagreed. The Court stated that "[a]lthough our prior cases have not stated a clear rule for determining when a plaintiff's interest is 'arguably within the zone of interests' to be protected by a statute, they nonetheless establish that we should not inquire whether there has been a congressional intent to benefit the would-be plaintiff." Id. at 488. According to the Court, "[t]he proper inquiry is simply 'whether the interest sought to be protected by the complainant is arguably within the zone of interests to be protected . . . by the statute.' Hence in applying the 'zone of interests' test, we do not ask whether, in enacting the statutory provision at issue, Congress specifically intended to benefit the plaintiff. Instead, we first discern the interests 'arguably . . . to be protected' by the statutory provision at issue; we then inquire whether the plaintiff's interests affected by the agency action in question are among them." Id. at 492. The Court found that the FCUA restricts membership in credit unions to definable groups, and, in so doing, "restricts the markets that every federal credit union can serve. . . . The link between . . . regulation of federal credit union membership and its limitation on the markets that federal credit unions can serve is unmistakable. Thus, even if it cannot be said that Congress had the specific purpose of benefiting commercial banks, one of the interests 'arguably . . . to be protected' by [the FCUA] is an interest in limiting the markets that federal credit unions can serve. This interest is precisely the interest of [banks] affected by the NCUA's interpretation. . . . As competitors of federal credit unions, [banks] certainly have an interest in limiting the markets that federal credit unions can serve, and the NCUA's interpretation has affected that interest by allowing federal credit unions to increase their customer base." Id. at 492-493.

4. Do the *FCUA* and *Bennett* cases serve to eviscerate any "zone of interests" requirement for standing? One might argue that they do for a variety of reasons: first, since the Supreme Court issued two decisions regarding "zone of interests" in two consecutive terms where it overturned federal court use of the doctrine to limit judicial review, the Court might be trying to send a message; and, second, it may make sense that the Court would eliminate a secondary limiting doctrine like the "zone of interests" test as it moved to rein in its definition of "injury in fact," and restrict standing as it seems to do in *Lujan, supra*. Despite these indications from the Court, however, some argue that circuit courts have continued to apply the zone of interest test in ways that have limited individuals' access to legal recourse on the basis of congressional intent. See Joseph S. Diedrich, Bostock v. Lexmark: Is the Zone of Interests Test a Canon of Donut Holes, 89 U. Cin. L. Rev. 814, 826-827 (2021).

E PRIMARY JURISDICTION

For judicial review to be available, the timing of the review action must be proper. Two principal doctrines have been developed to enable the question of timing to be answered: (1) primary jurisdiction and (2) exhaustion of administrative remedies. Primary jurisdiction and its relation to exhaustion are discussed in the California opinion below. The exhaustion doctrine is discussed in detail in the next section.

FARMERS INSURANCE EXCHANGE v. SUPERIOR COURT

826 P.2d 730 (Cal. 1992)

LUCAS, Chief Justice.

The People, through the Attorney General (real party in interest), filed suit against various insurers (petitioners) under the Unfair Practices Act (Bus. & Prof. Code, §§17000 et seq.). We granted review to decide whether this judicial action should be stayed under the doctrine of "primary jurisdiction" pending administrative action by the Commissioner of the Department of Insurance....

We conclude that in the absence of legislation clearly addressing whether a court may exercise discretion under the primary jurisdiction doctrine, a court may exercise such discretion and may decline to hear a suit until the administrative process has been invoked and completed. We hold that prior resort to the administrative process is required in the circumstances of this case and that the trial court abused its discretion in concluding otherwise.

I. FACTS AND PROCEDURE

The People filed a two-count complaint alleging petitioners violated sections 1861.02 and 1861.05 [of the California Insurance Code] ... by refusing to offer a "Good Driver Discount policy" to all eligible applicants.

In their first cause of action, the People claim that since November 1989, petitioners have violated the above provisions by: (i) refusing to offer and sell a Good Driver Discount policy to any person who meets the standards of section 1861.025; (ii) refusing to charge persons who qualify for the Good Driver Discount policy a rate "at least 20% below the rate the insured would otherwise have been charged for the same coverage"; (iii) unlawfully using the absence of insurance as a criterion for determining eligibility for a Good Driver Discount policy, and generally, for the setting of automobile insurance rates and premiums; and (iv) "unfairly discriminating in eligibility and rates for insurance for persons who qualify under the statutory criteria for a Good Driver Discount policy."

Under the first cause of action the People seek an order pursuant to Code of Civil Procedure section 526, enjoining petitioners from violating section 1861.02, subdivisions (b)(1), (b)(2), and (c), and section 1861.05, subdivision (a)....

Under the second cause of action the complaint seeks the injunctive relief described above pursuant to Business and Professions Code section 17204, a $2,500 civil penalty against each petitioner for each violation of law pursuant to Business and Professions Code section 17206, and "such other relief as this Court deems just and proper."

Petitioners demurred to both causes of action on the ground, inter alia, that the People's suit was precluded by their failure to pursue and exhaust administrative remedies....

As to the second cause of action ... the court overruled the demurrer, concluding that ... the People may proceed under the Business and Professions Code "even though there is a separate statutory scheme for enforcement of section 1861.02."

Petitioners sought a writ of mandate in the Court of Appeal challenging the propriety of this latter ruling. In an unpublished opinion, the Court of Appeal agreed with the trial court. It reasoned that "exhaustion of administrative remedies" is not required before an action under section 17200 of the Business and Professions Code may be prosecuted because (i) the People's second cause of action seeks a remedy that is "merely cumulative" to administrative remedies sought in the first count, and (ii) the courts can more promptly resolve the issues in this case than can the Insurance Commissioner.

As noted, we conclude prior resort to the administrative process is appropriate in these circumstances, and we therefore reverse the decision of the Court of Appeal....

1. Provisions for Administrative Hearings and Judicial Review

Section 1858 establishes an administrative scheme under which "[a]ny person aggrieved by any rate charged, rating plan, rating system, or underwriting rule... may" file a complaint with the Insurance Commissioner. (Id. subd. (a).) If, after considering the insurer's response, the commissioner finds the complaint states "probable cause" of a violation of the McBride Act, the commissioner "shall proceed as provided in Section 1858.1." (§1858, subd. (c).)

Section 1858.1 sets out procedures for the commissioner's investigation and resolution of the complaint. If the commissioner determines there is "good cause" to believe an insurer's rating scheme fails to comply with the requirements of the chapter, he or she "shall give notice in writing to that insurer, ... stating therein in what manner and to what extent that noncompliance is alleged to exist and specifying therein a reasonable time ... in which that noncompliance may be corrected, and specifying therein the amount of any penalty that may be due...." (Id. 1st par.) The section also sets out procedures to be followed by an insurer to contest the allegation of noncompliance, or, inter alia, to enter into a consent order. (Id. 2d par.)

Section 1858.2 sets out procedures for public hearings on disputed issues and requires the commissioner to issue a decision within 60 days after submission following a hearing. Sections 1858.3 through 1858.5 concern powers granted the commissioner, monitoring of complaints, and suspension of an insurer's license for noncompliance with the commissioner's orders. Sections 1858.07 and 1859.1 set out monetary penalties for an insurer's failure to comply with statutory rate-setting provisions, or the commissioner's orders.

Finally, section 1858.6 provides for judicial review following "[a]ny finding, ... ruling or order made by the commissioner under this chapter ... in accordance with the provisions of the Code of Civil Procedure." ...

III. THE PRIMARY JURISDICTION DOCTRINE

A. Development of the Doctrine

The judicially created doctrine of "primary jurisdiction" (also referred to as the doctrine of "prior resort" or "preliminary jurisdiction"), originated in Texas & Pac. Ry. v. Abilene Cotton Oil Co. (1907) 204 U.S. 426 (hereafter *Abilene*), and as explained below, most of the development of the doctrine has occurred in the federal courts.

1. Abilene

In *Abilene, supra*, 204 U.S. 426, a shipper sued a railroad in state court under the common law to recover alleged unreasonable amounts charged for transporting interstate freight. Such common law suits had been regularly entertained before enactment of the Interstate Commerce Act (Commerce Act) and creation of the Interstate Commerce Commission (ICC) in 1887. Under the Commerce Act, Congress granted the ICC power to hear such complaints by shippers, and to order reparations to those injured. Despite provisions of the Commerce Act allowing a litigant to elect between administrative enforcement of statutory rights and judicial enforcement of common law rights, the high court declined to allow the common law suit in the first instance. Instead, it ruled that in order to promote uniformity and consistency of rate regulations, the shipper

> must . . . primarily invoke redress through the Interstate Commerce Commission. . . . [If], without previous action by the Commission, power might be exerted by courts and juries generally to determine the reasonableness of an established rate, it would follow that unless all courts reached an identical conclusion a uniform standard of rates in the future would be impossible, as the standard would fluctuate and vary, depending on the divergent conclusions reached as to reasonableness by the various courts called upon to consider the subject as an original question.

The court concluded that the act should be construed to allow only those judicial actions that seek "redress of such wrongs as can, consistently with the context of the act, be redressed by courts without previous action by the Commission, and, therefore, does not imply the power in a court to primarily hear complaints concerning wrongs of the character of the one here complained of." . . .

2. Merchants

The doctrine of *Abilene, supra*, 204 U.S. 426, was refined and clarified in [Great N. Ry. v. Merchants Elev. Co. 259 U.S. 285 (1922)], another case in which a shipper attempted to press suit against a railway to recover asserted overcharges. Justice Brandeis, speaking for the court, allowed the state court suit to proceed because the issue presented in that case — i.e., the proper interpretation of a tariff — was one of law and neither involved disputed facts, nor required the exercise of expertise possessed by the ICC. The court explained,

> Preliminary resort to the Commission [is necessary when] the enquiry is essentially one of fact and of discretion in technical matters; and uniformity can be secured only if its determination is left to the Commission. Moreover, that determination is reached ordinarily upon voluminous and conflicting evidence, for the adequate appreciation of which acquaintance with many intricate facts of transportation is indispensable; and such acquaintance is commonly to be found only in a body of experts. But what construction shall be given to a railroad tariff presents ordinarily a question of law which does not differ in character from those presented when the construction of any other document is in dispute.

3. Western Pacific

In a third railroad shipping case, United States v. Western Pac. R. Co. (1956) 352 U.S. 59 (hereafter *Western Pacific*), the shipper (the United States government) filed suit in the Court of Claims to recover alleged overcharges. The issue presented was similar to that in *Merchants, supra*, 259 U.S. 285, i.e., the construction of a railroad tariff. Specifically, the question posed was whether shipments of steel bomb cases filled with napalm gel should be classified as "incendiary bombs" (subject to a high first-class tariff rate) or merely "gasoline in steel drums" (subject to a lower, fifth-class rate).

The high court considered the factors articulated in *Abilene, supra*, 204 U.S. 426, and *Merchants, supra*, 259 U.S. 285, i.e., (i) "the desirable uniformity which would obtain if initially a specialized agency passed on certain types of administrative questions" (*Western Pacific, supra*, 352 U.S. at p. 64), and (ii) the need to secure "the expert and specialized knowledge of the agencies involved." (Ibid.) The court asserted that the term "incendiary bomb," as used in the tariff regulations, posed a question of construction that "involves factors 'the adequate appreciation of which' presupposes an 'acquaintance with many intricate facts of transportation'" possessed by the ICC. . . . Accordingly, the court concluded, "in the circumstances here presented the question of tariff construction, as well as that of the reasonableness of the tariff as applied, was within the exclusive primary jurisdiction of the Interstate Commerce Commission." (*Western Pacific, supra*, 352 U.S. at p. 63.)

4. Nader

A more recent high court case illustrates both procedural and substantive aspects of the primary jurisdiction doctrine. In Nader v. Allegheny Airlines (1976) 426 U.S. 290 (hereafter *Nader*), the plaintiff filed a common law tort action for fraudulent misrepresentation against an airline that sold him a confirmed ticket on an overbooked flight, causing the plaintiff to miss his flight. Like the statute at issue in *Abilene*, supra, 204 U.S. 426, the relevant section of the Federal Aviation Act (49 U.S.C. §1381) provided, "'[n]othing contained in this chapter shall in any way abridge or alter the remedies now existing at common law or by statute, but the provisions of this chapter are in addition to such remedies.'" . . .

The United States District Court entertained the suit and entered judgment for the plaintiff, but the United States Court of Appeals for the District of Columbia, applying the primary jurisdiction doctrine, reversed and remanded for administrative findings on, inter alia, the common law claim. It took judicial notice that the Civil Aeronautics Board (Board) was then considering the same challenges to carriers' overbooking practices in an ongoing rulemaking proceeding, and held that before the plaintiff would be allowed to proceed with his misrepresentation action, the Board should be allowed to consider whether the challenged practices fell within its power to investigate complaints and issue cease-and-desist orders. . . . Accordingly, the court of appeals instructed the district court to *stay* further action on the plaintiff's misrepresentation claim pending the outcome of the rulemaking proceeding.

The high court reversed. Initially, it observed that there was no "irreconcilable conflict between the statutory scheme and the persistence of common-law remedies," and that "[u]nder the circumstances, the common-law action and the statute . . . may coexist."

The court then proceeded to apply the primary jurisdiction doctrine. It noted that under the administrative scheme at issue, individual consumers were "not even entitled" to initiate proceedings before the Board. The fact that the plaintiff in the case before it had no authority to bring an administrative action, however, did not resolve the court's primary jurisdiction inquiry. Instead, the court relied on *Western Pacific, supra,* 352 U.S. 59, and other primary jurisdiction cases, in determining whether "considerations of uniformity in regulation and of technical expertise . . . call for prior reference to the Board." It concluded the proposed misrepresentation action posed no challenge to uniformity of regulation and that "[t]he standards to be applied in an action for fraudulent misrepresentation are within the conventional competence of the courts, and the judgment of a technically expert body is not likely to be helpful in the application of these standards to the facts of this case." Accordingly, the court held prior resort to the administrative process was not required, and hence the plaintiff's "tort action should not be stayed pending reference to the Board. . . ."

B. The Primary Jurisdiction and Exhaustion Doctrines Compared

Petitioners assert throughout their briefs that the People should be required to "exhaust" their administrative remedies before pursuing their civil action in this case. As suggested above and explained below, the applicable principle in this case is the primary jurisdiction doctrine, not the exhaustion doctrine.

Petitioners' mischaracterization is understandable because courts have often confused the two closely related concepts. . . ." Both are essentially doctrines of comity between courts and agencies. They are two sides of the timing coin. Each determines whether an action may be brought in a court or whether an agency proceeding, or further agency proceeding, is necessary." (Schwartz, Administrative Law (1984) §8.23, p. 485.)

In *Western Pacific, supra,* 352 U.S. 59, the high court explained: "*'Exhaustion' applies where a claim is cognizable in the first instance by an administrative agency alone;* judicial interference is withheld until the administrative process has run its course. *'Primary jurisdiction,' on the other hand, applies where a claim is originally cognizable in the courts,* and comes into play whenever enforcement of the claim requires the resolution of issues which, under a regulatory scheme, have been placed within the special competence of an administrative body; in such a case the judicial process is suspended pending referral of such issues to the administrative body for its views."

As noted above, count 1 of the People's complaint presented a question of exhaustion of administrative remedies; the People attempted to litigate Insurance Code claims over which the Insurance Commissioner has been given exclusive jurisdiction without first invoking and completing the available administrative process set out in the Insurance Code. . . . By contrast, count 2 of the complaint — the only count before us now — presents a different issue. The Business and Professions Code claim in count 2 is "originally cognizable in the courts," and thus it triggers application of the primary jurisdiction doctrine.

C. Policy Considerations Underlying the Primary Jurisdiction and Exhaustion Doctrines

The policy reasons behind the two doctrines are similar and overlapping. The exhaustion doctrine is principally grounded on concerns favoring administrative autonomy (i.e., courts should not interfere with an agency determination until the agency has reached a final decision) and judicial efficiency (i.e., overworked courts should decline to intervene in an administrative dispute unless absolutely necessary). . . . As explained above, the primary jurisdiction doctrine advances two related policies: it enhances court decisionmaking and efficiency by allowing courts to take advantage of administrative expertise, and it helps assure uniform application of regulatory laws. . . .

No rigid formula exists for applying the primary jurisdiction doctrine. . . . Instead, resolution generally hinges on a court's determination of the extent to which the policies noted above are implicated in a given case. . . . This discretionary approach leaves courts with considerable flexibility to avoid application of the doctrine in appropriate situations, as required by the interests of justice.

IV. WHETHER THE LEGISLATURE HAS PRECLUDED APPLICATION OF THE PRIMARY JURISDICTION DOCTRINE IN ACTIONS FILED UNDER SECTION 17200 OF THE BUSINESS AND PROFESSIONS CODE

The People suggest that the Legislature, by establishing "cumulative" administrative (§1858 et seq.) and civil (Bus. & Prof. Code, §17200) "remedies" for the alleged violation of sections 1861.02 and 1861.05, has precluded courts from applying the primary jurisdiction doctrine in a case filed under the Business and Professions Code. . . . [W]e do not read the . . . cases as prohibiting a court from exercising its discretion under the primary jurisdiction doctrine merely because "alternative" or "cumulative" administrative and civil remedies are made available to a plaintiff. We conclude instead as follows:

If the Legislature establishes a scheme under which a court is prohibited from exercising discretion under the doctrine of primary jurisdiction, a court must honor the legislative scheme, and may not decline to adjudicate a suit on the basis that available administrative processes should first be invoked and completed. If, however, the Legislature does not preclude a court from exercising its discretion under the primary jurisdiction doctrine, a court may do so and, in appropriate cases, may decline to adjudicate a suit until the administrative process has been invoked and completed. . . .

VI. APPLICATION OF THE PRIMARY JURISDICTION DOCTRINE IN THIS CASE

Our analysis . . . informs the result in this case. First, . . . the Insurance Commissioner has at his disposal a "pervasive and self-contained system of administrative procedure" to deal with the precise questions involved herein.

Second, and more important, based on the allegations in the People's complaint, there is good reason to require that these administrative procedures be invoked here. As we explain below, we conclude that considerations of judicial economy, and concerns for uniformity in application of the complex insurance regulations here involved, strongly militate in favor of a stay to await action by the Insurance Commissioner in the present case.

In [a prior case], we reasoned that in light of the nature of the common law action involved in that case, the agency had no special expertise that would warrant prior resort to its procedures. By contrast, other courts have observed that questions involving insurance ratemaking pose issues for which specialized agency fact-finding and expertise is needed in order to both resolve complex factual questions and provide a record for subsequent judicial review.... A review of the allegations in the People's complaint demonstrates the "paramount need for specialized agency fact-finding expertise" in this case....

The gravamen of the People's action under section 17200 of the Business and Professions Code is alleged violation of three specific "Good Driver Discount policy" provisions of section 1861.02(b) and 1861.02(c), and the "unfairly discriminatory rates" provision of section 1861.05(a). In order to decide whether petitioners have violated the cited subdivisions of section 1861.02, it must be determined whether petitioners refused to offer discount policies to those who qualified for such a policy; refused to charge rates at least 20 percent below the rate that would otherwise have been charged; and used the absence of prior automobile insurance coverage, "in and of itself," to determine eligibility for a Good Driver Discount policy, or to establish rates and premiums. In order to decide whether petitioners have violated section 1861.05, it must be determined whether they employed an "unfairly discriminatory" rate. The resolution of these questions mandates exercise of expertise presumably possessed by the Insurance Commissioner and poses a risk of inconsistent application of the regulatory statutes if courts are forced to rule on such matters without benefit of the views of the agency charged with regulating the insurance industry.

First, in determining eligibility for Good Driver Discount policies, section 1861.02(b)(1) specifies that the criteria set out in section 1861.025 are to be used. That section in turn addresses the eligibility of persons who have been involved in accidents during the prior three years, and who were "principally at fault." (§1861.025, subd. (b)(1), (b)(4).) The statute further provides, as to both criteria, "[t]he commissioner shall adopt regulations setting guidelines to be used by insurers for their determination of fault for the purposes of [these] paragraph[s]." (§1861.025, subd. (b)(4); see Cal. Code Regs., tit. 10, ch. 5, subch. 4.7, §2632.13.1.) It seems clear to us that the Insurance Commissioner is best suited initially to determine whether his or her own regulations pertaining to eligibility have been faithfully adhered to by an insurer.

Similarly, the determination of whether a given Good Driver Discount policy comports with the "20 percent discount" provision of the statute also calls for exercise of administrative expertise preliminary to judicial review. Inevitably, analysis of the People's claim will require "a searching inquiry into the factual complexities of [automobile] insurance ratemaking and the conditions of that market during the turbulent time here involved." . . .

There is no reason to conclude otherwise in the present case; we think it is plain that a court attempting to determine whether a given Good Driver Discount policy meets the statutory 20 percent discount requirements should have the benefit of the Insurance Commissioner's expert assessment of that issue. In addition, we note that section 1861.02, subdivision (e), provides, "The commissioner shall adopt regulations implementing *this section* and insurers may submit applications pursuant to this article which comply with those regulations. . . ." (Italics added; see Cal. Code Regs., tit. 10, ch. 5, subch. 4.7, §2632.1 et seq.) As above, it seems clear that the Insurance Commissioner, rather than a court, is best suited initially to determine whether his or her own regulations pertaining to compliance have been faithfully adhered to by an insurer.

Finally, and for the same reasons, the determination whether petitioners employed rates that are "unfairly discriminatory" also calls for exercise of administrative expertise preliminary to judicial review. In practice, resolution of the "unfairly discriminatory rate" question will turn in many instances on determination of the above discussed rate-setting provisions of the Insurance Code. It is readily apparent that a court would benefit immensely, and uniformity of decisions would be greatly enhanced, by having an expert administrative analysis available before attempting to grapple with such a potentially broadranging and technical question of insurance law.

Accordingly, we reject the People's assertion that because eventual recourse to the courts is likely in this case, nothing is to be gained by requiring prior resort to the administrative process involved here . . . "even if . . . ultimate resort to the courts [is] inevitable, the prior administrative proceeding will still promote judicial efficiency by unearthing the relevant evidence and by providing a record which the court may review." In addition, we reject any suggestion that the interests of justice militate against a requirement of prior resort in this case. . . . The People do not assert that the administrative remedies available from the Insurance Commissioner are "inadequate," and we dismiss as unsupported conjecture the suggestion that prior resort to the administrative process will unduly delay or frustrate resolution of the issues presented in the People's complaint. . . .

Finally, we reject the People's unsupported and novel claim that because the Attorney General is the chief law enforcement officer of the state, actions filed by him should not be subject to the primary jurisdiction doctrine. The reasons supporting the doctrine apply to private citizens and the Attorney General alike, and the two classes of plaintiffs should be treated equally. The primary jurisdiction doctrine evolved for the benefit of courts and administrative agencies, and unless precluded by the Legislature, it may be invoked whenever a court concludes there is a "paramount need for specialized agency fact-finding expertise."

VII. CONCLUSION

We conclude, based on the complaint as it stands, that a paramount need for specialized agency review militates in favor of imposing a requirement of prior resort to the administrative process, and as noted above we reject any suggestion that the interests of justice militate against application of a prior resort requirement in this case.

Accordingly, the judgment of the Court of Appeal is reversed with directions to issue a writ of mandate directing the superior court to stay judicial proceedings in this case and retain the matter on the court's docket pending proceedings before the Insurance Commissioner . . . and to closely monitor the progress of the administrative proceedings to ensure against unreasonable delay of the People's civil action. . . .

NOTES

1. As the opinion indicates, primary jurisdiction is closely related to the rule requiring exhaustion of administrative remedies. Each determines whether an action may be brought in a court or whether an agency proceeding, or further agency proceeding, is necessary. The basic difference is that primary jurisdiction determines whether a court or an agency has initial jurisdiction; exhaustion determines whether review may be had of agency action that is not the last agency word on the matter.

2. Primary jurisdiction is a common law doctrine that allows a court to withdraw jurisdiction to avoid resolving a dispute, at least until the agency with the requisite expertise has spoken. The doctrine is generally used sparingly, with courts hesitant to cede away jurisdiction on otherwise properly raised issues. Although generally designed to invoke the "special competence" of an agency, it is not intended "to 'secure expert advice' from agencies 'every time a court is presented with an issue conceivably within the agency's ambit.'" Clark v. Time Warner Cable, 523 F.3d 1110, 1114 (9th Cir. 2008) (quoting Brown v. MCI Worldcom Network Servs., 277 F.3d 1166, 1172 (9th Cir. 2002)). Furthermore, primary jurisdiction "need not be applied simply because a complicated regulatory scheme applies to the subject matter before the court." Ctr. for Envtl. Law & Policy v. United States Fish & Wildlife Serv., No. 15-CV-0264, 2017 U.S. Dist. LEXIS 67630, at *15 (E.D. Wash. May 3, 2017).

3. The common law nature of the doctrine also means that the application can be varied. In a concurring opinion in Pharmaceutical Research and Mfrs. of America v. Walsh, 538 U.S. 644, 674 (2003), Justice Breyer made clear some of the discretion that courts could exercise in applying the doctrine. He noted that the doctrine could be raised by courts "on their own motion" and that they could stay the proceeding "for a limited time, if appropriate — to allow a party to initiate agency review."

4. The emphasis on agency expertise as a basis for primary jurisdiction led to the exception laid down in Great Northern Railway v. Merchants Elevator Co., 259 U.S. 285 (1922). Plaintiff there had shipped wheat from Iowa to Minnesota, where it was inspected and reconsigned to its ultimate destination. Under the railroad's tariff, there was a $5 per car charge for reconsignment, but there was an exception for grain "held . . . for inspection and disposition orders incident thereto at billed destination." The railroad imposed the $5 charge and the shipper, contending the exception applied, brought an action to recover the charge. The Court, in a noted opinion by Justice Brandeis, held that *Abilene* did not bar the court action. What construction should be given to the railroad tariff presented only a question of law. No fact was in controversy and there was no occasion for the exercise of administrative discretion. "The task to be performed is to determine the meaning of words of the tariff which were used in their ordinary sense and to apply that meaning to the undisputed facts. That operation was solely one of construction," and preliminary resort to the ICC was not necessary.

F EXHAUSTION OF ADMINISTRATIVE REMEDIES

COMMENTS

1. Exhaustion provides that "[w]here relief is available from an administrative agency, the plaintiff is ordinarily required to pursue that avenue of redress before proceeding to the courts; and until that recourse is exhausted, suit is premature and must be dismissed." Reiter v. Cooper, 507 U.S. 258, 269 (1993).

2. In many respects, the doctrine promotes both efficiency and allows for the application of agency expertise before judicial review. See Burger, C.J., dissenting in Moore v. East Cleveland, 431 U.S. 494, 524 (1977) ("Exhaustion [of administrative remedies] is simply one aspect of allocation of overtaxed judicial resources. . . . The exhaustion principle asks simply that absent compelling circumstances . . . the avenues of relief nearest and simplest should be pursued first."); see also Legalization Assistance Project v. INS, 976 F.2d 1198, 1203 (9th Cir. 1992) ("The purpose of exhaustion is to allow administrative agencies to complete their own decision-making procedures and to discourage premature judicial intervention.").

3. The historical roots of the doctrine were in equity. See John F. Duffy, Administrative Common Law in Judicial Review, 77 Tex. L. Rev. 113, 154 (1998). Nonetheless, the doctrine did not remain there. In *Myers*, the Court described the doctrine as a "long-settled rule of judicial administration. . . ." 303 U.S. at 50. As we will discuss, therefore, exhaustion may be required expressly by statute or rule, or by judicial fiat.

4. For a comparison between exhaustion and primary jurisdiction, see Daily Advertiser v. Trans-LA, 612 So. 2d 7, 27 (La. 1993):

> The distinction between primary jurisdiction and the exhaustion rule . . . is that primary jurisdiction applies when concurrent jurisdiction exists between the courts and the administrative agency; the exhaustion rule applies when exclusive jurisdiction exists in the administrative agency, and the courts have only appellate, as opposed to original, jurisdiction to review the agency's decision.

1. Application of the Exhaustion Doctrine

MCCARTHY v. MADIGAN

503 U.S. 140 (1992)

JUSTICE BLACKMUN delivered the opinion of the Court.

The issue in this case is whether a federal prisoner must resort to the internal grievance procedure promulgated by the Federal Bureau of Prisons before he may initiate a suit, pursuant to the authority of *Bivens v. Six Unknown Fed. Narcotics Agents*, 403 U.S. 388 (1971), solely for money damages. The Court of Appeals for the Tenth Circuit ruled that exhaustion of the grievance procedure was required. We granted certiorari to resolve a conflict among the Courts of Appeals.

I

While he was a prisoner in the federal penitentiary at Leavenworth, petitioner John J. McCarthy filed a pro se complaint in the United States District Court for the District of Kansas against four prison employees: the hospital administrator, the chief psychologist, another psychologist, and a physician. McCarthy alleged that respondents had violated his constitutional rights under the Eighth Amendment by their deliberate indifference to his needs and medical condition resulting from a back operation and a history of psychiatric problems. On the first page of his complaint, he wrote: "This Complaint seeks Money Damages Only."

The District Court dismissed the complaint on the ground that petitioner had failed to exhaust prison administrative remedies. Under 28 CFR pt. 542 (1991), setting forth the general "Administrative Remedy Procedure for Inmates" at federal correctional institutions, a prisoner may "seek formal review of a complaint which relates to any aspect of his imprisonment." §542.10. 2. . . . The general grievance regulations do not provide for any kind of hearing or for the granting of any particular type of relief.

Petitioner McCarthy filed with the District Court a motion for reconsideration under Federal Rule of Civil Procedure 60(b), arguing that he was not required to exhaust his administrative remedies, because he sought only money damages which, he claimed, the Bureau could not provide. The court denied the motion.

The Court of Appeals, in affirming, observed that because Bivens actions are a creation of the judiciary, the courts may impose reasonable conditions upon their filing. 914 F.2d at 1412. The exhaustion rule, the court reasoned, "is not keyed to the type of relief sought, but to the need for preliminary fact-finding" to determine "whether there is a possible Bivens cause of action." Ibid. Accordingly, "'although the administrative apparatus could not award money damages . . . , administrative consideration of the possibility of corrective action and a record would have aided a court in measuring liability and determining the extent of the damages.'" Ibid., quoting Goar v. Civiletti, 688 F.2d 27, 29 (CA6 1982) (emphasis in original). Exhaustion of the general grievance procedure was required notwithstanding the fact that McCarthy's request was solely for money damages.

II

The doctrine of exhaustion of administrative remedies is one among related doctrines — including abstention, finality, and ripeness — that govern the timing of federal-court decisionmaking. Of "paramount importance" to any exhaustion inquiry is congressional intent. Patsy v. Board of Regents of Florida, 457 U.S. 496, 501 (1982). Where Congress specifically mandates, exhaustion is required. But where Congress has not clearly required exhaustion, sound judicial discretion governs. Nevertheless, even in this field of judicial discretion, appropriate deference to Congress' power to prescribe the basic procedural scheme under which a claim may be heard in a federal court requires fashioning of exhaustion principles in a manner consistent with congressional intent and any applicable statutory scheme.

A

This Court long has acknowledged the general rule that parties exhaust prescribed administrative remedies before seeking relief from the federal courts. See, e.g., Myers v. Bethlehem Shipbuilding Corp., 303 U.S. 41, 50-51, and n. 9 (1938) (discussing cases as far back as 1898). Exhaustion is required because it serves the twin purposes of protecting administrative agency authority and promoting judicial efficiency.

As to the first of these purposes, the exhaustion doctrine recognizes the notion, grounded in deference to Congress' delegation of authority to coordinate branches of Government, that agencies, not the courts, ought to have primary responsibility for the programs that Congress has charged them to administer. Exhaustion concerns apply with particular force when the action under review involves exercise of the agency's discretionary power or when the agency proceedings in question allow the agency to apply its special expertise. McKart v. United States, 395 U.S. 185, 194 (1969). See also Bowen v. City of New York, 476 U.S. 467, 484 (1986). The exhaustion doctrine also acknowledges the commonsense notion of dispute resolution that an agency ought to have an opportunity to correct its own mistakes with respect to the programs it administers before it is haled into federal court. Correlatively, exhaustion principles apply with special force when "frequent and deliberate flouting of administrative processes" could weaken an agency's effectiveness by encouraging disregard of its procedures. McKart v. United States, 395 U.S. at 195.

As to the second of the purposes, exhaustion promotes judicial efficiency in at least two ways. When an agency has the opportunity to correct its own errors, a judicial controversy may well be mooted, or at least piecemeal appeals may be avoided. And even where a controversy survives administrative review, exhaustion of the administrative procedure may produce a useful record for subsequent judicial consideration, especially in a complex or technical factual context.

B

Notwithstanding these substantial institutional interests, federal courts are vested with a "virtually unflagging obligation" to exercise the jurisdiction given them. Accordingly, this Court has declined to require exhaustion in some circumstances even where administrative and judicial interests would counsel otherwise. In determining whether exhaustion is required, federal courts must balance the interest of the individual in retaining prompt access to a federal judicial forum against countervailing institutional interests favoring exhaustion. "Administrative remedies need not be pursued if the litigant's interests in immediate judicial review outweigh the government's interests in the efficiency or administrative autonomy that the exhaustion doctrine is designed to further." West v. Bergland, 611 F.2d 710, 715 (CA8 1979), cert. denied, 449 U.S. 821 (1980). Application of this balancing principle is "intensely practical," Bowen v. City of New York, 476 U.S. at 484, because attention is directed to both the nature of the claim presented and the characteristics of the particular administrative procedure provided.

C

This Court's precedents have recognized at least three broad sets of circumstances in which the interests of the individual weigh heavily against requiring administrative exhaustion. First, requiring resort to the administrative remedy may occasion undue prejudice to subsequent assertion of a court action. Such prejudice may result, for example, from an unreasonable or indefinite timeframe for administrative action. . . . Even where the administrative decisionmaking schedule is otherwise reasonable and definite, a particular plaintiff may suffer irreparable harm if unable to secure immediate judicial consideration of his claim. By the same token, exhaustion principles apply with less force when an individual's failure to exhaust may preclude a defense to criminal liability. Moore v. East Cleveland, 431 U.S. 494, 497, n. 5 (1977) (plurality opinion); McKart v. United States, 395 U.S. at 197.

Second, an administrative remedy may be inadequate "because of some doubt as to whether the agency was empowered to grant effective relief." Gibson v. Berryhill, 411 U.S. at 575, n. 14. For example, an agency, as a preliminary matter, may be unable to consider whether to grant relief because it lacks institutional competence to resolve the particular type of issue presented, such as the constitutionality of a statute. See, e.g., Moore v. East Cleveland, 431 U.S. at 497, n. 5; Mathews v. Diaz, 426 U.S. 67, 76 (1976). In a similar vein, exhaustion has not been required where the challenge is to the adequacy of the agency procedure itself, such that "'the question of the adequacy of the administrative remedy . . . [is] for all practical purposes identical with the merits of [the plaintiff's] lawsuit.'" Barry

v. Barchi, 443 U.S. 55, 63, n. 10 (1979). Alternatively, an agency may be competent to adjudicate the issue presented, but still lack authority to grant the type of relief requested. McNeese v. Board of Ed. for Community Unit School Dist. 187, 373 U.S. 668, 675 (1963) (students seeking to integrate public school need not file complaint with school superintendent because the "Superintendent himself apparently has no power to order corrective action" except to request the Attorney General to bring suit); Montana National Bank of Billings v. Yellowstone County, 276 U.S. 499, 505 (1928) (taxpayer seeking refund not required to exhaust where "any such application [would have been] utterly futile since the county board of equalization was powerless to grant any appropriate relief" in face of prior controlling court decision).

Third, an administrative remedy may be inadequate where the administrative body is shown to be biased or has otherwise predetermined the issue before it . . .

III

In light of these general principles, we conclude that petitioner McCarthy need not have exhausted his constitutional claim for money damages. As a preliminary matter, we find that Congress has not meaningfully addressed the appropriateness of requiring exhaustion in this context. Although respondents' interests are significant, we are left with a firm conviction that, given the type of claim McCarthy raises and the particular characteristics of the Bureau's general grievance procedure, McCarthy's individual interests outweigh countervailing institutional interests favoring exhaustion.

A

Turning first to congressional intent, we note that the general grievance procedure was neither enacted nor mandated by Congress. Respondents, however, urge that Congress, in effect, has acted to require exhaustion by delegating power to the Attorney General and the Bureau of Prisons to control and manage the federal prison system. See 18 U.S.C. §§4001(b) and 4042. We think respondents confuse what Congress could be claimed to allow by implication with what Congress affirmatively has requested or required. By delegating authority, in the most general of terms, to the Bureau to administer the federal prison system, Congress cannot be said to have spoken to the particular issue whether prisoners in the custody of the Bureau should have direct access to the federal courts.

Respondents next argue that Congress, by enactment of §7 of the Civil Rights of Institutionalized Persons Act, 94 Stat. 352, 42 U. S. C. §1997e, has articulated a policy favoring exhaustion of the prison grievance procedure prior to the filing of a constitutional claim against prison officials. Section 1997e imposes a limited exhaustion requirement for a claim brought by a state prisoner under Rev. Stat. §1979, 42 U.S.C. §1983, provided that the underlying state prison administrative remedy meets specified standards. Section 1997e has no direct application in this case. . . .

Section 1997e is not only inapplicable . . . but — by its own terms — cuts against respondents' claim that the particular procedure now at issue need be exhausted. First, unlike the rule of exhaustion proposed here, §1997e does not authorize dismissal of an action for failure to exhaust. Instead, it provides that the action is to be stayed for a maximum of 90 days. See §1997e(a)(1). Second, §1997e does not mechanically require exhaustion in every case where an acceptable state procedure is in place. Rather, it directs federal courts to abstain "if the court believes that such a [waiting] requirement would be appropriate and in the interests of justice." §1997e(a)(1). In other words, if an inmate fails to meet filing deadlines under an administrative scheme, a court has ample discretion to determine that exhaustion nonetheless should be forgone. Third, in contrast to the absence of any provision for the award of money damages under the Bureau's general grievance procedure, the statute conditions exhaustion on the existence of "effective administrative remedies." It is difficult to see why a stricter rule of exhaustion than Congress itself has required in the state prison context should apply in the federal prison context.

. . .

B

Because Congress has not required exhaustion [for claims like this], we turn to an evaluation of the individual and institutional interests at stake in this case. The general grievance procedure heavily burdens the individual interests of the petitioning inmate in two ways. First, the procedure imposes short, successive filing deadlines that create a high risk of forfeiture of a claim for failure to comply. Second, the administrative "remedy" does not authorize an award of monetary damages — the only relief requested by McCarthy in this action. The combination of these features means that the prisoner seeking only money damages has everything to lose and nothing to gain from being required to exhaust his claim under the internal grievance procedure.

The filing deadlines for the grievance procedure require an inmate, within 15 days of the precipitating incident, not only to attempt to resolve his grievance informally but also to file a formal written complaint with the prison warden. 28 CFR §542.13 (1991). Then, he must successively hurdle 20-day and 30-day deadlines to advance to the end of the grievance process. §542.15. Other than the Bureau's general and quite proper interest in having early notice of any claim, we have not been apprised of any urgency or exigency justifying this timetable. As a practical matter, the filing deadlines, of course, may pose little difficulty for the knowledgeable inmate accustomed to grievances and court actions. But they are a likely trap for the inexperienced and unwary inmate, ordinarily indigent and unrepresented by counsel, with a substantial claim. Respondents argue that the deadlines are not jurisdictional and may be extended for any "valid" reason. See 28 CFR §§542.13(b) and 542.15 (1991). Yet the regulations do not elaborate upon what a "valid" reason is. Moreover, it appears that prison officials — perhaps the very officials subject to suit — are charged with determining what is a "valid" reason.

All in all, these deadlines require a good deal of an inmate at the peril of forfeiting his claim for money damages. The "first" of "the principles that necessarily frame our analysis of prisoners' constitutional claims" is that "federal courts must take cognizance of the valid constitutional claims of prison inmates." Turner v. Safley, 482 U.S. 78, 84 (1987). Because a prisoner ordinarily is divested of the privilege to vote, the right to file a court action might be said to be his remaining most "fundamental political right, because preservative of all rights." Yick Wo v. Hopkins, 118 U.S. 356, 370 (1886). The rapid filing deadlines counsel strongly against exhaustion as a prerequisite to the filing of a federal court action.

As we have noted, the grievance procedure does not include any mention of the award of monetary relief. Respondents argue that this should not matter, because "in most cases there are other things that the inmate wants." This may be true in some instances. But we cannot presume, as a general matter, that when a litigant has deliberately forgone any claim for injunctive relief and has singled out discrete past wrongs, specifically requesting monetary compensation only, that he is likely interested in "other things." The Bureau, in any case, is always free to offer an inmate administrative relief in return for withdrawal of his lawsuit. We conclude that the absence of any monetary remedy in the grievance procedure also weighs heavily against imposing an exhaustion requirement.

The interests of judicial economy do not stand to be advanced substantially by the general grievance procedure. No formal factfindings are made. The paperwork generated by the grievance process might assist a court somewhat in ascertaining the facts underlying a prisoner's claim more quickly than if it has only a prisoner's complaint to review. But the grievance procedure does not create a formal factual record of the type that can be relied on conclusively by a court for disposition of a prisoner's claim on the pleadings or at summary judgment without the aid of affidavits.

C

In conclusion, we are struck by the absence of supporting material in the regulations, the record, or the briefs that the general grievance procedure here was crafted with any thought toward the principles of exhaustion of claims for money damages. The Attorney General's professed concern for internal dispute resolution has not translated itself into a more effective grievance procedure that might encourage the filing of an administrative complaint as opposed to a court action. Congress, of course, is free to design or require an appropriate administrative procedure for a prisoner to exhaust his claim for money damages. Even without further action by Congress, we do not foreclose the possibility that the Bureau itself may adopt an appropriate administrative procedure consistent with congressional intent.

The judgment of the Court of Appeals is reversed.

It is so ordered.

Chief Justice Rehnquist, with whom Justice Scalia and Justice Thomas join, concurring in the judgment.

I agree with the Court's holding that a federal prisoner need not exhaust the procedures promulgated by the Federal Bureau of Prisons. My view, however, is based entirely on the fact that the grievance procedure at issue does not provide for any award of monetary damages. As a result, in cases such as this one where prisoners seek monetary relief, the Bureau's administrative remedy furnishes no effective remedy at all, and it is therefore improper to impose an exhaustion requirement. . . .

NOTES

1. In his concurrence, Justice Rehnquist indicated that the Court could have relied solely on the absence of a provision for monetary awards from the Bureau of Prisons' administrative procedures to conclude that exhaustion was not required. Do you agree that the lack of availability of a particular remedy is sufficient, on its own, for courts to exercise discretion by waiving the exhaustion requirement? See Nelson v. Charles City Cmty. Sch. Dist., 900 F.3d 587, 593 (8th Cir. 2018) ("There are three exceptions to the exhaustion requirement. . . . If one of these exceptions applies, then a plaintiff is relieved of the obligation to exhaust her administrative remedies. . . ."). If so, why do you think the Court also relied on the burdensome nature of the administrative procedures themselves?

2. Note that Congress overrode the Court's decision in *McCarthy* by enacting the Prison Reform Litigation Act, specifically requiring exhaustion, in 1995.

3. The exceptions to non-mandated exhaustion are illustrated by the following questions:

(a) Should exhaustion be required when the available agency remedy cannot give plaintiff adequate relief? See Portela-Gonzalez v. Secretary of the Navy, 109 F.3d 74, 78 (1st Cir. 1997) ("[T]he futility exception is not available for the asking. Reliance on the exception in a given case must be anchored in demonstrable reality. A pessimistic prediction or a hunch that further administrative proceedings will prove unproductive is not enough to sidetrack the exhaustion rule."); Gardner v. School Bd., 958 F.2d 108, 112 (5th Cir. 1992) (exhaustion required because petitioners did not carry their burden to prove that the administrative remedy was futile). What if Congress intends otherwise? See Booth v. Churner, 532 U.S. 731, 741 (2001) (finding that Congress did not intend to create futility exception to exhaustion requirement for state prisoners in the Prison Litigation Reform Act of 1995 where agency lacked power to issue relief sought by prisoners). See also United States v. Alam, 960 F.3d 831, 835 (6th Cir. 2020) ("Alam requests that we innovate an equitable exception to this requirement to account for irreparable harm or futility. But the norm is to follow a mandatory rule unless the statutory exceptions apply."). Does the intent have to be explicit?

(b) When completing the administrative process will involve expense and delay? See Abbey v. Sullivan, 978 F.2d 37, 46 (2d Cir. 1992) ("It is the well-established rule 'that the mere trouble and expense of defending an administrative proceeding is insufficient to warrant judicial review . . . prior to the conclusion of the administrative proceeding. Other factors must be present in addition to this injury. . . .'" (citing Central Hudson Gas & Elec. Corp. v. EPA, 587 F.2d 549, 559 (2d Cir. 1978)).

(c) "When the aggrieved party can positively state what the administrative agency's decision in his particular case will be"? See Orion Corp. v. State, 693 P.2d 1369, 1378 (Wash. 1985), where the court said that to require exhaustion in such a case was "to require [plaintiffs] to pump oil from a dry hole."

(d) When the agency action will have a "chilling effect" on First Amendment rights? See Wolff v. Selective Service Local Bd., 372 F.2d 817 (2d Cir. 1967). But see New York Petroleum Corp. v. Ashland Oil, 757 F.2d 288, 293 (Temp. Emer. Ct. App. 1985) (*Wolff* does not apply where mere economic interests at stake).

(e) When the plaintiff claims that due process will be violated because the agency cannot function as an impartial tribunal? See Gibson v. Berryhill, 411 U.S. 564 (1973), where the Court stated, "the clear purport of appellees' complaint was that the State Board of Optometry was unconstitutionally constituted and so did not provide them with an adequate administrative remedy requiring exhaustion."

4. Should there be a further exception to exhaustion when the claim is made that the agency is acting without jurisdiction? The leading case on the rule that exhaustion is required even where it is claimed that the agency is acting without jurisdiction is Myers v. Bethlehem Shipbuilding Corp., 303 U.S. 41 (1938). The question there was whether a district court had equity jurisdiction to enjoin the National Labor Relations Board from holding a hearing upon a complaint filed by it against an employer alleged to be engaged in unfair labor practices. The employer had alleged that it was not engaged in interstate or foreign commerce and that the NLRB was therefore without jurisdiction over it. The employer contended that, since it denied that interstate or foreign commerce was involved and claimed that a hearing would subject it to irreparable damage, rights guaranteed by the federal Constitution would be denied unless it was held that the district court had jurisdiction to enjoin the holding of a hearing by the board. According to the Court, "The contention is at war with the long settled rule of judicial administration that no one is entitled to judicial relief for a supposed or threatened injury until the prescribed administrative remedy has been exhausted. That rule has been repeatedly acted on in cases where, as here, the contention is made that the administrative body lacked power over the subject matter." Under *Myers*, the established principle of federal administrative law is that the agency has exclusive initial power to determine its own jurisdiction. The agency is entitled to proceed to a conclusion without judicial interference; if it has mistaken its jurisdiction, the error can be corrected on judicial review. Under *Myers, the agency has initial jurisdiction to determine its own jurisdiction*; it "should make the initial determination of its own jurisdiction."

5. The state courts that have considered the matter refuse to follow the federal rule that exhaustion applies even to cases where agency jurisdiction is challenged. An oft-cited state case is Ward v. Keenan, 70 A.2d 77 (N.J. 1949), where the New Jersey court refused to follow *Myers.* Instead, it held that there was an exception to the exhaustion requirement when the jurisdiction of the agency was questioned on persuasive grounds. The New Jersey court relied on what it termed "the obvious reason that if the question of jurisdiction were resolved against the statutory tribunal the parties would be spared the vexation of a useless hearing." More recently, the Wyoming Supreme Court held that exhaustion of administrative remedies was not a valid rationale for dismissing a claim regarding drilling permits because the agency in question did not have jurisdiction to determine whether there was a civil trespass, a central issue in the permitting dispute. See Devon Energy Prod. Co. L.P. v. Grayson Oil Mill Operating, L.L.C., 458 P.3d 1201, 1211 (Wyo. 2020). Which rule is preferable, the federal rule applied in the *Myers* case or the rule followed in most state courts that have considered the matter, as stated in the *Ward* case?

6. Should exhaustion be required when plaintiff raises a constitutional issue? See State v. Superior Court, 524 P.2d 1281, 1290 (Cal. 1974):

> [S]ince an administrative agency is not the appropriate forum in which to challenge the constitutionality of the basic statute under which it operates, there seems little reason to require a litigant to raise the constitutional issue in proceedings before the agency as a condition of raising that issue in the courts. It would be heroic indeed to compel a party to appear before an administrative body to challenge its very existence and to expect a dispassionate hearing . . . on the constitutionality of the statute establishing its status and functions. We conclude that Veta should be permitted to challenge the constitutionality of the Act in this proceeding even though it failed to make such a challenge before the Commission.

Is the line drawn by the Iowa court in the following passage the proper one?

> "In administrative law cases generally there is some lingering confusion as to whether exhaustion will be required when the constitutionality of a statute is challenged on its face rather than as applied. . . . However, the emerging rule would appear to be that since the administrative remedy cannot resolve a constitutional challenge, exhaustion will not be required unless the administrative action might make judicial determination of the constitutional question unnecessary. See Public Utilities Commission v. United States, 355 U.S. 534, 539-540 (1958)." Metcalf v. Swank, 444 F.2d 1353, 1355-1356. We approve the "emerging rule" described in Metcalf v. Swank. But under the rule plaintiffs are still faced with the exhaustion requirement. In spite of their claim on appeal an examination of the petition clearly shows their challenge is to the ordinance "as applied," not "on its face."
>
> Plaintiffs were required to exhaust their administrative remedy before instituting their court challenge.

Matters v. City of Ames, 219 N.W.2d 718, 719-720 (Iowa 1974).

The Supreme Court considered this issue in Moore v. East Cleveland, 431 U.S. 494 (1977). The case involved a municipal housing ordinance that limited occupancy of a dwelling unit to members of a single family. The Court ruled that the ordinance violated due process since it defined "family" in such a way as to make it a crime for a grandmother to live with her grandson. Chief Justice Burger dissented on the ground that appellant had failed to exhaust her administrative remedies: Her deliberate refusal to use the administrative remedy provided by the city (by application for a variance to exempt her from the restriction of the ordinance) should foreclose her from pressing in court any constitutional objections to the zoning ordinance. According to the chief justice, the exhaustion rule is not inapplicable because a constitutional issue is raised.

The decision in *Moore* indicates that the majority of the Supreme Court now accept the rule that, where constitutionality of a statute or other act is challenged on its face rather than as applied, exhaustion should not be required. But see Reno v. American-Arab Antidiscrimination Committee, 525 U.S. 471 (1999) (five Justices refuse to apply constitutional exception to allow judicial review prior to agency deportation order because "an alien unlawfully in this country has no constitutional right to assert selective enforcement as a defense against his deportation"). For similar recent state holdings, see HOH Corp. v. Motor Vehicle Bd., 736 P.2d 1271, 1275-1276 (Haw. 1987) (explaining that agency findings rarely aid in determinations regarding the legal question of whether a statute is constitutional on its face); Kane County v. Carlson, 507 N.E.2d 482, 486 (Ill. Ct. App. 1987) (exhaustion "rule does not apply when a party challenges the constitutionality of a statute on its face"); but see Aranoff v. Bryan, 569 A.2d 466, 470 (Vt. 1989) (exhaustion required where challenge to statute as applied by agency). See also Peter A. Devlin, Jurisdiction, Exhaustion of Administrative Remedies, & Constitutional Claims, 93 N.Y.U. L. Rev. 1234, 1264 (2018) (asserting that facial challenges to the constitutionality of a statute "should be . . . exempt from exhaustion requirements" based on "the purposes of exhaustion, separation of powers principles, and . . . the constitutional avoidance canon [of statutory interpretation").

7. Can Congress impose exhaustion requirements for any claim? What about constitutional violations? See United States v. Clintwood Elkhorn Mining Co., 553 U.S. 1, 9 (2008) ("Further, Congress has the authority to require administrative exhaustion before allowing a suit against the Government, even for a constitutional violation.").

2. The Exhaustion Doctrine and the APA

APA §704. Actions Reviewable

. . . Except as otherwise expressly required by statute, agency action otherwise final is final for the purposes of this section whether or not there has been presented or determined an application for a declaratory order, for any form of reconsideration, or, unless the agency otherwise requires by rule and provides that the action meanwhile is inoperative, for an appeal to superior agency authority.

DARBY v. CISNEROS

509 U.S. 137 (1993)

JUSTICE BLACKMUN delivered the opinion of the Court.

This case presents the question whether federal courts have the authority to require that a plaintiff exhaust available administrative remedies before seeking judicial review under the Administrative Procedure Act (APA), 5 U.S.C. §701 et seq., where neither the statute nor agency rules specifically mandate exhaustion as a prerequisite to judicial review. At issue is the relationship between the judicially created doctrine of exhaustion of administrative remedies and the statutory requirements of §10(c) of the APA.

I

Petitioner R. Gordon Darby is a self-employed South Carolina real estate developer who specializes in the development and management of multifamily rental projects. In the early 1980s, he began working with Lonnie Garvin, Jr., a mortgage banker, who had developed a plan to enable multifamily developers to obtain single-family mortgage insurance from respondent Department of Housing and Urban Development (HUD). . . .

Darby obtained financing for three separate multiunit projects, and, through Garvin's plan, Darby obtained single-family mortgage insurance from HUD. Although Darby successfully rented the units, a combination of low rents, falling interest rates, and a generally depressed rental market forced him into default in 1988. HUD became responsible for the payment of over $6.6 million in insurance claims.

HUD had become suspicious of Garvin's financing plan as far back as 1983. In 1986, HUD initiated an audit but concluded that neither Darby nor Garvin had done anything wrong or misled HUD personnel. Nevertheless, in June 1989, HUD issued a limited denial of participation (LDP) that prohibited petitioners for one year from participating in any program in South Carolina administered by respondent Assistant Secretary of Housing. Two months later, the Assistant Secretary notified petitioners that HUD was also proposing to debar them from further participation in all HUD procurement contracts and in any nonprocurement transaction with any federal agency. . . .

Petitioners' appeal of the LDP and of the proposed debarment were consolidated, and an Administrative Law Judge (ALJ) conducted a hearing on the consolidated appeals in December 1989. The judge issued an "Initial Decision and Order" in April 1990, finding that the financing method used by petitioners was "a sham. . . ." The ALJ concluded, however, that most of the relevant facts had been disclosed to local HUD employees, that petitioners lacked criminal intent, and that Darby himself "genuinely cooperated with HUD to try [to] work out his financial dilemma and avoid foreclosure." In light of these mitigating factors, the ALJ concluded that an indefinite debarment would be punitive and that it would serve no legitimate purpose; good cause existed, however, to debar petitioners for a period of 18 months.

Under HUD regulations,

> The hearing officer's determination shall be final unless, pursuant to 24 CFR part 26, the Secretary or the Secretary's designee, within 30 days of receipt of a request decides as a matter of discretion to review the finding of the hearing officer. . . . Any party may request such a review in writing within 15 days of receipt of the hearing officer's determination. [24 CFR §24.314(c) (1992).]

Neither petitioners nor respondents sought further administrative review of the ALJ's "Initial Decision and Order."

On May 31, 1990, petitioners filed suit in the United States District Court for the District of South Carolina. They sought an injunction and a declaration that the administrative sanctions were imposed for purposes of punishment, in violation of HUD's own debarment regulations, and therefore were "not in accordance with law" within the meaning of §10(e)(B)(1) of the APA, 5 U.S.C. §706(2)(A).

Respondents moved to dismiss the complaint on the ground that petitioners, by forgoing the option to seek review by the Secretary, had failed to exhaust administrative remedies. The District Court denied respondents' motion to dismiss, reasoning that the administrative remedy was inadequate and that resort to that remedy would have been futile. . . .

The Court of Appeals for the Fourth Circuit reversed. . . . It recognized that neither the National Housing Act nor HUD regulations expressly mandate exhaustion of administrative remedies prior to filing suit. The court concluded, however, that the District Court had erred in denying respondents' motion to dismiss, because there was no evidence to suggest that further review would have been futile or that the Secretary would have abused his discretion by indefinitely extending the time limitations for review. . . .

II

Section 10(c) of the APA bears the caption "Actions reviewable." It provides in its first two sentences that judicial review is available for "final agency action for which there is no other adequate remedy in a court," and that "preliminary, procedural, or intermediate agency action . . . is subject to review on the review of the final agency action." The last sentence of §10(c) reads:

> Except as otherwise expressly required by statute, agency action otherwise final is final for the purposes of this section whether or not there has been presented or determined an application for a declaratory order, for any form of reconsideration, or, unless the agency otherwise requires by rule and provides that the action meanwhile is inoperative, for an appeal to superior agency authority. 5 U.S.C. §704.

Petitioners argue that this provision means that a litigant seeking judicial review of a final agency action under the APA need not exhaust available administrative remedies unless such exhaustion is expressly required by statute or agency rule. According to petitioners, since §10(c) contains an explicit exhaustion provision, federal courts are not free to require further exhaustion as a matter of judicial discretion.

Respondents contend that . . . even though nothing in §10(c) precludes judicial review of petitioners' claim, respondents argue that federal courts remain free under the APA to impose appropriate exhaustion requirements.

We have recognized that the judicial doctrine of exhaustion of administrative remedies is conceptually distinct from the doctrine of finality:

> [T]he finality requirement is concerned with whether the initial decisionmaker has arrived at a definitive position on the issue that inflicts an actual, concrete injury; the exhaustion requirement generally refers to administrative and judicial procedures by which an injured party may seek review of an adverse decision and obtain a remedy if the decision is found to be unlawful or otherwise inappropriate. Williamson County Regional Planning Comm'n v. Hamilton Bank, 473 U.S. 172, 193 (1985).

Whether courts are free to impose an exhaustion requirement as a matter of judicial discretion depends, at least in part, on whether Congress has provided otherwise, for "of 'paramount importance' to any exhaustion inquiry is congressional intent." . . . We therefore must consider whether §10(c), by providing the conditions under which agency action becomes "final for the purposes of" judicial review, limits the authority of courts to impose additional exhaustion requirements as a prerequisite to judicial review.

It perhaps is surprising that it has taken over 45 years since the passage of the APA for this Court definitively to address this question. . . .

This Court has had occasion, however, to consider §10(c) in other contexts. For example, in ICC v. Locomotive Engineers, 482 U.S. 270 (1987), we recognized that the plain language of §10(c), which provides that an agency action is final "Whether or not there has been presented or determined an application" for any form of reconsideration, could be read to suggest that the agency action is final regardless whether a motion for reconsideration has been filed. We noted, however, that §10(c) "has long been construed by this and other courts merely to relieve parties from the *requirement* of petitioning for rehearing before seeking judicial review (unless, of course, specifically required to do so by statute — see e.g., 15 U.S.C. §§717r, 3416(a)), but not to prevent petitions for reconsideration that are actually filed from rendering the orders under reconsideration nonfinal" (emphasis in original). Id. at 284-285.

In Bowen v. Massachusetts, 487 U.S. 879 (1988), we were concerned with whether relief available in the Claims Court was an "adequate remedy in a court" so as to preclude review in Federal District Court of a final agency action under the first sentence of §10(c). We concluded that "although the primary thrust of [§10(c)] was to codify the exhaustion requirement," 487 U.S. at 903, Congress intended by that provision simply to avoid duplicating previously established special statutory procedures for review of agency actions.

While some dicta in these cases might be claimed to lend support to petitioners' interpretation of §10(c), the text of the APA leaves little doubt that petitioners are correct. Under §10(c) of the APA, "[a] person suffering legal wrong because of agency action, or adversely affected or aggrieved by agency action within the meaning of a relevant statute, *is entitled to a judicial review thereof*." 5 U.S.C. §702 (emphasis added). Although §10(a) provides the general right to judicial review of agency actions under the APA, §10(c) establishes when such review is available. When an aggrieved party has exhausted all administrative remedies expressly prescribed by statute or agency rule, the agency action is "final for the purposes of this section" and therefore "subject to judicial review" under the first sentence. While federal courts may be free to apply, where appropriate, other prudential doctrines of judicial administration to limit the scope and timing of judicial review, §10(c), by its very terms, has limited the availability of the doctrine of exhaustion of administrative remedies to that which the statute or rule clearly mandates.

The last sentence of §10(c) refers explicitly to "any form of reconsideration" and "an appeal to superior agency authority." Congress clearly was concerned with making the exhaustion requirement unambiguous so that aggrieved parties would know precisely what administrative steps were required before judicial review would be available. If courts were available to impose additional exhaustion requirements beyond those provided by Congress or the agency, the last sentence of §10(c) would make no sense. To adopt respondents' reading would transform §10(c) from a provision designed to "'remove obstacles to judicial review of agency action,'" . . . into a trap for unwary litigants. Section 10(c) explicitly requires exhaustion of all intra-agency appeals mandated either by statute or by agency rule; it would be inconsistent with the plain language of §10(c) for courts to require litigants to exhaust optional appeals as well. . . .

III

. . . Respondents argue . . . that the law governing the exhaustion of administrative *appeals* prior to the APA was significantly different from §10(c) as petitioners would have us interpret it. Respondents rely on United States v. Sing Tuck, 194 U.S. 161 (1904), in which the Court considered whether, under the relevant statute, an aggrieved party had to appeal an adverse decision by the Inspector of Immigration to the Secretary of Commerce and Labor before judicial review would be available. It recognized that the relevant statute "points out a mode of procedure which must be followed before there can be a resort to the courts," id. at 167, and that a party must go through "the preliminary sifting process provided by the statutes," id. at 170. . . .

Nothing in this pre-APA history, however, supports respondents' argument that initial decisions that were "final" for purposes of judicial review were nonetheless unreviewable unless and until an administrative appeal was taken. The pre-APA cases concerning judicial review of federal agency action stand for the simple proposition that, until an administrative appeal was taken, the agency action was unreviewable because it was not yet "final." This is hardly surprising, given the fact that few, if any, administrative agencies authorized hearing officers to make final agency decisions prior to the enactment of the APA. . . .

The purpose of §10(c) was to permit agencies to require an appeal to "superior agency authority" before an examiner's initial decision became final. This was necessary because, under §8(a), initial decisions could become final agency decisions in the absence of an agency appeal. See 5 U.S.C. §557(b). Agencies may avoid the finality of an initial decision, first, by adopting a rule that an agency appeal be taken before judicial review is available, and second, by providing that the initial decision would be "inoperative" pending appeal. Otherwise, the initial decision becomes final and the aggrieved party is entitled to judicial review. . . .

IV

We noted just last Term in a non-APA case that

> appropriate deference to Congress' power to prescribe the basic procedural scheme under which a claim may be heard in a federal court requires fashioning of exhaustion principles in a manner consistent with congressional intent and any applicable statutory scheme. McCarthy v. Madigan, 503 U.S. 140, 144 (1992).

Appropriate deference in this case requires the recognition that, with respect to actions brought under the APA, Congress effectively codified the doctrine of exhaustion of administrative remedies in §10(c). Of course, the exhaustion doctrine continues to apply as a matter of judicial discretion in cases not governed by the APA. But where the APA applies, an appeal to "superior agency authority" is a prerequisite to judicial review *only* when expressly required by statute or when an agency rule requires appeal before review and the administrative action is made inoperative pending that review. Courts are not free to impose an exhaustion requirement as a rule of judicial administration where the agency action has already become "final" under §10(c).

The judgment of the Court of Appeals is reversed, and the case is remanded for further proceedings consistent with this opinion. *It is so ordered.*

NOTES

1. In United States v. Sing Tuck, 194 U.S. 161 (1904), discussed in the *Darby* opinion, petitioners were denied entry into the United States by an immigration inspector. Under the statute there was a right to appeal from the inspector's decision to the Secretary of Commerce and Labor. Instead of appealing, petitioners sought judicial review of the inspector's decision. The Court held that the attempt to bypass the administrative appeal could not succeed: "We are of opinion that the attempt to disregard and override the provisions of the statutes and the rules of the department, and to swamp the courts by a resort to them in the first instance, must fail. . . . [B]efore the courts can be called upon, the preliminary sifting process provided by the statutes must be gone through with."

According to United States v. Consolidated Mines & Smelting Co., 455 F.2d 432, 439-440 (9th Cir. 1971),

> [T]here appears to be little doubt that Congress intended to declare that failure to appeal administrative decisions to higher administrative authority would not preclude judicial review.... Thus it appears that the portion of the exhaustion doctrine in United States v. Sing Tuck, 194 U.S. 161 (1904) and pertinent here, has been abrogated by section 10(c) of the APA [5 U.S.C. §704]. The meaning of the statute clearly appears: Intraagency appeals are not a prerequisite to judicial review except to the extent statutes or appropriate agency rules command otherwise.

Does *Darby* adopt the Ninth Circuit's view? If it does, what room is left for the exhaustion doctrine in the *Sing Tuck*-type case? See Schreiber v. Cuccinelli, 981 F.3d 766, 786 (10th Cir. 2020) ("[N[othing in the APA's text — nor in *Darby*'s interpretation of it — indicates that a federal court may not require a party to have exhausted his administrative remedies . . . in an optional administrative appeal . . . *if* he actually elected to undertake such an appeal.").

2. Is a statutory scheme providing for administrative and judicial review exclusive? Where exclusivity is the rule, parties cannot challenge the agency through collateral actions in federal district court. Instead, legal arguments must be raised in the administrative proceeding where they can be addressed first by the agency and then by the U.S. Court of Appeals.

3. Exclusivity is generally treated as a matter of congressional intent. Intent, however, is inferred from the nature of the required proceedings. See Thunder Basin Coal Co. v. Reich, 510 U.S. 200, 216 (1994) ("We conclude that the Mine Act's comprehensive enforcement structure, combined with the legislative history's clear concern with channeling and streamlining the enforcement process, establishes a 'fairly discernible' intent to preclude district court review in the present case."). At the same time, however, the courts have grafted onto the doctrine a series of exceptions. Thus, in Free Enterprise Fund v. Public Co. Accounting Oversight Bd., 561 U.S. 477 (2010), the Court determined that Congress did "not intend to limit jurisdiction if 'a finding of preclusion could foreclose all meaningful judicial review'; if the suit is 'wholly collateral to a statute's review provisions'; and if the claims are 'outside the agency's expertise'" (quoting Thunder Basin Coal Co. v. Reich, 510 U.S. 200, 212-213 (1994)). In that case, the plaintiff sought to challenge the constitutionality of the PCAOB. A finding of exclusivity would have forced the firm to induce the PCAOB to bring an administrative action that could be appealed. This could occur, the Court noted, if the firm refused to provide documents as part of an investigation, incurred a sanction, and appealed the matter first to the Securities and Exchange Commission, then to the U.S. Court of Appeals. As the Court noted, "We normally do not require plaintiffs to 'bet the farm . . . by taking the violative action' before 'testing the validity of the law,' . . . and we do not consider this a 'meaningful' avenue of relief." How does this concept of exclusivity differ from exhaustion? Can this approach, first the inference of exclusivity, then the accompanying exceptions, be attributed to Congress, or does this doctrine represent a form of judicial "common law"?

4. The Securities and Exchange Commission has the authority to bring administrative proceedings for alleged violations of the federal securities laws. Appeal of a decision by an administrative law judge (ALJ) is to the full

Commission and from there appeal can be lodged in the U.S. Court of Appeals. See 15 U.S.C. §78y(a). Does the rule of exclusivity apply to a party in an administrative proceeding who wanted to challenge the constitutionality of the ALJ presiding over the hearing? For an answer, see Jarkesy v. SEC, 803 F.3d 9, 17 (D.C. Cir. 2015) (evaluating the SEC's statutory review scheme using the three *Thunder Basin* factors: (1) whether requiring initial administrative review would "foreclose all meaningful judicial review"; (2) whether the claim is "wholly collateral" to the relevant statute's review provisions; and (3) whether the claim is "outside of the agency's expertise").

3. Issue Exhaustion

What if a claimant properly exhausts administrative remedies but wants to raise issues not considered during the process?

SIMS v. APFEL

530 U.S. 103 (2000)

THOMAS, J., announced the judgment of the Court and delivered the opinion of the Court with respect to Parts I and II-A, and an opinion with respect to Part II-B, in which JUSTICE STEVENS, JUSTICE SOUTER, and JUSTICE GINSBURG join.

A person whose claim for Social Security benefits is denied by an administrative law judge (ALJ) must in most cases, before seeking judicial review of that denial, request that the Social Security Appeals Council review his claim. The question is whether a claimant pursuing judicial review has waived any issues that he did not include in that request. We hold that he has not.

I

In 1994, petitioner Juatassa Sims filed applications for disability benefits under Title II of the Social Security Act, 49 Stat. 622, 42 U.S.C. §401 et seq., and for supplemental security income benefits under Title XVI of that Act, 86 Stat. 1465, 42 U.S.C. §1381 et seq. She alleged disability from a variety of ailments, including degenerative joint diseases and carpal tunnel syndrome. After a state agency denied her claims, she obtained a hearing before a Social Security ALJ. See generally Heckler v. Day, 467 U.S. 104, 106-107 (1984) (describing stages of review of claims for Social Security benefits). The ALJ, in 1996, also denied her claims, concluding that, although she did have some medical impairments, she had not been and was not under a "disability," as defined in the Act. . . .

Petitioner then requested that the Social Security Appeals Council review her claims. A claimant may request such review by completing a one-page form provided by the Social Security Administration (SSA) — Form HA-520 — or "by any other writing specifically requesting review." 20 CFR §422.205(a) (1999).

Petitioner, through counsel, chose the latter option, submitting to the Council a letter arguing that the ALJ had erred in several ways in analyzing the evidence. The Council denied review. . . .

The Court of Appeals for the Fifth Circuit affirmed in an unpublished opinion. 162 F.3d 1160 (1998). . . . [I]t concluded that, under its decision in Paul v. Shalala, 29 F.3d 208, 210 (1994), it lacked jurisdiction because petitioner had not raised those contentions in her request for review by the Appeals Council. We granted certiorari, 528 U.S. 1018 (1999), to resolve a conflict among the Courts of Appeals over whether a Social Security claimant waives judicial review of an issue if he fails to exhaust that issue by presenting it to the Appeals Council in his request for review. . . .

II

A

The Social Security Act provides that "any individual, after any final decision of the Commissioner of Social Security made after a hearing to which he was a party, . . . may obtain a review of such decision by a civil action" in federal district court. 42 U.S.C. §405(g). But the Act does not define "final decision," instead leaving it to the SSA to give meaning to that term through regulations. See §405(a); Weinberger v. Salfi, 422 U.S. 749, 766 (1975). SSA regulations provide that, if the Appeals Council grants review of a claim, then the decision that the Council issues is the Commissioner's final decision. But if, as here, the Council denies the request for review, the ALJ's opinion becomes the final decision. See 20 CFR §§404.900(a)(4)-(5), 404.955, 404.981, 422.210(a) (1999). If a claimant fails to request review from the Council, there is no final decision and, as a result, no judicial review in most cases. See §404.900(b); Bowen v. City of New York, 476 U.S. 467, 482-483 (1986). In administrative-law parlance, such a claimant may not obtain judicial review because he has failed to exhaust administrative remedies. See *Salfi*, 422 U.S. at 765-766.

The Commissioner rightly concedes that petitioner exhausted administrative remedies by requesting review by the Council. Petitioner thus obtained a final decision, and nothing in §405(g) or the regulations implementing it bars judicial review of her claims.

Nevertheless, the Commissioner contends that we should require issue exhaustion in addition to exhaustion of remedies. That is, he contends that a Social Security claimant, to obtain judicial review of an issue, not only must obtain a final decision on his claim for benefits, but also must specify that issue in his request for review by the Council. (Whether a claimant must exhaust issues before the ALJ is not before us.) The Commissioner argues, in particular, that an issue-exhaustion requirement is "an important corollary" of any requirement of exhaustion of remedies. . . . We think that this is not necessarily so and that the corollary is particularly unwarranted in this case.

Initially, we note that requirements of administrative issue exhaustion are largely creatures of statute. Marine Mammal Conservancy, Inc. v. Department of Agriculture, 328 U.S. App. D.C. 253, 134 F.3d 409, 412 (CADC 1998). Our cases addressing issue exhaustion reflect this fact. For example, in Woelke & Romero Framing, Inc. v. NLRB, 456 U.S. 645 (1982), we held that the Court of Appeals lacked jurisdiction to review objections not raised before the National Labor Relations Board. We so held because a statute provided that "'no objection that has not been urged before the Board . . . shall be considered by the court.'" 456 U.S. at 665 (quoting 29 U.S.C. §160(e) (1982 ed.)). Our decision in FPC v. Colorado Interstate Gas Co., 348 U.S. 492 (1955), followed similar reasoning. See also United States v. L. A. Tucker Truck Lines, Inc., 344 U.S. 33, 36, n.6 (1952) (collecting statutes); Washington Assn. for Television and Children v. FCC, 229 U.S. App. D.C. 363, 712 F.2d 677, 681-682, and n.6 (CADC 1983) (interpreting issue-exhaustion requirement in 47 U.S.C. §405 (1982 ed.) and collecting statutes). Here, the Commissioner does not contend that any statute requires issue exhaustion in the request for review.

Similarly, it is common for an agency's regulations to require issue exhaustion in administrative appeals. See, e.g., 20 CFR §802.211(a) (1999) (petition for review to Benefits Review Board must "list the specific issues to be considered on appeal"). And when regulations do so, courts reviewing agency action regularly ensure against the bypassing of that requirement by refusing to consider unexhausted issues. See, e.g., South Carolina v. United States Dept. of Labor, 795 F.2d 375, 378 (CA4 1986); Sears, Roebuck and Co. v. FTC, 676 F.2d 385, 398, n.26 (CA9 1982). Yet, SSA regulations do not require issue exhaustion. (Although the question is not before us, we think it likely that the Commissioner could adopt a regulation that did require issue exhaustion.)

It is true that we have imposed an issue-exhaustion requirement even in the absence of a statute or regulation. But the reason we have done so does not apply here. The basis for a judicially imposed issue-exhaustion requirement is an analogy to the rule that appellate courts will not consider arguments not raised before trial courts. As the Court explained in Hormel v. Helvering, 312 U.S. 552 (1941):

> Ordinarily an appellate court does not give consideration to issues not raised below. For our procedural scheme contemplates that parties shall come to issue in the trial forum vested with authority to determine questions of fact. This is essential in order that parties may have the opportunity to offer all the evidence they believe relevant to the issues which the trial tribunal is alone competent to decide; it is equally essential in order that litigants may not be surprised on appeal by final decision there of issues upon which they have had no opportunity to introduce evidence. And the basic reasons which support this general principle applicable to trial courts make it equally desirable that parties should have an opportunity to offer evidence on the general issues involved in the less formal proceedings before administrative agencies entrusted with the responsibility of fact finding.

312 U.S. at 556.

As we further explained in *L. A. Tucker Truck Lines*, courts require administrative issue exhaustion "as a general rule" because it is usually "appropriate under [an agency's] practice" for "contestants in an adversary proceeding" before it to develop fully all issues there....

But, as *Hormel* and *L. A. Tucker Truck Lines* suggest, the desirability of a court imposing a requirement of issue exhaustion depends on the degree to which the analogy to normal adversarial litigation applies in a particular administrative proceeding. Cf. McKart v. United States, 395 U.S. 185, 193, 23 L. Ed. 2d 194, 89 S. Ct. 1657 (1969) (application of doctrine of exhaustion of administrative remedies "requires an understanding of its purposes and of the particular administrative scheme involved"); *Salfi*, 422 U.S. at 765 (same). Where the parties are expected to develop the issues in an adversarial administrative proceeding, it seems to us that the rationale for requiring issue exhaustion is at its greatest. *Hormel, L. A. Tucker Truck Lines*, and *Aragon* each involved an adversarial proceeding.... Where, by contrast, an administrative proceeding is not adversarial, we think the reasons for a court to require issue exhaustion are much weaker. More generally, we have observed that "it is well settled that there are wide differences between administrative agencies and courts," Shepard v. NLRB, 459 U.S. 344, 351, 74 L. Ed. 2d 523, 103 S. Ct. 665 (1983), and we have thus warned against reflexively "assimilating the relation of... administrative bodies and the courts to the relationship between lower and upper courts," FCC v. Pottsville Broadcasting Co., 309 U.S. 134, 144, 84 L. Ed. 656, 60 S. Ct. 437 (1940).

B

The differences between courts and agencies are nowhere more pronounced than in Social Security proceedings. Although "many agency systems of adjudication are based to a significant extent on the judicial model of decision making," 2 K. Davis & R. Pierce, Administrative Law Treatise §9.10, p. 103 (3d ed. 1994), the SSA is "perhaps the best example of an agency" that is not, B. Schwartz, Administrative Law 469-470 (4th ed. 1994). See id. at 470 ("The most important of [the SSA's modifications of the judicial model] is the replacement of normal adversary procedure by... the 'investigatory model'" (quoting Friendly, Some Kind of Hearing, 123 U. Pa. L. Rev. 1267, 1290 (1975))). Social Security proceedings are inquisitorial rather than adversarial. It is the ALJ's duty to investigate the facts and develop the arguments both for and against granting benefits, see Richardson v. Perales, 402 U.S. 389, 400-401 (1971), and the Council's review is similarly broad. The Commissioner has no representative before the ALJ to oppose the claim for benefits, and we have found no indication that he opposes claimants before the Council. See generally Dubin, Torquemada Meets Kafka: The Misapplication of the Issue Exhaustion Doctrine to Inquisitorial Administrative Proceedings, 97 Colum. L. Rev. 1289, 1301-1305, 1325-1329 (1997).

The regulations make this nature of SSA proceedings quite clear. They expressly provide that the SSA "conducts the administrative review process in an informal, nonadversary manner." 20 CFR §404.900(b) (1999). They permit — but do not require — the filing of a brief with the Council (even when the Council grants review), §404.975, and the Council's review is plenary unless it states otherwise, §404.976(a). See also §404.900(b) ("We will consider at each step of the review process any information you present as well as all the information in our records."). The Commissioner's involvement in the Appeals Council's decision whether to grant review appears to be not as a litigant opposing the claimant, but rather just as an advisor to the Council regarding which cases are good candidates for the Council to review pursuant to its authority to review a case sua sponte. See §§404.969(b)-(c); *Perales, supra,* at 403. The regulations further make clear that the Council will "evaluate the entire record," including "new and material evidence," in determining whether to grant review. §404.970(b). Similarly, the notice of decision that ALJ's provide unsuccessful claimants informs them that if they request review, the Council will "consider all of [the ALJ's] decision, even the parts with which you may agree" and that the Council might review the decision "even if you do not ask it to do so." App. 25-27. Finally, Form HA-520, which the Commissioner considers adequate for the Council's purposes in determining whether to review a case, see §422.205(a), provides only three lines for the request for review, and a notice accompanying the form estimates that it will take only 10 minutes to "read the instructions, gather the necessary facts and fill out the form." The form therefore strongly suggests that the Council does not depend much, if at all, on claimants to identify issues for review. Given that a large portion of Social Security claimants either have no representation at all or are represented by non-attorneys, see Dubin, *supra,* at 1294, n.29, the lack of such dependence is entirely understandable.

Thus, the *Hormel* analogy to judicial proceedings is at its weakest in this area. The adversarial development of issues by the parties — the "coming to issue," 312 U.S. at 556 — on which that analogy depends simply does not exist. The Council, not the claimant, has primary responsibility for identifying and developing the issues. We therefore agree with the Eighth Circuit that "the general rule [of issue exhaustion] makes little sense in this particular context." *Harwood,* 186 F.3d at 1042.

Accordingly, we hold that a judicially created issue-exhaustion requirement is inappropriate. Claimants who exhaust administrative remedies need not also exhaust issues in a request for review by the Appeals Council in order to preserve judicial review of those issues. The judgment of the Fifth Circuit is reversed, and the case is remanded for further proceedings consistent with this opinion. It is so ordered.

NOTES

1. The Court noted that the only issue was whether the claimant exhausted remedies by failing to raise issues with the Appeals Council, rather than with the administrative law judge. Would it have made any difference if the issues also had not been raised with the administrative law judge? The Court recently addressed this question in Carr v. Saul, 141 S. Ct. 1352 (2021). After SSA ALJs and the Appeals Council had denied petitioners' applications for benefits, petitioners from several circuits sought judicial review in the appropriate Courts of Appeals where they argued, for the first time, that they were entitled to a new hearing because the SSA ALJs had been unconstitutionally appointed. *Carr*, 141 S. Ct. at 1356-1357. The new argument stemmed from the Court's recent decision in Lucia v. SEC, ___U.S.___, 138 S. Ct. 2044 (2018), *supra* Chapter 1, holding the appointment process for SEC ALJs to be unconstitutional. Id. The SSA argued that, even if the appointment process for SSA ALJs was unconstitutional in light of *Lucia*, "petitioners had forfeited their Appointments Clause challenges by failing to raise them before the agency." Id. at 1357. The Court disagreed:

> Much of what the *Sims* opinions said about Appeals Council review applies equally to ALJ proceedings. . . . The SSA regulations that ensure informal, nonadversarial proceedings and plenary review apply as much to ALJs as to the Appeals Council. . . . Like the form supplied by the SSA to request Appeals Council review, the form to request an ALJ hearing provides roughly three lines for claimants to explain their disagreement with the agency's determination. . . . Last, as with the Appeal Council, SSA regulations provide no notice that claimants . . . must raise specific issues before the ALJ to preserve them for review in federal court.

Id. at 1359-1360 (internal quotation marks and citations omitted). While the Court admitted that "ALJ proceedings may be comparatively more adversarial than Appeals Council proceedings," it held that, at least in the context of Appointments Clause challenges, "two additional considerations tip[ped] the scales decidedly against imposing an issue-exhaustion requirement." Id. at 1360. First, the constitutional nature of the claims suggested that a court was the more appropriate forum in which to raise the issue. Id. at 1360-1361. Second, since SSA ALJs could not "remedy[] any defects in their own appointments," the Court viewed any issue exhaustion requirement as futile. Id. at 1361.

What do the decisions in *Sims* and *Carr* suggest are the most important factors in determining whether issue exhaustion is necessary? Could these decisions extend to other agencies? Should they?

2. The Court noted that issue exhaustion may be imposed as a matter of statute or regulation and in fact indicated that the Social Security Administration probably had the authority to adopt the appropriate regulation. Given this regulatory authority, why do courts sometimes impose a judicially created doctrine of issue exhaustion?

3. What happens when a plaintiff exhausts remedies for some issues in a complaint but not others? The issue was addressed in Jones v. Bock, 549 U.S. 199 (2007). The Court dealt with an exhaustion requirement imposed by Congress on claims brought by prisoners. The provision did not specifically address issue exhaustion. The Court noted that some lower courts had applied a doctrine of "total exhaustion," dismissing complaints unless all issues had been exhausted. The Supreme Court, however, rejected the doctrine of total exhaustion, noting that "[as] a general matter, if a complaint contains both good and bad claims, the court proceeds with the good and leaves the bad." Moreover, plaintiffs could avoid "total exhaustion" by filing multiple suits, each including a single claim. Discuss the pros and cons of "total exhaustion."

G RIPENESS FOR REVIEW

The ripeness doctrine exists to "ensure[] that a matter is suitable for judicial consideration, particularly that the facts have developed to the point where judicial involvement is appropriate, and there is enough potential for harm to the party challenging agency action that a court should consider the claims. In essence, ripeness addresses the question of whether review is premature." Bill Jordan, Ripeness and Standing — Maintain the Distinction, 39 Admin & Reg. L. News 17, 17 (2013). The Ninth Circuit has emphasized the importance of the "finality" of an agency action in determining whether that action is ripe for judicial review:

> "It is the imposition of an obligation or the fixing of a legal relationship that is the indicium of finality of the administrative process." . . . Indicia of finality include: the administrative action challenged should be a definitive statement of an agency's position; the action should have a direct and immediate effect on the day-to-day business of the complaining parties; the action should have the status of law; immediate compliance with the terms should be expected; and the question should be a legal one.

Mt. Adams Veneer Co. v. United States, 896 F.2d 339, 343 (9th Cir. 1990).

In *Abbott Laboratories*, a group of pharmaceutical manufacturing companies challenged certain drug labeling regulations on the ground that they exceeded the authority of the Commissioner of Food and Drugs. The Court granted certiorari to resolve the question of whether the action represented an "actual case or controversy" — that is, whether the case was ripe for judicial review.

ABBOTT LABORATORIES v. GARDNER

387 U.S. 136 (1967)

MR. JUSTICE HARLAN delivered the opinion of the Court.

. . .

A further inquiry must . . . be made. The injunctive and declaratory judgment remedies are discretionary, and courts traditionally have been reluctant to apply them to administrative determinations unless these arise in the context of a controversy "ripe" for judicial resolution. Without undertaking to survey the intricacies of the ripeness doctrine it is fair to say that its basic rationale is to prevent the courts, through avoidance of premature adjudication, from entangling themselves in abstract disagreements over administrative policies, and also to protect the agencies from judicial interference until an administrative decision has been formalized and its effects felt in a concrete way by the challenging parties. The problem is best seen in a twofold aspect, requiring us to evaluate both the fitness of the issues for judicial decision and the hardship to the parties of withholding court consideration. . . .

This is also a case in which the impact of the regulations upon the petitioners is sufficiently direct and immediate as to render the issue appropriate for judicial review at this stage. These regulations purport to give an authoritative interpretation of a statutory provision that has a direct effect on the day-to-day business of all prescription drug companies; its promulgation puts petitioners in a dilemma that it was the very purpose of the Declaratory Judgment Act to ameliorate. . . .

NOTES

1. As the *Abbott Laboratories* case shows, it does not matter whether the challenged agency act is a rule or order. Where a regulation requires an immediate change in conduct with penalties attached to noncompliance, the regulation is ripe for challenge. A different result would place in a dilemma those subject to substantive rules that they claim are invalid: either they must comply or take the even more costly alternative of risking serious criminal and/or civil penalties.

According to Justice Scalia, the cases "permit broad regulations to serve as the 'agency action,' and thus to be the object of judicial review directly, even before the concrete effects normally required for APA review are felt. . . . The major [example], of course, is a substantive rule which as a practical matter requires the plaintiff to adjust his conduct immediately. Such agency action is 'ripe' for review at once, whether or not explicit statutory review apart from the APA is provided. . . ." Lujan v. National Wildlife Federation, 497 U.S. 871, 891 (1990). See also Suitum v. Tahoe Regional Planning Agency, 520 U.S. 725 (1997) (reversing the circuit court in holding that an agency decision precluding building on land purchased for real estate development was ripe despite the arguments that there was no adverse effect against the petitioner because she had not yet attempted to transfer her rights to the land's development); Student Loan Marketing Ass'n v. Riley, 104 F.3d 397 (D.C. Cir. 1997) (holding that appeal of agency letter interpreting law as requiring petitioner to pay a 0.3 percent fee on securitized loans was final agency action because the letter required petitioner to abandon securitization plans or risk paying the fee).

2. What are the tests of ripeness? Compare the statement in Port of Boston Marine Terminal v. Rederiaktiebolaget, 400 U.S. 62, 71 (1970): "[T]he relevant considerations in determining finality are whether the process of administrative decisionmaking has reached a stage where judicial review will not disrupt the orderly process of adjudication and whether rights or obligations have been determined or legal consequences will flow from the agency action."

The prevailing trend in recent years has been in the direction of relaxing ripeness requirements. In the case just cited, the Federal Maritime Commission had issued an order stating that FMC approval was not necessary for a charge to be shifted from consignees to carriers by marine terminal operators. The Court declared that the

> argument that the order lacked finality because it had no independent effect on anyone and resembled an interlocutory court order denying a motion to dismiss a complaint has the hollow ring of another era. . . . Here there was no possible disruption of the administrative process; there was nothing else for the Commission to do. And certainly the Commission's action was expected to and did have legal consequences.

NATIONAL PARK HOSPITALITY ASS'N v. DEPARTMENT OF INTERIOR

538 U.S. 803 (2003)

THOMAS, J.

Petitioner, a nonprofit trade association that represents concessioners doing business in the national parks, challenges a National Park Service (NPS) regulation that purports to render the Contract Disputes Act of 1978 (CDA), 92 Stat. 2383, 41 U.S.C. §601 et seq. [41 U.S.C.S. §§601 et seq.], inapplicable to concession contracts. We conclude that the controversy is not yet ripe for judicial resolution.

I

The CDA establishes rules governing disputes arising out of certain Government contracts. The statute provides that these disputes first be submitted to an agency's contracting officer. §605. A Government contractor dissatisfied with the contracting officer's decision may seek review either from the United States Court of Federal Claims or from an administrative board in the agency. See §§606, 607(d), 609(a). Either decision may then be appealed to the United States Court of Appeals for the Federal Circuit. See 28 U.S.C. §1295, 28 U.S.C. §607(g).

Since 1916 Congress has charged NPS to "promote and regulate the use of the Federal areas known as national parks," "conserve the scenery and the natural and historic objects and the wild life therein," and "provide for [their] enjoyment [in a way that] will leave them unimpaired for the enjoyment of future generations." An Act to Establish a National Park Service, 39 Stat. 535, 16 U.S.C. §1. To make visits to national parks more enjoyable for the public, Congress authorized NPS to "grant privileges, leases, and permits for the use of land for the accommodation of visitors." §3, 39 Stat. 535. Such "privileges, leases, and permits" have become embodied in national parks concession contracts.

The specific rules governing national parks concession contracts have changed over time. In 1998, however, Congress enacted the National Parks Omnibus Management Act of 1998 (1998 Act or Act), Pub. L. 105-391, 112 Stat. 3497 (codified with certain exceptions in 16 U.S.C. §§5951-5966, 16 U.S.C.S. §§5951, establishing a new and comprehensive concession management program for national parks. The 1998 Act authorizes the Secretary of the Interior to enact regulations implementing the Act's provisions, §5965.

NPS, to which the Secretary has delegated her authority under the 1998 Act, promptly began a rulemaking proceeding to implement the Act. After notice and comment, final regulations were issued in April 2000. 65 Fed. Reg. 20630 (2000) (codified in 36 C.F.R. pt. 51). The regulations define the term "concession contract" as follows:

> A *concession contract (or contract)* means a binding written agreement between the Director and a concessioner. . . . Concession contracts are not contracts within the meaning of 41 U.S.C. §601 et seq. [(the Contract Disputes Act)] and are not service or procurement contracts within the meaning of statutes, regulations or policies that apply only to federal service contracts or other types of federal procurement actions.

36 C.F.R. §51.3(2002).

Through this provision NPS took a position with respect to a longstanding controversy with the Department of Interior's Board of Contract Appeals (IBCA). Beginning in 1989, the IBCA ruled that NPS concession contracts *were* subject to the CDA, see R & R Enterprises, 89-2 B.C.A., P 21708, pp 109145-109147 (1989), and subsequent attempts by NPS to convince the IBCA otherwise proved unavailing, National Park Concessions, Inc., 94-3 B.C.A., P 27104, pp 135096-135098 (1994).

II

Petitioner challenged the validity of §51.3 in the District Court for the District of Columbia. Amfac Resorts, L. L. C. v. United States Dept. of Interior, 142 F. Supp. 2d 54, 80-82 (2001). The District Court upheld the regulation, applying the deference principle of Chevron U.S.A. Inc. v. Natural Resources Defense Council, Inc., 467 U.S. 837 (1984). . . .

The Court of Appeals for the District of Columbia Circuit affirmed, albeit on different grounds. Amfac Resorts, L. L. C. v. United States Dept. of Interior, 350 U.S. App. D.C. 191, 282 F.3d 818, 834-835 (2002). Recognizing that NPS "does not administer the [CDA], and thus may not have interpretative authority over its provisions," the court placed no reliance on *Chevron* but simply "agreed" with NPS' reading of the CDA, finding that reading consistent with both the CDA and the 1998 Act. 282 F.3d at 835. . . .

III

Ripeness is a justiciability doctrine designed "to prevent the courts, through avoidance of premature adjudication, from entangling themselves in abstract disagreements over administrative policies, and also to protect the agencies from judicial interference until an administrative decision has been formalized and its effects felt in a concrete way by the challenging parties." Abbott

Laboratories v. Gardner, 387 U.S. 136, 148-149 (1967); accord, Ohio Forestry Assn. v. Sierra Club, 523 U.S. 726, 732-733 (1998). The ripeness doctrine is "drawn both from Article III limitations on judicial power and from prudential reasons for refusing to exercise jurisdiction," Reno v. Catholic Social Services, Inc., 509 U.S. 43, 57, n.18 (1993) (citations omitted), but, even in a case raising only prudential concerns, the question of ripeness may be considered on a court's own motion. Ibid. (citing Regional Rail Reorganization Act Cases, 419 U.S. 102,138, (1974)).

Determining whether administrative action is ripe for judicial review requires us to evaluate (1) the fitness of the issues for judicial decision and (2) the hardship to the parties of withholding court consideration. *Abbott Laboratories, supra*, at 149. "Absent [a statutory provision providing for immediate judicial review], a regulation is not ordinarily considered the type of agency action 'ripe' for judicial review under the [Administrative Procedure Act (APA)] until the scope of the controversy has been reduced to more manageable proportions, and its factual components fleshed out, by some concrete action applying the regulation to the claimant's situation in a fashion that harms or threatens to harm him. (The major exception, of course, is a substantive rule which as a practical matter requires the plaintiff to adjust his conduct immediately. . . .)" Lujan v. National Wildlife Federation, 497 U.S. 871, 891 (1990). Under the facts now before us, we conclude this case is not ripe.

We turn first to the hardship inquiry. The federal respondents concede that, because NPS has no delegated rulemaking authority under the CDA, the challenged portion of §51.3 cannot be a legislative regulation with the force of law. See Brief for Federal Respondents 15, n.6; Supplemental Brief for Federal Respondents 6. They note, though, that "agencies may issue interpretive rules 'to advise the public of the agency's construction of the statutes and rules *which it administers*,'" Brief for Federal Respondents 15, n.6 (quoting Shalala v. Guernsey Memorial Hospital, 514 U.S. 87, 99 (1995)) (emphasis added), and seek to characterize §51.3 as such an interpretive rule.

We disagree. Unlike in *Guernsey Memorial Hospital*, where the agency issuing the interpretative guideline was responsible for administering the relevant statutes and regulations, NPS is not empowered to administer the CDA. Rather, the task of applying the CDA rests with agency contracting officers and boards of contract appeals, as well as the Federal Court of Claims, the Court of Appeals for the Federal Circuit, and, ultimately, this Court. Moreover, under the CDA, any authority regarding the proper arrangement of agency boards belongs to the Administrator for Federal Procurement Policy. See 41 U.S.C. §607(h) ("Pursuant to the authority conferred under the Office of Federal Procurement Policy Act [41 U.S.C. §401 et seq., the Administrator is authorized and directed, as may be necessary or desirable to carry out the provisions of this chapter, to issue guidelines with respect to criteria for the establishment, functions, and procedures of the agency boards. . . ."). Consequently, we consider §51.3 to be nothing more than a "general statement of policy" designed to inform the public of NPS' views on the proper application of the CDA. 5 U.S.C. §553(b)(3)(A).

Viewed in this light, §51.3 does not create "adverse effects of a strictly legal kind," which we have previously required for a showing of hardship. *Ohio Forestry*

Assn., Inc., 523 U.S., at 733. Just like the Forest Service plan at issue in *Ohio Forestry*, §51.3 "does not command anyone to do anything or to refrain from doing anything; [it] does not grant, withhold, or modify any formal legal license, power, or authority; [it] does not subject anyone to any civil or criminal liability; [and it] creates no legal rights or obligations." Ibid.

Moreover, §51.3 does not affect a concessioner's primary conduct. . . . Unlike the regulation at issue in *Abbott Laboratories*, which required drug manufacturers to change the labels, advertisements, and promotional materials they used in marketing prescription drugs on pain of criminal and civil penalties, see 387 U.S., at 152-153, the regulation here leaves a concessioner free to conduct its business as it sees fit. See also Gardner v. Toilet Goods Assn., 387 U.S. 167, 171 (1967) (regulations governing conditions for use of color additives in foods, drugs, and cosmetics were "self-executing" and had "an immediate and substantial impact upon the respondents"). . . .

Petitioner contends that delaying judicial resolution of this issue will result in real harm because the applicability *vel non* of the CDA is one of the factors a concessioner takes into account when preparing its bid for NPS concession contracts. See Supplemental Brief for Petitioner 4-6. Petitioner's argument appears to be that mere uncertainty as to the validity of a legal rule constitutes a hardship for purposes of the ripeness analysis. We are not persuaded. If we were to follow petitioner's logic, courts would soon be overwhelmed with requests for what essentially would be advisory opinions because most business transactions could be priced more accurately if even a small portion of existing legal uncertainties were resolved. In short, petitioner has failed to demonstrate that deferring judicial review will result in real hardship.

We consider next whether the issue in this case is fit for review. Although the question presented here is "a purely legal one" and §51.3 constitutes "final agency action" within the meaning of §10 of the APA, 5 U.S.C. §704, *Abbott Laboratories*, *supra*, at 149, we nevertheless believe that further factual development would "significantly advance our ability to deal with the legal issues presented," Duke Power Co. v. Carolina Environmental Study Group, Inc., 438 U.S. 59, 82, 57 (1978); accord, *Ohio Forestry Assn., Inc.*, 523 U.S., at 736-737; *Toilet Goods Assn., supra*, at 163. While the federal respondents generally argue that NPS was correct to conclude that the CDA does not cover concession contracts, they acknowledge that certain types of concession contracts might come under the broad language of the CDA. Brief for Federal Respondents 33-34. Similarly, while petitioner and respondent Xanterra Parks & Resorts, LLC, present a facial challenge to §51.3, both rely on specific characteristics of certain types of concession contracts to support their positions. See Brief for Petitioner 21-23, 36; Brief for Respondent Xanterra Parks & Resorts, LLC, 20, 22. In light of the foregoing, we conclude that judicial resolution of the question presented here should await a concrete dispute about a particular concession contract. . . .

For the reasons stated above, we vacate the judgment of the Court of Appeals insofar as it addressed the validity of §51.3 and remand with instructions to dismiss the case with respect to this issue.

It is so ordered.

H SCOPE OF REVIEW

APA §706. Scope of Review

To the extent necessary to decision and when presented, the reviewing court shall decide all relevant questions of law, interpret constitutional and statutory provisions, and determine the meaning or applicability of the terms of an agency action. The reviewing court shall—

(1) compel agency action unlawfully withheld or unreasonably delayed; and

(2) hold unlawful and set aside agency action, findings, and conclusions found to be—

(A) arbitrary, capricious, an abuse of discretion, or otherwise not in accordance with law;

(B) contrary to constitutional right, power, privilege, or immunity;

(C) in excess of statutory jurisdiction, authority, or limitations, or short of statutory right;

(D) without observance of procedure required by law;

(E) unsupported by substantial evidence in a case subject to sections 556 and 557 of this title or otherwise reviewed on the record of an agency hearing provided by statute; or

(F) unwarranted by the facts to the extent that the facts are subject to trial de novo by the reviewing court.

In making the foregoing determinations, the court shall review the whole record or those parts of it cited by a party, and due account shall be taken of the rule of prejudicial error.

1. Substantial Evidence Rule

COMMENTS

1. How far should the reviewing court inquire into the merits of challenged agency action? Should the court assume only an appellate role, or should it act as though it were the tribunal of first instance in the case?

2. As we shall see, the scope of review is governed by the so-called substantial evidence rule. That rule has

> frequently been used by Congress and . . . consistently been associated with a review limited to the administrative record. The term "substantial evidence" in particular has become a term of art to describe the basis on which an administrative record is

> to be judged by a reviewing court. This standard goes to the reasonableness of what the agency did *on the basis of the evidence before it*, for a decision may be supported by substantial evidence even though it could be refuted by other evidence that was not presented to the decision-making body. . . . This sound and clearly expressed purpose would be frustrated if either side were free to withhold evidence at the administrative level and then to introduce it in a judicial proceeding. Moreover, the consequence of such a procedure would in many instances be a needless duplication of evidentiary hearings and a heavy additional burden in the time and expense required to bring litigation to an end.

United States v. Carlo Bianchi & Co., 373 U.S. 709, 715, 717 (1963). As the Court put it in another portion of the just-quoted opinion, "the reviewing function is one ordinarily limited to consideration of the decision of the agency or court below and of the evidence on which it was based." This rule gives way only if there is no agency record, Citizens to Preserve Overton Park v. Volpe, 401 U.S. 402 (1971), or if there is an express statutory provision for a trial de novo. Otherwise, "judicial review of agency action is limited to review of the record on which the administrative decision was based." Love v. Thomas, 858 F.2d 1347, 1356 (9th Cir. 1988).

3. The overriding consideration in fashioning the scope of review has been that of deference to the administrative expert. That theme certainly strikes a responsive chord in a society of insecure laymen. "The highly industrialized society in which we live has a great appetite for 'know-how.' Such a society elevates and aggrandizes the position of the expert. His is the voice with the ready answer. His opinions become the facts upon which lesser mortals — laymen — risk life and fortune." Rifkind, A Special Court for Patent Litigation? The Danger of a Specialized Judiciary, 37 A.B.A. J. 425 (1951). See Judge Neely, concurring in Monongahela Power Co. v. Public Service Comm'n, 276 S.E.2d 179, 189 (W. Va. 1981):

> I have very few illusions about my own limitations as a judge and from those limitations I generalize to the inherent limitations of all appellate courts reviewing rate cases. It must be remembered that this Court sees approximately 1,262 cases a year with five judges. I am not an accountant, electrical engineer, financier, banker, stock broker, or systems management analyst. It is the height of folly to expect judges intelligently to review a 5,000 page record addressing the intricacies of public utility operation.

Is such deference to the administrative expert consistent with the role of judicial review in controlling the legality of agency action?

"No lesson seems to be so deeply inculcated by experience of life as that you should never trust experts. If you believe doctors, nothing is wholesome; if you believe theologians, nothing is innocent; if you believe soldiers, nothing is safe." Manchester, The Last Lion: Winston Spencer Churchill — Visions of Glory 1874-1932, 523 (1983). There are increasing signs that the courts too have become uneasy at possible over-deference to administrative expertise. An oft-quoted statement is the following by Judge Bazelon in 1971:

> We stand on the threshold of a new era in the history of the long and fruitful collaboration of administrative agencies and reviewing courts. For many years, courts have treated administrative policy decisions with great deference, confining judicial

> attention primarily to matters of procedure. On matters of substance, the courts regularly upheld agency action, with a nod in the direction of the "substantial evidence" test, and a bow to the mysteries of administrative expertise. Courts occasionally asserted, but less often exercised, the power to set aside agency action on the ground that an impermissible factor had entered into the decision, or a crucial factor had not been considered. Gradually, however, that power has come into more frequent use, and with it, the requirement that administrators articulate the factors on which they base their decisions.
>
> Strict adherence to that requirement is especially important now that the character of administrative litigation is changing. As a result of expanding doctrines of standing and reviewability, and new statutory causes of action, courts are increasingly asked to review administrative action that touches on fundamental personal interests in life, health, and liberty. These interests have always had a special claim to judicial protection, in comparison with the economic interests at stake in a rate-making or licensing proceeding.
>
> To protect these interests from administrative arbitrariness, it is necessary . . . to insist on strict judicial scrutiny of administrative action.

Environmental Defense Fund v. Ruckelshaus, 439 F.2d 584, 597-598 (D.C. Cir. 1971).

UNIVERSAL CAMERA CORP. v. NLRB

340 U.S. 474 (1951)

MR. JUSTICE FRANKFURTER delivered the opinion of the Court.

The essential issue raised by this case . . . is the effect of the Administrative Procedure Act and the legislation colloquially known as the Taft-Hartley Act . . . on the duty of Courts of Appeal when called upon to review orders of the National Labor Relations Board.

The Court of Appeals for the Second Circuit granted enforcement of an order directing, in the main, that petitioner reinstate with back pay an employee found to have been discharged because he gave testimony under the Wagner Act, 29 U.S.C.A. §151 et seq., and cease and desist from discriminating against any employee who files charges or gives testimony under the Act. The court below, Judge Swan dissenting, decreed full enforcement of the order. 2d Cir., 179 F.2d 749. Because the views of that court regarding the effect of the new legislation on the relation between the Board and the courts of appeals in the enforcement of the Board's orders conflicted with those of the Court of Appeals for the Sixth Circuit we brought both cases here. . . . The clash of opinion obviously required settlement by this court.

I

Want of certainty in judicial review of Labor Board decisions partly reflects the intractability of any formula to furnish definiteness of content for all the impalpable factors involved in judicial review. But in part doubts as to the nature of the reviewing power and uncertainties in its application derive from history, and to that extent an elucidation of this history may clear them away. The Wagner Act provided:

> The findings of the Board as to the facts, if supported by evidence, shall be conclusive.

. . . This Court read "evidence" to mean "substantial evidence," . . . and we said that "[s]ubstantial evidence is more than a mere scintilla. It means such relevant evidence as a reasonable mind might accept as adequate to support a conclusion." Consolidated Edison Co. v. National Labor Relations Board, 305 U.S. 197, 229. Accordingly, it "must do more than create a suspicion of the existence of the fact to be established. . . . [I]t must be enough to justify, if the trial were to a jury, a refusal to direct a verdict when the conclusion sought to be drawn from it is one of fact for the jury." . . .

The very smoothness of the "substantial evidence" formula as the standard for reviewing the evidentiary validity of the Board's findings established its currency. But the inevitably variant applications of the standard to conflicting evidence soon brought contrariety of views and in due course bred criticism. Even though the whole record may have been canvassed in order to determine whether the evidentiary foundation of a determination by the Board was "substantial," the phrasing of this Court's process of review readily lent itself to the notion that it was enough that the evidence supporting the Board's result was "substantial" when considered by itself. It is fair to say that by imperceptible steps regard for the fact-finding function of the Board led to the assumption that the requirements of the Wagner Act were met when the reviewing court could find in the record evidence which, when viewed in isolation, substantiated the Board's findings. . . . This is not to say that every member of this Court was consciously guided by this view or that the Court ever explicitly avowed this practice as doctrine. What matters is that the belief justifiably arose that the Court had so construed the obligation to review.

Criticism of so contracted a reviewing power reinforced dissatisfaction felt in various quarters with the Board's administration of the Wagner Act in the years preceding the war. The scheme of the Act was attacked as an inherently unfair fusion of the functions of prosecutor and judge. Accusations of partisan bias were not wanting. The "irresponsible admission and weighing of hearsay, opinion, and emotional speculation in place of factual evidence" was said to be a "serious menace." No doubt some, perhaps even much, of the criticism was baseless and some surely was reckless. What is here relevant, however, is the climate of opinion thereby generated and its effect on Congress. Protests against "shocking injustices" and intimations of judicial "abdication" with which some courts granted enforcement of the Board's orders stimulated pressures for legislative relief from alleged administrative excesses.

The strength of these pressures was reflected in the passage in 1940 of the Walter-Logan Bill. It was vetoed by President Roosevelt, partly because it imposed unduly rigid limitations on the administrative process, and partly because of the investigation into the actual operation of the administrative process then being conducted by an experienced committee appointed by the Attorney General. It is worth noting that despite its aim to tighten control over administrative determinations of fact, the Walter-Logan Bill contented itself with the conventional formula that an agency's decision could be set aside if "the findings of fact are not supported by substantial evidence."

The final report of the Attorney General's Committee was submitted in January, 1941. The majority concluded that "[d]issatisfaction with the existing standards as to the scope of judicial review derives largely from dissatisfaction with the fact-finding procedures now employed by the administrative bodies." Departure from the "substantial evidence" test, it thought, would either create unnecessary uncertainty or transfer to courts the responsibility for ascertaining and assaying matters the significance of which lies outside judicial competence. Accordingly, it recommended against legislation embodying a general scheme of judicial review.

Three members of the Committee registered a dissent. Their view was that the "present system or lack of system of judicial review" led to inconsistency and uncertainty. They reported that under a "prevalent" interpretation of the "substantial evidence" rule

> if what is called "substantial evidence" is found anywhere in the record to support conclusions of fact, the courts are said to be obliged to sustain the decision without reference to how heavily the countervailing evidence may preponderate — unless indeed the stage of arbitrary decision is reached. Under this interpretation, the courts need to read only one side of the case and, if they find any evidence there, the administrative action is to be sustained and the record to the contrary is to be ignored.

Their view led them to recommend that Congress enact principles of review applicable to all agencies not excepted by unique characteristics. One of these principles was expressed by the formula that judicial review could extend to "findings, inferences, or conclusions of fact unsupported, upon the whole record, by substantial evidence." So far as the history of this movement for enlarged review reveals, the phrase "upon the whole record" makes its first appearance in this recommendation of the minority of the Attorney General's Committee. This evidence of the close relationship between the phrase and the criticism out of which it arose is important, for the substance of this formula for judicial review found its way into the statute books when Congress with unquestioning — we might even say uncritical — unanimity enacted the Administrative Procedure Act.

One is tempted to say "uncritical" because the legislative history of that Act hardly speaks with that clarity of purpose which Congress supposedly furnished courts in order to enable them to enforce its true will. On the one hand, the sponsors of the legislation indicated that they were reaffirming the prevailing "substantial evidence" test. But with equal clarity they expressed disapproval of the manner in which the courts were applying their own standard. The committee reports of both houses refer to the practice of agencies to rely upon "suspicion, surmise, implications, or plainly incredible evidence," and indicate that courts are to exact higher standards "in the exercise of their independent judgment" and on consideration of "the whole record."

Similar dissatisfaction with too restricted application of the "substantial evidence" test is reflected in the legislative history of the Taft-Hartley Act. The Bill as reported to the House provided that the

> findings of the Board as to the facts shall be conclusive unless it is made to appear to the satisfaction of the court either (1) that the findings of fact are against the manifest weight of the evidence, or (2) that the findings of fact are not supported by substantial evidence.

The bill left the House with this provision. Early committee prints in the Senate provided for review by "weight of the evidence" or "clearly erroneous" standards. But, as the Senate Committee Report relates, "it was finally decided to conform the statute to the corresponding section of the Administrative Procedure Act where the substantial evidence test prevails. In order to clarify any ambiguity in that statute, however, the committee inserted the words 'questions of fact, if supported by substantial evidence *on the record considered as a whole*. . . .'"

This phraseology was adopted by the Senate. The House conferees agreed. . . .

It is fair to say that in all this Congress expressed a mood. And it expressed its mood not merely by oratory but by legislation. As legislation that mood must be respected, even though it can only serve as a standard for judgment and not as a body of rigid rules assuring sameness of application. Enforcement of such broad standards implies subtlety of mind and solidity of judgment. But it is not for us to question that Congress may assume such qualities in the federal judiciary.

From the legislative story we have summarized, two concrete conclusions do emerge. One is the identity of aim of the Administrative Procedure Act and the Taft-Hartley Act regarding the proof with which the Labor Board must support a decision. The other is that now Congress has left no room for doubt as to the kind of scrutiny which a court of appeals must give the record before the Board to satisfy itself that the Board's order rests on adequate proof.

It would be mischievous word-playing to find that the scope of review under the Taft-Hartley Act is any different from that under the Administrative Procedure Act. The Senate Committee which reported the review clause of the Taft-Hartley Act expressly indicated that the two standards were to conform in this regard, and the wording of the two Acts is for purposes of judicial administration identical. And so we hold that the standard of proof specifically required of the Labor Board by the Taft-Hartley Act is the same as that to be exacted by courts reviewing every administrative action subject to the Administrative Procedure Act.

Whether or not it was ever permissible for courts to determine the substantiality of evidence supporting a Labor Board decision merely on the basis of evidence which in and of itself justified it, without taking into account contradictory evidence or evidence from which conflicting inferences could be drawn, the new legislation definitively precludes such a theory of review and bars its practice. The substantiality of evidence must take into account whatever in the record fairly detracts from its weight. This is clearly the significance of the requirement in both statutes that courts consider the whole record. Committee reports and the adoption in the Administrative Procedure Act of the minority views of the Attorney General's Committee demonstrate that to enjoin such a duty on the reviewing court was one of the important purposes of the movement which eventuated in that enactment.

To be sure, the requirement for canvassing "the whole record" in order to ascertain substantiality does not furnish a calculus of value by which a reviewing court can assess the evidence. Nor was it intended to negative the function of the Labor Board as one of those agencies presumably equipped or informed by experience to deal with a specialized field of knowledge, whose findings within that field carry the authority of an expertness which courts do not possess and therefore must respect. Nor does it mean that even as to matters not requiring expertise a court may displace the Board's choice between two fairly conflicting views, even though the court would justifiably have made a different choice had the matter been before it de novo. Congress has merely made it clear that a reviewing court is not barred from setting aside a Board decision when it cannot conscientiously find that the evidence supporting that decision is substantial, when viewed in the light that the record in its entirety furnishes, including the body of evidence opposed to the Board's view.

There remains, then, the question whether enactment of those two statutes has altered the scope of review other than to require that substantiality be determined in the light of all that the record relevantly presents. A formula for judicial review of administrative action may afford grounds for certitude but cannot assure certainty of application.

Some scope for judicial discretion in applying the formula can be avoided only by falsifying the actual process of judging or by using the formula as an instrument of futile casuistry. It cannot be too often repeated that judges are not automata. The ultimate reliance for the fair operation of any standard is a judiciary of high competence and character and the constant play of an informed professional critique upon its work.

Since the precise way in which courts interfere with agency findings cannot be imprisoned within any form of words, new formulas attempting to rephrase the old are not likely to be more helpful than the old. There are no talismanic words that can avoid the process of judgment. The difficulty is that we cannot escape, in relation to this problem, the use of undefined defining terms.

Whatever changes were made by the Administrative Procedure and Taft-Hartley Acts are clearly within this area where precise definition is impossible. Retention of the familiar "substantial evidence" terminology indicates that no drastic reversal of attitude was intended.

But a standard leaving an unavoidable margin for individual judgment does not leave the judicial judgment at large even though the phrasing of the standard does not wholly fence it in. The legislative history of these Acts demonstrates a purpose to impose on courts a responsibility which has not always been recognized. Of course it is a statute and not a committee report which we are interpreting. But the fair interpretation of a statute is often "the art of proliferating a purpose," . . . revealed more by the demonstrable forces that produced it than by its precise phrasing. The adoption in these statutes of the judicially-constructed "substantial evidence" test was a response to pressures for stricter and more uniform practice, not a reflection of approval of all existing practices.

To find the change so elusive that it cannot be precisely defined does not mean it may be ignored. We should fail in our duty to effectuate the will of Congress if we denied recognition to expressed Congressional disapproval of the finality accorded to Labor Board findings by some decisions of this and lower courts, or even of the atmosphere which may have favored those decisions.

We conclude, therefore, that the Administrative Procedure Act and the Taft-Hartley Act direct that courts must now assume more responsibility for the reasonableness and fairness of Labor Board decisions than some courts have shown in the past. Reviewing courts must be influenced by a feeling that they are not to abdicate the conventional judicial function. Congress has imposed on them responsibility for assuring that the Board keeps within reasonable grounds. That responsibility is not less real because it is limited to enforcing the requirement that evidence appear substantial when viewed, on the record as a whole, by courts invested with the authority and enjoying the prestige of the Courts of Appeals. The Board's findings are entitled to respect; but they must nonetheless be set aside when the record before a Court of Appeals clearly precludes the Board's decision from being justified by a fair estimate of the worth of the testimony of witnesses or its informed judgment on matters within its special competence or both.

From this it follows that enactment of these statutes does not require every Court of Appeals to alter its practice. Some — perhaps a majority — have always applied the attitude reflected in this legislation. To explore whether a particular court should or should not alter its practice would only divert attention from the application of the standard now prescribed to a futile inquiry into the nature of the test formerly used by a particular court.

Our power to review the correctness of application of the present standard ought seldom to be called into action. Whether on the record as a whole there is substantial evidence to support agency findings is a question which Congress has placed in the keeping of the Courts of Appeals. This Court will intervene only in what ought to be the rare instance when the standard appears to have been misapprehended or grossly misapplied.

II

Our disagreement with the view of the court below that the scope of review of Labor Board decisions is unaltered by recent legislation does not of itself, as we have noted, require reversal of its decision. This court may have applied a standard of review which satisfies the present Congressional requirement.

The decision of the Court of Appeals is assailed. . . . It is said . . . that the Board's order was not supported by substantial evidence on the record considered as a whole, even apart from the validity of the court's refusal to consider the rejected portions of the examiner's report.

The . . . contention is easily met. It is true that two of the earlier decisions of the court below were among those disapproved by Congress. But this disapproval, we have seen, may well have been caused by unintended intimations of judicial phrasing. And in any event, it is clear from the court's opinion in this case that it in fact did consider the "record as a whole," and did not deem itself merely the judicial echo of the Board's conclusion. The testimony of the company's witnesses was inconsistent, and there was clear evidence that the complaining employee had been discharged by an officer who was at one time influenced against him because of his appearance at the Board hearing. On such a record we could not say that it would be error to grant enforcement. . . .

We therefore remand the cause to the Court of Appeals. . . . We leave it free to grant or deny enforcement as it thinks the principles expressed in this opinion dictate.

Judgment vacated and cause remanded.

NOTES

1. In a 2005 case reviewing findings of fact made by the Federal Trade Commission, the Eleventh Circuit summarized the facts of *Universal Camera* and the Supreme Court's holding:

> [T]he ALJ found an employee was lawfully discharged for insubordination rather than his appearance at an NLRB proceeding. The factual testimony directly conflicted, and the ALJ's finding clearly relied on a credibility determination. The Board reversed the holding. On judicial review, the court of appeals hesitated to consider the ALJ's initial ruling because the Administrative Procedure Act gave the Board "all the powers it would have had in making the initial decision." 5 U.S.C. §557(b). Thus, the Second Circuit affirmed the Board's decision. The Supreme Court disagreed, and held that the plain language of the statute required a review of the record as a whole, which included the ALJ's decision.

Schering-Plough Corp. v. Federal Trade Comm'n, 402 F.3d 1056, 1063 (11th Cir. 2005).

2. The scope of review turns on the distinction between questions of law and questions of fact. "On questions of law, our review is de novo, with appropriate [administrative-law] deference to the agency's interpretation of the underlying statute. On questions of fact, however, we apply the substantial evidence standard." Wen Feng Liu v. Holder, 714 F.3d 56, 59 (1st Cir. 2013) (internal quotation marks and citations omitted). How does the challenged finding in *Universal Camera* fit into this classification?

According to the lower court, the NLRB had found that "the discharge was . . . for giving testimony hostile to the respondent at a hearing conducted by the Board to determine who should be the representative of the respondent's 'maintenance employees.'" Respondent employer had presented evidence to show that the discharge resulted from a bitter personal quarrel between the discharged employee and the company's personnel manager.

Note the difference between *questions* and *findings.* A case presents questions of law and questions of fact that must be answered by the agency concerned in reaching its decision. The agency makes findings of law and findings of fact that are the agency's answers to the questions presented. In discussing the scope of review, courts and commentators often use the terms as equivalents, referring interchangeably, for example, to review of questions of fact and fact findings.

3. Note how the APA, as interpreted in *Universal Camera*, expands the restricted pre-APA interpretation of the substantial evidence rule. What does the substantial evidence test mean under the *Universal Camera* approach? What is the quantum of evidence needed for *substantial* evidence today? An oft-cited answer is in Jaffe, Judicial Review: Substantial Evidence on the Whole Record, 64 Harv. L. Rev. 1233, 1239 (1951):

> [U]nderlying the vexed word "substantial" is the notion or sense of fairness. I would say, then, that the judge may — indeed must — reverse if as he conscientiously sees it the finding is not fairly supported by the record; or to phrase it more sharply, the judge must reverse if he cannot conscientiously escape the conclusion that the finding is unfair.

When is an agency finding unfair? Can a finding be fair when it is not reasonable in light of the evidence in the whole record? "The substantial evidence standard requires only that a reasonable person *could* have decided as the fact finder found: it does *not* require that a preponderance of the evidence supports the finding." Matter of Otero County Elec. Co-op., 774 P.2d 1050, 1053 (N.M. 1988). According to a recent Supreme Court decision, "[W]hatever the meaning of 'substantial' in other contexts, the threshold . . . is not high. Substantial evidence, this Court has said, is more than a mere scintilla. It means — and means only — such relevant evidence as a reasonable mind might accept as adequate to support a conclusion." Biestek v. Berryhill, 139 S. Ct. 1148, 1154 (2019) (internal quotation marks and citations omitted).

See also Blackmun, J., dissenting in Kremer v. Chemical Construction Corp., 456 U.S. 461, 491-492 (1982):

> When it affirms the agency's decision, the reviewing court does not determine that the [agency] was correct. . . . In affirming, the reviewing court finds only that the agency's conclusion "was a reasonable one and thus may not be set aside by the courts although a contrary decision 'may have been reasonable and also sustainable.'"

"Substantial evidence is a deferential standard, meaning that we cannot reverse the [agency] simply because we disagree with the [agency's] apprehension of the facts. . . . To obtain a reversal of the board's decision under this standard, the [petitioner] must show that the evidence he presented was so compelling that no reasonable fact-finder could fail to arrive at his conclusion. . . . The evidence must not merely support the [petitioner's] conclusion but must compel it." Silwany-Rodriguez v. INS, 975 F.2d 1157, 1160 (5th Cir. 1992).

4. The substantial evidence rule has been characterized as one of the "most stable and satisfactory features of our system of administrative law." See K. Davis & R. Pierce, Administrative Law (3d ed. 1996). However, the U.S. Supreme Court issued a decision in 1998 that seems to question the use of the substantial evidence test in some cases, favoring a harder look at administrative agency adjudication. In Allentown Mack Sales and Service v. National Labor Relations Board, 522 U.S. 359 (1998), the Court questioned the NLRB's affirmance of an ALJ's dismissal of three affidavits used by an employer to show that it had a "good faith reasonable doubt" that a union continued to enjoy majority support among employees. The issue was important in the case because the three affidavits were pivotal in making the "reasonable doubt" determination. A six-Justice majority opinion of the Court uncharacteristically challenged the ALJ and NLRB assessment, grounded in substantial reasoning, that the three affidavits should not be credited. The majority, in a sort of line-by-line review of the specific affidavits, found that the affidavits were substantially probative on the issue of reasonable doubt. The Court's re-review of the factual record in the case, and its reconstruction of the probity of witness evidence, would appear to fly clearly in the face of the substantial evidence rule.

After *Allentown*, the question was how federal courts would apply the decision, and, indeed, how often the Supreme Court would cite to the case in future decisions. Was the Court backing away from the substantial evidence standard and, if so, wouldn't the Court have been clearer about such an important shift? Such a stance seems inconsistent with the *Chevron* standard, *infra* page 730, which affords more deference to agencies but on questions of statutory interpretation. Shortly after the decision was issued, one commentator suggested that it was susceptible of two narrower interpretations: first, that the decision involved human behavior in the workplace, an area in which the six Justices in the majority may have felt quite competent themselves, thus according little deference to the agency in this particular situation; second, the case may have been limited to Court review of NLRB factfinding, support for this being found in the majority's scathing critique of the Board's patterns of behavior and an increasing hostility to the NLRB factfinding process by federal courts of appeals in general. See K. Davis & R. Pierce, Administrative Law Treatise 346-348 (3d ed.) (1999 Supp.).

More than 20 years after the decision in *Allentown*, some commentators have concluded that it did not significantly alter or abrogate the substantial evidence rule. For example, while acknowledging that the Court scrutinized NLRB's decision in a manner that was "more intense than has traditionally been applied to agency fact finding," Thomas Merrill noted that "[s]ubsequent decisions . . . , both of the Supreme Court and of lower courts, have not treated *Allentown Mack* as changing the established scope of review." Thomas Merill, Judicial Deference to Agency Action, 9 Engage: J. Federalist Soc'y Prac. Groups 16, 17 (2008). Still more recently, a study of federal circuit court decisions found no "systematic differences between cases" citing *Allentown* versus those citing *Universal Camera* in the context of the scope of review for the NLRB's findings of fact. Daniel B. Listwa & Lydia K. Fuller, Constraint Through Independence, 129 Yale L.J. 548, 576 n. 126 (2019). However, a recent decision from the Fourth Circuit relied largely on *Allentown* when it directly analyzed emails originally presented to the Federal Energy Regulatory Commission and concluded that the emails did not provide substantial evidence in support of the Commission's conclusion. See N.C. Dep't of Env't Quality v. Fed. Energy Regulatory Comm'n, 20-1655, 2021 WL 2763265, at *12 (4th Cir. July 2, 2021) ("When those emails are considered in their full context, however, they simply do not support FERC's . . . finding.").

5. Which party does the substantial evidence standard favor? See Allentown Mack Sales & Serv. v. NLRB, 522 U.S. 359, 377 (1998) ("The 'substantial evidence' test *itself* already gives the agency the benefit of the doubt, since it requires not the degree of evidence which satisfies the *court* that the requisite fact exists, but merely the degree that *could* satisfy a reasonable factfinder.").

2. Arbitrary and Capricious

CITIZENS TO PRESERVE OVERTON PARK v. VOLPE

401 U.S. 402 (1971)

Opinion of the Court by MR. JUSTICE MARSHALL . . .

[In a portion of the opinion not reprinted, the Court held that judicial review was available over the Secretary of Transportation's approval of construction of a highway through a public park, despite a statutory prohibition of such construction if a "feasible and prudent" alternative route exists.]

The growing public concern about the quality of our natural environment has prompted Congress in recent years to enact legislation designed to curb the accelerating destruction of our country's natural beauty. We are concerned in this case with §4(f) of the Department of Transportation Act of 1966, as amended, and §18(a) of the Federal-Aid Highway Act of 1968, 82 Stat. 823, 23 U.S.C. §138 (1964 ed., Supp. V) (hereafter §138). These statutes prohibit the Secretary of Transportation from authorizing the use of federal funds to finance the construction of highways through public parks if a "feasible and prudent" alternative route exists. If no such route is available, the statutes allow him to approve construction through public parks only if there has been "all possible planning to minimize harm" to the park.

Petitioners, private citizens as well as local and national conservation organizations, contend that the Secretary has violated these statutes by authorizing the expenditure of federal funds for the construction of a six-lane interstate highway through a public park in Memphis, Tennessee. . . .

Overton Park is a 342-acre city park located near the center of Memphis. The park contains a zoo, a nine-hole municipal golf course, an outdoor theater, nature trails, a bridle path, an art academy, picnic areas, and 170 acres of forest. The proposed highway, which is to be a six-lane, high-speed expressway, will sever the zoo from the rest of the park. Although the roadway will be depressed below ground level except where it crosses a small creek, twenty-six acres of the park will be destroyed. . . .

. . . In April 1968, the Secretary announced that he concurred in the judgment of local officials that I-40 should be built through the park. And in September 1969 the State acquired the right-of-way inside Overton Park from the city. Final approval for the project — the route as well as the design — was not announced until November 1969, after Congress had reiterated in §138 of the Federal-Aid Highway Act that highway construction through public parks was to be restricted. Neither announcement approving the route and design of I-40 was accompanied by a statement of the Secretary's factual findings. He did not indicate why he believed there were no feasible and prudent alternative routes or why design changes could not be made to reduce the harm to the park.

But the existence of judicial review is only the start: the standard for review must also be determined. For that we must look to §706 of the Administration Procedure Act, 5 U.S.C. §706 (1964 ed., Supp. V), which provides that a "reviewing court shall . . . hold unlawful and set aside agency action, findings, and conclusions found" not to meet six separate standards. In all cases agency action must be set aside if the action was "arbitrary, capricious, an abuse of discretion, or otherwise not in accordance with law" or if the action failed to meet statutory, procedural, or constitutional requirements. 5 U.S.C. §§706(2)(A), (B), (C), (D) (1964 ed., Supp. V). In certain narrow, specifically limited situations, the agency action is to be set aside if the action was not supported by "substantial evidence." And in other equally narrow circumstances the reviewing court is to engage in a de novo review of the action and set it aside if it was "unwarranted by the facts." 5 U.S.C. §§706(2)(E), (F) (1964 ed., Supp. V).

Petitioners argue that the Secretary's approval of the construction of I-40 through Overton Park is subject to one or the other of these latter two standards of limited applicability. First, they contend that the "substantial evidence" standard of §706(2)(E) must be applied. In the alternative, they claim that §706(2)(F) applies and that there must be a de novo review to determine if the Secretary's action was "unwarranted by the facts." Neither of these standards is, however, applicable.

Review under the substantial-evidence test is authorized only when the agency action is taken pursuant to a rulemaking provision of the Administrative Procedure Act itself, 5 U.S.C. §553 (1964 ed., Supp. V), or when the agency action is based on a public adjudicatory hearing. See 5 U.S.C. §§556, 557 (1964 ed., Supp. V). The Secretary's decision to allow the expenditure of federal funds to build I-40 through Overton Park was plainly not an exercise of a rulemaking function. . . . And the only hearing that is required by either the Administrative Procedure Act or the statutes regulating the distribution of federal funds for highway construction is a public hearing conducted by local officials for the purpose of informing the community about the proposed project and eliciting community views on the design and route. 23 U.S.C. §128 (1964 ed., Supp. V). The hearing is nonadjudicatory, quasi-legislative in nature. It is not designed to produce a record that is to be the basis of agency action — the basic requirement for substantial-evidence review. . . .

Petitioners' alternative argument also fails. De novo review of whether the Secretary's decision was "unwarranted by the facts" is authorized by §706(2)(F) in only two circumstances. First, such de novo review is authorized when the action is adjudicatory in nature and the agency factfinding procedures are inadequate. And, there may be independent judicial factfinding when issues that were not before the agency are raised in a proceeding to enforce nonadjudicatory agency action. . . . Neither situation exists here.

Even though there is no de novo review in this case and the Secretary's approval of the route of I-40 does not have ultimately to meet the substantial-evidence test, the generally applicable standards of §706 require the reviewing court to engage in a substantial inquiry. Certainly, the Secretary's decision is entitled to a presumption of regularity. . . . But that presumption is not to shield his action from a thorough, probing, in-depth review.

The court is first required to decide whether the Secretary acted within the scope of his authority. . . . This determination naturally begins with a delineation of the scope of the Secretary's authority and discretion. . . . As has been shown, Congress has specified only a small range of choices that the Secretary can make. Also involved in this initial inquiry is a determination of whether on the facts the Secretary's decision can reasonably be said to be within that range. The reviewing court must consider whether the Secretary properly construed his authority to approve the use of parkland as limited to situations where there are no feasible alternative routes or where feasible alternative routes involve uniquely difficult problems. And the reviewing court must be able to find that the Secretary could have reasonably believed that in this case there are no feasible alternatives or that alternatives do involve unique problems.

Scrutiny of the facts does not end, however, with the determination that the Secretary has acted within the scope of his statutory authority. Section 706(2)(A) requires a finding that the actual choice made was not "arbitrary, capricious, an abuse of discretion, or otherwise not in accordance with law." . . . To make this finding the court must consider whether the decision was based on a consideration of the relevant factors and whether there has been clear error of judgment. . . . Although this inquiry into the facts is to be searching and careful, the ultimate standard of review is a narrow one. The court is not empowered to substitute its judgment for that of the agency. . . .

NOTES

1. How does the scope of review without a record stated in *Overton Park* compare with that under the *Universal Camera* substantial evidence test?

2. The standard adopted by the Court, arbitrary and capricious, is the catch-all standard for agency actions not otherwise specifically addressed in other portions of §706. The standard applies to informal rulemaking, as well as rescissions and modifications of rules. See Motor Vehicle Mfrs. Ass'n v. State Farm Mut. Auto. Ins. Co., 463 U.S. 29, 41 (1983). Essentially, there has to be something inexplicable about the agency's decision, whether the failure to explain contrary evidence or the consideration of improper factors. See *Motor Vehicle Mfrs. Ass'n*, 463 U.S. at 43 ("Normally, an agency rule would be arbitrary and capricious if the agency has relied on factors which Congress has not intended it to consider, entirely failed to consider an important aspect of the problem, offered an explanation for its decision that runs counter to the evidence before the agency, or is so implausible that it could not be ascribed to a difference in view or the product of agency expertise.").

3. The standard has been described as "extremely narrow," see United States Postal Serv. v. Gregory, 534 U.S. 1, 7 (2005), and does not require perfection. Moreover, the doctrine is not intended to allow courts to substitute their judgment for that of the agency, even if a better result was possible. See FERC v. Electric Power Supply Association, 136 S. Ct. 760 (2016) ("The disputed question here involves both technical understanding and policy judgment. The Commission addressed that issue seriously and carefully, providing reasons in support of its position and responding to the principal alternative advanced. . . . It is not our job to render that judgment, on which reasonable minds can differ. Our important but limited role is to ensure that the Commission engaged in reasoned decisionmaking—that it weighed competing views, selected a compensation formula with adequate support in the record, and intelligibly explained the reasons for making that choice. FERC satisfied that standard.").

4. Despite the narrow nature, might the standard be applied broadly in practice? The system of notice and comment can generate thousands of comment letters. See Luis A. Aguilar, Shining a Light on Expenditures of Shareholder Money, Commissioner, Securities and Exchange Commission, Washington D.C., Feb. 24, 2012 (noting that the Commission has received "tens of thousands" of letters urging the consideration of a rule addressing the disclosure of political expenditures). How might this facilitate the ability of a court to characterize a rule as "arbitrary and capricious"? Similarly, rules often must be subject to a cost-benefit analysis. How might this facilitate a finding of arbitrary and capricious? For an example, see Business Roundtable v. SEC, 647 F.3d 1144, 1150, 1151, 1153 (D.C. Cir. 2011) (holding that the SEC's failure "to estimate and quantify the costs it expected companies to incur," its reliance on "relatively unpersuasive studies," and its decision to "arbitrarily ignore[]" certain effects were grounds, among others, to conclude that the agency's action was arbitrary and capricious).

5. Can a significant departure from long-standing agency positions be considered arbitrary? It can, at least if unexplained, see National Cable & Telecomms. Ass'n v. Brand X Internet Servs., 545 U.S. 967, 981 (2005) ("Unexplained inconsistency is, at most, a reason for holding an interpretation to be an arbitrary and capricious change from agency practice under the Administrative

Procedure Act."), or if failing to take into account the degree of reliance on the prior position. See Smiley v. Citibank (S.D.), N.A., 517 U.S. 735, 742 (1996) ("[C] hange that does not take account of legitimate reliance on prior interpretation may be 'arbitrary, capricious [or] an abuse of discretion.'" (internal citations omitted)); See also Christopher v. SmithKline Beecham Corp., 567 U.S. 142, 155-156 (2012) ("Petitioners invoke the [agency's] interpretation of ambiguous regulations to impose potentially massive liability on respondent for conduct that occurred well before that interpretation was announced. To defer to the agency's interpretation in this circumstance would seriously undermine the principle that agencies should provide regulated parties 'fair warning of the conduct [a regulation] prohibits or requires.'" (internal citations and quotation marks omitted)). *Overton Park* involved an agency's discrete decision to approve a proposed highway route. In that case, the decision had to be supported by a record that allowed a court to determine whether the decision was arbitrary and capricious. Can an agency also act in an arbitrary and capricious manner when it rescinds or modifies an existing rule or policy?

MOTOR VEHICLE MANUFACTURERS ASS'N v. STATE FARM

463 U.S. 29 (1983)

. . .

III

Unlike the Court of Appeals, we do not find the appropriate scope of judicial review to be the "most troublesome question" in these cases. Both the [National Traffic and Motor Vehicle Safety] Act and the 1974 Amendments concerning occupant crash protection standards indicate that motor vehicle safety standards are to be promulgated under the informal rulemaking procedures of the Administrative Procedure Act. 5 U.S.C. §553. The agency's action in promulgating such standards therefore may be set aside if found to be "arbitrary, capricious, an abuse of discretion, or otherwise not in accordance with law." 5 U.S.C. §706 (2)(A). . . . We believe that the rescission or modification of an occupant-protection standard is subject to the same test. Section 103(b) of the Act, 15 U.S.C. §1392(b), states that the procedural and judicial review provisions of the Administrative Procedure Act "shall apply to all orders establishing, amending, or revoking a Federal motor vehicle safety standard," and suggests no difference in the scope of judicial review depending upon the nature of the agency's action.

Petitioner Motor Vehicle Manufacturers Association (MVMA) disagrees, contending that the rescission of an agency rule should be judged by the same standard a court would use to judge an agency's refusal to promulgate a rule in the first place — a standard petitioner believes considerably narrower than the traditional arbitrary-and-capricious test. We reject this view. The Act expressly equates orders "revoking" and "establishing" safety standards; neither that Act nor the APA suggests that revocations are to be treated as refusals to promulgate standards. Petitioner's view would render meaningless Congress' authorization for judicial review of orders revoking safety rules. Moreover, the revocation of an extant regulation is substantially different than a failure to act. Revocation constitutes a reversal of the agency's former views as to the proper course. A "settled course of behavior embodies the agency's informed judgment that, by pursuing that course, it will carry out the policies committed to it by Congress. There is, then, at least a presumption that those policies will be carried out best if the settled rule is adhered to." Atchison, T. & S. F. R. Co. v. Wichita Bd. of Trade, 412 U.S. 800, 807-808 (1973). Accordingly, an agency changing its course by rescinding a rule is obligated to supply a reasoned analysis for the change beyond that which may be required when an agency does not act in the first instance.

In so holding, we fully recognize that "[regulatory] agencies do not establish rules of conduct to last forever," American Trucking Assns., Inc. v. Atchison, T. & S. F. R. Co., 387 U.S. 397, 416 (1967), and that an agency must be given ample latitude to "adapt their rules and policies to the demands of changing circumstances." Permian Basin Area Rate Cases, 390 U.S. 747, 784 (1968). But the forces of change do not always or necessarily point in the direction of deregulation. In the abstract, there is no more reason to presume that changing circumstances require the rescission of prior action, instead of a revision in or even the extension of current regulation. If Congress established a presumption from which judicial review should start, that presumption — contrary to petitioners' views — is not *against* safety regulation, but against changes in current policy that are not justified by the rulemaking record. While the removal of a regulation may not entail the monetary expenditures and other costs of enacting a new standard, and, accordingly, it may be easier for an agency to justify a deregulatory action, the direction in which an agency chooses to move does not alter the standard of judicial review established by law.

The Department of Transportation accepts the applicability of the "arbitrary and capricious" standard. It argues that under this standard, a reviewing court may not set aside an agency rule that is rational, based on consideration of the relevant factors, and within the scope of the authority delegated to the agency by the statute. We do not disagree with this formulation. The scope of review under the "arbitrary and capricious" standard is narrow and a court is not to substitute its judgment for that of the agency. Nevertheless, the agency must examine the relevant data and articulate a satisfactory explanation for its action including a "rational connection between the facts found and the choice made." Burlington Truck Lines, Inc. v. United States, 371 U.S. 156, 168 (1962). In reviewing that explanation, we must "consider whether the decision was based on a consideration of the relevant factors and whether there has been a clear error of judgment." Normally, an agency rule would be arbitrary and capricious if the agency has relied on factors which Congress has not intended it to consider, entirely failed to consider an important aspect of the problem, offered an explanation for its decision that runs counter to the evidence before the agency, or is so implausible that it could not be ascribed to a difference in view or the product of agency expertise. The reviewing court should not attempt itself to make up for such deficiencies; we may not supply a reasoned basis for the agency's action that the agency itself has not given. SEC v. Chenery Corp., 332 U.S. 194, 196 (1947). We will, however, "uphold a decision of less than ideal clarity if the agency's path may reasonably be discerned." For purposes of these cases, it is also relevant that Congress required a record of the rulemaking proceedings to be compiled and submitted to a reviewing court, 15 U.S.C. §1394, and intended that agency findings under the Act would be supported by "substantial evidence on the record considered as a whole." S. Rep. No. 1301, 89th Cong., 2d Sess., 8 (1966); H. R. Rep. No. 1776, 89th Cong., 2d Sess., 21 (1966).

■ ■ ■

State Farm establishes that the arbitrary-and-capricious standard extends to agency actions, including modifications and recissions of prior actions, and describes the reach of arbitrary and capricious review. The following case is an oft-cited example of how the Court has applied its holding in *State Farm* when confronting changes to an agency's rules, policies, and practices.

FEDERAL COMMUNICATIONS COMMISSION v. FOX TELEVISION STATIONS, INC.

556 U.S. 502 (2009)

JUSTICE SCALIA delivered the opinion of the Court, except as to Part III-E.

Federal law prohibits the broadcasting of "any . . . indecent . . . language," 18 U.S.C. §1464, which includes expletives referring to sexual or excretory activity or organs. . . . This case concerns the adequacy of the Federal Communications Commission's explanation of its decision that this sometimes forbids the broadcasting of indecent expletives even when the offensive words are not repeated. . . .

II.

This case concerns utterances in two live broadcasts aired by Fox Television Stations, Inc., and its affiliates prior to the Commission's *Golden Globes Order*. The first occurred during the 2002 Billboard Music Awards, when the singer Cher exclaimed, "I've also had critics for the last 40 years saying that I was on my way out every year." . . . The second involved a segment of the 2003 Billboard Music Awards, during the presentation of an award by Nicole Richie and Paris Hilton, principals in a Fox Television series called "The Simple Life." Ms. Hilton began their interchange by reminding Ms. Richie to "watch the bad language," but Ms. Richie proceeded to ask the audience, "Why do they even call it 'The Simple

Life?' Have you ever tried to get cow s*** out of a Prada purse? It's not so f***ing simple." ... Following each of these broadcasts, the Commission received numerous complaints from parents whose children were exposed to the language. . . .

The order asserted that both broadcasts under review would have been actionably indecent under the staff rulings and Commission dicta in effect prior to the *Golden Globes Order*—the 2003 broadcast because it involved a literal description of excrement, rather than a mere expletive, because it used more than one offensive word, and because it was planned, 21 FCC Rcd., at 13307, P22; and the 2002 broadcast because Cher used the F-Word not as a mere intensifier, but as a description of the sexual act to express hostility to her critics, *id.*, at 13324, P60. The order stated, however, that the pre-*Golden Globes* regime of immunity for isolated indecent expletives rested only upon staff rulings and Commission dicta, and that the Commission itself had never held "that the isolated use of an expletive . . . was not indecent or could not be indecent," 21 FCC Rcd., at 13307, P21. In any event, the order made clear, the *Golden Globes Order* eliminated any doubt that fleeting expletives could be actionably indecent, 21 FCC Rcd., at 13308, P23, 13325, P61, and the Commission disavowed the bureau-level decisions and its own dicta that had said otherwise, *id.*, at 13306-13307, PP20, 21. Under the new policy, a lack of repetition "weigh[s] against a finding of indecency," *id.*, at 13325, P61, but is not a safe harbor. . . .

In overturning the Commission's judgment, the Court of Appeals here relied in part on Circuit precedent requiring a more substantial explanation for agency action that changes prior policy. The Second Circuit has interpreted the Administrative Procedure Act and our opinion in *State Farm* as requiring agencies to make clear "'why the original reasons for adopting the [displaced] rule or policy are no longer dispositive'" as well as "'why the new rule effectuates the statute as well as or better than the old rule.'" 489 F.3d at 456-457 (quoting New York Council, Assn. of Civilian Technicians v. FLRA, 757 F.2d 502, 508 (2nd Cir. 1985); emphasis deleted). The Court of Appeals for the District of Columbia Circuit has similarly indicated that a court's standard of review is "heightened somewhat" when an agency reverses course. NAACP v. FCC, 682 F.2d 993, 998 (1982).

We find no basis in the Administrative Procedure Act or in our opinions for a requirement that all agency change be subjected to more searching review. The Act mentions no such heightened standard. And our opinion in *State Farm* neither held nor implied that every agency action representing a policy change must be justified by reasons more substantial than those required to adopt a policy in the first instance. That case, which involved the rescission of a prior regulation, said only that such action requires "a reasoned analysis for the change beyond that which may be required when an agency *does not act* in the first instance." 463 U.S. at 42 (emphasis added). Treating failures to act and rescissions of prior differently for purposes of the standard of review makes good sense, and has basis in the text of the statute, which likewise treats the two separately. It instructs a reviewing court to "compel agency action unlawfully withheld or unreasonably delayed," 5 U.S.C. §706(1), and to "hold unlawful and set aside agency action, findings, and conclusions found to be [among other things] . . . arbitrary [or] capricious," §706(2)(A). The statute makes no distinction, however, between initial agency action and subsequent agency action undoing or revising that action.

To be sure, the requirement that an agency provide reasoned explanation for its action would ordinarily demand that it display awareness that it *is* changing position. An agency may not, for example, depart from a prior policy *sub silentio* or simply disregard rules that are still on the books. See United States v. Nixon, 418 U.S. 683 (1974). And of course the agency must show that there are good reasons for the new policy. But it need not demonstrate to a court's satisfaction that the reasons for the new policy are *better* than the reasons for the old one; it suffices that the new policy is permissible under the statute, that there are good reasons for it, and that the agency *believes* it to be better, which the conscious change of course adequately indicates. This means that the agency need not always provide a more detailed justification than what would suffice for a new policy created on a blank slate. Sometimes it must — when, for example, its new policy rests upon factual findings that contradict those which underlay its prior policy; or when its prior policy has engendered serious reliance interests that must be taken into account. Smiley v. Citibank (South Dakota), N. A., 517 U.S. 735 (1996). It would be arbitrary or capricious to ignore such matters. In such cases it is not that further justification is demanded by the mere fact of policy change; but that a reasoned explanation is needed for disregarding facts and circumstances that underlay or were engendered by the prior policy. . . .

Judged under the above described standards, the Commission's new enforcement policy and its order finding the broadcasts actionably indecent were neither arbitrary nor capricious. First, the Commission forthrightly acknowledged that its recent actions have broken new ground, taking account of inconsistent "prior Commission and staff action" and explicitly disavowing them as "no longer good law." *Golden Globes Order*, 19 FCC Rcd., at 4980, P12. To be sure, the (superfluous) explanation in its *Remand Order* of why the Cher broadcast would even have violated its earlier policy may not be entirely convincing. But that unnecessary detour is irrelevant. There is no doubt that the Commission knew it was making a change. That is why it declined to assess penalties; and it relied on the *Golden Globes Order* as removing any lingering doubt. . . .

Moreover, the agency's reasons for expanding the scope of its enforcement activity were entirely rational. It was certainly reasonable to determine that it made no sense to distinguish between literal and nonliteral uses of offensive words, requiring repetitive use to render only the latter indecent. As the Commission said with regard to expletive use of the F-Word, "the word's power to insult and offend derives from its sexual meaning." *Id.*, at 13323, P58. And the Commission's decision to look at the patent offensiveness of even isolated uses of sexual and excretory words fits with the context-based approach we sanctioned in *Pacifica*, 438 U.S. at 750. Even isolated utterances can be made in "pander[ing,] . . . vulgar and shocking" manners, *Remand Order*, 21 FCC Rcd., at 13305, P17, and can constitute harmful "'first blow[s]'" to children, *id.*, at 13309, P25. It is surely rational (if not inescapable) to believe that a safe harbor for single words would "likely lead to more widespread use of the offensive language," *Golden Globes Order, supra*, at 4979, P9.

When confronting other requests for *per se* rules governing its enforcement of the indecency prohibition, the Commission has declined to create safe harbors for particular types of broadcasts. See In re Pacifica Foundation, Inc., 2 FCC Rcd., at 2699, P12 (repudiating the view that the Commission's enforcement power was limited to "deliberate, repetitive use of the seven words actually contained in the George Carlin monologue"); In re Infinity Broadcasting Corp. of Pa., 3 FCC Rcd., at 932, P17 ("reject[ing] an approach that would hold that if a work has merit, it is *per se* not indecent"). The Commission could rationally decide it needed to step away from its old regime where nonrepetitive use of an expletive was *per se* nonactionable because that was "at odds with the Commission's overall enforcement policy." *Remand Order, supra*, at 13308, P23.

The fact that technological advances have made it easier for broadcasters to bleep out offending words further supports the Commission's stepped-up enforcement policy. *Golden Globes Order, supra*, at 4980, P11. And the agency's decision not to impose any forfeiture or other sanction precludes any argument that it is arbitrarily punishing parties without notice of the potential consequences of their action.

C.

The Court of Appeals found the Commission's action arbitrary and capricious on three grounds. First, the court criticized the Commission for failing to explain why it had not previously banned fleeting expletives as "harmful 'first blow[s].'" 489 F.3d at 458. In the majority's view, without "evidence that suggests a fleeting expletive is harmful [and] . . . serious enough to warrant government regulation," the agency could not regulate more broadly. *Id.*, at 461. As explained above, the fact that an agency had a prior stance does not alone prevent it from changing its view or create a higher hurdle for doing so. And it is not the Commission, but Congress that has proscribed "any . . . indecent . . . language." 18 U.S.C. §1464.

There are some propositions for which scant empirical evidence can be marshaled, and the harmful effect of broadcast profanity on children is one of them. One cannot demand a multiyear controlled study, in which some children are intentionally exposed to indecent broadcasts (and insulated from all other indecency), and others are shielded from all indecency. It is one thing to set aside agency action under the Administrative Procedure Act because of failure to adduce empirical data that can readily be obtained. See, *e.g., State Farm*, 463 U.S. at 46-56 (addressing the costs and benefits of mandatory passive restraints for automobiles). It is something else to insist upon obtaining the unobtainable. Here it suffices to know that children mimic the behavior they observe — or at least the behavior that is presented to them as normal and appropriate. Programming replete with one-word indecent expletives will tend to produce children who use (at least) one-word indecent expletives. Congress has made the determination that indecent material is harmful to children, and has left enforcement of the ban to the Commission. If enforcement had to be supported by empirical data, the ban would effectively be a nullity.

The Commission had adduced no quantifiable measure of the harm caused by the language in *Pacifica*, and we nonetheless held that the "government's interest in the 'well-being of its youth' . . . justified the regulation of otherwise protected expression." 438 U.S. at 749 (quoting Ginsberg v. New York, 390 U.S. 629, 640 (1968)). If the Constitution itself demands of agencies no more scientifically certain criteria to comply with the First Amendment, neither does the Administrative Procedure Act to comply with the requirement of reasoned decisionmaking.

. . . [T]he agency's decision to consider the patent offensiveness of isolated expletives on a case-by-case basis is not arbitrary or capricious. "Even a prime-time recitation of Geoffrey Chaucer's Miller's Tale," we have explained, "would not be likely to command the attention of many children who are both old enough to understand and young enough to be adversely affected."*Pacifica, supra*, at 750, n. 29. The same rationale could support the Commission's finding that a broadcast of the film Saving Private Ryan was not indecent — a finding to which the broadcasters point as supposed evidence of the Commission's inconsistency. The frightening suspense and the graphic violence in the movie could well dissuade the most vulnerable from watching and would put parents on notice of potentially objectionable material. See In re Complaints Against Various Television Licensees Regarding Their Broadcast on Nov. 11, 2004 of the ABC Television Network's Presentation of the Film "Saving Private Ryan," 20 FCC Rcd. 4507, 4513, P15 (2005) (noting that the broadcast was not "intended as family entertainment"). The agency's decision to retain some discretion does not render arbitrary or capricious its regulation of the deliberate and shocking uses of offensive language at the award shows under review — shows that were expected to (and did) draw the attention of millions of children.

Finally, the Court of Appeals found unconvincing the agency's prediction (without any evidence) that a *per se* exemption for fleeting expletives would lead to increased use of expletives one at a time. 489 F.3d at 460. But even in the absence of evidence, the agency's predictive judgment basis in the (which merits deference) makes entire sense. To predict that complete immunity for fleeting expletives, ardently desired by broadcasters, will lead to a substantial increase in fleeting expletives seems to us an exercise in logic rather than clairvoyance. The Court of Appeals was perhaps correct that the Commission's prior policy had not yet caused broadcasters to "barrag[e] the airwaves with expletives,"*ibid.* That may have been because its prior permissive policy had been confirmed (save in dicta) only at the staff level. In any event, as the *Golden Globes* order demonstrated, it did produce more expletives than the Commission (which has the first call in this matter) deemed in conformity with the statute. . . .

Justice Breyer purports to "begin with applicable law," but in fact begins by stacking the deck. He claims that the FCC's status as an "independent" agency sheltered from political oversight requires courts to be "all the more" vigilant in ensuring "that major policy decisions be based upon articulable reasons." Not so. The independent agencies are sheltered not from politics but from the President, and it has often been observed that their freedom from presidential oversight (and protection) has simply been replaced by increased subservience to congressional direction. . . . Indeed, the precise policy change at issue here was spurred by significant political pressure from Congress. . . .

Regardless, it is assuredly not "applicable law" that rulemaking by independent regulatory agencies is subject to heightened scrutiny. The Administrative Procedure Act, which provides judicial review, makes no distinction between independent and other agencies, neither in its definition of agency, 5 U.S.C. §701(b)(1), nor in the standards for reviewing agency action, §706. . . .

NOTES

1. Section 706 of the APA governs the standard of review for agency decisions unless an alternative standard exists within the agency's enabling statute.

2. What exactly does it mean for an agency to act in an arbitrary and capricious fashion? Consider Massachusetts v. EPA, 549 U.S. 497 (2007), in which the Court held that EPA "offered no reasoned explanation for its refusal to decide whether greenhouse gases cause or contribute to climate change." 549 U.S. at 534. EPA had, however, "offered a laundry list of reasons not to regulate" in response to public comments on the issue, including "the existence of voluntary executive branch programs providing a response to global warming, . . . that regulating greenhouse gases might impair the President's ability to negotiate with 'key developing nations' to reduce emissions, . . . and that curtailing motor vehicle emissions would reflect 'an inefficient, piecemeal approach to address the climate change issue.'" Id. at 533. Despite recognizing that it had "neither the expertise nor the authority to evaluate these policy judgments," the Court concluded that EPA's failure to act was arbitrary and capricious. Id. at 533-534. Is this decision consistent with *State Farm* and *Fox*? Does it reflect the Court's description of the arbitrary and capricious standard in United States Postal Serv. v. Gregory as "extremely narrow?" Consider the fact that EPA offered its reason for declining to pursue rulemaking for greenhouse gases in the context of responses to public comment. Does the Court's decision in this case encourage agencies to seek and respond to public comments? Is this good policy?

3. The provision permits review of agency *actions*, a term that can also include agency inaction. See 5 U.S.C. §551(13) (including within the definition of agency action the "failure to act"). With respect to agency inaction, however, any action may only be maintained "where a plaintiff asserts that an agency failed to take a *discrete* agency action that it is *required to take*." Norton v. S. Utah Wilderness Alliance, 542 U.S. 55, 64 (2004). In that case, plaintiffs alleged that policies implemented by the Bureau of Land Management violated the agency's obligation to manage certain wilderness areas in a "manner so as not to impair the suitability of such areas for preservation as wilderness." The Court, in an opinion by Justice Scalia, rejected the claim, concluding that it did not meet the definition of "discrete agency action." As the Court explained:

> To take just a few examples from federal resources management, a plaintiff might allege that the Secretary had failed to "manage wild free-roaming horses and burros in a manner that is designed to achieve and maintain a thriving natural ecological balance," or to "manage the [New Orleans Jazz National] [H]istorical [P]ark in such a manner as will preserve and perpetuate knowledge and understanding of the history of jazz," or to "manage the [Steens Mountain] Cooperative Management and Protection Area for the benefit of present and future generations." . . . The prospect of pervasive oversight by federal courts over the manner and pace of agency compliance with such congressional directives is not contemplated by the APA.

4. The agency action must also be final. See APA §704. Thus, the provision generally does not permit challenge to intermediate rulings; a final resolution of the matter must occur first. In addition, actions by an agency may be preliminary or advisory and not qualify as final. See Dalton v. Specter, 511 U.S. 462, 469 (1994) (holding that an agency action requiring presidential review and approval is more like a "tentative recommendation" or the "ruling of a subordinate official" than a "final action" within the meaning of the APA).

5. The need for a final agency action has been much litigated. In Sackett v. EPA, 566 U.S. 120 (2012), the plaintiffs had filled in part of their property in anticipation of construction. The EPA asserted that the changes resulted in the "discharge of pollutant" and issued a compliance order requiring that the property be returned to its original state. Fines of up to $75,000 could be assessed for failing to do so. Plaintiffs had no right to appeal the determination within the agency. In arguing that this was not a "final" agency action, the government asserted that it was not final because the plaintiffs were notified of the right to "engage in informal discussions" with the EPA over the terms and requirements. Moreover, the EPA had not brought an action to collect any penalties. Was the agency action truly final? Take a look at the case for the answer.

Two recent opinions illustrate the Supreme Court's contemporary approach to review of agency actions alleged to violate the APA's prohibition against agency action that is arbitrary or capricious in violation of §706(2)(A). Both majority opinions are authored by Justice Roberts, and both address controversial agency action taken at the direction of former President Donald Trump. Both cases take a rigorous look at the factual underpinnings of the agency action; however, each considers the action through a different lens.

DEPARTMENT OF COMMERCE v. NEW YORK

588 U.S. ___ (2019)

CHIEF JUSTICE ROBERTS delivered the opinion of the Court.

The Secretary of Commerce decided to reinstate a question about citizenship on the 2020 census questionnaire. A group of plaintiffs challenged that decision on constitutional and statutory grounds. We now decide whether the Secretary violated the Enumeration Clause of the Constitution, the Census Act, or otherwise abused his discretion.

I.

A

In order to apportion Members of the House of Representatives among the States, the Constitution requires an "Enumeration" of the population every 10 years, to be made "in such Manner" as Congress "shall by Law direct." In the Census Act, Congress delegated to the Secretary of Commerce the task of conducting the decennial census "in such form and content as he may determine." The Secretary is aided in that task by the Census Bureau, a statistical agency housed within the Department of Commerce. . . .

There have been 23 decennial censuses from the first census in 1790 to the most recent in 2010. Every census between 1820 and 2000 (with the exception of 1840) asked at least some of the population about their citizenship or place of birth. . . .

In 2010, the year of the latest census, the format changed. . . . All households received the same questionnaire, which asked about sex, age, race, Hispanic origin, and living arrangements. The more detailed demographic questions previously asked on [a] long-form questionnaire, including [a] question about citizenship, were instead asked in the American Community Survey (or ACS), which is sent each year to a rotating sample of about 2.6% of households.

The Census Bureau and former Bureau officials have resisted occasional proposals to resume asking a citizenship question of everyone, on the ground that doing so would discourage noncitizens from responding to the census and lead to a less accurate count of the total population.

B

In March 2018, Secretary of Commerce Wilbur Ross announced in a memo that he had decided to reinstate a question about citizenship on the 2020 decennial census questionnaire. The Secretary stated that he was acting at the request of the Department of Justice (DOJ), which sought improved data about citizen voting-age population for purposes of enforcing the Voting Rights Act (or VRA) [in light of DOJ's view that citizenship data from the ACS was not ideal]. . . . [To avoid problems with that data,] DOJ . . . formally requested reinstatement of the citizenship question on the census questionnaire.

The Secretary's memo explained that the Census Bureau initially analyzed, and the Secretary considered, three possible courses of action. The first was to continue to collect citizenship information in the American Community Survey and attempt to develop a data model that would more accurately estimate citizenship at the census block level. The Secretary rejected that option because the

Bureau "did not assert and could not confirm" that such ACS-based data modeling was possible "with a sufficient degree of accuracy."

The second option was to reinstate a citizenship question on the decennial census. The Bureau predicted that doing so would discourage some noncitizens from responding to the census. That would necessitate increased "non-response follow up" operations — procedures the Bureau uses to attempt to count people who have not responded to the census — and potentially lead to a less accurate count of the total population.

Option three was to use administrative records from other agencies, such as the Social Security Administration and Citizenship and Immigration Services, to provide DOJ with citizenship data. The Census Bureau recommended this option, and the Secretary found it a "potentially appealing solution" because the Bureau has long used administrative records to supplement and improve census data. But the Secretary concluded that administrative records alone were inadequate because they were missing for more than 10% of the population.

The Secretary ultimately asked the Census Bureau to develop a fourth option that would combine options two and three: reinstate a citizenship question on the census questionnaire, and also use the time remaining until the 2020 census to "further enhance" the Bureau's "administrative record data sets, protocols, and statistical models." The memo explained that, in the Secretary's judgment, the fourth option would provide DOJ with the "most complete and accurate" citizen voting-age population data in response to its request.

The Secretary "carefully considered" the possibility that reinstating a citizenship question would depress the response rate. But after evaluating the Bureau's "limited empirical evidence" on the question — evidence drawn from estimated non-response rates to previous American Community Surveys and census questionnaires — the Secretary concluded that it was not possible to "determine definitively" whether inquiring about citizenship in the census would materially affect response rates. . . . Altogether, the Secretary determined that "the need for accurate citizenship data and the limited burden that the reinstatement of the citizenship question would impose outweigh fears about a potentially lower response rate."

C

Shortly after the Secretary announced his decision, two groups of plaintiffs filed suit in Federal District Court in New York, challenging the decision on several grounds. . . . The District Court consolidated the two cases. Both groups of plaintiffs are respondents here.

The Government moved to dismiss the lawsuits, arguing that the Secretary's decision was unreviewable and that respondents had failed to state cognizable claims under the Enumeration Clause and the Equal Protection Clause. The District Court dismissed the Enumeration Clause claim but allowed the other claims to proceed.

. . .

The District Court held a bench trial and issued findings of fact and conclusions of law on respondents' statutory and equal protection claims. After determining that respondents had standing to sue, the District Court ruled that the Secretary's action was arbitrary and capricious, based on a pretextual rationale, and violated certain provisions of the Census Act.

The Government appealed to the Second Circuit, but also filed a petition for writ of certiorari before judgment, asking this Court to review the District Court's decision directly because the case involved an issue of imperative public importance, and the census questionnaire needed to be finalized for printing by the end of June 2019. We granted the petition. . . .

[The Court's discussion of standing and of the Enumeration Clause are omitted.]

IV.

The District Court set aside the Secretary's decision to reinstate a citizenship question on the grounds that the Secretary acted arbitrarily and violated certain provisions of the Census Act. The Government contests those rulings. . . .

B

At the heart of this suit is respondents' claim that the Secretary abused his discretion in deciding to reinstate a citizenship question. We review the Secretary's exercise of discretion under the deferential "arbitrary and capricious" standard. §706(2)(A). Our scope of review is "narrow": we determine only whether the Secretary examined "the relevant data" and articulated "a satisfactory explanation" for his decision, "including a rational connection between the facts found and the choice made."

The District Court set aside the Secretary's decision for two independent reasons: His course of action was not supported by the evidence before him, and his stated rationale was pretextual.

The Secretary examined the Bureau's analysis of various ways to collect improved citizenship data and explained why he thought the best course was to both reinstate a citizenship question and use citizenship data from administrative records to fill in the gaps. He considered but rejected the Bureau's recommendation to use administrative records alone. As he explained, records are lacking for about 10% of the population, so the Bureau would still need to estimate citizenship for millions of voting-age people. Asking a citizenship question of everyone, the Secretary reasoned, would eliminate the need to estimate citizenship for many of those people. And supplementing census responses with administrative record data would help complete the picture and allow the Bureau to better estimate citizenship for the smaller set of cases where it was still necessary to do so.

The evidence before the Secretary supported that decision. As the Bureau acknowledged, each approach — using administrative records alone, or asking about citizenship and using records to fill in the gaps — entailed tradeoffs between accuracy and completeness. . . . Under either approach, there would be some errors in both the administrative records and the Bureau's estimates. . . .

The Bureau explained that the "relative quality" of the citizenship data generated by each approach would depend on the "relative importance of the errors" in each, but it was not able to "quantify the relative magnitude of the errors across the alternatives." The Bureau nonetheless recommended using administrative records alone because it had "high confidence" that it could develop an accurate model for estimating the citizenship of the 35 million people for whom administrative records were not available, and it thought the resulting citizenship data would be of superior quality. But when the time came for the Secretary to make a decision, the model did not yet exist, and even if it had, there was no way to gauge its relative accuracy. . . . The Secretary opted instead for the approach that would yield a more complete set of data at an acceptable rate of accuracy, and would require estimating the citizenship of fewer people.

The District Court overruled that choice, agreeing with the Bureau's assessment that its recommended approach would yield higher quality citizenship data on the whole. But the choice between reasonable policy alternatives in the face of uncertainty was the Secretary's to make. He considered the relevant factors, weighed risks and benefits, and articulated a satisfactory explanation for his decision. In overriding that reasonable exercise of discretion, the court improperly substituted its judgment for that of the agency.

The Secretary then weighed the benefit of collecting more complete and accurate citizenship data against the risk that inquiring about citizenship would depress census response rates, particularly among noncitizen households. In the Secretary's view, that risk was difficult to assess. The Bureau predicted a 5.1% decline in response rates among noncitizen households if the citizenship question were reinstated. It relied for that prediction primarily on studies showing that, while noncitizens had responded at lower rates than citizens to the 2000 short-form and 2010 censuses, which did not ask about citizenship, they responded at even lower rates than citizens to the 2000 long-form census and the 2010 American Community Survey, which did ask about citizenship. The Bureau thought it was reasonable to infer that the citizenship question accounted for the differential decline in noncitizen responses. But, the Secretary explained, the Bureau was unable to rule out other causes. . . .

The Secretary justifiably found the Bureau's analysis inconclusive. Weighing that uncertainty against the value of obtaining more complete and accurate citizenship data, he determined that reinstating a citizenship question was worth the risk of a potentially lower response rate. That decision was reasonable and reasonably explained, particularly in light of the long history of the citizenship question on the census.

Justice Breyer would conclude otherwise, but only by subordinating the Secretary's policymaking discretion to the Bureau's technocratic expertise. . . . He suggests that the Secretary should have deferred to the Bureau or at least offered some special justification for drawing his own inferences and adopting his own assumptions. But the Census Act authorizes the Secretary, not the Bureau, to make policy choices within the range of reasonable options. . . . It is not for us to ask whether his decision was "the best one possible" or even whether it was "better than the alternatives."

By second-guessing the Secretary's weighing of risks and benefits and penalizing him for departing from the Bureau's inferences and assumptions, Justice Breyer — like the District Court — substitutes his judgment for that of the agency.

. . .

V

We now consider the District Court's determination that the Secretary's decision must be set aside because it rested on a pretextual basis, which the Government conceded below would warrant a remand to the agency.

We start with settled propositions. First, in order to permit meaningful judicial review, an agency must "disclose the basis" of its action. Second, in reviewing agency action, a court is ordinarily limited to evaluating the agency's contemporaneous explanation in light of the existing administrative record. That principle reflects the recognition that further judicial inquiry into "executive motivation" represents "a substantial intrusion" into the workings of another branch of Government and should normally be avoided. Third, a court may not reject an agency's stated reasons for acting simply because the agency might also have had other unstated reasons. Relatedly, a court may not set aside an agency's policymaking decision solely because it might have been influenced by political considerations or prompted by an Administration's priorities. Agency policymaking is not a "rarified technocratic process, unaffected by political considerations or the presence of Presidential power." Such decisions are routinely informed by unstated considerations of politics, the legislative process, public relations, interest group relations, foreign relations, and national security concerns (among others).

Finally, we have recognized a narrow exception to the general rule against inquiring into "the mental processes of administrative decisionmakers." *Overton Park*. On a "strong showing of bad faith or improper behavior," such an inquiry may be warranted and may justify extra-record discovery. The District Court invoked that exception in ordering extra-record discovery here. Although that order was premature, we think it was ultimately justified in light of the expanded administrative record. Recall that shortly after this litigation began, the Secretary, prodded by DOJ, filed a supplemental memo that added new, pertinent information to the administrative record. The memo disclosed that the Secretary had been considering the citizenship question for some time and that Commerce had inquired whether DOJ would formally request reinstatement of the question. That supplemental memo prompted respondents to move for both completion of the administrative record and extra-record discovery. The District Court granted both requests at the same hearing, agreeing with respondents that the Government had submitted an incomplete administrative record and that the existing evidence supported a prima facie showing that the VRA rationale was pretextual.

The Government did not challenge the court's conclusion that the administrative record was incomplete, and the parties stipulated to the inclusion of more than 12,000 pages of internal deliberative materials as part of the administrative record, materials that the court later held were sufficient on their own to demonstrate pretext. The Government did, however, challenge the District Court's order authorizing extra-record discovery. . . .

We agree with the Government that the District Court should not have ordered extra-record discovery when it did. At that time, the most that was warranted was the order to complete the administrative record. But the new material that the parties stipulated should have been part of the administrative record — which showed, among other things, that the VRA played an insignificant role in the decisionmaking process — largely justified such extra-record discovery as occurred. . . . We accordingly review the District Court's ruling on pretext in light of all the evidence in the record before the court, including the extra-record discovery. . . .

The Government . . . contends that [the evidence showed] nothing objectionable or even surprising. . . . And we agree — to a point. It is hardly improper for an agency head to come into office with policy preferences and ideas, discuss them with affected parties, sound out other agencies for support, and work with staff attorneys to substantiate the legal basis for a preferred policy. The record here reflects the sometimes involved nature of Executive Branch decisionmaking, but no particular step in the process stands out as inappropriate or defective.

And yet, viewing the evidence as a whole, we share the District Court's conviction that the decision to reinstate a citizenship question cannot be adequately explained in terms of DOJ's request for improved citizenship data to better enforce the VRA. Several points, considered together, reveal a significant mismatch between the decision the Secretary made and the rationale he provided.

The record shows that the Secretary began taking steps to reinstate a citizenship question about a week into his tenure, but it contains no hint that he was considering VRA enforcement in connection with that project. The Secretary's Director of Policy did not know why the Secretary wished to reinstate the question, but saw it as his task to "find the best rationale." The Director initially attempted to elicit requests for citizenship data from the Department of Homeland Security and DOJ's Executive Office for Immigration Review, neither of which is responsible for enforcing the VRA. After those attempts failed, he asked Commerce staff to look into whether the Secretary could reinstate the question without receiving a request from another agency. The possibility that DOJ's Civil Rights Division might be willing to request citizenship data for VRA enforcement purposes was proposed by Commerce staff along the way and eventually pursued.

Even so, it was not until the Secretary contacted the Attorney General directly that DOJ's Civil Rights Division expressed interest in acquiring census-based citizenship data to better enforce the VRA. And even then, the record suggests that DOJ's interest was directed more to helping the Commerce Department than to securing the data. [A] December 2017 letter from DOJ drew heavily on contributions from Commerce staff and advisors. Their influence may explain why the letter went beyond a simple entreaty for better citizenship data — what one might expect of a typical request from another agency — to a specific request that Commerce collect the data by means of reinstating a citizenship question on the census. Finally, after sending the letter, DOJ declined the Census Bureau's offer to discuss alternative ways to meet DOJ's stated need for improved citizenship data, further suggesting a lack of interest on DOJ's part.

Altogether, the evidence tells a story that does not match the explanation the Secretary gave for his decision. In the Secretary's telling, Commerce was simply acting on a routine data request from another agency. Yet the materials before us indicate that Commerce went to great lengths to elicit the request from DOJ (or any other willing agency). And unlike a typical case in which an agency may have both stated and unstated reasons for a decision, here the VRA enforcement rationale — the sole stated reason — seems to have been contrived.

We are presented, in other words, with an explanation for agency action that is incongruent with what the record reveals about the agency's priorities and decisionmaking process.... Our review is deferential, but we are "not required to exhibit a naiveté from which ordinary citizens are free." The reasoned explanation requirement of administrative law, after all, is meant to ensure that agencies offer genuine justifications for important decisions, reasons that can be scrutinized by courts and the interested public. Accepting contrived reasons would defeat the purpose of the enterprise. If judicial review is to be more than an empty ritual, it must demand something better than the explanation offered for the action taken in this case.

In these unusual circumstances, the District Court was warranted in remanding to the agency, and we affirm that disposition. We do not hold that the agency decision here was substantively invalid. But agencies must pursue their goals reasonably. Reasoned decisionmaking under the Administrative Procedure Act calls for an explanation for agency action. What was provided here was more of a distraction.

The judgment of the United States District Court for the Southern District of New York is affirmed in part and reversed in part, and the case is remanded for further proceedings consistent with this opinion.

It is so ordered.

JUSTICE THOMAS, concurring in part and dissenting in part (joined BY JUSTICES GORSUCH and KAVANAUGH).

In March 2018, the Secretary of Commerce exercised his broad discretion over the administration of the decennial census to resume a nearly unbroken practice of asking a question relating to citizenship. Our only role in this case is to decide whether the Secretary complied with the law and gave a reasoned explanation for his decision. The Court correctly answers these questions in the affirmative. That ought to end our inquiry.

The Court, however, goes further. For the first time ever, the Court invalidates an agency action solely because it questions the sincerity of the agency's otherwise adequate rationale. Echoing the din of suspicion and distrust that seems to typify modern discourse, the Court declares the Secretary's memorandum "pretextual" because, "viewing the evidence as a whole," his explanation that including a citizenship question on the census would help enforce the Voting Rights Act (VRA) "seems to have been contrived." The Court does not hold that the Secretary merely had *additional*, unstated reasons for reinstating the citizenship question. Rather, it holds that the Secretary's stated rationale did not factor *at all* into his decision.

The Court's holding reflects an unprecedented departure from our deferential review of discretionary agency decisions. And, if taken seriously as a rule of decision, this holding would transform administrative law. It is not difficult for political opponents of executive actions to generate controversy with accusations of pretext, deceit, and illicit motives. Significant policy decisions are regularly criticized as products of partisan influence, interest-group pressure, corruption, and animus. Crediting these accusations on evidence as thin as the evidence here could lead judicial review of administrative proceedings to devolve into an endless morass of discovery and policy disputes not contemplated by the Administrative Procedure Act (APA).

. . .

The law requires a more impartial approach. Even assuming we are authorized to engage in the review undertaken by the Court — which is far from clear — we have often stated that courts reviewing agency action owe the Executive a "presumption of regularity." The Court pays only lipservice to this principle. But, the evidence falls far short of supporting its decision. The Court, I fear, will come to regret inventing the principles it uses to achieve today's result. I respectfully dissent from Part V of the opinion of the Court.

JUSTICE BREYER concurring in part and dissenting in part (joined BY JUSTICES BREYER, GINSBERG, SOTOMAYOR, AND KAGAN).

. . . I agree with the Court that the Secretary of Commerce provided a pretextual reason for placing a question about citizenship on the short-form census questionnaire and that a remand to the agency is appropriate on that ground. But I write separately because I also believe that the Secretary's decision to add the citizenship question was arbitrary and capricious and therefore violated the Administrative Procedure Act (APA).

There is no serious dispute that adding a citizenship question would diminish the accuracy of the enumeration of the population — the sole constitutional function of the census and a task of great practical importance. The record demonstrates that the question would likely cause a disproportionate number of noncitizens and Hispanics to go uncounted in the upcoming census. That, in turn, would create a risk that some States would wrongfully lose a congressional representative and funding for a host of federal programs. And, the Secretary was told, the adverse consequences would fall most heavily on minority communities. The Secretary decided to ask the question anyway, citing a need for more accurate citizenship data. But the evidence indicated that asking the question would produce citizenship data that is *less* accurate, not more. And the reason the Secretary gave for needing better citizenship data in the first place — to help enforce the Voting Rights Act of 1965 — was not convincing.

In short, the Secretary's decision to add a citizenship question created a severe risk of harmful consequences, yet he did not adequately consider whether the question was necessary or whether it was an appropriate means of achieving his stated goal. The Secretary thus failed to "articulate a satisfactory explanation" for his decision, "failed to consider . . . important aspect[s] of the problem," and "offered an explanation for [his] decision that runs counter to the evidence," all in violation of the APA. These failures, in my view, risked undermining public confidence in the integrity of our democratic system itself. I would therefore hold that the Secretary's decision — whether pretextual or not — was arbitrary, capricious, and an abuse of discretion. . . .

[Opinion of JUSTICE ALITO, concurring in part and dissenting in part, omitted.]

NOTES

1. What should be the role of politics in agency decisionmaking? While it would be naive in the extreme to expect that an agency could operate wholly outside of politics, should agencies attempt to limit political influences? For an evocative discussion of agency disclosure of the role of politics in agency decisionmaking, see Kathryn A. Watts, Proposing a Place for Politics in Arbitrary and Capricious Review, 119 Yale L.J. 2 (2009). Watts' position that agencies should consider and disclose political influences is not without critics. See Enrique Armijo, Politics, Rulemaking, and Judicial Review: A Response to Professor Watts, 62 Admin. L. Rev. 573 (2010); see also Shannon Roesler, Agency Reasons at the Intersection of Expertise and Presidential Preferences, 71 Admin. L. Rev. 491, 515, 554 (2019) (suggesting that Watts' argument fails to adequately account for the risk that agencies could characterize political decisions as technical and recommending that judges employ "hard-look review" practices to "keep political influence from swallowing expert judgment").

2. Upon finding that the agency's actions were pretextual, what remedy did the Court order? Owing to the tight timeline for printing the U.S. Census, there was little the Commerce Department could do here. Usually, though, when an agency decision is remanded, it is permissible for the agency to pursue the same policy, but only with a better record. In this case, but for the printing deadline, could the Commerce Department have attempted to develop a record that supported a less pretextual justification for the injection of a citizenship question into the census? The next case, Dep't of Homeland Security v. Regents of the Univ. of Cal., answers this question.

3. Chief Justice Roberts' majority opinion in the census case scrutinizes the agency decision as pretext. The opinion notes that "the evidence tells a story that does not match the explanation the Secretary gave for his decision," in that the "sole stated reason" for adding the citizenship question to the census "seems to have been contrived." Among the Court's concerns appears to be the role of judicial review. The Court noted that agencies must "offer genuine justifications for important decisions, reasons that can be scrutinized by courts and the interested public," or else judicial review may become "an empty ritual." Justice Thomas' dissent notes that the Chief Justice's scrutiny of the agency is "an unprecedented departure from our deferential review of discretionary agency decisions." Who has the better argument here?

4. Perhaps most important, what are the longer term implications for administrative law of the Court's 2019 term (along with the census case, consider the decisions in *Gundy, supra* p. 124, and Kisor v. Wilkie, 139 S. Ct. 2400 (2019), *infra* p. 755)? Is the Court's scrutiny of the agency here limited to the egregious circumstances? Or is Court precedent beginning to lay the groundwork for a system of judicial oversight in which agency explanations are subject to significant scrutiny rather than to great deference? Time will tell. However, a recent study suggests that increased judicial scrutiny of agency decisions during the Trump administration is related to agency failures rather than judicial philosophy. *See* Bethany A. Davis Noll, "Tired of Wining": Judicial Review of Regulatory Policy in the Trump Era, 73 Admin. L. Rev. 353, 414 (2021) ("The results from the study . . . demonstrate . . . that judicial ideology is not all to blame. Instead, . . . Trump Administration agencies acted in ways that were contrary to law, both by failing to provide a reasoned explanation for their actions and by ignoring their statutory mandates.").

DEPARTMENT OF HOMELAND SECURITY v. REGENTS OF THE UNIVERSITY OF CALIFORNIA

___U.S.___ 140 S. Ct. 1891 (June 18, 2020)

Chief Justice ROBERTS delivered the opinion of the Court.

In the summer of 2012, the Department of Homeland Security (DHS) announced an immigration program known as Deferred Action for Childhood Arrivals, or DACA. That program allows certain unauthorized aliens who entered the United States as children to apply for a two-year forbearance of removal. Those granted such relief are also eligible for work authorization and various federal benefits. Some 700,000 aliens have availed themselves of this opportunity.

Five years later, the Attorney General advised DHS to rescind DACA, based on his conclusion that it was unlawful. The Department's Acting Secretary issued a memorandum terminating the program on that basis. The termination was challenged by affected individuals and third parties who alleged, among other things, that the Acting Secretary had violated the Administrative Procedure Act (APA) by failing to adequately address important factors bearing on her decision. For the reasons that follow, we conclude that the Acting Secretary did violate the APA, and that the rescission must be vacated.

I

A

In June 2012, the Secretary of Homeland Security issued a memorandum announcing an immigration relief program for "certain young people who were brought to this country as children." Known as DACA, the program applies to childhood arrivals who [meet certain criteria]. . . . DHS concluded that individuals who meet these criteria warrant favorable treatment under the immigration laws because they "lacked the intent to violate the law," are "productive" contributors to our society, and "know only this country as home."

"[T]o prevent [these] low priority individuals from being removed from the United States," the DACA Memorandum instructs Immigration and Customs Enforcement to "exercise prosecutorial discretion[ ] on an individual basis . . . by deferring action for a period of two years, subject to renewal." In addition, it directs U.S. Citizenship and Immigration Services (USCIS) to "accept applications to determine whether these individuals qualify for work authorization during this period of deferred action," as permitted under regulations long predating DACA's creation. . . .

In November 2014, two years after DACA was promulgated, DHS issued a memorandum announcing that it would expand DACA eligibility. . . . In the same memorandum, DHS created a new, related program known as Deferred Action for Parents of Americans and Lawful Permanent Residents, or DAPA. That program would have authorized deferred action for up to 4.3 million parents whose children were U.S. citizens or lawful permanent residents. These parents were to enjoy the same forbearance, work eligibility, and other benefits as DACA recipients.

Before the DAPA Memorandum was implemented, 26 States, led by Texas, filed suit in the Southern District of Texas. . . . The District Court found that the States were likely to succeed on the merits of at least one of their claims and entered a nationwide preliminary injunction barring implementation of both DAPA and the DACA expansion.

[Additional procedure omitted] . . . For the next year, litigation over DAPA and the DACA expansion continued in the Southern District of Texas, while implementation of those policies remained enjoined.

Then, in June 2017, following a change in Presidential administrations, DHS rescinded the DAPA Memorandum. In explaining that decision, DHS cited the preliminary injunction and ongoing litigation in Texas, the fact that DAPA had never taken effect, and the new administration's immigration enforcement priorities.

Three months later, in September 2017, Attorney General Jefferson B. Sessions III sent a letter to Acting Secretary of Homeland Security Elaine C. Duke, "advis[ing]" that DHS "should rescind" DACA as well . . . [T]he Attorney General concluded that DACA shared the "same legal . . . defects that the courts recognized as to DAPA" and was "likely" to meet a similar fate. "In light of the costs and burdens" that a rescission would "impose[ ] on DHS," the Attorney General urged DHS to "consider an orderly and efficient wind-down process."

The next day, Duke acted on the Attorney General's advice. In her decision memorandum, Duke summarized the history of the DACA and DAPA programs, the Fifth Circuit opinion and ensuing affirmance, and the contents of the Attorney General's letter. "Taking into consideration the Supreme Court's and the Fifth Circuit's rulings" and the "letter from the Attorney General," she concluded that the "DACA program should be terminated."

B

Within days of Acting Secretary Duke's rescission announcement, multiple groups of plaintiffs . . . challenged her decision. . . .

The issues raised here are (1) whether the APA claims are reviewable, (2) if so, whether the rescission was arbitrary and capricious in violation of the APA, and (3) whether the plaintiffs have stated an equal protection claim.

II

The dispute before the Court is not whether DHS may rescind DACA. All parties agree that it may. The dispute is instead primarily about the procedure the agency followed in doing so.

The APA "sets forth the procedures by which federal agencies are accountable to the public and their actions subject to review by the courts." It requires agencies to engage in "reasoned decisionmaking," and directs that agency actions be "set aside" if they are "arbitrary" or "capricious," §706(2)(A). Under this "narrow standard of review . . . a court is not to substitute its judgment for that of the agency," but instead to assess only whether the decision was "based on a consideration of the relevant factors and whether there has been a clear error of judgment," Citizens to Preserve Overton Park, Inc. v. Volpe, 401 U.S. 402, 416, 91 S.Ct. 814, 28 L.Ed.2d 136 (1971).

But before determining whether the rescission was arbitrary and capricious, we must first address the Government's contentions that DHS's decision is unreviewable under the APA and outside this Court's jurisdiction.

A

The APA establishes a "basic presumption of judicial review [for] one 'suffering legal wrong because of agency action.'" That presumption can be rebutted by a showing that the relevant statute "preclude[s]" review, §701(a)(1), or that the "agency action is committed to agency discretion by law," §701(a)(2). The latter exception is at issue here.

[This section of the Court's reasoning, finding that the DACA program was more than a discretionary non-enforcement policy, is set out as a note following Heckler v. Chaney *supra* p. 624.].

. . .

III

A

Deciding whether agency action was adequately explained requires, first, knowing where to look for the agency's explanation. The natural starting point here is the explanation provided by Acting Secretary Duke when she announced the rescission in September 2017. But the Government urges us to go on and consider the June 2018 memorandum submitted by Secretary Nielsen as well. That memo was prepared after the D.C. District Court vacated the Duke rescission and gave DHS an opportunity to "reissue a memorandum rescinding DACA, this time providing a fuller explanation for the determination that the program lacks statutory and constitutional authority." According to the Government, the Nielsen Memorandum is properly before us because it was invited by the District Court and reflects the views of the Secretary of Homeland Security — the official responsible for immigration policy. Respondents disagree, arguing that the Nielsen Memorandum, issued nine months after the rescission, impermissibly asserts prudential and policy reasons not relied upon by Duke.

It is a "foundational principle of administrative law" that judicial review of agency action is limited to "the grounds that the agency invoked when it took the action." If those grounds are inadequate, a court may remand for the agency to do one of two things: First, the agency can offer "a fuller explanation of the agency's reasoning *at the time of the agency action*." This route has important limitations. When an agency's initial explanation "indicate[s] the determinative reason for the final action taken," the agency may elaborate later on that reason (or reasons) but may not provide new ones. Alternatively, the agency can "deal with the problem afresh" by taking *new* agency action. SEC v. Chenery Corp., 332 U.S. 194, 201, 67 S.Ct. 1760, 91 L.Ed. 1995 (1947) (*Chenery II*). An agency taking this route is not limited to its prior reasons but must comply with the procedural requirements for new agency action.

The District Court's remand thus presented DHS with a choice: rest on the Duke Memorandum while elaborating on its prior reasoning, or issue a new rescission bolstered by new reasons absent from the Duke Memorandum. Secretary Nielsen took the first path. Rather than making a new decision, she "decline[d] to disturb the Duke memorandum's rescission" and instead "provide[d] further explanation" for that action. . . . Contrary to the position of the Government before this Court, and of Justice Kavanaugh in dissent, the Nielsen Memorandum was by its own terms not a new rule implementing a new policy.

Because Secretary Nielsen chose to elaborate on the reasons for the initial rescission rather than take new administrative action, she was limited to the agency's original reasons, and her explanation "must be viewed critically" to ensure that the rescission is not upheld on the basis of impermissible "*post hoc* rationalization." *Overton Park*. But despite purporting to explain the Duke Memorandum, Secretary Nielsen's reasoning bears little relationship to that of her predecessor. Acting Secretary Duke rested the rescission on the conclusion that DACA is unlawful. Period. By contrast, Secretary Nielsen's new memorandum offered three "separate and independently sufficient reasons" for the rescission, only the first of which is the conclusion that DACA is illegal.

Her second reason is that DACA is, at minimum, legally *questionable* and should be terminated to maintain public confidence in the rule of law and avoid burdensome litigation. No such justification can be found in the Duke Memorandum. . . .

The policy reasons that Secretary Nielsen cites as a third basis for the rescission are also nowhere to be found in the Duke Memorandum. . . . They can be viewed only as impermissible *post hoc* rationalizations and thus are not properly before us.

The Government, echoed by Justice Kavanaugh, protests that requiring a new decision before considering Nielsen's new justifications would be "an idle and useless formality." Procedural requirements can often seem such. But here the rule serves important values of administrative law. Requiring a new decision before considering new reasons promotes "agency accountability," by ensuring that parties and the public can respond fully and in a timely manner to an agency's exercise of authority. Considering only contemporaneous explanations for agency action also instills confidence that the reasons given are not simply "convenient litigating position[s]." Permitting agencies to invoke belated justifications, on the other hand, can upset "the orderly functioning of the process of review," forcing both litigants and courts to chase a moving target. Each of these values would be markedly undermined were we to allow DHS to rely on reasons offered nine months after Duke announced the rescission and after three different courts had identified flaws in the original explanation.

Justice Holmes famously wrote that "[m]en must turn square corners when they deal with the Government." Rock Island, A. & L. R. Co. v. United States (1920). But it is also true, particularly when so much is at stake, that "the Government should turn square corners in dealing with the people." St. Regis Paper Co. v. United States (1961) (Black, J., dissenting). The basic rule here is clear: An agency must defend its actions based on the reasons it gave when it acted. This is not the case for cutting corners to allow DHS to rely upon reasons absent from its original decision.

B

We turn, finally, to whether DHS's decision to rescind DACA was arbitrary and capricious. As noted earlier, Acting Secretary Duke's justification for the rescission was succinct: "Taking into consideration" the Fifth Circuit's conclusion that DAPA was unlawful because it conferred benefits in violation of the INA, and the Attorney General's conclusion that DACA was unlawful for the same reason, she concluded — without elaboration — that the "DACA program should be terminated."

Respondents maintain that this explanation is deficient for three reasons. . . . [W]e focus our attention on respondents' third argument — that Acting Secretary Duke "failed to consider . . . important aspect[s] of the problem" before her.

Whether DACA is illegal is, of course, a legal determination, and therefore a question for the Attorney General. But deciding how best to address a finding of illegality moving forward can involve important policy choices, especially when the finding concerns a program with the breadth of DACA. Those policy choices are for DHS. . . .

[T]he Attorney General neither addressed the forbearance policy at the heart of DACA nor compelled DHS to abandon that policy. Thus, removing benefits eligibility while continuing forbearance remained squarely within the discretion of Acting Secretary Duke, who was responsible for "[e]stablishing national immigration enforcement policies and priorities." But Duke's memo offers no reason for terminating forbearance. She instead treated the Attorney General's conclusion regarding the illegality of benefits as sufficient to rescind both benefits and forbearance, without explanation.

That reasoning repeated the error we identified in one of our leading modern administrative law cases, Motor Vehicle Manufacturers Association of the United States, Inc. v. State Farm Mutual Automobile Insurance Co. . . .

Even if it is illegal for DHS to extend work authorization and other benefits to DACA recipients, that conclusion supported only "disallow[ing]" benefits. It did "not cast doubt" on the legality of forbearance or upon DHS's original reasons for extending forbearance to childhood arrivals. Thus, given DHS's earlier judgment that forbearance is "especially justified" for "productive young people" who were brought here as children and "know only this country as home," the DACA Memorandum could not be rescinded in full "without any consideration whatsoever" of a forbearance-only policy.

. . .

The Government acknowledges that "[d]eferred action coupled with the associated benefits are the two legs upon which the DACA policy stands." It insists, however, that "DHS was not required to consider whether DACA's illegality could be addressed by separating" the two. According to the Government, "It was not arbitrary and capricious for DHS to view deferred action and its collateral benefits as importantly linked." Perhaps. But that response misses the point. The fact that there may be a valid reason not to separate deferred action from benefits does not establish that DHS considered that option or that such consideration was unnecessary.

. . .

State Farm teaches that when an agency rescinds a prior policy its reasoned analysis must consider the "alternative[s]" that are "within the ambit of the existing [policy]." Here forbearance was not simply "within the ambit of the existing [policy]," it was the centerpiece of the policy: DACA, after all, stands for "*Deferred Action* for Childhood Arrivals." (emphasis added). But the rescission memorandum contains no discussion of forbearance or the option of retaining forbearance without benefits. Duke "entirely failed to consider [that] important aspect of the problem."

That omission alone renders Acting Secretary Duke's decision arbitrary and capricious. But it is not the only defect. Duke also failed to address whether there was "legitimate reliance" on the DACA Memorandum. When an agency changes course, as DHS did here, it must "be cognizant that longstanding policies may have 'engendered serious reliance interests that must be taken into account.'" It would be arbitrary and capricious to ignore such matters. Yet that is what the Duke Memorandum did.

. . .

To be clear, DHS was not required . . . to "consider all policy alternatives in reaching [its] decision." Agencies are not compelled to explore "every alternative device and thought conceivable by the mind of man." But, because DHS was "not writing on a blank slate," it *was* required to assess whether there were reliance interests, determine whether they were significant, and weigh any such interests against competing policy concerns.

. . . Acting Secretary Duke should have considered those matters but did not. That failure was arbitrary and capricious in violation of the APA.

■ ■ ■

We do not decide whether DACA or its rescission are sound policies. "The wisdom" of those decisions "is none of our concern." We address only whether the agency complied with the procedural requirement that it provide a reasoned explanation for its action. Here the agency failed to consider the conspicuous issues of whether to retain forbearance and what if anything to do about the hardship to DACA recipients. That dual failure raises doubts about whether the agency appreciated the scope of its discretion or exercised that discretion in a reasonable manner. The appropriate recourse is therefore to remand to DHS so that it may consider the problem anew. . . .

It is so ordered.

JUSTICE KAVANAUGH dissenting in part and in the judgment:

. . . The question before the Court is whether the Executive Branch acted lawfully in ordering rescission of the ongoing DACA program. To begin with, all nine Members of the Court accept, as do the DACA plaintiffs themselves, that the Executive Branch possesses the legal authority to rescind DACA and to resume pre-DACA enforcement of the immigration laws enacted by Congress. Having previously adopted a policy of prosecutorial discretion and nonenforcement with respect to a particular class of offenses or individuals, the Executive Branch has the legal authority to rescind such a policy and resume enforcing the law enacted by Congress. The Executive Branch's exercise of that rescission authority is subject to constitutional constraints and may also be subject to statutory constraints. The narrow legal dispute here concerns a statutory constraint — namely, whether the Executive Branch's action to rescind DACA satisfied the general arbitrary-and-capricious standard of the Administrative Procedure Act, or APA.

The APA's arbitrary-and-capricious standard requires that agency action be reasonable and reasonably explained. As the Court has long stated, judicial review under that standard is deferential to the agency. The Court may not substitute its policy judgment for that of the agency. The Court simply ensures that the agency has acted within a broad zone of reasonableness and, in particular, has reasonably considered the relevant issues and reasonably explained the decision.

The Executive Branch explained its decision to rescind DACA in two sequential memorandums by successive Secretaries of Homeland Security: the 2017 Duke Memorandum and the 2018 Nielsen Memorandum. The Duke Memorandum focused on DACA's perceived legal flaws. The Court today finds the Duke Memorandum insufficient under the APA's arbitrary-and-capricious standard.

But regardless of whether the Court is correct about the Duke Memorandum, the Nielsen Memorandum more fully explained the Department's legal reasons for rescinding DACA, and clarified that even if DACA were lawful, the Department would still rescind DACA for a variety of policy reasons. The Nielsen Memorandum also expressly addressed the reliance interests of DACA recipients. The question under the APA's deferential arbitrary-and-capricious standard . . . is whether the Nielsen Memorandum reasonably explained the decision to rescind DACA. Under ordinary application of the arbitrary-and-capricious standard, the Nielsen Memorandum — with its alternative and independent rationales and its discussion of reliance — would pass muster as an explanation for the Executive Branch's action.

Because it is a rule, the Nielsen Memorandum constitutes "agency action." §551(13). [It] was akin to common forms of agency action that follow earlier agency action on the same subject. . . . Courts often consider an agency's additional explanations of policy or additional explanations made, for example, on agency rehearing or reconsideration, or on remand from a court, even if the agency's bottom-line decision itself does not change.

Yet the Court today jettisons the Nielsen Memorandum by classifying it as a *post hoc* justification for rescinding DACA. *Ante*, at 1908-1909. Under our precedents, however, the *post hoc* justification doctrine merely requires that courts assess agency action based on the official explanations of the agency decisionmakers, and not based on after-the-fact explanations advanced *by agency lawyers during litigation* (or by judges). See, *e.g., State Farm*. . . .

Indeed, the ordinary judicial remedy for an agency's insufficient explanation is to remand for further explanation by the relevant agency personnel. It would make little sense for a court to exclude official explanations by agency personnel such as a Cabinet Secretary simply because the explanations are purportedly *post hoc*, and then to turn around and remand for further explanation by those same agency personnel. Yet that is the upshot of the Court's application of the *post hoc* justification doctrine today. The Court's refusal to look at the Nielsen Memorandum seems particularly mistaken, moreover, because the Nielsen Memorandum shows that the Department, back in 2018, considered the policy issues that the Court today says the Department did not consider.

To be sure, cases such as Overton Park v. Volpe . . . suggest that courts reviewing certain agency *adjudications* may in some circumstances decline to examine an after-the-fact agency explanation. But agency adjudications are "concerned with the determination of past and present rights and liabilities," and implicate the due process interests of the individual parties to the adjudication. Judicial review of an adjudication therefore ordinarily focuses on what happened during the agency's adjudication process of deciding that individual case.

Even if certain agency adjudications have a slightly more stringent restriction on *post hoc* explanations, the APA is "based upon a dichotomy between rule making and adjudication," and this case involves an ongoing agency rule that has future effect — the rescission of DACA. The Nielsen Memorandum implements and explains the rescission of DACA. I am aware of no case from this Court, and the Court today cites none, that has employed the *post hoc* justification doctrine to exclude an agency's official explanation of an agency rule. For purposes of arbitrary-and-capricious review, it does not matter whether the latest official explanation was two years ago or three years ago. What matters is whether the explanation was reasonable and followed the requisite procedures. In my view, the Court should consider the Nielsen Memorandum in deciding whether the Department's rescission of DACA satisfies the APA's arbitrary-and-capricious standard.

[A partial concurrence and partial dissent by JUSTICE SOTOMAYOR has been omitted.]

[A partial dissent and partial concurrence by JUSTICES THOMAS, and joined by JUSTICES ALITO and GORSUCH has been omitted.]

[A partial dissent and partial concurrence by JUSTICE ALITO has been omitted.]

NOTES

1. Justices in both the majority and dissent agree that the agency has authority to rescind DACA. Can you pinpoint precisely where the process the agency followed was "arbitrary and capricious" as it attempted to rescind DACA? What process would you have advised the agency to take (or avoid taking) to comply with procedural requirements and permissibly exercise authority to rescind the program?

2. The majority opined that "whether DACA is illegal is, of course, a legal determination, and therefore a question for the Attorney General." Shortly after the decision, Attorney General William Barr wrote to Acting Homeland Security Secretary Chad Wolf that he was rescinding the former determination that DACA was unlawful. What benefit might the Attorney General have seen to rescind the determination that DACA was unlawful? (Hint: the letter indicated that "I do not wish to maintain a determination as the Attorney General regarding DACA that might constrain the discretion you otherwise possess as Acting Secretary of Homeland Security. . . .")

COMMENTS: STATE SCOPE OF REVIEW

1. The Revised Model State APA states at §15(g)(5):

> The court may reverse or modify the decision if . . . the administrative findings, inferences, conclusions, or decisions are . . . clearly erroneous in view of the reliable, probative, and substantial evidence on the whole record.

Note the following comment by Professor Frank Cooper, one of the draftsmen of the Model Act:

> This standard does not permit the court to weigh the evidence, or to substitute its judgment for that of the agency on discretionary matters. But it does authorize the court to examine the whole record, and to reject as mere chaff testimony which is plainly unreliable or without probative force, and then to determine whether on the remaining evidence it must be concluded that the agency plainly erred.

2 Cooper, State Administrative Law 730 (1965).

Does the Model Act provision change the scope of review? Compare Ancheta v. Daly, 461 P.2d 531, 534 (Wash. 1969):

> In providing (1) that judicial review was under the provisions of the Administrative Procedure Act (RCW 34.04.130(1)), and (2) in changing subsection (e), conditioning judicial review upon a finding by the court that administrative action was "clearly erroneous in view of the entire record as submitted and the public policy contained in the act . . . " the legislature clearly intended a broader review of all the evidence.

State courts have increasingly tended to state the scope of review in terms of the substantial evidence rule, even where, as in the states that have adopted the Revised Model State APA, the legislature may have intended a somewhat broader scope. At the same time, state judges tend to be freer than their federal confreres in reversing agency decisions. The extent of review depends ultimately on the degree of deference shown toward the administrator.

2. The federal courts place more stress on agency expertise than do their state counterparts. This may reflect the higher caliber of personnel in Washington, D.C., or it may reflect only the greater reluctance of the states to yield to the claims of ever-expanding administrative power. Judges less willing to defer to agencies will not be deterred by any theory of limited review in reaching what they believe to be the just result. When they are persuaded agency decisions are wrong, state judges are readier to reverse, regardless of theoretical reasonableness under the substantial evidence rule.

3. Note that the Model State APA, approved in 1981, eliminates the "clearly erroneous" test and opts for the substantial evidence test of the Federal APA. §5-116(c)(7). Nonetheless, many states still adhere to the "clearly erroneous" standard.

3. Agency Delay

APA §706. Scope of Review

The reviewing court shall—

(1) compel agency action unlawfully withheld or unreasonably delayed;

HECKLER v. DAY

467 U.S. 104 (1984)

JUSTICE POWELL delivered the opinion for the Court.

The question presented is the validity of an injunction issued on behalf of a statewide class that requires the Secretary of Health and Human Services to adjudicate all future disputed disability claims under Title II of the Social Security Act, 42 U.S.C. §401 et seq., according to judicially established deadlines and to pay interim benefits in all cases of noncompliance with those deadlines.

I

Title II of the Social Security Act [Act] was passed in 1935. . . . Among other things, it provides for the payment of disability insurance benefits to those whose disability prevents them from pursuing gainful employment. . . . Approximately two million disability claims were filed . . . in fiscal year 1983. Over 320,000 of these claims must be heard by some 800 administrative law judges each year. To facilitate the orderly and sympathetic administration of the disability program of Title II, the Secretary and Congress have established an unusually protective four-step process for the review and adjudication of disputed claims. First, a state agency determines whether the claimant has a disability and the date the disability began or ceased. . . . Second, if the claimant is dissatisfied with that determination, he may request reconsideration of the determination. . . . Third, if the claimant receives an adverse reconsideration determination, he is entitled by statute to an evidentiary hearing and to a de novo review by an Administrative Law Judge [ALJ]. . . . Finally, if the claimant is dissatisfied with the decision of the ALJ, he may take an appeal to the Appeals Council of the Department of Health and Human Services [HHS]. . . .

In this class action, the named plaintiffs sought declaratory and injunctive relief from delays encountered in steps two and three above. The action was initiated by Leon Day in November 1978 after his disability benefits were terminated and he suffered substantial delays in obtaining a reconsideration determination and in securing a hearing before an ALJ.[1] . . . On the basis of the undisputed evidence, the District Court held that, as to all claimants for Title II disability benefits in Vermont, delays of more than ninety days from a request for hearing before an ALJ to the hearing itself were unreasonable. . . .

After the submission of additional evidence, the District Court considered motions for summary judgment concerning the reasonableness of delays in the reconsideration process. The additional evidence also was undisputed. It consisted of factual summaries of seventy-seven randomly selected disability cases submitted by the Secretary. . . . In twenty-seven of the seventy-seven cases, reconsideration determinations took longer than ninety days. In each of these twenty-seven, the District Court concluded that the delays were caused by agency inefficiencies and were not justified by the "necessary steps in the reconsideration process." . . . On the basis of this survey, the District Court concluded that, as a rule, delays of more than ninety days in making reconsideration determinations were unreasonable and violated the claimant's statutory rights. . . .

In November 1981, the District Court issued an injunction in favor of the statewide class that "ordered and directed [the Secretary] to conclude reconsideration processing and issue reconsideration determinations within ninety days of requests for reconsideration made by claimants." The injunction also required ALJs to provide hearings within ninety days after the request is made by claimants. Finally, it ordered payment of interim benefits to any claimant who did not receive a reconsideration determination or hearing within 180 days of the request for reconsideration or who did not receive a hearing within ninety days of the hearing request. The Court of Appeals for the Second Circuit affirmed. . . . We conclude that the legislative history makes clear that Congress, fully aware of the serious delays in resolution of disability claims, has declined to impose deadlines on the administrative process. Accordingly, we reverse the judgment below.

II

The Secretary does not challenge here the determination that §405(b) requires administrative hearings to be held within a reasonable time. Nor does she challenge the District Court's determination that the delays encountered in [this case] violated that requirement. She argues only that a statewide injunction that imposes judicially prescribed deadlines on HHS for all future disability

1. Day was forced to wait 167 days for a reconsideration determination. He received a hearing before the ALJ 173 days after his hearing request.

determinations is contrary to congressional intent and constitutes an abuse of the court's equitable power. . . .

The Secretary correctly points out that Congress repeatedly has been made aware of the long delays associated with resolution of disputed disability claims and repeatedly has considered and expressly rejected suggestions that mandatory deadlines be imposed to cure that problem. She argues that Congress expressly has balanced the need for timely disability determinations against the need to ensure quality decisions in the face of heavy and escalating workloads and limited agency resources. In striking that balance, the Secretary argues, the relevant legislative history also shows that Congress to date has determined that mandatory deadlines for agency adjudication of disputed disability claims are inconsistent with achievement of the Act's primary objectives, and that the District Court's statewide injunction flatly contradicts that legislative determination. We find this argument persuasive.

Congressional concern over timely resolution of disputed disability claims under Title II began at least as early as 1975. It has inspired almost annual congressional debate since that time. The consistency with which Congress has expressed concern over this issue is matched by its consistent refusal to impose on the Secretary mandatory deadlines for resolution of disputed disability claims. . . .

Bills proposing statutory deadlines have been proposed almost annually since 1975, and congressional concern over the delay problem has remained high. For example, in 1980 Congress directed the Secretary to submit a report recommending the establishment of appropriate and realistic deadlines for resolution of disputed SSA claims. It ordered the Secretary in doing so to consider "both the need for expeditious processing of claims for benefits and the need to assure that all such claims will be thoroughly considered and accurately determined." . . . The Secretary submitted a report in October 1980, suggesting deadlines of 150 days for reconsideration determinations and 165 days from hearing to post-hearing decision, both subject to certain exceptions. . . . The Secretary, however, cautioned Congress that budget and staff limitations and burgeoning workloads "mitigate against the Department meeting its proposed time limitation objectives in every instance." . . . Since receiving the Secretary's report, Congress has refused to impose mandatory deadlines on the Secretary, or to direct her to promulgate them herself.

Certainly in Congress the concern that mandatory deadlines would jeopardize the quality and uniformity of agency decisions has prevailed over considerations of timeliness. In its most recent comment on the subject, the House Committee on Ways and Means expressly disapproved mandatory hearing deadlines and indicated disagreement with recent judicial decisions imposing such time restrictions. . . .

> [The] Committee believes that a disability claimant is entitled to a timely hearing and decision on his appeal, but it also recognizes that the time needed before a well-reasoned and sound disability hearing decision can be made may vary widely

> on a case-by-case basis. . . . Establishing strict time limits for the adjudication of every case could result in incorrect determinations because time was not available to . . . reach well-reasoned decisions in difficult cases.

H.R. Rep. No. 97-588, pp.19-20 (1982). . . . In light of Congress' continuing concern that mandatory deadlines would subordinate quality to timeliness, and its recent efforts to ensure the quality of agency determinations, it hardly could have contemplated that courts should have authority to impose the very deadlines it repeatedly has rejected. . . . In light of the unmistakable intention of Congress, it would be an unwarranted judicial intrusion into this pervasively regulated area for federal courts to issue injunctions imposing deadlines with respect to future disability claims. Accordingly, we vacate the judgment of the Court of Appeals, and remand the case for further proceedings consistent with this opinion. It is so ordered.

JUSTICE MARSHALL, with whom JUSTICE BRENNAN, JUSTICE BLACKMUN, and JUSTICE STEVENS join, dissenting.

This case determines an issue of vital importance to the Social Security Administration, to disabled Vermont residents, and to federal courts. By failing to ground its opinion in the factual record of the case at hand, the majority has discarded a balanced remedy crafted to effectuate a federal statute. Far from intruding clumsily into a pervasively regulated area . . . the District Court fashioned a meaningful, carefully-tailored statewide remedy that mandated feasible, expeditious reconsideration determinations and hearings, that did not cause extra cost to the Secretary or reallocation to Vermont of resources from other States, and that did not harm other statutory goals such as quality and accuracy of decision making. Because that remedy is not expressly or impliedly prohibited by the Constitution or by statute, and is not an abuse of discretion, I would affirm the judgment of the Court of Appeals. . . .

The District Court ordered compliance with the prescribed time limits only after reviewing extensive responses to interrogatories in which the Secretary acknowledged not only that she was able to comply with those limits, but that it was her stated policy to do so. . . . The Secretary argued that the review process required some flexibility, and specified a variety of circumstances in which delay in completing a reconsideration or scheduling a hearing was justified. The District Court tailored its remedy to accommodate each of the Secretary's submissions. If a claimant offers new medical evidence, reports new medical treatment since the initial determination, agrees to undergo a consultative examination when the Secretary so suggests, causes a delay by failing to provide the information needed to reconsider the initial determination of non-disability, or otherwise causes a delay, the District Court ordered that the ninety-day limit on the time from a reconsideration request to issuance of the notice of the result be tolled. . . . Because the Secretary urged that it was frequently in the claimant's interest to delay, the court also tolled the time limit for any period of delay requested by the claimant or his representative. . . .

Finally, the remedy pertains only to the Secretary's statutory obligation to provide *hearings* within a reasonable time. The order places no time limit on the Secretary's issuance of decisions. . . . The order we are reviewing simply does not speak to decision making; it interprets and enforces only a claimant's right to a timely *hearing*. . . .

What insight can be gleaned from the recent history supports the proposition that the District Court's *statewide* prospective injunction setting time limits for reconsideration determinations and hearings, far from being inconsistent with "repeated congressional rejection of the imposition of mandatory deadlines on agency adjudication of disputed disability claims," . . . effectively accommodates Congress' concern that review of disputed disability determinations be both accurate and expeditious. While it is correct that Congress hitherto has not enacted a nationwide standard in statutory form, that inaction is relevant to the equitable remedy under review only if statutory nationwide time limits are functionally no different from time limits imposed by a court on the operations within one State. Clearly, they are not. A statutory response is inflexible, requires a concomitant commitment by Congress to provide the resources to enable the Secretary to comply with the standard across the nation, and is difficult to amend in response to changing experience. A court-ordered timetable is a flexible response to a particular factual record. It can be narrowly tailored to accommodate both the Secretary's obligation and the claimants' rights within the framework of resources and practices in a defined jurisdiction. . . . Congress' reluctance to establish nationwide time limits within which the Secretary must resolve disputed disability claims does not support the inference that Congress disapproves the exercise by federal courts of their equitable power to ensure that disability claimants in particular jurisdictions are not deprived of their statutory entitlements. If any aspect of the post-enactment legislative history of §205(b) of the Social Security Act bears directly on the problem before us, it is the fact that Congress has repeatedly reenacted the provision with the awareness that the courts had been ordering the Secretary to comply with time limits when necessary to prevent unreasonable delays in providing reconsiderations and hearings. There is thus no basis for the majority's conclusion that the equitable remedy ordered by the District Court in this case is barred by implication. . . .

The court's remedy . . . reflects its sensitivity to the special difficulties of administering the massive Social Security system, and to the challenges the Secretary faces in meeting the administrative goals of accuracy and promptness. . . . By exempting from its order circumstances in which the agency needed to gather medical evidence and reports, the court responded to the Secretary's concern that she not be forced to sacrifice accuracy for the sake of providing more expeditious hearings. By exempting circumstances in which the claimant failed to cooperate in the process or contributed to the delay, the court accommodated the Secretary's concern that she be permitted the degree of flexibility required in the best interests of the claimants as well as the agency. And, of course, a significant accommodation to the Secretary's concern for accurate determinations in the court's order is its total exemption of the decision making, as opposed to the information-gathering, process. There is no time limit whatsoever placed on ALJs' deliberations and issuance of decisions. ALJs have sufficient time to deliberate to ensure accurate decisions, and to schedule new consultative exams if additional evidence is required.

Finally, the consequences of the injunction are a further indication of the reasonableness of the court's interpretation of the statutory mandate.... During the twenty-eight months in which a hearing injunction has been in effect, the Secretary has met the standard in all but one case, without additional allocation of resources and subsequent adverse impact elsewhere in the Social Security Title II disability claims system.... This record suggests both that the injunction has not had the slightest impact on the Secretary's nationwide management of the disability review process, and that the injunction has had the desired effect of enforcing disabled Vermonters' rights to timely hearings....

NOTES

1. The mills of administrative justice grind slowly. In all too many agencies, the goal of dispensing speedy and inexpensive justice has proved to be more or less a will-o'-the-wisp. Those who have studied agencies have complained of the cumbersome and overtechnical nature of their adjudicatory process. Yet, despite the express APA provision empowering them to "compel agency action . . . unreasonably delayed," the courts have had difficulty in dealing with the problem.

2. Do you agree with the Court's answer to the problem of agency delay? What about the dissent's response?

3. The Court's reluctance to impose the judiciary as the hierarchical head of HHS on a matter normally relegated to administrative discretion is understandable. To compel an agency to follow a court-imposed timetable and pay interim benefits to people who may not be entitled to them is judicial activism pushed to an extreme. But what other remedy is available to ensure enforcement of the statutory requirement that hearings be held within a reasonable time?

4. The Doctrine of Statutory Deference

Once an agency sets out an interpretive position, whether as part of rulemaking or otherwise, courts have had to address the issue of deference. Ambiguous language can result in multiple interpretations. To the extent that courts do not give agency positions deference, they are in a position of having to decide what is often the "best" interpretation of the statutory or regulatory language at issue. The approach generally resolves the interpretive issue but is in many ways inflexible. Thereafter, the statute can be changed, for the most part, only after legislative amendment.

To the extent that the courts defer to agencies, they may allow for a suboptimal interpretation but one that is favored by the agency. Moreover, the interpretation of statutes and rules can change. A reasonable interpretation by the agency during one period does not preclude the agency from taking a different but reasonable interpretation at other times. Needless to say, the issue is not easily resolved. Moreover, the perspective of the courts shifts over time.

SKIDMORE v. SWIFT & CO.

323 U.S. 134 (1944)

MR. JUSTICE JACKSON delivered the opinion of the Court.

There is no statutory provision as to what, if any, deference courts should pay to the Administrator's conclusions. And, while we have given them notice, we have had no occasion to try to prescribe their influence. The rulings of this Administrator are not reached as a result of hearing adversary proceedings in which he finds facts from evidence and reaches conclusions of law from findings of fact. They are not, of course, conclusive, even in the cases with which they directly deal, much less in those to which they apply only by analogy. They do not constitute an interpretation of the Act or a standard for judging factual situations which binds a district court's processes, as an authoritative pronouncement of a higher court might do. But the Administrator's policies are made in pursuance of official duty, based upon more specialized experience and broader investigations and information than is likely to come to a judge in a particular case. They do determine the policy which will guide applications for enforcement by injunction on behalf of the Government. Good administration of the Act and good judicial administration alike require that the standards of public enforcement and those for determining private rights shall be at variance only where justified by very good reasons. The fact that the Administrator's policies and standards are not reached by trial in adversary form does not mean that they are not entitled to respect. This Court has long given considerable and in some cases decisive weight to Treasury Decisions and to interpretative regulations of the Treasury and of other bodies that were not of adversary origin.

We consider that the rulings, interpretations and opinions of the Administrator under this Act, while not controlling upon the courts by reason of their authority, do constitute a body of experience and informed judgment to which courts and litigants may properly resort for guidance. The weight of such a judgment in a particular case will depend upon the thoroughness evident in its consideration, the validity of its reasoning, its consistency with earlier and later pronouncements, and all those factors which give it power to persuade, if lacking power to control.

CHEVRON v. NATURAL RESOURCES DEFENSE COUNCIL

467 U.S. 837 (1984)

JUSTICE STEVENS delivered the opinion of the Court.

In the Clean Air Act Amendments of 1977, Pub. L. 95-95, 91 Stat. 685, Congress enacted certain requirements applicable to States that had not achieved the national air quality standards established by the Environmental Protection Agency (EPA) pursuant to earlier legislation. The amended Clean Air Act required these "nonattainment" States to establish a permit program regulating "new or modified major stationary sources" of air pollution. Generally, a permit may not be issued for a new or modified major stationary source unless several stringent conditions are met. The EPA regulation promulgated to implement this permit requirement allows a State to adopt a plantwide definition of the term "stationary source." Under this definition, an existing plant that contains several pollution-emitting devices may install or modify one piece of equipment without meeting the permit conditions if the alteration will not increase the total emissions from the plant. The question presented by these cases is whether EPA's decision to allow States to treat all of the pollution-emitting devices within the same industrial grouping as though they were encased within a single "bubble" is based on a reasonable construction of the statutory term "stationary source."

I

The EPA regulations containing the plantwide definition of the term stationary source were promulgated on October 14, 1981. 46 Fed. Reg. 50,766. Respondents filed a timely petition for review in the United States Court of Appeals for the District of Columbia Circuit pursuant to 42 U.S.C. §7607(b)(1). The Court of Appeals set aside the regulations. National Resources Defence Council, Inc. v. Gorsuch, 222 U.S. App. D.C. 268, 685 F.2d 718 (1982).

The court observed that the relevant part of the amended Clean Air Act "does not explicitly define what Congress envisioned as a 'stationary source,' to which the permit program . . . should apply," and further stated that the precise issue was not "squarely addressed in the legislative history." Id. at 273, 685 F.2d at 723. In light of its conclusion that the legislative history bearing on the question was "at best contradictory," it reasoned that "the purposes of the nonattainment program should guide our decision here." Id. at 276, n.39, 685 F.2d at 726, n.39. Based on two of its precedents concerning the applicability of the bubble concept to certain Clean Air Act programs, the court stated that the bubble concept was "mandatory" in programs designed merely to maintain existing air quality, but held that it was "inappropriate" in programs enacted to improve air quality. Id. at 276, 685 F.2d at 726. Since the purpose of the permit program — its "*raison d'être*," in the court's view — was to improve air quality, the court held that the bubble concept was inapplicable in these cases under its prior precedents. Ibid.

It therefore set aside the regulations embodying the bubble concept as contrary to law. We granted certiorari to review that judgment, 461 U.S. 956, (1983), and we now reverse.

The basic legal error of the Court of Appeals was to adopt a static judicial definition of the term "stationary source" when it had decided that Congress itself had not commanded that definition. . . . [W]e must determine whether the Court of Appeals' legal error resulted in an erroneous judgment on the validity of the regulations.

II

When a court reviews an agency's construction of the statute which it administers, it is confronted with two questions. First, always, is the question whether Congress has directly spoken to the precise question at issue. If the intent of Congress is clear, that is the end of the matter; for the court, as well as the agency, must give effect to the unambiguously expressed intent of Congress. If, however, the court determines Congress has not directly addressed the precise question at issue, the court does not simply impose its own construction on the statute, as would be necessary in the absence of an administrative interpretation. Rather, if the statute is silent or ambiguous with respect to the specific issue, the question for the court is whether the agency's answer is based on a permissible construction of the statute.

"The power of an administrative agency to administer a congressionally created . . . program necessarily requires the formulation of policy and the making of rules to fill any gap left, implicitly or explicitly, by Congress." . . . If Congress has explicitly left a gap for the agency to fill, there is an express delegation of authority to the agency to elucidate a specific provision of the statute by regulation. Such legislative regulations are given controlling weight unless they are arbitrary, capricious, or manifestly contrary to the statute. Sometimes the legislative delegation to an agency on a particular question is implicit rather than explicit. In such a case, a court may not substitute its own construction of a statutory provision for a reasonable interpretation made by the administrator of an agency.

We have long recognized that considerable weight should be accorded to an executive department's construction of a statutory scheme it is entrusted to administer, and the principle of deference to administrative interpretations

> has been consistently followed by this Court whenever decision as to the meaning or reach of a statute has involved reconciling conflicting policies, and a full understanding of the force of the statutory policy in the given situation has depended upon more than ordinary knowledge respecting the matters subjected to agency regulations. . . .
>
> . . . If this choice represents a reasonable accommodation of conflicting policies that were committed to the agency's care by the statute, we should not disturb it unless it appears from the statute or its legislative history that the accommodation is not one that Congress would have sanctioned.

United States v. Shimer, 367 U.S. 374, 382, 383 (1961). . . .

In light of these well-settled principles it is clear that the Court of Appeals misconceived the nature of its role in reviewing the regulations at issue. Once it determined, after its own examination of the legislation, that Congress did not actually have an intent regarding the applicability of the bubble concept to the permit program, the question before it was not whether in its view the concept is "inappropriate" in the general context of a program designed to improve air quality, but whether the Administrator's view that it is appropriate in the context of this particular program is a reasonable one. Based on the examination of the legislation and its history which follows, we agree with the Court of Appeals that Congress did not have a specific intention on the applicability of the bubble concept in these cases, and conclude that the EPA's use of that concept here is a reasonable policy choice for the agency to make. . . .

VII

In this Court respondents expressly reject the basic rationale of the Court of Appeals' decision. That court viewed the statutory definition of the term "source" as sufficiently flexible to cover either a plantwide definition, a narrower definition covering each unit within a plant, or a dual definition that could apply to both the entire "bubble" and its components. It interpreted the policies of the statute, however, to mandate the plantwide definition in programs designed to maintain clean air and to forbid it in programs designed to improve air quality. Respondents place a fundamentally different construction on the statute. They contend that the text of the Act requires the EPA to use a dual definition — if either a component of a plant, or the plant as a whole, emits over 100 tons of pollutant, it is a major stationary source. They thus contend that the EPA rules adopted in 1980, insofar as they apply to the maintenance of the quality of clean air, as well as the 1981 rules which apply to nonattainment areas, violate the statute.

Statutory Language

The definition of the term "stationary source" in §111(a)(3) refers to "any building, structure, facility, or installation" which emits air pollution. This definition is applicable only to the NSPS program by the express terms of the statute; the text of the statute does not make this definition applicable to the permit program. Petitioners therefore maintain that there is no statutory language even relevant to ascertaining the meaning of stationary source in the permit program aside from §302(j), which defines the term "major stationary source." We disagree with petitioners on this point.

The definition in §302(j) tells us what the word "major" means — a source must emit at least 100 tons of pollution to qualify — but it sheds virtually no light on the meaning of the term "stationary source." It does equate a source with a facility — a "major emitting facility" and a "major stationary source" are synonymous under §302(j). The ordinary meaning of the term "facility" is some collection of integrated elements which has been designed and constructed to achieve some purpose. Moreover, it is certainly no affront to common English usage to take a reference to a major facility or a major source to connote an entire plant as opposed to its constituent parts. Basically, however, the language of §302(j) simply does not compel any given interpretation of the term "source."

Respondents recognize that, and hence point to §111(a)(3). Although the definition in that section is not literally applicable to the permit program, it sheds as much light on the meaning of the word "source" as anything in the statute. As respondents point out, use of the words "building, structure, facility, or installation," as the definition of source, could be read to impose the permit conditions on an individual building that is a part of a plant. A "word may have a character of its own not to be submerged by its association." . . . On the other hand, the meaning of a word must be ascertained in the context of achieving particular objectives, and the words associated with it may indicate that the true meaning of the series is to convey a common idea. The language may reasonably be interpreted to impose the requirement on any discrete, but integrated, operation which pollutes. This gives meaning to all of the terms — a single building, not part of a larger operation, would be covered if it emits more than 100 tons of pollution, as would any facility, structure, or installation. Indeed, the language itself implies a "bubble concept" of sorts: each enumerated item would seem to be treated as if it were encased in a bubble. While respondents insist that each of these terms must be given a discrete meaning, they also argue that §111(a)(3) defines "source" as that term is used in §302(j). The latter section, however, equates a source with a facility, whereas the former defines "source" as a facility, among other items.

We are not persuaded that parsing of general terms in the text of a statute will reveal an actual intent of Congress. We know full well that this language is not dispositive; the terms are overlapping and the language is not precisely directed to the question of the applicability of a given term in the context of a larger operation. To the extent any congressional "intent" can be discerned from this language, it would appear that the listing of overlapping, illustrative terms was intended to enlarge, rather than to confine, the scope of the agency's power to regulate particular sources in order to effectuate the policies of the Act.

Legislative History

In addition, respondents argue that the legislative history and policies of the Act foreclose the plantwide definition, and that the EPA's interpretation is not entitled to deference because it represents a sharp break with prior interpretations of the Act.

Based on our examination of the legislative history, we agree with the Court of Appeals that it is unilluminating. The general remarks pointed to by respondents "were obviously not made with this narrow issue in mind and they cannot be said to demonstrate a Congressional desire. . . ." . . . Respondents' argument based on the legislative history relies heavily on Senator Muskie's observation that a new source is subject to the LAER [lowest achievable emission rate] requirement. But the full statement is ambiguous and, like the text of §173 itself, this comment does not tell us what a new source is, much less that it is to have an inflexible definition. We find that the legislative history as a whole is silent on the precise issue before us. It is, however, consistent with the view that the EPA should have broad discretion in implementing the policies of the 1977 Amendments.

More importantly, that history plainly identifies the policy concerns that motivated the enactment; the plantwide definition is fully consistent with one of those concerns — the allowance of reasonable economic growth — and, whether or not we believe it most effectively implements the other, we must recognize that the EPA has advanced a reasonable explanation for its conclusion that the regulations serve the environmental objectives as well. . . .

Our review of the EPA's varying interpretations of the word "source" — both before and after the 1977 Amendments — convinces us that the agency primarily responsible for administering this important legislation has consistently interpreted it flexibly — not in a sterile textual vacuum, but in the context of implementing policy decisions in a technical and complex arena. The fact that the agency has from time to time changed its interpretation of the term "source" does not, as respondents argue, lead us to conclude that no deference should be accorded the agency's interpretation of the statute. An initial agency interpretation is not instantly carved in stone. On the contrary, the agency, to engage in informed rulemaking, must consider varying interpretations and the wisdom of its policy on a continuing basis. Moreover, the fact that the agency has adopted different definitions in different contexts adds force to the argument that the definition itself is flexible, particularly since Congress has never indicated any disapproval of a flexible reading of the statute. . . .

Policy

The arguments over policy that are advanced in the parties' briefs create the impression that respondents are now waging in a judicial forum a specific policy battle which they ultimately lost in the agency and in the 32 jurisdictions opting for the "bubble concept," but one which was never waged in the Congress. Such policy arguments are more properly addressed to legislators or administrators, not to judges.

In these cases, the Administrator's interpretation represents a reasonable accommodation of manifestly competing interests and is entitled to deference: the regulatory scheme is technical and complex, the agency considered the matter in a detailed and reasoned fashion, and the decision involves reconciling conflicting policies. Congress intended to accommodate both interests, but did not do so itself on the level of specificity presented by these cases. Perhaps that body consciously desired the Administrator to strike the balance at this level, thinking that those with great expertise and charged with responsibility for administering the provision would be in a better position to do so; perhaps it simply did not consider the question at this level; and perhaps Congress was unable to forge a coalition on either side of the question, and those on each side decided to take their chances with the scheme devised by the agency. For judicial purposes, it matters not which of these things occurred.

Judges are not experts in the field, and are not part of either political branch of the Government. Courts must, in some cases, reconcile competing political interests, but not on the basis of the judges' personal policy preferences. In contrast, an agency to which Congress has delegated policy-making responsibilities may, within the limits of that delegation, properly rely upon the incumbent administration's views of wise policy to inform its judgments. While agencies are not directly accountable to the people, the Chief Executive is, and it is entirely appropriate for this political branch of Government to make such policy choices — resolving the competing interests which Congress itself either inadvertently did not resolve, or intentionally left to be resolved by the agency charged with the administration of the statute in light of everyday realities.

When a challenge to an agency construction of a statutory provision, fairly conceptualized, really centers on the wisdom of the agency's policy, rather than whether it is a reasonable choice within a gap left open by Congress, the challenge must fail. In such a case, federal judges — who have no constituency — have a duty to respect legitimate policy choices made by those who do. The responsibilities for assessing the wisdom of such policy choices and resolving the struggle between competing views of the public interest are not judicial ones: "Our Constitution vests such responsibilities in the political branches." . . .

We hold that the EPA's definition of the term "source" is a permissible construction of the statute which seeks to accommodate progress in reducing air pollution with economic growth. "The Regulations which the Administrator has adopted provide what the agency could allowably view as [an] effective reconciliation of these twofold ends. . . ."

The judgment of the Court of Appeals is reversed.

It is so ordered.

NOTES

1. According to Justice Scalia, *Chevron* is one of the most important administrative law decisions. Scalia, Judicial Deference to Administration Interpretations of Law, 1989 Duke L.J. 511, 512. "Under *Chevron* . . . , if a statute is unambiguous the statute governs; if, however, Congress' silence or ambiguity has 'left a gap for the agency to fill,' courts must defer to the agency's interpretation so long as it is 'a permissible construction of the statute.'" Stinson v. United States, 508 U.S. 36, 44 (1993). "This Court has consistently interpreted *Chevron* . . . as holding that courts must give effect to a reasonable agency interpretation of a statute unless that interpretation is inconsistent with a clearly expressed congressional intent." INS v. Cardoza-Fonseca, 480 U.S. 421 (1987). See Sierra Club v. Davies, 955 F.2d 1188 (8th Cir. 1992):

> When a court reviews an agency's construction of a statute the agency has been entrusted to administer, the court's analysis is two-fold. If Congress has spoken to the precise question at issue, the analysis is complete. This court, as well as the agency, must give effect to the unambiguously expressed intent of Congress (*Chevron* Prong I). . . . But where, as here, the court determines that Congress has not spoken directly to the issue, the court may not impose its own construction of the statute. Rather, the court's analysis is limited to whether the agency's construction of the statute was permissible. Since the agency was vested with policy-making power, it is authorized to fill in the gaps that may have been left by Congress and this court cannot substitute its judgment for that of the agency . . . unless the court finds the agency's construction inconsistent with the statutory mandate or that it frustrates the purpose of Congress (*Chevron* Prong II).

2. Note *Chevron*'s two prongs, or steps. Step I requires the court to determine whether the statute is ambiguous. "If the statute is unambiguous, then the court applies it as-written; 'that is the end of the matter.'" Arangure v. Whitaker, 911 F.3d 333, 337 (6th Cir. 2018).

If the court finds that the statute is ambiguous, however, it proceeds to Step II; it "defer[s] to the agency's construction if it is 'permissible'—i.e., 'within the bounds of reasonable interpretation.'" Id.

3. One commentator described *Chevron* as consisting of "false invocations of congressional intent." See Jack M. Beermann, The Turn Toward Congress in Administrative Law, 89 B.U. L. Rev. 727, 740 (2009). What does he mean by this interpretation? Do you agree?

4. How troubling is *Chevron*? Does it limit judicial review so much that it serves to vastly expand the power of the executive? See Breger, Comments on Bernard Schwartz' Essay, 5 Admin. L.J. 347, 371 (1991). Would it be appropriate to adopt an approach to judicial review that is highly deferential to agency positions? See Cass R. Sunstein, After the Rights Revolution, 142-143 (1990):

> [A] general rule of judicial deference to all agency interpretations of law would be unsound. Under the constitutional system, it is ordinarily for courts to say what the law is, and the case for deference to agency interpretations of law must therefore depend in the first instance on the law in the form of congressional instruction. If Congress has told courts to defer to agency interpretations, courts should do so. But many of the recent regulatory statutes were born out of legislative distrust for agency discretion; these statutes hardly call for deference to agency interpretations. As we have seen, they represent an effort to limit administrative authority through clear legislative specifications. A rule of deference in the face of ambiguity would be inconsistent with an appreciation, endorsed by Congress, of the considerable risks posed by administrative discretion. An ambiguity is not a delegation of law-interpreting power. *Chevron* elides the two.

5. Is there an argument that *Chevron* actually expanded the role of the courts? The U.S. Supreme Court has, at times, found that in this initial step *Chevron* deference is simply inappropriate, usually because there is some indication in the statute, however vague, that the legislature did not intend an agency's rulemaking authority to extend to the issue at hand. See, e.g., Gonzales v.

Oregon, 546 U.S. 243, 267 (2006) (refusal to recognize Attorney General's authority over physician-assisted suicide because Congress would surely have stated such an intent if it existed: "[Congress] does not, one might say, hide elephants in mouseholes."); FDA v. Brown & Williamson Tobacco Corp., 529 U.S. 120, 126 (2000) (refusal to recognize FDA authority over regulation of nicotine), abrogated on other grounds by Tobacco Control Act of 2009, 21 U.S.C. §387(a-1) (explicitly granting FDA regulatory authority over tobacco products). In other words, before applying *Chevron* deference courts must first determine whether Congress, in a broad sense, intended the agency to have authority, and therefore deference, over the subject matter at issue. In this sense, the court has the power to police the parameters of delegation. See also William S. Jordan III, *Chevron* and Hearing Rights: An Unintended Combination, 61 Admin. L. Rev. 249 (2009) (arguing that *Chevron* deference should not be applied to agency determinations about the applicability of APA formal adjudication provisions). Some have suggested, too, that *Chevron* deference should not apply ab initio to agency jurisdiction or other issues of agency self-interest. See, e.g., Ernest Gellhorn & Paul Verkuil, Controlling *Chevron*-Based Delegations, 20 Cardozo L. Rev. 989, 992 (1999); Cass R. Sunstein, Law and Administration After *Chevron*, 90 Colum. L. Rev. 2071, 2076 (1990).

6. Some view courts' initial determination of whether the *Chevron* analysis applies at all as "*Chevron* step zero." See Daniel J. Hemel & Aaron L. Nielson, Chevron Step One-and-a-Half, 84 U. Chi. L. Rev. 757, 759 (2017). Hemel and Nielson describe *Chevron* step zero as justified by the theory of implied delegation on which the *Chevron* decision is grounded; if Congress delegated to agencies the power to implement and, thus, to interpret a statute, "it is reasonable to think that there are some categories of interpretations for which Congress would not want the agency calling the shots." Id. at 774. The Supreme Court's decision in United States v. Mead Corp., *infra* p. 739, offers one example of such a category: when an agency issues a statutory interpretation through "informal procedures," the agency is not entitled to deference because "such interpretations do not have the force of law." Mary Holper, Failing Chevron Step Zero, 76 Brook. L. Rev. 1241, 1242 (2011). Some scholars view recent Court decisions as aggressive applications of *Chevron* step zero designed to undermine agency deference and, indeed, the administrative state itself. See Catherine M. Sharkey, Cutting in on the Chevron Two-Step, 86 Fordham L. Rev. 2359, 2413 (2019).

Others see additional steps in a *Chevron* analysis. For example, Cary Coglianese views the Court's decisions following *Chevron* as having created a "*Chevron* staircase," a term that describes a series of steps between steps I and II that identify "additional but necessary conditions that must be satisfied for a court to determine that Congress . . . delegated the agency primary authority to define ambiguous statutory terms, and thus for a court to award deference." Cary Coglianese, Chevron's Interstitial Steps, 85 Geo. Wash. L. Rev. 1339, 1361 (2017). These include determining whether Congress explicitly delegated the agency authority to fill statutory gaps, whether the ambiguous statute presents "extraordinary circumstances," and whether Congress gave the agency authority to engage in rulemaking or formal adjudication, among others. Id. The answer to these questions determines whether a court moves to step II (deferring to the agency if its interpretation is reasonable) or decides the meaning of the ambiguous statute itself. Id. at 1361-1362. Coglianese recognizes that his interstitial steps "share an important resemblance" to step zero. Id. at 1367. However, he suggests that engaging in these inquiries prior to applying step I results in unnecessary confusion and undermines step I's appropriate deference to the statute as written. Id. at 1367, 1369. In your opinion, when in a *Chevron* analysis should courts consider the extent to which Congress has delegated interpretive authority to an agency? Does it matter?

7. What about a position taken by the agency that is inconsistent with prior positions? Should that factor into whether a court accords deference to the agency position? Apparently not. In National Cable & Telecommunications Ass'n v. Brand X Internet Servs., 545 U.S. 967 (2005), the Court indicated that it made no difference in applying *Chevron* deference whether the agency had taken inconsistent positions in the past, even where those positions had been upheld by the courts. "The better rule is to hold judicial interpretations contained in precedents to the same demanding *Chevron* step one standard that applies if the court is reviewing the agency's construction on a blank slate: Only a judicial precedent holding that the statute unambiguously forecloses the agency's interpretation, and therefore contains no gap for the agency to fill, displaces a conflicting agency construction." Id. at 982-983.

8. Does the result change if the prior interpretation was by a court? In *Brand X*, the Court found that an earlier interpretation of an ambiguous statute did not bind the agency. But what happens when the earlier court finds that the statute is not ambiguous? Can an agency disagree, find otherwise, and adopt a different interpretation? In United States v. Home Concrete & Supply, 566 U.S. 478 (2012), a plurality of justices said no. In effect, they found that the earlier decision left "no gap to fill" and, as a result, Treasury's "gap-filling regulation cannot change [the earlier court's] interpretation of the statute."

9. *Chevron* applies in the case of ambiguities in the substance of a statute. What about interpretations that are jurisdictional? Does an agency receive deference in interpreting provisions that address the scope of its regulatory authority? In Arlington v. FCC, 569 U.S. 290 (2013), the Court dealt with a statute that required local authorities to rule on siting applications for wireless telecommunication towers "within a reasonable period of time after a request is duly filed." The FCC determined that a "reasonable period of time" was presumptively 90 days for some applications and 150 days for others. State and local governments challenged the interpretation. As a threshold matter, the Court had to determine whether *Chevron* applied. As Justice Scalia put it, "[t]he question here is whether a court must defer under *Chevron* to an agency's interpretation of a statutory ambiguity that concerns the scope of the agency's statutory authority (that is, its jurisdiction)." Id. at 296-297. He answered in the affirmative. "[T]he distinction between 'jurisdictional' and 'non-jurisdictional' interpretations is a mirage." Id. Instead, "the question in every case is, simply, whether the statutory text forecloses the agency's assertion of authority, or not." Id. The Chief Justice, in dissent, disagreed: "An agency cannot exercise interpretive authority until it has it; the question whether an agency enjoys that authority must be decided by a court, without deference to the agency." Id. at 312. What do you make of this disagreement? Who has the better argument? What are some potential concerns raised by the position taken by Justice Scalia?

UNITED STATES v. MEAD CORP.

533 U.S. 218 (2001)

JUSTICE SOUTER delivered the opinion of the Court.

The question is whether a tariff classification ruling by the United States Customs Service deserves judicial deference. The Federal Circuit rejected Customs' invocation of Chevron U.S.A. Inc. v. Natural Resources Defense Council, Inc., 467 U.S. 837 (1984), in support of such a ruling, to which it gave no deference. We agree that a tariff classification has no claim to judicial deference under *Chevron*, there being no indication that Congress intended such a ruling to carry the force of law, but we hold that under Skidmore v. Swift & Co., 323 U.S. 134 (1944), the ruling is eligible to claim respect according to its persuasiveness.

I

A

Imports are taxed under the Harmonized Tariff Schedule of the United States (HTSUS), 19 U.S.C. §1202. Title 19 U.S.C. §1500(b) provides that Customs "shall, under rules and regulations prescribed by the Secretary [of the Treasury,] . . . fix the final classification and rate of duty applicable to . . . merchandise" under the HTSUS. Section 1502(a) provides that "[t]he Secretary of the Treasury shall establish and promulgate such rules and regulations not inconsistent with the law (including regulations establishing procedures for the issuance of binding rulings prior to the entry of the merchandise concerned), and may disseminate such information as may be necessary to secure a just, impartial, and uniform appraisement of imported merchandise and the classification and assessment of duties thereon at the various ports of entry."[1] See also §1624 (general delegation to Secretary to issue rules and regulations for the admission of goods).

The Secretary provides for tariff rulings before the entry of goods by regulations authorizing "ruling letters" setting tariff classifications for particular imports. 19 C.F.R. §177.8 (2000). A ruling letter "represents the official position of the Customs Service with respect to the particular transaction or issue described therein and is binding on all Customs Service personnel in accordance with the

1. The statutory term "ruling" is defined by regulation as "a written statement . . . that interprets and applies the provisions of the Customs and related laws to a specific set of facts." 19 C.F.R. §177.1(d)(1) (2000).

provisions of this section until modified or revoked. In the absence of a change of practice or other modification or revocation which affects the principle of the ruling set forth in the ruling letter, that principle may be cited as authority in the disposition of transactions involving the same circumstances." §177.9(a).

After the transaction that gives it birth, a ruling letter is to "be applied only with respect to transactions involving articles identical to the sample submitted with the ruling request or to articles whose description is identical to the description set forth in the ruling letter." §177.9(b)(2). As a general matter, such a letter is "subject to modification or revocation without notice to any person, except the person to whom the letter was addressed," §177.9(c), and the regulations consequently provide that "no other person should rely on the ruling letter or assume that the principles of that ruling will be applied in connection with any transaction other than the one described in the letter," ibid. Since ruling letters respond to transactions of the moment, they are not subject to notice and comment before being issued, may be published but need only be made "available for public inspection," 19 U.S.C. §1625(a), and, at the time this action arose, could be modified without notice and comment under most circumstances, 19 C.F.R. §177.10(c) (2000).

Any of the 46 . . . port-of-entry Customs . . . offices may issue ruling letters, and so may the Customs Headquarters Office, in providing "[a]dvice or guidance as to the interpretation or proper application of the Customs and related laws with respect to a specific Customs transaction [which] may be requested by Customs Service field offices . . . at any time, whether the transaction is prospective, current, or completed," 19 C.F.R. §177.11(a) (2000). Most ruling letters contain little or no reasoning, but simply describe goods and state the appropriate category and tariff. A few letters, like the Headquarters ruling at issue here, set out a rationale in some detail.

B

Respondent, the Mead Corporation, imports "day planners," three-ring binders with pages having room for notes of daily schedules and phone numbers and addresses, together with a calendar and suchlike. The tariff schedule on point falls under the HTSUS heading for "[r]egisters, account books, notebooks, order books, receipt books, letter pads, memorandum pads, diaries and similar articles," HTSUS subheading 4820.10, which comprises two subcategories. Items in the first, "[d]iaries, notebooks and address books, bound; memorandum pads, letter pads and similar articles," were subject to a tariff of 4.0% at the time in controversy. 185 F.3d 1304, 1305 (C.A. Fed. 1999) (citing subheading 4820.10.20); see also App. to Pet. for Cert. 46a. Objects in the second, covering "[o]ther" items, were free of duty. HTSUS subheading 4820.10.40; see also App. to Pet. for Cert. 46a.

Between 1989 and 1993, Customs repeatedly treated day planners under the "other" HTSUS subheading. In January 1993, however, Customs changed its position, and issued a Headquarters ruling letter classifying Mead's day planners as "Diaries . . . , bound" subject to tariff under subheading 4820.10.20. That letter was short on explanation, App. to Brief in Opposition 4a-6a, but after Mead's protest, Customs Headquarters issued a new letter, carefully reasoned but never published, reaching the same conclusion, App. to Pet. for Cert. 28a-47a. This letter considered two definitions of "diary" from the Oxford English Dictionary, the first covering a daily journal of the past day's events, the second a book including "'printed dates for daily memoranda and jottings; also . . . calendars. . . .'" Id., at 33a-34a (quoting Oxford English Dictionary 321 (Compact ed. 1982)). Customs concluded that "diary" was not confined to the first, in part because the broader definition reflects commercial usage and hence the "commercial identity of these items in the marketplace." App. to Pet. for Cert. 34a. As for the definition of "bound," Customs concluded that HTSUS was not referring to "bookbinding," but to a less exact sort of fastening described in the Harmonized Commodity Description and Coding System Explanatory Notes to Heading 4820, which spoke of binding by "'reinforcements or fittings of metal, plastics, etc.'" Id., at 45a.

Customs rejected Mead's further protest of the second Headquarters ruling letter, and Mead filed suit in the Court of International Trade (CIT). The CIT granted the Government's motion for summary judgment, adopting Customs's reasoning without saying anything about deference. 17 F. Supp. 2d 1004 (1998).

Mead then went to the United States Court of Appeals for the Federal Circuit. While the case was pending there this Court decided United States v. Haggar Apparel Co., 526 U.S. 380 (1999), holding that Customs regulations receive the deference described in Chevron U.S.A. Inc. v. Natural Resources Defense Council, Inc., 467 U.S. 837 (1984). The appeals court requested briefing on the impact of *Haggar*, and the Government argued that classification rulings, like Customs regulations, deserve *Chevron* deference.

The Federal Circuit, however, reversed the CIT and held that Customs classification rulings should not get *Chevron* deference, owing to differences from the regulations at issue in *Haggar*. Rulings are not preceded by notice and comment as under the Administrative Procedure Act (APA), 5 U.S.C. §553, they "do not carry the force of law and are not, like regulations, intended to clarify the rights and obligations of importers beyond the specific case under review." 185 F.3d, at 1307. The appeals court thought classification rulings had a weaker *Chevron* claim even than Internal Revenue Service interpretive rulings, to which that court gives no deference; unlike rulings by the IRS, Customs rulings issue from many locations and need not be published. 185 F.3d, at 1307-1308.

The Court of Appeals accordingly gave no deference at all to the ruling classifying the Mead day planners and rejected the agency's reasoning as to both "diary" and "bound." It thought that planners were not diaries because they had no space for "relatively extensive notations about events, observations, feelings, or thoughts" in the past. Id., at 1310. And it concluded that diaries "bound" in subheading 4810.10.20 presupposed "unbound" diaries, such that treating ring-fastened diaries as "bound" would leave the "unbound diary" an empty category. Id., at 1311.

We granted certiorari, 530 U.S. 1202 (2000), in order to consider the limits of *Chevron* deference owed to administrative practice in applying a statute. We hold that administrative implementation of a particular statutory provision qualifies for *Chevron* deference when it appears that Congress delegated authority to the agency generally to make rules carrying the force of law, and that the agency interpretation claiming deference was promulgated in the exercise of that authority. Delegation of such authority may be shown in a variety of ways, as by an agency's power to engage in adjudication or notice-and-comment rulemaking, or by some other indication of a comparable congressional intent. The Customs ruling at issue here fails to qualify, although the possibility that it deserves some deference under *Skidmore* leads us to vacate and remand.

II

A

When Congress has "explicitly left a gap for an agency to fill, there is an express delegation of authority to the agency to elucidate a specific provision of the statute by regulation," *Chevron*, 467 U.S., at 843-844 and any ensuing regulation is binding in the courts unless procedurally defective, arbitrary or capricious in substance, or manifestly contrary to the statute (footnote omitted). See id., at 844,104 S. Ct. 2778; United States v. Morton, 467 U.S. 822, 834 (1984); APA, 5 U.S.C. §§706(2)(A), (D). But whether or not they enjoy any express delegation of authority on a particular question, agencies charged with applying a statute necessarily make all sorts of interpretive choices, and while not all of those choices bind judges to follow them, they certainly may influence courts facing questions the agencies have already answered. "[T]he well-reasoned views of the agencies implementing a statute 'constitute a body of experience and informed judgment to which courts and litigants may properly resort for guidance,'" Bragdon v. Abbott, 524 U.S. 624, 642 (1998) (quoting *Skidmore*, 323 U.S., at 139-140), and "[w]e have long recognized that considerable weight should be accorded to an executive department's construction of a statutory scheme it is entrusted to administer. . . ." *Chevron, supra*, at 844 (footnote omitted); see also Ford Motor Credit Co. v. Milhollin, 444 U.S. 555, 565 (1980); Zenith Radio Corp. v. United States, 437 U.S. 443, 450 (1978). The fair measure of deference to an agency administering its own statute has been understood to vary with circumstances, and courts have looked to the degree of the agency's care, . . . its consistency, . . . formality, . . . and relative expertness, . . . and to the persuasiveness of the agency's position, see *Skidmore, supra*, at 139-140. . . .

Since 1984, we have identified a category of interpretive choices distinguished by an additional reason for judicial deference. This Court in *Chevron* recognized that Congress not only engages in express delegation of specific interpretive authority, but that "[s]ometimes the legislative delegation to an agency on a particular question is implicit." 467 U.S., at 844. Congress, that is, may not have expressly delegated authority or responsibility to implement a particular provision or fill a particular gap. Yet it can still be apparent from the agency's generally conferred authority and other statutory circumstances that Congress would expect the agency to be able to speak with the force of law when it addresses ambiguity in the statute or fills a space in the enacted law, even one about which "Congress did not actually have an intent" as to a particular result. Id., at 845. When circumstances implying such an expectation exist, a reviewing court has no business rejecting an agency's exercise of its generally conferred authority to resolve a particular statutory ambiguity simply because the agency's chosen resolution seems unwise, see id., at 845-846, but is obliged to accept the agency's position if Congress has not previously spoken to the point at issue and the agency's interpretation is reasonable, see id., at 842-845; cf. 5 U.S.C. §706(2) (a reviewing court shall set aside agency action, findings, and conclusions found to be "arbitrary, capricious, an abuse of discretion, or otherwise not in accordance with law").

We have recognized a very good indicator of delegation meriting *Chevron* treatment in express congressional authorizations to engage in the process of rulemaking or adjudication that produces regulations or rulings for which deference is claimed. See, e.g., EEOC v. Arabian American Oil Co., 499 U.S. 244, 257 (1991) (no *Chevron* deference to agency guideline where congressional delegation did not include the power to "'promulgate rules or regulations'" (quoting General Elec. Co. v. Gilbert, 429 U.S. 125, 141 (1976))); see also Christensen v. Harris County, 529 U.S. 576, 596-597(2000) (Breyer, J., dissenting) (where it is in doubt that Congress actually intended to delegate particular interpretive authority to an agency, *Chevron* is "inapplicable"). It is fair to assume generally that Congress contemplates administrative action with the effect of law when it provides for a relatively formal administrative procedure tending to foster the fairness and deliberation that should underlie a pronouncement of such force (footnote omitted). Cf. Smiley v. Citibank (South Dakota), N.A., 517 U.S. 735, 741 (1996) (APA notice and comment "designed to assure due deliberation"). Thus, the overwhelming number of our cases applying *Chevron* deference have reviewed the fruits of notice-and-comment rulemaking or formal adjudication (footnote omitted). That said, and as significant as notice-and-comment is in pointing to *Chevron* authority, the want of that procedure here does not decide the case, for we have sometimes found reasons for *Chevron* deference even when no such administrative formality was required and none was afforded, see, e.g., NationsBank of N.C., N.A. v. Variable Annuity Life Ins. Co., 513 U.S. 251, 256-257, 263 (1995) (footnote omitted). The fact that the tariff classification here was not a product of such formal process does not alone, therefore, bar the application of *Chevron.*

There are, nonetheless, ample reasons to deny *Chevron* deference here. The authorization for classification rulings, and Customs's practice in making them, present a case far removed not only from notice-and-comment process, but from any other circumstances reasonably suggesting that Congress ever thought of classification rulings as deserving the deference claimed for them here.

B

No matter which angle we choose for viewing the Customs ruling letter in this case, it fails to qualify under *Chevron.* On the face of the statute, to begin with, the terms of the congressional delegation give no indication that Congress meant to delegate authority to Customs to issue classification rulings with the force of law. We are not, of course, here making any global statement about Customs's authority, for it is true that the general rulemaking power conferred on Customs, see 19 U.S.C. §1624, authorizes some regulation with the force of law, or "legal norms," as we put it in *Haggar*, 526 U.S., at 391 (footnote omitted). It is true as well that Congress had classification rulings in mind when it explicitly authorized, in a parenthetical, the issuance of "regulations establishing procedures for the issuance of binding rulings prior to the entry of the merchandise concerned," 19 U.S.C. §1502(a) (footnote omitted). The reference to binding classifications does not, however, bespeak the legislative type of activity that would naturally bind more than the parties to the ruling, once the goods classified are admitted into this country. And though the statute's direction to disseminate "information" necessary to "secure" uniformity, ibid., seems to assume that a ruling may be precedent in later transactions, precedential value alone does not add up to *Chevron* entitlement; interpretive rules may sometimes function as precedents, see Strauss, The Rulemaking Continuum, 41 Duke L.J. 1463, 1472-1473 (1992), and they enjoy no *Chevron* status as a class. In any event, any precedential claim of a classification ruling is counterbalanced by the provision for independent review of Customs classifications by the CIT, see 28 U.S.C. §§2638-2640; the scheme for CIT review includes a provision that treats classification rulings on par with the Secretary's rulings on "valuation, rate of duty, marking, restricted merchandise, entry requirements, drawbacks, vessel repairs, or similar matters," §1581(h); see §2639(b). It is hard to imagine a congressional understanding more at odds with the *Chevron* regime (footnote omitted).

It is difficult, in fact, to see in the agency practice itself any indication that Customs ever set out with a lawmaking pretense in mind when it undertook to make classifications like these. Customs does not generally engage in notice-and-comment practice when issuing them, and their treatment by the agency makes it clear that a letter's binding character as a ruling stops short of third parties; Customs has regarded a classification as conclusive only as between itself and the importer to whom it was issued, 19 C.F.R. §177.9(c) (2000), and even then only until Customs has given advance notice of intended change, §§177.9(a), (c). Other importers are in fact warned against assuming any right of detrimental reliance. §177.9(c).

Indeed, to claim that classifications have legal force is to ignore the reality that 46 different Customs offices issue 10,000 to 15,000 of them each year. . . . Any suggestion that rulings intended to have the force of law are being churned out at a rate of 10,000 a year at an agency's 46 scattered offices is simply self-refuting. Although the circumstances are less startling here, with a Headquarters letter in issue, none of the relevant statutes recognizes this category of rulings as separate or different from others; there is thus no indication that a more potent delegation might have been understood as going to Headquarters even when Headquarters provides developed reasoning, as it did in this instance.

In sum, classification rulings are best treated like "interpretations contained in policy statements, agency manuals, and enforcement guidelines." *Christensen,* 529 U.S., at 587. They are beyond the *Chevron* pale.

C

To agree with the Court of Appeals that Customs ruling letters do not fall within *Chevron* is not, however, to place them outside the pale of any deference whatever. *Chevron* did nothing to eliminate *Skidmore*'s holding that an agency's interpretation may merit some deference whatever its form, given the "specialized experience and broader investigations and information" available to the agency, 323 U.S., at 139, and given the value of uniformity in its administrative and judicial understandings of what a national law requires, id., at 140. See generally Metropolitan Stevedore Co. v. Rambo, 521 U.S. 121, 136 (1997) (reasonable agency interpretations carry "at least some added persuasive force" where *Chevron* is inapplicable); Reno v. Koray, 515 U.S. 50, 61 (1995) (according "some deference" to an interpretive rule that "do[es] not require notice and comment"); Martin v. Occupational Safety and Health Review Comm'n, 499 U.S. 144, 157 (1991) ("some weight" is due to informal interpretations though not "the same deference as norms that derive from the exercise of . . . delegated lawmaking powers").

There is room at least to raise a *Skidmore* claim here, where the regulatory scheme is highly detailed, and Customs can bring the benefit of specialized experience to bear on the subtle questions in this case: whether the daily planner with room for brief daily entries falls under "diaries," when diaries are grouped with "notebooks and address books, bound; memorandum pads, letter pads and similar articles," . . . and whether a planner with a ring binding should qualify as "bound," when a binding may be typified by a book, but also may have "reinforcements or fittings of metal, plastics, etc.," . . . (citations omitted). A classification ruling in this situation may therefore at least seek a respect proportional to its "power to persuade," *Skidmore*, supra, at 140; see also *Christensen,* 529 U.S., at 587; id., at 595 (Stevens, J., dissenting); id., at 596-597 (Breyer, J., dissenting). Such a ruling may surely claim the merit of its writer's thoroughness, logic, and expertness, its fit with prior interpretations, and any other sources of weight.

D

. . .

Since the *Skidmore* assessment called for here ought to be made in the first instance by the Court of Appeals for the Federal Circuit or the CIT, we go no further than to vacate the judgment and remand the case for further proceedings consistent with this opinion.

It is so ordered.

JUSTICE SCALIA, dissenting.

Today's opinion makes an avulsive change in judicial review of federal administrative action. Whereas previously a reasonable agency application of an ambiguous statutory provision had to be sustained so long as it represented the agency's authoritative interpretation, henceforth such an application can be set aside unless "it appears that Congress delegated authority to the agency generally to make rules carrying the force of law," as by giving an agency "power to engage in adjudication or notice-and-comment rulemaking, or . . . some other [procedure] indicati[ng] comparable congressional intent," and "the agency interpretation claiming deference was promulgated in the exercise of that authority." . . . What was previously a general presumption of authority in agencies to resolve ambiguity in the statutes they have been authorized to enforce has been changed to a presumption of no such authority, which must be overcome by affirmative legislative intent to the contrary. And whereas previously, when agency authority to resolve ambiguity did not exist the court was free to give the statute what it considered the best interpretation, henceforth the court must supposedly give the agency view some indeterminate amount of so-called *Skidmore* deference. Skidmore v. Swift & Co., 323 U.S. 134 (1944). We will be sorting out the consequences of the *Mead* doctrine, which has today replaced the *Chevron* doctrine, Chevron U.S.A. Inc. v. Natural Resources Defense Council, Inc., 467 U.S. 837 (1984), for years to come. I would adhere to our established jurisprudence, defer to the reasonable interpretation the Customs Service has given to the statute it is charged with enforcing, and reverse the judgment of the Court of Appeals.

NOTES

1. *Mead* limits the instances when courts should defer to agency decisions. What are the circumstances when deference will apply? When will deference not be accorded?

2. What are the consequences of limiting deference? See Raymond B. Yates, M.D., P.C. Profit Sharing Plan v. Hendon, 541 U.S. 1, 25 (2004) (Scalia, J., concurring) (noting that refusal to defer "deprives administrative agencies of two of their principal virtues: (1) the power to resolve statutory questions promptly, and with nationwide effect, and (2) the power (within the reasonable bounds of the text) to change the application of ambiguous laws as time and experience dictate. The Court's approach invites lengthy litigation in all the circuits — the product of which (when finally announced by this Court) is a rule of law that only Congress can change."). What do you think of this criticism?

3. Despite refusing to defer to the agency under *Chevron*, the Court in *Mead* still left open the possibility of a lower level of deference based upon agency experience and the need for uniformity — an analysis taken from the Supreme Court's decision in *Skidmore*. What do you make of this notion of varying levels of deference? For a discussion of the circumstances under which these and other levels of deference might apply, see Tercel Maria G. Mercado-Gephart, Deference in Wonderland: Into the Many Rabbit Holes of Chevron, Skidmore, and Auer Deference, 42 Okla. City U. L. Rev. 367 (2017).

4. The Court in *Mead* indicated that, in general, courts will give deference to rules adopted by agencies pursuant to their statutory authority and through notice and comment. What about nonlegislative rules? *Mead* left open the possibility that deference would apply to other agency pronouncements, something repeated in subsequent cases. See National Cable & Telecommunications Ass'n v. Brand X Internet Servs., 545 U.S. 967, 1004 (2005) (Breyer, J., concurring) ("It is not surprising that the Court would hold that the existence of a formal rulemaking proceeding is neither a necessary nor a sufficient condition for according *Chevron* deference to an agency's interpretation of a statute. It is not a necessary condition because an agency might arrive at an authoritative interpretation of a congressional enactment in other ways. . . . It is not a sufficient condition because Congress may have intended *not* to leave the matter of a particular interpretation up to the agency, irrespective of the procedure the agency uses to arrive at that interpretation."). Some cases, however, seem to suggest that the method used to adopt a position does matter in determining whether to apply deference. See Long Island Care at Home, Ltd. v. Coke, 551 U.S. 158, 165 (2007) (holding that a regulation was entitled to *Chevron* deference because the agency had conducted proper notice and comment procedures); Alaska Dep't of Envtl. Conservation v. EPA, 540 U.S. 461, 487 (2003) ("The Agency's interpretation in this case, presented in internal guidance memoranda, however, does not qualify for the dispositive force described in *Chevron*."). Is this the beginning of the "protracted confusion" predicted by Justice Scalia in his dissent?

5. States have been making distinctions with respect to deference along *Chevron* and *Skidmore* lines for some time prior to *Mead*. For example, in Yamaha Corp. v. State Board of Equalization, 960 P.2d 1031 (Cal. 1998), a majority of the California Supreme Court adopted the less deferential *Skidmore* approach in deciding what level of deference to give to a staff opinion of the State's sales tax collection agency. The Supreme Court distinguished between legislative rules, issued after prior notice and comment, and interpretive rules like the staff opinion in question. With respect to interpretive rules, the Court indicated that it was free to exercise independent judgment. The *Yamaha* case raises the question whether the *form* of agency action interpreting law should matter in applying *Chevron* deference.

Mead raised as many issues as it resolved. Nonetheless, the case seemed to make one point clear: use of notice-and-comment rulemaking with respect to substantive/legislative rules is entitled to deference under *Chevron*. Yet even this purportedly clear holding has been called into question.

KING v. BURWELL

576 U.S. 473 (2015)

CHIEF JUSTICE ROBERTS delivered the opinion of the Court.

The Patient Protection and Affordable Care Act adopts a series of interlocking reforms designed to expand coverage in the individual health insurance market. First, the Act bars insurers from taking a person's health into account when deciding whether to sell health insurance or how much to charge. Second, the Act generally requires each person to maintain insurance coverage or make a payment to the Internal Revenue Service. And third, the Act gives tax credits to certain people to make insurance more affordable.

In addition to those reforms, the Act requires the creation of an "Exchange" in each State — basically, a marketplace that allows people to compare and purchase insurance plans. The Act gives each State the opportunity to establish its own Exchange, but provides that the Federal Government will establish the Exchange if the State does not.

This case is about whether the Act's interlocking reforms apply equally in each State no matter who establishes the State's Exchange. Specifically, the question presented is whether the Act's tax credits are available in States that have a Federal Exchange.

. . .

II

The Affordable Care Act addresses tax credits in what is now Section 36B of the Internal Revenue Code. That section provides: "In the case of an applicable taxpayer, there shall be allowed as a credit against the tax imposed by this subtitle . . . an amount equal to the premium assistance credit amount." 26 U.S.C. §36B(a). Section 36B then defines the term "premium assistance credit amount" as "the sum of the *premium assistance amounts* determined under paragraph (2) with respect to all *coverage months* of the taxpayer occurring during the taxable year." §36B(b)(1) (emphasis added). Section 36B goes on to define the two italicized terms — "premium assistance amount" and "coverage month" — in part by referring to an insurance plan that is enrolled in through "an Exchange established by the State under [42 U.S.C. §18031]." 26 U.S.C. §§36B(b)(2)(A), (c)(2)(A)(i).

The parties dispute whether Section 36B authorizes tax credits for individuals who enroll in an insurance plan through a Federal Exchange. Petitioners argue that a Federal Exchange is not "an Exchange established by the State under [42 U.S.C. §18031]," and that the IRS Rule therefore contradicts Section 36B. Brief for Petitioners 18-20. The Government responds that the IRS Rule is lawful because the phrase "an Exchange established by the State under [42 U.S.C. §18031]" should be read to include Federal Exchanges. Brief for Respondents 20-25.

When analyzing an agency's interpretation of a statute, we often apply the two-step framework announced in *Chevron*, 467 U.S. 837, 104 S. Ct. 2778, 81 L. Ed. 2d 694. Under that framework, we ask whether the statute is ambiguous and, if so, whether the agency's interpretation is reasonable. *Id.*, at 842-843, 104 S. Ct. 2778. This approach "is premised on the theory that a statute's ambiguity constitutes an implicit delegation from Congress to the agency to fill in the statutory gaps." FDA v. Brown & Williamson Tobacco Corp., 529 U.S. 120, 159, 120 S. Ct. 1291, 146 L. Ed. 2d 121 (2000). "In extraordinary cases, however, there may be reason to hesitate before concluding that Congress has intended such an implicit delegation." *Ibid.*

This is one of those cases. The tax credits are among the Act's key reforms, involving billions of dollars in spending each year and affecting the price of health insurance for millions of people. Whether those credits are available on Federal Exchanges is thus a question of deep "economic and political significance" that is central to this statutory scheme; had Congress wished to assign that question to an agency, it surely would have done so expressly. . . . It is especially unlikely that Congress would have delegated this decision to the *IRS*, which has no expertise in crafting health insurance policy of this sort. See *Gonzales v. Oregon*, 546 U.S. 243, 266-267, 126 S. Ct. 904, 163 L. Ed. 2d 748 (2006). This is not a case for the IRS.

It is instead our task to determine the correct reading of Section 36B. If the statutory language is plain, we must enforce it according to its terms. . . . But oftentimes the "meaning — or ambiguity — of certain words or phrases may only become evident when placed in context." . . . So when deciding whether the language is plain, we must read the words "in their context and with a view to their place in the overall statutory scheme." . . . Our duty, after all, is "to construe statutes, not isolated provisions."

NOTES

1. This case arose over the interpretation of the Affordable Care Act, sometimes referred to as "Obamacare." ACA gave rise to a number of challenging interpretive issues that arguably arose out of the process by which the law was drafted and adopted. See *Burwell*, 576 U.S. at 491 (law contained "more than a few examples of inartful drafting" and did "not reflect the type of care and deliberation that one might expect of such significant legislation"). What is the proper role of the courts in these circumstances?

2. What uncertainty does this case create with respect to the application of *Chevron*? How might one make the case that *Chevron* deference should not apply to the adoption of substantive/legislative rules following notice and comment? Is this an instance of the application of Chevron step zero? See note 6, *supra* p. 737.

3. *King v. Burwell* is an example of what some have called the "major questions doctrine," under which "courts will presume Congress did not intend to delegate" issues of exceptional political and economic consequences to agencies "unless the statute is clear." Jonas J. Monast, Major Questions About the Major Questions Doctrine, 68 Admin L. Rev. 445, 447 (2016). When this doctrine applies, however, remains unclear. Id. at 448. For example, the Trump administration's EPA asserted that the Clean Power Plan, a rule promulgated under the previous administration, was beyond EPA's authority to enact because it would have had large economic impacts on the regulated community and affected electricity rates for every customer; thus, EPA argued, the major questions doctrine should have rendered the agency's prior interpretation illegal. Am. Lung Ass'n v. EPA, 985 F.3d 914, 959 (9th Cir. 2021). The Ninth Circuit disagreed, however, holding that the text of the Clean Air Act clearly gave EPA "not just the authority, but a statutory duty to regulate" the types of pollution and polluters at issue. Id. at 960. What does this holding suggest about the extent to which courts are willing to apply the major questions doctrine?

4. Ultimately the Court upheld the agency's interpretation. As a result, had the Court applied *Chevron* deference, the outcome of the case would have been the same. What difference does it make that the result was achieved without resort to *Chevron* deference? See Heidi Marie Werntz, Counting on Chevron?, 38 Energy L.J. 297, 348 (2017) ("[By refusing to apply *Chevron*], *King* locked in the Court's interpretation of the statute, preventing subsequent agency reinterpretation on this point.")

5. *Mead* and *King* are just two examples of cases in which the Court has limited the applicability of *Chevron* deference. Another is Encino Motorcars, LLC v. Navarro, 136 S. Ct. 2117 (2016), in which the Court considered whether the Department of Labor's revised interpretation of a statute defining workers exempt from overtime compensation rules was entitled to *Chevron* deference. The Court concluded that deference was not appropriate in this case because the agency's new interpretation violated "the basic procedural requirement[] of administrative rulemaking . . . that an agency must give adequate reasons for its decisions." Because the agency provided "barely any explanation" for its new regulation, the Court held that the statute "must be construed without placing controlling weight" on the document that enacted it. In Negusie v. Holder, 555 U.S. 511 (2009), the Court concluded that, although the agency's interpretations of its controlling statutes were typically entitled to *Chevron* deference, its "mistaken assumption" that a prior Court decision controlled was not an exercise of the agency's discretion to interpret the statute. Therefore, *Chevron* deference could not apply. The Court thus remanded the case to give the agency an opportunity for an "initial determination of the statutory interpretation question and its application to this case." There have, however, been cases in which the Court has extended at least some degree of deference despite circumstances that could have suggested otherwise. See, e.g., Dada v. Mukasey, 554 U.S. 1, 20-21 (2008) (affording "respectful consideration" to rules that had not yet taken effect); Federal Express Corporation v. Holowecki, 552 U.S. 389, 400 (2008) (allowing for *Skidmore* deference despite an agency's inconsistent application of a standard because "[s]ome degree of inconsistent treatment is unavoidable when the agency processes over 175,000 inquiries a year"); Wyeth v. Levine, 555 U.S. 555, 576-577 (2009) (holding that whether to defer to an agency on matters of constitutional interpretation could, in some instances, depend on the agency's "thoroughness consistency, and persuasiveness").

Given numerous decisions in which the Court has limited the application of *Chevron* deference, what is the state of *Chevron* today? In the following case decided in 2018, Justice Sotomayor finds no reason to apply *Chevron* deference because the statute at issue is unambiguous. While seemingly an unremarkable decision, many cite to Justice Kennedy's concurring opinion as strongly indicating that *Chevron* is in store for significant changes.

PEREIRA v. SESSIONS

585 U.S.___, 138 S. Ct. 2105 (2018)

JUSTICE SOTOMAYOR delivered the opinion of the Court:

Nonpermanent residents, like petitioner here, who are subject to removal proceedings and have accrued 10 years of continuous physical presence in the United States, may be eligible for a form of discretionary relief known as cancellation of removal. 8 U.S.C. §1229b(b)(1). Under the so-called "stop-time rule" set forth in §1229b(d)(1)(A), however, that period of continuous physical presence is "deemed to end . . . when the alien is served a notice to appear under section 1229(a)." Section 1229(a), in turn, provides that the Government shall serve noncitizens in removal proceedings with "written notice (in this section referred to as a 'notice to appear') . . . specifying" several required pieces of information, including "[t]he time and place at which the [removal] proceedings will be held." §1229(a)(1)(G)(i).

The narrow question in this case lies at the intersection of those statutory provisions. If the Government serves a noncitizen with a document that is labeled "notice to appear," but the document fails to specify either the time or place of the removal proceedings, does it trigger the stop-time rule? The answer is as obvious as it seems: No. A notice that does not inform a noncitizen when and where to appear for removal proceedings is not a "notice to appear under section 1229(a)" and therefore does not trigger the stop-time rule. The plain text, the statutory context, and common sense all lead inescapably and unambiguously to that conclusion.

I

B

In 1997, shortly after Congress passed IIRIRA [Illegal Immigration Reform and Immigrant Responsibility Act], the Attorney General promulgated a regulation stating that a "notice to appear" served on a noncitizen need only provide "the time, place and date of the initial removal hearing, where practicable." 62 Fed. Reg. 10332 (1997). Per that regulation, the Department of Homeland Security (DHS), at least in recent years, almost always serves noncitizens with notices that fail to specify the time, place, or date of initial removal hearings whenever the agency deems it impracticable to include such information. See Brief for Petitioner 14; Brief for Respondent 48-49; Tr. of Oral Arg. 52-53 (Government's admission that "almost 100 percent" of "notices to appear omit the time and date of the proceeding over the last three years"). Instead, these notices state that the times, places, or dates of the initial hearings are "to be determined." Brief for Petitioner 14.

In *Matter of Camarillo*, 25 I. & N. Dec. 644 (2011), the Board of Immigration Appeals (BIA) addressed whether such notices trigger the stop-time rule even if they do not specify the time and date of the removal proceedings. The BIA concluded that they do. *Id.*, at 651. It reasoned that the statutory phrase "notice to appear 'under section [1229](a)'" in the stop-time rule "merely specifies the document the DHS must serve on the alien to trigger the 'stop-time' rule," but otherwise imposes no "substantive requirements" as to what information that document must include to trigger the stop-time rule. *Id.*, at 647.

II

A

The Court granted certiorari in this case, 583 U.S. ___ (2018), to resolve division among the Courts of Appeals on a simple, but important, question of statutory interpretation: Does service of a document styled as a "notice to appear" that fails to specify "the items listed" in §1229(a)(1) trigger the stop-time rule?

As a threshold matter, the Court notes that the question presented by Pereira, which focuses on all "items listed" in §1229(a)(1), sweeps more broadly than necessary to resolve the particular case before us. Although the time-and-place information in a notice to appear will vary from case to case, the Government acknowledges that "[m]uch of the information Section 1229(a)(1) calls for does not" change and is therefore "included in standardized language on the I-862 notice-to-appear form." In fact, the Government's 2006 notice to Pereira included all of the information required by §1229(a)(1), except it failed to specify the date and time of Pereira's removal proceedings. Accordingly, the dispositive question in this case is much narrower, but no less vital: Does a "notice to appear" that does not specify the "time and place at which the proceedings will be held," as required by §1229(a)(1)(G)(i), trigger the stop-time rule?

In addressing that narrower question, the Court need not resort to *Chevron* deference, as some lower courts have done, for Congress has supplied a clear and unambiguous answer to the interpretive question at hand. See 467 U.S., at 842-843 ("If the intent of Congress is clear, that is the end of the matter; for the court, as well as the agency, must give effect to the unambiguously expressed intent of Congress"). A putative notice to appear that fails to designate the specific time or place of the noncitizen's removal proceedings is not a "notice to appear under section 1229(a)," and so does not trigger the stop-time rule.

JUSTICE KENNEDY concurring:

I agree with the Court's opinion and join it in full.

This separate writing is to note my concern with the way in which the Court's opinion in Chevron U.S.A. Inc. v. Natural Resources Defense Council, Inc., 467 U.S. 837 (1984), has come to be understood and applied. The application of that precedent to the question presented here by various Courts of Appeals illustrates one aspect of the problem.

The first Courts of Appeals to encounter the question concluded or assumed that the notice necessary to trigger the stop-time rule found in 8 U.S.C. §1229b(d)(1) was not "perfected" until the immigrant received all the information listed in §1229(a)(1). Guamanrrigra v. Holder, 670 F.3d 404, 410 (CA2 2012) (per curiam); see also Dababneh v. Gonzales, 471 F.3d 806, 809 (CA7 2006); Garcia-Ramirez v. Gonzales, 423 F.3d 935, 937, n. 3 (CA9 2005) (per curiam).

That emerging consensus abruptly dissolved not long after the Board of Immigration Appeals (BIA) reached a contrary interpretation of §1229b(d)(1) in Matter of Camarillo, 25 I. & N. Dec. 644 (2011). After that administrative ruling, in addition to the decision under review here, at least six Courts of Appeals, citing Chevron, concluded that §1229b(d)(1) was ambiguous and then held that the BIA's interpretation was reasonable. See Moscoso-Castellanos v. Lynch, 803 F.3d 1079, 1083 (CA9 2015); O'Garro v. United States Atty. Gen., 605 Fed. Appx. 951, 953 (CA11 2015) (per curiam); Guaman-Yuqui v. Lynch, 786 F.3d 235, 239-240 (CA2 2015) (per curiam); Gonzalez-Garcia v. Holder, 770 F.3d 431, 434-435 (CA6 2014); Yi Di Wang v. Holder, 759 F.3d 670, 674-675 (CA7 2014); Urbina v. Holder, 745 F.3d 736, 740 (CA4 2014). But see Orozco-Velasquez v. Attorney General United States, 817 F.3d 78, 81-82 (CA3 2016). The Court correctly concludes today that those holdings were wrong because the BIA's interpretation finds little support in the statute's text.

In according *Chevron* deference to the BIA's interpretation, some Courts of Appeals engaged in cursory analysis of the questions whether, applying the ordinary tools of statutory construction, Congress' intent could be discerned, 467 U.S., at 843, n. 9, and whether the BIA's interpretation was reasonable, *id.*, at 845. In Urbina v. Holder, for example, the court stated, without any further elaboration, that "we agree with the BIA that the relevant statutory provision is ambiguous." 745 F.3d, at 740. It then deemed reasonable the BIA's interpretation of the statute, "for the reasons the BIA gave in that case." *Ibid.* This analysis suggests an abdication of the Judiciary's proper role in interpreting federal statutes.

The type of reflexive deference exhibited in some of these cases is troubling. And when deference is applied to other questions of statutory interpretation, such as an agency's interpretation of the statutory provisions that concern the scope of its own authority, it is more troubling still. See Arlington v. FCC, 569 U.S. 290, 327, 133 S. Ct. 1863, 185 L. Ed. 2d 941 (2013) (Roberts, C. J., dissenting) ("We do not leave it to the agency to decide when it is in charge"). Given the concerns raised by some Members of this Court, see, *e.g.*, *id.*, at 312-328, 133 S. Ct. 1863, 185 L. Ed. 2d 941; Michigan v. EPA, 576 U.S. ___, ___, 135 S. Ct. 2699, 192 L. Ed. 2d 674 (2015) (Thomas, J., concurring); Gutierrez-Brizuela v. Lynch, 834 F.3d 1142, 1149-1158 (CA10 2016) (Gorsuch, J., concurring), it seems necessary and appropriate to reconsider, in an appropriate case, the premises that underlie *Chevron* and how courts have implemented that decision. The proper rules for interpreting statutes and determining agency jurisdiction and substantive agency powers should accord with constitutional separation-of-powers principles and the function and province of the Judiciary. See, *e.g.*, *Arlington*, *supra*, at 312-316, 133 S. Ct. 1863, 185 L. Ed. 2d 941 (Roberts, C. J., dissenting).

NOTES

1. Decided on the same day as *Periera* was another case touching on *Chevron*. The opinion in Wisconsin Central v. United States, 138 S. Ct. 2067 (2018), written by Justice Gorsuch, uses a statutory interpretation case to express that Chevron deference applies only when a statute contains a clear "gap" capable of more than one interpretation. Looking to the statute at issue, the Railroad Retirement Tax Act of 1937, the Court found it "clear enough . . . leaving no ambiguity for the agency to fill." In the absence of an ambiguity, there is no "gap" for the agency to fill and, consequently, no need for a court to grant an agency any deference.

2. When the opinion in *Pereira* was handed down toward the end of June 2018, many speculated that Justice Kennedy's concurrence calling for reconsideration of the *Chevron* doctrine may have been a parting shot authored by a soon-to-retire justice. See, e.g., Tony Mauro, A Kennedy Concurrence Fuels Speculation on *Chevron*'s Future — And His, National L. J. (June 21, 2018). In fact, Justice Kennedy announced his retirement soon after. It seems likely that with the appointment of conservative Justices Kavanaugh and Barrett, *Chevron* is in for a serious overhaul.

3. Scholars' views on the need for a *Chevron* overhaul vary considerably. For example, Craig Green squarely rejects constitutional arguments against *Chevron*, arguing that such critiques "represent a radical shift in constitutional principles" and have "potentially dire consequences for the administrative state as a whole." Craig Green, *Chevron* Debates and the Constitutional Transformation of Administrative Law, 88 Geo. Wash. L. Rev. 654, 694 (2020). Green's view focuses not on whether or how *Chevron* should be modified "through ordinary mechanisms of judicial pragmatism or political choice," but rather on the notion that any form of administrative deference could be held unconstitutional. Id. at 733. In contrast, Richard Murphy asserts that *Chevron* deference should be eliminated "not for being so strong as to destroy America's moral underpinnings and constitutional order, but instead for being so weak that it cannot be worth all the legal trouble it creates." Richard W. Murphy, Abandon *Chevron* and Modernize Stare Decisis for the Administrative State, 69 Ala. L. Rev. 1, 5 (2017). In place of the "contention regarding whether and how to implement deferential review" that *Chevron* has created, Murphy proposes a new limit on the precedential force of judicial opinions in which a court faced with an agency's new interpretation of a statute would be required to "determine the best available construction" without giving weight to its own conflicting precedent. Id. at 49. Still others do not believe that *Chevron* should be overruled, if only because such a decision would create "a large shock to the legal system, producing confusion, more conflicts in the courts of appeals, and far greater politicization of administrative law." Cass R. Sunstein, Chevron as Law, 107 Geo. L.J., 1613, 1670 (2019). However, Sunstein recognizes that there are significant problems with *Chevron*, including the quality of its reasoning and the complexity that its subsequent cases have created.

Id. at 1669. To resolve these issues, Sunstein recommends that three simple modifications be "formalized and entrenched": (1) ensure that judges seriously apply step I, proceeding to step II "only if the statutory provision is genuinely ambiguous"; (2) "emphasize the immense importance of Step Two" by ensuring that courts reject truly unreasonable interpretations of statutory terms; and (3) encourage the application of canons of statutory construction "to cabin the exercise of agency discretion." Id. at 1672-1678. Finally, some believe that even if *Chevron* is overruled, "judicial deference to administrative decisions will persist in roughly the same form." Lisa Schultz Bressman & Kevin M. Stack, *Chevron* Is a Phoenix, 74 Vand. L. Rev. 465, 466 (2021). Ultimately, this view is grounded in the seductive practicalities inherent in administrative deference. Id. at 479 ("[G] iven the complexity of statutory schemes, the specialized expertise and experience that implementing those schemes requires, and the sheer number of routine interpretive issues that the schemes involve, courts will confront the natural fault lines of their own competence as generalists and lawyers. They will have every incentive to find a way out. That way will have to involve a different form of judicial deference.").

5. The Doctrine of Regulatory Deference

Chevron and *Skidmore* deal with deference to an agency's interpretation of its enabling statute. What about an agency's interpretation of its own regulations?

KISOR v. WILKIE

588 U.S. ___; 139 S. Ct. 657 (2019)

JUSTICE KAGAN delivered the opinion of the Court with respect to Parts I, II-B, III-B, and IV, holding that *Auer* and *Seminole Rock* are not overruled.

This Court has often deferred to agencies' reasonable readings of genuinely ambiguous regulations. We call that practice *Auer* deference, or sometimes *Seminole Rock* deference, after two cases in which we employed it. See Auer v. Robbins, 519 U.S. 452 (1997); Bowles v. Seminole Rock & Sand Co., 325 U.S. 410 (1945). The only question presented here is whether we should overrule those decisions, discarding the deference they give to agencies. We answer that question no. *Auer* deference retains an important role in construing agency regulations. But even as we uphold it, we reinforce its limits. *Auer* deference is sometimes appropriate and sometimes not. Whether to apply it depends on a range of considerations that we have noted now and again, but compile and further develop today. The deference doctrine we describe is potent in its place, but cabined in its scope. On remand, the Court of Appeals should decide whether it applies to the agency interpretation at issue.

I

We begin by summarizing how petitioner James Kisor's case made its way to this Court. Truth be told, nothing recounted in this Part has much bearing on the rest of our decision. The question whether to overrule *Auer* does not turn on any single application, whether right or wrong, of that decision's deference doctrine. . . .

Kisor is a Vietnam War veteran seeking disability benefits from the Department of Veterans Affairs (VA). He first applied in 1982, alleging that he had developed post-traumatic stress disorder (PTSD) as a result of his participation in a military action called Operation Harvest Moon. The report of the agency's evaluating psychiatrist noted Kisor's involvement in that battle, but found that he "d[id] not suffer from PTSD." The VA thus denied Kisor benefits. There matters stood until 2006, when Kisor moved to reopen his claim. Based on a new psychiatric report, the VA this time agreed that Kisor suffered from PTSD. But it granted him benefits only from the date of his motion to reopen, rather than (as he requested) from the date of his first application.

The Board of Veterans' Appeals — a part of the VA, represented in Kisor's case by a single administrative judge — affirmed that timing decision, based on its interpretation of an agency rule. . . . The Court of Appeals for Veterans Claims, an independent Article I court that initially reviews the Board's decisions, affirmed for the same reason.

The Court of Appeals for the Federal Circuit also affirmed, but it did so based on deference to the Board's interpretation of the VA rule. See *Kisor v. Shulkin*, 869 F.3d 1360, 1368 (2017). Kisor had argued to the Federal Circuit that to count as "relevant," a service record need not (as the Board thought) "counter[ ] the basis of the prior denial"; instead, it could relate to some other criterion for obtaining disability benefits. *Id.*, at 1366. The Federal Circuit found the regulation "ambiguous" as between the two readings. *Id.*, at 1367. . . . "Both parties insist that the plain regulatory language supports their case, and neither party's position strikes us as unreasonable." *Id.*, at 1368. Because that was so, the court believed *Auer* deference appropriate: The agency's construction of its own regulation would govern unless "plainly erroneous or inconsistent with the VA's regulatory framework." *Ibid.* Applying that standard, the court upheld the Board's reading — and so approved the denial of retroactive benefits.

We then granted certiorari to decide whether to overrule *Auer* and (its predecessor) *Seminole Rock*. 586 U. S. ___, 139 S.Ct. 657(2018).

II

. . .

A

Begin with a familiar problem in administrative law: For various reasons, regulations may be genuinely ambiguous. They may not directly or clearly address every issue; when applied to some fact patterns, they may prove susceptible to more than one reasonable reading. . . . The subject matter of a rule "may be so specialized and varying in nature as to be impossible" — or at any rate, impracticable — to capture in its every detail. SEC v. Chenery Corp., 332 U.S. 194 (1947). Or a "problem[ ] may arise" that the agency, when drafting the rule, "could not [have] reasonably foresee[n]." *Id.*, at 202. Whichever the case, the result is to create real uncertainties about a regulation's meaning.

. . .

[T]ake the facts of *Auer* itself. An agency must decide whether police captains are eligible for overtime under the Fair Labor Standards Act. According to the agency's regulations, employees cannot receive overtime if they are paid on a "salary basis." 29 C.F.R. § 541.118(a) (1996). And in deciding whether an employee is salaried, one question is whether his pay is "subject to reduction" based on performance. *Ibid.* A police department's manual informs its officers that their pay might be docked if they commit a disciplinary infraction. Does that fact alone make them "subject to" pay deductions? Or must the department have a practice of docking officer pay, so that the possibility of that happening is more than theoretical? 519 U.S. at 459-462.

In each case, interpreting the regulation involves a choice between (or among) more than one reasonable reading. To apply the rule to some unanticipated or unresolved situation, the court must make a judgment call. How should it do so?

In answering that question, we have often thought that a court should defer to the agency's construction of its own regulation. For the last 20 or so years, we have referred to that doctrine as *Auer* deference, and applied it often. . . . Before the doctrine was called *Auer* deference, it was called *Seminole Rock* deference — for the 1945 decision in which we declared that when "the meaning of [a regulation] is in doubt," the agency's interpretation "becomes of controlling weight unless it is plainly erroneous or inconsistent with the regulation." 325 U.S. at 414. And *Seminole Rock* itself was not built on sand. Deference to administrative agencies traces back to the late nineteenth century, and perhaps beyond. See *United States v. Eaton*, 169 U.S. 331, 343 (1898) ("The interpretation given to the regulations by the department charged with their execution . . . is entitled to the greatest weight").

We have explained *Auer* deference (as we now call it) as rooted in a presumption about congressional intent — a presumption that Congress would generally want the agency to play the primary role in resolving regulatory ambiguities. See Martin v. Occupational Safety and Health Review Comm'n, 499 U.S. 144, 151-153 (1991). Congress, we have pointed out, routinely delegates to agencies the power to implement statutes by issuing rules. See *id.*, at 151. In doing so, Congress knows (how could it not?) that regulations will sometimes contain ambiguities. But Congress almost never explicitly assigns responsibility to deal with that problem, either to agencies or to courts. Hence the need to presume, one way or the other, what Congress would want. And as between those two choices, agencies have gotten the nod. We have adopted the presumption — though it is always rebuttable — that "the power authoritatively to interpret its own regulations is a component of the agency's delegated lawmaking powers." *Martin*, 499 U.S. at 151. Or otherwise said, we have thought that when granting rulemaking power to agencies, Congress usually intends to give them, too, considerable latitude to interpret the ambiguous rules they issue.

In part, that is because the agency that promulgated a rule is in the "better position [to] reconstruct" its original meaning. *Id.*, at 152. Consider that if you don't know what some text (say, a memo or an e-mail) means, you would probably want to ask the person who wrote it. And for the same reasons, we have thought, Congress would too (though the person is here a collective actor). The agency that "wrote the regulation" will often have direct insight into what that rule was intended to mean. . . . To be sure, this justification has its limits. It does not work so well, for example, when the agency failed to anticipate an issue in crafting a rule. . . . And the defense works yet less well when lots of time has passed between the rule's issuance and its interpretation — especially if the interpretation differs from one that has come before. . . .

In still greater measure, the presumption that Congress intended *Auer* deference stems from the awareness that resolving genuine regulatory ambiguities often "entail[s] the exercise of judgment grounded in policy concerns." *Thomas Jefferson Univ. v. Shalala*, 512 U.S. 504 (1994). . . .

And Congress, we have thought . . . is attuned to the comparative advantages of agencies over courts in making such policy judgments. Agencies (unlike courts) have "unique expertise," often of a scientific or technical nature, relevant to applying a regulation "to complex or changing circumstances." *Martin*, 499 U.S. at 151; see *Thomas Jefferson*, 512 U.S. at 512. Agencies (unlike courts) can conduct factual investigations, can consult with affected parties, can consider how their experts have handled similar issues over the long course of administering a regulatory program. See Long Island Care at Home, Ltd. v. Coke, 551 U.S. 158, 167-168 (2007). And agencies (again unlike courts) have political accountability, because they are subject to the supervision of the President, who in turn answers to the public. See Free Enterprise Fund v. Public Company Accounting Oversight Bd., 561 U.S. 477 (2010); Pauley v. BethEnergy Mines, Inc., 501 U.S. 680, 696 (1991) (discussing as a matter of democratic accountability the "proper roles of the political and judicial branches" in filling regulatory gaps). It is because of those features that Congress, when first enacting a statute, assigns rulemaking power to an agency and thus authorizes it to fill out the statutory scheme. And so too, when new issues demanding new policy calls come up within that scheme, Congress presumably wants the same agency, rather than any court, to take the laboring oar.

Finally, the presumption we use reflects the well-known benefits of uniformity in interpreting genuinely ambiguous rules. We have noted Congress's frequent "preference for resolving interpretive issues by uniform administrative decision, rather than piecemeal by litigation." Ford Motor Credit Co. v. Milhollin, 444 U.S. 555, 568 (1980). That preference may be strongest when the interpretive issue arises in the context of a "complex and highly technical regulatory program." *Thomas Jefferson*, 512 U.S. at 512. After all, judges are most likely to come to divergent conclusions when they are least likely to know what they are doing. . . . Consider *Auer* itself. There, four Circuits held that police captains were "subject to" pay deductions for disciplinary infractions if a police manual said they were, even if the department had never docked anyone. Two other Circuits held that captains were "subject to" pay deductions only if the department's actual practice made that punishment a realistic possibility. See *Auer*, 519 U.S. at 460. Had the agency issued an interpretation before all those rulings (rather than, as actually happened, in a brief in this Court), a deference rule would have averted most of that conflict and uncertainty. *Auer* deference thus serves to ensure consistency in federal regulatory law, for everyone who needs to know what it requires.

B

But all that said, *Auer* deference is not the answer to every question of interpreting an agency's rules. Far from it. As we explain in this section, the possibility of deference can arise only if a regulation is genuinely ambiguous . . . even after a court has resorted to all the standard tools of interpretation. Still more, not all reasonable agency constructions of those truly ambiguous rules are entitled to deference. As just explained, we presume that Congress intended for courts to defer to agencies when they interpret their own ambiguous rules. But when the reasons for that presumption do not apply, or countervailing reasons outweigh them, courts should not give deference to an agency's reading, except to the extent it has the "power to persuade." *Christopher*, 567 U.S. at 159 (quoting Skidmore v. Swift & Co., 323 U.S. 134 (1944)). We have thus cautioned that *Auer* deference is just a "general rule"; it "does not apply in all cases." *Christopher*, 567 U.S. at 155. And although the limits of *Auer* deference are not susceptible to any rigid test, we have noted various circumstances in which such deference is "unwarranted." *Ibid.* In particular, that will be so when a court concludes that an interpretation does not reflect an agency's authoritative, expertise-based, "fair[, or] considered judgment." *Ibid.* (quoting *Auer*, 519 U.S. at 462); cf. *United States v. Mead Corp.*, 533 U.S. 218, 229-231 (2001) (adopting a similar approach to *Chevron* deference).

We take the opportunity to restate, and somewhat expand on, those principles here to clear up some mixed messages we have sent. At times, this Court has applied *Auer* deference without significant analysis of the underlying regulation. At other times, the Court has given *Auer* deference without careful attention to the nature and context of the interpretation. And in a vacuum, our most classic formulation of the test — whether an agency's construction is "plainly erroneous or inconsistent with the regulation," *Seminole Rock*, 325 U.S. at 414 — may suggest a caricature of the doctrine, in which deference is "reflexive." Pereira v. Sessions, 585 U.S. ___, ___, 138 S. Ct. 2105, 2120 (2018) (Kennedy, J., concurring). So we cannot deny that Kisor has a bit of grist for his claim that *Auer* "bestows on agencies expansive, unreviewable" authority. But in fact *Auer* does no such thing: It gives agencies their due, while also allowing — indeed, obligating — courts to perform their reviewing and restraining functions. So before we turn to Kisor's specific grievances, we think it worth reinforcing some of the limits inherent in the *Auer* doctrine.

First and foremost, a court should not afford *Auer* deference unless the regulation is genuinely ambiguous. See Christensen v. Harris County, 529 U.S. 576, 588 (2000); *Seminole Rock*, 325 U.S. at 414 (deferring only "if the meaning of the words used is in doubt"). If uncertainty does not exist, there is no plausible reason for deference. The regulation then just means what it means — and the court must give it effect, as the court would any law. [I]f there is only one reasonable construction of a regulation . . . a court has no business deferring to any other reading, no matter how much the agency insists it would make more sense. Deference in that circumstance would "permit the agency, under the guise of interpreting a regulation, to create *de facto* a new regulation." See *Christensen*, 529 U.S. at 588. *Auer* does not, and indeed could not, go that far.

And before concluding that a rule is genuinely ambiguous, a court must exhaust all the "traditional tools" of construction. Chevron U.S.A. Inc. v. Natural Resources Defense Council, Inc., 467 U.S. 837, 843, n. 9 (1984) (adopting the same approach for ambiguous statutes). For again, only when that legal toolkit is empty and the interpretive question still has no single right answer can a judge conclude that it is "more [one] of policy than of law." *Pauley*, 501 U.S. at 696. . . . [A] court must "carefully consider[ ]" the text, structure, history, and purpose of a regulation, in all the ways it would if it had no agency to fall back on. Doing so will resolve many seeming ambiguities out of the box, without resort to *Auer* deference.

If genuine ambiguity remains, moreover, the agency's reading must still be "reasonable." *Thomas Jefferson*, 512 U.S. at 515. In other words, it must come within the zone of ambiguity the court has identified after employing all its interpretive tools. . . . Some courts have thought (perhaps because of *Seminole Rock*'s "plainly erroneous" formulation) that at this stage of the analysis, agency constructions of rules receive greater deference than agency constructions of statutes. See, *e.g.*, Ohio Dept. of Medicaid v. Price, 864 F.3d 469, 477 (CA6 2017). But that is not so. Under *Auer*, as under *Chevron*, the agency's reading must fall "within the bounds of reasonable interpretation." Arlington v. FCC, 569 U.S. 290, 296 (2013). And let there be no mistake: That is a requirement an agency can fail.

Still, we are not done — for not every reasonable agency reading of a genuinely ambiguous rule should receive *Auer* deference. . . . As explained above, we give *Auer* deference because we presume, for a set of reasons relating to the comparative attributes of courts and agencies, that Congress would have wanted us to. But the administrative realm is vast and varied, and we have understood that such a presumption cannot always hold. The inquiry on this dimension does not reduce to any exhaustive test. But we have laid out some especially important markers for identifying when *Auer* deference is and is not appropriate.

To begin with, the regulatory interpretation must be one actually made by the agency. In other words, it must be the agency's "authoritative" or "official position," rather than any more ad hoc statement not reflecting the agency's views. *Mead*, 533 U.S. at 257-259, and n. 6 (SCALIA, J., dissenting). That constraint follows from the logic of *Auer* deference — because Congress has delegated rulemaking power, and all that typically goes with it, to the agency alone. Of course, the requirement of "authoritative" action must recognize a reality of bureaucratic life. . . . [F]or example, we have deferred to "official staff memoranda" that were "published in the Federal Register," even though never approved by the agency head. But there are limits. The interpretation must at the least emanate from those actors, using those vehicles, understood to make authoritative policy in the relevant context. . . . If the interpretation does not do so, a court may not defer.

Next, the agency's interpretation must in some way implicate its substantive expertise. Administrative knowledge and experience largely "account [for] the presumption that Congress delegates interpretive lawmaking power to the agency." *Martin*, 499 U.S. at 153. So the basis for deference ebbs when "[t]he subject matter of the [dispute is] distan[t] from the agency's ordinary" duties or "fall[s] within the scope of another agency's authority." *Arlington*, 569 U.S. at 309 (opinion of BREYER, J.). This Court indicated as much when it analyzed a "split enforcement" scheme, in which Congress divided regulatory power between two entities. *Martin*, 499 U.S. at 151. To decide "*whose* reasonable interpretation" of a rule controlled, we "presum[ed] Congress intended to invest interpretive power" in whichever actor was "best position[ed] to develop" expertise about the given problem. *Id.*, at 149, 153. The same idea holds good as between agencies and courts. "Generally, agencies have a nuanced understanding of the regulations they administer." That point is most obvious when a rule is technical. . . . But more prosaic-seeming questions also commonly implicate policy expertise; consider the TSA assessing the security risks of pâté or a disabilities office weighing the costs and benefits of an accommodation. See *ibid.* Once again, though, there are limits. Some interpretive issues may fall more naturally into a judge's bailiwick. Take one requiring the elucidation of a simple common-law property term . . . or one concerning the award of an attorney's fee. When the agency has no comparative expertise in resolving a regulatory ambiguity, Congress presumably would not grant it that authority.

Finally, an agency's reading of a rule must reflect "fair and considered judgment" to receive *Auer* deference. *Christopher*, 567 U.S. at 155 (quoting *Auer*, 519 U.S. at 462, 117 S. Ct. 905). That means, we have stated, that a court should decline to defer to a merely "convenient litigating position" or "*post hoc* rationalizatio[n] advanced" to "defend past agency action against attack." And a court may not defer to a new interpretation, whether or not introduced in litigation, that creates "unfair surprise" to regulated parties. *Long Island Care*, 551 U.S. at 170. That disruption of expectations may occur when an agency substitutes one view of a rule for another. We have therefore only rarely given *Auer* deference to an agency construction "conflict[ing] with a prior" one. *Thomas Jefferson*, 512 U.S. at 515. Or the upending of reliance may happen without such an explicit interpretive change. This Court, for example, recently refused to defer to an interpretation that would have imposed retroactive liability on parties for longstanding conduct that the agency had never before addressed. See *Christopher*, 567 U.S. at 155-156. Here too the lack of "fair warning" outweighed the reasons to apply *Auer.Id.*, at 156.

■ ■ ■

The upshot of all this goes something as follows. When it applies, *Auer* deference gives an agency significant leeway to say what its own rules mean. In so doing, the doctrine enables the agency to fill out the regulatory scheme Congress has placed under its supervision. But that phrase "when it applies" is important — because it often doesn't. As described above, this Court has cabined *Auer*'s scope in varied and critical ways — and in exactly that measure, has maintained a strong judicial role in interpreting rules. What emerges is a deference doctrine not quite so tame as some might hope, but not nearly so menacing as they might fear.

III

That brings us to the lone question presented here — whether we should abandon the longstanding doctrine just described. In contending that we should, Kisor raises statutory, policy, and constitutional claims (in that order). . . . He must first convince us that *Auer* deference is wrong. And even then, he must overcome *stare decisis*. . . . [In the event Kisor fails at the first step][, n]one of his arguments provide good reason to doubt *Auer* deference. And even if that were not so, Kisor does not offer the kind of special justification needed to overrule *Auer*, and *Seminole Rock*, and all our many other decisions deferring to reasonable agency constructions of ambiguous rules.

A

[The Court goes on in this section to address Kisor's specific challenges to *Auer* deference: (1) that such deference is inconsistent with APA judicial review provision §706 (Court says: courts still use traditional methods of interpretation before getting to *Auer* deference and even then only defer if language is ambiguous); (2) such deference can be to interpretive rules that have not undergone notice and comment procedures (Court says: interpretive rules are not "binding," and courts ultimately make that call. Moreover, under *Auer* "a court may defer to only an agency's authoritative and considered judgments. No *ad hoc* statements or *post hoc* rationalizations need apply."); (3) agencies have an incentive under *Auer* to keep rules vague and then interpret them later (Court says: such action has not empirically been shown, regulated parties push hard for clarity, vagueness can result in adverse judicial rulings, and future administrations can easily re-interpret vague rules their own way); (4) *Auer* deference violates separation of powers principles (Court says: under *Auer* courts retain a grip on the interpretive function and understand that all exercises of agency power (legislative, executive, and judicial) are still just exercises of executive power pursuant to a statutory plan.)]

B

[The Court gives its reasons for refusing to overrule not just *Auer*, but its precedents extending back more than 75 years.]

IV

With that, we can finally return to Kisor's own case. You may remember that his retroactive benefits depend on the meaning of the term "relevant" records in a VA regulation. The Board of Veterans' Appeals, through a single judge's opinion, understood records to be relevant only if they relate to the basis of the VA's initial denial of benefits. By contrast, Kisor argued that records are relevant if they go to any benefits criterion, even one that was uncontested. The Federal Circuit upheld the Board's interpretation based on *Auer* deference.

Applying the principles outlined in this opinion, we hold that a redo is necessary for two reasons. First, the Federal Circuit jumped the gun in declaring the regulation ambiguous. We have insisted that a court bring all its interpretive tools to bear before finding that to be so. It is not enough to casually remark, as the court did here, that "[b]oth parties insist that the plain regulatory language supports their case, and neither party's position strikes us as unreasonable." 869 F.3d at 1368. Rather, the court must make a conscientious effort to determine, based on indicia like text, structure, history, and purpose, whether the regulation really has more than one reasonable meaning. The Solicitor General argued in this Court that the Board's reading is the only reasonable one. Perhaps Kisor will make the converse claim below. Before even considering deference, the court must seriously think through those positions.

And second, the Federal Circuit assumed too fast that *Auer* deference should apply in the event of genuine ambiguity. As we have explained, that is not always true. A court must assess whether the interpretation is of the sort that Congress would want to receive deference. The Solicitor General suggested at oral argument that the answer in this case might be no. He explained that all 100 or so members of the VA Board act individually (rather than in panels) and that their roughly 80,000 annual decisions have no "precedential value." He thus questioned whether a Board member's ruling "reflects the considered judgment of the agency as a whole." *Ibid.*; cf. *Mead*, 533 U.S. at 233 (declining to give *Chevron* deference to rulings "being churned out at a rate of 10,000 a year at an agency's 46 scattered offices"). We do not know what position the Government will take on that issue below. But the questions the Solicitor General raised are exactly the kind the court must consider in deciding whether to award *Auer* deference to the Board's interpretation.

We accordingly vacate the judgment below and remand the case for further proceedings.

It is so ordered.

CHIEF JUSTICE ROBERTS, concurring in part.

I join Parts I, II-B, III-B, and IV of the Court's opinion. We took this case to consider whether to overrule Auer v. Robbins, 519 U.S. 452 (1997), and *Bowles v. Seminole Rock & Sand Co.*, 325 U.S. 410 (1945). For the reasons the Court discusses in Part III-B, I agree that overruling those precedents is not warranted. I also agree with the Court's treatment in Part II-B of the bounds of *Auer* deference.

I write separately to suggest that the distance between the majority and JUSTICE GORSUCH is not as great as it may initially appear. The majority catalogs the prerequisites for, and limitations on, *Auer* deference: The underlying regulation must be genuinely ambiguous; the agency's interpretation must be reasonable and must reflect its authoritative, expertise-based, and fair and considered judgment; and the agency must take account of reliance interests and avoid unfair surprise. JUSTICE GORSUCH, meanwhile, lists the reasons that a court might be persuaded to adopt an agency's interpretation of its own regulation: The agency thoroughly considered the problem, offered a valid rationale, brought its expertise to bear, and interpreted the regulation in a manner consistent with earlier and later pronouncements. Accounting for variations in verbal formulation, those lists have much in common.

That is not to say that *Auer* deference is just the same as the power of persuasion discussed in *Skidmore v. Swift & Co.*, 323 U.S. 134 (1944); there is a difference between holding that a court ought to be persuaded by an agency's interpretation and holding that it should defer to that interpretation under certain conditions. But it is to say that the cases in which *Auer* deference is warranted largely overlap with the cases in which it would be unreasonable for a court not to be persuaded by an agency's interpretation of its own regulation.

One further point: Issues surrounding judicial deference to agency interpretations of their own regulations are distinct from those raised in connection with judicial deference to agency interpretations of statutes enacted by Congress. See Chevron U.S.A. Inc. v. Natural Resources Defense Council, Inc., 467 U.S. 837 (1984). I do not regard the Court's decision today to touch upon the latter question.

JUSTICE GORSUCH, with whom JUSTICE THOMAS joins, with whom JUSTICE KAVANAUGH joins as to Parts I, II, III, IV, and V, and with whom JUSTICE ALITO joins as to Parts I, II, and III, concurring in the judgment.

It should have been easy for the Court to say goodbye to Auer v. Robbins. In disputes involving the relationship between the government and the people, *Auer* requires judges to accept an executive agency's interpretation of its own regulations even when that interpretation doesn't represent the best and fairest reading. This rule creates a "systematic judicial bias in favor of the federal government, the most powerful of parties, and against everyone else." Nor is *Auer*'s biased rule the product of some congressional mandate we are powerless to correct: This Court invented it, almost by accident and without any meaningful effort to reconcile it with the Administrative Procedure Act or the Constitution. A legion of academics, lower court judges, and Members of this Court — even

Auer's author — has called on us to abandon *Auer*. Yet today a bare majority flinches, and *Auer* lives on.

Still, today's decision is more a stay of execution than a pardon. The Court cannot muster even five votes to say that *Auer* is lawful or wise. Instead, a majority retains *Auer* only because of *stare decisis*. And yet, far from standing by that precedent, the majority proceeds to impose so many new and nebulous qualifications and limitations on *Auer* that THE CHIEF JUSTICE claims to see little practical difference between keeping it on life support in this way and overruling it entirely. So the doctrine emerges maimed and enfeebled — in truth, zombified.

Respectfully, we owe our colleagues on the lower courts more candid and useful guidance than this. And judges owe the people who come before them nothing less than a fair contest, where every party has an equal chance to persuade the court of its interpretation of the law's demands. One can hope that THE CHIEF JUSTICE is right, and that whether we formally overrule *Auer* or merely neuter it, the results in most cases will prove the same. But means, not just ends, matter, and retaining even this debilitated version of *Auer* threatens to force litigants and lower courts to jump through needless and perplexing new hoops and in the process deny the people the independent judicial decisions they deserve. All to what end? So that we may *pretend* to abide *stare decisis*?

Consider this case. Mr. Kisor is a Marine who lost out on benefits for post-traumatic stress disorder when the court of appeals deferred to a regulatory interpretation advanced by the Department of Veterans Affairs. The court of appeals was guilty of nothing more than faithfully following *Auer*. But the majority today invokes *stare decisis*, of all things, to vacate that judgment and tell the court of appeals to try again using its newly retooled, multi-factored, and far less determinate version of *Auer*. Respectfully, I would stop this business of making up excuses for judges to abdicate their job of interpreting the law, and simply allow the court of appeals to afford Mr. Kisor its best independent judgment of the law's meaning.

The Court's failure to be done with *Auer*, and its decision to adorn *Auer* with so many new and ambiguous limitations, all but guarantees we will have to pass this way again. When that day comes, I hope this Court will find the nerve it lacks today and inter *Auer* at last. Until then, I hope that our judicial colleagues on other courts will take courage from today's ruling and realize that it has transformed *Auer* into a paper tiger.

NOTES

1. *Limited* Auer *deference?* The majority in *Kisor* upheld *Auer* but in so doing very carefully reiterated and expanded important limitations on the doctrine's application. Significantly, under *Kisor*, courts should apply *Auer* deference only if they determine that (1) a regulation is genuinely ambiguous after exhausting all traditional tools of interpretation, (2) the agency's interpretation is reasonable, and (3) the "character and context of the agency interpretation entitles it to controlling weight," because it reflects the official, expert, considered, and consistent judgment of the agency. Is this truly now a doctrine of deference? Review *Skidmore.* Are the *Skidmore* criteria required to persuade a court much different from all of the criteria now to be applied by courts before giving *Auer* deference to an agency decision? Is Roberts correct in his concurrence that there really is very little difference between the majority and the dissent in *Kisor*?

2. Despite Justice Kagan's pronouncement that the *Auer* deference doctrine remains "potent in its place," it is clear that courts have implemented *Kisor* as a significant change to *Auer* deference. For example, the Third Circuit recognized that its previous decision to give "binding effect" to a sentencing commission's interpretation of sentencing guidelines "may have gone too far in affording deference," specifically noting that after *Kisor*, "it is clear that [the commission's] interpretation is not warranted." United States v. Nasir, 982 F.3d 144, 158 (3rd Cir. 2020). The Court went on to state that *Kisor* limited the "uncritical and broad deference to agency interpretations of regulations" that *Auer* had demanded, restricting such deference to cases in which the regulation is "genuinely ambiguous." Id. Not only did the court find the plain text of the guidelines clear, precluding *Auer* deference and overturning its own precedent; the court also explained *Kisor*'s limits on deference as having the advantage of protecting separation of powers. *Id.* at 159. Similarly, the Eleventh Circuit concluded that the Department of Health and Human Services' interpretation of the regulatory term, "significant proposed policies," was not entitled to deference because "[a] careful reading" of the plain text, employing traditional tools of construction, sufficed to show its natural meaning. Callahan v. United States Dep't of Health & Hum. Servs., 939 F.3d 1251, 1258, 1260 (11th Cir. 2019). In this case, the court viewed the agency's interpretation as "the better" reading of the statute without relying on deference, an approach that the court described as illustrating "the truth and wisdom" of the *Kisor* decision. Id. at 1259. The Ninth Circuit has also employed *Kisor*'s "genuinely ambiguous" test, holding that the Bureau of Immigration Appeals' interpretation of a regulation was not entitled to deference because "the regulation's text, structure, history, and purpose" showed that the regulation was not genuinely ambiguous, and that its correct reading was contrary to the agency's. Rubalcaba v. Garland, 998 F.3d 1031, 1040 (9th Cir. 2021).

The D.C. Circuit has also ruled on agency regulatory interpretations under *Kisor*. In Nat'l Lifeline Ass'n v. Fed. Commc'ns Comm'n, the court held that the FCC's interpretation of its own regulation was "compelled by the terms of the rules": "Therefore, we need not 'defer' to the Commission's judgment, as if to suggest that there are other reasonable constructions of the rules. We simply reject Petitioner's position because it rests on an untenable interpretation of the rules." 983 F.3d 498, 511 (D.C. Cir. 2020). However, the court did not stop there; it also analyzed whether *Auer* deference under *Kisor* would have been appropriate if it had found the regulation to be genuinely ambiguous. Id. The court analyzed the factors that *Kisor* outlines to decide if an agency is entitled to deference with respect to a particular regulation, finding that the FCC's interpretation was an "authoritative and official position," that it implicated the agency's "policy expertise," and that it was issued after careful consideration. Id. at 511-512. The court thus held that if the regulation had been ambiguous, the FCC's reasonable interpretation would have been entitled to deference. Id. at 512.

What do these cases suggest about the nature of *Auer* deference under *Kisor*? If courts must engage in substantial exercises of textual interpretation before they can even consider conferring deference, does the *Auer* doctrine truly remain a doctrine of deference? What do you make of the Third Circuit's foray into justifying *Kisor* as protecting separation of powers? What about the D.C. Circuit's arguably superfluous analysis after deciding the regulation was not genuinely ambiguous?

3. *Self-delegation?* The majority addresses an argument made by Kisor, and offered up by former Justice Scalia in a number of prior cases, that *Auer* deference creates an incentive to agencies to keep its own interpretations intentionally vague, allowing the agency maximum flexibility in later determining the meaning and being afforded *Auer* deference in support of its later interpretation. Do you believe agencies will do this as a matter of strategy, or is the incentive always there for the agency to be as clear as it can be in promulgating regulations? The majority argues that despite the long existence of *Auer* deference there is no evidence of an agency acting in such a way: "As two noted scholars (one of whom reviewed thousands of rules during four years of government service) have written: '[W]e are unaware of, and no one has pointed to, any regulation in American history that, because of *Auer*, was designed vaguely.' Sunstein & Vermeule, 84 U. Chi. L. Rev., at 308." *Kisor*, 588 U.S. ___, at slip op. 24. Does this mean agencies will never "self-delegate"? See also Daniel E. Walters, The Self-Delegation False Alarm: Analyzing *Auer* Deference's Effects on Agency Rules, 119 Colum. L. Rev. 85 (2019) (empirical analysis of federal rules dataset running from 1982-2016 revealed no measurable increase in vagueness of agency writing in response to *Auer* deference; indeed, specificity arguably increased in this time period).

4. The majority's decision not to overrule *Auer* relied, in large part, on stare decisis. Chief Justice Roberts' concurrence, which represented the tie-breaking vote that kept *Auer* alive, also emphasized the importance of stare decisis. But given the significant limitations that *Kisor* places on *Auer* deference, was the court's refusal to reject its own precedent here a wise application of stare decisis? Some have argued that the Chief Justice's decision in *Kisor* primarily reflects his interest in maintaining "the reputation, credibility, and legitimacy of the Court as an institution" by avoiding overturning yet another example of "well-settled law," three such decisions having done just that over the 2018 and 2019 terms. Paul Warczak, Jr., The Cobra Effect: *Kisor*, Roberts, and the Law of Unintended Consequences, 54 Akron L. Rev. 111, 115-116 (2020). However, according to Warczak, the *Kisor* decision served only to harm the Court's reputation in light of the uncertainty its complex analysis creates for lower courts, agencies, and litigants alike. Id. at 151-152. He also invokes familiar arguments about the constitutionality of the *Auer* deference *Kisor* upheld to suggest that Roberts' attempt to maintain the Court's integrity through stare decisis will likely have the opposite effect. Id. at 156 ("Any stabilizing effects of abiding by stare decisis were more than offset by the destabilizing effects of the *Kisor* decision."). What do you make of these arguments? Do you agree that stare decisis can do more harm than good? Setting aside the questions of constitutionality, to what extent should the purported complexity of a *Kisor* analysis diminish its reputation and value?

CHAPTER 7 PROBLEM

Congress adopted legislation requiring that manufacturing companies disclose annually whether they used certain "conflict minerals" mined in the Democratic Republic of Westoria (DRW), a small country in Asia. Disclosure had to include a representation that by purchasing conflict minerals, the company was contributing to the humanitarian crisis in the region. Congress was concerned that these minerals were used to finance a brutal civil war in the country. Congress did not define "conflict minerals" in the statute, but the SEC has interpreted "conflict minerals" to mean "any valuable minerals whose purchase significantly serves to finance conflict in the DRW, including tungsten, tin, gold, and other derivatives." Congress anticipated that the threat of disclosure would cause companies to reduce their reliance on conflict minerals from that country. The statute provided that any action by the SEC for violation of the disclosure requirement "shall be final and conclusive, and not subject to further review in any court."

Although the provision did not require rulemaking by the SEC, the Association of Software Developers ("ASD") petitioned the agency to adopt a rule clarifying that the disclosure obligations applied to the use of minerals in neighboring countries. The ASD hoped that such a rule would force manufacturers to purchase more software in order to monitor the source of the relevant materials. After waiting six months, the SEC responded that it would move forward with rulemaking to address the issue. Six months later, however, following a change in the administration, the SEC issued a notice stating that the petition had been rejected and no rulemaking would be forthcoming.

Tele-Tex uses conflict minerals under the SEC definition but does not believe that the minerals are from DRW. As a result, Tele-Tex had not disclosed the use of the minerals. The SEC recently brought an action against the company alleging that, in fact, the minerals are from DRW and, in any case, serve significantly to finance conflict in the DRW. The SEC sought a substantial fine both for failing to disclose the use of the minerals and for failing to make the required representation about contributing to the humanitarian crisis. After a hearing, the administrative law judge imposed a $25 million fine for violations of both of these requirements.

Tele-Tex and the ASD have come to you for advice. Tele-Tex believes that it does not qualify under the statute as a manufacturing company and that the SEC definition is vague and outside the scope of the agency's authority. Although Tele-Tex sells products, they are assembled and not "manufactured." Moreover, the minerals are not from the DRW, as Congress required. In addition, Tele-Tex believes that the statement about a contribution to the humanitarian crisis violates the company's First Amendment rights. Tele-Tex wants to know if the company must appeal the ALJ's decision or whether it can seek immediate recourse in the U.S. Court of Appeals. Tele-Tex also wants to know if it can file an action in federal district court seeking to enjoin the SEC from going forward with the case. ASD would like to challenge the SEC's decision not to engage in rulemaking after having already said that it would. In considering this issue, consider whether ASD has standing to bring an action against the Commission.

APPENDIX A

Federal Administrative Procedure Act

TITLE 5, U.S. CODE

Chapter 5 — Administrative Procedure

§551. Definitions

For the purpose of this subchapter —

(1) "agency" means each authority of the Government of the United States, whether or not it is within or subject to review by another agency, but does not include —

(A) the Congress;

(B) the courts of the United States;

(C) the governments of the territories or possessions of the United States;

(D) the government of the District of Columbia; or except as to the requirements of section 552 of this title;

(E) agencies composed of representatives of the parties or of representatives of organizations of the parties to the disputes determined by them;

(F) courts martial and military commissions;

(G) military authority exercised in the field in time of war or in occupied territory; or

(H) functions conferred by sections 1738, 1739, 1743, and 1744 of title 12; chapter 2 of title 41; or sections 1622, 1884, 1891-1902, and former section 1641(b)(2), of title 50, appendix;

(2) "person" includes an individual, partnership, corporation, association, or public or private organization other than an agency;

(3) "party" includes a person or agency named or admitted as a party, or properly seeking and entitled as of right to be admitted as a party, in an agency proceeding, and a person or agency admitted by an agency as a party for limited purposes;

(4) "rule" means the whole or a part of an agency statement of general or particular applicability and future effect designed to implement, interpret, or prescribe law or policy or describing the organization, procedure, or practice requirements of an agency and includes the approval or prescription for the future of rates, wages, corporate or financial structures or reorganizations thereof, prices, facilities, appliances, services or allowances therefor or of valuations, costs, or accounting, or practices bearing on any of the foregoing;

(5) "rule making" means agency process for formulating, amending, or repealing a rule;

(6) "order" means the whole or a part of a final disposition, whether affirmative, negative, injunctive, or declaratory in form, of an agency in a matter other than rule making but including licensing;

(7) "adjudication" means agency process for the formulation of an order;

(8) "license" includes the whole or a part of an agency permit, certificate, approval, registration, charter, membership, statutory exemption or other form of permission;

(9) "licensing" includes agency process respecting the grant, renewal, denial, revocation, suspension, annulment, withdrawal, limitation, amendment, modification, or conditioning of a license;

(10) "sanction" includes the whole or a part of an agency—

(A) prohibition, requirement, limitation, or other condition affecting the freedom of a person;

(B) withholding of relief;

(C) imposition of penalty or fine;

(D) destruction, taking, seizure, or withholding of property;

(E) assessment of damages, reimbursement, restitution, compensation, costs, charges, or fees;

(F) requirement, revocation, or suspension of a license; or

(G) taking other compulsory or restrictive action;

(11) "relief" includes the whole or a part of an agency—

(A) grant of money, assistance, license, authority, exemption, exception, privilege, or remedy;

(B) recognition of a claim, right, immunity, privilege, exemption, or exception; or

(C) taking of other action on the application or petition of, and beneficial to, a person;

(12) "agency proceeding" means an agency process as defined by paragraphs (5), (7), and (9) of this section;

(13) "agency action" includes the whole or a part of an agency rule, order, license, sanction, relief, or the equivalent or denial thereof, or failure to act; and

(14) "ex parte communication" means an oral or written communication not on the public record with respect to which reasonable prior notice to all parties is not given, but it shall not include requests for status reports on any matter or proceeding covered by this subchapter.

(Pub. L. No. 89-554, Sept. 6, 1966, 80 Stat. 381; Pub. L. No. 94-409, §4(b), Sept. 13, 1976, 90 Stat. 1247.) . . .

§553. Rulemaking

(a) This section applies, according to the provisions thereof, except to the extent that there is involved—

(1) a military or foreign affairs function of the United States; or

(2) a matter relating to agency management or personnel or to public property, loans, grants, benefits, or contracts.

(b) General notice of proposed rule making shall be published in the Federal Register, unless persons subject thereto are named and either personally served or otherwise have actual notice thereof in accordance with law. The notice shall include—

(1) a statement of the time, place, and nature of public rule making proceedings;

(2) reference to the legal authority under which the rule is proposed; and

(3) either the terms or substance of the proposed rule or a description of the subjects and issues involved.

Except when notice or hearing is required by statute, this subsection does not apply.

(A) to interpretative rules, general statements of policy, or rules of agency organization, procedure, or practice; or

(B) when the agency for good cause finds (and incorporates the finding and a brief statement of reasons therefor in the rules issued) that notice and public procedure thereon are impracticable, unnecessary, or contrary to the public interest.

(c) After notice required by this section, the agency shall give interested persons an opportunity to participate in the rule making through submission of written data, views, or arguments with or without opportunity for oral presentation. After consideration of the relevant matter presented, the agency shall incorporate in the rules adopted a concise general statement of their basis and purpose. When rules are required by statute to be made on the record after opportunity for an agency hearing, sections 556 and 557 of this title apply instead of this subsection.

(d) The required publication or service of a substantive rule shall be made not less than 30 days before its effective date, except—

(1) a substantive rule which grants or recognizes an exemption or relieves a restriction;

(2) interpretative rules and statements of policy; or

(3) as otherwise provided by the agency for good cause found and published with the rule.

(e) Each agency shall give an interested person the right to petition for the issuance, amendment, or repeal of a rule.

(Pub. L. No. 89-554, Sept. 6, 1966, 80 Stat. 383.)

§554. Adjudications

(a) This section applies, according to the provisions thereof, in every case of adjudication required by statute to be determined on the record after opportunity for an agency hearing, except to the extent that there is involved—

(1) a matter subject to a subsequent trial of the law and the facts de novo in a court;

(2) the selection or tenure of an employee, except an administrative law judge appointed under section 3105 of this title;

(3) proceedings in which decisions rest solely on inspections, tests, or elections;

(4) the conduct of military or foreign affairs functions;

(5) cases in which an agency is acting as an agent for a court; or

(6) the certification of worker representatives.

(b) Persons entitled to notice of an agency hearing shall be timely informed of—

(1) the time, place, and nature of the hearing;

(2) the legal authority and jurisdiction under which the hearing is to be held; and

(3) the matters of fact and law asserted.

When private persons are the moving parties, other parties to the proceeding shall give prompt notice of issues controverted in fact or law; and in other instances agencies may by rule require responsive pleading. In fixing the time and place for hearings, due regard shall be had for the convenience and necessity of the parties or their representatives.

(c) The agency shall give all interested parties opportunity for—

(1) the submission and consideration of facts, arguments, offers of settlement, or proposals of adjustment when time, the nature of the proceeding, and the public interest permit; and

(2) to the extent that the parties are unable so to determine a controversy by consent, hearing and decision on notice and in accordance with sections 556 and 557 of this title.

(d) The employee who presides at the reception of evidence pursuant to section 556 of this title shall make the recommended decision or initial decision required by section 557 of this title, unless he becomes unavailable to the agency. Except to the extent required for the disposition of ex parte matters as authorized by law, such an employee may not—

(1) consult a person or party on a fact in issue, unless on notice and opportunity for all parties to participate; or

(2) be responsible to or subject to the supervision or direction of an employee or agent engaged in the performance of investigative or prosecuting functions for an agency.

An employee or agent engaged in the performance of investigative or prosecuting functions for an agency in a case may not, in that or a factually related case, participate or advise in the decision, recommended decision, or agency review pursuant to section 557 of this title, except as witness or counsel in public proceedings. This subsection does not apply—

(A) in determining applications for initial licenses;

(B) to proceedings involving the validity or application of rates, facilities, or practices of public utilities or carriers; or

(C) to the agency or a member or members of the body comprising the agency.

(e) The agency, with like effect as in the case of other orders, and in its sound discretion, may issue a declaratory order to terminate a controversy or remove uncertainty.

(Pub. L. No. 89-554, Sept. 6, 1966, 80 Stat. 384; Pub. L. No. 95-251, §2(a)(1), Mar. 27, 1978, 92 Stat. 183.)

§555. Ancillary matters

(a) This section applies, according to the provisions thereof, except as otherwise provided by this subchapter.

(b) A person compelled to appear in person before an agency or representative thereof is entitled to be accompanied, represented, and advised by counsel or, if permitted by the agency, by other qualified representative. A party is entitled to appear in person or by or with counsel or other duly qualified representative in an agency proceeding. So far as the orderly conduct of public business permits, an interested person may appear before an agency or its responsible employees for the presentation, adjustment, or determination of an issue, request, or controversy in a proceeding, whether interlocutory, summary, or otherwise, or in connection with an agency function. With due regard for the convenience and necessity of the parties of their representatives and within a reasonable time, each agency shall proceed to conclude a matter presented to it. This subsection does not grant or deny a person who is not a lawyer the right to appear for or represent others before an agency or in an agency proceeding.

(c) Process, requirement of a report, inspection, or other investigative act or demand may not be issued, made, or enforced except as authorized by law. A person compelled to submit data or evidence is entitled to retain or, on payment of lawfully prescribed costs, procure a copy or transcript thereof, except that in a nonpublic investigatory proceeding the witness may for good cause be limited to inspection of the official transcript of his testimony.

(d) Agency subpenas authorized by law shall be issued to a party on request and, when required by rules of procedure, on a statement or showing of general relevance and reasonable scope of the evidence sought. On contest, the court shall sustain the subpena or similar process or demand to the extent that it is found to be in accordance with law. In a proceeding for enforcement, the court shall issue an order requiring the appearance of the witness or the production of the evidence or data within a reasonable time under penalty of punishment for contempt in case of contumacious failure to comply.

(e) Prompt notice shall be given of the denial in whole or in part of a written application, petition, or other request of an interested person made in connection with any agency proceeding. Except in affirming a prior denial or when the denial is self-explanatory, the notice shall be accompanied by a brief statement of the grounds for denial.

(Pub. L. No. 89-554, Sept. 6, 1966, 80 Stat. 385.)

§556. Hearings; presiding employees; powers and duties; burden of proof; evidence; record as basis of decision

(a) This section applies, according to the provisions thereof, to hearings required by section 553 of 554 of this title to be conducted in accordance with this section.

(b) There shall preside at the taking of evidence —

(1) the agency;

(2) one or more members of the body which comprises the agency; or

(3) one or more administrative law judges appointed under section 3105 of this title.

This subchapter does not supersede the conduct of specified classes of proceedings, in whole or in part, by or before boards or other employees specially provided for by or designated under statute. The functions of presiding employees and of employees participating in decisions in accordance with section 557 of this title shall be conducted in an impartial manner. A presiding or participating employee may at any time disqualify him-self. On the filing in good faith of a timely and sufficient affidavit of personal bias or other disqualification of a presiding or participating employee, the agency shall determine the matter as a part of the record and decision in the case

(c) Subject to published rules of the agency and within its powers, employees presiding at hearings may—

(1) administer oaths and affirmations;

(2) issue subpenas authorized by law;

(3) rule on offers of proof and receive relevant evidence;

(4) take depositions or have depositions taken when the ends of justice would be served;

(5) regulate the course of the hearing;

(6) hold conferences for the settlement or simplification of the issues by consent of the parties or by the use of alternative means of dispute resolution as provided in subchapter IV of this chapter;

(7) inform the parties as to the availability of one or more alternative means of dispute resolution, and encourage use of such methods;

(8) require the attendance at any conference held pursuant to paragraph (6) of at least one representative of each party who has authority to negotiate concerning resolution of issues in controversy;

(9) dispose of procedural requests or similar matters;

(10) make or recommend decisions in accordance with section 557 of this title; and

(11) take other action authorized by agency rule consistent with this subchapter.

(d) Except as otherwise provided by statute, the proponent of a rule or order has the burden of proof. Any oral or documentary evidence may be received, but the agency as a matter of policy shall provide for the exclusion of irrelevant, immaterial, or unduly repetitious evidence. A sanction may not be imposed or rule or order issued except on consideration of the whole record or those parts thereof cited by a party and supported by and in accordance with the reliable, probative, and substantial evidence. The agency may, to the extent consistent with the interests of justice and the policy of the underlying statutes administered by the agency, consider a violation of section 557(d) of this title sufficient grounds for a decision adverse to a party who has knowingly committed such violation or knowingly caused such violation to occur. A party is entitled to present his case or defense by oral or documentary evidence, to submit rebuttal evidence, and to conduct such cross-examination as may be required for a full and true disclosure of the facts. In rule making or determining claims for money or benefits or applications for initial licenses an agency may, when a party will not be prejudiced thereby, adopt procedures for the submission of all or part of the evidence in written form.

(e) The transcript of testimony and exhibits, together with all papers and requests filed in the proceeding, constitutes the exclusive record for decision in accordance with section 557 of this title and, on payment of lawfully prescribed costs, shall be made available to the parties. When an agency decision rests on official notice of a material fact not appearing in the evidence in the record, a party is entitled, on timely request, to an opportunity to show the contrary.

(Pub. L. No. 89-554, Sept. 6, 1966, 80 Stat. 386; Pub. L. No. 94-409, §4(c), Sept. 13, 1976, 90 Stat. 1247; Pub. L. No. 95-251, §2(a)(1), Mar. 27, 1978, 92 Stat. 183; Pub. L. No. 101-552, §4(a), Nov. 15, 1990, 104 Stat. 2737.)

§557. Initial decisions; conclusiveness; review by agency; submissions by parties; contents of decisions; record

(a) This section applies, according to the provisions thereof, when a hearing is required to be conducted in accordance with section 556 of this title.

(b) When the agency did not preside at the reception of the evidence, the presiding employee or, in cases not subject to section 554(d) of this title, an employee qualified to preside at hearings pursuant to section 556 of this title, shall initially decide the case unless the agency requires, either in specific cases or by general rule, the entire record to be certified to it for decision. When the presiding employee makes an initial decision, that decision then becomes the decision of the agency without further proceedings unless there is an appeal to, or review on motion of, the agency within time provided by rule. On appeal from or review of the initial decision, the agency has all the powers which it would have in making the initial decision except as it may limit the issues on notice or by rule. When the agency makes the decision without having presided at the reception of the evidence, the presiding employee or an employee qualified to preside at hearings pursuant to section 556 of this title shall first recommend a decision, except that in rule making or determining applica tions for initial licenses—

(1) instead thereof the agency may issue a tentative decision or one of its responsible employees may recommend a decision; or

(2) this procedure may be omitted in a case in which the agency finds on the record that due and timely execution of its functions imperatively and unavoidably so requires.

(c) Before a recommended, initial, or tentative decision, or a decision on agency review of the decision of subordinate employees, the parties are entitled to a reasonable opportunity to submit for the consideration of the employees participating in the decisions—

(1) proposed findings and conclusions; or

(2) exceptions to the decisions or recommended decisions of subordinate employees or to tentative agency decisions; and

(3) supporting reasons for the exceptions or proposed findings or conclusions. The record shall show the ruling on each finding, conclusion, or exception presented. All decisions, including initial, recommended, and tentative decisions, are a part of the record and shall include a statement of—

(A) findings and conclusions, and the reasons or basis therefor, on all the material issues of fact, law, or discretion presented on the record; and

(B) the appropriate rule, order, sanction, relief, or denial thereof.

(d) (1) In any agency proceeding which is subject to subsection (a) of this section, except to the extent required for the disposition of ex parte matters as authorized by law—

(A) no interested person outside the agency shall make or knowingly cause to be made to any member of the body comprising the agency, administrative law judge, or other employee who is or may reasonably be expected to be involved in the decisional process of the proceeding, an ex parte communication relevant to the merits of the proceeding;

(B) no member of the body comprising the agency, administrative law judge, or other employee who is or may reasonably be expected to be involved in the decisional process of the proceeding, shall make or knowingly cause to be made to any interested person outside the agency an ex parte communication relevant to the merits of the proceeding;

(C) a member of the body comprising the agency, administrative law judge, or other employee who is or may reasonably be expected to be involved in the decisional process of such proceeding who receives, or who makes or knowingly causes to be made, a communication prohibited by this subsection shall place on the public record of the proceeding:

(i) all such written communications;

(ii) memoranda stating the substance of all such oral communications; and (iii) all written responses, and memoranda stating the substance of all oral responses, to the materials described in clauses (i) and (ii) of this subparagraph;

(D) upon receipt of a communication knowingly made or knowingly caused to be made by a party in violation of this subsection, the agency, administrative law judge, or other employee presiding at the hearing may, to the extent consistent with the interests of justice and the policy of the underlying statutes, require the party to show cause why his claim or interest in the proceeding should not be dismissed, denied, disregarded, or otherwise adversely affected on account of such violation; and

(E) the prohibitions of this subsection shall apply beginning at such time as the agency may designate, but in no case shall they begin to apply later than the time at which a proceeding is noticed for hearing unless the person responsible for the communication has knowledge that it will be noticed, in which case the prohibitions shall apply beginning at the time of his acquisition of such knowledge.

(2) This subsection does not constitute authority to withhold information from Congress.

(Pub. L. No. 89-554, Sept. 6, 1966, 80 Stat. 387; Pub. L. No. 94-409, §4(a), Sept. 13, 1976, 90 Stat. 1246.)

§558. Imposition of sanctions; determination of applications for licenses; suspension, revocation, and expiration of licenses

(a) This section applies, according to the provisions thereof, to the exercise of a power or authority.

(b) A sanction may not be imposed or a substantive rule or order issued except within jurisdiction delegated to the agency and as authorized by law.

(c) When application is made for a license required by law, the agency, with due regard for the rights and privileges of all the interested parties or adversely affected persons and within a reasonable time, shall set and complete proceedings required to be conducted in accordance with sections 556 and 557 of this title or other proceedings required by law and shall make its decision. Except in cases of willfulness or those in which public health, interest, or safety requires otherwise, the withdrawal, suspension, revocation, or annulment of a license is lawful only if, before the institution of agency proceedings therefor, the licensee has been given —

(1) notice by the agency in writing of the facts or conduct which may warrant the action; and

(2) opportunity to demonstrate or achieve compliance with all lawful requirements.

When the licensee has made timely and sufficient application for a renewal or a new license in accordance with agency rules, a license with reference to an activity of a continuing nature does not expire until the application has been finally determined by the agency.

(Pub. L. No. 89-554, Sept. 6, 1966, 80 Stat. 388.)

§559. Effect on other laws; effect of subsequent statute

This subchapter, chapter 7, and sections 1305, 3105, 3344, 4301(2)(E), 5372, and 7521 of this title, and the provisions of section 5335(a)(B) of this title that relate to administrative law judges, do not limit or repeal additional requirements imposed by statute or otherwise recognized by law. Except as otherwise required by law, requirements or privileges relating to evidence or procedure apply equally to agencies and persons. Each agency is granted the authority necessary to comply with the requirements of this subchapter through the issuance of rules or otherwise. Subsequent statute may not be held to supersede or modify this subchapter, chapter 7, sections 1305, 3105, 3344, 4301(2)(E), 5372, or 7521 of this title, or the provisions of section 5335(a)(B) of this title that relate to administrative law judges, except to the extent that it does so expressly.

(Pub. L. No. 89-554, Sept. 6, 1966, 80 Stat. 388; Pub. L. No. 90-623, §1(1), Oct. 22, 1968, 82 Stat. 1312; Pub. L. No. 95-251, §2(a)(1), Mar. 27, 1978, 92 Stat. 183; Pub. L. No. 95-454, title VIII, §801(a)(3)(B)(iii), Oct. 13, 1978, 92 Stat. 1221.)

Chapter 7 — Judicial Review

§701. Application; definitions

(a) This chapter applies, according to the provisions thereof, except to the extent that —

(1) statutes preclude judicial review; or

(2) agency action is committed to agency discretion by law.

(b) For the purpose of this chapter —

(1) "agency" means each authority of the Government of the United States, whether or not it is within or subject to review by another agency, but does not include—

(A) the Congress;

(B) the courts of the United States;

(C) the governments of the territories or possessions of the United States;

(D) the government of the District of Columbia;

(E) agencies composed of representatives of the parties or of representatives of organizations of the parties to the disputes determined by them;

(F) courts martial and military commissions;

(G) military authority exercised in the field in time of war or in occupied territory; or

(H) functions conferred by sections 1738, 1739, 1743, and 1744 of title 12; chapter 2 of title 41; or sections 1622, 1884, 1891-1902, and former section 1641(b)(2), of title 50, appendix; and

(2) "person", "rule", "order", "license", "sanction", "relief", and "agency action" have the meanings given them by section 551 of this title.

(Pub. L. No. 89-554, Sept. 6, 1966, 80 Stat. 392.)

§702. Right of review

A person suffering legal wrong because of agency action, or adversely affected or aggrieved by agency action within the meaning of a relevant statute, is entitled to judicial review thereof. An action in a court of the United States seeking relief other than money damages and stating a claim that an agency or an officer or employee thereof acted or failed to act in an official capacity or under color of legal authority shall not be dismissed nor relief therein be denied on the ground that it is against the United States or that the United States is an indispensable party. The United States may be named as a defendant in any such action, and a judgment or decree may be entered against the United States: Provided, That any mandatory or injunctive decree shall specify the Federal officer or officers (by name or by title), and their successors in office, personally responsible for compliance. Nothing herein (1) affects other limitations on judicial review or the power or duty of the court to dismiss any action or deny relief on any other appropriate legal or equitable ground; or (2) confers authority to grant relief if any other statute that grants consent to suit expressly or impliedly forbids the relief which is sought.

(Pub. L. No. 89-554, Sept. 6, 1966, 80 Stat. 392; Pub. L. No. 94-574, §1, Oct. 21, 1976, 90 Stat. 2721.)

§703. Form and venue of proceeding

The form of proceeding for judicial review is the special statutory review proceeding relevant to the subject matter in a court specified by statute or, in the absence or inadequacy thereof, any applicable form of legal action, including actions for declaratory judgments or writs of prohibitory or mandatory injunction or habeas corpus, in a court of competent jurisdiction. If no special statutory review proceeding is applicable, the action for judicial review may be brought against the United States, the agency by its official title, or the appropriate officer. Except to the extent that prior, adequate, and exclusive opportunity for judicial review is provided by law, agency action is subject to judicial review in civil or criminal proceedings for judicial enforcement.

(Pub. L. No. 89-554, Sept. 6, 1966, 80 Stat. 392; Pub. L. No. 94-574, §1, Oct. 21, 1976, 90 Stat. 2721.)

§704. Actions reviewable

Agency action made reviewable by statute and final agency action for which there is no other adequate remedy in a court are subject to judicial review. A preliminary, procedural, or intermediate agency action or ruling not directly reviewable is subject to review on the review of the final agency action. Except as otherwise expressly required by statute, agency action otherwise final is final for the purposes of this section whether or not there has been presented or determined an application for a declaratory order, for any form of reconsiderations, or, unless the agency otherwise requires by rule and provides that the action meanwhile is inoperative, for an appeal to superior agency authority.

(Pub. L. No. 89-554, Sept. 6, 1966, 80 Stat. 392.)

§705. Relief pending review

When an agency finds that justice so requires, it may postpone the effective date of action taken by it, pending judicial review. On such conditions as may be required and to the extent necessary to prevent irreparable injury, the reviewing court, including the court to which a case may be taken on appeal from or on application for certiorari or other writ to a reviewing court, may issue all necessary and appropriate process to postpone the effective date of an agency action or to preserve status or rights pending conclusion of the review proceedings.

(Pub. L. No. 89-554, Sept. 6, 1966, 80 Stat. 393.)

§706. Scope of review

To the extent necessary to decision and when presented, the reviewing court shall decide all relevant questions of law, interpret constitutional and statutory provisions, and determine the meaning or applicability of the terms of an agency action. The reviewing court shall—

(1) compel agency action unlawfully withheld or unreasonably delayed; and

(2) hold unlawful and set aside agency action, findings, and conclusions found to be—

(A) arbitrary, capricious, an abuse of discretion, or otherwise not in accordance with law;

(B) contrary to constitutional right, power, privilege, or immunity;

(C) in excess of statutory jurisdiction, authority, or limitations, or short of statutory right;

(D) without observance of procedure required by law;

(E) unsupported by substantial evidence in a case subject to sections 556 and 557 of this title or otherwise reviewed on the record of an agency hearing provided by statute; or

(F) unwarranted by the facts to the extent that the facts are subject to trial de novo by the reviewing court.

In making the foregoing determinations, the court shall review the whole record or those parts of it cited by a party, and due account shall be taken of the rule of prejudicial error.

(Pub. L. No. 89-554, Sept. 6, 1966, 80 Stat. 393.)

§1305. Administrative law judges

For the purpose of sections 3105, 3344, 4301(2)(D), and 5372 of this title and the provisions of section 5335(a)(B) of this title that relate to administrative law judges, the Office of Personnel Management may, and for the purpose of section 7521 of this title, the Merit Systems Protection Board may investigate, require reports by agencies, issue reports, including an annual report to Congress, prescribe regulations, appoint advisory committees as necessary, recommend legislation, subpena witnesses and records, and pay witness fees as established for the courts of the United States.

(Pub. L. No. 89-554, Sept. 6, 1966, 80 Stat. 402; Pub. L. No. 90-83, §1(3), Sept. 11, 1967, 81 Stat. 196; Pub. L. No. 95-251, §2(a)(1), (b)(1), Mar. 27, 1978, 92 Stat. 183; Pub. L. No. 95-454, title VIII, §801(a)(3)(B)(iii), title IX, §906(a)(12), Oct. 13, 1978, 92 Stat. 1221, 1225.)

§3105. Appointment of administrative law judges

Each agency shall appoint as many administrative law judges as are necessary for proceedings required to be conducted in accordance with sections 556 and 557 of this title. Administrative law judges shall be assigned to cases in rotation so far as practicable, and may not perform duties inconsistent with their duties and responsibilities as administrative law judges.

(Pub. L. No. 89-554, Sept. 6, 1966, 80 Stat. 415; Pub. L. No. 95-251, §2(a)(1), (b)(2), (d)(1), Mar. 27, 1978, 92 Stat. 183, 184.)

§3344. Details; administrative law judges

An agency as defined by section 551 of this title which occasionally or temporarily is insufficiently staffed with administrative law judges appointed under section 3105 of this title may use administrative law judges selected by the Office of Personnel Management from and with the consent of other agencies.

(Pub. L. No. 89-554, Sept. 6, 1966, 80 Stat. 425; Pub. L. No. 95-251, §2(a)(1), (b)(2), Mar. 27, 1978, 92 Stat. 183; Pub. L. No. 95-454, title IX, §906(a)(2), Oct. 13, 1978, 92 Stat. 1224.)

§5372. Administrative law judges

(a) For the purposes of this section, the term "administrative law judge" means an administrative law judge appointed under section 3105.

(b) (1) There shall be 3 levels of basic pay for administrative law judges (designated as AL-1, 2, and 3, respectively), and each such judge shall be paid at 1 of those levels, in accordance with the provisions of this section. The rates of basic pay for those levels shall be as follows:

AL-3, rate A 65 percent of the rate of basic pay for level IV of the Executive Schedule.
AL-3, rate B 70 percent of the rate of basic pay for level IV of the Executive Schedule.
AL-3, rate C 75 percent of the rate of basic pay for level IV of the Executive Schedule.
AL-3, rate D 80 percent of the rate of basic pay for level IV of the Executive Schedule.
AL-3, rate E 85 percent of the rate of basic pay for level IV of the Executive Schedule.
AL-3, rate F 90 percent of the rate of basic pay for level IV of the Executive Schedule.
AL-2 95 percent of the rate of basic pay for level IV of the Executive Schedule.
AL-1 The rate of basic pay for level IV of the Executive Schedule.

(2) The Office of Personnel Management shall determine, in accordance with procedures which the Office shall by regulation prescribe, the level in which each administrative-law-judge position shall be placed and the qualifications to be required for appointment to each level.

(3) **(A)** Upon appointment to a position in AL-3, an administrative law judge shall be paid at rate A of AL-3, and shall be advanced successively to rates B, C, and D of that level upon completion of 52 weeks of service in the next lower rate, and to rates E and F of that level upon completion of 104 weeks of service in the next lower rate.

(B) The Office of Personnel Management may provide for appointment of an administrative law judge in AL-3 at an advanced rate under such circumstances as the Office may determine appropriate.

(c) The Office of Personnel Management shall prescribe regulations necessary to administer this section.

(Pub. L. No. 89-554, Sept. 6, 1966, 80 Stat. 473, §5362; Pub. L. No. 95-251, §2(a)(1), (b)(1), Mar. 27, 1978, 92 Stat. 183; renumbered §5372 and amended Pub. L. No. 95-454, title VIII, §801(a)(3)(A)(ii), title IX, §906(a)(2), Oct. 13, 1978, 92 Stat. 1221, 1224; Pub. L. No. 101-509, title V, §529 [title I, §104(a)(1)], Nov. 5, 1990, 104 Stat. 1427, 1445.)

Amendments

1990 Pub. L. No. 101-509 amended section generally. Prior to amendment, section read as follows: "Administrative law judges appointed under section 3105 of this title are entitled to pay prescribed by the Office of Personnel Management independently of agency recommendations or ratings and in accordance with subchapter III of this chapter and chapter 51 of this title."

§7521. Actions against administrative law judges

(a) An action may be taken against an administrative law judge appointed under section 3105 of this title by the agency in which the administrative law judge is employed only for good cause established and determined by the Merit System Protection Board on the record after opportunity for hearing before the Board.

(b) The actions covered by this section are—

(1) a removal;

(2) (2) a suspension;

(3) a reduction in grade;

(4) a reduction in pay; and

(5) a furlough of 30 days or less;

but do not include—

(A) a suspension or removal under section 7532 of this title;

(B) a reduction-in-force action under section 3502 of this title; or

(C) any action initiated under section 1215 of this title.

(Added Pub. L. No. 95-454, title II, §204(a), Oct. 13, 1978, 92 Stat. 1137, and amended Pub. L. No. 101-12, §9(a)(2), Apr. 10, 1989, 103 Stat. 35.)

APPENDIX B

Freedom of Information Act

FREEDOM OF INFORMATION ACT

5 U.S.C. §552 (1996)

(a) (2) Each agency, in accordance with published rules, shall make available for public inspection and copying— . . .

(A) final opinions, including concurring and dissenting opinions, as well as orders, made in the adjudication of cases;

(B) those statements of policy and interpretations which have been adopted by the agency and are not published in the Federal Register;

(C) administrative staff manuals and instructions to staff that affect a member of the public;

(D) copies of all records, regardless of form or format, which have been released to any person under paragraph (3) and which, because of the nature of their subject matter, the agency determines have become or are likely to become the subject of subsequent requests for substantially the same records; and

(E) a general index of the records referred to under subparagraph (D);

unless the materials are promptly published and copies offered for sale. For records created on or after November 1, 1996, within one year after such date, each agency shall make such records available, including by computer telecommunications or, if computer telecommunications means have not been established by the agency, by other electronic means. [To the extent required to prevent a clearly unwarranted invasion of personal privacy, an agency may delete identifying details when it makes available or publishes an opinion, statement of, policy, interpretation,] staff manual, instruction, or copies of records referred to in subparagraph (D). [However, in each case the justification for the deletion shall be explained fully in writing,] and the extent of such deletion shall be indicated on the portion of the record which is made available or published, unless including that indication would harm an interest protected by the exemption in subsection (b) under which the deletion is made. If technically feasible, the extent of the deletion shall be indicated at the place in the record where the deletion was made. [Each agency shall also maintain and make available for public inspection and copying current indexes providing identifying information for the public as to any matter issued, adopted, or promulgated after July 4, 1967, and required by this paragraph to be made available or published. Each agency shall promptly publish, quarterly or more frequently, and distribute (by sale or otherwise) copies of each index or supplements thereto unless it determines by order published in the Federal Register that the publication would be unnecessary and impracticable, in which case the agency shall nonetheless provide copies of such index on request at a cost not to exceed the direct cost of duplication.] Each agency shall make the index referred to in subparagraph (E) available by computer telecommunications by December 31, 1999. [A final order, opinion, statement of policy, interpretation, or staff manual or instruction that affects a member of the public may be relied on, used, or cited as precedent by an agency against a party other than an agency only if—

(i) it has been indexed and either made available or published as provided by this paragraph; or

(ii) the party has actual and timely notice of the terms thereof.]

(3) **(A)** Except with respect to the records made available under paragraphs (1) and (2) of this subsection, each agency, upon any request for records which (i) reasonably describes such records and (ii) is made in accordance with published rules stating the time, place, fees (if any), and procedures to be followed, shall make the records promptly available to any person.

(B) In making any record available to a person under this paragraph, an agency shall provide the record in any form or format requested by the person if the record is readily reproducible by the agency in that form or format. Each agency shall make reasonable efforts to maintain its records in forms or formats that are reproducible for purposes of this section.

(C) In responding under this paragraph to a request for records, an agency shall make reasonable efforts to sear h for the records in electronic form or format, except when such efforts would significantly interfere with the operation of the agency's automated information system.

(D) For purposes of this paragraph, the term "search" means to review, manually or by automated means, agency records for the purpose of locating those records which are responsive to a request.

(4) **(A)**

(i) In order to carry out the provisions of this section, each agency shall promulgate regulations, pursuant to notice and receipt of public comment, specifying the schedule of fees applicable to the processing of requests under this section and establishing procedures and guidelines for determining when such fees should be waived or reduced. Such schedule shall conform to the guidelines which shall be promulgated, pursuant to notice and receipt of public comment, by the Director of the Office of Management and Budget and which shall provide for a uniform schedule of fees for all agencies.

(ii) Such agency regulations shall provide that—

(I) fees shall be limited to reasonable standard charges for document search, duplication, and review, when records are requested for commercial use;

(II) fees shall be limited to reasonable standard charges for document duplication when records are not sought for commercial use and the request is made by an educational or noncommercial scientific institution, whose purpose is scholarly or scientific research; or a representative of the news media; and

(III) for any request not described in (I) or (II), fees shall be limited to reasonable standard charges for document search and duplication.

(iii) Documents shall be furnished without any charge or at a charge reduced below the fees established under clause (ii) if disclosure of the information is in the public interest because it is likely to contribute significantly to public understanding of the operations or activities of the government and is not primarily in the commercial interest of the requester.

(iv) Fee schedules shall provide for the recovery of only the direct costs of search, duplication, or review. Review costs shall include only the direct costs incurred during the initial examination of a document for the purposes of determining whether the documents must be disclosed under this section and for the purposes of withholding any portions exempt from disclosure under this section. Review costs may not include any costs incurred in resolving issues of law or policy that may be raised in the course of processing a request under this section. No fee may be charged by any agency under this section —

(I) if the costs of routine collection and processing, of the fee are likely to equal or exceed the amount of the fee; or

(II) for any request described in clause (ii)(II) or (III) of this subparagraph for the first two hours of search time or for the first one hundred pages of duplication.

(v) No agency may require advance payment of any fee unless the requester has previously failed to pay fees in a timely fashion, or the agency has determined that the fee will exceed $250.

(vi) Nothing in this subparagraph shall supersede fees chargeable under a statute specifically providing for setting the level of fees for particular types of records.

(vii) In any action by a requester regarding the waiver of fees under this section, the court shall determine the matter de novo: Provided, That the court's review of the matter shall be limited to the record before the agency.

(B) On complaint, the district court of the United States in the district in which the complainant resides, or has his principal place of business, or in which the agency records are situated, or in the District of Columbia, has jurisdiction to enjoin the agency from withholding agency records and to order the production of any agency records improperly withheld from the complainant. In such a case the court shall determine the matter de novo, and may examine the contents of such agency records in camera to determine whether such records or any part thereof shall be withheld under any of the exemptions set forth in subsection (b) of this section, and the burden is on the agency to sustain its action. In addition to any other matters to which a court accords substantial weight, a court shall accord substantial weight to an affidavit of an agency concerning the agency's determination as to technical feasibility under paragraph (2)(C) and subsection (b) and reproducibility under paragraph (3)(B).

(C) Notwithstanding any other provision of law, the defendant shall serve an answer or otherwise plead to any complaint made under this subsection within thirty days after service upon the defendant of the pleading in which such complaint is made, unless the court otherwise directs for good cause shown. . . .

(E) The court may assess against the United States reasonable attorney fees and other litigation costs reasonably incurred in any case under this section in which the complainant has substantially prevailed.

(F) Whenever the court orders the production of any agency records improperly withheld from the complainant and assesses against the United States reasonable attorney fees and other litigation costs, and the court additionally issues a written finding that the circumstances surrounding the withholding raise questions whether agency personnel acted arbitrarily or capriciously with respect to the withholding, the Special Counsel shall promptly initiate a proceeding to determine whether disciplinary action is warranted against the officer or employee who was primarily responsible for the withholding. The Special Counsel, after investigation and consideration of the evidence submitted, shall submit his findings and recommendations to the administrative authority of the agency concerned and shall send copies of the findings and recommendation s to the officer or employee or his representative. The administrative authority shall take the corrective action that the Special Counsel recommends.

(G) In the event of noncompliance with the order of the court, the district court may punish for contempt the responsible employee, and in the case of a uniformed service, the responsible member.

(5) Each agency having more than one member shall maintain and make available for public inspection a record of the final votes of each member in every agency proceeding.]

(6) (A) Each agency, upon any request for records made under paragraph (1), (2), or (3) of this subsection, shall—

(i) determine within 20 days [(excepting Saturdays, Sun days, and legal public holidays) after the receipt of any such request whether to comply with such request and shall immediately notify the person making such request of such determination and the reasons therefor, and of the right of such person to appeal to the head of the agency any adverse determination; and

(ii) make a determination with respect to any appeal within twenty days (excepting Saturdays, Sundays, and legal public holidays) after the receipt of such appeal. If on appeal the denial of the request for records is in whole or in part upheld, the agency shall notify the person making such request of the provisions for judicial review of that determination under paragraph (4) of this subsection.]

(B)

(i) In unusual circumstances as specified in this subparagraph, the time limits prescribed in either clause (i) or clause (ii) of subparagraph (A) may be extended by written notice to the person making such request setting forth the unusual circumstances for such extension and the date on which a determination is expected to be dispatched. No such notice shall specify a date that would result in an extension for more than ten working days, except as provided in clause (ii) of this subparagraph.

(ii) With respect to a request for which a written notice under clause (i) extends the time limits prescribed under clause (i) of subparagraph (A), the agency shall notify the person making the request if the request cannot be processed within the time limit specified in that clause and shall provide the person an opportunity to limit the scope of the request so that it may be processed within that time limit or an opportunity to arrange with the agency an alternative time frame for processing the request or a modified request. Refusal by the person to reasonably modify the request or arrange such an alternative time frame shall be considered as a factor in determining whether exceptional circumstances exist for purposes of subparagraph (C).

(iii) As used in this subparagraph, "unusual circumstances" means, but only to the extent reasonably necessary to the proper processing of the particular requests —

(I) the need to search for and collect the requested records from field facilities or other establishments that are separate from the office processing the request;

(II) the need to search for, collect, and appropriately examine a voluminous amount of separate and distinct records which are demanded in a single request; or

(III) the need for consultation, which shall be conducted with all practicable speed, with another agency having a substantial interest in the determination of the request or among two or more components of the agency having substantial subject-matter interest therein.

(iv) Each agency may promulgate regulations, pursuant to notice and receipt of public comment, providing for the aggregation of certain requests by the same requestor, or by a group of requestors acting in concert, if the agency reasonably believes that such requests actually constitute a single request, which would otherwise satisfy the unusual circumstances specified in this subparagraph, and the requests involve clearly related matters. Multiple requests involving unrelated matters shall not be aggregated.

(C)

(i) Any person making a request to any agency for records under paragraph (1), (2), or (3) of this subsection shall be deemed to have exhausted his administrative remedies with respect to such request if the agency fails to comply with the applicable time limit provisions of this paragraph. If the Government can show exceptional circumstances exist and that the agency is exercising due diligence in responding to the request, the court may retain jurisdiction and allow the agency additional time to complete its review of the records. Upon any determination by an agency to comply with a request for records, the records shall be made promptly available to such person making such request. Any notification of denial of any request for records under this subsection shall set forth the names and titles or positions of each per on responsible for the denial of such request.

(ii) For purposes of this subparagraph, the term "exceptional circumstances" does not include a delay that results from a predictable agency workload of requests under this section, unless the agency demonstrates reasonable progress in reducing its backlog of pending requests.

(iii) Refusal by a person to reasonably modify the scope of a request or arrange an alternative time frame for processing a request (or a modified request) under clause (ii) after being given an opportunity to do so by the agency to whom the person made the request shall be considered as a factor in determining whether exceptional circumstances exist for purposes of this subparagraph.

(D)

(i) Each agency may promulgate regulations, pursuant to notice and receipt of public comment, providing for multitrack processing of requests for records based on the amount of work or time (or both) involved in processing requests.

(ii) Regulations under this subparagraph may provide a person making a request that does not qualify for the fastest multitrack processing an opportunity to limit the scope of the request in order to qualify for faster processing.

(iii) This subparagraphs shall not be considered to affect the requirement under subparagraph (C) to exercise due diligence.

(E)

(i) Each agency shall promulgate regulations, pursuant to notice and receipt of public comment, providing for expedited processing or requests for records—

(I) in cases in which the person requesting the records demonstrates a compelling need; and

(II) in other cases determined by the agency.

(ii) Notwithstanding clause (i), regulations under this subparagraph must ensure—

(I) that a determination of whether to provide expedited processing shall be made, and notice of the determination shall be provided to the person making the request, within 10 days after the date of the request; and

(II) expeditious consideration of administrative appeals of such determinations of whether to provide expedited processing.

(iii) An agency shall process as soon as practicable any request for records to which the agency has granted expedited processing under this subparagraph. Agency action to deny or affirm denial of a request for expedited processing pursuant to this subparagraph, and failure by an agency to respond in a timely manner to such a request shall be subject to judicial review under paragraph (4), except that the Judicial review shall be based on the record before the agency at the time of the determination.

(iv) A district court of the United States shall not have jurisdiction to review an agency denial of expedited processing of a request for records after the agency has provided a complete response to the request.

(v) For purposes of this subparagraph, the term "compelling need" means—

(I) that a failure to obtain requested records on an expedited basis under this paragraph could reasonably be expected to pose an imminent threat to the live or physical safety of an individual; or

(II) with respect to a request made by a person primarily engaged in disseminating information, urgency to inform the public concerning actual or alleged Federal Government activity.

(vi) A demonstration of a compelling need by a person making a request for expedited processing shall be made by a statement certified by such person to be true and correct to the best of such person's knowledge and belief.

(F) In denying a request for records, in whole or in part, an agency shall make a reasonable effort to estimate the volume of any requested matter the provision of which is denied, and shall provide any such estimate to the person making the request, unless providing such estimate would harm an interest protected by the exemption in subsection (b) pursuant to which the denial is made.

(b) This section does not apply to matters that are—

(1) (A) specifically authorized under criteria established by an Executive order to be kept secret in the interest of national defense or foreign policy and (B) are in fact properly classified pursuant to such Executive order;

(2) related solely to the internal personnel rules and practices of an agency;

(3) specifically exempted from disclosure by statute (other than section 552b of this title), provided that such statute. (A) requires that the matters be withheld from the public in such a manner as to leave no discretion on the issue, or (B) establishes particular criteria for withholding or refers to particular types of matters to be withheld;

(4) trade secrets and commercial or financial information obtained from a person and privileged or confidential;

(5) inter-agency or intra-agency memorandums or letters which would not be available by law to a party other than an agency in litigation with the agency;

(6) personnel and medical files and similar files the disclosure of which would constitute a clearly unwarranted invasion of personal privacy;

(7) records or information compiled for law enforcement purposes, but only to the extent that the production of such law enforcement records or information (A) could reasonably be expected to interfere with enforcement proceedings, (B) would deprive a person of a right to a fair trial or an impartial adjudication, (C) could reasonably be expected to constitute an unwarranted invasion of personal privacy, (D) could reasonably be expected to disclose the identity of a confidential source, including a State, local, or foreign agency or authority or any private institution which furnished information on a confidential basis, and, in the case of a record or information complied by criminal law enforcement authority in the course of a criminal investigation or by an agency conducting a lawful national security intelligence investigation, information furnished by a confidential source, (E) would disclose techniques and procedures for law enforcement investigations or prosecutions, or would disclose guidelines for law enforcement investigations or prosecutions if such disclosure could reasonably be expected to risk circumvention of the law, or (F) could reasonably be expected to endanger the life or physical safety of any individual;

(8) contained in or related to examination, operating, or condition reports prepared by, on behalf of, or for the use of an agency responsible for the regulation or supervision of financial institutions; or

(9) geological and geophysical information and data, including maps, concerning wells.

Any reasonably segregable portion of a record shall be provided to any person requesting such record after deletion of the portions which are exempt under this subsection. The amount of information deleted shall be indicated on the released portion of the record, unless including that indication would harm an interest protected by the exemption in this subsection under which the deletion is made. If technically feasible, the amount of the information shall be indicated at the place in the record where such deletion is made.

(c)

(1) Whenever a request is made which involves access to records described in subsection (b)(7)(A) and—

(A) the investigation or proceeding involves a possible violation of criminal law; and

(B) there is reason to believe that (i) the subject of the investigation or proceeding is not aware of its pendency, and (ii) disclosure of the existence of the records could reasonably be expected to interfere with enforcement proceedings,

the agency may, during only such time as that circumstance continues, treat the records as not subject to the requirements of this section.

(2) Whenever informant records maintained by a criminal law enforcement agency under an informant's name or personal identifier are requested by a third party according to the informant's name or personal identifier, the agency may treat the records as not subject to the requirements of this section unless the informant's status as an informant has been officially confirmed.

(3) Whenever a request is made which involves access to records maintained by the Federal Bureau of Investigation pertaining to foreign intelligence or counterintelligence, or international terrorism, and the existence of the records is classified information as provided in subsection (b)(1), the Bureau may, as long as the existence of the records remains classified information, treat the records as not subject to the requirements of this section.

(d) This section does not authorize withholding of information or limit the availability of records to the public, except as specifically stated in this section. This section is not authority to withhold information from Congress. . . .

TABLE OF CASES

Principal cases are indicated by italics.

N

O

P

Q

R

INDEX

B

C

D

G

H

I